International Directory of
COMPANY HISTORIES

International Directory of

COMPANY HISTORIES

VOLUME 107

Editor

Tina Grant

ST. JAMES PRESS
A part of Gale, Cengage Learning

Detroit • New York • San Francisco • New Haven, Conn • Waterville, Maine • London

GALE
CENGAGE Learning™

International Directory of Company Histories, Volume 107

Tina Grant, Editor

Project Editor: Miranda H. Ferrara

Editorial: Virgil Burton, Donna Craft, Louise Gagné, Peggy Geeseman, Julie Gough, Sonya Hill, Keith Jones, Lynn Pearce, Laura Peterson, Holly Selden, Justine Ventimiglia

Production Technology Specialist: Mike Weaver

Imaging and Multimedia: John Watkins

Composition and Electronic Prepress: Gary Leach, Evi Seoud

Manufacturing: Rhonda Dover

Product Manager: Jenai Drouillard

For product information and technology assistance, contact us at **Gale Customer Support, 1-800-877-4253.**
For permission to use material from this text or product, submit all requests online at **www.cengage.com/permissions.**
Further permissions questions can be emailed to **permissionrequest@cengage.com**

Gale
27500 Drake Rd.
Farmington Hills, MI, 48331-3535

LIBRARY OF CONGRESS CATALOG NUMBER 89-190943
ISBN-13: 978-1-4144-4103-0
ISBN-10: 1-4144-4103-7

This title is also available as an e-book
ISBN-13: 978-1-55862-770-3   ISBN-10: 1-55862-770-7
Contact your Gale, a part of Cengage Learning sales representative for ordering information.

BRITISH LIBRARY CATALOGUING IN PUBLICATION DATA
International directory of company histories, Vol. 107
Tina Grant
33.87409

Printed in the United States of America
2 3 4 5 6 7 13 12 11 10

Contents

Preface

The St. James Press series *The International Directory of Company Histories* (*IDCH*) is intended for reference use by students, business people, librarians, historians, economists, investors, job candidates, and others who seek to learn more about the historical development of the world's most important companies. To date, *IDCH* has covered more than 10,500 companies in 107 volumes.

INCLUSION CRITERIA

Most companies chosen for inclusion in *IDCH* have achieved a minimum of US$25 million in annual sales and are leading influences in their industries or geographical locations. Companies may be publicly held, private, or nonprofit. State-owned companies that are important in their industries and that may operate much like public or private companies also are included. Wholly owned subsidiaries and divisions are profiled if they meet the requirements for inclusion. Entries on companies that have had major changes since they were last profiled may be selected for updating.

The *IDCH* series highlights 25% private and nonprofit companies, and features updated entries on approximately 35 companies per volume.

ENTRY FORMAT

Each entry begins with the company's legal name; the address of its headquarters; its telephone, toll-free, and fax numbers; and its web site. A statement of public, private, state, or parent ownership follows. A company with a legal name in both English and the language of its headquarters country is listed by the English name, with the native-language name in parentheses.

The company's founding or earliest incorporation date, the number of employees, and the most recent available sales figures follow. Sales figures are given in local currencies with equivalents in U.S. dollars. For some private companies, sales figures are estimates and indicated by the abbreviation *est.* The entry lists the exchanges on which the company's stock is traded and its ticker symbol, as well as the company's NAICS codes.

Entries generally contain a *Company Perspectives* box which provides a short summary of the company's mission, goals, and ideals; a *Key Dates* box highlighting milestones in the company's history; lists of *Principal Subsidiaries, Principal Divisions, Principal Operating Units, Principal Competitors*; and articles for *Further Reading*.

American spelling is used throughout *IDCH*, and the word "billion" is used in its U.S. sense of one thousand million.

SOURCES

Entries have been compiled from publicly accessible sources both in print and on the Internet such as general and academic periodicals, books, and annual reports, as well as material supplied by the companies themselves.

CUMULATIVE INDEXES

IDCH contains three indexes: the **Cumulative Index to Companies**, which provides an alphabetical index to companies profiled in the *IDCH* series, the **Index to Industries**, which allows researchers to locate companies by their principal industry, and the **Geographic Index**, which lists companies alphabetically by the country of their headquarters. The indexes are cumulative and specific instructions for using them are found immediately preceding each index.

SPECIAL TO THIS VOLUME

This volume of *IDCH* contains an entry on Munir Sukhtian Group, an international conglomerate based in Jordan; Egis Gyogyszergyar Nyrt, a Hungarian developer and producer of generic branded pharmaceuticals used worldwide; and an update of KLM Royal Dutch Airlines, the world's oldest scheduled airline.

SUGGESTIONS WELCOME

Comments and suggestions from users of *IDCH* on any aspect of the product as well as suggestions for companies to be included or updated are cordially invited. Please write:

The Editor
International Directory of Company Histories
St. James Press
Gale, Cengage Learning
27500 Drake Rd.
Farmington Hills, Michigan 48331-3535

St. James Press does not endorse any of the companies or products mentioned in this series. Companies appearing in the *International Directory of Company Histories* were selected without reference to their wishes and have in no way endorsed their entries.

Notes on Contributors

Gerald E. Brennan
Writer and musician based in Germany.

M. L. Cohen
Novelist, business writer, and researcher living in Paris.

Ed Dinger
Writer and editor based in Bronx, New York.

Heidi Feldman
Writer and editor based in California.

Paul R. Greenland
Illinois-based writer and researcher; author of three books and former senior editor of a national business magazine; contributor to *The Encyclopedia of Chicago History*, *The Encyclopedia of Religion*, and the *Encyclopedia of American Industries*.

Robert Halasz
Former editor in chief of *World Progress* and *Funk & Wagnalls New Encyclopedia Yearbook*; author, *The U.S. Marines* (Millbrook Press, 1993).

Evelyn Hauser
Researcher, writer and marketing specialist based in Germany.

Frederick C. Ingram
Writer based in South Carolina.

Carrie Rothburd
Writer and editor specializing in corporate profiles, academic texts, and academic journal articles.

Christina M. Stansell
Writer and editor based in Louisville, Kentucky.

Frank Uhle
Ann Arbor-based writer, movie projectionist, disc jockey, and staff member of *Psychotronic Video* magazine.

A. Woodward
Wisconsin-based writer.

List of Abbreviations

€ European euro
¥ Japanese yen
£ United Kingdom pound
$ United States dollar

A
AB Aktiebolag (Finland, Sweden)
AB Oy Aktiebolag Osakeyhtiot (Finland)
A.E. Anonimos Eteria (Greece)
AED Emirati dirham
AG Aktiengesellschaft (Austria, Germany, Switzerland, Liechtenstein)
aG auf Gegenseitigkeit (Austria, Germany)
A.m.b.a. Andelsselskab med begraenset ansvar (Denmark)
A.O. Anonim Ortaklari/Ortakligi (Turkey)
ApS Amparteselskab (Denmark)
ARS Argentine peso
A.S. Anonim Sirketi (Turkey)
A/S Aksjeselskap (Norway)
A/S Aktieselskab (Denmark, Sweden)
Ay Avoinyhtio (Finland)
ATS Austrian shilling
AUD Australian dollar
Ay Avoinyhtio (Finland)

B
B.A. Buttengewone Aansprakeiijkheid (Netherlands)
BEF Belgian franc

BHD Bahraini dinar
Bhd. Berhad (Malaysia, Brunei)
BND Brunei dollar
BRL Brazilian real
B.V. Besloten Vennootschap (Belgium, Netherlands)

C
C. de R.L. Compania de Responsabilidad Limitada (Spain)
C. por A. Compania por Acciones (Dominican Republic)
C.A. Compania Anonima (Ecuador, Venezuela)
C.V. Commanditaire Vennootschap (Netherlands, Belgium)
CAD Canadian dollar
CEO Chief Executive Officer
CFO Chief Financial Officer
CHF Swiss franc
Cia. Compagnia (Italy)
Cia. Companhia (Brazil, Portugal)
Cia. Compania (Latin America [except Brazil], Spain)
Cie. Compagnie (Belgium, France, Luxembourg, Netherlands)
CIO Chief Information Officer
CLP Chilean peso
CNY Chinese yuan
Co. Company
COO Chief Operating Officer
Coop. Cooperative
COP Colombian peso

Corp. Corporation
CPT Cuideachta Phoibi Theoranta (Republic of Ireland)
CRL Companhia a Responsabilidao Limitida (Portugal, Spain)
CZK Czech koruna

D
D&B Dunn & Bradstreet
DEM German deutsche mark (W. Germany to 1990; unified Germany to 2002)
Div. Division (United States)
DKK Danish krone
DZD Algerian dinar

E
E.P.E. Etema Pemorismenis Evthynis (Greece)
EC Exempt Company (Arab countries)
Edms. Bpk. Eiendoms Beperk (South Africa)
EEK Estonian Kroon
eG eingetragene Genossenschaft (Germany)
EGMBH Eingetragene Genossenschaft mit beschraenkter Haftung (Austria, Germany)
EGP Egyptian pound
Ek For Ekonomisk Forening (Sweden)
EP Empresa Portuguesa (Portugal)

ESOP Employee Stock Options and Ownership
ESP Spanish peseta
Et(s). Etablissement(s) (Belgium, France, Luxembourg)
eV eingetragener Verein (Germany)
EUR European euro

F
FIM Finnish markka
FRF French franc

G
G.I.E. Groupement d'Interet Economique (France)
gGmbH gemeinnutzige Gesellschaft mit beschraenkter Haftung (Austria, Germany, Switzerland)
GmbH Gesellschaft mit beschraenkter Haftung (Austria, Germany, Switzerland)
GRD Greek drachma
GWA Gewerbte Amt (Austria, Germany)

H
HB Handelsbolag (Sweden)
HF Hlutafelag (Iceland)
HKD Hong Kong dollar
HUF Hungarian forint

I
IDR Indonesian rupiah
IEP Irish pound
ILS Israeli shekel (new)
Inc. Incorporated (United States, Canada)
INR Indian rupee
IPO Initial Public Offering
I/S Interesentselskap (Norway)
I/S Interessentselskab (Denmark)
ISK Icelandic krona
ITL Italian lira

J
JMD Jamaican dollar
JOD Jordanian dinar

K
KB Kommanditbolag (Sweden)
KES Kenyan schilling
Kft Korlatolt Felelossegu Tarsasag (Hungary)
KG Kommanditgesellschaft (Austria, Germany, Switzerland)
KGaA Kommanditgesellschaft auf Aktien (Austria, Germany, Switzerland)
KK Kabushiki Kaisha (Japan)
KPW North Korean won
KRW South Korean won
K/S Kommanditselskab (Denmark)
K/S Kommandittselskap (Norway)
KWD Kuwaiti dinar
Ky Kommandiitiyhtio (Finland)

L
L.L.C. Limited Liability Company (Arab countries, Egypt, Greece, United States)
L.L.P. Limited Liability Partnership (United States)
L.P. Limited Partnership (Canada, South Africa, United Kingdom, United States)
LBO Leveraged Buyout
Lda. Limitada (Spain)
Ltd. Limited
Ltda. Limitada (Brazil, Portugal)
Ltee. Limitee (Canada, France)
LUF Luxembourg franc

M
mbH mit beschraenkter Haftung (Austria, Germany)
Mij. Maatschappij (Netherlands)
MUR Mauritian rupee
MXN Mexican peso
MYR Malaysian ringgit

N
N.A. National Association (United States)
N.V. Naamloze Vennootschap (Belgium, Netherlands)
NGN Nigerian naira
NLG Netherlands guilder
NOK Norwegian krone
NZD New Zealand dollar

O
OAO Otkrytoe Aktsionernoe Obshchestve (Russia)
OHG Offene Handelsgesellschaft (Austria, Germany, Switzerland)
OMR Omani rial
OOO Obschestvo s Ogranichennoi Otvetstvennostiu (Russia)
OOUR Osnova Organizacija Udruzenog Rada (Yugoslavia)
Oy Osakeyhti ???? (Finland)

P
P.C. Private Corp. (United States)
P.L.L.C. Professional Limited Liability Corporation (United States)
P.T. Perusahaan/Perseroan Terbatas (Indonesia)
PEN Peruvian Nuevo Sol
PHP Philippine peso
PKR Pakistani rupee
P/L Part Lag (Norway)
PLC Public Limited Co. (United Kingdom, Ireland)
PLN Polish zloty
PTE Portuguese escudo
Pte. Private (Singapore)
Pty. Proprietary (Australia, South Africa, United Kingdom)
Pvt. Private (India, Zimbabwe)
PVBA Personen Vennootschap met Beperkte Aansprakelijkheid (Belgium)
PYG Paraguay guarani

Q
QAR Qatar riyal

R
REIT Real Estate Investment Trust
RMB Chinese renminbi
Rt Reszvenytarsasag (Hungary)
RUB Russian ruble

S
S.A. Sociedad Anónima (Latin America [except Brazil], Spain, Mexico)
S.A. Sociedades Anônimas (Brazil, Portugal)
S.A. Société Anonyme (Arab countries, Belgium, France, Jordan, Luxembourg, Switzerland)
S.A. de C.V. Sociedad Anonima de Capital Variable (Mexico)
S.A.B. de C.V. Sociedad Anónima Bursátil de Capital Variable (Mexico)
S.A.C. Sociedad Anonima Comercial (Latin America [except Brazil])
S.A.C.I. Sociedad Anonima Comercial e Industrial (Latin America [except Brazil])

S.A.C.I.y.F. Sociedad Anonima Comercial e Industrial y Financiera (Latin America [except Brazil])

S.A.R.L. Sociedade Anonima de Responsabilidade Limitada (Brazil, Portugal)

S.A.R.L. Société à Responsabilité Limitée (France, Belgium, Luxembourg)

S.A.S. Societe Anonyme Syrienne (Arab countries)

S.A.S. Societá in Accomandita Semplice (Italy)

S.C. Societe en Commandite (Belgium, France, Luxembourg)

S.C.A. Societe Cooperativa Agricole (France, Italy, Luxembourg)

S.C.I. Sociedad Cooperativa Ilimitada (Spain)

S.C.L. Sociedad Cooperativa Limitada (Spain)

S.C.R.L. Societe Cooperative a Responsabilite Limitee (Belgium)

S.L. Sociedad Limitada (Latin America [except Brazil], Portugal, Spain)

S.N.C. Société en Nom Collectif (France)

S.p.A. Società per Azioni (Italy)

S.R.L. Sociedad de Responsabilidad Limitada (Spain, Mexico, Latin America [except Brazil])

S.R.L. Società a Responsabilità Limitata (Italy)

S.R.O. Spolecnost s Rucenim Omezenym (Czechoslovakia

S.S.K. Sherkate Sahami Khass (Iran)

S.V. Samemwerkende Vennootschap (Belgium)

S.Z.R.L. Societe Zairoise a Responsabilite Limitee (Zaire)

SAA Societe Anonyme Arabienne (Arab countries)

SAK Societe Anonyme Kuweitienne (Arab countries)

SAL Societe Anonyme Libanaise (Arab countries)

SAO Societe Anonyme Omanienne (Arab countries)

SAQ Societe Anonyme Qatarienne (Arab countries)

SAR Saudi riyal

Sdn. Bhd. Sendirian Berhad (Malaysia)

SEK Swedish krona

SGD Singapore dollar

S/L Salgslag (Norway)

Soc. Sociedad (Latin America [except Brazil], Spain)

Soc. Sociedade (Brazil, Portugal)

Soc. Societa (Italy)

Sp. z.o.o. Spólka z ograniczona odpowiedzialnoscia (Poland)

Ste. Societe (France, Belgium, Luxembourg, Switzerland)

Ste. Cve. Societe Cooperative (Belgium)

T
THB Thai baht
TND Tunisian dinar

TRL Turkish lira
TWD Taiwan dollar (new)

U

U.A. Uitgesloten Aansporakeiijkheid (Netherlands)

u.p.a. utan personligt ansvar (Sweden)

V

V.O.f. Vennootschap onder firma (Netherlands)

VAG Verein der Arbeitgeber (Austria, Germany)

VEB Venezuelan bolivar

VERTR Vertriebs (Austria, Germany)

VND Vietnamese dong

VVAG Versicherungsverein auf Gegenseitigkeit (Austria, Germany)

W–Z

WA Wettelika Aansprakalikhaed (Netherlands)

WLL With Limited Liability (Bahrain, Kuwait, Qatar, Saudi Arabia)

YK Yugen Kaisha (Japan)

ZAO Zakrytoe Aktsionernoe Obshchestve (Russia)

ZAR South African rand

ZMK Zambian kwacha

ZWD Zimbabwean dollar

Actia Group S.A.

BP 74215, 25 Chemin de Pouvourville
Toulouse, F-31432 Cedex 04
France
Telephone: (33 05 61) 17 61 98
Fax: (33 05 61) 55 42 31
Web site: http://www.actiagroup.com

Public Company
Incorporated: 1986
Employees: 2,425
Sales: EUR 261.27 million ($326 million) (2008)
Stock Exchanges: Euronext Paris
Ticker Symbol: ATI
NAICS: 334515 Instrument Manufacturing for Measuring and Testing, Electricity and Electrical Signals; 334290 Other Communication Equipment Manufacturing; 334419 Other Electronic Component Manufacturing; 334519 Other Measuring and Controlling Device Manufacturing

■ ■ ■

Actia S.A. is a leading developer of specialized electronic equipment for the automotive and telecommunications markets. The company's largest division is its Automotive Division, which focuses on two main product groups: diagnostic systems; inspection systems; and onboard electronics. The group's diagnostic systems include specialized equipment designed to assist mechanics in the diagnosis and repair of automobiles. The company produces both brand-specific systems for Citroën, Peugeot, Renault, Mercedes, Fiat, BMW, and others, as well as the multiple-make Multi-Diag system. Through Actia Muller, the group produces a line of vehicle inspection products for light and heavy trucks and utility vans, including lifts, tire removal systems, and tire balancing systems. Onboard electronics is another major product category for the group, which focuses on developing a range of electronics systems, including dashboard systems; audio and video systems; measurement and control systems for trucks, buses, farm, and construction vehicles; and trains, boats, and airplanes produced in small and medium production runs. Altogether, Actia's Automotive Division generates more than 83 percent of the group's revenues, which topped EUR 261 million (US$ 326 million) in 2008. Actia's Telecommunications Division develops its own range of niche products for the telecommunications and broadcast industries, including onboard systems for aviation, military, and other uses. Founded in 1986, Actia has developed an international presence with subsidiaries in Brazil, Mexico, Spain, the Czech Republic, the Netherlands, the United Kingdom, the United States, and Tunisia. Exports account for more than 50 percent of the group's business. Actia is listed on the Euronext Paris stock exchange and is led by cofounders and majority shareholders Louis Pech and Pierre Calmels.

AUTOMOTIVE ELECTRONICS PIONEER IN 1978

Actia stemmed from the collaboration between two French companies, automotive giant Renault and electronics group Bendix, to develop early onboard electronic systems for automobiles and other vehicles. In 1978, the two companies created a joint venture, called

Renix SA. Renault remained the majority partner in the venture, with a 51 percent stake.

In 1980, Renix created a new Special Products Division. The new division specifically targeted development of onboard electronics for light trucks and similar vehicles, including buses and vans, developed in small- and medium-sized production runs. The incorporation of onboard electronics promised a variety of new functions and amenities, such as providing measurements of distance traveled, average speeds, fuel consumption, and later onboard communications and entertainment systems. The Special Products Division worked with its clients to design custom-built electronics systems.

The introduction of electronics in automobiles and other vehicles also led to the need to develop new diagnostic tools for their repair and maintenance. Working with Renault, the Special Products Division became one of the first to develop a specialized diagnostic tool, the XR25.

These operations, however, remained only a tiny sideline for both Renault and Bendix into the mid-1980s. Renault was the first to exit the business, selling its share of Renix to Bendix in 1985. The following year, however, Bendix itself was acquired by the U.S. company Allied Signal as that company pursued its European expansion. Allied Signal quickly restructured the Bendix group, disposing of a number of noncore business, including Renix's Special Products Division.

CREATING A NICHE
ELECTRONICS PLAYER IN 1986

Allied Signal's announcement of its intention to sell off the Special Products Division attracted the attention of two Toulouse-based entrepreneurs, Louis Pech and Pierre Calmels. Pech had launched his career in the late

1950s, after completing his business degree at Toulouse's École Supérieure de Commerce. Toulouse by then had become a major center for France's aviation and aeronautics industries, as well as the burgeoning high-technology sector. In 1960, Pech joined Ateliers Secma, a prominent developer of aircraft components that later became part of the Liebherr Group.

Pech rose quickly in Secma, and by 1961 he had become part of the team founding a new subsidiary, Microturbo. The new operation began developing starters and other jet engine system components. In 1963, Pech became Microturbo's commercial director, before moving up to deputy CEO. Pech remained with Microturbo through to the end of the 1980s.

By then, Pech had begun to develop plans to found his own company. Joining him was Calmels, who had begun working with Pech at Microturbo in 1968. Pech and Calmels developed a strong friendship, while Calmels advanced through Microturbo's ranks, becoming its technical director and ultimately its CEO. In the mid-1980s, however, both men decided to launch their own business.

Secma and its Microturbo subsidiary acquired publicly listed Labinal. As part of that purchase, both Pech and Calmels received stock in Labinal. In 1986, Pech and Calmels decided to sell their Labinal shares and use the proceeds to buy the Special Products Division from Allied Signal. The partners then named the company Actia.

At first, Actia focused on design and engineering of electronic automotive components. By 1988, the company had added its own manufacturing operations, buying another Toulouse-based company, Alcyon, that year. As one of the early players in the sector, Actia found itself in a prime position to take advantage of the surge in the use of onboard electronics in the automotive sector.

EXPANSION AND
DIVERSIFICATION IN THE 1990S

Through the second half of the 1980s, both Pech and Calmels remained at their positions with Microturbo. Actia's growth into the end of the decade permitted both to leave Microturbo and devote themselves full time to building the company. Pech left Microturbo first, in 1989, and immediately led Actia into telecommunications, a new high-growth sector. This was accomplished that same year by the acquisition of Sodielec, a producer of specialized electronic equipment for the telecommunications and broadcasting industries. Calmels joined the company full time in 1990.

Actia's move into telecommunications equipment came also as a means of strengthening its core automo-

KEY DATES

1978: Renault and Bendix form Renix to supply electronic components and systems for the automotive market.

1980: Renix creates a Special Products Division specialized in developing onboard electronic systems.

1986: Louis Pech and Pierre Calmels acquire the Special Products Division, which becomes Actia SA.

1989: The company acquires telecommunications supplier Sodielec and becomes Actielec.

1994: Actielec establishes subsidiaries in the United States and the United Kingdom.

2000: As part of an acquisition drive, Actielec merges with publicly listed Mors and becomes Actielec Technologies.

2003: Actielec acquires Muller Bern, a producer of vehicle inspection tools and systems.

2008: Actielec renames itself as Actia and establishes a subsidiary in Tunisia.

tive business. As Pech explained to *Les Echos:* "Our main activity remains automobile electronics, but as [the onboard mobile equipment] needs to communicate, we diversified into telecommunications in order to master that technology." Following the purchase of Sodielec, the company changed its name, becoming Actielec in 1989. Actia retained the name of the company's main automotive subsidiary.

Actielec entered a major expansion period, achieving annual growth rates of 20 percent and more. Part of this growth came from the company's strong commitment to research and development. At the same time, the company launched a long series of acquisitions, primarily small companies. These acquisitions, including the French Aixia, acquired in 1990, provided the company with an expanded technological base. At the same time, the company's acquisition drive took on an international form, enabling the company to accompany its major clients as they pursued their own international development strategies in the 1990s.

Actielec's first international extension came in 1991 with the acquisition of Tekne, based in the United Kingdom. The following year, the group added operations in Spain, strengthening its telecommunications division with the acquisition of Videobus there. The company also added businesses in Mexico, the Czech

Republic, and Germany that year. These purchases were followed by the creation of a number of dedicated foreign subsidiaries, including in the United States and the United Kingdom, in 1994.

GROWTH INTO THE TURN OF THE CENTURY

Actielec continued to develop its automotive diagnostic equipment, which grew into a major part of the company's operations. In 1989, for example, the company began working with Peugeot and Citroën, creating specialized diagnostic equipment for each brand. This resulted in the launch of the TEP92 and ELIT diagnostic systems for Peugeot and Citroën, respectively, in 1989. Into the next decade, the group began working with many of the major European automotive groups.

Actielec continued developing its technologies to meet the increasing complexity of automotive electronics systems in the late 1990s. This led the company to launch its next generation of diagnostic systems in 1998, including the Diag2000 for Peugeot, the Lexia for Citroën, and the NXR for Renault. While this equipment was used by the automaker's own dealer and repair networks, Actielec also targeted a presence on the factory floor. This led the company to develop its first diagnostic tools for the automotive production line as well.

At the same time, the company continued its strategy of acquisitions and foreign expansion. In the mid-1990s, the company completed a number of new French acquisitions, including Aton and Dateno in 1996, Berenisce in 1997, and Autotech and Techno in 1998. The company also added a dedicated Brazilian subsidiary in 1997, followed by subsidiaries in Italy and the Netherlands in 2000.

GOING PUBLIC IN 2000

Actielec achieved a major new milestone in 2000 when it agreed to merge with the publicly listed Mors Group. That company stemmed from a business founded in 1851, and, under brothers Louis and Emile Mors, became one of France's pioneering automakers. By 1906, Mors had begun a collaboration with André Citroën, who took over as head of the company while continuing to build what was to become one of France's largest automotive groups. By 1925, Mors had become part of Citroën, becoming a producer of automobile components. Mors later emerged as a public company focused on developing electronic components and systems for automotive applications.

Following the acquisition of Mors, Actielec changed its name to Actielec Technologies, with a listing on the Euronext Paris Stock Exchange. While the company maintained its telecommunications division, its focus turned more strongly toward its fast-growing automotive division.

The group's range of diagnostic equipment grew in 2001 with the development of a new high-performance computer, the Diag3G. The new computer was adopted by Fiat and DaimlerChrysler for their repair networks, and it was incorporated into each company's diagnostic systems. The following year, Actielec launched another successful product, the PassThru XS interface. The new product found clients in a wide range of major automakers, including Audi, BMW, Chrysler, Ford, General Motors, Honda, Jaguar, Mercedes-Benz, Mitsubishi, Porsche, Saab, Toyota, Volkswagen, and Volvo. The company also emerged as a leading player in the development of onboard electronics systems.

FOCUS ON THE AUTOMOTIVE MARKET IN THE NEW CENTURY

Actielec made its first move into Asia during the first decade of the 21st century, establishing a subsidiary in India in 2002. The following year, the group entered China as well, setting up operations in Shanghai. In 2004, the group set up a new subsidiary in Sweden, to develop its operations for the Nordic markets. Also that year, the company carried out a restructuring of its Telecommunications Division, merging all of those operations into the main Sodielec subsidiary. The group's international expansion continued into the end of the decade. In 2008, for example, the company launched a new production subsidiary in Tunisia.

However the company's Automotive Division, which accounted for more than 83 percent of its revenues at the end of the decade, remained the company's primary focus. In 2003, Actielec completed a new extension of that division with the acquisition of the Muller Bern Group, based in France. That company specialized in developing diagnostic and other tools and equipment for the vehicle inspection sector.

At the same time, Actielec prepared to roll out its first multi-make diagnostic system, launched as Multi-Diag in 2003. The Multi-Diag range targeted independent mechanics and the growing number of quick-service chains. The Multi-Diag provided these channels with a diagnostic tool capable of handling the wide variety of automotive makes and their electronic systems. The company also continued to develop specialized diagnostic equipment, such as the PP2000 diagnostic platform for Peugeot's Planet System diagnostic system, which rolled out in 2003. The following year, the company debuted its new generation Lexia3 system for Citroën.

With its Actia Automotive Division accounting for the vast majority of its revenues, the parent company decided to adopt once again the name Actia in 2008. The group's telecommunications subsidiary then took on the name Actia Sodielec. Both Pech and Calmels remained at the head of the company they had founded, and, through a shareholders' pact, continued to own a majority of the group. Actia had successfully established itself as one of the automotive sector's leading specialty electronics players, with sales of more than EUR 260 million ($326 million).

M. L. Cohen

PRINCIPAL SUBSIDIARIES

Actia Aixia; Actia Automotive; Actia de Mexico; Actia do Brasil; Actia Inc. (U.S.A.); Actia Muller; Actia NL (Netherlands); Actia Polska; Actia Sodielec SA; Actia UK; Actia Videobus (Spain); Atal (Czech Republic); Aton Systèmes; CIPI Tunisie.

PRINCIPAL DIVISIONS

Automotive; Telecommunications.

PRINCIPAL OPERATING UNITS

Automotive France; Automotive Europe; Automotive World; Telecommunications.

PRINCIPAL COMPETITORS

Rohde and Schwarz GmbH and Company KG; Continental; Stoneridge; RCS Communication Test Systems Ltd.; Schlumberger plc; ABB S.A.

FURTHER READING

"Actia Sets Sights on Tata's World Truck," *India Business Insight,* November 21, 2005.

"Actia Takes Over ATI, Actielec Floats," *Les Echos,* July 17, 2000, p. 22.

"Actielec Concrétise Sa Percée Asiatique," *MPS,* June 21, 2002.

"Actielec: L'Heure est au Recentrage sur Actia," *MPS,* March 26, 2004.

Dessort, Frédéric, "Face à la Crise, Actia Accentue Sa Diversification," *Mid e-News,* February 16, 2009.

"EBIM to Be Acquired by Actielec Technologies," *Les Echos,* March 12, 2001, p. 37.

Marcaillou, Laurent, "Louis Pech, un Bâtisseur Humaniste," *Les Echos,* January 29, 2003, p. 24.

"Mors Ready to Take Actielec," *Revue Hebdomadaire de l'Industrie Electrique & Electronique,* December 9, 1999, p. 8.

"Perspectives Prometteuses pour le Groupe Actielec Technologies," *MPS,* October 19, 2001.

Alexon Group PLC

40-48 Guildford Street
Luton, Bedfordshire LU1 2PB
United Kingdom
Telephone: (44 01582) 723131
Fax: (44 01582) 724158
Web site: http://www.alexon.co.uk

Public Company
Incorporated: 1904 as A. Steinberg & Co.
Employees: 5,751
Sales: £250.29 million ($359.1 million) (2008)
Stock Exchanges: London
Ticker Symbol: AXL
NAICS: 448120 Women's Clothing Stores; 315232 Women's and Girls' Cut and Sew Blouse and Shirt Manufacturing; 315233 Women's and Girls' Cut and Sew Dress Manufacturing

■ ■ ■

Alexon Group PLC is one of the pioneering names in the British women's clothing industry. The Bedfordshire, England-based group remains a prominent retailer and manufacturer of women's fashions. The company's operations focus primarily on branded concessions in third-party department stores and retail clothing stores. Alexon's retail business includes concessions in 860 outlets in the United Kingdom, as well as 143 concessions in continental Europe. The company also operates 80 Alexon retail stores directly. Alexon's brand family includes Alex & Co., Eastex, Dash, Ann Harvey, Kaliko, and Minuet Petite. Each brand targets a specific segment of the women's clothing market. Alex & Co. targets the career women's market, while Ann Harvey and Dash feature styles for the plus-size segment. Eastex adds fashions for older women, while Kaliko targets women in the 25- to 35-year-old segment. The company's youngest brand is Minuet, which features designs for smaller women.

Alexon has been restructuring its operations in the face of long-term difficulties in the British retail clothing sector. The company sold of its money-losing men's clothing subsidiary, Bay Trading, in April 2009. Alexon also operates a manufacturing division, MEAD. Alexon Group is listed on the London Stock Exchange and is led by CEO Jane McNally. The company posted revenues of £250.29 million ($359.1 million) in 2008.

PIONEERING WOMEN'S CLOTHING IN THE UNITED KINGDOM

In the late 19th century, the women's clothing market in England, specifically higher-end, fine tailored coats, was largely dominated by German imports. However, this situation began to change with the arrival of a number of Russian immigrants in the 1870s. Among them was Morris Cohen, who immigrated to England in 1877. Cohen had a background in tailoring for women, but his interest turned to marketing clothing designs. In 1880 Cohen began building a network of tailors to produce his designs, and wholesalers to introduce the finished garments into British shops.

Cohen's efforts paid off, and over the next decade he had built his own manufacturing facility, in Spi-

KEY DATES

1904: Alexander Steinberg sets up company producing women's coats in London.

1929: The company changes its name to Steinberg & Sons; the Alexon brand name is created.

1939: The company opens its first factory outside of London.

1948: Steinberg & Sons goes public on the London Stock Exchange.

1952: Steinberg & Sons acquires the girls' and infants' clothing division of George Williams & Co.

1967: The company begins developing the "shop within a shop" retail format.

1982: The company acquires 75 percent stake in Marks and Spencer supplier Claremount Garments.

1986: The company is renamed Alexon PLC.

1988: Alexon acquires Ellis & Goldstein, including its Eastex and Dash clothing brands.

1991: Alexon spins off Claremount as a separate publicly listed company.

1997: Alexon enters shoe retail, acquiring half of the Dolcis retail chain.

1999: Alexon enters men's clothing, buying Style Holdings; acquires youth fashions company Bay Trading.

2004: Alexon ends manufacturing in the United Kingdom, closing its last factory, in Hawthorne, South Wales.

2006: Alexon sells off money-losing Dolcis chain.

2009: Alexon places Bay Trading in liquidation.

talfields in the East End area of London. By the dawn of the 20th century, Cohen had emerged as a leading figure in the British clothing market. Cohen then began building the foundation for the emergence of a true British textile industry. Toward this end, he bought a number of properties in London's East End, which were then converted into textile workshops. These were rented out to a number of tailors, especially those focusing on women's clothing. From these workshops grew many of the largest names in the British clothing manufacturing industry in the 20th century.

Among them was Alexander Steinberg, who had immigrated to the United Kingdom to escape the Russian pogroms in 1898. Steinberg and his wife set up their business in one of Cohen's East End workshops.

By 1904 Steinberg had established his own company, A. Steinberg & Co., in London's Bow Lane, and began producing his own women's coat designs. Steinberg then began expanding his clothing range, adding women's suits and skirts, among other women's clothing items. Steinberg also later developed his own clothing brand, Dellbury Model.

TRANSFORMING THE BRITISH CLOTHING INDUSTRY

Steinberg brought his three sons, Joseph, Jack, and Philip (who later changed his last name to Stanbury) into the business, and in 1929 the company changed its name to Steinberg & Sons. The name change also led to the creation of a new clothing brand, Alexon, combining Steinberg's first name with "son." The Steinberg family then set out to build the company into one of the leaders in England's fast-growing textile sector. Through the 1930s, the company expanded its manufacturing operations, moving its headquarters to Aldersgate and opening three London-based factories with a total production surface of some 9,500 square feet.

The company also successfully built its Alexon and Dellbury Model brands into major national brands. Part of this success came through the company's pioneering introduction of what it called "petite sizing" for shorter women. The company then adopted the slogan "Alexon Size Right" for its popular brand.

The development of the Alexon brand name also played a role in transforming the British clothing industry. Previously, the bulk of British clothing manufacturing was distributed through a network of wholesalers. The strength of the Alexon brand, however, enabled the company to supply directly to retailers, and Steinberg grew into a major supplier to a number of the United Kingdom's leading clothing retailers, including Marks and Spencer Group p.l.c. (M&S) and Selfridges. Steinberg also played a role in building the growing reputation of the British textile industry on an international level. Through the end of the 1930s and into the 1940s, Steinberg successfully developed its own export operation.

Supporting this growth was the decision to add larger production facilities. For this, the company chose South Wales, which provided a number of advantages over the London area, including lower wages. In 1939 the company opened its first factory outside of London, in Treforest Trading Estate, Pontypridd, South Wales. That facility provided an addition 17,000 square feet of production space for the company.

POSTWAR EXPANSION

Like most of England's manufacturing sector, Steinberg's growth slowed during the years of World War II. Nevertheless, the Steinberg family, then led by Joseph Steinberg, played a major role in aiding the British utility manufacturing scheme to maintain the country's clothing supply for the duration. Steinberg also continued to build the reputation of its core Alexon and Dellbury Model brands. By the end of the 1940s, these brands had grown into two of the United Kingdom's most prominent women's clothing brands.

Steinberg & Sons took steps to grow even more strongly in the postwar era. Toward this end, the company incorporated as a limited liability company, Steinberg & Sons Ltd., in 1947. The following year, the company went public, listing on the London Stock Exchange. Alexander Steinberg remained the company's chairman, while his three sons took over the management of the family business.

By the late 1940s, the reconstruction process in the United Kingdom was well under way. The coming decades promised a new era of economic prosperity, not only in the United Kingdom, but across continental Europe and in North American markets as well. The Steinbergs correctly recognized opportunities for expansion in the postwar era.

In order to meet the growing demand for its clothing brands, the company launched construction of a new and larger factory in Pontypridd in 1948. The new factory, located in the village of Hawthorne, expanded the company's production capacity to more than 80,000 square feet. The opening of the new factory also led the company to nearly double its workforce. Production there was launched in 1950. Over the following years, the Hawthorne factory grew into one of the largest and most modern clothing factories in the United Kingdom, with more than 1,000 employees.

MOVING BEYOND WOMEN'S WEAR

Both of the company's brands grew strongly through the 1950s. The company's Dellbury Model brand became synonymous with high-quality British wool-based clothing. The Alexon Size Right brand also continued to reinforce the British textile industry's international reputation for quality products. Export sales boomed during the 1950s, despite the institution of tariffs and other trade barriers by a number of countries during this period. In order to meet the growing international demand for its products, the company acquired a new factory location on Southgate Road in London in 1951.

For most of its first half-century, Steinberg & Sons had focused on its manufacturing operations, building up a strong production arm for its range of women's outwear, and particularly coats, skirts, and suits. During the 1950s, the company recognized the need to develop a stronger marketing and distribution wing. This led the company to open its first retail showroom on London's Conduit Street in 1952. At the same time, the company updated its core clothing brands, which became known more simply as Alexon and Dellbury.

At the same time, the company made its first move beyond its core women's wear market. In 1952 Steinberg & Sons acquired the girls' and infants' clothing division of George Williams & Co. The new clothing lines were then rebranded under the Alexon and Dellbury names in 1953. Steinberg & Sons also expanded its foreign sales operations, opening a dedicated marketing subsidiary in the United States that year. These efforts helped the company achieve strong profit growth into the middle of the decade.

By 1955 Steinberg & Sons employed more than 2,000 people and had become one of England's leading clothing manufacturers. The company enjoyed particularly strong sales in the United Kingdom, which in turn led to a new extension of the group's South Wales production facility in 1956. On the other hand, the company's U.S. sales effort struggled to reach profitability, forcing the company to liquidate its U.S. subsidiary in 1957. Steinberg & Sons did not abandon that market, however; a new marketing unit was established in the United States in 1958.

APPETITE FOR ACQUISITIONS

Steinberg & Sons continued to seek growth in the United Kingdom. In 1957, for example, the company acquired a major stake in and management control of another clothing manufacturer, West Auckland Clothing Company. The purchase not only boosted the group's total production capacity but also enabled it to expand beyond its traditional focus on wool outerwear.

The company's appetite for acquisitions began to grow strongly at the end of the 1950s. In 1959, for example, the company completed a new purchase, of Tevaclo Ltd. This company then took over the group's youth and children's outerwear division. In 1960, Steinberg & Sons targeted N. Brenner Ltd., which produced its own women's clothing line under the Norman Hartnell Ready-to-Wear brand.

These acquisitions came as part of the company's effort to prepare itself for the entry of the United Kingdom into the European Common Market. Steinberg & Sons expected to profit from the reputation for high quality enjoyed by the British textile industry on the European continent. Steinberg continued to seek new acquisition opportunities. This led the company to acquire a 50 percent stake, as well as full management control, of Horrockses Fashions Ltd. in 1960.

In 1961, the company completed two new acquisitions, of Sol Levy Ltd., and of Freya Properties Ltd. These were followed by the purchase of The Essell Group of Companies, a manufacturer of handbags under the Essell, Pexella, and Chamelle brands. By the end of that year, Steinberg & Sons posted profits of more than £300,000, triple its profits of just five years before.

BECOMING ALEXON

By the middle of the 1960s, Steinberg & Sons had grown into one of the largest and most respected clothing manufacturers in the United Kingdom. The company then turned its attention more firmly to the retail front, and in 1967 the company began developing its "shop within a shop" retail concept. For this, the company placed in-store boutiques staffed with its own employees and featuring its brands in third-party retailers and department stores. Through the 1970s the company built up a network of more than 160 "shop within a shop" boutiques. At the same time, the group boosted its relationship with retailers, placing its brands in more than 2,000 clothing stores by the late 1970s. Meanwhile, the company also developed a division supplying unbranded garments to major retailers, and especially M&S. By the late 1970s, the company had also made its first tentative moves directly into the retail market, opening its first two Alexon stores.

Steinberg & Sons supported this growth by investing in distribution technology. Toward this end, in the mid-1970s the company built one of the largest computer-driven distribution facilities in the United Kingdom, in Milton Keynes. The company also invested in its manufacturing base, adding a new factory in Shannon, in the Republic of Ireland. That facility produced the company's Butte knitwear line, which became one of the leading knitwear producers in Europe. Leading the company by then was Anthony Stanbury, the third generation of the Steinberg family.

Control of the company was to pass from the Steinberg family's hands, however. In 1982 Steinberg acquired a 75 percent stake in another major M&S supplier, Claremount Garments. In 1983 Steinberg moved to acquire the remainder of Claremount, in a stock swap agreement that placed three of Claremount's executives on Steinberg's board as major shareholders. The Claremount executives, who originally continued to lead the

company's M&S contracting operations, soon took over the direction of the branded clothing lines. By 1986 the Steinberg family had exited the company, which was then renamed Alexon PLC.

Alexon completed several major acquisitions in the late 1980s, adding another prominent M&S supplier, Glasgow-based D&H Cohen, in 1987. The following year, the group purchased Ellis & Goldstein, which had started out in the same East End workshops as Steinberg at the beginning of the century, adding its Eastex and Dash clothing brands. While Eastex targeted the older women's market, the Dash brand targeted the high-volume, lower-priced categories. This meant, however, that Alexon had begun to emerge as a competitor for M&S. In order to avert this conflict, the company decided to demerge its contract manufacturing operation, spinning off Claremount as a separate public company in 1991.

REBOUNDING FROM DIFFICULTIES

Alexon entered a difficult period during the 1990s. The company was hit hard by the disastrous economy at the beginning of the decade. At the same time, the group's brands struggled to keep up with fast-changing trends in the clothing market. This period witnessed the rise of a growing number of highly international and very modern designer brands, which placed Alexon's own relatively traditional styles under increasing pressure.

Alexon attempted to respond by introducing a number of new brands, including Ann Harvey, for plus-size women, in 1993, and Kaliko, for younger women, in 1994. The company continued to struggle, and nearly went bankrupt by the middle of the decade. In 1995, however, Alexon found new financing, and a new chief executive officer, John Osborn, formerly head of the British Shoe Corporation. As Osborn described the company to the *Daily Mail*, Alexon was "near as dammit dead."

Osborn pushed through a revamping of most of the group's brands, placing an emphasis on youthful, chic fashions to draw back customers. The effort appeared to pay off, as the company's sales and profits grew again in the second half of the decade.

Alexon then targeted a new series of acquisitions to drive its growth into the next century. In 1997 the company ventured into shoe store operations, buying half of the money-losing Dolcis chain of stores from the British Shoe Corporation. The company then launched a major investment program, including spending £24 million to acquire full control of Dolcis in 1999, seeking to turn around its new division. Despite its efforts, however, Alexon was finally forced to abandon the shoe sector, selling the Dolcis chain for just £3 million in 2006.

SHARPENED FOCUS FOR THE 21ST CENTURY

In the meantime, Alexon struggled with another attempt to expand its business. In 1999 the company ventured into the men's retail clothing sector for the first time in its history, paying nearly £22 million to buy Style Holdings, including its 56-strong chain of Envy men's clothing stores, as well as a number of branded in-store concessions. Soon after that acquisition, Alexon acquired another company, Bay Trading, which focused on the youth fashions sector.

The move into these new markets quickly proved disappointing, as both Style Holdings and Bay Trading failed to become profitable in the new century. In 2008 the company appointed a new CEO, Jane McNally, to help restore the group's profit growth. Among McNally's first moves was to sell off Style Holdings to an investment group for just £1. By April 2009, Alexon pulled the plug on Bay Trading as well, placing that company in liquidation. By then, too, the company had been forced to shut down the last of its British manufacturing operations, ending production at the Hawthorne factory in 2004.

Alexon's core women's clothing brands continued to perform well, despite the intensely difficult trading conditions at the end of the decade. The company had successfully launched two new brands, Minuet Petite, a clothing line designed for smaller women shorter than five feet, four inches, introduced in 1999, and Alex & Co., replacing the Alexon brand, in 2000. The company's older brands, including Ann Harvey, Kaliko, Eastex, and Dash, continued to grow. As part of the group's new strategy under McNally, the company promised to reinvigorate its clothing and retail brands. As one of the oldest and best-known clothing names in the United Kingdom, Alexon looked for further growth opportunities in the future.

M. L. Cohen

PRINCIPAL SUBSIDIARIES

Alexon International Ltd.

PRINCIPAL DIVISIONS

Alexon Brands.

PRINCIPAL OPERATING UNITS

Alex & Co.; Eastex; Dash; Ann Harvey; Kaliko; Minuet; MEAD Manufacturing.

PRINCIPAL COMPETITORS

NEXT PLC; Arcadia Group Ltd.; Urban Outfitters U.K. Ltd.; Burberry Group PLC; Bhs Ltd.; New Look Retailers Ltd.; Lewis Trust Group Ltd.; Mothercare PLC.

FURTHER READING

"Alexon Group Puts Bay Trading Under Administration," *just-style.com*, April 26, 2009.

"Alexon Names Peacock's McNally as Next CEO," *just-style. com*, April 14, 2008.

"Alexon Shows a Leaner Style," *Times* (London), March 31, 1992, p. 20.

"Alexon to Sell Dolcis Chain," *just-style.com*, July 3, 2006.

Benoit, Bertrand, "Alexon Fashions New Style as It Steps into Dolcis," *Financial Times*, August 27, 1999, p. 19.

Braithwaite, Tom, "New Leaner and Fitter Look May Suit Alexon," *Financial Times*, April 3, 2007, p. 22.

———, "Slimmer Alexon Makes Progress," *Financial Times*, April 1, 2008, p. 22.

"Economy Sends Alexon Like-for-Like Down 12%," *just-style. com*, June 17, 2009.

Elder, Bryce, "Alexon Soars on Bay Trading Move," *Financial Times*, April 25, 2009, p. 22.

Gabb, Annabella, "Making It with M&S," *Management Today*, February 1992, p. 64.

Goff, Sharlene, "Alexon Finds Small Is Beautiful at Minuet," *Financial Times*, March 30, 2004.

Lemer, Jeremy, "Alexon Cuts Bay," *Financial Times*, April 25, 2009, p. 14.

Lockwood, Lisa, "Alexon Broadens Its Holdings," *WWD*, August 3, 1998, p. 14.

Skeel, Shirley, "New-Look Alexon Puts on the Style at £10m," *Daily Mail* (London), March 18, 1997, p. 57.

Urquhart, Lisa, "Focus on Young Women's Brands Bolsters Alexon," *Financial Times*, January 8, 2002, p. 23.

Altmeyer Home Stores Inc.

———————— ■ ————————

6515 Route 22
Delmont, Pennsylvania 15626-2402
U.S.A.
Telephone: (724) 468-3434
Toll Free: (800) 394-6628
Fax: (724) 468-3233
Web site: http://www.altmeyers.com

Private Company
Incorporated: 1941
Employees: 200
Sales: $61 million (2008 est.)
NAICS: 442299 All Other Home Furnishings Stores

■ ■ ■

Altmeyer Homes Stores Inc. is a family-owned and operated chain of 12 home furnishing stores in western Pennsylvania. The company also sells its wares online through Altmeyer's BedBathHome.com. Although the retail stores are much smaller than such competitors as Bed Bath & Beyond, generally in the 10,000-square-foot range as opposed to the 35,000-square-foot footprint of its rivals, the chain is a major player in its market, able to advertise and compete on price. Altmeyer's also prides itself on knowing its customers, making the best use of its limited space, and playing to its strengths. The company seeks to stock a product selection that satisfies customer needs without overwhelming them (and the shelves) with an excess of choice. The stores also do not have to devote as much space to

presenting ensembles, relying instead on sales staff to help customers coordinate their bedding.

Product categories include bath linens and such accessories as rugs, safety mats, shower hooks and liners, soaps and sponges, and toilet seats; curtains and drapes, as well as mini blinds and window shades; and tablecloths and linens. Home accent products include toss pillows, chair pads, slipcovers, wall tapestries, frames, floor and buffet lamps, as well as side tables, footstools, and bookshelves. Altmeyer's also carries area rugs, accent rugs, and door mats; bedding and memory foam mattresses and pillows; doilies and scarves; table protection products; organizer and storage products; outdoor patio covers; pet beds; and women's spa and sleepwear apparel. The company supplies store and Internet sales from its 32,000-square-foot headquarters and distribution center in Delmont, Pennsylvania, east of Pittsburgh in Westmoreland County. The company is owned by the Altmeyer family, and Rod Altmeyer, Sr., the son of the founder, serves as president. His children are also involved in the running of the business.

BASEMENT ORIGINS

The Altmeyer's chain was founded by George Altmeyer in 1941 in New Kensington, Pennsylvania, a Pittsburgh suburb. His was a success story once typical in the United States, the result of overcoming limitations through hard work. Born of modest circumstances and lacking a high school education, Altmeyer worked his way up in the retail industry and saved his money to one day start a company and fulfill a dream of owning his own business. He eventually became advertising and display manager for ready-to-wear at Hart's Department Store in New Kensington and supplemented his $50 a week salary by moonlighting with other area stores, writing ads and sometimes trimming show windows. By the time he was 37 years old, Altmeyer, despite supporting a wife and children, was able to save $4,000. With that stake he opened a small store in a New Kensington basement location, measuring 20 feet by 40 feet, far from the main business district in 1941.

Rather than open a ready-to-wear shop, a field he knew well, he decided to specialize in soft goods for the home rather than compete against his former employer, selling moderately priced table linens, bedding, curtains and draperies, and towels. However, it was not the best time to launch a soft goods business; by the end of the year the United States had entered World War II and the country was put on a war economy. All manner of materials were commandeered for military use, making it difficult to supply the stores, and purchasing home furnishings was hardly a priority for area families at the time. Nevertheless, Altmeyer, always known as the hardest worker in town, persevered, working in the store day and night to keep the business afloat.

MOVING TO THE SHOPPING DISTRICT

Altmeyer survived the war years, and in 1948 he was able to graduate from his basement shop to a larger corner space on Fourth Avenue, New Kensington's main shopping street. As the economy boomed during the postwar years, so did the population: returning servicemen married and started families at a record rate, leading to the development of suburbs and a surge in demand for the kind of soft goods for the home that Altmeyer's carried. Altmeyer followed his customers, and by the early 1950s was operating several small stores in the Pittsburgh area.

In 1951 Altmeyer was joined in the business by his son, Rod Altmeyer, Sr. The younger Altmeyer received the education his father did not, earning a degree in journalism from Ohio State University, in keeping with his desire not to spend his life in retail working in the

family business. After graduation, he enlisted in the army as a way to become part of the armed forces radio division in Korea. After completing his service, Rod Altmeyer returned home and went to work for an area radio and television station. Although he enjoyed the work, he found himself drawn to the family business and joined his father to learn all aspects of the operation.

The small Altmeyer's chain was enjoying some success in the early 1950s, due in part to being the only store of its kind in the market. George Altmeyer's old employer, Hart's Department Store, then decided to get involved in home furnishings. Having refrained from competing against Hart's in ready-to-wear, Altmeyer felt somewhat betrayed when Hart's entered home furnishings, and the two retail operations became bitter enemies in the Pittsburgh market in what was something of a David and Goliath battle. On the one hand was the well-entrenched Hart's chain that would grow to 15 stores in eight western Pennsylvania counties, and on the other was the Altmeyer family with their string of small shops. Despite the difference in size, and perhaps because of it, Altmeyer's was able to overcome the advantages held by its larger rival. While Altmeyer's lacked the general recognition of Hart's, its customers were well aware of all it had to offer.

FLAGSHIP STORE OPENS

Although half the size of a typical department store home furnishings section, Altmeyer's knew its customers and stocked accordingly. Rod Altmeyer in a 1990 interview with *HFD* provided an example of the store's approach: "If a customer wants a comforter and there are 200 comforters, she's going to buy one. If there are comforters and they're presented right, the customer is still going to buy one. We buy what we think is important." Altmeyer's opened a flagship store in 1960 that was 7,500 square feet in size, but generally the new Altmeyer stores were about 5,000 square feet in size. In the 1980s the company would try expanding some of the stores, but would find it difficult to make use of the extra space.

After George Altmeyer died around 1970 his son took over the business. Rod Altmeyer's wife, Judy, also played a major role in the business. She had been a secretary when they married, but soon asked to join the family business. She eventually became secretary-treasurer of the company and oversaw the personnel side of the business. Together they carried on what George Altmeyer began. While Altmeyer's continued to thrive, its chief rival, Hart's, began to falter. The chain that had been started in New Kensington by former street peddler and Russian immigrant Meyer Hart in 1910 to sell

```
┌─────────────────────────────────────────┐
│                                           │
│            KEY DATES                      │
│              ───■───                      │
│                                           │
│   1941:  George Altmeyer opens home       │
│          furnishings store in New         │
│          Kensington, Pennsylvania,        │
│          basement.                        │
│   1948:  Altmeyer's moves to larger       │
│          store.                           │
│   1951:  Rod Altmeyer, Sr., joins his     │
│          father in the business.          │
│   1960:  New flagship store opens.        │
│   1988:  Altmeyer's assumes four leases   │
│          of chief rival.                  │
│   1991:  Fire destroys company            │
│          headquarters.                    │
│   2006:  Judy Altmeyer dies.              │
│                                           │
└─────────────────────────────────────────┘
```

buttons and dry goods, and later expanded by his son Edwin who took the chain to shopping centers in the 1960s, was sold to its comptroller in 1982 and soon fell victim to a slump in the local economy. By 1987 the chain was in serious trouble. The New Kensington flagship store closed, followed by the shuttering of three other units. The leases of four other Hart's store were turned over to Altmeyer's in 1988 as the department store chain lapsed into bankruptcy and was liquidated. "My dad had been dead almost 20 years by then," Rod Altmeyer told *HFD*, "but he would have been happy to have seen that. It takes a long time to get that kind of satisfaction—sometimes you never get to see it at all."

FACING BIG-BOX COMPETITION

In addition to the four Hart's locations, Altmeyer's added a fifth store in 1988. By 1990 the chain was generating $12 million in annual revenues from 15 stores that saturated the Pittsburgh market, including all four of the area's major shopping centers, and reached as far southeast as Uniontown, Pennsylvania, and as far northwest as Youngstown, Ohio. Beside Hart's, another major competitor, Linen Center, had fallen by the wayside, leaving JC Penney as Altmeyer's only true competitor. That situation would change in the 1990s, however, as mass merchant retailer Wal-Mart made its mark in home furnishings, and big-box specialty retailers Bed Bath & Beyond and Linens 'n Things became players in the market.

In response, Altmeyer's adjusted its mix of stores, moving to larger formats to keep abreast of the times, while maintaining sight of what made the chain successful: knowing what the customers wanted, exhibiting good taste in the products it bought, and providing the kind of customer service that was a hallmark of the company and resulted in repeat business. A key to excellent customer service was the chain's ability to retain personnel and maintain continuity. "People have been here 20 years and don't want to leave," Rod Altmeyer explained to *HFD*. "We don't cut or lay off and they don't run or leave." Making those buying decisions by this time were the two sons of Rod Altmeyer, Rod, Jr., and Robert, who were being groomed to one day take over the family business.

FIRE DESTROYS HEADQUARTERS

Other than new competition, Altmeyer's had to contend with a different kind of challenge in January 1991 when the company headquarters and distribution center were destroyed in a ten-alarm fire. The company had built a 26,000-square-foot warehouse across the street that was not damaged, and despite losing everything the company was able to set up offices there immediately to continue the business. Altmeyer's also took the opportunity to modernize the stores, installing new lighting and fixtures, to avoid possible problems at its retail locations. Altmeyer's would later move its headquarters to a new distribution center located in nearby Delmont, Pennsylvania.

In 1994 trade publication *HFN* ranked Altmeyer's No. 24 on its list of the top home textile specialty retailers. Several of the companies listed ahead of it would disappear before the dawn of the new century while the Pittsburgh-area chain continued to fend off its larger rivals. In a concession to the times, Altmeyer's stores grew larger, averaging about 10,000 square feet, but were still far smaller than the 35,000 square feet of a typical Bed Bath & Beyond store. The company was also adept at following the market, closing stores in locations that could no longer support the business and opening new, larger units where conditions were more advantageous. In the big picture, however, Altmeyer's remained a small player and had to contend with large manufacturers that preferred to cater to the large retail chains. As a result, Altmeyer's had to seek vendors that appreciated what the chain could do, and because most vendors did not bother to make sales calls, family members had to spend an increasing amount of time visiting trade shows to make contacts.

In the 21st century further changes were made to the mix of Altmeyer's stores. A unit in Lower Burrell, Pennsylvania, was closed, as were the Ohio locations. The chain was down to 11 units but would grow to 12 with the addition of a new store in Johnstown, Pennsylvania, where Altmeyer's had once done business. A store in the Richland Mall closed in the 1990s. The company also kept pace by starting Altmeyer's

BedBathHome.com to sell its wares online. A transition to the third generation of family ownership was also well under way. In the fall of 2006 Judy Altmeyer died. Her husband remained president but sons Rod, Jr., and Robert were clearly ready to assume control and take the chain into the next phase of the company's history. Faced with a difficult climate in the early 2000s, with economic recession threatening all aspects of the retail sector, the new generation of Altmeyer leadership had their work cut out for them.

Ed Dinger

PRINCIPAL SUBSIDIARIES

Altmeyer's BedBathHome.com.

PRINCIPAL COMPETITORS

Bed Bath & Beyond Inc.; Linens 'n Things; Wal-Mart Stores, Inc.

FURTHER READING

Hollow, Michele C., "Proliferating in Pittsburgh," *Home Fashions Magazine,* September 1992, p. 47.

"Judy Altmeyer Remembered," *Home Textiles Today,* November 13, 2006, p. 12.

Kohn, Bernie, "Reorganization at Hart's Fails," *Pittsburgh Post-Gazette,* September 27, 1990, p. B1.

Leizens, Leticia, "Family Values; The Altmeyer's Chain Keeps Big Boxes at Bay by Adhering to Tradition," *HFN,* July 29, 2002, p. 12.

Trozzo, Sandy, "Fire Rips New Kensington Businesses," *Pittsburgh Post-Gazette,* January 25, 1991, p. C4.

Zutell, Irene, "For 50 Years, Personal Touch Fuels Altmeyer's," *Home Fashions Magazine,* December 10, 1990, p. 46.

Ascent Media Corporation

520 Broadway, 5th Floor
Santa Monica, California 90401-2420
U.S.A.
Telephone: (310) 434-7000
Fax: (310) 434-7001
Web site: http://www.ascentmedia.com

Public Company
Incorporated: 2008
Employees: 3,100
Sales: $600.6 million (2008)
Stock Exchanges: NASDAQ
Ticker Symbol: ASCMA
NAICS: 512191 Teleproduction and Other Postproduction Services; 512120 Motion Picture and Video Distribution

■ ■ ■

Ascent Media Corporation is a global operation that primarily puts the final touches on movies and television shows, offering its services to film studios, broadcast and cable television networks, independent producers, advertising agencies, and other content providers. The Santa Monica, California-based company splits its business between two divisions, Content Services and Network Services, which are further organized into groups.

Making up the Content Services Division are the Creative Services and Content Management groups. The former provides a wide range of digital media solutions to the film, television, and advertising industries, including sound design and mixing, color correction, file compression for DVD and Blu-ray creation, editing services, subtitling, visual effects, and daily rushes of shows in production (delivered electronically or physically). Content Management services include mastering services, such as foreign-language dubbing, subtitles, and duplication; digital archive creation and management, and library services; disaster recovery of content; and supply chain management services to provide studios and broadcasters with invoice and billing, order tracking, and other digital supply chain services.

Ascent's Network Services Division is composed of the Content Distribution and Systems & Technology Services groups, helping content providers to distribute and monetize their product, and providing consulting services to help them navigate the ever-shifting nature of digital media technology, including the design and construction of media facilities and the training of personnel. All told, Ascent Media maintains about 40 facilities around the world, covering North America, Europe, the Middle East, and the Asia Pacific market. Ascent Media is a public company listed on the NASDAQ.

LIBERTY MEDIA CORPORATION ESTABLISHES ASCENT MEDIA

The foundation for Ascent Media was laid by media mogul John C. Malone, the chairman and principal shareholder of Liberty Media Corporation. He started out in the 1970s as the president of cable TV equipment supplier Jerrold Communications, but by the time

COMPANY PERSPECTIVES

We blend breakthrough creative with emerging technologies to deliver some of the world's most advanced and innovative media solutions.

he was 32 he was named head of a cable operator, Denver-based Tele-Communications Inc. (TCI). After the cable markets were deregulated in 1984, Malone made his mark by snapping up programming assets, acquiring stakes in such cable channels as Black Entertainment Television, the Discovery Channel, and American Movie Classics, as well as an interest in Turner Broadcasting. He merged TCI with United Artists Cable International in 1991. Malone's operation was deemed too expansive by government regulators and in 1991 TCI spun off 14 cable systems and most of its programming assets to create Liberty Media, which was reacquired by TCI in 1994. In 1999 American Telephone and Telegraph Company (AT&T) bought TCI, and a variety of cable, programming, wireless telephone, and technology assets were combined to create Liberty Media Group with Malone as chairman.

Under AT&T's ownership Liberty Media at Malone's direction began quietly buying up Hollywood postproduction houses in a bid to consolidate what had always been a fragmented business. These boutique media services companies, as described by *Financial Times,* were "independent, thinly capitalized companies, often dependent on personal relationships between their principals and individual producers for business." They provided sound editing and mixing, film editing, special effects, film transfers, and DVD authoring. In 1999 Liberty Media acquired three of Hollywood's top postproduction houses, paying $263 million for Four Media Co., $92.5 million for Todd AO, and $70.3 million for Soundelux Entertainment Group. When the deals closed in May 2000, the combined operation assumed the name Liberty Livewire and was put under the day-to-day control of David Beddow, one of Malone's Liberty Media lieutenants. Malone could then direct work from Liberty Media's programming assets to Liberty Livewire, providing Todd AO, Four Media Co., and Soundelux with a decided edge over rival postproduction houses.

ACQUISITION SPREE

Through Liberty Livewire's principal subsidiaries, Malone bought smaller companies in the United State and the United Kingdom that serviced film, television, and

commercials and were ready to handle the task of encoding programming for Internet delivery as well. Todd AO, for example, added 102 Estudio, Chrysalis, Editworks, Filmatic, Hollywood Digital, Sound One, SVC Television, and Tele-Cine. In the meantime, Four Media acquired Anderson Video, Digital Magic, Digital Sound & Picture, Encore Hollywood, FilmCore, Pacific Ocean Post, Riot, TVI, TVO, and Video Symphony. Four Media also acquired United Kingdom-based Soho Group Ltd., a major addition to Liberty Livewire's global ambitions.

Moreover, content producers had to contend with digital technologies that while offering great advantages also made their products susceptible to piracy. Rather than hire scores of little companies around the world, Liberty Livewire believed that content providers would rather work with a giant company that could, for example, have a film ready in multiple languages for distribution on a specific release date. Getting to the market quickly, products could experience less loss of revenue from piracy and the producers could take better advantage of other revenue possibilities, such as DVDs, on a timely basis.

With a large war chest at its disposal, Liberty Livewire continued to roll up assets. Altogether, about 50 service companies, operating out of more than 60 facilities around the world, were acquired between 1999 and 2000, their combined annual revenues in excess of $500 million. In 2001 the company curtailed it acquisition spree in favor of digesting its purchases, helping the different subsidiaries work more efficiently together, making better use of digital technologies (a tapeless world being the ultimate goal), and expanding the services it had to offer to the producers of films, television shows, and commercials. Although it had about 6,000 clients, and nearly every entertainment and advertising company worked with a Liberty Livewire unit at some point in some fashion, there was little awareness in the marketplace about the true scope and scale of the company. To increase its visibility and drive further growth, Liberty Livewire in the fall of 2002 rebranded itself as Ascent Media Group, a company offering a full range of postproduction and distribution services on a global basis.

EMPHASIS ON DIGITAL TECHNOLOGY

The increasing importance of digital technology was reflected in 2003 when Ascent Media unveiled a suite of services that allowed film, television, and commercial clients to digitally manage their properties through the entire life cycle, from the creation of content to the distribution of the final product. The new offerings

KEY DATES

1999: Liberty Media begins acquiring top Hollywood postproduction houses.

2000: Liberty Livewire is created to house postproduction assets of Liberty Media.

2002: Liberty Livewire is rebranded as Ascent Media Group.

2005: Ascent Media is spun off as part of Discovery Holding Company.

2008: Ascent Media Corporation is spun off as independent public company.

included a Digital Screener Service that allowed clients to access footage in a digital vault rather than engage in a time-consuming search of tape or DVD libraries. The company's digital rights management (DRM) service streamlined regional DVD authoring, including alternate language dubbing. The Virtual Telecine service provided clients with high-resolution digital file masters. In addition, Ascent Media's Media Tracker service allowed advertising and marketing clients to store and deliver audio and video files via the Internet.

Also of note during the early part of the 21st century, AT&T spun off Ascent Media's parent company through a stock offering in 2002, leaving Liberty Media Group an independent public company. By 2004 Malone was considering spinoffs to unlock the value of the many components of Liberty Media, which management believed was not reflected in the price of its stock. In late 2004 the company packaged its international assets to create publicly traded Liberty Media International. A few months later, in March 2005, Liberty Media announced it was spinning off its 50 percent interest in Discovery Communications, which owned cable television's Discovery Channel, TLC, and Animal Planet. To sweeten the deal, Ascent Media was included. The result was Discovery Holding Company, which was headed by Malone as CEO. Liberty Media shareholders received one-tenth of a share of the new company for every share of Liberty Media they owned. The transaction was completed in July 2005.

Although technically Ascent Media had a new corporate parent, there was no change in the company's day-to-day affairs. It continued to invest in new technologies and advanced facilities. In 2005, for example, the company introduced a new remote calibration tool called Monitor Watch, which allowed clients to

see an exact match of an image on different monitors located far apart, connected by satellite transmission. In this way, a cinematographer working on location could participate in digital intermediate work conducted elsewhere.

RESTRUCTURING

In 2006 Ascent Media opened the doors of a new 100,000-square-foot facility called the Digital Media Data Center, which consolidated eight facilities into a single site that was the most advanced operation in the industry to date. Not only did the new facility and its cutting-edge electronic media technology increase productivity; product security, from conception to project completion, was greatly enhanced. A year later Ascent Media bolstered its broadcast transmission capabilities on both the East Coast and the West Coast by establishing an East Coast Network Origination Center in Stamford, Connecticut, to distribute such programming as the YES Network, the National Football League, the National Hockey League, and A&E Television Networks, and a West Coast Network Origination Center in Burbank, California, to distribute Classic Arts Showcase and other cable television programming.

To keep pace with its expansion, Ascent Media restructured its units to create a more cohesive operation. In late 2005 the Creative Sound Services Group, which included Todd AO, Soundelux, and Sound One, was integrated more closely with the Creative Services unit, which included, among others, Company 3, Riot, and FilmCore. A more significant change came in the summer of 2006 when Ascent Media divided its units between a pair of global operating divisions: Content Services and Network Services. It was a move that the company hoped would allow it to adapt more quickly to industry changes while developing an integrated suite of services that would more efficiently serve its clients, who had to contend with tighter release windows of its products.

Concurrent with the restructuring was the increased role of José Royo, the company's chief technology and strategy officer. His focus had been on digital services offered to major studio clients, and he had played a key role in working with Hewlett-Packard to create new worldwide digital media distribution channels. His new mandate was to help the divisions' technology teams to align the file-based systems of the Networks and Creative Services divisions. The importance of digital services and file-based operations as the industry moved away from physical media was underscored in 2008 when Royo was named CEO of Ascent Media Group.

For the previous two years an executive committee of top managers had led the company.

Later in 2008 Ascent Media and the Discovery Communications assets, the combination of which had always been a marriage of convenience, were split. An entity called Ascent Media Corporation was formed in May 2008 as a Discovery Holding Company subsidiary to contain Ascent Media Group, LLC, and in September of that year Ascent Media Corporation was spun off to Discovery Holding Company shareholders as an independent, publicly traded company. When the year came to a close, Ascent Media recorded revenues in excess of $600 million. Due to an ever-shifting media landscape the company faced an uncertain future, but with its global footprint and broad range of capabilities, it was well positioned to adapt to conditions in the years to come.

Ed Dinger

PRINCIPAL SUBSIDIARIES

Ascent Media Group, LLC.

PRINCIPAL COMPETITORS

Deluxe Entertainment Services Group, Inc.; LaserPacific Media Corporation; PostWorks.

FURTHER READING

"Ascent Media Develops Remote Monitor Calibration Tool," *Millimeter,* November 14, 2005.

"Ascent Media Group Restructures into Two Global Divisions," *CNW Group,* August 18, 2006.

"Ascent Media Group's New Digital Media Data Center," *Broadcasting Engineering,* April 1, 2006.

"Ascent Media Installs Bicoastal Automation Solutions to Support Its Growing Business," *Broadcast Engineering,* December 16, 2007.

Cane, Alan, "So Is Ascent on the Top," *Financial Times,* March 16, 2004, p. 2.

Friedman, Wayne, "Ascent Focusing on New Digital Strategy," *TelevisionWeek,* October 20, 2003, p. 14.

Giardina, Carolyn, "Ascent Media Group Taps Royo as CEO," *Hollywood Reporter,* February 13, 2008, p. 5.

Graser, Marc, "Ascent Stakes High Ground in Digital Post," *Daily Variety,* April 19, 2004, p. 8.

———, "Malone Can't Leave Biz Alone," *Variety,* April 3, 2000, p. 1.

Mermigas, Diane, "Liberty Media on a Roll," *Electronic Media,* April 17, 2000, p. 47.

Takaki, Millie, "Liberty Spreads Stateside, Overseas," *Shoot,* August 25, 2000, p. 1.

ASUSTeK Computer Inc.

150 Li-Te Road, Peitou
Taipei, 112
Taiwan
Telephone: (886 2) 2894 3447
Fax: (886 2) 2892 6140
Web site: http://www.asus.com

Public Company
Incorporated: 1990 as Hung-Shuo Computer Inc.
Employees: 3,456
Sales: $2.15 billion (2008)
Stock Exchanges: Taiwan
Ticker Symbol: 2357.TW
NAICS: 334111 Electronic Computer Manufacturing;
    334112 Computer Storage Device Manufacturing;
    334113 Computer Terminal Manufacturing;
    334119 Other Computer Peripheral Equipment
    Manufacturing

■ ■ ■

Based in Taipei, Taiwan, ASUSTeK Computer Inc. is a leading global technology company. It produces everything from computer components such as audio cards and motherboards (the main circuit board inside of a computer) to entire desktop computers, netbook and notebook computers, and servers/workstations. ASUSTeK also manufactures LCD monitors, mobile phones, optical storage devices, and webcams. ASUSTeK takes its name from the last letters of Pegasus, the winged horse that appears in tales of Greek mythology, which is meant to represent creative spirit, purity,

strength, and the ability to reach new heights. During the later years of the first decade of the 21st century, ASUSTeK motherboards were found in approximately one of every three desktop computers. The company's products have received thousands of awards, and the organization has been a regular in *Business Week*'s Info-Tech 100 ranking.

FORMATIVE YEARS

ASUSTeK traces its roots back to April 2, 1990, when the company was formed in the Beitou District of Taiwan's Taipei City by engineers who had worked for the Taiwan-based computer manufacturer Acer Inc. With initial paid-in capital of TWD 30 million, the new enterprise was initially named Hung-Shuo Computer Inc. After its formation, Hung-Shuo Computer quickly turned its focus to expanding its research and development department. First year sales totaled TWD 230 million, a figure that mushroomed to TWD 1.39 billion in 1991 and TWD 2.18 billion in 1992, by which time the company was producing more than 75,000 motherboards and computer interface cards per month.

During the company's early years, Taiwanese motherboard manufacturers often had to wait as long as six months to receive the latest computer processors developed by companies such as Intel Corp., which typically supplied their new processors directly to leading computer manufacturers such as International Business Machines Corporation (IBM). However, Hung-Shuo Computer was able to establish an informal relationship with Intel when it helped the company correct a design flaw related to its 486 motherboard.

A major leadership development took place in 1993, when an Acer Inc. research and development engineer named Jonney Shih was chosen to head Hung-Shuo Computer. Shih would play a key leadership role at the company for many years. In July 1994, Hung-Shuo Computer changed its name to ASUSTeK Computer Inc. The following month, the company formed subsidiaries in both Germany and the United States for the purposes of marketing, repair/maintenance, and service. ASUSTeK's factory in Taipei received ISO 9002 certification in December, at which time the company furthered its physical expansion by purchasing the Taoyuan Lu-Chu Plant, which came on-line the following year.

By the mid-1990s, motherboard manufacturers in Taiwan were developing cost-competitive motherboards that supported Pentium microprocessors from Intel Corp., Cyrix Corp., and Advanced Micro Devices Inc. In many cases, Taiwanese manufacturers were able to undercut companies like Intel in the motherboard category by as much as 20 percent. Although many of the motherboards produced by Taiwanese firms were similar in capabilities, which kept prices competitive, ASUSTeK developed a reputation for quality and was able to charge slightly more for its products. Revenues grew accordingly, increasing from TWD 3.36 billion in 1994 to TWD 7.87 billion in 1995.

BECOMING A PUBLIC COMPANY

In November 1996 ASUSTeK went public on the Taiwan Stock Exchange. That year, sales reached TWD 13.33 billion. In 1997 the company earned ISO 9002 certification for its Taoyuan Lu-Chu Plant. In April, it established the Nan-Kan Plant, which was located adjacent to its Lu-Chu Plant. By late 1997 ASUSTeK had expanded its product lineup beyond motherboards to include server products, book-sized personal computers (PCs), and notebook computers. As part of an effort to improve customer service, plans were formed to open a new RAM Center in Tokyo in November.

ASUSTeK experienced a flurry of recognition in 1998. In February, the company was designated as one of Taiwan's best-managed companies by *Asiamoney*. In April, ASUSTeK was included on *Finance Asia*'s list of Asia's strongest companies. In addition, *Business Week* ranked the company 18th in the world and first in Asia on its InfoTech 100 list. For the year, ASUSTeK's sales skyrocketed nearly 65 percent, reaching TWD 35.2 billion, with net income of TWD 11.56 billion.

In early 1999 ASUSTeK announced that technology leader Sony Corp. had selected it to supply all of its motherboards. The deal stood to raise ASUSTeK's motherboard production by approximately 250 percent. Around the same time, the company announced plans to part with approximately $194 million for the construction of a new factory in China that would manufacture both CD-ROM drives and motherboards. The milestone was significant in that the factory was ASUSTeK's first operation outside of Taiwan.

Chairman Jonney Shih, in the *Business Week* issue of June 14, 1999, provided some insight into ASUSTeK's corporate culture, explaining: "You have to have very strong inner strength in order to build outer strength, like market share and brand image. Our whole company culture is trying to maintain this kind of engineering spirit."

ASUSTeK rounded out the 1990s with good news and bad news. On the positive side, the company continued to receive recognition for its products. For example, the company's F7400 Notebook Computer surpassed similar devices manufactured by the likes of IBM, Acer, Compaq, and Toshiba in a review by *PC Magazine*. By late 1999 ASUSTeK manufactured more than one million motherboards per month, and had become Taiwan's leading manufacturer of graphic cards, with a monthly production of 500,000 units.

Several challenges also occurred in 1999. For example, ASUSTeK's web site was compromised by hackers, who defaced the company's home page with graffiti. Another major challenge occurred on September 21, 1999, when Taiwan was struck by a major earthquake. Although the company's facilities were spared from damage, the disaster affected the availability of food, water, and a consistent supply of electricity, thereby impacting manufacturing output.

KEY DATES

■

1990: The company is formed in the Beitou District of Taiwan's Taipei City as Hung-Shuo Computer Inc.

1993: Jonney Shih is chosen to lead the company.

1994: Hung-Shuo Computer changes its name to ASUSTeK Computer Inc.

1996: ASUSTeK goes public on the Taiwan Stock Exchange.

2004: Motherboard production swells to 42 million units, making ASUSTeK the world's leading manufacturer.

2007: The company spins off its contract manufacturing operations; a new enterprise named Pegatron is established for personal computer-related operations; Unihan is formed to handle non-PC operations.

2009: ASUSTeK reorganizes its operations into three business groups: Handheld, Systems, and Open Platform.

ENTERING THE 21ST CENTURY

Following the dawn of the new millennium, ASUSTeK began ramping up production of notebook computers. With an overall capacity to manufacture about 100,000 per month, production totaled 20,000 units in 1999. In 2000, this figure mushroomed to 400,000 units, a figure that was surpassed in the first quarter of 2001 alone, as the company sought to manufacture more than one million notebook computers that year.

During the early years of the decade, ASUSTeK and other Taiwanese companies were prepared for further expansion into mainland China. Physical expansion continued as ASUSTeK opened its new Beitou II Plant in May 2000. The company rounded out the year with sales of TWD 70.7 billion, up from TWD 49 billion the previous year. In late 2001, construction was completed on another plant in Taipei, followed by the Quay-Sun Plant in January 2003. ASUSTeK's new facilities supported the company's growing output. In the motherboard category alone, ASUSTeK shipped 17 million units in 2002; one of every six computers at that time included one of its motherboards. Sales continued to rise, with consolidated income growing from TWD 114.7 billion in 2002 to TWD 195.9 billion in 2003.

In 2004 ASUSTeK was honored with 1,048 global professional media and networking awards. Mother-

board production swelled to 42 million units, making the company the world's leading manufacturer. Several developments took place in 2005. In September of that year, ASUSTeK revealed plans to spin off its manufacturing operations within three years, following in the footsteps of competitors such as Acer. This was because the company was producing its own brand of notebook computers, and also manufacturing products on behalf of other customers, some of whom were concerned about potential competition-related issues involving the ASUSTeK brand.

Around the same time, a strategic alliance with Advantech Co. was announced, as part of an effort to seek new opportunities in the industrial computing sector. By late 2005, ASUSTeK's market value had grown to approximately $7.7 billion, and the company employed roughly 50,000 people throughout the world.

GROWTH AND CHANGE

ASUSTeK began 2006 by securing government approval to acquire Taiwan-based Askey Computer, the world's leading digital subscriber line (DSL) modem manufacturer, for $244 million. The deal was significant in that it allowed the company to unseat Motorola as the world's largest cable and DSL broadband modem supplier. Sales continued to increase, with consolidated income growing from TWD 357.8 billion in 2005 to TWD 560.24 billion in 2006.

Midway through 2007, the company continued to move forward with plans to spin off its contract manufacturing operations. Specifically, plans were formed to establish a new enterprise named Pegatron, responsible for PC-related operations. In addition, another business named Unihan was formed to handle non-PC manufacturing operations, including the production of networking equipment, game consoles, and PC cases. Tung Tzu-hsien, ASUSTeK cofounder and vice-chairman, was selected to serve as chairman of both new companies, while ASUSTeK cofounder Hsu Shih-chang would serve as president.

By 2007 the distinction between regular televisions and PCs began to dissolve as more consumers watched on-demand movies and other streaming video content via their computers. As part of an effort to ensure that its products rivaled or exceeded the viewing experience offered by televisions, ASUSTeK partnered with Pixel-works Inc. to develop high-quality video-processing technology.

In October, ASUSTeK essentially pioneered the netbook PC category (with screen sizes of ten inches or less and used mainly for web surfing and e-mail) when it unveiled an affordable minicomputer called the Eee PC. ASUSTeK expanded its product base once again in 2007. The December rollout of the BrightCam AF-200 and MF-200 marked the company's entrance into the optical field.

TECHNOLOGY LEADER

It also was in December 2007 that IBM filed a complaint against ASUSTeK and subsidiary ASUSTeK Computer International, alleging that the companies had infringed three of its patents pertaining to networking equipment, PC power supplies, and cooling fan controls.

As part of the patent dispute, which had been going on for three years, IBM filed a complaint with the International Trade Commission, asking it to ban the import of ASUSTeK's motherboards and other equipment. The complaint had significant implications beyond ASUSTeK, because the company manufactured laptop computers and components for other leading technology companies, including Dell. A resolution was still to be reached in 2009. ASUSTeK capped off 2007 with consolidated income of TWD 755.36 billion, an increase of 34.83 percent from the previous year.

Progress continued at ASUSTeK toward the end of the decade. In late 2008 the company revealed plans to eventually phase out production of its sub-ten-inch notebook computer, which would be replaced with a ten-inch Eee PC netbook priced at $200. In December, *Forbes* named the Eee PC as product of the year. The company moved forward with plans to sell 20 million netbook and notebook computers in 2009.

In early 2009, ASUSTeK cemented a deal with Garmin to manufacture Nuvifone smartphones for the Global Positioning System (GPS) equipment manufacturer, some of which would include a new open source (available for free to the public and software development community) operating system from Google named Android. Around the same time, word surfaced that ASUSTeK was considering the introduction of a notebook computer that also included Android.

In April 2009, ASUSTeK reorganized its operations into three business groups: Handheld, Systems, and Open Platform. Two months later, the company announced that it was developing a Disney-themed netbook computer called the Netpal. Priced at $350 and available in Magic Blue or Princess Pink, the computer would be sold through Amazon.com, DisneyStore.com, and Toys "R" Us. Features such as parental controls and

spill-proof keyboards served to make the devices popular with parents.

Paul R. Greenland

PRINCIPAL SUBSIDIARIES

AMA Corporation; AMA Holdings Ltd.; AMA Technology Corp.; Askey (Vietnam) Company Ltd.; Askey International Corp.; ASLink (H.K.) Precision Co. Ltd. (Hong Kong); ASLink Precision Co. Ltd. (Cayman Islands); Asus Computer Benelux B.V. (Netherlands); Asus Computer Corp. (British Virgin Islands); Asus Computer Czech Republic s.r.o.; Asus Computer GmbH (Germany); Asus Computer International (U.S.A.); Asus France Sarl; Asus Holland Holding B.V. (Netherlands); Asus Hungary Services LLC; Asus Iberica S.L. (Spain); Asus International Ltd.; Asus Japan InCorp.; Asus Korea Co. Ltd. (South Korea); Asus Middle East FZCO; Asus New Zealand Ltd.; Asus Polska Sp. z.o.o. (Poland); Asus Portugal Sociedade Unipessoal Lda. (Portugal); Asus Service Canada Inc.; Asus Technology (Vietnam) Co. Ltd.; Asus Technology Holland B.V. (Netherlands); Asus Technology Private Ltd. (India); Asus Technology Pte. Ltd. (Singapore); Asuschannel Corp. (British Virgin Islands); Asuspower Corp.; ASUSTeK (Hong Kong) Co. Ltd.; ASUSTeK (Suzhou) Co. Ltd. (China); ASUSTeK (UK) Ltd. (United Kingdom); ASUSTeK Holdings Ltd.; ASUSTeK Italy S.R.L.; ASUSTeK United Technology Co. Ltd.; Austek Computer (Singapore) Pte Ltd.; Azurewave (Cayman) Holding Inc. (Cayman Islands; 60.49%); AzureWave Technologies Inc. (58.09%); Azwave Holding (Samao) Inc. (58.09%); Big Profit Ltd.; Boardtek Computer (Suzhou) Co. Ltd. (China); Boardtek Holdings Ltd. (British Virgin Islands); Casetek Computer (Suzhou) Co. Ltd. (China); Central Tec Asia Ltd. (British Virgin Islands); Channel Pilot Ltd.; Chanshuo Technology (Shanghai) Co. Ltd. (China); Cotek Holdings Ltd. (British Virgin Islands); Deep Delight Ltd. (British Virgin Islands); Digitek Global Holdings Ltd.; Double Tech Ltd.; Dynalink International Corp.; Enertronix International Ltd.; Enertronix International Ltd.; Famous Star Investment Ltd.; Fengshuo Trading (Tongzhou) Co. Ltd. (China); Gongshou Electronic Technology (Shanghai) Co. Ltd. (China); Goodsmart International Ltd.; Guanshou Precision Industry (Suzhou) Co. Ltd. (China); Hesuo United Technology Co. Ltd.; Hua Sin Precision Co. Ltd.; Hua Wei Investment Co. Ltd.; Huacheng Chuangye Investment Co.; Huajie United Information (Shanghai) Co. Ltd. (China); Huamin Investment Co.; Huaqi Electronic Industry Co. Ltd.; Huaqian Trading (Shanghai) Co. Ltd. (China); HuaSyu Investment Co. Ltd.; Huaxiang Travel

Co. Ltd.; Huayong Investment Co. Ltd.; Hwa Yuh Investment Co. Ltd.; Junshuo Electronic Technology (Shanghai) Co. Ltd. (China); Kaedar Holdings Ltd.; Kaedar Trading Ltd.; Kaida Electronic (Kunshan) Co. Ltd. (China); Kaishuo Computer (Suzhou) Co. Ltd. (China); Kinsus Corp. (U.S.A.); Leading Profit Co. Ltd.; Lishuo Electronic (Huizhou) Co. Ltd. (China); Lishuo Electronic Co. Ltd.; Lusuo Resources Regeneration Co.; Magic International Co. Ltd.; Magicom International Corp.; Magnificent Brightness Ltd. (British Virgin Islands); Maintek Computer (Suzhou) Co. Ltd. (China); Metal Tradings Ltd.; Mobostar Technology Ltd.; North Tec Asia Ltd.; Openbase Ltd.; Pegatron Czech s.r.o. (Czech Republic); Pegatron Holding Ltd.; Pegatron Japan Inc.; Pegatron Mexico S.A. de C.V.; Pegatron Technology Service Inc. (U.S.A.); Pegatron USA; Powtek Holdings Ltd.; Protek Global Holdings Ltd. (British Virgin Islands); Shandong Lishuo Electronic Co. Ltd. (China); Shanghai Huawei Computer Co. Ltd. (China); Slitek Holdings Ltd.; South Tec Asia Ltd. (British Virgin Islands); Strong Choice Group Ltd. (British Virgin Islands); Suzhou Chongsheng Electronic Technology Co. Ltd. (China); Suzhou Lianshou Electronic Co. Ltd.; Suzhou Xuyong Electronic Technology Co. Ltd. (China); Systek Computer (Suzhou) Co. Ltd. (China); UNI Leader International Ltd.; Unihan Holding Ltd.; Unimax Holdings Ltd.; Weishuo Computer Co. Ltd.; West Tec Asia Ltd. (British Virgin Islands); Wujiang Weixing Property Co. Ltd. (China); Yangxun Electronic Technology (Shanghai) Co. Ltd. (China); Yaxu Computer Co. Ltd.; Yaxu Electronic Technology (Jiangsu) Co Ltd. (China); Yongsuo United International Co.; Yusuo Technology Co. Ltd.

PRINCIPAL OPERATING UNITS

Handheld; Systems; Open Platform.

PRINCIPAL COMPETITORS

Acer Inc.; Hon Hai Precision Industry Co. Ltd.; Inventec Corp.

FURTHER READING

"Asus to Penetrate Local Notebook Computer Market," *New Straits Times,* May 3, 2001.

Hille, Kathrin, "ASUSTeK Plans Spin-offs to Cut Brand Conflict," *Financial Times,* July 3, 2007.

Hille, Kathrin, and Kevin Allison, "IBM Seeks Import Ban on ASUSTeK," *Financial Times,* December 7, 2007.

"Jonney Shih, Chairman, ASUSTeK Computer, Taiwan," *Business Week,* June 14, 1999.

Marsh, Peter, and Kathrin Hille, "ASUSTeK to Spin Off Manufacturing Unit Electronic Goods," *Financial Times,* September 30, 2005.

"$200 Eee PC Netbook Expected in 2009; ASUSTeK CEO Jerry Shen Said His Company Also Would Begin to Phase Out Its Sub-10-Inch Netbooks that Sell for Less Than $500," *InformationWeek,* October 31, 2008.

Vance, Ashlee, "Taiwan Tech Firms Step Out of Shadows," *New York Times,* June 4, 2009.

Aubert & Duval S.A.S.

Tour Maine Montparnasse
33 Avenue du Maine
Paris, F-75755 Cedex 15
France
Telephone: (33 01) 44 10 24 00
Fax: (33 01) 44 10 24 01
Web site: http://www.aubertduval.com

Wholly Owned Subsidiary of Eramet S.A.
Incorporated: 1907
Employees: 3,719
Sales: EUR 863 million ($1.08 billion) (2008 est.)
NAICS: 331111 Iron and Steel Mills; 331112 Electro-
metallurgical Ferroalloy Product Manufacturing;
331419 Primary Smelting and Refining of Nonfer-
rous Metals (Except Copper and Aluminum)

■ ■ ■

Aubert & Duval S.A.S. is a world-leading producer of
largely nickel-based superalloys, special steels, and
aluminum and titanium alloys. The Paris, France-based
company is a subsidiary of Eramet S.A., one of the
world's leading nickel producers, and forms part of Eramet's Alloys Division. Aubert & Duval operates from
seven industrial sites in France. These include Interforge,
the site of a 65,000-ton closed-die press, the largest in
Europe and one of the largest in the world; and Issoire,
in the Puy-de-Dome region. The company's Airforge
subsidiary, near Toulouse, includes a newly installed
40,000-ton closed-die press developed to supply parts
and components for Airbus, among others. Other opera-

tions include Fortech, in Gennevilliers, and production
units in Ancizes, Imphy, and Firminy. The company also
operates two distribution centers, one in Heyrieux, and
one in Wuxi, in China. In 2009 the company announced the creation of a joint-venture partnership with
Kazakhstan's Ust Kamenogorsk Titanium and
Magnesium Plant (UKTMP) to build a EUR 47 million
titanium bar factory in Ancizes, scheduled to be
operational by 2011. Of Aubert & Duval's sales of EUR
863 million ($1.08 billion), 50 percent comes from
outside of France; 80 percent of the group's exports go
to European destinations. Members of the Duval family
are Eramet's leading shareholders; Edouard Duval is Eramet's chairman, and Georges Duval serves as Eramet's
vice-chairman as well as CEO of Eramet's Alloys
division. Aubert & Duval itself is led by CEO Xavier
Chastel.

STEEL FOUNDRY ORIGINS

Aubert & Duval started out as a Paris-based steel
foundry established by Pierre Aubert and brothers
Adrien and Henri Duval. The company set up its first
plant on Paris's Avenue de Republique in 1907. Aubert
& Duval initially focused on producing and tempering
steel. The growth of France's aviation industry led to
increased demand for specialty steels. These often
nickel-based steel alloys offered greater strength and
resistance at lighter weights. Aubert & Duval's entry
into this sector came in 1926, when the company
acquired an existing works in Ancizes from the
Compagnie d'Electrometallurgie d'Auvergne. That
company had been founded following World War I by
the Compagnie Hydro-Electrique to make use of excess

Your satisfaction. Our total commitment to your satisfaction. Stronger, longer lasting, better value for money, lighter, faster, safer. ... In your industry, you are constantly pushing back the frontiers. To guarantee the best overall performance of your products, you need to be able to rely on a trusted partner who can meet your requirements in terms of materials anywhere in the world. At Aubert & Duval, we provide you with highly reliable metallurgical solutions that have been developed, designed and processed in optimal conditions to ensure reliability and reproducibility.

electricity generated by a new hydroelectric dam. The Ancizes forge became one of the first in France to produce metals using new electric-arc technology. This permitted the site to concentrate in the production of specialty metals.

Aubert & Duval invested heavily in developing the Ancizes site in the years leading up to World War II. By the start of the war, the Ancizes forge, known as Aceries Aubert & Duval, employed more than 1,000 people. By this time, Aubert & Duval had also developed a new hardened steel surfacing treatment using the gas nitriding process. The new treatment played a significant role in engine development for French aircraft during World War II.

Aubert & Duval's emergence as a leading specialty metals producer came in the years following World War II. By 1945 the company had launched a new major investment program to expand its production levels and also to meet the increasing demands of the aeronautics and defense industries. The company's Ancizes foundry, and the Auvergne region in general, became the major focus of the group's operations. Over the next decades, the Ancizes site continued to expand its furnace capacity, while also adding laminating equipment.

NEW TECHNOLOGIES

Aubert & Duval also invested in new technologies. In 1957, for example, the company became the first in Europe to add a vacuum melting furnace, used for the production of superalloys. In 1961 the company complemented this technology with the construction of its first vacuum arc remelting furnace. These investments established Aubert & Duval as a major player in

France's specialty steel industry. As such, Aubert & Duval participated in most of the country's greatest technological and industrial achievements leading up to the dawn of the new century, including the development of the national nuclear power industry; the Ariane rocket program; the TGV, the French high-speed train system; as well as the construction and development of the Concorde and other Airbus aircraft. The company's involvement in the Concorde project, for example, came through its work with Snecma, which resulted in the development of a new alloy and the launch of production of turbine discs for the supersonic aircraft's engines in 1967.

Aubert & Duval's operations moved to a new level in 1973 as the company joined the Interforge (short for Société Internationale de Forge et de Matriçage) consortium, in partnership with three other French companies, Forgèal (later Fortech), Creusot-Loire, and Snecma. Aubert & Duval's stake in the joint venture initially stood at 13 percent. Interforge then launched construction of what was to become the largest and most modern closed-die forging press in Europe at that time. The new facility, called Interforge, was constructed at Forgèal's site in Issoire, near Ancizes, and featured a 65,000-ton press, making it one of the largest in the world as well. The Interforge facility launched production in 1975.

In the 1980s, Aubert & Duval boosted its research and development investment as part of its development of new specialty steels and components for the ambitious Airbus A320 project. Aubert & Duval's expansion also led the company to restructure its operations under a new holding company, called Société Industrielle de Materiaux Avancés (SIMA). The Duval family remained the leading shareholders of the new company, which then included Aubert & Duval as one of its subsidiaries.

JOINING ERAMET

The French government continued to control, directly or indirectly, much of the country's steel industry into the 1990s. During that decade, however, the government launched a major restructuring of the French steel industry. As part of that process, industrial giant Usinor agreed to sell most of its specialty steel businesses, including its operations in Fortech, Airforge, and Techphy, to SIMA in 1995.

Fortech had been founded as a steel foundry under the name Société pour le Forgeage et l'Estampage des Alliages Legers, or Forgèal. By the early 1970s the company's operations had grown to include more than 1,000 employees and included operations in Pamiers, near Toulouse, as well. Forgèal changed its name to Airforge in 1989; the following year, the company renamed

KEY DATES

1907: Pierre Aubert and brothers Adrien and Henri Duval establish the Aubert & Duval steel foundry in Paris.

1926: Aubert & Duval acquires Compagnie d'Electrometallurgie d'Auvergne, a specialty steel producer in Ancizes, France.

1957: The company is the first in Europe to build a vacuum melting furnace for the production of superalloys.

1973: Aubert & Duval joins the Interforge consortium in partnership with three other French companies.

1995: Aubert & Duval, as Société Industrielle de Materiaux Avancés, acquires Fortech, Airforge, and Tecphy from Usinor.

1999: Aubert & Duval agrees to be acquired by Eramet S.A.; Duval family becomes majority shareholders of Eramet.

2001: The company launches construction of a new EUR 100 million closed-die forging press in Pamiers.

2007: Pamiers press begins production.

2009: Aubert & Duval forms a joint venture with UKTMP of Kazakhstan to form a titanium bar production plant at Ancizes.

its Issoire facility as Fortech. The acquisition of Fortech gave SIMA majority control of the Interforge facility as well.

The integration of the production units, including a 4,500-ton forge in Firminy and Tecphy's alloy powder production facility in Clermont Ferrand, as well as Fortech and Airforge, established SIMA and the Duval family as world leaders in the production of specialty steels and superalloys. Airforge's location in Pamiers, a suburb of Toulouse, also placed SIMA in closer proximity to one of its major clients, Airbus. In 1998 SIMA carried out a restructuring exercise, placing Tecphy, Fortech, and Interforge under a new holding company, HTM.

The restructuring came ahead of the next milestone in Aubert & Duval's history. In 1999 the Duval family seized the opportunity to join in the privatization of France's state-owned steel industry, agreeing to be acquired by Eramet, one of the world's leading producers of nickel and manganese, both important

components of the metal alloy process. Following Eramet's acquisition of SIMA, the Duval family became Eramet's largest shareholders and quickly took over that company's leadership as well.

EXPANDING FOR THE FUTURE IN THE 21ST CENTURY

Eramet then regrouped its new specialty metals and alloys business into a dedicated Alloys division. In 2002, the company created a new subsidiary, Aubert & Duval Holding, under which were placed the group's superalloys, aluminum alloys, titanium alloys, and special steels production. Joining Aubert & Duval in the Alloys division was Erasteel, which focused on the high-speed steels segment.

As part of the larger group, Aubert & Duval launched a new and ambitious expansion program. In 2001 the company launched the first phase in development of a new 40,000-ton closed-die forging press in Pamiers. That project, which cost more than EUR 100 million, was completed in 2007, in time for Aubert & Duval's 100th anniversary celebration.

The new press represented an important part of Aubert & Duval's growth strategy for the new century, as the company targeted a doubling of its global market share to 20 percent by 2010. In order to achieve this objective, the company announced plans to spend as much as EUR 200 million through 2013 expanding its Ancizes operations as well. This investment included the construction of new 30-ton vacuum-melting furnace, the largest ever built to date, scheduled to be operation by mid-2010. The company thereby hoped to double production at the Ancizes site to 100,000 tons. The company also expected to double its revenues, to as high as EUR 1.7 billion, by 2015.

Aubert & Duval's expansion effort also developed as part of its partnership with Airbus. In 2009, the company reached an agreement with UKTMP, a world-leading manufacturer of titanium sponge based in Kazakhstan, to build a new titanium bar factory. The partnership agreement included the construction of a EUR 47 million, 40,000-square-meter facility in Ancizes. Construction of the new plant began in 2009, with production scheduled to begin in 2011. Through its strong investment program, Aubert & Duval was well positioned to remain the world's leading specialty alloys producer.

M. L. Cohen

PRINCIPAL SUBSIDIARIES

Airforge; Aubert & Duval Fortech; Aubert & Duval Holdings; Interforge.

PRINCIPAL OPERATING UNITS

Firminy; Gennevilliers; Imphy; Interforge; Pamiers.

PRINCIPAL COMPETITORS

GTR Inc.; ArcelorMittal; Cargill Inc.; BHP Billiton Ltd.; Nippon Steel Corp.; JFE Holdings Inc.; Tata Sons Ltd.; The Indian Iron and Steel Company Ltd.

FURTHER READING

Angel, Marina, "Aubert et Duval Mise sur l'Aéronautique avec Airforge," *L'Usine Nouvelle,* November 1, 2007.

———, "Aubert et Duval s'Etend avec le Site Airforge à Pamiers," *L'Usine Nouvelle,* October 20, 2007.

Barbier, Eric, "200 Millions pour les Ancizes d'Ici 2013," *La Montagne,* October 9, 2008, p. 3.

Colonna d'Istria, Geneviève, "Aubert et Duval: Une Nouvelle Presse," *L'Usine Nouvelle,* January 5, 2009.

———, "Une Usine Aubert et Duval aux Ancizes pour Fournir Airbus," *L'Usine Nouvelle,* April 10, 2009.

"Eramet Partenariat Stratégique dans le Titane au Kazakhstan," *CercleFinance,* February 8, 2008.

La Motte, J. M., "Une Période de Forte Croissante," *La Depeche,* February 19, 1999.

"Largest, Most Powerful Drop Forge," *Forging,* March–April 2008, p. 24.

Lucas, Thierry, and Laurence Demoulin, "Aubert et Duval Relève la Tête," *Les Echos,* April 7, 2005.

BW Group Ltd.

Suite 412 Washington Mall–Phase II
22 Church Street
Hamilton, HM11
Bermuda
Telephone: (441) 295 3770
Fax: (441) 295 3801
Web site: http://www.bwgroup.net

Private Company
Founded: 1935
Employees: 4,500
Sales: $682.3 million
NAICS: 483111 Deep Sea Freight Transportation

■ ■ ■

The BW Group Ltd. is one of the world's leading maritime companies. Based in Bermuda with most of its operational facilities located in Norway, the group is active in a variety of shipping activities through its subsidiaries BW Maritime, BW Offshore, and BW Gas. BW Maritime operates a fleet of 18 very large crude oil tankers, 14 tankers for chemicals and other liquid products, and 20 bulk cargo vessels. Its BW Fleet management division provides technical management of the combined BW Group fleet. BW Offshore provides offshore oil rigs and other offshore vessels to the oil and gas industry. BW Gas, the group's most important subsidiary, is a world leader in the transport of oil and gas. Its fleet of some 65 vessels includes 29 very large gas carriers and nine large gas carriers, together with 14 medium gas carriers and 13 liquefied natural gas

carriers. The BW Group is a Bermuda corporation. It has operation offices located in the Norwegian cities of Oslo and Arendal, as well as in Singapore.

The BW Group resulted from the merger of two major world shipping companies, Bergesen d.y. ASA of Norway and the World Wide Shipping. The two companies were both founded by giants of the international shipping industry, Bergesen by Sigval Bergesen and Worldwide by Yue-Kong Pao. Together the two formed one of the most significant firms for the seaborne transport of petroleum, gas, and dry-bulk cargos.

A TRADITIONAL NORWEGIAN SHIPPING COMPANY

The Bergesen name became well-known in the Norwegian shipping industry at the beginning of the 19th century after Berge Bergesen launched a successful shipping business in Stavanger, Norway. The work was in the blood of the Bergesens, and in the latter half of the century Berge's grandson, Sigval, started a shipping firm of his own. Sigval's son, in Norway known as Sigval Bergesen the Younger, followed his father's example, broke with the old firm, and founded his own, Bergesen d.y. in 1935. Within three years he had purchased three major tankers, the *Bergesund,* the *Charles Racine,* and the *Bergeland.* Norway tried to maintain neutrality during World War II, but it was invaded and occupied by the German army in the first year of the war. As a result, the activity of the Norwegian shipping industry was limited between 1940 and 1945. Even before the end of hostilities, however,

Sigval Bergesen was planning for the peace he knew would come. In 1942 he acquired a majority holding in Mekaniske Verksted, a Norwegian shipyard he intended to modernize once hostilities were over. The Rosenberg shipyard later contributed a great deal to Bergesen's postwar successes. Bergesen made other, more essential preparations as well. In May 1945, within weeks of the conclusion of fighting in Europe, Bergesen had signed contract for a new ship, and just five years later his company was operating four tanker vessels.

GROWTH IN THE POSTWAR ERA

Bergesen's shipping fleet continued to grow in the 1950s. By mid-decade the firm had established the essential business strategy that would enable it, unlike many of its competitors, to weather the economic storms that regularly rocked international shipping. Bergesen's approach was simple: it focused on shipping petroleum and it established long-term shipping contracts, known as charters, with major oil firms. Under the terms of a charter, an oil company agrees to hire a particular vessel for a particular period of time for a particular price. With its charter business, the firm was able to continue to ship cargo in periods when overcapacity in the industry led to precipitously falling income for most shippers. By the mid-1960s the Bergesen company had a fleet of nearly 20 tankers, with an average of 102,000 deadweight tons.

In the middle 1950s, Sigval Bergesen's son, Berge, started his own shipping line which specialized in the transport of dry-bulk cargo, such as grain, sugar, coal, or ore. Ten years later, however, the son's firm was in serious financial trouble. Bergesen d.y. ASA stepped in and took the firm and all of its ships over. The most important element was a charter for major iron ore shipments. That marked Bergesen ASA's first move beyond oil transport. By the time the 1970s started, Bergesen was among the largest shipping companies in the world. The decade was one of great challenges for the oil industry in general and for Bergesen in particular. The oil crisis that started in 1973 hit world shipping hard. As oil cargos disappeared, most companies found themselves on the brink of financial

ruin, forced to scrap much of their fleets. Bergesen, in contrast, with its long-term charters was not only stable, it was able to continue to grow. The crisis in world shipping would drag on for the better part of a decade. Bergesen, however, was virtually untouched by it.

The company was shaken by other, more individual incidents though. In January 1976, one of the its ships, the MS *Berge Istra,* an ore-bulk-oil (OBO) carrier, so called because it was a specialized vessel capable of carrying different types of cargo, disappeared without a trace one day in the Pacific Ocean while carrying iron ore from Brazil to Japan. Only two survivors were found some two weeks later. The cause of the disappearance was never officially established. Only four years later, however, another Bergesen OBO carrier, the MS *Berge Vanga,* disappeared under suspiciously similar circumstances, without a trace left in the ocean, without a single survivor, and without any official explanation. The company has steadfastly refused any comment on the incidents ever since. Experts theorize, however, that the ships were insufficiently cleaned and oil residues left in the ships caused explosions, which weighed down by their heavy iron ore cargo sank almost immediately. The accidents were a factor in a decline in the use of OBO vessels in the 1980s.

NEW OWNERS, NEW BUSINESS

Sigval Bergesen stepped down from the leadership of the company at the age of 83 years of age in 1976. He was succeeded by two of his grandsons, Petter C. G. Sundt and Morten Sig. Bergesen. One of the first moves of the new management was to move into another sector, the transport of liquefied petroleum gas (LPG). The expansion came when another Norwegian shipping company, Fearnley & Eger, got into financial trouble and was forced to cancel orders for six LPG transporters it was having built. Bergesen acquired the ships and made them the foundation of its new division. As the long-standing crisis in shipping was finally drawing to a close in 1984, Bergesen purchased a controlling interest in the *Berge Arrow* and *Berge Eagle,* two large LPG vessels. Four years later, a similar ship, the *Berge Sword,* was obtained. The move to LPG was a timely one. Oil was plentiful and inexpensive; companies transporting it had a difficult time recouping their costs. Gas, on the other hand, was profitable. Once again, Bergesen was able to charter the ships in its fleet, ensuring steady income over a long time.

In 1986 Bergesen's six shipholding firms were consolidated under the corporate umbrella Bergesen d.y. ASA, which had been reorganized into a holding

KEY DATES

1935: Bergesen d.y. ASA is founded.

1942: Bergesen acquires the Rosenberg Mekaniske Verksted shipyard in Norway.

1948: World Wide Steamship Company is founded by Yue-Kong Pao in Hong Kong.

1967: Company enters dry-bulk shipping sector.

1970: Rosenberg Mekaniske Verksted shipyard is sold to Kvaerner.

1976: Founder Sigval Bergesen d.y. retires at the age of 83.

1978: Company enters liquefied petroleum gas shipping sector.

1986: Bergesen d.y. ASA is reorganized into a holding company and listed on the Oslo Stock Exchange; Yue-Kong Pao resigns from the leadership of World Wide Steamship and is succeeded by Helmut Sohmen.

1996: Bergesen merges with the gas carrier, Havtor ASA.

1999: Scantank Offshore is acquired.

2000: World Wide Shipping acquires N&T Argonaut.

2003: Company is acquired by Helmut Sohmen; Bergesen is delisted from the Oslo Stock Exchange.

2005: Company is reorganized as Bergesen Worldwide Ltd., renamed Bergesen Worldwide Gas ASA and relisted on the Oslo Stock Exchange.

2007: Bergesen Worldwide Gas is renamed BW Gas.

2008: BW Group Ltd. is incorporated in Bermuda.

2009: BW Gas is taken private and delisted from the Oslo Stock Exchange.

company. Shortly afterwards, in September of the same year, the company went public after fifty years of family ownership. Before the month was out, however, a Norwegian competitor, Kosmos AS launched a hostile takeover attempt, bidding for 49.7 percent of Bergesen shares held by various members of the family. Petter Sundt and Morten Bergesen, who had the rights of first refusal for the stock, were able to head off the threat, accumulating some 80 percent of Bergesen stock themselves. One month later the pair sold most of their newly acquired shares mainly to institutional investors in Norway.

GROWTH DURING HARD TIMES

Bergesen continued its strong performance as the 1990s began. A measure of its business savvy in complicated times was its strength vis à vis its competitors. For example, in 1991 its operating result was nearly 80 percent higher than the year before, while competitors were reporting paper-thin earnings or taking losses. Experts maintained that the firm's strength was due to holding debt within reasonable limits, maintaining a great deal of liquid assets, the company's entry into LPG shipping, its aggressive pursuit of charters for its vessels, the level of technical standards if consistently maintained, and its control of operating costs. Still analysts warned of a possible downturn for Bergesen in the rest of the decade, accompanying a downturn in the oil and gas markets. By 1995 these predictions were coming true, with the company reporting losses, that were made even worse by the decline of the dollar.

The hard times were not enough to prevent Bergesen from acquiring the world's largest shipper of LPG, the Norwegian firm Havtor A/S in November 1995. Havtor controlled approximately ten percent of the world's total shipping business, with a fleet of about 48 ships, primarily small and medium-sized LPG carriers. Combined with Bergesen's large LPG vessels, 20 large tankers, and six dry-bulk ships, the new fleet made Bergesen a giant in the shipping world and far and away the international leader in LPG transport. The deal paid off almost immediately with the firm's operating profits shooting up in the first half of the following year.

NEW CARGO, NEW SERVICES, NEW OWNER

As the millennium turned, Bergesen set its sights on expansion into two new business sectors, liquified natural gas (LNG) and offshore services. Between 2000 and 2005 the company purchased 11 LNG vessels. The business took off in 2002 with the awarding of major charters from the company Nigeria LNG. Another smaller charter from Suez LNG followed in 2005. Bergesen moved into offshore services when it acquired the company Scantank Offshore in 1999, which became a division and eventually an independent subsidiary of the firm.

A new chapter in the company's history began in 2002 when Helmut Sohmen, the head of World Wide Shipping, reputed at the time to be the world's biggest private tanker firm, quietly began purchasing shares of Bergesen stock through his investment arm Tauro Co. Sohmen and his family acquired Bergesen outright in April 2003. World Wide had been founded as the World Wide Steamship Company in 1955 by Yue-Kong

Pao, after he moved from Shanghai to Hong Kong. He followed a strategy very similar to Bergesen, chartering his dry-bulk ships to companies in Japan and Hong Kong. In the mid-1960s Pao's company entered the oil shipping sector and as the result of its Far East charters became a major international shipping firm. By 1979 its fleet numbered 200 ships. It was the largest independently owned dry-bulk firm in the world. Pao had become so successful that he was knighted by Queen Elizabeth II in 1978. Pao retired in 1986 and the company was taken over by his son-in-law Dr. Helmut Sohmen. Just before acquiring Bergesen, Sohmen's company, by then renamed, had taken over a Swedish tanker company, N&T Argonaut.

Upon taking over Bergesen, Sohmen delisted the company from the Oslo Stock Exchange and established a new holding company, Bergesen Worldwide Ltd., in Bermuda. Bergesen's tankers were purchased by World Wide while Bergesen Worldwide kept control of the gas, dry-bulk, and offshore businesses. There was concern at time in Norway about the loss of one of its most significant shipping firms. Sohmen, however, kept Norwegian management in place and left the company's headquarters in Oslo. Restructuring continued during the succeeding years. In 2005 the company was re-branded as the BW Group. Its various division were spun off into independent subsidiaries, Bergesen Worldwide Gas, Bergesen Worldwide Offshore, and Bergesen Worldwide Shipping.

ON AND OFF THE OSLO STOCK EXCHANGE

In the middle of the first decade of the 2000s Bergesen Worldwide Gas, the firm's gas shipping subsidiary, possessed a fleet of approximately 67 gas transport vessels—including the world's biggest fleet of very large gas vessels—and another 11 ships under construction. In the wake of this success, when the subsidiary went public in 2005, the Bergesen name returned to the Oslo Stock Exchange. The Sohmen family retained a controlling interest in the company of close to 60 percent. The Sohmens intended to evaluate the offering and decide if other components of Bergesen Worldwide should follow the same path. In 2007 the entire Bergesen Worldwide Group underwent a rebranding, becoming the BW Group Ltd. Its subsidiaries were subsequently also renamed, BW Gas, BW Shipping, and BW Offshore.

BW GAS REDOMICILED IN BERMUDA

The Norwegian government passed a controversial new tax law in 2007 which had massive repercussions on

Norway's shipping industry, in particular the biggest players, such as BW Gas. The law, which was intended to bring Norwegian tax law in line with European standards, continued to give income tax breaks to companies based on total tonnage. However, to qualify for the exemptions, companies were required to pay back taxes on a decade's worth of untaxed profits. Abruptly BW Gas was faced with a tax bill of approximately $400 million. The company, with others in the industry, tried to fight the new law in court. In addition, however, the company was reincorporated in Bermuda as BW Gas Ltd. in July 2008, placing it outside the future reach of the Norwegian government. The company's operation base remained in Oslo, however, where it had access to its highly trained workforce. The Sohmen family was the main source of credit to BW Gas as it fought its way out from under the crippling debt. It made another public offering in early 2009 to raise new capital but it was generally ignored by the public and most shares in the end were purchased by World Nordic, a financial arm of the BW Group. By March the Sohmen family owned more than 90 percent of BW Gas shares and at the end of the month the announcement was made that the company would become a private firm once again. In June 2009 the company applied formally for delisting from the Oslo exchange.

Gerald E. Brennan

PRINCIPAL SUBSIDIARIES

BW Gas AS; BW Fleet Management AS; BW Fleet Management Pte Ltd; BW Gas Cyprus Ltd; BW Gas KK; BW Gas Pte Ltd; BW Shipping Philippines Inc; BW Shipping Managers Pte Ltd (India); LAPA Ltd (Latvia); World Nordic SE.

PRINCIPAL COMPETITORS

Anangel-American Shipholdings Ltd.; The Baltic Exchange, Ltd.; Braemar Shipping Services plc; BOURBON SA; Bronel Group Ltd.; Clarkson plc; I.M. Skaugen ASA; InterBulk Group plc; Leif Höegh & Co.; IMC Corporation; Exmar.

FURTHER READING

"Bergesen Bosses in Share Spree," *Lloyd's List,* October 2, 2002.

"Bergesen Officials to Raise Stake in Concern to 79.7%," *Wall Street Journal,* October 1, 1986.

Berrill, Paul, "Bergesen Finally Jettisons Its Defensive Family Structure," *Lloyd's List,* July 29, 1991, p. 2.

Bray, Julian, "Bergesen May Be Harmed by Votes Wrangle," *Lloyd's List,* December 14, 1995, p. 2.

———, "Bergesen Seizes LPG Carrier Top Spot with Havtor Merger," *Lloyd's List,* November 21, 1995.

Brown-Humes, Christopher, "Cash Reserves that Buoy Bergesen," *Lloyd's List,* November 12, 1990, p. 5.

"BW Gas $1.5bn Refinance Deal to Cover Oslo Tax Hit," *Lloyd's List,* April 29, 2008, p. 5.

Corkhill, Mike. "Independent Bergesen Blankets the Refrigerated Trades," *Lloyd's List,* July 8, 1997, p. 6.

Gray, Tony, "Bergesen Spends Tops Dollars 500m," *Lloyd's List,* June 27, 2000, p. 2

———, "Is Gas the Key to Sohmen's Oslo Raid?" *Lloyd's List,* April 26, 2002, p. 7.

———, "New Look Bergesen Makes Oslo Return as Gas Shipping Specialist," *Lloyd's List,* June 20, 2005, p. 2.

———, "Norwegian Aristocrats Bow to Bold Bid from Sohmen Dynasty," *Lloyd's List,* April 8, 2003, p. 3.

———, "Oslo Re-listing Could Value Bergesen in Excess of $1.5bn." *Lloyd's List,* June 20, 2005, p. 1.

———, "Sohmen Deal Set to Build on Success of Long-Term Strategy." *Lloyd's List,* April 9, 2003, p. 7.

———, "Sohmen Family Aims to Take BW Gas Private," *Lloyd's List,* March 30, 2009, p. 3.

———, "Sohmen Set to Put Assets to Work," *Lloyd's List,* April 11, 2003, p. 2.

"Heavy Losses Spur BW Gas and Maran to Go Their Separate Ways," *Lloyd's List,* May 15, 2008, p. 5.

Joshi, Rajesh, "Bergesen Changes Blend the Old with the New," *Lloyd's List,* June 12, 1998, p. 7.

———, "Family to Scale Down Role in Bergesen," *Lloyd's List,* April 24, 1998, p. 1.

Moloney, Sean, "Family Quarrel Puts Spotlight on Norwegian Shipping," *Lloyd's List,* September 24, 1992, p. 3.

"Shipowners Stunned by Oslo's $3.5bn Back Tax Plan," *Lloyd's List,* September 11, 2007, p. 1.

"Sohmen Family Takes Charge of Bergesen," *Lloyd's List,* April 25, 2003, p. 1.

Stokes, Peter, "Bergesen Group Shows Its Pre-eminence Among Independent Bulk Shipowners," *Lloyd's List,* October 28, 1991, p. 2.

"Two Bidders Compete for BW Gas Fleet," *Lloyd's List,* August 6, 2008, p. 1

Wallis, Keith, "Sohmen Buys into Norway Sea Giant," *Hong Kong iMail,* April 26, 2002.

Baldwin Technology
Company, Inc.

2 Trap Falls Road, Suite 402
Shelton, Connecticut 06484-0941
U.S.A.
Telephone: (203) 402-1000
Fax: (203) 402-5500
Web site: http://www.baldwintech.com

Public Company
Incorporated: 1984
Employees: 699
Sales: $236.3 million (2008)
Stock Exchanges: New York
Ticker Symbol: BLD
NAICS: 333293 Printing Machinery and Equipment
Manufacturing

■ ■ ■

Baldwin Technology Company, Inc., is a leading global supplier of process automation equipment for the printing and publishing industries. Its products include automatic cleaning systems, dampening and drying systems, and various accessories. The company's products are designed to improve workplace productivity, improve print quality, and improve the economic and environmental efficiency of printing equipment. The company has sales and service facilities in North America, Brazil, Japan, China, India, Singapore, Australia, and throughout Europe. Baldwin's customers include press manufacturers, printers, and publishers.

ORIGINS IN 1918

Baldwin Technology was started in 1918 and remained a fairly small company until 1950. It was begun by ex-printer and press service technician William Gegenheimer in his garage in Baldwin, New York. He invented a device, the Baldwin Press Washer, which unlocked the potential of offset printing by reducing the time required to clean printing presses from hours to minutes. A patent was granted for The Baldwin Press Washer in 1927, and in 1929 the company moved to Brooklyn, New York.

Over the coming decades, Baldwin's innovations would make offset lithography more efficient and profitable, accelerating the industry's growth and expanding its own market. Baldwin developed a reputation for listening to the needs of printers and developing innovative products to meet those needs.

SALES OF $1 MILLION IN 1950

Baldwin began to expand its product line when Harold W. Gegenheimer, son of the founder, joined the company in 1950. Harold Gegenheimer was a press designer and engineering manager. Sales reached the $1 million mark in 1950, and during the 1950s the company began to license its products for manufacture abroad.

Harold Gegenheimer became president of the company in 1961, chairman in 1971, and chairman of the executive committee in 1982. He retired in 1986. In 1987 the Harold W. Gegenheimer Endowment was established at Rochester Institute of Technology's School of Printing Management and Sciences. The endowment would enable students and faculty to pursue field research into the technological challenges facing the printing industry.

Wendell Smith joined the company in the 1960s, and in 1966 the company's headquarters was moved to Stamford, Connecticut. Together with Gegenheimer, Smith helped grow the company by expanding its product lines further and penetrating international markets. In the 1960s overseas affiliates were set up. Baldwin Japan was established when the company entered into a joint venture agreement in Japan in 1968, and Baldwin Gegenheimer GmbH was established in 1971 with offices in Augsburg, Germany. Japan and Germany would become Baldwin's strongest overseas markets.

In 1969 Baldwin began an aggressive program of acquisitions to expand its product lines. It acquired Korthe Engineering, which became the basis for Baldwin's web break detection and protection product line. In 1971 Baldwin added a signature handling and stacking product line when it acquired Graphic Engineers. In 1974 it acquired Sun Chemical Co.'s web control product line. In 1976 the Automatic Blanket Cleaner was introduced in Europe. Levimatic Packaging Systems was acquired in 1978, and in 1981 Baldwin acquired D&R Engineering's gluer product line.

SALES EXCEED $50 MILLION

In the early 1980s Baldwin was generating sales of $40 to $50 million. Through acquisitions and internal growth, sales approached $200 million by 1990. In 1983 Baldwin received a patent for an improved version of its Automatic Blanket cleaner, and in the following year the product won the InterTech Award from the Graphic Arts Technical Foundation. The award was given for a product expected to have a significant impact on the printing industry over the next five years.

Baldwin incurred its first loss in 1983, the result of losses at a computer software company, which was sold

the next year, and a large investment in establishing a manufacturing plant in Ireland. That same year a management buyout established Wendell Smith and his group as owners of the company. Smith became chairman of the board, president, and CEO. The following year Baldwin returned to the black, reporting a small profit on sales of $46 million.

In November 1984 the Baldwin Technology Company, Inc., was organized as a holding company to purchase the assets of Baldwin Technology Corporation and its wholly owned subsidiary, NB Technology Corporation (NBT). In March 1985 NBT was merged with Baldwin Technology Corporation, with Baldwin Technology Corporation surviving as a wholly owned subsidiary of Baldwin Technology Company. For fiscal year 1985 (ending June 30) Baldwin reported net income of $1.2 million on sales of $53 million. The next year net income improved to $1.9 million on sales of $61 million.

GOING PUBLIC, 1987

Baldwin became a publicly traded company on January 15, 1987. The initial public offering (IPO) raised approximately $10 million, which together with the company's record year in 1987 enabled it to pay off the $9 million in debt it had incurred during the management buyout of 1983. Sales improved dramatically to $75 million, while net income jumped to $3.2 million. Both were company records. Sales for 1988 were projected at $90 million. Following its IPO, Baldwin experienced a period of growing sales and income as well as new product development and a stronger market position. Baldwin was enjoying strong demand for its products from European and Far Eastern markets as well as a slight improvement in the U.S. market, which had been flat in recent years. Growth in the overseas market was due in part to Baldwin's becoming an increasingly important parts supplier to press manufacturers in Germany and Japan. The majority of the world's sheet-fed presses were produced in those two countries.

Non-U.S. operations were starting to contribute significantly to operating income. In 1985, non-U.S. operations contributed only $580,000 to operating income, while in 1987 they contributed $6.7 million, with U.S. operations contributing $4.3 million to operating profits. Sales were about evenly divided between the United States and overseas markets. International sales would continue to become more important to Baldwin. In 1988, 59 percent of the company's profits and 69 percent of its sales came from Japan and Germany. Additional areas for international growth included France, the Soviet Union, and China.

KEY DATES

■

1918: Ex-printer and press service technician William Gegenheimer establishes a company in his garage in Baldwin, New York.
1927: The Baldwin Press Washer is granted a patent.
1950: Sales reach $1 million.
1968: Baldwin Japan is established when the company enters into a joint venture agreement in Japan.
1969: Korthe Engineering is acquired.
1971: Baldwin Gegenheimer GmbH is established with offices in Augsburg, Germany.
1983: Baldwin receives a patent for an improved version of its Automatic Blanket cleaner.
1984: Baldwin Technology Company, Inc., is organized as a holding company.
1987: The company goes public.
1990: Misomex AB of Stockholm, Sweden, and its North American subsidiary, Misomex of North America, Inc., are acquired.
1997: Baldwin divests its Misomex unit.
1999: The company's largest customer, Goss Graphic Systems Inc., declares bankruptcy.
2006: Baldwin acquires Illinois-based Oxy-Dry Corp. for $18 million.

GROWTH THROUGH NEW PRODUCTS AND ACQUISITIONS

In early 1987 Baldwin introduced a patented newspaper blanket cleaner that operated at full press speed, eliminating the need for costly shutdowns to clean the press blankets. Baldwin also introduced an automatic signature bundler (ASB), which gathered high-speed press output to allow efficient handling in binding operations. The ASB solved a long-standing problem associated with high-volume, high-speed printing. It was aimed at directory and publications printers.

In late 1987 Baldwin acquired the Ultrasonic web break detection system from Beaudreau Electronic Inc, which detected web breaks. During the year Baldwin introduced a new family of newspaper press protection products and systems. These new on-press sensors and computer systems would guarantee that presses with the most complex web leads were fully protected from damage due to paper breaks.

During the previous 25 years, Baldwin enjoyed a compound annual growth rate of about 15 percent. The company was dependent on overall economic conditions and the changing levels of capital spending. For many customers, price was less of a consideration than such factors as a company's staying power, product quality, and level of customer support, areas in which Baldwin was strong.

Factors at work in the printing industry were also contributing to Baldwin's growth. Advances in press technology were resulting in higher press speeds, which created a need for more and better accessories and attachments to reduce down time and paper waste and to lower other costs. According to a 1988 analyst's report, Baldwin enjoyed a dominant 42 percent market share in press accessories and had room for growth in controls and material handling systems. Most of the companies competing against Baldwin were much smaller. Baldwin's new product development program was characterized by one analyst as "aggressive." In 1988 the company spent $1.9 million on research and $5.3 million on engineering and applications work. The company was spending about 10 percent of revenue on research and development efforts.

70TH ANNIVERSARY, 1988

Sales for 1988 rose to $95.5 million, and net income nearly doubled to $6.1 million. It was the company's 70th anniversary. In October 1988 Baldwin announced plans to acquire the Kansa Corp, based in Emporia, Kansas. Kansa manufactured newspaper inserters, padding machines, and other equipment for newspaper and commercial printers worldwide. The acquisition was completed in early 1989 for $4.5 million in cash and 400,000 shares of common stock valued at $2.9 million.

Baldwin also opened a 30,000-square-foot facility in Naugatuck, Connecticut, devoted to manufacturing the company's growing line of fountain solution control products and the Accu Spray Dampener, a newly developed product used on double-width newspaper presses. Fountain solution control systems controlled the supply, temperature, cleanliness, chemical composition, and other characteristics of water used in offset printing.

During 1988 Baldwin entered the thermographic and forms handling equipment business with the acquisition of Ecamo, S.A., a French corporation, for $1.6 million. It acquired its U.S. counterpart, Specialized Printing Machinery (SPM), in 1990. These operating units served small printers, a segment that would be particularly hard hit during the economic recession of the early 1990s. In 1992 both units were put up for sale.

In Baldwin's Pacific Asian market, company representatives attended ChinaPrint '88, a printing machinery exhibition, and made contacts with Chinese press manufacturers. A letter of intent was signed with China National Machinery and Equipment Import and Export Corporation and a proposed joint venture partner, Beijing Small Compressor Factory, to enter into a 75 percent company-owned joint venture for the manufacture of Baldwin products in the People's Republic of China.

WORLDWIDE GROWTH, 1989

In 1989 sales rose to $125.5 million, up 31.4 percent, and net income increased to $9.2 million, up 50.6 percent. Overall, the printing industry was continuing to expand into more sophisticated material handling as well as accessory and control equipment. Worldwide, printing was also continuing to grow. Baldwin Japan was the company's fastest-growing segment. It enjoyed a 51.1 percent increase in sales, mainly through existing product lines. In Europe, business grew 29.8 percent, with the strongest segment being sheetfed presses. After four years of stable sales, business in the United States also grew through new product introductions. These included additions to Baldwin's automatic blanket cleaners, web break detectors, rotary cutters, high-speed stackers, and other products. Baldwin's 15 percent annual compound growth rate was outpacing the growth of the printing industry.

During the year Baldwin acquired the remaining 29.4 percent interest in its Japanese subsidiary. Enkel Corporation of Sweden was acquired for $10 million in cash and $12.3 million worth of stock. Enkel made machinery for splicing and handling huge rolls of paper for web printers and converters. Stobb, Inc., a manufacturer of stacker/bundlers based in Clinton, New Jersey, was acquired for $3.7 million, which included the assumption of $2.4 million in liabilities.

During 1989 Baldwin was reorganized into three geographic sectors based on the worldwide printing market: the Americas, Europe Consolidated (including Africa), and Asia Pacific. Each geographic sector would have its own product development, manufacturing, and marketing capabilities. The new regional structure was designed to help the company keep in close touch with its customers. During 1989 the company applied for 44 patents.

GLOBAL ACQUISITIONS AND GEOGRAPHIC REORGANIZATION: 1990

In 1990 Baldwin's sales rose 45.8 percent to $183 million, and net income increased 31.4 percent to $12.1

million. While U.S. market conditions remained soft, the company was able to continue reporting record sales and income because of strong performance in its Asia Pacific and European regions. Each geographic segment of the business—Europe, the Americas, and Asia Pacific—accounted for about one-third of the company's sales. Business was also equally balanced between press manufacturers and printers. New product development was equally split between internal R&D and outside acquisitions.

Acquisitions in 1990 included Misomex AB of Stockholm, Sweden, and its North American subsidiary, Misomex of North America, Inc. The company was an international manufacturer of platemaking and other prepress equipment for the printing industry. It was headquartered in Sweden and also had operations in Germany, Great Britain, and the United States. Baldwin completed the acquisition on July 27, 1990, for $44 million in cash. The acquisition was financed through bank loans. Other acquisitions included SPM, which became Baldwin SPM, the U.S. sales counterpart to Ecamo.

During 1990 Baldwin raised $24 million in capital through a sale of stock, and the company's geographic reorganization was completed. Trading companies were established in the different regions to facilitate the exchange of product ideas and make importing and exporting products easier. During the year operating subsidiaries were established in Hong Kong and Beijing, China. An Australian subsidiary was established in 1991.

In 1991 Baldwin achieved its eighth straight year of record sales through acquisitions. Sales were $221.3 million, up 21 percent, but net income declined 43 percent to $6.9 million. While the decline in net income was attributed to a sluggish economy, the increase in sales was due primarily to the acquisition of Misomex.

A RECESSION BRINGS CHALLENGES

In 1992 a severe recession in global printing markets continued to impede Baldwin's financial performance. Sales rose one percent to $221.5 million. Income from continuing operations was $770,000, but the company took a special charge of $7.6 million for restructuring and discontinuing certain operations, resulting in a net loss of $6.9 million for the year. The recession was limiting the sales of new presses that might have been equipped with Baldwin products. The company was also experiencing intense pricing pressures that reduced and in some cases eliminated profitability on some products. Sales of new web presses, for example, were 50 percent below their 1989 level.

As a result of those recessionary conditions, Baldwin's acquisitions, Ecamo, Enkel, and Misomex, had to be downsized and restructured. Ecamo and its U.S. sales operation Baldwin SPM were discontinued at a cost of $5.9 million. Both units lost $1.8 million in 1992. These losses were offset somewhat by a 16 percent increase in net sales for Baldwin Asia Pacific in spite of a 30 percent decline in the Japanese printing press and accessory market. In an effort to trim costs, the company's workforce was reduced to 1,148 in 1992, down from a high of 1,390 employees in July 1990.

With the effects of the recession wearing off, Baldwin reported net income from continuing operations of $3.8 million for 1993, up from $770,000 for 1992. However, net sales declined by 2.6 percent to $215.8 million in 1993 from $221.5 million in 1992. In 1992 the company took a charge of $7.7 million for discontinued operations, which resulted in a net loss of $7.0 million for the year. Worldwide, the printing market was still a difficult one, according to chairman Wendell Smith.

At the end of 1993 Gerald Nathe was elected president. Wendell Smith retained chairmanship of the board and the title of CEO. In 1994 net income was $4.1 million, an increase of nine percent over net income of $3.8 million for 1993. Net sales declined by eight percent to $198 million. Asian operations were hampered by a strong yen and weak economic conditions in Japan. Order rates in Europe were improving, and the North American market was showing signs of increased business activity.

STREAMLINING FOR RECOVERY IN THE MID-NINETIES

In 1995 net income rose 37 percent to $5.7 million on record sales of $222.3 million. Baldwin's financial performance reflected continuing economic recovery in the company's key markets. The company was in the process of acquiring the Acrotec group of companies, which was expected to add about 10 percent to Baldwin's sales. The Acrotec acquisition was completed in October 1995, and its German operations would be merged with Baldwin Gegenheimer GmbH.

In 1996 net income was $2.4 million on sales of $259.3 million. It was a year of mixed results. Net sales set a new record, up 17 percent, but net income fell short of expectations due largely to restructuring charges. While the Americas and Asia Pacific operations were strong, sales in Europe were disappointing. The German operation was being restructured.

Several streamlining measures were taken during the year. In the United States, two Baldwin Graphic Products operations were consolidated in a single facility in Shelton, Connecticut, and two separate facilities were closed in Stamford, Connecticut. In Europe, the acquisition of Acrotec allowed the company to combine three sales operations for accessories and controls in the United Kingdom into one location. Other operations moved into new locations in Malmo, Sweden, and Tokyo, Japan.

In April 1997 Baldwin divested its Misomex unit, which was acquired in 1990. In the face of strong competition and a difficult technology to master, Misomex consistently lost money. Once the company decided to sell the unit, its stock price began to rise to the $5 per share range. The sale of Misomex to Kaber Imaging Inc. of Hudson, New Hampshire, was completed in July 1997 for $4 million and the assumption of certain liabilities. In other moves, the company downsized its German workforce by 15 percent and merged two separate businesses there, reducing plant capacity by 25 percent.

In 1997 Baldwin changed organizationally from a geographic orientation to a product market orientation. It reorganized its operations management from three geographic regions into two business areas: the Graphic Products and Control Group (press accessories and controls) and the Material Handling Group (splicer, in-line finishing, inserter and stacker bundler product lines). Baldwin companies from around the world with similar products, markets, and customer bases were put into similar groups. The reorganization was expected to facilitate technology transfers between business units and to enable the company to provide better customer service and respond more quickly to market changes.

IMPROVED SALES FORECAST FOR 1998

For 1997 Baldwin reported a net loss of just under $38 million on sales of $244.1 million, which included a one-time charge of $42.4 million for the Misomex sale. However, changes implemented during the year resulted in positive growth figures toward the end of the fiscal year. The company also had a higher order backlog than at the end of 1996. Improved sales were forecast for 1998 in Europe and Japan, where markets were expected to emerge from a prolonged recession.

In April 1997 Wendell Smith resigned as chairman of the board. President and CEO Gerald Nathe was elected to succeed him as chairman. Nathe had joined Baldwin Technology in 1990 as president of Baldwin Americas. In 1993, he became president of Baldwin Technology Company Inc., while continuing to serve as president of Baldwin Americas, and in 1995 he was elected CEO.

For the future, Baldwin identified print-on-demand, or distributed printing, as a new opportunity to be exploited through joint ventures. It would involve shorter print runs and printing only in black and white. Baldwin Technology was working with manufacturers of electronic printing engines, such as IBM, OCE, and Xerox, to build this area.

In an April 1998 interview in the *Wall Street Transcript,* Nathe was optimistic regarding the growth of print throughout the world. He said that Baldwin was also looking at new markets, such as packaging and print-on-demand. Nathe noted, "Packaging is a market that's changing to require more and more information on the package," and printing quality was becoming more important.

Among the trends Baldwin was watching was the rise of alternative media, to see whether they would replace printed material or generate the need for additional printed products. Software, for example, while it may displace some print products, required additional catalogs, magazines, and manuals. Baldwin was also carefully monitoring the growth rate of printing in lesser developed countries, which was generally outpacing the overall growth rate of such countries.

MOVING INTO THE NEW MILLENNIUM

The early years of the first decade of the 2000s proved challenging for Baldwin. The company's largest customer, Goss Graphic Systems Inc., declared bankruptcy in 1999. Company revenues dropped as a result and Baldwin was forced to initiate a series of cost-cutting efforts that included layoffs, plant closures, and the sale of unprofitable businesses. The company sold its Baldwin Stobb Division in 2000. Two years later it sold Baldwin Kansa Corp. Sales fell by 20 percent that year while the company posted a net loss of nearly $16 million.

With sales falling Baldwin began to consider a merger with Germany-based technotrans A.G. The company announced in late 2003 that technotrans had made a $2.50 per share offer for the company. Baldwin later declined the offer and soon found itself embroiled in a patent infringement lawsuit with the company. Baldwin had originally filed suit against technotrans in 2000 claiming the company infringed on its cooling combination patent. The Dusseldorf Higher Regional Court agreed and ruled in favor of Baldwin in 2002. Baldwin then filed suit in 2005 seeking nearly $41 million in patent infringement damages. Meanwhile, technotrans had filed its own suit, claiming Baldwin's lawsuit was invalid. In April 2009, the German Federal Supreme Court ruled in favor of Baldwin, upholding the validity of Baldwin's patent.

Meanwhile, sales and profits began to rise as demand for Baldwin's products increased. The company continued to bolster its international business by opening new offices abroad, a location in India in 2000 and its Italy office in 2005, and by forming key partnerships. During 2006 the company partnered with Switzerland-based Robatech to market Webtack contact gluing systems used in the web offset printing market. It also acquired Illinois-based Oxy-Dry Corp. for $18 million in late 2006. The company formed a distribution and manufacturing partnership with Thermal Care Inc. in 2007, which gave Baldwin rights to the AWS fountain solution and ink temperature control systems product line. It also acquired Hildebrand Systeme GmbH, a Swiss manufacturer of printing products.

The company had seen revenues increase from $179 million in 2006 to over $236 million in 2008. Net income also remained fairly steady during that period and the company posted a profit of $6.4 million in 2008. The company once again faced challenges however, as demand began to fall as a result the economic downturn in the United States and overseas. To deal with this Baldwin launched a number of initiatives including a 16 percent cut in its global workforce and additional cost cuts which would result in nearly $12 million in annual savings.

In June 2009 Baldwin announced it had secured $2.2 million in equipment orders from two Japanese newspaper publishers, Yomiuri Shimbun and Iwate Nichinichi Shimbun. Headed by President and CEO Karl S. Puehringer and Chairman Nathe, Baldwin was overcoming tough economic conditions through its lucrative international partnerships and stringent cost cutting efforts. While demand in several core markets remained weak, both Puehringer and Nathe believed Baldwin was on track for success in the years to come.

David Bianco
Updated, Christina M. Stansell

PRINCIPAL SUBSIDIARIES

Baldwin Americas Corporation; Baldwin Europe Consolidated Inc.; Baldwin Asia Pacific Corporation; Baldwin Technology India Private Limited; MTC Trading Company.

PRINCIPAL COMPETITORS

Heidelberger Druckmaschinen AG; Presstek Inc.; Scailex Corporation Ltd.

FURTHER READING

"Baldwin Earnings Triple in Third Quarter," *Business Wire,* May 6, 1998.

"Baldwin Extends Cost Saving Initiatives," *Wireless News,* April 15, 2009.

"Baldwin Implements Restructuring Plan," *Business Wire,* January 30, 2009.

"Baldwin Partners with Robatech for Contact Gluing Systems," *Editor & Publisher,* October 11, 2006.

"Baldwin Technology Company, Inc. Appoints New CEO," *Reuters Significant Developments,* June 13, 2007.

Baruzzi, Cara, "Baldwin Shrinks Shelton Operation," *New Haven Register,* December 29, 2006.

"CEO Interview: Baldwin Technology Company Inc. (BLD), Gerald Nathe," *Wall Street Transcript,* April 20, 1998.

Dawkins, Pam, "Baldwin Updates Layoff Numbers," *Connecticut Post,* April 8, 2009.

Dzikowski, Don, "Norwalk's Baldwin Technology on Rebound after Shedding Unit," *Fairfield County Business Journal,* September 29, 1997, p. 7.

"German Federal Supreme Court Rules for Baldwin in Patent Dispute with Technotrans," *Business Wire,* April 22, 2009.

Higgins, Steve, "Baldwin in Shelton Purchases Swiss Firm," *New Haven Register,* April 12, 2007.

Mastandrea, John, "Market-Dominant Baldwin Looks at Foreign Opportunities," *Fairfield County Business Journal,* November 21, 1988, p. 1.

Oster, Helen P., "Baldwin Reports Improved 1993 Earnings," *Business Wire,* August 26, 1993.

———, "Baldwin Reports Improved 1994 Earnings," *Business Wire,* August 22, 1994.

———, "Baldwin to Withdraw from Business Segment and Record Special Charge in Fourth Quarter," *PR Newswire,* June 25, 1992.

———, "Gerald A. Nathe Named Chief Executive Officer of Baldwin Technology Co. Inc.," *Business Wire,* October 18, 1995.

———, "Gerald A. Nathe Named President of Baldwin," *Business Wire,* August 5, 1993.

Troxell, Tom, "Baldwin Tech Makes Mark with Major Printers," *Intercorp,* May 27, 1988, p. 36.

Varnon, Rob, "Shelton, Conn.-based Technology Firm to Be Bought by German Firm," *Connecticut Post,* December 13, 2003.

Benninger AG

Fabrikstrasse
Uzwil, CH-9240
Switzerland
Telephone: (41 71) 955-8585
Fax: (41 71) 955-8747
Web site: http://www.benningergroup.com

Private Company
Incorporated: 1859 as Gebrüder Benninger Niederuzwyl
Employees: 650
Sales: CHF 220 million ($300 million) (2007 est.)
NAICS: 333292 Textile Machinery Manufacturing

■ ■ ■

Swiss-based Benninger AG considers itself the globally leading supplier of complete system solutions in the area of textile finishing, including washing, dyeing, bleaching, and mercerization. Benninger AG also manufactures installations for the impregnation and hot stretching processes of tire cord and conveyor belt fabrics and for other specialty yarns and textiles used in ropes, air bags, sails or paragliders. In addition the company offers automation consulting and engineering services. Headquartered in Uzwil in northern Switzerland, where the company's main production facilities are located, Benninger has additional production subsidiaries in Germany, India, and China. Contributing roughly 60 percent of the company's total revenues, Asia is Benninger's most important market, followed by Europe where about one-fifth of total sales originate. The company is owned by the Swiss private-equity firm Capvis.

EARLY SUCCESS WITH WEAVING MACHINES

One of the first industries that quickly adopted the stream of inventions of the 19th-century industrial revolution was the textile industry. Mechanization and steam-engine-driven power generation were the basis for the development of machines that began to replace the age-old spinning-wheels and hand looms. One of the centers of the emerging textile machine industry was located in eastern Switzerland where numerous manufacturers, founded in the first half of the 19th century, began to make a name for themselves. At one such firm, Joh. Jakob Rieter & Co., the brothers Heinrich, Jakob, and Ulrich Benninger started learning the craft of mechanical engineering.

After traveling the world for several years, the brothers returned to Switzerland and acquired a textile machine manufacturing and repair workshop in Uzwil near St. Gallen and the Bodensee, at the end of 1858. On February 7, 1859, Heinrich and Jakob Benninger officially registered their own company, Gebrüder Benninger Niederuzwyl. With the help of relatives and friends the two entrepreneurs raised the necessary capital and started building weaving machines. One of the first orders for 12 such machines came from a weaving company in nearby Sirnach which became a long-term customer of the Benninger brothers. In 1861 the Benninger brothers were asked to deliver several hundred mechanical weavers to a large weaving factory in Walenstadt.

To expand the business the Benningers bought a large piece of land where they not only built additional production facilities, but also grew produce to provide food for the family as well as for their workers. In 1862 Ulrich Benninger joined his brothers in the business. Due to the rapidly rising demand for mechanical weaving machines, the company flourished. In 1865 an additional hall housing a blacksmith's shop, a tool making and a painting workshop, a product display room, and the shipping department, was built in Uzwil. With this additional capacity the company was able to put out 50 weaving machines per month.

DIVERSIFICATION, SPECIALIZATION, AND GENERATION CHANGE

In addition to weaving machines, Gebrüder Benninger started manufacturing other machinery for the textile industry, such as sizing machines and winding machines. In 1869 the company began to specialize in embroidery machines which were in high demand not only in Eastern Switzerland, but also in France and England. After a fire had destroyed the Benninger brothers' main factory, an even larger one was built in its place as well as several residential buildings for the company's workforce in the early 1870s. In the middle of the decade the factory continued to expand its range of textile processing machinery to include finishing machines, industrial washing machines, milling machines and calendering machines. In addition to equipment for the textile industry, Gebrüder Benninger also manufactured machinery for other uses. After the company had invested a considerable sum in an on-site foundry, the Benningers' factory produced turbines, water wheels, mill works, sawmills, and belt drives.

In the second half of the 1870s the family enterprise entered a rather difficult period in its history. In 1876 the company was hit by flooding and had to spend a large sum to repair the damaged buildings. While demand began to slow down, an increasing number of customers failed to pay for the equipment they had received, bringing the Benninger brothers close to bankruptcy. Only with the financial help of a local bank was the company able to continue operations. To make up for the slowing demand in Europe, Gebrüder Benninger began to explore farther-away markets in Asia and South America where business contacts were made. In 1900 the company shipped its machinery outside of Switzerland for the first time.

The late 19th century also saw the first generation change at the company. After Jakob Benninger's early death in 1868, his son-in-law Jakob Vogt-Benninger joined the business in 1878. Ulrich Benninger's son Ulrich Jr. followed suit in 1884. The senior Benninger died five years later. Heinrich Benninger's son joined the family business in 1891. However, only four years later, both the company founder and the junior Benninger passed away within only four months. The company was transformed into a stock corporation and renamed Aktiengesellschaft Maschinenfabrik Benninger & Co. Uzwil in 1895.

FURTHER SPECIALIZATION AND NEW MANAGEMENT

Shortly after the turn of the 20th century, in 1902, the company was again heavily damaged by a large fire. The new brick buildings that replaced the burned-down ones remained the core of the Benninger factory for the next century, which brought about further specialization. Benninger's line of textile machines was slimmed down and refined. The company stopped making bobbing winding and winding machines and cotton weaving machines, but started making silk weaving machines. Around this time Benninger launched two pioneering products: a sectional warper and the first automatic jigger, or discontinuous dyeing machine. These gave the company a competitive edge, as they became bestsellers and were exported to many countries.

The production of turbines and water wheels became the company's second important product area in the early 1900s when electrification was a major driver of rapid industrialization. Benninger manufactured two types of turbines, Francis turbines and Pelton turbines, with a performance of up to 1,000 PS and also provided the necessary transmissions and pipeline systems. The

KEY DATES

1859: Heinrich Benninger founds a textile machinery manufacturing company in Uzwil.

1895: The company is transformed into the stock corporation Aktiengesellschaft Maschinenfabrik Benninger & Co.

1912: The company is renamed Maschinenfabrik Vogt und Schaad, vorm. Benninger & Co.

1946: Jakob Vogt-Benninger's son-in-law Eugen Peter is appointed to the board of directors.

1960s: A production license agreement with the Indian manufacturer Manekal is signed.

1978: Charles Peter succeeds his father as CEO and reestablishes family control.

1983: Benninger India Ltd. is founded.

1991: Zell-based sizing machine and tire cord manufacturing equipment maker Krückels is acquired.

1995: Benninger Textile Machinery Co. is established in China.

2001: The company takes over the wet finishing division of German textile machine tool manufacturer Kleinewefers.

2005: Benninger is acquired by the Swiss private-equity firm Capvis.

2007: The company acquires German wet finishing equipment manufacturer Küsters Textile.

2008: Benninger sells its weaving preparation division to the German textile machine manufacturer Karl Mayer.

turbine production helped level out the heavy fluctuations in the market for textile machines and generated one-third of Benninger's revenues. The company continued to expand this segment in cooperation with Mr. Schaad, an engineer and Benninger employee who became one of the company's executive directors in 1912 when the company was renamed Maschinenfabrik Vogt und Schaad, vorm. Benninger & Co. In addition the company produced conches, that is, machines for making chocolate.

Early in the 20th century the company also saw more family members enter the business. After Ulrich Benninger Jr.'s death in 1906, Jakob Vogt-Benninger's oldest son, Heinrich Vogt, joined the company as technical director. His brother Werner took over responsibility for the sales of weaving machines in 1914.

One year later Jakob Vogt-Benninger's son-in-law, Erhardt Bolter-Vogt, joined the management team.

FINANCIAL AND ECONOMIC CRISES AND WAR PRODUCTION

The beginning of World War I in 1914 suddenly cut the company off from its export markets. Business partner Schaad left the enterprise after disagreements over company strategy and Jakob Vogt-Benninger became the head of the newly formed family-controlled stock corporation. To make up for lost export business, the Benningers began to manufacture machinery for processing materials used in road construction, such as stone crushers and grinders. They soon realized, however, that it would take an enormous effort to compete with the already well-established manufacturers in that particular market. Instead Benninger started producing a variety of lathes for shafts and bolts, as well as thread milling machines which could also be used to manufacture ammunition and which were in high demand in Europe during the war years.

After the war ended Benninger saw increased demand for weaving machines; this led to production of as many as 120 units per month. With actual sales lagging behind production (about 70 machines were sold monthly in the postwar years) the company's inventory of unsold product began to increase. When, in addition, a number of customers failed to pay their bills in the early 1920s, Benninger struggled to maintain the necessary cash flow to keep the business running. By the late 1920s the company had overcome this critical situation, sold its inventory, and was putting out some four dozen weaving machines, two dozen warping frames, and a larger number of jiggers and mercerizing machines.

The 1930s ushered in another period of economic and political crises. In the wake of the Great Depression exports came to a halt again, mainly caused by the massive devaluation of some the world's major currencies which lost up to one third of their value against the Swiss franc, making Swiss products far too expensive on the world market. The critical situation lasted until 1936 when the Swiss franc was devalued as well. To put the business on a financially sound foundation again, Jakob Vogt-Benninger wrote off a significant share of the company's capital and opened the company to financial investors from outside the family to raise fresh capital. In 1946 Jakob Vogt-Benninger's son-in-law Eugen Peter was appointed to the board of directors. During World War II Benninger again produced thread milling machines which experienced high demand from manufacturers of ammunition.

RESTRUCTURING THE PRODUCT PORTFOLIO AFTER POSTWAR BOOM

After World War II Benninger experienced a surge in demand. Customers had to wait up to two years for the equipment they ordered and the effective price was calculated just before the production started to reflect current raw material costs. The incoming cash enabled Benninger to greatly expand production capacity in the late 1940s and early 1950s. The foundry was expanded and modernized, a new office building was added, the shipping department was enlarged, and a new assembly hall for textile machines was built.

At the same time, a rising number of competitors were trying to get a piece of the market, which put massive pressure on prices, especially for weaving machines. While Benninger had specialized in technologically refined silk weaving machines, the increasingly popular synthetic fibers could be manufactured by more common cotton weaving machines. In the mid-1950s Benninger discontinued its own production of weaving machines and issued a production license to an Italian manufacturer. The same path was taken with the company's line of jiggers, for which licensees were found in Germany, France, Argentina, and India. On the other hand, Benninger resumed the production of warping frames in 1963 which became one of the company's staple products. In the 1960s, the company's workforce had grown to about 580. By the end of the decade, Benninger was generating about CHF 30 million in annual sales.

GENERATIONAL CHANGE, TECHNOLOGY, AND QUALITY LEADERSHIP

The beginning of the 1970s also marked the beginning of a new era for Benninger. As the market for textile finishing machines further matured, the company had to find new ways to maintain their success in an increasingly competitive environment. In the wake of the first oil price shock of 1974 the company's sales dropped by roughly one-third. It was in this challenging environment that Eugen Peter's son Charles Peter joined the company as director of sales and in 1978 succeeded his father as CEO. He managed to buy back all company stock from financial investors until Benninger was once again a family-controlled business.

Under this new leadership the company intensified its marketing efforts, took steps towards globalization, and aimed for the highest-quality standards and for achieving technology leadership in its chosen markets. As the company's core markets moved from Europe and the United States to Asia, new sales offices were established around the globe while Benninger sales representatives received intensive training from the company.

The advent of microelectronics in the late 1970s and early 1980s changed the textile machine industry profoundly as electronic controls replaced the age-old mechanical principles. As technology leadership became a decisive competitive factor, Benninger invested in the development of innovative high-tech products. With the exception of weaving machines, the company offered a whole range of machine tools for all major textile processing needs. Innovative products such as the Supertronic and Ben-Matic electronic sectional warping machines that were introduced in the 1990s greatly increased warping speed, while saving costs at the same time.

Other innovative launches of the 1990s and first decade of the 2000s were the electronic creeling aid Benninger Creelmaster, the Ben-Matic washing machine, the Ben-Color steamer, the Ben-Bleach textile production system which combined desizing, scouring, and bleaching operations into a single process, and the wet-on-wet process of mercerizing fabrics. A steady stream of new, innovative textile machinery earned Benninger a growing share in the marketplace.

GLOBALIZATION, ACQUISITIONS, INVESTMENTS, DIVESTMENTS

As early as in the late 1960s and in the 1970s, long before globalization became a major trend, Eugen Peter had begun to build a foothold for Benninger in India. After a license agreement was signed with the Indian manufacturer Manekal, the latter began producing about 150 jiggers a year under the Benninger label. Under the leadership of Peter's son Charles, the company intensified its efforts to establish additional footholds outside of Switzerland and to move closer to the emerging markets in Asia and Eastern Europe. In 1979 the company set up a subsidiary in Italy where sectional warpers were produced. In 1992 a joint venture was established near Mumbai in India for the production of textile machines for wet finishing and woven products. In the early to mid-1990s Benninger also founded subsidiaries in Hong Kong and Shanghai in China, and a sales office in Moscow, Russia. By 2008, the company was generating roughly 60 percent of total revenues in Asia.

The 1991 a new Benninger division was opened to the automotive supplier market with the takeover of textile machine manufacturer Josef Krückels in Zell, Germany, which made installations for sizing machines and for the impregnation and hot stretching of tire cord and conveyor belt fabrics as well as for the treatment of other specialty yarns and textiles. After the turn of the 21st century Benninger significantly strengthened its textile wet finishing arm by way of new acquisitions. In 2001 the company took over the wet finishing division of the German textile machine tool manufacturer Kleinewefers Textilmaschinen GmbH in Krefeld.

Six years later Benninger acquired another German company and one of its main competitors in the wet finishing segment, Küsters Textile GmbH, with subsidiaries in Hong Kong and Shanghai. The global financial crisis of the later years of the first decade of the 2000s, however, caused a major drop in orders, which Benninger tried to offset by cutting costs and personnel. In 2008 the company sold its weaving preparation division to the German textile machine manufacturer Karl Mayer.

The new millennium also saw Benninger AG change hands. When Charles Peter's children showed no interest in taking over the management of the company, Benninger AG was sold to the Swiss private-equity firm Capvis in 2005. Benninger's in-house foundry, which had become a separate company division in 1980 and was spun off as Benninger Guss AG, an independent stock corporation, in 1997, remained in the hands of the family. In the increasingly consolidating market at the end of the first decade of the 2000s, Benninger AG saw its future in two major niche markets where the company had achieved a leading position: textile finishing and tire cord production.

Evelyn Hauser

PRINCIPAL SUBSIDIARIES

Benninger Zell GmbH (Germany); Küsters Textile GmbH (Germany); Benninger India Ltd.; Benninger Textile Machinery Co. Ltd. (China); Benninger AG Moscow Office (Russia).

PRINCIPAL COMPETITORS

Goller Textilmaschinen GmbH; Erbatech GmbH; Karl Menzel Maschinenfabrik GmbH & Co.

FURTHER READING

"Adding Stability," *Textile Month,* December 2004, p. 54.

"Benninger AG Takes over Küsters Textile GmbH in Zittau (D) with the Subsidiaries Küsters Far East Ltd. in Hong Kong and Küsters Shanghai Co. Ltd. (China)," http://www.texdata.com, November 2007.

"Benninger Holding," *Textile World,* October 1993, p. 85.

"Benninger: Injecta Open-Width Washer," *Textile World,* April 1993, p. 99.

Bollen, Manfred, and Erich Wiess, "Is Quality Affordable?" *Textile Month,* April 1997, p. 34.

Dennard, Jennifer, "Benninger to Install BEN-INDIGO System in Brazil," *Textile World,* June 2003, p. 46.

"Direct Success," *Textile Month,* September 2001, p. 18.

"Flexible Wet-on-Wet," *Textile Month,* February 2001, p. 16.

"High-Performance Direct Beaming with No Dust: Benninger's BEN-VAC System Dramatically Cuts Dust Generation in Direct Beaming Operations," *Textile Month,* April 1994, p. 49.

"India: Heinz Michel to Head Benninger Group," *TendersInfo,* February 13, 2009.

"Learning from the Best. Benninger Chief Daniel Hirschi's Plan for Company's Growth," *Textile Month,* April 2007, p. 16.

150 Jahre Benninger. Uzwil, Switzerland: Benninger AG, 2009, 100 p.

"Relaxed Elastic," *Textile Month,* August 2005, p. 72.

Rozelle, Walter N., "How Forstmann Optimizes Fancy Warp Preparation," *Textile World,* October 1994, p. 53.

Singh, Vijay, and George Alexander, "An Upswing in the Land of Gandhi: India's Economic Policy Attracts Swiss Investors," *swissBusiness,* September–October 1994, p. 52.

"Swiss Textile Machinery: Beyond Hardware. ... ," *Textile Month,* February 2004, p. 30.

Weiss, Erich, "Benninger: Ben-Bleach Desize/Scour/Bleach," *Textile World,* April 1997, p. 59.

Best Maid Products, Inc.

———■———

1401 South Riverside Drive
Fort Worth, Texas 76104
U.S.A.
Telephone: (817) 335-5494
Fax: (817) 534-7117
Web site: http://www.bestmaidproducts.com

Private Company
Incorporated: 1952
Employees: 250
Sales: $38.3 million (2008 est.)
NAICS: 311421 Fruit and Vegetable Canning

■ ■ ■

Best Maid Products, Inc., is a privately held food products company based in Fort Worth, Texas, serving both the retail and foodservice channels in about a dozen states, primarily in the southwestern United States. Retail products include a variety of jarred dill, kosher, sweet, and sour pickles, available whole as well as baby, spears, and chips; sweet and dill relish; and dressings, including the company's signature mayonnaise, salad dressing, sandwich spread, coleslaw dressing, tartar sauce, mustard, barbecue sauce, and Worcestershire sauce. These same products are packaged in larger quantities and distributed to foodservice chains and restaurants.

In addition to retail products sold under the Best Maid label, the company offers Del-Dixi Pickles, an old-line South Texas brand acquired in the 1960s that remains the top-selling supermarket brand in its

territory. Best Maid also does some business internationally, especially with its barbecue sauce. The company not only maintains its own processing plant, distribution facility, and fleet of delivery trucks, but also a large pickle tank yard in Mansfield, Texas, where cucumbers undergo a brining process in large vats before becoming pickles. Best Maid is owned and managed by the third and fourth generations of the Dalton family.

ORIGINS IN MAYONNAISE

The roots of Best Maid date back to the early 1920s to Mansfield, Texas, where Mildred Dalton baked pies and other pastries for her husband Jesse Otis Dalton to sell in the small Fort Worth grocery store he owned. In 1924, to make use of her leftover egg yolks, she began making mayonnaise. It proved so popular with friends and family that her husband began selling it at his store and soon customers were placing orders ahead of time to guarantee availability. Realizing they had a prize product on their hands, the Daltons formed Mrs. Dalton's Mayonnaise Company in 1926, a name that would eventually be changed as the company added product lines.

A small production facility was established in Fort Worth to produce mayonnaise and before long Mildred Dalton decided to use the mayonnaise to make a homemade sandwich spread that included pickle relish. The pickle relish was provided by an outside vendor, who soon raised his prices so high that the Daltons began growing cucumbers in the garden at their Mansfield home instead of purchasing them. The cucumber harvest was so large that in addition to making pickle relish the Daltons also began canning pickles in the mid-1930s. This pickle patch led to the creation of a full-scale pickle farm, including a pickle-curing tank yard that brought with it smells that were not a problem for many years when the area was remote. In time, however, as Mansfield developed, the tank yard was to become a point of contention with the neighbors.

To sell its mayonnaise, sandwich spread, and pickles, Best Maid developed a truck fleet to service small grocery stores in the area and also sold directly to consumers door-to-door. As the brand became better established the company began to take weekly orders and make deliveries on a regular basis. Helping to take those orders and make deliveries after school was one of the Dalton children, Garland "Son" Dalton, who had begun helping out in 1927 at the age of ten. His sister, Margie, would help in a different way. In 1940 a picture of her and Mildred Dalton was featured on Best Maid labels. In time her image evolved into a caricature known as "Smiley" that regularly adorned Best Maid materials.

POSTWAR EXPANSION

Despite difficult conditions during the Great Depression of the 1930s, Best Maid was able to establish a pickle farm in Mansfield and hang on until the economy recovered due to a surge in military spending caused by the entry of the United States into World War II in the 1941. The postwar economic boom drove sales, leading to the opening of new manufacturing facilities in 1946. As a result, the company had the capacity to expand distribution throughout Texas. In 1952 Best Maid was incorporated and moved its headquarters to Fort Worth where it established a new packing facility. In the mid-1950s a new tank yard facility was established in Mansfield to drive further growth.

In 1955, a third generation of the Dalton family became involved in Best Maid when Garland's son, Gary Dalton, went to work for the company. Starting out on the loading dock, he learned every aspect of the

business even as his own father was being groomed to succeed his grandparents. Five years later Garland's daughter, Patricia Dalton, went to work for Best Maid as well. After learning the production side of the business, she would turn her attention to accounting, eventually becoming chief financial officer. Another grandson of the founders, Dan Dalton, also joined Best Maid in 1964, finding his niche in sales.

During the postwar years Garland Dalton became president of Best Maid. In 1962 he was the key figure in the acquisition of Del-Dixi Foods Corporation, an Orange, Texas-based canned fruit and vegetable company that boasted one of the state's top pickle brands. Best Maid was then able to take advantage of its sales force to grow Del-Dixi in Texas and later establish it as a major regional brand in the Southwest. During this period Best Maid also kept pace with demand and changes in the industry. In 1965 the old wooden pickle tanks gave way to fiberglass. Other operations were also upgraded, so that by 1970 the Mansfield complex included five separate buildings housing Best Maid's administrative, manufacturing, warehousing, and shipping operations.

NEW LEADERSHIP

A changing of the guard took place during the 1970s. In 1976 Garland Dalton, nearing 60 years of age, was finally named chairman and chief executive officer. The business continued to grow under his leadership, resulting in further expansion of the company's facilities in the 1980s. Additional land near the plant was acquired in Mansfield in 1983, and three years later a new 125,000-square-foot warehouse distribution center opened. Dalton remained in charge until 1992 when he retired at the age of 75. By that time his children were more than ready to take the helm and had already assumed many of their father's responsibilities. President Gary Dalton, 54, became chairman and CEO, while his 52-year-old sister, Patricia Dalton, was named president and remained CFO. By this stage Best Maid products were being sold by supermarket chains and independent grocers, and convenience stores, and were being made available in restaurants and school cafeterias throughout 14 states. Moreover, the company was developing international sales. Shortly before Garland Dalton's retirement, Best Maid began exporting its barbecue sauce to the United Kingdom through brokers, and was eager to ship other product lines overseas. All told, revenues were growing at a strong pace. Although the company did not release sales numbers, it revealed that sales increased 18 percent in both 1990 and 1991.

KEY DATES

1924: Mildred Dalton develops mayonnaise recipe to use up leftover egg yolks.

1926: The Daltons form Mrs. Dalton's Mayonnaise Company to satisfy popular demand for Mildred's mayonnaise.

1952: Company incorporates and moves its headquarters to Fort Worth, Texas.

1962: Del-Dixi Foods Corporation is acquired.

1976: Garland Dalton is named chairman and CEO.

1986: A new 125,000-square-foot warehouse distribution center opens.

1992: Garland Dalton retires.

2000: Patricia Dalton retires and is replaced as president by fourth-generation family member Brian Dalton.

2008: Jesse Dalton line of barbecue sauces is introduced.

ENVIRONMENTAL CONCERNS

The new generation, concerned about the environment, soon put its own stamp on Best Maid. In 1993 a further plant expansion allowed Best Maid to begin packing pickles in recyclable plastic bags in addition to glass and plastic jars and other plastic containers. The new processing and bag-packing line also increased production capacity by about 20 percent. The new management team soon faced an environmental concern of a different sort: the unsightly pickle tanks and odors that emanated from them at the Best Maid pickle farm. To make pickles, raw cucumbers were stored for about two weeks in water and salt in large, open-air vats, each one capable of holding 1,000 bushels of cucumbers. This brining process resulted in a variety of aromas, some of which most people did not find pleasant. The pickle farm was by this time located in the heart of Mansfield's commercial district, which had expanded since the farm had been established six decades earlier and was zoned commercial in the early 1980s.

Concerns about the location of the pickle farm came to a head in 1996 when Best Maid filed a zoning request to expand the operation, increasing the number of brining vats from about 600 to 1,000. Mansfield city planners, however, had decided to construct a "sub-courthouse" across from the farm, which they hoped would be joined by stores and restaurants, resulting in a conflict and a public commotion. Added to the mix was

the fact that Gary Dalton was Mansfield's former mayor. That matter was resolved later in the year when the city decided against building the sub-courthouse in that location.

In November 1996 Mansfield's planning and zoning commission voted to approve Best Maid's expansion after the company agreed to some concessions, including the restriction of pickle vats to no more than 800 and the construction of a brick fence to keep the vats out of view.

BARBECUE SAUCES INTRODUCED IN THE 21ST CENTURY

In 1997 the tank yard expansion project was completed, allowing Best Maid to keep pace with growing demand for its pickle products. In that same year, the company began making plans to consolidate its operations, including the Mansfield pickle farm and Fort Worth condiment processing plant, to a 164-acre site in South Mansfield, away from the more commercial northwest Mansfield area where the tank yard had long been located. Best Maid also planned to move the Fort Worth processing plant to the new site to consolidate all of the company's operations. The proposed $20 million facility was designed to avoid problems with its neighbors by building in the middle of the property and maintaining a large buffer zone. Hydraulics would be used to flush cucumbers and brine from the vats rather than having the task performed by hand. Best Maid then sought county property tax abatements from the city of Mansfield. The request was turned down in January 1999 and the project was put on hold.

As Best Maid entered the new century, the Dalton family remained very much attached to the company. In 2000 Patricia Dalton retired and was replaced as president by fourth-generation family member Brian Dalton. While the company continued to rely on the same product lines that led to its success, Best Maid took steps to keep the brand fresh. In 2003 product labels received makeovers, as did truck trailer designs, which debuted on the highways a year later. A new processing building opened in 2005, and in the summer of 2008 the company introduced a line of barbecue sauces, based on the recipes of one of its founders and marketed under a new label: Jesse Dalton. The four initial flavors included Stockyard Stampede Texas Style BBQ Sauce, Guadalupe Smokehouse Smoke BBQ Sauce, Terlingua Creek Spicy Ancho BBQ Sauce, and Mustang Island Tropical Pepper BBQ Sauce. The sauces were carried by area Tom Thumb stores as well as Randalls supermarkets in Houston and Brookshire's stores in East Texas. There was every reason to expect the family business to continue to thrive in the Southwest for years to come.

Ed Dinger

PRINCIPAL SUBSIDIARIES

Dalton's Best Maid Products, Inc.

PRINCIPAL COMPETITORS

Del Monte Foods Company; H.J. Heinz Company; Pinnacle Foods Finance LLC.

FURTHER READING

Autrey, Jennifer, "Mansfield Has Dilly of Problem," *Fort Worth Star-Telegram,* June 10, 1996, p. 1.

———, "Mansfield Planners Approve Pickle Plant Expansion," *Fort Worth Star,* November 6, 1996, p. 2.

Cadwallader, Robert, "Best Maid Plans to Move Facilities to S. Mansfield," *Fort Worth Star-Telegram,* June 26, 1997, p. 1.

Carter, O. K., "Six Figures Make Mansfield History," *Fort Worth Star-Telegram,* April 6, 1997, p. 1.

Curry, Kerry, "Best Maid Moving to Mansfield," *Dallas Business Journal,* January 29, 1999, p. 1.

Wren, Worth, "Son, Daughter Replace CEO at Best Maid," *Fort Worth Star-Telegram,* May 26, 1992, p. 6.

Borghese Inc.

———————— ■ ————————

10 East 34th Street, Floor 3
New York, New York 10016
U.S.A.
Telephone: (212) 659-5300
Web site: http://www.borghese.com

Private Company
Incorporated: 1992 as Halston Borghese International
    Inc.
Employees: 60
Sales: $50 million (2008 est.)
NAICS: 325620 Toilet Preparation Manufacturing

■ ■ ■

Borghese Inc. is a New York City-based marketer of Italian cosmetics, skin care products, hair care products, spa products, and fragrances. The private company, headed by part owner Georgette Mosbacher, a well-known socialite and Republican Party fund-raiser, caters primarily to upscale department stores such as Bloomingdale's, Lord & Taylor, and Nordstrom. Cosmetics include lipsticks, lip glosses, lip pencils, mascaras, eye shadows, foundations, powders, blush, and bronzers. Skin care products include antiaging treatments, cleansers, moisturizers, masks, exfoliators, and sun care treatments. Borghese also offers body scrubs, hydrators, and hand and foot care products. Hair care products include shampoo, conditioner, and a conditioning mud treatment. Spa products and home spa products include contour scrubs and creams, skin renewal polish, facial pads, vitamin renewal kits, and gift sets. In addition,

Borghese's Men's Club unit offers face moisturizers, eye treatments, cleansing and restorative treatments, as well as body scrubs, lotions, and bath and shower gels. Borghese has also expanded into the mass market by developing a Borghese nail, hand, and foot care line under a licensing agreement with Del Laboratories, Inc., of Uniondale, New York.

ORIGINS

The woman behind the Borghese name was Princess Marcella Borghese. Born Marcella Fazi in Sicily, probably in 1911, she became in 1938 the second wife of Paolo Borghese, a widowed nobleman who was a prince and the Duke of Bomarzo as well as a descendant of a family that produced one pope. Then a princess, she lent her name to a cosmetics line in the 1950s. During that time, Revlon, Inc., was fending off competition in the department store sector from newcomer Estée Lauder and its upscale line of department store–only cosmetics as well as new exclusive lines introduced by other rivals, such as Coty's Dina Merrill brand, Max Factor's Geminesse, and Fabergé's Juliette Marglen.

It was Italian American businessman Gino di Grandi who recognized that an affiliation with Princess Marcella Borghese could help Revlon launch its own department store brand. In 1956 he introduced Princess Borghese to Charles Revson, Revlon's founder, leading a year later to her signing a licensing agreement with Revlon, allowing the company to manufacture, market, and sell cosmetics under her name. A Revlon subsidiary was formed in New York under the name Princess Marcella Borghese, Inc. For his efforts di Grandi receive a 10 percent commission on the income the princess received.

According to her obituaries, Princess Borghese was more than just a figurehead at the company that bore her name; the press reported that the cosmetics line was launched using old family recipes, some of them dating back to Pauline Bonaparte Borghese, Napoleon's sister. Borghese remained involved with the company until shortly before her death in 2002. Regardless, there was no doubt that the Italian cosmetics line found a place in upscale department stores. The initial products, lipstick and nail polish, made their debut in May 1958 on an exclusive basis at Bonwit Teller in Manhattan. Juliette Marglen leadership was not pleased with the newcomer's entry, however. Three months later the Fabergé subsidiary sued Princess Marcella Borghese Inc. and Charles Revson, alleging that in 1956 Revson discovered Marglen's business plans while exploring the acquisition of Fabergé and was using that knowledge to destroy Marglen by merchandising similar cosmetics through Princess Marcella Borghese.

NEW OWNERS

Over the years, Princess Marcella Borghese expanded its product offering, became available at other top-tier department stores, and ultimately emerged as the most successful of the department store brands launched in the 1950s. After Revson's death in 1975, department store distribution became less important, and the Princess Marcella Borghese line became a minor part of Revlon.

Ronald Perelman engineered a takeover of Revlon in 1985, and new management divested noncore assets to refocus the company on its beauty products. Reinvigorating Princess Marcella Borghese was part of that plan. The unit's research and development efforts were bolstered, and in the 1980s Princess Marcella Borghese helped to carve out the spa category. The Montecatini Cosmetic line, introduced during this period, used the Fango Mud and mineral waters of the princess's favorite spa, Terme di Montecatini.

The subsidiary remained a part of Revlon until January 1992 when it and the Halston fragrance and licensing operation were sold to a group of four Saudi investors who merged the assets to create a new company, Halston Borghese International Inc., also based in New York City. Assuming the chief executive officer position was Michael Marten, Revlon's former senior vice-president of corporate development, who planned to expand the Borghese brand beyond Hong Kong and Japan, where it was already marketed, to Europe, the Middle East, and Latin America.

Halston Borghese experienced a difficult start, its expansion plan proving too aggressive. In addition to the expense of moving into new geographic markets, the company spent heavily on the development of a pair of fragrances, Il Bacio for women and Catalyst for men. The company managed to build sales to $200 million in 1993 despite a crowded marketplace, but the high cost of materials that year crippled its finances. A new management team was installed in 1994, including industry veterans Ray Baliatico serving as CEO and Sherry Baker as president of the North American operations. Although Halston Borghese would continue to see growth in the Pacific Rim and Europe, the pace slackened as the company attempted to focus on the United States. Moreover, the new team hoped to modernize the image of the Borghese cosmetics line.

Halston Borghese fared no better under Baliatico and Baker than it had under Marten and his team. In July 1995 the company announced that it was looking for an outside investor with which to form a "strategic alliance," while not dismissing the possibility of selling the company, either whole or piecemeal. After two years at the helm Baliatico resigned as CEO in February 1996, followed a month later by Baker. At the same time there was a prospect of selling the Borghese cosmetics portion of the business to an investment group that included two sons of Princess Marcella Borghese. The deal soon fell through, however. In the end, the Saudi owners elected to sell the company's Halston and Nautica fragrance brands but retain Borghese.

CHANGE IN LEADERSHIP

Late in 1996 another industry veteran, Teresa Townsend, was installed as president and chief executive officer. One of her first moves was to shorten the brand name to Borghese and the corporate name to Borghese Inc. Retailer concerns about the brand were not placated by such surface changes, and Townsend spent a major part of a year paying visits to buyers across the country to assuage their anger over poorly executed promotions

KEY DATES

1957: Princess Marcella Borghese and Revlon Inc. create upscale Princess Marcella Borghese cosmetics line.

1992: Revlon sells Halston and Borghese brands to a group of investors who form Halston Borghese International Inc.

1996: The brand name is shortened to Borghese and the corporate name to Borghese Inc.

1999: Georgette Mosbacher becomes chief executive and part owner.

2005: Costco private-label line is introduced.

2008: Borghese enters licensing agreement with Del Laboratories to develop mass-market line.

and late shipments. Despite Townsend's best efforts, Borghese continued to lose money. In July 1999 Townsend resigned. Succeeding her as the head of the company was Georgette Mosbacher, who a year earlier had become involved with Borghese in an advisory role.

Mosbacher was a high-profile individual, both in the beauty industry and in the world of politics. Born Georgette Paulsin in Highland, Indiana, in 1947, she grew up under difficult circumstances. Her father, a pipe fitter and bowling alley owner, was killed in an automobile accident caused by a drunk driver when she was a child. While her mother worked as a travel agent, she helped earn money through babysitting at the age of nine, later ran a switchboard, tried her hand at sales, and took advantage of her beauty to land modeling jobs in Chicago. She worked her way through Indiana University and after graduating in 1969 took a job with a Detroit advertising agency. A year later she quit and moved to Los Angeles where her brother lived. It was there that Mosbacher posed as a journalist seeking an interview to meet the man she had already planned to marry: a real estate developer named Robert Muir, about 20 years her senior. The marriage lasted four years, and in 1977 Mosbacher moved to New York City.

Mosbacher went to work for the film production unit of Fabergé, and soon met the company's chairman, George Barrie. They became romantically involved and were married in 1980. Mosbacher learned the ins and outs of running a cosmetics company from Barrie, but he proved to be a hard-drinking, abusive man. They eventually divorced and Mosbacher moved to Houston, a city where she thought she could meet wealthy men. After a number of arranged dates, she met a suitable new partner in Robert Mosbacher, the twice-married owner of Mosbacher Energy Company. He was not as keen as she was on giving married life a third try, but he was eventually won over and the two were married in 1985.

MOSBACHER MAKES HER MARK IN WASHINGTON, D.C.

While focusing her attentions on wealthy men, she remained hard working and highly independent. Even before marrying Mosbacher, she was considering the purchase of an upscale cosmetics and skin care company, La Prairie, carried by only the best department stores. In 1988 she bought the company for $30 million to $35 million without using any of her husband's money, although he did introduce her to some investors in Germany and Japan. She was very much a hands-on executive at La Prairie, splitting her time between New York where her offices were and Washington, D.C., where Mosbacher was then based after being appointed secretary of commerce by President George H. W. Bush. Georgette Mosbacher and her flamboyant fashion soon made a mark in the nation's capital, known for a more conservative style. She became a media darling as well as a target of intense criticism; as a consequence, she toned down the way she dressed. She also became known as a Washington hostess and Republican Party fund-raiser, although in actuality she devoted much of her time to running her company and the dinner parties she held were just as likely to be connected to business or one of her favorite charities as politics.

In 1991 Mosbacher decided to sell La Prairie, which was acquired by Beiersdorf AG of Germany for about $45 million, an offer she said was too good to turn down. A year later Bush lost his reelection bid, and Robert Mosbacher left public service, returning to Houston. Marital problems eventually led to another divorce for Georgette Mosbacher. Although she had her own independent wealth as well as alimony from her husband, Mosbacher continued to work in the cosmetics field, forming a consultancy, Georgette Mosbacher Enterprises. In that capacity she was hired by Borghese and later when she was asked to run the company she accepted, her employment deal including a significant ownership position.

RESTRUCTURING PLAN LAUNCHED

Mosbacher believed the Borghese brand remained strong and the company's shortcomings were the result of a bloated organization. She soon initiated a restructuring plan that trimmed or eliminated most departments.

Research and development and testing were contracted out, and Borghese essentially became a sales and marketing operation. National advertising was eliminated, the savings invested in the company. The number of stock-keeping units (SKUs) was cut by more than half, while an effort was made to ensure that the top-selling products were also available in ample supplies. "We'll never have that level of cosmetics SKUs again," she told *WWD*. "We have three mascaras—black in waterproof and non-waterproof formulas, and brown. If you want blue mascara, you'll have to go somewhere else." In addition, Mosbacher cut the number of retailers that carried Borghese products from 1,000 to 500, and she negotiated better terms with the retailers that remained, more than willing not to ship her products to them if they could not make money.

Mosbacher had successfully turned around Borghese by the spring of 2001, when she decided the time had come to introduce the company's first new fragrance since she took charge, La Carezza D'Amore. Business had stabilized enough that in 2002 the company was able to reintroduce its Fango Active Mud for Hair and Scalp treatment to the U.K. market. A year later Borghese expanded its spa product offerings further with the introduction of the Spa-At-Home collection, whose exfoliating products and moisturizers targeted such specific areas as hair, eyes, and feet.

Rather than being limited to Borghese's traditional distribution channels, Mosbacher looked for new sources of income. In 2005 Borghese teamed up with warehouse club Costco to introduce a new line of private-label cosmetics under the Kirkland Signature name. In 2008 Borghese struck a deal to take its own brand into the mass market, forging a licensing agreement with Del Laboratories to introduce hand, foot, and nail items for sale in such drugstore chains as CVS, Longs Drug Stores, Rite Aid, and Walgreens. Major department stores remained the domain for Borghese's color cosmetics, however. Should the new mass market prove successful, Borghese planned to expand the brand into other categories, leading to a host of new opportunities for the venerable brand.

Ed Dinger

PRINCIPAL OPERATING UNITS

Skin Care; Color; Body/Hand; Spa; Hair Care; Men's Club.

PRINCIPAL COMPETITORS

Coty, Inc.; Elizabeth Arden, Inc.; Sephora USA.

FURTHER READING

Aktar, Alev, "Borghese Treats Itself to New Business Plan, Including Downsizing," *WWD*, September 24, 1999, p. 1.

Benson, Barbara, "Exec Retouches Firm's Foundation," *Crain's New York Business*, April 25, 1994, p. 31.

Edgar, Michelle, and Faye Brookman, "Borghese Partners with Del for Mass Items," *WWD*, January 18, 2008, p. 7.

"Former Revlon Brands Marketed by New Firm," *Chain Drug Review*, February 10, 1992, p. 2.

Hoppe, Karen, "Halston Borghese: Revamping, Retrenching, Revitalized," *Drug & Cosmetic Industry*, December 1994, p. 44.

"Italian Formulas Used in New Cosmetic Line," *New York Times*, March 28, 1958.

"Marcella Borghese; Princess, 90, Began a Line of Cosmetics," *New York Times*, February 8, 2002, p. A21.

"Mosbacher's Master Plan for Rebuilding Borghese," *WWD*, November 10, 2000, p. 6.

Naughton, Julie, "Borghese: Making Scents of Love," *WWD*, April 6, 2001, p. 11.

North, Marjorie, "'Feminine Force' Georgette Mosbacher Revives Failing Companies," *Sarasota Herald Tribune*, February 24, 2005, p. E3.

"Suit Accuses Revlon of Copying Cosmetics Made by Marglen," *New York Times*, August 15, 1958.

Bravo Health Insurance Company, Inc.

—■—

3601 O'Donnell Street
Baltimore, Maryland 21224
U.S.A.
Telephone: (410) 864-4400
Toll Free: (800) 291-0396
Web site: http://www.bravohealth.com

Private Company
Incorporated: 1995 as Elder Health, Inc.
Employees: 590
Sales: $532.7 million
NAICS: 524114 Direct Health and Medical Insurance
Carriers

■ ■ ■

Bravo Health Insurance Company, Inc., is a private healthcare company based in Baltimore, Maryland, specializing in providing healthcare benefits through several Medicare plans to elderly patients in Delaware, Maryland, Pennsylvania (Philadelphia and Pittsburgh), Texas (Dallas and Fort Worth, El Paso, Houston, and San Antonio), and Washington, D.C. These benefits include Medicare Advantage HMO options; Special Needs Plan to serve institutionalized patients as well as people who are eligible for both Medicare and Medicaid; Private Fee-For-Service plans, which provide patients with greater choice; Point of Service and Preferred Provider Organization plans to cover patients outside their networks; and Part D prescription plans to provide extra medication coverage. All told, the company serves more than 250,000 people and works

with more than 20,000 physicians. The company expects to expand its plan offerings to 46 states.

COMPANY FOUNDED: 1995

Bravo was founded in 1995 as Elder Health, Inc., put together by Baltimore-based venture-capital firm New Enterprise Associates (NEA). The inspiration for the company was supplied by one of the founding general partners, Charles Newhall, an advocate of pursuing opportunities in paradigm-shifting or rapidly growing markets. In the early 1990s healthcare clearly fit that bill, and according to *Forbes,* Newhall became convinced there were "big opportunities for companies specializing in monitoring the health of poor old folks, thus saving the government money that would otherwise be spent on expensive hospital visits and nursing home stays later on." To put flesh on the bones of this idea, NEA recruited a pair of seasoned executives to cofound Elder Health: David D. Carliner, a nursing home executive who had been in charge of prepaid healthcare initiatives with nursing-home company Genesis Health Ventures and became Elder Health's senior vice-president of development; and Michael R. Steele, who took over as president and chief executive officer of the new company. A University of West Florida graduate, Steele had held a number of top positions in the managed care field with such companies as Tampa Bay Health Plan Inc., Cigna/Equicor, and Travelers Health Company. NEA supplied $4.5 million in seed money, and three other venture firms contributed $12 million.

Elder Health started out as a for-profit health clinic that focused on the primary healthcare and day care of

```
┌─────────────────────────────────────────┐
│                                         │
│     COMPANY PERSPECTIVES                │
│              ───■───                     │
│                                         │
│   We will be a diversified, high growth company with │
│   no limits to our success by anticipating and fulfilling │
│   the health care needs of our customers. │
│                                         │
└─────────────────────────────────────────┘
```

poor, frail elderly persons who were enrolled in both Medicare and Medicaid. The first facility opened its doors in Baltimore in May 1995. The clinic served its patients by providing primary and preventive care. To accomplish this goal, both a nurse practitioner and a primary care physician were assigned to each patient. In addition to providing around-the-clock first-call coverage, the nurse served as case manager, arranging for social services as needed. Elder Health also provided transportation to ensure patients kept their medical appointments.

FUNDING ROUND IN 1999 RAISES $20 MILLION

A second Baltimore clinic opened in 1998, allowing Elder Care to serve about half of the city's Zip code areas. The company also began to deliver Medicaid and Medicare covered services to seniors on a set fee, essentially matching them with healthcare providers, through health maintenance organizations (HMOs) in Maryland, Florida, Pennsylvania, and Texas. It was a business model attractive to investors because, unlike assisted-living center and convalescent homes, Elder Health was not concerned with occupancy rates. In April 1999 the company was able to raise about $20 million in another round of funding, the original investors joined by the likes of General Electric Equity, a General Electric Capital Corp. subsidiary.

In the late 1990s Medicare HMOs enjoyed strong growth, peaking in 1999 when seven million seniors were enrolled. The federal government then cut reimbursement rates, making it difficult for HMOs to turn a profit and leading many to eliminate insurance products for the elderly. Not burdened by as much overhead, Elder Health continued to expand on a selective basis and achieved profitability in 2002 on revenues of $70 million. Also in 2002 subsidiary Elder Health Pennsylvania Inc. began operating a Medicare HMO in Philadelphia, which the company considered an attractive market because of its dense population, strong managed-care and long-term-care communities and Medicare reimbursement rates that were significantly higher than surrounding suburban communities. An

overhaul of Medicare in 2003 led to higher reimbursement rates, and in that year Elder Health expanded its coverage to include the counties surrounding Philadelphia: Bucks, Delaware, and Montgomery. In addition, Elder Health received permission to offer its SmartChoice Plus optional supplemental benefit plan in Philadelphia and Delaware counties.

WASHINGTON, D.C., MARKET ENTERED: 2004

To expand beyond Maryland and Pennsylvania, as well as meet regulatory capital requirements, Elder Health sought further financing. In 2003 it raised $16 million in another round of funding, which included NEA and other existing investors. For the year, revenues reached the $100 million level, a performance that led to an additional $52.5 million in financing in 2004. Not only were Medicare HMOs gaining greater favor with investors because of higher reimbursement rates, Elder Health was poised to benefit from extra payments for the frailer, sicker elderly, the company's focus, that were being phased in over the next few years. With the new funding, Elder Health in late 2004 began enrolling seniors in Washington, D.C. A few months later the company entered Pittsburgh, Pennsylvania's Allegheny County, another market that boasted high reimbursement rates.

Elder Health expanded on a number of fronts in 2005. In the spring the company grew its business in Maryland by reaching an agreement with Harford Primary Care to add its eight locations and 19 family practice and internal medicine physicians to its network in Harford County, Maryland. Later in the year, the Pennsylvania subsidiary assumed the Medicare business of AmeriChoice of Pennsylvania Inc., adding about 6,000 Medicare beneficiaries to become one of the largest Medicare HMOs in Pennsylvania. Elder Health entered the Texas market in 2005, establishing operations in Corpus Christi, El Paso, Houston, and San Antonio. Also in 2005 the company reached an agreement with the federal Centers for Medicare and Medicaid Services to offer prescription coverage as part of the federal government's new drug benefit. As a result revenues soared to the $350 million range, triple the previous year's total.

NEW CEO HIRED: 2006

Elder Health began a change in direction in 2005, starting with the departure of Steele as CEO. In July 2006 he was replaced by 30-year-industry veteran Jeffrey M. Folick, the former executive vice-president for Regional Health Plans and Specialty Companies with California-

KEY DATES

1995: Company founded as Elder Health, Inc., in Baltimore, Maryland.
1998: Second Baltimore clinic opens.
1999: Financing round raised $20 million.
2002: Company begins operating in Philadelphia, Pennsylvania.
2004: Company enters Washington, D.C., market.
2007: Elder Health changes name to Bravo Health.
2009: Membership tops 250,000.

based Health Net, a major managed healthcare company, and chief operating officer of PacifiCare Health Systems, where he was also president of the Medicare division. He quickly brought changes to Elder Health, laying off about 40 people, including members of the top management ranks. Folick brought in a new chief financial officer and several other new executives. Because so many members of the new executive team had experience with public companies, there was some speculation in the industry and the press that Elder Health was preparing to go public. While Folick did not entirely dismiss the possibility, he was clearly focused on growing the business in the short-term by moving beyond the focus on low-income Medicaid and Medicare beneficiaries, which accounted for only 18 percent of Medicare beneficiaries. He was especially interested in taking full advantage of the new federal drug benefit.

BRAVO HEALTH NAME ADOPTED: 2007

Another major step taken in 2006 was to rechristen the name of the Medicare Advantage and prescription drug plans to "Bravo by Elder Health." Given that graying baby boomers were becoming the target market, one that cherished a healthy, active lifestyle, the company no longer thought it wise to emphasize the word *elderly.* Thus, in the summer of 2007 Elder Health changed its name to Bravo Health, in keeping with the introduction of the Bravo brand a year earlier. By pursuing the prescription drug benefit business as well as the fast-growing private fee-for-service portion of the Medicare market, the branding effort became part of a larger strategy to make Bravo Health something of a one-stop shop for Medicare products. The prescription drug product was first rolled out in the mid-Atlantic regions, and in 2007 the program was expanded to eight other

states, including California, Florida, Illinois, New York, and Pennsylvania.

Folick sought to expand market share in cities where the company already operated, the goal to peel away affluent suburban seniors from their regular HMOs. In order to expand existing markets and enter new ones, Bravo Health pursued acquisition opportunities in the belief that people were reluctant to change health plans. It was, thus, easier to achieve growth externally than internally. In 2007, prior to the name change to Bravo Health, the company completed the first acquisition in its 11-year history by purchasing Senior Partners, the Medicare HMO subsidiary of Health Partners of Philadelphia Inc., jointly owned by seven Philadelphia hospitals, picking up about 23,000 new members.

To support ongoing growth, Bravo Health once again tapped the capital markets in the fall of 2007. In two separate rounds the company raised a total of $72 million. By the end of 2007 Bravo Health topped the 100,000 mark in members, about half of them enrolled in a prescription-only drug plan. The company enjoyed such strong growth that its membership rolls doubled in a matter of nine months, reaching 200,000 by July 2008. The addition of 50,000 new members in California for the Prescription Drug Plan was a major contributor to the increase.

Bravo Health continues to enjoy steady growth in 2009. At the start of the year, the company reached an agreement with Providence Hospital to become one of its approved healthcare providers in the Washington, D.C., area. Bravo Health also grew its business in Western Pennsylvania after plans for expansion into Washington and Westmoreland counties were approved. Around the same time, the company also received permission to market its Medicare Advantage plan in Dallas and Tarrant counties in the North Texas market, as well as the Fort Bend, Liberty, Chambers, and Montgomery counties in the Houston market. By the summer of 2009 Bravo Health had increased its membership in excess of 250,000.

The expansion of the membership ranks had been accompanied by an increase in employment over the previous three years, increasing from 300 to 570 people. In need of space, Bravo Health secured an additional 117,000 square feet at its Baltimore headquarters, providing enough space to accommodate more than 200 new hires in the years to come. There was every reason to believe that those extra employees would become necessary. Existing markets offered ample opportunities for continued growth, given that the baby boom generation was just beginning to swell the Medicare ranks. Moreover, they were expected to live longer and remain participants in Bravo Health plans for an extended period. There were also an abundance of new markets for Bravo Health to pursue near current operations as well as other parts of the country. Due to possible healthcare reforms initiated by a new administration in Washington, there was some degree of uncertainty in the future of Bravo Health, but because of its history of success, Bravo Health would in all likelihood find a way to prosper.

Ed Dinger

PRINCIPAL SUBSIDIARIES

Bravo Health, Inc.

PRINCIPAL COMPETITORS

CIGNA Corporation; Health Net, Inc.; Independence Blue Cross.

FURTHER READING

George, John, "Medicare HMO Drawn to Phila.," *Philadelphia Business Journal,* January 14, 2002.

Jaffe, Greg, "Start-Ups in Health Care Are Booming," *Wall Street Journal,* May 23, 1997, p. A9A.

Mamula, Kris B., "Baltimore Firm to Offer Medicare HMO Plan," *Pittsburgh Business Times,* May 2, 2005.

Mirabella, Lorraine, "Health Insurer to Add Office Space for 200 Jobs," *Baltimore Sun,* July 10, 2009.

Morse, Andrew, "Elder Health Draws $16M," *Daily Deal,* July 22, 2009.

Novack, Janet, "Paradigm Surfing," *Forbes,* November 4, 1996, p. 204.

Salganik, M. William, "Elder Health Buying a Medicare HMO in Pa.," *Baltimore Sun,* January 3, 2007.

———, "Investors Pump $52.5 Million into Baltimore Medicare HMO Elder Health," *Baltimore Sun,* December 9, 2004.

Schultz, Sue, "Elder Health Changes Name to Bravo Health," *Baltimore Business Journal,* July 25, 2007.

Werner, Ben, "Investors Ponder Market for Elderly," *Baltimore Business Journal,* May 7, 1999, p. 6.

Zibel, Alan, "New Execs, New Strategy for Elder Health," *Baltimore Business Journal,* August 7, 2006.

Bread Loaf Corporation

———— ■ ————

1292 Route 7S
Middlebury, Vermont 05753-8800
U.S.A.
Telephone: (802) 388-9871
Fax: (802) 388-3815
Web site: http://www.breadloaf.com

Private Company
Incorporated: 1968 as Bread Loaf Development
  Company
Employees: 100
Sales: $30 million (2008 est.)
NAICS: 236220 Commercial and Institutional Building
  Construction

■ ■ ■

Bread Loaf Corporation is a privately held planning, architecture, and building firm located in Middlebury, Vermont, named after the area's most prominent landmark, Bread Loaf Mountain. One of the largest full-service construction firms in Vermont, Bread Loaf serves a wide range of sectors, employing what it calls an Integrated Project Management approach that determines a client's goals and potential obstacles even before formal planning begins. Commercial projects include the corporate offices and warehouses of Ben & Jerry's Homemade, the Orvis Company headquarters and flagship store, the Littleton Coin Company headquarters, Vermont Federal credit branches in Burlington and Middlebury, and the Automaster BMW and Porsche dealerships.

Bread Loaf also serves the light industrial sector. Projects include a distribution center for the Vermont Country Store and a Teddy Bear Village at the headquarters of Vermont Teddy Bear Company, as well as facilities for Boston Scientific; Huber & Suhner, Inc.; Hypertherm, Inc.; Northeast Cooperatives, Inc.; and NRG Wind Systems. In the Resort Hospitality area, Bread Loaf projects include the Stratton Mountain Mid-Mountain Lodge and the Equinox Resort Avanyu Spa. Bread Loaf is also proficient in recreation projects, such as a community swimming pool and recreation center for Stowe, Vermont; an outdoor pool complex in Lebanon, New Hampshire; the renovation of a historic minor league baseball stadium in Nashua, New Hampshire; and a tennis center for Dartmouth College.

Over the years, Bread Loaf has also completed a variety of other projects at Dartmouth College. Additional higher education clients include Landmark College, Middlebury College, Saint Michael's College, the Catholic University of America, the University of Vermont, and Williams College. In addition, Bread Loaf works with communities on cultural and public institution projects, such as the Bennington Museum, the Montshire Museum, the Montshire Science Park, facilities for the Southern Vermont Arts Center, the Middlebury Police Department and town hall building, and a fire station and police station for Williston, Vermont. The firm's principal owner is its president and chief executive office, Maynard F. McLaughlin.

ORIGINS

Bread Loaf Corporation was founded in 1968 in Middlebury, Connecticut, by 26-year-old Ronald A.

Mainelli as Bread Loaf Development Company. It was initially devoted to residential projects, but soon shifted its focus to commercial and industrial projects. As a result, the name was changed to Bread Loaf Construction Company. In the 1970s the company expanded its capabilities to become one of the state's first design-build firms. In a natural progression, Bread Loaf began adding architects to its ranks by the end of the 1970s, instead of contracting with independent architecture firms. With an in-house design team saving clients time and money, Bread Loaf established the foundation on which its future success would develop.

Two key employees Mainelli hired to grow Bread Loaf were Maynard F. McLaughlin and John Leehman. The older of the two by 15 years was McLaughlin, a graduate of the Catholic University of America with a bachelor of science degree in civil engineering. He was in charge of estimates for Bread Loaf. Leehman, a 1970 graduate of Hobart and William Smith Colleges, joined Bread Loaf in 1972 after briefly running Boulder, Colorado-based InstraFrame Construction Company, a fast-track home builder. At Bread Loaf, Leehman was responsible for supervising construction sites.

By 1980 Bread Loaf was still a small concern, employing just 50 people, and not yet profitable. To keep growing, Mainelli was eager to make sure McLaughlin and Leehman stayed with the company, so he offered them stakes in the business. They each received a 4 percent interest at a cost of $3,500. Mainelli also took the precaution of making a buy-sell agreement between the three parties that maintained if any of the three men died, the estate of the deceased was obligated to sell his share of the stock to the company at a fixed price, based on the company's then book value of less than $500,000. An insurance policy was taken out on each man's life, based on his stake, to finance the stock buyback. In this way, Mainelli hoped to avoid the complications of dealing with the estate of a minority shareholder. His partners agreed but were hardly concerned about their estates at that moment. "We were all indestructible at that point," McLaughlin

told *Inc.* in 1990. "We saw the buy-sell as something Ron wanted, nothing more."

FOUNDER DIES IN CAR ACCIDENT

While the buy-sell agreement primarily served the interests of Mainelli, it also protected the existence of the company itself. This fact became all too evident late on the Friday evening of February 17, 1984, when the 42-year-old Mainelli was killed in a car accident. The buy-sell agreement that had been little more than an afterthought then provided the surviving partners with a structure to keep Bread Loaf alive. After a weekend of mourning, the partners returned to the office and were able to reassure employees about their jobs, because the buy-sell agreement required that the Mainelli estate sell its stock to the company, making McLaughlin and Leehman the sole owners and managing partners of Bread Loaf. Furthermore, because of the mechanism in place, they could also promise suppliers that they would be paid and clients that despite the loss of its founder Bread Loaf would complete projects as scheduled.

Because the company had taken on some of the highest-profile projects in its history, the loss of any of the partners would have caused enough press attention to ruin Bread Loaf's chances of securing further work. Therefore, the surviving partners paid a visit to every client, explaining the implications of the buy-sell agreement. The firm also placed local newspaper advertisements that laid out the succession plan in place while also announcing Mainelli's death. As a result of these efforts, the company retained its business under circumstances that would have devastated other companies of similar size.

Mainelli's wife had not been made aware of the arrangement, however, leading to some confusion at a difficult time for her. There were also some holes in the buy-sell agreement, including uncertainty about management succession. Because McLaughlin and Leehman were friends, they were able to work out a suitable arrangement. McLaughlin assumed the presidency while Leehman became executive vice-president. Titles aside, they shared management responsibilities and continued to fulfill the roles they had before Mainelli's death. They also took care to create a new buy-sell agreement, this one more thorough and revised on a regular basis to remain current with changing conditions. In essence, the new agreement required the estate of a deceased partner to sell his half-stake in the business to the company, paid for by term life insurance policies. In addition, it covered the prospects of disability (the buyout paid for by disability insurance) or the desire of a partner to cash out (paid for by cash flow from the company).

KEY DATES

1968: Ronald Mainelli founds Bread Loaf Development Company.
1984: Mainelli dies in car accident.
1989: Construction slump begins.
1995: Co-owner John Leehman sells back his stake in company.
1998: Company is renamed Bread Loaf Corporation.
2008: Building slump leads to layoffs.

McLaughlin and Leehman took ownership of a business that was generating a modest $4.5 million in annual revenues. It was an amount that would grow rapidly over the next few years as Vermont enjoyed a surge in construction activity. Some new clients taken on during this period were Dartmouth College and Vermont Country Store. One of the biggest challenges facing Bread Loaf was finding enough skilled employees as the firm's workforce more than tripled in a matter of five years. Leehman looked to other parts of the country to recruit employees, focusing on areas with climates similar to Vermont but whose market was depressed. He enjoyed some success in Denver, Colorado, where newspaper ads resulted in 30 candidates and four new hires.

SURVIVING TOUGH TIMES

Bread Loaf's revenues reached $27 million in 1989, but seeds of a construction slump had already been sown late in the year. A recession that enveloped the country in 1990 and 1991 only made the situation worse, and even when the United States as a whole began to recover, Vermont lagged behind. As a result, bidding for what projects became available was intense and profit margins were so slim that many Vermont construction companies sought work elsewhere or simply closed their doors.

Bread Loaf hung on despite tough conditions and tried to keep employees employed as long as possible. A rotating layoff system was implemented so that workers were employed two out of every three weeks. In this way, they maintained two-thirds of their salaries and kept their benefits, and the company achieved much-needed cuts in overhead. It was only a stopgap measure, however. Eventually the workforce had to be trimmed, and the ranks were thinned from a peak of 160 in 1989 to about 110 in the early 1990s.

Bread Loaf managed to land its share of projects as the slump continued in the early 1990s. These included a $12 million dormitory renovation project at Middlebury College, a $2.5 million hockey rink in Manchester, Vermont, and a $7.5 million Mack Molding plant in Arlington, Vermont. The mid-1990s also saw the departure of John Leehman, who took advantage of the buy-sell agreement to sell back his stake in Bread Loaf in 1995 to pursue new business interests. He became chief executive of an upscale women's fashion company, Dia, Ltd., and then joined the "total wellness" multilevel marketing company Nikken Inc.

To become a more rounded company and better able to compete, Bread Loaf added planning functions to its services. In addition to design and construction services, the company could then help clients in such areas as site selection, permit analysis, and cost options. This new capability led to the development of the company's proprietary Integrated Project Management process that brought together planning, design, and construction into a coordinated method. Because the company no longer considered itself a traditional construction company, it changed its name in 1998 from Bread Loaf Construction to Bread Loaf Corporation. A year later McLaughlin's son, Michael McLaughlin, joined the company. A Loyola College graduate with a degree in business administration, he became Bread Loaf's vice-president of business development and marketing.

Accompanying an economic boom in the second half of the 1990s was a return of the problem Bread Loaf had in finding sufficient numbers of skilled workers. Part of the problem was the previous construction slump, the duration of which dissuaded young people from turning to construction as a way to make a living. There was also a long-term trend of young people pursuing college and white-collar jobs rather than going into the trades. As a result, tradespeople of earlier generations were retiring but there was no one available to take their places, leading to a shortage of masons, electricians, and other skilled construction workers. In order to maintain the high quality of work, Bread Loaf had to refrain from bidding on some jobs because it did not want to risk its reputation by taking on more work than it could properly handle.

AN ABUNDANCE OF PROJECTS

As the 1990s came to a close, Bread Loaf completed a major addition for Mack Group in Arlington, Vermont; finished a new headquarters for the Orvis Company, Inc., the fly fishing equipment and outdoor clothing retail chain; constructed a new headquarters and distribution center for Littleton Coin Company; and completed the first phase of a headquarters and distribution facility project for Northeast Cooperatives. The firm's Integrated Project Management service was also proving popular with clients, and in the first year of the new century a majority of Bread Loaf's projects made use of it, including another phase of the Northeast Cooperatives contract, a new bakery for King Arthur Flour, and work on an operations center and administrative offices for Vermont Country Store. Design work for an Orvis flagship retail store was also begun in 2000 and construction the following year. Other repeat clients included Dartmouth College, which used Bread Loaf to build a new tennis facility and to complete laboratory upgrades. Although Dartmouth was a longtime client, these projects were the first on which Bread Loaf served as both architect and builder. The company also did work for Landmark College in 2000, and out of state it constructed manufacturing clean rooms, research and development facilities, and office renovations and additions for Boston Scientific in Glen Falls, New York, and Kendall Sheridan in Argyle, New York.

Vermont's economic boom continued, leading to further work for Bread Loaf in the new century as annual revenues approached $35 million, but the ongoing labor shortage did not allow the firm to fully exploit the flush times. By refusing to compromise quality in the pursuit of profits, Bread Loaf garnered a number of awards for the projects it completed in the first decade of the new century. Bread Loaf's work on the Bennington Museum won the coveted 2001 National Design-Build Award for Best Project under $5 million. A year later it received recognition for the Town Hall Theater in Middlebury as well as the Middlebury Natural Foods Co-op, winning the 2002 Vermont Public Space Merit Awards. In 2003 the Orvis flagship store received the Best Builder Award for New Construction from the Associated General Contractors of Vermont. Later in the decade Bread Loaf completed work on the Addison County solid waste transfer station that won the Silver Excellence in Solid Waste Management Award from the Solid Waste Association of North America.

Although residential construction remained strong in 2006, nonresidential construction began to dwindle. Bread Loaf remained busy, but conditions would continue to worsen. A credit crunch in the final months of 2008 made it more difficult to proceed with building projects. Bread Loaf was forced to make some layoffs but given its excellent track record there was every expectation that the firm would again weather the tough times and return to health as soon as the national and regional economies rebounded.

Ed Dinger

PRINCIPAL OPERATING UNITS

Commercial; Cultural and Public Institutions; Higher Education; Light Industrial; Recreation; Resort Hospitality.

PRINCIPAL COMPETITORS

Pizzagalli Construction Company; Engelberth Construction, Inc.; Neagley & Chase Construction Corporation.

FURTHER READING

Barnam, Ed, "Construction Roundup," *Vermont Business Magazine*, April 1, 1994.

Brokaw, Leslie, and Anne Murphy, "What It Takes," *Inc.*, November 1992.

"Construction Companies," *Vermont Business Magazine*, January 1, 1999.

Flagg, Kathryn, "Local Construction Work Dries Up, Builders Brace for Lean Times," *Addison County (Vt.) Independent*, December 18, 2008.

Fraser, Jill Andresky, "Life After Death," *Inc.*, February 1990, p. 90.

Kelley, Kevin, "Construction Boom Affected by Labor Crunch," *Vermont Business Magazine*, January 1, 2001.

Lammers, Teri, "The Effective and Indispensable Mission Statement," *Inc.*, August 1992, p. 75.

Mitchell, Tom, "Resuming Last Year's Trend, Vt. Construction off to a Strong Start in '06," *Rutland (Vt.) Herald*, March 27, 2006.

Bruce Oakley, Inc.

———■———

3700 Lincoln Avenue
North Little Rock, Arkansas 72114
U.S.A.
Telephone: (501) 945-0875
Toll Free: (800) 662-0875
Fax: (501) 945-6970
Web site: http://www.bruceoakley.com

Private Company
Incorporated: 1968
Employees: 180
Sales: $1.16 billion (2008)
NAICS: 484121 General Freight Trucking, Long-Distance, Truckload; 483211 Inland Water Freight Transportation

■ ■ ■

Family owned and operated Bruce Oakley, Inc., is a North Little Rock, Arkansas-based group of diverse companies involved in dry bulk commodity sales and transportation, serving customers that range from individual farmers to *Fortune* 500 companies. The flagship unit is Oakley Trucking, providing bulk transportation services in 48 states as well as Canada and Mexico. The 100 percent owner-operator fleet includes about 260 end-dump trailers with two-way tailgates capable of hauling bulk freight as well as palletized freight and bulk bags. In addition to grain and fertilizer, cargos include coke, scrap metal, and roofing granules. The fleet also includes about 185 pneumatic tank trailers, each with a hauling capacity of 2,000 cubic feet of dry bulk product

or as much as 24 tons, capable of bottom dropping their cargo or blowing it into silos or other storage facilities.

In addition, Oakley Trucking operates hopper bottom trailers to haul such dry bulk products as grain, feed, fertilizer, sand, roofing granules, soda ash, and phosphate. Terminals are maintained in North Little Rock; Reserve, Louisiana; and Inola, Oklahoma. Oakley Barge Line, Inc., transports bulk commodities in covered hopper barges throughout the inland waterways of the United States. Oakley maintains ports on the Arkansas River at North Little Rock; Pendleton, Arkansas; Morrilton, Arkansas; and Dardanelle, Arkansas. Oakley also maintains ports at Shreveport, Louisiana, on the Red River; and Caruthersville, Missouri, on the Mississippi River. The largest port is at North Little Rock, where the company also maintains its headquarters, and that port is capable of handling four barges simultaneously, while an on-site storage facility can hold 750,000 bushels of grain and 26,000 tons of fertilizer.

Another subsidiary, Oakley Fertilizer, Inc., makes use of these port facilities to act as an international wholesale distributor of bulk and bag fertilizers and salts. Oakley Grain, Inc., also takes advantage of the storage capacity of the North Little Rock, Pendleton, Morrilton, and Dardanelle ports to buy and sell grain, corn, and other feed products. Further storage is available at Beebe, Arkansas, served both by Oakley Trucking and Union Pacific Railroad. The operation also includes a fertilizer bagging facility and sells fertilizers and other farm supplies, including feed, fencing, salt, lime, baler twine, fencing materials, and veterinary supplies.

COMPANY PERSPECTIVES

Oakley Incorporated is dedicated to providing the best service among our diversified line of offerings. Whether you need Transportation services, Fertilizer, Dry Construction Goods, or Bagging Service, Oakley Inc. will meet your needs.

President of Bruce Oakley, Inc., is Dennis Oakley, son of the company's founder.

FOUNDER: DEPRESSION-ERA BORN

Bruce Oakley was born in El Paso, Arkansas, near Little Rock in the mid-1930s and raised on a farm. In addition to farming he became familiar with the trucking industry as a young man, for several years driving a milk truck for Central Arkansas Milk Producers. He went away from home in the early 1960s by joining the U.S. Navy, and upon his discharge he displayed the entrepreneurial skills that would serve him well later in life. After his stint in the navy he stayed in San Diego for a time, running a locker club. Not only did Oakley rent lockers to sailors for the storage of their belongings while they were at sea, he sold them clothing and other necessary items, including wedding rings.

COMPANY ORIGINS: 1968

In 1964 Oakley returned to Arkansas and resumed farming in El Paso, initially raising cows. As the price of grain increased, however, he decided to become a grower. He was not alone. Other area farmers also began raising grain, but they soon found it difficult to find someone to spread lime to fertilize their fields. Sensing an opportunity, in 1968 Oakley purchased a semi-dump truck and began making the 75-mile trip to Batesville, Arkansas, to purchase lime, which he then sold and spread for El Paso–area farmers.

With demand for his services growing, Oakley soon began hiring workers. Rather than make constant trips to Batesville, he built a fertilizer storage facility in El Paso. With that capacity in hand, he was able to set himself up as a fertilizer dealer. He then built a fertilizer facility a dozen miles away in Beebe, Arkansas, on the former site of a saw mill. The location was important because it had access to the railroad, allowing Oakley to buy fertilizer by the car load. Fertilizer was very much a seasonal business, however. To keep his workers and

trucks busy Oakley became involved in the grain business by the mid-1970s. To this point Oakley had financed his operations through loans obtained from the local Bank of Cabot, very much a small town institution. When Oakley began hedging to protect his investments in grain, the bank grew concerned and refused to lend him any further funds. Instead, Oakley took his business to Little Rock's First National Bank, which was more familiar with the fundamentals of grain dealing.

Oakley owned five or six trucks at this stage, and began contracting with truck owner-operators to expand the fleet. Again he grew his business interests to meet circumstances. To keep his truckers busy year-round and not just the spring hauling fertilizer or the fall hauling grain, Oakley looked for other products that needed to be moved in bulk. He turned to 3M Company, which had a plant in Little Rock, and began to haul 3M roofing granules. His trucks also hauled scrap metal and other commodities, and ventured farther from central Arkansas. In time, the trucking division would become the company's top revenue generator.

NORTH LITTLE ROCK PROPERTY ACQUIRED: 1977

Rail service in Beebe, in the meantime, was far from adequate, prompting Oakley to look to the river system in addition to trucks to move his goods. In 1977 he bought about 20 acres of land in North Little Rock, the site of the company's current headquarters, to gain access to the Arkansas River. The facility also served as a hub for his grain dealing, selling wholesale to dealers and eventually individual cooperatives. To establish a waterway business, Oakley took on a partner and bought a single used barge, which for the next two years or so constituted the company's entire fleet. Nevertheless, the barge business was strong enough that in 1980 Oakley was able to purchase six to eight new barges. He also looked to expand his waterway business by establishing his second Arkansas River location, building a port at Morrilton, Arkansas, some 60 miles northwest of Little Rock. Late in the 1980s, Oakley added another port on the Arkansas River at Dardanelle, Arkansas, bought out of bankruptcy from a bank.

DENNIS OAKLEY JOINS COMPANY: 1982

Bruce Oakley, Inc., enjoyed organic growth, as the success of one business led to ancillary opportunities. Fertilizer sales led to a trucking operation, which resulted in a grain business and general bulk hauling. A rail terminal was established to buy fertilizer and grain in bulk, but when rail service suffered, Oakley turned to the waterways, leading to the purchase of barges and the development of an inland waterway fleet. All the elements of the company were in place, as a result, when Oakley's son, Dennis Oakley, joined the family enterprise in 1982 at the age of 18. He was somewhat familiar with the business, having helped his father all his life, including baling hay on the farm when they kept cows. He went to work at the Beebe facility, doing whatever was necessary, including bagging fertilizer and running loaders.

Dennis Oakley also began learning the administrative side of the business his father had started and nurtured into a multifaceted operation. In the early 1990s Dennis Oakley succeeded his father as president of Bruce Oakley, Inc. The elder Oakley not only turned over the reins to his son to prepare for the company's succession to the next generation, he looked to spend more time with his family and pursue other interests. "He just enjoyed being busy," his son would later tell the *Arkansas Democrat Gazette.* In truth, however, Bruce Oakley never truly retired. He continued to come into the office on a regular basis, and until he died at the age of 70 in 2006 he went over the monthly accounting with his son.

Bruce Oakley imparted two bits of advice to his son, according to *Arkansas Business:* "Always do what you say you're going to do," and "Never bet the farm." Under Dennis Oakley's leadership, the company grew on every front in the 1990s. Increasing demand for grain and fertilizer drove the expansion of the trucking division, which became a 100 percent owner-operated fleet. In the late 1990s the company opened terminals in Reserve, Louisiana, and Inola, Oklahoma, as the trucking operation eventually covered the continental United States, Canada, and Mexico. During that time waterway hauling expanded as well. After adding a river terminal in Russellville, Arkansas, the company gained access to the Mississippi River in 1998 by purchasing a

fertilizer terminal at Caruthersville, Missouri, from Laroche Industries Inc. Capable of housing 20,000 short tons of dry capacity, the terminal opened up markets in Missouri, northeast Arkansas, and parts of Tennessee. Also as the 1990s came to a close, Bruce Oakley, Inc., built a terminal at Shreveport, Louisiana, providing access to markets in Louisiana and eastern Texas.

Generally unassuming, Bruce Oakley, Inc., took exception in the late 1990s to plans of the Arkansas legislature to make money available to develop public ports. The company objected and even hired a lobbyist to oppose the idea Oakley contended could result in an unlevel playing field for private port operators. The Port Priority Improvement Act passed, but because no tax revenues became available to fund the initiative, due to a sagging economy and more pressing funding priorities, the adverse impact of the measure did not materialize.

INTERNATIONAL DIVISION FORMED: 2003

In the new century, the company continued to expand its trucking fleet as well as its waterway business. In 2001 the company bought another port facility on the Arkansas River at Pendleton, Arkansas. The company also bought four or five new barges each year until high steel prices made such additions too cost prohibitive. Annual revenues increased to $178.5 million in fiscal 2003, a 35.6 percent increase over the previous year. In that same year Bruce Oakley, Inc., positioned itself for further growth through a new source of revenues, forming Oakley International to trade in fertilizer. The division was based in Savannah, Georgia, headed by a seasoned fertilizer trader named Jim Crawford. Taking advantage of business relationships Bruce Oakley, Inc., had developed over the years, the new division was able to arrange through trading companies a source of potash, a key fertilizer ingredient, from Russia. Previously, Bruce Oakley, Inc., had purchased potash locally, but the Russian potash was much less expensive. To help source the potash, Oakley International hired a Moscow resident as its representative.

International sales helped to increase annual revenues 42.9 percent to $255.1 million in fiscal 2004, but more instrumental in the improvement were fertilizer prices, which all but doubled that year. Revenues continued to grow at a strong rate, reaching $527 million in fiscal 2007. A year later grain prices doubled and fertilizer prices more than doubled, resulting in a 120 percent surge in revenues to $1.16 billion in fiscal 2008, a level that was unrealistic for the company to maintain once commodity prices settled. Going forward, the company simply planned to continue growing organically. To accommodate possible future expansion, it owned 25 acres next to the North Little Rock facilities, more than enough land needed in the foreseeable future.

Ed Dinger

PRINCIPAL SUBSIDIARIES

Oakley Barge Line, Inc.; Oakley Fertilizer, Inc.; Oakley Grain, Inc.; Bruce Oakley Trucking Inc.

PRINCIPAL COMPETITORS

American Commercial Lines Inc.; Bulkmatic Transport Company; Comcar Industries, Inc.

FURTHER READING

"Bruce Oakley, the Founder of Bruce Oakley Inc. of North Little Rock, a Diversified Bulk Cargo and Grain and Fertilizer Company, Died April 19," *Arkansas Business,* May 1, 2006, p. 11.

Hengel, Mark, "Commodity Prices Spur Bruce Oakley Revenue Growth," *Arkansas Business,* May 25, 2009, p. 16.

Henry, John, "Bruce Oakley Inc. Finds Ways to Grow by Land and Water," *Arkansas Business,* June 20, 2005, p. 1.

"LaRoche Sells Terminals," *Chemical Market Reporter,* August 17, 1998, p. 3.

Lovel, Jim, "Private Port Operators Oppose Waterways Plan," *Arkansas Business,* February 9, 1999, p. 16.

McGuffie, Deborah, "Right on the Job," *Fleet Owner,* November 2000, p. 30.

"A Welcome to Oakley International," *Fertilizer International,* September–October 2003, p. 68.

Woodworth, Hillary, "Businessman Oakley Dies at 70 in El Paso," *Arkansas Democrat-Gazette,* April 23, 2006, p. 26.

centrica

Centrica plc

———————■———————

Millstream
Maidenhead Road
Windsor, Berkshire SL4 5GD
United Kingdom
Telephone: (44 1753) 494-000
Fax: (44 1753) 494-001
Web site: http://www.centrica.com

Public Company
Incorporated: 1997
Employees: 32,817
Sales: £21.3 billion ($30.84 billion) (2008)
Stock Exchanges: London
Ticker Symbol: CNA
NAICS: 221210 Natural Gas Distribution; 221122
   Electric Power Distribution

■ ■ ■

Centrica plc is the largest energy supplier in the United Kingdom, serving 15.6 million gas and electricity clients in 2008. The company is involved in nearly every aspect of the energy industry including sourcing, generation, processing, storage, trading, supply, servicing, and energy conservation. Formed during the 1997 breakup of British Gas, Centrica inherited the gas supply portion of the business and the rights to the British Gas name. The company is focused on international expansion and has gained footholds in North America as well as continental Europe. Centrica operates as the third largest commercial supplier of power in the United States and has also expanded into Belgium, Germany, the Netherlands, Norway, Spain, Nigeria, Egypt, and Trinidad.

COMPANY PRECURSORS

Experiments using coal gas for lighting were performed in the late 18th century in England. William Murdock reportedly lit his home in Redruth, Cornwall, with gas in 1792. In the early years of the 19th century, when Britain was the world's first industrial nation, several factories made their own gas for lighting. The first gas company in the world to provide a public supply was the Gas Light and Coke Company of London, which received its charter in 1812. Gas for lighting proved both popular and profitable; by 1829, around 200 gas companies had been set up. Almost all of these companies relied on private capital; the first municipal gas department was set up in Manchester in 1817 by the police commissioners and was taken over by Manchester Corporation in 1843.

The first gas companies were established in a competitive climate; there were no restrictions on where a company might set up in business if the organizers could raise the capital and thought they could make a profit. In the early days it was by no means unheard of for two companies to serve the same street; in one notable case in South London no less than four competing companies had mains in the same street. However, people soon recognized that unbridled competition served neither the interests of gas companies nor their customers. Within London, where the problem was most severe, the Metropolis Gas Act of 1860 allocated each company its own district within which it had a monopoly. To prevent exploitation of captive customers, a statutory limit of 10 percent on dividends had been imposed by the Gasworks Clauses Act of 1847, but this limitation did not satisfy customers. Companies were enjoying monopoly powers and earning the maximum dividend; there was little incentive for them to cut prices despite increasing sales and improved technology. This form of statutory regulation thus proved ineffective in protecting the interests of the public.

In the mid-1870s competition began to offer customers the prospects of a better deal. At first the competition came from lighting oil. Persistent overproduction in the Pennsylvania oil fields in the United States meant there was a surplus over U.S. needs, which would then be shipped out and dumped cheaply on world markets, especially in the early 1870s. Oil lamps proved a popular alternative to gas. By the late 1870s, electricity was also beginning to emerge as a competitor for the gas lighting business. A practical arc lamp was produced in 1876, and Thomas Edison in the United States and Sir Joseph Swan in Britain independently produced the first incandescent lightbulbs in 1879–80. The gas industry responded in three ways: it attempted to improve the efficiency of its lamps, it looked for alternative markets, and it looked to its pricing structure.

COOKING WITH GAS

At the suggestion of George Livesey, chief engineer of the British South Metropolitan Gas Company and the foremost gas engineer of his generation, the sliding scale was introduced in 1875. Under his system, dividends and prices were linked inversely; that is, increased dividends could be paid if the price of gas came down, but if the price of gas rose, dividends had to be cut. Individual companies sought private legislation to permit them to introduce the sliding scale; by the year 1900, two-thirds of all gas sold was covered by this arrangement. Its fairness to customers depended

crucially on the datum price, or the price from which variations would be calculated. It was the good fortune of the gas companies that many technical improvements to cut costs were made after they adopted the sliding scale. Shares in the major gas companies were regarded as a very sound investment. Livesey also introduced a profit-sharing scheme for his workers in 1889; the bonus was linked to reductions in the price of gas. Similar copartnership schemes were set up by several of the larger gas companies, but few outside the industry adopted the concept.

When gas companies were looking for alternative uses for gas, they began to consider its use for cooking and heating in the home. The first geyser water heater was invented in 1868, and gas fires to heat individual rooms were developed in the 1880s. However, gas companies were more interested in persuading customers to use gas for cooking. Experimental gas stoves had been shown at the Great Exhibition of 1851, but they had made no headway against the popular coal-fired kitchen ranges that provided heat and hot water as well as facilities for cooking. By the 1870s there were gas stoves recognizably similar in layout to most modern stoves, with an oven below and burners above. As far as the gas managers of the time were concerned, the special advantage of the stove was that it was likely to be used more during the day than at night; it would therefore use off-peak gas. Lighting, of course, was still the predominant load.

For rational, promotional, and financial reasons, the installation of stoves could be subsidized from the profits on gas sales. As customers were disinclined to buy, they were supplied with basic, robust cast-iron stoves on inexpensive rental terms. By contrast, in the United States stoves were offered for sale, not rent, and were of lighter construction, well finished, and with attractive trim. This policy of supplying subsidized stoves was developed more extensively in Britain between 1890 and the 1920s than anywhere else in the world, and British companies sold more gas than the rest of Europe put together.

INTRODUCING THE PREPAYMENT METER

Despite the excitement engendered by the first incandescent electric lightbulbs, customers found them costly and unreliable. Gas saw a strong return to popularity in the 1890s, following the invention by an Austrian chemist of the Welsbach incandescent mantle, which increased fivefold the efficiency of gas for lighting. Gas was still very much a middle-class fuel; poorer people living in rented homes used coal, oil, and candles, and they could not afford to have gas installed,

KEY DATES

1812: The Gas Light and Coke Company of London receives its charter.

1926: The Electricity (Supply) Act brings about the restructuring of the electrical industry.

1948: The Gas Act is passed.

1949: The gas industry passes into public ownership on May 1.

1959: The first experimental shipment of liquefied natural gas arrives at Canvey Island in the Thames estuary; a huge discovery of natural gas in Holland leads to speculation that more might be discovered under the North Sea.

1967: A major conversion program begins that will convert appliances so that they can burn methane instead of coal gas.

1973: The Gas Council is replaced by the British Gas Corporation (BGC).

1986: BGC is privatized by the Gas Act.

1997: BGC splits into two separate companies: BG plc and Centrica plc.

1998: The British gas market opens fully to competition.

2000: Direct Energy Marketing Limited of Canada is purchased.

2001: Centrica moves into the continental European energy market through its purchase of a 50 percent share in Belgium's Luminus N.V.

2002: WTU Retail Energy and CPL Retail Energy, two providers based in south and west Texas, are acquired.

2004: Centrica buys its first U.S.-based power plant through the acquisition of Bastrop Energy Partners L.P.

2005: The company secures a 51 percent stake in Belgium's Société Publique d'Électricité (SPE).

even if they wanted to use it. This situation, however, was about to change dramatically.

The change was generally attributed to the invention in 1888 of the prepayment, penny-in-the-slot meter. This alone would not have brought about the spread of gas into working-class homes, however. The manager of the municipal Ramsgate gas undertaking, W. A. Valon, noted that half the houses in the town had no gas supply. He decided that instead of offering to

provide just the stove on easy terms, he would provide the whole gas installation—pipes, stove, and lights. As his new customers would pay for their gas in advance through a prepayment meter, there was no need to ask for a deposit as security. The profit on gas sales to poor homes was unlikely to be sufficient to pay for the installation costs, so there was a surcharge on the gas price for such customers, typically 25 percent, the prepayment supplement. The scheme spread like wildfire. In the words of Livesey, "This extension of gas supply to weekly tenants is the most extraordinary and remarkable development of the business that has ever been known." Between 1892 and 1912 the number of gas customers increased from two-and-one-half million to seven million, and sales doubled. The use of gas for cooking became more important than gas for lighting, as virtually all new customers were supplied with a stove.

This expansion of the industry was not accompanied by any structural change; it was still extremely fragmented. In 1914 there were some 1,500 suppliers of gas, two-thirds of whom had statutory monopoly powers within their areas of gas supply. There was little pressure toward amalgamation, in part because of high legal and consultancy fees, and also because of geography since supply networks could not easily be linked to achieve economies of scale. Another major factor was the split between the municipal and privately owned companies; about one-third of the industry was municipally owned. Each company could set its own technical standards and, because subsidized rental of appliances was almost universal, there was no independent appliance retailing network that might have encouraged harmonization of standards and appliance innovation.

COMPETING WITH ELECTRICITY

The interwar period was a difficult time for the gas industry. At the outbreak of World War I in 1914, ten times more homes had a gas supply than electricity. Although the number of gas customers continued to rise until 1939, the increase in gas sales slowed, while electricity sales grew sharply. The prepayment supplement had paid for so many homes to be equipped with gas lighting that the defense of the lighting business was a major preoccupation; it was feared that if electricity displaced gas for lighting, it would soon displace gas stoves and heaters. As a consequence, the industry was distracted and could not concentrate its efforts fully on displacing the huge stock of obsolete rented appliances and selling modern stoves, heaters, and water heaters in their place. The real value of the prepayment supplement—fixed in cash terms before 1914—fell, and cost increases meant there was no surplus for upgrading appliances.

Electric stoves were attractive and modern by contrast with the traditional rented gas stoves. Moreover, the gas industry had no answer to new types of electric appliances (vacuum cleaners, irons, and radios) which were sold aggressively through retailers and by door-to-door salesmen. These popular new items, and the convenience and cleanliness of electric lighting, ensured that householders came to regard electricity as a necessity. Many builders and customers, attracted by the idea of the all-electric house, saw no need to install gas; some councils with their own municipal electricity undertakings even sought to ban their tenants from using gas.

RESTRUCTURING THE GAS INDUSTRY IN THE MID-20TH CENTURY

The Electricity (Supply) Act of 1926 brought about the restructuring of the electrical industry, which until then had been as fragmented as gas. The government-appointed Central Electricity Board was charged with building a national grid. This initiative during the worst years of the Great Depression suggested that electricity was the key to a prosperous national future, and politicians of all parties were keen to jump on the electrical bandwagon. Nothing comparable was planned for gas. Under the leadership of David Milne-Watson of the Gas Light & Coke Company, the gas industry lobbied strongly for a "level playing field," but its pleas fell on deaf ears. By the late 1930s, people both within and outside the industry realized the existing structure could not survive without radical change. There was a need for some form of national framework for gas; those in the industry hoped that this would not mean state control.

These rumblings were muted during World War II, but thoughts on the future of the industry continued. A government committee under Geoffrey Heyworth proposed the compulsory purchase of all gas companies and the establishment of ten regions; regulation would be undertaken by commissioners, following the model of the electricity industry. His report was published in 1945, but by then a Labour government committed to the nationalization of the industry had been elected. There was little public concern or controversy, unlike the debates on the nationalization of coal, transport, electricity, or steel. Few might have given the industry much chance of survival, let alone expansion. Opposition came more from Conservative members of Parliament than from the industry.

Under the Gas Act of 1948, the industry passed into public ownership on May 1, 1949. Some £220 million of British Gas 3 percent stock—3 percent annual interest was payable on the face value of the stock—was issued as compensation to the former owners; 1,037 separate undertakings, previously under private or municipal ownership, were amalgamated into 12 area gas boards. Scotland and Wales each had their own board; Northern Ireland was outside the scope of the act. The Gas Council, a small central coordinating body, was established. Apart from its chairman and vice-chairman, this comprised the 12 area board chairmen. Most had held senior positions in the industry although other interests were presented; for example, one had a trade union and one a local government background.

The duties of the Gas Council were to advise the minister on gas matters and to promote the efficient exercise of their functions by the area boards; the central body had a small secretariat, of 159 members, one-third of whom dealt with publicity and another third with purchase of coal and the sale of coke. The main executive power rested with the boards, although capital investment programs had to be submitted through the council to the minister for approval. There were national arrangements for wage bargaining; close cooperation soon brought a measure of voluntary harmonization between the various boards over technical standards, commercial policy, and other areas of common interest. The industry was legally bound to take account of the interests of both workforce and customers through consultative arrangements.

FACING PROBLEMS

The new area boards settled down quickly but faced two long-term problems. Their public image was still that of an old-fashioned if not immediately moribund industry, and they were losing the battle for the domestic load to electricity. In the ten years after 1948, sales of gas increased by 20 percent; over the same period, sales of electricity more than doubled. Old rented stoves, heaters, and water heaters were not being replaced quickly with modern equipment, and the sales efforts of the boards were hindered at first by postwar material shortages and the export drive, and also by government purchase tax and restrictions on renting. The other problem was the price of gas, which no longer enjoyed its traditional advantage over electricity. While the price of electricity rose by 17 percent between 1950 and 1957, gas rose by 51 percent. The cost of high-grade coal for gas-making doubled between 1947 and 1957, whereas power stations could use cheaper grades.

Efforts to rebuild the market for gas appliances were urgently needed but less important than the need to reduce the relative price of gas, and the industry began to search for alternative methods of gas production. One path explored was the total gasification of coal, a process developed in Germany before the war. Another alternative which seemed to offer better prospects was the use of oil feedstocks for gas-making, either as an enricher of gas made by other processes or later by direct catalytic conversion of oil into gas. Britain, and notably the Gas Council's own scientists, were pioneers in the intense research efforts that resulted in several processes that could take any oil feedstock available in large quantity at low cost, especially naphtha and refinery waste gas, and convert it directly into usable gas. Major contracts were signed with oil companies to secure long-term supplies. For the first time in its history, during the 1960s the gas industry's fortunes were unshackled from coal.

MARKETING EFFORTS LEAD TO GROWTH

This technical breakthrough was matched by a change in marketing. Market research showed that gas still had a negative image by contrast with the strong modern image of electricity. W. K. Hutchison, the deputy chairman of the Gas Council, put himself at the head of the campaign to change the image of gas. In the words of the advertising agents, "The amiable, innocuous figure of 'Mr. Therm' around which the Gas Council's advertising had for many a year revolved, seemed too bland, too typecast to take up the challenge. ... And so it was that 'High Speed Gas, Heat That Obeys You' ... invited newspaper readers to realize how 'with it' they were to be using gas." This coincided with the arrival on the market of a new generation of stoves with timers and automatic ignition, and stylish and efficient gas heaters that quickly took over from coal the main task of heating living rooms. Showrooms were modernized and moved to prime locations.

The next stage was to attack the domestic central heating market, which was at the time being vigorously promoted by the oil companies. Gas was helped both by the arrival of natural gas and by the increases in OPEC oil prices beginning in 1973. It was also helped by the introduction of the Clean Air Act in 1956, which aimed to reduce the air pollution caused by coal-burning domestic fires. Natural gas enabled a significant reduction of smoke in the atmosphere. By 1989 more than 70 percent of all gas customers had gas central heating, a clear indication of the success of this campaign.

The 1960s saw other momentous changes that were to have even more far-reaching effects. Natural gas arrived in quantity for the first time in Britain. In its early days the Gas Council commissioned British Petroleum to act as operator to prospect for natural gas onshore; this search proved unsuccessful. The Gas Council was therefore particularly interested to hear of U.S. plans to ship liquefied natural gas (LNG) by tanker; cooling to very low temperatures reduces methane to a liquid, the volume of which is 1/600th of its gaseous state. The British government gave its approval to a trial to assess the practicality of the scheme, and the first experimental shipment arrived at Canvey Island in the Thames estuary in 1959. Gas Council proposals to proceed with import of LNG on a large scale ran into fierce opposition in government, predictably from the coal and oil lobbies. Approval was finally given by the British cabinet to a 15-year contract to buy gas from Algeria; two tankers shuttling back and forth would carry the equivalent of 10 percent of British gas output at that time. The two vessels came into service in 1964. To enable all parts of the country to take advantage of these supplies of natural gas, a high-pressure national grid was constructed, at first linking eight boards to Canvey Island. The grid network was 320 miles long in 1966–67; by 1976–77 the network extended 2,915 miles, and all boards were connected.

CONVERSION TO UNDILUTED NATURAL GAS

The liquefied methane project was running in parallel with another natural gas project. A huge discovery of natural gas in Holland in 1959 led to speculation that more might be discovered under the North Sea. The Gas Council was very keen to participate in the search and joined in partnership with experienced U.S. operators to explore, drill, and subsequently to produce gas and oil. The necessity for Gas Council involvement was questioned at the time as, under British law, all gas found in the United Kingdom had to be offered for sale to the council. The election of a Labour government in 1964 strengthened the hand of the Gas Council; it was positively encouraged to participate in North Sea activities.

Some of the early acreage allotted for exploration contained the huge Leman gas field. The council thus had invaluable information on the actual costs of finding and producing gas; it was able to negotiate prices based more on the costs of production (then two pence per therm, with 240 pence equaling £1) than on average revenue (16.5 pence) or the cost of seaborne gas from Algeria (6.5 pence). A whole series of discoveries soon proved that supplies of natural gas from the North Sea would meet British needs for a few decades at least. This raised the question of how best to use it. Up until then, natural gas had been converted into a coal-gas equivalent of only half the heat value of methane, volume for volume. There were enormous advantages to distributing methane without dilution; processing costs would be minimal, and the capacity of gas mains would be effectively doubled. Against this had to be set the cost of converting every appliance so that it could burn methane instead of coal gas. A survey of several thousand customers round the Canvey Island terminal in 1966 showed the great variety of equipment to be converted, three or four appliances per home on average. A large proportion were 15 years old or more. Ways had to be found to convert all these old appliances or to persuade customers, by offering generous terms, to buy new ones.

Despite the cost and potential problems, the advantages of complete conversion were overwhelming. This was an enormous technical, marketing, and public relations exercise. There was undoubted inconvenience, but considering the opportunities for error and complaint, most customers accepted the conversion with goodwill; it gave them a direct and personal opportunity to share in the excitement of the North Sea discoveries. Conversion was free and, for many, it provided an opportunity for old appliances to be brought up to date or replaced inexpensively; furthermore, North Sea gas was less expensive than the alternatives. The conversion exercise was, in the words of Sir Denis Rooke, chairman of British Gas from 1976 until 1989, "perhaps the greatest peacetime operation in the nation's history." The main conversion program began in 1967 and, 13 million customers later, the last home was converted in 1977. From 1912 until nationalization in 1940, sales had more than doubled. Between 1949 and the end of the conversion program they increased sixfold.

RESTRUCTURING

Until the early 1960s, the gas industry had managed to avoid the relentless tinkering by politicians that had bedeviled the other nationalized industries: coal, steel, transport, and electricity. It had not been perceived as having any long-term significance and had neither failed nor succeeded dramatically. With its involvement in North Sea exploration and consequently higher public profile, this situation changed. The government then thought seriously about establishing a production board along the lines of the Central Electricity Generating Board. The Gas Council persuaded the government that the existing arrangements were working harmoniously and suited the needs of the industry. As a consequence, the 1965 Gas Act, essential to clarify the powers of the council to buy gas in bulk and sell to its area board customers, left the basic structure untouched.

It was clear, however, that strong central leadership was necessary to enable the council to cope with the changes brought by natural gas; new headquarters departments were set up covering production and supply, marketing, and economic planning. Rooke, who had been a member of the team working on the import of LNG from its inception in 1957, became develop-

ment engineer, responsible for new production processes and planning an integrated supply system. Later, as member for production and supply, he played a crucial role in the technical changes in gas manufacture and distribution in the 1960s and 1970s. The arrangements under the 1965 act were temporary; a restructuring was necessary to place overall responsibility at the center. In 1973 the Gas Council was replaced by the British Gas Corporation (BGC), still state-owned, and the area boards set up in 1949 became regions under direct control of the BGC.

One outcome of the success of the North Sea search for gas was that the BGC became a producer of oil and thus became involved in international fuel markets. This situation did not survive the election of the Conservatives to power in 1979. BGC was required to sell its oil assets, spun off as Enterprise Oil; the proceeds went not to the industry but to the government. At this time the government also became concerned at the dominant position enjoyed by BGC in the business of the retail sale of appliances. The matter was referred to the Monopolies and Mergers Commission, which ruled that BGC's position in the market was against the public interest. The government drew back from enforcing a withdrawal from appliance trading; gas showrooms then served to deal with accounts and service queries as well as selling. Independent retailers began playing a larger part in appliance retailing than ever before in the history of the industry; even so, British Gas still had a turnover of £300 million from appliance trading in the early 1990s.

PRIVATIZATION

When the privatization of the industry was under consideration, some ministers were keen to introduce an element of competition and to break up the unified structure of the industry that had evolved since nationalization, largely in response to the availability of natural gas. Any breakup was opposed by Rooke, who lobbied strongly for the retention of the unified structure that had served the nation so well; his views ultimately prevailed, although the nationalized electricity industry was to be split up in its subsequent privatization. The BGC was privatized as a whole by the Gas Act of 1986 and returned to private ownership in what was then the largest company flotation ever undertaken. After a vigorous television advertising campaign to "Tell Sid" to buy shares, three million people became owners of British Gas plc shares. The advertising alone cost £25 million, much of it paid by the government; the total cost of the privatization, including fees, underwriting, and value-added tax, was £347 million.

As a private company, British Gas was no longer geographically restricted to the United Kingdom and U.K. offshore waters. The government, however, still preferred it to purchase its supplies from the U.K. sector of the North Sea for strategic and balance of payments reasons. Rooke retired in 1989 and was succeeded as chairman and chief executive by Robert Evans. The company made substantial investments in foreign oil and gas assets to strengthen its business worldwide. After its privatization, British Gas acquired interests in four exploration and production companies: Acre Oil and part of Texas Eastern North Sea were acquired to strengthen the company's oil and gas holdings in the North Sea's U.K. sector; some of Tenneco's subsidiaries were purchased, with exploration and production interests in a number of countries around the world; a 51 percent stake in Canada's Bow Valley Industries gave exposure to the North American energy market; and British Gas also bought Consumers Gas, Canada's largest natural gas distributor. It also continued to offer a consultancy service so that others could benefit from its expertise.

REGULATORY CHANGES

With privatization came the need to reinstate a regulatory organization to safeguard the public from the misuse of British Gas's monopoly position. The Office of Gas Supply, under a director general, monitored tariffs and commercial practices. In 1989 British Gas was obliged to formalize its charging structure for large non-domestic customers. It was also obliged to make its transmission network available to carry gas not sold directly; this allowed producers of gas to contract directly with customers for the sale of large quantities of gas. This regulatory change removed the monopoly of gas distribution that had been enjoyed by gas undertakings since the middle of the 19th century.

In the postwar years the position of the gas industry in the British fuel market had been totally transformed. From its perceived role as a minor player, it emerged as a major force in not only the United Kingdom but also in world energy markets. In the early 1990s it supplied more than half the energy used in British homes. It made enormous technical and commercial strides and demonstrated that the question of state ownership of the business for much of the period was irrelevant to its record of dynamism and success.

In the first years after privatization, British Gas enjoyed growing profits; its profit after tax in 1991 was £916 million. However, competition steadily ate away at the company's market share, and regulation curbed earnings in the early 1990s. By 1995 British Gas held only 35 percent of the gas market for industrial and commercial customers, down from 100 percent in 1990. The company's residential market share was in jeopardy with its opening to full competition to be completed in 1998.

Although customers' gas bills had fallen after British Gas was placed in the private sector, public sentiment had shifted in the mid-1990s against privatizing utilities. The utilities' high profits were criticized, and in 1995 the Labour Party proposed a one-time "windfall" tax, which would be taken only out of profits already realized. Adding fuel to the fire of the public's disapproval was the 67 percent pay raise given to British Gas's chief executive, Cedric Brown, in 1994. Continued criticism of Brown led to his retirement in 1996.

DIVIDING BRITISH GAS IN TWO CREATES CENTRICA

British Gas announced in 1996 its plan to split into two separate companies. One, eventually named BG plc, would take over the pipeline business, all foreign ventures, and the vast majority of British Gas's exploration and production assets. The other, dubbed Centrica plc, would control the retail business in the United Kingdom, two large gas fields off the coast of England, and the rights to the British Gas name. At the time, BG plc seemed to get the stronger end of the deal. The storage and pipeline business had been generating two-thirds of British Gas's profits and the international exploration assets were considered valuable.

Although the company cited a desire to better focus on specific businesses as the reason for the split, speculation was raised that the company was trying to force contract renegotiations with gas producers. Locked into contracts made in the 1980s, British Gas was paying almost double the going rate for gas in the mid-1990s, when BG's market share was falling. All of these contracts went to the cash-poor Centrica, effectively forcing renegotiation of these contracts. Indeed, by the end of 1997, Centrica had renegotiated all its major high-priced contracts, winning lower rates from such gas suppliers as Conoco and Elf Exploration.

Centrica's financial results for 1996 highlighted its weak position relative to its counterpart, BG. Profits after one-time charges relating to gas contract renegotiation and restructuring were $886 million for BG, whereas Centrica posted a loss of $1.2 billion. Although the company still saw a loss of £791 million after one-time charges in 1997, its renegotiated contracts and new products were encouraging. Centrica began a joint venture with Household Finance Corporation in creating a new financial product, the credit card Goldfish, which was well received. Centrica also created a new division to investigate possible new products and services, including savings accounts and home security. In 1999, the company acquired the Automobile Association (AA) in a £1.1 billion deal. All non-energy businesses, such as British Gas Trading, British Gas Services, and Home Energy Centres, were grouped in the new division.

In 1998 Centrica lost approximately one million households to 20 independent suppliers when its gas market was opened fully to competition. Centrica had new opportunities, however, from the partial opening of the European Union (EU) to gas competition, brought on by a 1997 directive from the EU energy ministers. Further opportunities had arisen by late 1998 when the British electricity market opened to competition. Centrica, with the well-known British Gas name, was in a good position to compete with the regional electric utilities. Advance transfers to British Gas Trading, Centrica's domestic gas supply subsidiary, numbered 400,000. By the end of 1998 the company had 850,000 electricity customers, and a few months later that number had climbed to nearly 1.5 million.

For the first time since the breakup, Centrica reported a profit in 1998: £89 million after exceptional charges. The company expanded its gas and oil field portfolio with the purchase in 1998 of PowerGen North Sea Limited. Further purchases of oil and gas assets were announced in 1999, from Dana Petroleum plc and British Borneo.

MOVING INTO THE 21ST CENTURY

Centrica spent the early years of the new millennium diversifying its portfolio and expanding its holdings, especially in North America and continental Europe. During 2000 the company branched out into telecommunications through a partnership with Vodafone Group plc. Its Goldfish financial services arm also inked a deal with Lloyds TSB's Internet banking unit. It also purchased Direct Energy Marketing Limited of Canada and launched its Direct Energy brand in the United States.

The company's acquisition strategy continued into 2001, highlighted by its purchase of a 50 percent share in Luminus N.V., a new Belgian energy supply business. The deal gave Centrica a foothold in the continental European energy market. The following year Centrica acquired WTU Retail Energy and CPL Retail Energy, two providers based in south and west Texas that served over 850,000 customers. It also doubled its customer

base in Canada through the purchase of the home and small business clientele of Enbridge Inc.

While the company focused heavily on expanding its energy-related holdings, it began to shutter some of its noncore businesses. The Goldfish Bank business was sold to Lloyds TSB in 2003. A private-equity group bought AA for approximately $3.2 billion in October 2004. Centrica sold Onetel Telecommunications Ltd. the following year. Meanwhile, the company continued to strengthen its international holdings. Centrica bought its first U.S.-based power plant in April 2004 through the acquisition of Bastrop Energy Partners L.P. It purchased a second facility in Texas, the Frontera Power Station, in December. The company added Dutch energy supplier Oxxio BV to its arsenal the following year. Shortly thereafter, Centrica secured a 51 percent stake in Belgium's Société Publique d'Électricité (SPE).

While Centrica had grown steadily over the past several years in global markets, its domestic image was under fire due to its high residential energy prices. In fact, by the end of 2006, nearly one million customers had left British Gas. The company had the highest prices in the U.K. energy market and customers had seen their gas bills climb by 91 percent since 2003. Sam Laidlaw, named CEO in July 2006, immediately set out to lower prices. Laidlaw implemented a cost restructuring plan that included job cuts and the closure of the Stockley Park, Middlesex, headquarters.

Centrica's plans for the future included additional growth in energy-related fields. During 2007 the company gained exploration rights in Trinidad and Tobago. It also focused on "green" energy and wind farm projects and created British Gas New Energy to offer environmentally friendly products and services. During 2008, Électricité de France SA (EDF) announced plans to acquire British Energy Group plc in a deal worth over $23 billion. Centrica stood to benefit from this purchase as EDF was expected to sell the company approximately one-quarter of British Energy upon completion of the acquisition. Negotiations continued into April 2009.

With gas prices reaching record levels in 2008, Centrica found itself operating in very difficult market conditions. The energy market in the United Kingdom as a whole experienced a decline in production, which left it subject to imports. The region imported nearly 40 percent of its gas in 2008 and that number was expected to rise significantly in the coming years. Thus, Centrica's plan to secure and provide other sources of energy, including wind power, nuclear, and LNG was critical. By focusing on diversification and international growth,

Centrica management believed it was well positioned for success in the years to come.

Francis Goodall
Updated, Susan Windisch Brown; Christina M. Stansell

PRINCIPAL OPERATING UNITS

British Gas Residential; British Gas Business; British Gas Services; British Gas New Energy; Centrica Energy; Centrica Storage; Direct Energy; European Energy.

PRINCIPAL COMPETITORS

E.ON UK plc; Iberdrola S.A.; RWE npower.

FURTHER READING

Barty-King, Hugh, *New Flame,* Tavistock: Graphmitre, 1984.

"BGT Powers Up for New Assault," *Marketing Week,* September 10, 1998, p. 3.

"British Gas. Hot Air?," *Economist,* February 10, 1996.

"British Gas Marks End of Restructuring," *Oil and Gas Journal,* March 10, 1997, p. 26.

"Centrica Completes Purchase of Texas Power Plant," *PR Newswire,* June 2, 2004.

"Centrica Crosses North Sea with Dutch Acquisition," *Upstream,* June 10, 2005.

Chantler, Philip, *The British Gas Industry: An Economic Study,* Manchester: Manchester University Press, 1938.

Cimilluca, Dana, and David Gauthier-Villars, "EDF Buys British Energy," *Wall Street Journal Europe,* September 24, 2008.

"Direct Energy Unveils Plan to Invest $10 Billion in Power and Gas Assets," *Global Power Report,* July 7, 2005.

Elliott, Charles, *The History of Natural Gas Conversion in Great Britain,* Royston: Cambridge Info. & Research Services with BGC, 1980.

Everard, Stirling, *The History of the Gas Light and Coke Company 1812–1949,* London: Benn, 1949.

Falkus, Malcolm, *Always Under Pressure: A History of North Thames Gas Since 1949,* London: Macmillan, 1988.

Harrison, Michael, "Centrica Plans $1.2bn Expansion into North America," *Independent* (London), September 7, 2001.

Hutchison, Sir Kenneth, *High-Speed Gas: An Autobiography,* London: Duckworth, 1987.

Report on the Gas Industry in Great Britain, London: Political and Economic Planning, 1939.

Rogers, Danny, "British Gas Unit Takes on Banks," *Marketing,* November 6, 1997, p. 1.

"A Tempting Target," *Economist,* December 9, 1995.

Williams, Trevor I., *A History of the British Gas Industry,* Oxford: Oxford University Press, 1981.

Williamson, David, "Centrica to Cut Power Bills After 1m Customers Dump Providers," *Western Mail,* December 16, 2006.

Cole Taylor Bank

———————■———————

9550 West Higgins Road, Suite 100
Des Plaines, Illinois 60018-4906
U.S.A.
Telephone: (847) 653-7978
Fax: (847) 459-5784
Web site: http://www.coletaylor.com

Wholly Owned Subsidiary of Taylor Capital Group Inc.
Incorporated: 1929
Employees: 500
Total Assets: $4 billion (2009 est.)
NAICS: 522110 Commercial Banking

■ ■ ■

Headquartered near Chicago, Cole Taylor Bank is a leading independent business bank. Specifically, the company specializes in serving family-owned businesses with revenues of $50 million or less. Cole Taylor's clients include medical, law, and accounting offices, as well as commercial real estate developers. A subsidiary of Taylor Capital Group, the company operated a network of nine banking centers as the first decade of the 2000s neared its end.

FORMATIVE YEARS

Cole Taylor Bank's history can be traced back to the 1920s, when the company originated as the Main State Bank in Chicago. L. Shirley Tark was named the bank's director in 1929, and provided leadership that allowed it to survive the stock market crash that year, which was

followed by the Great Depression. In fact, the bank was one of very few on the city's Northwest side to survive the many bank failures that occurred at that time.

In addition to dire economic conditions, Main State Bank faced other challenges during its formative years, including a number of robberies. For example, in mid-1932 four masked gunmen, two of whom wielded shotguns, robbed the bank and made away with $4,000.

Upon the request of federal regulators, Tark was named president of the bank in 1933. In January of the following year, the bank relocated from 2654 West North Avenue to a location on Milwaukee and Western avenues. At this time, deposits totaled approximately $700,000.

By the early 1940s, Tark held controlling interest in the bank, with 601.7 shares. Tark's future son-in-law, Sidney J. Taylor, began working at the bank as a clerk in 1946, after being discharged from the U.S. Army.

Progress continued during the 1950s. Taylor graduated from the University of Wisconsin's graduate business school in 1952, preparing him for a future leadership role. By late 1956, Main State Bank's surplus account totaled $2.4 million.

A major leadership change unfolded in 1960, at which time 36-year-old Taylor was named Main State Bank's president, becoming one of the youngest individuals in the nation to hold such a position. By this time, Taylor had honed his knowledge and experience by working in virtually every area of the bank.

Growth continued at Main State heading into the mid-1960s. By 1966 the bank's surplus account had grown to $5 million, and its lending limit totaled $900,000. In November 1967, the state commissioner of banks issued a permit allowing for the organization of the Main State Bank of Chicago. The new, proposed entity, organized by Taylor and several other individuals, was created as part of Main State Bank's merger with Mercantile Industries Inc.

OWNERSHIP CHANGES

An important development took place in 1969, when Taylor and Irwin H. Cole acquired Main State Bank from L. Shirley Tark. At the time of the deal, the bank's assets totaled $65 million. The bank moved forward with Taylor as chairman and chief operating officer.

In 1978 Chicago's Drovers National Bank, one of the oldest in the city, was declared insolvent following losses tied to bad loans. Taylor, along with Cole, acquired the bank, which was renamed Drovers Bank of Chicago.

By 1980 Main State Bank and Drovers Bank of Chicago had collective deposits of $257 million. Cole and Taylor essentially operated the two banks as one entity, to the degree allowed by state banking laws. Moving forward, Cole and Taylor revealed plans to acquire two or three additional banks during the next five years. By this time, Taylor's three sons, ages 25, 28, and 30, were working for the family business.

By 1982 Main State Bank had been renamed Main Bank of Chicago, which was part of the Cole Taylor Financial Group Inc. In addition to Main Bank, Cole Taylor Financial Group also held Drovers Bank of Chicago and the Lombard, Illinois-based Bank of Yorktown. The following year, the holding company added a discount brokerage service in partnership with Jerome Hickey & Associates Inc.

Changes continued in early 1984. At that time Cole Taylor Financial Group relocated its headquarters from Main Bank's North Milwaukee Avenue facility to Northbrook Place in Northbrook, Illinois. By August, Cole Taylor Financial Group also owned Skokie Trust &

Savings Bank and Ford City Bank, and had plans to acquire Wheeling Trust & Savings Bank.

By 1985 the banks of Cole Taylor Financial Group had assets exceeding $1 billion. The company served its customers from seven different locations. In September of that year, Taylor's son, Scott W. Taylor, was named president of Skokie Trust & Savings Bank.

More leadership changes unfolded in December 1986. At that time, Ford City Bank & Trust Co. President Bradley M. Stevens was named president of Cole Taylor Financial Group. In addition, Jeffrey W. Taylor became president and CEO of Main Bank, succeeding William C. Olsen, who assumed leadership of Ford City Bank.

FORMATION OF COLE TAYLOR BANK

The creation of Cole Taylor Bank was made possible at the end of the decade, with the passage of branch-banking legislation in 1989. Specifically, it became possible for separately named freestanding banks to become one bank with the same name and numerous locations. Cole Taylor Bank made state history by becoming the first branch-banking network in Illinois. At this time during the company's history, it began focusing heavily on retail banking.

By the early 1990s Cole Taylor Bank had nine locations throughout Chicagoland. The bank offered annuities, personal trust services, brokerage services, and more.

By 1993 the bank's assets totaled $1.4 billion. In September of that year, Cole Taylor Bank acquired the land trust business of Harris Trust and Savings Bank, acquiring 3,600 trust accounts. It also was in 1993 that a new finance business named Reliance Acceptance Corp. was established to offer subprime auto loans.

Progress continued during the mid-1990s. In 1994 Cole Taylor Financial Group Inc. went public. By September of that year, Cole Taylor Bank's assets totaled $1.6 billion. It also was in 1994 that Jeffrey Taylor succeeded his father, Sidney, as the organization's chairman.

By 1995 the Cole family had expressed an interest in selling Cole Taylor Bank to the highest bidder. Instead, the Taylors parted with more than $160 million in assets, stock, and cash, to buy out their former partners. Cole Taylor Financial Group agreed to spin off Cole Taylor Bank in mid-1996, and the deal was completed in February 1997.

With Bruce W. Taylor serving as president and CEO, Cole Taylor Bank ranked as the city's largest

KEY DATES

■

1920: The Main State Bank is formed in Chicago.

1929: L. Shirley Tark is named director and provides leadership throughout the Great Depression.

1946: Sidney J. Taylor begins working at the bank as a clerk.

1960: Taylor is named president.

1969: Taylor and Irwin Cole acquire Main State Bank from Tark.

1978: Drovers National Bank is acquired and, along with Main State Bank, becomes part of Cole Taylor Financial Group Inc., which begins acquiring other banks.

1989: The creation of Cole Taylor Bank is made possible with the passage of branch-banking legislation.

1994: Cole Taylor Financial Group Inc. goes public.

1997: Cole Taylor Financial Group spins off Cole Taylor Bank. Owned by the Taylor family, the bank becomes a subsidiary of Taylor Capital Group.

2001: Cole Taylor Bank begins focusing on commercial banking.

2002: Sidney Taylor dies; Taylor Capital Group goes public in October.

privately owned bank, with approximately 11 branches and 650 employees. It moved forward as a subsidiary of the holding company Taylor Capital Group which, with assets of $1.8 billion, was headed by Chairman and CEO Jeffrey Taylor.

Following the spinoff of Cole Taylor Bank, Cole Taylor Financial became Reliance Acceptance Group Inc., which filed for bankruptcy in February 1998. In August of that year, Cole family members and other former business partners filed a lawsuit, alleging that Taylor Capital did not pay enough for Cole Taylor Bank.

In mid-1998, Cole Taylor Bank relocated many of its small business lenders from Wheeling, Illinois, to a new downtown Chicago location, to put them in closer physical proximity to business customers such as physicians, attorneys, and accountants.

Later that year, a new Washington Street branch was established, which had no ATMs or bank teller lines. Instead, the branch focused on relationships with business owners, as well as high-income individuals. Tellers met with customers in seated locations, and conference rooms were available for private transactions. By October 1999, Cole Taylor Bank's assets had reached the $2 billion mark. The company served customers from 12 Chicago-area locations.

BUSINESS BANKING IN THE 21ST CENTURY

Cole Taylor Bank began the new millennium by forming Cole Taylor Insurance Services. Developed in partnership with Chicago-based Dann Insurance, the new business offered mortgage life insurance, homeowners insurance, and auto insurance.

In 2001 Cole Taylor Bank made a strategic shift and began focusing on commercial banking. By the early part of that year, approximately 70 percent of its loan portfolio comprised owner-operated businesses. At this time, many small banks were being acquired by larger banks. However, Bruce Taylor remained focused on keeping Cole Taylor Bank independent.

In mid-2001 Cole Taylor Bank was focused on expanding its correspondent banking business, which then provided services to approximately 50 smaller banks. In particular, Cole Taylor was focused on doing business with community banks in a 200-mile radius around Chicago, which were serving small and midsized businesses.

In April 2002, Sidney Taylor, who by this time was serving as chairman of Cole Taylor Bank's executive committee, died at age 79. That same year, Taylor Capital Group settled the lawsuit filed in 1998 by the Cole family and other former business partners. To cover the $64.5 million settlement, the company made an initial public offering of its stock in October. Plans were made to issue $2.8 million shares of stock, along with trust-preferred securities worth $40 million. The settlement had a negative impact on the company's net income in 2002, leading to a $41.4 million net loss.

In early 2003, Cole Taylor Bank agreed to sell its self-directed individual retirement account business to Millennium Trust Company LLC. That year, Taylor Capital Group's net income totaled $18.7 million. In an effort to gain more commercial customers, Cole Taylor Bank launched an advertising campaign positioning it as "Chicago's Business Bank."

Despite its efforts, Cole Taylor Bank's transition to commercial banking proved to be a difficult task because of cutthroat competition for business loans to middle-market firms. To improve its position, the company eliminated 7 percent of its workforce during the first half of the year and implemented other cost-cutting measures totaling approximately $2 million.

In keeping with the organization's continued strategy to become a business bank, Taylor Capital Group announced plans to sell Cole Taylor Bank's Broadview, Illinois-based banking center to Citizens Community Bank in November 2004.

LEADERSHIP CHANGES

A major development unfolded in mid-2006, when Cole Taylor Bank announced a major expansion of its commercial banking group. The expansion involved the addition of five vice-presidents and two senior vice-presidents. In November of that year, Bruce Taylor assumed the additional role of chairman and CEO of Taylor Capital Group. Jeffrey Taylor was then named executive managing director, market development and new ventures.

Developments continued as the bank headed into the end of the first decade of the 2000s. In early 2007, Cole Taylor Bank announced plans to relocate its commercial banking offices from 111 West Washington Street to 225 West Washington Street. By this time, Cole Taylor's assets exceeded $3 billion, and the organization ranked as one of Chicago's largest independent banks.

A major leadership change unfolded in January 2008, at which time Mark A. Hoppe was named president of Taylor Capital Group, as well as president and CEO of Cole Taylor Bank. Bruce Taylor continued to serve as chairman and CEO of Taylor Capital. It also was around this time that the organization nearly doubled the size of its commercial banking business, adding 30 staff members. Another leadership change followed in October 2008, when veteran banker John J. Lynch, Jr., was named vice-chairman of Cole Taylor Bank.

By 2009 Cole Taylor Bank was operating in a very difficult economic climate. In an effort to reduce overhead and improve the company's financial position, Taylor Capital Group announced that its executive team and board members would voluntarily reduce their compensation to the tune of about $300,000. Coupled with other salary cutbacks, the organization hoped to save some $2.2 million in 2009. Despite the challenging environment, Cole Taylor Bank approached the 21st century's second decade on a confident note, focused on continued growth as a commercial bank.

Paul R. Greenland

PRINCIPAL COMPETITORS

Great Lakes Bank N.A.; Old Second Bancorp Inc.; Parkway Bank and Trust Co.

FURTHER READING

Arndorfer, James B., "To the Taylors, Banking Is a Wonderful Life," *American Banker,* March 17, 1997.

Barnhart, Bill, "You Can Bank on Cole, Taylor Adding Holdings," *Chicago Tribune,* August 25, 1980.

Boylan, Anthony Burke, "Profile: Cole Taylor's Big Plan: Stay Independent by Thinking Small," *Crain's Chicago Business,* January 15, 2001.

"Cole Taylor Bank, a Subsidiary of Taylor Capital Group, Announces Major Expansion of Its Commercial Banking Group," *PR Newswire,* June 5, 2006.

"Cole Taylor Becomes Area's Largest Privately Held Bank; Split-off from Cole Taylor Financial Group Completed; Management Cites Commitment to Chicago Area Customers," *PR Newswire,* February 12, 1997.

"Commercial Bank Veteran Mark A. Hoppe Named President of Taylor Capital Group and President and Chief Executive Officer of Cole Taylor Bank," *PR Newswire,* January 30, 2008.

Daniels, Steve, "Cole Taylor Struggles to Improve; Not Catching On as 'Business Bank,'" *Crain's Chicago Business,* June 21, 2004.

Gruber, William, "He Banked on Banking," *Chicago Tribune,* January 30, 1978.

Jackson, Ben, "Taylor of Ill. Traces Loss to Lawsuit Settlement," *American Banker,* September 27, 2002.

"John J. Lynch Jr. Joins Cole Taylor Bank as Vice Chairman," *PR Newswire,* October 16, 2008.

Kleiman, Carol, "Outlander Is Given Fair Warning: Avoid the Family Business," *Chicago Tribune,* March 15, 1982.

"Main State Bank to Be Moved to Larger Quarters," *Chicago Daily Tribune,* January 7, 1934.

"New Main State Bank Gets Permit," *Chicago Tribune,* November 25, 1967.

Sluis, William, and Derrick Blakley, "Drovers National Fails; New Bank Is Organized," *Chicago Tribune,* January 20, 1978.

Colorado Group Ltd.

100 Melbourne Street
Brisbane, QLD 4001
Australia
Telephone: (61 07) 3877 3333
Fax: (61 07) 3877 3411
Web site: http://www.coloradogroup.com.au

Private Company
Incorporated: 1864 as Williams Shoes
Employees: 2,010
Sales: AUD 473 million ($310.8 million) (2007 est.)
NAICS: 424330 Women's, Children's, and Infants'
Clothing and Accessories Merchant Wholesalers;
424340 Footwear Merchant Wholesalers; 448110
Men's Clothing Stores; 448120 Women's Clothing
Stores; 448210 Shoe Stores

■ ■ ■

Colorado Group Ltd. is a leading operator of retail footwear and clothing chains in Australia. The Brisbane-based company operates several store formats, including upscale footwear brand Mathers; Williams the Shoemen, a general footwear chain; Colorado, featuring sports and outdoor shoes; and the designer-oriented Diana Ferrari retail format. The company has also rolled out a line of apparel and accessories under the Colorado Adventurewear line, and owns the JAG jeans and clothing brand and retail network. Altogether, Colorado operates more than 430 stores across Australia and New Zealand, and generates revenues of more than AUD 473 million ($311 million) per year. Formerly listed on the

Australian Stock Exchange, Colorado was acquired by private-equity group ARH Investments, the Australian arm of Affinity Equity Partners (AEP). The company, which traces its roots to 1864 but which took on its present name only in 1999, is led by CEO David Botta and Chairman Robert Dalziel.

ORIGINS

Colorado Group was the result of the merger of a number of prominent Australian footwear retailers. The earliest member of the group was the Williams Shoes chain, which became one of Australia's first footwear specialists in the 19th century. That company was founded in 1864 by the Williams family in Ballarat, in Victoria. The family had immigrated to Australia to take advantage of the opportunities offered by the region's ongoing gold rush.

Williams grew into one of Australia's leading shoe retailers into the 20th century, focusing primarily on the mid-market general shoe segment. The company incorporated as Williams Shoes Limited in 1954. The following year, the company went public, listing its shares on the Australian Stock Exchange.

Williams continued to grow strongly through the 1960s, developing the popular Williams the Shoemen store format. This growth caught the attention of Kinney World Trade Company of the United States. That company, which operated the Kinney Shoes retail network, had itself been acquired by the F.W. Woolworth Company earlier in the decade. Woolworth sought to accelerate its growth in the second half of the decade, leading to building an international presence. As part of that effort, Woolworth, through Kinney, acquired Williams Shoes in 1969. The company subsequently removed its stock exchange listing and changed its name to Kinney Shoes (Australia) Limited.

Kinney Shoes (Australia) went on to develop a number of other retail formats for the Australian and New Zealand market. In the mid-1970s, for example, the company introduced the popular Foot Locker sports shoe retail format to the Australian market. While Williams remained the Australian operation's flagship business, the company began targeting the development of a more expanded footwear portfolio in the late 1980s.

This led the group to acquire another major Australian footwear retailer, Mathers Enterprises Limited, in 1988. Mathers was founded by Bill Mathers, who had opened his own shoe store in Ipswich, in Queensland, with just AUD 100 in 1923. The growing prosperity of the post–World War II period led Mathers to expand its operations. This process started with a listing of the company's shares on the Australian Stock Exchange in 1951.

Mathers began opening a number of new stores during that decade, including a store at the Chermside Shopping Centre, the first regional shopping mall in Australia, in 1957. Mathers began expanding beyond the Queensland region at the beginning of the 1960s, starting with the purchase of four Shirley Jones stores in 1961. Two years later, the company added seven Vic Jen Jensens shoe shops as well.

The company moved into New South Wales in 1970, opening its first store there in Lismore. During that decade, Bill Mathers passed the leadership of the company to his son, Robert Mathers, who continued the retail chain's steady growth. Under Robert Mathers, the company completed its largest acquisition, buying the 79-store chain of Flints shoe stores in 1986.

NEW BRANDS

The growth of Mathers attracted the interest of Kinney Shoes (Australia), which bought the company in 1988. The following year, the Kinney Shoes (Australia) company moved its headquarters to Brisbane, in

Queensland. The addition of Mathers enabled the Australian company to extend its range of retail shoe offerings into the higher-price segments. At the same time, the company sought to capitalize on the growing interest in outdoor and hiking boots and shoes. In 1988 the company began developing its first Colorado shoe models. The choice of the name Colorado was meant to evoke the ruggedness symbolized in the Australian consumer's mind by that U.S. state.

The successful launch of the Colorado brand encouraged Kinney Shoes (Australia) to develop a dedicated retail format for the line. This led to the creation of the first Colorado Adventurewear stores in 1993. The Adventurewear concept quickly caught on with Australian consumers. By 1998 the company had opened more than 30 Colorado Adventurewear stores; this number quickly grew, nearing 55 stores by 2000.

By then, Kinney Shoes (Australia) had been broken up as Woolworth carried out a vast restructuring of its holdings leading to its own re-creation as the Venator group. In 1999 the Foot Locker operations were separated from the Australian subsidiary, which then changed its name to Colorado Group Ltd. By the end of the year, Venator had completed its sale of Colorado Group, listing all of the company's shares on the Australian Stock Exchange.

The choice of name was telling for the newly independent company's future strategy. Despite the fact that both the Williams and Mathers retail chains were larger, each with more than 120 stores at the beginning of the 21st century, the Colorado name provided greater future growth potential, and therefore greater attraction for investors. Among those attracted to the new company was Solomon Lew, a former director of Australia's Coles Myer group. Through his investment company, Australian Retail Investments, Lew quickly acquired a 15 percent stake in Colorado. By about 2005, Lew had raised his stake in the company to nearly 22 percent.

A SPATE OF ACQUISITIONS

Then led by Robin Webb, managing director, Colorado quickly sought to extend its retail operations beyond its reliance on the traditionally low-margin footwear market. The company went on a brief buying spree, starting with the purchase of Palmer Corporation Ltd. for AUD 13.8 million ($7.49 million) in 2001. Palmer controlled the internationally successful JAG jeans and clothing brand, which operated 30 stores in Australia. Palmer also held the Australian rights to the DKNY brand. After integrating the JAG operations, Colorado renamed Palmer as JAG (Aust) Pty Ltd. in 2003.

```
┌─────────────────────────────────────────┐
│                                         │
│            KEY DATES                    │
│            ─────●─────                   │
│                                         │
│  1864:  The Williams family founds the Williams │
│         Shoes retail shoe company in Balla- │
│         rat, Victoria, in Australia.    │
│  1923:  Bill Mathers opens a shoe store in Ipswich, │
│         Queensland.                     │
│  1951:  Mathers goes public on the Australian Stock │
│         Exchange.                       │
│  1955:  Williams Shoes goes public on the Australian │
│         Stock Exchange.                 │
│  1969:  Kinney World Trade Corporation, a │
│         subsidiary of Woolworth, acquires Williams │
│         Shoes, which becomes Kinney Shoes │
│         (Australia).                    │
│  1988:  Kinney Shoes (Australia) acquires Mathers │
│         and launches the Colorado shoe brand. │
│  1993:  The company launches the Colorado Adven- │
│         turewear retail store format.   │
│  2000:  Following the breakup of Woolworth's │
│         Australian holdings, Kinney Shoes (Australia) │
│         goes public as Colorado Group.  │
│  2001:  Colorado Group acquires Palmer Corporation │
│         and its JAG clothing brand.     │
│  2002:  Colorado Group acquires the Diana Ferrari │
│         shoe brand.                     │
│  2006:  AEP launches a hostile takeover offer for │
│         Colorado Group.                 │
│  2007:  AEP acquires 100 percent of Colorado Group │
│         through its subsidiary ARH Investments. │
│  2009:  Colorado Group avoids bankruptcy through a │
│         debt restructuring agreement.   │
│                                         │
└─────────────────────────────────────────┘
```

By 2002 Colorado Group had completed a second acquisition, of the designer shoe group Diana Ferrari. That company had been founded by the Kirkhope and Goodman families in 1979. The company, called the Diana Shoe Company, started out small, producing just 150 pairs of shoes per day, under the Rivers brand. Diana Shoe launched a new line of shoes, Supersoft, in 1983, the success of which enabled it to expand its operations. By the middle of the decade, the company's production had reached 4,000 pairs of shoes per day.

Diana Shoe also began expanding its brand range, developing a number of new brands, including the Diana Ferrari brand. At the end of the decade, the Goodman and Kirkhope families agreed to split up the company. As part of that agreement, the Kirkhopes

retained the Diana Ferrari brand, including the DF Supersoft line, as well as the group's women's shoes business.

Diana Ferrari continued to produce its shoes in Australia for much of the 1990s. Toward the end of the decade, however, the group decided to shift its production to China, forming a joint venture for this effort. In this way, the company raised its production output to 7,000 pairs of shoes per day and was able to meet the steady demand for its products; in the early years of the new century, the company claimed that some 40 percent of all Australian women owned a pair of its Diana Ferrari or Supersoft shoes. During this time Diana Ferrari also extended its operations to include a variety of handbags, belts, and other accessories.

TUMBLING SHARES

The Palmer and Diana Ferrari acquisitions allowed Colorado Group to post impressive growth figures in the first half of the decade. The company's bottom line was further aided by the rising strength of the Australian dollar and steady declines in production costs as China ramped up its low-cost manufacturing sector in the early part of the decade. The general economic optimism in Australia during this period also played an important role in Colorado Group's growth at this time. Through 2004, Colorado posted impressive gains, with profits rising by as a much as 50 percent per year.

Colorado Group's growth phase was cut short, however, as the Australian dollar fell sharply in 2005. Consumer spending dropped off as a result. In the meantime, Colorado's JAG division had been struggling to meet the group's growth targets, despite several attempts to redesign its stores and clothing range. By 2005 the group had begun to warn that its profit growth was slowing. Over the next year, the group issued three more profit warnings, finally revealing a drop of 30 percent for the 2005 year. Compounding the group's difficulties was Webb's sudden decision to resign from the company in July 2006.

As a result, the company's share price went into a tailspin, bottoming out at AUD 3.16. This left the company vulnerable to a takeover attempt. Australian Retail Investments had already begun reducing its exposure to the company, selling off its shareholding in the company starting in 2004.

Colorado at first appeared to become the target of retail clothing rival Just Group, which acquired a nearly 5 percent stake in the company in 2006. Just Group described its acquisition as "strategic," in the hopes that a breakup of Colorado would enable Just to take over parts of the company's brand stable.

NEW OWNERS

The difficult trading conditions in Australia at the time had led to a surge in private-equity interest in the country. Colorado Group became caught up in this trend, when ARH Investments, the Australian arm of Affinity Equity Partners (AEP), launched a hostile takeover of the company in 2006.

Colorado Group rebuffed ARH's initial offer. ARH began buying up a stake in the company, gaining nearly 14 percent by July 2006. ARH then countered with a new offer, for AUD 4.70 per share. By September, another 68 percent of Colorado's shareholders had agreed to sell out to ARH. However, the sale was temporarily blocked when Solomon Lew launched a bid to buy a blocking stake in Colorado. ARH was forced to raise its purchase price again, and in May 2007 agreed to buy out Lew's stake in the company for AUD 6.20. As a result, ARH and parent AEP gained full control of Colorado Group, which was then delisted from the Australian Stock Exchange.

The worsening economic climate in Australia and throughout the world continued to affect Colorado Group as it struggled to maintain both its sales and profits levels. At the same time, Colorado Group had begun to strain under its increasing debt burden which included some AUD 230 million in maturing debt. The global economic collapse of 2008 only exacerbated the company's difficulties. By 2009 this debt burden appeared ready to crush Colorado Group as the group fought to avoid bankruptcy. Finally in May of that year, the company reached an agreement with its banks to restructure its debt, avoiding liquidation proceedings. With a history dating back to the middle of the 19th century, Colorado Group hoped for brighter days ahead.

M. L. Cohen

PRINCIPAL DIVISIONS

Diana Ferrari; JAG; Williams the Shoemen; Mathers.

PRINCIPAL COMPETITORS

Billabong International Ltd.; Country Road Ltd.; Supre Proprietary Ltd.; Lowes-Manhattan Proprietary Ltd.; Jeanswest Investments (Australia) Proprietary Ltd.; Roger David Stores Proprietary Ltd.; RM Williams Holdings Ltd.

FURTHER READING

"Australia's Colorado Group About to Turn the Corner: Chairman," *AsiaPulse News,* March 22, 2007.

"Australia's Colorado to Bid for Palmer Corp," *AsiaPulse News,* December 20, 2000.

"Australia's Just Group Acquires Stake in Rival Colorado," *AsiaPulse News,* September 13, 2006.

"Colorado Accepts Revised Offer from Affinity," *just-style.com,* August 31, 2006.

"Colorado Group Poised for Private Equity Sale," *just-style.com,* May 29, 2007.

"Colorado Group to Continue Organic Growth Strategy," *Hardcopy,* September 5, 2000.

"Colorado to Roll out New Look," *Australiasian Business Intelligence,* April 7, 2005.

"Debt Plan on the Cards for Colorado," *Australiasian Business Intelligence,* May 27, 2009.

Downie, Stephen, "Jag's the Snag in Colorado's Climb," *Daily Telegraph,* March 20, 2005.

"If the Shoe Fits," *Australiasian Business Intelligence,* May 27, 2003.

"Venator Group," *Chain Store Age Executive with Shopping Center Age,* January 2000, p. 28.

"Venator Sells Australian, Canadian Subsidiaries," *Apparel Industry Magazine,* January 2000, p. 10.

Walker, Jacqui, "After Two Steps Forward, Colorado Pauses," *Business Review Weekly,* November 7, 2002, p. 42.

Cost Plus, Inc.

——————————■——————————

200 4th Street
Oakland, California 94607
U.S.A.
Telephone: (510) 893-7300
Fax: (510) 893-3681
Web site: http://www.worldmarket.com

Public Company
Incorporated: 1958
Employees: 6,251
Sales: $1 billion (2009)
Stock Exchanges: NASDAQ
Ticker Symbol: CPWM
NAICS: 452990 All Other General Merchandise Stores

■ ■ ■

One of the leading direct-import retailers in the United States, Cost Plus, Inc., operates approximately 270 Cost Plus World Market stores in 30 states. These stores specialize in home furnishings imported from more than 50 countries in Europe, Asia, and Africa. With the inventory of a specialty retailer and the prices of a mass merchandiser, Cost Plus built its reputation in San Francisco before expanding into Southern California and finally eastward, where the bulk of the company's stores were opening in the late 1990s. The chain more than doubled in size during the 1990s and continued to increase in size significantly during the early years of the new millennium. Cost Plus's sales surpassed the $1 billion mark in 2006, but growth quickly came to halt as a result of the difficult retail and economic climate in the

United States. After posting a loss of $102.7 million in fiscal 2009, the company announced plans to shutter 26 stores.

ORIGINS

Cost Plus's founder, William Amthor, did not intend to create a discount direct-import retail chain or even to open a single store; but he discovered San Franciscans had a penchant for just that sort of merchandise. His discovery occurred by chance in 1958 when he sold some extra rattan furniture he had stored in a warehouse. At the time, Amthor operated a small family-owned furniture store in San Francisco, but instead of displaying the rattan furniture in his store, he rented 4,000 square feet of warehouse space in the Fisherman's Wharf area of San Francisco. The rattan furniture sold quickly, convincing Amthor to start importing merchandise as a new business. He opened his first store devoted exclusively to imported merchandise later in 1958 and began importing wicker by the shipload. Amthor took the name for his new store from his pricing strategy. The imported goods were sold at cost, plus ten percent, the inspiration for a chain of stores that would become known as Cost Plus.

Amthor took frequent trips to foreign countries, looking for merchandise and hunting down the best bargains for an eclectic array of goods. During these trips, he established business relationships with vendors that Cost Plus would use 30 years later. The frequency of Amthor's trips established the company's founder as a "world traveler," words invariably used to describe the peripatetic retailer, and established Cost Plus as a

COMPANY PERSPECTIVES

Cost Plus World Market's business strategy is to differentiate itself by offering a large and ever-changing selection of unique products, many of which are imported, at value prices in an exciting shopping environment. Many of Cost Plus World Market's products are proprietary, or private label, often incorporating the Company's own designs, "World Market" brand name, quality standards and specifications, and typically are not available at department stores or other specialty retailers.

unique, exotic store, filled with an ever-changing selection of merchandise. Customers never knew what they might find at Cost Plus, and this mystery had a decided appeal, making a trip to Amthor's store similar to a treasure hunt.

The store's bazaar-style merchandising proved to be highly popular, its success spawning the establishment of additional stores. For years, the location of these new stores was restricted to the greater Bay Area, but the stores expanded, eventually, into Southern California. During this gradual expansion, which occurred during the 1960s and 1970s, the Cost Plus chain thrived, selling tiki torches, gauze dresses, wicker furniture, and a grab bag of other imported goods, all at discount prices.

By the 1980s, two and one half decades of expansion had created a flourishing regional chain. Midway through the decade, there were 24 Cost Plus stores in California and one in Arizona. The anchor of the chain was the company's flagship store in Fisherman's Wharf, a 40,000-square-foot unit that, despite being ten times larger than Amthor's original store, still exuded the atmosphere created by the chain's founder. Inside, amid housewares, clothing, and furniture, customers picked their way through a broad collection of merchandise, everything from an inexpensive wire whisk to a $1,000 brass buddha from India. The merchandising mix was unique, representing the efforts of the company's seven buyers who, like Amthor before them, traveled the globe looking for items in Indonesia, China, Thailand, Portugal, France, and a host of other countries.

The company's other stores were considerably smaller, averaging between 18,000 square feet and 20,000 square feet, but each contained as diverse a range of merchandise as the flagship store. The smaller stores, which averaged sales of $200 per square foot, were primarily located in shopping centers, next to other

retail tenants whose customer-drawing power proved to be a boon to Cost Plus's business. The expansion strategy had worked well, providing a welcome support system of sorts that eased Cost Plus's entry into new markets. By the end of 1986, the company was ready to open two more stores, one in San Dimas, California, and the other in Bakersfield, but troubles had begun to surface. As Cost Plus exited the mid-1980s, its consistent record of success began to unravel, prompting changes that ultimately led to the creation of the modern version of Cost Plus.

DECLINE AND RESURGENCE

The turning point in Cost Plus's financial performance occurred after a 1987 leveraged buyout engineered by Bechtel Investments (later renamed Fremont Group). In the wake of the ownership change, Cost Plus's formula for success was lost, and financial losses began to mount. The quality of the merchandise declined as the stores developed a reputation for being cluttered, rather than being rich in diversity. As time passed, the problems became more severe, leading to further escalating losses. One industry pundit remarked that Cost Plus offered "too much hunt and too little treasure," characterizing the rapid deterioration of the chain's former strength. By the beginning of the 1990s, the company had recorded five years of consecutive year-end deficits, an alarming record exacerbated by the $5.9 million loss posted for 1991. Clearly, changes needed to be made.

Help had arrived by the time the depressing financial figures for 1991 were released. Ralph D. Dillon, the former president and chief operating officer of Family Dollar Stores, had joined Cost Plus in 1990. It was Dillon's responsibility to muster a turnaround and revive the chain's former vitality. He began making changes in the way Cost Plus operated shortly after his arrival. The scope and the severity of the changes increased after control of the company was gained by Goldman Sachs and International Nederland Capital Corp. in 1994, but throughout the first half of the 1990s, the process of transforming Cost Plus into a healthy enterprise was under way. By the time the company entered the mid-1990s, it emerged as a different sort of retailer offering a subtly but significantly altered merchandise mix.

One of the first problems Dillon recognized was that Cost Plus had lost its focus on the proper merchandise for the stores to display. Accordingly, he launched a campaign to determine what product mix was most attractive to the chain's customers. Experiments with focus groups revealed that the typical Cost Plus customer, identified as a college-educated female between the ages of 25 and 55, desired a combination of

KEY DATES

1958: William Amthor opens his first store devoted exclusively to imported merchandise.
1987: Cost Plus is sold to a group of investors.
1990: Ralph D. Dillon is named CEO.
1994: Goldman Sachs and International Nederland Capital Corp. gain control of the company.
1996: Cost Plus goes public.
1998: Murray Dashe is named chairman, president, CEO.
1999: Cost Plus opens its 100th store.
2005: Dashe retires; Barry J. Feld is named his replacement.
2006: Sales surpass $1 billion; the company launches a major restructuring effort to shore up same-store sales.
2007: Cost Plus operates 298 stores in 34 states.
2009: With losses mounting, Cost Plus announces plans to close 26 stores.

home decor merchandise and gourmet food. Dillon reacted to the research by increasing the presence of home decor items, eliminating toys, and limiting the space devoted to jewelry and beverages. Along with these changes, the average square footage of the stores was decreased, reduced from 20,000 square feet to somewhere between the 16,000-square-foot and 18,000-square-foot range. Despite the smaller size, Cost Plus stores continued to display roughly the same amount of merchandise, using vertical merchandising to compensate for less retail space.

Once the proper merchandise mix was identified, Dillon refined the layout of the new, prototype Cost Plus, which was christened Cost Plus World Market. The objective was to eliminate the cluttered look that had developed during the late 1980s and create a more defined design, but the layout still had to retain the open-air market atmosphere that had characterized the chain since its birth. Cost Plus relied heavily on impulse purchases, so a balance had to be struck between an orderly design and one that was conducive to browsing.

To orient the customer, Dillon and his staff designed three featured areas. At the back of the store, an assortment of gourmet food and beverages composed Cost Plus's Marketplace section. One side of the store, identified by a rug wall, displayed decorative home furnishings, including textiles, pillows, and baskets. On the other side of the store, beneath a chair hung on the wall, functional home furnishings were displayed, such as furniture, glassware, and tabletops. These areas provided an easily recognizable structure to Cost Plus, serving as landmarks amid the sea of imported merchandise, but not at the expense of reducing the number of impulse purchases. The average Cost Plus customer spent 45 minutes in the store, nearly twice the time spent in a typical home store.

The changes were important, but just as significant were the characteristics that were left unchanged. Although the company greatly increased its reliance on home furnishings until they accounted for nearly 70 percent of a store's total inventory, the emphasis continued to be on stocking imported items, one of the company's original strengths. Cost Plus imported 90 percent of the home furnishings it sold, buying the merchandise in more than 40 countries in Europe, Asia, and Africa. Placemats, napkins, and rugs were shipped from India and Turkey. Wood and rattan furniture arrived from Italy, Thailand, and the Czech Republic.

Cost Plus buyers procured glassware and dinnerware from England and France, baskets from China, the Philippines, and Indonesia, and collectible home artifacts from Bali, Ghana, and Namibia. The diversity of the imported merchandise had not changed and neither had the grab-bag appeal of an ever-changing inventory—an integral part of the formula that created Cost Plus's "treasure hunt" attraction. Roughly 60 percent of the items on display were changed every 12-month period, while certain product types were changed more frequently, usually at a monthly rate. The interior of the store harkened back to Amthor's first years as well, retaining the warehouse "feel" of the earliest Cost Plus units. The floors were cement, ceilings were high, beams were exposed, and fixtures were plain, creating a spartan environment for what the company described as an "upscale, organized version of the Third World central market-place."

EXPANSION ACCELERATES

After the Cost Plus concept was refined and profitability was restored, Dillon was ready to usher in the most prolific era of expansion in the company's history, and add to the 38 stores in operation when he joined the company. The company expanded beyond its home territory in California and began opening stores in neighboring states, with the pace of expansion increasing after Goldman Sachs and International Nederland Capital Corp. assumed majority control over the company in 1994. By the end of 1995, there were 50 stores composing the Cost Plus chain, including 13 in the Bay area, more than 30 stores in California, and more than a dozen scattered in a ten-state territory.

In early 1996, after maintaining profitability for a three-year period and expanding at a modest pace, Dillon was ready to take the company to new heights. His confidence in the Cost Plus World Market concept was resolute, prompting him to develop ambitious plans for the company. First, he completed the company's initial public offering of stock in April 1996, raising $29.8 million to pay for past and future expansion. Several weeks later, Dillon announced that Cost Plus would open eight additional Cost Plus World Markets by the end of 1996 and 12 units the following year, hoping to reach nearly 90 units by the end of the decade. His long-term plan was much grander, a 300-unit chain collecting $1.5 billion in sales, exponentially higher than the $182 million Cost Plus generated in sales in 1995.

By the time Cost Plus converted to public ownership, expansion was under way in a number of new markets. New stores were being developed in Texas, Illinois, Missouri, and Wisconsin, and were established, as they had been for decades, in shopping centers where the presence of other retail tenants assured a steady stream of customers. As the company expanded eastward, its progress was made easier not only by situating its stores in established shopping centers, but also by its decades of experience in the business.

Other import retailers of Cost Plus's ilk such as Bombay Company, Euromarket Designs, and Pier 1 Imports had to contend with the often troublesome process of foreign-sourcing their merchandise, that is, coordinating supply and delivery of goods from distant markets. Delays and miscommunications were frequent, but Cost Plus avoided the problems that less experienced retailers had to contend with because of the company's long-established ties with overseas vendors, many of which stretched back two generations. This was one of Cost Plus's major strengths, enabling the company to expand eastward with relative ease. In October 1996, Dillon banked on this advantage when he announced plans for major expansion, projecting the opening of 35 stores by the end of the decade.

As Cost Plus entered the late 1990s, work was under way to reach Dillon's goal. Expansion pushed the company eastward into the Midwest, where Cost Plus World Market stores opened in Chicago, Detroit, and Cincinnati. By November 1997, when the company announced plans to open its first store in Indiana, the chain comprised 68 stores in a 12-state territory, including four stores in Chicago and three in Detroit. The company planned to open 15 stores in 1998, projecting an annual growth rate of between 15 percent and 20 percent as the end of the century approached. As the company prepared for the future, its record of success in the 1990s provided strong evidence that further expan-

sion would yield substantial growth. Between 1992 and 1997, revenues more than doubled, jumping from $121 million to $260 million. Net income increased more dramatically, swelling from $151,000 to reach $10 million. With these figures demonstrating the strength of the Cost Plus World Market concept, the company's future expansion suggested equally robust gains in the years ahead.

NEW CHALLENGES IN A NEW CENTURY

Cost Plus's growth continued at breakneck speed during the late 1990s and beyond. Dillon retired in early 1998, leaving retail veteran Murray Dashe at the helm. Under his leadership, Cost Plus opened its 100th store in 1999 and planned for additional expansion well into the new millennium. With sales and profits on the rise, the company opened 24 stores in 2000 and 23 new locations in 2001. Twenty-six new stores opened their doors in 2002 while 23 Cost Plus World Markets opened in 2003. Cost Plus began to expand into new markets during this time period as well, including Montana and South Carolina. By 2005, the company was operating 236 stores and had revenues of over $940 million.

Dashe announced his retirement in 2005, and the company named Barry J. Feld, a Cost Plus board member, his replacement. While sales surpassed the $1 billion mark in 2006 due in part to its increase in store count, the company began to experience an alarming trend. Its same-store sales (the marker for retail health) began to decline in 2005 and again in 2006. The company launched a major restructuring effort that year, focusing on revamping its merchandise mix as well as its marketing strategy. It stopped selling some of its higher-cost products in favor of its affordable, low-cost items and launched new ad campaigns in an attempt to lure customers back to its unique products, wine, and food.

As the company worked to shore up sales and profits, it received a bid from competitor Pier 1 Imports, who offered to buy the company in 2008 in a deal worth approximately $88.4 million. Cost Plus declined the offer, believing the timing was not right given the tough retail climate coupled with the progress it claimed to have made on its restructuring program. At this time, Cost Plus began to close unprofitable stores and move out of certain markets along with cutting 10 percent of its corporate workforce. In early 2009, the company announced that it planned to shutter 26 stores during the fiscal year.

With future expansion on hold and losses mounting, Cost Plus remained cautiously optimistic about its future. Demand in the U.S. retail sector fell sharply in

2008, and many retailers found themselves struggling amid the economic downturn. Cost Plus was no exception and believed it faced a tough road ahead. Intense competition, climbing debt, and weak sales were all challenges that Cost Plus would be forced to meet head on. Company management, however, stood firm in its belief that its restructuring over the past several years had left the company well positioned to battle the obstacles in its path. Cost Plus hoped to return to profitability by 2011.

Jeffrey L. Covell
Updated, Christina M. Stansell

PRINCIPAL SUBSIDIARIES

Cost Plus World Market.

PRINCIPAL COMPETITORS

Bed Bath & Beyond Inc.; Euromarket Designs Inc.; Pier 1 Imports Inc.

FURTHER READING

Barron, Kelly, "The Prince of Peddlers Murray Dashe Has Put New Life into Specialty Retailer Cost Plus," *Forbes,* October 18, 1999.

Blackwood, Francy, "Cost Plus Treks Across America: Eclectic Retailer Opening 35 Units as It Spreads East," *HFN—The Weekly Newspaper for the Home Furnishing Network,* October 21, 1996, p. 1.

Carlsen, Clifford, "Importer Maps Out Uncharted Territory," *San Francisco Business Times,* July 26, 1996, p. 4A.

Corral, Cecile B., "Furniture Drags Home at Cost Plus," *Home Textiles Today,* June 1, 2009.

"Cost Plus: Buddhas to Bakeware," *Chain Store Age Executive with Shopping Center,* September 1986, p. 36.

Duff, Mike, "Cost Plus Emerges As Home Player with Consumables Kick," *Discount Store News,* January 1, 2001.

Huesmann, Chris, "Cost Plus Inc. Shares Begin Trading with a Rise," *Knight-Ridder/Tribune Business News,* April 5, 1996, p. 4.

Key, Peter, "Cost Plus of Oakland, Calif., to Open Carmel, Ind., Store," *Knight-Ridder/Tribune Business News,* November 4, 1997, p. 11.

Konstam, Patricia, "California's Cost Plus World Market to Open San Antonio Store," *Knight-Ridder/Tribune Business News,* August 30, 1996, p. 8.

Sage, Alexandria, "Cost Plus Ahead of Curve Facing Recession," *Reuters News,* October 23, 2008.

Thomas, Larry, "Cost Plus Rejects Pier 1," *Furniture Today,* June 23, 2008.

Torres, Blanca, "Cost Plus Chooses New Chief Executive," *Contra Costa Times,* October 26, 2005.

Vincenti, Lisa, "Cost Plus Markets Intrigue," *HFN—The Weekly Newspaper for the Home Furnishing Network,* May 11, 1998, p. 1.

Youssef, Jennifer, "Cost Plus Kicks Off Closing Sale," *Detroit News,* February 15, 2008.

CROSSTEX
Crosstex Energy Inc.

2501 Cedar Springs, Suite 100
Dallas, Texas 75201
U.S.A.
Telephone: (214) 953-9500
Fax: (214) 953-9501
Web site: http://www.crosstexenergy.com

Public Company
Incorporated: 1996
Employees: 780
Sales: $4.91 billion (2008)
Stock Exchanges: NASDAQ
Ticker Symbol: XTXI
NAICS: 211111 Crude Petroleum and Natural Gas
    Extraction

■ ■ ■

Headquartered in Dallas, Texas, publicly traded Crosstex Energy Inc. is a leading independent midstream energy services company that owns Crosstex Energy L.P., a master limited partnership that trades separately under the symbol XTEX. Via this structure, Crosstex offers investors two different ownership options (common shares or partnership units). On the strength of more than 750 employees, Crosstex gathers, treats, processes, distributes, and markets natural gas. In addition, the company is also involved in the marketing of crude oil. Crosstex's operations span five states along the Gulf Coast, and include more than 5,000 miles of pipeline, approximately 160 gas treatment plants, 12 gas processing facilities, and four fractionation facilities.

Fractionation involves the removal and breakdown of natural gas liquids from the natural gas stream. As a result of this process, valuable byproducts such as ethane, natural gasoline, isobutane, propane, and butane, are broken down into their base components.

FORMATIVE YEARS

Crosstex traces its roots back to 1994, when the company was formed as a Comstock Resources subsidiary named Comstock Natural Gas Inc. (CNG). In turn, CNG had been established following Comstock Resources' acquisition of Ventana Natural Gas, a business formed in 1992. In 1995 CNG acquired the managing general partner interest, as well as a limited partner interest of 20.31 percent, in Crosstex Pipeline Partners Ltd. from a company named Sonat. The $1.5 million deal also included gas gathering systems in Harrison County, Texas.

A management buyout in December 1996 led to the establishment of Crosstex Energy, which took its name from CNG's Crosstex Pipeline. Included in the deal were interests in a processing plant, 85 miles of pipeline, and nine gathering systems, along with related marketing operations. From the very beginning, Crosstex was led by President and CEO Barry E. Davis. A native of Frisco, Texas, Davis graduated from Texas Christian University and began his professional career in banking before switching to the energy industry.

Crosstex Energy began the new millennium by incorporating in Delaware on April 28, 2000. The company proceeded to make several acquisitions during the early years of the new century. In a $10.63 million deal, GC Marketing Co. was acquired in September 2000. Crosstex parted with $30 million in April 2001 to acquire Tejas C Pipeline LP LLC and Tejas Texas Pipeline GP LLC. In October of that year, Millennium Gas Services Inc. was acquired for $2.12 million.

Midway through 2002, the company established the master limited partnership Crosstex Energy L.P., which began trading on the NASDAQ on December 12 under the symbol XTEX. This became the entity through which the company engaged in midstream natural gas operations. Specifically, Crosstex Energy L.P. received natural gas from producers' wells via its gathering systems, removed impurities, and finally sold and transported the end product to industrial customers, marketers, and utilities.

By this time the company had acquired some ten other companies over the course of three years, in deals collectively worth $60.6 million. Its operations had grown to include 125 employees, 49 natural gas treating plants, two processing plants, and more than 1,500 miles of pipeline. Crosstex ended 2002 by striking a deal with Devon Energy for the Vanderbilt System, which consisted of 200 miles of transmission and gathering pipelines near Houston, Texas. Early the following year, the company began selling natural gas in Florida. This new opportunity was made possible by the 2002 acquisition of approximately 70 miles of pipeline from Florida Gas Transmission.

EARLY GROWTH

A major deal with Duke Energy Field Services L.P. occurred in July 2003, when Crosstex acquired a variety of assets in Alabama, Mississippi, Louisiana, and Texas. The $67.35 million transaction included the AIM Pipeline System in Mississippi; a 12.4 percent stake in the Gaines County, Texas-based Seminole Gas Processing Plant; the Montgomery County, Texas-based Conroe Gas Plant and Gathering System; the Louisiana-based Cadeville and Aurora Centana systems; and the Alabama-based Black Warrior Pipeline System.

One final development in 2003 was the completion of an expansion project at the company's Gregory

processing plant in South Texas. In addition, Crosstex bolstered its ability to serve regional industrial customers by adding some 20 miles of pipeline to its gathering system. Crosstex had increased its assets by approximately 50 percent during 2003. Subsequently, the company saw its operations grow to include some 50 gas treating and processing plants, as well as 2,500 miles of pipeline.

In January 2004 Crosstex Energy Inc., which owned and controlled the general partner of Crosstex Energy L.P., made its initial public offering. The company offered 2.3 million shares of common stock and began trading on the NASDAQ under the symbol XTXI. In order to make its limited partnership units more accessible to investors, Crosstex Energy L.P. completed a two-for-one unit split in March 2004.

In April 2004 the company's Crosstex Louisiana Energy L.P. subsidiary acquired the LIG Pipeline Co. The $76.2 million deal, which included some 2,000 miles of transmission and gas gathering systems, essentially doubled the size of the company's pipeline network. Several LIG subsidiaries became part of Crosstex as part of the transaction, including Louisiana Intrastate Gas Company LLC, LIG Liquids Company LLC, LIG Inc., LIG Chemical Co., and the Tuscaloosa Pipeline Co.

By July 2004 Crosstex operated 4,500 miles of pipeline along the Gulf Coast, stretching from Mississippi to South Texas. In addition, the company operated 50 gas treating plants, as well as five processing plants. Crosstex Energy Inc. ended 2004 with revenues of $1.98 billion, up from $1.01 billion in 2003. Net income totaled $8.7 million, down from $13.4 million in 2003.

Midway through 2005, Crosstex revealed expansion plans for the company's Crosstex LIG pipeline. The company hired Kinder Morgan Energy Partners L.P. to construct a new, $225 million interstate pipeline between Northwest Louisiana and East Texas. In August Crosstex announced the largest deal in its history to date, when the company agreed to acquire the South Louisiana-based processing and liquids business of El Paso Corp. Concluded in November, the $486.4 million deal involved subsidiary Crosstex Energy Services L.P. acquiring El Paso Dauphin Island Company LLC, the Sabine Pass Plant Facility Joint Venture, and CFS Louisiana Midstream Company LLC.

REMARKABLE GROWTH

Davis continued to serve as Crosstex's CEO as the company headed into 2006. In January, the company

KEY DATES

1994: The company is formed as a Comstock Resources subsidiary named Comstock Natural Gas Inc.

1996: A management buyout in December leads to the establishment of Crosstex Energy.

2000: The company incorporates in Delaware.

2002: The master limited partnership Crosstex Energy L.P. is formed and begins trading on the NASDAQ under the symbol XTEX.

2004: Crosstex Energy Inc., which owns and controls the general partner of Crosstex Energy L.P., makes its initial public offering and begins trading on the NASDAQ under the symbol XTXI.

2006: CEO Barry Davis rings the NASDAQ opening bell in honor of the company's tenth anniversary.

2008: Crosstex announces plans to relocate its headquarters to the Dallas, Texas-based Harwood International Center.

2009: Crosstex agrees to sell its assets in Alabama, Mississippi, and South Texas to Southcross Energy LLC in a $220 million deal.

culture at Crosstex, commenting: "Crosstex's culture drives the company's success. Our culture enables our team to cultivate synergistic working relationships with fellow members of the Crosstex team, as well as our customers. Employees are empowered to think like owners and have mutual respect for their colleagues' talents. Crosstex is a strong company built to last. We are committed to excellence in all we do."

Crosstex rounded out 2006 by acquiring Cardinal Gas Solutions L.P.'s amine-treating operations in November. That month, the company also named Robert S. Purgason as executive vice-president and chief operating officer. By year's end, Crosstex's workforce had grown to include more than 600 employees, up from a staff of nine when the company was established ten years before. Crosstex L.P. capped off 2006 with distributable cash flow of $81.9 million, up from $64.6 million in 2005. The partnership recorded a net loss of $4.2 million, compared to net income of $19.2 million in 2005. Crosstex Energy Inc. reported net income of $16.5 million, down significantly from $49.1 million in 2005.

INDUSTRY LEADER

Growth continued in 2007. In April of that year, Crosstex's Louisiana Intrastate Gas Pipeline System expanded by 200 million cubic feet of gas per day following the completion of a $90 million expansion project. The following month, the company received an award from the Gas Processors Association, in recognition of an excellent safety record in 2006. In August 2007, Crosstex announced plans to build an $80 million, 29-mile natural gas pipeline in Johnson County, Texas. This development allowed the company to further its expansion in the Barnett Shale. Crosstex Energy L.P. rounded out the year by closing a public offering of 1.8 million common units.

By early 2008, Crosstex's growth had created cramped quarters at its Dallas headquarters facility. In April, the company announced that it was relocating to the city's Harwood International Center, where about 400 of its 700-member workforce would occupy five floors of office space. Around the same time, plans were made to construct a new, $80 million natural gas processing facility in North Texas. By adding some 200 million cubic feet of capacity, the new plant bolstered the company's daily capacity in the Barnett Shale field to about 485 million cubic feet. In mid-2008, Crosstex Energy L.P. and Crosstex Energy Inc. both elected President and CEO Davis to serve in the additional capacity of chairman.

In September, Crosstex literally weathered two potentially devastating storms. Over the span of several

announced plans to acquire 48 amine treating rental plants from a unit of Hanover Compression Co. In April, Crosstex finished construction of its $115 million North Texas Pipeline. Connected to the Barnett Shale, the nation's largest natural gas play, the pipeline gathered and transported gas through six counties in North Texas, spanning some 140 miles. Additional expansion in the Barnett Shale occurred midway through 2006. At that time the company's Crosstex Energy Services L.P. subsidiary acquired 250 miles of existing pipeline, as well as approximately 400 miles of planned pipeline, in a $480 million deal with Chief Holdings LLC.

Crosstex reached an important milestone in 2006, celebrating its tenth anniversary. During its first decade, the company had achieved remarkable growth. Operations had expanded from some 85 miles of pipeline to more than 5,000 miles. From the very beginning, the company was guided by President and CEO Davis, who rang the NASDAQ opening bell in honor of the occasion on October 20, 2006.

In the October 2006 issue of *Pipeline & Gas Journal,* Davis provided some insight into the corporate days, Hurricanes Gustav and Ike threatened the company's assets along the Gulf Coast. Fortunately, the resulting physical property damage was minimal. Crosstex's Sabine plant, as well as several offshore production platforms and pipelines serving its Bluewater and Pelican processing plants, sustained the most damage. In all, the company indicated that both hurricanes negatively impacted gross margins by nearly $23 million for the year. Crosstex L.P. ended 2008 with distributable cash flow of $180.2 million, up from $116 million in 2007. The partnership's net income totaled $10.8 million, down from $13.9 million in 2007. Crosstex Energy Inc. reported net income of $24.2 million for 2008, up significantly from $12.2 million the previous year.

By early 2009, Crosstex's operations had grown to include four fractionators, 12 processing plants, some 195 natural gas amine-treating plants, and 5,700 miles of pipeline. The company moved forward with a strong focus on growing the business in Louisiana and North Texas. In an effort to reduce its debt, which exceeded $200 million, Crosstex agreed to sell its assets in Alabama, Mississippi, and South Texas to Southcross Energy LLC. The $220 million deal, which closed in August, included some 1,400 miles of intrastate gathering and transmission lines in South Texas, as well as 780 miles of pipeline in Alabama and Mississippi. Based upon its successful track record and history of measured growth, Crosstex appeared to have good prospects for continued success in the second decade of the 21st century.

Paul R. Greenland

PRINCIPAL SUBSIDIARIES

Crosstex Acquisition Management L.P.; Crosstex Alabama Gathering System L.P.; Crosstex CCNG Gathering Ltd.; Crosstex CCNG Processing Ltd.; Crosstex CCNG Transmission Ltd.; Crosstex DC Gathering Company J.V.; Crosstex Energy GP L.P.; Crosstex Energy GP LLC; Crosstex Energy Services GP LLC; Crosstex Energy Services L.P.; Crosstex Energy L.P.; Crosstex Gulf Coast Marketing Ltd.; Crosstex Gulf Coast Transmission Ltd.; Crosstex Holdings GP LLC; Crosstex Holdings L.P.; Crosstex Holdings L.P. LLC; Crosstex LIG Liquids LLC; Crosstex LIG LLC; Crosstex Louisiana Energy L.P.; Crosstex Mississippi Industrial Gas Sales L.P.; Crosstex Mississippi Pipeline L.P.; Crosstex NGL Marketing L.P.; Crosstex NGL Pipeline L.P.; Crosstex North Texas Gathering L.P.; Crosstex North Texas Pipeline L.P.; Crosstex Operating GP LLC; Crosstex Pelican LLC; Crosstex Pipeline Partners Ltd.; Crosstex Pipeline LLC; Crosstex Processing Services LLC; Crosstex Seminole Gas L.P.; Crosstex Treating Services L.P.; Crosstex Tuscaloosa LLC; LIG Chemical GP LLC; LIG Chemical L.P.; LIG Liquids Holdings L.P.; Sabine Pass Plant Facility J.V.

PRINCIPAL COMPETITORS

DCP Midstream Partners LP; Kinder Morgan Energy Partners L.P.; TEPPCO Partners L.P.

FURTHER READING

"BRIEF: Dallas-Based Crosstex Moving Headquarters to Uptown," *Dallas Morning News,* April 1, 2008.

Bullion, Lew, "Crosstex Energy CEO Blends People and Financial Skills," *Pipeline & Gas Journal,* October 2006.

"Comstock Buys Properties," *Oil Daily,* August 3, 1995.

"Crosstex Celebrates 10 Years of Delivering Success," *Business Wire,* January 23, 2007.

"Crosstex Completes Acquisition of Processing and Liquids Business for $486.4 Million," *PR Newswire,* November 1, 2005.

"Crosstex Completes Sale of Mississippi, Alabama, and South Texas Assets," *Business Wire,* August 6, 2009.

"Crosstex Energy Enters Florida Gas Market," *PR Newswire,* January 23, 2003.

"Crosstex Energy Follows Plan for Rapid Growth," *Pipeline & Gas Journal,* February 2004.

"Crosstex Energy L.P. Units Began Trading on NASDAQ," *PR Newswire,* December 11, 2002.

Daktronics, Inc.

---

201 Daktronics Drive
Brookings, South Dakota 57006-5128
U.S.A.
Telephone: (605) 692-0200
Toll Free: (800) 843-5843
Fax: (605) 697-4700
Web site: http://www.daktronics.com

Public Company
Incorporated: 1968
Employees: 3,500
Sales: $581.9 million (2009)
Stock Exchanges: NASDAQ
Ticker Symbol: DAKT
NAICS: 339950 Scoreboards Manufacturing

■ ■ ■

Daktronics, Inc., is one of the world's largest suppliers of large format electronic display systems, including electronic scoreboards, computer programmable display systems, and large light-emitting diode (LED) video displays for sport, business, and government applications. In addition, the company markets integrated sound systems for sports facilities under the Sportsound brand name, as well as Vortek brand rigging and hoist systems for the entertainment market, including sports facilities and theaters.

Daktronics' displays communicate with millions of viewers in more than 100 countries worldwide. It is recognized globally as a technical leader with the capabilities to design, manufacture, install, and service complete systems displaying real-time data, graphics, animation, and video.

TECHNICAL ADVANCES SUPPORT BIRTH OF NEW COMPANY

Daktronics was founded in 1968 by Dr. Aelred Kurtenbach and Dr. Duane Sander, two professors of electrical engineering at South Dakota State University (SDSU) in Brookings. Kurtenbach received his B.S., M.S., and Ph.D. degrees in electrical engineering from the South Dakota School of Mines and Technology, the University of Nebraska, and Purdue University, respectively. His experience spanned the fields of communication engineering and control system design, technical services, computer systems, electrical engineering education, and small business management. Cofounder Sander began operating as a director and secretary of the company. He served as the dean of engineering at SDSU, where he taught electrical engineering courses and directed biomedical research projects since 1967.

The founders used the talents of the school's graduates, in 1970 producing and selling their first product, a voting display system for the Utah legislature. The founders sold shares to the public, marketing their offering as an opportunity for people in the community to invest in a new start-up. People in the area recognized the talent coming out of SDSU and responded favorably. Following up on a tip from the university's wrestling coach, they built a small scoreboard for school meets, a project that ultimately catapulted the company into the limelight, when a Daktronics scoreboard was employed at wrestling competitions during the 1976 Olympics.

COMPANY PERSPECTIVES

Though Daktronics may not be a household word, the company is recognized worldwide in its industry as the leading designer and manufacturer of electronic scoreboards, programmable display systems, and large screen video displays using light emitting diode (LED) technology.

Daktronics began using the technology developed from voting display systems, expanding production to include large scoreboards and commercial displays. Typical users of commercial displays included banks, shopping centers, auto dealers, hotels, retail stores, advertising companies, and casinos. Attuned to technical innovations of the time, the company incorporated microprocessor-based computers to process information provided by an operator, and to formulate the information for presentation on a display.

COMPUTER TECHNOLOGY DRIVES GROWTH

In the late 1970s the company began building computer-programmable information display systems utilizing standard modules or sections in a variety of systems. The use of modular sections allowed Daktronics to offer a broad range of standard as well as custom products. Daktronics' systems comprised two principal components, the display and the display controller. The display controller used computer hardware and software to process the information provided from the operator and formulated the information, graphics, or animation to be presented on the display.

The display controller then controlled each of the picture elements or "pixels" on the display to present the message or image. Data was transferred between the display controller and the displays for both local and remote display sites. Local connections used twisted pair cables, fiber optic cables, infrared links, or radio frequency. Both standard and cellular telephone connections were used to connect remote display locations, connections which were generally purchased from third parties. Prior to the use of computer programmable signage, which either emits or reflects light depending on the specific display technology, the large video display business was dominated by the small cathode ray tube-based product, and the suppliers were generally the same companies that were in the television set business.

PROVIDING SIGNS FOR WORLD-CLASS EVENTS

Daktronics quickly became an established leader in the niche of computer programmable signs and by 1977 the company had surpassed $1 million in annual sales, forcing it to double the size of its facilities. Daktronics secured a contract to provide nine large scoreboards for the 1980 Winter Olympic Games in Lake Placid, New York. During that period it also provided scoreboards for several large college installations.

The company continued to enhance its controller and display technology, acquiring the Glow Cube reflective display technology along with Star Circuits, a manufacturer of printed circuit boards. In the mid-1980s the company installed its first major league Scoreboard and provided systems to several other Olympic events as well as the Professional Golfers' Association tour.

On New Year's Eve, 1984, Daktronics installed its first large Starburst technology display at Caesars Palace in Las Vegas, Nevada, and later converted the World famous "Zipper" display at Times Square in New York City to Daktronics LED technology. In an interview with Sharon Phillips of the *Wall St. Corporate Reporter,* Kurtenbach stated, "We are building off the computer industry so there is definite expansion taking place. This is a growth-oriented business that addresses interesting applications."

ENTERING THE GLOBAL MARKET

During the 1990s Daktronics initiated a strategic business alliance with Omega Electronics, S.A., of Biel, Switzerland, a leading timing systems manufacturer and a company of SMH. The two companies planned to use each other's complementary core business positions, with Omega distributing Daktronics scoreboards and matrix displays for use in sport applications around the world. In return, Daktronics added Omega Electronics sports timing and photofinish products to its product offering for sale in the United States and Canada. Daktronics was counting on Omega Electronics' established presence and reputation to open up areas of the world that were very difficult and expensive to penetrate. Within months of the alliance, projects for Daktronics Scoreboard installations outside of North America included locations in Singapore, Egypt, France, Colombia, Switzerland, Portugal, India, and Scotland.

Another SMH company, Swiss Timing, the largest watchmaker in the world, contracted with Daktronics to provide more than 70 scoreboards for the 1996 Olympics to be held in Atlanta, Georgia. Everything from small, indoor reflective displays to large, outdoor

KEY DATES

1968: Daktronics is founded by two electrical engineering professors.
1969: The company completes its first stock offering.
1976: Daktronics scoreboards are first used in Olympic competition (wrestling).
1984: The company is restructured from a product-driven to a market-driven organization.
1987: Daktronics acquires circuit board manufacturer Star Circuits.
1994: Daktronics stock is traded on NASDAQ.
1999: Daktronics sets a record for annual orders with more than $100 million booked.
2006: The company announces its third two-for-one stock split in its history.
2009: Net sales reach $581.9 million, up from $499.7 million the previous year.

incandescent displays using low-energy lamp/reflector/lens technologies were included in the installations, with the most sophisticated displays located in the Olympic Stadium, site of the opening and closing ceremonies and track and field events. After the Olympics, the stadium and scoreboards were reconfigured for baseball, where the Atlanta Braves began playing in the 1997 season. New service offices were opened in Atlanta; Columbus, Ohio; and San Antonio, Texas, bringing the total number of Scoreboard Sales and Service offices to 11, as plans for further statewide openings were being considered.

Daktronics negotiated a multimillion-dollar contract with Artkraft-Strauss Sign Corporation to provide five large electronic displays and 24 digital clocks for installation in Times Square. Replacing the famous Zipper sign, the new 370-foot-long display used amber LEDs, controlled by the company's proprietary Venus 7000 software. The Venus control system was a Windows-based, large matrix control system that allowed customers to easily display text messages, colorful graphics and animation, statistics and data imported from other programs, out-of-town game scores, live video, and instant replays. Three of the displays were designed to scroll news headlines in 48-inch-high characters, for NASDAQ and New York Stock Exchange market information. The other two showed additional financial information, still graphics, animation, and video-sourced graphics in 256 different shades of color.

LIGHTING LAS VEGAS

Responding to the growth of the U.S. gaming industry, and because of the gaming industry's large use of programmable displays, the company developed special products for that market, a market of seemingly unlimited growth potential. In Las Vegas, new and bigger casinos continued to entice customers. In response to that growth, the company consolidated its marketing efforts to casinos to take advantage of contacts and experience with electric sign companies.

In addition to gaming growth in the Las Vegas area, Daktronics provided color displays to several riverboat and Native American casinos in other areas, and digital jackpot displays on billboards for the Oregon lottery. At dog and horse racetracks Daktronics' products were used to display odds, winners, track conditions, and other information.

GROWING CAPABILITIES

Despite sales growth in 1996, profits dropped from those of fiscal 1995, attributed to a $900,000 projected cost overrun on a contract to supply variable message signs to the New Jersey Department of Transportation and competitive conditions in other market segments. Company executives countered the loss by initiating a strategy to focus on product improvement and to slow down the growth pace. They planned to continue expanding sales and profits from standard products and to limit the increase of selling, general, and administrative costs, and to concentrate on returning to a profitable position in its custom technical contracting business. The company introduced a number of new standard products and expanded its manufacturing space to accommodate the final assembly of standard products. Additional sales and service staff were added to support that manufacturing facility.

Daktronics' sport market niches continued to provide some 70 percent of sales in 1997. The company reorganized its Engineering Departments into three product groups: Sports Products (primarily scoreboards and timing equipment); Data Trac/InfoNet (primarily text based displays); and Large Matrix (graphics/animation/video displays). The reorganization was intended to allow the company's technical employees to interact more effectively with the marketplace and to bring more appropriate products to the market in less time. The groups focused on standardizing smaller products and subassemblies that were used in building larger display systems.

Company management remained committed to offering a variety of different programmable display technologies for different customers. Many of Daktronics' competitors in the business markets produced only one type of display (lamp, LED, or reflective), limiting their offerings to customers, while Daktronics offered a solution for each unique situation. Management reasserted its desire to develop innovative products and updating existing ones will with new features, reducing costs when possible to maintain a competitive edge. Their strategy paid off with improved profit margins and a net income increase in 1998 of 125 percent over the previous year.

By May of that year company backlog exceeded $21 million, and executives were confident that strong growth would continue. Following the introduction of the ProStar family of RGB (red/green/blue) LED displays, which were enhanced in both resolution and color depth, executives felt confident that the company could compete favorably with industry giants such as Sony, Mitsubishi, Panasonic, and other large-screen video display companies.

NEW LEADERSHIP

Daktronics signed a multimillion-dollar contract with SMH to provide scoreboards, matrix displays, and technical support services at the 2000 Summer Olympics in Sydney, Australia. Daktronics had already installed equipment for certain venues at the site, including the International Aquatics Centre and the Sydney Showground. The equipment included more than 50 scoreboards and matrix displays to record scores, times, and other information at 34 different venues.

The company maintained its close relationship with SDSU, attributing much of the company's technical expertise to the institution's policy of ongoing training and education. Some 300 of the university's students were employed at Daktronics in various capacities in 1998. The company reimbursed tuition costs for work-related courses and internal education. According to company sources, many of the company leaders had previously worked at Daktronics as students. Additionally, Daktronics offered a few internships with other regional universities.

James Morgan took over as president and COO of the company in 1999, at a time when the company ranked as one of "The 100 Best Stocks to Own for Under $20," in the book of the same name by Gene Walden. Morgan earned his bachelor's and master's degrees in electrical engineering from SDSU and joined Daktronics in 1970 as a graduate student. Morgan designed the first company product, the Matside Wrestling Scoreboard, in 1971. His other accomplishments included leading the design, manufacturing, and

installation of the first Daktronics swim timing system, a control system for a municipal water treatment plant, various voting systems, and the first Daktronics outdoor electronic message center.

According to Jonah Keri of *Investor's Business Daily*, "A boom in new stadium construction, a greater focus on fan entertainment and corporations' heightened interest in sponsoring professional, college and high school sports has sent the Scoreboard industry through the roof." Daktronics' main rival in the scoreboard market was Trans-Lux Corporation, and it, too, attracted high-profile sports clients, contracting projects such as the Rose Bowl and the San Francisco Giants' Pacific Bell Park. Industry analysts predicted that superior product offerings by both Daktronics and Trans-Lux would enable them to be major contenders, with the other rival companies dropping off. Daktronics ended the 1990s on a high note, announcing a two-for-one stock split in December 1999.

GROWTH VIA ACQUISITIONS

The new millennium marked the beginning of an expansion period at Daktronics. In early 2000 the company bolstered its capabilities via the acquisition of the Tampa, Florida-based video production and video consulting company Keyframe Inc., and the Des Moines, Iowa-based video display company FibreLite. In 2001, the company acquired a Brookings, South Dakota-based large-screen video rental company named Sports Link Ltd., as well as an 80 percent stake in Servtrotech Inc.

Growth continued during the middle of the first decade of the 2000s. The Topeka-based audio systems company Dodge Electronics Inc. was acquired in November 2004, followed by Bristol, U.K.-based European Timing Systems Ltd. in December. In 2005, the company strengthened its Keyframe operation by snapping up a video production business in Clearwater, Florida, named Diamond P Studio.

Daktronics ended its 2006 fiscal year (April 2006) with $31.9 million in cash flow from operations. Several key developments occurred in early fiscal 2007. Daktronics announced the third two-for-one stock split in its history in May 2006. Shortly thereafter, the company formed a strategic partnership with New York-based Arena Media Networks, which then operated the nation's largest network of digital flat-panel displays in arenas and stadiums.

Several other developments took place during Daktronics' 2007 fiscal year. In addition to parting with $4 million for a 50 percent stake in FuelCast Media International, the company spent nearly $4.3 million to acquire New York-based Hoffend & Sons Inc., which produced scoreboard hoist systems and rigging systems used in theaters and arenas. Daktronics capped off its 2007 fiscal year with $15 million in cash flow from operations. The company paid out a $2 million dividend to shareholders, and announced capital expenditures of about $59 million. By September 2007, Daktronics had installed more than 450 digital billboards, giving the company status as a leading supplier within the industry. The following month, the company planned to begin shipping its Valo OT digital billboard, which offered features such as lower power consumption and reduced weight.

CHALLENGING TIMES

In November 2008, Daktronics faced a class-action lawsuit claiming that, between mid-November 2006 and early April 2007, the company had failed to disclose information regarding its operating expenses, the delay of several large orders, and problems the company was experiencing with its sports markets and digital billboard businesses. Together, these factors had caused Daktronics to revise its financial projections for 2008, and led to a decline in the value of its common stock.

By early 2009 Daktronics was in the process of upgrading or powering up display systems for several Major League Baseball teams, including the Cincinnati Reds, the Texas Rangers, the Pittsburgh Pirates, the New York Yankees, and the New York Mets. In addition, the company was planning to design and manufacture several LED video and scoring system upgrades at the Edward Jones Dome in St. Louis, Missouri, the home field of the National Football League's St. Louis Rams.

In May 2009, Daktronics ended its 2009 fiscal year with net sales of $581.9 million, up from $499.7 million the previous year. The company recorded net income of $26.4 million, compared to net income of $26.2 million in 2008. Moving forward, Daktronics forecast a noteworthy drop-off in sales and orders for its 2010 fiscal year, due to difficult economic conditions. Despite the challenging climate, the company's

prospects for continued success seemed good, given its position of industry leadership.

Terri Mozzone
Updated, Paul R. Greenland

PRINCIPAL SUBSIDIARIES

Daktronics Australia Pty Ltd.; Daktronics Beijing (China); Daktronics Canada Inc.; Daktronics France SARL; Daktronics Hoist Inc.; Daktronics Hong Kong Ltd.; Daktronics Media Holdings Inc.; Daktronics Shanghai Ltd. (China); Daktronics UK Ltd.; Daktronics GmbH (Germany); MSC Technologies Inc.; Star Circuits Inc.

PRINCIPAL COMPETITORS

LSI Industries Inc.; Mitsubishi Electric Corp.; Panasonic Corporation of North America.

FURTHER READING

"Daktronics Adopts Rights Plan," *Wall Street Journal,* November 25, 1998, p. C12.

"Daktronics Board Announces Annual Cash Dividend and Two-for-One Stock Split," *Business Wire,* May 25, 2006.

"Daktronics, Inc.," *First Coverage,* August 31, 1998, p. 3.

"Daktronics' New Digital Billboard Reaches Early Sales Milestone," *Wireless News,* September 19, 2007.

"Daktronics to Acquire Sports Link Large Screen Video Rental Company," *PR Newswire,* July 26, 2000.

"Edward Jones Dome to Feature New Daktronics Integrated Video & Scoring System," *GlobeNewswire,* March 3, 2009.

Keri, Jonah, "On Display, Daktronics Scoring Big Profits with Its High-Tech Scoreboards," *Investor's Business Daily,* August 31, 1999.

Koenig, Bill, "Indianapolis Motor Speedway Buys Television Screens," *Knight-Ridder/Tribune Business News,* December 16, 1998.

Oakley, Lawrence C., "Special Situation," *Conservative Speculator,* August 1998.

Vrcan, Lori, "Design a Pool, Keep It Running," *School Product News,* June 1983, p. 31.

Dollar Financial Corporation

———— ■ ————

1436 Lancaster Avenue, Suite 300
Berwyn, Pennsylvania 19312-1200
U.S.A.
Telephone: (610) 296-3400
Fax: (610) 296-7844
Web site: http://www.dfg.com

Public Company
Incorporated: 1979 as Monetary Management Corporation
Employees: 5,490
Sales: $572.2 million (2008)
Stock Exchanges: NASDAQ
Ticker Symbol: DLLR
NAICS: 522291 Consumer Lending

■ ■ ■

Dollar Financial Corporation is a financial services company based in Berwyn, Pennsylvania, a Philadelphia suburb. A public company listed on the NASDAQ, Dollar Financial serves what it calls "under-banked" consumers, lower- and middle-income people with an annual average salary of $26,000, most of whom lack a traditional checking account. The company operates a network of more than 1,200 stores in the United States, Canada, Ireland, and the United Kingdom, providing such services as check cashing, short-term consumer loans (including controversial payday loans), prepaid credit cards, money orders, and money transfers. Nearly 500 stores, about 60 of them franchised operations, operate in the United States, mostly in California and

Florida, under the Money Mart, Loan Mart, The Check Cashing Store, and American Payday Loans banners. Many of the stores also offer utility bill payment services and tax preparation.

About 460 Money Mart Stores, including 61 franchised stores, offer the same basic services as well as currency exchange in Canada. The more than 300 U.K. stores operate under the Money Shop name, and in addition to check cashing, cash advances, money transfer, prepaid credit cards, and currency exchange, they offer pawnbroking. The nine Money Shop units in Northern Ireland and the Republic of Ireland offer check cashing, money transfers, currency exchange, and gold and jewelry buying. Dollar Financial operates the second largest network of financial services stores in the United States, and the largest chains in Canada and the United Kingdom.

ORIGINS

Dollar Financial Group was created in 1979 as Monetary Management Corporation by the United States Banknote Company (USBN), a printer of paper currency, as a private distributor of government benefits in the Philadelphia area. The company expanded to Ohio, California, and Michigan in the mid-1980s, and in addition to distributing benefits the USBN centers offered check cashing services. The chain was incorporated as DFG Holdings, Inc., in April 1990, and a month later USBN sold the business to a private investor group affiliated with the Wall Street investment firm Bear, Stearns & Co. Inc. Serving as DFG's chief executive officer and chairman was Jeffrey Weiss, a Bear,

Stearns managing director who oversaw the firm's investment in small and midsized companies, for many of which he served as CEO and chairman. Also joining the board was another Bear, Stearns executive, Donald Gayhardt, who in 1993 left Bear, Stearns to become DFG's chief financial officer and executive vice-president.

In June 1994 Weiss and Gayhardt bought the company, now known as Dollar Financial, from Bear, Stearns. A year earlier the company had acquired the PenNet system, an electronic benefits transfer system, which distributed food stamps and other public benefits via magnetic cards in Pennsylvania. The system was then incorporated into Dollar Financial's Philadelphia-area check cashing stores as well as grocery stores in other parts of the state. Dollar Financial received a monthly fee from the state to operate and support the PenNet system.

By 1995 Dollar Financial, under the Check Mart banner (and "Almost A Bank" in Virginia), operated the second largest chain of check cashing stores in the United States and was the largest distributor of government benefits. The chain had done especially well establishing kiosk outlets in convenience stores, many of which were open 24 hours a day. In addition to check cashing they offered utility and other bill paying, money orders, money transfer, postal services and mailbox rentals, and copy and fax services.

PAYDAY LENDING

Dollar Financial also offered consumer loans, becoming involved in the increasingly popular, and controversial, payday loan business, which many critics called loan sharking, a predatory lending practice that took advantage of low-income customers. Proponents called it a "deferred presentment" service. A customer with an active checking account and proof of employment could write a postdated check to the lender for an amount that covered the loan plus a fee, generally $15 to $20 per $100 received, rather than an interest charge. The agency deposited the check on the date written, generally the day of the customer's next paycheck. All too often, however, the cash-strapped borrower fell into a refinancing trap and a second loan was taken out to cover the first, a "rollover" loan that created a vicious cycle for some borrowers who continued to pay fees but were unable to reduce the principal of the loan.

Payday lending was hardly new in the United States. In the late 1800s the practice thrived with "five for six" lenders whose customers borrowed $5 on Monday and repaid $6 when they received their pay on Friday or Saturday. The interest rate seemed modest in the context of a week, but at 20 percent per week it amounted to more than 1,000 percent per annum. These salary lenders, mostly found in northeastern cities, became known as loan sharks. They targeted lower-middle-class people who held steady jobs, but who lacked the assets to obtain a bank loan if they suffered a financial setback. Because they had jobs and families they were not likely to flee town. Lenders could also play on their Victorian sense of guilt about going into debt.

Some lenders hired a "bawler-out," usually a vocal woman, to visit a workplace to denounce and humiliate the negligent borrower. The primary goal of the loan shark was to extract as many payments as possible without having the principal of the loan reduced, thus creating "chain debt." Such high-cost lending became a major problem in the late 19th century. Not only were laws eventually enacted to combat loan sharking, charitable lending institutions and mutual savings and loan organizations arose to meet the credit needs of the middle class. Loan sharking, conducted by organized crime, continued to prey on people in the shadows of society, however.

ALLIANCE WITH EAGLE NATIONAL BANK EXPANDS PAYDAY LENDING

The payday lending business was reinvented in the 1980s following deregulation of the banking industry that lifted interest rate caps and the demise of traditional small loan providers. It enjoyed explosive growth in the early 1990s. To many, payday lending was a return to the days of loan sharking, but others portrayed the practice as filling a need, providing a service to people who were neglected by traditional banks, which were focused on more highly profitable areas than short-term loans to less-affluent people.

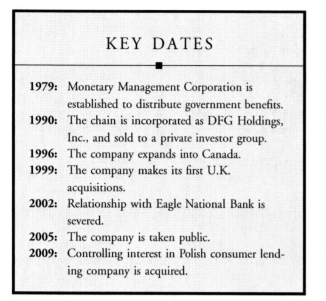

KEY DATES

1979: Monetary Management Corporation is established to distribute government benefits.
1990: The chain is incorporated as DFG Holdings, Inc., and sold to a private investor group.
1996: The company expands into Canada.
1999: The company makes its first U.K. acquisitions.
2002: Relationship with Eagle National Bank is severed.
2005: The company is taken public.
2009: Controlling interest in Polish consumer lending company is acquired.

By the end of the fiscal year ending June 30, 1996, Dollar Financial was operating about 425 outlets in 14 states, generating $91.7 million. A few months later, in November 1996, the company expanded into Canada by acquiring 36 company-owned Money Mart stores and 107 franchised locations. It was also around this time that Dollar Financial bolstered its domestic business through an alliance with Eagle National Bank of Upper Darby, Pennsylvania. With Eagle's imprimatur, Dollar Financial's check cashing units were able to make payday loans in states where they would not normally be allowed. As a small bank, Eagle found that the relationship with Dollar Financial provided it with the reach of a large bank that could maintain multiple branches. It was a mutually beneficial arrangement, but one that would last only six years.

By 2000 Eagle was making payday loans at 250 Dollar Financial outlets, but the partners were also receiving some unwanted attention. In January 1999 a San Diego, California, law firm filed a suit that charged Eagle with National Bank Act violations and Dollar Financial with racketeering law violations. The federal government also took notice of Dollar Financial's "Cash 'Til Payday Loans," which had grown in volume from $3 million the first year to $400 million in 2001, offered in 40 states through Dollar Financial outlets. The Office of the Comptroller of the Currency investigated that arrangement and found that Eagle had provided inadequate monitoring or control over loan origination, quality assurance, compliance, or auditing of Dollar Financial outlets. In some cases, Dollar Financial began operating stores and offering payday loans without Eagle's knowledge, let alone approval. Thus, in 2002 Eagle was ordered to stop funding Dollar Financial's payday loan business.

GROWTH AND ACQUISITIONS AT HOME AND ABROAD

Dollar Financial continued to grow its outlets in the United States and abroad in the late 1990s. The first Loan Mart units opened in fiscal 1998, and in February 1999 the company made its first U.K. acquisitions, buying five stores. In July 1999 Dollar Financial added 44 stores in the United Kingdom by purchasing the outstanding shares of Cash A Cheque Holdings Great Britain Limited. The year ended with the acquisition of Cash Centres Corporation Limited, which operated five company-owned stores and 238 franchise units in the United Kingdom. Also in December 1999 Dollar Financial bolstered its Canadian holdings through the purchase of Cheques R'Us, Inc., and Courtenay Money Mart Ltd., bringing into the fold another six stores, located in British Columbia. As a result of this activity, Dollar Financial's revenues increased from $121 million in fiscal 1999 to $165.8 million in fiscal 2000, of which nearly $100 million came from check cashing fees and another $35 million from consumer lending.

Further growth took place as the new decade arrived. In February 2000 the payday loan business of CheckStop, Inc., which operated in 150 independent document-transmitting outlets (mail stores and insurance offices) in 17 states, was acquired. The August 2000 purchase of West Coast Chequing Centres, Ltd., added another six stores in British Columbia. Later in the month, Dollar Financial acquired Fast 'n Friendly Check Cashing and its eight Maryland outlets. Also in August, Ram-Dur Enterprises, Inc., operator of five AAA Check Cashing Centers in Tucson, Arizona, was added. Dollar Financial closed calendar 2000 by acquiring Fastcash Ltd. and its 13 company-owned and 27 franchise stores in the United Kingdom.

GOING PUBLIC

Revenues increased to $195.5 million for the fiscal year ending June 30, 2001, and $202 million a year later. To pay down $200 million in debt taken on to grow the company, Dollar Financial issued $220 million in senior notes in late 2003. Little more than a year later, in January 2005, the company was taken public in a stock offering that raised $118 million. By this time, Dollar Financial operated a network of 1,122 locations, of which 650 were company-owned. The company also renewed its expansion efforts in 2005. Early in the year it acquired International Paper Converters, doing business as Cheque Changer Limited, as well as Alexandria Financial Services. In March 2005 Dollar Financial acquired We the People Forms and Service Centers USA, Inc., a legal-documentation preparation firm that operated through 170 franchise stores in 30 states and served the same low- and middle-income customers as Dollar Financial outlets. Two months later the five financial services stores in Arizona operated by Tenant Financial Enterprises, Inc., were added as well.

When fiscal 2005 came to a close on June 30, the company posted sales of $321 million. Consumer lending accounted for nearly half of the company's revenues, totaling $153 million compared to $128.7 million from check cashing fees. The disparity continued to grow over the next three years. Total revenues topped $572 million in fiscal 2008, but by this time consumer lending fees approached $300 million while check cashing fees approached the $200 million mark.

Along with greater rewards from payday lending came problems, however. A Canadian class-action suit filed in 2003 alleging violation of Canadian lending law was settled in early 2006, an agreement in which Dollar Financial admitted no wrongdoing. Also in 2006 the Federal Deposit Insurance Corporation pressured Wilmington, Delaware-based First Bank of Delaware into severing its payday lending partnership with Dollar Financial. A $515 million lawsuit in Canada received class-action status in early 2007. Begun in 2003, it alleged Dollar Financial and its payday loans charged fees and interest that exceeded Canadian law. Another settlement that allowed the company to avoid admitting guilt was reached in 2009.

Despite the stigma attached to payday lending, it remained a lucrative business, one of the few in the financial sector that was doing well in the early months of 2009. Unlike other companies that were scaling back, Dollar Financial looked to grow its operations, especially overseas. Four stores offering check cashing, payday loans, and pawnbroking services were acquired in Northern Ireland in the summer of 2009. In that same month a pair of 170-year-old pawnshops located in Edinburgh and Glasgow, Scotland, were added as well. Dollar Financial also extended its reach to the European continent by purchasing a controlling interest in a Polish consumer lender, Optima S.A. With ample growth

opportunities in the United States and abroad, there was every reason to expect Dollar Financial to continue to enjoy steady growth.

Ed Dinger

PRINCIPAL OPERATING UNITS

Money Mart; Loan Mart; The Check Cashing Store; American Payday Loans.

PRINCIPAL COMPETITORS

Advance America Cash Advance Centers, Inc.; Check Into Cash, Inc.; CNG Financial Corp.

FURTHER READING

Agosta, Veronica, "Small Banks Finding Profits Trump Payday Loans' Stigma," *American Banker*, August 9, 2000, p. 6.

Bergquist, Erick, "Dollar of Pa.'s IPO Raise $118 M," *American Banker*, January 31, 2005, p. 20.

———, "Payday Lender Buys Document Prep Firm," *American Banker*, March 9, 2005, p. 9.

Briggs, Rosland, "Check-Cashing Agencies Booming in Many Neighborhoods," *Philadelphia Inquirer*, February 8, 1997, p. A10.

Campbell, Colin, "Yes, It's a Good Time for Money Mart," *Maclean's*, February 16, 2009, p. 30.

"Fast-Growing 'Payday' Loan Business: Convenience or Legal Loan Sharking," *American Banker*, March 10, 1999.

Fernandez, Bob, "Regulators Order Upper Darby, Pa.-based Bank to Stop Payday-Loan Deal," *Philadelphia Inquirer*, January 4, 2002.

Huckstep, Aaron, "Payday Lending: Do Outrageous Prices Necessarily Mean Outrageous Profits?" *Fordham Journal of Corporate & Financial Law*, 2007, p. 203.

Mason, Todd, "Dollar Financial's Stock Falls," *Philadelphia Inquirer*, February 23, 2006.

Peterson, Christopher, *Taming the Sharks: Toward a Cure for the High-Cost Credit Market*, Akron, Ohio: University of Akron Press, 2004, 451 p.

Powell, Betsy, and Dale Anne Freed, "Payday Loan Victims Get $100 Million," *Toronto Star*, June 10, 2009, p. A01.

"Tapping a New Market," *Progressive Grocer*, July 1995, p. A14.

Eitzen Group

Bolette Brygge 1
Tjuvholmen
Oslo, 0252
Norway
Telephone: (47) 24 00 61 00
Fax: (47) 24 00 61 01
Web site: http://www.eitzen-group.com

Public Company
Founded: 1883
Employees: 1,082 shore-based and 5,300 seafarers (2008)
Sales: $412.06 million (2008)
Stock Exchanges: Oslo
Ticker Symbol: CECO
NAICS: 336611 Ship Building and Repairing; 488330 Navigational Services to Shipping; 483111 Deep Sea Freight Transportation; 483114 Coastal and Great Lakes Passenger Transportation; 488390 Other Support Activities for Water Transportation

■ ■ ■

The Eitzen Group comprises a number of diverse companies whose business focus is the ocean shipping trade. The most important company in the group is Camillo Eitzen & Co., which is active in bulk, gas, chemical, and petroleum shipment, as well as ship management and maritime services. The most important Camillo Eitzen subsidiaries active in these various sectors are Eitzen Bulk AS, Eitzen Gas AS, and Eitzen Tank AS. Another group member, Eitzen Maritime Services, provides a broad spectrum of technical and commercial services, crew staffing and manning, design, supervision and commissioning, port agency services, marine and offshore supplies, marine equipment, and spare parts, through its subsidiaries EMS Ship Management and EMS Ship Supply. EMS Insurance Brokers offers maritime insurance to the shipping industry. Eitzen Chemical ASA operates the world's largest fleet of chemical transport ships. The Eitzen Group is also involved in activities unrelated to cargo shipping. ACE link, for example, operates passenger ferries between Sweden and Denmark. Camillo Industry designs and produces valves and other parts for a variety of marine uses. All the companies in the Eitzen Group are owned, wholly or partly, by Eitzen Holding AS.

ORIGINS

Axel Camillo Eitzen was born in 1851 in Drøbak, Norway. Although from a middle-class family, Camillo, as he preferred to be known, decided to become a seaman and at the age of 16 he shipped out to sea aboard a local sailing ship. By the time he was 27, he had been given command of a ship, and when he was 39, he retired from seafaring altogether. He settled down in the Norwegian capital Christiania (later renamed Oslo), and set up a small company that produced safety supplies for ships. The business did well and two years later, in 1892, he had the wherewithal to purchase a ten-year-old ship-brokering firm. Eitzen would henceforth use 1883 as the date of his company's founding. He called his new company Camillo Eitzen Just Jacobsens Aftf (the successor of Just Nilsens).

Eitzen's new company owned a fleet of five ships that, like most of the Norwegian commercial fleet at the

COMPANY PERSPECTIVES

The Eitzen Group comprises a lot of different companies worldwide, both within shipping and non-shipping, and our common corporate culture is thus an important foundation for the organization. The Eitzen Group culture is based upon high ethical standards and our overall values and vision. We believe in a values driven culture, and promote leadership that encourage and inspire the employees, generating team spirit, loyalty, sustainable working environment and long-term growth. Being founded on the same common values, most companies within the Group still have their own business idea and customer promises adapted to their specific business area. A combination of the values, promises, business idea and vision is displayed in the Brand Platform. The brand platform is an important foundation for building a solid reputation focusing on responsibility, enhancing customer service and meeting internal and external expectations.

time, was nearing obsolescence. Eitzen was aware of the situation and decided to concentrate on the ship brokering side, that is, acting as an agent to bring together those with cargo and those with ships. Eitzen's new business was an immediate success; in 1896 alone Eitzen brokered 23 deals. He was also savvy enough to know the era of the sailing ship had passed; he recognized that steamships were the future and to compete in the shipping industry he would need a fleet of them. Eitzen himself knew nothing about the new technology, but Captain Henry Tschudi, a Swiss associate of his family, did. In 1894 Tschudi joined the firm as a full partner and the business was renamed Camillo Eitzen & Co.

Tschudi used his connections in Switzerland to assemble financing for the construction of the company's first steamship. Completed in 1896, it was profitable from the start and just six months later the firm placed an order for a second vessel. For the next 30 years steamships would remain the company's business focus. With them, Camillo Eitzen did business in the Americas, shipping primarily cattle and agricultural products. In 1900 an Eitzen ship was contracted to a Chinese merchant and became one of the first Norwegian vessels involved in the Far East trade. After initial resistance from investors, the individual holding companies that owned the Eitzen ships were con-

solidated into a single corporation in 1910. When Camillo Eitzen retired in 1913 the company was strong, both in operating its steamship fleet and pursuing ship-brokering contracts. Eitzen's son, Axel, succeeded him in 1914.

FALLING VICTIM TO BUSINESS CYCLES

With Norway neutral in World War I and trading with both sides, Camillo Eitzen & Co. was able to continue doing good business. After the war, the company placed an order for a large new ship, the *Rigi,* designed for deep-sea shipping. The ship was completed in 1921, but a major economic downturn struck most of Europe in the early 1920s and cut deeply into shipping. A seamen's strike in Norway combined with that to leave ships docked without cargo for ten months. To make matters worse for Eitzen, the *Rigi* turned out to be far more expensive than anticipated and in the end two-thirds of the costs were not covered by any bank financing and had to be paid from Eitzen's own coffers. By 1925 the shipping cycle had tipped in favor of those with cargo; there were too many ships serving the market. At first Eitzen's creditors let the *Rigi* continue to sail, hoping it would eventually earn back the money to cover its debts. By 1928 they had given up hope, and the ship was seized and put up for auction. The Eitzen subsidiary that operated it went out of business and, as stated in the company's chronicle, "the steamship era [at Eitzen] came to an end."

There may have been too many ships in commercial shipping in general at that time. However, there did exist a sector where growth was still possible, and that was oil shipping. In the 1920s the oil business was expanding dramatically. The oil tankers required were expensive, but once in place they could operate under lucrative, long-term charters with the oil firms. In 1928 Tschudi's son set off to enlist Swiss investors, just as his father had done some 30 years earlier. He found so much financing that the company was able to start construction on another tanker.

By the mid-1930s, the Eitzen firm comprised three shipping companies, Avanti, Navalis, and Tankrederi HTT. At that time Camillo Eitzen & Co. changed its name to Tschudi & Eitzen, reflecting Henry Tschudi's 25 years as senior partner. He passed away in April 1939 on the eve of World War II and was succeeded by his son, Felix Henry Tschudi.

SURVIVING WORLD WAR II

When World War II started in September 1939, Norway declared neutrality. However, its geographical

KEY DATES

1883: Just Nilsens Eftf is founded in Christiania, Norway.

1892: Just Nilsens Eftf is purchased by Camillo Eitzen.

1894: Camillo Eitzen enters partnership with Captain Henry F. Tschudi and renames company Camillo Eitzen & Co.

1913: Camillo Eitzen retires from active participation in the company.

1936: Name is changed to Tschudi & Eitzen.

1967: Company enters oil/bulk/ore (OBO) carrier market.

1969: Camillo Eitzen dies, leaving no direct heirs.

1980: Axel C. Eitzen joins company.

1987: Tschudi & Eitzen acquires Mosel Ore OBO carrier.

1992: Axel C. Eitzen becomes senior partner.

1994: Tschudi & Eitzen Shipping is listed on the Oslo Stock Exchange.

1997: East Asiatic Company of Copenhagen is acquired and reorganized as Tschudi & Eitzen Bulk.

1999: Sembawang Ship Management of Singapore is acquired.

2001: KiL Shipping of Copenhagen is acquired.

2003: Tschudi & Eitzen Holding is broken up and two new companies are formed, Camillo Eitzen & Co. AS and Tschudi Shipping Co. AS.

2004: Camillo Eitzen & Co. is listed on the Oslo Stock Exchange.

2006: Eitzen Chemical ASA is listed on the Oslo Stock Exchange.

position, commanding the North Atlantic as well as the North Sea, made it irresistible to the Nazis, and they invaded in April 1940. An organization was established in London to administer Norwegian commercial ships, five of them Tschudi & Eitzen ships, which had not fallen into German hands. Felix Tschudi tried to get one of the firm's ships surreptitiously out of the Swedish harbor it was docked in and out into the open sea, but the plan failed. Tschudi was arrested by the Gestapo and sent to a concentration camp, where he remained for the rest of the war. Eitzen also fell under suspicion. His son, a Royal Norwegian Air Force pilot, had fled to England. The Nazis seized his house, but Eitzen and his family were able to flee to neutral Sweden where they stayed until 1945.

When the war ended, Tschudi, age 48, and Eitzen, age 62, together with Eitzen's son Camillo, began rebuilding their company. They placed orders for new ships just before the Norwegian government introduced new licensing regulations that included a two-year moratorium on new shipbuilding. The 1950s were a period of growth and prosperity for the company; there was a relative shortage of ships worldwide. Tschudi & Eitzen had a new fleet together with lucrative charters that ran into the 1960s. However, another of the cyclical downturns in the shipping industry set in during the first years of the 1960s, just as most of Tschudi & Eitzen's charters expired. Between 1958 and 1961 the company's revenues plummeted from NOK 11.1 million to NOK 2.3 million. In 1961 Camillo Eitzen retired and was succeeded by his son, Axel.

WARS AND TANKERS

In the mid-1960s the firm invested in a fleet of a new, more versatile type of ship, known as OBO carriers, that could carry three types of cargo: oil, bulk cargos, or ore. Then in 1964, Tschudi & Eitzen believed it had found a use for the new vessels as well as a way out of its financial predicament when it concluded a contract with the Pakistani National Oil Company. However, the deal was plagued almost from the outset by ongoing legal disputes between the two parties, and when the contract expired in 1967, it was not renewed. The cancellation of the contract turned out to be a benefit for Tschudi & Eitzen, however, as shortly afterward the Six Day War between Israel and its Arab neighbors broke out. As a result, the Suez Canal was closed and demand for tankers escalated dramatically. With its OBO ships no longer bound by the Pakistani contract, Tschudi & Eitzen was able to use them for shipping other cargo. By the end of the decade, the firm's bookings were full again.

When Camillo Eitzen passed away in 1969 at the age of 58 without any children, the Eitzen family withdrew temporarily from active participation in the company's operations, and their 50 percent holding in Tschudi & Eitzen was placed under the control of a trustee. More than ten years would pass before an Eitzen took his place once again as a partner in the company. Other changes in the firm's leadership took place as the 1970s began. Felix Henry Tschudi retired and his son Henry Felix Tschudi took his place as the firm's sole partner.

Shipping was on the rise in the early 1970s, and Tschudi & Eitzen decided to invest in an enormous new oil supertanker with 485,000 deadweight tons capacity.

It would have been a highly cost-efficient vessel, assuming it could sail fully laden. However, eight days after the firm signed the contract with the Uddevalla shipyards in Sweden for the vessel, another war started in the Middle East. The Yom Kippur War threw world shipping, and oil shipping in particular, into total chaos. Again the Suez Canal was closed. Arab oil producers launched an embargo against the West, and oil prices suddenly quadrupled. Shipping capacity, on the rise since the late 1960s, was overextended, and there was much less cargo to be shipped.

Tschudi & Eitzen and the shipping industry as a whole entered a deep crisis that would drag on for the better part of 13 years. It hastily converted its OBO carriers for dry cargos. With no more use for the new tanker and no way to pay for such a ship, Tschudi & Eitzen asked the Swedish shipyard to cancel the construction contract. The shipyard objected and a court ordered Tschudi & Eitzen to pay $30 million in compensation. As a gesture of goodwill, however, Uddevalla offered to accept approximately $10.5 million of that amount as a down payment on future shipbuilding projects, an offer Tschudi & Eitzen accepted.

FIGHTING TO STAY IN BUSINESS

When 26-year-old Axel Camillo Eitzen, the nephew of the partner who had died 11 years earlier, joined the company as a partner in 1980, the shipping crisis seemed to be passing. It reasserted itself in 1983, however, and company income fell dramatically. Cost-cutting measures were introduced. The company switched from Norwegian to international crews, and reduced maintenance to minimal levels. The firm's problems were made worse by the drop in the value of the Norwegian krone in relation to the dollar and the deutsche mark. By 1986 the company's creditors had run out of patience. All the assets of five Tschudi & Eitzen companies were liquidated. Two ships were sold at a loss that year, and two more a year later. As the 1980s drew to a close, Tschudi & Eitzen was for all intents and purposes bankrupt.

Nevertheless, in the 1980s Tschudi & Eitzen had established a strong reputation for technical management of ships. With that expertise, it was able to participate in a special financing arrangement with banks for the construction of OBO vessels, whereby the firm acquired a 10 percent shareholding in the vessel and was awarded the contract as the ship's technical manager. By 1987, in the middle of its financial crisis, the firm had technical management contracts on 15 tankers and bulk carriers. It was Tschudi & Eitzen's only functioning business at that time. The firm started rebuilding its shipping fleet that same year when it was able to acquire a bargain-priced OBO carrier, the *Mosel Ore*, which Tschudi & Eitzen put into service shipping ore. The ship made money from the very start; $3,500 of its daily fee of $4,200 was profit. After one year of charter sailing, the *Mosel Ore*'s contract was extended for an additional three-year period. Tschudi & Eitzen was also aided by Norway's overhaul of its shipping regulations at the end of the 1980s, an action that stimulated the expansion of its shipping fleet.

NEW LEADERSHIP AND NEW UNCERTAINTIES

The shipping industry slumped once again around 1991. Revenues fell while ship maintenance and operation costs increased steadily. In 1992 the companies for Tschudi & Eitzen's recently built ships were consolidated into a new subsidiary, Tschudi & Eitzen Rederi AS. That company was, in turn, reorganized into Tschudi & Eitzen Holding one year later. The company passed into the hands of the next Tschudi & Eitzen generation in 1992 as well. Henry Felix Tschudi retired and was succeeded by his 32-year-old son, Felix Henry, and at the age of 38 Axel Eitzen became the company's senior partner. Eitzen and Tschudi seemed to complement one another well, the former with his engineering background and the latter with his maritime experience. However, they would ultimately disagree about the course the company should take, with momentous consequences for the company.

The latter half of the 1990s witnessed a genuine growth spurt at Tschudi & Eitzen. Midway through the decade, the company acquired Sibo, a Danish bulk shipper, that was then merged into Tschudi & Eitzen (T&E) Shipping, which subsequently became the first Tschudi & Eitzen company to be listed on the Oslo Stock Exchange. T&E Shipping then acquired another Danish shipper, Burwain Tankers International AS (BTI). By 1996, T&E Shipping, with 16 vessels, was one of the largest shipping firms on the Oslo exchange. Plans were afoot that year to merge all of its other individual ship companies into T&E Shipping, but shareholders opposed the addition of bulk and product carriers to its line of OBO carriers. Tschudi & Eitzen took over another company in December 1997 with the purchase of the East Asiatic Company of Copenhagen, a company Camillo Eitzen & Co. had done business with at the beginning of the 20th century. It was converted into another subsidiary called Tschudi & Eitzen Bulk.

Tschudi & Eitzen continued to make acquisitions worldwide up to 2003. These included individual ships, as well as shipping companies such as Gyda Shipping of Norway; Ove Skou and KiL Shipping, both of Denmark; International Transport Contractors (ITC) of the Netherlands; Sembawang Ship Management of Singapore; and Estonian Shipping Company, formerly the state shipping organization of Estonia. Together these companies brought Tschudi & Eitzen a breadth of service it had not possessed for years, including bulk carriers, OBOs, crude oil, product and chemical tankers, gas carriers, tugs and barges, as well as container and RORO (roll-on/roll-off) vessels designed to carry cars and trucks.

BREAKING UP AND GOING PUBLIC

Following the acquisition of Sembawang Ship Management in 1999, Axel Eitzen moved with his family to Singapore to oversee the reorganization of the company. They remained there until the end of 2002. There were enormous changes in store for Tschudi & Eitzen upon his return to Norway. Once back, he met with the company's board and demanded the end of the century-long Tschudi and Eitzen partnership. The demerger was not a new idea on Eitzen's part. He had, in fact, discussed the possibility with Felix Tschudi twice in the 1990s, only to be rebuffed. The strain on the partnership had its origins in the conflicting visions each man had for the firm. Tschudi wanted the firm to remain private, firmly in family hands. Eitzen, in contrast, wanted to take it public to raise money for new projects he had in mind. By the summer of 2003 a plan had been worked out for the breakup of Tschudi & Eitzen, and in November the formation of two new companies was announced, Camillo Eitzen & Co. AS and Tschudi Shipping Co. AS. Tschudi took over the Estonian shipping operation and the Dutch ITC subsidiary. Eitzen assumed control of the various Danish shipping operations. The OBO fleet and Singapore-based TESMA remained at first under joint control. The division of Tschudi & Eitzen was an amicable one.

In 2004, hoping to purchase Bergesen d.y.'s Igloo fleet of LPG/ethylene tankers, Axel Eitzen made the decision to take his company public. The negotiations for the purchase of the ships and the preparations for the initial public offering ran more or less concurrently. The acquisition of the ships was completed in March 2004 and the company was renamed Sigloo. The acquisition turned out to be a bargain. Thanks to the downturn in the shipping market at the dawn of the 21st century, the fleet, which had sold for $200 million in 1998, was acquired for only $75 million by Eitzen in 2004.

In June 2004 the stock offering, managed by Pareto Securities and Nordea Bank, was launched on the Oslo Stock Exchange. The offering of some 8.6 million shares raised $40 million, followed by a second offering in December, which raised another $36 million. With the new funds, Camillo Eitzen, then known as CECO, acquired the French shipping company, Navale Française, and the Spanish company, Naviera Quimica, for $37.3 million and $47 million respectively. CECO's acquisitions would henceforth reflect Axel Eitzen's desire to build a company with a central, unified, top-down organization that nonetheless pursued a diverse mix of commercial activities.

UPS AND DOWNS IN THE LATTER HALF OF THE DECADE

The company continued to expand in the latter half of the decade. Eitzen Maritime Services (EMS) was founded in April 2006. The foundation of the company was the Singapore operation, TESMA, which CECO had taken over in full from Tschudi the year before. Two months later, Eitzen Chemical was founded, following the acquisition of the French shipper Fouquet Sacop SA. In October 2006, two new acquisitions, Songa Shipholding and Sokana Chartering LLC, were merged into the company. One month later, Eitzen Chemical itself went public on the Oslo exchange.

Toward the end of the decade, Eitzen was feeling the pressure of weakening markets, in particular that for ethylene and chemicals shipments. Its fleet was aging as well, resulting in frequent repairs and layovers in dock. In February 2009 the company reported a 20 percent decline in revenues and the company was unable to meet the terms of its loan covenants. The losses continued in mid-2009, and Camillo Eitzen & Co. reported pretax losses of $403.49 million for 2008. As a remedy, the company canceled its new shipbuilding orders and planned a sell-off of assets. In July 2009, it remained in breach of its loan covenants, but had been granted a three-month reprieve by its banks to work out an acceptable financial strategy for the crisis.

Gerald E. Brennan

PRINCIPAL SUBSIDIARIES

Camillo Eitzen & Co. ASA; Eitzen Invest AS; ACE Link Holding AS; Eitzen Maritime Services ASA; Eitzen Chemical ASA; Eitzen Bulk; Eitzen Gas; Eitzen Tank; Eitzen Chemical (Denmark); Eitzen Chemical (Singapore); Eitzen Chemical (Spain); Navale Française; A.P. Møller-Mærsk; Odfjell ASA; Silja Oy Ab; TGE Marine AG.

PRINCIPAL COMPETITORS

AS Dampskibsselskabet TORM; Dampskibsselskabet NORDEN A/S; The Baltic Exchange, Ltd.; Braemar

Shipping Services Plc.; BW Gas AS; BP Shipping Limited; BOURBON SA; Bronel Group Ltd.; Clarkson PLC; I.M. Skaugen ASA; InterBulk Group plc.; Leif Höegh & Co.

FURTHER READING

Bakka, Dag, Jr., *Oceans of Opportunities,* Oslo: Dinamo Verlag, 2008.

"Camillo Eitzen Reports Q1 Net Loss of $5.9m," *ICIS News,* May 20, 2009.

Eason, Craig, "Eitzen Order Cancellations Reduce First Quarter Losses," *Lloyd's List,* May 21, 2009, p. 3.

"Eitzen Back in Black as Loss Swings to $27m Profit," *Lloyd's List,* November 19, 2007, p. 5.

"Eitzen Bulks Up as Freight Rates Soar," *Lloyd's List,* August 22, 2008, p. 12.

"Eitzen Doubles Profits After Fouquet Sale," *Lloyd's List,* November 16, 2007, p. 4.

"Eitzen in Breach of Loan Covenants," *Lloyd's List,* February 20, 2009, p. 5.

"Eitzen Maritime Snaps Up Seven Seas," *Lloyd's List,* June 10, 2008, p. 3.

"Eitzen Sells Fouquet to Sea-Invest for $322m," *Lloyd's List,* October 25, 2007, p. 1.

Gray, Tony, "Eitzen Gains Reprieve to Draw up Financial Plan," *Lloyd's List,* July 3, 2009, p. 3.

IT'S NOT JUST AN AIRLINE, IT'S ISRAEL

EL AL Israel Airlines Ltd.

—————— ■ ——————

Ben-Gurion International Airport
P.O. Box 4170100
Lod,
Israel
Telephone: (972 3) 971-6111
Fax: (972 3) 629-2312
Web site: http://www.elal.co.il

Public Company
Incorporated: 1948
Employees: 3,718
Sales: $1.93 billion (2007)
Stock Exchanges: Tel Aviv
Ticker Symbol: ELAL
NAICS: 481111 Scheduled Passenger Air Transporta-
tion; 481112 Scheduled Freight Air Transportation

■ ■ ■

EL AL Israel Airlines Ltd., formerly a state-owned entity, has approximately 40 Boeing jets in its fleet and carries 1.9 million passengers each year to nearly 40 destinations across the globe. EL AL operates as the State of Israel's designated carrier on most international flights to and from the country. The company went public on the Tel Aviv stock exchange in 2003 with Knafaim Arkia Holdings Ltd. securing a majority interest in 2005. Known for its high level of security, EL AL has thwarted hijack attempts and bomb threats since the 1960s. The only tarnish on its elite security record occurred in 1968 when an EL AL flight from Rome to Tel Aviv was hijacked by the Popular Front for the Libera-

tion of Palestine (PFLP). Seven crew members and five male Israeli passengers were held hostage in Algiers for five weeks. The event prompted EL AL to adopt extreme security measures that continue to be held in great regard throughout the airline industry.

TO THE SKIES IN 1948

EL AL was created as a symbol of Israel's national independence. Immediately after its founding on May 14, 1948, Israel found itself embroiled in a battle for survival with neighboring Arab states. The United States and most European countries subsequently imposed an embargo on all combatants. Although Israel's provisional government had already made establishing a civil airline a priority, President Chaim Weizmann's trip to Geneva gave the project impetus. The Israeli government wanted to fly him home in one of its own planes, but its military craft could not make the trip due to the embargo.

A four-engine C-54 military transport was repainted in civilian colors and outfitted with extra fuel tanks to make the ten-hour flight nonstop; the meandering flight path was also necessitated by the embargo. With a cabin full of fine furnishings, the first plane marked "EL AL Ltd./Israel National Aviation Company" departed Israel's Ekron Air Base on September 28, 1948. After returning from Switzerland the next day, the plane was stripped of its civilian luxuries and returned to military service.

Although the flight and its accompanying documentation were hastily arranged, the crew was adorned in tradition. Uniform insignia featured a flying camel, the mascot of early Jewish aviators, and the airline's name itself harkened back even further. Taken from the book of Hosea (11:7), EL AL means "to the skies." The Star of David was also incorporated into the airline's livery. Despite these trappings the airline had existed on paper only a couple of days and would not be formally incorporated until November 15.

Aryeh Pincus, a lawyer originally from South Africa, was chosen to lead the company, which faced significant challenges from the beginning. Airlifting imperiled Jewish refugees from Yemen and Iraq was among its earliest priorities. EL AL borrowed military aircraft until February 1949, when it bought several Douglas DC-4 aircraft (converted military C-54s) from American Airlines. After the necessary clearances were negotiated, the two planes flew to their home base, Lod Airport in Israel. EL AL's first scheduled flights, between Tel Aviv and Paris (refueling in Rome), started in July 1949. By the end of the year, the airline had flown passengers to London and Johannesburg as well. In the fall of 1950, EL AL acquired Universal Airways, founded by South African Zionists. A state-run domestic airline, Arkia, was also founded, with EL AL as half owner.

A CHALLENGING DECADE

The company began shipping freight to Europe using military surplus C-46 transports in 1950. It also initiated its first charter service to the United States; scheduled service soon followed. Disaster struck in February 1950, however, when one of EL AL's DC-4s was destroyed while attempting to take off in Tel Aviv. There were no casualties. Another DC-4 carrying cargo crashed into a Swiss hillside the next year, killing several crew members. In July 1955 an EL AL Constellation returning to Tel Aviv from Vienna was downed in flight by Bulgarian MiG-15 interceptors.

The newly acquired Constellations were superior aircraft with pressurized cabins that could fly above bad weather. However, they were noisy and unreliable, and challenged EL AL's ambitious timetables. In 1955 the airline placed a controversial order for two Bristol Britannia turboprops, a bold leap in both technology and cost for the fledgling carrier. EL AL became only the second airline to fly the Britannia after the British Overseas Airways Corporation.

In spite of the hopeful purchase, times were hard for the as-yet-unprofitable airline, as well as for the Israeli government. Both were pressed for qualified professionals, compounded by the challenges of taking on thousands of dispossessed immigrants amid hostile surroundings. During the Sinai War, Egypt blocked Israel's shipping lanes. After Israeli forces invaded the Sinai Peninsula, no foreign airlines would fly into the country. Having an independent civil airline remained an important government priority, and EL AL endured.

EL AL ended the decade with a capable new leader, Efraim Ben-Arzi, and the capacity to compete in the London–New York route with its swift and popular new Britannias—the fastest scheduled Atlantic crossing at the time. The company's bookings increased to impressive levels; the $18 million gamble on the new planes seemed to have paid off. Transatlantic passengers increased from 8,000 in 1957, before the turboprop service was introduced, to 32,000 in 1960. However, the de Havilland Comet 4, Boeing 707, and Douglas DC-8 jets, all introduced by 1959, soon eliminated the Britannia's speed advantage. The jet age had arrived.

REACHING NEW HEIGHTS IN THE JET AGE

EL AL posted its first profit in 1960. In order to remain competitive, EL AL began flying the new Boeing 707 jet. The airline promptly set records in June 1961 for longest nonstop commercial flight (New York to Tel Aviv) and speed (in 9.5 hours). A jet similar to the 707, the Boeing 720B, provided the power and endurance needed to carry the EL AL to Johannesburg via Tehran. Due to airspace restrictions, EL AL had previously been forced to lease jets from other airlines to complete the passage, which lasted 16 hours even with the 720B.

The speed and comfort offered by the Boeing 707 helped EL AL land more than half of all passengers flying into Israel. The company subsequently became the country's chief promoter of tourism; only a fraction of its passengers were business travelers. In spite of the high cost, jet service would boost company profits for years to come.

Egypt laid siege to Israel's Red Sea port of Elat in May 1967, prompting EL AL to evacuate tourists there. Its planes flew military support missions, and many of

KEY DATES

1948: EL AL is established.

1949: The company's first scheduled flights, between Tel Aviv and Paris, start in July.

1950: The company begins shipping freight to Europe using military surplus C-46 transports; charter service to the United States begins.

1960: EL AL posts its first profit.

1961: The airline sets a record for the longest nonstop commercial flight (New York to Tel Aviv).

1968: An EL AL flight from Rome to Tel Aviv is hijacked.

1971: EL AL's first 747 is delivered.

1980: A new route to Cairo opens.

1988: EL AL surpasses its old record by flying 7,000 miles from Tel Aviv to Los Angeles nonstop.

1991: More than a thousand Ethiopian Jewish immigrants are airlifted on a single EL AL Boeing 747.

2001: EL AL is the first airline allowed to make an international flight out of New York after the terrorist attacks of September 11.

2003: Company shares are offered to the public.

2004: EL AL is no longer a government-owned entity; Knafaim Arkia Holdings Ltd. acquires a 40 percent stake in EL AL.

2007: The company distributes a dividend to shareholders for the first time.

its staff were conscripted. In a month, actual hostilities were underway. Although they lasted only a week, the airline lost four of its pilots in battle. The only carrier serving Israel was EL AL, though it did modify its schedule to mostly night flights. After the Six-Day War, Israel controlled several new territories, including all of Jerusalem. After an intense public relations effort, tourism returned to Israel in unrelenting waves. Control of the Sinai gave the airline a direct route to Johannesburg, cutting flying time from Tel Aviv by nearly one-half.

In order to promote tourism, the Israeli government proposed lifting the five-year-old ban on incoming charter flights. Although EL AL was for the most part successful in fighting the charters, Chairman Ben-Arzi and President Col. Shlomo Lahat resigned in the wake of this vigorous political contest. Mordechai Ben-Ari,

previously the airline's commercial manager, was designated company president. EL AL began flying behind the Iron Curtain with scheduled visits to Bucharest commencing in 1968. Increased demand soon led to dedicated cargo flights to Europe and America. A catering subsidiary, Teshet Tourism and Aviation Services Ltd., was also formed in that year. EL AL posted annual profits of approximately $2 million in 1968 and 1969.

NEW CHALLENGES

During this time the airline was forced to reckon with an alarming new development that would remain a grave concern for commercial aviation: terrorism. An EL AL flight from Rome to Tel Aviv was hijacked to Algeria in July 1968; during the next two years attacks by Arab terrorists increased in violence. EL AL quickly began developing the tough, and expensive, security measures that would become its trademark, including staffing every flight with undercover armed guards and sealing the cockpit area. They proved effective on September 6, 1970, when operatives of the PFLP attacked four airliners in one day. While Pan Am, TWA, and Swissair saw their planes destroyed, EL AL's survived: the pilot plunged the aircraft 14,000 feet to help the crew gain the upper hand on the terrorists.

The stakes increased even more when EL AL began operating the colossal 400-seat Boeing 747 "jumbo jet." New facilities were needed to house and service the aircraft, which was twice as large as any of its predecessors. Although the first two jets sold for more than $30 million each, the accompanying preparations required another three times the investment. EL AL's first 747, resplendent in a new paint scheme, was delivered in May 1971.

As with its previous investments in new aircraft such as the Constellation and the 707, this purchase did not escape controversy. Critics believed it was simply too risky, given the enormous cost and the already serious threat of terrorism. However, traffic soared with the two 747s, and EL AL's relatively small operation (totaling just 12 jets) became one to emulate worldwide. A third 747 was delivered in 1973. The airline used it to introduce nonstop service from Tel Aviv to New York. At 13 hours against the prevailing winds, it was the longest scheduled flight in the world at that time.

FACING DIFFICULTIES

The success of the 747 service inspired plans for expansion, but they were truncated by the surprise attacks of October 1973 that launched the Yom Kippur War. Again EL AL aircraft and personnel were mobilized for the country's defense, and again all foreign airlines canceled flights to Israel. Although hostilities lasted only three weeks, EL AL was forced to contend with the effects for some time to come. All operations in Ethiopia were halted due to Arab political pressure there. The Arab oil embargo greatly increased the price of jet fuel.

Fighting between Cyprus and Turkey scared all other airlines out of the eastern Mediterranean again in July 1974, adding to EL AL's workload. In addition, EL AL was plagued with labor unrest. Although a tentative settlement was reached in February 1975, workers walked out for almost three weeks in October. This was repeated in April 1978, further damaging the company's reputation. The company averaged ten work stoppages a year.

In 1977 EL AL created a subsidiary to offer nonscheduled flights, EL AL Charter Services Ltd., later renamed Sun d'Or International Airlines Ltd. A global recession kept tourists home, and in 1975 EL AL failed to post a profit for the first time in a dozen years. Delays in replacing the Boeing 707 and 720 jetliners, relatively inefficient and too noisy for some European airports, did not help the bottom line. Miserable financial results and continuing labor strife prompted the Israeli government to install new management. Mordechai Hod, an air force commander, became president in 1977 but resigned less than two years later. Avraham Shavit, a manufacturing executive, was appointed board chairman, and eventually EL AL veteran Itzhak Shander was named president.

In Iran the situation was progressively deteriorating in 1978 with the rise of the Ayatollah Khomeini. Despite unstable local fuel supplies and little control tower support, EL AL dispatched additional 747s to fly thousands of emigrants out of that country. The company's facilities in Tehran were eventually either burned or confiscated. EL AL also scaled back certain operations elsewhere in the world. It canceled a money-losing route to Mexico City in 1979. Some progress was made, however, when a historically significant and popular new route to Cairo, EL AL's only Arab destination, opened in 1980.

RETURN TO PROFITABILITY

New management succeeded both in negotiating pay cuts and deflating the bloated workforce, which had reached 6,000 employees. Some poorly performing sales offices were closed. The Israeli government privatized the domestic carrier Arkia, in which EL AL had a 50 percent share. Morale was also turned around, and the airline's on-time record and customer service again earned world-class status. However, after an independent audit recommended further layoffs, labor troubles erupted again.

The government grounded EL AL after a flight steward strike in September 1982, canceling all but a handful of flight operations. The government appointed Amram Blum receiver, with ultimate authority for running the company. Rafi Harlev was named president. Employee and management representatives were able to produce an agreement under the glare of bankruptcy court. An end to strikes was negotiated, although a thousand more workers were to be furloughed.

The Israeli government provided EL AL with two new Boeing 737 midsize airliners and also agreed to purchase four state-of-the-art Boeing 767 long-range jets worth $200 million. EL AL could begin flying again in January 1983, but the damage seemed grave. For the fiscal year ending in April, the airline lost $123.3 million. However, its customers proved loyal and eager to return to the skies. Within several years the airline was again the model of productivity. Profitability returned in 1987, in spite of increased terrorism in Europe. The route system of the revived carrier expanded quickly. In May 1988 EL AL surpassed its old record by flying 7,000 miles from Tel Aviv to Los Angeles nonstop. Due to glasnost, flights to Poland and Yugoslavia were able to commence in 1989.

At the end of the decade, the airline seemed likely to recover from receivership, although increased terrorism again dampened tourism. In 1988 the carrier eked out a small $19 million profit on total revenues of $665 million. The government planned to sell about half of the company to employees and investors. EL AL operated 20 aircraft in 1990, including nine 747 jumbo jets, and had begun replacing its aging Boeing 707s with the state-of-the-art 757 model.

NEW PARTNERSHIPS

EL AL continued to operate profitably throughout the Gulf War by concentrating on cargo flights. However, cargo operations experienced one of the company's worst disasters in October 1992 when a 747 freighter crashed into a Dutch apartment building.

In cooperation with Aeroflot, EL AL conducted another airlift of Jewish refugees in January 1990. The airline transported more than 400,000 Soviet Jews from Moscow over the next three years. In May 1991 more than a thousand Ethiopian immigrants were airlifted on a single Boeing 747. In contrast, EL AL usually seated only ten passengers in the first-class section of these planes.

EL AL's reach stretched next to Asia, first with charter flights. Harlev boasted of the airline's exclusive "wall to wall" service: from the Western Wall to the Great Wall of China. The company also increased efficiency, investing in a 24.9 percent share of North American Airlines to give it flexibility in carrying passengers within the United States. In November 1995 EL AL entered its first code-sharing agreement, with American Airlines.

The Israeli government began adopting "open skies" policies in the mid-1990s, exposing the airline to severe competition at home. Approximately 40 scheduled airlines and 40 charter airlines served the market at the time. In 1996 Arkia and Royal Jordanian Airlines began connecting Tel Aviv with Amman. Nevertheless, after nearly ten consecutive years of profits, the airline emerged from receivership status in 1995. However, the next year EL AL posted the considerable loss of $83.1 million, due in part to a new wave of terrorism.

In order to keep all its planes in the sky, EL AL introduced "flights to nowhere;" passengers would enjoy various in-flight entertainments while circling the Mediterranean. It also promoted day trips for shopping in London or visiting newly accessible sites of religious importance in Eastern Europe. With routes connecting East and West and decades of experience flying the longest routes, EL AL hoped to develop Ben-Gurion Airport into a hub for intercontinental travel. The North American market remained responsible for nearly one-third of the carrier's revenues.

Harlev resigned in March 1996, frustrated by government privatization plans that had dragged on over a decade. Joel Feldschuh took over as president in October. EL AL carried nearly three million passengers per year and more than 270,000 tons of cargo on 27 jets, including three state-of-the-art Boeing 747-400s. The Israeli government planned to sell all shares of the company, not just 50 percent as previously planned, in the coming years.

THE 21ST CENTURY BRINGS CHANGE

The year 2000 proved challenging for EL AL. The company lost over $100 million after fuel prices and a sharp downturn in tourism brought on by Palestinian unrest wreaked havoc on its bottom line. In early 2001, the company announced that it would eliminate ten of its international routes, sell off some of its fleet, and cut jobs. It also sought government funds to cover costs related to security and the high cost of not flying planes on the Jewish Sabbath (*Shabbat*) which lasted from sundown on Friday through Saturday evening. The company's reputation for security, however, left it in an enviable position after the terrorist attacks on the United States on September 11, 2001. EL AL was the first airline allowed to leave U.S. airspace two days after the attacks. The company also experienced increased demand for its flights from New York to Tel Aviv.

At the same time, EL AL was preparing for significant change to its operating structure. Its initial public offering, which had been in the works for years, faced obstacles. Indeed, with over $900 million in debt and the airline industry in decline, the State of Israel had held off on listing the company until May 2003 when it offered 15 percent of the company on the Tel Aviv stock exchange. By June of the following year, EL AL was no longer a government-owned company as the State of Israel's holdings fell below 50 percent. On December 23, 2004, Knafaim-Arkia Holdings Ltd., headed by Izzy Borovich, increased its percentage of ownership to 40 percent. In January 2005, most of the company's board members were replaced by Knafaim appointees. EL AL President Amos Shapira stepped down that month.

Haim Romano was named CEO in March 2005. Under his leadership, the company launched the EL AL 2010 Strategic Plan, which included provisions related to improving customer service and shoring up profits. Rising fuel costs, increased competition, and the Second Lebanon War, which occurred in the summer of 2006 and caused a significant drop in Israeli travel, all had a negative effect on EL AL's bottom line.

Nevertheless, EL AL forged ahead with its Strategic Plan. While it posted a net loss in 2006, the company's profits rebounded in 2007, reaching $31.7 million. Sales also climbed to $1.93 billion that year, and the company paid its first dividend to shareholders. The company purchased two Boeing 777-200 aircraft that year and also signed a code-sharing agreement with American Airlines that allowed for continuation flights to over 20 destinations in the United States. With orders for additional aircraft made in 2008 and its first new destination (Brazil) announced in 2009, EL AL management was optimistic that the company was on target for success in the years to come.

Frederick C. Ingram
Updated, Christina M. Stansell

PRINCIPAL SUBSIDIARIES

Sun d'Or International Airlines Ltd.; Tammam; Air Consolidators Israel (50%); Catit; Superstar Holidays (UK); Borenstein Caterers (U.S.); Air Tour Israel (50%); Sabre Israel Travel Technologies (49%); Kavei Hufsha Israel (20%).

PRINCIPAL COMPETITORS

Air France-KLM S.A.; AMR Corp.; UAL Corp.

FURTHER READING

Blackburn, Nicky, "Ready for Takeoff?" *Jerusalem Post,* June 20, 2003.

"El Al Sees 60,000 Passengers/Year on Brazil Flight," *Reuters News,* March 23, 2009.

Goldman, Marvin G., *EL AL: Star in the Sky,* Miami: World Transport Press, 1990.

Grayeff, Yigal, "El Al CEO Amos Shapira Quits," *Jerusalem Post,* January 10, 2005.

Hill, Leonard, "Never on Shabbat," *Air Transport World,* June 1996, pp. 29–31.

Hornblower, Margot, "Disasters: Who Was to Blame?" *Time International,* October 19, 1992, p. 24.

Hughes, David, "Design, Checks Cited in Crash," *Aviation Week and Space Technology,* November 1, 1993, pp. 39–41.

Karp, Jonathan, "El Al's Airtight Security Is Now in Demand," *Wall Street Journal,* September 26, 2001.

Kestin, Hesh, "Buy Me, I'm EL AL," *Forbes,* November 27, 1989, pp. 42–43.

Morrocco, John D., "EL AL Plots Recovery Path to Privatization," *Aviation Week and Space Technology,* May 26, 1997, pp. 48–49.

Orme, William A., Jr., "Israel: EL AL Cuts Routes," *New York Times,* April 25, 2001.

———, "A Mirror of Israel's Divisions Prepares to Go 40% Public," *New York Times,* March 5, 1999.

Reichel, Arie, and John F. Preble, "The EL AL Strike in New York," *Journal of Management Case Studies,* Fall 1987, pp. 270–76.

Reingold, Lester, "EL AL: Instrument of National Purpose," *Air Transport World,* June 1992.

Sandler, Neal, "El Al: Cleared for Profit Takeoff," *Business Week,* July 5, 2004.

Sandler, Neal, and Andrea Rothman, "And You Thought US Airlines Had It Tough," *Business Week,* October 12, 1992.

Selwitz, Robert, "The Secret to EL AL's Success," *Global Trade and Transportation,* March 1994, pp. 23, 26.

Shapiro, Haim, "EL AL Offers 'Spiritual' Day Trips to Eastern Europe," *Jerusalem Post,* January 2, 1998, p. 1.

Sherman, Arnold, *To the Skies: The EL AL Story,* New York: Bantam, 1972.

Farnam Companies, Inc.

———————■———————

301 West Osborn Road
Phoenix, Arizona 85013-3921
U.S.A.
Telephone: (602) 285-1660
Toll Free: (800) 234-2269
Web site: http://www.farnam.com

Wholly Owned Subsidiary of Central Garden & Pet
* Company*
Incorporated: 1955 as Farnam Equipment Company
Employees: 300
Sales: $160 million (2005 est.)
NAICS: 325320 Pesticide and Other Agricultural
   Chemical Manufacturing

■ ■ ■

A wholly owned subsidiary of Central Garden & Pet Company, Farnam Companies, Inc., is best known for its horse care products. These include fly and pest control products, dewormers, hoof care products, leg care and liniments, nutritional supplements, and feed. In addition, Farnam offers stable supplies, rodent control products, grooming aids, and leather care products for boots, saddles, and tack. Farnam also serves the needs of cat and dog owners, marketing a variety of flea and tick control products, as well as dewormers, vitamins, aspirin, and shedding control, dental, behavior modification, joint care, and other products. All told, Farnam offers more than 4,000 products. Although Farnam products can be found in virtually every channel, the company primarily relies on a network of more than 16,000 independent retailers. Outside the United States, Farnam Companies International works through a network of distributors to sell Farnam products in more than 70 countries. In addition to its Phoenix facility, Farnam manufactures livestock products in Council Bluffs, Iowa, and horse care products in Omaha, Nebraska.

POST–WORLD WAR II ROOTS

Farnam Companies was founded in Omaha in 1946 by Mort Duff, an advertising man who became involved in the animal care industry by sheer chance when he accepted the patent for a back-rub insecticide dispenser for feed lot cattle, in lieu of payment for a delinquent account. He then started a cattle products mail order business called Farnam Equipment Company, a name that was drawn from the Omaha street on which his ad agency was located. Aside from the insecticide dispenser, Duff peddled such products as grain rollers. In 1949 he moved the company to Phoenix, Arizona, where he became involved in a number of other business ventures as well, including an advertising agency and real estate investments.

In 1953 Bill Johnson, a key employee who would stay with the company for half a century, was hired. He was one of just a handful of people who helped run the mail order business with Duff. Around that time, the company also began selling products directly to distributors. In 1954 Farnam added the Riteway Labs line of livestock remedies to its mail order offerings and a year later introduced its first livestock equipment catalog. In that same year, Duff incorporated the business.

ENTERING THE HORSE CARE FIELD

In 1957 Farnam entered the horse care market through the marketing of a fly repellent that could be mixed with water and sprayed on a horse. Its original name was Pyrenox, named for its primary active ingredient, pyrethrin. While using an ingredient as a brand name was common practice in the cattle industry, the company reasoned that horse enthusiasts might appreciate more enticing brand names. As a result, Duff and Johnson sought a new name, eventually settling on Repel-X, which they hoped customers would associate with the purpose of the product. The name change worked, and Repel-X became a perennial high-selling product for Farnam and laid the foundation for the company's success in the horse products sector.

Farnam was generating annual sales of less than $1 million in 1964 when Duff died. His son, Charles Duff, was just 21 years old and after completing the master of business administration program at the University of California at Los Angeles had taken a job with Ford Motor Company. He had been with Ford for only two months when his father died. He returned home to Phoenix to take over the family business but he was far from ready to take the reins. Johnson was well versed in all aspects of the company, however. He was able to split the administrative responsibilities with the younger Duff, handling sales, production, and the company's Omaha warehouse while allowing Charles Duff to focus on marketing and advertising and learning the business.

Spurred by the introduction of new products, Farnam enjoyed strong growth during the first decade after the death of its founder. The company also acquired Grand Champion horse grooming products from Rayette Faberge in 1968. As a result, sales increased to $12 million by 1973. Farnam continued to expand its horse products in 1977 when it established an important alliance with Merck Animal Health and began selling Equivet 14, a horse dewormer product. Also during that year, Farnam became involved in the pet care business, selling Country Dog products through feed stores. Farnam closed the 1970s by acquiring Merck's Top Form line of horse care products, important strategically because the horse care business was beginning to enjoy strong growth and Farnam was well positioned to take full advantage. In 1979 Farnam also diversified into the lawn and garden care market with the introduction of a dandelion control product called Killer Kane.

ACQUIRING ZIMECTERIN

Farnam broadened its scope in 1980 by entering the professional veterinary market with Furazolidone Aerosol, a product used to treat chronic skin infections, puncture wounds, and other flesh wounds. Four years later the company added a product that proved key to its success, Zimecterin, a horse deworming medicine. Merck had developed it for cattle but elected to sell the exclusive rights of a horse version to Farnam. Zimecterin became one of the top-selling horse products on the market, and at one time accounted for as much as 40 percent of Farnam's total sales, which increased from $19 million in 1981 to almost $70 million ten years later. The dog and cat products segment also experienced strong growth and by 1991 accounted for 15 percent of revenues. Farnam was active on other fronts as well in 1984. It added the Just One Bite rodenticide product through an alliance with LIPHA Tech. Farnam also expanded into the pet shop channel by acquiring Whitmire Pet Products. Three years later another alliance brought Speer flea and tick control products, adding another market for Farnam.

Farnam aggressively built up its horse care business in the 1990s. American Equine was acquired in 1990, followed in 1994 by the purchase of Horse Health Products, Inc., a subsidiary of Mallinckrodt Inc. A year later Equicare Horse Care Products was acquired from Sandoz International, and in 1997 Farnam bought the Vita Flex product line, advanced performance products for horses. Farnam expanded in other areas as well during this period, becoming involved in the livestock ear tag business in 1992 through an alliance with a New Zealand company. Farnam's veterinary product offerings were bolstered in 1994 with the addition of suture products through an alliance with Lukens Medical Corporation.

Surgical instruments were added through an alliance with Pilling Weck in 1998; also that year, veterinary products were broadened further through an alliance with medical technology company Becton, Dickinson and Company. In the meantime, the lawn and garden products segment added the product lines of Security Lawn and Garden Products in 1994, and in 1998 Farnam acquired Finale Weed Killer from the Scott's Miracle-Gro Company. The pet care segment also saw the 1996 introduction of the Bio Spot over-the-counter flea and tick control product.

KEY DATES

1946: Mort Duff starts Farnam Equipment Company in Omaha, Nebraska.
1949: Duff moves business to Phoenix, Arizona.
1957: Farnam enters horse care business.
1964: Duff dies; son Charles takes over the family business.
1980: Farnam enters professional veterinary market.
1984: Marketing rights to Zimecterin are acquired.
1994: Horse Health Products, Inc., is acquired.
2001: Rick Blomquist is named chief executive.
2006: Central Garden & Pet Company acquires Farnam.

NEW LEADERSHIP

As the new century dawned, Farnam continued to grow in all areas through product development, acquisitions, and alliances. In 2000 the company acquired Sure Nutrition, a premium line of horse products, and through an alliance with CEVA Santé Animale S.A. began distributing Feliway Pheromone Spray, a product used to dissuade cats from urine marking as well as scratching vertical surfaces, and a similar product for dogs to help reduce or eliminate destructive and other undesirable behaviors. A year later Happy Dog Toys was acquired, and Farnam introduced Continuex Daily De-wormer for horses and Endure Sweat-Proof Fly Spray for horses. It was also in 2001 that Farnam named a new chief executive officer, Rick Blomquist, who joined the company in 1981 after graduating from Northern Arizona University with a business degree. As a devoted horseman and animal rights advocate whose first job was working in a kennel for a veterinarian, Blomquist was well suited to the task of running an animal health care company.

Under the leadership of the new chief executive, Farnam continued to develop and acquire new products. In 2003 the company introduced IverCare, a sure-grip deworming syringe product, and purchased the Equi Aid brand of psyllium and daily deworming products. Two more company-developed products were unveiled in 2004: Comfort Zone Spray with D.A.P. to help dogs with stress-related behavior such as barking, chewing, and urinating due to visitors, car travel, adjusting to a new environment, and other causes; and ComboCare, a tapeworm product for horses and ponies that was also useful with other parasites. Another equine deworming product, IverEase, designed for feed use, was brought to

market in 2005. In that same year, the company entered the feed market for the first time, working with Land O'Lakes Purina Feed LLC to create the Platform line that included four categories to cover different ages and lifestyles: Pleasure, Performance, Mare & Foal, and Senior. In addition, Platform brand feed supplements were also developed, in keeping with a rise in popularity of supplements, mirroring in large degree what was happening in the human health care market. PetSmart and Tractor Supply Co. both agreed to carry the products on a national basis. In 2006 another equine tapeworm product, TapeCare Plus, was introduced. Farnam also looked to serve other needs of horse owners by acquiring the marketing rights in 2005 to Leather CPR, a cleaning and conditioning product for tack and other leather goods.

In 2003 Bill Johnson was recognized for his 50 years of service with Farnam, during which time he had held a number of top posts with the company. He received a cash bonus of $1 million from the grateful owners, the Duff and Bassham families. Although well past retirement age, Johnson expressed no interest in leaving the company, preferring instead to take advantage of his good health to keep on working.

COMPANY SOLD TO CENTRAL GARDEN & PET COMPANY

Johnson's protégé from 40 years earlier, Charles Duff, was by this time in his 60s and looking for an exit strategy from the business he had helped to grow into a company that in 2005 generated $160 million in sales. Once his intention was made known in the marketplace, Walnut Creek, California-based Central Garden & Pet Company was quick to make an attractive offer. A sales agreement was reached early in 2006 that called for Central Garden to pay $287 million for the business plus $4 million for Farnam's Phoenix headquarters.

Central Garden started out in 1955 as Central Garden Supply, a regional lawn and garden supply distributor. It was not until the late 1980s that the company, under the ownership of William E. Brown, began to grow into an industry powerhouse, driven by the necessity of making acquisitions in a rapidly consolidating industry or risk falling by the wayside. In 1991 it added a pet supplies distributor and in short order this segment was enjoying the fastest rate of growth. A year later Central Garden & Pet Company was formed to take Central Garden Supply public; due to a warehouse fire, however, the offering was postponed and not completed until July 1993. The company then used the money it raised and its stock to complete more acquisitions in both the lawn and garden and pet segments over the next decade, including Four Paws Products, Ltd., Inc., manufacturer of dog, cat, reptile, and small animal products; Sandoz Agro, Inc., maker of pet and veterinary products; Kaytee Products Incorporated, manufacturer of bird and small animal food; TFH Publications, Inc., which not only published pet books but also manufactured premium Nylabone dog chews. In the 21st century Central Garden became interested in expanding into the animal health business, and the acquisition of Farnam helped to accomplish this end.

Central was not looking for synergies so much as it hoped to acquire Farnam's leadership position in the equine market; products; research and development; and management talent. Despite the change in ownership Farnam continued to function as an independent operation under Blomquist's leadership. Farnam became a small, yet valued part of Central Garden, which posted nearly $1.4 billion in sales in 2005. Although a public company, Central Garden did not break out the performance of Farnam in its filings, but there was every indication that Farnam was doing well under its new ownership, and it was likely taking advantage of Central Garden's international network to grow overseas sales. The Farnam name was well entrenched in the market-place, and would likely remain a top brand in horse and pet care industry for years to come.

Ed Dinger

PRINCIPAL SUBSIDIARIES

Farnam Companies International.

PRINCIPAL COMPETITORS

Animal Health International, Inc.; Intervet/Schering-Plough Animal Health; MWI Veterinary Supply, Inc.

FURTHER READING

Lundeen, Tim, "Farnam Makes Entry into Feed Business," *Feedstuffs*, April 11, 2005, p. 9.

Reagor, Catherine, "Farnam Cos. Finds Niche with Animal Products," *Business Journal—Serving Phoenix & the Valley of the Sun*, November 11, 1991, p. 18.

"Sixty Years: Sharing Your Passion," *Between the Aisles*, Summer 2006.

Smith, Rod, "Central Saddles Up with Farnam," *Feedstuffs*, January 30, 2006, p. 7.

Snyder, Jodie, "A Firm with Horse Sense," *Arizona Republic*, July 23, 2001, p. 1D.

"The Story of Repel-X," *Between the Aisles*, Summer 2007.

Fellowes Inc.

1789 Norwood Avenue
Itasca, Illinois 60143
U.S.A.
Telephone: (630) 893-1600
Fax: (630) 893-1683
Web site: http://www.fellowes.com

Private Company
Incorporated: 1917 as The Bankers Box Company
Employees: 2,700
Sales: $700 million (2007 est.)
NAICS: 322211 Corrugated and Solid Fiber Box
   Manufacturing; 42213 Industrial and Personal
   Service Paper Wholesalers; 337214 Office Furniture
   (Except Wood) Manufacturing; 421420 Office
   Equipment Wholesaling

■ ■ ■

Fellowes Inc. is a leading global manufacturer of workspace products designed to enhance security, organization, and productivity. These products include paper shredders, records storage boxes, desk accessories, space organization products, protective cases through its role as a Body Glove brand licensee, and media labeling products. Founded in 1917 by Harry Fellowes, the privately held, family-owned and operated company is headquartered in Itasca, Illinois. Originally known as The Bankers Box Company, Fellowes has grown to employ more than 2,700 people throughout the world with operations in 15 countries.

THE BANKERS BOX COMPANY: 1917

A chance meeting in an elevator between Harry Fellowes and Walter Nickel in 1917 is where the Fellowes story begins. The two gentlemen were small businessmen who worked in the same office building. Harry learned that Nickel had been called up for duty in World War I and needed to sell his business, a start-up company that made inexpensive corrugated boxes used for storing bank records. Harry found the idea intriguing because of the record-keeping requirements brought about by the newly enacted federal income tax. Consequently, before the elevator had reached the lobby, Harry Fellowes had purchased the company for $50. Thus The Bankers Box Company was born. Harry assembled the sturdy file-like boxes on his kitchen table at night and went out to peddle them during the day.

In May 1938 Harry's sons, John E. and Folger Fellowes, joined the company, traveling to the West Coast on sales calls. Some 20 years later, during the 1950s, John and his brother took over the management of the business from their father, with the goal of building the company into a strong national manufacturer. While Folger established the company's customer base and was in charge of sales and marketing, John managed the internal operations of purchasing, manufacturing, and administration, overseeing new product developments and new locations, increasing production and efficiency with each move, tailoring each new manufacturing location to regional customer needs, culminating in Fellowes' current one million-square-foot location just outside of Chicago, Illinois.

John recognized the company's global opportunities and led the company through a decade of overseas expansions during the 1960s and 1970s, opening subsidiaries in the United Kingdom, Australia, and Canada, as well as four regional U.S. manufacturing plants, which were added to provide faster service and lower freight costs for customers across the country. Building upon this foundation, the company later developed businesses in Germany, Belgium, the Netherlands, Luxembourg, France, and Japan, including exports to more than 60 additional countries. By 1972 the company was a major manufacturer of office products. In 1998, John was still involved with Fellowes as vice-chairman, as an active member of the board, and as its principal stockholder, even though he had turned the reins over to his two sons, James and Peter. John died in 2007.

In 1969, when third-generation Fellowes family member James began working for the company, total revenues were somewhere around $4 million per year. Under his guidance as CEO—along with brother Peter as chief operating officer—the company increased its revenues at an estimated 14 percent annually from 1980 to 1994, with total revenue somewhere around $220.4 million in 1994 and a net income of about $9.2 million.

INDUSTRY CHANGE AND PAPER SHREDDERS: 1980–90

By 1980 total revenues reached approximately $31 million. During that decade, the office products industry changed radically. Manufacturers were challenged as office technology advancements changed the way people worked and the products they needed to support that work. In addition, increased foreign competition, consolidation within distribution channels, and rapid expansion of retail outlets began to present remarkable challenges to the manufacturers who supplied the distribution channels. Fellowes Manufacturing's answer to those challenges was to devote its

energy and resources to planning carefully for the future. For example, early on Fellowes envisioned the computer as being the center of workplace activity. That led Fellowes to envision many products that related to the computer-based work environment of the 1990s. Consistent with the company's vision of the computer-based work environment, noticing that the computer environment was information-intensive and realizing that information in the wrong hands represented a significant risk for businesses and individuals, James Fellowes led his company into the paper shredder business.

In 1982 the company started selling, as an original equipment manufacturer (OEM), five general office shredders, which were manufactured by other companies, under their own brand name with moderate success. Nonetheless competition soon sprang up, and the large, expensive ($1,500–$4,500) shredders quickly faced a shrinking market share. By the end of the decade the Fellowes line of general office shredders had evolved to eight machines with sales of more than $7 million per year. Nevertheless, although it was a thriving business for Fellowes at the time, the company was learning that its products, and those of its competitors, were not meeting consumers' needs effectively.

Listening to its customers complain about the inconvenience and distraction of leaving their workstation to shred documents, the company's vision changed. The new plan: to design and manufacture a shredder so inexpensive that anyone handling sensitive information could shred documents at their workstation and to decentralize the shredding function in the same way that computers were being decentralized in the 1980s through personal computers. In 1990 Fellowes introduced the world's first "personal shredder," making it convenient and affordable (starting at about $149) for the first time for anyone to have one at their workstation.

The company also began marketing its products through the office "superstores" that were sprouting across the United States, such as Office Depot, OfficeMax, and Staples, as well as in chains such as Kmart, Target, and Wal-Mart, rather than through the big office machine dealers or wholesalers traditionally used in the industry. Prices for personal shredders continued to fall (by more than 60 percent from 1990 to 1999), creating stronger demand for shredders. By mid-1999 Fellowes was the leading brand of shredders in the world, growing from $8 million in sales in 1990, to account for 18 percent of the company's total sales in 1994, and to some $40 million in 1995, which represented more than half of the estimated $75 million market.

The company shipped more than 1,300 interbranch shipments with a total weight in excess of 32 million

```
┌─────────────────────────────────────────────────┐
│                                                  │
│                 KEY DATES                        │
│              ──────────◆──────────               │
│                                                  │
│  1917:  Harry Fellowes pays $50 for a company    │
│         that makes inexpensive corrugated boxes  │
│         used for storing bank records.           │
│  1938:  Harry's sons, John E. and Folger         │
│         Fellowes, join the company.              │
│  1969:  James Fellowes becomes the third         │
│         generation to work for the family        │
│         business.                                │
│  1982:  The company begins to sell office paper  │
│         shredders.                               │
│  1983:  Bankers Box changes its name to Fellowes │
│         Manufacturing.                           │
│  1990:  Fellowes introduces the world's first    │
│         personal shredder.                       │
│  1998:  The company completes the acquisition of │
│         French binding and laminating company    │
│         Lamirel.                                 │
│  2001:  John Fellowes II joins the family        │
│         business; GoNeo LLC is acquired.         │
│  2005:  A paper shredder with SafeSense          │
│         technology is launched.                  │
│  2007:  The company establishes two new joint    │
│         ventures in Russia and China.            │
│  2008:  The Intellishred Series, a new           │
│         generation of personal paper shredders   │
│         that claim to be 100 percent jam proof,  │
│         makes its debut.                         │
│                                                  │
└─────────────────────────────────────────────────┘
```

pounds in 1990. Looking for a more efficient way to provide better service and to meet the needs of its plants and its customers, the following year the company changed its distribution system from rail to trucking, employing carrier CRST Inc. of Cedar Rapids, Iowa, to handle the load.

OTHER PRODUCT DEVELOPMENT: 1994–97

While the shredder lent prominence to the Fellowes name, and the company's original business (record storage equipment) accounted for 45 percent of sales during 1994, the new market was in computer accessories. In December 1994 the company introduced several new organizational products and computer accessories, including its new "Wild Things" line of multicolored computer accessories, its "Box Options" line of multipurpose corrugated storage products, and "Neat Ideas" portable organizers, all at the School and Home Office Products Association show in New Orleans. Computer accessories accounted for nearly 37 percent of

the company's total revenue in 1994.

In January 1995, in an effort to continue to expand beyond office organization products and to increase its strength in new business segments, Fellowes acquired C-2 Office Gear Inc., a $21 million Chicago-based manufacturer of computer covers, mouse pads, wrist rests, keyboard protectors, laptop carrying cases, and molded products, as well as a license for a line of Looney Tunes products, for an undisclosed price.

At the 1997 Consumer Electronics Show, the company introduced a handheld computer input device, called Tracker. The device was a result of a joint venture between Fellowes and Fujitsu Takamisawa, a Japanese producer of high-end technology. The Tracker used Fujitsu's proprietary Non-Contact Magnetic Field Detection method for "effortless and accurate" cursor control. The device, which contained no moving parts, was designed for both right-handed and left-handed operation. The two-button device was released in both IBM PS/2 and Microsoft compatible formats.

NEW CORPORATE LOOK

In October 1998, to take advantage of its brand equity in the Fellowes name, the company unified the packaging of its products under a newly redesigned black, white, and yellow corporate logo. That year, the company, which was ranked 469th on *Forbes'* "Private 500" list, expanded its product line by 147 new products, including such breakthrough products as the first Memoflex gel for ergonomic support, as well as new media storage products, glare filters, copyholders, licensed mouse pads, dust covers, and computer cables, all of which were added to enrich the company's offerings. In addition, the company expanded its line of Looney Tunes licensed computer accessories and audio storage products, including an embroidered CD player case, Tweety-at-the-Beach mouse pad, and character-themed CD jewel cases. By May 1999 the company offered the industry's most extensive line of computer accessories, with roughly 350 unique products and more than 2,000 stock-keeping units within 17 different product categories. Also early that year, the company completed the acquisition of French binding and laminating company Lamirel.

In April 1999 the company received a 1998 Sears Partner in Progress Award. The award was given each year by Sears, Roebuck and Co. to a select group of vendor companies who supplied Sears with quality products and services on several levels and for various achievements.

By the end of the 20th century Fellowes Manufacturing remained a family-run firm as Harry's grandsons, James and Peter Fellowes, continued to build the global business, driven by a strong commitment to excellence. In mid-1999 the company had 1,500 employees worldwide, and seven foreign subsidiaries, marketing products in more than 60 international markets. As it had in the past, the office products industry would continue to evolve, and the company fully anticipated adapting new strategies to prepare for the future. The company cited as an example the trend toward increased mobility in the workforce. New product lines would accurately reflect this development as Fellowes continued to heed the most important voice in the industry, the consumer's.

MOVING INTO THE NEW CENTURY

Fellowes Inc. (the company having dropped "Manufacturing" from its name) continued expanding well into the new millennium. The company made a significant addition to its product arsenal when it acquired GoNeo LLC in 2001. GoNeo was the licensee of the Body Glove brand, which offered protective casing solutions for portable consumer electronics including cell phones and eventually, the iPod. John Fellowes II, the fourth generation of Fellowes, joined the family business that same year.

Along with adding new products to its line up through acquisition, Fellowes continued to redesign its existing product offerings. During 2005 it launched a paper shredder that had what the company called its SafeSense technology, which would automatically shut the shredder down when hands were too close to the paper opening. The Good Housekeeping Institute gave the new Fellowes Powershred DS1 its "All Star" rating in 2006 and in 2007, the company was a recipient of Chicago's Innovation Award for the new Powershred. During 2008 the company debuted its Intellishred Series, a new generation of personal paper shredders that claimed to be 100 percent jam proof. Paper jams were consumers' leading complaint about paper shredders at the time and Fellowes expected to see high demand for this new product.

Strong demand for the company's products left Fellowes in an enviable position among office supply manufacturers. A January 2008 *Chicago Daily Herald* article described the company's current situation claiming, "Still spry at 90, Fellowes Inc. is growing with constant product innovations and expansion into foreign markets." Indeed, during 2007, the company established a joint venture in Moscow, Russia, to expand its distribution capabilities in the country. It also formed Fellowes China that year to take advantage of strong growth in that region. Its China-based shredder

manufacturing facility was thought to be the largest in the world.

As the Chicago-area's 48th largest privately owned company, Fellowes seemed to be on track for continued success. Sales surpassed $700 million in 2007 and demand for the company's products remained strong in international markets. At this time the company had subsidiaries in 15 countries and distributor and licensing partnerships with firms in 10 other countries. While the weak economy in the U.S. threatened to derail its domestic revenue growth in 2008 and 2009, chairman and CEO James Fellow remained confident that Fellowes products would continue be found on store shelves well into the future.

Daryl F. Mallett
Updated, Christina M. Stansell

PRINCIPAL COMPETITORS

ACCO Brands Corporation; Cummins-American Corp.; Escalade Inc.

FURTHER READING

"Answer Sheet," *Times Union,* June 11, 2008.

"Anti-Glare Screens Get Rave Reviews," *Modern Office Technology,* May 1990, p. 26.

Brindza, Stephen, "Inactive Filing Seems Valuable," *Modern Office Technology,* July 1988, p. 88.

Crown, Judith, "Office Products Firm Likes High-Tech Fallout," *Crain's Chicago Business,* April 24, 1995, p. 45.

"Fellowes," *Discount Store News,* October 26, 1998, p. 41.

"Fellowes Accessories Bow," *HFD,* December 6, 1993, p. 83.

"Fellowes Acquires California-Based GoNeo," *PR Newswire,* June 18, 2001.

"Fellowes Establishes a Joint Venture in Russia," *M2 Presswire,* October 8, 2007.

"Fellowes' Looney Tunes Office Accessories," *HFN,* October 16, 1995, p. 100.

"Fellowes: New Swivel Arm Holder," *HFD,* September 21, 1992, p. 168.

"Fellowes Readies Instant-Win Promo," *HFN,* September 14, 1998, p. 62.

"Fellowes Receives Sears 1998 Partner in Progress Award," *PR Newswire,* April 19, 1999, p. 3136.

"Fellowes Screens to Cut Glare Set," *HFD,* August 2, 1993, p. 76.

"Fellowes Targets Home Offices," *HFD,* June 7, 1993, p. 80.

"Fellowes Unveils Work Station Line," *HFD,* June 8, 1992, p. 124.

"Fellowes Upgrades Shredder," *HFD,* July 20, 1992, p. 87.

Fondiller, David S., "Better Shred Than Read," *Forbes,* September 11, 1995, p. 186.

Garbato, Debby, "Fellowes Refocusing on Home Office Market," *HFD,* November 30, 1992, p. 58.

————, "Fellowes Sells Closet Mates," *HFD,* November 30, 1992, p. 56.

Greenberg, Manning, "Fellowes Finds Own Path to Home Office Profits," *HFD,* November 2, 1992, p. 107.

Hill, Dawn, "Fellowes Acquires C-2 to Add Clout in Computer Accessories," *HFN,* January 23, 1995, p. 51.

Milfeld, Becca, "A Need for Paper Documents Still Propels Fellowes," *Chicago Daily Herald,* January 9, 2008.

Nelton, Sharon, "The Benefits That Flow from Quality," *Nation's Business,* March 1993, p. 71.

"New Fellowes Finance Chief," *HFN,* February 10, 1997, p. 46.

"Powershred DS1 Wins Endorsement," *Sarasota Herald-Tribune,* January 27, 2006.

"Revolutionary Paper Shredder Puts an End to Consumers' Number One Complaint," *Product News Network,* February 26, 2008.

Scelsi, Paul, "A Mode Change for the Better," *Chilton's Distribution,* May 1991, p. 56.

"The Scoop," *HFN,* January 16, 1995, p. 204.

Shear, Barbara, "Color and Variety Add Luster to Accessories: Manufacturers Are Striving to Produce Desktop Products That Are Attractive and Functional," *Office,* October 1991, p. 16.

Stankevich, Debby Garbato, "Fellowes to Unveil File Organizer That Fits into RTA Shelving Units," *HFD,* August 2, 1993, p. 65.

Stemgold, Mark, "Fellowes Manufacturing Inc.," *New York Times,* October 26, 1998, p. C9.

Troy, Terry, "Fellowes Inks Dan River Pattern Pact," *HFD,* January 27, 1992, p. 81.

"WARNING: Is Your Tax-Time Garbage a Buffet for Identity Thieves? Timely Advice for Anyone Filing Taxes in 1998," *PR Newswire,* April 7, 1999, p. 5323.

"Wrapper Doubles Output of Office Products," *Packaging Digest,* January 1994, p. 72.

Ferrellgas Partners, L.P.

7500 College Park Boulevard, Suite 1000
Overland Park, Kansas 66210
U.S.A.
Telephone: (913) 661-1500
Fax: (913) 792-7985
Web site: http://www.ferrellgas.com

Public Company
Incorporated: 1939 as A.C. Ferrell Butane Gas Company
Employees: 3,508
Sales: $2.29 billion (2008)
Stock Exchanges: New York
Ticker Symbol: FGP
NAICS: 454312 Liquefied Petroleum Gas (Bottled Gas)
   Dealers

■ ■ ■

Ferrellgas Partners, L.P., is the second largest retail propane marketer in the United States, with annual sales of nearly 850,000 billion gallons and a customer base of over one million in all 50 states and Puerto Rico. The company is also the largest provider of propane by branded tank exchange through its Blue Rhino Corp. subsidiary. The company's distribution business transports propane to retail distribution outlets and then into tanks on its customers' property. In addition, Ferrellgas manages a transportation fleet consisting of 5,000 bulk, transport, and delivery trucks. The company also is involved in the trade of propane and natural gas, the marketing of wholesale propane, the storage of liquid natural gas, and the marketing of chemical feedstock.

Propane, or liquefied petroleum gas, is used by nearly 60 million people in the United States to fuel furnaces, water heaters, air conditioners, outdoor grills, fireplaces, dryers, and range tops. It is also estimated that propane is used on over 660,000 farms in the United States.

EARLY HISTORY

In 1939 A.C. Ferrell Butane Gas Company opened its doors in Atchison, Kansas, as a family-owned and operated gas business. A.C. Ferrell opened his business in the devastated Dust Bowl and during the Great Depression. Facing strong odds that his new venture would fail, he nevertheless forged ahead with confidence. The fortitude shown by the company's founder established a precedent for intelligent risk-taking that the company would come to regard as its hallmark. Ferrell's maternal grandfather, E. E. Samson, was a Skelgas bottle dealer in the early days of the Skelgas era, and that influence may have informed his decision as well. Ferrell and his wife initially had set out to make their livelihood through farming in Valley Falls, Kansas, but moved to the city with the hopes of securing a better standard of living.

According to their son, Jim Ferrell, in the Winter 1999 Ferrell company publication, *Flame,* the husband and wife team optimized their individual talents to make the business work. A. C. Ferrell acted as salesman, and Mabel ran the business operations. She managed the money, collected the bills, kept the books, and ran the business out of their home from 1939 until the end of World War II. To make ends meet, A. C. Ferrell took on second and even third jobs. During the war, he worked as a part-time fireman, a part-time police officer, and for the railroad.

COMPANY PERSPECTIVES

Americans have relied on Ferrellgas for their home, business, and agricultural propane needs. Throughout our history, we've prided ourselves on being not only propane industry leaders, but good neighbors to the approximately 1 million Customers we serve nationwide.

The end of World War II generated a rebirth of business. Americans were weary of rations and lean times, and pent-up demand made consumers hungry for modern conveniences. This translated into opportunity for the Ferrells. The founder began selling gas refrigerators, floor furnaces, and electric milking machines during this time, and even used a trailer outfitted with a complete kitchen as a marketing tool. He would back the trailer up close to a prospective buyer's back door and leave it there for the buyer to become familiar with and use. The notion worked; the consumer became hooked. When Ferrell returned, he managed to sell a whole new kitchen, similar to the one the consumer had been using in the trailer.

The business grew, and the Ferrells purchased a building in Atchison to house their first office. Mabel Ferrell continued to run the business while A. C. Ferrell drove the company truck, delivered propane, and handled sales. In 1947 the company established its first plant, located across the river in Missouri and on land leased from the railroad. By 1952 the company had approximately 12 employees, primarily farmers and men returning home from the war. That same year, Mabel died, leaving A. C. Ferrell without a business partner and creating a significant gap in the business operations.

THE NEXT GENERATION
EXPANDS THE BUSINESS

A. C. Ferrell continued the business, however, incorporating in 1954 as Ferrell Companies, Inc. He attempted to diversify the business by selling furniture and televisions, but that proved unsuccessful, and by 1965 the business focused solely on the sale of propane and some related equipment. The employee count dwindled to fewer than four, and only a slight positive cash flow due to depreciation kept the business going.

In 1963 James E. (Jim) Ferrell, the founder's son, received a degree in business from the University of Kansas and returned home to help his father stabilize

the business. This was only to be temporary, as he was in the U.S. Army and intended to make the military his career. However, Ferrell found that the company's problems would involve more time to resolve than he originally had anticipated. Giving up his military aspirations in 1965, he devoted himself wholeheartedly to the propane business his parents had started. Not satisfied with merely stabilizing and managing a small company, Ferrell was determined to grow the business. The latter determination marked the beginning of a growth era for the company that would continue through to the next millennium.

In 1965 Jim Ferrell changed the company's name to the more modern-sounding Ferrellgas. Within two years, he had borrowed $14,000 from a propane supplier, in return for a contract to purchase all his propane from that company, and used the money to purchase J & J Propane in Rushville, Missouri, located just over the state line from Atchison. Ferrell quickly recognized that to grow, he needed a bigger market. Therefore, in 1969, he formed Propane Industrial to serve the larger Kansas City industrial market. Around this time, Coffey Oil & Gas, in Platte City, Missouri, went on the auction block, and Ferrell seized the opportunity, purchasing Coffey and moving his office to that location, just outside of Kansas City. The Coffey Oil & Gas acquisition alone doubled sales for Ferrellgas.

In 1973 the next growth opportunity presented itself with the acquisition of Leavitt Propane in Kearney, Missouri. The company once again more than doubled sales and once again moved its main office to the new location. This acquisition was significant for two reasons: Leavitt operated in three states—Iowa, Kansas, and Missouri; and with Leavitt, Ferrellgas entered the wholesale business. During this time, Ferrell employed the husband-and-wife-team approach so successfully initiated by his parents; Ferrell's wife, Zibbie, came to work at Ferrellgas, keeping the books and working on collections.

Ferrellgas was faced with a significant challenge in the early 1970s. During the OPEC oil embargo, U.S. oil prices skyrocketed, and the U.S. government reacted with legislative controls that distorted the marketplace. Ferrellgas's response was to avoid traditional supply sources in favor of small producers and to enter the storage business to help offset flagging sales.

In 1977 Ferrellgas purchased Kathol Petroleum, renaming it Indian Wells Oil Company. This acquisition gave the company a natural gas liquids extraction plant, a field of gas wells, and an introduction to Wall Street, the latter being the result of the involvement of Indian Wells in several drilling partnerships with financiers,

KEY DATES

1939: A.C. Ferrell Butane Gas Company opens for business in Atchison, Kansas.

1947: The company establishes its first plant.

1965: Founder's son, Jim Ferrell, steps in to help stabilize and eventually expand the company; company is renamed Ferrellgas.

1981: New headquarters are established in Liberty, Missouri.

1994: Ferrellgas converts from a privately owned company to a master limited partnership traded on the New York Stock Exchange.

1998: The company initiates an employee stock ownership plan.

1999: Ferrellgas acquires Thermogas, making it the nation's largest propane retailer.

2002: ProAm Inc. is acquired.

2004: The company merges with Blue Rhino Corporation.

designed to fund the drilling necessary to feed the plant. Indian Wells was sold three years later for a profit.

UNPRECEDENTED GROWTH

Proceeds from the Indian Wells sale helped the company acquire portions of Buckeye Gas Products Company in Nebraska and Iowa in 1984. Two years later, in 1986, Ferrellgas purchased the remainder of Buckeye and converted the company from a regional propane supplier to a national company.

The success of the business resulted in the company outgrowing its offices in Kearney. Therefore, in 1981, company headquarters moved to the Building One site in Liberty, Missouri. Ferrell chose Liberty because of its proximity to Kansas City. Building Two was constructed in 1983 and by 1986 both buildings were occupied to capacity.

In 1994 after several more large and small acquisitions, Ferrellgas converted from a privately owned company to a master limited partnership (MLP) traded on the New York Stock Exchange. Such a partnership organization combined features of general and limited partnerships with those of publicly traded corporations. Specifically, with most limited partnerships, one group of partners, the general partners, managed a business or investment while another group, the limited partners, raised any capital required by the business. With MLPs,

one could issue publicly traded securities to raise capital. For tax purposes, these securities were referred to as partnership units rather than corporate shares even though they were traded like stock. The move to form an MLP was unprecedented in the propane gas industry, giving the company greater financial flexibility and enhancing its capacity to grow. After the formation of the MLP, the company acquired 50 high-quality independent retail propane companies. Among these deals was the 1996 purchase of Skelgas, for which Ferrell's grandfather had been a bottle dealer in the 1920s.

In 1997 Ferrellgas purchased the North Carolina Propane Gas Co. Inc., the second largest propane dealer in North Carolina. Also vying, unsuccessfully, for that purchase was Ferrellgas competitor Thermogas Co., a subsidiary of Mapco Inc. and The Williams Cos. Inc., both based in Tulsa. Soon after the acquisition, Ferrellgas brought a lawsuit against Thermogas, alleging that the latter had hired away employees from the North Carolina propane dealer in an attempt to learn proprietary information about Ferrellgas. The lawsuit was quickly settled out of court, and Ferrellgas would eventually be on friendlier terms with Thermogas.

INTRODUCING EMPLOYEE OWNERSHIP

In 1998 Ferrellgas became the first in its industry to form an employee stock ownership plan (ESOP) when Ferrell sold parent Ferrell Companies, Inc., to employees, resulting in approximately 50 percent ownership. Approved by Congress in 1974, and regulated by the U.S. Department of Labor and the Internal Revenue Service, the ESOP was a form of a long-term savings plan that gave tax breaks to business owners in return for assisting employees in purchasing company stock. The Ferrellgas ESOP distinguished itself from other company plans by not requiring employees to make payroll deductions to participate. The company arranged a $160 million financing package to purchase its 50 percent stake in the enterprise.

The decision to enact an ESOP at Ferrellgas was Ferrell's. He was preparing to retire and had no heirs to groom for the leadership role. He recalled in a 1999 interview for the company magazine *Flame:* "I knew I would much rather have the ownership changed in this way, with an ESOP, rather than see it merged into another company. It was the right thing to do." This structure remained in effect well into the new millennium. At the end of 2007, Ferrellgas employees indirectly owned over 20 million common units of the partnership.

In late 1999, Ferrellgas became the nation's largest propane marketer in terms of retail volume when it purchased its Tulsa-based competitor Thermogas for $432.5 million; in the years to come the company would vie for the top spot with competitor AmeriGas Partners L.P. The company's largest acquisition to date, Thermogas added 1,400 employees and 330,000 residential, industrial/commercial, and agricultural customers to the company's client base, while also giving Ferrellgas a presence in Michigan and other upper-midwest states. Before the acquisition, Ferrellgas had been ranked as the nation's second largest propane retailer; thereafter, it was first, with a workforce of 6,000 in more than 700 retail locations in 45 states and the District of Columbia.

As the company looked forward to continued years of growth, a new management team began to take over. With Jim Ferrell less involved in the day-to-day operations of the company, serving as chairman of the board, the role of president and CEO was held by Danley K. Sheldon, who had been instrumental in taking the company public in 1994, when he was chief financial officer at Ferrellgas. Rounding out the management team in June 2000, Ferrellgas brought in Patrick Chesterman as vice-president and chief operating officer. All agreed that the company's plan for the future focused on continued growth. Such growth would be achieved, according to company literature, through a combination of acquisitions, efforts to bolster client base, and retaining the loyalty of long-standing customers through superior products and service.

MOVING INTO THE 21ST CENTURY

Indeed, the growth through acquisition policy continued well into the new millennium. During 2002 the company added propane retailer ProAm Inc. to its arsenal. The deal added nearly 42 million gallons to Ferrellgas's company sales, over 70,000 customers in seven states, and allowed the firm to enter new markets. During 2003 Ferrellgas purchased six propane companies including Suburban Propane Partners, which marked its 65th acquisition since its public offering in 1994. The growth of the company forced it to begin upgrading its transportation assets. Also in 2003 the company launched a fleet renewal effort that included the purchase of 400 new trucks.

The company's most significant purchase of this period came in 2004 when it made a play for Blue Rhino Corp. Blue Rhino, established in 1994 by Billy Prim, was operating as the largest branded propane tank exchange provider in the country. It began to look for a buyer in 2003 after determining the costs of operating as a public entity were too high. Ferrellgas agreed to acquire and merge with the company in 2004 for $343

million. Upon completion of the deal, Blue Rhino was delisted from the NASDAQ and became a wholly owned subsidiary of Ferrellgas.

With Blue Rhino under its wing, Ferrellgas immediately strengthened its foothold in the branded propane tank exchange service arena. Blue Rhino's portable tank exchange was available at over 32,000 retail locations including home improvement centers, mass merchants, hardware retailers, grocery stores, and convenience stores. The union positioned Ferrellgas as the largest provider of propane by branded tank exchange. It stood as the second largest marketer of propane in the United States, just behind competitor AmeriGas. AmeriGas had been pursuing a similar growth-through-acquisition strategy and claimed the number one slot in 2001 with its purchase of the retail propane distribution businesses of Columbia Energy Group.

Additional acquisitions included Puget Sound Propane and Yankee Gas in 2006. The company also increased its presence in central California and southern Texas in 2008. The company achieved record financial results in 2007 with net earnings reaching $34.8 million. Net income fell in 2008, which the company attributed in part to the significant rise in the wholesale price of propane. Nevertheless, Ferrellgas management, led by Chairman and CEO Ferrell and President and Chief Operating Officer Steve Wambold, was optimistic that the company was on track for success in the years to come.

Ana Garcia Schulz
Updated, Christina M. Stansell

PRINCIPAL SUBSIDIARIES

Ferrellgas Partners Finance Corporation; Ferrellgas L.P.; Ferrellgas Finance Corporation; Ferrellgas Real Estate Inc.; Ferrellgas Receivables LLC; Blue Rhino Canada Inc.; Blue Rhino Global Sourcing Inc.; Uni Asia Ltd.

PRINCIPAL COMPETITORS

AmeriGas Partners, L.P.; Energy Transfer Partners L.P.; Suburban Propane Partners L.P.

FURTHER READING

Bogoslaw, David, "Ferrellgas Eyes Further Mkt Growth in Blue Rhino Buy," *Dow Jones Newswires*, February 9, 2004.

"Ferrellgas Partners L.P. Acquires Puget Sound Propane and Yankee Gas," *PR Newswire*, January 3, 2007.

Kovski, Alan, "Warm Winter Chills Sellers of Heating Fuels," *Oil Daily*, February 26, 1998, p. 1.

Louis, Brian, "Blue Rhino Sale Ok'd," *Winston-Salem Journal*, April 21, 2004.

———, "Propane Products Company Blue Rhino Began Attempts to Sell Itself Last Year," *Winston-Salem Journal*, March 4, 2004.

———, "Winston-Salem, N.C.-based Propane Company Sold Due to Cost of Regulation," *Winston-Salem Journal*, February 18, 2004.

Meyer, Gene, "Ferrellgas Says It Has Settled Lawsuits," *Kansas City Star*, September 21, 1999, p. D6.

———, "Ferrellgas Workers Act as if They Own the Business. And They Do," *Kansas City Star*, September 22, 1998, p. E19.

"Risks Pay Off for A.C. Ferrell," *Flame: A Quarterly Publication for All Ferrell Employees and Their Families*, Winter 1999.

"Transformation," *Truck Fleet Management*, November 1999, p. 16.

Walsh, Patrick, "The Ferrellgas Solution Renaissance, a Rebirth," *Propane Canada*, November 1, 2006.

Wilson, Charles E., "Bobtail Upgrade," *Modern Bulk Transporter*, August 1, 2003.

fieldale farms corporation

Fieldale Farms
Corporation

555 Broiler Boulevard
Baldwin, Georgia 30511
U.S.A.
Telephone: (706) 778-5100
Fax: (706) 776-3191
Web site: http://www.fieldale.com

Private Company
Incorporated: 1972
Employees: 4,800
Sales: $750 million (2008 est.)
NAICS: 311615 Poultry Processing

■ ■ ■

Fieldale Farms Corporation is one of the largest family-owned and operated poultry producers in the world. The company provides whole birds, cut-up chicken parts, and boneless and skinless chicken parts. Fieldale also manufactures breaded and marinated ready-to-cook and fully-cooked chicken products. The company is northeast Georgia's largest privately owned company and one of that region's major employers. As is common of the industry, controversies involving a variety of environmental and ethics issues associated with chicken production are a part of the company's history.

HATFIELD AND THE ARRENDALE
BROTHERS

Long before an interstate was completed in the 1980s, making the northeastern corner of Georgia a popular

recreation spot and a way-point for vacationers headed to the Smoky Mountains of Tennessee and North Carolina, the Arrendale brothers began the business that would become Fieldale. Tom and Lee Arrendale were born in Rabun County, in the tip of the state near the joint border with North and South Carolina, in the 1920s. Tom attended Lakemont Consolidated High School, later studying at Georgia Tech, and during World War II, he served in the Army Air Corps. After he returned to north Georgia, he began a career in the poultry business as Lee's partner. In January 1946, the Arrendale brothers went into business together growing live broilers, and eventually they would become involved in chicken processing as well.

The Arrendales had their operation in Clarkesville, county seat of Habersham County; further south lay Gainesville, a much larger town that served as the county seat of Hall. In the early 1950s, Joe Hatfield moved to Gainesville, and also became involved in the poultry industry, working first in the processing and then the marketing areas. He and several partners established a processing company that they called Gainesville Fryers. Throughout the 1950s, Hatfield with Gainesville Fryers, and the Arrendale brothers with their farms and processing facilities, continued to prosper. However by the end of the decade, the poultry industry entered a slump, and both the Arrendales and Gainesville Fryers were hit by potentially hard times. By the beginning of the 1960s, all three men faced difficult choices.

RALSTON PURINA AND THE FOUNDING OF FIELDALE

In 1961 Tom and Lee Arrendale made what must have been a difficult decision, opting to sell their business to Ralston Purina. The latter, a large and well-known company with interests in many geographic and commercial areas, had begun to move into the northeast Georgia poultry processing business, and in September 1961, the Arrendales sold all their interests to Ralston Purina. At around the same time, Hatfield and his associates reached a similar decision, and they too sold their company to Ralston Purina. Not only that, but all three men went to work for their former companies' new owner.

Thus Tom Arrendale became the general manager for Ralston Purina's Clarkesville operations, while Lee took the general manager's position for their Gainesville facilities. Hatfield, on the other hand, was assigned the job of general manager of southeastern poultry operations. During the 1960s, Ralston Purina's poultry enterprises in the area expanded, and partly on the strength of its lucrative north Georgia business, by the latter part of the decade it became the world's largest producer of broilers.

In 1971 the company's leadership decided to sell off all its poultry operations in the United States. Learning of this, Hatfield and the Arrendale brothers, along with other associates, decided to take advantage of the opportunity to gain a sizable share in the broiler operation, and purchased the entire northeast Georgia operations of Ralston Purina. The three entrepreneurs had been forced to sell their companies and go to work for a large corporation; now, almost exactly a decade later, they were about to take control once again, this time of a larger company. Combining parts of both last names, they dubbed their corporation "Fieldale," and began operations under that name in February 1972.

GROWTH AND JOBS

The three businessmen, already leaders in their communities, became some of the wealthiest men in the northeast region of Georgia. They were recognized for their contributions: Tom Arrendale, for instance, won numerous awards from local organizations, and became a member of the board of directors of a prominent local bank. Fieldale had emerged as the largest of the homegrown local businesses, and its economic impact was enormous.

Poultry, always more viable than traditional farming in a mountainous area that did not have particularly rich soil for growing crops, provided numerous jobs in the surrounding counties. First there were the farmers, who grew chickens in large chicken houses; then there were also the employees in the processing plants. Thus poultry could be said to span a variety of businesses from agricultural to industrial, and from the viewpoint of owners, it was an extremely lucrative enterprise. From the perspective of potential employees, some in white-collar positions and many more in blue-collar processing jobs, it meant employment; and there were far more people outside the company, including the affiliated chicken farms, who benefited from their relationship with Fieldale.

Circumstances in the 1980s seemed to coalesce to Fieldale's benefit. A trend toward health-consciousness had made chicken an increasingly more popular source of protein, as opposed to beef and pork. Waves of immigration, a result of the spread of Communism in Southeast Asia, and later an economic crisis in the Texas oil industry, respectively brought large numbers of Laotians and Mexicans to the region. In many cases, these people were willing to work at jobs unpopular among the area's mostly white population of U.S. citizens, either because these jobs paid poorly, or because they involved unpleasant activities, or both. Hence in 1996, the *Atlanta Journal and Constitution* reported that chicken-processing jobs, which seldom paid more than $6.50 an hour, were mostly filled by Mexican and South American immigrants. "I don't think anyone says, 'After graduation, I want to get a job in the blood room at Fieldale,'" a Hall County Chamber of Commerce spokeswoman told the *Atlanta Journal and Constitution*.

Nevertheless, to high school students and unskilled workers, jobs in the processing plants such as the one in Cornelia, near company headquarters in Baldwin, represented an opportunity that might not have existed elsewhere. Clearly Fieldale was having a strong economic impact on the community; in the 1990s, however, the region's growing prosperity ironically helped to raise concerns about the environmental impact Fieldale was having on northeast Georgia.

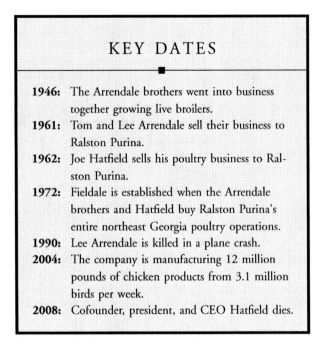

KEY DATES

1946: The Arrendale brothers went into business together growing live broilers.

1961: Tom and Lee Arrendale sell their business to Ralston Purina.

1962: Joe Hatfield sells his poultry business to Ralston Purina.

1972: Fieldale is established when the Arrendale brothers and Hatfield buy Ralston Purina's entire northeast Georgia poultry operations.

1990: Lee Arrendale is killed in a plane crash.

2004: The company is manufacturing 12 million pounds of chicken products from 3.1 million birds per week.

2008: Cofounder, president, and CEO Hatfield dies.

TROUBLES IN 1990

The company suffered two blows in 1990, the first of which came early in the year, when Lee Arrendale was killed in a plane crash. Later a nearby school, as well as a road, were named in his honor; and in 1994 the local rotary club would award; "W. Lee Arrendale Award for Vocational Excellence."

The other blow of 1990 came later in the year. On December 1, 1990, the *Journal and Constitution* ran an exposé on alleged dumping of wastewater by a Fieldale facility in the tiny community of Murrayville, in Hall County. In October, the state of Georgia had fined the company $100,000 for illegal discharge of "thousands of gallons of sewage" into streams that ultimately fed into Lake Lanier, one of the north Georgia region's largest lakes, and a popular recreation spot.

Chicken processing is messy work, and the paper reported that for every chicken processed by the plant, "three gallons of clay-colored water—dyed by blood, guts and millions of feathers" was produced as well. This wastewater was supposedly treated, then sprayed onto pasture land for fertilizer. According to several former employees, however, the water was actually being dumped, sometimes under cover of night, into Lake Lanier. Fieldale executives responded that it was true that their plant, which was processing a million chickens a week, had reached its legal waste disposal limit. Because of high production rates, they said, they were nearly at capacity in their 115-acre disposal field; but, they claimed, they had not exceeded capacity. After being fined in October 1990, the company had cut production levels. "We have these [production] lines up

there because they make us money," the plant's wastewater manager told the paper. "When they're sitting idle, they lose us money. I'd say that's a gesture of good faith right there."

The charges of illegal waste disposal activities, according to Fieldale executives, came from disgruntled ex-workers with ulterior motives; in fact one of the two former employees making the charges had been fired for fighting. But scientists and state officials had confirmed signs of heavy environmental impact. Biologists who studied the lake, which among other things is a source of drinking water for metropolitan Atlanta, reported that the area near the plant was "aging" faster than any other section along the shores of Lake Lanier.

After complaints by neighbors, an official with the Georgia Department of Natural Resources had conducted an inspection, and found the company guilty of violations, which had resulted in the $100,000 fine. Fieldale, which had invested $2 million in a new treatment system in 1989, had applied for permits from the county and state to expand its disposal fields. Neighbors, officials, scientists, and certainly the company's leadership hoped the problem would be alleviated.

CONTINUING CONTROVERSY

In 1993 Fieldale ran into another problem, but this time the accusation was dirty politics rather than dirty water. Tom Arrendale, whose company had contributed $10,000 to the election campaign of Governor Zell Miller in 1990, had paid to fly two state legislators, along with Georgia Agricultural Commissioner Tommy Irvin, to Daytona, Florida, for the Daytona 500 auto race. When the media learned of this, they raised an uproar at the apparent attempt to buy influence; but according to a loophole in the state law, the three officials were not legally required to report that they had been the beneficiaries of Arrendale's hospitality.

The "loophole" had been left in the law because, as the newspaper stated, members of the Georgia General Assembly had held that "People such as bank presidents and hardware-store owners ... ought to be able to take their local legislators to lunch without having to register as lobbyists and file disclosure forms." However according to the Atlanta paper's editorial, Arrendale had taken advantage of the law to woo the legislators, one of whom was the head of the state's Environmental Protection Division. Since he was technically not a lobbyist, neither Arrendale nor the public officials were required to report the Daytona junket.

The editorial at least judged as true the claim by Arrendale and the officials that they discussed no politics on the trip: "Talking politics on such trips is considered impolite, because it shatters the fragile illusion that it's an outing among friends. It is only later that friends begin to help each other, as friends are wont to do." In December 1993, another editorial called on the state's general assembly to "Close the Fieldale Farms Loophole," and said that doing so had become legislators' "top ethics-reform priority" in 1994.

Nor was this the end of Fieldale's troubles in the 1990s. Years before, Arrendale and Hatfield might never have imagined that their company would get attention from the *New York Times,* but when it happened, it was not pleasant. Under the heading "Chicken Farm's Food Is Banned," the paper reported that certain school districts had banned use of food provided by Fieldale Farms after one of its shipments was found to contain bone and cartilage.

In 1996 the company made headlines in another prominent national paper, the *Wall Street Journal,* but again the reasons were not good. This time the cause was a lawsuit filed by the company against Franklin County, Georgia, because the latter had established an environmental ordinance which was more stringent than existing state law to keep a Fieldale plant out. Throughout Georgia and beyond, businesspeople, government officials, and citizens' groups took notice of the lawsuit, which would determine much about the relative powers of businesses, local governments, and state governments. Economic growth in the region, it turned out, had created a prosperous local economy in which people could afford to have concerns for the environment, and not merely their pocketbooks: "Franklin County officials say that 10 years ago they never would have considered passing an environmental ordinance." However at the time, thanks to growing prosperity in north Georgia—prosperity for which, ironically, Fieldale could claim some share of the credit—Franklin County was keeping Fieldale out in favor of the cleaner, better-paying jobs being offered by auto-plant supply manufacturers, including makers of windshield wipers and exhaust systems.

COMING OF AGE WITH ITS COMMUNITY

Around the same time as the *Wall Street Journal* article, in April 1996, the *Journal and Constitution*'s "Southern Economic Survey" reported what appeared to be a telling fact. The town of Gainesville, in preparation for hosting visitors to Olympic rowing events on Lake Lanier that summer, was painting over the water tower in the center of town, thus obscuring the slogan it had carried for a quarter of a century: "Poultry Capital of the World." Gainesville still had a strong interest in poultry, its mayor told the paper, "but we're so much more than that."

Clearly the news from Gainesville and Franklin County indicated that north Georgia was coming of age, and was more resistant to the influence of Fieldale and other firms involved in the region's large chicken processing industry. Just as Fieldale had benefited from social changes in the 1980s, it seemed to be suffering from changes in the 1990s, particularly a growing concern for the environment, worries over the health hazards posed by chicken, and the growth of north Georgia from an out-of-the-way mountain region to an adjunct of metro Atlanta.

Reports of the eclipse of the poultry industry were highly exaggerated. In its economic survey, the *Journal and Constitution* went on to report that in Hall County, the poultry industry alone, of which Fieldale, ConAgra, and other companies were a part, put $145 million into the county's economy. In addition "This one-county poultry farm income," according to Abit Massey, executive director of the Georgia Poultry Federation, "is larger than the combined statewide income for peaches, pecans, apples, blueberries, grapes, and onions." This claim is impressive, particularly considering that the first of the fruits named is the one most commonly associated with Georgia.

Further proof of Fieldale's stability was offered by its continued growth. In 1994 the trade journal *Feedstuffs* reported that Fieldale and another company were spurring a "building boom" in the Southeast, and that Fieldale planned to build 110 broiler houses in Georgia and South Carolina within a short time. In 1995 in its survey of Georgia's leading private companies, the *Journal and Constitution* reported that sixth-place Fieldale Farms had contracts with 700 chicken growers in two states, and that it operated three processing plants, four hatcheries, and a feed mill.

FIELDALE IN THE 21ST CENTURY

Scandal and controversy followed Fieldale into the new millennium. By that time, the demand for organic food, the fastest-growing segment of the agriculture industry, was increasing and new legislation was being passed related to food label requirements. During 2003 Georgia Representative Nathan Deal, at the prompting of Fieldale, included language in a new federal spending bill that would allow Fieldale to label its chickens as organic, even after feeding them nonorganic food. Consumer watchdog groups protested vehemently and Senator Patrick Leahy from Vermont and Senator Olympia Snowe from Maine quickly sponsored a bill to eliminate the provision. The language was eventually repealed after a new rider was attached to the bill that benefited Senator Ted Stevens and his constituents in Alaska. The new legislation stipulated that all wild-caught seafood, especially Alaskan salmon, was to be considered organic.

At the same time, the company and members of the poultry industry in Georgia were working to change legislation that would allow for the establishment of poultry farms in Oconee and other northwest South Carolina counties. An article published in the *Columbia State* in 2006 described residents' concerns with chicken farms in their communities claiming, "If not properly managed, poultry farms can produce powerful odors and send manure-polluted runoff into creeks. Tens of thousands of birds live on the farms, clustered in barns, where they produce tons of waste." Despite citizen outcry, plans were in the works to establish poultry farms in these areas of South Carolina.

Amid the negative publicity, Fieldale continued to grow its business in a highly competitive industry. By 2004 the company was manufacturing 12 million pounds of chicken products from 3.1 million birds per week. It had 500 contract chicken growers and annual sales of nearly $465 million. It was selling over 250 products in more than 50 countries across the globe. During 2005 the company announced a $45 million expansion project at its processing facility in Georgia.

Fieldale faced challenges in 2008 when the price of chicken feed, especially corn, skyrocketed. Feed corn was being used to produce ethanol, which was driving up the price of corn for meat farmers. Corn, which historically had cost approximately $2 per bushel, had risen to $8 per bushel in 2008 and was hovering at $4 bushel in mid-2009. The industry was also experiencing an oversupply of chicken, which forced the company to cut production by 5 percent in April 2008.

Cofounder, president, and CEO Joe S. Hatfield died that year at the age of 84. While the National Chicken Council mourned his passing and publicly lauded Hatfield as a leader and innovator in the development of the U.S. poultry industry, the company he created along with the Arrendale brothers had remained subject to public criticism throughout its history. Despite the controversy, Fieldale Farms stood secure its position as one of the largest family-owned poultry processors in the world.

Judson Knight
Updated, Christina M. Stansell

PRINCIPAL COMPETITORS

Pilgrim's Pride Corporation; Sanderson Farms Inc.; Tyson Foods Inc.

FURTHER READING

Allen, Elizabeth, "New Federal Organic Food Rules Place Extra Burden on Texas Farmers, Ranchers," *San Antonio Express-News*, May 21, 2003.

Ashby, John K., "What's in a Name?" *Food Processing*, July 1, 2003.

Brown, Robert H., "Broiler House Construction Up in Southeast," *Feedstuffs*, March 28, 1994, p. 19.

"Close the Fieldale Farms Loophole," *Atlanta Journal and Constitution*, February 22, 1993, p. A18.

Fretwell, Sammy, "Residents Fear the Smell of Chickens," *Columbia (S.C.) State*, April 16, 2006.

Higginbotham, Mickey, "Southern Economic Survey, Poultry and Pluto: Gainesville No Longer Puts All Its Eggs in One Basket," *Atlanta Journal and Constitution*, April 14, 1996, p. H12.

Jaffe, Greg, "Southeast Journal: Suit Targets Local Laws on Pollution," *Wall Street Journal*, June 12, 1996, p. SI.

"Passing of Joe Hatfield, Co-Founder, President and CEO of Fieldale Farms," *Targeted News Service*, June 23, 2008.

"Running A-Fowl of the Ethics Law," *Atlanta Journal and Constitution*, February 18, 1993, p. A14.

Sonnier, Cheramie, "Chicken Industry Looks at Issues Facing Consumers," *Baton Rouge Advocate*, June 11, 2009.

Stock, Robert W., "Chicken Farm's Food Is Banned," *New York Times*, May 11, 1995, p. Bl.

Teegardin, Carrie, "Workers: Poultry Plant Often Dumped Sewage," *Atlanta Journal and Constitution*, December 1, 1990, p. Al.

Young, Barbara, "Elements of Success," *National Provisioner*, January 2004.

First Niagara Financial
Group Inc.

6950 South Transit Road
Lockport, New York 14094-6333
U.S.A.
Telephone: (716) 625-7500
Toll Free: (800) 201-6621
Fax: (716) 625-8405
Web site: http://www.fnfg.com

Public Company
Incorporated: 1998
Employees: 1909
Sales: $384.3 million (2008)
Stock Exchanges: NASDAQ
Ticker Symbol: FNFG
NAICS: 551111 Offices of Bank Holding Companies

■ ■ ■

Based in Lockport, New York, about 30 miles from Buffalo, First Niagara Financial Group, Inc., is a NASDAQ-listed publicly traded holding company for First Niagara Commercial Bank and several other financial services subsidiaries. With more than $11.5 billion in assets and more than $6 billion in deposits, New York–chartered First Niagara Bank maintains about 115 branches in 21 counties in upstate New York and in late 2009 was expected to add 57 branches western Pennsylvania and another 83 branches in eastern Pennsylvania through a pair of acquisitions. The community bank serves consumers and businesses, offering consumer checking and savings accounts, commercial deposit products, residential and commercial real estate loans, commercial

business loans and leases, consumer loans, and such wealth management products as stocks, bonds, mutual funds, and annuities. Other group subsidiaries include First Niagara Funding, Inc., a real estate investment trust that originates and holds much of the bank's commercial real estate and business loans; and First Niagara Risk Management, Inc., a full-service insurance agency and employee benefits consulting firm.

QUIET FIRST CENTURY FOR A SMALL-TOWN BANK

First Niagara Commercial Bank was established as Farmers & Mechanics Savings Bank in Lockport in 1870, chartered by the New York State Legislature on May 11 of that year. The bank was founded by 15 Lockport residents, including Jason Collier, who became the first president. He served just two years before being succeeded by James Jackson Jr., whose tenure spanned 20 years. The bank enjoyed steady growth, enough to support the construction of a new headquarters in Lockport in 1905. During its first century the small-town bank offered customers a safe place to deposit their savings, but little else in the way of financial services.

In 1967 the bank became Lockport Savings Bank; six years later it finally opened a second branch in town. Soon after Norman Sinclair took the reins and began to guide Lockport Savings into a new era.

Sinclair was well familiar with the heritage of the bank, having started his career with Farmers & Mechanics in 1942 as a runner. At the time, New York State was home to 113 mutual savings banks, many of them serving single small towns. Sinclair worked his way up

---

COMPANY PERSPECTIVES

■

First Niagara's values are the fundamental principles that surround and guide our relationships, partnerships, teamwork and performance as we interact with our employees, customer, communities and shareholders.

through the ranks at Farmers & Mechanics, and later Lockport Savings. After taking charge in 1975 he began expanding the bank beyond Lockport and Niagara County, keeping pace with a changing world in community banking. In 1984 the bank formed LSB Realty, Inc., to invest in real estate development projects, mostly residential.

Sinclair was in reality a transitional figure. Perhaps his most important contribution to what would become First Niagara Financial Group was the hiring of his successor, William E. Swan. The son of a bus driver and a waitress, Swan earned a degree in sociology in 1969 from western New York's St. Bonaventure University, a hotbed for college basketball. Swan served as the team's Indian mascot and became a lifelong, ardent supporter of the school, a commitment that would lead to dire consequences later in his life.

Swan had grown up wanting to become a social worker, but a summer job as a caseworker apprentice in the Erie County welfare department soured him on the idea. Instead, after graduation Swan went to work at a Manufacturers and Traders Trust Company branch and learned the banking business. In time he became vice-president of the lending division and then in 1984 was named administrative vice-president and regional executive. In November 1987, however, his position was eliminated, and because there were no senior level positions available he found himself out of work. The 42-year-old was not unemployed for long: Sinclair reached out to Swan to encourage him to apply for the senior executive vice president post at Lockport Savings.

SINCLAIR RETIRES, SWAN TAKES CHARGE

Swan was hired and Sinclair began grooming him to take his place. Sinclair retired in June 1989. Soon after Swan took over as president and chief executive officer, Lockport Savings began to expand, opening a pair of branches in 1989 in North Tonawanda and Clarence, the latter the bank's first branch in Erie County.

Although these branches had been planned under Sinclair's watch, they were in keeping with Swan's more aggressive approach to running Lockport Savings. Another Erie County branch followed in 1991 in Cheektowaga.

Lockport Savings expanded beyond its core deposit-taking and mortgage business as well. In 1991 it acquired the life insurance portfolio of Permanent Savings Bank and Goldome Savings Bank to become the largest SBLI (savings bank life insurance) servicer in the state. Lockport Savings also began to charge fees for the first time in its history, something that his predecessor had found an anathema but was now considered a standard source of revenues for a modern bank.

Growth continued in the mid-1990s. Lockport Savings turned to nontraditional branch locations in 1993, opening a pair of supermarket branches in Niagara Fall and West Amherst, New York, both of which proved successful. A telephone service center was established in 1995. In that same year, to keep pace with the bank's steady expansion, a new administrative center opened in Pendleton, New York.

The bank also initiated a strategy to crack the $1 billion mark in assets that called for continued growth in Erie County, including the opening of five branch offices in suburban Buffalo, further internal growth, and possible acquisitions. Lockport Savings reached Buffalo itself by opening its first branch in the city in May 1997. Also in that year it formed LSB Funding, Inc., a real estate investment trust to own mortgage loans the bank originated, and LSB Associates, Inc., a subsidiary to sell annuities and mutual funds as well as life insurance products.

NIAGARA BANCORP FORMED, TAKEN PUBLIC 1998

In order to grow further, it was necessary for the old-time thrift to convert to a stock savings bank. Rather than be owned by its depositors, the bank would be owned by shareholders. In this way, the bank could tap the capital markets and also have its stock available to make acquisitions. To achieve this goal, a holding company called Niagara Bancorp Inc. was formed. A controlling interest of shares would be issued to Niagara Bancorp MHC (mutual holding company), and the balance would be sold to the public after bank customers, officers, and other insiders had a chance to buy shares at a reduced rate. The conversion process was completed at the end of March 1998, and a month later Niagara Bancorp stock became available to the general public and began trading on the NASDAQ. All told, the 15-branch bank raised $135 million to help finance further growth.

KEY DATES

1870: Farmers & Mechanics Savings Bank is established.
1967: The bank becomes Lockport Savings Bank.
1973: A second branch opens in Lockport.
1989: William Swan is named chief executive.
1998: First Niagara Financial Group is formed to take Lockport Savings public.
2000: Lockport Savings is renamed First Niagara Bank.
2003: Swan's suicide rocks First Niagara.
2005: Hudson River Bancorp is acquired.
2009: First Niagara agrees to acquire two Pennsylvania Bank holding companies.

Before the decade came to a close, another five branches opened or were about to, including one in a suburb of Rochester, New York. A loan production office was opened in Rochester in 1999, followed by a full-service branch. Niagara Bancorp acquired a major Western New York full-service insurance agency, Warren-Hoffman & Associates Inc. in 1999, as well as an employee benefits affiliate, NOVA Healthcare Administrators. A deal was also reached to acquire Empire National Leasing, a equipment lease financing company, and Empire National Auto Leasing, Inc. The deals closed at the start of 2000.

More in keeping with its regional and national aspirations, Lockport Savings Bank changed its name to First Niagara Bank in 2000, and Niagara Bancorp became First Niagara Financial Group, Inc. While those changes received regulatory approval, First Niagara continued to expand. In the first quarter of the year, it acquired Albion Banc Corp, the holding company of Albion Federal Savings and Loan Association and its two branches in Orleans County, New York.

Later in 2000 First Niagara completed the acquisition of CNY Financial Corporation for $87.9 million to add banking offices in Cortland, Homer, and Cortlandville, New York, and a loan production office in Ithaca, New York. First Niagara also paid $80.3 million for Iroquois Bancorp Inc., the holding company for Cayuga Savings Bank and Homestead Savings, which operated 11 branches in Cayuga, Oneida, and Oswego counties. In addition, First Niagara acquired Buffalo-based investment adviser Niagara Investment Advisors Inc., which focused on equity, fixed-income, and balanced portfolio accounts, serving a wide variety of clients.

SECONDARY STOCK OFFERING: 2002

First Niagara devoted much of 2001 to digesting the acquisitions of the prior year. Having depleted the money raised from its initial public offering of stock, First Niagara held a secondary offering in 2002 to raise funds to support further expansion. The offering netted $390.9 million, which was put to use in 2003 with the acquisition of Finger Lakes Bancorp, Inc., the holding company of Geneva, New York-based Savings Bank of the Finger Lakes. Its seven branch locations helped First Niagara fill out its footprint in Cayuga and Tompkins Counties and gain a presence in Ontario and Seneca counties. In a deal that closed on January 1, 2004, First Niagara paid $356.6 million in cash and stock for Troy Financial Corp., holding company for the Troy Savings Bank and Troy Commercial Bank, which combined for $1.2 billion in assets and 21 offices.

By the time the Troy Financial deal was completed, First Niagara was operating under the leadership of a new chief executive, the change the result of tragic circumstances. In addition to guiding First Niagara through a period of unprecedented growth, William Swan was helping to lead his beloved St. Bonaventure University as chair of the school's board of trustees. In June 2002 St. Bonaventure was rocked by a basketball scandal when a Georgia junior college transfer was ruled ineligible to play because, instead of the associate's degree required for eligibility, he possessed only a welding certificate from Coastal Georgia Community College. St. Bonaventure's president, Robert J. Wickenheiser, had decided the player was eligible despite the advice of his athletic department and without consulting the National Collegiate Athletic Association, college sports' ruling body. Swan was made aware of Wickenheiser's decision but opted not to interfere in the day-to-day running of the university. It was a decision that proved devastating, as a scandal over the matter erupted in March 2003.

ST. BONAVENTURE SCANDAL RESULTS IN SWAN'S DEATH

Swan and Wickenheiser exacerbated the situation by not publicly addressing the matter for almost a week, although Swan took time off from the bank to attempt to find a resolution behind the scenes. The basketball coach was soon fired and the athletic director was also forced to resign. Wickenheiser stayed on, however, and Swan was reelected as chairman in June 2003.

Nevertheless, Swan remained troubled by the scandal. In the summer he penned an article for the *Trusteeship* magazine called "The REAL March Madness," in which he admitted that he questioned his handling of the matter countless times. Although he declared he was at peace with his actions, he was clearly unsettled. One early evening in August 2003 Swan's wife found her 55-year-old husband hanging in the basement of their East Amherst home. He left behind a suicide note lamenting the way he had left down St. Bonaventure and his colleagues, and begging the forgiveness of his family.

Swan's death caused the price of First Niagara stock to plummet, but it began to rebound as it became quickly apparent that the matter had nothing to do with the health of the bank, something the police had initially indicated but subsequently rescinded. Swan was replaced by Paul K. Kolkmeyer, who took over as interim president and chief executive until assuming the posts on a permanent basis. Kolkmeyer had been with First Niagara since 1975, when he was hired as chief financial officer.

MOVING BEYOND TRAGEDY WITH NEW EXPANSION: 2005

After overcoming the shocking loss of Swan, the man who had been the driving force behind the rapid growth of First Niagara, the bank resumed its pattern of expansion at the beginning of 2005 with the completion of the $580 million cash and stock acquisition of Hudson River Bancorp. Based in Hudson, New York, it was the holding company for Hudson River Bank & Trust Co. and Hudson River Commercial Bank. The deal brought 50 branches in eastern New York to First Niagara, providing it with a strong foundation in the fast-growing Albany area. In one stroke First Niagara became the No. 3 bank in terms of market share in the Capital District and the seventh largest bank in upstate New York.

Although investors were pleased with First Niagara's geographic growth, they were concerned about high expenses and low return on equity, resulting in a stagnant stock price. Kolkmeyer launched a cross-selling initiative to increase profits by encouraging existing customers to do more business with First Niagara and its subsidiaries. The efforts failed to bear fruit quickly enough, and in December 2006 Kolkmeyer was abruptly fired. His chief financial officer, John Koelmel, was then installed as CEO. Given the difficult conditions facing the banking industry in general, he faced a difficult task.

FIRST NIAGARA ACCEPTS TARP MONEY: 2008

Under Koelmel, First Niagara in 2008 acquired Great Lakes Bancorp, holding company for Greater Buffalo Savings Bank, which maintained banking offices in Erie, Chautauqua, and Niagara counties. Later in the year First Niagara was able to raise $108.8 million in a secondary stock offing despite market worsening conditions. The federal government responded by making funds available to banks through the Troubled Asset Relief Program (TARP). First Niagara opted to participate and received $184 million of capital in exchange for stock.

With nearly $300 million in fresh capital, First Niagara was poised for further expansion. In 2009 it agreed to a pair of deals which, pending regulatory approval, would take First Niagara into Pennsylvania. They included National City Corp. with 57 branches in Pittsburgh and western Pennsylvania, and Harleysville National Corp., a Philadelphia-area banking company with 83 branches in nine eastern Pennsylvania counties northwest of Philadelphia. With the successful completion of these deals, First Niagara would be poised to become a player in the mid-Atlantic market. In anticipation of its new stature, First Niagara updated its corporate logo. Rather than portray itself as a community bank, First Niagara redesigned its logo to compare more favorably with the competitors it would face on a larger stage.

Ed Dinger

PRINCIPAL SUBSIDIARIES

First Niagara Bank; First Niagara Funding, Inc.; First Niagara Risk Management, Inc.

PRINCIPAL COMPETITORS

HSBC USA Inc.; PNC Financial Services Group; M&T Bank Corporation.

FURTHER READING

Bridger, Chet, "'Our People Are Just Devastated,'" *Buffalo News,* August 22, 2003, p. B4.

Epstein, Jonathan D., "First Niagara Buys 57 Branches," *Buffalo News,* April 8, 2009.

——, "First Niagara Changes Its Logo," *Buffalo News,* June 26, 2009, p. D7.

——, "First Niagara to Grow 50% After Philly Bank Purchase," *Buffalo News,* July 28, 2009.

——, "Koelmel Tries to Shake First Niagara from Its Doldrums," *Buffalo News,* June 17, 2007, p. B9.

Harlin, Kevin, "First Niagara Financial Group Tries to Stem Fears Concerning Chief's Death," *Albany (N.Y.) Times Union,* August 25, 2003.

Hartley, Tom, "Bank Poised for Expansion," *Business First of Buffalo,* December 10, 2001, p. 1.

————, "Lockport Savings Bank Investing in Erie County," *Business First of Buffalo,* December 11, 1995, p. 4.

————, "Lockport Savings Builds Empire," *Business First of Buffalo,* April 21, 1997, p. 1.

————, "Lockport Savings' New Boss," *Business First of Buffalo,* January 1, 1990, p. 10.

————, "Lockport Savings Undertakes Search for Headquarters Space, *Business First of Buffalo,* January 30, 1995, p. 3.

Manning, James Hilton, *Century of American Savings Banks,* New York: B.F. Buck & Company, 1917.

Reosti, John, "First Niagara on the Prowl for Fill-In Acquisitions," *American Banker,* July 1, 2001.

Warner, Gene, "Banker Found Dead in His Home," *Buffalo News,* August 21, 2003, p. A1.

Fives S.A.

———■———

27-29 Rue de Provence
Paris, F-75009
France
Telephone: (33 01 45) 23 75 75
Fax: (33 01 45) 23 75 71
Web site: http://www.fivesgroup.com

98% Owned by F.L. Investco S.A.S.
Incorporated: 1861 as Parent, Schaken, Caillet et Cie
Employees: 5,679
Sales: EUR 1.35 billion ($1.7 billion) (2008)
NAICS: 551112 Offices of Other Holding Companies

■ ■ ■

Fives S.A. is one of the world's leading industrial engineering groups. The Paris-based company designs, manufactures, and installs industrial equipment, machinery, and systems. The company's wide range of competencies enables it to provide everything from single components to full production lines to entire factories on a turnkey (i.e., ready to use) basis for the automotive, logistics, cement, metals, sugar, energy, and other industries. Fives (pronounced "feeve") operates through a network of more than 60 subsidiaries in 30 countries on six continents. The operations of Fives are carried out through a number of specialized companies. These include Fives Cinetic (automotive and logistics); Fives Stein and Fives DMS (steel, metals, and glass); Fives Solios (aluminum); Fives Celes (heating and cooling); Fives Cail (sugar); Fives Cryogenic (heat exchanges and pumps); Fives Industries (heavy industrial equip-

ment); Fives Nordon (piping systems for the energy and other industries); and Fives Pillard and Fives North American (industrial combustion equipment for the energy and mining industries).

More than 80 percent of the operations of Fives comes from outside of France, and nearly 65 percent from outside of Europe. The group's operations are well balanced among its Metals, Automotive/Logistics, Energy, and Cement divisions, which combined to produce a total of EUR 1.35 billion ($1.7 billion) in 2008. Formerly a public company, Fives is controlled by private-equity investors, through holding F.L. Investco, which owns more than 98 percent of the company. Leading Fives is Chairman Frédéric Sanchez.

BUILDING FRANCE'S INDUSTRIAL INFRASTRUCTURE

The Fives group of companies emerged in the second half of the 19th century as important components in the construction of France's industrial infrastructure. The earliest part of the group was Société des Anciens Établissements Cail, which was founded in 1812. Cail was a major producer of sugar processing machinery and equipment, one of France's most important industries during the period. Throughout the century, Cail expanded its scope of expertise, supplying mechanical and industrial equipment to a wide range of industries, as well as to the great French engineering projects of the day.

Paris-based Cail became an important factor in the development of a new company founded in Lille in 1861 by Basile Parent and Pierre Schaken, who had

COMPANY PERSPECTIVES

Our expertise: designing and supplying process equipment, production lines and plant facilities on a "turnkey basis" for major industrial players, all over the world. Our experience in industrial engineering and in managing large projects overseas is unique. Thanks to the quality of our teams and our knowledge of the groundwork, we are recognized for our ability to manage projects as a whole within the deadlines and in compliance with the performance guarantees. Our multi-sector expertise gives us a wide-range vision of the industry which provides a continuous source of innovation for our R&D department. We are willing to share this accumulated experience with our customers and are always in search of new industrial solutions combining technology, safety and profitability.

been awarded a contract to produce rails and locomotives for the Grand Central railroad company in 1854. Parent and Schaken opened a factory in the Fives neighborhood of Lille and began operations as Parent, Schaken, Caillet et Cie. The company also built a second factory in Givors, in France's Rhone region. The company changed its name to Compagnie de Fives-Lille in 1865, and then reincorporated as a limited liability company in 1868.

Cail and Fives-Lille collaborated closely through the 1860s, forming the joint-venture partnership J.F. Cail, Parent, Schaken, Houel, Caillet, Paris et Fives-Lille. The partnership was hugely successful, and joined in the construction of many of France's major public works projects of the day. The construction of the Busseau Viaduct Bridge became one of the partnership's first achievements, completed in 1863. The reputation of the company soon enabled it to participate in major public works projects around the world, including in Russia and Egypt. Steam locomotives and trams were another company specialty, and the joint venture became a major supplier to railroads around the world.

The joint venture between Cail and Fives-Lille came to an end in 1870. Fives-Lille by then had expanded its name, officially becoming Compagnie de Fives-Lille pour Constructions Mécaniques et Entreprises in 1868. The outbreak of war in 1870 provided the company with a new market, as it turned its production to the manufacture of weapons and arma-

ments and other equipment to support the French war effort. Following the war, the company resumed its production of locomotives, establishing itself as a major name in the world export market. At the same time, the end of the partnership with Cail permitted the company to begin producing its own machinery and equipment for the sugar processing industry as well.

MERGERS FUEL GROWTH

Fives-Lille continued to expand its range of operations through the end of the 19th century and into the beginning of the 20th century. Among the company's major markets at the dawn of the 20th century were the production of machinery and equipment for public works projects. In the years leading up to World War I, Fives-Lille was among its region's major employers, with more than 3,000 workers. The war and its aftermath cut short the company's growth, however. The company struggled to rebuild its operations and its workforce. By the early 1920s, Fives-Lille once again resumed its expansion. The company then refocused its business around three primary areas: public works, railroads, and sugar factories.

In the 1930s, Fives-Lille added a new dimension to its operations, buying Société des Etablissements Dalbouze & Brachet in 1933. That company had been founded in the early 19th century. By the 1930s, the company, based in Puteaux, near Paris, had specialized in the production of cement manufacturing equipment. Under Fives-Lille, this unit later took on the name of FCB Ciment.

World War II and the Nazi occupation of France brought a new period of difficulty for Fives-Lille. However, the postwar reconstruction period offered new growth opportunities for the company. At the same time, Fives-Lille and Cail began to move closer to a merger. The two companies had continued to collaborate on a number of projects over the decades since their partnership. During the 20th century, the companies had also held talks on the possibility of merging their businesses. These talks finally came to fruition in 1958. The newly merged business then took on the name of Société Fives-Lille-Cail.

ACQUIRING SCALE

The merged company quickly proved its place among the world's leading engineering groups, as it completed the construction of the Atchinsk cement plant in the Soviet Union's Siberia region. That plant became the world's largest cement plant at that time, with a total production of 5,700 tons per day. Fives-Lille also

KEY DATES

1861: Parent, Schaken, Caillet et Cie is founded and forms a joint venture with Société des Anciens Établissements Cail to produce locomotives and industrial machinery and equipment.

1865: Parent, Schaken, Caillet et Cie changes its name to Compagnie de Fives-Lille.

1870: The joint venture between Cail and Fives-Lille comes to an end.

1933: Fives-Lille acquires cement plant specialist Société des Etablissements Dalbouze & Brachet.

1958: Fives-Lille and Cail merge to form Fives-Lille-Cail.

1973: Fives-Lille-Cail merges with Babcock-Atlantique, forming Fives-Cail-Babcock.

1983: The company changes its name to Groupe Fives-Lille.

1987: Fives-Lille acquires Stein-Heurtey group.

2001: Industri Kapital acquires 98 percent of Fives-Lille.

2004: Barclays Private Equity France backs management buyout of Fives-Lille.

2006: Charterhouse Capital Ltd. acquires Fives-Lille.

2007: The company changes its name to Fives S.A.

2008: Fives acquires the North American Manufacturing Company.

completed another nine cement production facilities in the next decade, in Brazil, Iraq, and Turkey. The company remained a prominent player in the infrastructure market as well, participating in a number of large-scale projects, including the Tancarville Bridge in 1959, the Garigliano Bridge in 1966, and the Massena Bridge in 1970.

During the 1960s, Fives-Lille-Cail went on an expansion drive, completing a number of significant acquisitions. These included Applevage, acquired in 1963, and Bréguet and Bréguet-Sauter-Harlé in 1966. The group's acquisition drive helped it expand its range of expertise as the company moved toward positioning itself as a provider of "turnkey" (that is, ready to use) industrial facilities. In 1968, the company acquired Pillard EGCI, a company founded in 1920 to produce fuel oil-burning boilers. The company later grew into a major producer of boilers and furnaces for the glass and cement industries, as well as for food processing and other heat treatment processing applications.

Fives-Lille-Cail reached a major milestone in 1973 when the company agreed to merge with Babcock-Atlantique, a manufacturer of industrial boilers and heating systems. The company then took on the name Fives-Cail-Babcock, more popularly known as FCB. FCB then became one of France's leading manufacturers of heavy machinery and equipment. The company also expanded into the steel and metals industry, operating foundries and factories in Fives, Denain, Ivry, La Courneuve, and elsewhere. The company continued its acquisition drive through the 1970s and 1980s, boosting its existing operations while adding competencies in a widening array of industries. The company's businesses grew to include operations in the food processing, port handling, minerals, steel, glass, aluminum, and other markets.

DIVERSIFYING AND RESTRUCTURING

This diversification led the company to change the name of its holding company back to Compagnie de Fives-Lille in 1980, and then to Groupe Fives-Lille in 1983; FCB became the name of one of the company's subsidiaries. Through the 1980s, Fives-Lille continued to target new acquisitions to build up its existing businesses and to extend its range of operations.

In 1984, the company acquired a producer of large-scale industrial equipment, which had been founded as Dujardin in 1867 to produce steam-driven equipment. That company later added diesel engines and compressors, before being acquired by Vallourec in 1972. Under Fives-Lille, the company would become known as Fives Industries.

In 1987 the company acquired Stein-Heurtey, a company founded in the middle of the 19th century to produce furnaces and heat treatment equipment for the steel and glass industries. Stein acquired Heurtey, developer of the aperiodic generator in 1980, and then acquired Celes, which had been founded in 1967 to build one of the first aperiodic generators. Through the Stein-Heurtey acquisition, Fives-Lille also added EFTA, a designer of mechanical and automation equipment. Also in the 1980s, Fives-Lille bought DMS, based in Lille and founded in 1963 to produce tubing factories for Vallourec. Fives-Lille acquired full control of DMS, which was placed under FCB, in 1986.

Fives-Lille's diversification effort enabled it to benefit from the booming industrial sector during the 1980s. The group's presence across a broad range of industries also helped to protect it amid the collapse of the building market at the end of the 1980s and the global economic recession at the beginning of the 1990s. Nevertheless, the difficult economic period led to a decade-long restructuring effort, starting in 1987. As part of that process, Fives-Lille refocused its operations around a number of core businesses. The company also began phasing out much of its existing manufacturing businesses, as it began its transition toward becoming an industrial engineering company.

During the 1990s, Fives-Lille targeted the fast-growing developing markets for its own growth. The company scored success in the Middle East, for example, when it received an order to carry out a major expansion of a cement plant for Qatar Cement Company in 1994. Also in that year, Fives-Lille moved to take advantage of the booming Chinese infrastructure and industrial market, opening a commercial office in Beijing.

NEW OWNERS IN THE 21ST CENTURY

As the economy picked up again in the mid-1990s, Fives-Lille targeted new expansion efforts. The company's Cinetic group, which operated in both the automotive and logistics sectors, took form during the decade and into the next, as the company transferred a number of its existing business, including EFTA, into a new Automotive Business Division. In 1999, Fives-Lille acquired the automation division of Ingersoll-Rand, a producer of automated assembly and production systems for the automotive industry. Cinetic also took over Rouchaud Gendron, part of Celes, which formed the basis for what would become the Cinetic Machining division.

In 2000, Fives-Lille completed several new acquisitions, including U.K.-based Fletcher Smith, active in the sugar industry, and Italy's Giustina, a producer of grinding machines for the automotive industry. Also that year, Fives-Lille merged its cement business with that of fellow French cement engineering specialist Technip, thereby becoming a leading global player in the cement engineering sector, with a market share of nearly 4 percent.

Fives-Lille had long been a public company, with French banking giant Paribas among its reference shareholders. In 2001, however, Paribas agreed to sell out its stake in the company to private-equity group Industri Kapital, which subsequently launched a full-scale takeover of Fives-Lille. The group's ownership changed hands again in 2004, when Barclays Private Equity France backed a EUR 300 million management buyout. In 2006, Barclays itself sold Fives-Lille to U.K.-based Charterhouse Capital Ltd.

During this time, Fives-Lille completed several more notable acquisitions. The company acquired Landis, the grinding machine business of U.S.-based UNOVA (later renamed Intermec Inc.), in 2005. This was followed by the acquisition of Sandvik Sorting, boosting the group's logistics operations, in 2007. In 2008, the company became one of the world's leading producers of field combustion systems and high-temperature burners when it acquired North American Manufacturing Company. By then, the company had simplified its name, becoming Fives S.A. and rebranding most of its primary businesses in 2007. With a history reaching back to the middle of the 19th century, Fives had become one of the world's leading and most integrated industrial engineering companies.

M. L. Cohen

PRINCIPAL SUBSIDIARIES

F.L. Metals; Fives Cail; Fives Cail KCP Ltd. (India); Fives Cinetic; Fives Cinetic Srl; Fives Cryomec AG (Switzerland); Fives FCB; Fives Fletcher Ltd. (UK); Fives North American Combustion Inc. (U.S.A.); Fives Pillard; Fives Stein; Fives Stein (Shanghai) Industrial Furnace Co. Ltd. (China); FL Industries Inc. (U.S.A.); Fletcher Smith Inc. (U.S.A.); Nordon; North American Mfg. (Canada) Inc.; Pillard Feuerungen GmbH (Germany); Solios Environment Inc. (U.S.A.); Solios Environnement.

PRINCIPAL DIVISIONS

Automotive Logistics; Cement; Energy/Sugar; Metals.

PRINCIPAL OPERATING UNITS

Fives Cail; Fives Cinetic; Fives Pillard; Fives Stein; Nordon.

PRINCIPAL COMPETITORS

Robert Bosch GmbH; Itochu Corp.; Dover Corporation; Hudong Zhonghua Shipbuilding (Group) Company Ltd.; Leggett and Platt Inc.; Georg Fischer AG; ZF Lenksysteme GmbH; Sulzer AG; TRUMPF GmbH and Company KG.

FURTHER READING

"Acquisition of Fives-Lille by Charterhouse Cleared," *European Report,* July 26, 2006.
"Commission Clears Acquisition of Landis by French Engineering Firm," *European Report,* December 10, 2005, p. 217.

"Fives-Lille Buys Ingersoll Rand's Operation," *Les Echos,* November 23, 1999, p. 16.

"Fives-Lille Group," *European Venture Capital Journal,* September 2006, p. 50.

"Fives-Lille in Secondary Buyout," *European Venture Capital Journal,* September 2004, p. 17.

"French Take Qassim Cement Plant Contract," *MEED Middle East Economic Digest,* April 8, 1994, p. 29.

"Technip, Fives-Lille Could Team Up," *Les Echos,* February 23, 2000, p. 18.

The Foundation for National Progress

———■———

222 Sutter Street, Suite 600
San Francisco, California 94108
U.S.A.
Telephone: (415) 321-1700
Fax: (415) 321-1701
Web site: http://www.motherjones.com

Nonprofit Company
Founded: 1975
Employees: 22
Total Assets: $1.5 million (2007)
NAICS: 511120 Periodical Publishers; 519130 Internet Publishing and Broadcasting and Web Search Portals

■ ■ ■

The Foundation for National Progress is a nonprofit organization and publisher of *Mother Jones* magazine and also maintains that publication's web site presence, motherjones.com. Named for a feisty feminist union organizer named Mary Harris Jones, *Mother Jones* is a left-liberal political magazine that specializes in hard-nosed investigative journalism in the tradition of Upton Sinclair. Over the years, *Mother Jones* has built its reputation as a responsible journal that exposes corruption and works for social justice, covering topics such as racial discrimination, women's rights, environmental justice, and the plight of migrant farm workers. Although initially it focused on fomenting radical political activism, the magazine has gradually softened its image, expanding its coverage to include lifestyle topics, such as media, technology, travel, and marketing and advertising. In addition to issuing *Mother Jones,* The Foundation for National Progress also supports a program for new journalists called The Ben Bagdikian Fellowship Program.

RADICAL ROOTS AND A QUICK RISE TO THE TOP

In 1974, just after the Watergate scandal broke, effectively demonstrating that investigative journalism could change the course of history, Adam Hochschild and Jeffrey Klein met with a group of inspired journalists in the living room of Paul Jacobs to plan their own magazine, *Mother Jones.* Seemingly overnight, alternative newspapers with a strong progressive bent were springing up across the United States, not only in the wake of Watergate, but also as the U.S. civil rights and antiwar movements were winding down.

Until then, powerful politicians had been the main targets of investigative journalism. *Mother Jones* would be the first print journal to expand investigations to multinational corporations. The magazine's founders were ambitious; they wanted the magazine to be politically influential, which meant it needed to be well written and expertly designed so that it could reach a larger audience than traditional left-leaning periodicals. To keep *Mother Jones* independent of corporate influence, they started a nonprofit organization in 1975, the Foundation for National Progress (FNP), to publish the magazine using donations from its board members and readers, supplementing its income with advertising and subscriptions.

Two years after its conception, the founders' vision was finally realized. In 1976, the printer delivered the first issue of *Mother Jones* to its 17 employees in their cramped office located above a McDonald's in San Francisco. However, it was not until about a year and a half after it was launched that *Mother Jones* finally took off. In 1977, the magazine published "Pinto Madness," an exposé of the Ford Pinto, the best-selling subcompact car in the United States at the time, which tended to explode when it was rear-ended. The article became famous, winning numerous awards and getting national news coverage.

A few years later, in 1979, *Mother Jones* ran a groundbreaking article on how tobacco could be as addictive as some illegal narcotics. It soon followed this story with an exposé on "dumping," the corporate practice of selling medicines, pesticides, and other products banned as unsafe in the United States to third world countries. These pieces and others like them sought to change the way people thought about corporate power, galvanize the population into action, and help establish important legislation.

THE ORGANIZATION COMES UNDER PRESSURE

Attention-grabbing stories, prestigious awards, and an ambitious direct-mail campaign all contributed to a large circulation for a liberal-progressive magazine. In 1979, three years after it was launched, the circulation of *Mother Jones* had reached 238,000. In 1980, at the height of the magazine's success, the Internal Revenue Service (IRS) began an investigation into the nonprofit status of *Mother Jones,* claiming that it owed back taxes on its advertising revenue even though it consistently ran at a deficit.

At the same time, *Mother Jones* also experienced its first major staff upheaval. During the magazine's first

four years, founders Hochschild and Klein worked as the two top editors. In 1981, however, when the magazine decided to appoint its first editor-in-chief, Klein was passed over. Deirdre English was appointed to the position and Klein resigned.

Although the IRS dropped its case against *Mother Jones* in 1983, the magazine grappled with huge legal bills. These financial worries were compounded by falling subscriptions. By 1984, the circulation of *Mother Jones* had dropped to 170,000. Two years later, it dropped further to 150,000. By comparison, however, this figure was still quite high for a political magazine: the *Nation* had a circulation of 69,000, while the *Progressive* had a circulation of 55,000.

By 1985, the magazine seemed to be making a slight comeback. Its total income was up slightly from the previous year, with ad revenues composing a significant 36 percent of its total $3 million in revenues. Annual donations totaled about $500,000. To increase the economic viability of the magazine, publication was reduced from ten to nine times a year.

APPEALING TO A BROADER AUDIENCE

At the time, the reader base for *Mother Jones* was wealthy members of the baby-boom generation, not the hippies and yippies that most advertisers assumed. As a further bid for increased circulation, in 1986 the magazine underwent a redesign to be more reader-friendly; pages were reformatted, and the magazine's overall focus shifted from advocating radical activism to providing information to its readers. "We're still going to be hard hitting, but our investigative stuff will be more subtle, more behind-the-scenes about how power works in this country," Don Hazen, publisher of *Mother Jones* at that time, said in a 1986 *Advertising Age* article. During this time, English resigned and Michael Moore took the helm. Moore remained in charge for only three issues, however, before being fired.

By 1988, circulation had climbed to 176,000. Nevertheless, the magazine wanted to further broaden its appeal by becoming more of a general-interest magazine. To this end, *Mother Jones* underwent another redesign far more radical than the last. While previous covers tended to feature people from far outside the mainstream, the new covers featured celebrities such as Susan Sarandon, Sam Donaldson, and Spike Lee. Additionally, the magazine added more lifestyle columns, including pieces about culturally sensitive travel and ethical investing. "Our goal is to make *Mother Jones* a bigger voice out there in the world and the pulse of

KEY DATES

1975: The Foundation for National Progress, the nonprofit organization that publishes *Mother Jones*, is founded.

1976: *Mother Jones* publishes its first issue.

1977: The article "Pinto Madness" breaks the story of the Ford Pinto's exploding gas tank.

1979: Circulation reaches 238,000.

1980: The Internal Revenue Service (IRS) starts an investigation into the nonprofit status of *Mother Jones*.

1981: Deirdre English becomes the magazine's first editor-in-chief.

1983: The IRS drops its investigation.

1986: Michael Moore is appointed editor-in-chief; he leaves after three issues.

1991: Circulation drops to a record low of 110,000.

1992: Jeffrey Klein, one of the magazine's founding editors, becomes editor-in-chief.

1993: *Mother Jones* becomes the first general-interest magazine to establish an Internet presence by launching *Mother Jones Interactive*.

1997: Circulation hits 145,000.

1998: Klein resigns.

2004: The circulation of *Mother Jones* reaches 236,000.

2006: Budget constraints cause the magazine to undergo a round of layoffs; Clara Jeffery and Monika Bauerlein are appointed co-editors-in-chief.

2007: *Mother Jones* opens a Washington, D.C., bureau.

2009: Circulation is steady at 230,000; the magazine is nominated for three National Magazine Awards.

popular culture," said Lila Purinton, associate publisher and advertising director, in a 1990 *Advertising Age* article.

Combined with an aggressive direct-mail campaign, *Mother Jones* saw an immediate spike in subscriptions and an increase in newsstand sales of 17 percent. Total circulation hovered at 200,000. However, the magazine did not attract major advertisers, and ads fell to a mere 10 percent of total revenues. To make *Mother Jones* more viable economically, in 1989 publication was further reduced to bimonthly.

RETURNING TO HARD-HITTING INVESTIGATIVE ROOTS

By 1991, circulation had dropped to 110,000, a historic low. Some members of the board felt that the magazine had strayed too far from its roots, and in an attempt to return to the magazine's hard-hitting investigative journalistic style, Klein was invited in 1992 to return to the magazine and become its editor-in-chief. Klein accepted and immediately began featuring topics such as the politics of breast cancer, big money in politics, and the rise of Newt Gingrich. By 1992, circulation had climbed slightly to 122,000. In an attempt to further expand its audience and reach, *Mother Jones* launched its web site in 1993, becoming the first general interest magazine to publish on the Internet.

Over the next several years, circulation climbed moderately. By 1997, it was at 140,000, and *Mother Jones* was ready to release its fourth redesign. Once again, the goal was to expand readership outside its base, represented by readers averaging 49 years of age, with a graduate degree and an annual household income of $63,600. *Mother Jones* was hoping to appeal to a younger audience, in the 18- to 34-year-old age range, which then composed only 15 percent of its subscribers. This group did not identify with the 1960s radicalism associated with the magazine. To attract them, the magazine added coverage on media and technology, as well as advertising and marketing. *Mother Jones* also hoped to attract more lucrative advertising deals, including Apple Computer, Volkswagen, and Timberland Co., whose products this group bought. At the time, most ads were for alternative products, such as folk music CDs and herbal dietary supplements.

REGAINING A SIGNIFICANT READERSHIP

Right before the relaunch in 1998, Klein resigned, creating a significant buzz in the publishing world. Controversial editorial decisions he had made during his six-year tenure—including an issue that focused on spirituality in America and another that focused on race—caused some board members to argue that he was veering too far outside of the political mission of *Mother Jones*.

With the search on to find Klein's replacement, the new design launched in September 1998. Immediately, *Mother Jones* saw an upswing in sales. "Our ad revenue is up substantially, and the last two issues of '98 were record issues for us," Jay Harris, publisher of *Mother Jones*, said in a 1999 *Print* interview. By 1999, *Mother Jones* had found Klein's replacement, Roger Cohn, who was given free rein to dramatically remake the style and content of *Mother Jones* again.

Two years later, *Mother Jones* won a National Magazine Award for General Excellence, its first in more than 20 years. At the time, circulation was moderately on the rise with readership reaching 165,000. Most significantly, the magazine's fastest-growing demographic was the college-educated 25- to 34-year-old age group, which had previously eluded it. Traffic on its web site was improving with 1.25 million page views per month.

The ongoing economic downturn had little effect on the publication. While many news organizations were reeling, *Mother Jones* was able to retain its entire staff. Moreover, from 1997 to 2000, advertising revenue had climbed by 50 percent. By 2002, circulation had climbed to 194,000. Thanks in part to the lack of popularity of the Bush administration, the first issue of 2003 sold 29,000 copies at the newsstand, a record for the magazine. Its cover featured an illustration of George W. Bush wearing a cowboy hat and riding his horse off a cliff. In 2004, circulation was almost at a record high, reaching 236,000.

BECOMING MORE MAINSTREAM

As the magazine celebrated its 30th anniversary, *Mother Jones* was struggling with budget issues. Its circulation was down 6 percent, and there was a decline both in subscriptions and in newsstand sales. Donations were down as well. Prior to the late 1990s relaunch, about 35 percent of the magazine's money came from philanthropic sources, 15 percent came from advertising, and 50 percent from subscriptions and newsstand sales. When finances ran low, board members historically had stepped in to provide additional funding, many of them dipping into their own pockets.

Such philanthropy did not happen this time around. For the first time in the magazine's history, five staff members were laid off. Right before the layoffs, the editor-in-chief, Russ Rymer, who had been hired a year before, resigned. In his place, longtime senior editors, Clara Jeffery and Monika Bauerlein, were appointed to the magazine's helm.

However, after this initial belt tightening, as news organizations across the country were shutting down foreign bureaus and reducing staff, *Mother Jones* opened a Washington, D.C., bureau and hired eight employees in 2007. "Publishing six times a year is our biggest problem and our biggest asset because everyone else tries to compete in 24/7, and it leaves a lot of gaps and a hunger for something different," said Bauerlein in a 2006 *San Francisco Chronicle* article. While the magazine focused on long-term investigative pieces, the Washington bureau had the task of breaking daily news on MotherJones.com, thus filling a coverage gap and

keeping *Mother Jones* relevant.

In 2009, as the recession deepened, income for *Mother Jones* stayed moderately steady, although advertising revenues had plummeted (dropping 23 percent in 2008), and some big donations that the magazine depended on did not come through. However, to the surprise of editors, who had expected the downturn to take a more significant toll, small donations and subscriptions held strong. Overall, revenue percentages broke down much as they had throughout the history of *Mother Jones,* with 50 percent coming from grants and donations, 15 percent from advertising, and 35 percent from circulation. The magazine avoided layoffs or reducing its ambitious projects; the Washington bureau stayed open, the web site was redesigned, and all major fund-raising initiatives remained on track. Only some salaries and expenses were trimmed to control costs.

As the news and publishing industries experienced significant changes, grappling with shrinking budgets, staff cuts, and multinational ownership, journalistic circles were increasingly interested in nonprofit, endowed journalism; *Mother Jones* sought to provide a real-life laboratory. "We've been hearing from more and more people, 'How does that work?' 'What's it like being a nonprofit?'" Bauerlein said in a 2009 *New York Times* article. Increasingly, the editors of *Mother Jones* evangelized for the nonprofit model at industry seminars as a way to prevent investigative journalism from becoming extinct.

Overall, *Mother Jones* was on an upswing, thanks in part to the leadership of the co-editors, Jeffery and Bauerlein, who kept the magazine's focus on deep investigative journalism. Web site editors also talked about continuing to build up a MotherJones.com community, providing visitors with new tools to help them organize around important issues. Surprisingly to some, *Mother Jones* even began to have an important voice in the mainstream; its Washington bureau chief, David Corn, was a regular commentator on MSNBC.

Mother Jones continued to be operated under the auspices of the nonprofit Foundation for National Progress, lead by Jay Harris. This company also oversaw the business of The Media Consortium, a network of progressive independent journalism organizations, the mission of which was to promote honesty, fairness and accuracy in American journalism.

Carrie Rothburd

PRINCIPAL DIVISIONS

Mother Jones Magazine; MotherJones.com; The Ben Bagdikian Fellowship Program; The Media Consortium.

PRINCIPAL COMPETITORS

The Nation Company L.P.; Salon Media Group Inc.; The New Republic Inc.; The Progressive Magazine.

FURTHER READING

Arango, Tim, "Mother Jones Tests Nonprofit Model in Race to Survive the Recession," *New York Times,* March 7, 2009, p. C 1.

Armstrong, David, "Mother Jones: 20 Years Old and Still Rebelling," *San Francisco Chronicle,* February 4, 1996, p B 1.

Coates, Ta-Nehisi, "Four More Years?" *Village Voice,* August 17, 2004, p. 24.

Emert, Carol, "Culture Clash/*Mother Jones* Magazine's Liberals at Odds," *San Francisco Chronicle,* August 29, 1998, p. D 1.

Hochschild, Adam, "The First 25 Years," *Mother Jones,* May/June 2001, p. 51.

Pruzan, Todd, "Mother Goosed," *Print,* July/August 1999, p. 41.

Steinberg, Brian, "*Mother Jones* Gets New Look for Walk on Madison Avenue—Magazine Hopes Makeover Will Enhance Its Appeal to Corporate Advertisers," *Wall Street Journal,* August 25, 1998, p. 1.

Walljasper, Jay, "Radical, Mama!" *Utne Reader,* November/December 1998, p. 89.

Freese and Nichols, Inc.

———————— ■ ————————

4055 International Plaza, Suite 200
Fort Worth, Texas 76109-4895
U.S.A.
Telephone: (817) 735-7300
Fax: (817) 735-7491
Web site: http://www.freese.com

Private Company
Incorporated: 1977
Employees: 411
Sales: $69.6 million (2008)
NAICS: 541330 Engineering Services

■ ■ ■

Freese and Nichols, Inc., is a privately held Fort Worth, Texas-based engineering, architectural, and environmental science services firm. Clients, located in Texas and throughout the Southwest, include municipalities, water suppliers, colleges and universities, transportation authorities, military and government agencies, and manufacturers. Freese's engineering services center around water and wastewater treatment, dam design, and hydrology, but also include structural engineering, transportation planning, and streets and highways.

On the architectural side, the firm designs a wide variety of buildings as well as offering interior design, and historical restoration and preservation services. Freese's environmental science services include environmental impact assessments, pollution prevention and permitting, and contamination assessment and

remediation. In addition, Freese offers such construction services as cost estimating, project scheduling, and value engineering, as well as management services. Branch offices are located in Austin, Corpus Christi, Dallas, Denton, Garland, Houston, Lubbock, Pearland, McKinney, San Antonio, and Tyler, Texas.

19TH-CENTURY ROOTS

Although his name is no longer associated with the firm, the founder of Freese and Nichols was John Blackstock Hawley, who was born in Red Wing, Minnesota, in 1866, the son of a doctor who died when Hawley was just 12 years old. Overcoming hardship he was able to find odd jobs to work his way through the University of Minnesota, graduating in 1887 with a degree in science and civil engineering. He then went to work as a construction engineer for the St. Paul, Minnesota, water board to help build a reservoir. After two and a half years he turned to private practice in Chicago, engaged in hydraulic and sanitary engineering as a member of the firm of Harrison & Hawley. In 1891 he accepted a post with a Chicago construction firm, McArthur Brothers Company. In that same year, he was assigned by his new employer to prepare a proposal for a new municipal water system in Fort Worth, Texas. McArthur Brothers would win the contract, and Hawley would never leave Fort Worth.

When Hawley completed his responsibilities in the building of the Fort Worth water system, he elected to make the city his home and set up a private practice, becoming the first water and sewer consulting engineer in the state. Fort Worth kept him busy designing and overseeing the construction of three nearby channel dams on the Trinity River, built to address Fort Worth's growing need for water. His efforts resulted in him being named city engineer in 1897, a post Hawley would hold for the next decade, building roads and bridges while still being allowed to take on outside work, some of which took him far from Fort Worth as his reputation grew. Hawley completed a drainage project in New Orleans, Louisiana, helped in the development of a sewage system for Havana, Cuba, and in 1906 paid a visit to Panama to advise a syndicate of contractors about bidding on the Panama Canal project.

Hawley resigned as city engineer of Fort Worth in 1907 to focus on his water supply and sewage practice. Ten years later he developed an international reputation when he was commissioned major of engineers by the U.S. Army as it became involved in World War I, providing Hawley with the opportunity to display his skill on a larger stage. Not only did Hawley receive commendations for his work from both the United States and France, he retained his wartime rank, and for the rest of his life was known as Major Hawley.

FREESE JOINS FIRM: 1922

Following the war, Hawley took on partners and associates to grow his practice. In 1921 he combined his practice with that of Edward E. Sands of Houston, so that the resulting firm of Hawley & Sands operated with branch offices in both Fort Worth and Houston. A year later Hawley hired a young man named Simon Wilke Freese, the 21-year-old son of a building contractor who despite his youth possessed years of practical construction experience. He was also a graduate of the Massachusetts Institute of Technology (MIT) after transferring there from Southern Methodist University in Dallas. Sands died from what was described as a cerebral tumor in 1923, ending the partnership of Hawley & Sands. In 1927 Hawley made Freese a partner, the young associate having more than adequately proven his

abilities and worth, resulting in the firm taking the name Hawley & Freese.

In that same year Freese made partner, Marvin C. Nichols joined the firm to serve as supervising engineer for the firm's work on dams, disposal plants, water filtration plants, paving, and other projects. Born near Fort Worth, Nichols had earned a civil engineering degree from the University of Texas at Austin in 1918. Over the next decade he worked as a county engineer while taking time off to earn a master of science degree from the University of Illinois. A year after joining Hawley & Freese, Nichols had become such a valuable addition to the firm that he too was named partner, and the firm took the name Hawley, Freese and Nichols.

HAWLEY RETIRES: 1937

Hawley retired in November 1937, and the following year the firm was reorganized as Freese and Nichols, although Hawley's name remained on his office door and he spent most days there in pursuit of his many scientific and engineering interests. Hawley died of a heart attack in 1940. By that time the United States was once again preparing for war, which was already raging in Europe and the South Pacific, and Freese and Nichols was kept busy providing engineering services for the many army and navy posts located in Texas, favored by the military because of its mild weather and secure central location. In 1941 alone the firm was involved in the design of Camp Bowie, Camp Hulen, Camp Swift, Camp Barkeley, and the Houma Blimp Base. Also during World War II, Freese became a major in the Specialists Reserve Corps of the U.S. Army. Later, as a lieutenant colonel following the surrender of Germany, he was sent to Germany to lend his expertise as the Allies studied that country's industry and economy in preparation for the postwar years.

A number of changes took place at Freese and Nichols following the war. Looking to expand into the Gulf Coast area, the firm allied itself with a Houston engineer, Nathaniel P. Turner Jr., who became managing partner of a separate Houston company, Freese, Nichols and Turner. The era also saw Nichols's sons, Robert L. and James R., join the firm. Robert began working there in 1948 and made partner in 1950, the same year that his brother James came to Freese and Nichols. James Nichols made partner in 1956. Freese's son, Lee B. Freese, joined the firm as well in 1958 after graduating from MIT like his father.

A major client during this period was the Colorado River Municipal Water District, for which Freese and Nichols, starting in 1949, served as consulting engineers, a post the firm would continue to hold into

KEY DATES

1894: John B. Hawley starts consulting engineering firm in Fort Worth, Texas.
1922: Simon Freese joins Hawley.
1927: Freese is named partner; Marvin Nichols joins firm.
1928: Nichols is named partner.
1937: Hawley retires.
1950: Robert Nichols is named partner.
1956: James Nichols is named partner.
1969: Marvin Nichols dies.
1988: Simon Freese retires.
1991: First non-engineer becomes firm's chief executive.
2000: Morrison Hydrology Engineering is acquired.

the next century. Due to the Cold War stand-off between the United States and the Soviet Union, the country invested heavily in the construction of an interstate highway system, primarily for military reasons. Freese and Nichols received its share of contracts in this effort during the 1950s, designing more than 40 bridges for what would become part of Highway 30.

In 1959 the Houston operation broke off as a separate engineering firm, becoming Turner, Collie and Braden, Inc. The Fort Worth company, in the meantime, took on another new partner, S. Gardner Endress, and became Freese, Nichols and Endress. It was also at the end of the decade that the firm began work on a series of major government water supply projects throughout Texas, spurred in large measure by a major drought that had lasted from 1950 until the spring of 1957. Especially hard hit was Fort Worth, which would invest in the construction of the largest lake engineered by the firm, the Cedar Creek Reservoir, completed in 1965. A year later work was completed on another Freese, Nichols and Endress–designed lake, the Greenbelt Reservoir, constructed for the Red River Authority. Other lake projects completed in the 1960s include the Hubbard Creek Reservoir located in the Brazos River basin; and the White River Reservoir, upriver from the Hubbard Creek Reservoir.

AUSTIN BRANCH OPENS: 1968

By the end of the 1960s the firm was also becoming involved in environmental engineering in response to the nation's growing concern over the effects of pollution on the earth, air, and water. It was hardly a difficult

transition for the firm to make. Robert Nichols, in fact, had been a member of the Water Pollution Control Federation since 1948. Because federal and state governments were passing legislation related to the environment, Freese, Nichols and Endress in 1968 opened a branch office in Austin, the Texas state capital. The firm expanded into other types of projects as well. In 1969 it won a contract to develop airport utilities and roads for the Dallas–Fort Worth International Airport. The end of the decade also brought the conclusion of an era at the firm. In April 1969 Marvin Nichols passed away. He was so well respected in the state that just hours after his death the Texas Legislature passed a resolution to name a dam and reservoir planned for northeast Texas as the Marvin C. Nichols Dam and Reservoir.

As the new decade dawned, the senior partner, Simon Freese, was into his 70s. In 1972 he celebrated his 50th year as a working engineer. He stayed on even as Endress retired in 1973 and the firm reverted to the Freese and Nichols name. The partnership came to an end when the firm was incorporated as Freese and Nichols, Inc., in 1977, with Simon Freese serving as chairman and James Nichols as president. Three years later the firm restructured its operation to keep pace with the increasing complexity of the projects the company was now taking on. Engineering and Project Management divisions were established, and within the divisions departments were formed. In 1982 Construction Services was added as another operating division. A third branch office was then opened in Arlington, Texas, in 1984 to specialize in land development and site planning services. There was no lack of projects for Freese and Nichols in the 1980s as the infrastructure of Texas was showing the effects of time, resulting in manifold repair and improvement contracts for military bases, highway bridges and viaducts, dams, and water treatment facilities. The firm also took on a number of new projects throughout the state.

FIRST NON-ENGINEER NAMED CEO: 1991

Simon Freese relinquished the chairmanship to 65-year-old James Nichols in 1988, and 62-year-old Robert Nichols became president of the firm. Two years later Simon Freese died at the age of 89. Given that the Nichols brothers were both at or beyond retirement age, the question of the firm's future direction took on greater significance. There were only a limited number of Texas reservoir projects in the planning stages and the future funding of any was far from certain. Not only did the firm need a fresh sense of direction, the brothers decided that the management ranks needed to be reorganized to position Freese and Nichols for continued success.

In 1989 the firm for the first time appointed two nonprincipals to the board of directors in an advisory capacity to provide an outside perspective. In 1991 one of those board members, Robert L. Herschert, was tapped to take over as president and chief executive officer, becoming the first non-engineer to lead the firm. Not only did Herschert possess strong management skills, he had experience working with engineers, having served as city manager of Fort Worth from 1978 to 1984 and previous stints as city manager of Camden, Arkansas, and assistant city manager of Fairborn, Ohio, and Kansas City, Missouri.

Under Herschert's direction, Freese and Nichols conducted a thorough self-assessment, resulting in some business areas on which the firm elected to focus, including dam evaluation and repair, waste treatment, and aviation. One example of these points of emphasis coming together was at the Fort Worth Alliance Airport where the firm was able to take advantage of its experience in water treatment and aviation to land a major contract designing a $15 million industrial wastewater-treatment plant for American Airlines.

Freese and Nichols also made use of its reputation in designing municipal sewage plants to become involved in the hazardous-waste field, serving as a consultant on spills and remediation. Another significant change that took place under Herschert came in 1993 when for the first time in its history, Freese and Nichols maintained its headquarters outside downtown Fort Worth, taking up space in the International Plaza building in southwest Fort Worth, the change made necessary by the firm's strong growth in recent years.

FREESE AND NICHOLS TURNS 100

Freese and Nichols celebrated its 100th anniversary in 1994. Under its new structure and management team, the firm looked to a second century of building upon a reputation of excellence while expanding to new markets and increasing its range of services. Freese and Nichols's position in the Texas water planning field remained strong. In 1998 the firm was contracted to provide half of the state's 16 regions with water planning services under Senate Bill I. The work of Freese and Nichols was also recognized by various parties. In 1996 the firm received a national American Society of Civil Engineers' Outstanding Civil Engineering Achievement Award nomination, and in that same year won the Outstanding Civil Engineering Award from state of Texas for the O.H. Ivie Project. Always enjoying an excellent work environment, Freese and Nichols in 1997 was honored with the Tarrant Enterprise Award for Employee Motivation and Retention. The firm also received local recognition. In 1999 it received the Mayor's Export Award for its success in exporting its services.

Freese and Nichols continued to expand the scope of its work in the new century. In 2000 it was part of a consulting team to win a contract for a major automated people mover project at the Dallas–Fort Worth International Airport. In that same year, the firm merged with the Arlington, Texas-based firm Morrison Hydrology Engineering, a company with more than 30 years of experience in the hydraulic and hydrologic field. To take full advantage of its reputation to grow revenues, Freese and Nichols opened a score of offices across Texas in the early 2000s. According to the *Dallas Morning News,* the firm posted sales of $43.2 million in 2005, garnering it No. 169 on the newspaper's list of the Top 200 private firms in the Dallas–Fort Worth area. Even as Freese and Nichols sought to grow new practice areas, it continued to provide its traditional water services in its home territory, revisiting problems with which John Hawley was well familiar. In 2007, for example, Freese and Nichols received a new contract to do work on the Trinity River. Although the firm would not outlive the waters of Texas, it would undoubtedly receive more than its share of the work in harnessing and cleaning those waters in the years to come.

Ed Dinger

PRINCIPAL DIVISIONS

Engineering; Architecture; Environmental Science.

PRINCIPAL COMPETITORS

AECOM Technology Corporation; LopezGarcia Group Inc.; The PBSJ Corporation.

FURTHER READING

Baker, Max B., "$1.7 Million OK'd for Team Creating Trinity Blueprint," *Fort Worth Star-Telegram,* September 6, 2007, p. B4.

Freese, Simon W., D. L. Sizemore, and Joe Pickle, *A Century in the Works,* Austin: Texas A&M Press, 1994, 456 p.

Leach, Mark S., "Freese and Nichols Leaving Downtown," *Fort Worth Star Telegram,* October 29, 1992, p. 1.

Mason, Todd, "Freese and Nichols Pushing to New Heights Under New Management," *Fort Worth Star-Telegram,* November 29, 1992, p. 1.

Piller, Dan, "Freese and Nichols Greets Future with New Offices, Larger Vistas in Engineering," *Fort Worth Star-Telegram,* April 4, 1994, p. 14.

GL Events S.A.

BP 40, Route d'Irigny
Zone Industrielle Nord
Brignais, F-69530
France
Telephone: (33 04) 72 31 54 54
Fax: (33 04) 72 31 54 99
Web site: http://www.gl-events.com

Public Company
Incorporated: 1978 as Polygone
Employees: 2,738
Sales: EUR 605.7 million ($814.9 million) (2008)
Stock Exchanges: Euronext Paris
Ticker Symbol: GLTN.PA
NAICS: 713990 All Other Amusement and Recreation
Industries

■ ■ ■

GL Events S.A. is a major integrated player in the global events services industry. Based in the greater Lyon community of Brignais, France, GL Events operates across the full range of events services, including venue management and operation, the rental, supply and installation of fixtures and equipment, and the organization of major trade shows, fairs, exhibitions, congresses, conventions, and related events. GL Events operates through three primary divisions: Organization, Venues, and Services.

The group's Events Organization division holds a portfolio of 200 proprietary trade fairs and other events, in both the business-to-business and business-to-consumer categories worldwide. These include events such as the Habitat and Tradexpo Paris salons, the Lyon International Fair, the Bologna Motor Show in Italy, the Biennial International Book Fair in Brazil, and Construma in Hungary. In total, the group provided organizational services to more than 2,600 events throughout the world in 2008. The Venue Management division operates 29 major venues in France and elsewhere around the world. Among the sites managed by GL Events are Eurexpo in Lyon; the Parc Floral in Paris; the CCIB Convention Center in Barcelona, Spain; Hungexpo in Budapest, Hungary; Square in Brussels; Lingotto Fiere in Turin, Italy; the Battersea Evolution in London; Rio Centro in Rio de Janeiro; the Pudong Expo in Shanghai, China; and La Venue, in New York.

The group's Events Services division spans the full range of events services from the design phase through equipment and fixture rental, information technology (IT) management, and installation. GL Events is listed on the Euronext Paris Stock Exchange. Founder Olivier Ginon remains the company's president. Through his control of holding company Polygone SA, Ginon also controls the majority of GL Events. In 2008 the company posted revenues of EUR 605.7 million ($814.9 million).

ORIGINS IN LYON

GL Events was founded in 1978 by Olivier Ginon, who abandoned his law studies to form a company providing events services in the French city of Lyon. Joining Ginon in the business were three school friends, Olivier Roux, Jacques Danger, and Gille Gouédard-Comte. The

COMPANY PERSPECTIVES

As a publicly traded company, GL events has an obligation to meet its CSR commitments. Two major priorities have been defined by Group Human resources. First, successfully attract, motivate and retain talent. In other words, provide all employees opportunities to evolve and develop their expertise and skills. Secondly, fight against all forms of discrimination: age, gender, religion ... and promote the integration of population segments in difficulty (young jobseekers without schooling, the long-term unemployed ...). The notion of social progress however does not only concern Group employees. It also applies to the suppliers with which GL events shares its vision and values to promote and improve the application of the principles of ethical conduct. CSR (Corporate Social Responsibility) is also deployed outside the scope of the company's business operations, and includes a social dimension that is frequently very important. Since its creation, GL events has consistently focused on respecting its environment by notably working in collaboration with associations or individuals to promote a wide range of initiatives.

partners named their business Polygone Services. By 1981 the young company had completed its first major event, the installation of a computer show in Lyon's Part-Dieu shopping center.

Led by Ginon, Polygone Services grew quickly while focusing on providing installation services: setting up stands, tents, and related fixtures required for exhibitions, trade shows, conferences, and similar events. By 1984 the company was operating on a national level, providing installation services for a number of major exhibitions and trade shows. Among the company's early clients were such trade show organizations as Europack, Infora, and Première Vision.

The company was not without its setbacks, however. In the summer of 1988, a fire broke out in the company's warehouse, destroying all of the materials and equipment that had been prepared for the events of the coming fall season. Ginon spent the month of August visiting suppliers across Europe and succeeded in gathering the supplies needed to fulfill the company's events contracts. By the end of the 1980s, Polygone

Services had grown into the leading French provider of events installation services.

Ginon then prepared to lead the group to the next level. In 1989 the company reached an agreement to merge with Groupe Cré-Rossi, led by Hubert-Jean Vial. That company held the leading European spot as a provider of rental furniture, fixtures, floor covering, and other equipment and accessories required by events operations. The merged group took on a new name, Générale Location. Polygone then became a holding company, with a 64 percent stake in Générale Location, while Vial retained 36 percent of the group.

A PERIOD OF GROWTH

Générale Location had by this time achieved the scale it needed to become an important partner for France's major events organizers. The company signed on a new series of important clients, including Paris Exhibition Committee, Blenheim/Miller, and CEP Communication. By 1990, Générale Location had completed its first acquisition, buying up the assets of rival Chenel, which had run into financial difficulties. That company nevertheless remained a prominent player in the events installation market, with a specialty in large-scale trade shows, such as the Foire de Paris. Chenel added more than FRF 136 million in revenues to Générale Location's sales, which then topped FRF 553 million (approximately $100 million). Also in 1990, Générale Location made its first move outside of France, acquiring Cologne, Germany-based furniture rental company EMP GmbH.

Back in France, the company followed the Chenel purchase with the 1992 takeover of the Vachon Group, a company that specialized in renting furniture, props, and antiques, such as automobiles and other items, for the film, television, advertising, photography, and events markets. In 1993 the company took over Pichot Exposition, which provided fitting services for exhibitions. Pichot was then merged with Chenel. The combination of the two companies added nearly FRF 130 million to Générale Location's total revenues.

Générale Location continued to supply its services exclusively to third-party events producers into the mid-1990s. In 1995, however, the company began positioning itself as an events organizer as well. The company claimed two major projects that year, the European Summit in Cannes, and the Summit of French-Speaking Heads of State in the Republic of Benin in Western Africa.

The company also reinforced its services business at the middle of the decade, creating a new subsidiary, GL Image, in 1996. This company specialized in servicing

KEY DATES

1978: Olivier Ginon and partners found Polygone Services to provide event installation services.
1981: The company completes its first major event.
1989: Polygone merges with Groupe Cré-Rossi, becoming Générale Location.
1995: Générale Location launches a new division providing event organization services.
1998: Générale Location goes public on the Paris Stock Exchange's Secondary Market and then enters the venue management sector.
2003: The company changes its name to GL Events.
2009: GL Events reorganizes its operations into three divisions.

major client accounts by providing high-end exhibition stands. Also in 1996, Polygone bought out Vial's stake in Générale Location, giving Polygone control of 99.99 percent of Générale Location's shares.

More acquisitions followed through the end of the decade. In 1997 the company acquired Decorama, a company that provided stands, signage, and fittings for institutions, corporations, and museums. The company also made a new move into the international market, setting up GL Middle East in Dubai and acquiring that country's Eastern Exhibition Services Ltd. The acquisition marked the company's first international events services subsidiary.

In France, the company's position as a market leader was confirmed when it was named the official provider of events services for the 1998 World Cup in Paris. The company then completed a new acquisition to boost its service offerings, buying Profile, a company that specialized in providing hosts and hostesses and interpreters. By the end of 1997, Générale Location's sales neared FRF 750 million (approximately $125 million).

GOING PUBLIC

Générale Location geared up for more growth toward the dawn of the new century. In 1998 the company went public, listing its shares on the Paris Stock Exchange's Secondary Market. By then, the company had completed a new acquisition, of Ranno Enterprise, boosting its exhibition installation services. The purchase of Ranno not only added FRF 60 million to

the group's annual sales, it also marked a new step toward the company's goal of building a fully national network. Générale Location had also begun to expand its international presence. In 1999 the company teamed up with a local partner to launch operations in Hong Kong. The company's share of the venture, GL Furniture Asia, stood at 60 percent.

The company's public offering in 1998 also enabled the company to prepare to add the third element of its organizational strategy, venue management. In this way, the company intended to create a fully integrated events operation, capable of offering a full range of services from event fittings to the hosting of the events themselves. The effort got off to a strong start, as Générale Location acquired a 51 percent stake in Secil, which managed the Lyon Convention Center.

The company experienced a setback in 1999, however, when its attempt to take over Paris Expo, a publicly listed company, was outbid by Parisian property group Unibail. Générale Location, which had built up a 23.52 percent stake in Paris Expo, ultimately agreed to sell its stake to Unibail in 2000, realizing a profit of some FRF 150 million on the deal.

Générale Location instead hit the acquisition trail again, buying Hong Kong's Team Legend and Belgium's Fair Line in 2000. The company also picked up three French companies that year. At the same time, the company's events organization division booked a number of high-profile events, including the Summit for the European Heads of State. The company's emergence as a global player was highlighted especially when it received the contract to provide services to the Sydney Olympic Games.

BECOMING GL EVENTS

The company sales continued to increase steadily through this period, topping EUR 235 million ($200 million) in 2001. Générale Location also continued its international expansion, buying two U.K. companies, Owen Brown and Package Organisation, that year. The following year, the company acquired Toulouse Expo, which held the management contract for the Toulouse Exhibition Center. That purchase was soon followed by the award of the management concession for the Pierre Baudis Convention Center, also in Toulouse. By 2003, the company's venue portfolio expanded with the additions of Floral Park in Paris and the Grande Halle d'Auvergne. In October of the year, in recognition of the group's transformation into a multifaceted, internationally operating company, Générale Location changed its name to GL Events.

New acquisitions helped reinforce the group's operations in 2004. The company bought Market Place, a Paris-based provider of event organization and communication services. The company also acquired Temp-A-Store in the United Kingdom, a specialist in leasing and sales of temporary structures founded in 1972. Through 2005 GL Events continued to strengthen its venue management wing, acquiring a majority stake in Italy's Padua Exhibition Center, and then purchasing Chorus, which managed a small exhibition center in Vannes, France. The company also entered Hungary, winning its bid to acquire Hungexpo in partnership with that country's Trigranit group.

GL Events won the concession for the Riocentro Convention Center in Rio de Janeiro in 2006. The company also entered the Chinese market that year, setting up an office in Shanghai and winning the concession for the city's Pudong Expo. In 2007 the company boosted its Italian presence, acquiring the Turin Lingotto Fiere Exhibition Center. The company also acquired Italy's leading events services group that year, Promotor International.

By 2009 the venue management portfolio of GL Events had reached 29 major venues worldwide. In recognition of the importance of these operations, GL Events restructured into three main divisions, Events Organization, Venue Management, and Events Services. At just 50 years of age, Olivier Ginon stood at the head of one of the world's leading events services companies, with operations around the world and annual revenues of more than EUR 600 million ($800 million).

M. L. Cohen

PRINCIPAL SUBSIDIARIES

Action Développement; GL Events Audiovisual; GL Events Cité Centre de Congrès Lyon; CCIB Catering (Spain); Générale Location Canada; Générale Location Espana; GL Events Asia (Hong Kong); GL Events Algérie; GL Events Belgium; GL Events China; GL Events Hong Kong; GL Events Hungaria Rt; GL Events Portugal; GL Events Suisse; GL Events USA; GL Middle East (Dubai); Hungexpo (Hungary); Sodes Inc. (U.S.A.).

PRINCIPAL DIVISIONS

Organization; Venues; Services.

PRINCIPAL COMPETITORS

La Française des Jeux S.A.; Club Mediterranee S.A.; Euro Disney S.C.A.; Compagnie des Alpes S.A.; Rodriguez Group S.A.; NRJ Group S.A.; Paris Saint Germain Football S.A.; Compagnie du Mont-Blanc S.A.

FURTHER READING

Besses-Boumard, Pascale, "Générale Location Veut Créer avec Paris Expo un Leader en Europe," *Les Echos,* January 2000, p. 15.

Dedieu, Franck, "Les 15 Patrons les Plus Influents," *L'Expansion,* September 1, 2005.

"French GL Events Agrees to Buy Alice Evenements," *ADP News France,* July 13, 2009.

"French Organizer GL Events Posted Revenues of EUR 294 Million in the First Half of 2008," *Tradeshow Week,* September 1, 2008, p. 4.

"GL Events Ajoute à Son Portefeuille Six Salons Industriels," *CercleFinance,* February 8, 2008.

"GL Events in France Has Acquired Temp-a-Store, a UK Company that Sells and Rents Temporary Structures for Storage and Warehousing," *European Rental News,* September 2004, p. 11.

"GL Events' New Division Offers Interiors Work," *Marketing Event,* January 23, 2006, p. 5.

"GL Events: Polygone Passe sous 2/3 Droits de Vote," *CercleFinance,* October 18, 2007.

"GL Events Reçoit la Concession de l'Arena à Rio de Janeiro," *CercleFinance,* December 4, 2007.

"GL Events to Invest EUR 20m in Hungexpo by 2009," *Hungarian News Agency,* July 6, 2005.

"GL Events Veut Investir dans la Restauration," *Reuters,* December 11, 2008.

Lafay, Denis, "Portrait Olivier Ginon," *Acteurs de l'Economie,* June 2008.

"NEC's French Link-up Hailed as 'Milestone,'" *Marketing Event,* February 14, 2007, p. 6.

"Olivier Ginon, Président de GL Events, Distingué en Rhône-Alpes," *Strategies,* January 28, 2008.

Great Dane L.P.

602 West Lathrop Avenue
Savannah, Georgia 31415
U.S.A.
Telephone: (912) 232-4471
Fax: (912) 944-2497
Web site: http://www.greatdanetrailers.com

Private Company
Incorporated: 1931 as The Steel Products Company
Employees: 3,892
Sales: $422.8 million (2008 est.)
NAICS: 336212 Truck Trailer Manufacturing

■ ■ ■

Great Dane L. P. is one of North America's largest truck trailer manufacturers. The Savannah, Georgia-based private company offers refrigerated trailers, a category Great Dane pioneered, including the Multi-Temp line that provides three separate temperature-controlled compartments and an ambient section to accommodate a variety of hauls. Dry freight trailers include Classic stainless steel and aluminum trailers, the damage resistant P-Series, the SSL trailer that employs a single-sided laminate interior lining, and the Composite line that features composite panel technology. Great Dane also offers semi-insulated trailers, platform trailers for hauling machinery and steel, deep-drop furniture vans, shallow-drop electronic vans, and open top trailers for hauling produce. Production facilities are located in Brazil, Indiana; Danville, Pennsylvania; Greenville, Mississippi; Huntsville, Tennessee; Jonesboro, Arkansas; Ke-

wanee, Illinois; Terre Haute, Indiana; and Wayne, Nebraska. Great Dane is owned by CC Industries, Inc., a Chicago-based investment group controlled by Henry Crown and Company.

ORIGINS IN STEEL FABRICATION

Great Dane traces its history to the 1900 formation of Savannah Blowpipe Company in Savannah, Georgia, which focused on dust and chip collecting equipment used in sawmills, planing mills, and furniture plants. The company soon began fabricating light structural steel and steel plant products, developing an expertise that would be used to produce truck trailers as the automotive age evolved. In 1930 Savannah Blowpipe manufactured its first trailer. A year later the company changed its name to something more encompassing than Savannah Blowpipe, incorporating as The Steel Products Company.

The company decided to focus on truck trailers, which was to be a field destined for steady growth as the United States developed a national highway system. Leading the design effort was the company's Greenville, South Carolina, plant, which boasted an established trailer man, his name forgotten, who began applying the Great Dane name to the Steel Products trailers. Apparently he had become familiar with the breed as work dogs in Belgium, where they were renowned for their strength and stamina, qualities that he felt were also appropriate to truck trailers. The name stuck, leading to the evolution of a brand that would overshadow the more mundane Steel Products name. Also of note in the 1930s, Chris Hammond, Jr., joined the company. He

COMPANY PERSPECTIVES

Great Dane Trailers will provide equipment and service to the transportation industry. We will fully satisfy our customers by setting the standard for quality, innovation and leadership. We will be the preferred supplier in our industry by delivering exceptional value to our customers. We will generate a return on investment that is sufficient to assure continuous improvement in quality and market growth as well as professional opportunities and financial security for our employees.

would eventually become president and chairman of the board and be succeeded by his son, Chris "Kit" Hammond III.

REFRIGERATED TRAILER DEVELOPMENT

Steel Products proved to be proficient in recognizing and meeting the needs of new trends and changing regulations. With the introduction of highway weight laws, the company turned to high-tensile steel to produce lighter tank and van trailers, introduced in 1938. The country was soon involved in World War II and Steel Products played its part by manufacturing about 12,000 trailers for military use. In the early 1940s Steel Products also turned its attention to the development of refrigerated trailers, which became increasingly necessary as haulers carried perishable products greater distances. The company's first effort combined a wet ice bunker containing a 300-pound block of ice and a fan powered from outside the van to cool produce inside. It was not until 1947 that Steel Products introduced its first mechanically refrigerated trailers. Also in the late 1940s the company introduced an aluminum van trailer, resulting in a refrigerated aluminum trailer that in the 1950s became extremely popular for hauling Florida produce.

By the mid-1950s Steel Products was operating in 18 states through 31 sales offices. In 1958 the company embraced it recognizable brand name more fully, renaming itself Great Dane Trailers, Inc. Moreover, the company began to eschew all structural steel products, devoting itself solely to aluminum construction. As the 1950s came to a close, Great Dane redesigned all of it van and tank trailers to make use of lightweight aluminum, and as customers began to accept the aluminum products the company was able to complete its withdrawal from structural steel construction.

In the 1960s Great Dane used its expertise in building van and tank trailers to become involved in the emerging intermodal freight hauling market, as shippers sought to achieve efficiencies by making use of containers that could be hauled by ship, train, and truck without the delay of unnecessary loading and unloading. Great Dane sold its first piggyback trailer that could be hauled by train in 1961. Two years later Great Dane became further involved in the intermodal field when it won its first maritime container order.

EXPANSION PROGRAM

By the mid-1960s Great Dane was well established in the eastern half of the United States, maintaining sales operations in 24 states. Demand for trailers was strong, spurred by the development of a vast interstate highway system. The government in the 1950s and 1960s, during the heart of the Cold War with the Soviet Union, had determined such a system was a vital defense consideration, but it also benefited long distance haulers. To keep pace, Great Dane initiated a $2 million expansion program in 1966 to double trailer production. A second manufacturing plant was added in Memphis, Tennessee, in 1972 through the acquisition of Arrow Trailers. This facility would eventually become the home for all of Great Dane's platform trailer construction. In 1975 the Brazil, Indiana, manufacturing facility was opened as well, and three years later a refrigerated trailer production line was added to almost double the plant's production capacity.

The extra capacity was put to good use in the 1980s when Great Dane enjoyed strong growth. Not only did the company continue to invest in trailer technology; it also added to its capabilities through external means. In 1988 Great Dane acquired the Wayne, Nebraska, plant of Timpte Trailers, which two years earlier had begun to build trailers for Great Dane. Great Dane also acquired Timpte's refrigerated trailer division, including the Super Seal refrigerated trailer line. As a result, Great Dane then offered the industry's broadest range of refrigerated trailers.

Following a recession in the early 1990s, Great Dane resumed expansion. A new dry van plant opened in Terre Haute, Indiana, in 1995 and an adjacent parts distribution center was added as well. By this time the parent company, Great Dane Holdings Inc., was generating more than $1 billion in annual sales through 17 company-owned branches and 51 independent dealers, as well as about two dozen parts-only dealers. Also contributing to the balance sheet was Checker Motors, a

KEY DATES

1900: Savannah Blowpipe Company is founded.
1930: Savannah Blowpipe manufactures its first truck trailer.
1931: The company is incorporated as The Steel Products Company.
1947: Steel Products introduces its first mechanically refrigerated trailers.
1958: The Steel Products Company is renamed Great Dane Trailers, Inc.
1961: Great Dane sells its first piggyback trailer that could be hauled by train.
1972: Manufacturing plant in Memphis, Tennessee, is added through the acquisition of Arrow Trailers.
1975: Brazil, Indiana, plant opens.
1997: Great Dane Trailers is sold and merged with Pines Trailers to create Great Dane Limited Partnership.
2002: Two manufacturing plants are acquired from Strick Trailer Corporation.
2005: Kit Hammond retires as president.
2009: The company's original plant in Savannah is closed.

sheet-metal stamping company serving the North American automotive industry.

SALE AND MERGER

Great Dane Holdings was put up for sale in the summer of 1996. Later in the year the South Charleston Stamping and Manufacturing plant in West Virginia was sold for $165 million to United Kingdom conglomerate The Mayflower Corporation. What remained of Great Dane Holdings was then bought by Stamford Capitol Group, a private investment group, in mid-December. A short time later, in early 1997, Stamford sold Great Dane Trailers Inc. to CC Industries of Chicago, which simultaneously arranged to merge Great Dane with another trailer manufacturer, family-owned Pines Trailer Limited Partnership. Founded in Chicago in 1950, Pines Trailer operated production plants in Kewanee, Illinois, and Greenville, Mississippi, the latter in operation since 1970 and purchased in 1990. The combined company, under the leadership of Chief Executive Officer C. F. "Kit" Hammond in Savannah, took the name Great Dane Limited Partnership and comprised two divisions, Great Dane Trailers and Pines Trailers. Great

Dane was clearly the better-known brand and in time the operations were all organized under the Great Dane name.

In the late 1990s Great Dane integrated its operations and upgraded its branch locations in time for its 100th anniversary. The company also looked to the future, redesigning its refrigerated trailers and platform trailers, and introducing a pair of new freight van trailers. The SSL dry freight van was unveiled in 2002, boasting steel-lined interior walls to provide greater cargo protection. Great Dane was also soon in the market for acquisitions to spur further growth. In early 2002 Great Dane bought a pair of manufacturing plants, located in Danville, Pennsylvania, and Abbeville, South Carolina, from Strick Trailer Corporation. Up until this time, Great Dane's reach was mostly limited to the Southeast and Midwest. The new plants opened up markets in the Northeast and Canada. In 2004 Great Dane acquired a plant in Huntsville, Tennessee, from Wabash National Corporation. After some upgrades it opened a year later, focusing on flatbed production.

Great Dane also continued to build up its service capabilities during this time. The new Charlotte, North Carolina, branch that opened in the summer of 2003 included a high-tech paint booth, an expanded parts warehouse, and additional service bays to become the prototype for future Great Dane branch locations, capable of selling new and used trailers and providing a complete range of services. Soon following in this vein were branch locations in Lancaster, Pennsylvania, and Dallas, Texas.

KIT HAMMOND RETIRES

In 2004 Kit Hammond prepared to turn over day-to-day responsibilities. He relinquished the presidency and retired at the end of 2005. The Hammond family did not sever its ties to Great Dane, however. Chris Hammond IV was employed by the company, serving as vice-president of dealer sales. Despite the changes in the management ranks, research and development efforts continued to keep Great Dane in the vanguard of trailer innovation. In 2004 and 2005 the company unveiled five new products. They included three new trailers and a pair of liner innovations. The trailers included the Freedom line of flatbeds; the Super LT refrigerated trailer, designed specifically for the eastern United States and Canadian long-haul markets; and the i-Van versatile semi-insulated freight van that was ideally suited for such temperature-sensitive loads as chemicals and candy.

To accommodate the manufacturing needs of the i-Van, the Brazil, Indiana, plant was retooled to include the necessary special foam presses and modular assembly needs. The Brazil plant also manufactured the Super LT van, as did the Savannah plant. The new Huntsville plant was upgraded to produce the Freedom line as well as other flatbed trailers. The first of the interior products, PunctureGuard, featured a thermoplastic material that resisted splintering and other damage often caused by forklift loading and unloading. It was soon followed by ThermoGuard, a glass-reinforced thermoplastic that included an additional layer to protect a refrigerated trailer's insulation barrier.

In addition to the introduction of new materials, Great Dane upgraded the onboard communication capabilities of its trailers to add further value to trucking companies. At the heart of the systems was the Meritor WABCO Enhanced Central Easy-Stop Trailer ABS ECU, employing InfoLink to provide communications between tractor-trailers and trucking command centers to provide such information as malfunction status, diagnostics, trailer mileage, vehicle identification number, and trailer suspension weight. The system could also monitor brake lining wear, trailer air reservoir supply pressure, trailer suspension weight, and the activation of backup lights, alarms, and steer axle lockouts.

Another watershed moment for Great Dane arrived in early 2009 when the company's original plant in Savannah was closed, eliminating 270 jobs. The facility was no longer an efficient plant site. Great Dane began searching for another site to build a new plant, but indicated a desire to retain its corporate offices in Savannah, including accounting, marketing, customer service, a research and development lab, and engineering department. Until a new plant could be built, the Savannah's plant production of refrigerated trailers was split between the Wayne and Brazil plants. While the plant closing may have represented the passing of an era, there was every reason to expect that Great Dane trailers would continue to enjoy strong sales for many years to come.

Ed Dinger

PRINCIPAL SUBSIDIARIES

Great Dane Trailers, Inc.

PRINCIPAL COMPETITORS

Lufkin Industries, Inc.; Utility Trailer Manufacturing Company; Wabash National Corporation.

FURTHER READING

Cochran, Charles, "Great Dane's Savannah President Steps Down," *Savannah Morning News,* January 28, 2004, p. 5C.

"Great Dane Introduces New Refrigerated Trailer," *Fleet Equipment,* June 2004, p. 42.

"Great Dane Trailers Closes Savannah Plant," *Fleet Equipment,* December 2008, p. 18.

"Great Dane Trailers to Stop Manufacturing in Savannah," *Trailer/Body Builders,* November 11, 2008.

Solomon, Loyall, "Trailer Manufacturers Hitch Up," *Augusta (Ga.) Chronicle,* January 3, 1997, p. C10.

Weber, Rick, "Great Dane Closes Savannah Plant, Takes a Look Back at Rich History of Trailer Production," *Trailer/Body Builders,* February 1, 2009.

Green Mountain Coffee Roasters, Inc.

33 Coffee Lane
Waterbury, Vermont 05676-1529
U.S.A.
Telephone: (802) 244-5421
Toll Free: (888) 879-4627
Fax: (802) 244-5436
Web site: http://www.greenmountaincoffee.com

Public Company
Incorporated: 1981
Employees: 1,220
Sales: $500.3 million (2008)
Stock Exchanges: NASDAQ
Ticker Symbol: GMCR
NAICS: 311920 Coffee and Tea Manufacturing

■ ■ ■

Green Mountain Coffee Roasters, Inc., operates as a leader in the specialty coffee industry, buying coffee beans from over 60 countries in Asia, Africa, and South America. The company sells over 100 varieties of whole bean and ground coffees as well as hot cocoa, teas, Keurig single-cup brewers, and K-cup single-portion packs. The company's products can be found online and in a variety of retail outlets including Wal-Mart stores throughout the United States and Canada. Green Mountain's Specialty Coffee Business Unit oversees the activities of Green Mountain Coffee, which includes the Green Mountain, Newman's Own Organics, and the Tully's Coffee brands. Its Keurig Business Unit manufactures single-cup brewing systems used in offices, homes, and hotels. Green Mountain has experienced significant growth since its purchase of Keurig Inc. in 2006. Sales rose from $225.3 million in 2006 to over $500 million in 2008. The company shipped 24.6 million pounds of coffee in 2006; it sold over 32 million pounds of coffee, tea, and hot cocoa and shipped over one billion K-cups in 2008.

HAZY ORIGINS

In 1971 Green Mountain's founder Robert Stiller had helped launch E-Z Wider, a maker of rolling papers. E-Z Wider offered smokers wider papers, so they did not have to lick and splice two papers together to make bigger joints. As the high-flying days of the 1970s came to a close, Stiller and his partner Burton Rubin sold the company to English tobacconist Rizla for $6.2 million. Then, one day while lounging at a Vermont ski resort, Stiller found a cup of coffee so good that he bought the company. At the time, Green Mountain was a small specialty store, begun in 1981, which sold to the public and a few restaurants. Stiller bought out the owners, prospective snowbirds, for $200,000. The couple went to Florida to start another coffee business.

The specialty coffee industry had been growing at 7 percent to 10 percent a year since the late 1960s. Nevertheless, Stiller discovered that competition was keener in coffee than in cigarette papers. Green Mountain floundered for four years, competing at the highest end of the market: prized Arabica beans (as opposed to the lower-quality Robusta variety). Although he turned a profit on retail sales, Stiller had a hard time persuading restaurants to pay premium prices. Eventu-

We create the ultimate coffee experience in every life we touch from tree to cup—transforming the way the world understands business.

ally, however, his company's coffee would be served at some of the Northeast's finest restaurants.

Free samples, distributed through such charitable organizations as the Kiwanis club, helped spark demand. The company was making money by 1985. Advertising in gourmet magazines helped build a mail-order business. Promotions continued with high-end products such as Muesli cereal. Stiller persuaded a doubtful convenience store owner to let him sell coffee there, competing with Dunkin' Donuts across the street. Attention to details not only kept the sales flowing, it increased traffic to the gas station. Stiller took this to the next level, placing Green Mountain coffee in Mobil Corporation's 1,000 stores nationwide. Green Mountain similarly segued an opportunity to sell cups of fresh coffee at a supermarket chain into shelf placement.

EMPHASIS ON THE ENVIRONMENT

In 1989 Green Mountain Coffee Roasters employees formed an environmental committee to steer it on conservation issues. The company cut its refuse in half through a recycling program and switched to oxygen-whitened filters, deemed less hazardous than standard bleached filters. It began selling these Green Mountain Earth Friendly Filters to the public soon after. In 1990 Green Mountain introduced Rain Forest Nut–flavored coffee to sponsor the cause of rain forest preservation. It divided 10 percent of net profits between Conservation International and The Rainforest Alliance.

Stiller focused on streamlining operations and applying contemporary principles of quality manufacturing. In 1991 he invested in a $30,000 computerized roaster at the company's store in Winooski, Vermont. The company began a database management program to keep beans moving in clients' stores. In the fiscal year 1991, Green Mountain boasted seven retail outlets, plus 1,000 wholesale clients. Sales were $11 million, producing profits of $200,000.

Serving 2,400 wholesale accounts, Green Mountain had sales of about $10 million in 1993. The holding company Green Mountain Coffee, Inc., was formed and

an initial public offering was completed in September. Green Mountain opened its ninth store, in Waterbury, Vermont, in December. It was selling 80 varieties of coffee, roasting 25 different types of Arabica beans.

A link-up with a large New England foodservice distributor helped solidify Green Mountain's position among restaurants and institutions. Jordan's Food Corporation, based in Maine, reported that it had been fielding customer requests for the brand. Wholesale continued to account for most of Green Mountain's business, although its retail chain then operated in Vermont, New Hampshire, Maine, Connecticut, and upstate New York.

Green Mountain continued to tout its environmental consciousness. In 1994 it joined the national Buy Recycled! Alliance. Aside from using paper with recycled content for its letterhead and invoices, the company reduced its roasting emissions. Its Stewardship line of coffee proclaimed "respect for the land and workers." These beans came from specially inspected farms in Mexico, Hawaii, Peru, Guatemala, and Sumatra. Locally, the company sponsored "Dr. Trash," who lectured children about environmental responsibility. Another interesting mascot was "The Green Mountain Coffee Buster," who became something of a celebrity for serving rush hour Boston commuters five-second cups of coffee. The company also gave away its bean chaff and burlap bags to gardeners.

Social causes were supported as well. Apart from standard charities such as the United Way, Salvation Army, and Red Cross, Coffee Kids Conservation International worked to improve living conditions for children in coffee-producing areas. Customers were invited to contribute through coin drops and the sale of gift boxes.

EXPORTING TO CANADA AND TAIWAN

Green Mountain began exporting to Canada and Taiwan in 1994. This brought in revenues of $80,000 the first year. Frosts in Brazil, where Green Mountain did not buy coffee, sent the worldwide price of coffee up, prompting the company to raise its own prices by 30 percent. Sales for 1994 were about $22 million; the company lost nearly $3 million. The next year produced an income of $179,000 on sales of $34 million. Green Mountain Coffee Roasters became the launch customer for sophisticated, Windows-based roasting control software developed by Praxis Werke, Inc., in New Jersey. In addition to providing unprecedented consistency, the software also promised reduced costs and greater safety.

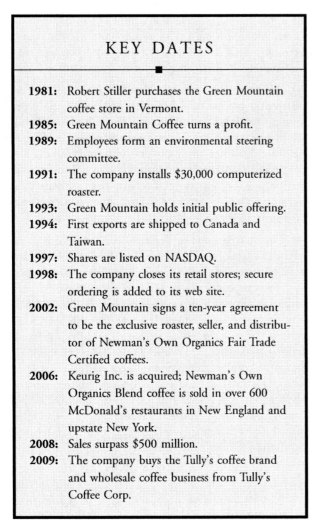

KEY DATES

1981: Robert Stiller purchases the Green Mountain coffee store in Vermont.

1985: Green Mountain Coffee turns a profit.

1989: Employees form an environmental steering committee.

1991: The company installs $30,000 computerized roaster.

1993: Green Mountain holds initial public offering.

1994: First exports are shipped to Canada and Taiwan.

1997: Shares are listed on NASDAQ.

1998: The company closes its retail stores; secure ordering is added to its web site.

2002: Green Mountain signs a ten-year agreement to be the exclusive roaster, seller, and distributor of Newman's Own Organics Fair Trade Certified coffees.

2006: Keurig Inc. is acquired; Newman's Own Organics Blend coffee is sold in over 600 McDonald's restaurants in New England and upstate New York.

2008: Sales surpass $500 million.

2009: The company buys the Tully's coffee brand and wholesale coffee business from Tully's Coffee Corp.

In 1996 Green Mountain sponsored a study of the comparative economic benefits of traditional shaded coffee growing systems with full-sun systems. Traditionally, coffee plants were raised in the shade of trees. New sun-resistant hybrids offered higher yields but were more reliant on synthetic pesticides and fertilizers.

The company announced an assault on national supermarket chains in June 1996. By the end of the year, its retail stores had increased to 12, in Vermont, Connecticut, Illinois, Maine, Massachusetts, New Hampshire, and New York. Its wholesale clients by then included Weight Watchers International and the L.L. Bean Catalog.

Business Express was one of the first airlines to offer Green Mountain coffee. By October 1996, Green Mountain Coffee was also being served on more than a hundred Delta Express flights per day. Enthusiastic Delta Shuttle customers helped Green Mountain land the Delta Express contract. The next month, Amtrack added the brew, putting it in the cups of even more commuters. While two million passengers flew Delta

Express each year, 11 million rode Amtrack's Northeast trains. Midway Airlines added Green Mountain Coffee in 1997. The carrier's reputation for customer satisfaction enhanced the roaster's own reputation.

Green Mountain started 1997 in a big way. It signed up as exclusive supplier to The Coffee Station, Inc. The retailer had been in business since only 1994 but already operated the largest specialty coffee stores in the United States: Its two locations in New York's World Trade Center served more than 7,500 customers a day. The Coffee Station operated 25 other locations in downtown areas in Los Angeles, Atlanta, Charlotte, and Seattle. The agreement brought the Green Mountain brand to one million consumers.

TRADING ON THE NASDAQ

In March 1997, Green Mountain's shares began trading on the NASDAQ National Market System, instead of the SmallCap Market System and the Boston Stock Exchange; Green Mountain's 1996 income qualified it for the listing. The company earned $1.26 million on revenues of $38.35 million for the fiscal year ending September 28. Sales had increased 145 percent during the three previous years.

In 1997 the growing company licensed PeopleSoft software for manufacturing and accounting applications. The cost of implementing the new system was reported as about $1.5 million. A year later, Green Mountain reported good results. The company's information technology personnel praised the new efficiency it brought to communicating with suppliers and distribution centers. Bar coding and online inventory tracking were two key features speeding the process. Electronic data interchange also was becoming a prerequisite for doing business with large customers such as grocery chains.

Green Mountain struck a deal with office supplies discounter Staples Inc. in May 1997. This put the coffee in 600 office superstores throughout North America and in the Staples mail-order catalog and marked a major step in penetrating the office coffee market. The company revamped its packaging, beckoning patrons to "Sip and relax—you're on Green Mountain time."

In September 1997, Green Mountain made another significant move into the office market by teaming with Poland Spring Natural Spring Water Co. (a subsidiary of the Perrier Group of America). Poland Spring's existing distribution network brought Green Mountain Coffee to thousands of offices in the Northeast. In the first year of the five-year agreement, Green Mountain expected to ship more than one million pounds of coffee through this channel. Coffee and bottled water were the fastest-growing categories in the beverage industry at that time. Although a regional brand, Poland Spring sold more bottled water than anyone else in the country. Poland Spring's sales were $248 million in 1996.

EXITING RETAIL

According to Stiller, Green Mountain remained passionate about its social and environmental responsibilities. In April 1998, as one of its Earth Day tie-ins, the company introduced "bird-friendly" coffees grown without synthetic fertilizers or pesticides. It expanded its support of its Coffee Kids micro-lending projects in Mexico.

With wholesale trade booming, Green Mountain announced plans to leave retail entirely in May 1998. The company kept its mail-order business operational, devoting energy to its new consumer online business, which, although it accounted for only a fraction of sales, was deemed promising because of the unprecedented convenience it offered customers. Sales through www. greenmountaincoffee.com increased fivefold within four months of the introduction of secure online ordering in 1998. Green Mountain aimed to have 30 percent of its 5,000 resellers order online by 2000. The company promoted the site on www.CNN.com.

Green Mountain distributed its first corporate gifts catalog in the fall of 1998. Businesses had long turned to the company to remember their clients, vendors, and friends at the holidays. The catalog offered volume discounts on gift baskets, mugs, and Vermont products. It also introduced filtered hospitality packs for in-room coffee service at hotels. The company continued to use brewed cups as a tool to introduce itself to new customers.

The American Skiing Company picked Green Mountain Coffee for its resorts in November 1998. The group operated nine resorts that had more than five million visits per year; the coffee was to be served at its six eastern resorts during the first winter of the five-year contract. Maine-based American Skiing was the largest alpine ski, snowboard, and golf resorts operator in the United States. It had previously served Starbucks coffee.

In late 1998, Mobil Corporation's On the Run shops became the first national convenience store chain to offer certified organic coffee. To match the pace of hurried shoppers, espresso-based drinks were not offered, only brewed, to-go cups of plain coffee. Since most households did not own coffee grinders, whole beans were not sold, either. The program brought Green Mountain certified organic coffee to 283 stores in the United States and more than 300 abroad.

About 70 percent of coffee was purchased in supermarkets, making this segment a key priority for future growth, as Stiller reported to shareholders in 1999. In the previous year, Green Mountain had been able to expand its supermarket distribution from 180 to more than 500 stores. Stop & Shop and Shaw's were two chains that had added Green Mountain coffee.

Another area for growth was the overseas market, particularly Great Britain. Green Mountain teamed with the Scottish company Banana Brothers to open outlets offering juice, soup, and coffee. The first debuted in Glasgow in September 1999. Green Mountain also was developing mobile coffee bars for shopping centers and examining acquisition targets. Exports were worth about $500,000 a year at the time.

In September 1998, Green Mountain had begun buying back about $500,000 of its shares, feeling they were undervalued. In the five years prior, the company averaged a growth rate of 30 percent a year, with international sales nearly doubling.

EXPANSION IN THE 21ST CENTURY

Green Mountain experienced significant growth during the early years of the new millennium. With over 7,000 wholesale customers, the company was selling enough coffee to fill ten million cups each week. Throughout its expansion, the company remained dedicated to commitment to the environment, social causes, and fair trade. Approximately 5 percent of the company's operating income was spent on charitable and nonprofit ventures each year. During 2000 the company partnered with TransFair USA to purchase fair-trade coffee from farmers in Peru, Mexico, and Sumatra. The company agreed to have all of its certified organic coffees also certified by TransFair, a nonprofit monitoring agency providing independent, third-party certification for fair-trade products in the United States. By 2006 Green Mountain controlled nearly 10 percent of the fair-trade coffee market.

During 2001 the company added the Frontier Organic Coffee brand to its arsenal. During 2002, Green Mountain signed a ten-year agreement to be the exclusive roaster, seller, and distributor of Newman's Own Organics Fair Trade Certified coffees. This deal proved quite lucrative. Beginning in 2006, Newman's Own Organics Blend coffee was sold in over 600 McDonald's restaurants in New England and upstate New York.

In 2006 the company purchased Keurig Inc., a manufacturer of single-cup brewing systems used both in homes and offices. The Keurig system used K-cups, specialized one-serving cups used exclusively with the Keurig machine. Before the deal, Green Mountain owned 33.2 percent of Keurig and Green Mountain coffee was found in a large portion of K-cups. With the single-cup coffee market growing from $111 million in 2006 to $176 million in 2007, Keurig was well positioned with a 59 percent market share.

With Keurig under its belt, Green Mountain experienced a dramatic rise in both revenue and net income. It benefited from every K-cup sold, earning a five-cent royalty on each third-party cup—a K-cup that did not have Green Mountain coffee in it. Sales climbed from $161.5 million in 2005 to $500.2 million in 2008. Net income grew from $8.9 million to $22.3 million during the same time period. Despite a weak U.S. economy, Green Mountain appeared poised for financial success in 2009 as well. Indeed, profits for the first quarter of fiscal 2009 skyrocketed by 392 percent over the previous year's quarterly results. The company shipped 357 million K-cups during the first quarter in 2009, a 55 percent increase over 2008 results.

To support its rapid growth, the company opened a new production center in Essex, Vermont, in 2007. An additional facility began operation in Knox County, Tennessee, the following year. Stiller, the company's leader since 1981 and *Forbes* magazine's 2001 "Entrepreneur of the Year," turned over the reins of day-to-day operations to Lawrence J. Blanford in 2007 while remaining chairman. Green Mountain's growth continued under the leadership of the new president and CEO. In early 2009, the company purchased the Tully's coffee brand and wholesale coffee business from Tully's Coffee Corporation for just over $40 million. The company also began selling the Keurig brewing systems and K-cups at over 3,000 Wal-Mart stores that year. If demand for single-cup brewers remained strong, Green Mountain was well positioned for success in the years to come.

Frederick C. Ingram
Updated, Christina M. Stansell

PRINCIPAL SUBSIDIARIES

Green Mountain Coffee Roasters, Inc.; Keurig Inc.

PRINCIPAL OPERATING UNITS

Specialty Coffee Business; Keurig.

PRINCIPAL COMPETITORS

The Folgers Coffee Company; Sara Lee Food and Beverage; Starbucks Corporation.

FURTHER READING

Alpert, Bill, "Green Mountain Coffee: Too Hot to Hold?" *Barron's,* June 1, 2009.

Barrett, Jennifer, "Something Brewing; Green Mountain, a Specialty-Coffee Roaster, Is Betting a Whole Lotta Beans on a One-Cup Machine Maker," *Newsweek,* October 2, 2006.

"Fill'er Up with Gas and Organic Coffee," *Specialty Coffee Retailer,* December 1998, p. 8.

Grover, Mary Beth, "Hippie Redux," *Forbes,* December 9, 1991, pp. 326, 328.

Jacobs, April, "Business Process Software Pays Off," *Computerworld,* August 31, 1998, pp. 33–37.

Kelly, Brad, "Acquisition Brings Coffee Roaster the Sweet Smell of Success," *Investor's Business Daily,* April 25, 2008.

Marcel, Joyce, "Planting a Seed, One Cup at a Time," *Vermont Business Magazine,* July 1, 2007.

Marcum, Ed, "Green Mountain Coffee Plant to Expand," *Knoxville News-Sentinel,* January 29, 2009.

Sinanoglu, Elif, "Wake Up and Smell the $5 French Roast," *Money,* November 1994, p. 223.

"U.S. Coffee Giant Lifts Lid on Joint Venture Chain," *LeisureWeek,* August 12, 1999, p. 4.

Grupo Carso, S.A. de C.V.

Miguel de Cervantes Saavedra 255
Col. Ampliacion Granada
Mexico City, D.F. 11520
Mexico
Telephone: (555) 328-5800
Fax: (555) 606-1584
Web site: http://www.gcarso.com.mx

Public Company
Incorporated: 1980 as Grupo Galas, S.A.
Employees: 78,904
Sales: 64.88 billion pesos ($6.86 billion) (2007)
Stock Exchanges: Mexico City
Ticker Symbol: GCARSOA1
NAICS: 551112 Offices of Other Holding Companies

■ ■ ■

Grupo Carso, S.A. de C.V., is one of Latin America's largest industrial conglomerates with holdings in three main business areas: Industrial, Construction and Infrastructure, and Commercial. Grupo Condomex, the industrial arm, offers products related to mining, construction, energy, and telecommunications. Carso Infraestructura y Construcción, S.A. de C.V. (CICSA), is responsible for the company's infrastructure and construction operations, and Grupo Sanborns oversees the company's commercial operations including the opening of the first Saks Fifth Avenue in Mexico during 2007. Grupo Carso's founder, Carlos Slim Helú, is believed to be one of the richest men in the world, with a fortune estimated at $59 billion in early 2009. The name Carso is a fusion of Slim's first name and that of his deceased wife, Soumaya.

FORGING AN EMPIRE

Carlos Slim Helú, who made his first stock purchase at the age of 12, built his fortune without connections to Mexico's closely knit business elite. The son of a Lebanese immigrant who became successful in business, Slim received a degree in civil engineering at the National Autonomous University of Mexico. By then, he had a net worth of $400,000, which he used in 1965 and 1966 to purchase and further develop a brokerage house, real estate firm, construction company, and soda bottling plant. In 1976 he bought a 60 percent share of Galas de México, a small printer of cigarette pack labels, for $1 million. Slim acquired a majority stake in Cigarros la Tabacalera Mexicana (Cigatam), Mexico's second largest producer and marketer of cigarettes, in 1981.

During the years that followed the collapse of the peso in 1982, Slim bought controlling interests in many Mexican companies cheaply, mainly using Cigatam's revenues. These included the mining firm Empresas Frisco for only $50 million; Industrias Nacobre, a manufacturer of copper products; and a majority share in the retail and restaurant chain Sanborn Hermanos.

During the 1990s Slim's Grupo Carso expanded its holdings still further and took over management of privatized Teléfonos de México (Telmex), the nation's telephone monopoly; Telmex was spun off into another holding company in 1996. In 1997 Grupo Carso purchased a majority share of the department store chain Sears Roebuck de México. (Independently of

```
┌─────────────────────────────────────────┐
│                                         │
│              KEY DATES                  │
│                 ■                       │
│  ─────────────────────────────────────  │
│                                         │
│  1965:  Carlos Slim Helú begins to buy  │
│         various companies.              │
│  1976:  Slim acquires a 60 percent      │
│         share of Galas de México.       │
│  1981:  Cigarros la Tabacalera          │
│         Mexicana is purchased.          │
│  1990:  Grupo Carso's stock becomes     │
│         publicly traded on the Bolsa    │
│         de Valores Mexicanas; the       │
│         company and two foreign         │
│         partners acquire about 20       │
│         percent of the equity of        │
│         Teléfonos de México.            │
│  1992:  The company acquires 51         │
│         percent of Grupo Condumex.      │
│  1993:  Grupo Carso raises its stake    │
│         in Sanborns to 67 percent.      │
│  1997:  Grupo Carso purchases a         │
│         majority share of the           │
│         department store chain Sears    │
│         Roebuck de México.              │
│  2004:  Slim's son, Carlos Slim         │
│         Domit, takes over as chairman.  │
│  2005:  Carso Infraestructura y         │
│         Construcción, S.A. de C.V.,     │
│         makes its initial public        │
│         offering.                       │
│  2007:  The company sells its stake in  │
│         CompUSA.                        │
│                                         │
└─────────────────────────────────────────┘
```

Grupo Carso, Slim also created Grupo Financiero Inbursa, which became Mexico's fourth largest financial group.)

Slim stressed cost control in his business empire, which he managed, with only about a dozen staff members, from an unpretentious two-story house in Mexico City. His approach was to let each subsidiary run its own affairs but to look for savings and synergies between different group members without, however, any special deals or favors. When he acquired a company, he dismissed the management and sold corporate headquarters, moving his own people into nondescript offices at the production sites. These, according to the head of an executive search firm, were "unswervingly loyal, capable people" recruited by relatives and friends of relatives and "willing to put up with the mercurial nature of the boss." The labor force was reduced, sometimes provoking strikes, and unprofitable lines of business were dropped, but investment in new machinery rose sharply.

Although Grupo Carso's stock became publicly traded on the Bolsa de Valores Mexicanas, Mexico's stock exchange, in 1990, about 60 to 65 percent of the shares were retained by Slim and his immediately fam-

ily—his wife and six children, three of whom worked for the group. The stock had risen tenfold by early 1994. When the value of the peso fell by more than half in dollar terms in December 1994, Grupo Carso was not badly hurt because only $130 million, or 12 percent, of its debt was denominated in dollars.

CIGARETTES, MANUFACTURING, AND INDUSTRIAL ACQUISITIONS

Cigatam was founded in 1907. By 1919 this company and its associate, El Buen Tono, with whom it merged in 1960, produced more than half of the tobacco consumed nationally. Its share of the market subsequently was considerably reduced by new rivals, however. In the mid-1970s Philip Morris held 27 percent of the stock, while a government body held 36 percent. After absorbing the fourth and fifth largest tobacco companies in Mexico, Cigatam moved into second place, behind Cigarrera La Moderna, with 34 percent of tobacco production in 1976 and 25 percent of sales.

Cigatam's brands in 1995 included Marlboro, Mexico's best-selling cigarette since 1990, and Benson & Hedges, both manufactured and marketed under license from Philip Morris. Cigatam accounted for 26 percent of Grupo Carso's revenues in 1994 and 17 percent in the first quarter of 1997. Grupo Carso acquired 51 percent of Grupo Condumex in 1992 for 818 billion pesos (about $264 million) and subsequently increased its share to 96 percent. Founded in 1952, this company was engaged in the electro manufacture of cables and wires, the production of plastic pipe and other products, and the manufacture of auto parts. Its holdings included 48 percent of Cobre de Mexico, which was founded in 1943 and refined and produced cathodes used to make cable. Following Grupo Carso's takeover, the number of Condumex subsidiaries was cut from 52 to 25, the labor force was reduced by 30 percent, and the company's luxurious headquarters was sold. Grupo Carso acquired Latincasa, a manufacturer of cable for the construction, telecommunications, and energy sectors, in 1997. Since Latincasa held 9 percent of Cobre de Mexico, Condumex's share in the enterprise increased to 57 percent. Condumex was the biggest revenue earner in Grupo Carso during the first quarter of 1997, accounting for 31 percent of its sales.

Industrias Nacobre was founded in 1950. Grupo Industrial Carso, a predecessor of Grupo Carso, acquired a majority share in the enterprise in 1987 and subsequently almost all the rest. Through subsidiaries it was making copper and steel pipes and tubes and also auto parts and accessories. In 1992 Nacobre also acquired 78 percent of the shares of Grupo Aluminio,

Mexico's largest aluminum producer, including a 44 percent interest purchased from the Aluminum Co. of America for $50 million. This stake was soon increased to 98 percent. In 1995 Industrias Nacobre was manufacturing copper and copper-alloy products for the construction, automotive, and electrical industry and, through Grupo Aluminio, aluminum sheet, foil, and ingots. It was also producing polyvinyl chloride pipe in 1997. Nacobre accounted for 15 percent of Grupo Carso's sales in the first quarter of 1997.

MINING, TIRES, AND MORE

Empresas Frisco was founded in 1924. Grupo Industrial Carso acquired a majority interest in the 1980s. At this time it was operating mines producing silver, gold, copper, lead, and zinc from extracted ores, and also chemical products such as hydrofluoric acid. With two partners, it opened what was described as the world's largest silver mine in 1982 and bought out the remaining partner in 1993. Empresas Frisco, which was also producing molybdenum, accounted for 6 percent of Grupo Carso's revenues in the first quarter of 1997.

Compania Hulera Euzkadi, Mexico's largest tire maker, was producing about 2.5 million tires in 1981, when it had four plants in Mexico. B.F. Goodrich Co. held a 35 percent interest in the firm. Grupo Carso acquired Goodrich's share in 1991 for about $35 million and 50.06 percent of the outstanding shares in January 1993. Also in January 1993, Grupo Carso acquired General Tire de México, a unit of Germany's Continental AG, for $40 million. Euzkadi and General Tire were merged into Corporación Industrial Llantera, which had four plants turning out Euzkadi, General Tire, and Continental tires. This company held about 30 percent of the Mexican tire market. Corporación Industrial Llantera accounted for 8 percent of Grupo Carso's sales in the first quarter of 1997.

Grupo Carso acquired majority ownership of the tile maker Porcelanite in 1990. This investment was assigned to an associated company, but in 1995 Grupo Carso increased its equity stake to 83 percent and made it a subsidiary. Porcelanite accounted for 4 percent of Grupo Carso's sales in the first quarter of 1997. Another tile maker, P&M Tile Inc., was established in 1994 as a joint venture by Mannington Mills Inc. and Inmuebles Cantabria, another Grupo Carso subsidiary.

A tissue products company, Fábricas de Papel Loreto y Peña Pobre, was acquired by Grupo Galas in the 1980s. In July 1997 Grupo Carso agreed to sell to Procter & Gamble de México, a subsidiary of Procter & Gamble Co., a manufacturing plant in Apizaco and the company's Lypps, Pampys, and other toilet tissue brands

for about $170 million. All other facilities with the Loreto y Peña Pobre name were to continue as a part of Grupo Carso.

RETAIL STORES

Walter and Frank Sanborn were Americans who opened a drugstore in Mexico City in 1903 and named their company Sanborn Hermanos in 1909. The business later became a chain of stores offering meals and a variety of goods. A group of unidentified Mexican investors bought Walgreen Co.'s 46 percent share of the business in 1984. Grupo Industrial Carso subsequently acquired majority control of Sanborn Hermanos, which had 30 stores in 1989, and Grupo Carso raised its stake to 67 percent by 1993. Under Grupo Carso's management the business continued to expand. In 1997 there were 89 full-service Sanborns and 39 Sanborns Café restaurants. The company also owned ten Mix-Up record stores and 12 other outlets and prepared to test its units in the United States before the end of the year. Sanborn Hermanos contributed 12 percent to Grupo Carso's sales in the first quarter of 1997.

Sears, Roebuck de México was established in 1945 as a wholly owned subsidiary of Sears, Roebuck & Co. and opened its first department store in 1947. The company revolutionized retailing in Mexico but subsequently had difficulty meeting growing competition and fell into the red. Despite a resurgence in the late 1980s, the company was losing money again in the mid-1990s. Grupo Carso acquired a 60 percent share from the parent company in 1997 and set about rehabilitating the chain by updating the stores.

TELMEX HOLDING

In December 1990 Grupo Carso and two foreign partners, Southwestern Bell and France Telecom, acquired about 20 percent of the equity (and 51 percent of the voting shares) of Teléfonos de Mexico (Telmex), the nation's telephone monopoly, from the government for $1.76 billion. Grupo Carso put up $860 million and received operating control of the company, with Slim becoming its chairman. His Condumex acquisition gave Grupo Carso control of a major supplier of the materials needed for a network of new fiber-optic cable to upgrade the outdated telephone system, while Nacobre was producing the needed copper and copper alloy.

Under Slim's management, Telmex surpassed the government's target for line expansion and reduced the average wait for a telephone hookup more than sixfold. Repairs that used to take months were being completed in 24 hours. By the autumn of 1995 Telmex had spent $10 billion on plants and equipment, completely rebuilding its long distance network, adding more than three million new lines, and laying 8,400 miles of fiberoptic cable. Grupo Carso's 8.4 percent share in Telmex was spun off into a separate holding company in 1996.

Grupo Carso was a major investor in International Wireless Inc., which in 1996 purchased the Prodigy online service from International Business Machines Corp. and Sears, Roebuck & Co. for close to $250 million in cash and stock. The other major investor was Greg Carr, co-chairman of Cambridge, Massachusetts-based International Wireless, a closely held concern investing in cellular phone properties in Mexico, Asia, and Africa. The new owners planned to make Prodigy available outside the United States in other languages and use its communications network to expand its Internet-access business. International Wireless merged its operations with Prodigy's, and renamed the combined company Prodigy Inc. A Spanish-language version of the online service was eventually launched in the Mexican market. Prodigy went public in 1999.

Grupo Carso also held a one-third interest in Corporación Moctezuma, an international cement consortium founded in 1982. Spanish and Italian investors held the other two-thirds. Among the company's holdings was Cementos Portland Moctezuma, a Mexican firm founded in 1942. Corporación Moctezuma contributed 175 million pesos ($50 million) to Grupo Carso's sales in 1994. Orient Star Holdings was a Grupo Carso subsidiary established in the United States in 1994. Its principal activity was the trading of shares and securities of issuers in the United States.

GRUPO CARSO MOVES INTO THE 21ST CENTURY

By the early years of the new millennium, Slim had created a formidable conglomerate involved in nearly every aspect of Latin American business. In fact, a July 2000 *Financial Times* article claimed, "Every time Mexicans eat a croissant or visit their bank, every time they use the telephone or light a cigarette, the chances are that Carlos Slim is making money. He probably even sold them the clothes on their back." Indeed, with holdings across a broad array of industries, Grupo Carso stood as Latin America's largest industrial conglomerate. Slim's companies made up one-third of the Mexican stock exchange and Slim's total holdings accounted for over 5 percent of Mexico's gross domestic product.

Most of Grupo Carso's investments paid off handsomely and the founder was known for his ability to capitalize on unique opportunities. For example, during 1997 Slim purchased a 3 percent stake in Apple Computer. Approximately one year later, after the return

of Steve Jobs and the launch of the iMac computer, Apple's stock jumped from $17 to $100 per share. Telmex, which had previously operated as an unprofitable state-owned entity, had a $50 billion market capitalization in 2000 and was one of the most profitable telecommunications firms in the world. Slim's America Movil SAB stood as Latin America's largest mobile phone provider.

Some of Grupo Carso's ventures failed to pay off, however. During 2000 the company acquired the majority interest in CompUSA for over $800 million. By 2001 plans were in the works to spin off the unprofitable retailer; in 2007, CompUSA was sold to Gordon Brothers Group LLC who immediately set out to sell most of the stores. At the same time, the company sold its investment in the U.S. operations of the Prodigy Internet company.

During 2004 Slim passed the reins of Grupo Carso over to his son, Carlos Slim Domit. Under his leadership, Grupo Carso continued to strengthen and streamline its business operations. In October 2005 CICSA made its initial public offering. During 2007 the conglomerate began a restructuring effort that focused on three core areas—Industrial, Construction and Infrastructure, and Commercial. Grupo Condomex, the industrial arm, offered products related to mining, construction, energy, and telecommunications. CICSA was responsible for the company's infrastructure and construction operations, and Grupo Sanborns oversaw the company's commercial operations, including the opening of the first Saks Fifth Avenue in Mexico during 2007.

At the same time, Grupo Carso reduced its ownership in Cigatam and divested its Porcelanite operations. It also sold off holdings related to the manufacture of automotive rings and cylinder liners. During fiscal 2007, sales and profits were on the rise, indicating that the company's strategy was paying off.

With many U.S. companies floundering as a result of an economic downturn, analysts speculated that Slim would begin to make strategic U.S. purchases, which included a stake in the New York Times Co. Rumored to be either the richest or second richest man in the world, Carlos Slim Helú and his investments would no doubt continue to play a big role in the future of Grupo Carso.

Robert Halasz
Updated, Christina M. Stansell

PRINCIPAL SUBSIDIARIES

Grupo Sanborns S.A. de C.V.; Grupo Condumex S.A. de C.V.; Carso Infraestructura y Construcción, S.A. de

C.V.; Grupo Calinda, S.A. de C.V.; Inmuebles Cantabria, S.A. de C.V.

PRINCIPAL DIVISIONS

Industrial; Construction and Infrastructure; Commercial.

PRINCIPAL COMPETITORS

Grupo Industrial Saltillo S.A.B. de C.V.; Grupo México S.A.B. de C.V.; Wal-Mart de México, S.A.B. de C.V.

FURTHER READING

Button, Graham, Christopher Palmeri, and Kerry A. Dolan, "'There's Lot's of Opportunity,'" *Forbes*, January 30, 1995, pp. 46–47.

Case, Brendan M., "Two Firms Complete CompUSA Spinoff," *Dallas Morning News*, July 10, 2002.

Crawford, Leslie, "The Big Draw for Cigarette Companies," *Financial Times*, July 28, 1997, p. 19.

Dolan, Kerry A., "Rooting for the Home Team," *Forbes*, September 11, 1995, pp. 121–23.

González Sierra, José, *Monopolio del humo*, Xalapa: Universidad Veracruzana, 1981, pp. 23–39.

"Grupo Carso: The Slim Alternative," *Euromoney*, May 1993, pp. 118, 120.

"Grupo Carso to Test Sanborn Units in U.S.," *WWD*, May 1, 1997, p. 9.

Kandell, Jonathan, "Carlos Slim Bets Big on Mexico—Again," *Institutional Investor*, June 1995, pp. 98–102, 105.

Mandel-Campbell, Andrea, "A Mexican with the Midas Touch," *Financial Times*, July 10, 2000.

Mehta, Stephanie N., "Carlos Slim," *Fortune*, August 20, 2007.

"Mexico Company—Grupo Carso Slims Down," *Economist Intelligence Unit*, October 4, 2001.

Poole, Claire, "El Conquistador," *Forbes*, September 16, 1991, pp. 68, 72.

"Profits Fall, but Outlook Is Good at Carso," *El Financiero*, June 2–8, 1997, pp. 17, 25.

"The Rise and Rise of Possibly the Richest Man You've Never Even Heard Of," *Daily Telegraph*, January 24, 2009.

Sandberg, Jared, "Prodigy Owner on First Day Asserts Control," *Wall Street Journal*, July 30, 1996, p. B6.

Smith, Geri, "Mexico's No-Frills Mogul," *Business Week*, March 7, 1994, pp. 62–64.

Torres, Craig, "Group's Spinoff Move Triggers Worry Over Telefonos de Mexico," *Wall Street Journal*, January 12, 1996, pp. C1–C2.

Watson, Julie, "New York Times Offers Prestige to Mexican Billionaire Looking to Expand into US Market," *Associated Press Newswires*, January 20, 2009.

Ziegler, Bart, "IBM, Sears Sell Prodigy for $250 Million in Cash and Stock to Investor Group," *Wall Street Journal*, May 13, 1996, p. B2.

Grupo Sanborns, S.A. de C.V.

Avenida Calvario, No. 106 Tlalpán
Mexico City, D.F. 14000
Mexico
Telephone: (525) 325-9900
Fax: (525) 573-2756
Web site: http://www.sanborns.com.mx

Wholly Owned Subsidiary of Grupo Carso, S.A. de C.V.
Incorporated: 1907 as Sanborn Hermanos
Employees: 45,120
Sales: 31 billion pesos ($2.85 billion) (2007 est.)
NAICS: 452110 Department Stores; 722110 Full-
Service Restaurants

■ ■ ■

As one of the largest retail groups in Mexico, Grupo Sanborns, S.A. de C.V., operates over 400 stores under the Sanborns, Dorian's, Dax, Mas, Sanborns Café, The Coffee Factory, Café Caffe, Sears, Pier 1, and Saks Fifth Avenue names. It also operates a chain of almost 80 Mixup music stores in Mexico. The company is a subsidiary of Grupo Carso, S.A. de C.V., one of Latin America's largest industrial conglomerates. Grupo Carso's founder, Carlos Slim Helú, is believed to be one of the richest men in the world, with a fortune estimated at $59 billion in early 2009.

ORIGINS AS A FAMILY BUSINESS

Walter Sanborn, a young American newly licensed as a pharmacist, traveled to Mexico in 1898 and took a job in the Mexico City apothecary shop run by an old German named Schmidt. Four years later his brother Frank came down for a visit and was equally fascinated by the country. In 1903 the brothers opened their own drugstore in Mexico City. "We decided that Mexico couldn't be a land of manana and a land of opportunity at the same time," Frank recalled in an interview many years later. "We decided we'd have to work just as hard here as we would at home, and we decided we were here to stay, not to make a quick fortune, but to build our homes and lives. That makes a difference in the attitude of people here just as it would in our hometown."

The business, founded as Farmacía América, became Sanborn Hermanos in 1907 (*hermanos* is the Spanish word for "brothers"). One of the first decisions was to eliminate the 15 percent commission that doctors charged for directing prescriptions to a pharmacist. Most of Mexico City's doctors refused to deal with them, but a few agreed because, Walter said, he promised them "not only quality, but service you have never seen before." At the time, it took hours and sometimes even days for medicine to reach the patients from drugstores. The Sanborns used bicycle messengers to provide the city's first quick free delivery service. By the early 1940s the company estimated it had filled nearly three million prescriptions.

The Sanborn brothers not only had to overcome the reluctance of Mexico City's doctors to direct prescriptions to their pharmacy but also the virtual monopoly that three German firms held over the drug business in Mexico. Besides importing German and American brands, they produced low-cost imitations of others and sold them at a discount. The Sanborn broth-

KEY DATES

1903: Brothers Walter and Frank Sanborn establish Farmacía América.

1907: The company adopts the name Sanborn Hermanos.

1946: The Sanborns sell their business to the Walgreen Co.

1953: Sanborns opens a four-story, $5 million store on Mexico City's swank Paseo de la Reforma.

1984: Walgreen sells its 46.9 percent share in Sanborns to a group of Mexican investors for $30 million.

1990: Carlos Slim Helú has a controlling share in Sanborns.

1993: Grupo Carso, owned by Slim, raises its stake in Sanborns to 67 percent.

1997: The company acquires an 84.9 percent stake in Sears, Roebuck & Co.'s Mexican operations.

1999: Grupo Sanborns goes public on the Mexican stock exchange.

2006: The company is taken private by Grupo Carso.

2007: Grupo Sanborns opens the first Saks Fifth Avenue in Mexico City.

ers brought in American brands and refused to discount but offered guarantees of quality. "We missed a lot of sales, but once we'd won a customer, we never lost him," Frank recalled.

One of the German firms then played its trump card: It placed an enormous order with an American manufacturer for a brand Sanborns was importing, an order big enough to supply all Mexico for more than a year. Frank Sanborn took a train to New York and convinced the manufacturer that the Germans planned to divide the goods among themselves and flood Mexico's pharmacies with them at discount prices until Sanborns was driven out of business, and then return to their old practices, which favored German brands over American ones.

BEYOND THE PHARMACY

The Sanborns were not content to run a pharmacy. They started to serve lunch to their employees to keep them from going home for the siesta and soon began serving sandwiches to their customers as well. In 1910

they sent to the United States for a soda fountain, which was still a novelty even there. The milk supply needed for ice cream and malteds was unsafe, but the brothers found a few healthy cows and imported Mexico's first cream separator along with the soda fountain to serve what they claimed was the first scoop of ice cream south of the border. Sanborns did so well catering to the Mexican sweet tooth that the brothers brought in a herd of tested cattle, thereby becoming fathers of Mexico's modern dairy industry. They rented more space to accommodate trade, and the soda fountain grew into a restaurant.

The decade that followed the Mexican revolution of 1910, during which the country was plunged into bloodshed and anarchy, was a difficult one for Sanborns. The store was smashed by soldiers in 1914, when the brothers evacuated their U.S. workers, but it survived as a kind of neutral zone in which Sanborn employees were forbidden to talk politics and the same ban was "tactfully impressed" on its patrons. In 1919 the brothers decided the political situation was stable enough to move into the House of Tiles, a stone palace covered with blue tiles in the heart of downtown, which had just been vacated by the Jockey Club. It had been built in 1596 for a Spanish aristocrat and had later served as the Russian and Japanese embassies and as a dormitory for homeless newsboys. A Mexican later recalled that the opening of the new Sanborns in 1921 "was like a rebirth of optimism in the city. Other businessmen, too, decided the revolutions were over, and money that had been hidden for ten years began to circulate again."

EXPANDING SCOPE

The Sanborns restored the House of Tiles and commissioned the celebrated painter José Clemente Orozco to produce a mural facing the great stairway. Waitresses were dressed in the colorful costumes of the Tehuantepec Indians. Politicians, civil servants, journalists, and businessmen—the movers and shakers of Mexican society—gathered in the restaurant. Churchgoers began dropping in for breakfast after Mass, and Sanborns even became home for debutante teas. By the end of World War II almost two million people were visiting the two-story tiled palace each year.

Sanborns entered a new endeavor in the early 1920s, when Frank Sanborn found he could not locate a competent silversmith even though Mexico led the world in silver production. While another American, William Spratling, was reviving the art and craft of silverwork in Taxco, Sanborns stimulated the trade by using workmen to fashion silver to the company's own designs. By the early 1940s the company's annual sales volume from silverwork came to $250,000. Ten years later Sanborns was the biggest silver shop in Mexico.

By this time Walter Sanborn was long retired and Frank was administering the business with the help of his two sons, Frank, Jr., and Jack. The tile-clad patio restaurant served 3,500 customers a day, and there was a cocktail lounge as well. In addition to silverwork, Sanborns, then the biggest crafts shop in Mexico, was selling the output of some 1,300 native craftsmen in wood, wool, glass, pottery, stone, metal, leather, and feathers. The second floor offered furs, gowns and accessories, men's suits, and household goods. There was a post office and information bureau for tourists. A second Sanborns had been opened in Monterrey.

Sanborns was a considerable wholesaling and manufacturing concern as well. The company was Mexico's largest drug manufacturer, with a modern factory. There was also a toilet-goods plant. In addition, the company was serving as the Mexican wholesaler for nearly 30 U.S. manufacturers. Sanborns held the manufacturing and distribution rights to several major U.S. drug and cosmetic lines, including Hinds hand cream, Listerine, Prophylactic brushes, and the products of the American Safety Razor Corp. Its annual sales volume came to close to 20 million pesos ($4 million). The company had between 700 and 800 employees.

UNDER WALGREEN
MANAGEMENT

In 1946 the Sanborns sold their business, which at this time included a second Mexico City outlet in the Hotel Del Prado (a victim of the 1985 earthquake), to the Walgreen Co. drugstore chain for about $2.5 million. By Mexican law, the purchaser was required to form a Mexican corporation in which at least 51 percent of the stock was owned by Mexican citizens. In the mid-1960s this controlling interest was in the hands of a group headed by two of the nation's biggest industrial and financial tycoons, Carlos Trouyet and Julio Lacaud. The Walgreen Co. received a share of the profits and ran the enterprise under a long-term management contract. It was the chain's only venture outside the United States. A Sanborns plant manufacturing chocolates, candy, and other comestibles was added around 1950.

Sanborns opened a four-story, $5 million store in 1953 on Mexico City's swank Paseo de la Reforma, next to the U.S. embassy. This store included, in addition to a restaurant and soda fountain, a big drug department, cosmetics, clothing and accessories, household goods, arts and crafts, photographic equipment and supplies, and a bakery. It also included a plush cocktail lounge. The structure, with 98,000 square feet of floor space,

was leased to Sanborns on a rent-plus-profit-sharing basis.

In the ensuing 20 years Sanborns grew into a chain of eight stores, all of them in Mexico City except the Monterrey outlet. Three of the Sanborns stores had cocktail lounges. About 45 percent of the chain's sales came from restaurants and lunch counters. Only four of the outlets maintained drug departments, because with prices controlled by the government and discount stores glutting the market, the company had decided the business was no longer profitable. Sanborns had displays of U.S. magazines, money exchange booths, and the kind of trinkets and sombreros that attracted tourists, but the tourist trade made up only about 15 percent of the company's business.

ANOTHER CHANGE IN
OWNERSHIP

More than 10 percent of income for Sanborns at this time came from wholesaling popular priced Sanborns-labeled products to other stores. These consisted mainly of toiletries, coffee, ice cream, and candy, with candy the leading single item sold in all the stores. Sanborns was still making its own candy and selling more than 100 tons a month in its own stores and through the wholesaling operation. The Sanborns manufacturing line also included shampoo, cold cream, and cologne (Mexico's top seller), and it was licensed to produce four items under the Walgreen name: a henna hair rinse, a shampoo, a cleaning fluid, and an aftershave lotion. The company was no longer manufacturing and distributing U.S. products under other licenses except to bottle Eye-Gene, an eyewash, and to distribute Mentholatum and Tampax. "Most of the companies that once licensed us now have moved in with their own manufacturing operations after the market was developed for them," explained general manager James Mitchell.

Sanborns opened a store in Acapulco in 1966 and one in Puebla in 1969, bringing to 12 its number of outlets. Also in 1969, it completed construction of a large modern complex that included a laboratory, warehouse, commissary, and laundry. In 1971 the number of stores reached 17, including three new Mexico City outlets, one of them in the Plaza Satelite, a shopping mall. A second Acapulco store opened in 1973. By this time the company's arts and crafts offerings included sculpture and paintings. Sanborns acquired the 18 units in five Mexican cities of the Denny's restaurant chain in 1976. A year later the company ranked 71st in sales among Mexican-based companies, with 1.29 billion pesos (about $58 million) in revenues.

Sanborns had revenues of 2.98 billion pesos (about $130 million) and net income of 255.8 million pesos (about $11.3 million) in fiscal 1980 (the year ended June 30, 1980), when it operated 44 retail outlets (including the Denny's chain), of which 14 were outside Mexico City. However, the 1982 Mexican economic crisis so reduced the value of the peso that the Walgreen Co. lost faith in the chain's ability to return a significant profit in dollars. In 1984 the company sold its 46.9 percent share in Sanborns to a group of Mexican investors for $30 million. The company had been selling shares on the Bolsa de Valores, Mexico City's stock exchange, since 1956, and most of the shares not held by Walgreen belonged to banks and mutual funds. The purchasers of Walgreen's stock were not disclosed, but by 1990 Slim had a controlling share of the company through the firm Galas de México, in which he held majority control.

GOING PUBLIC

After the Walgreen Co. sold out, Mitchell was replaced as general manager of Sanborns by Juan Antonio Pérez Simón, who also assumed the title of president. Sanborns continued to turn a healthy profit. In 1991 it had net income of 81.04 billion pesos ($26.9 million) on net sales of 990.54 billion pesos ($328.4 million). By the early 1990s a large portion of Slim's assets were in the holding company Grupo Carso, which owned a two-thirds share of Sanborns. Sanborns was selling books as well as magazines (and would soon become the largest bookseller in Mexico) and audio products such as stereo systems. Some 90 percent of company sales were coming from the Sanborns chain, with the rest from Denny's. The company's assets included a significant amount of real estate.

By 1995 Carlos Slim Domit, son of Carlos Slim Helú, had become general director of Sanborns, replacing Pérez, who became chairman of the board of directors. Despite the devaluation of the peso in December 1994, resulting from a flight of capital abroad, and the devastating economic crisis that followed, Sanborns continued to be profitable. In 1995 it had net income of 158.1 million pesos ($23.2 million) on net sales of 2.28 billion pesos ($335.3 million). The long-term debt was 142.9 million pesos ($21 million) at the end of 1995. By then the Denny's units had been converted into more upscale Sanborns Café coffee shops. The company also had taken a majority interest in the Mixup and Discolandia music store chains. There were 86 Sanborns units and 35 Sanborns Café units at the end of 1995. During the first quarter of 1997 Sanborns accounted for 12.1 percent of the consolidated revenues of Grupo Carso and 7.4 percent of its operating profit. The company acquired an 84.9 percent stake in Sears, Roebuck & Co.'s Mexican operations later that

year. During 1999 the company, then known as Grupo Sanborns, went public on the Mexican stock exchange.

MOVING INTO THE 21ST CENTURY

Grupo Sanborns entered the new millennium on solid ground as a subsidiary of Grupo Carso. By this time, Slim Helú controlled a formidable conglomerate that was involved in nearly every aspect of Latin American business. In fact, a July 2000 *Financial Times* article claimed, "Every time Mexicans eat a croissant or visit their bank, every time they use the telephone or light a cigarette, the chances are that Carlos Slim is making money. He probably even sold them the clothes on their back." Indeed, with holdings across a broad array of industries, Grupo Carso stood as Latin America's largest industrial conglomerate. Slim's companies made up one-third of the Mexican stock exchange and Slim's total holdings accounted for over 5 percent of Mexico's gross domestic product. Under such an auspicious thumb, Sanborns enjoyed success in the retail world.

One of the company's missteps, however, came with its 2000 purchase of the majority interest of CompUSA in a deal worth over $800 million. While the company hoped to turn around the troubled U.S. retailer, its efforts failed and plans were in the works for a spin off by 2002. In 2007 CompUSA was sold to Gordon Brothers Group LLC who immediately set out to sell most of the stores.

Meanwhile, Grupo Sanborns continued with its growth strategy. In late 2004 the company added the Dorian's chain of department stores. In 2005 the company acquired three stores operated by J.C. Penney Company Inc. in Mexico and planned to change their name to Dorian's. Later that year, the company expanded into Central America by opening two stores in El Salvador. It also opened its first Oakley store in Mexico City.

Grupo Carso, the parent company of Grupo Sanborns, took the company private in 2006 when its shares were removed from the Mexican stock exchange. This move did little to dampen the company's expansion efforts. In 2007 Grupo Sanborns opened the first Saks Fifth Avenue in Mexico. In total, the company opened eight new Sanborns stores that year along with six new Sears locations and five new music stores. Mexico's economy, which weakened in 2008 and 2009, was hit especially hard due to escalating drug violence and the 2009 outbreak of the swine flu. To contain the epidemic, many businesses and government operations were shuttered in Mexico City in April of that year. While the retail environment remained challenging during this time, Grupo Sanborns stood well positioned among its competitors in the retail industry.

Robert Halasz
Updated, Christina M. Stansell

PRINCIPAL COMPETITORS

Controladora Comercial Mexicana, S.A.B. de C.V.; Organización Soriana, S.A.B. de C.V.; Wal-Mart de México, S.A.B. de C.V.

FURTHER READING

"A Chain Plus Personality," *Business Week,* August 1, 1953, pp. 76–77.

"Grupo Sanborns Opens First Oakley Store in Mexico," *Latin America News Digest,* June 27, 2005.

Hanrath, Alexander, "Slim's Carso Spins Off CompUSA Holdings," *Financial Times,* July 12, 2002.

Mandel-Campbell, Andrea, "A Mexican with the Midas Touch," *Financial Times,* July 10, 2000.

"Mexican Venture," *Business Week,* June 8, 1946, pp. 80–81.

"Mexico: Carso to Buy Sanborns off Bolsa," *El Financiero,* August 8, 2006.

"Mexico's 'Drug Store' Changes Prescription," *Business Week,* May 15, 1965, pp. 72–73, 76.

Moin, David, "Saks Opens in Mexico," *Women's Wear Daily,* November 29, 2007.

Orlandi, Lorraine, "Mexico's Sanborns Takes Retailing into 21st Century," *Reuters News,* February 21, 2001.

Poole, Claire, "El Conquistador," *Forbes,* September 16, 1991, pp. 68, 72.

Pozas, Ricardo, and Matilde Luna, eds., *Empresas y las empresarios en Mexico,* Mexico City: Editorial Grijalbo, 1991, pp. 337–54.

"Sanborns Completes Purchase of JC Penney," *Corporate Mexico,* February 25, 2005.

Scully, Michael, "Pan America's Crossroads Store," *Pan American,* January 1942, pp. 8–11.

Smith, Geri, and Stephanie Anderson, "Slim's New World," *Business Week,* March 6, 2000.

"Walgreen Sells Stake in Sanborn of 46.9% for $30 Million Total," *Wall Street Journal,* September 18, 1984, p. 20.

Guyenne et Gascogne

Guyenne et Gascogne S.A.

60, avenue du capitaine Resplandy
Bayonne, 64 100
France
Telephone: (33 05) 59 44 55 00
Web site: http://www.guyenneetgascogne.com

Public Company
Incorporated: 1913 as Société Succursaliste S.A.
    d'Approvisionements Guyenne et Gascogne
Sales: $731.7 million (2008)
Stock Exchanges: Euronext Paris
Ticker Symbol: GG
NAICS: 445110 Supermarkets and Other Grocery
    (Except Convenience) Stores

■ ■ ■

Guyenne et Gascogne S.A. is a retail group with a primary focus on food products through the company's hypermarkets, supermarkets, and grocery stores. Based in Bayonne, France, Guyenne et Gascogne concentrates largely on the country's southwest region through its franchise relationship with world's second-largest retailer, Carrefour S.A. The company is also present throughout much of Spain through its partial ownership of Centros Comerciales Carrefour S.A. During 2008 Guyenne et Gascogne operated six Carrefour hypermarkets and 28 Champion supermarkets and Carrefour Market stores in southwest France. Its Sogara subsidiary oversaw 13 Carrefour hypermarkets in the same region. Centros Comerciales Carrefour operated 168 Carrefour hypermarkets, 98 Carrefour Express Supermarkets, and 11 local urban Carrefour City stores. In 2008 the company's sales surpassed $731 million, generating net profit of $44.8 million.

FOUNDED IN 1913

Guyenne et Gascogne started out in the small grocery business in Bayonne, in the far southwest of France, in 1913. The company, called the Société Succursaliste S.A. d'Appro visonnements Guyenne et Gascogne, developed a network of traditional groceries, with emphasis on fresh foods and regional culinary specialties, in the village centers of the region and also established itself as a neighborhood grocer in the area's larger urban centers. While many of the company's stores served a year-round public, Guyenne et Gascogne also began catering to the important vacation trade in its coastal region. The French (and European) summer vacation typically extended over several weeks, and the French vacationer typically returned year after year to a favorite location. Guyenne et Gascogne became a fixture for many such vacationers, opening and extending its branch stores to include seasonal groceries serving local campsites, caravan parks, and other vacation villages during the summer months.

By the mid-1960s, however, Guyenne et Gascogne recognized that its customers' purchasing habits were changing. France was by then in the midst of the so-called Thirty Glorious Years of its post–World War II economic boom. As in much of the western world, the mainstreaming of the automobile was under way, and the newly mobile consumer no longer needed to depend on the proximity of local merchants including butchers, bakers, and grocers or area farmers' markets for their purchases.

Developments in food refrigeration and the creation of the frozen food segment appealed to a population rapidly abandoning tradition in favor of convenience. The supermarket (and later the hypermarket variant) with larger selections, frozen and refrigerated foods and other products, and economies of scale providing lower prices, quickly succeeded in taking a growing share of the food distribution industry, even though French consumers were typically more loyal to the small store concept than their counterparts in other countries.

JOINT VENTURE WITH
CARREFOUR S.A.

In 1966 Guyenne et Gascogne, while not abandoning its chain of small grocers, nevertheless looked toward the new large surface area format to maintain the company's viability in the changing consumer market. That year the company joined with Carrefour S.A., which itself grew to become a dominant force in France's retail food distribution industry, to form the 50-50 joint venture Sogara S.A. The joint venture's mission was to build, acquire, and/or manage supermarkets and hypermarkets under the Carrefour name and others. The Sogara joint venture eventually would take Guyenne et Gascogne beyond its southwestern market, but, with stores focusing on larger urban markets, such as Bordeaux and Toulouse, the Sogara hypermarkets complemented, rather than directly competed with, Guyenne et Gascogne's village and neighborhood-based small markets.

The company also would move into hypermarket and supermarket exploitation on its own, with hyper-

markets participating in the Mammouth chain, created in 1969, and creating its own "brand name" of supermarkets under the Squale name. In these areas, too, the company reinforced its activities in its home region and, eventually, much of the southern French provinces.

Eyeing further growth in the 1970s, Guyenne et Gascogne went public in 1973, listing on the Bordeaux stock exchange. Four years later the company transferred its listing to the Paris stock exchange. By then the company had acquired a number of new supermarkets and in 1974 expanded its hypermarket category, as a 50 percent partner in the joint venture Grandes Superficies S.A., into the Spanish market. In 1978, through Sogara, the company acquired two new Carrefour hypermarkets, located in Angouleme and La Rochelle, farther north, but still close to the country's western coast.

Guyenne et Gascogne began the 1980s by simplifying its name; the company also made several acquisitions, purchasing majority control of supermarket and hypermarket distributors Solodis, Société Civile Agricole du Chateau Puycardin, and Somondex. Guyenne et Gascogne also expanded its regional concentration, opening stores in the Lot and Dordogne departments. During the decade the company increased its participation in its subsidiaries, eventually controlling nearly 100 percent of Solodis. This became a primary subsidiary under which the company would group and later absorb its other hypermarket and supermarket subsidiaries including Somondex, Soldilial, Sodiso, and Jondis. In 1988, however, the company fully absorbed its Solodis subsidiary, grouping its hypermarket and supermarket activities directly under the parent company.

A REGIONAL PRESENCE IN THE
EARLY NINETIES

By the start of the 1990s Guyenne et Gascogne was posting consolidated sales of more than FRF 5 million. Roughly half of the company's revenues came through its own directly controlled hypermarkets, supermarkets, and small branch grocers, with its participation in Sogara representing a nearly equal percentage of its sales. The company's transformation from a chain of branch stores to an important regional developer and exploiter of large surface format stores was dramatic: By then, the chain of Guyenne et Gascogne grocers, which numbered 83 permanent stores and 26 seasonal stores, accounted only for slightly more than 6.5 percent of the company's total sales.

Hypermarkets, excluding the company's participation in the Sogara Carrefour, had become the company's primary revenue generator, with its eight Mammouth

KEY DATES

1913: Guyenne et Gascogne starts out in the small grocery business in Bayonne, in the far southwest of France.

1966: The company joins with Carrefour S.A. to form the 50-50 joint venture Sogara S.A.

1973: Guyenne et Gascogne goes public.

1974: The company expands into Spain.

1988: The company fully absorbs its Solodis subsidiary, grouping its hypermarket and supermarket activities directly under the parent company.

2000: Carrefour becomes the largest retailer in Europe through its merger with Promodès.

2008: Guyenne et Gascogne's partnership with Carrefour is renewed.

hypermarkets (branded within the Paridoc buying central) providing nearly 74 percent of the parent company's annual revenues. The company's hypermarkets were positioned as shopping complexes with a variety of small shops anchored by the Carrefour centerpiece stores, which themselves featured extended product assortments including the standard supermarket categories, but also extensive selections of clothing, audio and computer equipment, automobile and gardening supplies, housewares and appliances, and other consumer goods.

Guyenne et Gascogne's Squale supermarkets, which numbered 18 in the company's home region, contributed a further 19 percent of annual sales. In Spain, the company's position was strengthened by the fusion of its 50 percent subsidiary Grandes Superficies with Centros Commerciales Pryca, creating Spain's largest network of hypermarkets, grouped under Sogara. Guyenne et Gascogne's participation in Pryca was fixed at 10 percent. Meanwhile, as Sogara expanded, Guyenne et Gascogne's share of the joint venture slipped below 50 percent.

SURVIVING RECESSION YEARS

The 1990s would mark difficult economic conditions in France and in much of Europe. The recession that began during the early years of the decade would become a prolonged crisis, reaching into the middle of the decade. Nonetheless, Guyenne et Gascogne had taken a number of steps that enabled it to meet the recession with some success.

The modernization of its distribution facilities, including investments in its computerized inventory, warehousing, distribution, and pricing systems helped the company increase its margins while controlling its pricing structure, countering the drop-off in consumer spending. During the 1990s, in addition, the company began shifting its supermarkets from its Squale name to the Paridoc-controlled Atac franchise. At the same time, Guyenne et Gascogne continued to invest in Sogara's expansion, regaining a 50 percent participation in the joint venture.

The sole weak point in Guyenne et Gascogne's position came with its 1993 attempt to counter the incursion of the so-called hard discounters into France with a purchase of a 20 percent participation in Europa Discount Sud-Ouest, and that chain of deep discount supermarkets. In 1996 Guyenne et Gascogne sold back its share of Europa Discount, which had grown to 16 stores, and exited the hard discounter market. Meanwhile, the company was also forced to close several of its branch grocers; Guyenne et Gascogne remained committed to the format, however, and in 1997 more than 100 permanent and seasonal grocers continued to bear the company's name and history.

SOGARA JOINT VENTURE GROWS IN IMPORTANCE

The transformation of the Squale stores into Atac stores would continue into the mid-1990s. The company acquired several new supermarkets, while closing others that did not meet the requirements for the Atac format. By 1997 Guyenne et Gascogne's supermarket activities included 15 Atac stores and only three Squale stores.

The 1990s also would mark the increasing importance of the Sogara joint venture and its growing number of Carrefour hypermarkets, with new sites added in Toulouse, Bordeaux, and Niort bringing the total to 12 stores by 1997. By year-end 1996 the Sogara participation would account for nearly two-thirds of Guyenne et Gascogne's total revenues.

Hypermarkets in general continued to provide the motor for the company's growth, with the company's chain of six Mammouth hypermarkets accounting for more than 62 percent of Guyenne et Gascogne's sales excluding its Sogara and Pryca participations. By then, too, the Guyenne et Gascogne branch stores represented only slightly more than 5 percent of the company's own revenues. Yet the groceries, which had come to play an important role in the commercial life of many villages, continued to add a significant, if symbolic, reminder of Guyenne et Gascogne's more than 80-year history.

CHANGES HEADING INTO THE NEW MILLENNIUM

Guyenne et Gascogne's operating structure began to change during the late 1990s due in part to several mergers taking place in France's consolidating supermarket industry. Carrefour had purchased supermarket operator Comptoirs Modernes in 1998 and then followed that with the $16.3 billion merger with Promodès, an operator of nearly 6,000 hypermarkets, supermarkets, convenience stores, and discount stores found throughout Europe. The deal, which was finalized in 2000, secured Carrefour's position as the largest retailer in Europe and the second largest in the world.

Meanwhile, Guyenne et Gascogne ended its distribution agreement with Paridoc and switched to the Carrefour central purchasing division. Competitor Groupe Auchan S.A. had acquired Docks de France in 1996, which added the Mammouth and Atac chains to Auchan's coffers. Guyenne et Gascogne began converting its Mammouth hypermarkets into Carrefour stores shortly thereafter.

By 2000 there were rumors that Carrefour had set its sights on acquiring Guyenne et Gascogne. The company denied these claims, opting to remain independent to pursue its own growth strategy. As one of the last remaining French regional retailers, the company stood by its decision not to merge and continued to experience steady growth while rebranding many of its stores under the Carrefour banner. The Beau family remained in control of just over 20 percent of the company.

Net profits dropped in 2005 but rebounded the following year after Sogara launched a divestment program to unload unprofitable businesses. During 2006 Guyenne et Gascogne invested nearly EUR 4.5 million to revamp company headquarters after a fire three years prior destroyed the facility. The company and Carrefour extended their partnership in 2008, which led to many of the company's Champion supermarkets adopting the Carrefour name. It spent EUR 23.8 million that year to upgrade its facilities and expand some of its stores.

Both sales and profits rose in 2008, a sure sign the company was successfully battling increased competition from discounters and online stores as well as weak economic conditions plaguing its French and Spanish operations. Led by chairman Bertrand de Montesquiou and CEO Jean Boutsoque, Guyenne et Gascogne appeared to be on track for success in the years to come as its lucrative partnership with retail giant Carrefour remained firmly in place.

M. L. Cohen
Updated, Christina M. Stansell

PRINCIPAL SUBSIDIARIES

Sogara S.A. (50%); Centros Comerciales Carrefour S.A. (8.232%).

PRINCIPAL COMPETITORS

Groupe Auchan S.A.; Casino, Guichard-Perrachon; METRO AG.

FURTHER READING

Daneshkhu, Scheherazade, "Duran Places His Trust in Stores Restructuring Plan," *Financial Times,* June 26, 2008.

"France: Guyenne et Gascogne's Goals," *Points de Vente,* January 26, 2000.

"France: Review of Guyenne et Gascogne," *LSA,* May 10, 2002.

"Guyenne et Gascogne and Carrefour Partnership," *Business Wire,* November 20, 2008.

"Guyenne et Gascogne Chief Ponders Beau Link," *Reuters News,* September 26, 2003.

"Guyenne et Gascogne Posts Drop in Profit for 2005," *Les Echos,* March 22, 2006.

"Guyenne et Gascogne Profit Edges Up to EUR 31.77m in 2008," *French News Digest,* March 18, 2009.

"Guyenne et Gascogne Rebuilds Headquarters," *Les Echos,* July 24, 2006.

"Guyenne et Gascogne Sees Increase in Profit," *Les Echos,* March 21, 2007.

"Guyenne et Gascogne Takes Carrefour Fascia," *Eurofood,* July 2, 1998.

"Small French Retailers Switch Alliance," *Eurofood,* October 9, 1997.

Hearth & Home Technologies

———■———

7571 215th Street West
Lakeville, Minnesota 55044
U.S.A.
Telephone: (952) 985-6000
Toll Free: (888) 427-3973
Fax: (952) 985-6001
Web site: http://www.hearthtech.com

Wholly Owned Subsidiary of HNI Corporation
Incorporated: 1927 as Heatilator Company
Employees: 2,800
Sales: $424 million (2008 est.)
NAICS: 334140 Heating Equipment (Except Electric and Warm Air Furnaces) Manufacturing

■ ■ ■

A subsidiary of office furniture maker HNI Corporation, Hearth & Home Technologies (HHT) is one of the world's top hearth manufacturers. Based in Lakeville, Minnesota, the company offers a variety of gas, wood, pellet, and electric fireplaces and stoves, as well as fireplace inserts, gas logs, and mantels. Brands include Heat & Glo, Heatilator, Quadra-Fire, and Harman Stoves. Hearth & Home also manufactures outdoor fireplaces and patio campfires. New home builders and homeowners renovating existing structures are HHT's primary customers. The products are mostly sold through independent dealers who either buy directly from the company or through an intermediate distributor. Manufacturing is done at plants in Iowa, Minnesota, Washington, and Pennsylvania.

ORIGINS

Hearth & Home's oldest brand is Heatilator, applied in 1927 to a revolutionary air circulating fireplace invented by Charles LeVerne Carpenter, founder of Chemical Toilet Corporation in Syracuse, New York. A subsidiary, the Heatilator Company, was formed to house the business, which continued to be a leader in the hearth industry for years to come. In 1946 the company introduced the first factory-built fireplace system, making traditional masonry work unnecessary. The parent company, in the meantime, changed its name to San-Equip, Inc., in 1930, and Vega Industries in 1955. Manufacturing for Heatilator products was moved to Mt. Pleasant, Iowa, in 1964. HON Industries acquired Vega's fireplace division in 1981.

HON Industries was founded in Des Moines, Iowa, in 1944 by friends C. Maxwell Stanley, Clement T. Hanson, and H. Wood Miller, their plan being to establish a manufacturing company that would employ servicemen when they returned home from World War II. They anticipated a period of high unemployment, and while that did not materialize, they were correct in their belief that the country would enjoy a construction boom. As a result, they focused on the home market and pursued such products as home freezers and steel kitchen cabinets; this focus was reflected in their choice of the Home-O-Nize Company name. The company proved adept at pursuing opportunities as they rose and dropping product lines that failed to work, such as the kitchen cabinet venture and efforts to manufacture a mechanical corn picker.

The company had better luck with office products, which grew out of an effort to make use of scrap aluminum left over from making aluminum hoods used in installing commercial gas in homes and businesses. These scraps were used to make beverage coasters with the names of businesses stamped on them for promotional purposes, as well as metal file boxes. It was the success of these green metal boxes that led to the company's greater involvement in office products, sold under the HON label. The company added steel cash boxes and steel drawer card cabinets and became involved in furniture through acquisitions. In 1968 the Home-O-Nize Company changed its name, becoming HON Industries, Inc. Although the focus of HON was on entering other sectors in the office products and office furniture industry, it achieved some level of diversity by acquiring the Heatilator operation in 1981.

HEAT-N-GLO ACQUIRED

Under HON's ownership, Heatilator continued to be a leading company in the hearth industry and remained on the cutting edge of technology. In 1991 the Mt. Pleasant subsidiary introduced the Heatilator E Series, which surpassed the Heatilator Mark 123 fireplace (introduced in 1968) as the highest selling fireplace in the history of the hearth industry at that time. Heatilator's NOVUS line of four-sided gas fireplaces was unveiled in 1995 and became the best-selling line in that sector as well. Heatilator also offered stoves for sale.

To fortify its position in the natural gas fireplace market, HON completed a major acquisition in 1996, purchasing Heat-N-Glo Fireplace Products Inc. of Savage, Minnesota, to create the largest hearth products manufacturer in North America to date. Heat-N-Glo was established by brothers Ronald and Daniel Shimek in 1975. Ronald Shimek was a physicist who helped design missile guidance systems for Unisys and started Heat-N-Glo as a hobby. In the 1970s while visiting the Breezy Point Resort in Pequot Lakes, Minnesota, he became fascinated with a freestanding glass-walled gas fireplace.

Taken aback by the $2,000 price tag of adding one to his home, Shimek decided to build one on his own. Soon he assembled a prototype made from hardware glass. It was a far-from-perfect design, however. The flame blew out and Shimek almost burned down his house. Undeterred, he worked out the design flaws and his younger brother, Daniel, a chemicals purchasing manager for 3M, was so impressed that he told Ronald he would sell the fireplaces if Ron would make them. Thus, the two brothers launched Heat-N-Glo as a sideline to their careers, turning out fireplaces in Ron's garage.

Heat-N-Glo enjoyed steady growth, and by 1986 the company was generating $3 million in annual sales, allowing both brothers to quit their jobs to focus all of their attention on the business. Moreover, two other brothers, Steven and Gerald, joined the management team. In 1987 Heat-N-Glo made its mark in the hearth industry when it introduced one of the first self-contained natural gas-burning fireplaces. It relied on direct vent technology that could use a metal pipe pointed in any direction, including downward to vent through the floor.

HEARTH TECHNOLOGIES IS FORMED

The advantages were manifold. Because there was no need for a chimney, homeowners could save on installation and locate fireplaces virtually anywhere in the house. The lack of a chimney, which pulled down cold air into the space below, also created a more energy-efficient house. Outfitted with a thermostat, the fireplace became a virtual space heater by heating the air in a chamber above the fireplace and blowing it back into the room. Because the fireplaces burned natural gas, they were also a good choice for communities such as Seattle and Albuquerque that imposed "no-burn" days to curtail smog caused by burning wood in a fireplace, or cities such as Las Vegas and Denver that limited new homes to natural gas or Environmental Protection Agency–certified wood burning units.

To placate purists, the new natural gas fireplaces included realistic ceramic logs, sound systems that emulated the crackle of real wood, valves that could mimic the sudden surge of a wood fire, and filters that could permeate a room with the smell of burning pine or cedar. The new fireplaces became even more useful with the introduction of remote controlled units in 1988.

By 1990 Heat-N-Glo sales reached $20 million and continued to climb, spurred by further innovations, such as the introduction of the wall heater fireplace in

KEY DATES

1927: First air circulating fireplace is marketed under Heatilator name.

1975: The Shimek brothers establish Heat-N-Glo company.

1981: HON Industries acquires Heatilator.

1987: Heat-N-Glo introduces direct vent gas fireplace.

1996: HON Industries acquires Heat-N-Glo and merges it with Heatilator to form Hearth Technologies.

2000: Several fireplace companies are acquired.

2002: Ronald Shimek retires as president.

2007: Harman Stove Co. is acquired.

1991 and a four-sided gas fireplace, the "Coffee Table," in 1995. By 1996 sales reached $100 million, as natural gas fireplaces were growing in popularity with consumers. To gain a larger stake in the field, HON acquired Heat-N-Glo in October 1996 for $76 million in cash and stock and merged it with Heatilator, which boasted annual sales of about $60 million. The Heatilator subsidiary then took the name Hearth Technologies Inc., comprising the Heatilator Division and the Heat-N-Glo Division, the latter led by Daniel Shimek as president. The two fireplace companies were well suited, combining Heat-N-Glo technology with Heatilator's proficiency in manufacturing.

Hearth Technologies retained its edge in innovation during the second half of the 1990s. Technology introduced in 1997 permitted venting from the top or rear of a fireplace without compromising the sealed combustion chamber. In that same year, zone heating technology provided users with greater heating flexibility and comfort. Firebrick technology was introduced in 1998, adding a more realistic looking ceramic fiber firebox to direct vent gas units. In 1999 the company introduced the first outdoor gas log sets to allow the placement of outdoor fireplaces, followed by the addition of zero-clearance gas fireplaces for the patio.

ACQUISITION SPREE

Hearth Technologies solidified its place in the hearth and stove market in 2000 through the acquisition of several companies, including American Fireplace Co., Allied Fireside Inc., Madison Fire Place Inc., Minocqua Fireplace Co., and Fireplace & Spa Inc. A year later Hearth Technologies restructured its operations. Instead

of being organized around brands, the company divided its operations among three groups: Manufacturing, Sales and Marketing, and distribution under the Hearth Services banner. Other changes were soon in store as well. Hearth Technologies changed its name to Hearth & Home Technologies (the parent company also became HNI Corporation). At the end of 2002 Ronald Shimek retired as president, leaving behind a company that had grown sales to more than $500 million. Retirement did not suit Shimek for very long, however, and he bought the grill division of his former company to create a new venture, Fire Stone Home Products, which later took the Outdoor GreatRoom Company name.

In addition to external growth achieved through acquisitions, HHT continued to drive sales through innovative new products in the early years of the new century. Fireplaces were designed for specific rooms, such as bathrooms and kitchens. The Crescent model, for example, was designed for kitchen use and included a flip-down warming shelf. In 2001 the Patio Gourmet grill was added to allow cooking on outdoor gas fireplaces, followed a year later by the IntelliFire Plus electronic ignition system that eliminated the need for a pilot light, and the see-through, draft-assisted Gateway gas fireplace that offered enhanced venting capabilities.

In 2003 Heat-N-Glo unveiled the Escape, a direct vent fireplace with no exposed sheet metal, thus creating a look indistinguishable from a traditional masonry fireplace. HHT products were then able to take advantage of the HRV200 heat recovery ventilation system, introduced in 2004, to allow the intake of fresh air into a home while exhausting an equal amount of stale air. Also in 2004, Heat-N-Glo brought out the Cyclone, which produced a large burning swirl inside a glass container to create what the company called a "wall art" fireplace.

MAINTAINING A COMPETITIVE EDGE

Not only did HHT produce cutting-edge products, it also manufactured them in a safe and efficient manner, especially important because it allowed the company to maintain a competitive edge in a saturated marketplace. For its achievements in this regard, HHT won the 2005 Shingo Prize, called by *Business Week* "the Nobel Prize of manufacturing." Over the years several HHT products also won the Vesta Award, a fireplace industry honor for design and technology excellence.

HHT also continued to purse external growth as opportunities became available. The company was especially aggressive in acquiring distributors, such as Buck Stoves West Inc. of Northern California, added in

March 2005. A year later HHT added to its Southern California business by acquiring Riverside-based Fireplace Distributors, supplementing two other Southern California distribution operations owned by HHT. The company also sought to help independent dealers grow their businesses, instituting in 2006 a new Retail Partnership Program that allowed them to tap into HHT's marketing, merchandising, and training practices. This was especially important as business conditions began to adversely impact the fireplace industry in 2006. A year later HHT acquired Harman Stove Co., a manufacturer of stoves that relied primarily on wood pellets as fuel. A mild winter coupled with rising wood prices and moderate oil prices crippled that company, which became available to HHT for $29.75 million.

A far greater problem than a mild winter was the decrease in new home starts. After reaching a peak of about $520 million, HHT saw annual sales drop to $462 million in 2007. The slump led to temporary layoffs to allow the company to work through some inventory. In 2008 sales dipped another 8 percent to $424 million. It was a trend that would likely reverse itself when the economy rebounded and builders and remodeling homeowners returned to the market for new fireplaces.

Ed Dinger

PRINCIPAL OPERATING UNITS

Harman Stoves; Heatilator; Heat & Glo; Quadra-Fire.

PRINCIPAL COMPETITORS

Travis Industries, Inc.; Lennox International Inc.; Monessen Hearth Systems Company.

FURTHER READING

Aronovich, Hanna, "Fanning the Flames," *US Business Review,* January–February 2005, p. 218.

Dochat, Tom, "Stove Maker Hopes Sale Will Help Company Grow," *Harrisburg (Pa.) Patriot-News,* September 27, 2007.

Ellis, Kristine, "Dan Shimek: Owner & President, the Outdoor-GreatRoom Company," *Casual Living,* March 1, 2009, p. 16.

"Hearth & Home Technologies Expands in Southern California," *Casual Living,* February 2006, p. 57.

"Hearth Technologies Realigns Units," *Air Conditioning, Heating & Refrigeration News,* February 19, 2001, p. 5.

"Heatilator: Quality Training Provides Top Support," *Professional Builder and Remodeler,* August 1993, p. 77.

"Heat-N-Glo Carries Its Long Tradition of Innovation into the Next Millennium," *Builder,* January 2000, p. 330.

"Hon to Acquire Company," *Burlington (Iowa) Hawk Eye,* July 31, 1996.

Palmeri, Christopher, "Hot Product," *Forbes,* December 30, 1996, p. 98.

Parker, Dick, and Melinda Rogers, "The Heat Is On," *Minneapolis (Minn.) Star Tribune,* June 9, 2003, p. 1B.

Straumnais, Andris, "Fire in Their Eyes and Their Products," *Corporate Report–Minnesota,* December 1990, p. 25.

Herlitz AG

Am Borsigturm 100
Berlin, 13507
Germany
Telephone: (49 030) 4393 0
Fax: (49 030) 4393 3262
Web site: http://www.herlitz.de

Public Company
Founded: 1904
Employees: 2,289
Sales: EUR 301.8 million ($387 million) (2008)
Stock Exchanges: Frankfurt
Ticker Symbol: HEZ
NAICS: 322231 Die-Cut Paper and Paperboard Office
  Supplies Manufacturing; 322233 Stationery, Tablet,
  and Related Product Manufacturing; 42212
  Stationery and Office Supplies Wholesalers

■ ■ ■

Herlitz AG is one of Germany's leading manufacturers and distributors of office and paper supplies, writing instruments, greeting cards, and gift wrap. Under the Herlitz brand name, the company offers high-quality office and school supplies. Schoolchildren form the company's core clientele with more than one-third of them in Germany using Herlitz products. Since 2007 the Herlitz brand has also included a line of quality business-to-business office supplies. The company's Falken brand is its line of lower-priced office supplies and included items such as file folders, binders, notebooks, plastic document sleeves, and other products.

Susy Card is the firm's line of greeting cards and gift wrap. The company also offers wholesale/retail logistic services through its eCom Logistik division and software for inventory management and product distribution through Mercoline. Herlitz has production facilities in the Berlin area, as well as in Peitz, Germany; Most, Czech Republic; Przezmierowo, Poland; Buftea, Romania; and Droylsden, England. Its subsidiaries are located in the Netherlands, Great Britain, Finland, France, Poland, Hungary, the Czech Republic, Slovakia, Bulgaria, Greece, Russia, Switzerland, and Romania. The German market accounted for 57 percent of Herlitz' total revenues in 2008; 23 percent came from the rest of Western Europe, while the rest of the world accounted for 20 percent of sales.

SELLING STATIONERY IN THE GERMAN CAPITAL

Herlitz AG, like so many other tradition-rich German industrial enterprises, was founded around the dawn of the 20th century, when the Second German Empire under Kaiser Wilhelm II was at its high point. In September 1904, Carl Herlitz, a 37-year-old bookseller, founded a company to distribute stationery supplies, such as paper and pens. The company was launched from the four-room apartment where Herlitz and his wife lived in Berlin.

The city was undergoing explosive growth at the time and Herlitz was able to take advantage of it. It was, at first, an early form of the just-in-time supply chain with few products were kept on hand in the apartment at any one time, and everything Herlitz did have in stock was stored under his bed in the room of the apartment which also served as the company's operational headquarters. His customers were many small stationery shops in the capital and the towns in the surrounding countryside.

By the end of World War I, in 1920, Herlitz had three sons. He moved the family and the business to a larger apartment in the same suburban Berlin neighborhood. The office and warehouse were equipped with the high-technology office equipment of the day, namely a telephone and a typewriter. Since typewriter ribbons were so hard to come by, however, it was used for only the most important jobs. Deliveries were made not by horse-drawn carriage they were brought into the center of Berlin on the city's electric streetcar line. They were then distributed by handcart to the approximately 100 stationery shops in Berlin. Carl Herlitz made a regular visit to the industry's annual trade fair in Leipzig and took pains to keep his customers informed of and hopefully supplied with novel and innovative office supplies. So much so that his clientele began referring to him as their *Neuheiten-Onkel* or "Uncle Novelty." It was absolutely necessary strategy though if he were to compete with the larger stationery wholesalers in Berlin at the time.

SURVIVING THE GREAT DEPRESSION

By the end of the 1920s, the Carl Herlitz GmbH was an established midsized Berlin company, with a workforce that hovered around ten employees. Nonetheless, the decade had provided it a constant series of challenges. In 1923 runaway inflation eventually saw the value of the Mark decrease by millions in the course of a single day, wrecking many other companies. When the Great Depression came, it hit Germany particularly hard. Herlitz was forced to introduce strict cost-saving

measures and cut personnel to the bare bones to survive the economic crisis.

Sixty-eight-year-old Carl Herlitz' health was in decline when he retired in 1935 (he would die just four years later), and the management of the company was taken over by his middle son, Günter. Times were still hard then. In its way, the company and its six employees was a German version of the poor man in the United States selling pencils on the street corner. In this case, though, the company was selling rubber bands in cellophane packages of 20, each packed by hand. At the same time it continued to introduce new products, however, for example an early form of cellophane tape, which Herlitz was among the first firms to sell. As the 1930s drew on, the company rented a proper office and warehouse space closer to the center of Berlin. Günter Herlitz also oversaw the expansion of Herlitz' distribution channels to large cities near Berlin, such as Neuruppin, Potsdam, and Wittenberge. Herlitz service and expertise had also won the confidence of the companies whose products it distributed and some responded by awarding Herlitz exclusive distribution rights in the Berlin metropolitan area.

When World War II began in September 1939, it brought six years of hardship to Berlin and the Herlitz company. Günter Herlitz and his brother Walter were drafted almost immediately into the German army. Their mother in Berlin was required to take over the day-to-day management of the company. On the material front, the war brought shortages of raw materials and finished products; on the military front, it brought bombing raids to Berlin on an almost daily basis from 1943 onwards. These struck Herlitz regularly. Their downtown office and warehouse was completely destroyed by bombs in November 1943. Afterward the company moved in with another firm in another part of town and a little over a year later was bombed out once again in one of the most destructive raids of the war.

POSTWAR RECOVERY IN WEST BERLIN

Although the war ended in May 1945, Günter Herlitz did not return until the following July, and the rebirth of the Herlitz company occurred slowly. The first years of the war were marked by shortages in nearly every phase of life. They were particularly severe in the paper industry. The company was reduced to producing vases from the shells of lightbulbs, bags from old string, toys from old pieces of wood and fabric, in short, everything, it seemed, but stationery supplies. The company truck, with which deliveries had been made since the mid-1930s, had apparently also been destroyed in the bombing. Günter was able, though, to get his hands one

KEY DATES

1904: Founded by Carl Herlitz in Berlin.

1935: Founder Carl Herlitz resigns and is succeeded by his son Günter Herlitz as company head.

1943: Company offices and warehouse are destroyed in a bombing raid.

1948: Goods are flown in from West Germany during the Berlin Airlift.

1960: Production of notebooks and pads starts in Berlin Schöneberg.

1977: Herlitz is listed on the Berlin Stock Exchange.

1978: Greeting card company Paul Zoeke Glückswunschkarten GmbH & Co. KG is acquired.

1984: McPaper office supply store chain is founded.

1987: Greeting card producer Susy Card GmbH & Co. KG is acquired.

1988: Günter Herlitz steps down from day-to-day management of the company.

1994: Company acquires shares in AO Wolga paper factory in Russia.

1996: Firm is reorganized.

1998: McPaper chain is sold to the German Post Office.

1999: Subsidiaries Herlitz Falkenhöh AG Wohnungen and Herlitz Merchandising GmbH are sold.

2001: Bank consortium takes over ownership of about 70 percent of Herlitz.

2002: Herlitz goes into receivership.

2005: Company is acquired by Advent International Corporation.

of the rarest of postwar commodities, a bicycle, and to get a permit for it from the Russian administrators of the eastern sector of the city on the condition that it be used "exclusively for business purposes." With it, the company was once again able to start delivering goods throughout Berlin and nearby outlying areas. Then, to everyone's astonishment, the truck was recovered from underneath the rubble of the old company headquarters and eventually restored to running condition.

In 1948 the three Western occupation forces, the United States, Great Britain, and France, voted to unite their zones in West Berlin into a single economic unit that used the newly inaugurated deutsche mark as its official currency. In reaction, the Soviet military in East Germany, which completely surrounded Berlin geographically, closed off all lines of supply, including

rail, water, and road, into West Berlin. That launched the beginning of the Berlin airlift in June 1948, in which the United States and Britain transported thousands of pounds of food, coal, and other supplies into West Berlin every day. Twenty wholesalers in the city were also allowed to transport their products into the city on the planes. Herlitz was one of them.

Around the same time, he moved the company from its old building in the Russian zone across town into the American zone. The move had to be carried out surreptitiously because the Russian officials in East Berlin would not have allowed the firm to take its goods from the east zone. As a result, Herlitz employees made daily trips on the Berlin subway, smuggling the company's stock into the American sector.

EAST BERLIN UPRISING INTERRUPTS PRODUCTION

The Russian blockade of West Berlin did not end for nearly a year. In May 1949 goods, including office supplies, could once again be delivered to Berlin unhindered. That, along with the introduction of the deutsche mark, marked the beginning of the so-called *Wunderwirtschaft* in West Germany, the German Economic Miracle of the 1950s. Herlitz profited from it as much as any West German company, and soon the company was supplying paper and writing supplies to nearly half of the approximately 2,000 stationery and office supply stores in and around Berlin.

Notebooks and pads of paper came from a small bindery, a subcontractor located not far from the East Berlin sector boundary (the Berlin Wall would not be built for another 12 years). Most of the bindery's employees were residents of the Russian sector of the city. That created problems for Herlitz in June 1953 when a popular uprising against the communist regime in East Germany started in the Russian sector. While it was being put down by the Russian army, many of East Berlin employees were not able to get to their jobs in West Berlin. Work in the bindery ground to a halt. In response, Herlitz was forced to purchase three pieces of secondhand machinery so it could produce its own pads and notebooks temporarily in small, jury-rigged factory in another part of the city.

A PRESENCE IN WEST GERMANY, EUROPE, AND THE UNITED STATES

By 1955 Herlitz had revenues of about DEM 2.2 million and was distributing some 60 tons of paper products annually. An attempt to set up facilities in

West Germany, separated from Berlin by more than 100 miles of East German territory, failed. In 1960, however, the company won a foothold there nonetheless, thanks to a popular series of notebooks and drawing pads decorated with pictures of animals and sports stars. Growth was breathtakingly rapid in the 1960s thanks in part at least to generous subsidies provided by West Germany to companies located in West Berlin. At the beginning of the decade the company's annual revenues stood at DEM 4.2 million. By 1964 they had more than doubled, reaching DEM 8.7 million. Over the next five years they nearly tripled, amounting to DEM 23 million in 1969.

Hoping to fund further growth, Herlitz went public in 1972. Two years later the company put its first assembly line into operation, producing standard A4 sized notebooks. That marked Herlitz's move beyond distribution into production as well. From that point on its activities as a distributor would compose only about 10 percent of its revenues. In the company started exporting its products to other European markets in 1977. To oversee that activity, it founded the subsidiary Herlitz International Trading AG. The venture was a success and the following year the firm's revenues topped DEM 121 million. As the 1980s got underway, Herlitz continued to expand. Between 1978 and 1987 no fewer than nine companies, makers of greeting cards, writing instruments, paper, gift wrap, and office supplies were acquired. An American subsidiary, Herlitz Inc. was established in Dallas, Texas, in 1981 and a year later the paper good production was launched there.

Internal growth in Berlin proceeded apace as well. In 1979 the firm purchased a large piece of property in northwest Berlin. Over the following decade, one of the world's largest, state-of-the-art warehouses and distribution centers would be constructed on the site. Production in Berlin was consolidated in a new factory in the Tegel area of the city; where the firm's administrative headquarters were also set up.

NEW LEADERSHIP, EXPANSION MANIA, AND THE START OF HARD TIMES

The year 1988 was a watershed for Herlitz AG. That year, with revenues totaling DEM 642 million and a product line encompassing more than 10,000 items, Günter Herlitz stepped down from active management after 53 years at the firm's helm. Herlitz' three sons Heinz, Peter, and Klaus had been brought into the management team in the 1960s and 1970s. Following with the departure of their father matters began to slowly crumble at the company. For one thing, the long-standing economic situation in Berlin, established by the

Cold War and the desire of the West German government to attract business to the island city, changed dramatically.

The fall of the Berlin Wall was greeted with jubilation, by Herlitz as much as anyone, and the company distributed free notebooks and pens to East Berliners entering the city for the first time. Nonetheless, soon the subsidies companies in West Berlin had enjoyed for 20 years would be discontinued completely.

The first small sign of problems came in 1990, when the American subsidiary (it had been the Herlitz sons who had pushed for expansion into North America) had to be closed. Herlitz entered the slippery slope in earnest in the first half of the 1990s, however, when the company leadership was overcome by an expansion mania that had little connection to Herlitz' resources or its expertise. In 1992, for example, it jumped into the Berlin real estate market with the establishment of Herlitz Falkenhöh AG Wohnungen. The subsidiary planned to build some 1,400 homes, apartments, and offices in a large subdivision in northwest Berlin. The construction of a large, new Herlitz factory and office complex near the Falkenhöh site at a cost of some DEM 350 million was also begun. Five years later, the real estate development would be far below full occupancy and much of the new Herlitz complex would be rented to outsiders or vacant.

Another failed project was the development a modern shopping mall and office building near the company's Berlin-Tegel headquarters, which in the end cost Herlitz more than DEM 850 million. In 1995, when practically all business eyes in Europe were looking towards expansion into the former Soviet bloc, the firm purchased AO Volga, a paper manufacturer in Russia, for $12 million. What Herlitz did not realize at the time of the acquisition was that the factory was balanced precariously on the edge of bankruptcy. When the scales tipped, AO Volga had to be abandoned. The adventure cost Herlitz more than $100 million.

INTO THE RED AND INTO BANKRUPTCY

After steady growth every year since the late 1940s, the expansion mania finally pushed Herlitz into the red in 1995. The company was reorganized the following year and the upper management team was shaken up. A strategic decision was taken in 1997 to return the company to its core business focus on office supplies and stationery products, but it seemed to come too late. That year Klaus Herlitz resigned from the company board and Peter Herlitz stepped down as CEO. Soon no member of the Herlitz family would be active in the company. At year's end losses of DEM 101 million. Berlin, the city that had supported Herlitz with generous subsidies during the Cold War years, also felt the brunt of the changes in the firm. Only half of the Herlitz workforce was still composed of Berliners. The rest were scattered across eastern Europe and China.

By the end of the 1990s Herlitz had undergone a thorough housecleaning. It had sold off most of its non-core businesses including real estate subsidiary Herlitz Falkenhöh AG, the foreign trade subsidiary Herlitz International Trading, the McPaper retail chain, and Herlitz Merchandising GmbH, a producer of sports fan merchandise. The money continued to flow out of the firm however. In 2000 the firm reported losses of DEM 100.7 million against total business of DEM 958 million. The company's debts amounted to some DEM 700 million. A bailout plan was put together the following year by a consortium of banks led by Deutsche Bank and the Berliner Kommerzbank, determined that the company not go under. They assumed ownership of about 67 percent of the company shares. In spring 2002 the company nonetheless was forced to start bankruptcy proceedings in Berlin.

A strict cost-cutting regimen was introduced. More employees were laid off until the number worldwide had dipped to about 3,000, down from 5,000 in the early 1990s. The firm's new owners set about looking for a buyer for Herlitz, one with fairly deep pockets and willing to invest in the company. One problem was that the market for office supplies and stationery was changing. Herlitz was a top-of-the-line brand and hence expensive. The public and retailers, however, were demanding the least-expensive paper and writing products available. Additional pressure came from rising prices for the raw materials Herlitz needed for its production. The company was being squeezed from both sides.

FINDING A NEW OWNER

The Esselte Group, a Swedish office supplies maker, expressed interest in acquiring Herlitz in spring 2003. The deal fell through though when the two sides were unable to come to terms on a price. In 2005, however, an American venture-capital firm, Advent International Corp., acquired 65 percent of the company from the bank group. Advent subsequently made an attempt to purchase the 35 percent of the shares held by private investors but shareholders showed little interest in selling, a sign Advent interpreted as optimism about Herlitz' future. Advent called its investment in Herlitz a middle-term project. Its goal was to reorganize the company, not to break it up, restore it to good financial health once again, and then to make a hopefully lucrative a stock offering.

The restructuring proved to be a tougher project than Advent anticipated. After a short period back in the black, Herlitz announced losses in both 2006 and 2007. In the latter year, it managed to boost its revenues for the first time in some ten years. However, the new owners were more interested in boosting profit rather than business. As an antidote plans were laid to focus on promoting the company's own product lines, the Herlitz brand and the Falken budget brand. Herlitz had looked eastward for rescue in the Eastern European markets.

By 2009, however, the effects of the global finance crisis were making themselves felt in that part of the world, with dropping sales and eastern currencies falling badly in relation to the euro. With a large portion of its annual income coming from purchases for schoolchildren in Germany, the company was also concerned about the effects Germany's falling birthrate would have on performance in coming years. The worst might be behind it, but for Herlitz the future was still full of questions.

Gerald E. Brennan

PRINCIPAL SUBSIDIARIES

eCom Logistics; Mercoline; Herlitz OY (Finland); Herlitz Hellas A.E. (Greece); Herlitz UK Ltd.; Herlitz Benelux B.V. (Netherlands); Herlitz Bulgaria EooD (Bulgaria); Herlitz Spolka zo.o. (Poland); DELMET PROD srl (Romania); Herlitz România S.A.; Herlitz Slovakia s.r.o.; Herlitz Hungária Kft. (Hungary); Susy Card GmbH; eCom Logistik GmbH & Co. KG; Mercoline GmbH; Convex Schreibwaren-Handels GmbH; PBS Papeterie Service GmbH; ANCO Boutique GmbH; Falken Office Products GmbH; HGG Verwaltungsgesellschaft mbH; Herlitz Papierverarbeitungs GmbH.

PRINCIPAL COMPETITORS

Esselte Leitz GmbH & Co KG; Corporate Express US, Inc.; International Paper Company; Manutan International; Office Depot International (UK) Ltd.; Quill Corporation; S.P. Richards Company; United Stationers Inc; Smead Manufacturing Company.

FURTHER READING

"Als er die Zügel locker ließ, war es um Herlitz geschehen," *Die Welt*, February 8, 2003, p. 14.

"Der unaufhaltsame Fall von Herlitz," *Die Welt*, December 21 1999.

Gericke, Ulli, "Herlitz-Banken haben 130 Mill. Euro zum Überleben beigesteuert," *Börsen-Zeitung*, June 18, 2003, p. 12.

"Herlitz Buys into Volga," *Moscow Times,* October 10, 1996.

"Herlitz Has Been Through the Worst," *Borsen-Zeitung,* October 29, 1998, p. 8.

"Herlitz Restructuring Yet to Pay Off Paper," *Handelsblatt* (English version), August 30, 2001.

"Herlitz Saved from Bankruptcy for Now," *Handelsblatt* (English version), May 9, 2001.

Hobday, Nicola, "Capital Management in Herlitz Hunt," *Daily Deal,* August 29, 2002.

Hooson, Ben, "German Herlitz to Sell Stake in Volga Paper," *Moscow Times,* March 7, 1997.

100 Jahre Herlitz, Berlin, 2004. Available at: http://www.herlitz. de/fileadmin/Bilder/Bilder-Produkte/Unternehmen/Konzern/ 100_Jahre_Herlitz.pdf.

"Vor fast 100 Jahren von einem Buchhändler gegründet," *Die Welt,* April 4, 2002, p. 34.

"World Bank Affiliate Boosts Investment in Russian Paper Plant," *BBC Summary of World Broadcasts,* March 10, 1995.

Hersha Hospitality Trust

———— ■ ————

44 Hersha Drive
Harrisburg, Pennsylvania 17102
U.S.A.
Telephone: (717) 236-4400
Fax: (717) 774-7383
Web site: http://www.hersha.com

Real Estate Investment Trust
Incorporated: 1998
Employees: 24
Sales: $264.8 million (2008)
Stock Exchanges: New York
Ticker Symbol: HT
NAICS: 525930 Real Estate Investment Trusts

■ ■ ■

Hersha Hospitality Trust is a Harrisburg, Pennsylvania-based real estate investment trust (REIT) that specializes in the ownership of hotel properties. Its portfolio at the end of 2008 included 58 wholly owned properties and interests in 18 others. All told, these properties include more than 9,500 rooms. Hersha operates primarily under franchise licenses from such major hotel chains as Marriott International (Marriott, Residence Inn, Spring-hill Suites, Courtyard by Marriott, Fairfield Inn, and TownePlace Suites brands), Hilton Hotel Corporation (Hilton, Hilton Garden Inn, Hampton Inn, and Homewood Suites brands), Intercontinental Hotel Group (Holiday Inn, Holiday Inn Express, and Holiday Inn Express & Suites brands), Global Hyatt Corporation (Hyatt Summerfield Suites and Hawthorn Suites

brands), Starwood Hotels (Four Points by Sheraton and Sheraton Hotels brands), and Choice Hotels International (Comfort Inn, Comfort Suites, Sleep Inn, and Mainstay Suites brands).

Hersha tends to locate its hotels in central business districts and suburban office markets in the northeastern United States and West Coast cities where it operates, including the Boston metropolitan area; Connecticut; the New York City metropolitan area; New Jersey; the Philadelphia metropolitan area and central Pennsylvania; Wilmington, Delaware; the Washington, D.C., metropolitan area; Virginia and North Carolina; San Francisco, California; and Scottsdale, Arizona. Hersha Hospitality Trust is part of the Hersha Group of companies, which is majority shareholder of the REIT and includes Hersha Construction and Hersha Hotel Supply. Hersha Trust was founded by its chairman, Hasu P. Shah, and named for his wife, Hersha.

IMMIGRANT FOUNDER

Born in India, Hasu Shah immigrated to the United States from Bombay in 1960 to further his education. Although his father had borrowed money to pay for his chemical engineering studies at Tennessee Technological University, the 20-year-old Shah arrived with just $60 in his pocket. After receiving his bachelor of science degree, he went to work as a chemist for the New Jersey state police. In 1968 he moved to Harrisburg, Pennsylvania, taking a position in the state's Department of Environmental Resources. Shah continued his education, earning a master's degree in engineering administration from Pennsylvania State University in

1974. Along the way he made money on the side by acquiring foreclosed homes and then renovating and renting them out.

In 1978 he sold his properties to raise enough money to return to India to set himself up in business there. Against his family's wishes, he sold his car, house, and furnishings, and relocated everyone to India, where he planned to purchase a pharmaceutical company. As a precaution, Shah left behind much of their possessions in boxes and did not quit his job, taking a leave of absence instead. It proved to be a wise decision, because at the last moment the deal was scuttled, and soon he, his wife, and two sons were flying back to Harrisburg.

Shah returned to his state position. Rather than abandoning his dream of running his own business, however, Shah put the $45,000 that remained of his savings to use by purchasing an 11-room motel in nearby Middletown, Pennsylvania. During the day his wife ran the motel, and he assumed the night shift, sleeping in his clothes to meet the needs of his guests while preparing for the next day at the office. Less then a year later Shah was able to acquire a second motel, and he began to trade up, again following the formula of buying undervalued properties and renovating them. In 1984 he bought the run-down 125-room Nationwide Inn in the historic Shipoke area in Harrisburg, Pennsylvania, later renamed the Riverfront Inn. This was to be the foundation of Hersha Enterprises Ltd., a company Shah named after his wife. In 1985 he was able to quit his day job and devote all of his time to the hotel business.

ADDING MAJOR BRANDS

Shah turned his attention to major hotel brands. In 1990 he spent $500,000 to completely renovate the Riverfront Inn to gain a Quality Inn franchise. In this way, he would be able to take advantage of Quality Inn's referral network to attract more upscale business to his location in Shipoke, a row house neighborhood that had become newly gentrified. The old Nationwide Inn had once catered to railroad workers, but even as a Quality Inn franchise the property struggled to bring in a new demographic. Shah hoped to make the hotel more visible by erecting a 65-foot Quality Inn sign that could be seen from Interstate 83, but the idea caused an uproar in the community, which feared that other tall signs would follow and mar the historic look of the area. In the end, rather than alienate his neighbors, Shah relented.

The Quality Inn Riverfront was not Shah's only interest, however. Hersha continued to add properties, mostly under the Holiday Inn banner. By 1997 the company controlled 14 hotels in Pennsylvania, generating about $20 million in annual revenues. Shah and some Indian partners also looked to bring the Holiday Inn name to their home country, but once again Shah found it far more difficult to do business in his native country than in the United States. He had a handshake deal to purchase some property near the Bombay airport, but the contract never arrived. After three months of waiting, he learned that a rival Hong Kong group had made a much higher bid, prompting Shah to walk away from the deal.

In 1998 Shah packaged his hotel properties into a real estate investment trust (REIT). Congress had created REITs in 1960 as a real estate investment vehicle similar to mutual funds. They could be taken public and their shares (units) traded like stocks. Because REITs were required by law to pay out at least 95 percent of their taxable income to shareholders each year, their ability to raise funds internally was limited. Moreover, third parties had to be engaged to operate or manage the properties. As a result, REITs were not especially popular during their first 30 years of existence. It was not until the Tax Reform Act of 1986 that REITs gained some attraction. In the early 1990s, when traditional sources of real estate investment dried up and the marketplace was glutted with available properties due to a period of overbuilding, REITS came into their own, most of them focusing on alternative sectors of the real estate market.

Hersha Hospitality Trust was formed in May 1998, incorporated in Maryland for tax purposes. It was taken public in January 1999 and shares began trading on the American Stock Exchange. The proceeds of the offering were used to acquire ten hotel properties owned by Hersha Enterprises and affiliates. They included five Holiday Inn franchised units, two Hampton Inn hotels, two Comfort Inns, and one Clarion Suites property. Altogether, the portfolio boasted nearly 1,600 rooms. They were managed by Hersha Hospitality Management, L.P., on a lease basis. Other members of the Hersha group of affiliated companies included Hersha

KEY DATES

1984: Hasu P. Shah purchases run-down 125-room hotel in the Shipoke neighborhood of Harrisburg, Pennsylvania; forms Hersha Enterprises Ltd. to own hotel properties.

1990: The Shipoke property is completely renovated to gain a Quality Inn franchise.

1998: Shah packages his hotel properties into a real estate investment trust named Hersha Hospitality Trust.

1999: Hersha Hospitality Trust is taken public, trading on the American Stock Exchange.

2005: Succession plan is put into effect.

2008: Hersha receives New York Stock Exchange listing.

Development Corporation, Hersha Construction Services, and Hersha Interiors & Supply.

DECADE CLOSES WITH MULTIPLE ACQUISITIONS

Hersha Hospitality Trust soon expanded its slate of hotel properties. In August 1999 a newly opened 60-room Comfort Inn located near John F. Kennedy International Airport in Jamaica, New York, was added, followed a month later by the purchase of a pair of two other Hersha-affiliated properties: a 77-room Clarion Inn & Suites hotel in Harrisburg and a 72-room Hampton Inn in Danville, Pennsylvania. Three more hotels owned by Hersha affiliates were then acquired in February 2000, including a 110-room Hampton Inn & Suites located in Hershey, Pennsylvania; a 107-room Best Western in Indiana, Pennsylvania; and a 76-room Comfort Inn in McHenry, Maryland. During the rest of 2000, Hersha acquired five more hotels, one of which, a Sleep Inn in Coraopolis, Pennsylvania, had been owned by a Hersha affiliate. The other four were purchased in May from Nobel Investment Group, Ltd. The properties included Comfort Suites and Holiday Inn Express operations in Duluth, Georgia, and a pair of Hampton Inn hotels in Newman and Peachtree City, Georgia.

Hersha increased revenues from $25.7 million in 1999 to nearly $33 million in 2000. Nonetheless, despite this strong performance, the REIT did not receive much attention from Wall Street, which at the time was focused on Internet and high-technology stocks. To provide itself with the financial wherewithal to maintain growth, Hersha engineered a $22 million refinancing with Lehman Brothers in the spring of 2000.

The following year was turbulent for everyone involved in the hospitality and travel industries, due to the adverse impact of the terrorist attacks of September 11, 2001, in New York City and Washington, D.C. Occupancy rates dipped and Hersha's total revenues fell to $31.4 million, leading to a net loss of more than $1 million. Considering the environment, however, it was a performance that proved the resiliency of the Hersha business model that focused on midpriced hotels. During the year, Hersha made adjustments to its portfolio. The company sold the Shipoke property as well as the Comfort Inn in McHenry, Maryland, and a Holiday Inn in Pennsylvania. In the meantime, Hersha acquired three other hotels: an 87-room Sleep Inn and 69-room Mainstay Suites in King of Prussia, Pennsylvania, and a 79-room Holiday Inn Express in Long Island City, New York.

SECOND STOCK OFFERING FUELS GROWTH

Difficult economic conditions continued in 2002 and did not begin to improve until the end of 2003. During this time, Hersha acquired a 72-room Mainstay Suites hotel in Frederick, Maryland, and a Doubletree Club at JFK International Airport in New York City. A more important development came in June 2003 when a partnership was forged with CNL Hospitality Properties Inc., which invested about $20 million in the company and teamed up with Hersha to buy a Hampton Inn in the Chelsea neighborhood of Manhattan in New York City. Moreover, In October 2003 Hersha conducted a secondary share offering that netted $77 million, earmarked to support the company's plan to move into large metropolitan markets. Other acquisitions in 2003 included a Hilton Garden Inn in Edison, New Jersey; a Hampton Inn in Newark, New Jersey; and a Hilton Garden Inn in Glastonbury, Connecticut.

With the economy improving, Hersha began to grow at a more accelerated rate in 2004, adding several new properties and joint venture interests in others. A 96-room Holiday Inn Express was added in Hartford, Connecticut, in January 2004, followed a month later by a 55 percent stake in a Four Points by Sheraton at Boston's Logan International Airport. A 125-room Residence Inn in Framingham, Massachusetts, was added in March, and a 73-room Comfort Inn in Frederick, Maryland, in May. July brought three acquisitions: a 50 percent joint-venture interest in a 130-room Courtyard by Marriott in Ewing-Hopewell, New Jersey; a 120-room Residence Inn in Greenbelt, Maryland; and a 109-room Fairfield Inn in Laurel, Maryland.

A year later, Hersha remained active, adding 20 hotels with more than 2,700 rooms in key markets the company hoped would drive future growth: Boston, New York City, Philadelphia, Hartford, and Washington, D.C. In 2006 the company was even more aggressive, acquiring interests in another 24 hotels with more than 3,500 rooms, including a new brand, Hyatt Summerfield Suites, part of a strategy of establishing a strong presence in the extended-stay sector. As a result of this activity, total revenues increased to $70 million in 2005 and $137.6 million in 2006. To support the company's growth, Hersha issued new stock, raising $202 million in funds.

SUCCESSION PLANS TAKE SHAPE

While expanding the portfolio at a rapid pace, Hersha also took steps to put a management succession plan in place in 2005. Shah stepped down as chief executive officer in December 2005, succeeded by one of his sons, Jay H. Shah, who had served as president and chief operating officer since 2003, positions that were then assigned to another son, Neil H. Shah. Their father continued to serve as chairman of the board.

One market of particular importance to Hersha's future was metropolitan New York City. Rather than affiliating their properties with major chains, the company looked to develop and operate independent properties in addition to its budget brands. The company opened a hotel in Manhattan at Lexington Avenue and East 48th Street in the shadow of several major hotels, including the famous Waldorf-Astoria. In 2008 Hersha opened its first boutique hotel, the Nu Hotel, located in downtown Brooklyn on Smith Street and Atlantic Avenue. Smith Street by the time was emerging as a place for trendy bars and eateries, close to a number of upscale Brooklyn neighborhoods and easily accessible from Manhattan by subway.

Hersha purchased seven properties in 2007 and another six hotels in 2008. Total revenues increased to $241.3 million in 2007 and nearly $265 million a year later. In May 2008 Hersha was listed on the New York Stock Exchange. Due to softening business conditions, the company eased up on its expansion efforts and began to trim its portfolio of some noncore properties. A poor economy led to the sale of three properties in July 2009, including a Mainstay Suites and a Comfort Inn in Frederick, Maryland, and a Four Points hotel in Revere, Massachusetts. Nevertheless, Hersha remained well positioned to enjoy sustained long-term growth.

Ed Dinger

PRINCIPAL SUBSIDIARIES

44 New England Management Company; Hersha Hospitality, LLC; Hersha CNL TRS, Inc.

PRINCIPAL COMPETITORS

Innkeepers USA Trust; Jameson Inns, Inc.; Supertel Hospitality, Inc.

FURTHER READING

Carroll, Pat, "From the Depths of a Seedy Riverside Motel, Stock Has Risen to a $50 Million Enterprise," *Harrisburg (Pa.) Patriot-News,* January 31, 1999, p. D1.

Dochat, Tom, "Deal Provides Hersha with More Impact," *Harrisburg (Pa.) Patriot-News,* June 22, 2003, p. U11.

———, "Hotel Investment Trust Hersha Makes Reservation with New York Stock Exchange," *Harrisburg (Pa.) Patriot-News,* May 5, 2008.

———, "Hotel Operator Thrives in New Home," *Harrisburg (Pa.) Patriot-News,* February 1, 2007, p. C1.

Raghavan, Sudarsan, "50 Years of Independence: Still in Tune with India After Rags to Riches in PA," *Philadelphia Inquirer,* August 15, 1997, p. A1.

Turkel, Stanley, "From Ragas to Riches: Part 2," *Lodging Hospitality,* March 15, 2003, p. 42.

Wysocki, Bernard, Jr., "Elite U.S. Immigrants Straddle Two Cultures," *Wall Street Journal,* May 12, 1997, p. B1.

Holland Casino

Postbus 355
Hoofddorp, NL-2130 AH
Netherlands
Telephone: (31 023) 565 95 65
Fax: (31 023) 565 95 00
Web site: http://www.hollandcasino.nl

State-Owned Company
Incorporated: 1976
Employees: 4,795
Sales: EUR 700.1 million ($875 million) (2008 est.)
NAICS: 713210 Casinos (Except Casino Hotels)

■ ■ ■

Holland Casino is more formally known as De Nationale Stichting tot Exploitatie van Casinospelen in Nederland (National Foundation for the Operation of Casino Games in the Netherlands). The state-owned company was established by the Dutch government as the sole license-holder authorized to operate gaming casinos in the Netherlands. Holland Casino operates 14 casinos throughout the country, in Amsterdam, Breda, Eindhoven, Enschede, Groningen, Leeuwarden, Nijmegen, Rotterdam, Scheveningen, Utrecht, Valkenburg and Venlo, and Zandvoort. The company also operates a casino in Schiphol Airport reserved exclusively for air travelers. Holland Casino's gambling business covers nearly 520 tables, accounting for 40 percent of group revenues, and nearly 7,400 slot machines, which generate 49 percent of the company's sales.

In addition to providing a legal gambling alternative, Holland Casino's mandate includes the enforcement of a responsible gambling policy. Guests to the casinos are monitored for the frequency of their visits. For frequent gamblers, the company provides preventive information and conducts prevention interviews. Frequent gamblers also face limits on the number of visits, as well as temporary exclusion from the group's casinos.

Holland Casino has been faced with increasing competition from the rise of online gambling offered by web sites outside of the Netherlands. The Dutch government has resisted the company's request for authorization to develop its own online gambling operation. Due to increasing competition and the economic downturn, Holland Casino has seen its attendance figures drop in the 21st century. In 2008, the company's revenues fell 7.5 percent to EUR 700 million ($875 million). The company's operating profit that year slipped by 83 percent, to EUR 14.3 million. Holland Casino is led by CEO D. F. Flink and Chairman B. Staal.

ESTABLISHING A NATIONALIZED CASINO MONOPOLY

Calls to legalize gambling, and specifically table games, in the Netherlands appeared as early as the 1930s. However, stiff opposition from religious groups meant that several decades were to pass before the Dutch returned to the idea of legalized gambling. A number of problems associated with gambling had become clear by the 1970s. With no legal outlet available, gaming enthusiasts turned toward illegal gambling operations.

COMPANY PERSPECTIVES

Our mission. Mission statement of Holland Casino. Our casinos are congenial places of entertainment where our guests can play a range of exciting games for monetary stakes in a safe, exhilarating setting. The four core values of Holland Casino's Mission Statement: All guests can expect a warm welcome and the highest standards of hospitality. They are assured of a fair game, with something to appeal to everyone. We provide an excellent service to players and non-players alike. Our staff display courtesy and respect to all guests. They are continually honing their professional skills. Modern working conditions encourage them to provide the best possible service at all times. We answer a social need by offering casinos with a varied range of games to address our guests' requirements. We are constantly alert to signs of problem gambling and do everything possible to obviate or reduce the risks.

We maintain our continuity by achieving good profitability levels. We invest in staff and equipment to keep our casinos up to date and attractive. In doing so, we also guarantee security of employment.

This in turn brought about the risk of encouraging development of criminal organizations.

Gambling had also come to be recognized for its social toll. While the majority of people viewed gambling as a recreational activity, a growing number of people had begun to display signs of gambling addiction. The loss of income and other social consequences were viewed as detrimental to society as a whole. Meanwhile, illegal gambling swallowed up an increasing amount of financial resources. Furthermore, a rising number of people were traveling to Belgium, where casino gambling was authorized, causing a further exit of revenues which might otherwise have flowed back into the country's treasury.

In 1974, the Dutch government drafted new legislation calling for the creation of a national, licensed casino system. The government created a new body, called De Nationale Stichting tot Exploitatie van Casinospelen in Nederland (National Foundation for the Operation of Casino Games in the Netherlands). The new state-owned foundation, which later became more popularly known as Holland Casino, was then granted

the first (and only) license to operate casinos in the Netherlands in December 1975.

Holland Casino was charged not only with constructing and operating casinos, but also with promoting and enforcing the government's policies toward the social aspects of casino gambling. Thus, the company became responsible for protecting gamblers by ensuring the fairness of its casino operations. Holland Casino was also responsible for developing and carrying out methods to identify and prevent problem gambling. The company was further charged with helping to prevent illegal gambling operations and the concomitant crime. Holland Casino also provided an additional source of tax income and other revenues for the Netherlands.

OPENING THE FIRST CASINO

Holland Casino established its headquarters in Schiphol, near the international airport, in 1976. The company then launched construction of its first casino, in the seaside resort town of Zandvoort. The new establishment opened for business in October of that year. The new Dutch casino differed markedly from its flashier cousins in the United States, as would the ones to follow. While Holland Casino's establishments included restaurants and nightclubs, they remained generally small, with a subdued, even serious, atmosphere. Minimum age requirements were set at 18, and dress codes, including jackets and ties for male patrons, were enforced.

By 1977, work had been completed on the group's second casino, which opened in Valkenburg in May of that year. The company also began developing plans to open a casino in Scheveningen, another major seaside resort town. Scheveningen, which had seen its glory days in the years before World War II, had been slated for a $300 million redevelopment. The opening of a casino became a prominent part of that effort. Holland Casino chose the Kurhaus, a landmark hotel built in 1885, which was refurbished and expanded at a cost of $40 million. The Scheveningen casino, which opened in 1979, became the company's largest, with 24 roulette and blackjack tables.

Holland Casino moved its headquarters to Hoofddorp in 1984. The move corresponded with the group's plans to open several more casinos through the end of the decade. While the initial casinos had been placed in resort areas, the company at this time targeted a presence in the country's city centers. The first of the new wave of casinos opened in Rotterdam in 1985, and was followed by the introduction of a casino in Amsterdam in 1986. In that year the company also added its first electronic gaming machines. Unlike gaming tables,

KEY DATES

1975: The Netherlands government establishes a casino monopoly, De Nationale Stichting tot Exploitatie van Casinospelen in Nederland, also later known as Holland Casino.
1976: Holland Casino opens its first casino in Zandvoort.
1984: Holland Casino moves its headquarters to Hoofddorp.
1985: Holland Casino introduces electronic gaming machines in its casinos and begins opening its first city center casinos.
1995: A casino reserved exclusively for air travelers opens at Schiphol Airport.
2004: Holland Casino receives permission to add two new casinos.
2008: The Dutch parliament rejects Holland Casino's request to launch an online gaming web site.

however, Holland Casino did not hold a monopoly over the installation of the new slot machines. As a result, these quickly spread throughout the country.

COUNTERING GAMBLING ADDICTION AND ILLEGAL GAMBLING

This proliferation came at a cost, however, as a rising number of people, including a growing number of young people, began to exhibit signs of gambling addiction. The rise in people seeking help for this problem brought about new demands for Holland Casino to fulfill the preventive side of its corporate mission. For this, Holland Casino teamed up with VAN, the Dutch amusement machine industry organization, and Jellinek Consultancy, part of the Jellinekhuis, the Amsterdam Institute for Addiction Research, to form a prevention plan.

The partnership resulted in a series of measures that included the creation of brochures, posters, and other informational formats. The company also committed to posting information about the odds of winning at its casinos. Employees, as well as others in contact with gamblers and the amusement gaming field, were to be given training in handling compulsive gamblers and their problems. Holland Casino also committed to developing a national system for identifying potential problem gamblers at its casinos.

The company set up a program providing information and counseling services for frequent gamblers and also pledged to limit access to certain customers, including imposing temporary bans on entry into its casinos. Toward this end, the company set up a computer database and established identification requirements for potential customers.

Holland Casino also continued its expansion program, in part as a means to fulfill its mission to help counter the illegal gambling market. By creating a wide network of legally operated and strictly controlled casinos, the company hoped to reduce the attractiveness of illegal gaming. Through the end of the 1980s, the company completed several new casinos, including Breda in 1987, Groningen in 1988, and Nijmegen in 1989. Nevertheless, by the beginning of the 21st century, there remained an estimated 40 to 50 illegal casinos still in operation in the Netherlands.

The company also began redeveloping some of its existing casinos, starting with the original Zandvoort casino, which reopened for business in 1988. The company also officially adopted the brand name Holland Casino that year.

FACING PROBLEMS

Further expansion of Holland Casino's network was put on hold during the difficult recession years of the early 1990s. The company nonetheless continued to refurbish a number of existing properties, including the Amsterdam casino, which reopened in 1991. The following year, the group completed a similar expansion of its Rotterdam site. By 1993, the company had launched construction of its first new casino in four years, opening a site in Eindhoven that year. The group also began developing a new casino at Schiphol Airport. This establishment, which opened in 1995, was reserved exclusively for air travelers.

Holland Casino continued to refurbish its existing casino network, including the Scheveningen and Valkenburg casinos in the mid-1990s, and continuing with the Breda casino in 2003. The company had opened two new casinos by then, in Utrecht in 2000 and in Enschede in 2002. This marked the end of the group's original mandate, which called for the company to operate just 12 casinos.

Pressure began to build on the Dutch government to abandon its restrictive gambling policies. This came in part because of the apparent hypocrisy of the government's gambling legislation. The government moved to reduce the number of slot machines in the country, while at the same time authorizing an increase in the number of lotteries in the country. The existence of legal casinos had failed to eliminate the growth of an illegal casino circuit. Holland Casino was faced with a major new rival in the form of online gambling and the growing number of gaming web sites based outside of the Netherlands. Additionally, the European Union had begun to place pressure on member countries that refused to abandon their various gambling, lottery, and casino monopolies.

The Dutch government addressed the question in 2000, commissioning a report that concluded with the necessity for the revision of the country's gambling legislation. The report proposed that the government allow the construction of new casinos, while transitioning toward a liberalized, and privatized, casino market.

EXPANDING THE NETWORK

The government initially rejected the report's conclusions. By 2004, however, the Dutch government, while confirming its commitment to maintaining the Holland Casino monopoly, recognized the need to allow further expansion of the company's casino network. As a result, the group received permission to add two new casinos, in Venlo in 2006, and Leeuwaarden in 2007. Holland Casino also launched plans to develop five more casinos to expand its network fully to a national level.

The state-owned group faced mounting pressure from its online rivals, which continued to drain off Dutch players and their revenues to the foreign-based sites. In order to head off the competition, Holland Casino petitioned the government to allow it to develop its own online gaming site. A bill was introduced to the Dutch parliament proposing the creation of a temporary online gaming site on a trial basis. This bill was defeated in 2008.

However, the European Commission continued to place pressure on the Netherlands to liberalize its gambling market. As the *International Herald Tribune* reported in 2008, the commission claimed that the country had done little to eliminate illegal and compulsive gambling, and instead only exacerbated these problems with "new addictive games, intensive and increasing advertising and [the] absence of concrete measures against gambling addiction."

The failure to win authorization to add online operations only added to Holland Casino's difficulties.

As the Dutch economy went into a tailspin along with the rest of the world, the company was faced with a sharp downturn in visits. By the beginning of 2008, visits to the company casinos had decreased by more than 500,000, a drop of nearly 7 percent, over the previous year. The company's revenues had also slipped, down to EUR 700 million ($$875 million), while its operating profit lost 83 percent over the previous year. Holland Casino would have to gamble on the future extension of its casino network to help it face the growing competition for Europe's gaming revenues.

M. L. Cohen

PRINCIPAL DIVISIONS

Table Games; Slot Machines; Gaming and Non-Gaming Tips; Catering; Other Revenue.

PRINCIPAL OPERATING UNITS

Northeast Region; Northwest Region; Central Region; Southwest Region; South Region.

FURTHER READING

Green, Marian, "Atronic Kicks Off Mega Millions in 13 Holland Casino Properties," *Slot Manager,* July–August 2007, p. 11.

"Holland Casino 'Mega Millions Jackpot' with First Prize of at Least One Million Euros," *PR Newswire,* April 23, 2007.

"Holland Rejects Gambling Bill," *World Entertainment News Network,* April 2, 2008.

"Irish Investors Are on a Safe Bet with EUR 63m Dutch Casino," *Irish Independent,* June 27, 2007.

"Netherlands: Holland Casino Signs Network Contract with Axians," *TendersInfo,* August 26, 2008.

"Players Spending Less, and Holland Casino Is Feeling the Pinch," *IGWB: International Gaming & Wagering Business,* June 2008, p. 16.

"Profits Down 83 Percent in a Very Bad Year for Holland Casino," *Casino Journal,* June 2009, p. 18.

"Regulator Warns EU Gambling Firms; Greece and Netherlands Told to Stop Competition Restrictions," *International Herald Tribune,* February 29, 2008.

Strauss, Karyn, "Dutch Casinos Go Cashless with G&D," *Hotels,* May 2006, p. 68.

Hongkong Electric Holdings Ltd.

Hongkong Electric Centre
44 Kennedy Road
Hong Kong,
People's Republic of China
Telephone: (3 852) 2843-3111
Fax: (3 852) 2537-1013
Web site: http://www.hec.com.hk

Public Company
Incorporated: 1889 as Hongkong Electric Company Ltd.
Employees: 2,000
Sales: HKD 12.77 billion ($1.65 billion) (2008)
Stock Exchanges: Hong Kong
Ticker Symbol: 0006
NAICS: 221112 Fossil Fuel Electric Power Generation;
221122 Electric Power Distribution; 541330
Engineering Services

■ ■ ■

Hongkong Electric Holdings Ltd. (HEH) is the holding company for one of the world's oldest electric utility companies, the Hongkong Electric Co. Ltd. The utility firm generates, transmits, and distributes power to over 560,000 customers on Hong Kong and Lamma islands. HEH, which also oversees the operations of Hongkong Electric International Ltd. (HEI) and engineering consultancy firm Associated Technical Services Ltd. HEI, created in 1997, has energy-related investments in Australia, Thailand, the United Kingdom, Canada, mainland China, and New Zealand. Asian billionaire Li

Ka-shing and his family control just under 40 percent of the company through Cheung Kong (Holdings) Ltd.

19TH-CENTURY ORIGINS

Hongkong Electric traces its beginnings to Sir Paul Chater, a native of Calcutta who arrived in the British colony of Hong Kong in 1864 to become a clerk with the Bank of Hindustan. By 1870 Sir Paul had left the bank to form his own brokerage house and was on his way to becoming one of Hong Kong's most prominent *taipans,* or merchants. Sir Paul made his early fortune through property, developing a number of commercial sites in and around Hong Kong Island's Core Central business district, and throughout the 1870s, he developed the Hong Kong harbor, providing portside facilities for the colony's expanding trading base.

In 1888 Sir Paul and two fellow members of the ruling Legislative Council were granted a government contract to form an electric company. The men agreed to provide streetlights and to pump water to the Peak, a residential district rising high atop Hong Kong Island. The company chose a site at Wanchai that it had purchased from the government to build its first power station. A year later, upon the incorporation of the Hongkong Electric Company Ltd., shares were offered to the public on the Hong Kong Stock Exchange.

In the meantime, Sir Paul was busy incorporating another company that would eventually prove to be an asset for Hongkong Electric. The new venture, the Hongkong Land Investment and Agency Company, was organized to reclaim land for new developments on Hong Kong Island. One of the company's particular projects was the 57-acre Praya Reclamation Project in the Central District.

Eventually the government canceled its contract for water to be pumped up to the Peak, but Hongkong Electric was still to supply the electricity for streetlights. The company had already ordered two steam-driven generating units from Britain, each with a generating capacity of 50 kilowatts. The Wanchai Power Station was brought on line at 6:00 P.M. on December 1, 1890. By 1896 the company was flourishing, and Hongkong Electric was able to declare its first dividend. An amount totaling HKD 12,000 was paid out to the company's shareholders that year.

EARLY 20TH-CENTURY DEVELOPMENTS

Supplying electricity to new property developments built by Sir Paul became a successful venture. One such development, the Queen's Hotel, which opened on the Praya reclamation site in 1898, was supplied with energy to drive the first electric elevators installed in Hong Kong. The elevators (four in all) sped up and down the structure at 200 feet per minute and operated on a DC electricity supply from Hongkong Electric's first substation.

Rather than taking up precious land of which Hong Kong Island had little to spare in 1905, Hongkong Electric adopted a policy of installing supply cables underground. The company continued to maintain this policy, although the plan did encounter difficulties in its early stages when white ants began eating into the cable coverings.

In 1909, the first lightbulbs using metal filaments were installed in residential and commercial buildings on the island. The new bulbs emitted far more light than those previously used, which had filaments made of bamboo. A year later electricity was made available to the western areas of Hong Kong Island and the fashionable Peak residential district.

In 1914 Hongkong Electric decided to expand from its original Wanchai Power Station after the plant's generating capacity became overloaded. A second power station, a coal-fired facility, was to be built at North Point, a rural area that was suited for such a plant. A site of approximately 125,000 square feet was purchased for a cost of HKD 37,500.

By 1916 sales revenue for Hongkong Electric had topped HKD 1 million. Three years later, the new North Point Power Station was brought on line with an initial capacity of 3,000 kilowatts, while the Wanchai Power Station was put on standby. In 1925 an out-of-town substation was opened at Shaukiwan. That same year the supply voltage was changed from 100 to 200 volts. The change involved more than the throw of a switch; 240,000 lightbulbs were issued free to the company's customers, and all manner of appliances had to be converted or exchanged. A year later the company, as well as Hong Kong Island, lost a guiding light when Sir Paul Chater died.

The Japanese occupation of Hong Kong, beginning in 1941, had huge consequences for Hongkong Electric. Following the invasion, the North Point Power Station was shut down and abandoned in December. Although the *Times* of London reported in 1942 that the North Point Power Station had been attacked and destroyed by American bombers, the plant was again generating power two months after the liberation of the island in August 1945.

RAPID GROWTH IN POSTWAR ERA

Demand for electricity began to grow markedly with the influx of Chinese immigrants following the rise of the Communist regime in China in 1949. In an effort to keep up with the demand the North Point Power Station was refitted and a 20-megawatt generating unit, the company's largest at the time, was installed in 1955. Three years later, to meet the still-growing demand, the transmission network voltage was upgraded from 6,600 to 33,000 volts with the installation of an even larger 30-megawatt generator at the newly commissioned North Point "B" station.

By 1964, Hongkong Electric had decided that the North Point Power Station, in addition to having become an environmental hazard in its then-residential site, would not have sufficient capacity to meet

KEY DATES

1889: The Hongkong Electric Company Ltd. incorporates.

1890: The Wanchai Power Station is brought on line at 6:00 P.M. on December 1.

1914: Hongkong Electric decides to expand from its original Wanchai Power Station after the plant's generating capacity becomes overloaded.

1919: The North Point Power Station is brought on line with an initial capacity of 3,000 kilowatts.

1968: The first unit at Ap Lei Chau Power Station begins generating power.

1979: Hongkong Electric is regulated through a Government Scheme of Control Agreement (SCA).

1981: The company signs an agreement with China Light & Power (CLP), connecting the two systems.

1982: The company completes construction of the Lamma Power Station.

1985: Hongkong Land Holdings Ltd. divests its stake in Hongkong Electric to Hutchison Whampoa Ltd., thereby placing the utility in Asian business magnate Li Ka-shing's sphere of influence.

1997: Hutchison Whampoa's 35.01 percent share of Hongkong Electric is transferred to Cheung Kong Infrastructure (CKI).

2000: The company acquires Powercor Australia Ltd.

2006: Construction begins on a gas-fired facility in Thailand's Ratchaburi Province; Hong Kong's first wind power station begins operations.

2008: A new SCA is signed.

projected future demand. In order to build a new oil-fired power station, the company purchased a plot of land on Ap Lei Chau Island. In 1966, as construction continued on the Ap Lei Chau station, North Point "C" station—computerized and oil-fired—was brought on line with a 60 megawatt unit, bringing the network's voltage up to 66,000 volts. In 1968 the first unit at Ap Lei Chau Power Station began generating power.

By this time demand for electricity in Hong Kong was growing exponentially. A 125-megawatt generator,

manufactured by the Japanese company Mitsubishi, was brought on line at Ap Lei Chau. Over the course of the next ten years, another six identical units were installed, bringing the entire network transmission voltage to 132,000 volts.

In response to community concern that the company's three smokestacks were offensive due to their resemblance to the joss sticks used in the rituals of ancestor worship and funerals, Hongkong Electric built a fourth stack. Because the additional smokestack was not necessary at that time, it went unused.

In 1978 the company began planning another new power station, purchasing a site on Lamma Island at Po Lo Tsui. Hongkong Electric made a strategic move when, in response to the OPEC (Organization of Petroleum Exporting Countries) hold on the oil market and the subsequent steep increase in prices, the company decided to equip the new plant with dual-firing capabilities. Therefore, the facility could be run on either coal or oil, as circumstances warranted.

Beginning in 1979, Hongkong Electric was regulated through a Government Scheme of Control Agreement (SCA) in an effort to guarantee equity between the company's customers and stockholders and the Hong Kong Island community. In a cooperative effort, in 1981 the company signed an agreement with China Light & Power (CLP), connecting the two systems. With the ability to transfer up to 480 megawatts, the companies could operate more efficiently in addition to having reserves available for times of peak demand. Moreover, this agreement preserved the monopoly enjoyed by each of the firms; CLP was the exclusive generator of electricity to Kowloon and Hongkong Electric supplied the Hong Kong, Lamma, and Ap Lei Chau islands. These schemes of control also established profit based on capacity; in 1995, the maximum allowable profit was 15 percent of fixed assets.

SETTING RECORDS

A world record was established in 1982 with the completion of the Lamma Power Station, constructed in just under three and a half years. The first unit to go on line, a 250-megawatt coal-fired generator, brought the transmission network voltage up to 275,000 volts.

The 1980s brought Hongkong Electric several more milestones. First, in 1983, the company topped the 1,000-megawatt mark in maximum demand. In 1985 work was completed on the Wanchai Zone Substation, the first substation built in the Far East on a modular basis, saving both time and expense during construction. Then in 1986, the second phase of the 275-kilovolt submarine cable network, transmitting energy from the Lamma Power Station to Hong Kong Island, was brought on line. This completed the highest-capacity submarine cable network anywhere in the world to date.

In 1987 a second coal-fired generator with a 350-megawatt capacity, went on line at the Lamma Power Station. The was the company's largest unit, representing a generating capacity 7,000 times greater than Hongkong Electric's first unit, originally installed at Wanchai Power Station.

In 1989 the company recorded that demand for electricity in Hong Kong had exceeded 1,000 megawatts during every month of the year. After six 125-megawatt generators were transferred from Ap Lei Chau to Lamma, where they were to be operated by gas turbines, the Ap Lei Chau Power Station was shut down.

The Lamma Power Station was by this time using both coal and oil firing to remain flexible in its fuel use; however, the use of coal far outweighed that of oil. Coal consumption in 1988 was 2.3 million tons and was expected to increase at an average yearly rate of 5 percent. The station contained a jetty alongside the facility from which coal could be unloaded out of oceangoing vessels. To operate and monitor all the generating units, the Lamma station also contained a Central Control Room that acted as the nerve center of the complex. Complex data processing systems helped personnel keep a running tab on energy output and control the generating units for accuracy, efficiency, and economy.

INCREASING PRODUCTIVITY

In 1988 the company constructed and opened a 3.1-kilometer tunnel between Wah Fu and Kennedy Road to house its 275-kilovolt transmission network. The tunnel replaced the laying of 275-kilovolt cables in busy urban areas, thereby avoiding disrupting traffic or ruining the environment. Over the course of the decade, the company increased productivity from 1.4 million kilowatt hours per employee annually in 1980 to 2.57 million by 1992. That factor helped multiply Hongkong Electric's net income from HKD 611.1 million in 1981 to HKD 2.34 billion in 1991.

During the 1980s Hongkong Land Holdings Ltd. reasserted its historic link to Hongkong Electric. Originally founded by Sir Paul Chater during the 1870s, this property development company had grown to rank among the world's largest property management companies. In an effort to weather the recessionary conditions on Hong Kong Island, Hongkong Land began to diversify its holdings, taking a one-third interest in Hongkong Telephone and a similar stake in Hongkong Electric.

However, Hongkong Land did not maintain its investment in Hongkong Electric for long; in 1985 it divested the stake to Hutchison Whampoa Ltd., thereby placing the utility in Asian business magnate Li Ka-shing's sphere of influence. A child of Chinese immigrants, Li started out in the 1950s making artificial flowers. By the time he took his stake in Hongkong Electric, this tycoon known as *chiu yan,* or Superman, reigned over a HKD 390 billion ($50 billion) empire. His flagship company, Cheung Kong (Holdings) Ltd., built and managed toll roads, toll bridges, power stations, and other infrastructure throughout Asia. It owned a controlling interest in Hutchison Whampoa, which in turn held a substantial stake in Hongkong Electric.

FACING UNCERTAINTIES

Hongkong Electric's executive management was soon replete with Hutchison expatriates. Simon Murray acted as chairman from 1985 to 1993, when he was succeeded by Hutchison director George Magnus. At that time, Canning Fok Kin-ning advanced to managing director. In 1994, Magnus laid out a rather simple formula for HEH's continued growth, telling Gareth Hewett of the *South China Morning Post* that "the redevelopment of buildings on established land and the creation of new buildings on existing and future reclaimed land, together with continual increases in domestic per capita electricity consumption, all add to Hong Kong Island's increasing demand for electricity." Increasing demand would require greater capacity, which in turn would drive Hongkong Electric's ever-growing profits. Indeed, Hongkong Electric completed a HKD 15 billion program of capital expenditure from 1990 through the end of 1994. The utility's profits grew from just under HKD 2 billion in 1990 to over HKD 4 billion in 1995.

However, Magnus's neat formula did not add up in the mid-1990s, when capacity began to outstrip demand. As manufacturers moved to mainland China, overall sales of electricity flattened and peak power usage began to decline during this period. By 1996, CLP was operating at 50 percent overcapacity and was forced by the government to postpone HKD 1.8 billion in capital expenditures. Although Hongkong Electric also experienced overcapacity during this period, it forecast that growing demand would require that a new power station be on line by 2003. Its proposal for a new power station on Po Toi Island was met with opposition from consumer groups and environmentalists, who questioned the need for additional capacity when CLP had generating power to spare.

As the July 1997 deadline approached for the United Kingdom to hand Hong Kong over to Chinese rule, Li reorganized his empire. He transferred Hutchison Whampoa's 35.01 percent share of Hongkong Electric to the recently formed Cheung Kong Infrastructure (CKI). Run by Li's eldest son, Victor, this firm managed Asian infrastructure investments. Li told the *Financial Times* (London) that "the reorganisations reflects our intention to increase our total investment in infrastructure." A second restructuring in May made CKI part of Hutchison Whampoa. One benefit to Hongkong Electric from the new arrangement was the creation of an international subsidiary in charge of power projects throughout Asia-Pacific. This key growth vehicle made its first acquisition in June, when it took a 25 percent stake in a Thai power plant project.

With its SCA up for review in 1998, Hongkong Electric faced the possibility of dramatic change. Possibilities included a merger with or purchase of capacity from China Light & Power; complete takeover by Li Ka-shing's Cheung Kong group; or a simple maintenance of the status quo. In the end, the SCA was reviewed in 1998 and 1999 with little change to Hongkong Electric's core operations.

MOVING INTO THE 21ST CENTURY

Hongkong Electric focused on international expansion as well as on providing reliable and environmentally friendly sources of power during the early years of the new millennium. As global economies slowed, the company was also forced to cut costs while improving productivity. As part of its growth efforts, the company partnered with Cheung Kong Infrastructure Holdings Ltd. and added the electricity distribution business of Australia's ETSA Holdings to its arsenal in late 1999. In September 2000, the company strengthened its foothold in that region with the purchase of Powercor Australia Ltd. Hongkong Electric then invested in Australia's CitiPower in 2002.

In early 2006, the company began construction on a gas-fired facility in Thailand's Ratchaburi Province, marking Hongkong Electric's first power-generation investment outside of Hong Kong. The facility began operations in June 2008. In October 2007, the company once again partnered with CKI to purchase Canada's TransAlta Power LP. The two companies teamed up again the following year when they made a play for New Zealand's Wellington electricity network from Vector Ltd. In November 2008, the company increased its stake in the United Kingdom's Northern Gas Networks from 19.9 percent to 35.1 percent.

As part of its efforts to add renewable energy sources to its holdings, the company launched Lamma Winds, Hong Kong's first wind power station, in February 2006. It also invested in wind farm projects in China. The wind farm project in Dali, Yunnan Province, began commercial operation in January 2009, while a wind farm in Leting, Hebei Province, was scheduled to go on line later that year.

There was much speculation about the future of the electricity market in Hong Kong during the time period leading up to the slated expiration of the SCA in 2008. There was intense debate regarding the deregulation of the region's energy market. Critics of the SCA claimed the existing plan encouraged a "build more-charge-more-and-earn-more" mentality, as reported in an April 2004 *South China Morning Post* article. After months of public discussion and heated negotiations, the company eventually signed a new SCA in January 2008 that took effect January 1, 2009, and would extend for a period of ten years at a lower rate of return than the previous agreement. The new agreement allowed for a 9.99 percent rate of return on average net fixed assets and an 11 percent rate of return on renewable energy fixed assets. The SCA also included provisions related to emission reduction, energy efficiency and investment in renewable energy, and service quality. According to the company, the new SCA would benefit customers by providing a reliable and secure energy supply at reasonable prices.

The new SCA's lower rate of return, however, was expected to affect Hongkong Electric's earnings. Accordingly, the company continued to look for ways to bolster its international business to offset the impact. In February 2009, the company announced plans to acquire a 45 percent stake in three power plant joint ventures in China. With a solid expansion strategy in place, lucrative overseas investments, and a record of reliability and profitability, Hongkong Electric Holdings appeared to be on track for success in the years to come.

Etan Vlessing
Updated, April Dougal Gasbarre;
Christina M. Stansell

PRINCIPAL SUBSIDIARIES

The Hongkong Electric Company Limited; Hongkong Electric International Limited; Associated Technical Services Limited.

PRINCIPAL COMPETITORS

CLP Holdings Limited; Guangdong Investment Limited; Hong Kong and China Gas Company Limited.

FURTHER READING

Chetham, Andrew, "Utilities Merger 'A Profitable Proposal,'" *South China Morning Post*, April 16, 1997, p. 14.

"Chinese Utility Helping Parent Buy TransAlta," *Toronto Star,* October 31, 2007.

Clayton, Dusty, "HK Electric Net Rises 8.7 pc," *South China Morning Post,* March 8, 1996, p. 1.

Cottrell, Robert, "HK Land Buys 20 Percent of HK Electric," *Financial Times* (London), April 27, 1982, p. 21.

Criswell, Colin, *The Taipans of Hong Kong,* Oxford: Oxford University Press, 1981.

Hewett, Gareth, "Hongkong Electric's Star Shines Brightly," *South China Morning Post,* March 4, 1994, p. 1.

Highlights of the Electric Years, Hong Kong: The Hongkong Electric Co. Ltd., 1992.

"HKE Aims to Double Gas-Fired Power Output," *Standard,* May 11, 2007.

"HK Electric Opens Bangkok Power Plant for Full Operation," *NewsTrak Daily,* June 5, 2008.

"Hongkong Electric Holdings Ltd.: Finances Are Completed to Build Central Thailand Power Plant," *Wall Street Journal,* December 30, 2005.

"Hong Kong's Supermen Prepare for China," *Financial Times* (London), January 14, 1997, p. 25.

"Li Ka-shing Stays Ahead of the Game," *Financial Times* (London), January 7, 1997, p. 20.

Lucas, Louise, "HK Power Groups Study Co-Operation Deal," *Financial Times* (London), December 10, 1996, p. 32.

————, "Power Policy Kept on Low Heat," *Financial Times* (London), September 16, 1996, p. 6.

100 Years of Energy, Hong Kong: The Hongkong Electric Co. Ltd., 1990.

Porter, Barry, and Dusty Clayton, "Lucrative Signs of a Powerful Union," *South China Morning Post,* November 5, 1995, p. 3.

Ridding, John, and Louise Lucas, "Beijing Buys £1.3 Billion Stake in Top HK Power Supplier," *Financial Times* (London), January 29, 1997, p. 1.

Tsang, Denise, "Power Study Sparks Debate on Options," *South China Morning Post,* April 30, 2004.

Yung, Chester, "Power Struggles in Electricity Market," *Standard,* March 27, 2006.

Horserace Totalisator
Board (The Tote)

Westgate House
Wigan, WN3 4HS
United Kingdom
Telephone: (44 01942) 824211
Fax: (44 01942) 820 040
Web site: http://corporate.totesport.com

Private Company
Incorporated: 1928
Employees: 2,057
Sales: £2.91 billion ($5.5 billion) (2008 est.)
NAICS: 713990 All Other Amusement and Recreation
    Industries

■ ■ ■

The Horserace Totalisator Board, more popularly known as The Tote, holds the monopoly concession on pool betting for the United Kingdom's horse-racing circuit. A totalisator refers to a system of gathering all bets into a common pool from which jackpots are then distributed equally among all winners. The Tote receives a levy based on the total number of bets. The Tote's profits are in turned distributed out to the horse-racing industry to support and encourage its growth. The Tote operates at all of the United Kingdom's racetracks, as well as from its own national network of more than 600 betting shops. The company also accepts bets through its web sites, a telephone call center, and through third-party betting shops.

The Tote has also developed a variety of betting products, including its mainstay totewin and toteplace games, and toteswinger, introduced in 2008. In addition to horse-race betting, the Tote also operates in other gambling markets, including online casinos and events betting. The Tote is described as a "non-departmental public body," but the company operates as a privately held corporation under government supervision. The Labour government of the later years of the first decade of the 2000s has committed itself to breaking up the Tote's pool-betting monopoly and privatizing the company. In 2008, however, amid the economic recession, the sale of the Tote was placed on hold. The Tote was founded in 1928 by Winston Churchill. In 2008, the company posted sales of £2.91 billion ($5.5 billion). Trevor Beaumont is the group's chief executive officer.

CHURCHILL FOOTNOTE IN 1928

Horse racing had long been one of the United Kingdom's favorite sports traditions, and many of the country's most popular racing tracks had been in place since before the 20th century. Betting, however, remained illegal amid an overall antigambling climate in the early decades of the century. This situation gave rise to a growing number of illegally operating bookmakers in the years following World War I. The lack of a legal structure inevitably led to abuses and rising criminality, which in turn reflected poorly on horse racing itself.

In the late 1920s, Winston Churchill, then Chancellor of the Exchequer, turned his attention to the problems stemming from horse-race betting. In 1928, Churchill led the passage of the Racecourse Betting Act, which created the Racecourse Betting Control Board. The new body then received the national monopoly for

COMPANY PERSPECTIVES

The tote is one of the principal betting organisations in Britain, with more than 3,500 employees, over 500 shops, a major presence on all of the 60 racecourses in Britain, as well as internet and telephone betting facilities. Totesport offers a comprehensive multi-channel means of betting on sports from across the globe—everything from golf through to the Superbowl. Present on all British racecourses, totepool is the only pool betting operation on horseracing in Britain.

accepting on-course bets through a totalisator, or betting pool, system.

The board's mission was not only to provide a legal outlet for gambling on horse racing. Its primary purpose became the support of the horse-racing industry itself by turning over its profits toward "purposes conducive to the improvement of breeds of horses or the sport of horseracing." These purposes include funding prize money awards, as well as improvements to racecourses.

The Tote, as the body later became known, was unique in its status as a private corporation that was not owned but nonetheless controlled by the British government. The Tote organized its first betting pool in March 1929, and by that summer had launched pool betting operations at the country's major horse-racing events, including the July course at Newmarket. The Tote quickly established its on-course betting services across the country's horse-racing tracks. The Racecourse Betting Act, however, applied specifically to strictly on-course, cash-only bets.

As a result, the Tote generated far lower profits than had been hoped. The illegal bookie circuit continued to flourish, particularly through the provision of off-course and credit-based betting. In 1930, however, a new group of horse-racing enthusiasts joined together to form Guardian Pari-mutuel Ltd. to develop a system of betting clubs to provide credit-based betting into the Tote's betting pools. The new group, which later changed its name to Tote Investors Ltd., successfully petitioned the government for the right to the off-course, credit-based concession. By 1932, there were several hundred tote clubs operating across the United Kingdom. The new clubs provided gamblers not only with a locale for placing bets, but also to listen to broadcasts of the races, while sharing a drink with other gamblers.

NEW WAYS TO BET

This new source of revenue enabled the Tote to fulfill its original brief. By 1933, the company had begun to contribute its growing profits to the horse racing industry. Initially, the Tote was responsible not only for collecting bets, but also for distributing its profits. Among the company's first contributions were grants given to the Hunters' Improvement Society. Other industry related groups, including horse breeders, and the racetracks themselves, benefited from the Tote's profits. As such, the Tote was credited with playing an important role in establishing the United Kingdom as one of the world's major horse racing centers.

Profits rose strongly as the Tote developed a range of betting pool products. The first of these were the Win and Place pools, later rebranded as totewin and toteplace, respectively. Both were introduced in 1929. In 1930, the Tote introduced its Daily Double, which remained a popular pool for more than half a century, before being discontinued in 1985. That year also saw the discontinuation of another popular pool, the Daily Treble, introduced in 1939.

Other pools had shorter life spans, such as the Straight Forecast pool, launched in 1933 and ended in 1939. During the 1960s, the company introduced the Quadpool, which lasted just one year, shutting down in 1966. Similarly, the Tricast, launched in 1970, was abandoned in 1973.

By then, the Tote and gambling in the United Kingdom in general had undergone a number of significant changes. Chief among these was the passage of the Betting Levy Act of 1961. The new legislation stripped the Tote of its profits distribution function, which was turned over to a newly created Levy Board. The Tote also lost its monopoly on horse-race betting, as the Levy Act legalized the opening of betting parlors. The new betting shops were also permitted to accept bets on horse racing.

EXPANDING OPERATIONS IN THE SEVENTIES

The Tote nonetheless retained its dominant position in horse-race pool betting. The legislation also allowed the Tote to begin operating its own betting shops for the first time. In 1962, therefore, the company took over Tote Investors Ltd., giving it control of the United Kingdom's off-course and credit betting circuits as well. The company had direct ownership of its own network of betting shops which grew to 130 by the late 1980s.

However, the Tote's brief remained strictly limited to the horse racing circuit. This left the company at a

KEY DATES

1928: Winston Churchill leads the creation of the Racecourse Betting Control Board (later the Horserace Totalisator Board, or "the Tote") as part of the Racecourse Betting Act.

1930: Guardian Para-Mutuel Ltd. (later Tote Investors Ltd.) is founded to provide off-course credit-based betting services.

1962: The Tote acquires Tote Investors Ltd., adding its High Street betting shop network.

1972: The Tote is authorized to accept bets on all sports events.

1986: The Tote introduces computerized bet-taking services.

1993: The Tote launches the Tote Direct betting machine partnership with Coral.

1997: The Tote is authorized to offer bets on non-sports events.

2001: The British government announces its plan to privatize the Tote.

2005: The Tote acquires nearly 80 betting shops from William Hill.

2008: The British government rejects a takeover bid for the Tote.

distinct disadvantage, as a new range of betting parlors and companies arose to compete for the gambling market. The 1960s saw the growth of the first major U.K. gambling companies, such as William Hill and Ladbrokes. These companies expanded rapidly, establishing nationally operating networks of betting parlors offering a full range of betting services, including horse racing. In contrast, the Tote could offer only access to its betting pools.

By the early 1970s, the Tote was struggling to keep pace with the competition. Profits slipped sharply and by 1972, the company was in the midst of a deep financial crisis. At last, the British government stepped in and authorized the Tote to expand its brief to accept bets at starting prices (the more common type of betting on horse racing) in addition to its tote pools. At the same time, the Tote was authorized to accept bets on other sports events for the first time. This led to the creation of a new division, Tote Bookmakers, in 1973.

Horse racing remained the group's primary focus, however. During the 1970s and into the 1980s, the Tote continued to introduce new betting pools. These included the Placepot, in 1977, and the Top Three

Jocket Pool, launched at Ascot in 1979. In 1983, the company introduced the short-lived Super Double and Super Treble for the Scottish racing market. These were both discontinued during the same year.

NEW MARKETS IN THE NINETIES

In order to sharpen its competitive edge, the Tote launched a modernization effort starting in the mid-1980s. The company introduced computer technology in 1986, adding a system adapted from one originally developed by the Hong Kong Jockey Club. By the end of the decade, the Tote had installed a full-fledged computer betting system. This enabled the company to achieve dramatic reductions in the time it took for customers to place bets. As a result, the Tote achieved a surge in revenues, and profits, during the decade.

The Tote also introduced other amenities into its off-course betting clubs. Chief among these was the launch of televised broadcasts of its races, with the introduction of a live television service in 1986. In 1992, the company teamed up with Coral, then one of the fastest-growing U.K. gambling groups, to launch a new electronic machine-based service, Tote Direct. This service enabled Coral customers to place bets directly on the Tote from Coral's shops. Tote Direct was later joined by Ladbrokes, which agreed to provide access to the Tote's pools in exchange for a 21 percent commission in 1997. Other betting groups, including William Hill, later joined Tote Direct as well.

These developments helped increase the Tote's revenue streams, while also expanding its reach. The Ladbrokes deal, for example, extended the group's reach to more than 3,500 betting shops. The Tote's own operations were growing as well. In 1993, the company extended its opening hours to include weekday evenings. Two years later, the group added betting services on Sunday as well.

Then, in 1997, the Tote received authorization from the government to enter the events betting market. This singularly British market allowed gamblers to place bets on an infinite range of often outlandish and unusual events, beyond traditional horse-race and sports betting.

PRIVATIZATION DRIVE AT THE TURN OF THE 21ST CENTURY

The extension of the Tote's operations coincided with increasing calls for the corporation's "privatization" despite the fact that the Tote had never, in fact, been owned by the British government. The corporation had long faced a challenge over its monopoly on horse-race betting pools, yet somehow had survived the wholesale privatization of British industry during the Margaret Thatcher era.

Calls for the abolition of the Tote's monopoly and its sale to private investors had begun to appear in the late 1980s, however. Paradoxically enough, it took the arrival of a new Labour government in the late 1990s for the privatization effort to take root. The privatization of the Tote was adopted as part of the Labour government's official manifesto. In 2001, the company published its commitment to sell off the Tote (despite the fact that the government did not actually own the company) to a racing trust. In the process, the Tote was expected to convert its operations to a commercial basis.

Legislation for the change in the Tote's status was adopted in 2004. The new legislation established a framework for the transformation of the nearly 80-year-old company. All of the Tote's assets and operations were to be transferred to a new company to be established by the government. This company was then to be sold off to a consortium based in the racing industry. The Tote's monopoly was then to be abolished, and instead replaced by a seven-year exclusive contract. At the end of that seven-year period, other companies were then to be permitted to bid for the right to operate horse-race betting pools.

NEW TECHNOLOGIES IN THE NEW CENTURY

Discussions as to the Tote's value helped hinder progress toward the sale of the company through the middle of the decade. The value of the company and its well-placed network of High Street betting shops ranged widely, with some suggesting the company's worth to be as high as £700 million ($1.3 billion). By the middle of the decade, however, the British government had settled on a value of £400 million for the company.

The government then invited a consortium of racing interests, including the Racecourse Holdings Trust, the Race Course Association, the Racehorse Owners Association, as well as the Tote's management and staff, to bid for the company. Yet the consortium's final bid for the company reached just £310 million. Claiming that accepting the bid would violate European Union rules, the British government was forced to reject the bid in March 2008. By the end of the year, as the British economy spiraled into a deep recession, the government announced the planned sale of the Tote had been placed on hold.

Despite the uncertainty over its ownership, and over its continued control of its betting pool monopoly, the Tote had continued to expand its operations during the

first decade of the 2000s. The company went online in 2002, launching its tote BetXpress Internet betting service.

The company also joined in another fast-growing online gambling market, operating online casinos. The Tote's casino debuted in 2005. Originally based in Curacao, the company transferred the casino's registration to the Channel Islands in 2008. In this way, the company was allowed to launch a direct advertising campaign in England. Other online operations included the launch of the company's iGaming network, providing a range of fixed-odds betting services based on such popular board games as Clue, Monopoly, and Wheel of Fortune.

The Tote also expanded its betting shop network during the decade. In 2005, the company acquired nearly 80 shops, in two separate deals, from William Hill, following that company's acquisition of rival Stanley Leisure group. The acquisitions helped boost the group's total network to nearly 540 shops by the end of that year. By the end of the decade, the company's network had grown past 600 shops.

The Tote also rolled out a number of new betting products during the decade. These included Totescoop6, Toteswinger, and Win-only, Place and Show pools. The Tote also developed new partnerships, including one with TurfTV, a major provider of racing broadcasts and data services in the United Kingdom. The deal placed TurfTV programming in the Tote's national betting shop network. Once known as the "nanny goat" of British gambling, the Tote had transformed itself into a modern player competing among the United Kingdom's top gambling groups in the 21st century.

M. L. Cohen

PRINCIPAL SUBSIDIARIES

Tote Bookmakers Ltd.

PRINCIPAL DIVISIONS

Totesport; Totepool.

PRINCIPAL OPERATING UNITS

Totewin; Toteplace; Totesuper7; Toteeachway; Totescoop6; Toteplacepot; Totejackpot; Totequadpot; Toteexacta; Totetrifecta; Toteswinger.

PRINCIPAL COMPETITORS

William Hill plc; Camelot Group plc; Pearson PLC; Littlewoods Shop Direct Group Ltd.; Mitchells and Butlers PLC; Emap Ltd.; Sportingbet plc.

FURTHER READING

Clark, Neil, "A Nanny Goat Under Threat," *Guardian* (London), November 6, 2006, p. 31.

Dobson, David, "Horses for Courses," *Which Computer?* June 1991, p. 138.

"Government Rejects Racing Consortium Bid for the Tote," *M2 Presswire,* March 5, 2008.

Gunther-Bushell, Matthew, "Tote's Days Look to Be Numbered," *Western Mail,* June 2, 2003, p. 20.

McSmith, Andy, "The Tote for Sale? All Bets Are Off," *Observer,* June 21, 1998, p. 18.

"New Basis for the Sale of the Horse-Race Totalisator Board ('The Tote') Announced," *Europe Intelligence Wire,* December 15, 2006.

Randall, Jeff, "Tote Heads for Row on Privatisation Plans," *Sunday Times,* April 9, 1989.

"Totalbet.com Introduces Online Tote Pool Betting," *Internet Business News,* September 8, 2000.

"Tote Seeks Chief Marketer to Lead Shops Expansion," *Marketing,* October 17, 2002, p. 4.

Woolf, Marie, "Can the Pool Make a Bigger Splash?" *Observer,* February 23, 1997, p. 7.

Huy Fong Foods, Inc.

————————■————————

5001 Earle Avenue
Rosemead, California 91770
U.S.A.
Telephone: (626) 286-8328
Fax: (626) 286-8522
Web site: http://huyfong.com

Private Company
Incorporated: 1980
Employees: 20
Sales: $20 million (2009 est.)
NAICS: 311941 Mayonnaise, Dressing, and Other
    Prepared Sauce Manufacturing

■ ■ ■

Huy Fong Foods, Inc., makes jalapeno pepper-based sauces. The company is best known for Tuong Ot Sriracha (Sriracha Hot Chili Sauce), a spicy, garlicky condiment sold in a clear plastic squeeze bottle with a green top and popularly known as "rooster sauce" after the distinctive logo it sports. Other Huy Fong products include the chunkier Chili Garlic Sauce and Sambal Oelek, which omits garlic for a pure chili taste. Although the company does no advertising, its products have become a staple at Asian restaurants around the United States and abroad, with Sriracha also found on the shelves of mass-market chains such as Wal-Mart and in the kitchens of restaurants ranging from Applebee's to those offering haute cuisine. The firm is owned and managed by founder David Tran and members of his family.

ORIGINS IN VIETNAM

Huy Fong Foods was founded in Los Angeles in 1980 by David Tran, but the company's roots can be traced several years earlier to the war-torn country of Vietnam. Tran, an ethnic Chinese, was born near Saigon in 1945, his grandfather having settled there in the late 1800s. In 1975 Tran began making spicy sauces from peppers his older brother grew on a small farm, using family members to bottle them in Gerber baby food jars obtained from American soldiers. The lids were decorated with a drawing of a rooster, Tran's astrological sign according to Chinese tradition, and the sauces were sold to middlemen who distributed them to small shops and food vendors. His most popular sauce, which mixed peppers with oil and a ginger-like root called galangal, was used in *Pho,* the classic meat-and-noodle soup, or on roasted dog. The business was not very successful, however, as most locals preferred using fresh peppers in their cooking.

The Vietnam War ended that same year, and afterward the country's population of ethnic Chinese felt a growing sense of persecution under the new government. Tran decided to convert most of his assets into gold pieces and began sending family members overseas in small groups, so at least some might make it out if a ship were seized. In 1978 Tran traveled to Hong Kong with 3,000 other refugees in the hold of a run-down Taiwanese freighter called the *Huy Fong.* The entire family managed to reach safety as well, and after spending time in a United Nations refugee camp, Tran made it to Boston and then in January 1980 settled in Los Angeles, where a brother-in-law lived.

SETTING UP SHOP IN CHINATOWN

Casting about for a way to support his family, Tran noticed that the quality of imported chili sauces sold in Los Angeles's Chinatown was mediocre, and he quickly decided to make his own. He approached a bank to borrow $200,000, anticipating a return of $1 million, but was turned down. Scaling back the plan, he scraped together $50,000 from family savings to found Huy Fong Foods in a 2,500-square-foot shop in Chinatown, which he rented for $700 per month. The company's first product was Thai-style Pepper Sate Sauce, which Tran produced in a 50-gallon mixer. Distributing it in a van to local restaurants and stores, the new company took in $2,300 the first month, and sales grew steadily thereafter.

Capitalizing on his initial success, Tran added several other products and in 1983 developed Tuong Ot Sriracha, or Sriracha Hot Chili Sauce. He was inspired by the impending 1984 Los Angeles Olympics, according to an interview in the *New York Times*, as well as the Heinz 57 ketchup bottle, which gave him the idea of creating a Tran 84 that he could sell to a wider audience. The new product was a variation on a style thought to have originated in the southern Thai coastal region of Sri Racha, which used garlic, hot chili peppers, and a touch of sugar to create a unique blend that added a distinctive flavor as well as spiciness. Sriracha sauce was especially popular in the Vietnamese community, but was also used by other Asian cuisines that favored spicy food including Chinese, Korean, and Thai.

Although Tran had spent only a couple of days creating the formula, testing variations on family and friends until he found one they all liked, the new sauce would prove to be the company's biggest hit, and in the next few years became a staple at Asian restaurants and groceries around the United States. Packaged in a clear plastic squeeze bottle with a green top, and decorated with a white drawing of a rooster and information in Chinese, Vietnamese, Thai, English, French, and Spanish, the sauce lent a pleasing touch of heat and flavor to a multitude of dishes. Unlike most other products made primarily for an Asian clientele, it would begin to develop a following in the broader marketplace as diners who saw it on their tables in restaurants sought it out for home use.

MOVING TO ROSEMEAD

As sales grew, in 1987 the company moved its operations from Los Angeles to suburban Rosemead, where a 68,000-square-foot production facility was established. In 1990 Huy Fong trademarked the rooster logo used on its bottles, and six years later it boosted capacity further by purchasing the former Wham-O toy factory on the same block as its plant.

The main ingredient of Huy Fong sauces was jalapeno peppers, which were grown under contract for the company on farms north of Los Angeles and on land it owned near San Diego. After shipment to Rosemead the peppers were quickly processed into a pulp on machines that had been modified by the company's founder, who had taught himself to cut and weld metal and maintained a repair shop on-site. After the pulp was de-stemmed, washed, dried, and chopped, it was mixed with salt, vinegar, and a preservative and put into 50-gallon vacuum-sealed plastic drums. The pepper crop was largely harvested in the fall, which kept the company especially busy for two months processing and storing it.

Pepper mash formed the basis of the firm's entire product line, which at this time included Sambal Oelek, almost purely peppers; a thicker Chili Garlic Paste; spicy Sambal Badjak, which added onions; its original Pepper Sate sauce; and top seller Sriracha. The latter was produced in vats, where pureed jalapeno mash was combined with a large quantity of garlic powder and smaller amounts of sugar and xanthan gum thickener to create a sauce that was roughly the same color as ketchup, though slightly more viscous. After blending, it was injected into bottles using other Tran-modified equipment. The simple ingredients were relatively inexpensive (Tran had chosen red ripe jalapenos over other pepper varieties because they were easier to harvest), and a 17-ounce bottle cost only about two dollars, but the distinctive result impressed customers and food critics alike, some of whom hailed it as the best sauce of its type.

```
┌─────────────────────────────────────────────┐
│                                             │
│              KEY DATES                      │
│                   ■                         │
├─────────────────────────────────────────────┤
│  1980:  Vietnamese immigrant David Tran     │
│         begins making hot sauce in Los      │
│         Angeles.                            │
│  1983:  Sriracha Hot Chili Sauce is         │
│         introduced.                         │
│  1987:  Company moves operations to Los     │
│         Angeles suburb of Rosemead.         │
│  1990:  Huy Fong trademarks the rooster     │
│         logo used on its bottles.           │
│  1996:  Huy Fong buys former Wham-O         │
│         factory to expand operations.       │
│  1999:  The company voluntarily recalls     │
│         42,300 cases of Sriracha sauce that │
│         had fermented after bottling.       │
│  2001:  Huy Fong is selling six million     │
│         pounds of chili-based sauces        │
│         annually and has revenues of about  │
│         $12 million.                        │
│  2009:  David Tran's 33-year-old son        │
│         William is serving as president.    │
│                                             │
└─────────────────────────────────────────────┘
```

RECALL IN 1999

In September 1999 the company voluntarily recalled 42,300 cases of Sriracha sauce that had fermented after bottling, causing gas buildup that could potentially spray sauce when opened. Some bottles managed to make it to store shelves, however, which prompted the Hawaii Department of Health to issue an advisory. The fermentation was later attributed to problems with garlic that had been used in several batches. The recall was managed by Tran's son William, who was then serving as the firm's director of operations.

By 2001 Huy Fong was selling six million pounds of chili-based sauces annually and had revenues of about $12 million. The company was concentrating on its top sellers, and had stopped making Pepper Sate and Sambal Badjak. Even though Huy Fong had never advertised, its products were found around the United States and were also exported to some foreign markets including the Far East. Huy Fong produced the leading Sriracha sauce on the market, which according to industry expert Dave DeWitt had become as dominant as the McIlhenny Company's Tabasco brand in its segment. Eight members of the Tran family were working for the company at this time.

With success came competition, and by then Huy Fong had begun to discover that other companies were closely mimicking its logo and bottle design. The firm took action to stop such operators, hiring private investigators and suing former customers who had begun purchasing counterfeit versions of Sriracha. Although the design might look the same, the sauce could taste very different, and beyond losing sales the firm was worried about harm to its reputation from poorly produced fakes, some of which were possibly even unsafe to eat.

During the latter half of the decade the cult following of Huy Fong Sriracha sauce continued to grow. Prominent chefs used it in their dishes, a Facebook group devoted to it claimed 120,000 members, and some fans went so far as to get rooster tattoos. Mainstream restaurant chains also began to incorporate it in their recipes, with Applebee's mixing it with mayonnaise to accompany shrimp, and Roly Poly squirting it on wrap sandwiches. It was also available at a wider range of retail outlets than ever before, including Wal-Mart and Kroger. Despite these breakthroughs, its primary market continued to be Asian restaurants and groceries, which accounted for some 80 percent of sales.

By 2009 Huy Fong was selling approximately ten million bottles of Sriracha sauce per year, with the company's offerings consisting of just three products that also included Chili Garlic Sauce and Sambal Oelek in addition to Sriracha. David Tran's 33-year-old son William had been appointed as president, and other family members held key positions as well.

Nearly three decades after David Tran began selling hot sauce in Los Angeles's Chinatown, Huy Fong Foods, Inc., had grown into the leading maker of Asian-style hot sauces in the United States. The firm's signature offering, Tuong Ot Sriracha (Sriracha Hot Chili Sauce), had developed a cult following far beyond its original customer base in the Asian community, and was embraced by chain restaurant kitchens and celebrity chefs alike. With new customers discovering it every day, and ownership and management still under the control of its founding family, continued success appeared likely.

Frank Uhle

PRINCIPAL COMPETITORS

Kosol-Ampa Co. Ltd.; Nr. Instant Produce Co. Ltd.; Lee Kum Kee International Holdings Ltd.; Suree Interfoods Co. Ltd.; Foodex Co. Ltd.; Chokguakul Co. Ltd.; Sea World Cold Storage Co. Ltd.; Chuew Huad Co. Ltd.; Thai Theparos Food Products Public Co. Ltd.

FURTHER READING

Chute, David, "Fire in the Bowl," *Los Angeles Magazine,* April 2001, p. 72.

Edge, John T., "A Chili Sauce to Crow About," *New York Times,* May 20, 2009, p. D1.

"Enforcement," *Food Chemical News,* April 3, 2000.

"Explosive Chili Sauce Prompts Health Advisory," *Associated Press,* January 11, 2000.

Hopkins, Brent, "Putting the Heat On," *Los Angeles Daily News,* February 2, 2005.

Martin, Chuck, "Sriracha Sauce Hot 'Korean Ketchup,'" *Cincinnati Enquirer,* October 31, 2001.

Nakamura, Eric, "The Famous Hot Sauce Factory Tour!" *Giant Robot,* Issue 9, 1997, pp. 32–33.

Silverstein, Clara, "Special Sauce," *Boston Globe,* May 24, 2006, p. C2.

Sytsma, Alan, "A Rooster's Wake-Up Call," *Gourmet,* February 8, 2008.

IDEXX Laboratories, Inc.

One IDEXX Drive
Westbrook, Maine 04092
U.S.A.
Telephone: (207) 556-0300
Fax: (207) 556-4286
Web site: http://www.idexx.com

Public Company
Incorporated: 1983
Employees: 4,700
Sales: $1.02 billion (2008)
Stock Exchanges: NASDAQ
Ticker Symbol: IDXX
NAICS: 325413 In Vitro Diagnostic Substance Manufacturing; 334516 Analytical Laboratory Instrument Manufacturing

■ ■ ■

IDEXX Laboratories, Inc., provides diagnostic testing and information technology solutions for the animal health care industry as well as products used to test drinking water and milk quality. Its largest business segment is its Companion Animal Group, which secures over 80 percent of company revenues. This segment serves over 50,000 veterinary practices across the globe. IDEXX provides a variety of veterinary diagnostic products including in-house diagnostic tests and instruments, and also offers laboratory services and practice management software. IDEXX also provides microbiology testing products used to test drinking water and milk. The company has over 60 offices across the globe

and employs over 100 scientists. IDEXX's revenues surpassed $1 billion in 2008.

ORIGINS

In the early 1980s David E. Shaw, having just turned 30, was commuting every week from Maine to Agribusiness Associates, Inc., an international management consulting firm in the affluent Boston suburb of Wellesley Hills, Massachusetts. The travel was draining, and Shaw began to think of other ways to live. As a consultant, he began to notice untapped markets that could be pursued from Maine. As he told the *Boston Globe,* "I saw opportunities in animal health that were not being served well. I got tired of the commute to Massachusetts and liked living in Maine, so I started with the poultry industry, seeing that the initial investment would be small and the time to market shorter." In 1983 IDEXX was incorporated, and soon afterward the new company began operations. Shaw had some difficulty in luring employees to rural Maine for his start-up company, but as the company's success grew it also drew a pool of talented employees.

The early years of IDEXX were accompanied by enormous growth in the biotechnology field, and the field was highly competitive from the start. Typically it took several years for a company to develop a new product, since funds for research, testing, and marketing had to be raised. Often development funds were raised from pharmaceutical companies that in return wanted to own a share of the biotechnology company, and as a result, many biotechnology companies (most of which had fewer than 150 employees) were taken over by

COMPANY PERSPECTIVES

IDEXX's strategy is to drive growth through investment in innovative technologies that create new products and advance existing offerings to support improvements in our customers' businesses. Our long-standing mission is to be a great company by creating exceptional long-term value for our employees, customers, and stockholders through worldwide leadership in our businesses.

larger companies in the process. For products intended for human use, a company also had to go through an elaborate approval process at the U.S. Food and Drug Administration (FDA), and then, even if this approval was granted, companies could not predict whether products would be successful or prove disappointing when they finally reached the marketplace. In this turbulent atmosphere, IDEXX had the advantage of being able to avoid waiting for FDA approval for its early products, since IDEXX products were aimed at the veterinary and agricultural markets, rather than for human medical use.

EARLY FOCUS ON TESTING

In its earliest years IDEXX concentrated on two key product lines. In 1985 IDEXX introduced systems that government agencies and businesses could use to test for the presence of contaminants in foods and food processing facilities. The following year it began to sell diagnostic and detection products for use by veterinarians in their offices. By the mid-1990s, IDEXX also sold tests with which government agencies and businesses could detect contaminants in drinking water (introduced in 1993) and began to offer commercial veterinary laboratory testing, consultation, and advisory services to veterinarians (introduced in 1994). IDEXX internally referred to its products and services as falling into two specialized areas, Animal Health, and Food and Environmental. Testing kits sold by IDEXX ranged in price from $25 to $4,000 each; testing instruments and systems were priced from $1,000 to over $70,000 each.

IDEXX's products relied heavily on such sophisticated biotechnologies as immunoassay technology, employing tests based on antibody-antigen reactions. Most simply explained, antigens are foreign substances such as viruses or bacteria that enter a body; through its immune system, the body produces antibodies in hopes of eliminating the antigen. Several IDEXX

products relied on DNA probe technology, in which a single-stranded DNA molecule is introduced into a test sample. If a particular organism is present in the sample, the DNA molecule will combine with it to form a double-stranded molecule.

During the 1980s and 1990s IDEXX developed numerous inexpensive test kits for use by veterinarians, to detect diseases common among household pets, such as heartworm disease, feline immunodeficiency virus (sometimes called "feline AIDS"), feline leukemia, and canine parvovirus. Veterinarians recommended regular testing for many of these diseases, making such products quite profitable. IDEXX also developed a test for equine infectious anemia, important in that federal law required that horses be tested for this disease before being taken across state lines. The company also developed a wide variety of much more costly instrument-based testing systems: one to analyze enzyme levels in animals' blood; a second to measure electrolytes (sodium, potassium, and chloride); a third to evaluate blood components; and a fourth to measure hormones. IDEXX created software that linked these four systems, allowing veterinarians to produce a profile report within their own offices, rather than having to rely on commercial testing laboratories. Brand names of tests marketed by IDEXX included SNAP, CITE, VetLite, and QBC Vet Autoread.

ADDING VETERINARY
LABORATORY SERVICES

In the mid-1990s, following acquisition of several testing laboratories, IDEXX began to offer veterinary laboratory services in the United States, England, and Japan. Veterinarians who needed more sophisticated testing than was possible in their offices sent samples to IDEXX facilities and received reports. Through its subsidiary Cardiopet, IDEXX provided specialized consultation services to veterinarians in the United States, Canada, and 11 other countries. Veterinarians could telephone Cardiopet during a patient's visit and receive immediate interpretation of test results in areas such as radiology, dermatology, and cardiology.

IDEXX instrument-based systems were used by government agencies and industrial laboratories to test large numbers of samples, allowing diagnosis and monitoring of diseases in poultry and livestock. Of particular interest, given the concern about salmonella poisoning in the late 1990s, were IDEXX's "Flock-Chek" testing system and software, which could be used to test poultry for this contaminant.

IDEXX also created many products used to measure the safety of drinking water, dairy products, poultry, and

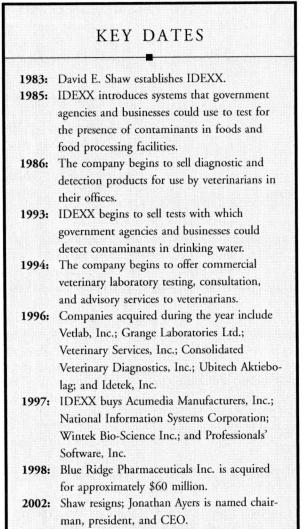

KEY DATES

1983: David E. Shaw establishes IDEXX.

1985: IDEXX introduces systems that government agencies and businesses could use to test for the presence of contaminants in foods and food processing facilities.

1986: The company begins to sell diagnostic and detection products for use by veterinarians in their offices.

1993: IDEXX begins to sell tests with which government agencies and businesses could detect contaminants in drinking water.

1994: The company begins to offer commercial veterinary laboratory testing, consultation, and advisory services to veterinarians.

1996: Companies acquired during the year include Vetlab, Inc.; Grange Laboratories Ltd.; Veterinary Services, Inc.; Consolidated Veterinary Diagnostics, Inc.; Ubitech Aktiebolag; and Idetek, Inc.

1997: IDEXX buys Acumedia Manufacturers, Inc.; National Information Systems Corporation; Wintek Bio-Science Inc.; and Professionals' Software, Inc.

1998: Blue Ridge Pharmaceuticals Inc. is acquired for approximately $60 million.

2002: Shaw resigns; Jonathan Ayers is named chairman, president, and CEO.

2008: Sales surpass $1 billion.

processed meat. Dairy farmers, government laboratories, and food companies all made use of these detection products, as numerous contaminants could be detected with IDEXX products, including *Escherichia coli* (*E. coli,* which could be found in both food and water and was responsible in the late 1990s for well-publicized food poisoning incidents in beef products), salmonella (a bacteria that could lead to fatal food contamination), aflatoxins, and dangerous antibiotic residues in food products.

Among IDEXX's entries into this area were its Lightning, SimPlate, and Acumedia testing products. The Lightning testing system, introduced in 1995, was used to test the cleanliness of processing surfaces and other equipment in food processing plants. The SimPlate product line, introduced the following year, was used by food quality managers to determine the total

level of *E. coli* and other contaminants in food products. In 1997 IDEXX acquired Acumedia, a company that manufactured more than 300 products used for bacteria detection in foods; these products were being integrated with other IDEXX testing devices in the late 1990s. IDEXX also maintained the Food Safety Net, a network of products and testing and consulting services.

ACQUISITIONS AND INTERNATIONAL EXPANSION

Through the mid-1990s, IDEXX completed several major acquisitions of other biotechnology and testing companies. Major acquisitions included: VetTest S.A., a veterinary clinical testing business; Environetics, Inc., producer of the Colilert water testing product line; AMIS International Company, KK, a Japanese veterinary laboratory business; and Cardiopet Incorporated, a veterinary consulting service.

During 1996 and 1997, IDEXX's acquisitions accelerated, and it became the owner of several additional veterinary reference laboratory businesses, plus manufacturers of detection and diagnostic tests. Companies acquired during 1996 included: Vetlab, Inc., a Texas operator of two veterinary reference laboratories; Grange Laboratories Ltd., operator of veterinary reference laboratories in the United Kingdom; Veterinary Services, Inc., operator of veterinary reference laboratories in Colorado, Illinois, and Oklahoma; Consolidated Veterinary Diagnostics, Inc., operator of veterinary reference laboratories in California, Nevada, and Oregon; Ubitech Aktiebolag, a Swedish manufacturer and distributor of livestock diagnostic test kits; and Idetek, Inc., a California company that manufactured and distributed detection tests used by the food, agricultural, and environmental industries.

In 1997 IDEXX placed a similar focus on acquiring its competitors. It acquired Acumedia Manufacturers, Inc., a Maryland manufacturer of dehydrated culture media used for bacteria detection; National Information Systems Corporation, a Wisconsin company that supplied computer systems for veterinary practice management; Wintek Bio-Science Inc., a company in Taiwan that distributed diagnostic products to veterinarians and hospitals; and Professionals' Software, Inc., an Illinois company also engaged in supplying practice management computer systems to veterinarians. IDEXX also entered into an agreement with Fuisz Technologies, a Virginia company that had developed technology for rapidly dissolving tablets, allowing IDEXX to adapt this technology for veterinary use. Its largest acquisition to date came in 1998, when it bought Blue Ridge Pharmaceuticals Inc. in a $60 million deal. The purchase gave IDEXX a foothold in the veterinary pharmaceutical market, which was valued at $7 billion in 1998.

In 1991 only 21 percent ($6.5 million) of IDEXX's revenues came from sales outside of the United States. By 1996, that figure had risen to 34 percent ($91.5 million). The company attributed this rise largely to the expansion of its sales force in other countries; by 1996 it maintained foreign sales offices in Australia, France, Germany, Italy, Japan, New Zealand, the Netherlands, Spain, and the United Kingdom. However, these foreign operations were not without risk. IDEXX had to deal with regulatory approvals and patent processes for its products that differed from country to country, import and export tariffs, and economic fluctuations in foreign countries. The latter factor became particularly important in late 1997, when economies in both Europe and the Pacific Rim region (Australia, Japan, Taiwan, and other Asian countries) became shaky and IDEXX's revenues there dropped substantially. This drop contributed to an overall decrease in revenues to IDEXX for the first nine months of 1997, an abrupt halt to its rapid growth in the preceding years.

PATENT LAWSUITS CONCERNS

As the biotechnology industry was marked by rapid change and heavy dependence on legal protection for a company's products such as licenses, patents, and copyrights, it was common for companies to charge each other with infringement of product patents. The resulting lawsuits often proved very expensive, complicated, and time consuming. In the mid-1990s IDEXX found itself involved in several of these lawsuits. The two most important of these involved the Millipore Corporation and the Barnes-Jewish Hospital of St. Louis.

In 1993 IDEXX had acquired Environetics, Inc., which already had a lawsuit pending against Millipore Corporation, charging that Millipore had infringed its patented technology for detecting *E. coli* and other contaminants in food and water. Two years later, IDEXX added a second lawsuit against Millipore for similar infringements. The two lawsuits were finally settled in December 1997, when Millipore agreed to halt sales of the products that were the subjects of the lawsuits.

In May 1995, the Barnes-Jewish Hospital of St. Louis filed a lawsuit against IDEXX, claiming that IDEXX's canine heartworm diagnostic products had infringed one of the hospital's patents. Although IDEXX claimed that the hospital's patent was invalid, it eventually decided to settle the case out of court in September 1997, paying the hospital $5.5 million. (Fol-

lowing this settlement, the hospital then sued IDEXX's chief competitor in the heartworm diagnostic business, Synbiotics Corporation of California.) While the lawsuit was pending, IDEXX had spent a great deal of time and funds to develop products to replace the ones challenged by the hospital.

CHANGES IN LEADERSHIP

IDEXX experienced massive growth during the mid-1990s. Between 1994 and 1995, its total revenues increased 49 percent, from $126.4 million to $188.6 million. Its international revenues almost doubled during that single year, rising from $34.3 million to $65 million. From 1995 to 1996, growth was almost as impressive. Revenues in 1996 increased another 42 percent, to $267.7 million; international revenues in 1996 increased 41 percent, to $91.5 million. Growth in Europe and Japan was a key factor in these increases. In 1996 revenues in the Pacific Rim region rose more than 135 percent.

However, 1997 saw a halt to such large-scale growth. The combination of the settlement paid in the Barnes-Jewish Hospital lawsuit, the costs of acquiring new companies, and drastically reduced sales in economically troubled Europe and Japan resulted in a third-quarter 1997 loss for IDEXX, a reversal of the large rise in profits the company had come to expect. Indeed, IDEXX posted losses in both 1997 and 1998.

In November 1997, CEO Shaw announced that Erwin F. Workman, Jr., president and chief operating officer of IDEXX since 1993 and an employee since its first year in business, would be replaced by Jeffrey J. Langan, a 20-year employee of the Hewlett-Packard Company. Workman would take over operations in the products divisions and would focus on research and development activities. Langan was named CEO in early 1999 but his tenure proved short-lived. He resigned later in the year and Shaw resumed CEO responsibilities.

IDEXX IN THE 21ST CENTURY

By 2000 IDEXX's financial performance was back on track. The company's Animal Health business segment enjoyed steady growth as the company worked to launch new products and grow its business through key acquisitions. It also expanded its water testing arm by acquiring U.K.-based Genera Technologies Ltd., a company focused on creating products that detected cryptosporidium in drinking water. IDEXX's pharmaceutical division also was bolstered by the FDA's approval and subsequent launch of its first pharmaceutical product, ACAREXX Otic Suspension, a treatment for ear mites in cats. IDEXX sold its Acumedia business that year, ending its involvement in the food product testing market.

In early 2002, founder David Shaw resigned from the company and named Jonathan Ayers his successor. Sales and profits continued to rise as the company launched successful new products. The company's Laser-Cyte machine, the first major diagnostic instrument to be fully designed and manufactured by IDEXX, made its debut in 2002, and by 2003, it had installed almost 1,300 machines in veterinary offices. The new LaserCyte used laser technology that enabled veterinarians to analyze an animal's blood to diagnose disease and illnesses. IDEXX launched a total of 12 new products in 2004. Acquisitions for the year included several reference labs and Dr. Bommeli AG, a Swiss manufacturer of animal diagnostic reagents.

By 2005 revenues had grown to $635 million. The company's Companion Animal Group—formerly known as its Animal Health division—accounted for 82 percent of overall revenues that year. Growth continued at a rapid pace and by 2007 revenues had climbed to $923 million. During 2008 the company launched several next-generation versions of its Catalyst Dx and SNAPshot Dx testing instruments that were part of its IDEXX Vetlab in-house diagnostic instruments product line. The Catalyst Dx was used to analyze an animal's blood chemistry while the SNAPshot Dx screened for liver and thyroid disease.

Company revenues surpassed $1 billion in 2008. The company sold its ACAREXX and SURPASS veterinary pharmaceutical products business that year to focus on its core Companion Animal operations. While it had enjoyed a rapid rate of growth over the past several years, IDEXX expected its growth to slow somewhat as the U.S. economy continued to weaken in 2009. Much of the company's business was dependent upon pet owners taking their companion animals for annual checkups, vaccines, tests, and so forth. With the rate of unemployment rising in certain parts of the country, many pet owners were forced to reduce pet health care costs and some were even forced to give up their family pets. While IDEXX was cognizant of economic conditions, its strong growth and product development during the early years of the 21st century left it well positioned to face future challenges.

Gerry Azzata
Updated, Christina M. Stansell

PRINCIPAL SUBSIDIARIES

Beijing IDEXX-Yuanheng Laboratories Co. Ltd. (China); Cardiopet Inc.; Diavet Labor AG (Switzer-land); Genera Technologies Ltd. (UK); IDEXX Computer Systems, Inc.; IDEXX Distribution, Inc.; IDEXX Europe B.V. (Netherlands); IDEXX GmbH (Germany); IDEXX Holding GmbH (Germany); IDEXX Holdings, Inc.; IDEXX Laboratories B.V. (Netherlands); IDEXX Laboratories Canada 1, ULC; IDEXX Laboratories Canada 2, ULC; IDEXX Laboratories Canada Corporation; IDEXX Laboratories Canada LP; IDEXX Laboratories Italia S.r.l.; IDEXX Laboratories, KK (Japan); IDEXX Laboratories Limited (UK); IDEXX Laboratories (NZ) Ltd. (New Zealand); IDEXX Laboratories Pty. Ltd. (Australia); IDEXX Laboratories (Proprietary) Ltd. (South Africa); IDEXX Laboratories (Shanghai) Co. Ltd.; IDEXX Laboratories, S. de R.L. de C.V. (Mexico); IDEXX Laboratorios, S.L. (Spain); IDEXX Laboratories Sp. z o.o. (Poland); IDEXX Laboratories SPRL (Belgium); IDEXX Laboratories Inc. Taiwan R.O.C.; IDEXX Operations, Inc.; IDEXX Pharmaceuticals, Inc.; IDEXX Real Estate Holdings, LLC; IDEXX Reference Laboratories, Inc.; IDEXX Reference Laboratories Ltd. (Canada); IDEXX SARL (France); IDEXX Switzerland AG; IDEXX UK Acquisition Limited (UK); Institut Pourquier SAS (France); Laboratoire IDEXX SARL (France); OPTI Medical Systems, Inc.; OPTI Medical Systems GmbH (Germany); Syracuse Bioanalytical, Inc.; Vet Med Lab ApS (Denmark); Vet Med Lab (UK) Ltd; Vet Med Labor GmbH (Germany); Vet Med Labor GmbH (Austria).

PRINCIPAL COMPETITORS

Eli Lilly and Company; Heska Corp.; VCA Antech Inc.

FURTHER READING

Canfield, Clarke, "IDEXX CEO Resigns After Short Tenure," *Portland (Me.) Press Herald*, July 23, 1999.

Drury, Allan, "For New IDEXX CEO, Learning Is a Constant," *Portland (Me.) Press Herald*, February 17, 2002.

Gondo, Nancy, "'97 Acquisition Made IDEXX a Long-Term Play," *Investor's Business Daily*, August 27, 2008.

"IDEXX Releases Key Product Upgrades," *Portland (Me.) Press Herald*, April 3, 2008.

Murphy, Edward D., "Founder of IDEXX to Leave—Again," *Portland (Me.) Press Herald*, January 25, 2002.

Ramanathan, Anuradha, "Pet Firms Feel Pain as Man and Best Friend Separate," *Reuters News*, January 2009.

Rosenberg, Ronald, "New Businesses Move Maine Ahead," *Boston Globe*, June 2, 1996, p. 79.

Shanahan, Mark, "Income, Revenue Increase; The Westbrook Biotech Firm's Strong Performance Occurs Even with a Delay in a Key New Product," *Portland (Me.) Press Herald*, July 16, 2002.

Industrias Peñoles, S.A. de C.V.

Moliere No. 222 Colonia Polanco
Mexico City, D.F. 11540
Mexico
Telephone: (555) 279-3000
Fax: (555) 279-3014
Web site: http://www.penoles.com.mx

Public Company
Founded: 1887 as Compañía Minera de Peñoles
Employees: 7,862
Sales: 44.73 billion pesos ($4.35 billion) (2007)
Stock Exchanges: Mexico
Ticker Symbol: PENOLES
NAICS: 212231 Lead Ore and Zinc Ore Mining; 212221 Gold Ore Mining; 212222 Silver Ore Mining; 331419 Primary Smelting and Refining of Nonferrous Metal

■ ■ ■

Industrias Peñoles, S.A. de C.V., operates as a mining group with operations in smelting and refining nonferrous metals as well as chemical production. The company, part of Mexico's Grupo BAL, is the world's leading producer of refined silver, metallic bismuth, and sodium sulfate. Peñoles also stands as the number one producer of refined gold, lead, and zinc throughout Latin America and is one of Mexico's largest net exporters. The company's mining facilities include: Fresnillo, the world's richest silver mine; La Ciénega, Mexico's richest gold mine; La Herradura, Mexico's largest gold mine; Naica, the largest lead-producing mine in Mexico; and Francisco I. Madero, the largest zinc mine found in Mexico. Peñoles also operates the fourth largest metallurgical facility in the world as well as the largest sodium sulfate production complex.

ORIGINS AND INITIAL GROWTH

The Compañía Minera de Peñoles was founded in 1887 to exploit the silver-lead mines at Mapimi in the state of Durango that had been discovered by the Spanish in 1598. During the late 19th century the Durango-Mapimi Mining Co. of Council Bluffs, Iowa, united the principal mines and smelted some 20 tons of ore a day but was unable to make a profit. Operating with capital provided by a Spanish investor, Charles Reidt made a major new strike. The Compañía Minera de Peñoles was organized in 1887 to exploit this deposit and by 1892 had opened a smelter to treat the ores. Large scale operations began during 1893 and 1894, when the company introduced electricity and built a railroad to connect the mines and smelter, a task that involved construction of a suspension bridge.

By 1903 Peñoles was the largest independent base metal enterprise in Mexico, producing lead, silver, and arsenic. Its revenues rose from 673,000 pesos ($336,500) in 1893 to more than four million pesos ($2 million) in 1899. The profits were immense for Peñoles and its backers, Minerales y Metales, S.A., and the German-controlled American Metal Co.; the enterprise yielded dividends of 100,000 pesos ($50,000) per month on a total capitalization of only 250,000 pesos ($125,000). With its profits Peñoles and its subsidiary, the Mexican Metal Co., bought mines in other areas of northern Mexico and was strong enough to survive the chaos of the 1910–17 Mexican Revolution.

Minerales y Metales was merged in 1920 into Peñoles, which in turn became a wholly owned subsidiary of American Metal in 1923. Using its cash reserves, American Metal had acquired additional properties during the revolution, including smelters in Torreón and Monterrey and their rail connections. Most of the ore treated at these facilities came from the Mapimí area, but these mines were being depleted, and the Mapimí smelter was eventually abandoned. With the end of this supply, the Torreón and Monterrey smelters turned to custom work for other clients. Peñoles, however, had many other mining properties by this time, including a silver-lead deposit in Santa Eulalia and coal mines at Agujita, both purchased during the revolution.

Despite mixed results, Peñoles retained its ranking in the 1920s as the second largest mining company in Mexico. Ore from Santa Eulalia and Santa Barbara in the state of Chihuahua was shipped to Torreón. The company took over a pyritic copper ore deposit in the state of Guerrero that was difficult to refine and solved the problem, building a 300-ton mill. The Monterrey smelter had to cast around for business, however, because Peñoles lead ores in the area were being depleted and ventures in the states of Durango, Guanajuato, Oaxaca, and Zacatecas were unsuccessful. The Torreón smelter was closed in 1932 because of falling lead and silver prices during the Great Depression.

MEXICAN OWNERSHIP

Compañía Metalúrgica de Peñoles was formed after World War II to lease the smelting and refining plants of Compañía Minera de Peñoles. San Francisco Mines of Mexico Ltd. (37.5 percent owned by American Metal) received the contract to smelt and refine the lead and copper production of both Peñoles companies. The two were merged by 1961, when American Metal (later American Metal Climax, Inc.) sold a 51 percent interest in Metalúrgica Mexicana Peñoles, S.A. (Met-Mex Peñoles), to Mexican nationals Raúl Baillères and José A. García. The sale was mandated by a law requiring all mining companies in Mexico to be majority owned by Mexicans. Baillères was a founder of the first mining financial institution, Crédito Minero y Mercantil, S.A., in 1934, and had 15 years of experience in managing the buying and selling of nearly all the gold, silver, and mercury in the country.

American Metal Climax sold the remaining 49 percent to Baillères and García in 1965 for about $10 million. Peñoles thereby became the first major mining and smelting company in Mexico to be completely Mexican-owned, although Bernard Rohe, a U.S. citizen, remained its chief executive officer until 1983. The company had diversified into industrial chemicals, organizing a subsidiary to produce sodium sulfate in 1963. Peñoles became a public company in 1968, when it first offered shares on the Bolsa, Mexico's stock exchange. Beginning in 1969, it also began borrowing heavily from U.S. banks to finance a massive, eight-year, $500-million, exploration and development program.

By 1977 Industrias Peñoles had raised its estimated mineral reserves more than tenfold and had opened enough new silver mines to enable Mexico to pass the Soviet Union as the world's leading producer of that metal. It was the twelfth largest company in Mexico that year, with sales of 6.89 billion pesos (about $313 million), compared with only $92 million in 1972, and income more than three times the $5 million 1972 level. The company also expanded the scope of its activities by acquiring Refractarios Mexicanos, S.A. de C.V., in 1973.

EXPANDED PRODUCTION

By 1980 Industrias Peñoles was producing gold, silver, lead, zinc, copper, cadmium, bismuth, sodium sulfate, sulfuric acid, magnesium oxide, fluorspar, granular refractories, and refractory bricks. Net sales came to 21.7 billion pesos ($947.6 million) in 1980, when net income was 1.8 billion pesos ($78.6 million). This was an exceptionally strong year, as silver prices reached a record $50.35 an ounce. By early 1982 silver had sunk to $4.50 an ounce, and that year an international payments crisis sent the peso into free fall. At first glance, this seemed a recipe for disaster for Peñoles, but the company was selling most of its products abroad for dollars and incurring its costs in devalued pesos. Record profits enabled it to reduce its foreign debt of $208 million in 1983 to $141 million at the end of 1985. That year it had net sales of $597.3 million and net profit of

KEY DATES

■

1887: The Compañía Minera de Peñoles is established to exploit the silver-lead mines at Mapimi.

1903: Peñoles is the largest independent base metal enterprise in Mexico, producing lead, silver, and arsenic.

1920: Minerales y Metales, S.A., is merged into Peñoles.

1923: The company becomes a subsidiary of American Metal Co.

1961: American Metal sells a 51 percent interest in Peñoles to Mexican nationals Raúl Bailléres and José A. García.

1965: American Metal sells the remaining 49 percent of Peñoles to Bailléres and García.

1968: Peñoles goes public.

1973: Refractarios Mexicanos, S.A. de C.V., is acquired.

1990: A joint venture with U.S. Cyprus Minerals Corp. and a venture capital affiliate of Banamex is established for one of the richest ore deposits in Mexico.

1994: Peñoles starts gold mining operations in Durango.

1997: Peñoles purchases a 51 percent share in Peru's largest metallurgical complex, state-owned La Oroya.

2006: The Milpillas copper mine in Sonora begins production.

2008: Peñoles combines its silver and gold mining assets into Fresnillo plc, which is then spun off on the London Stock Exchange.

$10.5 million, of which chemical production accounted for about 40 percent. The company had added barite to its product mix during this period.

By 1986 the position of Peñoles was strong enough to consider new acquisitions. That year it bought out Bethlehem Steel's 40 percent share of its Met-Mex Peñoles metals processing subsidiary. The company remained a majority partner in mining ventures with AMAX (the former American Metal Climax) and two other companies. Its other joint ventures included one with the Finnish firm Outokumpu in zinc mining and with A.P. Green Refractories to manufacture refractory materials with its magnesium oxide production.

Outside of Mexico, Peñoles had a sodium sulfate joint venture in Spain, a refractories plant in Argentina, an acquisition in France from Vielle Montaign, large acquisitions in Japan, and trading companies in New York City and São Paulo, Brazil. Alberto Bailléres, the company chairman, held 20 percent of its stock in 1987.

CONTINUED GROWTH

Net sales reached two trillion pesos ($663 million) in 1991, and net profit was 129.6 billion pesos ($42.9 million). A joint venture with U.S. Cyprus Minerals Corp. and a venture capital affiliate of the giant financial services firm Banamex was established in 1990 for one of the richest ore deposits in Mexico—about 8.5 million metric tons of minable reserves, principally zinc, silver, and lead. During 1993 Peñoles increased its stake in this joint venture, Minera Bismark, S.A., to 90 percent by acquiring Cyprus's 40 percent holding. It assumed full ownership of the enterprise in 1995. Peñoles withdrew from the manufacture of refractories in 1994 by selling properties, including its share in the joint venture with Green, to subsidiaries of the U.S. company Indresco, Inc., for $75 million. This sector of its business accounted for $71 million in sales the previous year.

In 1994 Peñoles started gold mining operations in Durango through a subsidiary, Minera Mexicana La Ciénega, and opened a mine producing zinc and silver in the state of Mexico, in participation with a Japanese firm, through 51 percent owned Minera Tizapa. In 1995 it opened a lead and zinc mine named La Negra in the state of Querétaro through Minera Cápela, a wholly owned subsidiary. Also in 1995, Peñoles incorporated subsidiaries in Peru and Argentina to explore and exploit mining concessions.

Because it was selling a high percentage of its goods abroad, Peñoles remained profitable despite the economic crisis that gripped Mexico following the devaluation of the peso in December 1994. Net sales dropped from 3.73 billion pesos in 1994 ($1.07 billion) to 5.75 billion pesos ($845.6 million). Net income, however, rose from 28.8 million pesos ($8.2 million) to 1.01 billion pesos ($148.5 million). Export sales represented 60 percent of the 1995 total, with the United States accounting for 62 percent of export sales and Japan for 16 percent. The long-term debt fell from 2.09 billion pesos ($597 million) to 1.86 billion pesos ($273.5 million). Alberto Bailléres remained chairman of the board. In addition to his holdings in Peñoles, Bailléres controlled the insurer Grupo Nacional Provincial and had an estimated net worth of $1.8 billion in mid-1996.

During 1996 Industrias Peñoles announced it would invest $70 million in a new silver-rich mining project in the state of Zacatecas, with the start up date scheduled sometime in 1998. This mine had proven reserves of 23.2 million metric tons of mostly silver ore, with some zinc, lead, and copper. Also in 1996, Industrias Peñoles agreed to pay $160 million to take full control of the Rosario companies, primarily producing silver, gold, lead, and zinc, from its joint venture partner Alumax Inc. This company had been spun off from AMAX in 1993, when AMAX was acquired by Cyprus Minerals, which then became Cyprus AMAX Minerals Co.

MET-MEX PEÑOLES AND OTHER SUBSIDIARIES

Peñoles purchased a 51 percent share in Peru's largest metallurgical complex, state-owned La Oroya, in 1997 for $194 million. The complex, consisting of smelters and refineries to produce copper, lead, zinc, gold, and silver, from ores, was expected to add nearly $500 million to the company's revenues and just under $50 million in operating income. Its chief liability was that La Oroya was one of the most environmentally damaged mining sites in Peru. Also in 1997, a consortium composed of Industrias Peñoles and Grupo Acerero del Norte purchased for $23 million a 25-year operating concession on the previously government-owned, 442-mile Coahuila-Durango railway line.

The heart of Industrias Peñoles was Met-Mex Peñoles, which operated the Torreón complex. This subsidiary of Metales Peñoles accounted for 72 percent of its 1994 revenues. It was 7 percent owned by U.S. interests. Also important was Compañía Fresnillo, a 60 percent owned subsidiary of Minas Peñoles producing lead, zinc, and other metal concentrates. The other 40 percent was U.S. owned. Fresnillo's revenues came to 20 percent of the parent company's total in 1994. Another subsidiary of Minas Peñoles was Compania Minera Las Torres. Founded in 1966, it had 45 percent U.S.-Canadian participation in 1985, but this fell to 14 percent in 1995. The revenues of Las Torres came to 5 percent of the parent company's total in 1994. Silver accounted for some 35 percent of the revenues of Industrias Peñoles in the mid-1990s. Lead and zinc accounted for another 31 percent, and gold accounted for 13 percent.

In the mid-1990s Minas Peñoles, the company's mining group, was producing gold, silver, lead, zinc, copper, and tungsten through six operating companies. Metales Peñoles, the Metals Group, was operating the Torreón complex, which consisted of a lead smelter, zinc plant, lead-silver refinery, two sulfuric acid plants, and cadmium, bismuth, ammonium sulfate, antimonium trioxide, cadmium oxide, and liquid sulfur dioxide plants, through Met-Mex Peñoles. Through Quimicos Industriales Peñoles, its Chemicals Division, the company operated four companies in the inorganic chemicals area, producing magnesium oxide and sodium sulfate from brines; magnesium oxide from seawater and chemical lime; and other chemical products, such as fertilizers, some of which were obtained using raw materials from Met-Mex.

MOVING INTO THE 21ST CENTURY

The early years of the new millennium proved challenging for Peñoles as the mining industry experienced consolidation amid a global economic slowdown in the metals market. Gold, silver, and zinc prices all fell in 2001, forcing the company to focus on cost cutting efforts. While it opened its Francisco I. Madero zinc mine that year, Peñoles opted to suspend operations at its Rey de Plata zinc mine due to falling zinc prices. The company shuttered its El Monte and Los Torres mines the following year.

The efforts of Peñoles to focus on its core operations and control costs paid off as metal prices began to improve in 2002. With production levels reaching record highs that year, the company secured net sales of over $1 billion. Growth continued in 2003 when sales topped out at $1.2 billion. Peñoles also continued to invest heavily in exploration and development during this period, which led to increased reserves at its Fresnillo silver mine as well as its La Ciénega gold mine. It continued to develop its Milpillas copper mine in Sonora, which opened in August 2006. At the same time, it completed construction on the Termoeléctrica Peñoles electric generation plant, which began to provide electric energy to Peñoles facilities in 2004 and resulted in significant energy cost savings.

By focusing on exploration and development and investing in profitable mines and projects, Peñoles began to benefit handsomely from positive market conditions in the mining industry. The company secured record sales and profits in 2004 and 2005 as the prices of silver, gold, lead, and zinc rose significantly due to increased demand in China, India, and the United States. As part of its strategy to shed unprofitable ventures, the company sold its Mezcala gold project in 2005 and its Pinos Altos gold project in early 2006.

The company invested $62.7 million in exploration during 2006 in Mexico and Latin America, focusing on Chihuahua, Guanajuato, Durango, Sonora, and Chiapas in Mexico, as well as developing projects in Peru and

Chile. Peñoles invested $87.2 million in exploration in 2007, its largest investment in exploration in its history up to that time. With the price of metals continuing to rise, the company posted record financial results with revenues reaching $4.35 billion in 2007. Production levels continued to rise as well. During 2007 the company produced 46.6 million ounces of silver; 388,554 ounces of gold; 194,058 tons of zinc; 62,082 tons of lead; 12,318 tons of copper; and 6,386 tons of copper cathodes.

During 2008 Peñoles made a strategic move when it combined its silver and gold mining assets into Fresnillo plc. The company then spun off Fresnillo plc on the London Stock Exchange in May 2008, marking the first time a Mexican company listed on the London exchange. Peñoles retained a 77 percent stake in Fresnillo and hoped to capitalize on the rising prices of precious metals. While the company remained subject to high raw material costs, increasing labor costs, and fluctuating metal prices, the profitable mining holdings of Peñoles left it in an enviable position among its competitors. As a member of Grupo BAL and headed by one of Mexico's richest men—Alberto Baillères, Peñoles appeared to be on track for success in the years to come.

Robert Halasz
Updated, Christina M. Stansell

PRINCIPAL DIVISIONS

Exploration; Mining; Metals-Chemicals; Infrastructure.

PRINCIPAL COMPETITORS

Barrick Gold Corporation; Dowa Holdings Co. Ltd.; Grupo México S.A.B. de C.V.

FURTHER READING

"Alumax Selling Rosario Stake," *American Metal Market,* May 29, 1996, p. 2.

"American Metal Climax Sells Its 49% Interest in Peñoles of Mexico," *Wall Street Journal,* July 22, 1965, p. 8.

Bernstein, Marvin D., *The Mexican Mining Industry, 1890–1950,* Albany: State University of New York, 1964.

Bream, Rebecca, "Mexico's Fresnillo to List in London," *Financial Times,* April 12, 2008.

"Chile: Peñoles Keen on Mining in Chile," *Estrategia,* July 31, 2008.

Dorfman, John R., "If Any Stock Can Be Said to Have Silver Lining, This Mexican Mining Concern Just Could Be It," *Wall Street Journal,* March 3, 1992, p. C2.

"Industrias Peñoles Finds a Silver Lining in the Plight of the Peso," *Business Week,* November 28, 1983, p. 76.

"Industrias Peñoles: Mining Mexican Silver with U.S. Money," *Business Week,* August 21, 1978, pp. 110–12.

"Mexican Comparison," *Mining Journal,* December 22, 1995, p. 487.

"Mexican to Make Waves on the Footsie," *Daily Mail,* August 28, 2008.

"Mexico's Industrial Groups," *Business Latin America,* April 27, 1987, p. 132.

"Peñoles Gains a Foothold in Peru," *El Fianciero International Edition,* May 5–11, 1997, p. 17.

"Peñoles Obtained Record Production in 2002," *Corporate Mexico,* February 28, 2003.

Scrutton, Alistair, "Peñoles Wins Peruvian Mining Bid," *Financial Times,* April 22, 1997, p. 33.

Smith, Arthur, "Prospecting by Peñoles Expected to Yield Rich Silver Find in Mexico," *American Metal Market,* April 13, 1976, pp. 1, 13.

Thomson, Adam, "Mexican Miners' Strike Set to Persist," *Financial Times,* March 3, 2006.

IOI GROUP

IOI Corporation Bhd

Two IOI Square, IOI Resort
Putrajaya, 62502
Malaysia
Telephone: (60 603) 894 78888
Fax: (60 603) 894 32266
Web site: http://www.ioigroup.com

Public Company
Incorporated: 1972
Employees: 30,000
Sales: MYR 14.665 billion ($4.09 billion) (2008)
Stock Exchanges: Kuala Lumpur
Ticker Symbol: 9027-W
NAICS: 311225 Fats and Oils Refining and Blending; 113210 Forest Nurseries and Gathering of Forest Products

■ ■ ■

IOI Corporation Bhd (IOI) is the world's largest integrated palm oil producer. IOI controls nearly 150,000 hectares of oil palm plantations across 80 estates. These are located primarily in the East Malaysian states of Sabah and Sarawak, as well as on the Malaysian Peninsula. Beginning in 2007, IOI has also extended its plantation operations into Indonesia. IOI is also one of the most efficient palm oil producers, achieving average per-hectare yields of more than six metric tons. The Plantation Division generated 59 percent of group profits in 2008.

IOI's Resource-Based Manufacturing Division comprises the company's palm oil refining and ole-ochemicals production. The company operates four refineries (three in Malaysia and one in Rotterdam, Netherlands) with a total refining capacity of 3.35 million metric tons. The group's Oleochemicals business unit produces fatty acids, fatty esters, glycerin, and soap noodles for the food, plastics, detergents, and other industries. The company's manufacturing capacity of 710,000 metric tons makes it the leading vegetable-based oleochemicals producer in the world. The Specialty Oils and Fat Manufacturing unit, carried out primarily through subsidiary Loders Croklaan, is a leading producer of food-grade palm oil products, with production plants in Canada, Egypt, Malaysia, and the United States.

In addition to its palm oil operations, IOI Corporation is one of Malaysia's leading property development companies, through its 76 percent stake in publicly listed IOI Properties Bhd. This company also operates a number of hotels and resort complexes. IOI Corporation is listed on the Kuala Lumpur Stock Exchange. Founder Lee Shin Cheng is the group's executive chairman. In 2008 IOI's revenues reached MYR 14.65 billion ($4.1 billion).

ORIGINS

Lee Shin Cheng, born in 1935, grew up on one of Malaysia's many rubber plantations in Jeram, Kuala Selangor. An ethnic Chinese, Lee's father operated a small grocery shop on the plantation. At the age of 11, Lee left school and began selling ice cream from a bicycle cart to help his impoverished family. Lee returned to school four years later, however, completing his high school education.

COMPANY PERSPECTIVES

Our Vision. Our Vision is to be a leading corporation in our core businesses by providing products and services of superior values and by sustaining consistent long-term growth in volume and profitability. We shall strive to achieve responsible commercial success by satisfying our customers' needs, giving superior performance to our shareholders, providing rewarding careers to our people, cultivating mutually beneficial relationship with our business associates, caring for the society and the environment in which we operate, and contributing towards the progress of our nation.

Lee's interest turned to the plantation sector, which remained the region's main industry as it emerged from British colonial domination. Lee's initial attempt to enter the industry was rebuffed when he was refused a job because he did not speak English. Lee persisted, however, and at the age of 22 landed a job as a field supervisor at a palm plantation for a different palm oil company.

This first job laid the foundation for the depth of experience that enabled Lee to emerge as one of the world's most powerful palm oil producers. Lee developed his own, intensively hands-on production methods. Lee also recognized the importance of developing methods for increasing the yields of palm plantations. Indeed, with an oil-per-hectare content far superior to other vegetable oil crops, such as soybean, rapeseed, and sunflower, palm oil provided major potential as a global commodity crop.

Even after the creation of an independent Malaysia in the late 1950s, Europeans continued to control most of Malaysia's rubber and palm plantations. This situation began to change in the 1970s as the Malaysian government passed legislation enforcing the transfer of ownership of much of the country's industries and resources to Malaysian citizens. While the government's actions favored the ethnic Malay population, a large number of ethnic Chinese also rose to prominence during this period.

Lee Shin Cheng's chance came in the early 1980s. Lee had formed his own company in 1975. In 1982 Lee used his small company to launch a takeover of an existing public company, Industrial Oxygen Incorporated (IOI). That company had been founded in 1969 and functioned as a distributor of oxygen and other industrial gases. The company incorporated in 1972 and then went public on the Kuala Lumpur Stock Exchange in 1980.

BUILDING A PALM PLANTATION PORTFOLIO

While Lee maintained IOI's gas distribution business, his own business interest remained focused on the palm oil sector. The company made its start in the industry in 1983, when it acquired an existing plantation business, Perusahaan Mekassar. The purchase gave the company control of two palm estates, Bukit Dinding and Sabai. The company continued buying palm plantations, adding estates in Mekassar, Triang, and Pukin in 1985. In June of that year, the company made its first major acquisition, buying up Syarimo SB and its 27,000 hectares of land in Kinabatangan Sabah. By then, IOI had also acquired its first palm oil mill, in Pukin, with a production capacity of 30 metric tons per hour.

Lee was then able to put into practice the planting, cultivation, and harvest techniques he had developed over the course of his career. In particular, Lee became well known for his extremely hands-on approach. Despite leading the company, Lee was known to spend a great deal of time among—and even speaking to—the trees in the company's plantations. As Lee told the *Business Times,* "My trees are my girlfriends. Each one has her own characteristics. If one produces well, I will tell her 'I love you.'" Lee's efforts paid off, as his plantations began to outpace the industry average for oil yields.

Lee also began investing in property development, buying three companies in 1984. These acquisitions formed the basis of the future IOI Properties, one of the leading property development groups in Malaysia. The successful growth of IOI Properties helped fund Lee's investments in the palm oil industry. By 1985 Lee had restructured the group's operations, reforming IOI as a holding company and transferring the original Industrial Oxygen business into a new subsidiary.

IOI completed several more plantation purchases through the end of the decade. In 1988 the company acquired the Swee Lam Estate. The following year, it added estates in Bukit Leelau and Detas. In 1990 IOI acquired 12 new palm plantations owned by Dunlop Estates Bhd. The new properties provided IOI with nearly 28,000 hectares of additional crop. The Dunlop acquisition also boosted IOI's industrial operations, adding two oil mills and two rubber factories, as well as a research center.

EXPANDING LAND BANK

Research became an important component of IOI's growth, as the company launched its own palm plant

KEY DATES

1969: Industrial gas distributor Industrial Oxygen Incorporated (IOI) is founded.
1975: Lee Shin Cheng forms his own company.
1980: IOI goes public on the Kuala Lumpur Stock Exchange.
1982: Lee Shin Cheng takes over IOI.
1984: IOI begins investing in property development, buying three companies.
1990: IOI acquires Dunlop Estates Bhd and its 12 plantations.
1995: The company is renamed IOI Corporation.
1997: IOI launches vertical integration effort, acquiring a stake in Palmco (later IOI Oleochemicals) to enter oleochemicals production.
2002: IOI acquires Loders Croklaan, leading producer of palm oil-based ingredients for the food industry.
2006: IOI acquires the Pan Century group and becomes the world's leading oleochemicals producer.
2007: Through joint ventures with Harita Group, IOI acquires more than 227,000 hectares of land in Kalimantan, Indonesia.
2009: IOI begins planting in Indonesia; the company announces its intention to buy out minority shareholders in IOI Properties.

breeding program. By the 1990s, the company had succeeded in developing its own high-yield palm variety, known as DXP IOI. The company created a breeding estate, known as the Regent Estate, in Negri Sembilan. By the dawn of the new century, the estate boasted 60 mother trees capable of producing more than six million seeds per year. The company's nursery then became an important provider of palm seedlings, not only for IOI's own growing list of plantations, but for many of its major rivals as well.

Plantation purchases continued throughout the 1990s. IOI's expansion program favored "brownfield" sites, that is, existing agricultural lands, rather than carrying out the clear-cutting of Malaysia's forests. This policy was reinforced by the Malaysian government, which imposed a moratorium on further destruction of the country's forests at the beginning of the 21st century. Instead, IOI began converting existing rubber, cocoa, and other plantations into higher-yield palm plantations.

Among the group's acquisitions during the decade were Morisem Estates in 1993; Permodalan Plantations, a cocoa estate operation in Sabah, in 1995; and five plantations through the acquisition of Ladang Sabah Estates in 1998. The new series of acquisitions enabled the company to dispose of its lower-yielding plantations. A number of these were transferred to the group's property arm for conversion into residential, commercial, and resort developments. By the end of the 1990s, IOI's total land bank neared 160,000 hectares across 78 estates.

IOI also expanded its industrial operations during the 1990s. The company commissioned or acquired a number of palm oil mills, including the Bukit Leelau Mill, built by the company in 1992, with a capacity of 30 metric tons per hour. In 1993 the Morisem Estate acquisition added a mill with a capacity of up to 60 metric tons per hour. The company built a similar mill, at Baturong, in Sabah, in 1996. By 1998 the company had commissioned three more large-capacity mills, in New Gomali, Leepang, and Syarimo.

VERTICAL INTEGRATION

By this time, the company had exited its original industrial gas business. In 1995, in recognition of the group's new, more diversified operations, the company changed its name to IOI Corporation. The company's fast-growing real estate development wing was also renamed, as IOI Properties.

By the late 1990s, IOI had set its sights on developing vertically integrated operations. The group took a major step in this direction with the purchase in 1997 of a 32 percent stake in Palmco, a leading publicly listed oleochemicals producer in Malaysia. Also in that year, IOI commissioned its first palm oil refinery, in Sandakan, Sabah. IOI continued to build up its shareholding in Palmco. By 2003 the company succeeded in gaining majority control. Palmco was then renamed IOI Oleochemicals Industries Bhd. In 2006 IOI completed its acquisition of IOI Oleochemicals, which was then delisted from the Kuala Lumpur Stock Exchange.

IOI's industrial operations expanded again in 2002, through the purchase of Netherlands-based Loders Croklaan from Unilever. Loders Croklaan, which traced its origins to the late 19th century, had grown into one of the world's leading suppliers of food-grade palm-based products, with operations in the United States and Europe, as well as Malaysia. Following the purchase, IOI announced plans to build the world's largest palm oil refinery in Rotterdam to supply booming demand from the European market. The facility, with a capacity of 200,000 metric tons per year, was completed in 2005.

IOI's Oleochemicals Division grew again in 2006. In that year, the company acquired the Pan Century group, including its edible oils and oleochemicals operations. The acquisition raised IOI to the leading position among the world's top oleochemicals producers.

BECOMING A GLOBAL LEADER

By this time the world's leading integrated palm oil group, IOI continued its expansion through the end of the decade. The company purchase ten plantations in Johor and Sabah in 2003, adding nearly 25,000 hectares of planted land. In 2006 the company paid MYR 21 million to buy the Rinwood Pelita Plantation, as well as its subsidiary Rinwood Quarry.

By the end of the decade, IOI had become the dominant palm oil plantation group in Malaysia, with more than 150,000 planted hectares under its control. However, IOI was faced with the limited prospects of further expansion in Malaysia due to the government-imposed protection of the country's forests. At the same time, a number of new players, most notably Indonesia, had begun to emerge to challenge Malaysia's palm oil leadership.

These factors led IOI to begin seeking to extend its plantation operations beyond Malaysia. To this end, the company formed two joint ventures with Indonesia's Harita Group to bid for plantation land in Indonesia. The bids were successful, and by 2007 IOI had gained control of 227,340 hectares of cultivatable land in Kalimantan. IOI's share of the new plantation stood at 67 percent. By 2009 the company had prepared 83,000 hectares for planting.

IOI's palm oil operations remained strong despite the global economic downturn at the end of the decade. This was due to the surge in demand for vegetable oils in general, particularly as developing markets incorporated vegetable oils and margarine into their diets. At the same time, the use of palm oil as a biofuel had become increasingly attractive, further stimulating demand. The strength of the palm oil market helped shield IOI's other operations, particularly its property wing, which struggled with the collapse of the building market. The difficult trading conditions led IOI to announce its interest in buying out the minority shareholders of IOI Properties in 2009.

By then, Lee Shin Cheng had become one of Malaysia's wealthiest people, overseeing one of the world's largest integrated vegetable oil corporations. At 69, Lee remained an active, hands-on manager of the business empire he had founded less than 30 years before, representing one of Malaysia's most successful rags-to-riches stories in the 21st century.

M. L. Cohen

PRINCIPAL SUBSIDIARIES

IOI Edible Oils S.B.; IOI Oleochemical Industries S.B.; IOI Properties Bhd; Loders Croklaan Group B.V.

PRINCIPAL DIVISIONS

Plantation; Resource-Based Manufacturing; Property.

PRINCIPAL OPERATING UNITS

Oil Palm Cultivation & Milling; Commodity Trading; Refinery & Trading; Refinery & Oleochemicals; Refinery, Specialty Fats & Lipid Nutrition; Real Estate Development & Investment; Hotel & Resort Development.

PRINCIPAL COMPETITORS

Sime Darby Bhd; Genting Bhd; FFM Bhd; Kuala Lumpur Kepong Bhd; FELDA Holdings Bhd; PGEO Group Sdn Bhd; Felda Palm Industries Sdn Bhd; PPB Group Bhd; PGEO Edible Oils Sdn Bhd; Mewah-Oils Sdn Bhd.

FURTHER READING

Barrock, Leela, "For IOI, Can the End Justify the Means?" *Edge*, April 24, 2002.

"Branding Malaysian Palm Oil," *Star*, July 4, 2009.

De Guzman, Doris, "Divining IOI's Palmfuture," *ICIS Chemical Business*, August 6, 2007.

Fong, Kathy, "IOI Corp Going Global with Loders Acquisition," *Star*, August 31, 2002.

Gatsiounis, Ioannis, "Pumping Palm Oil," *Forbes Global*, June 18, 2007, p. 30.

"Homegrown Business with a Global Reach," *Star*, December 22, 2006.

"IOI Betting That There Will Be Recovery in Palm Oil Prices," *Star*, July 15, 2009.

"IOI Corp Plans Second US Plant," *Edge*, December 13, 2007.

"IOI Corp Shares Fall on News of Rights Issue Plan," *Business Times* (Malaysia), July 25, 2009.

"IOI Corp: Worst Over for Plantation Sector," *Business Times*, July 2, 2009.

"IOI Has the Edge," *Star,* November 9, 2002.

"IOI, Largest Oil-Palm Grower, Targets Acquisitions," *Bloomberg,* February 22, 2007.

"IOI Puts Its Vision into Practise," *Euromoney,* March 2006, p. 143.

Ismail, Zaidi Isham, "IOI Plans to Build Biodiesel Plant," *Business Times* (Malaysia), December 14, 2005.

Ooi Tee Ching, "IOI Chairman's Passion for His Oil Palms," *Business Times* (Malaysia), October 31, 2005.

"The Winning Edge," *New Straits Times,* July 1, 2001.

KappAhl

KappAhl Holding AB

———■———

Box 303, Idrottsvaegen 14
Mölndal, S-431 24
Sweden
Telephone: (46 031) 771 55 00
Fax: (46 031) 771 58 15
Web site: http://www.kappahl.com

Public Company
Founded: 1953 as Kappaffären
Employees: 4,500
Sales: SEK 4.62 billion ($608.7 million) (2008)
Stock Exchanges: Stockholm
Ticker Symbol: KAHL
NAICS: 448120 Women's Clothing Stores

■ ■ ■

KappAhl Holding AB is a leading clothing retailer based in Sweden with a focus on the Nordic region. Based in Mölndal, near Göteborg, KappAhl operates 300 stores in Sweden, Finland, Norway, Poland, and, since 2009, in the Czech Republic. KappAhl stores feature a full range of company-designed clothing and accessories for women, children, and men. However, the company focuses its marketing effort especially on women in the age 30 to 50 market segment who, according to the company, "buy for all members of the family." Sales of women's clothing lead the group's revenues, representing 58 percent of the company's SEK 4.62 billion ($609 million) in 2008. Children's clothing adds 27 percent, while men's clothing follows with 15 percent. KappAhl has long differentiated itself from competitors by

developing a strong value-for-money reputation. KappAhl is listed on the Stockholm Stock Exchange. The company is led by CEO Christian W. Jansson and Chairman Finn Johnsson.

BASEMENT BEGINNINGS

KappAhl stemmed from a small business selling raincoats founded by Per Olof Ahl in Göteborg in 1953. Ahl produced his own coat designs, selling them in a basement store called Kappaffären ("Raincoat Shop"). From the outset, Ahl sought to sell high-quality, affordably priced coats. Word quickly spread of the new store, and soon customers were waiting in long lines to make their purchases. By the end of 1954, Ahl's shop sold more than 400 coats each day, reaching total yearly revenues of SEK 4.5 million.

Ahl incorporated the company as KappAhl and began expanding the range of coats as well as adding sales beyond the Göteborg market. For this, Ahl himself often loaded up busses with his raincoats, making sales trips around the country. The success of these trips encouraged Ahl to build a network of shops throughout Sweden. This led the company to open its first store in Stockholm in 1956. The company also experimented with a men's clothing format, called Herman, opening a first store in Göteborg in 1959. However, women's clothing remained the major focus. By 1963, the company operated 25 stores, generating sales of SEK 50 million.

KappAhl attracted strong media attention throughout the 1960s, further stimulating the company's growth. The company continued to expand its store network, reaching 50 stores by 1972. These were stocked with an ever-expanding range of clothing, with the company targeting especially the women's fashion market. Nevertheless, coats, such as the launch of a highly successful green loden coat in 1967, continued to play a prominent role in the company's success. KappAhl grew into one of the best-known clothing brands in Sweden, and could claim that one out of every four women in Sweden owned one of its coats. In the early 1970s, sales topped SEK 100 million for the first time.

ADDING CHILDREN'S WEAR

KappAhl's success was cut short by the economic turmoil of the 1970s. The sudden decline in consumer spending cut deeply into the company's sales. The company continued to struggle through the early years of the decade. By the mid-1970s, however, KappAhl once again resumed its expansion, adding another five stores. The 1970s also marked the company's first entry into sales of children's clothing with the addition of a dedicated children's department in 1978.

During the decade, KappAhl also began shifting production of its garments outside of Sweden for the first time. The significant cost reductions enabled the company to maintain a strong profit record, despite the devaluation of the Swedish kroner and a new drop in consumer spending at the end of the 1970s. The difficult economic climate gave way to social turmoil, as the country was hit by a series of strikes.

KappAhl had nevertheless maintained a strong investment effort, building a new central distribution facility in Mölndal, a town outside of Göteborg, in

1981. The new warehouse, considered the most modern in Europe at the time, helped KappAhl to maintain control of its costs. In this way, the company was able to retain its longstanding commitment to quality clothing at reasonable prices.

The success of the children's department led KappAhl to explore other market segments. In 1980, for example, the group created a new department dedicated to youth fashions, called Intact. Two years later, the company also became one of the first in Sweden to begin offering plus-size fashions. These efforts helped drive up sales volume and revenues broke the SEK 500 million mark. This growth came despite the addition of just two more stores. Renewed growth, however, encouraged the company to continue its expansion. By 1985, KappAhl had opened its 69th store, boosting total sales past SEK 1 billion for the first time.

The small size of the Swedish market led KappAhl to begin preparing its international expansion at mid-decade. The company's first move was into Switzerland, where it opened its first store in 1985. The company's move into the Swiss market proved only temporary, however. Unable to replicate its success at home, the company withdrew from that market before the end of the decade.

NEW OWNERS

Instead, the company targeted expansion closer to home, entering Norway in 1988. By 1990, the company had added operations in Finland as well. The Norwegian market became especially important for the company, growing into its second largest market after Sweden, and representing 28 percent of total group sales by the end of the first decade of the 21st century. Finland also proved a successful market for the company, ultimately generating 12 percent of company revenues.

The beginning of the 1990s marked a new era for the company. Founder Per Olof Ahl took ill in 1988, turning over leadership of the company to his son, Pieter, that year. KappAhl's days as a family-owned business were numbered, however. Amid the new economic downturn at the beginning of the 1990s, Pieter Ahl decided to sell the company to Swedish cooperative giant Kooperativa Foerbundet (KF, the Swedish Cooperative Union).

As part of one of Sweden's largest corporate groups, KappAhl continued to expand its operations through the recession years of the early 1990s. By 1993, as the company celebrated its 40th anniversary, the KappAhl retail network topped 130 stores and sales had reached the SEK 2 billion mark. By this time, KappAhl had grown into Sweden's second largest clothing retailer.

KEY DATES

1953: Per Olof Ahl opens the Kappaffären (Raincoat Shop) in Göteborg, Sweden.

1956: KappAhl begins its national expansion, opening a store in Stockholm.

1972: The KappAhl retail network tops 50 stores.

1978: KappAhl adds a children's clothing department to its stores.

1988: KappAhl begins Scandinavian expansion, opening a store in Norway.

1990: The Ahl family sells KappAhl to Kooperativa Foerbundet (KF).

2004: KF sells KappAhl to Nordic Capital and Accent Equity Partners.

2006: KappAhl goes public on the Stockholm Stock Exchange.

2009: KappAhl opens its first new Czech store in Prague.

Toward the middle of the decade, however, KappAhl's fortunes seemed to be on the decline. The company faced the onslaught of a new breed of internationally operating, fashion-forward clothing chains, epitomized by such names as Zara, Benetton, the Gap, Elite, and H&M. KappAhl's relatively small size and somewhat staid image left the company struggling to compete, but the company fought back in the second half of the decade. KappAhl devised a new marketing strategy, focused on the "KappAhl Family" concept. The company fixed its primary target solidly on women aged 30 to 50 who, as the company claimed, "buy for all members of the family."

However, the new strategy quickly backfired; the new format failed to attract new customers and the stores continued to lose existing customers. By the early years of the new century, KappAhl had not only lost its second-place position in the Swedish clothing market, it had become, in the words of *Dagens Industri,* "a second-rate chain."

RETRENCHING AND REVAMPING

Compounding KappAhl's problems were difficulties in pursuing its international expansion. In 1997, the company attempted to enter the Danish market, buying that country's MacCoy clothing chain. The move failed to generate results, however, and by 2002, the company was forced to exit Denmark. Similarly, in 2001, KappAhl targeted a move into the Czech Republic, opening its first store in Prague. The company quickly pulled the plug on that subsidiary, winding up operations there in 2002.

Nevertheless, the group had achieved some success in its international operations. In 1999 the group expanded its Norwegian presence, buying that country's Adelstein retail group. KappAhl also made a successful entry into Poland, opening its first two stores there in 1999. The lack of strong domestic players in that country enabled KappAhl to build its network there, and by the end of the first decade of the 21st century the company operated 20 stores throughout Poland.

Faced with growing difficulties at the beginning of the 21st century, KappAhl brought in new management under CEO Christian Jansson in 2002. The company immediately suspended further international expansion while it worked to revitalize its existing operations. New emphasis was placed especially on consolidating the group's Scandinavian presence.

The company also worked at revamping its clothing designs and labels. While KappAhl remained the company's core clothing brand, it also began developing a number of new specialized brands for the new century. For women, these included the Bodyzone underwear, intimates, and swimwear range; Xlnt, for plus-size fashions; Soft, a "comfortable" clothing line; and Creem lingerie. By 2009 the company had added another women's clothing brand, Number One, described by the company as "classic modern style with a preppy feel."

KappAhl also worked on revitalizing its other clothing collections. The children's and youth departments featured such brands as Kaxs, Lab Industries, and Comp. In the men's department, the group developed designs under the Madison Avenue, Redwood, Body Zone, and U.S. Polo Assn. brands.

These efforts helped restore the group to profitability by 2003. The return to financial health also led to the sale of the company by KF, which had been engaged in a streamlining effort to refocus its operations around its core supermarket business. In 2004 KF sold KappAhl to private equity investors Nordic Capital and Accent Equity Partners.

TARGETING THE INTERNATIONAL MARKET

Under its new owners, KappAhl returned to its retail network expansion. By 2006 the company had added 20 new stores, with contracts in place for 20 additional stores in the second half of the decade. Through the end of the decade, the company boosted its store network to 300, including 138 stores in Sweden, 87 stores in

Norway, 46 stores in Finland, as well as its 20 stores in Poland. This new momentum also led the company to the stock market, where it completed a listing on the Stockholm exchange in February 2006.

The public offering provided the company with the financial backing for the launch of a new and highly ambitious target. In 2007 the company launched a takeover offer for Swedish rival Lindex. The proposed acquisition offered the potential for KappAhl to develop into a major multinational and multibranded retail group, with more than 600 stores and revenues of more than SEK 9 billion. However, the unsolicited takeover offer, a share and debt-based deal worth SEK 7 billion ($1.02 billion), was considered hostile by Lindex. Soon after, Lindex instead agreed to be acquired Finland's Stockmann, which bid SEK 7.98 billion ($1.2 billion) for the company.

KappAhl was forced to content itself with a less dramatic expansion drive into the end of the decade. By 2008, the company had put into place plans to open nearly 60 new stores, including 24 stores in Poland alone. KappAhl also began preparations to return to the Czech Republic, a market that had been growing strongly during the decade, and particularly since joining the European Union in 2004.

The company opened its first new Czech store in Prague in 2009. The company also expected to open a new store in Brno, the country's second largest city, by October of that year, followed by several more stores throughout the country in late 2009 and through 2010. These openings fit in with KappAhl's overall strategy to maintain a new store opening rate of as many as 25 stores per year in the new century.

M. L. Cohen

PRINCIPAL SUBSIDIARIES

Detaljhandel Logistik AB; Fastighets AB (Sweden); KappAhl Åland AB; KappAhl AS (Norway); KappAhl Czech Republic s.r.o; KappAhl Far East Ltd (Hong Kong); KappAhl Fastighets AB (Sweden); KappAhl OY (Finland); KappAhl Polska Sp.zo.o; KappAhl Sverige AB.

PRINCIPAL OPERATING UNITS

Bodyzone; Creem; KappAhl; Number One; Soft; XLNT.

PRINCIPAL COMPETITORS

Kooperativa Foerbundet (KF); Lindex AB; Nilson Group AB; MQ Retail AB; JC AB; Intersport Sverige AB; Peak Performance Production AB; Naturkompaniet AB.

FURTHER READING

Anderson, Robert, "Stockmann Cash Offer for Lindex Trumps KappAhl," *Financial Times,* October 2, 2007, p. 20.

"KappAhl Acquires Companies," *Europe Intelligence Wire,* November 29, 2006.

"KappAhl Buys SEK 447m Headquarters," *just-style.com,* May 29, 2008.

"KappAhl: Eleven New Stores in Three Months," *Europe Intelligence Wire,* December 4, 2006.

"KappAhl Expands into Czech Republic," *just-style.com,* April 16, 2009.

"KappAhl Makes $1.02bn Offer for Rival Lindex," *just-style.com,* August 14, 2007.

"KappAhl the Leading Nordic Fashion Retailer Achieved New Records in Sales and Profitability," *Europe Intelligence Wire,* April 12, 2007.

"Kooperativa Foerbundet to Divest KappAhl Chain to Nordic Capital and Accent Equity Partners," *Nordic Business Report,* October 28, 2004.

"Lindex Tells Shareholders to Reject KappAhl Bid," *just-style.com,* August 22, 2007.

Sieczkos, Anna, "Swedish Value for Money," *Czech Business Weekly,* May 20, 2009.

"Will Swedish Conquer Czech Fashion?" *Europe Intelligence Wire,* April 27, 2009.

Kyushu Electric Power Company Inc.

———————■———————

1-82 Watanabe-dori 2-chome
Chuo-ku
Fukuoka, 810-8720
Japan
Telephone: (+81 92) 761-3031
Fax: (+81 92) 733-1435
Web site: http://www.kyuden.co.jp

Public Company
Incorporated: 1951
Employees: 12,466
Sales: ¥1.48 trillion ($14.79 billion) (2008)
Stock Exchanges: Tokyo Osaka Fukuoka
Ticker Symbol: 9508
NAICS: 221122 Electric Power Distribution; 221111 Hydroelectric Power Generation; 221113 Nuclear Electric Power Generation

■ ■ ■

The Kyushu Electric Power Company Inc. (KEPCO) operates as Japan's fourth largest electric power company (EPC). KEPCO supplies power to over 8.45 million customers and has 193 power generation facilities capable of producing 19.716 million kilowatts. With six nuclear reactors in its arsenal, nuclear energy accounts for approximately 40 percent of KEPCO's operations. The company also operates ten oil, coal, and liquefied natural gas (LNG) power facilities, 35 internal combustion power generating facilities, five geothermal power stations, and 138 hydroelectric power facilities. KEPCO serves customers in the Kyushu region of Japan, which

includes seven prefectures: Fukuoka, Saga, Nagasaki, Kumamoto, Oita, Miyazaki, and Kagoshima. Electric power makes up the bulk of KEPCO's sales. The company has various interests in other energy-related businesses as well as information technology and telecommunications.

EARLY HISTORY

KEPCO was incorporated along with the eight other regional EPCs in May 1951, but the story of its foundation goes back to the start of the Allied occupation of Japan in 1945. Japan's energy-intensive military-industrial complex, centered on the production of steel, ships, and munitions, had been largely eradicated by the start of the occupation. Although the nuclear bomb aimed at one of Kyushu's major shipyards, Nagasaki, had failed to destroy the industrial target, conventional bombing of other industrial sites in northern Kyushu had caused enormous damage. Because part of Kyushu's electricity-generating facilities had survived the war relatively unscathed, the first year of occupation saw an energy surplus in the region. This pattern was mirrored throughout the country.

As the process of reconstruction gathered pace, demand for electricity increased dramatically and soon exceeded supply. The General Headquarters (GHQ) of the Allied powers feared that an expansion of electricity production under the surviving and highly centralized wartime structure of the Japan Electricity Generation and Transmission Company (JEGTCO) and the local distribution companies could be a step in the direction of rearmament because the structure itself had been an

COMPANY PERSPECTIVES

Kyushu Electric Power's mission is to enlighten our future towards a comfortable and environment-friendly lifestyle today and for generations to come.

integral factor in Japan's military expansion in the first place. In 1948 GHQ decided to dismantle the centralized JEGTCO structure and replace it with regionally based, vertically integrated electricity generation and distribution companies. After a certain amount of disagreement between GHQ and the fledgling Japanese government regarding the precise structure, status, and organization of the new companies, the government acted to establish the EPCs by implementing the Electricity Utility Industry Reorganization Order and the Public Utilities Order.

On May 1, 1951, operating rights and facilities of the state-run Kyushu branch of JEGTCO and the Kyushu Electric Power Distribution Company were taken over by the newly created Kyushu Electric Power Company. KEPCO's first president was Tokujiro Sato, and under government decree the new company was given the task of generating and supplying electric power to the entire Kyushu district including outlying islands. The company's start-up capital was ¥760 million.

While the demand for electricity had caught up with supply in the late 1940s thanks to rapid reconstruction, the manufacturing economy of Kyushu was given a second boost by demand for components and material support for the war raging on the Korean Peninsula. The resulting surge in demand for electricity from local industry stimulated KEPCO to seek the immediate stabilization and expansion of its generating capabilities, and the company turned to the United States for assistance. The latest technology was imported for Kyushu's first Arch-Type dam—an arch-shaped concrete structure across a valley, facing up the valley when seen in plan—at the Kamishiba hydroelectric power (HEP) station. In addition, the company imported a model plant—bought off-the-shelf, and of a tried and tested design—from the United States, which was built at Karita, and work was undertaken to expand and strengthen the high-voltage distribution trunk lines and other installations in the central and northern parts of Kyushu.

POSTWAR GROWTH

In April 1957 a new 220,000-volt trunk line was inaugurated to enhance distribution of electricity to the industrial centers of Kyushu where demand was starting to outstrip KEPCO's ability to distribute electricity, and to allow further expansion of electricity consumption in the future. By the end of the 1950s, as a result of the incorporation of new technology and plants, KEPCO had managed to double its generating capacity while increasing its thermal efficiency (a measure of the conversion rate from thermal energy to electrical energy in a generating system) from 20 percent to over 30 percent.

By the early 1960s demand for electricity in Kyushu was increasing by over 10 percent per year, fueled by industrial demand from heavy industry in the north of the island, from the rapidly expanding small business sector, and from private consumers. The latter were using more electricity for lighting and heating, and in the summer months for air conditioning. By the mid-1960s the annual peak demand for electricity in Kyushu, with its warm climate, had switched from winter to summer as a direct result of the growing use of air conditioning.

In the past KEPCO and its predecessor had relied on local coal production to generate electricity, but by the late 1950s oil had started to appear a far cheaper and more flexible alternative. In 1955 Kyushu had produced 23 million tons of coal or 43 percent of Japan's coal output, much of it for the energy industry. However, as the switch to oil-fired power stations proceeded, local coal production was progressively cut back. By 1988 Kyushu produced slightly more than four million tons of coal.

In the meantime, new generating facilities were tending to use imported oil and coal. While HEP had accounted for a large proportion of generating capacity in the first half of the century in Kyushu, its relative importance had started to decline by the early 1960s. This was due not only to the availability of less expensive alternative sources of energy, but because technological advancements had brought the cost of building thermal power stations substantially below that of HEP equivalents.

In August 1968 KEPCO achieved 3,000 megawatts (MW) of electricity production for the first time, and with demand still rising year by year, further oil and coal powered facilities were inaugurated. In July 1969 a large crude oil powered thermal power station opened at Oita. In the same year KEPCO strengthened its international standing by establishing a technical exchange agreement with the Korea Electric Power Co.

KEY DATES

1951: Kyushu Electric Power Company (KEPCO) incorporates as the Japanese electric power industry returns to private ownership.

1968: KEPCO achieves 3,000 megawatts of electricity production for the first time.

1969: A large crude oil powered thermal power station opens at Oita.

1975: The Genkai No. 1 Nuclear Power Station is inaugurated.

1977: KEPCO enters into a long-term contract to 2000 for the supply of liquefied natural gas from North Sumatra.

1995: Changes in the Electricity Utilities Industry Law allow for competition in the electricity generation and supply market.

2000: The retail sector of Japan's electric power industry begins to deregulate.

2001: KEPCO partners with Japan Telecom Co. Ltd., Korean Telecom Corp., and NTT Communications Corp. to construct the Korea-Japan Cable Network.

2009: KEPCO submits construction plans for a 1,590-megawatt advanced pressurized water reactor at the Sendai nuclear facility.

OVERCOMING HARDSHIP DURING THE OIL CRISIS

In early 1973, with Kiyoshi Kawarabayashi in the position of president, KEPCO was looking toward further steady, and by international standards, spectacular, growth in the foreseeable future. The outbreak of war in the Middle East in mid-1973 and the subsequent quadrupling of oil prices imposed by the Organization of Petroleum Exporting Countries hit Japan harder than any other Organization for Economic Cooperation and Development country because of the country's heavy dependence on Middle Eastern oil. The immediate effect on KEPCO was to raise the price of fuel for its oil-powered thermal generating plants. This resulted in financial difficulties in the short term because the company, like the rest of Japan's EPCs, was not free to pass the higher fuel rates on to its industrial and domestic consumers without approval from the Ministry of International Trade and Industry (MITI).

In December 1973 the Japanese government introduced measures to enforce conservation of electric power, but it was not until later the following year that MITI finally consented to allowing a 48 percent electricity rate rise for KEPCO and the other EPCs. Although it alleviated short-term financial pressures on the generation industry as a whole, the first sharp rise in the price of electricity in 20 years failed to benefit the power companies in the medium term because the price of oil continued to rise.

Furthermore, as higher charges were passed on to the large energy-intensive manufacturing sector in Kyushu, a chain of events was set underway leading to a wholesale restructuring of the Kyushu economy away from energy-intensive industrial production. This in turn stimulated KEPCO to reappraise its customer base and eventually concentrate on the non-manufacturing sector (consumption by offices and the retail and service sectors) to make up the shortfall in demand from heavy industry.

The oil price hikes that continued throughout the 1970s stimulated a major reappraisal of resource security at the national level. While individual power companies and oil companies were able to meet their requirements for oil by paying inflated prices in spot markets around the world, it soon became apparent that Japan needed to diversify its supply of energy away from the Middle East and away from oil. Although a number of projects had been in the planning phase for some time, the events of 1973 and 1974 added urgency to strategic decision making in Tokyo and at KEPCO's head office in Fukuoka. In July 1974 the Electric Power Resource Development Adjustment Council in Tokyo approved construction of a second nuclear plant at Genkai in northwest Kyushu with a planned capacity of 559,000 kilowatt (kW). In October 1975 Genkai No. 1 Nuclear Power Station was inaugurated and in December 1975 the Taihei thermal power station started operations.

NUCLEAR POWER SUCCESS

While the Japanese economy languished in recession in the mid-1970s, KEPCO was achieving encouraging results at its Genkai No. 1 Nuclear Power Station. The pressurized water reactor (PWR) set a Japanese record for trouble-free running by operating for 367 days without an unscheduled break, much to the pleasure of the then president of KEPCO, Saburo Nagakura. In addition to the nuclear development program, LNG-fired thermal energy was actively pursued as an efficient and clean alternative to oil. In 1977 KEPCO entered into a long-term contract to 2000 for the supply of LNG from North Sumatra.

By the end of the 1970s the rich geothermal resources of the island of Kyushu were also being used by KEPCO to complement its conventional generating facilities. In June 1977 Hachobaru geothermal power station opened, and in April 1980 it achieved an output of 55,000 kW, making it the largest of its type in the country. The company was also actively developing its geothermal sites on the Hakusan and Kirishima volcanic plateaus. Together, KEPCO's geothermal facilities accounted for half of Japan's geothermal energy production.

Although there had been some easing of electricity prices in 1978, in 1980 KEPCO was forced to raise its rates again by a further 46 percent. This was a result of further steep rises in the price of oil in the aftermath of the Iranian revolution. By this stage, however, KEPCO's prospects of a secure and stable energy supply were looking better than they had for a number of years. Despite the widespread alarm in Japan caused by the Three Mile Island nuclear accident in Pennsylvania in 1979, KEPCO took several steps toward becoming one of Japan's major generators of nuclear power.

In 1980 the Nuclear Safety Commission held public hearings concerning the construction of the No. 2 Sendai nuclear plant and in the same year MITI started hearings about the construction of the Genkai No. 3 and No. 4 PWR projects. These new nuclear plants would be the first of their type in Japan and were designed so that they could quickly adjust their generation to changes in demand in the daytime and at night. Their planned generation capacity was 1,180 MW each, with operations scheduled to begin in 1997.

The Electric Power Development Company (EPDC) was founded jointly by the Japanese government and the power companies immediately after the end of World War II for the purpose of propelling the nation's power resource development. KEPCO worked with EPDC to build a large coal-powered power station at Matsuura, Nagasaki Prefecture. With a planned capacity of 2,000 MW, the Matsuura No. 2 coal-fired generating plant opened in 1997, also in collaboration with EPDC. KEPCO was also building two coal-powered units at Reihoku with a planned combined output of 1,400 MW.

KEPCO's chairman at this time, Tetsuya Watanabe, was heading a company with better future prospects than it had enjoyed for many years. The leader of the Kyushu business community was also leading Japan's other EPCs in the development of new energy resources. Despite opposition from the antinuclear lobby, particularly after nuclear accidents at Three Mile Island and Chernobyl, Ukraine, the company managed to commission a nuclear program that accounted for 41 percent of its electricity production, twice the national average. With an electricity monopoly in Kyushu and a highly diversified generation base, the company stood

well positioned for changes that would take place in Japan's energy industry.

MOVING TOWARD DEREGULATION

During the 1990s, the electricity industry in Japan began its deregulation process. In 1995 changes in the Electricity Utilities Industry Law allowed competition to enter into the electricity generation and supply market. Then in 1996, a wholesale electric power bidding system enabled nonelectric power companies to sell electricity to electric power companies. In March 2000, retail sales of electricity were partially deregulated, allowing large-lot customers, those demanding large amounts of electricity, to choose their power supplier. The retail sector continued the deregulation process in April 2005.

The intent of deregulation in Japan was to foster competition, which in turn would lower the electricity costs in the country. The deregulation, however, was slow to change Japanese industry and during 2001 KEPCO and the other regional companies still controlled 99 percent of the market. In fact, only six Japanese-based companies other than the original regional power companies supplied power to large customers including retail stores and office buildings. This accounted for a 0.2 percent share of the overall market.

During Japan's deregulation process, the nation as a whole was suffering due to an economic downturn. Demand for electric power fell, leaving KEPCO to focus on developing new sources of income and revenue. In 1995 it created Astel Kyushu Corp., a personal handy-phone service provider. This unit was eventually shuttered in 2000, however, as most Japanese consumers began to use regular cellular phones. KEPCO also partnered with Japan Telecom Co. Ltd., Korean Telecom Corp., and NTT Communications Corp. in 2001 to construct the Korea-Japan Cable Network, a high-bandwidth underwater optical-fiber cable system that would be used to broadcast the 2002 FIFA World Cup games, which were cohosted by South Korea and Japan. KEPCO also made investments in a natural gas–fired facility in Mexico as well as a geothermal power project in the Philippines.

FOCUSING ON NUCLEAR POWER IN THE 21ST CENTURY

During the early years of the new millennium, public sentiment in Japan remained hostile toward the development of nuclear power due to fatal accidents and several scandals. For much of the 1990s, however, Japan's industry had aggressively focused on shifting from expensive and polluting coal-fired plants to nuclear power, which was considered more environmentally friendly. Because of concerns over the safety of these nuclear facilities, Japan's government was urged by its citizens to rethink its expansion efforts, cut back on its nuclear development plans, and find alternative sources of power.

Despite negative public opinion, nuclear power generation remained at the forefront of Japan's energy policy. Japan's Energy Policy and Strategy, set forth by the Ministry of Economy, Trade and Industry (METI) in 2006, established a goal of increasing Japan's nuclear power generation to at least 40 percent of Japan's total energy production by 2030. METI believed this strategy would reduce its reliance on Middle Eastern oil as well as provide a "greener" form of energy.

In 2000 KEPCO submitted a request for environmental studies related to the construction for a 1,590 MW advanced pressurized water reactor at the Sendai nuclear facility. In 2009 the company submitted its construction plans for the reactor. KEPCO hoped to gain approval and begin construction in 2013. At the same time, it announced plans to launch Japan's first plutonium-thermal (pluthermal) operation at its No. 3 reactor at Genkai in August 2009. Pluthermal power generation used mixed-oxide fuel, which was made from recycled nuclear fuel.

Along with its efforts to increase its production capacity, KEPCO continued to look for ways to take advantage of deregulation measures. In 2006 the company became one of the first Japanese utility firms to supply electricity outside of its traditional boundaries when it provided service to a large supermarket in Hiroshima. At the same time, it focused on cutting costs to improve profitability. Fuel prices reached record levels in 2008, forcing the company to take further action to preserve its bottom line. Despite rising costs, KEPCO management, led by President Toshio Manabe, believed the company had a solid strategy in place and could weather any volatile conditions that came its way.

Stephen Christopher Kremer
Updated, Christina M. Stansell

PRINCIPAL SUBSIDIARIES

Oita Co-operative Thermal Power Co., Inc.; Tobata Co-operative Thermal Power Co., Inc.; Kyushu Rinsan Co., Inc.; Nishi Nippon Plant Engineering and Construction Co., Ltd.; Kyuden Sangyo Co., Inc.; West Japan Engineering Consultants, Inc.; Nishigi Kogyo; Nishi Nippon Environmental Construction Co., Inc.; Plazwire Co., Ltd.; Nishigi Surveying and Design Co., Ltd.; Kyudenko Corporation Affiliated Company; Nishi Kyushu Kyodo Kowan Co., Ltd.; Kyuken Corporation; Kyuki Corporation; Nishi Nippon Airlines Co.; Kyushu Kouatsu Concrete Industries Co., Ltd.; Kyushu Meter & Relay Engineering Corporation; Koyou Denki Kogyo Co., Ltd.; Contex; Kyuhen Co., Ltd.; Seishin Corporation; Nishi Nihon Denki Tekkou Co., Ltd.; Japan Australia Uranium Resource Development Co., Ltd.; Kyuden International Corporation; Oita Liquefied Natural Gas Company, Inc.; Kitakyushu Liquefied Natural Gas Company Inc.; Nishi Nippon Environmental Energy Company, Incorporated.; Pacific Hope Shipping Limited; Nagashima Windhill Co., Ltd.; Fukuoka Energy Service Co., Inc.; Miyazaki Biomass Recycling Co., Ltd.; Washiodake Wind Power Co., Ltd.; Amami Oshima Wind Power Co., Ltd.; Kyuden Ilijan Holding Corporation; Fukuoka Clean Energy Co., Ltd.; Kyushu Cryogenics Co., Ltd.; Electricidad Aguila de Tuxpan, S.de R.L.de C.V.; Kyushu Telecommunication Network Co., Inc.; J-Re-Lights Co., Ltd.; Kyuden Good Life Company, Inc.

PRINCIPAL COMPETITORS

Chubu Electric Power Company Inc.; The Kansai Electric Power Company Inc.; Tokyo Electric Power Company Inc.

FURTHER READING

History of the Electric Power Industry in Japan, Tokyo: Japan Electric Power Information Center, 1988.

Hosoe, Tomoko, "Nuclear, LNG Vie to Meet Japan's Energy Needs," *Oil and Gas Journal,* October 1, 2007.

"Korea Telecom, Japan Firms to Lay Korea-Japan Undersea Fibre Optic Cables," *Asia Pulse,* March 27, 2001.

"Kyushu Electric Power Submitted Nuclear Power Plant Expansion Plan to Local Governments," *Electric Daily News,* January 9, 2009.

"Kyushu Electric Set to Launch Pluthermal Power Generation," *Asia Pulse,* March 9, 2009.

Nicholls, Tom, "Nuclear May Leave Gap in Market for Gas," *Petroleum Economist,* May 2, 2003.

Sato, Shigeru, "Price of Electricity in Japan Falls Ahead of Market Liberalization," *Asian Wall Street Journal,* October 15, 2004.

Thomas, Steve, and Chris Cragg, *Japan Power Station Fuel Demand to 2000,* London: Financial Times Business Information, 1987.

Ladish Company Inc.

5481 South Packard Avenue
Cudahy, Wisconsin 53110
U.S.A.
Telephone: (414) 747-2611
Fax: (414) 747-2963
Web site: http://www.ladishco.com

Public Company
Incorporated: 1905
Employees: 1,380
Sales: $469.5 million (2008)
Stock Exchanges: NASDAQ
Ticker Symbol: LDSH
NAICS: 332111 Iron and Steel Forging; 332116 Metal
Stamping; 336412 Jet Propulsion and Internal
Combustion Engines and Parts, Aircraft,
Manufacturing

■ ■ ■

Ladish Company Inc. is a supplier of highly engineered forgings, castings, and machined components for jet engines and other aerospace and industrial applications. The company's engine business accounts for just over 50 percent of revenues while its aerospace division secures approximately 26 percent of sales. Ladish's industrial unit, comprising heavy construction, mining equipment, and railway power, shores up the remaining revenues. The company has operations in California, Connecticut, Oregon, and Wisconsin. Its 2005 purchase of Zaklad Kuznia Matrycowa, a Polish metal forger, also gave Ladish a foothold in the European market.

ORIGINS

According to Ladish's official time line, Herman W. Ladish bought a steam hammer in 1905, setting himself on the track to become "Axle Forger to the Industry." Expansion, both in facilities and in product offerings, continued through the 1930s, when Ladish spent $1 million upgrading its plant in 1935 and began doing its own machining. New products included aircraft brake drums.

During the war years, components for critical U.S. aircraft originated at Ladish's forge, including struts for B-26 bombers and propeller shafts for P-51 Mustangs. The company also supplied engine crankcases. In addition, it developed advanced, high-strength alloys and installed new hammers for forging them.

The company's patented D6 tool steel found its way into early rocket motors. By the end of the 1950s, Ladish had installed the world's largest counterblow hammer. The company was employing about 7,000 people in four plants.

A new plant was added in Kentucky in 1966, as the company continued to supply the space program. Ladish built a factory in Arkansas in 1975 to make industrial supplies. It continued to upgrade its Cudahy forging operation, making it larger and hotter. It produced steel-alloy forgings for use in nuclear equipment and oil wells.

Ladish was forced to contend with a strike in April 1979. While Ladish used alternate employees to keep its production lines moving, its clients such as General Electric searched for alternate sources. At the same time, two critical metals, titanium and cobalt, were in short supply. The strikes at Ladish and at Fafnir Bearing Co., another engine parts supplier, were settled in September.

CHANGING HANDS: 1981

In July 1981, Armco Inc. of Middletown, Ohio, announced that it was buying a 53 percent interest in privately owned Ladish after highly secret negotiations. The stock acquisition agreement was originally worth $221 million, later upped to $286 million after ACF Industries of New York made its own offer. ACF already had purchased a 5 percent interest in Ladish in June. ACF increased its bid to $324 million in cash and stock in August. In preparation for the deal, the rather secretive Ladish revealed that it had sales of $486.3 million in 1980, surprising many analysts. Its earnings were $11.5 million.

This bidding war came at a slow period for the U.S. forging industry. Italy, West Germany, and Japan were beginning to develop considerable competition abroad. At home, Ladish was edged out of the leading independent producer slot by Wyman-Gordon of Worcester, Massachusetts, which posted 1980 sales of $550 million. Like the companies vying for control of Ladish, Wyman-Gordon was also bullish, however, investing $12.5 million in new tooling.

In November 1981, Armco received government approval for its takeover bid, then valued at $286 million worth of stock. Ladish's forging operation tied in nicely with Armco's alloy steel production and promised opportunities for further expansion. However it could not keep its prize acquisition for long. Struggling financially after years of losses in steel, oil-field equipment, and specialty materials, Armco sold Ladish to Owens Corning Corporation in 1985, along with Armco's other aerospace subsidiaries, Hitco (reinforced composites) and Oregon Metallurgical Corporation (titanium), in which Armco had an 80 percent share. The total purchase price was $415 million.

Although the Hitco expertise that initially attracted Owens Corning seemed like a good fit, some analysts wondered how well the other acquisitions, such as Ladish, would work with Owens Coming's existing businesses, centered around the stagnant construction industry. The new businesses gave Owens Corning an entry into the aerospace market but also exposed it to the vagaries of defense spending.

Within two years, Owens Corning sold Ladish as it came under threat of a hostile takeover. Owens Corning, in fact, divested its entire Aerospace and Strategic Materials Group. An investment group, including members of Ladish management, then bought the company for $236 million. Investment bankers Gibbons, Green and van Amerongen and Salomon Brothers Inc. financed the deal.

OVERCOMING CRISES

The early 1990s were catastrophic for the aviation industry. The Persian Gulf War stifled world tourism and a global recession compounded difficulties. Privately owned Ladish experienced its worst losses ever and was losing market share rapidly. In 1992 Ladish closed its Los Angeles forging operation as a result, eliminating 188 jobs. The closing left the company with three facilities, in Wisconsin, Kentucky, and Arkansas.

Payments on the buyback debt ($110 million in junk bonds) forced Ladish into bankruptcy in 1993. It emerged from bankruptcy protection in April. Although just two months in Chapter 11, Ladish suffered a lasting stigma, given the industry's preference for long-term contracts.

Ladish lost between $15 million and $20 million a year in 1994 and 1995, on sales of $122 million and $115 million, respectively. Lagging a few years behind its larger competitors, the company embarked upon a massive competitiveness campaign. After turning to outside consultants for guidance, it initiated many of the employee empowerment measures popular at the time. Ladish kept employees notified of financial and marketing information via e-mail memos and periodic staff meetings. It also started an incentive payment plan.

The company employed "synchronous manufacturing" techniques of controlling work flow throughout its plants. Process improvements included reducing batch sizes. "Process mapping" involved input from all levels of production workers with the aim of removing unnecessary steps. Speaking to *Aviation Week & Space Technology*, a company executive characterized "the speed issue" as the key to improving costs as well as performance. Ladish also attempted to coordinate such improvements across the whole supply chain, from vendors to customers.

KEY DATES

1905: Herman W. Ladish buys a steam hammer.

1935: The company launches a $1 million upgrading and modernization program at its plant.

1966: Ladish builds a new plant in Kentucky.

1975: The company builds a new factory in Arkansas.

1981: Armco Inc. of Middletown, Ohio, announces that it is buying a 53 percent interest in privately owned Ladish.

1985: Armco sells Ladish to Owens Corning Corporation.

1987: Ladish is sold to an investment group.

1993: The company spends two months under Chapter 11 bankruptcy protection.

1997: Stowe Machine Co. Inc. is acquired.

1998: Ladish goes public.

2005: Zaklad Kuznia Matrycowa is acquired.

2008: Aerex Manufacturing Inc. and Chen-Tech Industries Inc. are acquired.

Ladish teamed with Paramount, California-based Weber to enter new markets. Weber's 35,000-ton hydraulic press was more than twice the size of any of Ladish's. Weber aimed to capitalize upon Ladish's position in the jet engine forging market. Although in this instance another company brought a unique piece of equipment to the deal, Ladish was already the sole source for several products, such as certain massive rocket engine parts. Ladish had some of the industry's largest presses and hammers.

GOING PUBLIC: 1997

Kerry L. Woody was named president in 1996. The company employed 1,075 at the time. Annual sales were $162 million, with profits of $2.1 million. During the year, Ladish sold its industrial products division to Trinity Industries for $36.5 million to better focus on its core business. The company bought Stowe Machine Co., Inc., in Windsor, Connecticut, for $9.5 million. That site employed 40, making jet engine components. Rival Wyman-Gordon bought Cameron Forged Products from Cooper Industries, reducing the number of competitors but making Wyman, already the industry leader, an even larger player. Shortly after Ladish's Kentucky plant flooded in March 1997, the company announced that it was selling its pipe fittings division, which also included a plant in Arkansas.

As a result of Ladish's competitiveness regimen, by 1997 the company was acting like a lean, world-class supplier. Lead times and on-time deliveries improved drastically, and the company handled its raw materials inventories more efficiently as well. In addition, the aircraft industry as a whole was facing a boom time. A thousand employees enjoyed profit-sharing bonuses averaging $2,000 as a result of the improvements. The workforce had been cut in half during Ladish's retooling.

In late 1997, the company announced plans to sell some of its stock on the market to raise capital and to enhance shareholder liquidity. Some shares, given to creditors in its bankruptcy settlement, already had been trading over the counter. The initial public offering (IPO) was initially planned for $60 million worth of shares, later increased to $115 million.

The $86 million IPO in March 1998 raised $29 million. Ladish President Woody told the *Business Journal of Milwaukee* that the company had finally "arrived." Several months later, however, one of the major investing groups disbanded, sending share prices tumbling.

Ladish spent $1.6 million to upgrade its 15,000-ton hydraulic forging press in May 1998. By August it was planning a stock buyback and looking for other machining and forging companies to acquire to increase its product line and make its stock more attractive. At this time, the company was practically debt-free and aiming for 40 percent growth by 2000, mostly through acquisitions. Although the Asian financial crisis had begun to affect sales at Boeing and Airbus, sales of helicopters and business and regional jets were increasing. The company also had a steady business in replacement parts.

The booming commercial aviation market in the late 1990s kept suppliers working at full capacity. This led many to focus on improving on-time performance rather than worry about market share, according to a Ladish market survey. Manufacturers also chose to enter longer agreements with fewer vendors.

Ladish announced that it was cooperating with the Chinese aviation industry in 1998. It arranged to buy 1,200 tons of titanium ingot from Sino-Titanium. In July 1998, Ladish teamed with Falk Corporation to build a 30-ton gear for an Army Corps of Engineers hydroelectric power facility.

Concerned the company was being undervalued in the stock market, Ladish management announced that the company was buying back more shares in August 1998, further increased by 50 percent the following May. The company also instituted a poison pill plan in September 1998 to ward off potential takeover attempts.

On December 2, 1998, Boeing announced that it was cutting production 25 percent and laying off 48,000 workers. The worse-than-expected news worried suppliers on all levels of the still recovering aviation industry. To further compound Ladish's difficulties, the firm's 10,000-ton thermal press broke down later that month. The press was down for nearly three months, costing several million dollars in repairs and millions more in lost revenues. Afterward, Ladish was able to boast higher efficiency from the repaired equipment. The company also suffered the loss of partner Weber Metal's huge 38,000-ton press, however, which was down due to a cracked cylinder. The joint venture had just begun to show results, accounting for 4 percent of Ladish's total 1998 revenue.

Ladish posted profits of about $24 million a year in 1997 and 1998. Annual sales had climbed past $200 million. By early 1999, Ladish was reporting drastically reduced earnings, in part due to its press failure. Earnings continued to fall into the second quarter. As business slowed, Ladish offered its aging workforce retirement incentives. It then brought back apprenticeship programs to deal with a generational shortage of skilled labor. Despite all this, Ladish continued to invest for the future, buying precision machiner Adco Manufacturing of South Windsor, Connecticut. Adco employed about 30 people and was to be folded into Stowe.

MOVING INTO THE 21ST CENTURY

Ladish experienced significant growth during the early years of the new millennium despite a rocky start to the decade. Titanium, a key component in aerospace equipment, was in short supply, leaving many vendors unable to supply parts. To make matters worse, terrorist attacks against the United States on September 11, 2001, caused a sharp decline in demand for airline parts. With revenues and earnings falling, Ladish and its competitors found themselves retooling their strategies and cutting costs.

The market soon began its slow recovery and Ladish benefited from several acquisitions, which were designed to bolster its business both at home and abroad. In 2000 the company added Wyman-Gordon Titanium Castings LLC to its arsenal, renaming it Pacific Coast Technologies Inc. The company made its first international purchase in 2005, acquiring Zaklad Kuznia Matrycowa for $11.3 million. The Polish metals forging company operated as a supplier to the automotive, mining, and railway industries and gave Ladish a European presence.

With the aerospace industry in full swing, Ladish focused on strengthened this portion of its business. In 2006 it purchased Valley Machining Inc., a Wisconsin-based supplier of precision machined components to aerospace material companies. It also set plans in motion to add a third isothermal press, which forged super alloys into jet aircraft engine parts, to its Cudahy facility.

Despite concerns about the shrinking supply of titanium and the high cost of raw materials, Ladish announced in 2007 that it planned to construct a new investment casting foundry in Mexico that would produce titanium aerospace components. One year later it acquired Aerex Manufacturing Inc., bolstering its titanium machining capacity. It also purchased California-based Chen-Tech Industries Inc., a forger of jet engine parts, later that year.

During 2008 the company posted revenues $469.5 million and profits of $32.2 million. Its business was hit hard in 2009 as the global economic recession began to impact nearly every market it served. With demand falling, profits plunged by 90 percent during the second quarter of the year. At this time, the company announced plans for the new plant in Mexico were on hold and it also implemented several rounds of layoffs. While the company believed it well positioned to weather the difficult climate, it remained cautious about expansion and growth in its near future.

Frederick C. Ingram
Updated, Christina M. Stansell

PRINCIPAL SUBSIDIARIES

Ladish Forging, LLC; Chen-Tech Industries, Inc.; Pacific Cast Technologies, Inc.; Zaklad Kuznia Matrycowa Sp. z o.o. (Poland); Stowe Machine Co., Inc.; Aerex LLC; Valley Machining, Inc.; Zaklad Obrobki I Procesow Specjalnych Sp. z o.o. (Poland); Metallum Corporation.

PRINCIPAL COMPETITORS

Barnes Group Inc.; Goodrich Corporation; Titanium Metals Corporation.

FURTHER READING

"Aerospace Purchasers Take Broad, Long-Term View," *Purchasing,* October 9, 1997.

Camia, Catalina, and Dale D. Buss, "Owens-Corning to Buy Armco Business in Aerospace Materials for $415 Million," *Wall Street Journal,* August 19, 1985, p. 1.

Elliott, Alan R., "Demand for Aerospace Gear Has Parts Supplier in Expansion Mode," *Investor's Business Daily,* June 26, 2006.

Gallun, Alby, "Area Aircraft Suppliers Hold Breath for Boeing Cuts," *Business Journal of Milwaukee,* December 14, 1998.

———, "Bucyrus, Ladish Emerge from Chapter 11 Shadow," *Business Journal of Milwaukee,* March 10, 1997.

———, "Firms Face Mass Retirements As Work Force Ages," *Business Journal of Milwaukee,* March 1, 1999.

———, "Ladish Files to Become Public Company," *Business Journal of Milwaukee,* December 29, 1997.

———, "Stock Buyback Plans: Investment Tools or Smoke Screens?" *Business Journal of Milwaukee,* September 14, 1998.

———, "Stock Offering Helps Ladish Take Off," *Business Journal of Milwaukee,* April 13, 1998.

Haflich, Frank, "Ladish May Nix Sales of Scrap; Plant on Hold," *American Metal Market,* February 11, 2009.

———, "Ladish's Aerex Buy Adds Titanium Capacity," *American Metal Market,* July 17, 2008.

"Ladish Backs Away from IC Project in Mexico," *Foundry Management & Technology,* March 1, 2009.

"Ladish Building Titanium Plant in Mexico," *Weekly Business of Aviation,* December 17, 2007.

"Ladish Forges Ahead As Aerospace Rallies," *Milwaukee Journal Sentinel,* December 2, 1996.

"Ladish Seeks Close Ties with Rocket Designers," *Space News,* June 2, 1997.

Lank, Avrum, "Stock Sale Could Net Ladish Co. of Cudahy, Wis., $35 Million," *Milwaukee Journal Sentinel,* December 24, 1997.

Mullins, Robert, "Ladish to Sell Fittings Division," *Business Journal of Milwaukee,* March 24, 1997.

Rohan, Thomas M., "A Hush-Hush Deal for a Secretive Company," *Industry Week,* July 27, 1981, p. 17.

Savage, Mark, "Cudahy, Wis.-based Jet Engine Parts Maker Ladish Co. Plans Stock Buyback," *Milwaukee Journal Sentinel,* August 26, 1998.

Schlesinger, Jacob M., "Owens-Corning to Sell Ladish Unit for $236 Million," *Wall Street Journal,* January 21, 1987, p. 1.

Schmid, John, "Ladish Buys Polish Forging Firm," *Milwaukee Journal Sentinel,* November 22, 2005.

"'Strategic Buyers' Having Hard Time Finding Good Deals," *Business Journal-Milwaukee,* April 24, 1998.

Velocci, Anthony L., Jr., "Aerospace Suppliers Preoccupied with Possible Cyclical Downturn," *Aviation Week & Space Technology,* May 31, 1999, p. 64.

———, "Ladish Turnaround: Lesson for Industry," *Aviation Week & Space Technology,* June 9, 1997, pp. 70–71.

———, "Survey Highlights Conflicting Priorities Among Suppliers," *Aviation Week & Space Technology,* August 10, 1998, p. 66.

Wetmore, Warren C., "Supplier Strikes Worry Engine Makers," *Aviation Week & Space Technology,* July 23, 1979, p. 22.

Langer Juice Company, Inc.

16195 Stephens Street
City of Industry, California 91745-1718
U.S.A.
Telephone: (626) 336-1666
Web site: http://www.langers.com

Private Company
Incorporated: 1975 as L&A Juice Company, Inc.
Employees: 300
Sales: $190 million (2008)
NAICS: 312100 Beverage Manufacturing

■ ■ ■

Langer Juice Company, Inc., generally known as Langers, is a family owned and operated beverage company based in City of Industry, California. Langers offers about 200 different products, including a wide variety of 100 percent shelf-stable fruit juices and blends, juices enhanced with nutrients and supplements, fresh refrigerated juices, organic juices, sugarless juices, frozen juices, sparkling juices, flavored waters, cocktail mixes, vegetable juices, and gourmet sodas. Langers also offers apple sauce and apple butter, both manufactured on a contract basis. Langers produces beverages at its main 140,000-square-foot plant in City of Industry, as well as production facilities in Bakersville and Healdsburg, California. Langers' primary customers are grocery and club stores in the all of the United States, Latin America, and Asia. Distribution is handled by six strategically located facilities in California, Iowa, New York, Oregon, and Texas. The company is headed by its founder, Nathan Langer, who in his 80s remains president. His sons David and Bruce serve as vice presidents and handle most of the day-to-day responsibilities.

FOUNDER: POST–WORLD WAR II IMMIGRANT

Nathan Langer was born in Poland. He came to the United States after World War II and settled in Houston, Texas, where he worked as a dental technician, for which he had been trained in Poland. Langer and his wife were both health enthusiasts, and in 1960 they moved to San Diego to open a retail shop, investing in commercial presses to make and serve fresh squeezed carrot juice, a drink popular in Europe. The store, known as Veg-o-juice, proved popular, leading to the introduction of other vegetable juices, followed by the first fruit juice: grape.

In the early 1960s Langer began to deliver fresh, refrigerated juices in quart and half-gallon plastic bottles to San Diego–area health food stores, resulting in a venture called L&A Juice, the initials drawn from Langer's last name and that of an associate who made the deliveries. The Langers began selling apple butter as well.

For family reasons the Langers decided to move to Los Angeles around 1965. The retail operation was discontinued but health food store deliveries of vegetable and fruit juices continued in San Diego, and from Los Angeles the company could service all of Southern California. Production was conducted at a downtown facility that also served as a warehouse and contained

COMPANY PERSPECTIVES

We make juice. We drink a lot of juice as well. In fact, we taste every batch before the Langer label reaches the bottle.

the company's administrative offices. Langers remained here until the late 1970s when the operations were moved to Downey, California.

In the meantime the business was incorporated as L&A Juice Company, Inc., in 1975. The new facility allowed the company to add hot-fill capabilities to produce pasteurized bottled juices. The first of these products were pineapple-coconut and apple-boysenberry blends. These new shelf stable products were sold to health food stores in 32-ounce bottles under the L&A brand and in 64-ounce bottles to supermarkets using the "Health Aide" brand. (Health Aide remained in use until 1988 when the Langers brand name was adopted.) As this product line expanded to include other flavors in the late 1970s, carrot juice and the other vegetable juices were phased out.

SECOND GENERATION JOINS COMPANY

By this time a second generation of the Langer family was becoming involved in the family business. Both David and Bruce Langer worked summers at the company during high school and college. David had always been interested in the business and after graduating from college in 1977 he joined his father. Younger brother Bruce had other plans, attending law school and considering a career in government, eventually working for a judge during one summer in Washington, D.C. He too, however, decided to make Langers a career, taking a full-time position in 1985.

Around the time Bruce Langer joined his father and brother, the company reached a major turning point in its evolution. The new-age beverage category was gaining strength, including flavored seltzers. In March 1985 Langers introduced the 5th Avenue Seltzer line in Southland supermarkets. It proved extremely popular, leading to the introduction of additional flavors and geographic expansion for Langers. Carried by Kmart and Target, independent distributors, and supermarket chains, 5th Avenue Seltzer achieved distribution in about 25 states. The Downey space, only large enough to accommodate a single production line, was unable to keep up with demand, leading Langers to hire contract

bottlers in Minnesota and Georgia to make up the difference.

CITY OF INDUSTRY PLANT OPENS: 1988

Even without the addition of 5th Avenue Seltzer, Langers was overextended at the Downey facility. As a result, the family searched for a large parcel of land on which to build a new plant. Because the Los Angeles area was so heavily developed, the company looked eastward, eventually buying property in City of Industry. Here a 140,000-square-foot plant was opened in 1988. The company subsequently changed its name from L&A Juice Co. to Langer Juice Company, Inc. The company was poised to expand throughout the United States.

The new City of Industry plant permitted Langers to take advantage of an opportunity in the marketplace. A new technology had become available that allowed juice to be pasteurized in a polyethylene terephthalate (PET) bottle. Previous plastic bottles could not withstand the heat involved in the process and would melt. Langers was quick to embrace the new material and became the first company in the West to switch to PET in 1989. At the time, apple juice and cranberry juice were sold in 48-ounce glass containers. Langers introduced a 64-ounce PET container of apple juice that disrupted the category.

The advantages of the new container were obvious. Unlike glass it would not break, and given that the core market for apple juice were children the safety issue was extremely important. Consumers also appreciated the value of a 64-ounce size versus a 48-ounce product. The new container allowed Langers to distinguish itself from the other apple juice brands. Langers was able to convince the chains that it made sense to carry Langers' plastic bottled apple juice as a contrast to the glass-bottle apple juice brands they typically carried.

The key to Langers' success with apple juice in the new PET container was the product itself. Consumers may have tried Langers apple juice because of the safety factor and the value, but they continued to buy it only because of the good taste and excellent quality. As a small company, Langers' only goal was to have an apple juice that ranked higher than No. 5 in sales. As long as it outsold somebody on the shelf, the company knew the brand could survive. The company was so small at this stage that it did not subscribe to Nielsen's marketing data. Only when a former broker called to offer his congratulations did Langers learn that it had become the top-selling apple juice in Southern California.

KEY DATES

1960: Nathan Langer begins selling carrot juice in San Diego.
1965: The Langer family moves to Los Angeles.
1985: Fifth Avenue Seltzer product introduced.
1988: Company moves to City of Industry, California.
1991: Plastic gallon containers of apple juice introduced.
1998: Name changed to Langer Juice Company, Inc.
2000: Hollywood tie-in promotions begin.
2003: Frozen juice products introduced.
2009: Disney cobranding program begins.

PLASTIC GALLON CONTAINERS OF APPLE JUICE INTRODUCED: 1991

The next major development that shaped Langers' growth took place around 1991 when the company began using a plastic gallon bottle that was hot-fillable. Langers became the first company in the West to introduce apple juice in a plastic gallon jug. Until that time apple juice in that quantity was sold in glass bottles with a finger ring handle on the narrow neck. The glass was heavy and the handle unwieldy. As a result supermarkets created displays of the product only around Halloween, as much a nod to tradition as anything else.

Langers lighter, easier-to-handle gallon-size apple juice changed everything. Virtually overnight, the company's sales of gallon jugs of apple juice dramatically increased to an 80 percent share of the Southern California market. Moreover, supermarkets promoted the product in displays throughout the year, not just during the fall, so that Langers not only seized a large part of the market for gallon jug apple juice sales, it made the market larger.

Langers used the new 64-ounce PET containers for other juices in the early 1990s, as the old 48-ounce glass bottles became obsolete in the marketplace. Using its success with PET and plastic gallon containers as a springboard, Langers expanded into other categories and entered new parts of the country. Langers moved into northern Arizona, Colorado, Oregon, Utah, and Washington State. Later in the decade the company spread to the Midwest and Southwest. As a result distribution facilities were established to support regional sales.

NEW JUICES AND EXPANSION INTO MEXICO IN THE NINETIES

In the mid-1990s the company introduced a line of 100 percent cranberry juice blends, tropical blends, and a baby juice line. Near the end of the decade Langers brought out Langers 100, enhanced 100 percent fruit juices containing vitamins, minerals, and antioxidants. When it was reported that regular drinking of wine helped to prevent heart disease, Langers added grape seed extract to some drinks to take advantage of the so-called French Paradox. The new products and expanded territory helped to drive annual sales to about the $50 million mark by the end of the decade. There was also a name change to the corporation, which became Langer Juice Company, Inc., in January 1998.

Langers expanded its operations to Mexico in the late 1990s, taking over an apple juice concentrating plant in a mountainous area conducive to apple growing. After the facility had been built, its owners abandoned it. Through an intermediary, the Mexican government, in an effort to help the area's farmers, contacted Langers about taking over the plant. Langers agreed and operated it until selling the facility in 2002.

FIRST HOLLYWOOD PRODUCT TIE-IN: 2000

Langers' proximity to Mexico led to that opportunity for growth, but a more important opening came about in 2000 because of nearby Hollywood. At that time a production company contacted Langers about a tie-in arrangement with the *Bear in a Big Blue House* children's television program. Langers promoted the television show on its packaging and Web site, and produced a freestanding newspaper insert to sell both the juice and the show. To spur sales a promotion was created that sent a kids' cup shaped like a bear to children whose parents sent in three proofs of purchase.

Not only did this increase consumer awareness of Langers, as well as *Bear in the Big Blue House,* other Hollywood production companies and studios took notice and began contacting Langers about other tie-in possibilities. In 2000 tie-ins were done with the video/DVD release of *The Flintstones in Viva Rock Vegas* and the Baby Einstein educational series. Langers' first theatrical promotion took place with 20th Century Fox's *Ice Age*. Langers would also become involved in tie-ins with video games, which was potentially important because youngsters who like a product often become lifelong customers.

EXPANSION IN THE UNITED STATES AND BEYOND

Langers grew on multiple fronts in the new century. In 2002 a push began to take the brand to the rest of the United States. The company entered the New England market and then spread to the mid-Atlantic and southeastern markets. It also established itself in Alaska and Hawaii and later in the decade spread to other parts of the world through a relationship with Costco, reaching markets in Central America, Asia, Korea, Japan, the Philippines, and Australia. Popular low-carb diets that frowned upon fruit juices hurt sales to a limited extent, but caused only minor damage. Sales continued to grow at a strong pace, topping $100 million in 2002.

Langers continued to add new product categories as well. In 2003 it entered the frozen juice category, once again using innovation as a way to enter a market. Rather than use a composite can that relied on a cardboard body and metal end caps, Langers offered a proprietary octagonal PET container. Not only was it resealable, it could be thawed in a microwave oven unlike composite containers. It also did not leak as did cardboard when the juice was thawed, and it was 100 percent recyclable.

In 2007 Langers introduced the nonalcoholic No Worries mixer line. A year later the company returned to its roots by once again offering vegetable juice and blends, as well as a line of fresh, refrigerated juice that was carried by the Ralph's supermarket chain. Langers acquired a plant in Healdsburg, California, to make carbonated juices and the new line of Langers Gourmet Sodas in 12-ounce cans, introduced in 2009.

Another major development was a cobranding relationship forged with The Disney Company. To target young children and tweens, Langers produced 32-ounce and 64-ounce juices cobranded with such Disney titles as *Cars, Hannah Montana,* and *High School Musical.* Langers also replaced its baby juice line with products bearing the likenesses of Winnie-the-Pooh, Tigger, and Mickey Mouse. Late in 2009 Langers introduce a line of 6.75-ounce juice pouches that featured Disney's *Fairies, Cars,* and *High School Musical.* Given its relationship with Disney and strong reputation in the marketplace, Langers was well positioned to enjoy continued strong growth for years to come.

Ed Dinger

PRINCIPAL SUBSIDIARIES

Langer Farms, LLC; Sonoma Beverage Company, LLC.

PRINCIPAL COMPETITORS

Mott's LLP; Ocean Spray Cranberries, Inc.; Tropicana Products, Inc.; Apple & Eve L.L.C

FURTHER READING

Finnigan, David, "Langers Juice, Ralphs, Burger King Chill with Family-Focused Ice Age," *Brandweek,* November 19, 2001, p. 14.

Lapin, Lisa A., "Small Southland Firms Start a Trend Flavored Seltzer," *Los Angeles Times,* October 20, 1986, p. 1.

Popp, Jamie, "Building on a Healthy Foundation," *Beverage Industry,* June 2003, p. 28.

"Split Line Doubles Output," *Packaging,* July 1990, p. 44.

LOEHMANN'S

Loehmann's Holdings Inc.

---

500 Halsey Street
Bronx, New York 10461
U.S.A.
Telephone: (718) 409-2000
Fax: (718) 518-2766
Web site: http://www.loehmanns.com

Private Company
Incorporated: 1930 as Charles C. Loehmann Corporation
Employees: 1,784
Sales: $550 million (2008 est.)
NAICS: 448120 Women's Clothing Stores; 448110 Men's Clothing Stores; 44815 Clothing Accessories Stores

■ ■ ■

Loehmann's Holdings Inc. is a retailer of designer and brand name women's and men's clothing, shoes, and accessories with approximately 60 stores in 16 states. It is best known for its Back Room, which offers high-end designer and couture clothing sold at discount prices. Loehmann's filed for Chapter 11 bankruptcy protection in 1999 and emerged the following year. Dubai-based Istithmar PJSC purchased the company in 2006.

ORIGINS AS A FAMILY RUN DISCOUNTER

The Loehmann's retail chain was founded in 1930 by Charles C. Loehmann. The company's spiritual matriarch, however, was Loehmann's mother, Frieda Loehmann. Mother of three children, she became the family breadwinner in 1916 when her husband, a flutist with a symphony orchestra, developed a paralyzed lip. Mrs. Loehmann was a coat buyer for a fashionable department store until 1921, when, with $800 in cash, she and her son Charles opened a women's specialty clothing shop named the Original Designer Outlet below their Brooklyn apartment. "Mama" Loehmann got her merchandise by driving to the garment district on Manhattan's Seventh Avenue in a black limousine and filling it with designers' seasonal overstocks at a fraction of the traditional wholesale price, paying from a wad of cash she kept in what designer Bill Blass called her "voluminous black bloomers."

Mrs. Loehmann continued to descend daily on the garment district until two weeks before her death in 1962, and the store was doing an estimated $3 million in annual sales at the time. Her one flaw, according to a manufacturer who was one of her suppliers, was that "she thought Brooklyn was the beginning and end of the world." Her son Charles had different ideas. After his mother rejected the notion of expansion, he opened a women's clothing store on Fordham Road in the borough of the Bronx in 1930 and incorporated the enterprise as the Charles C. Loehmann Corp.

Loehmann's gained fame as a discounter, but of high-fashion, first quality merchandise, made possible by purchasing manufacturers' overruns and "broken lots"—groups of garments in a limited range of sizes and colors. The store also kept its costs down by paying cash

COMPANY PERSPECTIVES

Loehmann's continues to distinguish itself as a preeminent, upscale, off-price specialty retailer for name brand designer fashions. Couture and designer fashions plus current, in-season merchandise and frequent new arrivals, all at prices 30% to 65% less than department store prices, still serve as hallmark features of Loehmann's, attracting generations of fashion-savvy women and men to a shopping experience unlike any other.

for these "odd lots" on the day it ordered them. These were then taken from the manufacturer's plant, processed and ticketed at the company warehouse, and delivered to the store, sometimes all on the same day. As a result, a woman might be able to buy a couturier-designed dress for as little as one-third the price at a competing store, with the only difference being that the manufacturer's label had been removed from the garment.

Loehmann's also saved on overhead by hanging most of the clothing on ordinary pipe racks and making women try clothing on in "community" dressing rooms. The chaos that occurred when a desirable shipment arrived was recalled by one woman as "female bonding" and discussed more graphically by Erma Bombeck in her book *Everything I Know About Animal Behavior I Learned at Loehmann's*. The company also saved money by not offering credit, delivery, or alterations, seldom accepting returns, and restricting advertising to the mailing of announcements.

It was not until 1951 that Loehmann's felt ready to open a store outside of New York City. Three such stores were opened during the 1950s, and by 1964, when the company went public, it was operating four stores in New York, one in Connecticut, and one in New Jersey. These establishments, specialty stores for women, sold dresses, coats, suits, sweaters, blouses, skirts, slacks, shorts, separates, raincoats, and bathing suits. Net sales rose from $9 million in 1961 to $15.1 million in 1964; net profit rose from $288,315 in 1961 to $532,712 in 1964. After shares were first offered on the American Stock Exchange in 1964, Charles Loehmann and his wife, Anita, continued to hold a majority of the stock for about a decade. George J. Greenberg succeeded Charles as president of the company, which was renamed Loehmann's Inc.

ADDING STORES

Before the 1960s ended, Loehmann's had added ten more stores. The company entered Massachusetts in 1965, Maryland in 1967, and Pennsylvania and Virginia in 1968, and it opened a store in Los Angeles in October 1969. The flagship Bronx store remained by far the largest, however, and the company also built a new Bronx corporate headquarters and warehouse in 1968. The new Loehmann's stores were much like the earlier ones, located away from high-rent areas and with furnishings kept to a minimum. Moreover, the company was careful to make sure that the stores were a sizable distance from major fashion retailers normally carrying the same merchandise lines. Net sales passed $37 million in 1970, while net income was reported at $1.1 million.

After the Los Angeles store proved successful, Loehmann's opened its first midwestern outlet in a Chicago suburb and its first southern store in Atlanta. The company also experimented with seven lower-line Charley's Place outlets but converted them into conventional Loehmann's stores in 1972 when the profit margin proved too small. By the spring of that year there were 27 stores in the chain. In 1975, when Loehmann's boasted 31 stores in 12 states, the company broke precedent by beginning to advertise in local newspapers. Still, advertising expenditures in 1976 came to less than 1 percent of sales.

Five categories of women's sportswear were accounting for 62 percent of Loehmann's sales in 1977. That year Greenberg discussed the company's activities among a group of financial analysts. He noted that Loehmann's blouses could be purchased for as low as $8.98 and that its dresses retailed for as much as $700; the company also carried a wide variety of furs and had sold sables and minks for as much as $12,000. Loehmann's was still striving to process goods in its warehouse and get them to its stores within 48 hours and was turning around its merchandise 12 to 13 times a year, as compared to six to eight for a regular retailer. The company, said Greenberg, was doing "considerable" purchasing outside Seventh Avenue, particularly in Philadelphia, Baltimore, and Los Angeles, but also overseas.

CHANGES IN OWNERSHIP

Loehmann's net sales reached a record $159.7 million in fiscal 1980, and its net income came to a record $6.5 million. In April 1980 there were 48 stores (all but two leased) in 21 states. More than half were in shopping centers, including 19 in "Loehmann's Plaza" locations. At the instigation of the Loehmann family, which still held 37 percent of the stock, the company agreed in

KEY DATES

1921: Charles C. Loehmann and his mother, Frieda, open a clothing shop called the Original Designer Outlet.

1930: Charles Loehmann opens a women's clothing store on Fordham Road in the Bronx and incorporates the enterprise as the Charles C. Loehmann Corp.

1962: Frieda Loehmann dies.

1964: The company goes public.

1975: Loehmann's is operating 31 stores in 12 states; the company begins to advertise in local newspapers.

1980: The company accepts a purchase offer of about $68 million from AEA Investors Inc.

1983: Loehmann's is sold to Associated Dry Goods Corp.

1986: May Department Stores Co. buys Associated Dry Goods.

1988: The chain is sold to an affiliate of a Spanish firm, Entrecanales y Tavora S.A., and a venture capital arm of Donaldson, Lufkin & Jenrette Securities Corp.

1996: Loehmann's goes public again.

1999: The company files for Chapter 11 bankruptcy protection.

2000: The company emerges from Chapter 11 as Loehmann's Holdings Inc.

2004: Crescent Capital Investments Inc. buys Loehmann's.

2006: Dubai-based Istithmar PJSC acquires Loehmann's.

Despite its growth in scale, however, Loehmann's had achieved only modest growth in average sales per store during the mid-1980s and had actually slipped in this category during 1987. A new president and chief executive officer, Allan R. Bogner, closed 13 marginal stores, established a policy of accepting credit cards and personal checks, and hired a trendy New York advertising agency to conduct a $4 million campaign. During 1988 the 77 Loehmann's stores had sales of $334 million. In the summer of 1988, however, the chain was sold again to an affiliate of a Spanish firm, Entrecanales y Tavora S.A., and a venture capital arm of Donaldson, Lufkin & Jenrette Securities Corp., for a reported $170 million. The new owners took the firm private in a leveraged buyout.

OVERCOMING CHALLENGES

In its first full year under new management, Loehmann's closed more underperforming stores while expanding rapidly across the nation and achieved an average same-store increase in sales of 18.7 percent. The owners used the profits to buy back about $30 million of the loans they had taken out and the high yielding "junk" bonds they had issued to pay for the company. Loehmann's lost $4 million in fiscal 1989 (the year ended February 3, 1990). Its sales remained essentially stagnant during the next three years, in which it lost $1.1 million, $6.5 million, and $783,000, respectively. Some sources suggested in 1992 that Loehmann's had sacrificed some of its mystique by venturing into mainstream retailing and stocking many lesser-known brands. By then the 83-store chain was accepting returns as well as credit cards, was leaving the manufacturers' labels in the clothing, and even began offering its own private label clothing. In March 1992 Bogner was replaced as president by Robert Friedman, a veteran Macy's executive.

Friedman steered Loehmann's toward an even more conventional department store atmosphere, putting up signs in the stores that emphasized manufacturers' names, displaying clothing on mannequins, and even giving customers the option of trying on clothes in private dressing rooms. The company also added shoes, lingerie, hosiery, hats, and accessories such as jewelry, perfume, and sunglasses to its offerings. Loehmann's circulated its own credit card and offered an Insiders Club for special discounts. Nevertheless, sales continued to drop in 1993. In October of that year the company completed a financial reorganization, repurchasing $30 million of its notes and selling $55.7 million of new bonds, with no repayment of principal required until 1997.

September 1980 to accept a purchase offer of about $68 million from AEA Investors Inc. Greenberg continued to serve as chairman and president of the company.

Three years later, this investment group sold Loehmann's to Associated Dry Goods Corp., operator of 14 department store chains, for $96 million. During 1983 the company had posted sales of about $260 to $270 million and extended its operations to 61 stores in 25 states. Along with the rest of Associated Dry Goods, Loehmann's passed in 1986 to May Department Stores Co. By 1988 the number of Loehmann's had grown to 82 in 26 states. That year the original Bronx store was closed, giving way to a 35,000-square-foot outlet, the largest in the chain, in a converted skating rink.

Loehmann's lost a record $12.2 million in fiscal 1993 on net sales of $373.4 million, down by $16 million. In 1994 the company lost $1.5 million on net sales of $392.6 million. The company was burdened with heavy interest payments—$18.2 million in fiscal 1994—on its considerable debt. During fiscal 1995 net sales dipped to $386.1 million, and the company lost $15 million, after taking a $15.3 million charge to close 11 small, underperforming stores.

GOING PUBLIC AGAIN

Loehmann's went public again in May 1996, raising $60 million after expenses by selling common stock at $17 a share. The proceeds were used to redeem preferred stock held by the investors and to help refinance the company's long-term debt load. Just before going public, the company also sold $100 million worth of junk bonds at 11.875 percent in annual interest, due in 2003, in order to redeem $130 million worth of notes, some of which were at even higher rates. This enabled the company to reduce its interest costs in fiscal 1995 to $13.4 million.

Many analysts agreed with the editor and publisher of a research service who said Loehmann's had lost its way by reducing sales of designer and "bridge" merchandise (apparel just below designer category) to only one-third of overall inventory. Company executives countered that the chain's traditional niche was ill suited to the expansion they planned: seven new stores in 1996 and seven to ten each in 1997 and 1998. Investors did step up to buy the company's stock, lifting the price of the initial offering to $22.25 by day's end. In October 1996 a secondary stock offering raised $63.8 million for insiders who chose to sell. One month later, Loehmann's common stock reached a peak of $30.25 a share.

On opening day in October 1996, Loehmann's new five-story, 60,000-square-foot Manhattan store on 16th Street and Seventh Avenue was mobbed by frenzied shoppers contending for such merchandise as Giorgio Armani bustiers marked down from $2,810 to $750 as well as upscale goods by Jones New York and DKNY in the $100 to $500 range. By August 1997 the number of new Loehmann's stores opened since the beginning of 1996 had reached 13, raising the total to 77. Many, like the Manhattan one, were in high-rent downtown districts where Loehmann's rarely had been located in the past. For fiscal 1996 the company reported record revenues of $417.8 million and net income of $4.5 million after a $7.1 million write-off on early extinguishment of debt.

LOSSES CONTINUE

During the spring of 1997, however, bad news returned in the form of escalating costs and falling sales. Management attributed the results to its inexperience with large stores in major downtown locations, while observers pointed to the competition Loehmann's faced from the more than 1,900 stores nationwide then competing in the off-price category for designer apparel overruns. Donna Karan International Inc. and Anne Klein & Co., for example, formerly good Loehmann's suppliers, were directing their surplus production to their own outlet stores. Some of Loehmann's own employees suggested that as little as 2 percent to 10 percent of the chain's merchandise on hand was designer clothing, although Friedman maintained that the level remained at 30 percent. At the end of July 1997, shares of Loehmann's common stock were selling for only $6.625. The company's long-term debt was $107.9 million at the end of March 1997.

In October 1997 Loehmann's introduced merchandise for men, including dress shirts, ties, sportswear, and some designer collection items such as jackets and pants, in 15 of its stores. (Tailored clothing and shoes were not offered.) Design collections included Ralph Lauren, Donna Karan, Calvin Klein, and DKNY. Friedman said the chain's desired merchandise mix was 60 percent women's apparel; 20 percent accessories, intimate apparel, and shoes; and 20 percent menswear, compared to its existing merchandise mix of 80 percent women's apparel and 20 percent accessories, intimate apparel, and shoes. Management intended to have menswear in 55 Loehmann's stores by the end of 1998.

Loehmann's announced in February 1998 that, of its existing 86 stores, it was planning to close ten, which combined were losing an estimated $900,000 a year. The company reported a loss of $15.6 million in the fourth quarter of fiscal 1997, including a $9 million restructuring charge to cover closing costs. The company put expansion plans on hold as intense competition continued to eat away at company revenues. The company posted a loss of $5.1 million in fiscal 1999 while it secured almost no sales growth. With debt climbing, Loehmann's was forced to file for Chapter 11 bankruptcy protection in May 1999. Its stock was delisted from the NASDAQ shortly thereafter.

EMERGING FROM BANKRUPTCY IN THE 21ST CENTURY

The company emerged from Chapter 11 in October 2000 as Loehmann's Holdings Inc. The company's first foray into expansion after its emergence was the opening of a stand alone shoe store in San Francisco in 2003.

The store proved to be an instant success and two additional stores were opened in New York and New Jersey in 2005.

Loehmann's changed hands more than once during the early years of the new millennium. Crescent Capital Investments Inc., a U.S.-based investment subsidiary of First Islamic Investment Bank, acquired Loehmann's in 2004. Crescent, renamed Arcapita Inc., sold Loehmann's to Dubai-based investment firm Istithmar PJSC in a $300 million deal in 2006. Istithmar, the investment arm of the government of the United Arab Emirates, quickly set plans in motion to significantly increase the company's store count. A new flagship store opened its doors in the famed Ansonia building on the Upper West Side of Manhattan in 2007, as did a store on State Street in Chicago.

Chairman and CEO Friedman retired in 2008 after 16 years of directing Loehmann's. Jerald Politzer, a longtime retail executive, was named his replacement and faced distinct challenges. While Istithmar had originally set forth ambitious expansion plans, the declining U.S. economy and intense competition once again wreaked havoc on the company's strategy as well as its bottom line. It closed its Philadelphia location in 2008, just two years after its grand opening.

With sales of women's apparel down across the industry, Loehmann's was forced to retool. In an attempt to lure younger customers, it focused on carrying brands including Juicy Couture, Theory, and True Religion. By this time, the average age of its customer was 35 years old, down from 55 in the past. It also revamped its merchandise mix, adding more accessories, shoes, intimate apparel, and children's wear to its store shelves.

Istithmar, which had added Barneys New York Inc. to its growing arsenal of U.S. companies in 2007, believed the Loehmann's chain had solid growth potential despite the challenging economic climate. Sluggish retail sales in 2009, however, had cast a cloud over Loehmann's future expansion efforts. While a cash-rich parent could prove valuable to Loehmann's in the years to come, CEO Politzer was charged with leading Loehmann's into what would no doubt prove to be a challenging period in its history.

Robert Halasz
Updated, Christina M. Stansell

PRINCIPAL COMPETITORS

Filene's Basement Inc.; Ross Stores Inc.; TJX Companies Inc.

FURTHER READING

Clark, Evan, "Politzer Said New CEO at Loehmann's," *Women's Wear Daily*, April 16, 2008.

Curan, Catherine, "Loehmann's Scrambles to Beat Chapter 11," *Crain's New York Business*, May 17, 1999.

Dribben, Melissa, "Low-Cost Fashion Stalwart's Last Sale," *Philadelphia Enquirer*, April 28, 2008.

Furman, Phyllis, "Loehmann Races Against Time," *Crain's New York Business*, March 30, 1991, pp. 1, 37.

Hemlock, Doreen, "As Retail Rebounds, Investors Snap Up Loehmann's," *New York Times*, May 12, 1996, Sec. 3, p. 3.

"Loehmann's Agrees to Be Purchased; Price Is $68 Million," *Wall Street Journal*, September 26, 1980, p. 7.

"Loehmann's, Inc.," *Wall Street Transcript*, October 6, 1969.

"Loehmann's, Inc.," *Wall Street Transcript*, July 11, 1977.

"Loehmann's Styles Smart Advance Selling High Fashion at Low Cost," *Barron's*, January 23, 1967, pp. 22, 28.

Moin, David, "Loehmann's CEO to Retire," *Women's Wear Daily*, November 30, 2007.

Palmieri, Jean E., "Calling All Men to Loehmann's," *Daily News Record*, October 13, 1997, pp. 12, 16.

———, "Loehmann's in High Gear," *DNR*, February 5, 2007.

Schiro, Anne-Marie, "Tough Balancing Act at Loehmann's," *New York Times*, October 30, 1993, pp. 37, 50.

"A Shopping Cult Goes National," *Business Week*, April 29, 1972, pp. 20–21.

Simmons, Jacqueline, "Loehmann's Plans IPO to Refinance Debt, Redeem Series A Preferred Stock," *Wall Street Journal*, October 3, 1995.

Span, Paula, "A Shrine to Bargains," *Newsweek*, March 21, 1988, p. 81.

Steinhauer, Jennifer, "Bargain Hunting? Keep Looking," *New York Times*, July 30, 1997, pp. DI, D8.

Verdon, Joan, "Have We Got a Deal for You," *Record* (Bergen County, N.J.), March 30, 2007.

———, "Seeing if the Shoe Fits," *Record* (Bergen County, N.J.), September 16, 2005.

Yaeger, Deborah Sue, "In Women's Clothing, Dean of Discounters Is Still Loehmann's," *Wall Street Journal*, July 6, 1976, pp. 1, 24.

Zaczkiewicz, Arthur, "Loehmann's Sold for $300M," *Women's Wear Daily*, July 18, 2006.

Lojas Renner S.A.

Avenue Joaquim Porto Villanova 401
Porto Alegre, Rio Grande do Sul 91410-400
Brazil
Telephone: (55 51) 2121-7045
Fax: (55 51) 2121-7161
Web site: http://www.lojasrenner.com.br

Public Company
Incorporated: 1965
Employees: 9,647
Sales: BRL 2.83 billion ($1.54 billion) (2008)
Stock Exchanges: São Paulo
Ticker Symbol: LREN
NAICS: 452111 Department Stores (Except Discount
    Department Stores); 522210 Credit Card Issuing;
    522220 Sales Financing; 522291 Consumer
    Lending

■ ■ ■

Lojas Renner S.A. operates a retail chain for consumer products that include clothing and shoes, accessories such as perfume and cosmetics, and general home appliances. It is the second largest retail chain for clothing in Brazil. Some of the merchandise it stocks consists of its own proprietary brands. In addition, the company is engaged in credit card management and other financial activities through its subsidiaries.

ORIGINS

Antônio Jacob (A.J.) Renner descended from German immigrants to Rio Grande do Sul, Brazil's southernmost state, where his father owned grain mills and a meatpacking plant. The energetic A.J. eventually came to own a number of enterprises, most of which were based on the state's raw materials, and the Renner group dominated the state economically. Among its enterprises was the largest industrial plant in southern Brazil for some decades, one that enabled Renner to lead Brazil in producing ready made clothing.

Lojas Renner began its existence in 1922 as a store in Porto Alegre, the state capital. It originally functioned as a point of sale for the Renner group's textiles and clothing. In 1940, the mix of products was amplified and Lojas Renner began to operate as a department store chain. By 1962 there were eight stores, all in Rio Grande do Sul. In 1965 the A.J. Renner group opted to separate the various companies that it owned, with the store chain becoming Lojas Renner S.A. Two years later, this company began offering shares of stock on the São Paulo exchange. In 1990 the Brazilian economy experienced one of its two worst years since the Great Depression. The following year, stockholders trying to sell their shares on the exchange were scarcely able to collect $1 million in all. This impelled a restructuring of Lojas Renner.

In 1992, after the second straight year of losing money, the Renner family, which still owned 60 percent of the voting capital, decided to turn the enterprise over to professional management. José Galló, a seasoned retail executive, was hired as director-superintendent. "To reposition Renner was the great challenge of my life," he later told Suzana Naiditch of the Brazilian business magazine *Exame* for a 1995 article.

COMPANY PERSPECTIVES

Mission: To be the biggest and best department store chain in the Americas for the medium/upper segment of consumers, with competitiveness and excellence in our rendered services, enchanting and innovative.

FOCUS ON FASHION

Lojas Renner at this time was a department store chain selling general merchandise, clothing, furniture, and home appliances. Galló decided to orient it toward fashion, and particularly women's fashion, to attract customers willing to pay a premium for designer labels. Instead of waiting for the manufacturers to come to him, he hired executives who proposed partnerships. Everything was negotiable, including payments on credit and the development of new products. "We sold quality goods, but at competitive prices," he told Naiditch.

To attract middle-class shoppers, who represented 80 percent of the chain's customers but were hard pressed by the recession, Lojas Renner emphasized self-service. Some $500,000 was invested on creating a new logo to replace the one that was more than 20 years old. A new promotional campaign was launched featuring the buzzword *encantamento* (enchantment), a concept still employed in the company's mission statement in the first decade of the 21st century.

Renner established the first focus group for Brazilian retail. The chain's prices, services, qualities, and defects were compared to the competition. "Enchantment meters"—electronic devices with colored lights—were installed at the exit of each store to ask shoppers if they were satisfied with their experience. If dissatisfied, they were invited to make suggestions.

Among other amenities offered by Lojas Renner was a bell in the fitting room that allowed a customer to summon a sales attendant to try a different size or item. A "pre-checkout checkout" during busy periods featured staffers scanning purchases with handheld calculators. The line then moved faster because when the customer reached the cashier, all he or she needed to do was make payment. Lojas Renner first offered its own credit card in 1973. By 1999, 87 percent of its sales were by credit card. Store machines made installment payments easy; customers inserted a blank check that was processed and, after being returned for signature, placed back in the machine.

By the end of 1995 Renner's shares were worth 89 times what they had been four years earlier. Three more stores had opened, and the chain had entered the neighboring state of Santa Catarina. Lojas Renner premiered in São Paulo, Brazil's wealthiest and most populous state, the following year. The company had revenues of $253 million in 1997. By late 1998 there were a total of 21 Lojas Renner outlets in six states and Brasília.

J.C. PENNEY ACQUIRES LOJAS RENNER

J.C. Penney Brasil Investimentos Ltda., the Brazilian subsidiary of the U.S.-based department store chain, acquired control of Lojas Renner in December 1998 by paying an estimated $60 million for the 63 percent of the voting capital and 27 percent of the shares held by the Renner family. Penney subsequently purchased almost all the other outstanding shares. Galló was named president of the company.

Although Brazil was again in the throes of an economic recession, J.C. Penney made major investments in the chain, which grew to 35 stores in 1999 and 54 by the end of 2002. These outlets were almost all units of 3,000 square meters (about 32,000 square feet) in shopping centers of cities with more than 400,000 inhabitants. Sales reached BRL 750 million ($318 million) in 2001, but because of the expenses incurred by expansion, Lojas Renner did not become profitable again until 2003.

During this period Lojas Renner was locked in battle with two other fashion conscious retail chains: C&A, owned by a European-based multinational, and Lojas Riachuelo. The company continued to concentrate its efforts on selling clothing and accessories such as watches and cosmetics to young shoppers while dispensing with home items such as kitchen utensils. It also invested further in its proprietary credit card, which had 6.5 million holders in 2004, making it the third largest shopping card network in Brazil. A Renner charge card was available to shoppers with family income as low as $150 per month. An interest-free plan allowed them to make payments as small as $5 a month.

Lojas Renner's sales volume reached BRL 1.3 billion ($542 million) in 2004. There were 64 stores in 2005, when J.C. Penney sold the company for about BRL 1 billion ($435 million), mostly by selling shares on the São Paulo exchange. This was a precedent setting transaction, for it had been the practice in Brazil to sell to another firm rather than to test the public marketplace. In order to maintain what journalists called the "pulverization" of the shares, a company statute directed that any shareholder who acquired more than one-fifth of the capital would have to buy the rest of the

KEY DATES

1922: Lojas Renner begins as a store in Porto Alegre, capital of Rio Grande do Sul.

1940: Previously selling only textiles and clothing, Lojas Renner becomes a department store.

1962: There are eight Lojas Renner department stores, all in Rio Grande do Sul.

1967: As Lojas Renner S.A., the company makes its initial public offering of stock.

1973: Lojas Renner introduces its own company credit card.

1992: After two years in the red, family-run Lojas Renner brings in professional managers.

1995: Shares of company stock are worth 89 times what they were worth in 1991.

1998: The number of Lojas Renner stores reaches 21 in six states and Brasília.

1999: J.C. Penney completes its purchase of Lojas Renner's stock.

2005: J.C. Penney sells the 64-store chain for about BRL 1 billion (about $435 million).

2008: With 110 stores, Lojas Renner is the second largest clothing-oriented department store chain in Brazil.

stock at a price slightly above market value. Shares of Lojas Renner rose by 150 percent over the next eight months.

Galló remained in charge of Lojas Renner but had 900 shareholders looking over his shoulder rather than one boss thousands of miles away. Every week about 50 shareholder consultants arrived at company headquarters in Porto Alegre, seeking information about the profitability of the enterprise. Galló was also subject to closer inspection by the new board, which could exercise effective control over the shares held by the company executives. Furthermore, the new board met monthly rather than twice a year as before.

COMMITMENT TO FINANCIAL SERVICES

Nevertheless, Galló relished what he regarded as an opportunity to make decisions with fewer constraints. Lojas Renner doubled its investment spending in 2006. During the year it opened 15 new stores, six of them in three states of Brazil's poverty-stricken northeast, where the chain was present for the first time.

Galló also committed the company to a larger role in financial services, not only in financing store sales but also in making personal loans and selling insurance. He told an interviewer in 2007 that Lojas Renner had decided to offer these products because only about 34 percent of the economically active population of Brazil had bank accounts. Some 13.6 million Renner credit cards were outstanding in 2008.

Lojas Renner launched its first stores in the states of Amazonas, Paraíba, and Sergipe in 2007, when it opened 14 outlets in all, bringing the total to 95. This made it the second largest clothing-oriented department store chain in Brazil. By the end of 2008, there were 110 stores in all regions of the country. All but seven were located in shopping centers. Revenues rose by only 12 percent during the year, compared to 22 percent in 2007, 26 percent in 2006, and 19 percent in 2005. The drop in sales growth was attributed to the effects of the world economic crisis on consumer spending in Brazil and affected other retailers as well.

Lojas Renner's sales rose by 2.7 percent in the first half of 2009, better than expected in view of the economic downturn. Because of the unsettled conditions, Lojas Renner had withdrawn from an announced purchase of Lojas Leader, a retail chain based in Rio de Janeiro with 39 stores. Nevertheless, it was planning to launch eight more stores in 2009, and five had opened their doors by midyear. Eight more were foreseen in 2010, and the long-range goal was to have 170 to 180 outlets in place.

The leading retailer of perfumes in Brazil, Lojas Renner was also planning to sell perfumes and watches over the Internet, in collaboration with the virtual store Sack's, its principal rival in the perfume segment. In its own stores Renner was selling more than 20 imported perfume brands, including Kenzo, Burberry, Givenchy, and Ralph Lauren. On its web site, Lojas Renner listed the following departments: clothing and accessories, cosmetics, perfumes, shoes, intimate apparel, beach and surf, sports, and watches.

A new hybrid credit card, developed in collaboration with Visa and MasterCard, was scheduled for introduction at the beginning of 2010. Furthermore, Lojas Renner had asked Brazil's central bank for permission to open a finance company during 2010. Aberdeen Asset Management plc held 16 percent of the shares of common stock of Lojas Renner at the end of 2008.

Robert Halasz

PRINCIPAL SUBSIDIARIES

Dromegon Participações Ltda.; Renner Administradora de Cartões Ltda.

PRINCIPAL COMPETITORS

C&A Modas Ltda.; Lojas Riochuelo S.A.

FURTHER READING

Caplen, Brian, "Riding with the Gaucho," *Euromoney,* October 1999, p. 38.

Cordioli, Andrea, "Renner anda mais rápido segundo o director-presidente do grupo," *Jornal do Commercio,* May 2, 2007.

———, "Renner mira novas compras de olho na baixa renda," *Jornal do Commercio,* July 29, 2009.

"JC Penney's Irregular Brazilian Fit," *Business Latin America,* May 24, 2004, p. 7.

Johnson, Tom, "Look Who's in Control Now," *Institutional Investor,* December 2006.

Jordan, Miriam, "Penney Blends *Two* Business Cultures," *Wall Street Journal,* April 5, 2001, p. A15.

Koike, Beth, "Renner planeja operação on-line para vender perfumes e relógios," *Valor Econômico,* July 3, 2009.

Mano, Cristiane, "A ditadura da moda," *Exame,* October 16, 2002, pp. 50–52.

Naiditch, Suzana, "A JCPenney chegou," *Exame,* December 16, 1998, p. 20.

———, "A JCPenney na bolsa," *Exame,* May 25, 2005, p. 54.

———, "O dono nem sempre faz falta," *Exame,* December 6, 2006, pp. 80–81.

———, "O xodó das bolsas quer dar o troco," *Exame,* December 6, 1995, pp. 59–60.

Neder, Vinicius, "Dispersão do control acionário aumenta poder du administração pode reduzir fiscalização sobre ela," *Jornal do Commercio,* March 13, 2006.

Onaga, Marcelo, "Empresas sem dono," *Exame,* February 1, 2006, pp. 56–57.

Maïsadour S.C.A.

Route de St. Sever
Haut Mauco, F-40280
France
Telephone: (33 05 58) 05 84 84
Fax: (33 05 58) 05 84 99
Web site: http://www.maisadour.com

Cooperative Company
Incorporated: 1973
Employees: 3,200
Sales: EUR 895 million ($1.15 billion) (2008)
NAICS: 424910 Farm Supplies Merchant Wholesalers; 111140 Wheat Farming; 111150 Corn Farming; 111219 Other Vegetable (Except Potato) and Melon Farming; 111998 All Other Miscellaneous Crop Farming; 112990 All Other Animal Production; 424510 Grain and Field Bean Merchant Wholesalers

■ ■ ■

Maïsadour S.C.A. is a leading, integrated agro-industrial company focused on the southwest region of France. Maïsadour has built up a fully integrated network of businesses with interests spanning the full range of food production, from seeds to cereals and vegetable production to processed foods to distribution. The company operates along two broad business lines, Upstream, including Cereals Production and Agricultural Supplies, Seeds, Vegetables, Animal Production, and Animal Nutrition; and Downstream, including Gastronomic Products of the southwest region and its wholesale and retail distribution operations. The group's upstream operations account for 57 percent of annual revenues, which topped EUR 895 million ($1.15 billion) in 2008.

The group's brands include Ovalie agricultural and crop protection products; Maïsadour Semences, an internationally operating seed producer; Primland fresh vegetable production; the Maïsadour chain of 38 retail gardening centers; and Delpeyrat, the leading producer of southwest region prepared foods, including foie gras, hams, and other processed and ready-to-eat products under the Delpeyrat, Montagne Noir and other brands. The company also operates vegetable processing partnerships with Bonduelle for canned vegetables and Ardo for frozen vegetables. Maïsadour has also developed a network of foreign subsidiaries, in Belgium, Germany, Hungary, Italy, Morocco, Poland, Portugal, Romania, Russia, Spain, and Ukraine. Founded in 1936, Maïsadour remains wholly owned by its farmer members. The company is led by president Michel Prugue.

FROM WHEAT TO CORN AT MID-CENTURY

Despite its name, Groupe Coopératif Maïsadour started off as a wheat farmers' cooperative, Coopérative de Blé des Landes, in the Landes region along France's southwest coast. That cooperatives's extension into other cereals and grains came in the postwar period, as the French government encouraged the use of newly developing intensive agricultural techniques. Among the government's objectives was the stimulation of industrial livestock production. In order to fulfill this objective, the government encouraged large swaths of French farmers to convert their large areas of farmland to the production of corn and other grains. In response to the new diversity of crops, the Landes cooperative changed its name to Coopérative des Cérales des Landes.

Like many of France's large-scale farming cooperatives, the Landes cooperative began diversifying its operations in the postwar period. Starting in 1959, the company began investing in agricultural supplies to provide fertilizers, crop protection products, and the equipment and machinery needed by both its own network of farmers and others.

The Landes cooperative's diversification effort continued into the late 1960s, when it opened its first agricultural supplies center, called LISA, for Libre-Services Agricoles. These centers catered largely to the professional farming and gardening markets. In 1973, the cooperative launched a food processing business as well.

BECOMING MAÏSADOUR IN 1973

The extension of the group's activities beyond farming led the cooperative to adopt a new name, Maïsadour, in 1973. This name also featured a new retail format inaugurated by the company in the late 1970s, a chain of consumer-oriented retail gardening centers called Maïsadour. By the end of the 1970s, the company operated 18 Maïsadour stores, all located in the Landes region.

Also during the 1970s, the group developed its own seed production subsidiary. This division quickly grew into a major European seed producer. By the turn of the century, Maïsadour Semences had added subsidiaries in Portugal and Italy, and claimed the Western European leadership in the production of maize and sunflower seeds.

Maïsadour began branching out into vegetable production in the 1980s. This activity began, appropriately enough, with the development of the cooperative's own sweet corn production line in 1983. Maïsadour then began marketing its corn under the Le

Valdour brand in partnership with the Avril Group. In 1988, the company deepened its involvement in the vegetable sector, creating a fresh vegetables production line in Hern. That unit launched operations with carrots before adding other vegetable varieties.

DIVERSIFYING IN THE NINETIES

Into the 1990s, the group added its own animal feed operation, buying Société Descal. Maïsadour also extended its vegetable operations, adding a frozen vegetable unit, Aquitaine Légumes Surgelés. That business operated in partnership with Belgium-based Ardorvries, distributing its products under the Ardo brand.

Maïsadour continued to seek new extensions to its operations as it developed into a diversified and vertically integrated agro-industrial group. The company entered animal production in 1993 when it came to the rescue of struggling poultry products group Les Fermiers Landais. The purchase of that company, in partnership with Unigrains and Arrivé, gave Maïsadour control of 40 percent of Les Fermiers Landais. Maïsadour also acquired the right to first refusal in the event Arrivé, which later acquired 60 percent of Les Fermiers Landais, decided to sell its share.

Following the rescue of Les Fermiers Landais, Maïsadour launched its own poultry farming business in 1994. The company also began investing in one of the southwest region's most well-known traditional foods, foie gras, acquiring the Sarrade foie gras brand.

During the 1990s, Maïsadour's distribution operations continued their own evolution. The company reoriented all of its retail operations into the more consumer-oriented Maïsadour format. At the same time, Maïsadour began extending its retail business beyond the Landes region for the first time, opening stores in other southwest departments, including the Gironde, Gers, and Pyrénées-Atlantiques. Into the next century, the Maïsadour chain grew to 38 locations. At the same time, the company added its first retail lawnmower and gardening equipment centers under the Vert Loisirs name.

ADDING FOOD PROCESSING IN 1998

Maïsadour's next major diversification move came in 1998, when the company acquired regional foods producer Delpeyrat, a major producer of foie gras. Delpeyrat had been founded in 1890 in Sarlat, in the Perigord region, and developed a range of regional specialties, including foie gras and confit de canard. Delpeyrat moved its operations to the Landes region,

KEY DATES

1936: A group of wheat farmers in the French southwest form the Coopérative de Blé des Landes.

1948: The cooperative changes its name to Coopérative des Cérales des Landes as its farmers begin to emphasize corn production.

1959: The cooperative begins to diversify, adding agricultural supply operations.

1969: The cooperative opens its first agricultural and garden supply and equipment center, LISA.

1973: The cooperative changes its name to Maïsadour.

1983: The company creates a sweet corn packaging joint venture, Le Valdour.

1990: Maïsadour acquires animal nutrition group Descal.

1993: Maïsadour acquires 40 percent of poultry products group Les Fermiers Landais and launches poultry farming operations.

1998: Maïsadour acquires Delpeyrat, a leading foie gras producer.

2007: Delpeyrat acquires Montagne Noir, producer of cured meats.

2009: Delpeyrat announces intention to acquire full control of Les Fermiers Landais and launches a bid to acquire the Marie processed foods brand.

which by then accounted for more than 30 percent of France's total foie gras production. Under Maïsadour, Delpeyrat was merged with Sarrade, becoming France's number two foie gras producer.

Delpeyrat struggled somewhat into the first decade of the 2000s, however, facing intense competition from the number one player, Labeyrie, and from smaller foie gras producers as well. The company shut down its remaining operations in Sarlat, transferring all of its business to the Landes region, spending EUR 15 million renovating its processing facility in Saint Pierre du Mont. Maïsadour was forced to come to Delpeyrat's aid that year, injecting EUR 7.6 million into the food processing operations. A collapse in the foie gras market in 2003 brought Delpeyrat into new difficulties; this time Maïsadour pumped EUR 24 million into the company.

This latest capital injection helped Delpeyrat turn the corner. By 2005, the company had launched a new expansion drive, buying Le Canard du Midi that year. The following year, Delpeyrat launched a new fresh-cooked ready meal operation, called Delpeyrat Traiteur. As part of that effort, the company acquired Agen-based Le Magicien Vert that year. The following year, Delpeyrat extended its product range with Montagne Noir, the leading producer of Bayonne ham, as well as cured sausage products, from Spain's Campofrio group. Maïsadour also boosted its presence in the market for duck and goose products through the creation of the joint venture MVVH SA, in partnership with Vivadour and Val de Sevre Holding. Maïsadour's stake in MVVH stood at 86 percent.

SOUTHWEST AGRO-FOOD LEADER IN THE NEW CENTURY

Maïsadour continued building up its Delpeyrat subsidiary into the end of the decade, adding two new companies, Muller and Chevallier in 2008. Maïsadour, which had established a number of subsidiaries in other European markets, also saw Delpeyrat as its vehicle for expansion farther abroad.

At the beginning of 2008, for example, the company opened a production and distribution subsidiary in China, to supply Delpeyrat branded foie gras and other products in time for that summer's Olympic Games in Beijing. In October 2008, the company acquired, through MVVH, Excel, a France-based foie gras producer that held the market leadership in Canada. MVVH also expanded its cured meats operations, buying another Bayonne ham brand, Chevallier.

Elsewhere, the cooperatives' other business units grew strongly as well. In 2005, the company teamed up with Vivadour, a Gers-based cooperative controlled by Maïsadour, and Euralis to enter a canned sweet corn partnership with Bonduelle, one of France's leading canned and frozen vegetable producers. The company also teamed up with Vivadour to form Ovalie Agrofourniture to supply crop protection and other agricultural products. Then in 2008, Maïsadour, Vivadour and another company, Gascoval, merged their animal nutrition operations together to form Sud-Ouest Aliment.

Maïsadour closed out 2008 with sales of EUR 895 million ($1.15 billion), with plans to top the EUR 1 billion mark before the end of 2009. Toward this end, the company continued to seek new acquisitions, particularly in the fast-growing processed foods sector. In June 2009, the company joined with French frozen fish leader Findus to launch a buyout offer for Marie, a leading prepared foods brand in France owned by U.K.-based Uniq. The addition of the Marie line would transform Delpeyrat into one of France's leading ready-meal producers.

While awaiting that decision, Maïsadour had already prepared its next expansion move. At the beginning of the summer of 2009, French poultry products leader LDC announced its decision to acquire Arrivé, by then number four on the market. The acquisition excluded, however, Les Fermiers Landais, allowing Maïsadour to exercise its right to acquire the company. The company announced it intended to do this in August 2009, while suggesting it would then seek a distribution partnership with LDC. The addition of Les Fermiers Landais would help solidify Maïsadour's position as the leading agro-industrial player in the French southwest region.

M. L. Cohen

PRINCIPAL SUBSIDIARIES

A.G.A. SAAT (Germany); Agralia; Agrar Semillas (Spain); Delpeyrat SA; Duran Cereales; Fermiers Landais; Maïsadour Belgium; Maïsadour Deutschland; Maïsadour Hongrie; Maïsadour Maroc (Morocco); Maïsadour Polska; Maïsadour Romania; Maïsadour Russia; Maïsadour Semences SA; Maïsadour Sementes (Portugal); Maïsadour Semsnces (Italy); Maïsadour Ukraina; Maisica; Nutricia; Soleal; Sud-Ouest Aliment; Unio.

PRINCIPAL DIVISIONS

Animal Nutrition; Distribution; Grains-Agro Supplies; Regional Food Processing and Distribution; Seeds; Vegetables.

PRINCIPAL COMPETITORS

Union InVivo; Terrena S.C.A.; Fenaco; Provimi S.A.; Société Coopérative Agricole et Agro-Alimentaire S.C.A.; Centrale Coopérative Agricole Bretonne S.C.A.; Union Régionale de Coopératives Agricoles; Groupe Limagrain Holding S.A.

FURTHER READING

Broustet, Bernard, "Maïsadour Recapitalise Sa Filiale Delpeyrat," *Les Echos,* October 2003, p. 22.

Cougard, Marie-Josée, "Le Duo Delpeyrat-Findus sur les Rangs pour Acheter Marie," *Les Echos,* June 23, 2009.

"French Delpeyrat Buys Loeul et Piriot's Catering Business," *ADP News France,* August 20, 2009.

"French Maïsadour Aims to Gain Full Control of Fermier Landais," *ADP News France,* August 14, 2009.

"Holding Giant for French Foie Gras Producers," *Europe Intelligence Wire,* January 26, 2005.

"Maïsadour ne Cesse de Grossir," *Points de Vente,* November 20, 2006.

"Maïsadour Veut Récupérer Fermier Landais," *La Tribune,* August 14, 2009.

"Maïsadour Vise le Milliard d'Euros de Ventes Cette Année," *Les Echos,* October 8, 2008.

Maréchal, Caroline, "Maïsadour, le Sud-Ouest d'Abord," *Points de Vente,* October 13, 2008.

Manna Pro Products, LLC

———————————■———————————

707 Spirit 40 Park Drive, Suite 150
Chesterfield, Missouri 63005
U.S.A.
Telephone: (636) 681-1700
Toll Free: (800) 690-9908
Fax: (636) 681-1799
Web site: http://www.mannapro.com

Private Company
Incorporated: 1985
Employees: 210
Sales: $85 million (2008 est.)
NAICS: 311111 Dog and Cat Food Manufacturing;
    311119 Other Animal Food Manufacturing

■ ■ ■

Manna Pro Products, LLC, is a privately held animal nutrition and animal health products company based in Chesterfield, Missouri, near St. Louis, that caters largely to "lifestyle farmer customers" or people who farm as a hobby or appreciate rural styling. The company's signature product is Calf-Manna, a concentrated supplement formulated for a variety of species, including horses, cattle, rabbits, and hogs. Manna Pro also serves the equine market through a diverse line of other supplements, feeds, and treats, as well as stall refresher, odor neutralizer, and fly control products. Manna Pro's cattle products include feed, supplements, and such specialty products as calf milk replacer. In addition, Manna Pro offers rabbit feed and supplements; goat feed, supplements, and dewormer; poultry feed, grit,

oyster shells for calcium, and conditioner supplements; and a broad range of products specifically formulated for young animals. Manna Pro also offers cat and dog foods, sold under the Hearty and Country Cousin labels.

The company runs a decentralized operation. Plants and distribution facilities, essentially run as independent profit centers serving different regions of the country, are strategically located in California, Colorado, Florida, Georgia, Kansas, Ohio, and Pennsylvania. They produce pelleted and textured feeds and pressed blocks, as well as supplements, although one plant might specialize in a particular product that it provides for sale to other regional operations. Manna Pro products are sold through a network of more than 2,500 feed dealers and more than 4,000 retail stores in the United States, Canada, Mexico, Japan, and several European countries.

ORIGINS IN EVAPORATED MILK

Manna Pro grew out of the Carnation Company Milling Division. The well-known Carnation evaporated milk brand was developed by the Pacific Coast Condensed Milk Company of Kent, Washington, bought out of bankruptcy in 1899 by grocer Elbridge Amos Stuart and a business partner who sold out a short time later. The evaporation process was new and Stuart believed important because it provided sanitary milk at a time when the freshness of milk was often questionable. He found a ready market in prospectors who at the time were heading to Alaska for the Yukon gold rush and looking for reliable provisions. In 1907, in seeking out the perfect name for the product, Stuart settled on "Carnation," which he had originally stumbled across as a cigar brand.

A farmer's son, Stuart was not merely interested in developing a memorable brand, he was well aware that in order to sell a quality milk product it was important to ensure the health of the cows producing it. To this end, he provided his supplying dairy farmers with purebred bulls to improve the genetics of their herds and increase milk production. He also took care to provide the cows with proper nutrition. Stuart's focus on good treatment of the dairy herd also led to one of the most recognizable taglines in advertising history: "Carnation Condensed Milk, the milk from contented cows."

The focus on quality feed led to the establishment of a milling division. In 1929 Carnation acquired the Albers Brothers' Milling Company, which in addition to animal feed produced cornmeal and oatmeal. The division also grew through the acquisition of Lancaster, Pennsylvania-based John W. Eshelman & Sons, which had been established in 1842, making it the oldest animal feed company in the country. In 1931 the Carnation Company Milling Division developed the first dry pelleted calf feed in the United States, part of the company's effort to create a nutritional feed to further enhance the health of dairy cows. The new product was named Calf-Manna. While the development of calves was indeed improved with the feed, it was soon discovered that Calf-Manna was also an ideal supplement for lactating cows. Moreover, Calf-Manna proved to be an effective supplement for beef cattle, as well as horses, swine, deer, rabbits, and poultry. In time, Calf-Manna would be fed more to horses than any other animal. Because of its widespread appeal, Calf-Manna became the signature product of the Carnation Company Milling Division.

MANNA PRO PURCHASES MILLING DIVISION

Stuart died in 1944 and his family maintained control of Carnation for the next 40 years. In addition to evaporated milk the company developed the popular Friskies pet food line and Contadina tomato products.

In November 1983, Dwight L. Stuart, a descendant of the founder, resigned as president due to health reasons, and in early 1984 decided to sell his stock in the company. Word spread in the investment community, leading to Swiss food conglomerate Nestlé S.A. expressing an interest in buying the entire company. The timing and fit were right, and by the fall of 1984 Nestlé reached an agreement to acquire the Carnation Company for about $3 billion.

The milling division was not considered a core unit for Carnation's new owners and in May 1985 Nestlé announced that it was for sale. In that same year, a group of former Carnation executives formed Manna Pro Products, LLC, to acquire the milling division, the name drawn from the unit's flagship Calf-Manna product. In February 1986 the $35.5 million purchase was completed and Manna Pro became an independent, privately held company based in Los Angeles. It consisted of 11 mills on the mainland of the United States as well as a Hawaii operation, originally called Honolulu Milling and acquired by Carnation's Albers unit in 1956. The Hawaii operation manufactured animal feed and also included a grain elevator and acted as both a retail and wholesale farm supply distributor, although the core of the business was its bulk feed business.

By the end of the 1980s Manna Pro decided to move away from bulk feed in favor of higher margin, value-added specialized bagged products. As a result, in 1989 the company decided to sell the Hawaii division as well as a milling unit in Portland, Oregon, which was also geared toward bulk feed. In January 1990 the sale of the Portland business was completed, followed a month later by the sale of the Hawaii division. Manna Pro then consisted of eight feed mills strategically located across the country at York, Pennsylvania; Tampa, Florida; Chamblee, Georgia; Circleville, Ohio; Kansas City, Kansas; Chilton, Wisconsin; Denver, Colorado; and Fresno, California.

KANSAS PUBLIC EMPLOYEES RETIREMENT SYSTEM GAINS MAJORITY CONTROL

Later in 1990 Manna Pro moved its headquarters from Los Angeles to Clayton, Missouri, near St. Louis. It was a more central location than Los Angeles for the type of business in which Manna Pro was involved. Moreover, the company president, L. R. Chapman, lived there. Chapman had run a management consulting firm in Clayton, joining Manna Pro in 1988. Also in 1990, the Kansas Public Employees Retirement System acquired a controlling interest in Manna Pro, taking a 70 percent stake.

KEY DATES

1899: Grocer Elbridge Amos Stuart enters evaporated milk business.
1929: Carnation acquires Albers Brothers' Milling Company.
1931: Carnation introduces Calf-Manna.
1984: Nestlé S.A. reaches an agreement to acquire the Carnation Company for about $3 billion.
1985: A group of former Carnation executives form Manna Pro Products, LLC.
1986: Manna Pro acquires Carnation Company Milling Division from Nestlé.
1990: Kansas Public Employees Retirement System acquires controlling stake in Manna Pro.
1997: Andrew Bresler is named chief executive.
2004: Manna Pro executives buy out Kansas Public Employees Retirement System.
2006: Group of St. Louis investors acquires company.
2008: Bresler retires as CEO.

Since breaking away from Carnation, Manna Pro had pursued a decentralized approach, allowing each milling unit to act independently to better serve its section of the country. The strategy began to pay off in the 1990s. Initially considered a disappointing performer for the Kansas Public Employees Retirement System, Manna Pro in 1994 generated record profits. The Kansas City mill, for example, had been losing money, but the general manager was given the latitude to turn around the business. "I basically run a company," general manager Robert Wagner told the *Kansas City Star* in explaining his authority. "The mission is turning a profit for our stockholders and turning out a quality product for our customers."

To better serve the midwest market, the plant invested $750,00 in an expansion in the early 1990s, doubling warehouse capacity and increasing the mill's pelleted feed capacity by 60 percent with the installation of a new pelleting system. The operation was then robust enough that the Chilton operation became superfluous and was closed, leaving seven mill locations to supply the United States as well as Canada and other foreign markets.

In the 1990s Manna Pro continued to pursue more profitable value-added products, eschewing commodity grain products that were purely price driven in the marketplace and, as a result, low in margin. In keeping with this strategy, in November 1998 Manna Pro unveiled a comprehensive horse feeding system branded the Super Horse program, intended to spur the use of a variety of Manna Pro products. In essence, the feeding program suggested a menu of feeds and supplements from which owners could pick, depending on the life stage and other needs of their horses. Products in the program contained Calf-Manna and other supplements.

NEW CEO HIRED

In 1997 Andrew Bresler was named Manna Pro's chief executive officer. A veteran from pet food giant Ralston Purina Company, he had served as the director of marketing for Ralcorp Holdings after Ralston spun off the business in the 1990s. Manna Pro closed the decade posting annual sales of $62 million in 1999. A year later an agreement was reached to sell the company to a Boston-based private-equity fund, Capital Resource Partners, which planned to combine Manna Pro with Dalton, Ohio-based Buckeye Nutrition, a 90-year-old maker of animal feeds with about half the annual sales of Manna Pro, to create a new company. The deal was slated to close in January 2001, but negotiations fell apart over undisclosed issues and the deal was called off.

The acquisition offer from Capital Resource Partners had been unsolicited, and Manna Pro had little difficulty in carrying on as an independent business. In the new century the company furthered its move toward the value-added realm, each year introducing ten or more new specialty products, helping to offset a decline in its traditional feed business. Sales dipped to $59 million in 2001 but the mix began to shift. About 40 percent of the company's products were then intended for small animals. Sold under the Small World, Hearty, and Country Cousin labels, the dog, cat, and other animal foods were sold at such retailers as Wal-Mart and PetSmart. Annual sales fell further to $58 million in 2003.

OWNERSHIP CHANGES

In 2004, 22 Manna Pro executives led by Bresler bought out Kansas Public Employees Retirement System in a stock purchase arrangement that was expected to be completed within three years. No significant changes took place within the company, but revenues began to rebound in 2004, totaling $59.9 million. A year later they reached $60.7 million. The introduction of scores of value-added products bore fruit, as revenues surged 18 percent to $71.8 million in 2006. Also in 2006 Manna Pro's manager-owners sold the company to four unnamed private investors from the St. Louis area. One of them, Edward Ryan, became known because he took on the role of chairman of the board.

More new products were introduced in 2007, such as a daily horse supplement called Max-E-Glo, which helped to drive sales to $77 million in 2007. Price increases in wheat, corn, and soybeans that were passed on to customers were another factor in higher sales. The cost of raw materials remained high in 2008, again resulting in higher product prices that played a role in the 10.4 percent increase in Manna Pro revenues to $85 million for the year. New products such as Apple Blasts and Carrot Blasts expanded the company's horse snack line, also adding to the bottom line. Given the spike in wheat, corn, and soybean prices, the emphasis on this type of value-added products was key to keeping Manna Pro profitable.

Bresler retired as CEO at the end of 2008 after 11 years at the helm. He was replaced by 42-year-old John Howe, who had been with the company for the past seven years after serving as vice-president of national accounts for Spectrum Brands. He also had eight years of experience in sales and customer marketing with Ralston Purina. In 2008 he was named Manna Pro's president as Bresler began to groom him as his successor. He was taking over a company that in offering value-added products that catered to the lifestyle farmer market had found a profitable niche. There was every reason to expect Manna Pro to enjoy success in this approach in the foreseeable future.

Ed Dinger

PRINCIPAL COMPETITORS

Animal Health International, Inc.; Farnam Companies, Inc.; MWI Veterinary Supply, Inc.

FURTHER READING

Chang, Diane, "Manna Pro Corp., #144," *Hawaii Business,* August 1987, p. 121.

"Clayton to Get Manna Pro," *St. Louis Post-Dispatch,* April 24, 1990, p. 5C.

Desloge, Rick, "Buckeye Nutrition Scraps Plan to Buy Manna Pro," *St. Louis Business Journal,* January 26, 2001, p. 6A.

———, "Howe Taking Reins of Manna Pro Expansion," *St. Louis Business Journal,* August 11, 2008.

———, "Manna Pro Sells Animal Feed Business to Capital Resource Partners of Boston," *St. Louis Business Journal,* October 2, 2000, p. 1.

Everly, Steve, "Robert Wagner Has Turned Fortunes Around at Manna Pro in KCK," *Kansas City Star,* April 11, 1995, p. D16.

Forest, Stephanie A., "Manna Pro Selling Off Its Hawaii Operations," *Pacific Business News,* November 6, 1989, p. 1.

Long, Victoria Sizemore, "Expansion of Plant Unveiled," *Kansas City Star,* September 3, 1994, p. B1.

"Manna Pro's Managers Buy Out Company," *St. Louis Business Journal,* September 1, 2004.

Sterngold, James, "Nestlé Planning to Pay $3 Billion to Acquire Carnation Company," *New York Times,* September 4, 1984.

Marisol S.A.

Rua Bernardo Dorndusch 1300
Jaraguá do Sul, Santa Catarina 89256-901
Brazil
Telephone: (55 47) 3372-6013
Fax: (55 47) 3372-6144
Web site: http://www.marisolsa.com.br

Public Company
Founded: 1964
Employees: 6,293
Sales: BRL 452.9 million ($246.14 million) (2008)
Stock Exchanges: São Paulo
Ticker Symbol: MRSL
NAICS: 315228 Men's and Boys' Cut and Sew Other Outwear Manufacturing; 315291 Infants' Cut and Sew Apparel Manufacturing; 315999 Other Apparel Accessories and Other Apparel Manufacturing; 316219 Other Footwear Manufacturing; 551112 Offices of Other Holding Companies

■ ■ ■

Marisol S.A. is a holding company that, through its subsidiaries, is engaged in the manufacture of yarn, the production of textiles, and the retail sale of casual wear and intimate apparel. It also sells such other textile products as bed linens, tablecloths, and bath towels. Marisol also sells shoes. The company is especially strong in children's wear and has the capacity to produce 12 million pieces of children's clothing and 2 million pairs of children's shoes each year. It has a number of exclusive franchises and an international market, with subsidiaries in Italy and Mexico.

THE FIRST THREE DECADES: 1964–89

Marisol was founded in 1964 by Pedro Donini to make beach hats, choosing the Marisol name as a combination of sea (*mar*) and sun (*sol*). With the addition of a small knitwear factory in 1968, it became a textile firm. Production moved to a larger site in its home town, Jaraguá do Sul, in 1975. Its corporate name, until 2000, was Marisol S.A. Indústria do Vestuário.

Marisol struggled through the 1970s, a decade in which dozens of Brazilian textile firms failed. However, it buttressed its finances by taking in two partners and went public in 1974. This enabled the firm to buy capital goods allowing it to finish as well as manufacture its goods in Jaraguá do Sul. The company also employed some 400 workers in eight nearby sewing units.

At the same time Marisol found new markets, producing knitwear for children, T-shirts, and shorts. In 1982 the firm's production rose by almost 80 percent, and its number of employees almost tripled. Sales agencies were opened in seven states, and in 1983 the number of points of sale for Marisol products rose from 5,000 to 13,000. Some 75 percent of its production was destined for youngsters below the age of 14.

RESTRUCTURING THE ENTERPRISE: 1990–93

The situation changed at the end of the 1980s, as Brazilian clothing manufacturers began to feel the effects of Asian competition. Marisol's revenues fell from $124.6 million in 1990 to only $66.9 million in 1992.

Donini held 44 percent of Marisol's stock in 1991, when a Marisol shareholder with 23 percent of the voting capital decided to sell his stock. This threatened Donini's control of the firm, because Malwee Malhas Ltda., a competitor of Marisol, held one-third of its shares. Donini then persuaded his younger brother Vicente, an executive at Weg S.A., the largest Latin American manufacturer of electric motors, to buy the shares on sale. Vicente became vice president of Marisol and was charged with turning the company around.

There was much to do. Production was in nine factories, each with its own administration. Employees not directly tied to production composed 40 percent of the total. Donini cut employment by one-quarter, reduced the number of plants to six, and contracted out nonproductive activities. He also eliminated two company brands that were performing poorly. The reduction in expenses allowed Marisol to cut its prices, which were too high for the market. As a result, revenues increased by almost 50 percent in 1993.

Around this time Donini came under the spell of an Israeli physicist named Eliyahu Goldratt, who had written a work of business management in the form of a novel. Applying Goldratt's theory of restrictions, Donini reduced the production cycle and inventories and began preparing Marisol to compete for sales outside Brazil.

The theory of restrictions, for Donini, enabled him to identify and eliminate bottlenecks that were strangling production. On the cutting floor, for example, production moved faster than the next stage, stamping, could deal with, so that every day unfinished clothing piled up, slowing the whole process. According to the theory of restrictions, this lack of coordination was the result of a failure to communicate. To resolve such matters, 30 technicians were dispatched to work at the side of the machines. By 1997 another Marisol plant had been closed.

The push to do more business abroad began in 1992, when Marisol formed an association with a Bolivian distributor to sell the company's products there door to door. This alliance brought in $500,000 in the next year and led to direct sales in Mexico and Argentina as

well. Exports, which came to $6.5 million in 1992, reached $9 million in 1993. Vicente bought his brother's shares in 1995 and assumed the presidency.

RETURNING TO PROSPERITY: 1994–99

Marisol had annual sales of $100 million in 1994 and 15,000 active accounts. It was exporting to 20 countries, especially Germany, Bolivia, and Paraguay. There were four brands: Marisol for children, teenagers, and men's sportswear; Criativa for women's fashions; Lilica Ripilica for girls; and Tigor T. Tigre for boys.

The company's raw material was undyed yarn, which was kept in stock only a week to control costs. Production was only to fill orders. Marisol was earmarking 10 percent of its profit to its employees. In addition to its medical plan, it offered financial assistance for night school and college courses and compensated its employees for child care.

Marisol reached $167.8 million in revenues in 1996, when it was the only major Brazilian clothing manufacturer whose profit exceeded 10 percent of sales. This allowed the company to reduce its debt by one-third. By that year seventh in sales, Marisol was chosen in 1997 by the business magazine *Exame* as the best company in the clothing sector.

Marisol opened a plant in Pacatuba, Ceará, in northeastern Brazil in 1998 for adult garments. This factory for Marisol's cheaper brands was willing, when it later hired more workers, to take on a large number of applicants without any experience whatever. Wages in Ceará were averaging about 30 to 40 percent lower than in São Paulo. The average age of the Pacatuba employees in 2006 was only 23, and 70 percent of them were women.

NEW REVENUE STREAMS: 2000–01

Marisol entered retailing in 2000 by opening three stores in shopping centers in Porto Alegre, the capital of the state of Rio Grande do Sul, where it sold children's clothing under its Lilica Ripilica and Tigor T. Tigre brands. Donini's objective was to open 60 franchised Lilica & Tigor stores in 37 cities of southern Brazil by 2003 and 240 before 2005. Thirty had opened by the end of 2002.

This endeavor did not please Marisol's existing retail customers. Donini sought to convince them that the company would not be competing with them but merely establishing a new sales channel for two of its brands. The retailers were invited to become franchisees of these company products. In any case, Marisol

KEY DATES

1964: Marisol founded to produce beach hats.
1968: Marisol founds a small knitwear factory to become a textile firm.
1974: Marisol takes in two partners and goes public.
1982: Marisol's output leaps by 80 percent, to 250 metric tons per month.
1992: The company's sales have fallen by almost half in two years.
1993: By cutting costs Marisol has been able to lower prices and raise sales by half.
1996: A double-digit profit margin has allowed Marisol to cut its debt by one-third.
2000: Marisol enters retailing by opening three stores and also begins making shoes.
2003: With ten stores in operation, Marisol is the largest clothing company in Lebanon.
2006: Marisol introduces One Store as a network for small retailers.
2008: The company is resurgent and expansion minded after two disappointing years.

proceeded with plans to reorient the enterprise toward more profitable lines of goods. Those lines considered dispensable were eliminated, with three factories closed and 800 workers laid off.

On the other hand, footwear was seen as a vehicle for profit. Marisol began making shoes for children, having bought two factories, and was offering complementary lines of shoes and accessories, such as socks, for children. Another shoe factory opened in 2001 in Novo Hamburgo, Rio Grande do Sul, an important manufacturing center for footwear.

MARISOL IN 2002–03

At the end of 2002, children's wear constituted 70 percent of Marisol's production. Knitwear accounted for 65 percent and socks and shoes, 35 percent. Knitwear production was vertically integrated, but woven garments were made from purchased finished fabrics. Six production sewing units, five of them within a 30-mile radius of Jaraguá do Sol, made garments for children. These units were composed of small teams paid by the piece. All of the company's products were aimed at the "A" and "B" socioeconomic levels (the top 10 percent of the population). Marisol had, for 13 consecutive years, won a prize regarded as the "Oscar" of retail business.

Despite Marisol's success, management had realized by 2001 that the company had almost saturated the domestic market and that for growth it had to look to exports, which in 2002 accounted for 5 percent of sales. Marisol entered a partnership in Lebanon that was given the right to sell the company's products throughout the Arab world. There were ten stores in Lebanon, making this partnership the nation's largest clothing company.

EXPANSION AND CONTRACTION

The Marisol brand for adults and Lilica Ripilica brand for children were by far the most popular company brands in 2005, when Marisol S.A. entered the youth market for the first time by acquiring Pakalolo, which had been a leader in teenage fashion in the 1980s and 1990s and at one time had fielded 240 outlets.

Marisol also pursued its export program, establishing, by late 2005, eight Lilica & Tigor stores in Lebanon and Portugal. Of its projected revenues of BRL 500 million ($200 million) in 2005, 8 percent was expected to come from foreign sales. The goal for 2010 was 20 percent. "Exclusive stores guarantee the visibility of our brands," Donini told Suzana Naiditch of *Exame* in 2005. "It is a way of keeping them from falling by the wayside." The alternative of turning over the company's products to foreign retailers carried the risk of neglect and competition from cheap Chinese goods.

By this time Giuliano Donini, Vicente's younger son, was playing a leading part in Marisol. Director of marketing since 2001, he had repositioned Lilica Ripilica in the marketplace to attract wealthier consumers and had taken the brand abroad. By late 2006 there were 130 franchised Lilica & Tigor units in Brazil and 15 in other countries. Among those opened in Europe was one on Milan's Spanish Steps, next to the wares of companies such as Prada S.p.A., and another in Madrid.

Also in 2006, Giuliano introduced One Store, a network to allow small retailers to compete with large chains by diversifying their mix of products, bargaining with suppliers, and improving management and communications. Participating retailers committed themselves to pay royalties of 5 percent on their sales, and half the stock in their stores was to consist of Marisol's eight brands. The goal was to have 40 member stores in the state of São Paulo by the end of the year and 400 in Brazil by 2010.

Donini also purchased 75 percent of Rosa Chá Studio Ltda., noted for its line of swimsuits, in 2006. This company had 18 owned and franchised stores for its goods and was turning out 350,000 units a year in Bom Retiro, São Paulo, and through contractors, but production from the latter was terminated and redirected to Jaraguá do Sul.

The long haired, bearded 31-year-old heir to the presidency challenged the appearance expected of a business executive. He scorned business attire, wearing faded jeans and sporting giant silver rings on his fingers. Nonetheless, he was favored over his older brother, Giorgio, who was the company's industrial director. "The older brother is in charge of a very important part of the business, but Giuliano has the type of personality that Marisol needs at this moment," an important customer told Naiditch for a 2006 article in *Exame*.

Giorgio, like his father, was enamored of a concept: in this case what was called "lean manufacturing" but resembled Goldratt's theory of restrictions. He had organized a team of specialists seeking to reduce the time needed to manufacture Marisol's products and thereby save the company money.

Both brothers had been carefully groomed for the job since 2001 by the U.S. consulting firm Keseberg & Partners and were considered equally competent. Giuliano had earned a master's degree in business administration in the United States and had served as a market analyst and an administrator of one of the shoe factories. When in Brazil, he spent three days a week in the company's office in São Paulo, putting in 14 hours a day. The other two working days were at its headquarters in Jaraguá do Sul.

Giuliano's rise to the top was interrupted in 2007, however, by his father's decision to restructure Marisol, closing some plants and eliminating some brands. Revenues had risen only 3 percent in 2006, and profits had remained stagnant at what was deemed a disappointing 6 percent of revenues. Ebitda (an acronym for profit before taxes, debt, depreciation, and amortization), regarded as the main indicator of operational efficiency, fell almost 40 percent. The results for 2007 were even worse. Revenues fell by more than 4 percent and profits to a minuscule BRL 9.5 million ($5 million). The One Store chain had only 17 outlets at the end of the year.

MARISOL IN 2008–09

Giuliano Donini assumed the presidency of Marisol in March 2008 and resumed the company's program of expansion. One Store grew markedly in size. Rosa Chá opened a small store and showroom in Manhattan. Marisol purchased the remainder of the shares in Rosa Chá and took a half-interest in BPK S.A., operator of a retail chain of 13 Blue Pink outlets for layettes and babies' articles. Donini's objective was to field 40 Blue Pink stores by the end of 2009, most of them franchised.

Marisol ended the year with a revenue gain of almost 8 percent over the 2007 total. The company's

net profit more than doubled, reaching BRL 21.3 million ($11.6 million). Ebitda more than doubled. Exports, however, came to less than 4 percent of the total.

Marisol was divided into three business units: consumer, premium, and luxury. Consumer consisted of lower-priced items sold in a large number of stores that carried many brands. This unit consisted of the Marisol, Pakalolo, and Babysol brands and the One Store network. Marisol was a brand of comfortable, colorful clothes and shoes for children through age 12. Pakalolo was aimed at youths seeking clothing with style, personality, and modernity. Babysol was a brand of clothing, shoes, and accessories for infants and children under three years of age. It also included a line of layettes and such items as baby bottles, pacifiers, and strollers. There was also a Babysol network of stores selling these items and directed to children up through age six.

The premium unit was focused on products of higher aggregate value and made with a higher standard of quality. Aimed at more demanding customers seeking up-to-date fashion, it included the Lilica Ripilica and Tigor T. Tigre brands and their franchised stores. Lilica Ripilica sought to dress children with delicacy, authenticity, and, above all, with the richest tendencies of children's fashion. Tigor T. Tigre's products were intended to be "cool" as well as fashionable. Lilica & Tigor was the name for franchised stores selling these brands exclusively.

The luxury unit consisted of brands directed at a demanding public seeking products that stood out from the commonplace, manufactured in small amounts and often characterized by artisanal details. These brands included Rosa Chá and Stereo. With the departure of Amir Slama, the previous Rosa Chá owner and designer, noted clothing stylist Alexandre Herchcovitch was given a two-year contract to be its creative leader. This brand was aimed at men as well as women aware of fashion as a form of expression. Stereo was a brand for faded jeanswear.

Marisol had, at the close of 2008, 147 franchised Lilica & Tigor stores in Brazil and 19 abroad, mostly in shopping centers, selling Lilica Ripilica and Tigor T. Tigre brand products exclusively. Marisol company products were also in more than 15,000 points of sale displaying similar products by many manufacturers. One Store had 80 outlets in 11 states and the federal district of Brasília. Rosa Chá had 23 franchised units in Brazil and three in other countries, including one in Miami. Abroad, Marisol's products were also available in Chile,

Colombia, Costa Rica, Italy, Peru, Portugal, and Spain. Marisol's plants were in Jaraguá do Sol, Novo Hamburgo, and Pacatuba. The company also maintained a studio in São Paulo.

Marisol's goal for 2009 was to expand and consolidate the company's three franchised networks, to acquire the remaining 50 percent of the Blue Pink network, and to make the company more agile and competitive. It foresaw investments of BRL 34.3 million in 2009, mainly using its own resources, to modernize its factories and bring information technology up to date. GFV Participações Ltda., which appeared to be a Donini family enterprise, owned 40 percent of Marisol's shares of common stock in 2008. Three pension and investment funds owned another 46 percent, with the remaining shares in the hands of the public at large.

Robert Halasz

PRINCIPAL OPERATING UNITS

Consumer; Luxury; Premium.

PRINCIPAL SUBSIDIARIES

Marisol Calçados Ltda.; Marisol Europe S.R.L. (Italy); Marisol Franchising Ltda.; Marisol Indústria Têxtil Ltda.; Marisol Indústria do Vestuário Ltda.; Marisol México, S.A. de C.V. (Mexico); Marisol Nordeste S.A.; OneService Serviços Comerciais Ltda.; Rosa Chá Studio Ltda.

PRINCIPAL COMPETITORS

Malwee Malhas Ltda.

FURTHER READING

Barone, Vanessa, "Grupo Marisol organiza rede para crescer no varejo," *Valor Econômico,* June 14, 2006.

Costa, Flávio, "Uma lição que dá lucros," *Exame,* July 6, 1994, pp. 71–72.

Des Marteau, Kathleen, "Brazil Building for the Future," *Bobbin,* March 1995, pp. 106, 108.

Furtado, Thais, "A vitória de quem cedo madruga," *Exame Melhores e Maiores,* July 1997, pp. 144, 146.

Gusmão, Marcos, "Educar para crescer," *Exame,* supplement, August 30, 2006, p. 133.

Jurgenfeld, Vanessa, "Com lucro maior, Marisol pode fazer aquisições," *Valor Econômico,* May 21, 2009, p. B4.

———, "Marisol controla Rosa Chá em nova empresa," *Valor Econômico,* April 6, 2006.

———, "Marisol prepara expansão da rede Blue Pink," *Valor Econômico,* November 27, 2008.

Lloyd, Brenda, "Brazilian Knitwear Companies Gear Up for Global Market," *Knitting Times,* February 1995, p. 39.

Naiditch, Suzana, "Da cabeça aos pés," *Exame,* March 7, 2001, pp. 88–90.

———, "Lojas em Nova York, Beirute e Lisboa," *Exame,* September 14, 2005, pp. 58–59.

———, "Por que a sucessão atrasou," *Exame,* March 12, 2008, pp. 80–82.

———, "Um presidente diferente," *Exame,* November 22, 2006, pp. 64–65.

Neves, Regina, "Pakalolo volta como PKL, de olho no novo público teen," *NoticiasFinancieras,* June 14, 2005, p. 1.

"Sem medo da recessão," *Exame,* January 4, 1987, p. 58.

Tait, Niki, "Profiles of Five Leading Textile and Apparel Companies in Brazil," *Textile Outlook International,* May/June 2003, pp. 155–75.

Meridian Industries Inc.

———■———

100 East Wisconsin Avenue, Suite 2750
Milwaukee, Wisconsin 53202-4110
U.S.A.
Telephone: (414) 224-0610
Fax: (414) 224-9544
Web site: http://www.meridiancompanies.com

Private Company
Incorporated: 1943 as Myron E. Schwartz Inc.
Employees: 1,100
Sales: $300 million (2008 est.)
NAICS: 313312 Textile and Fabric Finishing (Except Broadwoven Fabric) Mills

■ ■ ■

Milwaukee, Wisconsin-based Meridian Industries Inc. is a privately held diversified manufacturing concern with five operating companies: Aurora Specialty Textiles Group, Inc.; Kent Elastomer Products, Inc.; Kleen Test Products Corporation; Majilite Corporation; and Meridian Specialty Yarn Group, Inc. Aurora, which takes its name from the site of its headquarters (Aurora, Illinois) is a textile finisher, involved in the preparation, coating, dyeing, and technical finishing of woven as well as nonwoven fabrics. In effect, it is a one-stop shop for its customers. Aurora processed products are used for print media in T-shirts, pressure-sensitive adhesive tapes, and dyed and finished fabrics used in apparel, tote bags, bedding, and wall coverings. In addition to Aurora, the company maintains a plant in Travelers Rest, South Carolina. Also based in a city that provides its name,

Kent Elastomer Products of Kent, Ohio, produces low durometer tubing and dip-molded products used in the medical, dental, laboratory, industrial, food and beverage, and sports and recreation markets at three plant locations in Ohio. Kleen Test Products, Meridian's original business, is a major contract manufacturer of wet wipes and dryer sheets. The company's capabilities also include die cutting for the production of medical supplies, cosmetic and beauty products, and household cleaning products; jar and tube filling; coating and laminating for materials used to make gift wrap and paper plates; confectionary packaging; and specialty packing. Manufacturing is done at eight Wisconsin plants. Majilite Corporation is a Dracut, Massachusetts-based maker of specialty performance fabrics and coated substrates used to make athletic footwear, upholstery, wall coverings, and fashion accessories. Manufacturing is done at two plants in Massachusetts. The final Meridian operating company, Meridian Specialty Yarn Group, Inc., operates a pair of plants. The Valdese, North Carolina, facility specializes in package dyeing, while the Ranlo, North Carolina, plant is involved in novelty yarn spinning. Meridian is headed by Chief Executive Officer Bruce Eben Pindyck. He and his wife, Ellen, own the company, founded by her father.

KLEEN TEST FOUNDED: 1943

The original Meridian company, Kleen Test, was founded in Milwaukee in 1943 as a filter manufacturer by Myron Edward Schwartz and was originally named Myron E. Schwartz Inc. After he died in 1948, his wife took charge of the company. She then married Sidney

H. Rogovin, who ran the company while she raised their family for seven years. Upon Rogovin's death, she once again became president of Myron E. Schwartz Inc. It was in the late 1950s that Kleen Test Products, Inc., name was adopted.

Bruce Pindyck joined the family in 1968 when he married Mary Ellen Schwartz. Born in New York City in 1945, he was the son of Sylvester Pindyck, a well-known lawyer who specialized in immigration and made his name in the 1930s as a special assistant to the U.S. attorney general. At the time of his marriage, the 23-year-old Bruce Pindyck was a student at Columbia School of Law. Later in 1968, his father passed away as did his wife's mother. Ellen Pindyck and her sister inherited Kleen Test, but Pindyck and his wife were in no position to move to Milwaukee to be actively involved in the running of the business, although he became an officer and a board member. Responsibility for running Kleen Test was left to a general manager. Pindyck graduated from Columbia Law School in 1970, and a year later received a master's degree in business administration; his wife also earned a degree from Columbia Law School in 1973. While Ellen finished up her education, Bruce went to work at the law firm Olwine, Connelly, Chase, O'Donnell & Wehyer, where he stayed until 1980. Pindyck then became assistant general counsel for Peat, Marwick, Mitchell & Co., and in 1983, he became partner at Hollyer, Jones, Pindyck, Brady & Chira, serving as a securities litigator.

KENT LATEX ACQUIRED: 1979

While Bruce and Ellen Pindyck were pursuing their law careers in New York, their business interests in Milwaukee continued to evolve. Kleen Test began acquiring other companies, such as Majilite, which had been founded in Boston in the 1940s and in the 1970s relocated to South Lowell, Massachusetts. Kent Latex Products was acquired in 1979. It had been established in Ohio in 1960 to specialize in the manufacturing of dipped natural rubber latex tubing. The business enjoyed steady growth, leading to the building of a new plant in Winesburg, Ohio. Because of these additions, Meridian Industries was established in 1980 to house the growing stable of subsidiaries. By the early 1980s, the company was generating about $35 million in annual sales.

PINDYCK FAMILY TAKES CONTROL: 1984

In February 1984, Bruce and Ellen Pindyck bought out her sister's interest and gained complete control of Meridian Industries. A short time later, the company's president quit and the remaining manager asked Bruce Pindyck to assume control. Without taking a title, Pindyck attempted to run Meridian and continue to practice law, but it was simply too much work to handle. As a result, he quit Hollyer, Jones, and he and his family moved to Milwaukee, where he could devote all of his attention to Meridian.

Pindyck provided a great deal of latitude to managers running the subsidiaries, and he was more than willing to cede credit for success. "I want them to believe they're running their own businesses," he told *Business Journal-Milwaukee*. While he received daily reports from all Meridian subsidiaries and paid regular visits to all of the plants, he made no attempt to run any of the operations. Instead, he kept watch over the interests of the entire group, reluctant to take on debt and devoted to the idea of self-financing through cash flow. "If I have to spend $100,000 for a piece of machinery for Kleen Test," he provided as an example to *Business Journal-Milwaukee*, "I look to see if Meridian as a whole can afford to do that." Nevertheless, Pindyck was more than willing to invest in the growth of the subsidiaries. In 1988, Kent Latex added extrusion equipment to expand into soft, flexible, thermoplastic tubing. Pindyck also looked for opportunities to make complementary acquisitions. Aurora Bleachery, a company in operation for more than 100 years, was added. In 1990, Meridian acquired Belmont Dyers of Belmont, North Carolina, which was involved in package dyeing and winding for natural and synthetic yarn.

LABOR PROBLEM: 1990

Another key to the success of Meridian was the development of long-term relationships with major industrial customers as well as employees. In 1980, the Kleen Test operation had to contend with employees at the Brown Deer, Wisconsin, plant who voted to join the Amalgamated Clothing and Textile Workers Union of America. About 22 union supporters were subsequently terminated, leading to some picketing outside the plant. Kleen Test contested the union certification for two years, but according to Pindyck, the problems between the two sides were settled "amicably," and the Brown

KEY DATES

1943: Myron Schwartz founded Myron E. Schwartz Inc., later known as Kleen Test Products.
1948: Schwartz dies.
1979: Kent Latex Products acquired.
1980: Company takes the name Meridian Industries.
1984: Schwartz's daughter Ellen and her husband, Bruce Pindyck, buy company.
1990: Belmont Dyers acquired.
1998: Plant in Travelers Rest, South Carolina, acquired.
2001: Astro Dye works acquired.
2003: Belmont plant closed.
2004: Majilite expansion completed.

Deer plant was unionized in 1991. At the other Kleen Test plant in Port Washington, Wisconsin, hundreds of workers were laid off in 1991 after Kleen Test lost a major customer.

Despite the loss of business at Kleen Test and tough economic times at the start of the 1990s, Meridian's five subsidiaries combined to post sales of $127.4 million in 1992, and a year later sales were in the $140 million range. Meridian was also in the market for further acquisitions. In 1995, Kleen Test acquired a 70,000-square-foot plant in Milwaukee from W.H. Brady Co. Later in the decade, it invested in new equipment to take advantage of a surging lamination market. A new state-of-the-art coater/laminator was installed in 1998, allowing Kleen Test to add such capabilities as the lamination of metalized films to lightweight papers and board stock. Also in the 1990s, the company added to its mid-Atlantic operations by acquiring a pair of companies to complement Belmont, both of which produced dyed yarns: Franklin Dyed Yarn of Greenville, South Carolina, and Valdese Manufacturing of Valdese, North Carolina. In 1998, Aurora Bleachery acquired the Travelers Rest, South Carolina, plant of Kreiger Corporation, which a year earlier had filed for bankruptcy and suspended its operations. Also of note during the decade, Majilite moved its headquarters from Lowell to Dracut, Massachusetts, along with its dry warehouse and laboratory testing facilities.

In fiscal 1997, the year ending on October 31, Meridian posted sales in the $275 million range, placing it at No. 32 among Wisconsin's 100 largest private companies, according to the annual list compiled by ac-

counting firm Arthur Andersen. In explaining his success, Pindyck told the *Milwaukee Journal-Sentinel,* "I have a game plan. I want to continue what we've been doing, growing and nurturing this business." He also credited Meridian's executives, adding "I try to surround myself with talented people." Pindyck continued to grow Meridian into the new century while also pursuing a long-range plan of nurturing the next generation of leaders to ensure future continuity.

BELMONT PLANT CLOSES: 2003

At the start of the new century, Belmont Dyers, Franklin Dyed Yarn, and Valdese Manufacturing were brought together to form the Meridian Specialty Yarn Group (MSYG). In 2001, the subsidiary acquired Astro Dye Works, producer of space dyeing yarns and twisting novelty items at facilities located in Calhoun, Georgia. The marketplace was changing, however, as MSYG's business was adversely impacted by low-priced imported yarns. As a result, the unit in the spring of 2003 cut 70 jobs at the Belmont plant and another 56 at Valdese Manufacturing. Business was so poor that by the fall of 2003, Meridian decided to close the Belmont plant, moving its operations to Valdese. A dozen of the remaining 33 Belmont employees were able to transfer to Valdese as well. As part of Meridian, MSYG was strong enough to take advantage of poor conditions to make an acquisition in August 2004, when it bought the novelty yarn assets of Bessemer City, North Carolina-based Atlantic Spinners Inc. The deal greatly enhanced MSYG yarn design capabilities. The Atlantic Spinner personnel and other assets were then incorporated into the Valdese operation.

Kent Elastomer, in the meantime, acquired Precision Latex, Inc., a manufacturer of dip-molded tubing and custom-dipped products. Precision's rubber molding operations were then folded into Kent Elastomer. A year later, the company moved the operations to a new modern plant in Mogadore, Ohio. Kent Elastomer completed another acquisition in 2006, buying the dip-molded product line from Hospira, Inc. As a result, the company added synthetic polyisoprene to its line of nonlatex materials.

Other Meridian subsidiaries were looking to expand in the new century. In 2005, Kleen Test filed plans with the city of Port Washington to construct seven new buildings, altogether adding 700,000 square feet of space. The seven buildings were slated to open over the course of five to ten years. Aurora Specialty Textiles continued to operate out of its two plants and expanded its offerings in the new century to include the Deco-print line of printable textiles to supplement the company's already extensive range of fabrics and canvases. Majilite also enjoyed growing demand for its products. To keep pace, the company established a Commission Services Group in 2002. The company had outgrown its manufacturing space, and in 2002, Majilite made plans to move its manufacturing operations from a 48,000-square-foot space in Lowell to Dracut, where the company's headquarters was slated to expand by 57,000 square feet. The construction was completed in 2004, and the manufacturing operations relocated to Dracut. The expanded facility would also receive some acclaim in 2009 for installing a 400-kilowatt solar power system that included more than 2,800 solar panels on the roof, making it the largest building in Massachusetts with an installation of this kind.

Meridian was generating about $300 million in annual sales by 2009, ten times what the company posted when Bruce Pindyck took the helm. He was approaching retirement age. However, as long as he remained in charge, there was every reason to expect Meridian to adapt to changing conditions and continue to prosper.

Ed Dinger

PRINCIPAL SUBSIDIARIES

Aurora Specialty Textiles Group, Inc.; Kent Elastomer Products, Inc.; Kleen Test Products Corporation; Majilite Corporation; Meridian Specialty Yarn Group, Inc.

PRINCIPAL COMPETITORS

Georgia-Pacific LLC.; Kimberly-Clark Corporation; The Procter & Gamble Company.

FURTHER READING

Edquist, Peg Masterson, "Pindyck Pilots Meridian's Subsidiaries Like a Proud, Private Parent," *Business Journal–Milwaukee*, May 29, 1993.

Gunn, Erik, "Union Voting Sparks Battle at Kleen Test," *Milwaukee Journal*, April 2, 1990.

O'Brien, Matt, "Majilite to Expand Headquarters," *1590 Broadcaster* (Lowell, Mass.), June 13, 2002.

Pierman, Sue, "Meridian Industries Weaves a Fabric of Success," *Milwaukee Journal-Sentinel*, October 13, 1997, p. D3.

Shaughnessey, Dennis, "Pioneering Solar-Panel Agreement Lets Dracut Firm Manufacture Another Kind of Product—Clean Power," *Lowell (Mass.) Sun*, January 11, 2009.

Sussman, Lawrence, and Joel Dresang, "Kleen Test Plans Expansion in Port," *Milwaukee Journal-Sentinel*, May 24, 2005, p. D1.

MITRE Corporation

─────────■─────────

202 Burlington Road
Bedford, Massachusetts 01730-1420
U.S.A.
Telephone: (781) 271-2000
Fax: (781) 271-2271
Web site: http://www.mitre.org

Nonprofit Company
Incorporated: 1958
Employees: 7,000
Sales: $1.24 billion (2008)
NAICS: 541710 Research and Development in the Physical, Engineering, and Life Sciences; 541380 Testing Laboratories; 561210 Facilities Support Services; 928110 National Security

■ ■ ■

MITRE Corporation is a private, independent nonprofit organization that provides engineering and information technology services for government agencies. Its areas of expertise include: systems analysis; aviation systems, safety, and security; command and control; cybersecurity; enterprise systems engineering; global networking; healthcare technology; homeland security; intelligence, surveillance, and reconnaissance; and large-scale enterprise transformation. It manages four federally funded research and development centers (FFRDCs) that are sponsored by the Department of Defense, the Federal Aviation Administration (FAA), the Internal Revenue Service (IRS), the Department of Veterans Affairs (VA), and the Department of Homeland Security.

It maintains facilities in Bedford, Massachusetts, and McLean, Virginia, and has 60 sites across the globe. MITRE celebrated its 50th anniversary in 2008. The company was awarded the Secretary of Defense Medal for Outstanding Public Service that year.

AN ELECTRONIC SYSTEMS PIONEER

MITRE was formed in 1958 as a federally funded "think tank," with its staff detached from the Massachusetts Institute of Technology's Lincoln Laboratories, which had been established by the Pentagon in 1951. Some 480 laboratory personnel were transferred to the new organization, whose first task was to develop the nation's first automated, real-time air defense system for the U.S. Air Force, which had been unable to find a for-profit company to do the job. Later, in 1989, Charles S. Zrabet, president and chief executive officer at the time, recalled MITRE's beginnings: "They wanted a dedicated laboratory that had the multi-disciplines of radar, computers, and communications. It was a new technology, and there was no expertise for this anywhere."

In its early years MITRE played a vital role in helping design electronic systems that detected and tracked Soviet-bloc missiles and aircraft and intercepted communications. It played a major part in designing the hardened, underground North American Air Defense facilities intended to protect against a possible nuclear attack by enemy aircraft and/or ballistic missiles. In order to process and interpret information quickly for military purposes, MITRE, together with the Electronic

Systems Division (ESD) of the U.S. Air Force Systems Command, came to possess, by 1962, one of the most powerful computers in the world. The computer was an IBM 7030 that, including peripheral equipment, covered a space the equivalent of a basketball court. Also in 1962, MITRE and ESD sponsored the first congress of information system sciences ever held.

During the Vietnam War, MITRE endured criticism by opponents of the war for its role in developing a so-called electronic fence, composed mainly of acoustics and sensors, that was supposed to help pinpoint the movement of Vietcong and North Vietnamese forces into South Vietnam. Despite the unpopularity of the war and the doomsday scenarios of the Cold War era, Zrabet told a reporter in 1985 that in his many years at MITRE he could not remember a time when an employee left due to objections to the moral or political nature of the organization's work.

Not all of MITRE's work was related to the military, however. During the 1960s it began to work on systems used for civilian air-traffic control. As electronic command and control systems proliferated, in 1963 the organization established a Washington-area office in addition to its Bedford facility. This new office was later moved to McLean. Because the technology it developed for the military was also useful for civilian applications, MITRE helped civil agencies develop information systems for transportation, medicine, law enforcement, space exploration, and environmental remediation. In 1971, for example, it began developing a two-way, interactive cable-television system.

NEW PROJECTS AND GOALS

Throughout the 1970s and 1980s, MITRE continued to work on air defense and other command, control, communications, and intelligence (C3I) systems used by Department of Defense clients. C3I networks were frequently referred to as the brains or nervous systems of weaponry. They consisted of command centers on both the ground and in airplanes, the radar and satellites scanning the battlefield, and the communications equipment linking the other components. MITRE also

became heavily involved in satellite communications technology, and in the late 1980s was working on Millstar, a system designed to provide worldwide communications for the military which was not only invulnerable to enemy efforts to jam it, but also capable of surviving nuclear attack.

On the one hand, to preserve the credibility of the country's defense against nuclear attack, it was essential that the C3I systems function so that the military could counter any enemy first strike with a retaliatory attack. These systems had to be able to distinguish a real strike from, for example, blips on the radar screen that turned out to be geese. In addition, nuclear weapons sites had to be protected from entry by unauthorized personnel, which might include thieves or terrorists. Thus, during the 1970s a four-year research effort by MITRE and ESD scientists established automatic speech, handwriting, and fingerprint verification systems to screen all personnel and deny access to would-be intruders.

During the late 1980s MITRE was also taking part in projects to replace the federal telecommunications system, design a new computer system for the Securities and Exchange Commission, upgrade medical information systems for the National Institutes of Health, and store radiological images on computer tape rather than film for Georgetown Hospital. MITRE also designed the Federal Bureau of Investigation's (FBI) National Crime Information Center.

Military projects, however, remained MITRE's bread and butter. Its heyday was during the Reagan administration's buildup of the 1980s, when one of the military's highest priorities became improving command and control systems so that the United States retained the capacity to retaliate against a massive nuclear strike. By the end of the decade MITRE was exploring sensor technology to cope with radar-evading stealth aircraft.

MITRE's revenues doubled between 1980 and 1984, reaching $287 million by the end of that period, when the workforce rose to 5,000. The company actually outgrew its own facilities in Bedford and had to move its operations into several leased buildings. MITRE's revenues then rose to $463 million in 1988, when it had 5,800 employees and $62 million in a reserve fund. As the Cold War came to a close at the end of the decade, military spending began to decline and competition for contracts became fiercer. Commercial engineering firms argued that they could do MITRE's work at a lower cost. They complained about the organization's lack of public accountability, particularly its freedom from the federal government's competitive bidding process and its exemption from taxes. They also resented MITRE's power over for-profit companies in its capacity to help review proposals from such contractors and to monitor how well the work was carried out.

FAA AND MILITARY FOCUS

Amid the uncertainties of a new decade, MITRE continued to collaborate closely with the Air Force's (renamed) Electronic Systems Center (ESC) at Hanscom Air Force Base. In 1994 MITRE and ESC personnel were engaged in laboratory simulations intended to improve the capabilities of Joint-STARS aircraft to use both onboard and offboard sensors in providing a synthesized picture of the battlefield. Two years later, a journalist visiting the Air Force base received a demonstration of three-dimensional, virtual-reality imaging techniques that might be used to meet a variety of military needs. These ranged from allowing planners to configure an air command center in the field to using robotics to assist surgeons in performing simple operations from a remote site. The visualization lab also created a computer model of a section of Seoul, South Korea, in a 24-hour period as a demonstration of what could be done quickly to aid forces conducting a hostage rescue mission.

MITRE continued to count on steady work from the FAA. In 1993 this agency awarded the organization

a new three-year, $222 million contract to continue operating its Center for Advanced Aviation System Development (CAASD), which had been created in 1990, in McLean and to provide support for further development of the National Airspace System. MITRE also held contracts to help upgrade the federal government's telephone network and apply a Defense Department navigation system to commercial aviation. Meanwhile, MITRE offered its services to help the military clean up bases and was working with the FBI to improve the National Crime Information Center by, among other things, developing a system to send mug shots directly to police patrol cars.

About 70 percent of MITRE's work, however, remained in C3I applications for the military. As one of ten federally funded research and development centers scheduled to lose $100 million of $1.35 billion in government funds, the organization reacted by laying off 300 employees in October 1994. In response to objections raised by members of Congress and the Defense Department, MITRE also cut back on some of its federally funded expenses and canceled holiday parties for executives. It continued to give employees generous relocation allowances, however, and provided automobiles to company officers for personal use. In 1996 a government audit described $4.7 million of $5.3 million in management expenses incurred during fiscal 1994 as "unnecessary and in some cases extravagant."

MITRE disarmed its critics in January 1996 by divesting itself of $70 million worth of federal nonmilitary contracts. This work was spun off to Mitretek Systems Inc., a new nonprofit organization dedicated to research for nonmilitary federal agencies and state and local governments in such areas as environmental remediation and telecommunications. In 1998 MITRE established the IRS and the VA's FFRDC, the Center for Enterprise Modernization (CEM). The CEM worked to develop modern systems within the IRS and the VA, along with Department of Treasury, the Department of Health and Human Services, the U.S. Census Bureau, and the Federal Judiciary.

NEW CHALLENGES AND AN ANNIVERSARY

In April 2000, leadership at the company changed as Martin C. Faga was named president and CEO upon the retirement of Victor DeMarines. Shortly after Faga's appointment, MITRE and the FAA signed a new ten-year contract for the CAASD FFRDC, which had been established in 1990. MITRE also launched the MITRE Aviation Institute in 2001 and released its Collaborative Virtual Workspace technology to the public.

Immediately following the terrorist attacks against the United States on September 11, 2001, MITRE employees began searching for victims at the World Trade Center site using cell phone detection methods. It also sent crews out to the Pentagon to assess the damage and restore communication functions. MITRE's workload increased significantly after 2001, with government spending rising sharply as a result of military action in Afghanistan and Iraq. In 2002 the Transportation Security Administration (TSA) selected MITRE to provide support on credentialing and prescreening systems. The company also worked to establish the Partnership for Public Warning, which designed national warning message standards, protocols, and priorities. MITRE began working for the Department of Homeland Security in 2003.

During 2004 MITRE worked with the IRS on their launch of the newly modernized E-File system, which allowed taxpayers to file yearly taxes electronically. Two years later, its work with the TSA came to fruition when the TSA rolled out its Registered Traveler program, which allowed passengers who passed a TSA security threat assessment to receive expedited security screening at airports. In June 2006 Faga retired leaving Al Grasso in control of the growing MITRE empire. Grasso commented on the rise in demand for MITRE's services in a March 2007 *Wall Street Journal* article, claiming, "There is no doubt that post-9/11 there is more growth than we have experienced historically." Indeed, revenues surpassed $1 billion for the first time in 2006.

The company celebrated its 50th anniversary in 2008. It was awarded the Secretary of Defense Medal for Outstanding Public Service that year. Along with receiving acknowledgment for its contributions to public service and national security, MITRE was named by *Fortune* magazine as one of the "100 Best Companies to Work For" in 2009, marking the eighth consecutive year it was named to the list. The company established the Homeland Security Systems Engineering and Development Institute in 2009. This newly created FFRDC supported the Department of Homeland Security and its efforts related to protecting the United States against terrorist threats as well as providing recovery efforts after national disasters and national emergencies.

Robert Halasz
Updated, Christina M. Stansell

FURTHER READING

Black, Chris, "Audit Hits Firm's Use of US Funds," *Boston Globe*, January 26, 1996, p. 37.

Day, Kathleen, "The Think Tank That Went Out for a Spin," *Washington Post*, February 23, 1996, p. B1.

Debons, Anthony, and Esther E. Horne, "NATO Advanced Study Institutes of Information Science and Foundations of Information Science," *Journal of the American Society for Information Science*, September 1997, pp. 794–803.

"Grasso New Mitre President," *Air Traffic Management*, Winter 2006.

Gwynne, Peter, "Fail Safe," *Newsweek*, January 17, 1977, p. 42.

Hughes, David, "Mitre, Air Force Explore Data Fusion for Joint-STARS," *Aviation Week & Space Technology*, March 7, 1994, pp. 47–51.

———, "USAF Finds C3I Uses for Virtual Reality," *Aviation Week & Space Technology*, March 18, 1996, pp. 50–52.

Lewis, Diane, "Mitre Plans to Lay Off 300 Workers with Nearly Half of Cuts in Bedford," *Boston Globe*, October 12, 1994, p. 43.

Marcus, Jon, "Defense-Oriented MITRE Adjusts, Finds Work with the FBI," *Boston Globe*, April 13, 1993, p. 47.

"The MITRE Corporation Purchases Simulation Software from Boeing Subsidiary Preston Aviation Solutions," *PR Newswire*, February 6, 2002.

"MITRE Named to Fortune's '100 Best Companies to Work For' List for Eighth Straight Year," *Business Wire*, January 29, 2009.

Stein, Charles, "Mitre Booms As Military Takes Brains over Brawn," *Boston Globe*, April 23, 1985, p. 27.

Sugawara, Sandra, "The Mighty Voice of Mitre," *Washington Post*, August 20, 1989, p. HI.

Wilgoren, Debbi, "Mitre Corp. Picks Insider As New CEO," *Washington Post*, March 2, 1990, p. 10.

Wysocki, Bernard, Jr., "Private Practice: Is U.S. Government 'Outsourcing Its Brain'?" *Wall Street Journal*, March 30, 2007.

Movado Group, Inc.

650 From Road
Paramus, New Jersey 07652-3507
U.S.A.
Telephone: (201) 267-8000
Fax: (201) 267-8070
Web site: http://www.movadogroupinc.com

Public Company
Incorporated: 1961 as North American Watch Company
Employees: 1,600
Sales: $460.9 million (2009)
Stock Exchanges: New York
Ticker Symbol: MOV
NAICS: 334518 Watch, Clock, and Part Manufacturing

■ ■ ■

Movado Group, Inc., is a leading manufacturer, marketer, and distributor of watches. The company is an amalgamation of several historic fine watchmakers, including the Swiss Movado and Concord companies, and it also makes watches under the brand names Ebel and ESQ. It also has licensing agreements to make watches under the Coach, HUGO BOSS, Juicy Couture, Lacoste, and Tommy Hilfiger brands. The company operates several retail Movado stores, which sell its watches as well as jewelry and gifts. Perhaps its most recognizable product is the Movado Museum Watch. The watch's black, numberless face is adorned only with a single dot at 12 o'clock. Founder Gerry Grinberg, long considered a visionary in the watch industry, died in January 2009.

EARLY YEARS

Several roots led to the current Movado Group. In the United States, the company dates back to 1961, with the founding of the North American Watch Company. This company was run by Gedalio Grinberg, an immigrant from Cuba. He owned 50 percent of the company, in partnership with a Swiss watchmaker and a consortium of three U.S. businessmen. In 1969, North American Watch became the parent company of Concord, an old Swiss watchmaker. It was the U.S. distributor for two other Swiss watches, Piaget and Corum, as well. Concord was founded in Biel, Switzerland, in 1908. The company made fine luxury watches and was especially noted for its skill in producing ultrathin designs. Since its beginnings, Concord was associated with some of the world's leading jewelers, including Tiffany's and Cartier, for whom it designed private-label watches. Another unique design from Concord was a watch with a coin for a face. Its first coin watch premiered in 1946, and collectors clamor for these unusual and distinctive watches.

An even older company was Movado, which dates back to 1881. This company was at first the workshop of a young Swiss, Achille Ditesheim, who moved with his family from Alsace, France, to the village of La Chaux-de-Fonds in the Swiss Jura Mountains in 1876. In 1881 at age 19, Ditesheim set himself up in business with six craftsmen to manufacture watches. His small workshop grew quickly, so that by 1897 it employed 80 watchmakers. It had become one of the largest watch manufacturers in all Switzerland and was noted for its technological sophistication. Early for its time, Ditesheim's company used electricity and advanced

COMPANY PERSPECTIVES

Our mission is to be the leading company in the watch industry by: building strong brands with the most sought-after images, and offering products with the best design, quality and value in their categories; treating everyone with respect, and making integrity the core of our actions and relationships; striving to have employees, vendors and retailers feel like they are part of the same team; providing the best possible services to our retailers and consumers, and recognizing their importance to our continued success; and constantly striving for excellence. We believe our people are critical to the achievement of this goal, and their continuous development is essential to and increasing sales and profits from year to year, ensuring the security and growth of our company, and providing a reasonable return to our shareholders.

machinery in place of the simple hand tools of other watchmakers. Ditesheim gave his company the name Movado in 1905, choosing a word meaning "always in motion" in the then-flourishing international language of Esperanto.

Movado was always an admired innovator in technology and design. In 1912, its Polyplan watch pioneered a curved design, with movements specially engineered to conform to an elongated case that followed the plane of the wearer's wrist. Movado's designs also won top awards at the Paris, Brussels, and Liège world expositions. The company became internationally prominent, and by 1920, Movado was making more than 700 different wristwatch models. Two of its most famous watches from the 1920s were the Valentino and the Ermeto. The Valentino was inspired by the glamorous star of the silent screen Rudolph Valentino. It was encased in sensuous snakeskin. The Ermeto was a hand-held watch in a small box, the forerunner of the travel clock. Opening the case revealed the timepiece, and the motion automatically wound the watch. It was an ingenious design that the company promoted with extensive advertising. Movado produced its Ermeto watch in a variety of styles, including etched gold or silver, and several enameled versions such as a striking black-and-white checkerboard design. The more luxurious Ermeto watches were trimmed with precious stones.

Movado continued to produce complicated and innovative watches in ensuing decades. In the 1930s, the company manufactured one of the first digital watches, and as early as 1935, Movado was making water-resistant watches in both round and rectangular styles. In 1945, the company debuted the world's first automatic winding wristwatch. This was called the Tempomatic. By 1956, the Tempomatic had been retooled into the Kingmatic. This was an automatic watch designed to be extremely rugged, and it was one of Movado's bestsellers in the 1950s and 1960s. Movado's signature Museum Watch was first manufactured for sale in 1962. An American artist, Nathan George Horwitt, designed the stark, black, numberless dial watch in 1947, and in 1960, Horwitt donated his prototype to the Museum of Modern Art in New York. Movado agreed to produce the Horwitt watch in 1962, and it went on to become one of the world's best-selling dial designs.

NORTH AMERICAN WATCH:
1969–1979

In 1969, Grinberg's North American Watch Company purchased the Swiss watchmaker Concord. This was an interesting moment in the history of watch technology because in 1968 Swiss watchmakers first developed the quartz watch. These watches combined an integrated circuit with a battery-powered quartz crystal that oscillated at thousands of vibrations per second. The resulting watch was more accurate than the meticulously handcrafted mechanical watches the Swiss were so famed for making. It took only a few years for the technology to spread to other countries. In the United States, Texas Instruments began selling plastic quartz watches for under $10. Although lower-cost and perhaps not as fashionable, they were every bit as functional as an expensive mechanical watch. K. Hattori & Co., a Japanese company, began promoting its Seiko brand watches by 1972, cutting deeply into Swiss market share. While nearly 40 percent of watches on the U.S. market in 1971 were imported from Switzerland, by 1976 fewer than 20 percent were Swiss.

Consequently, North American Watch, which also distributed the Swiss Piaget and Corum brands, had rather limited corporate success in the early 1970s. Swiss watches were falling out of vogue. In 1976, North American Watch had sales of $8.1 million, and its net income was a mere $209,000. This led Grinberg to adopt a new marketing strategy in 1977. While other Swiss watchmakers had shied away from the new quartz technology, Grinberg asked that 90 percent of his watches have quartz works. By comparison, the prestigious Rolex company was making only about 15 percent of its watches with quartz works in the late 1970s. Thus, the watches had the latest technological

KEY DATES

1881: Achille Ditesheim establishes a watchmaking business.
1905: Ditesheim gives his company the name Movado.
1935: Movado begins making water-resistant watches in both round and rectangular styles.
1945: Movado debuts the world's first automatic winding wristwatch.
1961: Gedalio Grinberg establishes The North American Watch Company.
1962: Movado's signature Museum Watch is manufactured for sale.
1969: North American Watch becomes the parent company of Concord, an old Swiss watchmaker.
1983: North American Watch buys Movado.
1988: The company opens its first freestanding Movado store, on Madison Avenue in New York City.
1993: The company goes public.
1996: North American Watch adopts the Movado Group name.
1999: Movado sells its Piaget line.
2000: The Corum business is sold.
2004: Movado buys the Ebel luxury watch brand.
2009: Founder Grinberg dies.

advantage, yet North American's products remained classic in other ways. They were gold, studded with diamonds, and had no alarms or calculators. They were the old-fashioned luxury Swiss watches in every way but the inside.

Then Grinberg upped North American's ad spending. In 1977, the company spent $1.4 million on advertising, and by 1980, it was spending $6 million annually. In another unusual move, North American eschewed the standard print ads and went to television. The company wished to reach out to middle-income Americans, who would see owning a gold Swiss watch as both status symbol and investment. The watches were expensive, ranging from about $400 in 1980 to as much as $60,000 for the Concord Delirium, and North American tried to market them as hedges against inflation. Few middle-income Americans could plunk down $60,000 for a watch in 1980, but there were apparently many who would pay up to $10,000 for a model from the more moderate Concord Nine Line collection. Grinberg's revamping of North American was successful almost immediately. From the sluggish figures of 1976, sales went up almost sixfold by 1980. The company pulled in $45 million in sales for 1980, with profits of $3 million. Although previously not a serious competitor, it found itself outselling some of the larger and better-known names in Swiss watches.

EXPANDING PRODUCT LINES: 1980–1989

Although the percentage of watches imported from Switzerland to the United States continued to plummet, hanging just above 6 percent in 1981, North American Watch did not suffer. It spent more each year on advertising, dedicating some $14 million in 1982. Sales were still soaring in the early 1980s, reaching close to $86 million in 1982. North American competed with more than a dozen different brands that made up the luxury watch market in the United States in the early 1980s, and the company was recognized within the industry as the most successful Swiss watch distributor. In 1983, North American added another Swiss watch brand to its portfolio, Movado. After its great success earlier in the century, Movado was ailing. In fact, the company was losing money at the time of the acquisition. But it was a good match for North American Watch, forming the least expensive end of its four brands. Movado watches were priced from around $200 to $2,500, while Concord watches ran from around $500 to $10,000. Piaget and Corum, the two brands North American distributed but did not own, were even more expensive.

North American Watch made the most of Movado. The black Museum Watch was well known, and the company expanded the line to include dozens of variants. There were at least 24 different watches being sold under the name Movado Museum Watch in 1986, and some of these were a far cry from the gaunt simplicity of Horwitt's original design. One watch even had numbers on the dial, and it was ringed with diamonds. The name "Museum Watch" had a certain cachet that the company's advertising exploited as well as it could. The Museum of Modern Art, which displayed the original Horwitt watch, even put up a disclaimer in 1984, noting that "the Movado watch is not a Museum of Art watch, nor is there any connection between the Museum of Modern Art and the Movado Watch Corporation." Sol Flick, a lawyer for North American Watch countered that the "museum" in "Museum Watch" might refer to any museum. "It could be the Museum of Natural History," he said in a November 1986 *Consumer Reports* article.

Nevertheless, North American's advertising continued to make references to the Museum of Modern Art. Capitalizing on the name even further, the company set up a division in 1987 called Movado Museum Designs International Ltd. This new division was to develop products such as desk accessories, luggage, jewelry, leather goods, and handbags for sale in department stores that also handled Movado watches. In 1988, the company opened its first freestanding Movado store, on Madison Avenue in New York City.

North American Watch made a move into another luxury category, luggage, in the late 1980s. In 1987, it bought Wings, a formerly chic luggage maker that was losing money. Similar perhaps to Movado, Wings had been a glamorous brand through the 1950s and 1960s, but sales had sagged afterward and the company had not been able to market itself effectively. North American bought the company and then went back into its design history and brought out new versions of old classics. In keeping with its retro feel, a Wings ad for 1988 was a reshot version of one from 1953. North American Watch promoted its new line heavily, allocating approximately $1 million of its total ad budget in 1989 for Wings.

BECOMING MOVADO IN 1996

In the early 1990s, North American Watch continued to promote its products heavily through advertising, both in print and on television. For years the company had relied on an in-house advertising agency, although by the late 1980s North American also used outside agencies. Romantic, virtually wordless television ads were designed by Ogilvy & Mather to appeal to a worldwide audience, because the company had growing sales in Asia, the Middle East, Latin America, and Europe.

In 1992, North American introduced a new line of high-performance watches geared for sports enthusiasts and active people. At first called Esquire, the company shortened the name to ESQ in 1995. The watches were less expensive than North American's other Swiss watches and were different in design, with lots of features packed on the dial. This gave North American a good product spread, with watches in every segment of the market except for the very cheapest. Then on September 30, 1993, North American Watch Company raised cash by going public. The company wanted to expand more into retailing, among other things, and the stock offering was expected to bring an influx of money. Apparently, the company did not make as big a splash as it had expected. Even though its sales and profits had been increasing at respectable rates, the name North American Watch was not well known. As a result, in 1996 the company officially adopted the name of its best-known brand and became the Movado Group, Inc.

The newly named company rolled out plans to expand its product line and to court new markets, principally in Japan, Hong Kong, and Taiwan. Movado also signed an agreement with Coach, a well-known luxury luggage maker, to produce a line of Coach watches. In an interesting mix, this got the luggage maker's name on watches just as Movado was trying to extend its brand name onto luggage, jewelry, and accessories. The company intended to put the Movado name on a bigger variety of items for its stand-alone Movado boutiques. Although in 1997 Movado's sales were principally through independent jewelers, jewelry chains such as Zales, Helzberg, and Sterling, or through premium department stores, including Saks, Macy's, and Neiman Marcus, it had opened a small line of retail outlet stores.

These 16 stores across the United States sold its discontinued merchandise, as well as samples and factory seconds. The New York Movado boutique was still the only one of its kind, while a second store the company operated sold only Piaget watches and jewelry. In 1998, Movado announced that it would open three new boutiques, with plans for four more the next year. The stores sold Movado brand jewelry and accessories as well as watches, with 500 products at a range of price levels. The new stores aimed to draw in the kind of customers who bought Movado watches, though the boutiques were emphatically not merely watch shops. The famous black face of the Museum Watch was transferred onto a wall clock that faced the store entrance, and the kind of spare, modern design epitomized by the Museum Watch was meant to carry through to the whole store. The 1998 stores opened in malls in Short Hills, New Jersey, and in White Plains, New York, while the third, in Rockefeller Center in Manhattan, replaced the first retail space the company had opened in New York ten years earlier.

Financially, Movado was doing very well in the late 1990s. Sales climbed steeply, from $161 million in 1995 to $237 million in 1998. Net income also kept pace. Movado continued to spend heavily on advertising worldwide. The company's strategy for the future hinged on reaching farther into international markets with its core brands and expanding its move into retailing. By 1998, just under 17 percent of the company's sales were international, up from 14 percent in 1997. In the same period, its domestic sales grew almost 11 percent. Movado signed a new licensing agreement, expanding into clocks through the Linden company. Linden was a leading clock maker, and it agreed to develop, produce, and distribute clocks with the Movado name. The company was anxious to refine and improve the stores it opened in 1998, viewing them as prototypes for future rollouts of boutiques in malls across the United States and then internationally. With surging sales and an increasingly recognized brand name and design style, Movado seemed ready to handle more growth and expansion into the next century.

MOVADO IN THE NEW MILLENNIUM

Movado began to focus on expanding its manufactured watch brands as it entered the new millennium. It sold its venerable Piaget line in 1999 and followed that sale with the 2000 disposal of its Corum business. Grinberg's son, Efraim, took over as CEO in 2001 while his father remained chairman.

In 2004, the company bolstered its luxury watch business by purchasing the Ebel SA brand from LVMH Moët Hennessy Louis Vuitton SA in a $47.3-million deal. The purchase was its first since 1983 and revealed the company's plans to strengthen its foothold in the luxury market. It quickly set out to revamp Ebel's operations and cut nearly 35 percent of its workforce in an attempt to restore Ebel's profitability. It also updated the Ebel Classic line and renamed it Classic Wave. It launched Ebel's new Brasilia line based on a design from the 1960s.

The company posted record sales in 2004 for the second consecutive year. Movado experienced financial success thanks to the expansion of its brand arsenal. The company made significant moves during this time period to strengthen its licensing business. It added the Tommy Hilfiger brand to its holdings in 2001. This was followed by the Hugo Boss brand in 2006, and Juicy Couture and Lacoste brands in 2007.

Founder Gerry Grinberg, the first recipient of the Jewelry Information Center's Lifetime Achievement Award in 2003, was slated to step down from the chairman position on January 31, 2009, leaving son Efraim at the head of the company. The elder Grinberg died in early January, and industry leaders mourned the passing of what many considered to be a visionary. When asked in October 2008 by *Women's Wear Daily* what prompted him to enter the business he claimed, "Watches measure time and I have always been fascinated by what a person does with their time." This fascination led to the creation of one of the leading watch companies in the world with sales of just over $460 million in fiscal 2009.

The company faced challenges in 2009 though, as sales declined for the first time since 2002. The slowdown in the global economy took its toll on the watch and jewelry industry as a whole as consumers slowed their purchases of luxury items. The company hoped that its cost cutting measures and growth in new markets including China would bolster its bottom line. In April, the company announced it was eliminating its quarterly dividend and negotiating new loan agreements. The future would, no doubt, bring challenges for Movado but the company believed it was well positioned to overcome any obstacles that may come its way.

A. Woodward
Updated, Christina M. Stansell

PRINCIPAL SUBSIDIARIES

MGI International, Ltd.; North American Watch Service Corporation; Movado Group of Canada, Inc.; MGI Luxury Trading Shanghai Ltd.; Movado International, Ltd.; Movado Group Delaware Holdings Corporation; Movado LLC; MGI Luxury Group UK Ltd.; MGS Distribution Ltd. (UK); SwissWave Europe SA (France); MGI-TWC SAS (France); Movado Deutschland GmbH; Concord Deutschland GmbH; MGI Luxury Group GmbH (Germany); MGI-TWC GmbH (Germany); MGI Luxury Asia Pacific Ltd. (Hong Kong); SwissAm Products Ltd. (Hong Kong); MGI Japan Co., Ltd.; MGI-TWC BV (Netherlands); EWC Marketing Corp.; Movado Retail Group, Inc.; MGI Luxury Singapore Pte. Ltd.; Movado Watch Company, SA (Switzerland); MGI Luxury Group, SA (Switzerland); Concord Watch Company, SA (Switzerland); Ebel Watches SA (Switzerland).

PRINCIPAL COMPETITORS

LVMH Moët Hennessy Louis Vuitton SA; Compagnie Financière Richemont SA; The Swatch Group Ltd.

FURTHER READING

Bailey, Ellen Askin, "Hugo Boss, Movado Sign Watch Pact," *DNR,* December 20, 2004.

Barmash, Isadore, "Fighting the Recession by Spotting Some Fads and Inventing Others," *New York Times,* November 17, 1991, p. F5.

"Battling for Luxury Watches," *New York Times,* June 5, 1984, p. D5.

Chabbott, Sophia, "Movado's Gerry Grinberg Reflects on His Life and Times," *Women's Wear Daily,* October 6, 2008.

"Coach, Movado: Timely Pair," *WWD,* December 1, 1997, p. 12.

Dougherty, Philip H., "Ogilvy Puts Romance in Concord Watch Ads," *New York Times,* April 21, 1987, p. D27.

———, "Ogilvy Turns Seductive for Watches," *New York Times,* May 2, 1988, p. D11.

Elliot, Stuart, "Movado Group Hires an Outside Agency to Reset the Luxury Face of Its Concord Watch," *New York Times,* October 27, 1998, p. C7.

Green, Barbara, "Movado Group Buys Ebel," *National Jeweler,* February 1, 2004.

Hessen, Wendy, "The Book on Movado," *WWD,* October 28, 1996, p. 11.

McLean, Bethany, "A Timely Move," *Fortune,* October 14, 1996, p. 296.

"Movado Group's Earnings Increase 41.7% in Quarter," *WWD,* April 6, 1998, p. 17.

"Movado Raises $32.2M," *WWD,* October 23, 1997, p. 22.

"Movado's Gedalio 'Gerry' Grinberg Dies," *National Jewelry Network,* January 5, 2009.

"Movado's Net Rose 13% in Latest Period, Helped by Strong Sales," *Wall Street Journal,* December 11, 1996, p. C19.

"Movado Strategies: Boutiques, Diversification, Sales Penetration," *Jewelers Circular Keystone,* December 1997, p. 28.

Neiss, Doug, "Movado Forms New Division to Develop Complements of Museum Watch," *HFD,* August 10, 1987, p. 48.

Newman, Jill, "Movado Opens First New York Unit," *WWD,* December 16, 1988, p. 6.

"North American Watch: Selling Jewelry Rather Than Time," *Business Week,* January 14, 1980.

Roman, Monica, "What's with the 10 Grand Watch?—Big Biz!" *Daily News Record,* March 25, 1983, p. 15.

Rozhon, Tracie, "Movado's Chief Insists the Wristwatch Has a Future," *New York Times,* October 27, 2007.

Schuster, William George, "Movado Group Has 'Banner Year,'" *Jewelers Circular Keystone,* June 1, 2004.

———, "Movado: The New Jeweler," *Jewelers Circular Keystone,* June 1998, p. 328.

Simon, Ellen, "Movado Group Profit Rises 24 Percent," *Knight-Ridder/Tribune Business News,* March 31, 1997.

Stern, Aimee L., "Upgrading 'Wings' to First-Class Status," *Adweek's Marketing Week,* March 6, 1989, p. 74.

"What's in a Name? The Movado Museum Watch," *Consumer Reports,* November 1986, p. 694.

MTD Products Inc.

5965 Grafton Road
Valley City, Ohio 44280-9329
U.S.A.
Telephone: (330) 225-2600
Fax: (330) 273-4617
Web site: http://www.mtdproducts.com

Private Company
Founded: 1932 as Modern Tool & Die Company
Employees: 6,400
Sales: $1.03 billion (2008 est.)
NAICS: 333112 Lawn and Garden Tractor and Home
    Lawn and Garden Equipment Manufacturing

■ ■ ■

A private company based in Valley City, Ohio, near Cleveland, MTD Products Inc. is a manufacturer of outdoor power equipment produced under several brands. They include Yard-Man, maker of walk-behind mowers, lawn tractors, string trimmers, garden cultivators, and handheld leaf blowers; White Outdoor, offering garden equipment similar to Yard-Man along with snow throwers; Yard Machines, which manufactures power garden equipment and snow throwers as well as edgers for sidewalk and driveway construction; Troy-Bilt mowers, tillers and cultivators, leaf blowers, chippers, snow throwers, and other power products; and Bolens power garden equipment and log splitters. MTD products are carried by mass retailers, hardware stores, home improvement centers, farm supply stores, and independent dealers. Over the years MTD has also

manufactured a wide variety of private-label and store-brand lawn mowers and tractors for such companies as Ace Hardware, Home Depot, JCPenney, Kmart, and Montgomery Ward. Manufacturing operations are maintained in Ohio, Arizona, Kentucky, and Mississippi. In addition, the company manufactures and markets outdoor power equipment around the world through MTD International.

DEPRESSION-ERA ROOTS

MTD Products traces its lineage to 1932 when cousins Theodore Moll and Emil Jochum along with fellow immigrant Erwin Gerhard formed a partnership to purchase the assets of a Cleveland business called Modern Tool & Die Company. Jochum was born in the late 1890s in western Germany where he learned the blacksmith craft from an uncle, became an apprentice at a tool-and-die shop, and eventually graduated from engineering school. He immigrated to Cleveland in 1928. Around the same age, his cousin Theo Moll, born in Herborn, Germany, was the only son of a Lutheran minister who died when Theo was just three years old. Thus, at an early age he was forced to work to help support his family. After completing his schooling he worked at a wire factory and later served as a maintenance employee at a German coal mine. With a loan from an aunt in Wisconsin, Moll was able to immigrate to the United States at the age of 19. He too came to Cleveland and found work as a tool and die maker at Easy-On Cap Co.

With initial capital of $4,500, the immigrant partners operated out of a fourth-floor location in the

COMPANY PERSPECTIVES

Our commitment is to provide our customers with the Quality, Dependability and Value that they need and want by using each of our talents to the fullest, improving our skills, maintaining and upgrading our facilities and product innovation for the purpose of producing steady employment opportunities for all of our people and a fair return for our shareholders.

Whitney Power Block Building in Cleveland, supplying tools and dies for Standard Products, an auto parts maker. After generating $25,000 in sales during its first year, Modern Tool & Die was able to purchase its own die-cutting tools and a rolling machine, allowing it to produce window channels for Standard Products. The company produced its first consumer product in 1935, a tooling, stamping, and painting recording registry for Egry Register. A year later Modern Tool & Die began producing automobile radiator grills and heater blower housings. As the company increased its work for automakers, it leased new space and by the end of the decade transferred its operations there.

In 1941 Modern Tool & Die acquired a facility on West 130th Street in Cleveland, which would become its longtime home and was large enough to accommodate the company's strong growth. When the United States entered World War II the country began devoting its manufacturing resources to the production of military materials. With virtually no auto industry to support, Modern Tool & Die did tool and die work for companies such as Goodyear, assembling wing fixtures for the aircraft the giant rubber producer was then manufacturing. Later Modern Tool & Die put its expertise to use in other ways, such as stamping out mess kits used by soldiers in the field. It was also during this period that the partnership was dissolved and Modern Tool & Die was incorporated. Theo Moll became president of the firm, while Jochum and Gerhard were named vice-presidents. (Gerhard later left the company.)

LAWN MOWERS INTRODUCED

After the war, Modern Tool & Die returned to the stamping of automotive parts but became increasingly more involved in consumer products, such as stamped-steel television cabinet housings and household appliance stampings. In 1952 it acquired majority interest in Midwest Industries, Inc., a maker of wheeled goods in

which the company had invested during the previous decade. Modern Tool & Die then began producing children's bicycles and tricycles, kiddie cars, and playground equipment. The country was undergoing a baby boom as returning servicemen and servicewomen and their spouses had settled in the new suburbs to raise families. Many of them also planted gardens, and Modern Tool & Die began to tap into this market in 1954 by manufacturing wheelbarrows for Sears, Roebuck. Positive feedback from customers led to additional gardening equipment, and in 1958 a turning point was reached when the company introduced a walk-behind, gas powered, 18-inch rotary lawn mower. A year later a riding mower was introduced.

During the 1960s Modern Tool & Die expanded its slate of outdoor power equipment. In 1963 the company introduced a vertical rotary tiller, battery-powered walk-behind mowers, and snow throwers. The company also continued to upgrade its riding mowers, leading in 1967 to the introduction of its first full frame lawn tractor. By the end of the decade a line of hydrostatic and transaxle garden tractors was also in production. To support further research and development efforts, the company opened a new technical center in Valley City, Ohio, in 1969.

During the 1960s Modern Tool & Die also grew through acquisitions. The company expanded into Canada through the purchase of Sehl Engineering Ltd. in 1962. Four years later Cleveland-based Industrial Plastics Company was acquired. Other purchases during this period included Columbia Manufacturing Company, the Modern Line Plant in Indianola, Mississippi, and the Liverpool Industrial Park in Valley City. Because of the many changes that had taken place over the years, Modern Tool & Die was renamed MTD Products Inc. in 1969. Ed Stell was named president while Moll became chairman and Jochum vice-chairman of the board.

ACQUISITIONS AND EXPANSION

MTD expanded on a number of fronts in the 1970s. Industrial Plastics moved its manufacturing operations to the Liverpool Industrial Park in 1971, and later transmission manufacturing was moved to a new Cleveland plant. The assets of the Yard-Man Company were acquired in 1975 from Montgomery Ward. MTD opened a new corporate headquarters in Valley City at the end of the decade. Throughout the 1970s MTD also extended its line of outdoor power equipment. Moreover, the company expanded beyond North America. In 1970 MTD acquired a German company, Ventzki GmbH, providing a platform for European sales. In 1976 MTD became the first company to sell

KEY DATES

1932: Immigrants Theo Moll, Emil Jochum, and Erwin Gerhard form a partnership to acquire assets of Modern Tool & Die Company.

1954: Company begins making wheelbarrows for Sears, Roebuck.

1958: Company manufactures first lawn mower.

1969: Modern Tool & Die is renamed MTD Products Inc.

1970: Ventzki GmbH is acquired.

1981: Cub Cadet line of mowers and garden tractors is acquired.

1997: MTD Pro Line is introduced.

1998: Last of original partners, Jochum, retires.

2000: Ryobi Outdoor Power Equipment is acquired.

2001: Garden Way, Inc., is acquired.

2007: Jochum dies at age 102.

rear discharge lawn tractors in Europe, marketed under the Ventzki brand.

MTD's commitment to outdoor power equipment deepened in the 1980s. The Cub Cadet line of walk-behind and riding mowers and lawn tractors was acquired in 1981 from International Harvester, which would continue to market the MTD-produced farm and garden tractors. MTD also developed a dealer direct line of outdoor power equipment through the establishment of White Outdoor Products Company. Columbus, Indiana-based Hartup Tool Inc. was acquired in 1984, followed two years later by the purchase of Aircap Industries of Tupelo, Mississippi. To enhance its do-it-yourself parts business, MTD acquired Arnold Industries. Also in the 1980s MTD constructed a 160,000-square-foot manufacturing facility in Brownsville, Tennessee, which in 1985 began producing Cub Cadet riding mowers as well as automotive parts. At the end of the decade the MTD Technical Center added a 50,000-square-foot expansion to accommodate dealer training and customer service operations.

MTD expanded its European footprint as well in the 1980s, acquiring an interest in E.P. Barrus of the United Kingdom, and built upon the business in the following decade. In 1991 a branch office was opened in France, followed by a branch in Austria two years later. Gutbrod AG of Germany was acquired in 1996, and its headquarters in Saarbrücken-Bubingen became MTD International's European central office. Originally involved in motorcycles, Gutbrod began producing

compact tractors in 1962 and snow throwers in 1983. Additional MTD branches opened in Hungary in 1996, and Sweden and Denmark in 1997. A central warehouse was established in Valmont, France, in 1998. During this period MTD looked to other parts of the world as well, establishing a retail operation in Australia in 1991.

SHIFT IN FOCUS

The 1990s was a time of transition for MTD in a number of ways. It exited the automotive parts business in 1999, selling that operation for $20 million in cash and another $20 million in stock to Shiloh Industries Inc., in which MTD held a large stake. Shiloh was a supplier of steel blanks, stampings, and processed steel to automotive, appliance, and other industrial manufacturers. Over the years Shiloh and MTD had been involved in a number of joint ventures, dating back to 1960. The joint ventures were brought together in 1993 as a publicly owned configuration of Shiloh Industries, in which MTD held a 36 percent interest and the public about 28 percent. In 1997 MTD made a bid to acquire all of the outstanding shares but eventually withdrew its offer and then sold its automotive parts division to Shiloh.

Even before the divestiture, MTD had been shifting its focus to its many outdoor power equipment brands. In the 1990s the company became especially interested in the mass market. Not only did it penetrate that market deeper through the sale of products to such retailers as Ace Hardware, Home Depot, Lowe's, Sears, and Wal-Mart, MTD manufactured a large number of private-label equipment. In addition to the mass market, the company introduced its MTD Pro line in 1997. In keeping with its shifting focus, MTD developed a parent brand strategy, positioning MTD as a house of brands, which were linked together by a "sprig" design incorporated into each brand's logo.

The 1990s was also marked by the death of Moll, at age 91. Despite his advanced age, Jochum continued to work at MTD, finally retiring in 1998 when he was well into his 90s. He lived until November 2007, dying at home five days before his 103rd birthday. The two men had always been religious, known to pray before important business meetings, and at their behest MTD established the Jochum-Moll Foundation to support Christian-oriented educational, healthcare, and welfare programs.

EXPANDING OPERATIONS IN THE 21ST CENTURY

MTD further expanded its European operations in the new century. Production capacity was increased in Germany, and a factory was established in Hungary in

2000 to manufacture lawn mowers. Sales offices and subsidiaries were added in Italy and Switzerland in 2001, and Benelux and Poland in 2002. The Poland branch served as a platform for the growth of the distribution network in Eastern Europe. In 2006 MTD began manufacturing lawn equipment for sale in Europe under the Massey Ferguson label. Further production expansion was completed at the Saarbrücken plant in 2007. The extra capacity would be put to use as MTD looked further eastward, opening branches in Bulgaria and Russia in 2009.

On the domestic front, MTD added to its stable of brands early in the new century. The company added handheld products through the 2000 acquisition of Ryobi Outdoor Power Equipment. A year later Garden Way, Inc., and its Troy-Bilt and Bolens brands were purchased as well. To support the growth of the company, MTD expanded a distribution center in Verona, Mississippi, and built a new one in Shelby, Ohio. In 2005 the Mower MD Service Center concept was introduced, providing repair services to the mass market for outdoor power equipment. A deteriorating economy and a slump in housing sales, however, hurt the demand for lawn and garden equipment and forced MTD to retrench in the latter half of the decade. Due to overcapacity, a plant in Kitchener, Ontario, Canada, was closed in late 2008, and in the summer of 2009 the Brownsville, Tennessee, plant was shuttered as well. Nevertheless, MTD, well established in the market, was likely to weather these difficult conditions and resume growth as the economy improved.

Ed Dinger

PRINCIPAL SUBSIDIARIES

MTD International.

PRINCIPAL COMPETITORS

The Black & Decker Corporation; Briggs & Stratton Power Products Group, LLC; Deere & Company.

FURTHER READING

Buranick, Alana, "Emil Jochum, Co-Founded MTD Products," *Cleveland Plain Dealer,* November 17, 2007, p. B3.

Flint, Troy, "Production Will Stop at MTD Plant," *Cleveland Plain Dealer,* April 18, 1998, p. 1C.

Ford, Tom, "Shiloh Acquires MTD Unit with Eyes on Growth," *Crain's Cleveland Business,* June 28, 1999, p. 4.

Gerdel, Thomas W., "MTD Products Woos Shiloh Industries for $19 a Share," *Cleveland Plain Dealer,* June 17, 1997, p. 1C.

Hailman, Lydia, "Ohio-Based Manufacturer to Expand Verona, Miss., Distribution Center," *Northeast MS Daily Journal* (Tupelo), July 15, 2004.

Hardin, Angela Y., "MTD Ready to Ride with Sears Deal," *Crain's Cleveland Business,* February 15, 1999, p. 2.

Hunter, Ned B., "Last Day Brownsville Cub Cadet," *Jackson (Tenn.) Sun,* July 29, 2009.

"Shiloh Industries Inc.: MTD Withdraws Its Offer to Acquire All of Concern," *Wall Street Journal,* August 14, 1997, p. B4.

Vishnevsky, Zina, "Theo Moll, 91, Helped Start MTD Products," *Cleveland Plain Dealer,* May 29, 1996, p. 9B.

Mutuelle Assurance des Commercants et Industriels de France (Macif)

———■———

2 et 4 rue Pied de Fond
Niort, F-79037 Cedex 9
France
Telephone: (33 05 49) 09 44 32
Fax: (33 05 49) 09 44 98
Web site: http://www.macif.fr

Mutual Company
Incorporated: 1960
Employees: 8,100
Sales: EUR 4.96 billion ($6.2 billion) (2008)
NAICS: 524126 Direct Property and Casualty Insurance
Carriers; 524113 Direct Life Insurance Carriers;
524114 Direct Health and Medical Insurance Car-
riers

■ ■ ■

Mutuelle Assurance des Commercants et Industriels de France, more commonly known as Macif, is a major French insurance group, and one of the country's leading providers of personal insurance products and services. The company claims the French lead in car insurance, with a 14 percent share of the market, and is the leading home insurance provider, with more than three million policies. Macif is also the country's leading provider of boat and yacht insurance. A mutual company owned by its more than 4.6 million policyholders, Macif serves as a holding company and central organizational body for a network of 11 independently operating regional companies. Together these regional bodies operate 535 agencies and 43 call centers throughout France. The company's operations are conducted largely through four primary subsidiaries: Macif-Mutualité, focused on the Health and Prevention market; Mutavie, the company's life insurance and savings provider; Macif Gestion, providing savings and investment management services; and Macifilia, which focuses on providing group and transport insurance. Automotive insurance accounts for 40 percent of the group's total revenues of EUR 4.96 billion ($6.2 billion) in 2008. Life insurance and savings accounts for 35 percent; Health and Prevention adds 11.5 percent; and home insurance adds 10 percent to total revenues. In 2009 Macif agreed to create a common holding company in cooperation with two other major French mutual insurance companies, Maif and Matmut. The new body is expected to be operational at the end of the year. Gérard Andreck is the company's CEO.

AUTO INSURANCE BEGINNINGS IN 1960

The French government passed new legislation in 1958 requiring automobile owners to purchase automotive insurance. While many of France's existing insurance groups began providing automotive insurance, the legislation nonetheless provided new opportunities for developing insurance services. However, the provision of automotive insurance became especially the province of the mutual insurance market. A number of existing mutual companies, including Mutuelle Assurance des Instituteurs (Maif), began offering automotive insurance

COMPANY PERSPECTIVES

Macif comprises 11 self-managing regions administered by regional committees. Macif is not a stock company with shareholders to reward. Decision-making is in the hands of the policyholders, who directly elect regional delegates to represent them. Macif insures individuals, the self-employed, associations and works committees. Its comprehensive range of products covers every eventuality. Macif is not just an insurer, but a socially responsible player. It fulfills its role by promoting full employment, social cohesion and risk prevention.

at this time. Niort was already home to many of France's mutual benefit societies, including the Maif.

These companies tended to focus on specific industries. In Maif's case, its policyholders came from the teaching profession, which had been one of the earliest and most active proponents of mutual benefit societies in France. The success of the Maif and others inspired a group of Niort-area retailers and business leaders to establish their own mutual benefit society. That company received government approval in 1960 and took on the name of Mutuelle Assurance des Commercants et Industriels de France, or Macif. Jacques Vandier, a graduate of the prestigious École Polytechnique, was named the company's first CEO.

The Macif began issuing its first automotive insurance policies that year. The company ran into trouble in 1962 when it was forced to turn to its policyholders to help shoulder the burden of a large number of accident claims that year. The situation led Vandier to recognize the need to institute risk-based selection methods for its potential policyholders. In this way, the company was able to minimize the number of claims, while at the same time greatly reducing the number of non-payers.

With fewer claims Macif was able to return a greater share of its profits to its policyholders. These payouts quickly attracted the interest of other customers, and by 1967 Macif had signed on its 100,000th policyholder. Through the 1960s Macif developed a number of innovations for the automotive insurance market, most notably the "constat aimable." This was an accident report form in which both parties involved in an accident agreed upon a description of the events, thereby greatly simplifying the insurance claims process.

ADDING PRODUCTS AND SERVICES IN THE SIXTIES AND SEVENTIES

The year 1967 marked Macif's first diversified venture when the company joined in the creation of Socram, in partnership with a number of other mutual benefit insurance groups, to provide automotive loans to their members. Socram stood for "Société de credit des sociétés d'assurances à caracte mutuel."

Into the 1970s, Macif continued developing innovative products and services for its policyholders. The company developed a solidarity fund, Fonsomacif, to aid policyholders in need of assistance for emergencies not covered by their insurance policies. That program was launched in 1969. The following year Macif became the first automotive insurance group in France to institute a *bonus-malus* system, establishing several categories of policy rates according to various criteria, including age, gender, and car type. The new system helped reduce the cost of automotive insurance for a great number of the group's policyholders.

With rates as much as 30 percent lower than its competitors, Macif grew quickly, becoming a nationally operating insurance group. Other initiatives further enhanced the company's reputation. In the early 1970s, for example, the French government began lowering speed limits along the country's highways and roads, achieving a dramatic reduction in automotive accidents. Concurrently the Arab oil embargo of 1973 caused a sharp increase in gasoline prices, reducing automobile usage and further reducing the number of accidents. Maif then decided to pay out the resulting profits to its policyholders.

NEW STRUCTURE IN 1987

The major Niort-based mutual benefit insurance groups, including Maif, Maaf, and Macif, joined together again at the end of the 1970s and into the early 1980s. The companies created Mutavie in 1979 to offer life insurance and savings products for its members. In 1980 the mutuals formed their own automobile assistance service to rival those provided by the country's for-profit insurance companies. The new company, called Inter Mutuelles Assistance, or Ima, began business in 1981. Macif's share of the new company stood at 27.14 percent.

Macif was behind another automotive insurance industry initiative, proposing that automobile owners be required to post proof of their possession of automobile insurance on their windshields. This proposal was taken up by the government in 1986. It was aimed at reducing the number of noninsured drivers on the road by making them more readily identifiable. In the meantime

KEY DATES

■

1960: A group of Niort-area retailers and industrialists join together to found Mutuelle Assurance des Commercants et Industriels de France as a mutual insurance society.

1967: Macif joins in the creation of Socram, a provider of automobile loans.

1979: Macif becomes a founding partner of Mutavie, a life insurance and savings provider.

1981: Macif becomes a founding member of Inter Mutuelles Assistance.

1987: Macif adopts a new regional structure based on 11 autonomously operating regions.

1998: Macif creates a mutual fund investment subsidiary, Macif Gestion.

2004: Macif enters Poland, establishing Macif Życie TUW.

2009: Macif announces plans to create a combined holding company with partners Maif and Matmut.

Macif enjoyed continued growth. The company had gradually been expanding its range of policyholders. A traveling salespeople's union joined with the initial group of retailers and industrialists in creating Macif. Membership was soon opened up to these companies' management and employees as well. Over the next decade Macif began admitting members from the various trade unions, before developing specialized products and services for the self-employed sector.

By the end of the 1970s the company counted nearly 1.3 policyholder members. By the end of the 1980s the group's membership had more than doubled, topping 3.2 million in 1989. In order to coordinate its impressive expansion, Macif had begun taking steps to develop a new organizational structure in the middle of the 1970s. In 1975 the company instituted a new delegate-based decision-making process under which policyholders elected delegates to represent them at a national conference.

The first of these took place in Monte Carlo in 1981, a meeting that set the stage for the creation of a new national organization based on a network of regional divisions. By 1985 the company's membership had voted to complete the regionalization of the company's operations, resulting in the formation of 11 independently operating regional companies, coordinated by the Macif's Niort-based headquarters.

The new organization took effect in 1987, the same year Jacques Vandier became Macif's chairman after nearly three decades during which he helped build the company into one of France's leading automotive insurance providers. The company then named Jean Simmonnet, who had worked alongside Vandier since 1963, as the society's CEO.

DIVERSIFYING IN THE NINETIES

As a nonprofit mutual benefit society, Macif recognized that part of its responsibility lay in helping to prevent accidents. In keeping with this spirit the company began developing a number of prevention programs in 1987. This initiative resulted in the creation of the first workshops for young drivers with the possibility of lowering premiums as an incentive to participate in 1989. In the late 1990s the company developed a new series of workshops for drivers over the age of 65.

During the 1990s Macif had begun to diversify its operations. The process began in 1989 when the company's Loir-Bretagne region launched a cooperation agreement with a health insurance mutual in the region. The company also became a founding partner of EURESA, a group created in 1990 to promote the mutual society model to other European countries. Partners in Euresa included P&V in Belgium, Folksam in Sweden, Unipol in Italy, LB Group in Denmark, and DEVK Versicherungen in Germany.

The company invested in the property development market, founding subsidiary Trema and launching the development of shopping centers in France, Italy, and Spain. In 1996 the company teamed up with U.S.-based Hines, which purchased a 50 percent stake in the Trema and took over the management of its shopping centers.

Macif created a new investment subsidiary, Macif Gestion in 1998. Macif Gestion became one of the first in France to develop mutual fund portfolios based on ethical criteria. The following year, Macif added a number of new insurance products, including policy payment guarantees in case of unemployment, and policy guarantees for the replacement of stolen or lost keys.

CREATING A MUTUAL INSURANCE GIANT

In the meantime Macif had begun a new process toward expanding its membership. In 1995 the company established a new subsidiary, Macifilia, offering insurance products for public servants and members of the liberal professions. In 1996 Macif then changed its own charter, formally extending membership to other professions. Anyone in France could become a policyholder with the Macif. The move helped the group achieve new growth in its membership. By the end of the first decade of the 2000s, Macif counted more than 4.6 million members.

Macif continued rolling out new business lines into the turn of the 21st century. In 2001 the company created Macif Mutualité and began offering personal accident and life protection insurance, as well as personal and group health insurance policies. The company also created Macif Sourds in 2003 to provide insurance products and services specifically designed for the deaf and hard of hearing.

Macif also began to take its first steps into international markets, acquiring stakes in a number of foreign counterparts. These included a 24.5 percent stake in Atlantis Seguros, of Spain, and a shareholding in Greece's Syneteristik. Many of Macif's international moves came through its participation in Euresa. In 2004 Macif entered Poland directly, establishing Macif Życie TUW. The company hoped to establish the mutual society model as a counterpart to the often customer-unfriendly operations of the private insurance sector there. The company entered Algeria later in the decade, forming a cooperation agreement with that country's CAR insurance company in 2008.

Macif began targeting an entry into the booming *bancassurance* market in the first decade of the 2000s as well. In 2004 the company teamed up with Maif and bank Caisses d'Epargne to provide banking and insurance products to the noncorporate sector. That partnership resulted in the creation of the CEMM holding company in 2005.

The partnership with Maif also set the stage for talks to build a wider partnership among France's major mutual benefits societies. In 2009 Macif, together with Maif and Matmut, announced that they had agreed to form a new holding company that would enable the companies to combine forces while still maintaining their independent operations. The new company, targeted to be in place by the end of 2009, was expected to become a new major force in the French insurance industry, with combined revenues of EUR 9 billion ($11.6 billion). From a small group of Niort-based retailers, Macif had grown into one of France's leading insurance companies in the new century.

M. L. Cohen

PRINCIPAL SUBSIDIARIES

Altima; Atlantis Seguros S.A. (Spain; 24.5%); Compagnie Foncière Macif; Foncière de Lutèce; GCE Assurances; Groupe IMA (27.14 %); Macif Participations; Macif Życie TUW (Poland); Macifilia; Macif-Mutualité; Mutavie; Siem; Syneteristik (Greece); Themis.

PRINCIPAL DIVISIONS

Pôle Dommages; Pôle Epargne; Pôle Sante/Prévoyancé; Pôle Gestion d'Actifs.

PRINCIPAL OPERATING UNITS

Centre; Centre Europe; Centre Ouest Atlantique; Gâtinais Champagne; Île de France; Loir-Bretagne; Nord Pas de Calais; Picardie; Provence Méditerranée; Rhône-Alpes; Sud-Ouest Pyrénées; Val de Seine.

PRINCIPAL COMPETITORS

AXA Group; CNP Assurances; La Garantie Mutuelle des Fonctionnaires; Assurances Générales de France S.A.; BNP Paribas Assurance S.A.; La Mutuelle du Mans Assurances; La Mondiale Société d'Assurance Mutuelle sur la Vie et de Capitalisation; Mutuelle Assurance des Instituteurs de France; MAAF Assurances S.A.; Mutuelle Assurance des Travaileurs Mutualistes SAM.

FURTHER READING

"Algeria: CAR and MACIF Seal Agreement," *IPR Strategic Business Information Database*, April 9, 2008.

Denis, Pascale, "La Macif Lancerait une Filiale Bancaire en Avril," *Le Point*, January 12, 2009.

"French Insurer Takes Majority Share of Cambodian Company," *America's Intelligence Wire*, September 17, 2004.

"French Mutual Insurers Consider Banking Partnerships," *Europe Intelligence Wire*, May 8, 2004.

"Hines and French Insurance Giant Macif Form Partnership to Own and Manage Seven Shopping Centers in Europe," *PR Newswire*, August 9, 1996.

Huijgen, Annelot, "La Macif se Lance dans la Vente d'Assurances Auto sur Internet," *Agefi*, June 19, 2008.

"La Macif Cree une Filiale en Pologne," *Le Figaro*, November 2, 2004.

Landrot, Antoine, "La Maif Mise sur l'Assurbanque pour Limiter Sa Dépendance à l'IARD," *Agefi*, May 29, 2009.

Lemoine, Sandrine, "Mutavie Défend Encore le Monosupport en Euros," *Agefi*, May 4, 2007.

"Matmut-Macif-Maif: L'Assurance d'un Géant," *Liberation*, March 24, 2009.

Pilla, David, "French Insurers to Invest in Cambodia Market," *AM Best Newswire*, September 20, 2004.

Urbajtel, Stéphane, "Le Vrai Pouvoir des Mutuelles," *L'Express*, January 7, 2008.

Naked Juice Company

935 West 8th Street
Azusa, California 91702
U.S.A.
Telephone: (626) 812-6022
Toll Free: (877) 858-4237
Fax: (626) 334-6439
Web site: http://www.nakedjuice.com

Private Company
Incorporated: 1984
Employees: 400
Sales: $182 million (2007 est.)
NAICS: 311421 Fruit and Vegetable Canning

■ ■ ■

A subsidiary of PepsiCo Inc., Naked Juice Company is an Azusa, California-based beverage company specializing in 100 percent juices, juice blends, and juice smoothies, fortified with proteins, vitamins, herbs, and probiotics. Sub-brands include Bare Breeze, Super Food, Protein Zone, Pure Juice, and Well Being. Flavors include Berry Blast, a combination of strawberries, raspberries, and blackberries; Cherry Pomegranate Power; Watermelon Chill, watermelon juice accented with lime; Green Machine, a blend of apple and kiwi juices fortified with nutrients; Blue Machine, a blackberry, blueberry, and banana blend; Gold Machine, a combination of golden kiwi, pineapple, and passion fruit; and Red Machine, combining raspberry, strawberry, and pomegranate juices.

Depending on the flavor, Naked Juice products are available in ten-ounce, 15.2-ounce, 32-ounce, and 64-ounce plastic bottles. Naked Juice products are found in North America and the United Kingdom in supermarket produce aisles as well as refrigerated sections, and are also sold in health food stores, health clubs, club stores, and specialty retailers. Because the juices do not rely on preservatives and must be refrigerated, Naked Juice maintains a chilled-distribution network, and also allows customers to pick up orders directly from its plants or warehouses.

BEACH ORIGINS

The idea for Naked Juice was conceived in 1983 by friends James Rosenberg and David Bleeden, new college graduates and members of the same rock band. According to Bleeden, they started hawking juice as a way to make money while pursuing their musical careers, inspired by Rosenberg's father who saw a Juice King machine advertisement in the *Wall Street Journal.* They set up shop in the back of the Chipper Wish Hoagie Shop in Venice, California, to sell fresh juice towel-to-towel on Santa Monica beach and nearby Venice Beach. To ensure a supply of the best fruits, the partners rose at 3:00 A.M. to visit the Los Angeles Produce Market. They then squeezed their juices at the hoagie shop before it opened, stashed the product in a backpack filled with ice, and made the rounds of the area beaches, selling the juice at a dollar a glass.

In January 1984 the Naked Juice Company was formed. While the company would later attribute its name to the raw fruits used to make its natural

COMPANY PERSPECTIVES

We're dedicated to creating the best, all-natural 100% juices and juice smoothies, made from the finest bare-naked fruits, with no added sugar and no preservatives—ever.

products, eschewing concentrates and purees, Bleeden claimed they coined the name because he and Rosenberg liked to sunbathe naked. Also helping to grow the business was a high school friend of Rosenberg, Danny Rubenstein. Demand for the juices grew steadily, leading to the company's first major account, Gelson's Market. Soon the number of juice items increased to 25, of which ten were organic. Because consumers in the 1980s were not yet willing to pay extra for organic juices, the number of organic products was trimmed to just the two most popular juices. As Naked Juice grew in popularity in Southern California, a San Diego division was also established.

In 1991 Naked Juice was sold to Chiquita Brands International, which tucked the brand into California Day-Fresh Foods, a fresh food manufacturer and distributor that would also include the Chiquita and Ferraro's juice lines. A few years later Rosenberg and some of his former colleagues at Naked Juice returned to the fresh juice business, producing fresh juices exclusively for Gelson's supermarkets and later establishing Juice Harvest Corporation.

In the meantime, Naked Juice under corporate ownership steered a more traditional course. Market research, including surveys and in-store testing, was used to take the brand to the nutraceutical area, combining fresh juices with herbs, vitamins, and other supplements to stake a claim in the functional food category. The Green Machine product, for example, included 11 supplements, so-called superfoods, and in short order became the top-selling blended juice in the history of California Day-Fresh Foods at that time. In addition to blended juices and 100 percent orange juice and apple juice, Naked Juice developed vegetable juices, smoothies, and fortified shakes. The brand also expanded beyond Southern California, stretching its market the length of the West Coast.

PRIVATE INVESTMENT COMPANY ACQUIRES NAKED JUICE BRAND

In 2000 California Day-Fresh Foods and the Naked Juice brand were acquired by North Castle Partners

LLC, a private investment company with offices in San Francisco and Greenwich, Connecticut, that targeted middle-market companies involved in healthy living and aging, including consumer health, personal fitness, and nutrition companies. Earlier in 2000 Castle Partners had taken private Saratoga Beverage Group Inc., a publicly traded juice and spring water company, and used it as the platform for a mergers and acquisitions vehicle in the refrigerated juice category. In addition to Naked Juice, North Castle purchased Wiman Beverage Co. Inc., M.H. Zeigler and Sons Inc., Orchard Island Juice Co., Hansen's Smoothies, and Fantasia Juice Co. In the summer of 2001 North Castle formed the Ultimate Juice Company to house these beverage brands and opened corporate offices in New Jersey. From the outset, Naked Juice was considered the flagship property, a "mega-brand" that management believed could be used just as well to sell smoothies as juice. To emphasize their nutritional content, the products were recast as Naked Food-Juice and marketed as good tasting convenient meals in a bottle.

Ultimate Juice was eager to extend the Naked Juice brand to the Midwest and then the Northeast. In September 2001 the brand made its debut in the key New York City market. Helping the company in an indirect manner with its national rollout of the brand later in the fall was Coca-Cola Co.'s acquisition of Odwalla Inc., a California fresh juice manufacturer. The deal helped Ultimate Juice and its Naked Juice brand by bringing more attention to the fresh juice category. It also led to speculation that as the largest remaining independent premium juice company with about $100 million in annual revenues, Ultimate Juice was a likely acquisition target for PepsiCo, to counter the move made by its longtime corporate rival. Nothing came of that possibility at the time, however.

Ultimate Juice continued its national rollout of Naked Food-Juice in February 2002, entering Boston, Massachusetts, and Portland, Maine, both areas that had well developed juice markets, in particular the campuses of Harvard University, the Massachusetts Institute of Technology, and Northeastern University. Later in the year Ultimate Juice took the Naked Food-Juice brand to two more new markets, Seattle, Washington, and Portland, Oregon, although the original Naked Juice brand had long ago been introduced to the Northwest.

ULTIMATE JUICE BECOMES NAKED JUICE

By this time, superpremium juices were driving growth in the juice category, and Naked Juice was the fastest-growing superpremium juice brand. As a result, it was no surprise that North Castle Partners decided to focus

KEY DATES

1983: James Rosenberg and David Bleeden begin selling fresh juices on Southern California beaches.
1984: Naked Juice Company is formed.
1991: Company is sold to Chiquita Brands International.
2000: Naked Juice is sold to North Castle Partners LLC.
2001: North Castle forms the Ultimate Juice Company to house beverage brands.
2003: Ultimate Juice changes its name to Naked Juice Company.
2007: Naked Juice is sold to PepsiCo.
2008: Starbucks Coffee begins carrying Naked Juice products.

all of its resources on the Naked Juice brand. In 2003 Ultimate Juice changed its name to the Naked Juice Company and later in the year moved its corporate offices from New Jersey to its Southern California roots, bringing together finance, human resources, and operations in Glendora, and consolidating manufacturing at a pair of California facilities in Glendora and Azusa. Moreover, seven new products were being readied for national introduction in November 2003, including three new soy smoothie drinks. To help broaden distribution channels and grow market share, the new products also boasted an extended shelf life of 60 days.

A new management team led by Chief Executive Officer Monty Sharma was installed in 2004 and took steps to reposition the Naked Juice brand, shifting away from the Naked Food-Juice and meal in a bottle idea while growing distribution and overseeing a number of new product launches, including 12 in 2005 and 2006, most of them the result of customer input and feedback. Naked Juice increased sales to about $150 million by 2006 and continued to take steps to maintain further growth. In response to the growing popularity of energy drinks, the company introduced its own entries in the category in the spring of 2006: Strawberry Kiwi Kick and Orange Mango Motion. Both smoothie products included 43 milligrams of caffeine per serving, drawn from green tea extract and guarana. They would be followed by Black & Blueberry Rush and Cherry Pomegranate Power. Naked Juice also became the first company to bring to market a 100 percent juice product including probiotic and prebiotic supplements to help promote a healthy digestive tract and more robust immune system. Although they had been popular in Europe for many years, probiotics had been mostly limited to dairy items in North America.

Naked Juice opened a pair of direct-store delivery centers in Sacramento and Seattle in 2006, driving strong sales increases in these two key markets. Also to keep pace with strong demand for Naked Juice products, the company added 64,155 square feet of climate-controlled distribution space to its operation, an amount that would grow to more than 87,000 square feet by the start of 2007. All told, Naked Juice was shipping six million bottles of juice each month at that time.

PEPSICO BUYS NAKED JUICE

While Naked Juice had not caught the notice of PepsiCo after Coca-Cola purchased Odwalla a few years earlier, its performance since that time clearly piqued PepsiCo's interest by 2006. In November of that year, North Castle Partners agreed to sell the brand to PepsiCo for an estimated $450 million, or three times annual sales. The acquisition was completed in early 2007. For PepsiCo the addition of Naked Juice and its portfolio of 25 fortified drinks was part of a strategy to add businesses offering health food choices. Just prior to the Naked Juice acquisition, PepsiCo purchased Izze Beverages, which offered a line of natural, sparkling fruit juices. Both became part of PepsiCo's Quaker Oats, Tropicana, and Gatorade division.

While part of a giant corporation, Naked Juice continued to remain close to its customers. Marketing programs were conducted in ten markets each year to permit taste testing with consumers and one-on-one interaction with "brand ambassadors." The Naked Juice web site created the "Naked Juice Nation" space in 2008 to further facilitate dialogue with customers. Even though it had the deep pockets of PepsiCo to draw on, the company also continued to pursue guerrilla marketing campaigns, such as staging tongue-in-cheek The Fruit Will Set You Free "protests," in which people dressed in fruit costumes gathered on city streets to chant and demand the end of free radicals, sugar, and preservatives in juice.

Having PepsiCo as its owner brought advantages to Naked Juice beyond financial ones. In 2008 Naked Juice reached an agreement with Starbucks Coffee Co. to provide its juice products to the chain's more than 7,000 outlets. Naked Juice had sales of $182 million in 2007, a 26 percent improvement over 2006, and with the Starbucks alliance, and taking further advantage of PepsiCo's far-flung distribution network, was well positioned to maintain robust sales increases in the years to come. Long-term trends also favored Naked Juice. As the population of the United States aged, the demand for healthful food products was expected to enjoy steady growth for years to come.

Customers were also becoming increasingly concerned about the world's environment. To maintain its brand position, one that focused on natural and organic products, Naked Juice looked to incorporate eco-friendly packaging. In 2009 the company began the switch to post-consumer recycled polyethylene plastic containers, starting with 32-ounce bottles, and expected to complete the conversion to the new materials in 2010. The move, the company estimated, would save about 57,000 barrels of oil each year, a statistic that would likely be trumpeted to consumers as Naked Juice supported the image it had been honing for more than a quarter of a century.

Ed Dinger

PRINCIPAL SUBSIDIARIES

Naked Juice Co. of Glendora, Inc.

PRINCIPAL COMPETITORS

Hansen Natural Corporation; Odwalla, Inc.; South Beach Beverage Company, Inc.

FURTHER READING

"The Benefits of Helping Businesses Rise with the Green Tide," http://www.greenbiz.com/print/14093.

Chammas, Charifah, "Smoothie Move: Naked Juice Bumps Odwalla from Starbucks," *Los Angeles Business Journal,* March 17, 2008, p. 3.

Fuhrman, Elizabeth, "Baring It All: Naked Juice Brings on the Innovation," *Beverage Industry,* October 2007, p. 26.

Furfaro, Danielle T., "Eyes on Ultimate After Juice Deal," *Albany (N.Y.) Times Union,* November 2, 2001, p. E6.

Hein, Kenneth, "North Castle Forms Ultimate Juice As Main Squeeze for Beverage Brands," *Brandweek,* August 13, 2001, p. 14.

Horovita, Bruce, "2 Food Companies Go All-Out with Recycling," *USA Today,* July 9, 2009, p. B2.

Lowe, Marianne, "Smoothies Thirst for Beach Roots," *Inland Valley Daily Bulletin,* October 14, 2003.

Picarella, Michael, "Naked Juice Co-Creator Acquires a New Firm," *Agoura Hills (Calif.) Acorn,* September 11, 2003.

Tanaka, Rodney, "PepsiCo to Buy Naked Juice," *San Gabriel Valley Tribune,* November 22, 2006.

Newegg Inc.

16839 East Gale Avenue
City of Industry, California 91745
U.S.A.
Telephone: (909) 395-9046
Toll Free: (800) 390-1119
Fax: (909) 395-8907
Web site: http://www.newegg.com

Private Company
Incorporated: 2001
Employees: 1,500
Sales: $2.1 billion (2008 est.)
NAICS: 454113 Mail-Order Houses; 334119 Other
   Computer Peripheral Equipment Manufacturing

■ ■ ■

Based in City of Industry, California, Newegg Inc. is the nation's second largest online-only retailer. The company offers a selection of approximately 40,000 technology-related products, which it markets via an easy-to-use web site that includes customer ratings and reviews, product photos, specifications, and other details to support informed buying decisions. Toward the end of the first decade of the 21st century, Newegg served a customer base that included 12 million registered users at Newegg.com. Ranging from novices to advanced technology enthusiasts, the company's customers continually give the company top ratings for customer service. Newegg has a reputation for shipping products quickly from its warehouses, which spanned more than one million square feet. In addition to www.newegg.

com, Newegg also operates the web sites www.biz.newegg.com, www.newegg.com.cn, www.newegg.ca, and www.neweggbusiness.com.

FORMATIVE YEARS

Newegg emerged from a personal computer vendor named ABS Computer Technologies, which had formed in 1990. Much like Dell Inc., ABS manufactured build-to-order computer systems but focused on upper-end users. Over time, ABS began receiving customer requests for computer components, as opposed to entire systems. Because ABS's operations were geared toward selling entire computer systems, several of its employees decided to create a new company. Howard Tong, an engineer who had joined ABS in 1998, technology executive Fred Chang, and programmer Ken Lam used $1,000 to establish Newegg in January 2001. The company would later become known as one of the largest minority-owned businesses in Los Angeles County.

Newegg's name was inspired by the symbol of an egg, which represented the concepts of birth and unlimited potential. Specifically, the company explained that the name "Newegg" signified "new hope for e-commerce during a period when e-commerce businesses were struggling to remain in existence." Success came quickly for Newegg. After only a few months of operations, the company was profitable. By 2003 Newegg employed a workforce of 1,000 people. That year, the company expanded its product offerings to include consumer electronics, including flat-screen televisions and digital cameras. Another important development in 2003 was the establishment of operations on the East

Coast. These included a 50,000-square-foot warehouse in Edison, New Jersey, as well as a 75,000-square-foot bulk-order warehouse in Cranberry, New Jersey.

In 2004 the company began rolling out a variety of improvements to its web site. In addition to better search technology, the site's layout was enhanced, and navigation was streamlined. It also was in 2004 that Newegg established a subsidiary named Rosewill Inc. to manufacture private-label computer hardware and peripherals, which it planned to market exclusively via Newegg.com. Newegg's advertising expenditures totaled roughly $10 million in 2004, up significantly from $3.4 million the previous year. At that time, the company launched its first print and outdoor advertisements developed by an outside agency.

In August 2004 Newegg strengthened its senior leadership team by naming Jerry Kanaly as chief financial officer of Newegg.com. One final development occurred in December, when the company revealed plans to establish a global product management center in Taiwan. Roughly 80 percent of Newegg's products were manufactured in Taiwan and China. Sales totaled $980 million in 2004, supported by a strong customer following. Customer satisfaction was bolstered by the company's ability to ship products quickly. Newegg accomplished this by stocking its own inventory instead of relying upon shipments from suppliers and listing items for sale only if they were in stock.

EARLY GROWTH

Along with satisfied customers and growing sales, Newegg was generating considerable recognition during the middle of the decade. For example, in its 2004 Shoppers' Choice Awards, *Computer Shopper* ranked the company as the best overall place to shop online, and also best in three specific categories (core components,

digital gear, and software). More leadership changes took place in 2005. Early in the year, Ken Lam, U.S. CEO of Newegg.com, was promoted to the role of vice-chairman. In addition, Strategic Officer Simon Hsieh was promoted to global CEO. By this time, the company was generating 25,000 orders per day, nearly one-third of which were from first-time customers.

Midway through the year, Newegg bolstered its operations in Asia as part of a strategy to enhance customer support and establish direct buying relationships. In Chengdu, China, a new customer support operation was formed. In addition, the company secured three floors of office space in Shanghai to house its management information system, information technology, marketing research, human resources, customer support, product marketing, and corporate planning departments and benchmarking facilities.

Efforts to improve customer service continued in 2005. In September, the company announced plans to partner with technology company 14 Commerce, in an effort to roll out a preferred account program. Around the same time, a relationship was established with the alternative payment solutions company Bill Me Later. This allowed customers to purchase items without providing account or credit card information.

By November 2005, approximately 500,000 visitors frequented Newegg.com every day. The company served customers from five warehouses in California, one in Memphis, Tennessee, and two in New Jersey. Putting a premium on customer service, Newegg offered assistance via online chat and a toll-free phone line. The company rounded out the year with sales of $1.3 billion. Heading into the second half of the decade, Newegg's customer base continued to grow, reaching six million during 2006. In August of that year Newegg announced that it had cemented a deal with Brightpoint Inc., which agreed to supply the company with wireless devices and accessories.

OPERATIONAL EVOLUTION

As Newegg grew, the company looked to third parties for assistance with certain aspects of its operations. For example, although the company had once handled e-mail marketing to its customers internally, this task became difficult when Newegg's customer mailing list surpassed the 500,000 mark. A solution was found in San Francisco, California-based Loyalty Lab, a provider of customer relationship management tools, which began handling the company's marketing-focused e-mail communications.

Another new partner was Grand Rapids, Michigan-based Dematic Corp., which was tapped to provide an

KEY DATES

2001: Newegg is established.

2003: The company expands its product offerings to include consumer electronics, including flat-screen televisions and digital cameras.

2004: A subsidiary named Rosewill Inc. is formed to manufacture private-label brand computer hardware and peripherals.

2005: Sales reach $1.3 billion.

2007: Newegg introduces a new online community named Eggxpert.com and also expands into the mobile wireless arena.

2008: NeweggMall.com marks the company's expansion into general merchandise sales.

2009: The company ranks as the nation's second largest online-only retailer, with sales of more than $2 billion.

automated material handling system for a new distribution center the company planned to open in Edison in 2007. It also was in 2006 that Newegg cemented an agreement with the on-demand e-commerce and fulfillment solutions provider Vcommerce, which agreed to provide Newegg with a back-end fulfillment solution that synchronized customer orders with the company's drop-ship fulfillment processes. By this time, Newegg's product selection had grown to include some 60,000 stock-keeping units.

Newegg quickly caught on with consumers in search of good deals on consumer electronics. The 2006 holiday shopping season, in particular, provided ample evidence of this. On the Friday and Monday after Thanksgiving, known as Black Friday and Cyber Monday, the company broke the previous year's sales record as gift buyers and others snapped up flash drives and large hard drives capable of storing photos and other files.

Newegg continued to receive positive industry recognition. The company capped off 2006 by securing a place on *Internet Retailer*'s Top 10 Web Sites list. Specifically, Newegg.com was named the tenth highest-grossing online retailer. With more than 12 million unique visitors coming to its site every month, Newegg surpassed Walmart.com, QVC.com, and Best Buy in online sales that year. Among web-only retailers, Newegg was second only to Amazon.com.

Newegg ushered in 2007 by announcing the addition of several senior managers. Bernard Luthi joined

the company as vice-president of merchandising. Rick Quiroga was named vice-president of finance. Ed Johnson was appointed vice-president of human resources. Finally, Ron Bester was named vice-president of consumer electronics. Fred Chang led the company as chairman and CEO. In 2007 the *Los Angeles Business Journal* named Newegg as the third largest minority-owned business in Los Angeles County, based on 2006 revenues of $1.5 billion, up from $1.3 billion in 2005.

EXPANDED OFFERINGS

Midway through 2007, Newegg introduced a new online community named Eggxpert.com. In addition to a newsletter, the community included a free technology database called Eggipedia, which included new entries contributed by users, as well as the company's existing product information. Eggxpert.com also included the Eggxpert Blog Community, providing a forum for members to share their ideas.

In August, Newegg announced its entry into the mobile wireless arena. At that time, the company established a partnership with AT&T and became one of its authorized dealers. Newegg significantly enhanced its operations on the East Coast in September 2007, when its new 380,100-square-foot distribution center opened in Edison. The new distribution center included a conveyor platform and a pick-to-light system that provided a greater degree of automation. For example, instead of a manual process where workers searched throughout the distribution center for inventory, orders were routed to appropriate inventory areas. Technology also allowed the company to pack and ship orders more efficiently. In all, the amount of time required to process an order was reduced by approximately 15 to 20 percent.

By the latter part of 2007, Newegg's workforce had swelled to include 1,800 employees, 800 of whom were located in China and focused on handling management information systems. The company ended the year with revenues of $1.9 billion, an increase of $400 million from 2006.

During the second half of the decade, Newegg showed appreciation for its customers in a number of ways, including an annual sweepstakes that saw one winner drive away in a Mini Cooper S worth nearly $27,000. Other winners received flash drives, portable DVD players, digital cameras, iPods, and Bluetooth headsets.

Customer satisfaction continued to be high at Newegg. Based upon measurements from the firm Fore-See Results, which measured customer satisfaction for Newegg.com based upon the American Customer

Satisfaction Index, customers often gave ratings of 89 or 90 on a 100-point scale. In 2008 Newegg's satisfaction scores ranked in the top 1 percent among all clients of ForeSee Results.

INDUSTRY LEADER

Newegg had become one of the nation's largest privately held companies by 2008. At that time, the company had about 8.7 million registered users at Newegg.com. Along with a growing customer base, the company's workforce continued to expand, reaching 2,200 people. The company continued its evolution by rolling out NeweggMall.com. The new site applied certain aspects of the company's online retailing approach to general merchandise, such as auto parts, garden supplies, diamonds, apparel, furniture, and even makeup. In all, the new site initially offered 15,000 different products. One major difference between Newegg.com and NeweggMall.com was that general merchandise was not stocked in the company's own warehouses, as was the case with consumer electronics and computer components.

Despite difficult economic conditions, Newegg was able to achieve double-digit sales growth during the 2008 holiday season. The company headed into 2009 with more than 11 million registered users at Newegg.com. Newegg kicked off 2009 on a high note. For the sixth consecutive year, Newegg.com was named the Overall Best Place to Buy Online by *Consumer Shopper Magazine*. In addition, the National Retail Federation ranked the company sixth for Overall Best Customer Service.

In May 2009, Newegg filed a trademark infringement and unfair competition lawsuit against Kohl's Corp. in the U.S. District Court for the Central District of California. Specifically, the lawsuit focused on Kohl's use of the slogan, "The More You Know, the More You Kohl's," which Newegg felt infringed upon its trademarked slogan, "Once You Know, You Newegg."

By 2009 Newegg's Rosewill private-label subsidiary was producing more than 530 items, which were sold at Newegg.com and Newegg.ca. These included everything from keyboards and mice to power supplies and networking routers and switches. Rosewill had operations located in Shanghai, China; Taipei, Taiwan; and Southern California.

Newegg headed toward the second decade of the 21st century on solid footing. In only eight years' time, the company had grown to become the nation's second largest online-only retailer, with sales of more than $2 billion. Based on its winning retail approach and strong customer base, Newegg's prospects for the future seemed very bright.

Paul R. Greenland

PRINCIPAL DIVISIONS

Newegg Canada; Newegg China; Newegg Logistics; Newegg Taiwan; Newegg Tech; Newegg.com Inc.; NeweggMall; Rosewill Inc.

PRINCIPAL COMPETITORS

CDW Corp.; PC Connection Inc.; Systemax Inc.

FURTHER READING

Berman, Jeff, "Newegg.com Cooks up a New Model," *Logistics Management*, June 1, 2009.

Holmes, Kim, "Executive Finds Happiness with Incubation of Newegg," *Los Angeles Business Journal*, February 21, 2005.

Lee, Booyeon, "Online Retailer Drops PC Focus for New Venture: Computer-Centric Newegg Branches out with Amazon-Style Site," *Los Angeles Business Journal*, June 9, 2008.

"Newegg.com Carves Niche as Web Retailer," *San Gabriel Valley Tribune*, March 15, 2008.

Potkewitz, Hilary, "NewEgg.com Hatches Growth with Tech-Savvy Customers," *Los Angeles Business Journal*, March 27, 2006.

"Where the Tech Buffs Shop: NewEgg.com Has Carved Out a Loyal Following Among Shoppers Looking for the Latest Computer Gear," *Business Week Online*, November 18, 2005.

NOLAND
A WinWholesale Company

Noland Company

80 29th Street
Newport News, Virginia 23607
U.S.A.
Telephone: (757) 928-9000
Fax: (757) 928-9170
Web site: http://www.noland.com

Wholly Owned Subsidiary of WinWholesale Inc.
Incorporated: 1919 as Newport Plumbing & Mill Supply Company
Employees: 1,300
Sales: $600 million (2008 est.)
NAICS: 421720 Plumbing and Heating Equipment and Supplies Wholesalers; 421730 Air Conditioning Equipment and Supplies Wholesalers; 421610 Electrical Apparatus and Equipment, Wiring Supplies and Construction Materials Wholesalers; 421830 Industrial Machinery and Equipment Wholesalers

∎ ∎ ∎

Noland Company is a wholesale distributor of mechanical equipment and supplies. The company's product line includes plumbing, air conditioning, water systems, electrical, and industrial items. Noland Company serves customers, primarily the construction industry and industrial manufacturing, in 75 locations across the eastern and southern United States. Noland was acquired by WinWholesale Inc. in 2005 and operates as a subsidiary of the company.

THE EARLY YEARS: A SELF-MADE MAN SEIZES OPPORTUNITIES

Beginning with his departure from an orphanage at the age of 11, L. U. "Casey" Noland, founder of Noland Company, was the quintessential self-made man. At a young age, he went to Baltimore, where he worked at various jobs and eventually attained employment at a steelworks. He then found an apprenticeship with a plumber, which led to employment at the Newport News, Virginia, shipyard. Noland later took a position at an engineering firm, where he became vice-president at just 26 years of age. It was in 1915, however, that he truly began to make his mark. At that time, Noland and T. B. Clifford took advantage of new economic opportunities created by the advent of World War I, and formed a mechanical contracting business called the Noland-Clifford Company.

The Noland-Clifford Company did well but had difficulty procuring plumbing supplies. Locally, supplies were scarce and so most had to be shipped from Baltimore. Rather than purchase supplies on an as-needed basis, as most contractors did, the company began to stock an inventory of regularly required materials. It was when other local contractors began to seek supplies from Noland-Clifford's stash that Casey Noland recognized a need for a wholesale distributor in the Newport News area.

Thus, the Newport Plumbing & Mill Supply Company was formed in 1919. By the time the company incorporated as Noland Company in 1922, Noland had opened branches in Roanoke, Virginia, and Goldsboro and Winston-Salem, North Carolina. The company prospered, selling modern bathtubs, sinks, toilets, and related supplies. It continued to open new branches throughout the southeastern states. Noland's philosophy of strong sales support involved sales training, good employee benefits, and the incentive of a share in the company's profits.

Growth had its obstacles, but Noland was always up to the challenge. For example, when a railroad embargo halted shipments of supplies to the West Palm Beach branch during the Florida building boom, Noland resolved the problem by acquiring a 3,000-ton steamship to transport supplies to West Palm Beach. In doing so, Noland Company became the only plumbing, heating, and mill supplier in Florida. When the land boom later collapsed, Noland shipped the inventory from Florida to a new branch in Washington, D.C. As the business expanded and became more difficult to manage, Noland purchased a three-seat plane to speed travel to distant company branches.

Noland Company survived and even thrived during the Great Depression. In 1930 the company opened four new branches, filling what need existed as other companies failed. The only year the company experienced a financial loss due to the hard times was in 1932. Later, as President Franklin Roosevelt's civil service programs expanded access to electricity, Noland Company started an electrical supply department in 1938 and added refrigeration supplies to its product line in 1940. Company headquarters were moved to a larger facility in downtown Newport News, a few blocks from the original office. During the postwar home-building boom, Noland Company continued to thrive, providing plumbing, electrical, and other supplies to construction contractors. By 1952 Noland Company encompassed 25 branch units with 1,000 employees, and annual sales reached $50 million.

POSTWAR ERA

Upon the death of Casey Noland in 1952, L. U. Noland, Jr., took over the company's operations. The company continued to grow as Noland, Jr., emphasized customer service and satisfaction. His efforts, in fact,

culminated in *Supply House Times* naming the Noland Company "Wholesaler of the Year" in 1960.

In the early 1960s, the company diversified its wholesale supply offerings, with central air conditioning equipment becoming a significant new source of sales in the hot and humid southern states. The company upgraded its warehousing facilities, transferring operations to new modern buildings that allowed for more efficient operations. Noland included showrooms at many of the new buildings to display luxury plumbing fixtures and home lighting.

Noland Company became a public company with an initial offering of stock in 1967. Proceeds from the sale of stock funded acquisitions and electronic data processing. In the late 1960s, the company began implementation of the computer-based Branch Data System, which automated daily paperwork. The move streamlined purchase orders, vendor invoices, price changes, billing, and accounts receivables. After several years of branch level implementation, all branches were linked to a mainframe computer in 1978, enabling accessibility to information from distant branch locations for analysis at the central corporate office. The system provided managers with sales and inventory reports on a daily basis, allowing them to better serve branch units from the supply warehouses. In conjunction with computerized inventory tracking, Noland also implemented the "First In, First Out" inventory method in 1974 to reduce the impact of inflation on profit.

Expansion in the 1970s centered primarily on the states of Tennessee, Arkansas, and Alabama. In 1971 Noland acquired two units of the Amstar Division of American Standard, one located in Knoxville, Tennessee, and the other in Birmingham, Alabama. Soon thereafter came the purchase of Amstar Supply Company in Little Rock, Arkansas, in 1972. The company expanded more acquisitions and branches in 1978, as three single-unit wholesale outlets were purchased near existing Noland outlets that had growth potential. The new locations were Superior Supply in West Memphis, Arkansas; Savannah, Tennessee; and Annapolis, Maryland. The new branches were located in Mechanicsville, Maryland; Mountain Home, Arkansas; and Columbus, Mississippi. In early 1979, the company acquired Southern Supply in Jackson, Tennessee. With 61 branches in 11 southeastern states, 1979 sales reached $272 million.

Meanwhile, Noland continued its program to modernize, expand, and renovate its facilities. In 1978 four branch units were replaced by newer, larger facilities, while six others were expanded and a new warehouse-office-showroom opened in Atlanta. Also, a sales and service center opened in Roanoke, Virginia,

KEY DATES

1919: Newport Plumbing & Mill Supply Company is established.
1922: The company's name is changed to Noland Company.
1938: Noland adds an electrical supply department.
1952: L. U. Noland, Jr., becomes president.
1960: Noland is named "Wholesaler of the Year" by *Supply House Times*.
1967: Noland Company becomes a public company with an initial offering of stock.
1978: Implementation of Branch Data System significantly improves inventory control.
1991: Noland experiences its first net loss since the Great Depression.
1995: International expansion begins in Latin America.
1999: State-of-the-art inventory technology is implemented.
2003: A new distribution logistics center opens near Richmond, Virginia.
2005: Noland is acquired by WinWholesale Inc.

and the company's new Drilling Equipment Branch completed its first full year of operations in 1978, selling and repairing new and used well drilling rigs. A 70,000-square-foot main facility was completed in Norfolk in 1979.

Upgrading branch facilities produced a favorable response from the industry, as a survey of manufacturers' representatives voted 26 of the company's 44 showrooms onto the blue-ribbon list of better plumbing showrooms in *Supply House Times* magazine. Of the 26 showrooms, 12 were named "Best in Territory."

OVERCOMING FINANCIAL CHALLENGES

The 1980s proved to be financially uncertain years as sales and earnings fluctuated. The high rate of inflation and high interest rates discouraged home building and industrial production, which were Noland Company's key markets. The company took preventive measures and lowered its operating expenses, including staff cutbacks, to offset declining sales in 1980. The company halted capital expenditures for new equipment, branch expansion, and facilities upgrades, with the exception of those already in progress. Luckily, it was around this

time that the Branch Data System, in its second full year of operation, began to realize effective stock management and reduced inventory costs.

As economic conditions improved, the company resumed its expansion and improvement programs. The company acquired Tropical Supply Company in 1981, which had five branches in southeast Florida. In 1983 the company expanded its product line to include maintenance and repair parts, and implemented a new advertising program designed to highlight the company's showroom outlets. Noland Company added 12 new branches through both acquisition and new start-ups, but at the same time closed two small stores in 1984.

Noland also resumed its facilities improvement in the mid-1980s, remodeling eight branches in 1984 and seven branches in 1985. The company also built a new 84,000-square-foot facility in Frederick, Maryland. New facilities in Richmond included the Pipe, Valve, and Fitting Center and the Virginia Regional Distribution Center/Industrial. The latter facility was designed to serve the special requirements of the DuPont Company, including just-in-time delivery to area factories. This led to improvements in computer tracking of inventory.

The company also implemented a number of new technologies to improve customer service in the mid-1980s. The Customer Direct Order Entry System, a computer-to-computer ordering system, was introduced in 1982 and attracted large industrial customers. To facilitate faster counter service at its branches, the company invested in the Advanced Counter Computer System of electronic cash registers. The Counter Area Merchandising Program added self-service racks for tools, repair parts, and other frequently required items. The company also added industrial automation products to its supply line, primarily for customers in Nashville and Montgomery. The efforts to improve customer satisfaction proved valuable as *Supply House Times* once again named Noland Company "Wholesaler of the Year" in 1985.

Expansion continued with the June 1985 acquisition of Mars Plumbing Repair Parts and Mars Plumbing Supply Company; the latter supplied pipe, valves, and fittings to utility and mechanical contractors and industrial manufacturers through nine branches in San Antonio, Texas. With 17 new branches overall, Noland recorded its third year of record earnings in 1985, at $6.5 million. Sales at that time reached $380.9 million, representing an increase of 13.4 percent over those of 1984.

A THIRD GENERATION LEADS NOLAND

Sales and earnings continued to fluctuate as the third generation of the founding family assumed leadership of the company when L. U. Noland III became chairman of the board and CEO in 1987. Competitive pricing lowered profit margins and a slowdown in the economy led to a reduction in sales. The company responded by closing its unprofitable units, reducing the total number of branches to 94 in 1989; by laying off some of its employees; and by decreasing its inventory. Furthermore, a high rate of bankruptcy among the company's customers in the construction industry led to losses from uncollectible accounts payable. In 1991 Noland Company experienced a 10.3 percent decline in sales, to $384.5 million, and its first net loss since the Great Depression.

As the 1990s continued, however, modest improvements in the economy resulted in slow growth in the construction and industrial manufacturing industry. Noland lowered operating expenses by reducing its sales staff, thus increasing the average sales per employee and its gross profit margins. In 1992 sales reached $492.1 million. Sales of air conditioners and supplies did well at this time, but business in the company's other departments declined.

In 1994 the company experienced a 15 percent increase in sales of industrial maintenance, repair, and operating supplies through a systems-oriented sales and service approach. Noland Company added six new branches through both acquisition and new store openings. While Maryland branches served the company's Pennsylvania markets, it operated for the first time within Pennsylvania with an acquisition in Hanover. Noland Company's conservative control of expenses improved profit margins from 18.7 percent in 1992 to 19.6 percent in 1994. This resulted in impressive gains in 1994 in net income and sales, which reached $440.2 million.

The up and down trend of the 1990s continued in 1995, however, as lower-than-expected sales in the company's major markets (housing construction and industrial production) resulted in a 20.5 percent decline in earnings. Although the company's sales had actually risen 6.7 percent that year, excess stock had hurt the company financially. Sales in the air conditioner/refrigeration department made a significant contribution to total revenue. The dramatic increase resulted from Noland Company's entry into the export market in Latin American countries. Operating a new branch in Miami, Noland International sought exclusive distributors in Latin America.

The company continued to expand in profitable markets throughout the decade. Noland Company acquired two plumbing supply houses in Clearwater and Tampa, which increased the number of branches in Florida to 18, and gave Noland a branch in every major Florida market. The acquisition of Raub Supply Company added seven locations in Pennsylvania and Virginia, as well, raising the company's total number of branch locations to 107 in 14 states.

CHANGES AND IMPROVEMENTS

The company again designed a new branch computer system to improve inventory turnover and reduce excess inventory. The new system used bar-coding technology instituted at company warehouses and branch units in 1990. With implementation of the new system at 55 branches in 1995, excess inventory declined $1.7 million.

In the late 1990s, L. U. Noland III implemented a reorganization strategy to stabilize earnings and sales. Reorganization involved changes in staffing at both the sales and management levels. The company altered its approach to sales, shifting to a commission-based program with no salary. The sales staff was reduced from 333 to 250 people, which resulted in relocating employees to other positions in the company. L. U. Noland III also renewed the company's emphasis on employee training for all areas of the company. Its new headquarters included a multimedia training center, Noland University, to provide the continual development of new classes. Four regional management positions were added to address problems early, rather than wait for problems to reach the corporate office. The company also replaced branch credit managers with area credit managers, providing better controls and less bad-credit losses.

Noland Company continued to build on its success through new and time-tested methods. In 1999 the company decided to withdraw from the Texas market, and closed its six unprofitable branches to focus instead on the profitable southern and southeastern markets. The company updated and improved its inventory management strategy with state-of-the-art technology for more precise monitoring and forecasting. The system, implemented in 1999 for one-third of the company's branch units, included a Stock Locator System and Systematic Cycle Counting in all warehouses.

The company also instituted an Internet-based catalog to facilitate business-to-business sales; at the same time, promotions for the company's 35 Bath & Idea Centers resulted in a 22 percent increase in showroom sales. A central Industrial Distribution Center opened in 2000 to improve service to the company's industrial integrated supply accounts.

FACING CHALLENGES IN THE 21ST CENTURY

The early years of the new millennium proved challenging for Noland. Falling demand in its electrical and industrial segment forced the closure of its Industrial Distribution Center in 2002. At the same time, however, the company announced plans to construct a new $8.4 million Distribution Logistics Center near Richmond, Virginia, in an attempt to streamline its supply chain and cut costs. The new facility opened its doors in 2003.

Meanwhile, the company began to focus heavily on its air conditioning business. In 2000 it secured the distribution rights for Ruud Air Conditioning equipment and supplies in several Florida markets. The company's strategy paid off in 2003, when air conditioning sales increased by 10 percent. While overall company sales were down, Noland secured a 30 percent increase in net income over the previous year thanks in part to its cost-cutting efforts. Company sales increased in 2004, with growth in all three of the company's business segments—plumbing, air conditioning, and electrical/industrial.

By this time, intense competition was plaguing the marketplace and forcing companies to quickly expand or partner with larger entities. Noland opted for the latter and announced that Ohio-based WinWholesale Inc. had offered to purchase the company in 2005. Noland III and WinWholesale CEO Rick Schwartz had become familiar with each other through meetings at annual trade shows over the years and Schwartz eventually approached Noland III about selling the company. Noland Company's CEO agreed, and accepted WinWholesale's offer over six other bids.

WinWholesale, a firm with over 430 wholesale distribution companies in 41 states, was looking to expand into the southeastern United States and Noland was a perfect fit. Upon completion of the $250 million deal WinWholesale secured a position as the nation's fourth largest wholesaler.

As part of the Win Group of Companies, Noland operated as a private entity with little change to its overall business model. It benefited from being part of a larger organization and continued to strengthen its product line. In 2008 Noland partnered with Nordyhe, a subsidiary of Nortek Inc., to exclusively sell the Nu-Tone Heating and Cooling products line. While Noland's family business roots were a thing of the past, it appeared as though its new partnership with WinWholesale left it well positioned for future growth opportunities.

Mary Tradii
Updated, Christina M. Stansell

PRINCIPAL COMPETITORS

Ferguson Enterprises Inc.; HD Supply Inc.; Watsco Inc.

FURTHER READING

Blackwell, John Reid, "Noland to Build Distribution Center in Prince George County, Va.," *Richmond Times-Dispatch,* November 6, 2002.

Davis, Michael, "WinWholesale Completes Stock Buyout of Noland," *Virginian-Pilot,* May 20, 2005.

Glynn, Matt, "Virginia-Based Noland Co. Expects an Even Better Year," *Knight-Ridder/Tribune Business News,* April 24, 1997.

Noland Company: A Blend of Traditional Strengths and Progressive Changes, Newport News: Noland Company, 1990.

"Noland Company Reports 1993 Earnings of $3.3 Million," *PR Newswire,* February 18, 1994.

"Noland Company Reports Lower '95 Earnings," *PR Newswire,* February 23, 1996.

"Noland Reports Record Earnings for 1999," *PR Newswire,* February 21, 2000.

Roberson, Jason, "CEO's Small Talk Led to Big Deal," *Dayton (Ohio) Daily News,* April 17, 2005.

Shean, Tom, "A Rich History," *Virginian-Pilot,* April 14, 2005.

NRJ Group S.A.

—————— ■ ——————

22 rue Boileau
Paris, F-75203 Cedex 16
France
Telephone: (33 01) 40 71 40 00
Fax: (33 01) 40 71 40 40
Web site: http://www.nrjgroup.fr

Public Company
Founded: 1984
Employees: 1,865
Sales: EUR 331.3 million ($473.7 million) (2008)
Stock Exchanges: Euronext Paris
Ticker Symbol: NRJ
NAICS: 515112 Radio Stations; 515120 Television
 Broadcasting

■ ■ ■

NRJ Group S.A. is a leading French radio broadcaster. Since the dawn of the 21st century, NRJ (pronounced "energy") has also been developing as a full-scale media group, with operations in television broadcasting, Internet, music distribution, events planning, mobile telephony, and other areas. NRJ's French radio offering focuses on its four main radio brands: NRJ, France's "number one hits" station, with more than ten million listeners per week; Rire & Chansons, which mixes music and humor; Cherie FM, an easy listening format targeting female listeners; and Nostalgie, a "golden oldies" format. Each week, the company reaches more than 28 million listeners in France. The company has also rolled out the NRJ music format on an international level, with stations broadcasting in Austria, Belgium, Bulgaria, Denmark, Finland, Germany, Lebanon, Norway, Russia, Sweden, Switzerland, Ukraine, and, since 2009, Canada.

NRJ's television division operates through France's digital terrestrial television broadcasting format and is led by flagship NRJ 12, a national broadcaster featuring general programming. The company also operates the music-oriented NRJ Hits, and two local channels, NRJ Paris and 7L TV. NRJ's Internet operations, which include web sites for its major radio and television brands, boast monthly visitor rates of 5.1 million per month. NRJ has reduced its exposure to the mobile telephony market, while remaining a partner in the virtual operator NRJ Mobile. The company is also active in events planning and theatrical productions; music publishing through the NRJ Music label; and broadcast services through subsidiary Towercast. NRJ is listed on the Euronext Paris stock exchange. Founder and Chairman Jean-Paul Baudecroux controls 72.6 percent of the group's shares. In 2008, the company generated total revenues of EUR 331.3 million ($474 million).

ORIGINS IN FM

NRJ Group was the brainchild of Jean-Paul Baudecroux, born in 1946. Baudecroux's father, who died when Baudecroux was 11 years old, was chemist Paul Baudecroux, inventor of the first indelible lipstick, Rouge Baiser. Baudecroux displayed little passion for his studies, and never completed his high school diploma. Baudecroux at first went to work for the family's cosmetics business; however, in 1965 he traveled to the United States, where

COMPANY PERSPECTIVES

Mission. A multimedia Group. Radio, Television, Internet, Mobile Telecommunications and Entertainment. A key radio player in France, with operations in a further 12 countries, NRJ Group works as an editor, producer and broadcaster, while marketing its own media spaces. It is capitalising on the strength of the radio media and its brands (NRJ, Nostalgie, Cherie Fm, Rire & Chansons), as well as its marketing expertise and commercial strength to deploy new media—television, internet and mobile telephony—in order to follow and anticipate changes in consumption trends and offer overall solutions for its customers.

he completed a course in management training. Baudecroux then took a marketing job with Revlon in the United States. In 1972, Baudecroux returned to France to set up his first business, Elysées 12-12, a telephone call center providing information and reservation services for Parisian restaurants. That business provided Baudecroux with his first success as an entrepreneur.

In the 1980s, Baudecroux became interested in the opportunities offered by the introduction of FM radio in France. While France had been a pioneer in radio broadcasting in the 1920s, the country's airwaves had remained commercial-free and tightly controlled by the government. The few state-owned broadcasters were limited largely to a general format, mixing news, talk, and popular music. This situation, similar to other European radio markets, stimulated the growth of pirate broadcasters, which transmitted into the country from beyond France's borders. These broadcasters usually displayed a lack of professionalism, and their transmissions were often difficult to capture.

The arrival of François Mitterrand's Socialist government in 1981 promised to liberalize the radio market, as the government prepared to authorize the creation of privately owned radio broadcasters for the first time. In anticipation of this event, Baudecroux decided to establish his own radio station in 1981. Baudecroux initially targeted the female listening audience. He quickly changed his mind, however, and instead began developing a youth-oriented radio format. Baudecroux called his station Nouveau Radio Jeunesse (French for "New Youth Radio"), which provided the initials NRJ—pronounced "energy."

PARIS RADIO PIONEER

Baudecroux installed his transmitter in the former maid's room atop his family's home on rue Telegraphe, on the Buttes-Chaumont in Paris. As Baudecroux liked to claim, NRJ started out with a "transmitter in the bathtub" and "the antenna posed in the window." NRJ nevertheless enjoyed a number of advantages. For one, its location atop one of Paris's hills provided access to unobstructed transmission to much of the city. For another, Baudecroux was backed by his family's wealth, which enabled him to purchase the most modern and powerful transmitters available at that time.

Because commercial radio broadcasts had not been legalized at the time, NRJ originated as an association, formed by Baudecroux and partners Max Guazzini, Jean-Pierre d'Amico, and a number of volunteers. The station launched its first broadcast in July 1981. Like many early FM radio stations, NRJ operated on an amateurish basis; disc jockeys played music from their own collections, and often filled the studio with their friends during broadcasts. The station's youth-oriented format and the strength of its transmission enabled NRJ quickly to build a large listenership in the Paris area. By 1983, the station claimed the largest audience in its segment.

The Socialist government's initial goal of liberalizing the radio market was to encourage the creation of locally based, nonprofit radio stations largely devoted to community service. However, the pressure to allow the broadcasting of advertisements began to build, particularly after the creation of the country's first commercial television broadcasters. The legalization of commercial radio finally came in 1984.

In preparation for this moment, Baudecroux recognized the need to transform the chaotic atmosphere of the early NRJ into a more professionally structured business. Baudecroux, who had continued to run Elysées 12-12, took direct control of NRJ, forcing out d'Amico and Guazzini, and the company incorporated as NRJ Régies. Baudecroux brought in Ted Fergusson, who had run Radio Alabama in the United States, to transform the FM radio association into a commercial radio broadcaster.

BECOMING A COMMERCIAL BROADCASTER

Fergusson imposed a new, more rigorous style on the station. Disc jockeys were expected to play music only from the station's own collection, especially following play lists based on hits of the day. NRJ also eliminated a great deal of the between-song chatter, increasing the number of songs played per hour. These were separated by slick, recorded jingles promoting NRJ itself.

KEY DATES

1981: Jean-Claude Baudecroux founds the NRJ radio station as an association, broadcasting from his family's home in Paris.

1984: NRJ incorporates as a limited liability company and begins commercial radio broadcasts.

1985: NRJ adds its first franchise stations, in Bordeaux and Lyon.

1987: NRJ launches a second radio format, Cherie FM.

1988: NRJ launches its third radio format, Rire & Chansons; the company goes public on the Paris Bourse and launches its first international radio stations in Switzerland and Belgium.

1998: NRJ acquires its fourth radio format, Nostalgie.

2000: NRJ regroups all of its operations under a new holding company, NRJ Group.

2005: NRJ launches a diversification drive, introducing television broadcasting, mobile telephone, Internet, and events planning operations.

2007: NRJ adds two more television stations, NRJ Hits and 7L.

2009: NRJ begins its exit from the mobile telephone sector as it slips into losses for the first time.

The new regime proved immediately successful, and the station's audience soared. NRJ's fast-growing audience also attracted the station's first advertisers. The influx of revenues in turn permitted the station to install still more powerful transmission equipment, extending its reach. By the end of 1984, NRJ's powerful broadcasts brought it into conflict with the authorities, which charged the company with overreaching its permitted frequencies. As punishment, the government attempted to impose a one-month broadcast suspension on the company. NRJ called on its audience for support, sparking a demonstration by more than 100,000 people in Paris. The suspension was lifted after just one day.

Baudecroux then set out to build a national radio network. In 1985, he sold Elysées 12-12 to focus solely on building NRJ. Baudecroux brought in a new partner that year, Alain Weill, to help build the company's

network. For this, Baudecroux took his inspiration from the franchise concept of the fast-food industry. Weill was sent out to recruit broadcasters for the NRJ format. Rather than recruit radio professionals, NRJ instead brought in people with no prior radio experience, a tactic that permitted Baudecroux and Weill to maintain tighter control over the NRJ brand and format. By the end of 1985, the company had signed on its first provincial franchisees, in Lyon and Bordeaux.

Control remained an important facet of NRJ's strategy through the 1980s. In 1986, the company created Sogetec (later known as Towercast), which began installing radio and television transmission towers throughout France. Sogetec also became one of the first to invest in new satellite transmission technologies. The company built up a network of more than 500 towers in strategic locations throughout the country. The transmission towers not only supported NRJ's own broadcasts, but also provided a source of revenues as a provider of transmission services to third-party broadcasters, and later, mobile telephone operators.

EXPANDING BRAND PORTFOLIO

NRJ continued to develop its network of local NRJ-branded radio stations through the 1980s and 1990s. At the same time, the company also sought to build a portfolio of broadcast brands. In 1987, Baudecroux revisited his original radio target market, creating the easy listening Cherie FM station designed to attract a female audience. Toward this end, the company acquired an existing radio station, Gilda, operating in the Parisian region, which was then converted to the Chérie format.

For his next target Baudecroux turned to the male audience. The company developed a new format for this, mixing topical humor with popular music. The new radio format was given the name Rire & Chansons (Laughter & Song), and the company went in search of a new radio broadcaster acquisition. This came in 1989, when NRJ acquired Pacific FM. That network of stations was then converted to the Rire & Chansons format. Also in that year, NRJ went public, listing on the Paris Bourse secondary market.

In the 1990s, NRJ held three markedly different radio formats, designed to attract their own audiences and advertisers. By then, NRJ had grown into one of France's most powerful radio broadcast groups, easily outpacing rival Europe 1. By the mid-1990s, the company had begun to close in on French leader France Inter. In the meantime, Baudecroux had also begun to export the NRJ format. The company spotted new opportunities as a number of other European countries began liberalizing their radio broadcasting sectors in the late 1980s and into the 1990s.

By 1989, NRJ had established its first international NRJ franchises, in Switzerland and Belgium. The company next entered Germany, establishing its first radio station in Berlin in 1991. By 1993, the company had added three more German stations, and had also become the first private broadcaster to gain a license in Sweden. The company expanded rapidly in that country, and by 1995 had set up a network of more than 15 radio stations. NRJ continued to build up its presence in the Scandinavian market, adding its first station in Finland in 1995, and then entering Norway in 1998 and Denmark in 2000.

While NRJ's international operations focused exclusively on building its hits-oriented NRJ format, the company's French base added its fourth format in 1998. In that year, the company acquired an existing radio network, Nostalgie, focused on the "golden oldies" segment. NRJ quickly revitalized Nostalgie, placing the emphasis on up-tempo rock music from the era of the 1960s to the 1980s. Nostalgie rapidly claimed the leadership in its broadcast segment.

BUILDING A 21ST CENTURY MEDIA GROUP

NRJ's radio ambitions soon ran into legislation that limited the reach of French broadcasters to just 150 million potential listeners, forcing the company to abandon its bid to acquire Radio Monte Carlo in 2000. Instead, NRJ began developing a new strategy, designed to transform the company from a radio broadcaster to a multifaceted media group. One of the company's first moves in this direction was the creation of its own record label, NRJ Music, in 1999.

NRJ restructured in 2000, bringing all of its operations under a new holding company, NRJ Group. The company then transferred its listing to the primary board of the Paris Bourse in preparation for setting in motion its new diversification strategy. Baudecroux began seeking new media horizons in the 21st century, including television broadcasting and the fast-growing Internet market.

NRJ's true diversification came in 2005. In that year, the company created a new subsidiary, NRJ Events. This company, which developed and promoted events such as concerts and shows, provided strong ties with the group's existing operations. Among the major successes of NRJ Events was the 2005–06 production of "Le Roi Soleil," a Broadway-style musical theater performance featuring catchy, hit-oriented music. With strong airplay of its songs on the NRJ radio network,

"Le Roi Soleil" became a major hit for the company.

NRJ Group then turned its attention to another major ambition, entering the television broadcast market. The introduction of digital terrestrial television (known as TNT in France) provided the company with the opportunity, as it secured its first two licenses in 2005. By the end of that year, the company had rolled out its flagship channel, NRJ 12, a general format featuring series, films, game shows, and music, broadcasting on a national level. Also in 2005, NRJ made a move into the mobile telephone market, launching the virtual operator NRJ Mobile. A virtual operator did not own its own transmission infrastructure, but instead rented bandwidth from full-fledged operators. NRJ also established a major presence in the Internet, building up its own network of web sites for its various radio and television brands.

FACING DIFFICULTIES

NRJ's radio division in the meantime had continued its own strong growth. In 2002, the company laid claim to the leadership in the French radio market for the first time. Through the end of the decade, however, NRJ faced growing competition, notably from RTL, which again grabbed the lead, and state-owned rival France Inter.

In 2007, the company extended its television broadcast operations, adding the music oriented NRJ Hits channel, as well as 7L, a local broadcaster based in Montpellier. The company also launched its first web-based radio broadcasts, in conjunction with a reformatting of its web sites. However, the economic downturn at the end of the decade caught up with the company by 2008. The company was forced to reduce its exposure to the mobile telephone market, dropping its stake in money-losing NRJ Mobile in 2009 to just 10 percent. At the same time, NRJ was confronted with a drop in audience levels and advertising revenues at its radio networks. The group's international operations also began losing money. By the end of 2008, revenues had slipped back to EUR 331 million ($474 million). The company slipped into losses for the first time in its history.

To make matters worse, in 2009 NRJ slipped back into third place, behind rival France Inter. In response to the group's difficulties, founder Baudecroux, who had begun preparing his retirement from the company in the middle of the decade, returned to take active control of its direction. Baudecroux announced the group's interest in acquiring new television licenses, targeting in particular Télé Lyon Métropole (TLM). Baudecroux hoped to recapture the spirit of NRJ's early days, when the upstart radio station had emerged as one of the most dynamic players in France's media industry.

M. L. Cohen

PRINCIPAL SUBSIDIARIES

CanalMusic SA (Luxembourg); Capitec OY (Finland); Cherie FM Réseau SAS; Cherie FM SAS; Energy Zürich (Radio Z AG) (Switzerland; 49%); Gilda SARL; Nostalgie SA (Belgium); NRJ 12 SARL; NRJ Belgique SA; NRJ Events SARL; NRJ Finland OY; NRJ Global SAS; NRJ Holding Suisse SA (Switzerland); NRJ International Operations GmbH (Germany); NRJ Media AB (Sweden); NRJ Nordic AB (Sweden); NRJ Norge AS (Norway); NRJ SAS; Radio Nostalgie Réseau SAS; Radio Nostalgie SAS; Radio NRJ GmbH (Germany); Régie Networks Belgique SA; Rire & Chansons SAS; Sonopar Participations SAS; SW Radiodiffusion SAS.

PRINCIPAL DIVISIONS

Rire & Chansons; NRJ; Cherie FM; Radio Nostalgie.

PRINCIPAL OPERATING UNITS

Regies; Secteurs Annonceurs; Diffusion.

PRINCIPAL COMPETITORS

Lagardere Active SAS; Société Nationale de Radiodiffusion Radio France; DI Group SA; Radio France Internationale SA; NextRadioTV SA; Société pour l'Édition Radiophonique SA.

FURTHER READING

Bouchara, Olivier, "Jean-Paul Baudecroux, Fondateur d'NRJ," *L'Expansion,* September 15, 2008.

Bouton, Remi, "Centralised NRJ Creates New European 'Network,'" *Music & Media,* June 26, 1999, p. 1.

———, "NRJ to Launch Ambitious New E-Commerce Division," *Music & Media,* September 18, 1999, p. 3.

"Jean-Paul Baudecroux Aimerait Racheter TLM," *Zonebourse. com,* April 28, 2009.

"Jean-Paul Baudecroux Reprend les Manettes de NRJ," *Stratégies,* May 22, 2008.

Legrand, Emmanuel, "NRJ Shares Ratings Crown with France Info," *Music & Media,* July 26, 2003, p. 1.

———, "Viva la Radio," *Billboard Radio Monitor,* October 15, 2004, p. 16.

"Le Mobile et l'International Font Plonger NRJ dans le Rouge," *Stratégies,* March 26, 2009.

Manceau, Jean-Jacques, "NRJ Explore d'Autres Fréquences," *L'Expansion,* March 1, 2006.

"NRJ Group (France) Is Pronounced 'Energy' by the Millions of European Teens Tuning into the Growing Radio Company's Pop Fluff," *Forbes Global,* October 27, 2003, p. 42.

"NRJ to Launch French Digital TV Channel," *Music & Media,* November 2, 2002, p. 3.

Pasold, Lisa, "NRJ Displaces RTL as French Leader," *Music & Media,* November 30, 2002, p. 1.

Signouret, Muriel, "NRJ Arrive en Zone Rouge," *Stratégies Magazine,* April 2, 2009.

———, "NRJ Soigne sa Locale avec Google," *Stratégies,* June 4, 2009.

NTK Holdings Inc.

———— ■ ————

50 Kennedy Plaza
Providence, Rhode Island 02903-2360
U.S.A.
Telephone: (401) 751-1600
Fax: (401) 751-4610
Web site: http://www.nortek-inc.com

Private Company
Incorporated: 1967 as Nortek, Inc.
Employees: 8,800
Sales: $2.27 billion (2008 est.)
NAICS: 332322 Sheet Metal Work Manufacturing;
333415 Air Conditioning and Warm Air Heating
Equipment and Commercial and Industrial
Refrigeration Equipment Manufacturing; 335228
Other Major Household Appliance Manufacturing

■ ■ ■

NTK Holdings Inc. operates as a holding company for
Nortek, Inc., a leading international, diversified
manufacturer and distributor of building products for
residential, light commercial, and commercial
applications. From its headquarters in Providence,
Rhode Island, Nortek and its subsidiaries operate within
four principal segments: Residential Ventilation
Products; Home Technology Products; Residential Air
Conditioning and Heating (HVAC) Products; and
Commercial HVAC.

These subsidiaries manufacture and sell a wide
variety of building products in key categories, such as
kitchen range hoods and other spot-ventilating products,

heating and air conditioning systems, lighting controls,
indoor air-quality systems, and specialty home entertainment products primarily in the United States, Canada,
and Europe. Nortek's products are designed to meet the
needs of professionals in the manufactured home, new
construction, and remodeling markets as well as those of
individual contractors, wholesalers, and do-it-yourself
customers. The company is the largest supplier of
kitchen range hoods in North America. Thomas H. Lee
Partners L.P. and members of Nortek's management
team acquired Nortek in August 2004.

ORIGINS

Ralph R. Papitto began his career as an entrepreneur in
1956 by founding Glass-Tite Industries, Inc., later
known as GTI Corporation, a manufacturer of
electronic semiconductor components. On July 24,
1967, Papitto founded Nortek, Inc., (named in part
after Norma, his first wife) in Cranston, Rhode Island,
and took the company public in September. His
purpose, as stated in Nortek's 1967 annual report, was
to form "an alliance of companies with long records of
successful growth." Within a Nortek alliance, Papitto
believed these companies could operate from "a larger
perspective ... and better cope with technical, financial,
production, and marketing problems." Thus, Papitto
based his business philosophy on "strong internal
growth and external growth with strong companies in
carefully selected industries."

Papitto quickly implemented this business
philosophy. On November 20, 1967, Nortek purchased
Kinetic Instrument Corp. and Kaybe Machine and

Instrument Corp.; in December he acquired Nursery Plastics, Inc., and Young Designs, Inc. Kinetic produced high-performance elements such as small gears, gyroscope yokes, wave guides, and microwave insulators for space-age technologies. Kaybe was a recognized manufacturer of large multiple-needle stitching machines and the innovator of quilting patterns used by textile firms. Nursery Plastics and Young Designs, on the other hand, worked with educators, pediatricians, and child psychologists to manufacture items for developing the coordination, and memory retention of small children.

During 1968 Nortek acquired four organizations. The first two were Vitta Corporation, originator of a new dry-plating method that used flexible tapes in the electronics industry primarily to transfer thin layers of precious metals to surfaces without causing any molecular change; and Providence-based Domestic Credit Corporation, which conducted several banking activities. In December Nortek purchased American Flexible Conduit Co., Inc., and its two associated companies (all of which Papitto bought after his retirement). Nortek also acquired the Massachusetts-based Duro Group of seven companies engaged in dyeing, finishing, printing, and distributing textiles. By year-end 1968, Nortek reported net revenues of $23.70 million compared to revenues of $13.62 million in fiscal 1967. Internal growth of operating units during 1968 averaged 15 percent, compared to a growth of 9 percent in the Gross National Product Index of that year.

In an interview included in Nortek's 1968 annual report, Chairman Papitto told financial analyst James D. Kilpatrick that Nortek's rapid growth was largely due to the application of the multi-market company concept. Most medium-sized companies in the United States, said Papitto, were "convinced of the merits of becoming public companies" but feared that lack of sufficient resources would prevent them from performing successfully as public companies responsible to shareholders. Papitto persuaded companies to join multi-market Nortek, a parent organization that would give them the resources for meeting public company responsibilities of growth through new opportunities for "planning,

research, risk-taking, and expansion." Papitto explained that Nortek's business strategy was one of "planned growth through balanced diversification."

EARLY EMPHASIS ON REAL ESTATE

In 1969 Nortek was listed on the American Stock Exchange and was one of the most actively traded issues of that year. Initially, the company focused on three major areas: land sales and development; consumer and industrial products; and financial services. Nortek purchased Vermont-based Rock of Ages Corporation and its granite quarries. Rock of Ages was the leader of the memorialization industry (monuments, markers, mausoleums, memorials) in North America. In Nortek's 1969 annual report, Papitto quoted data from *U.S. News & World Report* indicating that from 1959 to 1969 land prices "soared 95 percent while common stocks, by contrast, rose only 18 percent in the same period, in terms of the Dow Jones Industrial average."

In sync with the trend to buy land, Nortek acquired the Webb Realty Group of five associated companies that were among the fastest-growing organizations in the land development business in Florida (where they created planned communities) and also acquired large acreage for community developments in New England, Arizona, Nebraska, and Michigan. The growth of consumer reliance on installment credit fostered Domestic Credit Corp.'s diversification into financing and mortgaging services. Net sales and operating revenues for fiscal 1969 totaled $43.75 million, compared to $23.70 million (as restated for pooling of interests) in fiscal 1968.

The Webb Realty Group sold mobile homes and reported record revenues. In 1971 Domestic Credit Corp. relocated to Cranston, Rhode Island, and offered all financial services, except checking and trust functions. Domestic's operations complemented those of the Webb Group; financial services were a necessary dimension for full-service land sales and development, including the financing and development of mobile home communities. Nortek also acquired Arizona-based Mastercraft Homes, Inc., which had a strong growth record as a builder of homes. Despite the soft economy that prevailed in 1971, Nortek reported revenues of $30.81 million for that fiscal year.

STRENGTHENING CORPORATE MANAGEMENT

During 1972–73, Nortek reduced overhead costs, raised selling prices, and increased sales. Substantial debt was

KEY DATES

1967: Ralph R. Papitto founds Nortek, Inc.

1969: Nortek is listed on the American Stock Exchange.

1971: A Nortek subsidiary reports record sales of mobile homes.

1980: Nortek sets plans in motion to enter the building-products industry.

1985: Nortek relocates its headquarters to Providence, Rhode Island.

1989: Housing starts drop sharply for the third consecutive year.

1990: Chairman Papitto retires in favor of Nortek President Richard L. Bready.

1993: Nortek management restructures operations and revises its business strategy.

1999: Nortek launches plans to sell eight businesses and acquire seven major companies; company posts record sales.

2003: Kelso & Company L.P. acquires Nortek in a $1.6 billion deal.

2004: Thomas H. Lee Partners, L.P., and members of company management purchase the company.

2005: NTK Holdings is formed as a holding company for Nortek.

eliminated by the company's withdrawal from real estate and land development activities. Nortek divested itself of both Nortek Properties, Inc. (formerly the Webb Group), and Mastercraft Homes, Inc.; continued to nurture the growth of its other subsidiary companies; and strengthened corporate management. Richard J. Harris joined the company as manager of corporate accounting, thereby initiating a career path that would bring him to serve as vice-president, treasurer, and chief financial officer beyond 2000. At the end of fiscal 1973, Nortek reported net earnings of $1.43 million, compared to $1.14 million in 1972.

An energy crisis, shortages of raw materials, high interest rates, government controls, and accelerating inflation created an adverse economic environment during 1974–75. Nortek strengthened its senior management team with the appointment of Richard L. Bready (who became president and CEO in 1990) as vice-president and treasurer. A growing demand for Duro Group's fabrics allowed it to recover from the 1974 turndown of the textile industry. Rock of Ages

continued to upgrade its procedures and, according to Nortek's 1975 annual report, "was particularly proud of the unique 27x30-foot bas-relief granite sculpture completed for installation on the facade of the giant Libby Dam in Montana." For fiscal 1975, Nortek posted net sales of $62.42 million, an increase of 28 percent over 1974.

Although net sales for 1976 peaked at $72.71 million, net earnings dropped to $82,000, reduced by settlement of litigation for a seven-year-old lawsuit and reorganization of Nortek's Cable and Wire Division. Nortek sold its marginally profitable finance subsidiary, Domestic Credit Corporation, and merged its new acquisition, Minnesota-based Manufacturers Systems, Inc. (MSI), into a Nortek subsidiary. MSI manufactured and distributed a wide variety of metal products for heating and cooling systems. During 1977 harsh winter weather severely affected the quarrying operations of Nortek's Rock of Ages subsidiary and the worldwide oversupply of copper caused continued erosion in the selling prices and gross profit margins of the Cable and Wire Division. Nevertheless, despite adverse economic conditions in many of Nortek's primary markets, none of Nortek's operating divisions experienced losses during 1978–79. Net sales for fiscal 1979 rose to $117.96 million while net earnings grew to $3.75 million.

ADAPTING TO A CHANGING ECONOMY

The 1980s, according to the Kingwood College Library web site, was "an era of hostile takeovers, leveraged buy-outs, and mega-mergers that spawned a new breed of billionaires." For many people, binge buying and running up credit were the order of the day during this decade, which began with double-digit inflation. President Ronald Reagan (1981–89) "obtained legislation to curb inflation, stimulate economic growth, increase employment, strengthen the military and renew national self confidence." The recession of 1981–82 slowly gave way to relative prosperity as corporations adapted to a changing economy.

Higher prices for supplies and raw materials, rising wage levels, additional fringe benefits, and other costs that Nortek could not completely pass along to customers had a negative impact on net earnings. Furthermore, reduced demand for exports of higher-margin rough granite and price fluctuations in copper adversely affected the profitability of Rock of Ages and of the Cable and Wire Division.

It was at this time that Nortek, with subsidiaries in various types of businesses, entered the building products industry with the acquisition of Miami-based

Glassalum Engineering Corp. and of Glassalum Installations, Inc. These companies engineered, manufactured, and installed glass and aluminum exteriors for multistory commercial buildings and condominiums and brought in a $16 million backlog of orders. In January 1981, Nortek further strengthened its position in the building products industry by acquiring Wisconsin-based Broan Mfg. Co., Inc., a manufacturer of built-in home products, and the largest manufacturer of kitchen range hoods; Broan products were used in new construction and in renovation projects.

Nortek's investment in building products did not pay off immediately but did serve as the seed from which Nortek would grow. High interest rates on mortgages slowed down the demand for housing in 1981–82. In the mid-1980s, however, according to Carl Horowitz's analysis of housing in the 1980s, the United States "had 102.7 million dwellings in 1987, a 49.5 percent increase over the 68.7 million dwellings in 1970." The increase was due in part to a recovering economy and a shift in population brought on by baby boomers who, "by the close of the 1980s, were in the 35–54 age group, had established their own households." "During the 1980s," according to the April 29, 1990, issue of the *Boston Globe*, Nortek "bought or sold more than a dozen companies, including makers of aerospace fasteners, bicycle spokes, aircraft landing gear, brass nuts and plastics."

FACING PROBLEMS

Nortek continued to diversify through acquisitions, mainly Linear Corporation and Nordyne Inc. At first, Nortek financed acquisitions with commercial bank debt. Early in the 1980s, however, "the company was introduced to a different way of raising money: selling high-yield, high-risk debt, known as junk bonds," according to Neil Downing in the *Providence Journal-Bulletin*. These bonds gave Nortek millions of dollars for acquisitions. "Nortek issued junk bonds to help pay for one or two big acquisitions, which never materialized. While searching for deals, Nortek invested a lot of the proceeds from the bond sales in other companies' junk bonds or in junk-bond mutual funds," Downing noted. At the end of the decade, the company's profits suffered from the 1987 stock market crash, which devastated Nortek's junk bond portfolio. For several years after early 1988, Nortek made no significant material acquisitions.

Furthermore, by 1989 Nortek had other problems. Housing starts had begun to plummet in 1986 and by 1989 were down for the third consecutive year nationwide and at their lowest level since the 1981–82 recession. "Resales of existing homes were at a five-year low," wrote Biddle for the *Boston Globe*. Nortek had to settle two court cases and resolve allegations brought by the Securities and Exchange Commission. For fiscal 1989, the company posted a $12.5 million loss on sales of $1.08 billion, the company's largest net loss and, ironically, its largest net sales in about ten years. All was not gloom and doom, however: Nortek had begun to evolve as a manufacturer of building products, to cut operating costs, and to restructure.

Since its founding in 1967, Nortek had owned a granite quarry, a land development company, and a lamp manufacturer. It had bought and sold dozens of companies, including those involved in textiles, toys, banking, and aerospace. A significant number of acquisitions made in a relatively short time rapidly increased the company's debt. Relatively high interest rates, problems in the savings-and-loan industry, and a sudden downturn in the housing market slowed sales of building products. Nortek found it difficult to service its debt on a continuing basis. By 1990 Nortek shares had plunged to $2.875 per share, compared to a range before the October 1987 crash of $12 to $16 per share.

CHANGES IN LEADERSHIP

In November 1990, Papitto retired in favor of his longtime associate, Nortek President Bready, who succeeded him as the company's chief executive officer. Bready came into his new position to face $350 million in short- and long-term debt, including $170 million in junk bonds. Nortek's stock had dropped down to less than $2 a share.

Nortek's growth had been generated largely by strategic acquisitions and mergers, and by the success of its product groups. The profitability of these groups was significantly impacted between 1986 and 1991 by a decline of 43.8 percent in new housing starts as well as by harsh economic conditions, particularly in the Northeast, California, and Canada. Construction of residential housing increased about 20 percent during 1990–94 but remained below the levels of the mid-1980s. President and CEO Bready led Nortek management through a restructuring of operations and a revision of Nortek's business philosophy in 1993. The company reduced production costs and overhead levels, improved the efficiency and productivity of its operations, and showed operating earnings despite a slow economy. Net sales decreased to $744.11 million in 1993 but net losses that had spiraled to $38.1 million in 1990 were down to $20.8 million in fiscal 1993, although 1993 sales were $55.87 million lower than those of the preceding year.

During an interview with Don DeMaio for the *Providence Business News*, Chairman Bready commented that since 1990, Nortek had sold nine businesses, reduced the workforce by 15 percent, and "cost-reduced the entire delivery system." Bready explained Nortek's revised business philosophy: "We want to have one of the best products in the industries that we're in and the lowest delivered cost. You have to have continuous improvement in both the product and your costs. If you don't have that, somebody else will," he emphasized. At year-end 1994, Nortek posted net earnings of $17.8 million and had accumulated $100 million in cash reserves.

As a diversified manufacturer of residential and commercial building products, in 1995 Nortek operated within three principal product sections: the Residential Building Products Group, the HVAC Products Group, and the Plumbing Products Group. To strengthen the Residential Building Products Group, during the last quarter of 1995, Nortek acquired Texas-based Rangaire Company (kitchen range hoods and lighting fixtures); the capital stock and related entities of Italy-based Best S.p.A. (kitchen range hoods); and the stock of Venmar Ventilation Inc. (continuous ventilation systems and energy-recovery ventilators), headquartered in Quebec, Canada. These acquisitions expanded Nortek's product lines, advanced its indoor air-quality technology, and moved the company into new global markets.

In mid-1994 Nortek had experienced significant increases in the cost for raw materials as well as fewer demands for building products. Although these negative factors increased in fiscal 1995 Nortek posted net earnings of $15 million on sales of $776.21 million. In 1996 Nortek's operations were stimulated by an increase in housing starts throughout the United States and Canada. Cost increases subsided and Nortek began to reap increased benefits from the turnaround strategy that Chairman Bready and his team had set in place in the early 1990s; namely, development of a strong core group of businesses; divestiture of units that did not fit the core; reduction of debt-servicing costs; and initiation of a rigorous but realistic system of cost reductions and controls. Nortek became one of the largest suppliers of custom-designed commercial HVAC products in the United States. Fiscal 1996 net sales grew to $969.80 million and net earnings to $22 million.

CONTINUED REORGANIZATION

Because of continuing losses in the Plumbing Products Group, Nortek adopted a plan to discontinue this group and reorganized the company into three segments: Residential Building Products; Air Conditioning and Heating Products; and Windows, Doors, and Siding. The August acquisition of New York-based Ply Gem Industries, Inc., a leading manufacturer and distributor

of specialty building products for the home improvement industry and a major supplier to national do-it-yourself retail home centers, represented a quantum leap in growth for the company and raised it to national leadership ranks in the building products industry. Ply Gem operated two principal product groups targeting the residential and light-commercial markets: Windows, Doors, and Siding; and Specialty Products and Distribution. Ply Gem was phased into one of Nortek's wholly owned subsidiaries. Nortek's sales for fiscal 1997 peaked at $1.13 billion and net earnings were $21.2 million.

During 1998 Nortek sold eight businesses, some of which were considered nonstrategic assets that had come with the purchase of Ply Gem. In July, from London-based Williams plc, Nortek acquired Ohio-based Nu-Tone, Inc., which specialized in intercom systems and home theater systems. In October Nortek acquired Pennsylvania-based Napco Inc., which owned factories for the production of quality vinyl siding, aluminum building products, and vinyl windows within a few miles of each other. Napco's siding business was combined with Nortek's Variform siding subsidiary, and Napco's window fabrication operations were merged with Nortek's Great Lakes Window Inc. subsidiary, according to the September 7, 1998, issue of *Plastic News*. All of Nortek's core businesses were profitable in fiscal 1998, principally as a result of acquisitions and higher sales for superior-level, built-in ventilation products in North America. Net sales for fiscal 1998 rose to $1.74 billion, a 53 percent increase over those of 1997; net earnings increased to $35 million, a 65 percent rise over those for 1997.

A SPATE OF ACQUISITIONS

During 1999 the company acquired seven companies, among which was Webco, Inc., a designer and manufacturer of custom air-handling equipment for industrial, institutional, and commercial customers. To expand its presence in the windows and doors marketplace, Nortek also purchased three businesses from United Kingdom-based Caradon plc: Georgia-based Peachtree Doors and Windows, a national supplier of premium residential windows, entry doors, and patio doors that targeted custom and high-end home markets; Pennsylvania-based Thermal-Gard, which made premium replacement windows, patio doors, and sunrooms; and Alberta, Canada-based CWD Windows and Doors, a leading provider of complete window and door systems for new homes in western Canada.

Next came Nortek's purchase of Multiplex Technologies, Inc., a manufacturer of high-performance, multiroom video distribution equipment for the home.

In October Nortek acquired Kroy Building Products, Inc., a market leader in vinyl fencing, railing profiles, and vinyl decking systems for residential and commercial applications. In early December Nortek acquired Xantech Corporation, a manufacturer of residential infrared remote-control systems for extending control of VCR, cable, satellite, and stereo systems to multiple rooms throughout an entire household.

Fiscal 1999 was the second consecutive year for which Nortek reported record financial results. Net sales for the year rose to $1.99 billion, a 15 percent increase from the $1.74 billion for 1998. Net earnings peaked at $49 million, a 41 percent increase from the $35 million reported for 1998.

As 2000 unfolded, Chairman Bready commented in a letter to Nortek shareholders that Nortek was poised "to benefit from generally favorable economic conditions. Low inflation, near full employment, strong liquidity and strong consumer confidence continued to help Americans fulfill their dream of home ownership and improved home amenities through extensive home remodeling and expansion."

MOVING INTO THE 21ST CENTURY

Nortek entered the new millennium on solid ground. Its sales and balance sheet were solid and it continued to look for ways to expand while trimming costs and shoring up profits. During 2001 Ply Gem exited the wood window market through the sale Peachtree Doors and Windows and SNE Enterprises. The proceeds were used to pay down Nortek's debt.

By this time, Nortek had become an attractive target and various private-equity firms began making bids for the company. In 2002 Kelso & Company L.P. made a play for the company by partnering with Chairman and CEO Bready, who owned 25 percent of Nortek's voting stock, to buy Nortek. Kelso's $1.6 billion bid won out and the deal was finalized in early 2003.

Nortek, which began operating as a private company, came under the corporate umbrella of NTK Holdings in 2005 when that holding company was formed. Changes continued for Nortek when Kelso announced plans to sell off its windows, doors, and siding business in late 2003. Ply Gem was eventually sold for $560 million. Kelso opted to sell its holdings in Nortek in 2004 in a $1.75 billion arrangement that gave Bready and other Nortek management control of nearly 33 percent of the company while Thomas H. Lee Partners L.P. purchased the remainder of the firm.

Although the housing market had been strong at the start of the new millennium, it experienced a sharp decline as the U.S. and global economies weakened. High material costs and a slowdown in sales left Nortek focused on trimming costs while bolstering its product offerings during this period. The company acquired 11 companies in 2006 including upscale range hood manufacturer Zephyr Corp. Additional acquisitions followed in 2007, including: Aigis Mechtronics LLC, a camera housing manufacturer serving the closed-circuit television market; HomeLogic LLC, a software and hardware designer for in-home control systems used for audio and theater systems; bath cabinet manufacturer Solar of Michigan; and two metal suppliers in Poland and Italy.

Unstable market conditions forced the cancellation of Nortek's public offering in 2007. With the housing market in a nosedive the company was forced to move production to lower-cost regions. Plants were shuttered in Los Angeles, Illinois, and Ohio. A new facility opened in Mexico in 2008. With sales falling and significant losses in 2008, Nortek management expected the next few years to be challenging. The company retained the Blackstone Group and Weil, Gotshal & Manges as advisers in June 2009 to analyze the company's financial position going forward.

Gloria A. Lemieux
Updated, Christina M. Stansell

PRINCIPAL SUBSIDIARIES

Nortek Inc.; Best S.p.A.; Broan-NuTone LLC; Broan-NuTone Canada Inc.; Broan-NuTone Storage Solutions LP; NuTone Inc.; Pacific Zephyr Range Hood, Inc.; Venmar Ventilation Inc.; Zephyr Corporation; Aigis Mechtronics, Inc.; ELAN Home Systems, L.L.C.; Gefen, Inc.; GTO, Inc.; HomeLogic LLC; Imerge Limited; Linear LLC; LiteTouch, Inc.; Magenta Research Ltd.; Niles Audio Corporation; OmniMount Systems, Inc.; Operator Specialty Company, Inc.; Panamax Inc.; Secure Wireless, Inc.; SpeakerCraft, Inc.; Sunfire; Xantech Corporation; Nordyne Inc.; Nordyne International, Inc.; Cleanpak International, Inc.; Eaton-Williams Group Limited; Governair Corporation; Huntair, Inc.; Mammoth-Webco, Inc.; Temtrol, Inc.; Venmar CES, Inc.; Ventrol Air Handling Systems Inc.

PRINCIPAL OPERATING UNITS

Ventilation Products; Home Technology Products; Residential Air Conditioning and Heating (HVAC) Products; Commercial HVAC.

PRINCIPAL COMPETITORS

Carrier Corporation; Johnson Controls Inc.; Lennox International Inc.

FURTHER READING

"American Cultural History: 1980–89," http.www. kingwoodcollegelibrary.com/subjects.html#history.

Arditi, Lynn, "Nortek Sold for 2nd Time in Two Years," *Providence Journal,* July 20, 2004.

Biddle, Frederic M., "Why Wall Street Doesn't Believe Nortek Anymore," *Boston Globe,* April 29, 1990, p. 69.

Cecil, Mark, "Kelso Wants to Unload Large Nortek Division," *Mergers & Acquisitions Report,* October 20, 2003.

Davis, Paul, "Nortek Eyes New Strategy After Loss of $19.9 Million," *Providence Journal-Bulletin,* November 4, 1992.

DeMaio, Don, "Bready: Improve Product and Cost = Nortek Success," *Providence Business News,* September 15, 1995.

Downing, Neil, "Parting Shots: Nortek's Feisty Founder Defends Junk Bonds, Calls Company Sound," *Providence Journal-Bulletin,* November 4, 1990, p. F1.

———, "Trouble at Nortek: A Predator's Fall; Nortek Growth Strategy Flounders in Red Ink," *Providence Journal-Bulletin,* April 29, 1990.

Horowitz, Carl F., "Washington's Continuing Fiction: A National Housing Shortage," August 22, 1990, http://www. heritage.org/library/categories/healthwel/#bg783.html.

Kosman, Josh, "Kelso to Acquire Nortek for $1.6B," *Daily Deal,* June 22, 2002.

"Nortek Changes Its Name," *Wall Street Journal,* November 21, 2002.

"Nortek Division Sells Two Millwork Subsidiaries to Pay Debt, Sharpen Focus," *National Home Center News,* October 8, 2001.

"Nortek IPO Withdrawn As Earnings Lag," *Providence Journal,* November 13, 2007.

"NTK Holdings, Inc., and Nortek, Inc., Retain Advisors," *PR Newswire,* June 17, 2009.

Sheahan, Matthew, "Nortek Puts New Wrinkle in Deal, Prices $750M," *Bank Loan Report,* May 19, 2008.

Urey, Craig, "Consolidation & Merger of Corporations: Napco, Inc.; Nortek, Inc.," *Plastic News,* September 7, 1998.

The NutraSweet Company

10 South Wacker Drive
Chicago, Illinois 60606
U.S.A.
Telephone: (312) 873-5000
Toll Free: (800) 323-5321
Fax: (312) 873-5050
Web site: http://www.nutrasweet.com

Private Company
Incorporated: 1985
Employees: 417
Sales: $470 million (2008 est.)
NAICS: 325199 All Other Basic Organic Chemical Manufacturing; 311999 All Other Miscellaneous Food Manufacturing

■ ■ ■

The NutraSweet Company is one of the world's largest producers of aspartame, an artificial sweetener found in over 5,000 products. The company sells its sweetener—considered to be nearly 200 times sweeter than sugar—to food and beverage manufacturers in more than 100 countries. NutraSweet is consumed by 250 million people across the globe. Monsanto Company sold NutraSweet to J.W. Childs Equity Partners II, L.P., in 2000 in a $440 million deal.

EARLY HISTORY

NutraSweet, one of the world's largest manufacturers of the sweetening product known as aspartame, originated as a single product manufactured by the drug company G.D. Searle & Co. Aspartame was discovered in 1965 when a Searle scientist was testing combinations of amino acids for a potential ulcer drug. When the scientist put a finger in his mouth, he found that one of the mixtures, a combination of aspartic acid and phenylalanine, tasted like sugar. Aspartame proved to be over 180 times as sweet as sugar, and unlike other artificial sweeteners such as cyclamates and saccharin, it did not have a bitter or metallic aftertaste.

Receiving approval from the U.S. Food and Drug Administration (FDA) to market aspartame proved a lengthy process. The FDA approved aspartame in 1974, only to change its mind in 1975 when a psychiatrist claimed it caused brain damage in animals. Further tests showed no evidence of neurological damage. After lengthy studies were completed, aspartame finally received FDA approval in 1981. By that time the sweetener had received approval in France, Luxembourg, and Belgium, and was being sold in those countries.

Searle initially marketed aspartame as a tabletop sweetener, packaged in individual serving packets, under the Equal brand name. Aspartame was also used in cereals and desserts under the NutraSweet brand name. The big money in sweeteners was in low-calorie drinks, however, and Searle received approval to include aspartame in carbonated beverages in 1983. By that point, aspartame was already being used in 40 products in 22 countries, including soft drinks in Canada. Sales of aspartame reached $74 million in 1982, when Searle decided to create the NutraSweet brand name. It also created a NutraSweet business group to manage the sweetener. One of the group's first moves was an

COMPANY PERSPECTIVES

Since its introduction in 1981, millions of people worldwide have enjoyed and continue to enjoy more than 5,000 products containing NutraSweet brand sweetener. As the world's premier sugar substitute, NutraSweet offers great taste and virtually no calories. With regulatory approvals in more than 100 countries on six continents, NutraSweet is the most widely recognized and tested sweetening ingredient in the world.

introductory advertising campaign that offered consumers coupons worth five free NutraSweet-containing gum balls. The company received two million coupons in the first year.

BUILDING A BRAND

Some U.S. soft-drink companies were slow to use aspartame because it cost $90 a pound versus $4 a pound for saccharin, according to an August 1, 1983, article in *Newsweek*. Aspartame also lost its sweetness if stored for too long in warm temperatures. Blends had a shelf life of about eight months, while products using pure NutraSweet tended to lose their sweetness in about six months. However, the beverage market was fiercely competitive, and when manufacturers perceived the use of NutraSweet as a marketing advantage, given the appeal of its taste in soft drinks, they began using it in large quantities. Searle allowed some soft-drink manufacturers to mix aspartame and saccharin to hold their costs down.

In the meantime, Searle worked to increase aspartame production, which could not meet demand at that time. In 1983 construction began on a $100 million aspartame plant in Georgia. Sales of low-calorie powdered drink mixes using NutraSweet were booming as the entire diet-foods sector grew dramatically. Searle's pharmaceutical arm had long been suffering mediocre sales, and NutraSweet's profits were accounting for more and more of its total revenue.

With aspartame becoming a crucial ingredient in the products of other manufacturers, Searle began a campaign to build public recognition for it. When it created the name NutraSweet in 1982 a logo (a red and white swirl) was designed to go along with it. Searle spent $40 million advertising NutraSweet, and got food manufacturers to display the NutraSweet logo on

products that used it. The trademark demand was initially unpopular with retailers of products made with NutraSweet, although some changed their minds when they found that promoting NutraSweet as an ingredient increased demand for their products. Searle's initial ad campaign focused on the number and variety of products that used NutraSweet and the fact that they displayed the red swirl. The move was partly designed to put pressure on soft-drink manufacturers and others that used a blend of NutraSweet and saccharin. The firm also wanted to lock up the artificial sweetener market for NutraSweet before its aspartame patent expired in 1992.

In 1985 Searle was bought by Monsanto, which combined the NutraSweet and Equal operations into the NutraSweet Company, a wholly owned subsidiary of Monsanto. NutraSweet sales amounted to over $700 million in 1985.

NEW PRODUCT DEVELOPMENT

In 1986 NutraSweet began a $30 million advertising campaign to push the fact that it was made from natural ingredients, not artificial ones like saccharin and cyclamates. The television ads, which featured views of fruits and vegetables, used the theme, "Nature doesn't make NutraSweet, but NutraSweet couldn't be made without it." The print ads, which appeared in major national magazines, focused on the fact that NutraSweet was digested in the same way as fruit or milk.

By 1986 NutraSweet was marketed in over 50 countries, including Germany, where the product had finally been granted approval that year. The company was awaiting approval in France, Spain, and Italy, however, and its patents in several European markets were about to expire. Aware that it was essentially a one-product company, NutraSweet was pouring research dollars into developing new sweeteners and other food products. In the meantime, it received approval from the FDA to use NutraSweet in juice drinks, breath mints, tea beverages, and frozen novelties. These four new product categories had total annual sales of about $6 billion a year, giving NutraSweet huge new market opportunities.

According to *New York Times* contributor Eben Shapiro, when NutraSweet's European patents expired in 1987, the firm took strong competitive measures, cutting prices by over 60 percent, down to $27 a pound. As a result it continued to hold on to most of its market share, though profits in Europe tumbled.

NutraSweet unveiled its first serious attempt at product expansion in January 1988 with an all-natural fat substitute named Simplesse. Simplesse was made of egg whites or milk proteins that were heated until they

KEY DATES

1965: Aspartame is discovered by a G.D. Searle & Co. scientist.

1974: The Food and Drug Administration (FDA) initially approves aspartame.

1975: The FDA withdraws its approval when a psychiatrist claims aspartame causes brain damage in animals.

1981: Aspartame receives final approval from the FDA.

1982: The NutraSweet brand name is created; Searle receives approval to include aspartame in carbonated beverages.

1985: Searle is purchased by Monsanto Company.

1988: NutraSweet introduces an all-natural fat substitute named Simplesse.

1992: NutraSweet's patent on aspartame expires.

2000: J.W. Childs Equity Partners II, L.P., buys NutraSweet.

2002: Neotame gains FDA approval.

2004: Craig R. Petray is named CEO.

2007: NutraSweet partners with American Sugar Refining Inc. to manufacture and produce a new tabletop version of NutraSweet.

coagulated, and then shaped into tiny beads that simulated the texture of fat. The fatlike proteins were discovered in 1979 by a chemist working on alternative uses for the byproducts of cheese making. In 1985 NutraSweet had bought the rights from John Labatt Ltd., a Canadian beer and food concern, and spent another two years perfecting the product.

Simplesse was introduced at a press conference at which the company asserted Simplesse did not need FDA approval since it was made from natural ingredients. The next day, however, the FDA commissioner announced that Simplesse would be seized unless it was submitted for review. NutraSweet Chair Robert B. Shapiro quietly announced that Simplesse would be submitted after all. The attempt to skirt FDA review was largely an effort to beat competitors to market. Procter & Gamble had already submitted a fat substitute for review and others were close behind.

Simplesse had only 15 percent of the calories of fat. When exposed to heat, however, it became tough. It was therefore limited to the $15 billion dairy, cheese, and salad dressing markets. Procter & Gamble's Olestra was a synthetic chemical that had no calories because the body did not digest it. Heat did not change Olestra, and it therefore could be used to cook foods. Olestra, however, raised more health concerns than Simplesse, which like NutraSweet claimed to be digestible in the manner of the natural ingredients from which it was made. Other Simplesse competition came from products made from starch, although these too could not be heated.

OVERCOMING COMPETITION

NutraSweet's artificial sweetener market was also hit with increasing competitive pressure. By 1989 Pfizer and Hoechst Celanese Corp. were almost ready with competing products, while Kraft General Foods Group and Procter & Gamble were working on them as well. NutraSweet had 65 percent of the market, and its years of advertising its red swirl trademark had paid off in high consumer recognition. Its competitors were aware of this, however, and countered with huge advertising budgets of their own. Pfizer spent $30 million on its introductory campaign for its Alitame sweetener, said to be 2,000 times sweeter than sugar. Johnson & Johnson's sucralose, which was derived from sugar, had the advantage of being stable enough to be used in baked and frozen products.

A potential benefit to NutraSweet's competitors was the dislike many food makers had for the NutraSweet Company. NutraSweet had acquired a reputation for arrogance as it built its huge business quickly. It had charged premium prices and advertised directly to consumers even though, in its first couple of years, it could not produce enough aspartame to meet demand. Despite criticism over these moves, NutraSweet began marketing Simplesse in similar ways even before it had FDA approval.

The FDA finally approved Simplesse in 1990. By this time, Kraft Foods was well on the way to developing a Simplesse-based low-fat mayonnaise. In an attempt to broaden its base, NutraSweet kept the rights to use Simplesse in frozen products for itself. Shortly after the approval of Simplesse, it brought out the Simple Pleasures line of frozen desserts, putting NutraSweet into competition with its own customers. Simple Pleasures ice cream cost as much as premium ice cream and had half the calories and less than 10 percent of the fat. Industry observers reported that its taste was not up to that of premium ice creams such as Häagen-Dazs. Simple Pleasures ice cream was also competing with low-fat frozen yogurt, which had about the same caloric content and was already popular.

FACING PATENT EXPIRATION

Robert E. Flynn became NutraSweet's top executive in 1990, taking on the mission of preventing a drop in earnings when the aspartame patent expired. He immediately began trying to improve relationships with clients. When NutraSweet announced a $20 million ad campaign in 1991, it was targeted to support the products of customers using NutraSweet. Flynn also began cutting NutraSweet prices. Company sales reached $933 million in 1990, but Simple Pleasures reportedly contributed only $12 million of that.

Although Simplesse was being approved for use in countries outside the United States, it was falling short of expectations. Kraft, for example, sold back its rights to Simplesse, and brought out its own fat-free mayonnaise. NutraSweet continued working on products using Simplesse, including cheesecake and frostings, and released an ice cream that used Simplesse and NutraSweet. To strengthen the company's bottom line, Flynn stressed reducing the cost of producing aspartame and laid off 12 percent of the firm's 1,700-person workforce.

Nevertheless, the firm faced trouble because of its expiring patents. Coca-Cola Co. and Pepsi-Cola Co. reportedly accounted for about 80 percent of NutraSweet's sales. Both were expected to produce aspartame themselves within a few years of the patent expiration, according to Tom Pirko, the president of a food and beverage consulting firm, who was quoted in a 1991 *Advertising Age* article. With Simple Pleasures not selling well, NutraSweet finally decided to sell the Niles, Illinois, plant where Simple Pleasures products were manufactured. The move improved relations with customers, since NutraSweet resumed its role as an ingredient supplier rather than a potential competitor. NutraSweet instead concentrated on producing a second generation of artificial food ingredients. It worked on methods of eliminating cholesterol and fat from egg yolks and removing high-calorie sucrose from orange juice.

In 1991 NutraSweet announced work on a new product called Sweetener 2000, an artificial sweetener 10,000 times as sweet as sugar. The sweetener was more stable than aspartame, with an indefinite shelf life and the ability to be used in baking. In the meantime, Johnson & Johnson's sucralose, which was not approved in the United States, seemed to be approaching the market. Despite the prestige of having the NutraSweet logo on its cans, major soft-drink companies were expected to consider dropping NutraSweet in favor of sucralose, which had an indefinite shelf life. The new sweetener would enable the companies to advertise their products as "new and improved." NutraSweet thus found itself in a race to come up with its own new and improved ingredients before decreasing aspartame profits devoured its bottom line. Throughout the 1990s, the company was a serious competitor in the artificial ingredients arena but the heady days of the mid-1980s were gone. In 1999 *BrandWeek* magazine named NutraSweet one of the top 100 brands of the century.

MOVING INTO THE 21ST CENTURY

Facing intense competition and additional products entering the marketplace, NutraSweet found itself constantly focused on research and development of new products. It began to develop Neotame, a sweetener that was 8,000 times sweeter than sugar and 40 times sweeter than NutraSweet. Neotame gained FDA approval in 2002 as well as approval from the World Health Organization and 14 countries in Asia, Latin America, and Europe.

The company experienced a change in ownership when Monsanto sold NutraSweet to J.W. Childs Equity Partners II, L.P., in 2000 in a deal worth $440 million. Craig R. Petray was named CEO in 2004 and under his leadership NutraSweet continued to pursue new product development. It opened a new beverage laboratory, dubbed the NutraSweetSpot, in Chicago where it worked to replace high-fructose corn syrup with alternative sugar substitutes in beverages.

Competing product Splenda, made from sucralose, hit store shelves during this period and began to threaten NutraSweet's control of the diet beverage market, where the company garnered 75 percent of its sales. NutraSweet remained the artificial sweetener of choice in Diet Coke and Diet Pepsi, however, the two leading diet sodas in the industry. In fact, demand for aspartame was increasing by 4 percent to 5 percent per year, forcing NutraSweet to ramp up production in its Georgia-based facility in 2005 and 2006. Nevertheless, NutraSweet started to look for ways to enter the sucralose market. It sought partnerships with companies in China and India during 2005 and began to pursue production opportunities that would not infringe upon Splenda's patent rights.

Throughout aspartame's history, it was forced to fend off concerns about its use and associated health risks including cancer. During 2005 these fears were once again pushed to the forefront when a new study published by the European Ramazzini Foundation in Italy claimed there was an increased risk of lymphoma and various cancers in rats that consumed the equivalent of four to five 20-ounce bottles of diet soda per day. The National Cancer Institute published its own study in 2006 and found no increased risk of cancer in people who consumed artificial sweeteners. While both institutions backed their claims, there continued to be conflicting opinions regarding the health risks associated with consumption of aspartame and other artificial sweeteners.

Despite health concerns raised by certain consumer advocacy groups, demand for artificial sweeteners and healthful alternatives to sugar remained high. NutraSweet partnered with American Sugar Refining Inc. to manufacture and produce a new tabletop version of NutraSweet in 2007. In the coming years, NutraSweet also hoped to launch a new natural sweetener along with newer, better-tasting versions of its existing sweeteners. CEO Petray summed up the company's focus in a June 2008 *Grocery Headquarters* article: "We understand that consumers' sweet preferences vary, so we're developing innovative formulas and blends to meet all of those needs."

Scott M. Lewis
Updated, Christina M. Stansell

PRINCIPAL COMPETITORS

Cumberland Packing Corporation; Johnson & Johnson; Merisant Worldwide Inc.

FURTHER READING

"Aspartame: The Newest Weapon for Diet Soda Rivals," *Business Week,* July 18, 1983.

Berk, Christina Cheddar, "NutraSweet to Increase Production," *Wall Street Journal,* April 6, 2005.

Clark, Matt, "A Sweet Sugar Substitute," *Newsweek,* July 27, 1981.

Cordeiro, Anjali, "Food Firms Seek Sweet Success," *Wall Street Journal,* August 15, 2007.

Dagnoli, Judann, "NutraSweet Rivals Stirring," *Advertising Age,* June 26, 1989.

Kantrowitz, Barbara, "A Heavyweight Fuss over the New Fake Fat," *Newsweek,* March 5, 1990.

Liesse, Julie, "Bitter Future for NutraSweet?" *Advertising Age,* May 27, 1991, p. 33.

McCann, Joseph E., *Sweet Success: How NutraSweet Created a Billion Dollar Business,* Homewood, Ill.: Business One Irwin, 1990.

O'Neil, Molly, "First Low-Calorie Substitute for Fats Is Approved by U.S.," *New York Times,* February 23, 1990.

Pauly, David, "Sweet Dreams for Searle," *Newsweek,* August 1, 1983.

Petre, Peter, "Searle's Big Pitch for a Tiny Ingredient," *Fortune,* September 3, 1984.

Ryan, Kate, "Splenda's Cola Sales May Be Slim," *Crain's Chicago Business,* February 21, 2005.

Schiller, Zachary, and James E. Ellis, "NutraSweet Sets Out for Fat-Substitute City," *Business Week,* February 15, 1988.

Shapiro, Eben, "NutraSweet's Bitter Fight," *New York Times,* November 19, 1989.

"Should You Sour on Aspartame?" *Tufts University Health & Nutrition Letter,* September 1, 2007.

Therrien, Lois, "NutraSweet Tries Being More of a Sweetie," *Business Week,* April 8, 1991.

Turcsik, Richard, "Sweet Reinvention," *Grocery Headquarters,* June 1, 2008.

Ward, Andrew, "NutraSweet Seeks Taste of Sucralose Market," *Financial Times,* September 25, 2005.

Warner, Melanie, "Study Finds No Cancer Link to Sweetener," *New York Times,* April 8, 2006.

"What's New with NutraSweet," *Beverage World,* August 15, 2004.

Witsil, Frank, "Monsanto Sells NutraSweet," *Augusta Chronicle,* May 31, 2000.

OAO Gazprom

Nametkina 16
V-420
Moscow, 117997
Russia
Telephone: (495) 719-3001
Fax: (495) 719-8333
Web site: http://www.gazprom.com

Public Company
Incorporated: 1993 as RAO Gazprom
Employees: 376,300
Sales: $72.41 billion (2007)
Stock Exchanges: Russian
Ticker Symbol: GAZP
NAICS: 211111 Crude Petroleum and Natural Gas Extraction; 211112 Natural Gas Liquid Extraction; 213111 Drilling Oil and Gas Wells; 213112 Support Activities for Oil and Gas Field Operations; 221210 Natural Gas Distribution; 486210 Pipeline Transportation of Natural Gas; 541710 Research and Development in the Physical, Engineering, and Life Sciences

∎ ∎ ∎

OAO Gazprom is one of the largest energy companies in the world and the largest company in Russia. It controls 17 percent of the world's known natural gas reserves and accounts for nearly 25 percent of Russia's tax revenues. Through a network of over 100 subsidiaries, Gazprom is active in all areas of the gas industry, including exploration, extraction, processing, storage,

transportation, and marketing. In 2008 Gazprom produced 549.7 billion cubic meters of gas. Gazprom was privatized in 1993, although the state holds a 50 percent stake in the company and controls a significant number of the seats on the board of directors. This fact has contributed to an unusually high degree of political involvement at Gazprom. Historically, the company is alleged to have received special treatment from the Kremlin, and, in return, to use its considerable influence and assets for the government's benefit. Not only does Gazprom have tremendous importance for the economy of the Russian Federation, foreign dependence on Russian gas, especially in countries of the former Soviet Union, allows Gazprom to be used externally as a diplomatic tool. The company's history is peppered with incidents of apparent cooperation with the Kremlin as well as power struggles when interests clashed. As of 2008, Gazprom's natural gas reserves were 33.1 trillion cubic meters. In U.S. dollars, the value of the company's reserves was $230.1 billion.

NATURAL GAS IN THE SOVIET ERA

Many of the pipelines and facilities controlled by Gazprom were developed in the Soviet era under a succession of state gas ministries. Russia's natural gas reserves were first exploited on a large scale shortly after World War II, when an 843-kilometer (km) pipeline was constructed from Saratov, on the lower Volga River, to Moscow. The success of the Saratov-Moscow project led to more pipeline construction in the 1950s, with the development of a localized network around Leningrad and Moscow as well as pipelines stretching into Ukraine and Central Asia. The majority of homes in the largest cities in the U.S.S.R. were soon connected to the natural gas network, decreasing the country's reliance on wood and coal for energy and lessening the burden on the railroad system.

In the late 1960s the gas industry made a major advance by beginning to tap the huge natural gas reserves in western Siberia. Despite the challenges of working in frigid conditions, a pipeline was successfully constructed in the 1960s from the Urengoi gas field to Moscow. By 1983, western Siberia was producing more than half of the U.S.S.R.'s natural gas, and in 2000 Siberian gas fields accounted for more than 70 percent of natural gas production in Russia.

Exports to Western Europe got their start in 1970, when a Soviet export agency signed a contract to supply natural gas to the West German company Ruhrgas. The first Russian gas reached Germany in 1973. The second Western firm to buy Russian gas was Fortum of Finland, which initiated contracts in the 1970s. Exports, especially to Germany, increased through the succeeding decades. In 1982 Soyuzgasexport, the exporting arm of the gas ministry, signed a contract to construct a 5,000 km pipeline from the Urengoi gas field to the West German border. The pipeline was projected to carry 40 billion cubic meters of gas a year to Western Europe.

In the 1980s the development of west Siberian gas fields continued with the opening of the extensive Yamburg reserve. Explorations showed many large untapped gas reserves in the area. As experimental projects relating to crude oil and nuclear power faltered, the U.S.S.R.'s massive natural gas resources took on increased importance. By the time of the breakup of the U.S.S.R. in 1991, it was clear that natural gas would be critical in fulfilling Russia's future energy needs, as well as in supporting the nation's new capitalist economy.

POST U.S.S.R. PRIVATIZATION

In 1989 the Ministry of the Gas Industry was transformed into the state gas concern "Gazprom," the name "Gazprom" coming from a contraction of the Russian words for "gas industry." Minister Viktor Chernomyrdin, who had risen from a position as a machinist, became chairman and CEO of the state concern.

After the breakup of the Soviet Union in 1991, government decrees effected the privatization of Gazprom. A November 5, 1992, presidential edict called for the formation of a company to explore and produce gas and to build pipelines. Articles of association for the company were approved by the Council of Ministers on February 17, 1993, and the Russian joint stock company (RAO) Gazprom was formed. A condition of privatization was that the government retained a 40 percent share in the company. Gazprom workers received 15 percent of shares and 28 percent went to people living in Russia's gas-producing regions.

Meanwhile, Chernomyrdin became President Boris Yeltsin's prime minister in 1992 and picked Rem Vyakhirev to succeed him as Gazprom CEO. Chernomyrdin was rumored to have used his political position to grant Gazprom certain tax breaks and unusual privileges during the privatization process. For example, Gazprom retained the right of first refusal, meaning it had the first opportunity to purchase any of its shares that came on the market. In addition, all sales of shares were to be approved by Gazprom management. *U.S. News & World Report* suggested that Chernomyrdin may have received large amounts of stock in exchange for these concessions, although both Vyakhirev and Chernomyrdin denied the allegation. In any case, the privatization process set a precedent for close ties between the state and the gas industry.

The newly formed RAO Gazprom inherited all the assets of the former gas ministry. Various subsidiary production, transportation, and service amalgamations became Gazprom daughter enterprises. The mammoth company produced 578 billion cubic meters of gas in 1993, more than twice the combined output that year of Royal Dutch/Shell, Exxon, Mobil, Amoco, British Petroleum, Chevron, and Texaco. However, because of secrecy surrounding the company's financial situation, financial analysts were unable to pinpoint the value of the company. Gazprom clearly had extensive assets, but its market capitalization was low.

DEALING WITH OUTSTANDING DEBT

Another blight on Gazprom's financial standing was difficulty receiving payments. Many customers inside Russia and in the former Soviet republics were insolvent, leading to large amounts of outstanding debt. Gazprom, while still a state concern in 1992, had attempted to address this problem by cutting off gas to Ukraine. The

KEY DATES

1946: Saratov-Moscow pipeline begins era of "big gas."

1966: Opening of Urengoi field marks the start of west Siberian exploitation.

1973: First Russian gas reaches Germany.

1989: The Ministry of the Gas Industry becomes state concern "Gazprom."

1993: The state concern is privatized as RAO Gazprom.

1995: First shareholders meeting is held.

1998: Gazprom changes its name and status from a Russian joint stock company (RAO) to an open joint stock company (OAO).

1999: Major sections of the Yamal-Europe pipeline are inaugurated.

2000: First junction of the Blue Stream pipeline is welded.

2001: Alexei Miller replaces Vyakhirev as CEO.

2005: The state's interest in Gazprom grows to 50.002 percent; Gazprom pays $13 billion for a majority interest in Sibneft.

2008: Dmitry Medvedev is elected president of Russia; Victor A. Zubkov takes over as chairman of Gazprom.

2009: The company signs a 20-year agreement to supply oil to China in exchange for $25 billion in loan guarantees; construction on the Sakhalin-Khabarovsk-Vladivostok gas transmission system begins.

plan backfired, since Russia's major pipeline to Europe ran through Ukraine, so Ukrainians took for themselves gas that was meant for German customers. Customers inside the Russian Federation, such as electrical utilities, were also unable to pay debts. Gazprom often took in-kind payments in return for gas, accepting anything from vacations and healthcare services for its employees to meat packaging plants and textile factories.

Without hard cash payments, it was difficult to finance new projects. For example, Gazprom had completed a feasibility study for the development of gas fields on the Yamal Peninsula, in western Siberia, in 1988. The company hoped to build a Yamal-Europe pipeline along a northern route, running 4,107 km from Yamal through Belarus and Poland to Germany. The pipeline would bypass Ukraine and reduce that country's control over exports to Europe. In an attempt

to raise funds, the government in 1994 granted Gazprom permission to sell one-quarter of state-owned shares, or 9 percent of total shares, to foreign investors. The venture failed, however, because investors found Gazprom to be overvalued under the terms of the offering. Gazprom did make some profitable international connections in 1994. In a partnership with Gaz de France, the French company agreed to assist in the modernization of Russia's natural gas technology and transportation systems. In addition, a contract with Fortum confirmed the supply of Russian gas to Finland for 20 years.

In May 1995 Gazprom held its first shareholders meeting. The board of directors was elected and PricewaterhouseCoopers was chosen to be the firm's auditor. In some respects, Gazprom occupied an enviable position as it developed into a privatized company. The company had an estimated 1.5 trillion cubic feet of gas reserves, a natural monopoly in Russia, and control of much of Europe's export market. Despite these advantages, Gazprom's revenues in 1994 were only $13 billion, compared to $100 billion for the smaller Exxon. Another cause for concern was a deteriorating infrastructure. A November 1995 study, reported in *Oil and Gas Journal*, cited the need for more than $3 billion to improve inefficient compressor stations, leaking valves, corroding pipes, and inadequate environmental protections. Vigilant development was needed to keep Gazprom on a stable course.

INCREASING INTERNATIONAL PARTNERSHIPS

As Gazprom entered 1996 it still faced the tough problem of financing maintenance and construction while having difficulty collecting payments from customers. About 85 percent of the payments from customers in Ukraine and Russia were more than 90 days in arrears. Foreign investors and customers abroad once again seemed to be the most promising source of capital. In October Gazprom offered 1.15 percent of its shares for sale as American Depositary Receipts. The offering was oversubscribed by five times. The company also signed contracts with the Italian firm Eni and with Warsaw to bring Siberian gas to Italy and Poland. The proceeds from these deals helped finance the much-desired Yamal-Europe pipeline, the first sections of which were opened in Poland and Germany in November. Some of Gazprom's funds, however, were spent to further political ends as the company generously supported Yeltsin's successful 1996 reelection campaign.

The following year brought conflicts with both the Russian and the U.S. governments. Gazprom owed the

Russian government $2.6 billion in back taxes, and the International Monetary Fund had been pressuring Yeltsin to reduce Gazprom's monopoly status as a condition for receiving loans. The two sides reached a compromise in April, when Gazprom agreed to pay a portion of the back taxes, yield its monopoly on gas fields, and divest nonessential operations to independent companies. Separate divisions were created within the company for such activities as production, transportation, and investment, in the hopes that it would encourage competition. In return for those concessions, Gazprom was allowed to continue voting the government's stake in the company.

The conflict with Washington related to a contract between Total S.A. in France, Petronas of Malaysia, and Gazprom to develop parts of the South Pars oil field in the Persian Gulf. Washington claimed that the contract violated U.S. sanctions against European firms that helped Iran develop energy projects. The conflict was resolved when the United States waived the sanctions in May 1998 with the understanding that no companies would assist Iran in developing weapons.

International partnerships in 1997 included the formation of North Transgas Oy, a 50-50 venture with Fortum of Finland to build a northern European pipeline that would take gas to central Europe under the Baltic Sea. After exploratory work, a definite route for the pipeline was chosen by the end of 1999. Gazprom also signed its first formal agreement with Royal Dutch/Shell to jointly develop the Zapolyarnoe field in western Siberia. Finally, in December 1997, the groundwork was laid for the momentous Blue Stream project, which would bring gas to Turkey via a pipeline under the Black Sea. An agreement was signed between the Russian and Turkish governments to supply Turkey with $25 billion worth of Russian gas between 2001 and 2005.

CHANGE IN NAME AND STATUS

Gazprom found its first Norwegian partners in 1998, when in May it signed a protocol to work together with Statoil and Norsk Hydro to look for hydrocarbon deposits in the Pechora Sea. That summer the Russian economy crashed and the ruble collapsed. Despite $16.1 billion in sales, Gazprom lost $7 billion in 1998. Nevertheless, the company's size and its extensive assets helped it survive the crash in much better shape than many other Russian companies. Gas production for the year was 554 billion cubic meters, slightly higher than the previous year. Gazprom also further opened its doors to international investors in 1998, when at the annual shareholders meeting it voted to change its name and status from a Russian joint stock company (RAO) to an open joint stock company (OAO). Ruhrgas AG, a longtime customer in Germany, bought 2.5 percent of Gazprom's shares. The following year Ruhrgas increased its stake to almost 4 percent.

As Gazprom entered 1999 it was still having trouble collecting payments and finding the funds to develop new gas fields and construct new pipelines. The depletion of the mainstay Yamburg and Urengoi fields in western Siberia, as well as the continued disappearance of gas from Ukraine pipeline, put pressure on the company to pursue new projects. Although Gazprom lost $2.8 billion in 1999, several positive steps were taken in the course of the year. In February loans were secured for the Blue Stream pipeline to Turkey, and the Italian firm Eni became Gazprom's partner in the project. The pipeline was planned to extend 373 km over land from Izobilnoye to a Russian port on the Black Sea, and then continue for 396 km under the Black Sea.

In September 1999 the Polish and Belorussian sections of the crucial Yamal-Europe pipeline were inaugurated. By bypassing Ukraine and giving Gazprom an alternate route to the German pipeline grid, the project was expected to make gas deliveries to Western Europe more flexible and easier to direct. In 2000, 14 billion cubic meters of gas were exported along the route, bringing valuable hard currency into Russia's economy.

NEW MANAGEMENT FOR THE 21ST CENTURY

The transition into the new millennium at Gazprom was marked by political involvement, struggles with the government, and allegations of mismanagement. In 1999 the Kremlin made a move to increase its control over Gazprom. At the annual shareholders meeting in June, former Prime Minister Chernomyrdin was chosen to resume his post as chairman of the board, replacing Vyakhirev, who would remain CEO. Chernomyrdin then demanded that the board of directors be reelected, since the state, despite holding a 38 percent stake in Gazprom, was represented by only four out of 11 directors. A new election, which followed in August, gave the government five seats.

More scandals and political involvement clouded Gazprom's business dealings in 2000. Articles in *Business Week* and the *Economist* reported that minority shareholders were concerned that their investments were being depleted by mismanagement and asset stripping. Many of the allegations centered on dealings with Itera, a Florida-based company that acted as a broker for gas export sales. Leaders at Gazprom were suspected of holding large shares in Itera and therefore giving the firm sweetheart deals. In one case, Gazprom paid taxes to a Siberian regional administration in the form of gas valued at a low price. The local administration sold the gas to Itera at the same low price. Itera then made $1.8 billion by selling the gas abroad for up to 30 times the original price. President Yeltsin initiated investigations into these activities, but Itera denied that it was receiving any free assets from Gazprom. Minority shareholders were also concerned that investment at Gazprom was poorly planned, that upper management was transferring assets to relatives, and that money was spent on unnecessary luxury items. At a board meeting, for example, management agreed to buy a yacht club in the port of Astrakhan.

In January 2000 Yeltsin abdicated his post to Vladimir Putin, who was then reelected in March. Many of Putin's actions appeared targeted at reducing the power of Yeltsin-era business oligarchies. In May 2000 Gazprom Chairman Chernomyrdin was replaced by Dmitry Medvedev, an official with fairly close ties to the new government. A more radical change followed in the summer of 2001. At the June shareholders meeting, longtime CEO Vyakhirev was replaced with the relatively unknown Alexei Miller. Miller had worked loyally with Putin in the St. Petersburg administration and also served two years as deputy energy minister. He promised to raise the market capitalization of Gazprom and guarantee the full disclosure of investments.

SHAKE-UPS AND SCANDALS

Vyakhirev retained some influence at Gazprom, as he was elected chairman of the board. However, stockholders apparently believed that reform had a much better chance since the state had more control through Miller. Gazprom's shares rose 10 percent on the London Stock Exchange following news of the switch in leadership.

Also under Putin, Gazprom was mixed up in the struggle between the government and NTV, the only independent television network in Russia. NTV was known for its open criticism of Putin and candid reporting of such events as the war in Chechnya and the *Kursk* submarine accident. Gazprom owned a 46 percent stake in NTV's parent company, Media Most, and was suspected of acting as an agent of the Kremlin when, in the summer of 2000, it demanded that the media company sell shares to settle millions of dollars in debt to Gazprom. There was some talk of foreign investors helping settle Media Most's debt, but no deals were realized. In April 2001 Gazprom seized control of NTV in a boardroom coup, tossing out the station director. NTV journalists launched a strike, fearing that the era of independent reporting was over. At the July 2001 an-

nual meeting of NTV, Gazprom representatives made no appearance. Exiled media tycoon Vladimir Gusinsky sold his remaining shares of Media Most to Gazprom and in the end, Gazprom sold a 49 percent stake in its media assets to a Russian bank, Evrofinance.

Against the backdrop of these shake-ups and scandals, Gazprom projects advanced. The first junction of the Blue Stream pipeline was welded in February 2000. Then CEO Vyakhirev announced that two more parallel pipelines would be built starting in 2003 to increase export capacity to Turkey. The Blue Stream project thwarted U.S. companies, who had hoped to bypass Russia with a pipeline from Turkmenistan to Turkey.

In other international partnerships, Gazprom signed a memorandum in June to work together with Wintershall AG of Germany on the Prirazlomnyi deposit in the Barents Sea. Wintershall had worked with Gazprom on projects in Germany since 1990. In September Wintershall and Gazprom joined in a consortium with Ruhrgas, Gaz de France, and the Italian gas transportation firm Snam to build a pipeline across Poland to Slovakia. In the spring of 2001 work began on the Zapolyarnoe deposit near Yamal, a joint venture with Royal Dutch/Shell. Finally, in August Gazprom and Royal Dutch/Shell agreed to pool their resources to try to win a contract to build a pipeline linking the western Xinjiang region in China to Shanghai on the east coast. Despite concerns over management style at Gazprom, foreign investors could not ignore the tremendous potential of Russia's natural gas reserves. Gazprom forged ahead with the projects necessary to ensure its continued place as a leader in the world gas industry.

SUCCESS AND GOVERNMENT INVOLVEMENT

The year 2003 proved to be successful for Gazprom. The company reached record revenue and net profit levels and its share price was skyrocketing. With gas production rising along with gas prices, Gazprom stood on solid ground. The government, certainly aware of the company's growing importance in the world's oil and gas arena, increased its stake in the company in 2005 through a complex deal in which OAO Rosneftegaz (Rosneft) purchased a 10.74 percent stake in Gazprom. In addition, Gazprom was involved in Russia's largest takeover to date when it bought a 72.663 percent stake in Sibneft for $13 billion. By the end of 2005, the Russian Federation controlled over 30 percent of its oil industry.

Gazprom celebrated its 15th anniversary in 2008, the same year Medvedev was elected Russia's president.

One of Medvedev's first actions as president was to secure Putin's position as prime minister of Russia. Victor A. Zubkov, the former prime minister of Russia and at that time first deputy prime minister, was named Gazprom's chairman in June 2008. The elections proved to most outsiders that Gazprom and its ties to the Russian Federation were clearly intact. A May 2008 *New York Times* article summed up the relationship between the government and Gazprom claiming, "in today's Russia, the line separating big business and the state is becoming so fine that it's almost nonexistent."

Meanwhile, the company worked to sell off many of its noncore assets and focused on several international projects that would create Eurasian gas transmission systems. These included the Yamal-Europe gas pipeline, the Blue Stream and Nord Stream gas pipeline, the South Stream gas pipeline, and the Pre-Caspian gas pipeline. Gazprom was also focused on developing offshore hydrocarbon fields in Venezuela, Vietnam, India, and Libya. Another area of focus was developing its oil fields in the Arctic, which would be both expensive and highly complex due to frigid temperatures.

In January 2009 Gazprom stopped exporting natural gas to Europe for nearly two weeks during a price dispute with Ukraine. Shortages were experienced throughout Europe, which depended on Russia for nearly 40 percent of its imported fuel. The action further weakened Russia's relationship with the West, which had been damaged when Russia sent troops into Georgia, a former Soviet republic, in August 2008. The altercation with Ukraine fueled Gazprom's decision to begin focusing on exporting to Asian countries. At the time, the company's largest gas markets in terms of sales were Germany, Turkey, Italy, the United Kingdom, and France. Gazprom hoped to add Asian countries to that list in the future.

In February 2009 the company signed a 20-year agreement to supply oil to China in exchange for $25 billion in loan guarantees. At the same time, Gazprom's first liquefied natural gas plant on Sakhalin Island began operations. In July of that year, Gazprom celebrated the start of construction on the Sakhalin-Khabarovsk-Vladivostok gas transmission system slated for initial completion in 2011. The system would supply gas to Eastern Russia and provide exporting opportunities to the Asia Pacific region.

By 2009 oil prices had fallen sharply and threatened to weaken Russia's economy as well as derail Russia's budget. Nevertheless, Gazprom management was optimistic about the company's future success as a leader in the global energy market. Indeed, with daily crude oil and natural gas production surpassing that of Saudi Arabia, Gazprom's importance to the industry was evident. The company hoped to surpass Exxon Mobil Corp. as the world's largest publicly traded company by 2014.

Sarah Ruth Lorenz
Updated, Christina M. Stansell

PRINCIPAL DIVISIONS

Exploration and Production; Transmission; Gas, Gas Condensate, and Oil Processing; Marketing and Gas Distribution; Peripheral Activities.

PRINCIPAL COMPETITORS

Centrica plc; OAO LUKOIL; N.V. Nederlandse Gasunie; BP p.l.c.

FURTHER READING

"Bad Vibes: Russian Media," *Economist,* February 3, 2001, p. 3.

"Big Outlays Seen Required for Gas Pipelines in Russia," *Oil and Gas Journal,* November 27, 1995, p. 31.

Birchenough, Tom, "Gazprom Exec No-Shows As NTV Row Brews," *Variety,* July 9, 2001, p. 16.

"Blue Stream Contracts Signed," *Pipeline & Gas Journal,* January 2000, p. 14.

Bush, Jason, and Anthony Bianco, "Why Russians Love Gazprom," *Business Week,* July 31, 2006.

Caryl, Christian, "Putin's Gas-Patch Putsch," *Newsweek International,* June 11, 2001, p. 21.

Chazan, Guy, "Gazprom Sells 49% of Media Assets," *Wall Street Journal,* September 27, 2002.

Dettmer, Jamie, "European Dependence on Russia's Gazprom," *Insight on the News,* August 6, 2001, p. 13.

"The Eighth Sister: Emerging Multinationals," *Economist,* October 15, 1994, p. 93.

"Firms Plan Black Sea Pipe," *Oil Daily,* February 5, 1999.

Fuhrman, Peter, "Robber Baron," *Forbes,* September 11, 1995, pp. 208–12.

"Gassing Away at Gazprom: Gazprom's Shoddy Governance," *Economist,* December 23, 2000, p. 6.

"Gazprom Buys Sibneft in Top Russian Deal," *Oil Daily,* September 25, 2005.

"Gazprom Frets over Gas Prices amid Expansion," *Oil and Gas Journal,* November 8, 1999, pp. 28–32.

"Gazprom on the Grill," *Business Week,* December 4, 2000, p. 62.

"Gazprom Re-elects Chernomyrdin," *Oil Daily,* August 27, 1999.

"Gazprom Resurgent," *Oil and Gas Journal,* April 21, 1997, p. 32.

"Gazprom, Shell Close to Deal," *Oil Daily,* May 18, 2000.

"Gazprom, Shell to Team Up," *Oil Daily,* August 2, 2001.

"German Gas Concern to Buy More Gazprom Shares," *ITAR/TASS News Agency,* May 19, 1999.

"Giving an Inch: Russia's Energy Monopolies," *Economist,* February 1, 1997, p. 66.

Heath, Michael, "Investors Jubilant at Vyakhirev Ouster," *Russia Journal,* June 1–7, 2001.

Klebnikov, Paul, "Sorcerer's Apprentice," *Forbes,* September 22, 1997, pp. 52–55.

Korchemkin, Mikhail, "Russia's Huge Gazprom Struggles to Adjust to New Realities," *Oil and Gas Journal,* October 18, 1993.

Kramer, Andrew E., "As Gazprom Goes, So Goes Russia," *New York Times,* May 11, 2008.

———, "Russia Cuts Gas, Europe Shivers," *New York Times,* January 7, 2009.

———, "Russia, Looking Eastward, Opens a Gas Plant to Supply Asian Markets," *New York Times,* February 19, 2009.

———, "Russia Restores Gas to Ukraine," *New York Times,* January 21, 2009.

Larina, Ekaterina, "Putin Topples Gazprom's Vyakhirev," *Russia Journal,* June 1–7, 2001.

LeVine, Steve, and Owen Matthews, "The Presidential Pipeline," *Newsweek International,* September 13, 1999, p. 31.

"Norwegian: Agreement to Explore Offshore Field in Pechora Sea," *Oil and Gas Journal,* October 20, 1997, p. 44.

"Reporting Russia's Gas Industry," *Petroleum Economist,* May 1996, pp. 64–72.

Surovtsev, Dmitry, "Gazprom Follows Unique Course to Privatization," *Oil and Gas Journal,* March 25, 1996, pp. 62–65.

Thoenes, Sander, and Alan Cooperman, "What Are Comrades For?" *U.S. News & World Report,* December 11, 1995, pp. 58–61.

"Turkey–Blue Stream," *APS Review Gas Market Trends,* May 1, 2000.

"U.S. Waives Sanctions on South Pars Field," *Oil and Gas Journal,* May 25, 1998, p. 18.

Wilson, David Cameron, "Russian Gas in 1993," *Petroleum Economist,* September 1994, pp. 58–60.

"Wintershall, Gazprom Create JV," *Oil Daily,* June 9, 2000.

Orbital Sciences Corporation

———■———

21839 Atlantic Boulevard
Dulles, Virginia 20166
U.S.A.
Telephone: (703) 406-5000
Fax: (703) 406-3502
Web site: http://www.orbital.com

Public Company
Incorporated: 1982 as Space Systems Corporation
Employees: 3,400
Sales: $1.17 billion (2008)
Stock Exchanges: New York
Ticker Symbol: ORB
NAICS: 336414 Guided Missile and Space Vehicle
 Manufacturing; 336415 Guided Missile and Space
 Vehicle Propulsion Unit and Propulsion Unit Parts
 Manufacturing; 334511 Search, Detection, Naviga-
 tion, Guidance, Aeronautical, and Nautical System
 and Instrument Manufacturing

■ ■ ■

Orbital Sciences Corporation designs, manufactures, operates, and markets a broad range of space and rocket systems. Its business operations are grouped into three categories: Satellites and Space Systems; Advanced Space Programs; and Launch Vehicles. The company's Satellite and Space Systems arm develops and manufactures small and medium-sized geosynchronous Earth orbit satellites used for communications and broadcasting as well as for exploration and research.

Orbital's Advanced Space Programs unit oversees its operations in human-rated space systems as well as national security space systems. The company also develops a variety of space launch vehicles including rockets that deliver satellites into orbit and missile defense rockets that carry intercept vehicles used to destroy hostile ballistic missiles used against the United States and its allies. The company's primary customers are the National Aeronautics and Space Administration (NASA), the Department of Defense, and various commercial and academic space programs. Since its inception in 1982, the company has delivered approximately 900 satellites, launch vehicles, and space-related systems to its clients.

THE EARLY YEARS

The foundation for Orbital Sciences Corporation was laid in 1980, when David Thompson, Bruce Ferguson, and Scott Webster met at Harvard Business School and worked together on a NASA-sponsored study of commercial space applications. They submitted their study to NASA in 1981 and subsequently won the Space Foundation Prize for Space Business Research.

On April 2, 1982, Space Systems Corporation (SSC) was incorporated in Delaware to develop, manufacture, test, and market commercial space transportation systems. On September 30, 1983, a year after the initial start-up, Orbital Research Corporation (ORC) was incorporated as a wholly owned subsidiary of SSC to be the managing general partner of Orbital Research Partners L.P., which was formed on October 20, 1983, for the purpose of designing, developing, and commercially marketing an orbit transfer vehicle, to become known as the Transfer Orbit Stage (TOS) Vehicle. The company signed an agreement with NASA for the company's first space product, the TOS Vehicle, and reached a production agreement with Martin Marietta Corporation. That same year, the company secured $2 million in venture capital and opened its first office in Vienna, Virginia, near Washington, D.C., with 12 employees and had opening year revenues of $100,000.

The next year the company's board of directors grew to include prominent figures in the space industry, academia, and finance. The company also raised $50 million from outside investors to finance development of the TOS Vehicle. The number of employees rose to 20 and revenues hit $2 million.

The year 1985 saw the company's design, development, and marketing efforts for the TOS Vehicle move into high gear, with 25 employees and $3 million in revenues. The company entered into the Minuteman CFE Contract with the U.S. Air Force for the production of 20 Minuteman Rocket Consolidated Front End (altitude control, telemetry, and flight termination) modules, for approximately $33.2 million. In June, the company's Space Data Division entered into the Phase I Starbird Contract with the U.S. Air Force to develop and launch the Starbird launch vehicle and related products and services for approximately $17.8 million.

In 1986 the company moved to a new headquarters in Fairfax, Virginia, and NASA signed a $35 million contract for the first TOS Vehicle and an option for a second. The company had 40 employees and $6 million in revenues.

RAPID GROWTH

In 1987 Antonio Elias conceived of a revolutionary, air-launched rocket, later named *Pegasus* in an employee

contest, designed to place small satellites into low-Earth orbit. The company also began investigating a system for collecting data from remote locations using satellites in low-Earth orbit, which evolved into the company's Orbital Communications Corporation (ORBCOMM) commercial communications subsidiary. Additionally, in March, the company signed the NASA TOS Vehicle Contract for the Mars *Observer* and the Advanced Communications Technology Satellite (ACTS) mission for approximately $78.6 million and signed a Mars *Observer* and ACTS production subcontract with Martin Marietta. A TOS Vehicle flight activation contract was also signed with Martin Marietta for approximately $6.3 million. Continuing to grow, the company had 50 employees and revenues jumped to $25 million.

In 1988 the Defense Advanced Research Project Agency (DARPA) signed the DARPA Pegasus Contract, the first Pegasus contract for the purchase of one Pegasus launch vehicle with an option for an additional five launches for approximately $36.3 million. The company and Hercules Inc. agreed to jointly develop and produce *Pegasus,* with Hercules, the subcontractor, investing $32 million in the company. The company also broadened its rocket business and manufacturing capabilities by acquiring the stock of Arizona-based Space Data Corporation, one of the world's leading suppliers of suborbital rockets. The $17.5 million deal was achieved through a merger of Space Data into a wholly owned subsidiary of Orbital Sciences, organized for that purpose. The company's revenues grew to $35 million as 300 new employees were added to the company with the acquisition, jumping the number up to 400 employees total.

The company began construction of a new facility in Chandler, Arizona, in 1989 to house the company's expanding rocket production line and support staff. It entered into a contract with DARPA to supply a ground-launched Taurus rocket and launch services for approximately $10 million, with an option for an additional four launches for another $58.4 million. Also during this time, the Extended Range Interceptor (ERINT) Contract was signed with the U.S. Army Strategic Defense Command, which provided for the design, development, fabrication, analysis, testing, and delivery of launch systems and services required for five launches of the ERINT target system for approximately $15.6 million, with an option for three additional launches for a total of approximately $5.4 million.

In July 1989 the company's Space Data Division entered into the Phase II Starbird Contract with the U.S. Air Force to develop and launch the Starbird launch vehicle and related products and services for approximately $12.6 million. The employee count that

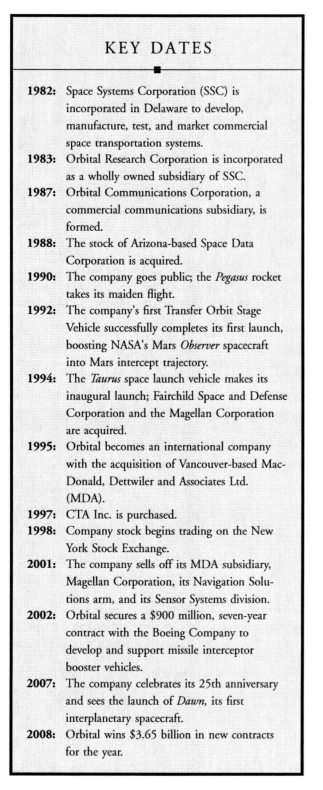

KEY DATES

1982: Space Systems Corporation (SSC) is incorporated in Delaware to develop, manufacture, test, and market commercial space transportation systems.

1983: Orbital Research Corporation is incorporated as a wholly owned subsidiary of SSC.

1987: Orbital Communications Corporation, a commercial communications subsidiary, is formed.

1988: The stock of Arizona-based Space Data Corporation is acquired.

1990: The company goes public; the *Pegasus* rocket takes its maiden flight.

1992: The company's first Transfer Orbit Stage Vehicle successfully completes its first launch, boosting NASA's Mars *Observer* spacecraft into Mars intercept trajectory.

1994: The *Taurus* space launch vehicle makes its inaugural launch; Fairchild Space and Defense Corporation and the Magellan Corporation are acquired.

1995: Orbital becomes an international company with the acquisition of Vancouver-based Mac-Donald, Dettwiler and Associates Ltd. (MDA).

1997: CTA Inc. is purchased.

1998: Company stock begins trading on the New York Stock Exchange.

2001: The company sells off its MDA subsidiary, Magellan Corporation, its Navigation Solutions arm, and its Sensor Systems division.

2002: Orbital secures a $900 million, seven-year contract with the Boeing Company to develop and support missile interceptor booster vehicles.

2007: The company celebrates its 25th anniversary and sees the launch of *Dawn*, its first interplanetary spacecraft.

2008: Orbital wins $3.65 billion in new contracts for the year.

year was up to 475 and revenues reached $80 million. In addition, the company won numerous awards in 1989, including the DARPA Outstanding Technical Performance Award, the American Astronautical Society Space Commerce Award, and the Space Foundation Commercial Space Award.

GOING PUBLIC

In 1990 the company faced some of its largest and most significant challenges since its foundation but also witnessed a number of impressive space "firsts." In April the company became the first commercial space company to open its financial future to public participation through the successful completion of an initial public offering of $32.5 million of its common stock on the NASDAQ.

It also celebrated the initial launch of its *Pegasus* rocket. The highly successful maiden flight made the air-launched space booster the world's first privately developed Earth-to-space vehicle. Initial launches were conducted of several other of the company's major suborbital rocket systems, including the Minuteman Missile Consolidated Front End, Starbird suborbital vehicle, and High Performance Booster. In addition, three important space experiments were conducted by the company, including the Ultra-Violet Bow Shock flight, the Excede III scientific probe, and the Two-Axis Pointing System mission, the first two on suborbital vehicles and the latter on the space shuttle, for a total of eight successfully completed space missions for the year.

In 1990 the company filed the world's first license application with the Federal Communications Commission (FCC) for the operation of a network of small low-Earth orbit spacecraft to provide global satellite services of commercial messaging and data communications services via the company's ORBCOMM subsidiary.

The company also signed a contract with the Strategic Defense Initiative Organization (SDIO) in January to provide suborbital launch vehicles and related services in connection with the SDIO Flight Test Services Program (the FTSP Contract) for approximately $34.8 million, with options totaling another $14.9 million.

The Chandler, Arizona, facility opened and the number of employees jumped to 725; Orbital achieved significant improvements in its financial position, with recorded revenues of $100 million, a 25 percent increase over 1989 sales. Awards received in 1990 included the National Air and Space Museum Trophy, the National Space Society Space Pioneer Award, the Space Business Roundtable Commercial Space Industry Award, and the Washington Technology and Popular Science New Product of the Year Awards.

PURSUING A COMMUNICATIONS NETWORK

In 1991 the company was established as the preeminent supplier of small launch vehicles by winning an $80 million NASA contract for Pegasus launches and another launch contract from the U.S. Air Force that included up to 40 Pegasus launches. The company was also selected by NASA to build *SeaStar,* the world's first privately owned environmental monitoring satellite with a commitment for $44 million in image purchases over five years.

The company's ORBCOMM mobile data communications network proposal made important technical and regulatory progress with the FCC and the World Administrative Radio Conference's agreement to allocate the global radio spectrum. ORBCOMM signed agreements with 12 potential user equipment suppliers and international service licensees.

Top management was strengthened with the addition of former NASA Deputy Administrator James R. Thompson and former McDonnell Douglas executive Donald W. Tutwiler. Orbital turned in its best financial performance to that time in 1991, with revenues of $135 million, exceeding by 5 percent the company's 30 percent target of increase over 1990 revenues. The company raised $65 million in a secondary public offering of stock. In addition, awards received in 1991 included the Virginia Outstanding Industrialist of the Year Award, the Via Satellite Executive of the Year Award, and the National Medal of Technology Citation, the last presented by President George H. W. Bush and U.S. Commerce Secretary Robert Mosbacher.

Orbital continued its rapid growth in 1992, with revenues of $175 million, representing a 29 percent increase over 1991 revenues. In September, the company's first TOS Vehicle successfully completed its first launch, boosting NASA's Mars *Observer* spacecraft into Mars intercept trajectory. The *Observer* would reach Mars in August 1993 and begin providing a wealth of scientific information on Earth's nearest planetary neighbor to assist the 1997 launches of several more Mars missions. Of the company's ten space missions in 1992 (bringing the number of successfully completed missions to 27 in three years of launch operations), five involved new vehicles, a very high proportion for the industry.

Progress continued on the company's ORBCOMM low-Earth orbit mobile satellite communications project, with the signing of 17 companies in 19 countries prepared to offer ORBCOMM services upon receipt of regulatory approvals and deployment of the satellites in 1993 and 1994. The Capabilities Demonstration Satel-lite was successfully launched in February and began providing valuable information on the planned design and operation of ORBCOMM satellites.

The company also created two new subsidiaries in 1992. The first was Orbital Imaging Corporation (ORBIMAGE), to consolidate the company's Earth-viewing satellite remote sensing initiatives, including the SeaStar ocean color monitoring service, which began service in 1993. The second was Orbital Environmental Systems Group, to focus on meteorological products and satellite tracking systems.

An L-1011 carrier aircraft was purchased by the company to be used with its Pegasus launch vehicle program, the total contract for backlog exceeded $1 billion for the first time in the company's history, and the number of employees climbed to 1,150.

ACQUISITIONS FOR EXPANSION

In 1993 Orbital carried out 16 space missions, all successfully, including two flights of the *Pegasus* space vehicle, 11 flights of suborbital rockets, one mission of the TOS Vehicle, and two missions of communications satellites and research payloads. February saw the launch of the first prototype satellite in the ORBCOMM two-way messaging and mobile data communications system, beginning the final phase of space and ground technology development for the revolutionary global PCS network. The network operations simulation was run through end-to-end successfully.

In June, Orbital created an equal partnership called ORBCOMM Development Partners L.P. with Teleglobe Mobile Partners, an affiliate of Teleglobe Inc., one of the world's largest intercontinental telecommunications carriers, for the design and development of the low-Earth orbit satellite system. Teleglobe Mobile invested $85 million in the project and provided not only financing but also international service distribution. Orbital agreed to construct and launch satellites for the ORBCOMM System and to construct the satellite control center, the network control center, and four U.S. gateway Earth stations.

The ORBIMAGE subsidiary made more progress on the SeaStar project, as well as beginning new projects ranging from satellite-based atmospheric lightning detection to high-resolution imaging for mapping the land surfaces of Earth.

In September, the company acquired the Pomona, California-based Applied Science Operation business unit of the Perkin-Elmer Corporation for approximately $5.8 million to produce and market sophisticated space sensors and ground-based analytical instruments primarily for agencies of the U.S. government and commercial aerospace companies. The 200 new employees based in Pomona brought the number of employees to 1,350.

The company achieved substantial financial improvements in 1993 as revenues climbed to $195 million, a 9 percent increase over 1992. The company also moved its corporate headquarters to Dulles, Virginia.

GLOBAL SATELLITE NETWORK LICENSING

Of the nine successful space missions conducted in 1994, one was the inaugural launch of the company's *Taurus* space launch vehicle, which took place from Vandenberg Air Force Base in California and another was the maiden voyage of the PegaStar small satellite platform. The APEX satellite, built for the U.S. Air Force by the company's satellite group, was successfully launched aboard a *Pegasus* rocket and operated flawlessly while in orbit. The only failure for the year was the first use of the new *Pegasus XL* enhanced-performance rocket, but the total number of successful missions jumped to 40 in 1994.

The ORBCOMM system also made progress that year, receiving a full construction and operating license from the FCC, the first ever granted to a commercial low-orbit satellite network, in October, culminating a four-year crusade the company led to "rezone" the desired radio frequencies needed, both in the United States and around the world. ORBCOMM received the only VHF/UHF license for a global satellite network, providing over 600 kilohertz of primary spectrum in the United States and extended its network of domestic resellers of ORBCOMM services for markets such as trucking, marine, and energy facilities, and expanded its international distribution of services to nearly 70 countries.

In August, the company acquired Fairchild Space and Defense Corporation from Matra Aerospace Inc., part of the Matra-Hachette Group, for approximately $71 million. As a result, Orbital substantially expanded its spacecraft design and production capability and added advanced electronics and satellite-aided vehicle management networks to the product lines. The acquisition also brought 800 new employees to the company.

December saw the acquisition of Magellan Corporation in a merger, bringing personal satellite navigation and communications technologies to the company. The world's leader in the manufacture of consumer-level Global Positioning System (GPS) products, Magellan also produced $40 million per year of inexpensive, handheld satellite navigators, with the potential to expand into ORBCOMM messaging

devices and automotive positioning equipment. Orbital also gained over 150 employees with the acquisition, boosting the total number to 2,100. Revenues climbed to $225 million, a 17 percent increase over 1993.

ACHIEVING A MAJOR GOAL

For Orbital, 1995 was the year the company achieved its longstanding goal of developing or acquiring all the core technologies and product lines necessary to position the company as the industry's only complete provider of space systems infrastructure. Orbital became an international company with the acquisition of Vancouver-based MacDonald, Dettwiler and Associates Ltd. (MDA), the world leader in the design and integration of ground stations for remote sensing satellites. The addition of MDA's products enabled the company to offer full end-to-end space mission capabilities. Nearly 800 additional employees were added to the company's ranks with the acquisition. Magellan introduced the world's first handheld personal GPS navigator to retail for under $200.

Orbital successfully completed 11 major rocket launches, including a Pegasus launch carrying the first two ORBCOMM satellites, the first ORBIMAGE satellite, called MicroLab, and the first successful launch of the *Pegasus XL* in March. The entire ORBCOMM global mobile data communications network was tested and Teleglobe Mobile invested an additional $75 million in the project. The company employee base grew to 2,700 and revenues were at $364 million, a jump of 21 percent over 1994.

In 1996, following a 1995 failure, the Pegasus program returned to flight with four consecutive, near-perfect *Pegasus XL* launches, including NASA's Total Ozone Mapping Sensor mission, for which Orbital's Pomona facility supplied the space sensor payload. Orbital was selected by NASA for a $60 million contract to build the X-34 hypersonic vehicle. The project would test key technologies leading to reusable launch vehicles, the industry's next step to making space travel less costly and more easily accessible. Magellan sold a record 300,000 GPS navigation units through over 10,000 U.S. retail outlets and in 80 countries worldwide.

In February, ORBCOMM initiated the world's first commercial service for global mobile data communications provided by low-Earth orbit satellites. ORBCOMM also raised an additional $170 million. The satellite mobile telephones the company marketed quickly became one of the top-selling products used with the existing Inmarsat geosynchronous satellite system.

By 1996 the company had completed 82 space missions spanning some seven years of operations. The management was strengthened with the addition of Frank Salizzoni, former president and chief operating officer of U.S. Airways, and Janice Obuchowski, a former administrator of the National Telecommunications and Information Agency. For the first time, Orbital's total backlog of contract orders and options exceeded $2 billion and overall revenue increased to $461 million, a 27 percent increase from 1995. During 1997 the company purchased CTA Inc., adding its space systems business and its geosynchronous communications satellite technology into its fold. The following year, Orbital began trading on the New York Stock Exchange.

OVERCOMING CHALLENGES IN THE 21ST CENTURY

Orbital's growth hit a snag as revenues began to slow and profits took a nosedive in 2000. The company lost its NASA contract for the Orbital X-34 prototype space launch cargo vehicle. At the same time, its ORBCOMM unit was struggling with high costs. Unable to secure necessary financing, the subsidiary was forced to file for Chapter 11 bankruptcy protection in 2000. Orbital quickly began to revamp its operating strategy as a result. In an attempt to reduce its debt load by nearly $100 million, the company launched a restructuring effort designed to refocus on its core operations in space technology, satellites, rockets, and related systems. As part of this effort, the company sold off its MDA subsidiary as well as Magellan Corp. and its Navigation Solutions arm in 2001. It also jettisoned its Sensor Systems division that year.

The company's fortunes slowly began to turn and it appeared as though the new strategy was paying off. During 2002 Orbital secured a $900 million, seven-year contract with the Boeing Company to develop and support missile interceptor booster vehicles. The contract was the largest in company history at the time. Its first two interceptor booster vehicles for Boeing were launched the following year. Providing missile interceptor booster vehicles became a major focus for Orbital during this period. Defense-related business accounted for nearly 40 percent of revenues in 2007 while commercial and civil space operations continued to shore up the remainder of company sales. Orbital had also secured a position as a subcontractor for NASA's Orion Crew Exploration Vehicle, which would eventually replace NASA's space shuttle program.

In 2005 the company completed its 500th mission since its inception in 1982. Orbital landed over $1.7 billion in new orders in 2006, marking the fifth consecutive year of new orders in excess of $1 billion. The company celebrated its 25th anniversary in 2007 and saw the launch of *Dawn*, its first interplanetary spacecraft, which was slated to complete an eight-year, three billion mile flight to the asteroid belt between Mars and Jupiter.

During 2008 the company completed its restructuring with the sale of Transportation Management Systems for $42.5 million. With sales and profits on the rise, Orbital had overcome the earlier financial challenges and was once again on the fast track for growth. New contracts were coming in at breakneck speed. The company secured a $1.9 billion NASA contract to provide cargo transportation services to and from the International Space Station. Overall, the company landed $3.65 billion in new contracts for the year.

The company experienced a setback in 2009 when NASA's Orbiting Carbon Observatory, a satellite designed to measure carbon dioxide levels in Earth's atmosphere, crashed shortly after launch. Initial reports cited the failure of the *Taurus XL* rocket. Orbital launched an internal investigation into the failure in March. The company had experienced record growth in recent years, and Orbital management remained cautiously optimistic regarding the future of the company. Although the company stood on solid financial ground, it continued to remain subject to fluctuations in government spending in both the defense and space sectors. Nevertheless, Orbital's turnaround during the early years of the new millennium left it well prepared for future challenges.

Daryl F. Mallett
Updated, Christina M. Stansell

PRINCIPAL COMPETITORS

The Boeing Company; Lockheed Martin Corporation; Northrop Grumman Corporation.

FURTHER READING

Abrams, Doug, "Orbital Seeks O.K. to Send Up 20 Small Satellites," *Washington Business Journal*, March 26, 1990, p. 14.

———, "Star Wars Showers Contracts on 2 Area Firms," *Washington Business Journal*, August 10, 1992, p. 3.

Anselmo, Joseph C., "NASA Gives Orbital Second Shot at X-34," *Aviation Week & Space Technology*, June 17, 1996, p. 31.

———, "Ocean-Monitoring Satellite Generates First Images," *Aviation Week & Space Technology*, October 20, 1997, p. 83.

———, "Pegasus XL Launches from the Canary Islands," *Aviation Week & Space Technology*, April 28, 1997, p. 67.

Asker, James R., "ORBCOMM Satellites to Use Unique Disk Shape," *Aviation Week & Space Technology,* September 27, 1993, p. 49.

———, "Orbital Sciences Becomes First Commercial Space Firm to Go Public," *Aviation Week & Space Technology,* April 30, 1990, p. 27.

Bodenheimer, Matt, "Orbital Sells Off Pomona, Calif.-based Sensor Division for $20 Million," *Knight-Ridder/Tribune Business News,* August 13, 2001.

"Boon for Baby Birds," *U.S. News & World Report,* June 13, 1988, p. 10.

Brokaw, Leslie, "Rocket Man," *Inc.,* March 1990, p. 25.

Carey, John, "A Small Step for Man—A Tiny One for Industry," *Business Week,* August 12, 1991, p. 46.

Greer, Jim, "Rocket Man: Space Booster Going into Orbit," *Houston Business Journal,* March 25, 1991, p. 1.

Kulman, Linda, "The Final Frontier," *U.S. News & World Report,* May 5, 1997, p. 16.

"Lagardere to Sell Fairchild to Orbital for Cash and Stock," *Wall Street Journal Europe,* June 2, 1994, p. 4.

Mack, Toni, "Pies in the Sky: How Three Recent B-School Graduates Plan to Push $50 Million of Investors' Cash into Heavenly Orbit," *Forbes,* March 26, 1984, p. 41.

Marcial, Gene G., "Orbital Isn't Lost in Space," *Business Week,* November 7, 1994, p. 130.

"The Next Frontier; As Orbital Sciences Turns 25, Its Co-Founder Reflects on Successes and Mistakes and Looks Ahead to Reinvigorated Space Age," *Aviation Week & Space Technology,* April 2, 2007.

Olgeirson, Ian, "Space Race Heats Up in the Suburbs," *Denver Business Journal,* July 18, 1997, p. 3A.

"Orbital Begins Taurus Failure Investigation," *Satellite News,* March 4, 2009.

"Orbital Sciences Corp.," *Wall Street Journal,* August 6, 1997.

"Orbital to Reduce Debt $100 Million by Unloading Units," *Satellite News,* May 28, 2001.

"Spacecraft Sports 'Out-of-This-World' Composite," *Design News,* September 8, 1997, p. 48.

Orscheln Farm and Home LLC

---■---

101 West Coates Street
Moberly, Missouri 65270
U.S.A.
Telephone: (660) 263-4335
Toll Free: (800) 577-2580
Fax: (660) 269-3500
Web site: http://www.orschelnfarmhome.com

Private Company
Incorporated: 1960
Employees: 1,150
Sales: $323 million (2008 est.)
NAICS: 422910 Farm Supplies Wholesalers

■ ■ ■

Orscheln Farm and Home LLC is a private company based in Moberly, Missouri, that operates a chain of more than 150 farm stores under the Orscheln Farm and Home banner. Mostly found in Missouri and Kansas, stores are also located in Arkansas, Illinois, Indiana, Iowa, Kentucky, and Nebraska, primarily in small to midsize cities. In addition to farming supplies, Orscheln stores and the company's catalog operation offer livestock and pet feeds; animal health products; hardware, electrical, and plumbing supplies; lawn and garden products; automotive parts and tires; housewares and toys; and work and western wear. Some stores also stock sporting goods.

Unlike many rural retailers, Orscheln has found a way to successfully compete against Wal-Mart, mostly by adhering to a narrower focus, offering higher-end

merchandise while also carrying some of the same merchandise as Wal-Mart, and providing strong customer service as well as a more personal experience than the giant retailer can offer. In some cases, Orscheln has taken over former Wal-Mart stores. Not only has Orscheln continued to expand its number of stores, it has moved into more suburban markets, and to appeal to hobbyist farmers and others has adjusted its product mix accordingly. The chain is owned and operated by the Orscheln family, which also controls about a dozen other business interests in manufacturing, formulated products, property management, and hospitality and recreation. Orscheln Management Co. provides accounting, human resources, and other administrative support service to Orscheln Farm and Home and its sister companies.

DANCE HALL ORIGINS

The members of the Orscheln family were originally farmers who by chance became serial entrepreneurs, forever adjusting to changing circumstances and seizing opportunities as they arose. The founders of the family enterprises were brothers Ed and William Orscheln. They grew up on a farm near Tipton, Missouri, and left in 1919 to buy a farm for themselves near Sturgeon, Missouri. They soon found that conditions beyond their control, including weather and commodity prices, made farming a difficult proposition. As teenagers they had earned spending money by hauling a portable dance floor on a hay wagon for local hoedowns; this had proved so popular that the brothers decided to open a dance hall. Called Orscheln Heights, the dance hall developed a following and soon was hosting dances

COMPANY PERSPECTIVES

Though our numbers have grown, the Orscheln Family values and traditions remain the same. It is our goal and responsibility to honor the tradition and achievements of my grandfather and uncle by ensuring that Orscheln Farm and Home continues to meet the needs of our rural customers as well as those of a new generation of Americans seeking a touch of the rural lifestyle, no matter where they live.

three or four times a week. Many potential patrons, however, lacked a way to reach the dance hall. To meet this need, the brothers bought a Model T pickup truck in 1924, installed benches in the back, and began transporting people from miles around to Orscheln Heights.

Another opportunity came along when a grocer in Renick, Missouri, paid William Orscheln to bring him a box of bread from a bakery in Moberly, Missouri. William began soliciting other business along the dance hall route, and in time the delivery service became more lucrative than the bus business and the benches were removed to accommodate more freight. A year later a second truck was purchased and a third brother, Al, was hired as a driver. William managed the fledgling trucking operations while Ed oversaw the farm and their sister Jo took care of the books. The family's willingness to pursue new ventures paid off in the 1930s, a difficult time to do business given the Great Depression that encompassed the entire decade. The dance hall business had done well and Orscheln Heights became a regular stop for many of the top bands of the day, but the advent of the jukebox depressed the live music business, and in 1936 Orscheln Heights closed.

TURNING PROBLEMS INTO OPPORTUNITIES

The trucking business then became the heart of the Orscheln enterprises, but the family continued to develop new business ventures by turning problems into opportunities. When the truck fleet experienced persistent difficulties with failing parking brakes, Al Orscheln in 1938 designed an overcenter parking brake that made use of a pull-up handle and magnified leverage to lock the brakes in place, which he built in the repair shop and installed on one of the trucks. The new brake was a major improvement over what had been available from truck manufacturers. A year later a patent

was received, but several years passed before the parking brake was made available to trucks outside the Orscheln fleet. Finally, in 1946, the family incorporated the Orscheln Brake Lever Manufacturing Company and began selling the brake system, which in the 1950s became optional equipment for International Harvester trucks. General Motors trucks soon followed suit and in the late 1960s the Dodge truck made the Orscheln brake lever standard equipment.

The Orscheln family divided its varied business interests among its members in the early 1960s. Four of the brothers, Ed, Ted, Al, and Louie, received the trucking company, while William and his sons Gerald and Don assumed control of the remaining ventures, including the brake lever company, an equipment dealership, a real estate company, and a newly launched retail operation: Orscheln Farm and Home. The first store opened in 1960 in Sedalia, Missouri, to supply rural families with the products they needed for farming and ranching, and to support a general rural lifestyle.

In the mid-1960s, Gerald Orscheln, who earned a degree in business from Missouri Valley College, was put in charge of Orscheln Farm and Home to grow the business. The elder brother, Don, took charge of the brake lever company. Both were also involved in any number of ventures over the next 20 years, abandoning those that failed and nurturing the winners. The brothers also brought their own children into family enterprises, but unlike the family members that took over the trucking business, this branch of the family eschewed outright nepotism. Orscheln Brothers Truck Line Company employed many family members and friends of the family without regard for qualifications, a policy that caught up to the company in the 1970s. What had once been the largest trucking company serving the market between Kansas City and Chicago faltered and in the 1970s folded.

COMPETING AGAINST WAL-MART

William's side of the Orscheln family took a more circumspect approach to hiring family members, insisting that they first gain experience working elsewhere or by starting their own businesses. Don's son, Barry Orscheln, for example, started his own commercial leasing business in the 1970s and in 1986 sold it to Chase Manhattan Bank. He stayed with Chase for a year to meet a commitment of the sale, and then in 1987 became the chief financial officer of the Orscheln Group. Three years later he became president. Don's other son, Bob, helped in 1983 to launch Orbseal, maker of sealants and adhesives that muffled sound from auto components. Orbseal became a major supplier to U.S. automakers and eventually expanded to

KEY DATES

■

1919: Brothers William and Ed Orscheln leave home to buy a farm for themselves near Sturgeon, Missouri.

1946: The family incorporates the Orscheln Brake Lever Manufacturing Company.

1960: First Orscheln Farm and Home store opens in Sedalia, Missouri.

1987: Barry Orscheln joins company as chief financial officer.

1998: New distribution center opens in Moberly, Missouri.

2002: Company acquires 26 Quality Stores through bankruptcy auction.

2003: Gerald Orscheln dies.

2009: The chain tops the 150-unit mark and generates about $325 million in annual sales.

Australia and Europe. In 2004 the company was sold to Henkel International, a German conglomerate.

Orscheln Farm and Home enjoyed steady growth over the years, especially in small towns in Missouri and Kansas. Several years after the first store opened in Sedalia, the fledgling chain opened its ninth store in Columbia, Missouri, in almost the precise center of the state. Columbia and Topeka, Kansas, became the company's largest markets. As was the case with other Orscheln businesses, the retail operation was adept at adjusting to the times. When the core market for basic farm equipment and supplies started to deteriorate, the stores added items that catered more to hobbyist farmers and other rural consumers.

Long serving the needs of livestock, it was a natural transition to develop in-store "One Stop Pet Shops" to carry a full range of pet food and pet care supplies. The chain also found a way to coexist with Wal-Mart, unlike so many other rural retailers who simply closed their doors. Not only did Orscheln Farm and Home carve out its own niche to fend off Wal-Mart, it often acquired former Wal-Mart stores, taking advantage of Wal-Mart's growth to save money on new facilities and maintain its competitive edge. In many markets the Orscheln Farm and Home store was located next to the local Wal-Mart.

Another example of the chain's flexibility was the transition from work clothing to work and western wear, as epitomized by the glove category. The stores had traditionally carried work gloves, which appealed to

blue-collar men who preferred jersey models almost exclusively on the basis of price. By the 1990s the various glove offerings at Orscheln stores broadened as the ranks of farm workers and laborers thinned. Aimed both at men and women, products included gloves for garden hobbyists, ski gloves, winter gloves, and beginning in 1997, men's dress leather gloves.

GROWTH THROUGH ACQUISITION

By 1998 the Orscheln Farm and Home chain numbered nearly 90 stores in eight states. Traditionally the chain had produced its own circulars and radio spots in-house, but at this time an advertising agency, Kupper Parker Communications, was hired to develop a comprehensive strategy for appealing to both the core farm customer and the increasingly important general consumer. The company also looked to develop some direct-mail capabilities and engage in some television advertising.

To support sales growth the company opened a new state-of-the-art warehouse and distribution center in Moberly in 1998. By the start of the new century it supported 88 Orscheln Farm and Home stores in eight states. Missouri with 36 units was the most represented, followed by Kansas with 24 stores, Iowa with 15, Oklahoma's seven stores, Nebraska's three stores, and single locations in Arkansas, Kentucky, and Texas. The chain enjoyed a major growth spurt in 2002, taking advantage of the misfortunes of Muskegon, Michigan-based Quality Stores Inc.

Quality had been the largest farm store operator with 300 locations in 30 states, following the 1999 merger with Central Tractor Farm and Country of Iowa, but the chain grew too large too quickly, and in November 2001 was forced to seek federal bankruptcy protection. At the same time, it announced that it planned to concentrate on the 178 stores it operated in 11 states east of the Mississippi River and sell its 133 stores west of the river to help satisfy the demands of creditors. Nashville-based Tractor Supply Co. bought the lion's share, 85 stores, to become the country's largest farm supply retailer, while Orscheln Farm and Home bought 26 Quality Stores at auction for $6.5 million. Of that number, 18 stores were located in Nebraska, where Orscheln had a limited presence.

The Quality Stores deal allowed the Orscheln chain to penetrate the Nebraska market in a single stroke without incurring the cost of constructing new buildings. The other Quality Stores included four units in Kansas, three in Colorado, and a single store in Iowa. The Moberly distribution center was large enough to supply the new addition, although the Colorado stores were located too far away and were divested. Later in

2002 Orscheln Farm and Home grew further through external means by converting ten units of Indiana's Big Blue Stores Inc. to the Orscheln format. In this way, Orscheln was able to expand into Indiana for the first time.

In June 2003 Gerald Orscheln died at the age of 76 after an extended battle with Parkinson's and Alzheimer's diseases. He had played a key role in setting the direction of the Orscheln chain and nurturing it through the early years. By this time the next generation of the family was in control and President Stephen Chick handled day-to-day responsibilities. The chain continued to expand at a steady pace, topping the 150-unit mark and generating about $325 million in annual sales by 2009. Given its proven ability to adapt to changing conditions, Orscheln Farm and Home would likely continue to prosper for many years to come.

Ed Dinger

PRINCIPAL COMPETITORS

The Home Depot, Inc.; Southern States Cooperative, Incorporated; Tractor Supply Company.

FURTHER READING

"Diversifying at Orscheln," *Discount Store News,* July 15, 1996, p. 32.

Friedman, Steve, "Orscheln Purchases 26 Outlets," *Columbia (Mo.) Daily Tribune,* January 8, 2002.

———, "Orscheln Speeds Toward New Horizons," *Columbia (Mo.) Daily Tribune,* June 1, 2002.

———, "Orscheln to Take Over Indiana Chain," *Columbia (Mo.) Daily Tribune,* October 4, 2002.

Harris, Joe, "Orscheln Is a Little Bit of Everything," *Festus (Mo.) News Democrat Journal,* April 20, 2005.

"Obituary: Jerry Orscheln," *Columbia (Mo.) Daily Tribune,* June 30, 2003.

OrthoSynetics Inc.

---

545 South Nolen Drive, Suite 300
Southlake, Texas 76092
U.S.A.
Toll Free: (888) 622-7645
Fax: (817) 977-6707
Web site: http://www.orthosynetics.com

Private Company
Incorporated: 1994 as Orthodontic Centers of America,
    Inc. (OCA)
Employees: 3,092
Sales: $129.9 million (2008 est.)
NAICS: 621210 Offices of Dentists

■ ■ ■

OrthoSynetics Inc., known until 2007 as Orthodontic Centers of America, Inc. (OCA), is a leading provider of orthodontic and dental practice services. Specifically, the company helps orthodontic and dental practices handle the nonclinical side of their business. Toward the end of the first decade of the 21st century the company served approximately 350 practices, lending a hand in areas such as insurance services, real estate, information technology, financial reporting, human resources, billing and collections, marketing, and purchasing/procurement.

ORIGINS

Dr. Gasper Lazzara spent more than 25 years practicing as an orthodontist before he decided to embark on a career as an entrepreneur. In 1980, Lazzara joined forces with another orthodontist and two optometrists associated with Pearle Vision Center, a company that was rapidly turning optometry into an efficient, profit-producing enterprise geared for volume business. Lazzara intended to achieve the same results in orthodontics, and he gathered the financial resources to pursue his entrepreneurial dream. Pearle Vision invested $700,000 in Lazzara's enterprise, start-up money that was enriched by the contribution of $75,000 from each of the active partners. With $1 million in seed money, Lazzara and his partners opened 16 dental practices in Florida, establishing the offices within shopping malls. The business foundered, forcing the dissolution of the partnership forged to create the enterprise. Lazzara had failed but he was not willing to let his first mistake dash his dreams of becoming a successful entrepreneur.

Lazzara made his next bid to infuse economies of scale into the practice of orthodontics in 1985. For his second venture, Lazzara enlisted the help of his longtime accountant, Bartholomew Palmisano, Sr., whose unwavering attention to fiscal matters would underpin Lazzara's innovative approach to the business of straightening teeth. Lazzara used a combination of his personal savings and bank loans to purchase two orthodontic offices in Jacksonville, Florida, which would serve as the proving ground for Lazzara's business strategy in 1985 and for his company's other orthodontic ventures in the years to come. The heart of Lazzara's plan was consolidation of the orthodontic industry. At that time, the U.S. orthodontic industry was highly fragmented, with 90 percent of the approximately 9,000 practicing orthodontists acting as sole practitioners.

DEVELOPING A BUSINESS STRATEGY

Eventually, Lazzara hoped to bring a significant portion of the thousands of orthodontic offices in operation under the banner of one management company, a company that would later become known as OCA, and then OrthoSynetics. His plan was based on the theory that if one central organization provided a full range of management services to a host of satellite offices, then the individual offices would realize increased operational efficiency and greater profits, achieving results better than would be achieved as separate businesses. Freed from the responsibilities of managing the business side of their practices, orthodontists, Lazzara concluded, could devote more time to attending to patients, thereby increasing their business volume.

Moreover, a systematic approach to dealing with the operational aspects of an orthodontic practice would yield greater efficiency, Lazzara contended, with office design, inventory control, staff bonuses, and other aspects of the business standardized in a fashion similar to that of successful franchise organizations. Further, with advertising and marketing resources emanating from a central organization, individual orthodontists could expect greater promotional support for their practice than they could provide on their own. Lazzara hoped to prove his point in Jacksonville; if he succeeded, he could begin consolidating the industry, establish his own satellite offices, and create a powerful force in the multibillion-dollar U.S. orthodontic industry.

As Lazzara fleshed out the details of his business strategy, the future of his entrepreneurial dream hinged on the results achieved with the pilot Jacksonville practices. Lazzara and Palmisano needed to produce quantifiable results, figures that the pair could use to convince orthodontists of the financial gains to be made

by joining a central management organization. Accordingly, Palmisano set up a computer system capable of monitoring the operational functions of the two offices and charting their productivity. With the information gleaned from Palmisano's electronic scrutiny, fundamental changes were made. Inventories were reduced and invoicing procedures were more tightly controlled, causing patients to pay their bills more promptly. Within a year, the partners could point to tangible results. The operating profit margins of the two practices increased from 10 percent to 30 percent; Lazzara and Palmisano were in business.

Lazzara expanded his network of affiliated orthodontic centers at a measured pace during his first years in business. By the beginning of the 1990s, nine more orthodontic practices had affiliated themselves with Lazzara's management services program. The pace of expansion accelerated from there, with 20 more orthodontic centers joining the fold during the next two years, giving Lazzara a total of 31 centers by the end of 1991. At this point in the company's development, all but five of the orthodontic centers were located within the offices of general dentists. During 1992, when 16 more centers became affiliated practices, Lazzara began implementing a strategy to relocate all of the company's affiliated centers to freestanding locations, preferring either shopping centers or professional office buildings as site locations.

REORGANIZATION FOLLOWED BY PUBLIC OFFERING

As Lazzara's network of affiliated orthodontic centers prepared to enter the mid-1990s, the corporate structure of the organization underwent significant change. The reorganization, executed on October 18, 1994, marked the debut of OCA as the corporate banner for the affiliated centers. Before October 1994, there were two management entities that oversaw the business operations of the affiliated centers, which, following the reorganization, were referred to as OCA's predecessor entities. In October 1994, OCA was formed to acquire the two predecessor management entities and all of the assets and liabilities of the predecessor operating entities—the orthodontic centers previously affiliated with the two management entities. In the wake of the structural changes, OCA, with Lazzara serving as the company's chief executive officer and Palmisano serving as its chief financial officer, became the single managerial concern governing the business operations of all of the company's orthodontic centers. Two months later, Lazzara completed OCA's initial public offering (IPO), selling 26 percent of the company to the public and netting $18 million from the stock sale.

By the time of OCA's IPO, there were 46 affiliated orthodontists operating 75 OCA offices, each run according to the detailed specifications formulated by Lazzara and Palmisano. OCA mandated a screening process, excluding cases that required elaborate braces attached to the back of teeth or patients with jaw joint problems. "We only do bread-and-butter orthodontics," Lazzara explained in a May 20, 1996, interview with *Forbes* magazine. In the same interview, Palmisano offered his perspective. "The most expensive cost is an idle staff," he remarked. Within an OCA center, responsibilities were clearly defined for each staff member, enhancing efficiency. If no patients were scheduled for a particular day, the center's staff was trimmed to include only a receptionist who answered incoming telephone calls. OCA specified the layout and design of its orthodontic centers, among myriad other details, and offered staff bonuses, with awards based on how successfully each office controlled inventory and brought in new patients.

RAPID GROWTH

In exchange for adhering to the operational criteria dictated by OCA and sharing revenue with OCA, affiliated orthodontists reaped the benefits of OCA's services.

For its constituents, OCA developed and implemented an aggressive marketing program that by far exceeded the means of orthodontists who served as sole practitioners. The company used local and national television, radio and print advertising, and internal marketing promotions, spending an average of nearly $70,500 per year for each affiliated orthodontist on direct marketing costs and advertising. In comparison, the typical independent orthodontist spent an average of $4,400 per year on marketing and advertising.

Because of the considerable gulf separating the marketing budgets of OCA affiliates and independent orthodontists, Lazzara possessed a powerful recruitment tool to induce practicing orthodontists to ally themselves with OCA. On average, an OCA doctor saw 77 patients per day during the mid-1990s versus the industry average of 42 patients per day. Further, affiliated orthodontists in practice for at least a year generated 512 new cases per year, compared with the industry average of 170 new patients per year for non-OCA orthodontists. For the consumer, there was an inducement to use OCA as well. At $2,770, OCA fees during the mid-1990s for straightening teeth were 20 percent below the national average.

The cumulative effect of the perquisites for orthodontists and consumers alike made OCA an attractive alternative to the traditional orthodontic practice. Consequently, the company was poised for national expansion, an inherent aspect of Lazzara's strategy and one that he financed by selling stock in OCA to the public. Following the company's IPO at the end of 1994, Lazzara sold the public another 34 percent in 1995, raising $82 million, and completed another public offering in April 1996, selling 12 percent of OCA for $75 million.

Against the backdrop of Lazzara's efforts to raise capital, OCA expanded vigorously. Between the end of 1994 and the end of 1996, the number of OCA centers more than tripled, increasing from 75 to 247, spreading out to cover 28 states. Of the 247 centers composing OCA at the end of 1996, 134 were developed by the company (at an average cost of $230,000) and 113 were existing orthodontic practices whose assets were acquired by the company.

INTERNATIONAL EXPANSION AND DIVERSIFICATION

The aggressive pace of expansion during the mid-1990s continued unabated during the late 1990s, elevating OCA to the leadership position in its industry. There were other companies in the orthodontic industry pursuing strategies similar to OCA's business plan, but strident growth kept the company's rivals at bay. In 1997, 1998, and 1999, Lazzara added at least 100 new centers each year to his network, giving the company 537 centers by the end of 1999, more than seven times the total recorded five years earlier. The company's prodigious growth extended its geographic coverage into 43 states, but the most dramatic aspect of OCA's expansion during the latter half of the 1990s occurred overseas. Beginning in 1998, Lazzara began expanding internationally, developing orthodontic centers in Japan and Puerto Rico. By the end of 1998, OCA managed six centers in Japan and two centers in Puerto Rico. In 1999, the company expanded aggressively in Japan by adding 18 more centers, bolstered its presence in Puerto Rico by developing three additional centers, and completed its entry into Mexico by establishing two centers. By the end of the decade, Lazzara was exploring additional expansion opportunities in Canada, England, and Spain.

OCA's physical expansion during the late 1990s was coupled with the expansion of its operational scope, as Lazzara steered the company in a new business direction. Lazzara signed an agreement with BriteSmile, Inc., a developer and manufacturer of teeth-whitening technology and related products. Under the terms of the agreement, OCA conducted a pilot program in 1999 that incorporated BriteSmile's systems into OCA centers in Jacksonville and in Tucson, Arizona. In a related venture, OCA started the trial operation of a cosmetic dental center in Jacksonville in 1999. The experimental center, designed to resemble a boutique or a spa rather than a dental office, offered cosmetic services such as teeth-whitening services and porcelain teeth laminates.

As OCA prepared for the new millennium, the company faced tantalizing expansion opportunities. Despite the prolific growth of OCA and the expansion of other companies similar to OCA, less than 10 percent of practicing orthodontists were affiliated with practice management companies. Moreover, among the handful of major practice management companies, OCA was demonstrating marked superiority, particularly in relation to one of its main rivals, Apple Orthodontix, Inc. Apple Orthodontix filed for protection from its creditors under Chapter 11 of the U.S. Bankruptcy Code in January 2000. The company's misfortune proved to be OCA's gain, as Lazzara signed a definitive agreement to acquire up to 47 orthodontic practices affiliated with Apple Orthodontix.

LEADERSHIP CHANGES AND ACCOUNTING CONTROVERSY

Lazzara stepped down as CEO in July 2000. Although he remained with the company as chairman and

revealed plans to provide the company with strategic guidance, day-to-day leadership was transitioned to Palmisano, who had been serving as co-CEO for two years. Lazzara's continued involvement with the company proved to be short-lived, however. He ultimately left after he and Palmisano had differing views about OCA's strategy.

During the early years of the 21st century, OCA's network of orthodontic centers grew to nearly 600, staffed by approximately 400 orthodontists and 2,300 support personnel. Revenues totaled $295 million in 2000, with earnings of $63 million. By early 2001, Palmisano, Sr., had been joined in the leadership suite by his son Bartholomew Palmisano, Jr., who served as chief financial officer, and later chief operating officer. Also in 2001, OCA relocated its corporate headquarters from Ponte Vedra Beach, Florida, to Louisiana.

It was around this time that OCA began attracting attention for its unusual accounting methods. For example, patients of its affiliated orthodontic centers were allowed to make interest-free monthly payments over the course of their 26-month treatment. OCA required its orthodontists to pay the company 24 percent of the total treatment amount during the first month. If the practice was not able to pay, OCA accepted an IOU and recorded the 24 percent figure on its books anyway.

In 2001 the Securities and Exchange Commission (SEC) required OCA to change its accounting methods, which did not comply with SEC accounting guidelines. OCA was forced to restate its revenues and earnings for 2000. OCA's unusual accounting methods ultimately resulted in lawsuits from the company's shareholders, who claimed that its financial statements were misleading. Subsequently, OCA began recording equal revenue amounts over the span of orthodontic contracts.

OCA experienced high turnover of its chief financial officers during the early years of the decade. In addition to Bartholomew Palmisano, Jr., John C. Glover also held this position. When he resigned, Thomas J. Sandeman assumed the role in October 2002. Looking to the future, Palmisano, Sr., pledged that the company would do a better job of explaining its accounting procedures to the public. In October 2002 the U.S. District Court for the Eastern District of Louisiana dismissed a class-action securities fraud lawsuit against OCA and its senior management. Specifically, the court ruled that there were insufficient facts to support claims that OCA had violated federal securities laws.

FACING DIFFICULT TIMES

Midway through 2001, OCA agreed to acquire its largest competitor, Torrance, California-based OrthAlliance

Inc. The deal, worth approximately $55.7 million, was finalized in 2002. OCA began 2003 by securing a three-year, $125 million line of credit to support future expansion, as well as a stock buyback initiative. While this was a positive development, the company had struggled following its acquisition of OrthAlliance. Closing OrthAlliance's headquarters, combining the cultures of both organizations, and getting former OrthAlliance customers on board with OCA's approach had been challenging. In addition, OCA found itself contending with approximately 50 lawsuits that customers had filed against OrthAlliance over contract-related issues.

By mid-decade OCA served some 365 affiliated practices, which cared for more than 490,000 patients. Difficult times led the company to file for Chapter 11 bankruptcy protection in March 2006. By May of that year, Palmisano, Sr., had been terminated as CEO, and temporarily succeeded by Chief Restructuring Officer Michael Gries. OCA emerged from bankruptcy on January 26, 2007, when the company's reorganization plan was approved by the U.S. Bankruptcy Court. OCA's old stock was canceled, and new stock was issued to Silver Point Capital, OCA's senior lender.

OCA moved forward as a privately owned company with new management. Chris Roussos was named the company's new CEO in 2007. Midway through the year OCA changed its name to OrthoSynetics, which was intended to symbolize the organization's new culture and vision. In addition to Roussos, other new senior leaders included Chief Information Officer Tim Tiffin and Chief Financial Officer Cathy M. Green.

Several improvements were made in late 2007. OrthoSynetics established a new data center and co-location facility in Dallas, Texas, in September. The following month, the company introduced a new web site that included features intended to improve customer service.

OrthoSynetics began 2008 by opening new regional offices in Dallas and Atlanta, Georgia. The latter location was intended to serve as a part-time operational base for Roussos and Tiffin. It also was in early 2008 that former Chief Operating Officer and Chief Financial Officer Palmisano, Jr., was fined $100,000 and banned from serving as the director of a publicly traded company for ten years. The penalties followed a suit filed in U.S. District Court by the SEC, which charged that Palmisano, Jr., had manipulated the company's accounting systems on 18 occasions between 1998 and September 2001.

After implementing a new leadership team and making numerous improvements, OrthoSynetics strengthened its sales team in 2008, preparing the company for further growth. In early 2009 President and CEO Roussos was named chairman of the board. The company was prepared to move forward in a difficult economic climate, with a commitment to helping its affiliated practices operate as efficiently as possible.

Jeffrey L. Covell
Updated, Paul R. Greenland

PRINCIPAL COMPETITORS

American Dental Partners Inc.; Castle Dental Centers Inc.; InterDent Inc.

FURTHER READING

Basch, Mark, "CEO of Ponte Vedra Beach, Fla.-based Orthodontic Company Resigns," *Florida Times Union*, August 1, 2000.

———, "Dental Group to Be More Open on Finances," *Florida Times Union*, November 25, 2002.

———, "Florida-Based Orthodontic Centers of America Sets Goal," *Knight-Ridder/Tribune Business News*, May 21, 1996.

———, "Florida's Orthodontic Centers of America Reports Rise in Earnings," *Knight-Ridder/Tribune Business News*, November 1, 1996.

———, "Three Jacksonville, Fla., Company Stocks Stood Out in 1995," *Knight-Ridder/Tribune Business News*, January 1, 1996.

Butler, Elisabeth, "Orthodontist Chain Struggles to Revive Stock After Merger," *New Orleans CityBusiness*, January 13, 2003.

"Chris Roussos Appointed Chairman of the Board of Ortho-Synetics," *PR Newswire*, March 17, 2009.

Dolan, Kerry A., "Braces for the Masses," *Forbes*, May 20, 1996, p. 260.

Elliott, Alan, "Orthodontic Centers of America Inc./Ponte Vedra Beach, Florida Orthodontic Firm Sinks Teeth into Growth," *Investor's Business Daily*, November 22, 2000.

Freedman, Michael, "Streetwalker," *Forbes*, February 7, 2000, p. 194.

Messingill, Teena, "BriteSmile Teeth-Whitening Centers Move Headquarters to California," *Knight-Ridder/Tribune Business News*, November 1, 1999.

"OCA Inc. Files Chapter 11 to Address Financial and Operational Challenges," *Business Wire*, March 16, 2006.

"OrthoSynetics Launches New Name; Renews Commitment to Customer Service," *PR Newswire*, June 6, 2007.

Robertshaw, Nicky, "Orthodontics Centers Move into Memphis' Three Local Offices for Florida MSO," *Memphis Business Journal*, December 1, 1997, p. 1.

Panavision Inc.

―――――■―――――

6219 De Soto Avenue
Woodland Hills, California 91367-2602
U.S.A.
Telephone: (818) 316-1000
Fax: (818) 316-1111
Web site: http://www.panavision.com

Wholly Owned Subsidiary of MacAndrews & Forbes Holdings Inc.
Founded: 1954
Employees: 1,211
Sales: $250 million (2008 est.)
NAICS: 333315 Photographic and Photocopying Equipment Manufacturing; 532490 Other Commercial and Industrial Machinery and Equipment Rental and Leasing

■ ■ ■

With both Oscar and Emmy awards under its belt, Panavision Inc. is a leading designer, manufacturer, and renter of film and digital camera systems for the motion-picture and television industries. Its products, which include cameras, lenses, and lighting equipment, are considered by many to be the finest in cinematography and have been used in films ranging from *Lawrence of Arabia* and *Ben-Hur* to *Iron Man* and *Batman: The Dark Knight.* Panavision's products have also been used for television shows including *CSI, Desperate Housewives, Law & Order, Lost,* and *24.* In 2009 and since 1990, 13 of the Oscars for Best Cinematography have been awarded to cinematogra-

phers who used Panavision cameras and lenses during the filming process. Billionaire investor Ronald Perelman purchased a majority interest in Panavision in 1998 and took the company private in 2006.

HUMBLE BEGINNINGS IN A LOS ANGELES CAMERA STORE

Panavision started in Los Angeles in 1954 in a camera store owned and operated by Robert Gottschalk. Besides being a camera retailer, Gottschalk also was an inventor of photography-related innovations. His first major breakthrough was his design and perfection of a camera lens that did not distort images in wide-screen motion pictures. He officially introduced the first Panavision lens in 1957. Ten years later Gottschalk sold Panavision to Kinney Corporation, a predecessor company of Time Warner. Despite the sale, Gottschalk remained active in Panavision. He went on to invent the Panaflex camera, a mobile unit that was lighter and more portable than earlier camera models.

After Gottschalk died in 1982, a variety of owners bought and sold Panavision most notably Ted Field, the grandson of Marshall Field, founder of the eponymous U.S. retail chain. Field bought Panavision in 1985 from Warner Communications for $52 million. Shortly after purchasing the company, Field bought out his investment partners, giving him total control of the enterprise. Under his direction, Panavision played a role in the production of many financially successful motion pictures, including *Outrageous Fortune, Critical Condition,* and *Revenge of the Nerds.* Field sold the company in

September 1987 to Britain's Lee International for $142 million.

In 1988 Warburg Pincus Capital Company assumed control of Panavision. The capital company invested $60 million to keep Panavision solvent. Yet the company struggled financially when camera production dropped from 25 to a mere 15. Panavision spent the next five years securing its place in the industry, returning to profitability in 1993.

In 1994 Panavision led the investment group that established Panavision New York, a dealership with the right to inventory and rental of the company's cameras and lenses in the northeastern United States. The new company's president, Peter Schnitzler, CFO, Ira Goodman, and general counsel, Charles Hopfl, comprised the remainder of the investment group. Goodman explained the significance of Panavision's role in the New York-based company to *SHOOT:* "Panavision actually being a minority owner of Panavision New York, they actually enter into a franchise/leased agreement … which gives us the right to rent Panavision cameras to production companies."

Panavision relocated its headquarters from Tarzana, California, to the Warner Center in Woodland Hills, California, in 1995. Relocation "was necessitated by our company's continued success and growth," President John S. Farrand told the *Los Angeles Business Journal.* "This new facility will allow us to bring our manufacturing, rental, and administrative operations under one roof."

MODERN INNOVATIONS

In the spirit of Gottschalk, Panavision introduced a new camera system in 1996. The system was the company's enhanced version of an innovative lens created by Jim Frazier, an Australian camera operator. Frustrated by conventional lenses, Frazier developed a Deep Focus Lens System that had an almost infinite depth of field. The camera operator's system then kept objects in the foreground and background in focus. The Panavision/Frazier Lens System, however, augmented the original

design. Panavision's system focused images in the same way as Frazier's, but also included a swivel tip to allow filming at various angles and the ability to rotate images in the lens. Observers considered the Deep Focus system to be one of the foremost optical innovations since the zoom lens.

Panavision's small optics shop launched another innovation that greatly pleased cinematographers. In 1996 Panavision used the Tecnara MST modular RAA head to manufacture lens barrels to the exact specifications of professional camera operators. By this time, approximately 90 percent of all Hollywood productions used the company's cameras. Each of the top ten motion pictures of 1995 including *Batman Forever, Apollo 13, Die Hard with a Vengeance,* and *Ace Ventura: When Nature Calls* were filmed using Panavision systems. In 1996, nine of the ten leading box-office successes used Panavision cameras and equipment, notably *Independence Day, Mission: Impossible, Twister, Ransom, The Rock,* and *A Time to Kill.*

In addition to financial success, motion pictures filmed with Panavision systems also earned acclaim for cinematography within the industry. From 1954 through 1995, the company won 14 awards from the Academy of Motion Picture Arts and Sciences. During the 1990s, the Academy recognized Panavision with two Oscars and 17 awards for scientific and technical achievement. In fact, in that decade two of every three Oscar nominees for best cinematography filmed their works with Panavision systems, and five of every six Oscar-winning cinematographers filmed their productions with Panavision cameras.

Panavision was equally successful on the small screen, providing cameras and equipment for the most watched television series of the 1990s. *Friends, Seinfeld, Fraser,* and *ER* were all filmed with Panavision equipment. "There is no question that Panavision has a dominant place in the industry," noted Christopher Dixon, an analyst with Paine Webber, in *Going Public: The IPO Reporter.*

Panavision was also renowned for the level of customer service it provided through its rental facilities and agent network. The company offered its customers 140 technicians and 160,000 square feet of factory space in which to develop new equipment. For the 1997 Hollywood blockbuster *Titanic,* for example, Panavision designed a special camera for filming underwater. Similarly, for the movie *JFK* the company engineered cameras that mounted on the hoods of cars and trucks.

In total, Panavision manufactured 35 camera systems in 1996. With strong sales that year, the company initiated a recapitalization and its initial public offering (IPO) of stock. In November 1996, Panavision

KEY DATES

1954: Panavision gets its start in a camera store owned by Robert Gottschalk.
1957: The first Panavision lens makes its debut.
1967: Panavision is sold to Kinney Corp.
1985: Ted Field buys Panavision from Warner Communications for $52 million.
1987: Field sells the company to Britain's Lee International for $142 million.
1988: Warburg Pincus Capital Company assumes control of Panavision.
1996: The company introduces the Panavision/ Frazier Lens System; Panavision goes public.
1997: Panavision acquires the Film Services Group of Visual Action Holdings PLC, a London-based company, for $61 million in cash.
1998: Ronald Perelman acquires a majority interest in the company.
2004: The company launches its Genesis Digital Camera system.
2006: Perelman takes Panavision private.

offered 2.8 million shares of stock at $17 per share. The stock sales brought the company $47.6 million for the repayment of debt and the generation of working capital, and the company decreased its annual interest expenses to $3.9 million. Within seven days of the IPO, Panavision stock jumped to $22.25 per share. Panavision manufactured no less than 80 cameras in 1997. Owing to this increase in sales and the successful IPO, Panavision's earnings rose from $13 million in 1996 to $18 million.

NEW TECHNOLOGIES

This new climate prompted the company to seek acquisitions, as well as to continue the development of new photographic innovations. In June 1997, Panavision acquired the Film Services Group of Visual Action Holdings PLC, a London-based company, for $61 million in cash. The purchase of this enterprise solidified Panavision's foothold in camera rental operations throughout the world, including the United Kingdom, France, Australia, New Zealand, Singapore, Malaysia, and Indonesia. Panavision also expanded its U.S. camera rental operations when it assumed Visual Action operations in Atlanta, Chicago, and Dallas.

In 1997 Panavision introduced the Panavision Take 1 Digital Video Assist, which combined digital and opti-

cal technologies for quick editing, optical effects, and bridging special effects and postproduction operations. Other features of the new system included multi-camera recording, random access searching, and instant playback. Panavision released a second innovation in 1997 as well. Its Millennium camera system launched a new generation of Panaflex camera systems. This 35-millimeter sync-sound film camera system used optical and electronic technologies, materials, and coatings. With optical and video viewfinders, the system featured custom-designed and manufactured optics with advanced coatings, in addition to a full-field view finding system. The camera's enhanced light path created brighter, clearer images, and its light weight made the system versatile. For example, the studio quiet camera operated as a Steadicam and converted quickly to a handheld camera.

In 1997 Panavision faced the future prepared to manufacture additional camera systems and accessories in response to the growing feature film and television commercial markets in North America and the United Kingdom and elsewhere in Europe. From 1992 until 1996, feature film production in North America grew from 104 to 124 films annually, more than a 19 percent increase. Likewise, independent filmmaking on this continent increased from 246 in 1992 to 367 films in 1996. Europe produced 500 feature films in 1996 alone. The growth in feature film production offered many opportunities for Panavision, because each motion picture could require as many as ten cameras, 40 lenses, and a variety of video cameras and focusing devices—as much as $600,000 in equipment.

Similarly, Panavision expected television production to increase beyond 1997. The company prepared for greater opportunities in television as more cable channels, new networks, and increased video distribution took hold in North America. The privatization of network channels in Europe, as well as the growth of satellite networks there, also pointed to an increase in television production abroad. In 1997 Panavision estimated that revenues from commercial television production grew 61 percent since 1992, while episodic television production-related revenues increased 75 percent in those five years.

Panavision's plan was to capitalize on this growth-oriented environment. As Farrand and William C. Scott, chairman and chief executive officer of the company, wrote in Panavision's 1996 annual report: "In 1997 and beyond, we intend to take advantage of this growth in worldwide demand for filmed entertainment by leveraging our superior brand name, extensive distribution network, increased design and manufacturing capacity, and strategic financial position."

PERELMAN TAKES CONTROL

Billionaire investor Ronald Perelman launched a $600 million takeover of Panavision in 1998. Perelman secured a 72 percent interest in the company, making himself and his firm, MacAndrews & Forbes Holdings Inc., the majority shareholder. Panavision soon began to struggle under a mountain of debt, and with losses growing, Perelman orchestrated a deal that garnered criticism from many investors. Perelman sold his stake in Panavision to M&F Worldwide Corporation, a licorice-flavorings company he owned. Shareholders were outraged, claiming the deal caused M&F Worldwide's share price to fall when it was forced to borrow $90 million to finance its purchase of Panavision. Shareholders filed suit against Perelman and in late 2002 a Delaware state court judge approved a $128 million pact in which the sale of Panavision stock to M&F Worldwide would be reversed.

Meanwhile, Panavision was focused on developing new digital technologies while continuing to bolster its television business. In 2004 it launched the Genesis Digital Camera System, which was used in films including *Scary Movie 4* and *Superman Returns*. By 2006 nearly 20 percent of company revenues stemmed from the rental of digital equipment while traditional film equipment rentals shored up the remainder of rental revenues. Although many movie producers were slow to embrace the new digital technology, Panavision believed using digital cameras would eventually become commonplace. Rental for the company's Genesis digital camera was estimated to be nearly $3,000 per day, almost twice the cost of renting a traditional film camera. The company claimed, however, that using one of its digital cameras would save an estimated $600,000 in film costs and processing activities for big-budget movies.

The company secured a $345 million credit line to finance new product development in 2006. Shortly thereafter, Perelman announced he was taking the company private. Panavision faced several challenges during this period, including increased competition as well as a writers' strike in Hollywood, and the overall economic downturn that led to the production of fewer movies. At the same time, television producers were forced to cut costs and many turned to less-expensive digital cameras offered by Panavision's competitors. In fact, television embraced digital technology much more quickly than the movie industry. Nearly every television pilot made in 2009 was shot using digital equipment. Although Panavision rented digital cameras including its Genesis model, it was falling behind the competition with its costly product offerings. Even though most of the television series *ER* had been filmed using Panavi-

sion equipment, the final six episodes of the series were filmed using a less-expensive digital camera called the Red One, made by Oakley Inc. founder Jim Jannard.

Furthermore, Panavision's leadership had been inconsistent. Bob Beitcher, CEO of Panavision since 2003, was ousted by Perelman in 2009 and replaced by industry executive William M. Campbell in April of that year. Campbell stepped down just three months later and William C. Bevins, an executive who headed several other Perelman-owned entities, took the helm.

With competition eating into company revenues and profits, Panavision was forced to revamp its strategy. Newly elected CEO Bevins commented on the company's direction in a July 2009 *Hamilton Spectator* article. "We decided to redouble our efforts to develop product for the digital marketplace," he claimed. "We can't rent what people don't want."

Charity Anne Dorgan
Updated, Christina M. Stansell

PRINCIPAL SUBSIDIARIES

Lee Filters USA; Panavision New York; Panavision GP Inc.; Panavision International, L.P.; Panavision Remote Systems LLC; Panavision Federal Systems, LLC; Panavision U.K. Holdings, Inc.; TFN Lighting Corporation; LPPI, LLC; Panavision U.K LP; Panavision Europe Ltd.; Lee Lighting Ltd.; Samuelson Group Ltd.; Lee Filters Limited; Camera Bellows Ltd.; Panavision Polska z.o.o.; Camera Rentals Ireland Ltd.; Panavision NZ Ltd.; Film Facilities Ltd. (New Zealand); Panavision Lighting NZ Ltd.; Panavision Alga Techno Eurl (France); Cinecam Sarl (France); Technovision France SAS; Panavision Marseille Sarl (France); Panavision Australia Pty. Ltd.; Panavision Asia Pacific Pty. Ltd.; John Barry Group Pty. Ltd.; Panavision Lighting Asia Pacific Pty. Ltd.; Panavision Asia Pte. Ltd. (Singapore); Panavision Luxembourg Sarl; Panavision Canada Holdings Inc.; Panavision (Canada) Corporation.

PRINCIPAL COMPETITORS

Ballantyne of Omaha Inc.; Eastman Kodak Company; Production Resource Group LLC.

FURTHER READING

Bary, Andrew, "Deep Focus: Panavision's Debt Is Putting Perelman in an Unflattering Light," *Barron's,* May 6, 2002.

Berton, Brad, "Panavision Signs $20 Million Long-Term Lease," *Los Angeles Business Journal,* July 10, 1995, p. 11.

"Creative Optics Shop Takes Aim at Tough Problems," *Modern Machine Shop,* January 1996, p. 134.

"Firm Commitment IPOs Issued in November: Panavision Inc.," *Going Public: The IPO Reporter,* December 16, 1996.

Giardina, Carolyn, "Panavision N.Y. Obtains General Camera Corporation," *SHOOT,* June 17, 1994, p. 1.

Gubernick, Lisa, "Behind the Scenes," *Forbes,* June 2, 1997, p. 108.

Kirsner, Scott, "Studios Shift to Digital Movies, but Not Without Resistance," *New York Times,* July 24, 2006.

Newcomb, Peter, "Divided We Stand: At Thirty-two, Ted Field Has $260 Million and a Burning Ambition to Emerge from the Shadow of Older Half-Brother Marshall V," *Forbes,* October 26, 1987, p. 68.

Norris, Floyd, "Panavision's Star Is Falling," *Milwaukee Journal Sentinel,* November 26, 2000.

"Panavision Inc.," *Venture Capital Journal,* January 1, 1997.

"Panavision Records Public Offering," *Going Public: The IPO Reporter,* December 2, 1996.

Riley-Katz, Anne, "Going Private and Digital Panavision's Focus," *Los Angeles Business Journal,* May 1, 2006.

Soter, Tom, "Depth of Field," *SHOOT,* October 6, 1995, p. 36.

Verrier, Richard, "Panavision No Longer Hollywood's Golden Girl," *Los Angeles Times,* July 25, 2009.

Woodward, Sarah, "Beitcher Outlines Panavision's Plans," *SHOOT,* June 20, 2003.

Perkins & Marie Callender's Inc.

6075 Poplar Avenue, Suite 800
Memphis, Tennessee 38119-4709
U.S.A.
Telephone: (901) 766-6400
Fax: (901) 766-6482
Web site: http://www.mcpies.com

Private Company
Incorporated: 1964 as Marie Callender's Pie Shops, Inc.
Employees: 16,300
Sales: $582 million (2008 est.)
NAICS: 722110 Full-Service Restaurants

■■■

Perkins & Marie Callender's Inc., owned by investment group Castle Harlan, Inc., operates the Perkins Restaurant & Bakery and Marie Callender's Restaurant & Bakery chains. Perkins operates over 480 full-service restaurants in 34 states and five Canadian provinces. The company's Foxtail Foods division manufactures pies, pancake mix, cookie dough, and muffin batter used by in-store bakeries and third-party customers. Marie Callender's, purchased in 1999 by Castle Harlan, operates 130 Marie Callender's restaurants and one East Side Mario's restaurant in the United States and Mexico. Marie Callender's frozen entrée products are also sold in supermarkets throughout the United States. Castle Harlan acquired Perkins in 2005 and merged it with Marie Callender's the following year.

PERKINS POST–WORLD WAR II ORIGINS

The Perkins chain was founded by William Smith, but it takes its name from Ohioans Mat and Ivan Perkins. Smith launched his first Smitty's pancake house in Seattle, Washington, in 1957, featuring his own special pancake recipe. The Perkins brothers adopted Smith's recipes and took them to Silverton, Ohio, a suburb of Cincinnati, in 1958, where they opened the first Perkins Pancake House. While similar in all but name, the two restaurant concepts were separately owned and operated throughout the 1950s, 1960s, and most of the 1970s. Franchises under both the Smitty's and Perkins names were sold throughout the Midwest.

Although the food at Perkins was low-priced—checks averaged $1 per person in the early 1960s—it was not a run-of-the-mill pancake house. The menu included more than two-dozen different kinds of pancakes and waffles prepared by chefs wearing white hats. Pancake choices included the standard buttermilk cakes, as well as potato, banana, curried tuna, "toad-in-the-hole," and Swedish varieties. Waffles were made with strawberries, coconut, butter pecan, and many other nontraditional ingredients. The Perkins brothers added sandwiches to their menu in the early 1960s. Restaurants were decorated in a colonial theme, featuring lantern-style light fixtures and Early American furnishings.

In 1967 Wyman Nelson, a major franchisee headquartered in Minneapolis, Minnesota, began to emerge as a leader of the rather loosely knit organization. That year he expanded service to 24 hours a day, seven days a week, and changed the name of all his restaurants throughout the state to Perkins Cake & Steak to reflect the addition of a dinner menu to the restaurant's offerings. Nelson also mounted an advertising campaign to publicize the changes. Over the course of the next several years, Nelson gradually took over the Smitty's and Perkins chains. In 1969 he purchased the right to develop the dining concept throughout Minnesota. Seven years later, he acquired a nationwide license to the Perkins concept. He completed his consolidation effort in 1978 with the outright purchase of the Perkins trademark and flour distribution rights.

HOLIDAY CORP. ACQUIRES PERKINS

Less than a year after Nelson's consolidation, Perkins Cake & Steak, Inc., was itself acquired by Holiday Corp., parent company of Holiday Inn, Inc. The purchase was part of Holiday's diversification into both restaurants and casinos at that time. By 1981 Perkins had 258 restaurants in 29 states. In 1983 the hotel chain moved the headquarters of Perkins to Memphis, Tennessee, where the main office of Perkins would remain through the early years of the new millennium. Although it remained marginally profitable, Perkins did not fare particularly well under its new ownership structure. James Scarpa of *Restaurant Business* described the chain as "dated and disorganized" in a 1990 article, particularly noting its "downscale coffee shop look."

The ownership of Perkins transferred again in the mid-1980s, when restaurateur Donald N. Smith, a member of Holiday's board of directors, took the 312-unit chain private. At the time, Perkins was netting only $3 million on revenues of $103 million. Smith (no rela-

tion to the founder), however, believed the restaurant chain had excellent potential for growth and profitability. Smith's resume included executive positions with several well-known restaurant chains. He was credited with developing Pizza Hut's Pan Pizza and Personal Pan Pizza and launching McDonald's breakfast menu. As CEO of Burger King in the late 1970s, he doubled profits on a 50 percent increase in chainwide sales.

With the cooperation of Holiday Corp., Smith formed an investment group dubbed Tennessee Restaurant Company (TRC) and purchased the chain for about $70 million in 1985. In 1986 he transformed the company into a limited partnership, selling a minority stake to the public. A portion of the funds raised was invested in remodeling and an almost complete overhaul of the menu. New and renewed units featured ceramic tile, green neon, and a solarium. One important and lasting addition to the menu was the Perkins in-store bakery, launched in 1986. The restaurant made omelets, rather than pancakes, the new featured breakfast item, and put a stronger emphasis on the lunch menu, adding cheese melt sandwiches and specialty salads. The changes boosted check averages, same-store sales, overall revenues, and corporate profitability. By the end of the decade, Smith had tripled the company's net to $9.7 million on a 50 percent increase in sales to $150 million.

GROWTH TARGETED FOR PERKINS

Having stabilized the chain, Smith focused on expansion in the early 1990s, hoping to double the number of restaurants by 1995. The growth plan for Perkins, dubbed the "1-95 Strategy," concentrated new units in the vicinity of this major East Coast thoroughfare. The chain also opened its first international restaurant in Ontario, Canada, Smith's native province, in 1988. Although it had dozens of company-owned units, Perkins continued to emphasize franchising as its key growth vehicle during this period. Corporate restaurants were used as testing grounds for new menu, decor, and marketing ideas.

Driven in large part by expansion, sales for Perkins increased by more than 40 percent from $180.5 million in 1990 to $252.8 million in 1996. However, the company's bottom-line performance did not match that top-line growth rate. In fact, net income declined from a high of $15.4 million in 1992 to less than $10 million in 1995 before recovering somewhat to $13.5 million in 1996. The erratic profitability of the company was matched by an unstable stock price. Shares in the helped rebound shares to $13.81 by that September. The deal was finalized in December of that year.

PERKINS EMPHASIZES FEEDING FAMILIES

The 1996 annual report of Perkins outlined a multifaceted program for future growth. All the initiatives were tested in company programs and slated to be adopted in franchises in the late 1990s. A new round of remodeling continued the chain's upscale trend. Company-owned sites refurbished during 1995 and 1996 featured garden rooms, "libraries" with bookcase wallpaper, sports-themed rooms, and sunrooms. Perkins arranged financing to assist its franchisees in the renovation process. New market research and customer satisfaction surveys were adopted as well. Perkins even tackled the difficult task of improving productivity in a service business. It combined backroom efficiencies, manager incentives, and a new scheduling system to increase the number of customers served per hour of labor. A closely related program sought to reduce turnover and thereby trim hiring and training costs.

Still led by David Smith in 1997, the management of Perkins hoped to parlay its bakeries into increased traffic, increased sales, and even new dining concepts. The company started testing stand-alone bakeries and cafés in 1995. Both formats were designed to adapt Perkins to food courts in a wide variety of settings, from malls to colleges to military bases.

The family orientation of Perkins sharpened its focus on serving children, and in 1996 the company began testing KidPerks, a program that incorporated a menu expansion and new entertainment options. In place of the coloring page and crayons typically offered to placate children while they waited for dinner to be prepared and served, KidPerks offered handheld computer games, comic books, and Etch A Sketch toys, as well as free popcorn to quiet growling stomachs. Successful KidPerks programs were in place at company-owned restaurants throughout Minnesota, Nebraska, North Dakota, Oklahoma, Tennessee, and Wisconsin during this time. As it prepared to enter the new millennium, Perkins Family Restaurants was hopeful of pulling out of its earnings slump and returning to profitable growth.

MARIE CALLENDER'S SOUTHERN CALIFORNIA ORIGINS

Marie Callender's was founded in Long Beach, California, in 1948 when Marie Callender was encouraged by husband Cal and son Don to pursue the

KEY DATES

1948: Marie Callender's is founded in Long Beach, California.
1957: William Smith launches his first Smitty's pancake house in Seattle, Washington.
1958: The Perkins brothers adopt Smith's recipes and take them to Silverton, Ohio, where they open the first Perkins Pancake House.
1964: Marie Callender's opens its first retail pie and coffee shop in Orange, California.
1978: Wyman Nelson buys the Perkins trademark and flour distribution rights.
1979: Perkins "Cake & Steak," Inc., is acquired by Holiday Corp., parent company of Holiday Inn, Inc.
1985: Donald Smith forms an investment group named Tennessee Restaurant Company and purchases Perkins for about $70 million.
1986: Perkins launches an in-store bakery; Marie Callender's is sold to Ramada International for over $80 million.
1988: Perkins opens its first international location in Canada.
1989: Ramada sells Marie Callender's to Wilshire Restaurant Group.
1997: The Restaurant Company (TRC) takes Perkins private.
1999: Castle Harlan Partners III L.P. acquires Wilshire Restaurant Group.
2005: Castle Harlan adds Perkins to its holdings when it acquires TRC.
2006: Perkins and Marie Callender's merge to form Perkins & Marie Callender's Inc.

limited partnership, which started trading publicly in 1989 at around $13, grew to over $15 late in 1993 before plunging to less than $8 in late 1994.

Steady dividend payouts helped boost the stock back over the $13 mark early in 1997, but that was before stakeholders learned that the partnership would become subject to corporate taxation beginning in 1998. In June 1997 the company announced that tax payments would likely reduce or even eliminate partnership dividends, news that sent the company's already battered shares into a midyear slide to about $10. The late 1997 offer by TRC (by this time known as The Restaurant Company) of $14 per share to take the company private

American dream and roll her prodigious pie-making skills into profits. Marie was a South Dakota native who had moved to Southern California and married at the age of 17. She worked in the food service industry at a delicatessen prior to making the decision to sell the family car for $700, using the funds to rent a converted World War II Quonset hut that would become the site of the first Marie Callender's bakery. The remaining cash funded a down payment on a small oven, refrigerator, rolling pin, and various baking utensils.

Marie was soon in business, baking whole pies for wholesale customers. Seats were removed from a 1936 Ford sedan to make room for the stacks of pies that would be delivered to local restaurants. All three family members worked 13-hour shifts once orders that originally numbered ten per day swelled to 40 per day. Within two years, the business had grown to 200 pie requests per day, a volume that necessitated the purchase of a truck and a mixer.

Fifteen years later, the business had grown substantially to the extent that several thousand pies per day were created for several restaurants. Although production had grown considerably by 1963, profits were less than desirable, prompting Don Callender to begin formulating plans for the construction of a retail pie and coffee shop, which was opened in Orange, California, in 1964. In that same year the company incorporated and was renamed Marie Callender's Pie Shop, Inc. The retail business at that time sold only whole pies that were made fresh daily, priced at 95 cents each. By offering free slices of pie and coffee the new restaurant enticed many new customers. The Marie Callender's formula proved so successful that soon a second small retail shop was opened in La Habra, then another in Anaheim, California.

The company expanded into other menu items in 1969, beginning with hamburgers, ham stacked sandwiches, salads, chili and cornbread, and grew to include a wide variety of home-style meals. A year later the family-owned business had grown to a chain of 26 restaurants located primarily in Southern California. Then a franchise restaurant was opened in Houston and another in Las Vegas. Cal became the full-time financial manager, while Don continued with expansion plans. Don was concerned with creating a comfortable, homey image for the company, one in keeping with the associations people made with home-baked pie.

Stylistically, the restaurant interiors imitated a cozy English country decor. Don expressed concern for the integrity of Marie Callender's architectural design, emphasizing that their restaurants should not have a "cookie cutter" look or feel, and opted to build businesses that were varied in their architectural ambiance,

reflecting a niche between the casual and family dining sector. Finally, in 1986, having fulfilled goals and imminent expansion plans, Don negotiated the sale of the family chain to Ramada International for over $80 million.

ANOTHER CHANGE IN OWNERSHIP FOR MARIE CALLENDER'S

According to Kelly Barron of the *Orange County Register,* following Ramada's buyout of Marie Callender's, "the hotel operator did little to build upon the chain's homespun image and 25 varieties of fresh-baked pies." Don Callender sued Ramada and the management at Marie Callender's contending that "they breached a contract allowing him to stay in operations," according to Barron. The suits were settled in 1994, ending Don Callender's involvement in the chain. Following unsuccessful attempts to develop the company, Ramada sold its share of the debt-laden chain in 1989 to the Wilshire Restaurant Group, a shell company made up of insurance companies and individuals, who added another $60 million to the debt load.

The Wilshire Group began to concentrate efforts on improving employee training and service. Despite their efforts, interest payments overwhelmed profits and the company defaulted on its loans. Management began courting investors to either buy or recapitalize it. In 1993 Saunders, Karp, and Megrue, LP, a New York-based firm, bought a majority interest (68 percent) in the company with an investment of $30 million. Existing management owned 15 percent, leaving a 17 percent ownership by other investors. The firm had other resources with additional holdings in Mimi's Café and the apparel retailer Charlotte Russe. Marie Callender's restructured its debt after obtaining a new $15 million credit line.

Under the new leadership, Leonard H. Dreyer was promoted to president and chief executive of Marie Callender's, which at that time consisted of 145 units. Launching an effort to repair the damaged chain, Dreyer closed several underperforming stores and opened no new ones. According to Melinda Fulmer of the *Orange County Business Journal,* at the point when Wilshire Restaurant Group bought the chain from Ramada, industry onlookers commented that "Marie Callender's had the smell of death" about it, due in part to bad franchisee relations, erratic store density, and heavy debt from the leveraged buyout.

Streamlining operations, the new management sold its frozen food line to Conagra Inc. for about $140 million. Dreyer implemented ways to cut costs, tightened quality controls, and strengthened relations with franchisees. He focused on what made the restaurant work in the early days and added menu items to keep up with evolving tastes and trends. Under its newly focused direction, Marie Callender's once again maintained its market share with reported 1993 revenues of $240 million.

MARIE CALLENDER'S EXPANDS MENU OFFERINGS

In homage to the quality of products originated by "the" Marie Callender, Dreyer continued to endorse and use her original pie recipes for most of the 33 varieties of pies it made. Fulmer of the *Orange County Business Journal* reported that "Dreyer never met the lady who spawned the chain of restaurants, who died of cancer last year (1995) at age 88." The company kept their core menu but added new items in an attempt to attract a broader customer base, recognizing that competitors were offering extensive menus, including specialty desserts. Marie Callender's expanded its pie line in time for the 1994 holiday season, with the introduction of its superpremium pies, satin pies described by the company as "one up on silk pies." Offering desserts not readily available at home or elsewhere, they unveiled a superpremium pumpkin version on a white chocolate base, and a peanut butter pie on a dark chocolate base.

Sales heated up when the company began offering fresh-roasted and carved-to-order turkey, rather than the precooked turkey previously offered. The company attempted to offer something for everyone: veggie burgers for vegetarians, low-fat items for the weight-conscious, and traditional fare for average consumers. They added sliced turkey breast sandwiches with choices including roasted sweet peppers, romaine lettuce, and roasted garlic mayonnaise on focaccia; turkey Caesar salad; and a turkey luncheon with apple-walnut stuffing, giblet gravy, mashed potatoes, and vegetables.

The company continued to grow at a steady pace, boosted by customer loyalty and the home-cooked image. Fulmer reported in the *Orange County Business Journal,* "the chain comes closer to white tablecloth restaurants than competitors Coco's, Carrows, and Denny's, with their made-from-scratch foods and ambiance … but customers are reluctant to pay the price associated with this quality." The company found it difficult to exceed the $10 price point, although overhead costs, particularly real estate prices, continued to rise.

As part of its new marketing strategy the company began to explore the advantages of building smaller units. Some of the larger flagship units were 15,000 square feet in size, but the newer prototypes were designed at an average of 5,000 square feet. In addition

to scaling down their regular formats, the company also began operating the even smaller format Best of Marie's concept in food courts that were typically located in malls and universities. The food court concept was an attempt to expand the market base to include 20-year-olds. Although the Best of Marie's outlets were not widely profitable, they functioned as a marketing tool for the larger restaurants.

MARIE CALLENDER'S COURTS YOUNGER CLIENTELE

As part of their major expansion plan Wilshire Restaurant Group purchased the restaurant chain East Side Mario's from PepsiCo in 1997. Gerald Tanaka, president of Mario's, became senior vice-president of Marie Callender's and helped implement a restaurant concept he termed as "lighter, brighter, more casual than our traditional dining rooms," according to Don Nichols of *Restaurant Business.* Attempting to attract younger clientele, the company modernized its "look" and opened ten new locations in California, Nevada, Oregon, and Texas. Newer units could seat approximately 175 people, with one-third of the space sectioned in a café setting. Geographic locations in smaller markets with less competition, such as Waco, Texas, were considered. Also, in addition to the regular Callender's menu items, the cafés served beer, wine, gourmet coffees, and espresso.

A food-to-go counter was expanded to attract young double-income families, which immediately produced an average 20 percent of revenue, including pie takeouts. Tanaka told Don Nichols of *Restaurant Business,* "East Side Mario's is newer and sexier, but it wouldn't make sense for us to focus all of our attention on it." He added, "Marie Callender's is a stable concept with a long history of success that we can grow nationally and internationally."

Marie Callender's unexpectedly came into the limelight in connection with a sensationalist news story. It was discovered that prior to their mass suicide, members of the San Diego-based Heaven's Gate cult had apparently eaten their last meal at a Carlsbad, California, Marie Callender's, which landed the company on popular national television shows such as *Jenny Jones* and *Extra.* The national coverage coincided with the largest expansion undertaken by Marie Callender's in a decade.

Management continued to assess the company's position and the reasons for its steady but relatively slow growth of 5 percent to 10 percent since 1995, despite the fact that surveys showed that 85 percent of consumers recognized the Marie Callender's name. One of the internal challenges facing the chain involved the lack of an advertising agreement among its franchisees, making funding and approval for advertisements unnecessarily difficult. Also, the differing designs in restaurant layout complicated the uniformity of menu presentation, especially in locations with counter seating, which limited menu options. Dreyer began spending a great deal of time visiting restaurants and talking to employees to get a ground-level perspective. In order to remain competitive the company continued searching for smaller regional chains that could be converted to Marie Callender's restaurants, particularly in the Midwest and Southeast.

CASTLE HARLAN PARTNERS ACQUIRES MARIE CALLENDER'S

Complementing his strategic financial aptitude, Dreyer's unique personal style served as an inspiration to company employees. Dreyer told Fulmer of the *Orange County Business Journal,* "I believe that from the top down it's got to be an environment that nurtures the employee," adding, "If they're not happy, the customer won't be happy." Known for his offbeat humor, Dreyer built a reputation in the industry for his antics which included appearing in costume at business presentations.

The company celebrated its 50th anniversary in 1998, while planning for 12 more full-service stores in the Pacific Northwest, Texas, and the Southeast. Adapting to the times, Marie Callender's developed home-style takeout meals targeting busy two-job families. For the future, Dreyer indicated the possibility of raising additional capital by taking the company public. The company hoped to see annual revenue growth rise to the 10 to 15 percent level. According to Fulmer, Dreyer said that an offering "would be the exit strategy majority-owner Saunders, Karp & Megrue, L.P., eventually is looking for. If they could find a buyer out there that would make sense to buy Marie Callender's, they might," he continued, "But the more likely strategy would be an initial public offering. We realize that the public marketplace is where you get the most value out of the company." Ultimately, however, private-equity group Castle Harlan Partners III, L.P., acquired the Wilshire Restaurant Group in 1999, adding Marie Callender's to its growing arsenal of midsized companies.

A NEW COMPANY FOR THE 21ST CENTURY

Marie Callender's spent the early years of the new millennium operating as a Castle Harlan entity. During 2005 Castle Harlan added Perkins to its holdings when it acquired TRC in a deal worth approximately $245 million. Both Marie Callender's and Perkins were operating on solid ground and had reputable brand names. Castle Harlan opted in 2006 to merge the two businesses to create Perkins & Marie Callender's Inc. Joseph Trungale, the president and CEO of TRC, held the same position at the newly created company.

Perkins & Marie Callender's experienced cost savings immediately after merging. The company saved nearly $10 million just by combining purchasing, human resources, general administration, and technology functions. In addition, the company saved nearly $2 million per year in food costs due to its increased buying power. While certain home office functions were combined, company management stressed there would not be a consolidation of the unique brands. "We recognized the integrity of both brands and are not blending operations teams, recipes, or marketing strategies. But we are sharing the best practices of both," Trungale explained to *Nation's Restaurant News* in August 2007.

Under Trungale's leadership, both Perkins and Marie Callender's hoped to strengthen their foothold in their own geographic markets. Perkins launched a revamped menu in 2007 that featured a new line of Breakfast Scramblers and Lunch Wraps. However, the weak U.S. economy affected the restaurant industry as a whole, and Perkins & Marie Callender's bottom line felt the pinch. Sales fell in 2007 and then again in 2008 while the company posted a net loss of $16.3 million in 2007 and then $52.9 million in 2008.

Eight Perkins franchised locations, three Marie Callender's franchised locations, and one Marie Callender's company-owned restaurant were shuttered in 2008. Nevertheless, the company continued with slow expansion and a total of four Perkins restaurants and one Marie Callender's franchised restaurant opened their doors during the year. While management expected a very slow rebound in dining sales, Perkins & Marie Callender's remained focused on trimming costs while providing a high-quality dining experience for all of its guests in the years to come.

April Dougal Gasbarre
Updated, Terri Mozzone; Christina M. Stansell

PRINCIPAL COMPETITORS

Denny's Corporation; DineEquity Inc.; VICORP Restaurants Inc.

FURTHER READING

Abelson, Reed, "Perkins Family Restaurants LP," *Fortune,* July 3, 1989, p. 112.

Anreder, Steven S., "Color Me Green," *Barron's,* December 21, 1981, pp. 29–30.

Barron, Kelly, "Going Sky-High with Pie," *Orange County Register,* May 6, 1997, p. 1.

———, "Marie Callender's Restaurant Chain Enjoys Strong Recovery, Expansion," *Knight-Ridder/Tribune Business News,* May 6, 1997.

Bonham, Roger D., "Perkins Pancake House," *Restaurant Management,* December 1960, pp. 33–35.

Carlino, Bill, "Perkins Deploys Dinner Program, Unit Redesign," *Nation's Restaurant News,* June 20, 1994, p. 7.

Cobb, Catherine R., "Combination Leads to Big Savings for Marie Callender's and Perkins," *Nation's Restaurant News,* August 13, 2007.

Fulmer, Melinda, "No Pie in the Sky," *Orange County Business Journal,* April 22–28, 1996.

Goldfield, Robert, "Marie Callender's Prowls Metro Area for Restaurant Sites," *Business Journal–Portland,* January 31, 1997, p. 8.

Hardesty, Greg, "Orange, Calif.-based Marie Callender's Restaurant Chain Is Up for Sale," *Knight-Ridder/Tribune Business News,* September 18, 1998.

Jennings, Lisa, "Perkins, Callender's Bake Up Merger," *Nation's Restaurant News,* April 24, 2006.

Keegan, Peter O., "Upscale Dinner Rollout Fuels Perkins' Profit Leap," *Nation's Restaurant News,* November 15, 1993, p. 14.

Liddle, Alan, "Marie Callender's Concern Mulls Sale, Alternatives," *Nation's Restaurant News,* September 28, 1998, p. 3.

Marie Callender's Corporate History, Long Beach, Calif.: Marie Callender's Restaurant & Bakery, Inc., 1998.

"Marie Callender's Exec. Dreyer Feted for His Spirit of Giving," *Nation's Restaurant News,* May 19, 1997, p. 39.

Nichols, Don, "Checking the Callender: A 29-Year-Old Concept Gets an Update," *Restaurant Business,* May 1, 1997, p. 26.

"Perkins, Marie Callender's Finalize Consolidation," *Food & Beverage Close-Up,* May 3, 2006.

"Perkins Winds Up 1996 with Profits of $13.52M," *Nation's Restaurant News,* February 24, 1997, p. 12.

Prewitt, Milford, "Perkins Turnaround Leads to Expansion Drive," *Nation's Restaurant News,* November 6, 1989, pp. F14–F17.

"The Restaurant Company Announces Name Change," *PR Newswire,* August 23, 2006.

Riell, Howard, "Smith, Investors to Acquire 80% of Perkins," *Nation's Restaurant News,* April 29, 1985, p. 1.

Scarpa, James, "Perkins Gears for Growth," *Restaurant Business,* January 1, 1990, pp. 60–62.

Strauss, Karen, "Family-Dining Chains Scramble," *Restaurants & Institutions,* July 15, 1993, pp. 90–92.

Thompson, Stephanie, "Marie Callender's: CME Takes a Homey Brand on the Board," *Brandweek,* March 9, 1998, p. R11.

Townsend, Rob, "The Midscale Advantage: Menu, Service and Value," *Restaurants & Institutions,* August 21, 1991, pp. 26–30.

Walkup, Carolyn, "Winter Sellers Warm Season's Profits," *Nation's Restaurant News,* November 21, 1994, p. 63.

Petrof spol. S.R.O.

Brnenska 371
Hradec Králové, 500 06
Czech Republic
Telephone: (420) 495 712 111
Fax: (420) 495 267 158
Web site: http://www.petrof.com

Private Company
Incorporated: 1908
Employees: 200
Sales: $23.4 million (2006 est.)
NAICS: 339992 Musical Instrument Manufacturing

■ ■ ■

Petrof spol. S.R.O. is one of the world's most renowned names in piano manufacturing. Founded in 1864, Petrof has survived its share of ups and downs over the course of its history. In the 21st century, Petrof has returned to the ownership of the founding Petrof family, led by Zuzana Ceralova-Petrofova. Petrof produces high-quality, high-end grand pianos and upright pianos under its own name. The company also develops midpriced and entry-level pianos under the Rösler, Scholze, and Weinbach brands. These are produced for the company in China by Hailun; since 2009, Hailun also distributes Petrof's main piano line in China.

Petrof's own production takes place at its factory in Hradec Králové. That facility features nearly 131,000 square meters of production space. The production facility also features workshops in which the company produces many of its own piano components, including keyboards, hammers, strings, resonance boards, and other metal parts and components. Petrof also holds a majority stake in Piana Tyniste, the largest producer of piano cases in Europe. In 2009, faced with the ongoing economic crisis, Petrof converted part of its business to the production of high-end furniture and fitted kitchens. Zuzana Ceralová-Petrofová is both the company's president and its largest shareholder, with 77 percent of the company.

FOUNDING A PIANO DYNASTY

Antonin Petrof was born in 1839 in Koniggratz, Hradec Králové, in what would later become the Czech Republic. Petrof's family was involved in woodworking and piano manufacturing; his father was a carpenter, and his uncle, Johann Heitzmann, built pianos in Vienna. Antonin Petrof's own interest turned to piano building, and in 1857 he moved to Vienna, becoming an apprentice at his uncle's workshop. Petrof later worked for two other noted Viennese piano makers, Ehrbar and then Schweighofer. In 1864, Petrof decided to launch his own business. For this he returned to Hradec Králové and his father's workshop. By the end of that year, Petrof had completed his first piano, a concert grand piano incorporating piano construction techniques developed in Vienna.

Soon after, Petrof converted the Hradec Králové workshop into a piano factory and completed construction of his first standard grand piano. Over the next decades, Petrof traveled extensively, promoting his piano construction while also studying the new construction techniques and technologies being developed in

Europe's bustling piano industry. Petrof himself developed a reputation as an innovator. In 1875 he became one of the first to incorporate a cast-iron frame, which provided much better resistance against the massive tension produced by the piano's strings, into his design. Petrof also borrowed from the English piano industry to develop his own action, the mechanism allowing a keystroke to be repeated rapidly. By 1881, the company had also begun to construct its own keyboards.

Petrof was also among the first to invest in industrial production capacity, setting up a second, larger factory outside of Hradec Králové in 1874. The expansion in capacity allowed the company to achieve economies of scale, a strategy further backed by a drive to establish the company's export operations. In 1877, Petrof began exporting to nearby Hungary, establishing a dedicated subsidiary there three years later.

BUILDING A REPUTATION

The new factory also enabled Petrof to expand his production into a newly developing piano type, the upright piano. The new design, which replaced the previous square piano design, revolutionized the piano industry by making pianos both more affordable and small enough to be placed in a greater variety of homes. Petrof's own upright piano production began in the early 1880s.

By the final years of the 19th century, Petrof had become one of the most well respected piano builders in Europe. The company's instruments became particularly prized in Vienna, and in 1895 the company established offices there, including a warehouse and service facility. In 1899, Petrof became the official piano supplier to the Imperial Court. By then, the company had produced more than 13,000 pianos.

Antonin Petrof brought his three sons, Jan, Antonin, and Vladimir, into the business. In 1908, the business incorporated as a limited liability company. In 1914, the year before he died, Petrof turned over control of the company to his sons, dividing the company equally among them. Vladimir, the youngest son, took over the leadership of the company. The company had made significant progress in its production since the beginning of the new century, and by 1915 had sold more than 30,000 pianos.

Petrof was one of the survivors of a major shakeout in the international piano industry at the dawn of the 20th century. In the late 1890s, Europe numbered some 300 piano makers. By the outbreak of World War I, just a few dozen remained. Petrof's investment in industrial production techniques, coupled with its strong reputation for quality, played an important role in its survival. Petrof's production slowed during World War I. Following the war, however, Petrof's reputation enabled it to expand the scope of its exports, and its first pianos were shipped to China and Australia starting in 1920. These were supported by the company's new office, opened in London in 1919.

NATIONALIZATION

The 1920s saw a new rise in demand for pianos, and particularly for newly developed player pianos. These pianos, driven by electro-pneumatic and other motorized mechanisms, played notes read from music rolls. Petrof invested in developing its own player piano models, starting in 1924. While short-lived, the boom in demand allowed the company to expand its production capacity. The company also launched its first exports to Japan and South America during this time.

The player piano faded quickly, however, as the first radios appeared in the late 1920s. The company instead fell back on its traditional piano production. This activity was boosted by an association with the U.S.-based Steinway piano company. In 1928, the two companies formed a partnership to open a showroom in London. Also in that year, the third generation of Petrofs, Dimitrij, Eduard, and Eugene, entered the company.

The Depression era brought new difficulties for Petrof, and for the piano industry as a whole. In order to survive, Petrof converted large parts of its manufacturing capacity to new products, including railway sleeper cars. The company's pool of highly skilled craftsmen, essential for its piano production, provided it with this kind of flexibility. The years of World War II provided a new trial for the company, which was hit hard by the German occupation of Czechoslovakia starting in 1938. The company's piano

---

KEY DATES

1864: Antonin Petrof begins building pianos in Hradec Králové.

1877: Petrof begins exporting pianos to Hungary.

1899: Petrof opens a subsidiary in Vienna and becomes the official supplier to the Imperial Court.

1914: The second generation of the Petrof family takes over the company.

1928: Petrof and Steinway form a partnership to open a showroom in London; the third generation of Petrofs enters the business.

1948: Petrof is nationalized by Czech government; Petrof family is removed from management.

1965: Petrof is renamed Czechoslovak Musical Instruments Hradec Králové.

1991: Jan Petrof becomes president of the company and launches privatization process.

2001: The Petrof family, under Zuzana Ceralova-Petrofova, completes a leveraged buyout of the company.

2008: Petrof forms a U.S. distribution subsidiary.

2009: In response to the economic crisis, Petrof begins producing furniture and fitted kitchens in addition to pianos.

---

production tapered off again, and the company was forced to convert part of its production to the manufacturing of munitions boxes for the German war effort.

Furthermore, the Communist takeover of Czechoslovakia in 1948 led to the nationalization of the country's industrial sector, including Petrof. The piano company was confiscated by the government, and the Petrof family—branded as "enemies of the people"—was removed from the company's management. For the next 40 years, the Petrofs lived in their home next to the factory but were allowed no involvement in its operations.

SURVIVING UNDER COMMUNISM

The Petrof name represented an important source of foreign currency, as well as international prestige, for the Communist government. Under its new managers, the company's production capacity increased steadily. Other prominent Czech brands were brought into the Petrof stable, including Rösler; Scholze, a company founded in 1876; and Weinbach, founded in 1884. The company

appeared to flourish in the 1950s, adding its own development operations for new upright and grand piano designs in 1954. This effort produced the Petrof Mondial model, winner of the 1958 gold medal at the Brussels Expo.

However, Petrof soon fell prey to the poor production standards that marked much of the Communist bloc in the second half of the 20th century. In 1965, the Petrof company was renamed Czechoslovak Musical Instruments Hradec Králové. The following year, the company shifted its upright piano production to factories in Liberec and Jihlava. The Hradec Králové factory itself was outfitted with new production line technology, and began producing upright pianos beginning in 1970.

The company's production increased, at the expense of quality, as managers were obliged to perform to production quotas. Most of the company's production during this period was directed toward the Soviet Union, not to musicians, but as bartering tools for oil and natural gas and other products. Before long, Petrof was producing more than 10,000 upright pianos and more than 800 grand pianos per year, and in 1989 the company's completed its 450,000th piano since its founding.

RETURNING TO THE FAMILY

The Hradec Králové facility received a further expansion in 1989, in the form of a new production line for grand pianos. By then, the company had begun to benefit from the loosening economic policies of the Czech and Soviet governments during the 1980s. In 1985, the company signed an agreement with a young U.S. company, Geneva International, which gained the exclusive distribution rights for Petrof's pianos in the United States. Geneva presented Petrof's pianos as high-quality, lower-priced European-made alternatives to the Asian-built pianos then capturing a significant share of the U.S. market.

The nonviolent Velvet Revolution of 1989 in Czechoslovakia, which brought an end to Communist regime, brought new hope to the Petrof family. In 1991, Jan Petrof, of the family's fourth generation, reclaimed the company's presidency. The company itself remained the government's property, however. The privatization of the company proceeded very slowly. This was because a dispute arose between the Petrof family and the Czech government, which claimed that the piano company's operations had been vastly expanded under Communist rule. In the end, the Czech government valued the Petrof family's share of the company at just 4 percent of what the family claimed. Nevertheless, in 2001, in a leveraged buyout for 71 percent of the company launched by fifth-generation family member Zuzana Ceralová-Petrofová, the family regained control of the piano company.

Petrof had made a number of improvements in the 1990s. In 1994, the company opened its own research and development center. The company opened a new subsidiary, Továrna na pianina, in Hradec Králové in 1997. Petrof also enjoyed strong demand from the United States, which came to account for 30 percent of its total piano sales. By the end of the decade, the company's production had reached 15,000 grand and upright pianos per year. The Petrof name had become internationally recognized, with sales reaching more than 70 countries. Petrof's research and development effort paid off as well, with the development of a new magnetically accelerated action. The new technology was patented in 2003, and incorporated into the company's pianos the following year.

SURVIVING A NEW CRISIS

Petrof once again faced difficulties, however. Piano manufacturing had made a new shift at the start of the 21st century, with an increasing amount of production taking place in China. Petrof found itself struggling to compete against the lower prices and fast-rising quality of this new generation of Asian imports. At the same time, Petrof was hit hard by the successful resurrection of the Czech economy, as the country joined the European Union in the middle of the decade. The growing strength of the Czech crown actually cut sharply into Petrof's profits, and by 2004 the company teetered on the brink of bankruptcy.

Petrof managed to stave off liquidation by carrying out a drastic restructuring. This effort resulted in the shutting down of all of the company's factories except for its main Hradec Králové facility. The company also made steady cuts to its payroll. From 1,000 workers at the start of the decade, the group's workforce had shrunk to just 200 in 2009. During this time, the company also shifted production of its Rösler, Scholze, and Weinbach brands to China, contracting with that country's Hailun company.

The company also came into conflict with its U.S. distributor, prompting the company to break its distribution contract with Geneva International. Geneva then launched and lost a lawsuit against Petrof. Following the court's decision in 2008, Petrof established its own U.S. subsidiary, Petrof USA LLC, to take over its distribution there. In the meantime, however, the Petrof name had virtually disappeared from U.S. showrooms.

By 2008, amid the global economic crisis, Petrof's piano production had shrunk to just 1,500 annually, including 800 grand pianos. In order to ensure its survival, the company took a lesson from its own history by directing its skilled workforce to products other than pianos. In 2009 Petrof announced that it was converting half of its workforce to the production of high-end furniture and fitted kitchens. The new effort appeared to get off to a strong start, as the company quickly attracted a clientele, largely of wealthy Russian customers.

Petrof nevertheless continued to seek new markets for its piano production. In June 2009, the company reached an agreement with Hailun to import its high-end Petrof piano line to China. Having survived the ups and downs of nearly 150 years, Petrof was determined to remain one of the most prestigious names in the worldwide piano industry in the 21st century.

M. L. Cohen

PRINCIPAL SUBSIDIARIES

Petrof USA LLC; Piana Tyniste a.s.; Továrna na pianina a.s.

PRINCIPAL COMPETITORS

Yamaha Corp.; Young Chang Co.; Jiujiang Instrument Factory; Kaman Corp.; Roland Corp.; Guangzhou Pearl River Piano Group Ltd.; Kawai Musical Instruments Manufacturing Company Ltd.; Steinway Musical Instruments Inc.; Matth. Hohner AG; Samick Musical Instruments Company Ltd.; Baldwin Piano Inc.

FURTHER READING

Barrett, Andy, "Petrof Expands into Luxury Furniture," *Musical Instrument Professional,* May 21, 2009.

Cameron, Rob, "Famous Czech Piano-maker Switches to Kitchens to Survive Crisis," *Radio Praha,* April 22, 2009.

"Ceralova Gains Majority Stake in Czech Piano Maker Petrof," *Czech Business News,* April 19, 2004.

"Crisis Manager Moucka to Leave Troubled Piano Maker Petrof," *Europe Intelligence Wire,* April 23, 2004.

"Czech Piano Maker Petrof Wins CZK Mln Contract in U.S.," *Czech Business News,* February 7, 2005.

"Geneva International and Petrof Forge Closer Relationship," *Music Trades,* June 2004, p. 48.

"Geneva Int. Files Suit Against Petrof Piano," *Music Trades,* August 2007, p. 34.

Hulpachová, Markéta, "Dueling Lawsuits Accompany End of Petrof-Geneva Partnership," *Prague Post,* August 8, 2007.

"In Troubled Musical Waters," *Europe Intelligence Wire,* November 20, 2006.

Palmieri, Robert, and Margaret W. Palmieri, "Czechoslovakia-Piano Industry," in *Piano: An Encyclopedia,* New York: Routledge, 2003, pp. 102–103.

"The Petrof Piano Saga," *Music Trades,* January 2009, p. 112.

"Petrof Pianos Unveils Pasat B Grand Piano," *Music Trades,* March 2006, p. 186.

"Piano Maker Petrof Back in Black in 2005," *Europe Intelligence Wire,* June 21, 2006.

"Piano Maker Petrof Doubles 2007 Profit to Kc 24m," *Europe Intelligence Wire,* September 9, 2008.

"Pianos Cannot Be Sold Through the Internet," *Europe Intelligence Wire,* November 22, 2004.

Smidova, Zuzana, "A Somber Note," *Prague Business Journal,* September 29, 2003.

"Troubled Piano Maker Petrof Agrees with Biggest Buyer on Supplies," *Czech News Agency,* May 3, 2004.

Piper Jaffray Companies

———————■———————

800 Nicollet Mall, Suite 800
Minneapolis, Minnesota 55402-7020
U.S.A.
Telephone: (612) 303-6000
Fax: (612) 303-8199
Web site: http://www.piperjaffray.com

Public Company
Incorporated: 1969
Employees: 1,045
Sales: $345.1 million (2008)
Stock Exchanges: New York
Ticker Symbol: PJC
NAICS: 523110 Investment Banking and Securities
   Dealing; 523999 Miscellaneous Financial Invest-
   ment Activities

■ ■ ■

Minneapolis-based Piper Jaffray Companies operates as a middle market investment firm offering investment banking services, institutional securities, and asset management. The company is involved in a variety of industries ranging from aircraft finance and education to health care and real estate. Piper Jaffray was acquired by U.S. Bancorp in 1998 and spun off as an independent firm in 2003. The company sold its Private Client Services business in 2006 to focus on its middle market investment banking activities. Piper Jaffray has offices throughout the United States and in Hong Kong, London, and Shanghai.

ORIGINS

In 1892 a former cashier named George Bishop Lane arrived in the thriving northern prairie town of Minneapolis to start a commercial paper business. Over the preceding century, commercial paper had become a means by which needy merchants could more easily get loans for short-term operating capital in exchange for their signature on a six- to eight-month promissory note. These notes were then turned over to a note dealer, who typically sold them to financial institutions like banks, who in turn used this "commercial paper" as a short-term investment.

To George Lane, it seemed clear that the promissory notes generated by Minneapolis's growing grain elevator and milling industry represented a sizable potential market. Therefore, he began participating in commercial paper transactions with major Minneapolis merchants such as Cargill Elevator Company (the forerunner of agricultural giant Cargill Inc.). Lane established George B. Lane, Commercial Paper and Collateral Loans & Co. in Minneapolis in 1895. In 1899 he enlisted George Lang to help him manage his growing volume and within eight years he had handled more than $16 million in commercial paper transactions.

ENTER C. PALMER JAFFRAY AND HARRY PIPER: 1913–29

In 1913, as Lane's business continued to thrive, C. Palmer Jaffray and Harry Piper, the sons of a prominent Minneapolis banker and a leading entrepreneur, respectively, decided to leave their steady but dull jobs at the First National Bank of Minneapolis and strike out

COMPANY PERSPECTIVES

We create and implement superior financial solutions for our clients. Serving clients is our fundamental purpose. We earn our clients' trust by delivering the best guidance and service. Great people are our competitive advantage. As we serve, we are committed to these core values: always place our clients' interests first; conduct ourselves with integrity and treat others with respect; work in partnership with our clients and each other; maintain a high-quality environment that attracts, retains and develops the best people; and contribute our talents and resources to serve the communities in which we live and work.

on their own. Only a year out of Yale University where their shared Minnesota backgrounds had sparked a close friendship, Jaffray and Piper soon formed Piper, Jaffray and Company, a commercial paper house whose first clients included growing enterprises like Archer Daniels Midland and Pillsbury. Harry Piper quickly emerged as the young firm's salesman and deal maker—the risk taker and entrepreneur who drummed up new business—and Palmer Jaffray became the numbers man, the financial wizard who understood the banking industry and the ins and outs of running a business.

As World War I raged in Europe, George Lane began to take admiring note of his new competitors. Already in his fifties, he needed new blood to keep his business competitive, and in 1917 he persuaded Piper and Jaffray to merge their firm with his to form Lane, Piper, and Jaffray, Inc. Despite the Great War's devastation, it spurred a mighty economic boom in the United States, where between 1915 and 1920 alone gross national product doubled to $80 billion. A brief recession in 1920–21, however, made it difficult for midwestern grain companies to secure loans from banks, and Lane, Piper, and Jaffray stepped into the breach by persuading small town banks throughout Minnesota and the Dakotas to lend these firms the needed capital.

The economic boom resumed stronger than ever in 1922 and, seeing the growing profits to be made on Wall Street, Lane, Piper, and Jaffray expanded from commercial paper to investment banking. Between 1922 and 1929 they underwrote the stocks and bonds issued for the public stock market by such emerging companies as Minneapolis-Honeywell, Cream of Wheat, Minnesota Mining and Manufacturing (3M), Munsing-wear, and Greyhound. Since new companies were not required to

disclose their financial operations at that time, Lane, Piper, and Jaffray had to determine their clients' financial stability through diligent spadework. This scrupulous concern for the facts led them to establish one of the first statistics and research departments in the U.S. investment banking industry.

Showing a willingness to embrace new technologies, Piper and Jaffray also joined with two competitors to participate in a national wire service system for stock transactions. The system enabled them to boast in ads that they could complete a transaction with New York "in less than 10 minutes." While many Americans were allowing the giddy growth of the Roaring Twenties to color their investing judgment, Lane, Piper, and Jaffray kept an even keel, and in one year alone they declined the stock underwriting applications of 692 new firms. In part as a result of such caution, by mid-decade Lane, Piper had offices in four Minnesota cities and Fargo, North Dakota, and had purchased an interest in the Chicago firm, Rickards, Roloson & Company. It also expanded its investment products portfolio, adding municipal and construction bonds, debenture, and notes for public utilities to its stable.

THE GREAT CRASH AND AFTER: 1929–40

In late October 1929 the irrational exuberance that had seen the volume of shares traded on Wall Street rise 500 percent in only seven years was dealt a fatal blow when stocks on the New York Stock Exchange began a precipitous and protracted swoon that liquidated $30 billion in investors' wealth in a matter of a few weeks. Investors who had bought their stocks on margins of only 10 to 25 percent cash were ruined when their brokers demanded they make good on their outstanding balances. Many stockholders had no savings outside of their investments, and roughly 25 million of them were ruined almost overnight. Banks across the country failed, businesses were wiped out, and unemployment reached crisis proportions.

Despite its conservative underwriting practices, Lane, Piper was also hit hard and was soon posting a negative net worth. Although the First National Bank of Minneapolis loaned Lane, Piper the money to stay in business and the firm's focus on commercial paper and underwriting rather than speculative trading softened the blow, the Great Depression began to hammer farm commodity prices and Lane, Piper's commercial paper business revenues plummeted from $45.2 million in 1929 to $8.6 million in 1932.

Convinced that it had survived the brunt of the crash's clout, in 1931 Lane, Piper presciently purchased

KEY DATES

1895: George Lane establishes George B. Lane, Commercial Paper and Collateral Loans & Co., a commercial paper brokerage based in Minneapolis.

1913: H. C. Piper, Sr., and C. P. Jaffray establish their own commercial paper business called Piper, Jaffray & Co.

1917: George B. Lane merges with Piper, Jaffray & Co. to form Lane, Piper & Jaffray.

1931: The company buys Hopwood & Company.

1971: Piper Jaffray goes public.

1974: The company reorganizes itself into a public holding company called Piper Jaffray Inc.

1986: Piper Jaffray moves its stock listing from the Midwest and Chicago exchanges to the NASDAQ.

1995: The company begins to pay out more than $100 million to settle class-action lawsuits related to losses incurred by a derivatives-based fund.

1998: U.S. Bancorp completes its acquisition of Piper Jaffray.

1999: The company changes its name to U.S. Bancorp Piper Jaffray.

2003: Piper Jaffray is spun off as an independent firm.

2006: The company sells its Private Client Services branch.

the nearly bankrupt Minneapolis brokerage house, Hopwood & Company (founded in 1914). Hopwood's selling point was its seat on the New York Stock Exchange, which offered the newly christened Piper, Jaffray & Hopwood a way to enter the broader securities market in expectation of the day—if it ever returned—when Wall Street would no longer be a dirty word.

In 1933 Congress took a step toward ensuring that day's arrival by passing the Securities Act of 1933, which required companies offering public stock to submit their books to the public scrutiny of certified accountants and by forming the Securities and Exchange Commission to regulate exchanges and brokers. Fueled by federal funds for public works projects, the municipal bond industry began to turn around in the mid-1930s, and Piper Jaffray aggressively pursued the "muni" market with cities, counties, and school districts across the country. It also began to make money hedging the

sale of commodities, that is, offsetting the sale of one commodity against a future sale as a way of countering fluctuations in prices. By 1935 it was posting modest, if temporary, profits, and by 1937 assets totaled $2.8 million.

WORLD WAR II AND POSTWAR GROWTH

During World War II, Piper Jaffray benefited from America's economic resurgence by financing the Minnesota-based firms that supplied the U.S. military. It also contributed to the war effort by selling war bonds, and although U.S. sales of commercial paper fell dramatically during the war, in Minnesota they grew. By 1944 Piper Jaffray's commercial paper revenues had climbed to $18.2 million. Moreover, by 1945 its net profits, which had been a meager $1,000 in 1940, rose to $177,000. With the war's end in sight, Piper Jaffray opened a new office in Great Falls, Montana, reflecting its long-standing presence in that region's brokerage and municipal bond markets.

As Minnesota corporations ramped up for the postwar economy, Piper Jaffray teamed with Wall Street investment powerhouse Goldman Sachs to handle their multimillion-dollar stock offerings. In 1946 Harry Piper's son, Harry "Bob" Piper, Jr., joined the firm as a runner in the cashier's "cage." He worked his way up the ladder by winning investment accounts for the firm and by the early 1950s had been named a partner. In 1949, as the great 16-year postwar bull market began, Piper Jaffray opened a new office in Billings, Montana.

With the U.S. economy booming, the stock market underwent a major transformation. More and more major companies offered stock (more than 9,000 separate public offerings took place during the decade), the modern mutual fund was born, and institutional investors' share of the stock market rose to an unprecedented 25 percent. Despite these changes, Piper Jaffray remained a traditional firm dominated by informal decision making and training methods, a close-knit family spirit, and a hard-working culture. Nevertheless, in 1954 it set a precedent that few other firms in the industry could match when it appointed Ruth Cranston as its first female partner.

It also improved the speed with which it placed customers' orders on Wall Street by replacing its New York telegraph connection with a teletype, cutting transaction delays from 15 minutes to one minute. By the late 1950s Piper Jaffray's traditional handwritten ledger system for recording transactions had also been replaced by a mechanical keypunch accounting system and the company had invested in its first mainframe computer, setting the stage for its rapid adoption of computing innovations in the coming years.

THE "GO-GO" ERA: 1960–70

In 1963, with revenues well more than $3 million, the Minneapolis Tribune celebrated the half-century-old partnership of founders Harry Piper, Sr., and Palmer Jaffray, both in their seventies, by touting their firm as "the largest locally owned entity in the Upper Midwest." In 1964 Piper Jaffray installed its first Stockmaster, an electronic stock monitoring system that replaced the now antiquated magnetic tape stock ticker system, Quotron. More important, Piper Jaffray acted on expansion plans set in motion in the 1950s by acquiring Minneapolis-based Jamieson & Co. (founded in 1939). The purchase doubled Piper Jaffray's revenues and size and extended its territory to Duluth, to Eau Claire, Wisconsin, and to unpenetrated regions of the Dakotas. These new branches added to the opening in Rapid City, South Dakota (1962), and were followed in 1967 by four- or five-broker offices in Omaha, Nebraska, and Bismarck, North Dakota.

In 1968 Piper Jaffray acquired the Wausau, Wisconsin-based over-the-counter (OTC) securities firm Altenburg & Gooding and a year later the company opened an OTC trading office in New York and Harry Piper, Jr., became Jaffray's chairman and CEO. Piper Jaffray's formation of a formal Corporate Finance department in the late 1960s also signaled its intent to take on the complicated paperwork it had traditionally farmed out to Goldman Sachs. In 1969 Piper also took a step toward becoming a public stock itself when it incorporated, giving its principals the limited financial liability they would need to remain independent as they grew the business.

GROWTH: 1971–79

The technology, military, and aerospace boom of the 1960s had fueled a growing market that enriched many U.S. investment firms, which increasingly sought to expand through acquisition. Piper Jaffray found itself among this fast-growing lot, and throughout the 1970s it absorbed smaller, middle- and small-market investment firms. To fund this expansion, it first had to raise capital. In 1971, therefore, it held its first public stock offering, raising some $5.7 million, which during the next decade helped it acquire the faltering securities giant Goodbody & Company as well as firms in Minnesota, Iowa, and the Pacific Northwest. It also opened new territories by launching offices in Lincoln,

Nebraska, and in Appleton, Madison, and Milwaukee, Wisconsin.

In 1972 Harry Piper, Jr., told the *Wall Street Journal* that by 1977, "20 to 25 percent of our business may be in things we now do modestly or not at all." In the early 1970s most of Piper Jaffray's business still revolved around buying and selling stock, trading municipal and corporate bonds, and underwriting stock offerings, but Harry Piper declared that the company would attempt to increase its business with institutional investors (then only 8 percent of sales) and establish a corporate finance department that would rival the biggest Wall Street operations. In July 1972 Piper Jaffray endured much unwelcome publicity when Harry Piper's wife, Virginia, was kidnapped by an unknown group demanding $1 million in ransom. Harry Piper provided the money, and three days later Virginia was found tied to a tree near Duluth, Minnesota, dazed but alive. (Neither the ransom nor the kidnappers ever surfaced.)

Although the recession of 1973–74 pummeled Piper Jaffray's bottom line and stock, its newly enlarged Corporate Finance department began to establish a profitable new business for the firm—mergers and acquisitions (M&A). By the end of the decade Piper's M&A activity exceeded $760 million. Corporate Finance also entered the private placement market (in which firms raised capital by selling financial instruments to private investors) and the new venture capital market, underwriting the initial public offerings (IPOs) of new-breed companies such as supercomputer maker Cray Research.

In 1974 Piper Jaffray reorganized itself into a public holding company, Piper Jaffray Inc., which became the parent company of the operational broker/dealer business, Piper, Jaffray & Hopwood. A year later it established an employee stock ownership trust (ESOT) to encourage its employees to identify more closely with the company's fortunes. When it attempted to raise capital for the ESOT through six public stock offerings, however, some of its shareholders claimed Piper Jaffray's offer price was too low and sued (a jury ruled in their favor in 1981).

In 1978 Piper Jaffray continued its tradition of technological innovation by installing the $4 million "Piper Pipeline," an electronic information and stock monitoring system that gave its customers the same real-time access to Wall Street data as the most sophisticated Manhattan brokerage. The same year, to help keep the Minnesota Vikings football team from leaving town, Piper Jaffray stage-managed a last-minute agreement to construct a new domed stadium for the Twin Cities, for which it oversaw the bond sale.

THE THIRD GENERATION:
1980–89

By 1981 Piper Jaffray boasted more than 55,000 clients, 37 offices in 11 states, and annual revenues of $50.4 million, a more than threefold increase over 1971. In 1983 Harry Piper, Jr.'s son, Addison ("Tad"), who like his father had started his career in the firm's cashier's "cage," was named CEO. When the Hartford Insurance Group paid $29.3 million for 309,000 Piper Jaffray shares (25 percent of the firm's total shares) the same year, Piper Jaffray suddenly found itself with a new income stream, insurance products.

Between 1980 and 1985 Piper Jaffray opened new offices in Denver, Kansas City, and Green Bay, Wisconsin, positioning itself to ride the bull market that began in 1982. Piper Jaffray's Fixed Income department, which handled public and private bond issues for state and local public institutions, was enjoying the success, meanwhile, that the Corporate Finance department had begun enjoying in the 1970s; by 1985 Piper Jaffray was managing or co-managing almost 250 bond issues a year with a total value of some $3.2 billion.

The firm moved into the new 42-story Piper Jaffray Tower in 1985 and in October of the same year opened a new "Piper Capital Management" operation to offer mutual funds and manage the money of pension funds, public asset funds, and large individual accounts. Within eight months Capital Management's portfolio had grown to more than $125 million in assets and by mid-1988 to almost $1.5 billion. In 1986 Piper Jaffray moved its stock listing from the Midwest and Chicago exchanges to NASDAQ and in 1987 introduced its first mutual funds. Early the same year it also unveiled a comprehensive five-year corporate plan, christened "Vision 1992," that set ambitious goals for growing retail sales, expanding Piper Capital Management and its fixed-income/public finance markets, and gaining leadership in equity capital markets (the new umbrella term for Corporate Finance, equity trading, and institutional equity sales). Many of the firm's departments were reorganized and unified to streamline the company's operations and emphasize its customer-driven philosophy.

On Black Monday, October 22, 1987, the Dow Jones index dropped a stomach-churning 508 points, wiping out an estimated $500 billion in market value in the span of seven hours. Just as the 1929 crash had left Piper with fewer scars than many of its competitors, however, so again in 1987 Piper Jaffray emerged intact. Its computerized data and reporting systems had handled the surge in trading volume smoothly, its employees had pulled the extra hours needed to calm frantic customers and process mountains of paperwork,

and its banking allies had extended the financial resources needed to cover the transaction costs that some its customers were unable to ante up. Moreover, Piper Jaffray had refused to join the general panic, seeing the sell-off as an opportunity to market some of its favorite stocks at bargain-basement prices. As the "me decade" closed, Piper Jaffray could boast annual revenues of almost $200 million, a new institutional sales office in London, and a new fiduciary trust services subsidiary, Piper Trust Company. Best of all, *Forbes* magazine named Piper Jaffray first among all U.S. investment bankers for its post-IPO performance during the decade.

GROWTH IN THE NINETIES:
1990–94

By the 1990s Piper Jaffray had established itself as one of the largest regionally based brokers in the United States, with a reputation for expertise in food, agricultural, and medical technology industry stocks. In August 1990 Harry Piper, Jr., died, symbolically completing the passing of the baton of leadership to his son Tad that had begun in the 1980s. With one dramatic exception, Tad Piper's stewardship of the firm in the 1990s seemed to quicken the company's financial and geographic growth and range of investment products. In 1990 Piper Jaffray opened offices in Denver and Los Angeles, expanded its line of mutual funds to 17, and began installing the latest generation of computerized real-time investment data systems. Known as Stockmate, the $3.5 million system used a satellite data feed and a mainframe computer to give its far-flung offices the capability to make ever faster and more accurate trades. Its 1991 year-end revenues stood at $267.8 million, a threefold increase in less than a decade.

In 1992 Piper Jaffray ranked as the fifth largest security underwriter in the nation and before the year was out it had added securities firms in Kansas City and San Francisco to its roster of strategic acquisitions. It also opened offices in Tucson and Phoenix, Arizona, and reorganized itself into three new core businesses: Individual Investor Services, Capital Markets (including equity and fixed income investment products), and Investment Management Services (encompassing Piper Capital Management and Piper Trust). In a reflection of its new identity it also dropped "Hopwood" from its corporate name, officially closing a six-decade-old chapter in its history.

By 1993 Piper Jaffray had 78 retail offices in 17 states and five straight years of record-setting growth. Moreover, with its tradition of multimillion-dollar annual charity giving and its reputation for conservative, ethical, customer-loyal investing (it had refused to participate in the hostile takeover craze of the 1980s), the firm's stature as it approached its centennial year celebration seemed secure.

SURVIVING A DERIVATIVES-BASED LOSS AND LAWSUITS: 1994–97

In 1994, however, a little understood investment vehicle known as derivatives dealt a serious blow to Piper Jaffray's fortunes. Worth Bruntjen, one of the architects of Piper's Capital Management operation and the manager of its successful Institutional Government Income Portfolio (a short-term bond mutual fund) had attempted to boost his funds' returns by using derivatives, a financial instrument in which the return is tied to—or "derived" from—the performance of another instrument such as currencies, commodities, or bonds. Because the link between these interwoven instruments can be so substantial and so complex, the unexpected collapse of a derivative's underlying assets can quickly balloon into an enormous, snowballing loss.

Bruntjen had invested as much as 90 percent of his funds' $3.5 billion assets into such derivatives (in his case, derivatives based on residential mortgages grouped together as securities) and exacerbated his risk by borrowing to fund his purchases. Bruntjen's derivatives were based on his expectation that interest rates would decline, as they had in 1990 and 1991. When they began to rise in 1994, however, Bruntjen's funds rapidly accumulated a roughly $700 million paper loss, an embarrassment that one industry insider called "one of the most incredible debacles in the financial services industry."

To add to its injury, Piper had marketed Bruntjen's funds as conservative investments for the risk-averse. When the funds' investors learned of the catastrophe they filed suit against Piper for misleading shareholders and making "monumental purchases of highly speculative securities." Amidst front-page coverage in the *Wall Street Journal,* Piper's carefully built reputation as the "little old lady of brokerage firms" seemed about to vanish. Tad Piper told the press, "We do not believe we have done anything wrong," but later admitted, "We got caught in a market that we thought we understood." Piper Jaffray then closed the funds to new investors and added an additional $10 million to "show faith in the fund."

The lawsuits wound their way through the courts with Piper Jaffray claiming all the while that it had fully disclosed all the funds' risks and investment tactics in its prospectuses and investors maintaining they had been defrauded. Beginning in 1995 it began paying out more than $100 million in settlements, and in 1996 the National Association of Securities Dealers (NASD) levied a $1.125 million fine against it for its marketing practices in connection with the funds. In October 1997 the last class-action lawsuit was settled for $24 million. Piper Jaffray could begin rebuilding its reputation anew.

BECOMING PART OF U.S. BANCORP: 1997–99

With its expensive class-action lawsuits in its past, Piper Jaffray began to look for ways to grow in the quickly consolidating banking industry. For the first time since before the Great Depression, banks and brokerage houses were allowed to merge, giving way to large financial concerns with operations in both banking and investment activities. U.S. Bancorp, the 15th largest commercial bank in the United States, made a $730 million play for Piper Jaffray in 1997. U.S. Bancorp was interested in Piper Jaffray's retail and institutional brokerage services as well as its investment banking and merger and acquisition assets. Piper Jaffray hoped its new parent would provide the scale and funds necessary to expand its business. The deal was completed in 1998 and the company changed its name to U.S. Bancorp Piper Jaffray one year later.

The company underwent several changes during the early years of the 21st century. Its parent grew significantly through its 2001 merger with Firstar Inc. The $18.9 billion stock swap that created the eighth-largest bank holding company in the United States. Meanwhile, Piper Jaffray remained a small part of the company and accounted for just 1 percent of U.S. Bancorp's net income. During 2002, the company earned only $106,000 on net revenues of $729 million.

U.S. Bancorp and Piper Jaffray decided to part ways in 2003 and the company was spun off as an independent entity trading on the New York Stock Exchange. Left on its own, Piper Jaffray focused on its full-service retail brokerage services and its investment banking activities that catered to medium-sized companies in the consumer, financial, healthcare, and technology industries. The company acquired Vie Securities LLC in 2004, giving it access to Vie's algorithm-based electronic execution services.

While the company hoped to remain out of the spotlight, it once again fell victim to bad press when it was fined $25 million in 2003 for providing biased stock information. The company revamped its research and investment banking business as a result. It also was fined $2.4 million by the NASD (now known as the Financial Industry Regulatory Authority) for IPO spinning, or selling hot, or highly profitable, IPO stocks to its investment banking clients. During 2005 Piper Jaffray was banned from providing bond issue services to the state of Minnesota until 2007 after it was revealed that a Piper Jaffray employee violated contribution rules related to Governor Tim Pawlenty's campaign.

NEW STRATEGY FOR INVESTMENT BANKING GROWTH: 2006–09

Despite these setbacks, Piper Jaffray revamped its strategy to grow its investment banking business. During 2006 the company sold its brokerage sales business, known as its Private Client Services division, to UBS Financial Services Inc. The company planned to use the nearly $500 million in proceeds from the sale to fuel its expansion efforts. Indeed, during 2007 the company made two key acquisitions. In September, it added investment management firm Fiduciary Asset Management LLC to its holdings in a $66 million deal. One month later, it completed the purchase of Goldbond Capital Holdings Limited, a Hong Kong-based investment bank. By that time, Piper Jaffray had offices in Hong Kong, London, and Shanghai.

While Piper Jaffray remained shielded from the subprime mortgage crisis in the United States, the tough global economic climate did force the company to focus on cutting costs while positioning itself as an international investment firm. During 2008 the company posted a $183 million loss due in part to a slowdown in public offerings in the U.S. and volatility in U.S. equity markets. While market conditions were expected to remain challenging during 2009, Piper Jaffray and its management team remained confident the company had solid strategy in place to experience growth and success in the years to come.

Paul S. Bodine
Updated, Christina M. Stansell

PRINCIPAL SUBSIDIARIES

Piper Jaffray & Co.; PJI Arizona, Inc.; Piper Jaffray Ltd. (UK); PJC Nominees Ltd. (UK); Piper Jaffray Financial Products Inc.; Piper Jaffray Financial Products II Inc.; Piper Jaffray Financial Products III Inc.; Piper Jaffray Funding LLC; Piper Jaffray Lending LLC; Piper Jaffray Private Capital Inc.; Piper Jaffray Private Capital LLC; Piper Jaffray Private Equity Funds Group I, LLC; Piper Jaffray Ventures Inc.; Piper Ventures Capital Inc.; PJC Capital LLC; Piper Jaffray Foundation; Piper Jaffray Investment Management Inc.; Piper Jaffray Investment

Management LLC; Fiduciary Asset Management, LLC; Piper Jaffray MENA (LP) Inc.; PJC Consumer Partners Acquisition I, LLC; PJC Capital Management LLC; Piper Jaffray Green Fund LLC; PJC Merchant Banking Partners I, LLC; Piper Jaffray Asia Holdings Ltd. (Hong Kong); Piper Jaffray Asia Ltd. (Hong Kong); Piper Jaffray Asia Securities Ltd. (Hong Kong); Piper Jaffray Asia Futures Ltd. (Hong Kong); Piper Jaffray Asia Management Services Ltd. (Hong Kong); Piper Jaffray Value Creation Fund (Cayman Islands); Piper Jaffray Asia Asset Management Ltd. (Hong Kong); Goldbond Fund Management (Cayman) Ltd.; Grandward Investments Ltd. (Hong Kong); Goldbond Capital (China) Ltd.; Goldbond Hualu Investment Consultants Ltd. (Hong Kong).

PRINCIPAL COMPETITORS

Arlington Asset Investment Corporation; Deutsche Bank Alex. Brown; Jeffries Group Inc.

FURTHER READING

Barshay, Jill J., "Piper Jaffray Settles Last Derivatives Class-Action Suit," *Minneapolis Star-Tribune,* October 16, 1997.

Barshay, Jill J., and David Phelps, "Housecleaning Eased Piper Sale," *Minneapolis Star-Tribune,* December 17, 1997.

Johnson, Robert, "Piper Jaffray Sees Slightly Higher Profit for Year, Citing Small-Investor Activity," *Wall Street Journal,* June 8, 1990.

Knecht, G. Bruce, "Minneapolis Investors Are Hurt by Local Firm They Knew As Cautious," *Wall Street Journal,* August 26, 1994, pp. Al, A5.

——, "Piper Jaffray's Foiled Manager Is Used to Risk," *Wall Street Journal,* September 1, 1981, pp. Cl, C17.

——, "Piper Manager's Losses May Total $700 Million," *Wall Street Journal,* August 25, 1994, pp. Cl, C19.

Lee, Thomas, "Bold Ambitions; A New, Smaller Piper Jaffray Hopes to Break into the Ranks of Top Investment Banks," *Minneapolis Star-Tribune,* August 21, 2006.

McGough, Robert, "Piper Jaffray Acts to Boost Battered Fund," *Wall Street Journal,* May 23, 1994, pp. Cl, C17.

Merrick, Amy, "Firstar Agrees to Acquire U.S. Bancorp," *Wall Street Journal,* October 5, 2000.

Nelson, Rick, "Less Proves More in Piper Suit," *Corporate Report Minnesota,* October 1995.

"Piper Jaffray Actions Manipulated Prices of Stock, Jury Finds," *Wall Street Journal,* May 8, 1981.

Piper Jaffray Companies, *Celebrating a Century of Service, 1895–1995,* Minneapolis: Piper Jaffray Companies, 1994.

"Piper Jaffray Pushes Diversification Plans," *Wall Street Journal,* September 19, 1972.

St. Anthony, Neal, and Dee DePass, "U.S. Bank Details Piper Spinoff Plans," *Minneapolis Star-Tribune,* June 26, 2003.

Shields, Yvette, "Piper Banned from Minnesota Until 2007," *Bond Buyer,* December 9, 2005.

Skinner, Liz, "Piper Jaffray Aims for Global Growth," *Investment News,* October 22, 2007.

PKZ Burger-Kehl and Company AG

In der Luberzenstrasse 19
Urdorf, CH-8902
Switzerland
Telephone: (41 044) 736 33 33
Fax: (41 044) 736 33 00
Web site: http://www.pkz.ch

Private Company
Founded: 1881
Employees: 495
Sales: CHF 226.7 million ($200 million) (2008 est.)
NAICS: 448110 Men's Clothing Stores; 448150 Clothing Accessories Stores

■ ■ ■

PKZ Burger-Kehl and Company AG is one of Switzerland's leading clothing retailers. The Urdorf-based company operates 55 retail stores under four brand formats, which are primarily focused on the upper-middle price range. PKZ is the group's oldest and flagship retail network, having been introduced in 1891. PKZ stores focus on men's clothing, including the company's own designs, at 28 locations throughout Switzerland. Feldpausch, acquired by the company in 1997, is the group's women's fashions chain. Blue Dog is PKZ's youth-oriented retail format. Blue Dog operates as in-store boutiques, with 20 shops in the PKZ chain and six shops in the Feldpausch chain. The company's youngest retail format is Burger, launched in 2002 with a store on Zurich's Bahnhofstrasse. Burger focuses on Swiss designer fashions for both men and women. The Kehl-Burger family has been in control of PKZ since its founding in 1881. Philippe Olivier Burger is the company's president. PKZ remains a privately held company, with sales of CHF 226.7 million ($200 million) in 2008.

FOUNDING A SWISS CLOTHING DYNASTY

Paul Kehl founded Switzerland's first clothing factory, or at least the first to incorporate industrial production practices, in Winterthur in 1881. The company met with rapid success and by 1884 had moved to a larger factory in Zurich, on that city's Bahnhofstrasse. Demand for Kehl's clothing grew steadily, and by the beginning of the 1890s, Kehl had developed his own brand, PKZ, which stood for Paul Kehl Zurich, which he trademarked in 1891. Also in that year, Kehl branched out into retail for the first time, opening his first Paul Kehl Zurich (PKZ) store in Zurich.

Kehl's manufacturing and retail businesses both focused on the menswear market. Kehl's retail concept was based on providing a full range of quality men's clothing. Kehl emphasized service, assisting the store's customers in purchases of complete outfits, including accessories. The company's commitment to service and high quality paid off, and by 1896 the company had opened its first retail branches. By the dawn of the 20th century, the company operated stores in Basel, Winterthur, Lucerne, Lausanne, St. Gallen, and Geneva, as well as in Zurich.

Kehl was joined in the business by his son-in-law, Karl Burger, who took over the company after Kehl's death in 1910. Burger continued to build the group's reputation and its sales. By 1928, the company had moved its production to a new factory, on the Bederstrasse, in Zurich Enge. Part of the company's growth came from a move into the export market, as the PKZ brand achieved an international reputation.

FOCUS ON RETAIL

Burger brought his two sons, Walter and Rudolf into the family business in 1928. The brothers took over as heads of the company after Karl Burger died in 1935. Walter Burger became especially involved in running the business, leading its growth into the postwar period. During the war, the company had expanded its manufacturing base, building a new factory in Massagno.

The postwar years represented a new boom period for PKZ. Demand from the international markets was particularly strong, and by the mid-1950s, PKZ had built up an international network of 300 wholesale distributors. In this way, PKZ's clothing grew into a well-known international men's clothing brand. The company also continued to open retail stores throughout Switzerland. By the beginning of the 1970s, PKZ operated 15 stores.

PKZ encountered some obstacles during the 1970s. The economic crisis caused by the Arab oil embargo and the subsequent rise in oil prices led to a number of dramatic consequences. In particular, the Swiss franc soared in value. As a result, PKZ's export market collapsed at the beginning of the decade. The company, which employed 1,500 people by the mid-1950s, was also hurt by the fast-rising labor costs in Switzerland.

The company was forced to make a decision, and in 1975 PKZ shut down its two factories. PKZ then focused its operations around its retail clothing chain. The company continued to develop its own clothing designs, turning to other manufacturers for their production. PKZ's retail operations also remained strong, boosted by such advertising slogans as "L'habit fait l'homme; PKZ, le gentleman" (Clothing makes the man; PKZ, the gentleman). The new slogan became part of the group's new marketing strategy, launched in 1977, which targeted the upper-middle price segment.

MODERNIZING THE BRAND

Walter Burger began preparing his succession in the early 1980s, buying out his brother's stake in the company in 1983. In 1984, Burger brought his son, Olivier, into the family business. By the mid-1980s, the younger Burger had taken over the company's direction, and had acquired a two-thirds stake in the company from his parents. Following the death of his father in 1993, Olivier Burger became the company's chairman, and later increased his stake in the company to 80 percent.

Olivier Burger had studied retailing, with a focus on the fashion industry, at the University of St. Gallen, before moving to Canada in the 1970s. There, Burger founded his own company focused on women's fashions. Olivier Burger's experience in the Canadian clothing market proved invaluable for PKZ's strong growth into the 21st century.

Under its new and more youthful management, PKZ launched a new strategy designed to rejuvenate the company's somewhat staid image, as well as to cut its operating costs. One of the first steps Olivier Burger took was to move the group's headquarters to less expensive quarters in Urdorf, on the outskirts of Zurich.

At the same time, Burger began introducing a number of retail features that, while quite commonplace in North America, represented retail innovations in Switzerland. Among these was the company's decision to display clothing items grouped around central themes, rather than along garment types. The company also began developing a multibranded approach, bringing in many of the noted designer brands in its upper-middle price segment, including Diesel and Hugo Boss.

Behind the scenes, the company radically shortened its design and ordering policies. Instead of maintaining a large and expensive inventory, the group began developing and sourcing its designs in smaller quantities on a more frequent schedule. This enabled the company to reduce its warehousing costs and lower its risk of unsold stock, while also allowing it to respond more quickly to

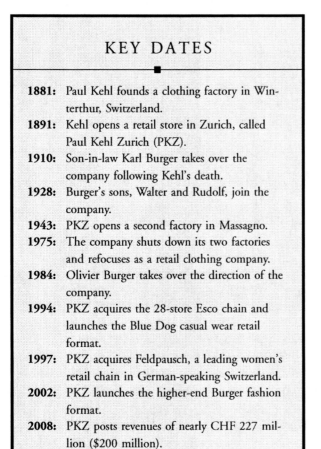

KEY DATES

1881: Paul Kehl founds a clothing factory in Winterthur, Switzerland.

1891: Kehl opens a retail store in Zurich, called Paul Kehl Zurich (PKZ).

1910: Son-in-law Karl Burger takes over the company following Kehl's death.

1928: Burger's sons, Walter and Rudolf, join the company.

1943: PKZ opens a second factory in Massagno.

1975: The company shuts down its two factories and refocuses as a retail clothing company.

1984: Olivier Burger takes over the direction of the company.

1994: PKZ acquires the 28-store Esco chain and launches the Blue Dog casual wear retail format.

1997: PKZ acquires Feldpausch, a leading women's retail chain in German-speaking Switzerland.

2002: PKZ launches the higher-end Burger fashion format.

2008: PKZ posts revenues of nearly CHF 227 million ($200 million).

consumer trends. As a result, the company was able to transform its image from a conservative, "papa's" brand into a more modern one.

ACQUIRING A BRAND PORTFOLIO

PKZ targeted the expansion of its retail empire in the 1990s, in part to maintain a position among the Swiss market's retail clothing leaders. The decade was marked by the arrival of a number of foreign competitors into Switzerland, notably mass-market retailers such as H&M, Zara, and C&A. This period was also marked by the rise of a number of high-end boutiques and brands, such as Zegna and Armani. In response, PKZ adjusted its own clothing range, focusing more sharply on the upper-middle price range.

In order to maintain its competitiveness, PKZ sought to expand its retail network. The company achieved a major milestone in reaching this goal in 1994, when it acquired the 24-store chain of Esco men's clothing shops. The acquisition allowed PKZ to establish itself as the leading men's clothing shop specialist in Switzerland. The integration of the Esco

business, and the conversion of its stores, was completed in 1996.

By then, PKZ had launched another prong of its growth strategy, developing its own portfolio of retail brands. In 1994, the company introduced a new casual wear concept, Blue Dog. That brand, which included the development of an in-store boutique-style corner shop concept, caught on quickly with PKZ's customers. By 1996, the company had opened 12 Blue Dog boutiques.

Next, PKZ sought to move beyond the men's clothing market and establish a presence in the far larger women's clothing market. For this, the company purchased one of Switzerland's leading women's fashions brands, Feldpausch, in 1997. Willy Feldpausch had founded that company in 1927, with a store in Basel. By 1933, Feldpausch had opened a second store in Zurich, before expanding throughout German-speaking Switzerland. By the time of its acquisition, Feldpausch had grown into a chain of ten stores.

In the 1990s, however, Feldpausch had been struggling to maintain its growth, in part because of a series of management changes. Its acquisition by PKZ raised industry observers' eyebrows as well because of the company's inexperience in the women's fashions market. Nevertheless, Olivier Burger counted on his earlier experience in women's fashion in Canada, as well as the strong background in women's clothing retailing of a number of his management team.

SWISS CLOTHING RETAIL LEADER IN THE 21ST CENTURY

The company quickly integrated Feldpausch into its own corporate culture, while converting Feldpausch's smaller F-branded stores to its Blue Dog retail format. The Blue Dog brand then began its own expansion beyond men's wear, developing its own women's clothing range as well.

PKZ's expansion strategy paid off strongly for the company. By 1998, PKZ's revenues topped CHF 100 million for the first time. At the same time, Olivier Burger was rewarded with the title of Entrepreneur of the Year in 1998. By the early years of the new century, the company's total sales had more than doubled, with sales topping CHF 220 million by 2001. PKZ could then claim to be Switzerland's fastest-growing retail group.

Nevertheless, PKZ, as with the rest of the Swiss retail clothing industry, saw its sales slip steadily through the middle years of the decade. This was in part because of the dramatic drop in clothing prices themselves, as imports from China flooded the market at the beginning of the decade. As a result, PKZ saw its sales fall back to CHF 195 million by 2004. However, the company's cost-reduction efforts enabled the group to maintain its profits.

PKZ's commitment toward investing a significant share of its profits into its retail network also played an important role in helping the company to maintain its position among Switzerland's retail leaders. Through the decade, the company continued its strong investment program, which included the refurbishing of each of its retail stores every five to six years. In this way, the company developed a reputation for its modern and trendy retail formats.

PKZ had taken note of retail developments elsewhere in Europe and the United States in the new century. The multibrand retail format had become increasingly popular. In 2001, PKZ decided to launch its own multibrand format, combining the Blue Dog Men, Blue Dog Women, and Feldpausch retail brands into a single store, with the first of this new concept opening in Zoug in 2001.

The new formats included the group's latest retail foray, the creation of the higher-end Mr. Burger men's clothing store format in 2002. The first Burger store opened in 2002. While initially a men's format, the company expanded the brand to include women's clothing as well.

PKZ numbered among Switzerland's top four clothing retailers in the middle of the decade, and was the country's largest Swiss-based retailer. The company took steps to solidify this position. Marketing played a major role in this effort, including the launch of the group's own magazine in 2005. Published four times a year,

with plans to distribute 500,000 copies, the company's magazine was said to have the largest circulation of any Swiss magazine. After nearly 130 years, PKZ represented one of the top Swiss clothing brands.

M. L. Cohen

PRINCIPAL OPERATING UNITS

Blue Dog; Burger; Feldpausch; PKZ.

PRINCIPAL COMPETITORS

Bally Schuhfabriken S.A.; Bon Genie-Grieder Les Boutiques; Herren Globus AG.

FURTHER READING

"Bienvenue dans l'Univers de la Mode!" *Adress-Magazin,* September 1, 2008.

"Cent Vingt-cinq Ans pour PKZ," *Luxes par Bilan,* May 31, 2006, p. 20.

"Des Affiches Qui N'ont Pas Pris un Pli," *Le Temps,* June 6, 2006.

Duarte, Florence, "PKZ, 125 Ans de Pied en Cape," *Type,* June 30, 2006, p. 44.

"PKZ Ouvre Son Premier Magasin 'Femmes,'" *La Liberté,* November 18, 2005.

"PKZ Passt Sich Stark Dem Zeitgeist an," *Bieler Tagblatt,* November 21, 2005.

Portmann, Jutta, "Unternehmerportrait von Ph. Olivier Burger der PKZ Burger-Kehl & Co. AG," *KMU Doktorandenseminar,* June 2, 2005.

Richard, Martin, "Fashion's Phantom and Masculinity's Mystery: The Posters of PKZ," *Journal of Popular Culture,* Winter 1997, p. 69.

"Tout Pour les Hommes," *Adress-Magazin,* February 27, 2009.

Rawlings Sporting Goods Company

---■---

510 Maryville University Drive, Suite 110
St. Louis, Missouri 63141
U.S.A.
Telephone: (314) 819-2800
Fax: (314) 819-2988
Web site: http://www.rawlings.com

Wholly Owned Subsidiary of Jarden Corporation
Founded: 1887
Employees: 935
Sales: $173.71 million (2002 est.)
NAICS: 339920 Sporting and Athletic Goods
    Manufacturing; 421910 Sporting and Recreational
    Goods and Supplies Wholesalers; 451110 Sporting
    Goods Stores

■ ■ ■

Rawlings Sporting Goods Company is a leading marketer and manufacturer of baseball equipment and other sporting goods products. Rawlings makes the official baseball and helmet used in Major League Baseball (MLB) games and the official baseball used in National Collegiate Athletic Association (NCAA) baseball championship games. Rawlings became the official sponsor of the National Federation of State High School Associations for baseballs, softballs, basketballs, footballs, soccer balls, and volleyballs in 2002. Rawlings was acquired by K2 Inc. in 2003 and then became a subsidiary of Jarden Corp. in 2007, after the consumer products concern acquired K2 in a $1.2 billion deal.

SPORTING GOODS PIONEER

Rawlings Sporting Goods Company was founded in 1887 by George and Alfred Rawlings, brothers who opened a small store in St. Louis, Missouri. Its first catalog characterized the company as "Dealers in Fishing Tackle, Guns, Baseball, Football, Golf, Polo, Tennis, Athletic and General Sporting Goods." The store soon went up in flames, so the Rawlings brothers got into manufacturing in 1898 in partnership with Charles W. Scudder, who put up the money.

Rawlings Manufacturing Co. introduced the first shoulder pads for football players in 1902, a fiber-and-felt model named "Whitley's Armor Clothing" after an executive. It designed the first all-weather football; began outfitting baseball's St. Louis Cardinals with team uniforms in 1906; and first provided baseballs to a professional league in 1907.

Bill Doak, a Cardinals pitcher, designed the first modern baseball glove in 1919, when he separated the thumb and forefinger with a few strands of rawhide to form a deep pocket. Doak took the idea to Rawlings, which manufactured it and made it a bestseller for more than 25 years. Harry Latina, who joined the company in 1922, was dubbed the "Glove Doctor" for devising such models as the Deep Well Pocket (1930), Trapper (1940), and V-Anchored Web (1950). He took out some 30 patents for features such as adjustable thumb and pinky loops, the V-anchored web, and the "Edge-u-cated" heel.

Latina's son Rollie assumed his father's job in 1961 and retained it until 1984.

Rawlings was the fourth largest sporting goods concern in the United States in 1954, with sales of about $12 million. The following year Rawlings was sold for $5.7 million in stock to A.G. Spalding & Bros., Inc., then the second largest sporting goods company in the nation. In addition to baseball gloves, balls, and shoes, and protective football equipment, Rawlings at this time was producing equipment and supplies for badminton, basketball, bowling, boxing, golf, softball, tennis, track, volleyball, and wrestling. In 1957 the company introduced the prestigious Rawlings Golden Glove Award to recognize fielding excellence for the best MLB players at each position.

Following a review of the Spalding acquisition, the Federal Trade Commission charged that the deal represented a violation of antitrust laws and in 1960 ordered Spalding to divest itself of Rawlings. Spalding took the case to court but lost and in 1963 sold the firm, which had been renamed Rawlings Sporting Goods Co., to a group of private investors for about $10.3 million in cash and notes. John L. Burns, the new chairman and chief executive officer, said sales at Rawlings had exceeded $20 million in 1962 and that the company had not lost money in any year of its existence.

Then renamed Rawlings Corp., the company was the only privately owned sporting goods manufacturer in the United States. It retained headquarters in St. Louis and had eight factories, including three in Puerto Rico. Most had been built within the previous decade. Rawlings discontinued athletic footwear in 1967 after losing business to more advanced German molded-shoe models. Also a factor was a ban placed on the importation of kangaroo hide, which the company had been using to produce cleated athletic footwear; Rawlings had been making cleated shoes since the 1890s.

CHANGES IN OWNERSHIP

Rawlings had annual sales of about $20 million and six manufacturing plants (four in Missouri and two in Puerto Rico) when it was sold in 1967 to Automatic Sprinkler Corp. of America, which changed its name to A-T-O Inc. in 1969. This conglomerate made the company a division under its prior Rawlings Sporting Goods name. In 1970, 12 major league teams were wearing Rawlings-made uniforms, including the Pittsburgh Pirates, clad in the division's newly introduced double-knit nylon-and-cotton uniforms. The American Basketball Association was using the red, white, and blue ball made by Rawlings. A-T-O said that in just one year Rawlings had become the largest manufacturer of quality hockey equipment in the United States. Rawlings also was making golf and tennis equipment.

Early in 1971, A-T-O acquired Adirondack Industries, best known for its baseball bats but also an important producer of toboggans and winter toys as well as archery bows and hockey sticks. The Adirondack operation was combined administratively with the Rawlings division. Earnings slumped for Rawlings in the early 1970s but recovered following a restructuring in the middle of the decade that stressed advertising and marketing. The company claimed to have achieved 20 percent annual sales growth between 1975 and 1978. Rawlings Golf was established in 1976 as a separate A-T-O division. Its products consisted of clubs, balls, shoes, bags, gloves, and Toney Penna custom equipment.

Rawlings raised its baseball profile in 1977, when it replaced Spalding as the supplier of baseballs to the major leagues. This contract amounted to 30,000 dozen Haitian-produced balls a year, not counting additional special balls for the World Series and the All-Star Game. In addition, in 1979 Rawlings was the chief source of baseballs for the amateur market, accounting for about one-third of the annual sale of some 1.2 million dozen baseballs. Rawlings also had taken the lead from Wilson Sporting Goods Co. in the baseball glove business, with a market share between 28 and 30 percent and more than 50 percent of the gloves sold to professional players. Adirondack bats were less prominent, because of the longtime dominance of Hillerich & Bradsby Co.'s Louisville Sluggers. Nevertheless, Adirondack bats held 15 to 20 percent of the (strictly wooden bat) professional market and 25 percent of the amateur market.

A-T-O was renamed Figgie International, Inc., in 1981. By 1983 Adirondack was no longer making toboggans. The Rawlings Sporting Goods division had added soccer balls to its line of products. Rawlings Golf was manufacturing and distributing clubs under both the Toney Penna and Rawlings brand names, and it was

KEY DATES

1887: George and Alfred Rawlings open a small store in St. Louis, Missouri.
1898: The Rawlings brothers go into manufacturing in partnership with Charles W. Scudder.
1902: Rawlings Manufacturing Co. introduces the first shoulder pads for football players.
1906: The company begins outfitting baseball's St. Louis Cardinals with team uniforms.
1907: Rawlings provides baseballs to a professional league for the first time.
1919: Bill Doak, a Cardinals pitcher, designs the first modern baseball glove.
1922: Harry Latina, eventually dubbed the "Glove Doctor," joins the company.
1955: Rawlings is sold for $5.7 million in stock to A.G. Spalding & Bros., Inc.
1957: The company introduces the prestigious Rawlings Golden Glove Award.
1963: Spalding is forced to sell Rawlings to a group of private investors.
1967: Rawlings is sold to Automatic Sprinkler Corp.
1987: Rawlings is designated the "Official Uniform and Protective Equipment Supplier to Major League Baseball."
1994: Rawlings goes public.
2002: Rawlings becomes the official sponsor of the National Federation of State High School Associations for baseballs, softballs, basketballs, footballs, soccer balls, and volleyballs.
2003: K2 Inc. acquires Rawlings.
2007: Jarden Corp. buys K2; Rawlings becomes part of Jarden's Outdoor Solutions division.

also distributing balls, bags, shoes, and gloves. This division had been discontinued by 1986, however.

Baseball equipment accounted for half of sales for Rawlings in 1985. It was still the sole supplier of major league baseballs, which were still being hand-stitched in Haiti. The bats (then renamed Adirondack Rawlings bats) were being made—along with Sherwood hockey sticks—in Dolgeville, New York, from timber logged in the Adirondack Mountains, with the plant heated from wood shavings. Most baseball gloves sold in the United States at that time were being manufactured in the Far East, but Rawlings maintained three plants in Missouri,

plus a Tennessee facility that produced leather for some of the gloves and covers for the baseballs.

UPS AND DOWNS

By 1990 Rawlings was one of only two companies manufacturing baseball gloves in the United States. Hides from steers raised in Missouri were taken to a Chicago leather company, where they were tanned and sorted. Each animal yielded two hides, one from each side, with each hide providing enough material for almost four gloves. From Chicago the hides were being shipped to a Rawlings plant in Ava, Missouri, where all of the company's professional baseball gloves, most of its baseball helmets, and most of its footballs were produced.

Rawlings resumed manufacturing athletic footwear in 1989, with made-in-Taiwan baseball, softball, and football shoes featuring both metal and rubber cleats for natural and artificial surfaces. The top-of-the-line series came in kangaroo hide—again legal for some species—while two lower-priced series came in leather and synthetic material. Rawlings dropped the football shoes in 1991, however, because of poor sales. The company opened a baseball manufacturing plant in Costa Rica in 1987 and closed its Haitian factory in 1990 because of political instability. It had discontinued Haitian-based production of baseball gloves in 1986 and clothing in 1989.

In 1987 Rawlings was designated the "Official Uniform and Protective Equipment Supplier to Major League Baseball," the first company to earn that recognition. Its five-year contract as the supplier of team uniforms for major league baseball and licensed apparel such as replica jerseys and T-shirts was not a success for the company, however, and was not renewed. Also in 1987, Rawlings balls were selected as the "Official Basketball and Football for NCAA Championships," and the company became the exclusive licensee for a complete line of NCAA retail basketballs, footballs, and accessories.

Net revenues at Rawlings dropped from $145 million in 1991 to $135.8 million in 1992. Although the company had record net income of $7.1 million in the latter year, industry observers said it was experiencing manufacturing and distribution problems that made it unable to develop and market goods to sports retailers on a timely basis. The end of the MLB licensed apparel contract was a blow to the company's clothing division, which accounted for about one-fourth of company sales and had been targeted for growth to offset the flat sales of hard goods. In an effort to turn things around, the company appointed its fifth president in the last six years, and the ninth in the last 11 years, in 1992.

GOING PUBLIC

Sales remained stagnant and profits dropped in the next two years. Rawlings executives later blamed a lack of investment by parent Figgie International, Inc., forcing the firm to limit production of some products and to cancel certain customer orders. In 1994 Figgie put Rawlings up for sale to the public, collecting $127 million, including a one-time cash dividend. The newly independent company assumed debt equivalent to 60 percent of its capital. Another new chief executive officer, Carl Shields, assumed the helm that year and vowed to make changes. Figgie, he said in the March 1995 issue of *Bobbin,* had been "a metal-bending, heavy manufacturing-type company that never did understand how to operate in a consumer goods industry."

Accordingly, Rawlings fielded a new management team whose objective was to emphasize apparel, tripling sales in this category during the next three years without investing in new facilities. During this period the company began selling "hotel wear," spruced-up sweat suits and similar items that athletes might wear while lounging around a hotel or traveling to a game. Rawlings did not neglect its traditional baseball market, however, renewing its contract to make major league baseballs through 2000, and in 1994 becoming the exclusive supplier of baseballs to the 18 minor leagues through 2000.

To increase sales in Canada, its largest foreign market, Rawlings in 1997 purchased Daignault Rolland, primarily a manufacturer of hockey equipment, although it also made baseball equipment for Canada only. Later in the year Rawlings also purchased the Victoriaville line of hockey equipment, used by more than 150 professional hockey players, from California Pro Sports Inc. for $14 million. Rawlings had reentered the hockey business previously by contracting with other companies to make pads and some kinds of gloves endorsed by St. Louis Blues star Brett Hull. The company also announced that it would soon resume offering products for volleyball and soccer.

NEW PRODUCTS

In 1998 Rawlings started production in Taiwan of the Radar Ball, a baseball with a built-in microchip and display unit for measuring the speed of a pitch. It introduced a new aluminum bat less prone to dents and cracking, and had also developed one that could be customized by adding up to eight ounces of weights and counterweights. Some analysts, however, contended that the company remained overly dependent on baseball, a stagnating source of revenue whose sales in fiscal 1997 (the year ended August 31, 1997) came to $80.8 million, $7.5 million less than the previous year. Annual net revenues for the company as a whole during fiscal years 1995 through 1997 ranged between $144.1 million and $149.7 million, while net earnings ranged between $4.6 million and $5.5 million. The company's long-term debt was $32.6 million at the end of fiscal 1997. Sales for 1999 reached $165.4 million.

In 1997 Rawlings signed a five-year contract with Host Communications Inc., the nation's leading sports marketer. Host vowed to raise the company's visibility in the marketplace by such comparatively inexpensive means as working its contacts with coaches' organizations and the amateur sports contests that Host was sponsoring around the world. Bull Run Corp., a holding company that owned 30 percent of Host, had acquired 10 percent of stock in Rawlings and had purchased warrants to buy an even larger share of the company.

By the end of the 1990s, Rawlings believed itself to be the leading supplier of baseballs, baseball gloves, and baseball protective equipment in North America. It was offering 14 types of baseballs and more than 125 styles of gloves, ranging in retail price from $5.99 to $159.99 for the Heart of the Hide series. Rawlings also was selling 20 different types of basketballs, 22 types of footballs, football shoulder pads, other protective gear, and accessories. The acquisition of the Victoriaville hockey business added hockey sticks and protective equipment to supplement the full line of protective hockey equipment the company had developed in 1996. Rawlings also had licensing agreements with 16 companies in the United States to use the brand name on various products and with the ASICS Corp. in Japan for use of the Rawlings name on all types of baseball equipment, team uniforms, and practice clothing. In 1999 Rawlings was named the official baseball supplier to the NCAA Baseball World Series and tournament through 2004.

Rawlings was manufacturing baseball gloves, batting helmets, footballs, and injection-molded accessories in Ava, Missouri; wooden baseball bats in Dolgeville, New York; apparel in Licking, Missouri; tanned leather in Tullahoma, Tennessee; hockey sticks in Daveluyville, Quebec; hockey protective equipment in Montreal; and hockey goaltender equipment in London, Ontario. The balance of its products (accounting for three-quarters of net revenues) was being manufactured by third parties in various Asian countries and Mexico. Of the company's net revenues in fiscal 1999, baseball equipment accounted for 56 percent; basketball, football, and volleyball equipment for 19 percent; apparel, 13 percent; hockey, 5 percent; licensing, 4 percent; and miscellaneous, 4 percent.

CHANGES IN THE 21ST CENTURY

Rawlings experienced several changes in ownership during the early years of the new millennium. The company's search for a buyer began in 2000 when it announced that it was in the early stages of merger talks with Bull Run. Rawlings asked Bull Run to make a cash offer for the firm, but Bull Run declined. Sales from 2000 to 2002 remained relatively flat. The company secured modest profits in 2001 and 2002 after posting a $13 million loss in 2000. The company shuttered its hockey manufacturing operations in 2000 and sold Victoriaville (Vic Hockey) in 2001. Rawlings became the official sponsor of the National Federation of State High School Associations for baseballs, softballs, basketballs, footballs, soccer balls, and volleyballs in 2002. It lost its exclusive basketball supplier status for the NCAA Men's and Women's tournament championship games that same year.

By 2002 Rawlings had been in talks with investor Dan Gilbert, the company's largest investor and owner of Quicken Loans Inc., as well as Huffy Corp. and Russell Corp. Sports manufacturer K2 Inc., however, made the most attractive offer, at $9 per share, in November 2002. K2 manufactured a variety of sporting equipment including skis, snowboards, bikes, and in-line skates but was looking to bolster its team summer sports business. It saw the supplier contracts and licensing business of Rawlings as potentially very lucrative. K2 Chairman and CEO Dick Heckmann explained his rationale for the union to the *St. Louis Business Journal* shortly after the announcement, "The simple fact is Rawlings is too small to be an independent company, and scale is everything in this business. The Rawlings brand has a lot of legs to it, and in the right setting with the right parent, it could have significant growth to it." The stock-swap deal, valued at approximately $115 million, was finalized in March 2003. K2 also acquired Worth Inc., a Rawlings competitor, that year.

Under the leadership of the new parent company, Rawlings set out to develop new products. The company launched its first line of softball bats made from graphite-composite material in 2003 and had plans in the works to develop a new line of baseball bats made from a special alloy by Liquidmetal Technologies Inc. Rawlings acquired Texas-based ABC Helmet Co. in 2003. Two years later, it relocated company headquarters from Fenton, Missouri, to St. Louis. During 2007 Jarden Corp. acquired K2 in a $1.2 billion deal. K2, along with Rawlings, became part of the consumer products firm's Outdoor Solutions division.

This division secured $2.5 billion in sales and $298 million in earnings in 2008, figures that bode well for the future growth and development of Rawlings.

Robert Halasz
Updated, Christina M. Stansell

PRINCIPAL COMPETITORS

Amer Sports Corp.; Easton-Bell Sports Inc.; Hillerich & Bradsby Co.

FURTHER READING

Cancelada, Gregory, "Los Angeles Firm Hopes to Score with Buyout of Rawlings Sporting Goods," *St. Louis Post-Dispatch*, May 6, 2003.

———, "New Parent Firm to Pump Life into Fenton, Mo.-based Sporting Goods Store," *St. Louis Post-Dispatch*, March 27, 2003.

Cedrone, Lisa, "Rawlings Scores with New Lineup," *Bobbin*, March 1995.

Fikes, Bradley J., "Carlsbad's K2 Sold in $1.2B Deal," *North County (Calif.) Times*, April 26, 2007.

Garrison, Chad, "Behind the Scenes of Rawlings, K2 Merger," *St. Louis Business Journal*, December 27, 2002.

———, "K2 Combines Sales Teams at Rawlings Headquarters," *St. Louis Business Journal*, January 16, 2004.

———, "Rawlings Talked to Huffy, Russell Before K2 Deal," *St. Louis Business Journal*, January 31, 2003.

"Jarden Corporation Completes Acquisition of K2 Inc.," *PR Newswire*, August 9, 2007.

LaMarre, Thomas E., "Squeeze Play," *Nation's Business*, November 1985, p. 87R.

Marshall, Christy, "Rawlings' Baseball Line Hits Grand Slam," *Advertising Age*, April 16, 1979, pp. 22, 62.

"Playing to Win," *St. Louis Commerce*, September 1991, p. 6.

"Rawlings Sporting Goods Says Acquisition Talks Failed," *New York Times*, January 14, 2000.

Sanford, Robert, "Glove Affair," *St. Louis Post-Dispatch*, May 8, 1994, pp. E1, E5.

Stamborski, Al, "Challenges Force Rawlings to Learn How to Innovate," *St. Louis Post-Dispatch*, February 22, 1998, pp. E1, E8.

Stichnoth, Matthew M., "Baseball and Beyond," *New York Times*, March 15, 1998.

Wessling, Jack, "Rawlings Re-Enters Athletic Footwear After 22 Years," *Footwear News*, September 4, 1989, p. 26.

Wulf, Steve, and Jim Kaplan, "Glove Story," *Sports Illustrated*, May 7, 1990, pp. 73–76.

Riviana Foods Inc.

2777 Allan Parkway
P.O. Box 2636
Houston, Texas 77019-2141
U.S.A.
Telephone: (713) 529-3251
Fax: (713) 529-1866
Web site: http://www.riviana.com

Wholly Owned Subsidiary of Ebro Puleva, S.A.
Incorporated: 1986
Employees: 2,752
Sales: $458.7 million (2008)
NAICS: 311212 Rice Milling

■ ■ ■

Riviana Foods Inc. is one of the largest processors, distributors, and marketers of rice products in the United States. The company buys rough or green rice from independent growers and processes it at plants located in Arkansas, Minnesota, Tennessee, and Texas. Riviana's familiar brands include Mahatma, Success, Carolina, Minute, and Gourmet House. Under these names, Riviana sells an array of processed rice in different grains and types, including dried, instant, prepared, boil-in-a-bag, and brown rice. The company also provides various supermarket and grocery chains with rice under private labels and food manufacturers with bulk rice for an array of processed foods, including multigrain bars. Riviana became a wholly owned subsidiary of Ebro Puleva S.A., the largest food processing firm in Spain, in 2004.

ORIGIN AND EARLY
DEVELOPMENT: 1910–30

By 1910 American rice growers and millers faced a serious problem: a market glut created by overproduction and a price that had bottomed out. The industry was plagued by its haphazard, inefficient system of small, independent mills, which were driving milling costs up and quality down. In 1911, looking for a solution for Louisiana rice producers, a consortium of millers merged to become Louisiana State Rice Company.

The move was spearheaded by Frank A. Godchaux, Sr., the general manager of two mills in rural Louisiana. The consortium soon chartered Louisiana State Rice Milling Company of New Orleans (LSRMC), created to improve both the efficiency of the mills and the quality of their rice. It combined the assets of more than 30 of the state's 70 rice mills. LSRMC had tough going in its early years. It was unable to eliminate depressed prices resulting from excessive production, lower-cost foreign competition, and a frustrating lack of domestic interest in rice as a food staple. In 1916 it reorganized as the Louisiana State Rice Milling Company, Inc. (LSRMCI), still hoping to solve the problems nagging the industry. LSRMCI combined 12 Louisiana mills, but it quickly added two mills in both Arkansas and Texas. It could not shake off the industry's doldrums, however, and struggled for several years. Its one bright point was the 1919–20 season, when it recorded a promising surplus of about $320,000. However, it would not prove as successful again until the mid-1930s, despite its valiant efforts to promote its product domestically. By 1924 the company had divested several marginal and idle properties, leaving a cluster of six mills in south-central Louisiana, one in Arkansas, and a California subsidiary.

In 1925 LSRMCI also began standardizing its rice merchandising, marketing its best-quality short-grain Blue Rose rice in 100-pound packets, soon to be sold under the Water-Maid brand name. In that same year, Godchaux and some associated investors acquired a controlling interest in the company, and Godchaux's son, Frank A. Godchaux, Jr., entered the business. Over the next four years, the Godchauxs sold the California subsidiary and got their finances in good enough shape to survive the economic debacle that started in 1929.

THE DEPRESSION AND WAR
YEARS: 1930–45

The Great Depression hit the rice industry hard. It devastated export sales, forcing American farmers and mills to hold surpluses that in turn caused prices to plummet, leaving the industry in total disarray. Under the Roosevelt administration there were efforts to bail farmers and millers out through price supports, but many of the New Deal initiatives were delayed by legal entanglements. By 1935 the industry faced the unhappy prospect of having the largest unsold surplus in its history. The government responded by imposing a processing tax designed to curtail milling enough to stabilize the industry, but, delayed by the Supreme Court, it went into effect too late to help the industry.

Through careful management, LSRMCI fared better than many of its competitors. It survived and even prospered some during the 1930s. It managed by redoubling its marketing efforts. It also introduced the popular Mahatma brand, its name for its finest long-grain rice. But there was luck, too; unlike many other banks, LSRMCIs banks remained solvent through the bad years.

In the 1936–37 season, Frank A. Godchaux, Jr., replaced his father as president of LSRMCI and took charge of managing the company's operations. He ran into immediate difficulties the following year, when farmers held their crops with the futile hope that economic conditions at both home and abroad would improve, forcing prices up. Nonetheless, LSRMCI weathered this and other problems to become, by the early 1940s, the best managed operation in the industry.

World War II brought its own special problems. Both the Lend-Lease and Selective Service Acts had a negative impact on the rice industry, as did the closing of foreign markets. Unable to make solid market projections, LSRMCI had to pass up an opportunity to purchase its chief competitor, the Standard Rice Milling Company, after that company's president and principal stockholder, W. R. Morrow, died. The war convinced the Godchauxs that greater attention should be given to marketing packaged rice for household table use. It also brought a major account with Kellogg, which used LSRMCI's Water Maid rice for its famous Rice Krispies cereal.

RECOVERY AND MERGER: 1946–65

LSRMCI had serious postwar problems, including government allegations of price control and mandatory set aside violations. Competition was also picking up. In 1946 the Champion Rice Milling Company emerged, soon becoming the River Brand Rice Mills, Inc. It purchased the Southern Rice Sales Co. and several other enterprises. Southern, founded in 1911 by Julius R. Ross, had proved a troublesome marketing rival of LSRMCI since it had begun packaging and selling rice under the Carolina and River Brand names in the late 1920s. Combining that marketing ability and the milling capacity of four mills, River quickly became a major headache for LSRMCI, demanding as much attention as commodity-market fluctuations, consumer tastes, and federal regulations.

The competition spurred greater marketing efforts by LSRMCI. To promote its sales, the company put more funds into advertising, which, in the 1950s, included television spots and the publication of free recipe books that garnered national attention. In 1950 Frank A. Godchaux III joined the company and was soon named vice-president, charged with sales. He faced toughening competition, especially from Uncle Ben's Converted Rice, which, thanks to its ads on the Garry Moore television show, was quickly growing in popularity. In spite of the increasing success of converted and "minute" rices, and America's emerging fast-food lifestyle, LSRMCI doggedly pursued the principle that rice was an economy food and delayed marketing value-added lines.

KEY DATES

■

1911: A consortium of millers merge to become Louisiana State Rice Company.

1916: The company reorganizes as the Louisiana State Rice Milling Company, Inc.

1935: The rice industry has the largest unsold surplus in its history.

1964: River Brand Rice Mills and the company form Food Engineering International, a jointly owned and financed research and development company.

1965: The two companies merge under the River name—later changed to Riviana Foods Inc.

1970: Riviana purchases Central American food processing and distribution properties from W.R. Grace & Co., including Pozuelo S.A. in Costa Rica and Alimentos Kern de Guatemala, S.A.

1976: Colgate-Palmolive Company buys Riviana.

1986: Investors launch a buyout of Riviana's holdings.

1995: The company goes public.

2004: Riviana is acquired by Ebro Puleva S.A.

2006: The Minute rice brand becomes part of Riviana's holdings.

2008: The company breaks ground on a rice processing, packaging, and warehouse facility in Memphis.

The 1950s proved a troublesome decade for LSRMCI. It faced decreasing profit margins and stagnant sales. However, these factors did stimulate company efforts to improve its efficiency, largely through modernizing and centralizing billing and accounting operations. Some relief came in the late 1950s, when new government programs permitted commercial rice stocks to qualify for subsidies, even when exported. It was a timely measure, for in 1961, after the Castro regime came to power in Cuba, the punitive trade embargo closed one of LSRMCIs more lucrative markets.

By the early 1960s, Frank A. Godchaux III was pressing for innovations geared to America's new love affair with quick and easy foods. The company introduced Mahatma Yellow Rice, using real saffron, and sped up its research on a freeze-dried method of producing a quick-cooking rice. It was also trying to find a more effective milling method of removing rice hulls,

research in which River Brand Rice Mills was also engaged. In 1964 the two companies pooled their efforts, forming Food Engineering International (FEI), a jointly owned and financed research and development company.

By that year, almost total control of the company's day-to-day operations had passed to Frank A. Godchaux III and his brother, Charles R. Godchaux. Frank became president after his grandfather's death in 1965. Surrounded by an older management team mostly recruited by their grandfather, the younger Godchauxs grew concerned about the company's future prospects and began merger negotiations with River Brand, their FEI partner. They felt that, in tandem, the two companies could compete successfully in the domestic table-rice market then dominated by Uncle Ben's and Minute rice brands. On September 2, 1965, through a stock-exchange arrangement, the two companies merged under the River name—later changed to Riviana Foods Inc.—with Frank A. Godchaux III as chairman of its board. Riviana soon began aggressive marketing in the convenience food market through both expansion and diversification.

DIVERSIFYING AND THE COLGATE MERGER: 1966–76

Riviana first started streamlining its operations by centering its milling and packaging facilities in Houston, Memphis, and Abbeville, Louisiana. It also looked for new export markets, especially in South Africa, where it owned Quix-Riviana Foods (Pty) Ltd. But most importantly, Riviana started acquiring other food-product companies. These included the Pangburn Company, a candy maker and marketer; the Austex Foods Division of Frito-Lay, Inc., which processed convenience-food items such as tamales and chili; the Hill's Packing Company, a processor and seller of pet foods; Hebrew National Kosher Foods, a processor of meat products; the Romanoff Caviar Company, which marketed imported and domestic caviar and manufactured dehydrated, granulated instant beef and vegetable and chicken flavored products under the MBT brand name; and several small restaurant chains and delicatessens, including Trim's, a chain of Mexican food restaurants in Texas.

Riviana's expansion also necessitated organizational changes. The company soon established four operating divisions: the Grocery Products, Specialty Foods, International, and Retail Divisions. Each of these operated as a profit center with full authority over the policies of the subsidiaries under its control. All divisions prospered and grew, especially those milling and marketing rice products, the demand for which greatly escalated during the Vietnam War. The company also pursued new foreign markets. In 1970 it purchased Central American food processing and distribution properties from W.R. Grace & Co., including Pozuelo S.A. in Costa Rica and Alimentos Kern de Guatemala, S.A., producers and marketers of a wide variety of foods.

In the domestic market, diversification produced promising results, but Riviana's staple remained rice, which accounted for about 50 percent of its sales. Overall, sales between 1965 and 1970 climbed from about $30 million to almost $145 million. By 1968, Riviana's success had gained it a listing on the New York Stock Exchange. It also attracted the attention of Colgate-Palmolive Company's CEO, David R. Foster, who had begun his own campaign of aggressive diversification. In June 1976, Colgate bought Riviana by trading 1.1 shares of Colgate for each share of Riviana common, a sale amounting to about $180 million. Theoretically, Riviana was to continue as a quasi-independent division under its own management, thus Riviana viewed the merger as an opportunity for even faster growth. Reality would soon dampen those expectations.

AN END TO COLGATE'S
OWNERSHIP: 1976–86

Larger sales gains from the merger with Colgate simply failed to materialize. Both domestic and international economic problems slowed the sale of rice products, although Riviana's subsidiaries did well, particularly Hill's Pet Food, Hebrew National, and the Central American operations. In 1977 Riviana reorganized, hoping to reverse steadily declining rice sales. It created Riviana Rice USA, a new division in control of domestic rice sales and marketing, with Charles R. Godchaux as president. Frank A. Godchaux III also reorganized his division, Riviana International Inc. However, stiff competition from nonprofit farmer-owned cooperatives continued to erode the company's market share and force prices down. In 1978 Riviana attempted to gain back its lost ground by more aggressive pricing and by building a new parboil plant, strategies that worked to a very limited degree and still left Riviana struggling to maintain its financial equilibrium.

In 1979 Foster, in ill health, resigned as Colgate's CEO and chairman. Colgate then began selling off what Foster himself had called "rundown acquisitions." Over the next two years, it sold off all of Riviana's domestic subsidiaries except Hill, leaving only Hill's Pet Nutrition, Riviana Rice USA, and Riviana International intact. Then, in 1980 Riviana struck a new nadir. In ill health, the company's president and CEO resigned. While Hill's remained quite profitable, Riviana, with just a 7 percent market share, was losing out to the rice

cooperatives. Other problems followed. The company lost a major mill in Memphis to fire in 1983 and took a temporary market beating when national publicity argued that a long-used crop fumigant was contaminating its rice products. Facing the possibility of Colgate's selling off what remained of Riviana's holdings, the Godchauxs began organizing an investment group to purchase the company back.

In 1986, operating as Lastarmco, Inc., controlled by the Godchauxs, the investors bought all of Riviana's holdings except the Hill's subsidiary. The basic price Lastarmco paid in a complex agreement was $23.9 million. The new company was incorporated as a private company, Louisiana State Rice Milling Company, Inc. (LSRM), and merged with Lastarmco. In 1987 its name changed to Riviana Foods Inc. The Godchaux family held about 62 percent of new company's stock, and Frank A. Godchaux III and Charles R. Godchaux served, respectively, as chairman and vice-chairman of the board of directors.

PROMISE AND GROWTH: 1987–99

With net sales of $244 million and a $9.3 million profit in 1987, Riviana quickly demonstrated renewed promise. It benefited from supportive farm legislation and the rising per capita consumption of rice in the United States, which, in 1991, at 20.5 pounds a year, was almost three times what it had been in 1961. Determined to reduce its dependency on the volatile bulk-rice commodities market, the company continued to pursue an increased share of the convenient instant rice market then dominated by General Foods. In 1988 it built a new research and development facility in Houston, and the next year opened its new Food Service Kitchen at the Houston Technical Center, where it tested food service equipment with consumer rice products. Riviana also entered a 1989 agreement with Riceland Foods, Inc., the nation's leading rice processor. Named Rivland Partnership, the joint enterprise set out to make and market rice flour from a new facility in Jonesboro and within a year was dominating that market.

There were still problems in Riviana's reemergence as an industry leader. After four years of growth, in 1994 Riviana's net income dropped, despite an increase in sales. The company then decided to go public once again, and in December 1995 requested the Securities and Exchange Commission's permission to offer 21.6 percent of its privately owned common stock. At the same time, Riviana's operational leadership passed to Joseph Hafner, the company's president and CEO, but the Godchauxs continued to hold a controlling interest in the company.

In 1995 Riviana's sales reached $427 million, returning the company to its projected levels of sales and profits. In fact, its net income, at $19.13 million, rocketed to 71 percent over the previous year's net. The company continued with slow but steady increases in both figures into 2000. It also undertook some new steps toward broadening its markets. For example, in 1997 Riviana began working with Tiger Oats Ltd. in South Africa, with plans to market value-added rice products there. Increasingly dependent on its lines of packaged rice for its profits, Riviana would continue its aggressive search for additional convenience-food markets.

Because domestic rice consumption was continuing to rise, Riviana expected to fare well into the next century. In the United States, it sold its branded and private-label rice products to all but one of the top 20 supermarket chains in 1999. Only its Central American subsidiaries were going through an unstable period, plagued by destructive weather, economic problems, and political unrest. Hafner remained optimistic, however, confident that the region would stabilize and that Riviana would be able to use its branded-market position as a base for the introduction of new lines and upgraded packaging. Further expansion and product development enhanced Riviana's presence, both at home and abroad.

CHALLENGES IN THE 21ST CENTURY

With profits climbing, Riviana continued its growth strategy during the early years of the new millennium. It acquired Germany's Euryza Reis GmbH as well as adding the Gourmet Brand label to its brand arsenal. During 2003 it purchased the Rice Specialties business of ACH Food Companies Inc., a $24 million deal. The company also launched a new joint venture in the United Kingdom that year with Ebro Puleva S.A., a large food processing firm based in Spain. Riviana and Ebro had partnered together on many ventures and the two companies jointly owned Herto N.V., the Rice-growers' Co-operative Ltd. of Australia, Belgium-based Boost Nutrition C.V., and the recently acquired Euryza.

By that time, Riviana's impressive profit growth had begun to falter and sales were falling due to the increasing popularity of low-carbohydrate diets. Companies involved in the production of high-carbohydrate products, including Riviana, were largely affected and saw profits slide as consumers began to shy away from their products. According to market research firm AC-Nielsen, sales of fresh bread in the U.S. fell by 2.5 percent in 2003 while pasta fell by 4.6 percent, and instant rice dropped by a significant 8.2 percent. Concerned with this new trend, CEO Hafner told the

Houston Chronicle in early 2004, "We and other affected food marketers have yet to come up with an effective strategy to counteract these debatable diet plans."

Determined to secure its position as a leading rice company, Riviana decided to partner with its longtime European ally. In September 2004 the company became a wholly owned subsidiary of Ebro Puleva in a deal worth approximately $380 million. As a result of the acquisition, Ebro gained a substantial foothold in the U.S. and became the largest rice company in the world, controlling nearly 30 percent of the rice market in Europe. Riviana, meanwhile, stood to gain from Ebro's considerable size and global reach.

Hafner retired in 2005 after 33 years of service with Riviana. W. David Hanks, a longtime Riviana executive, was named his replacement. His tenure as CEO was short-lived and he announced his retirement in early 2006. Bastiaan de Zeeuw, a Riviana executive since 1984, took the helm and continued to focus on the company's expansion efforts. While Riviana shuttered its rice milling, storage, and drying facilities based in Louisiana in 2006, it broke ground on a new 400,000-square-foot rice packaging and processing plant in Memphis in 2008.

Ebro acquired the Minute Rice brand from Kraft Foods Global Inc. in 2006. Minute became part of Riviana's portfolio and gave the company a foothold in the Canadian market where the Minute brand held a strong position. Ebro also purchased New World Pasta Company that year, which secured Ebro's position as not only the largest rice company in the world, but the second-largest pasta maker. While Riviana's fortunes remained subject to consumer demand, rice was, in fact, the world's most consumed cereal grain, humankind's third-largest food crop, and a staple in the diet of nearly two-thirds of the world's population. Riviana, well positioned under Ebro's solid corporate umbrella, was confident it was on track for success in the years to come.

John W. Fiero
Updated, Christina M. Stansell

PRINCIPAL COMPETITORS

American Rice Inc.; The Connell Company; Mars, Inc.

FURTHER READING

"Board Approves Buyback of 1 Million Shares," *Wall Street Journal*, August 31, 1998, pp. B3, B2.

Buss, Dale, "Spilling the Beans: Better Dehydration Technologies Pave the Way for New Legions of Legumes," *Food*

Processing, December 1996, p. 65.

"Ebro Puleva Buys Kraft's Minute Rice Brand and Assets," *Market News Publishing,* July 28, 2006.

"Ebro Puleva Completes Acquisition of Riviana," *PR Newswire,* September 5, 2004.

Elder, Laura Elizabeth, "The Riceman Cometh," *Houston Business Journal,* March 8, 1996, p. 16A.

Hensel, Bill, Jr., "Stop Dieting? Fat Chance!" *Houston Chronicle,* January 23, 2004.

Moore, John Robert, *Grist for the Mill,* Lafayette: Center for Louisiana Studies, 1999.

Moreno, Jenalia, "Second Helping of Texas Rice," *Houston Chronicle,* July 24, 2004.

Pybus, Kenneth R., "Riviana Foods Returns to Wall Street with New IPO," *Houston Business Journal,* January 6, 1995, p. 1.

"Riviana Buyout Makes Puleva World Rice Leader," *El Pais,* August 28, 2004.

"Riviana Foods' CEO to Retire," *Just-Food,* April 1, 2005.

"Riviana Foods to Sell Louisiana Facilities," *Delta Farm Press,* March 3, 2006.

Rubio's Restaurants, Inc.

1902 Wright Place, Suite 300
Carlsbad, California 92008
U.S.A.
Telephone: (760) 929-8226
Toll Free: (800) 354-4199
Fax: (760) 929-8203
Web site: http://www.rubios.com

Public Company
Incorporated: 1985
Employees: 3,700
Sales: $179.3 million (2008)
Stock Exchanges: NASDAQ
Ticker Symbol: RUBO
NAICS: 722211 Limited-Service Restaurants

■ ■ ■

Rubio's Restaurants, Inc., operates, franchises, or licenses a chain of more than 190 Rubio's Fresh Mexican Grill restaurants, most of which are located in Southern California, where the company was founded, but also in Arizona, Nevada, Colorado, and Utah. Rubio's Fresh Mexican Grill restaurants offer soft-shell tacos, quesadillas, made-to-order burritos, salads, and seafood from the Baja California region of Mexico, including Rubio's signature World Famous Fish Taco, as well as char-grilled mahi mahi and sautéed shrimp. Menu favorites include Chopped Chicken Salad, Big Burrito Especial, Grilled Mesquite Shrimp Burritos, Grilled Mahi Mahi Tacos & Burritos, Steak Street Tacos, and Carnitas Street Tacos, which are accompanied by fresh salsa, beans, guacamole, and chips.

CREATING A MARKET FOR RUBIO'S SIGNATURE FISH TACO

According to Ralph Rubio's own account, Rubio's Baja Grill resulted from a challenge made by his father Ray (Rafael) "to get off his surfboard and make something of his life." It was 1982, and although Ralph had no business experience of note, he did have a good recipe for making what became the chain's signature menu item—its fish taco. He had gotten the recipe at a taco shop in San Felipe, a fishing village in Baja California, where, in the mid-1970s, he and other student friends from San Diego State University used to take their spring break. After sampling the fare at the shop, Ralph knew that he had found a very tasty and unique Mexican dish. He wangled the recipe from Carlos, the obliging counterman, took it home and began making fish tacos for family and friends.

With the financial backing and business acumen of his father and the help of his brother Robert, Ralph Rubio bought a small building in the Mission Bay section of San Diego and, in January 1983, began making and selling his unique tacos under a sign reading "Rubio's. The Home of the Fish Taco." Before opening that first Rubio's, Ralph Rubio had only limited experience in managing a restaurant. He had started working as a waiter in 1978, largely to have daytime hours free for the beach, but it was only after making his deal with his father that he got some managerial experience as an assistant manager at the Pier Company restaurant in Seaport Village.

Thus Rubio's had an unassuming but fairly risky start for a restaurant chain that by 1999 had sold more than 35 million fish tacos. The family, using Ray Rubio's initial investment of $30,000, bought the building at a "distressed" sale for $16,000. Previously a hamburger grill, it was little more than a stand, but it would do. Not knowing whether the business would take hold, the Rubios started out frugally. In order to save money while learning and building the business, Ralph elected to move back into to his parents' home.

The careful start soon paid off. The fish taco became a favorite treat for the crowd of young surfers in the neighborhood, and the initial unit's success soon encouraged expansion plans. In fact, from the outset the Rubios began reinvesting the company profits, building a chain, first in San Diego, then beyond. Expansion, however, was slow and cautious at first. It was three years before the company opened its second restaurant, located on College Avenue near San Diego State University. In the next year, 1987, it added another unit. It also reached $1.6 million in sales. By that time, Ralph Rubio had moved out of the kitchen. Although he continued to do his own marketing and advertising, his principal concern was management, making sure that the company in its growth made the right decisions.

EXPANDING INTO NEW MARKETS DESPITE DECADE-END RECESSION

In 1988, the company added three more Rubio's Deli-Mex restaurants, as they were then called. Although the chain was still relatively small, consisting of just six units, it had started moving into new market areas. Rubio's opened one of its units in San Marcos, an inland community that provided a test of the company's chance of catching on in a locale where residents had no knowledge of Baja cuisine and demographically differed from beach areas where younger and more active people tended to congregate, a group more willing to try novel foods.

Believing that the San Diego market, though very profitable, was almost saturated, Ralph Rubio had adopted a strategy of opening additional units first throughout San Diego County and then in North County, Orange County, and Los Angeles, which offered a much larger market potential than San Diego. Original plans called for buying land for the new units, but Rubio felt that commercial property in promising locales often sold at prohibitive prices, which forced the company to continue leasing land at its new sites. Initially, Rubio's tried to finance its expansion from its profits, but when its rate of growth picked up, it had to rely on bank loans. That slowed growth somewhat, as did the recession of the late 1980s.

1992–98: ACCELERATED GROWTH

Growth of Rubio's in the 1990s greatly accelerated. At the end of 1992, the chain consisted of 16 restaurants employing about 300 people. These had combined sales of $8.9 million. Also, they were still wholly under the family's control, but continued growth was clearly going to make a strict family-management impractical if not impossible. When the chain grew to 26 locations, during 1996, the company began extensive recruiting outside the family.

Over the next four years, the company worked to put together a strong executive team and solid board of directors. Ralph Rubio remained at the company's helm as president and CEO, and after his father's retirement in 1999, he also became chairman of the company's board. Many new members of the team brought important experience from their previous work at other fast-food and other retail chains. They included Chief Operating Officer Stephen J. Sather, Chief Financial Officer Joseph Stein, Chief Marketing Officer Bruce Frazer, and Director of Real Estate Ted Frumkin.

Among other things, they faced some stiffening competition from other chains. At least in Southern California, the fish taco was becoming popular enough to attract tough players, even the fast-service, Mexican-food giant, Taco Bell, which started offering its own version of the famous fish taco in mid-decade.

The greatest challenge, coping with success, was a happy one. In 1995, Rubio's Baja Grill units numbered 23. By the end of the following year, they had increased to 31, in 1997 to 43, and in 1998 to 59. That represented an annual average growth rate of nine units between 1995 and 1998. The strong sales in the same period justified the accelerated expansion. Same-store increases in sales hit double digits in both 1997 (18 percent) and 1998 (10.4 percent). Those figures prompted Rubio's decision to go public, which it did in 1999, when it made its first stock offering of 3.15 million shares of common stock, traded on the NASDAQ, priced at $10.50 per share.

KEY DATES

1983: Ralph Rubio's family begins business at a stand in Mission Bay area of San Diego.
1986: Expansion begins with opening of second restaurant; Rubio's sells its one-millionth fish taco.
1991: Company expands into Orange County.
1997: Restaurants become Rubio's Baja Grills and expand into Phoenix and Las Vegas markets.
1999: Company goes public.
2000: Rubio's opens its 100th Rubio's Baja Grill.
2001: The first franchised Rubio's restaurant, in Fresno, California, opens.
2002: Rubio's Restaurants does away with the Rubio's Baja Grill brand name and replaces it with Rubio's Fresh Mexican Grill.
2009: Locations exceed 190.

Prior to that, financing had been achieved through private placements of Rubio's stock, made possible because of the company's solid reputation. The fact that in 1993 the U.S. Small Business Administration had named Rubio's California's most successful entrepreneurial business helped. Between 1995 and 1997, the company privately placed convertible preferred stock totaling $17.6 million.

GOING PUBLIC

Through its initial public offering in 1999, the company raised an additional $23.4 million, allowing it to finance the opening of 31 new restaurants, giving it a total of 90 Rubio's Baja Grill locations. It also tapped into four new markets: Denver, Salt Lake City, Sacramento, and Tucson. With that single-year 50 percent increase in its total number of units, Rubio's primary challenge was to maintain the quality of its operation. Its special development and operations teams accomplished that feat with no major difficulties.

Rapid growth carried risks, of course. Among other things, the company could not afford to invest in property for its new Baja Grills during its accelerating expansion. As a result, the company continued to lease all of its restaurant locations, with, of course, the sole exception of its initial unit. Its plans for expansion into the next century called for the continued leasing of property. To keep the expense of adding new restaurants down, the company was determined to operate within very specific cost and size limits. Historically, Rubio's

restaurants ranged between 1,800 and 3,600 square feet in size, with its smallest units located in food courts. New plans called for selecting sites for units with a footprint ranging between 2,000 and 2,400 square feet, with an average start-up cost of about $380,000.

Ways to ensure efficiency and economize without sacrificing quality in food or service became the study of Rubio's growing managerial team throughout the 1990s. For example, in 1998, Rubio's hired Paul Wartenberg as director of information technology. He joined the company from CKE Restaurants, parent company to two fast-food chains. His job was to ensure that Rubio's, in adapting computer technology to its expansion needs, took no costly false steps. Other moves were made to achieve cost-cutting efficiency. Among other steps, in the winter of 2000, Rubio's signed a contractual agreement with Alliant Foodservice Inc., which provided centralized distribution of all food and paper products to the company's chain of restaurants.

Starting in 2000, the company also initiated a franchise program to help its expansion into new markets. The stratagem called for partnering with other chain operators. Plans also called for opening 36 new restaurants in 2000 and 41 more in 2001, mostly in the company's existing markets, where brand recognition was high and was being regularly reinforced through radio and television advertising.

A milestone was reached on March 27, 2000, when, in Pasadena, Rubio's Restaurant Inc. opened its 100th Rubio's Baja Grill. At that time, Ralph Rubio indicated that the achievement was just the beginning of the company's efforts to create a nationwide chain.

By the end of 2000, Rubio's operated 124 locations. In December, the company announced that it had inked its first franchise agreement, paving the way for S&A Enterprises to open eight new locations in Portland, Oregon.

2001–03: A NEW IMAGE

Growth continued in 2001. Midway through the year, Jim Pardini opened the first franchised Rubio's restaurant in Fresno, California, to be followed by a second location in Bakersfield, California, in December. Franchising became an increasingly important aspect of Rubio's strategy around this time. In October 2001, for example, the company shuttered 11 company-owned locations in Las Vegas, Denver, and Salt Lake City, and announced plans to find franchisees to take over all of its company-owned restaurants outside of Arizona and California.

Rubio's revenues grew to $111.5 million in 2001. The company opened a total of 18 new restaurants that year, pushing its base of company-owned sites to 133. In addition to the two franchised locations operated by Pardini, S&A Enterprises planned to open its first Portland location in the spring of 2002. Despite efforts to reposition itself as a destination for a variety of chicken and beef items, consumer research revealed that many consumers still viewed Rubio's as a fish taco restaurant. For this reason, the company scaled back national expansion plans in early 2002 and decided to concentrate efforts on strengthening its image as a Mexican steak and chicken quick-service restaurant within its main markets of Arizona and California.

As part of its repositioning efforts, the company began experimenting with new packaging, new menu portions and prices, and a new menu board. Franchise plans were put on hold until a new restaurant prototype could be developed. In September 2002, Seattle Coffee Co. executive Sheri Miksa was hired as Rubio's president and chief operating officer. Ralph Rubio continued to serve as chairman and CEO. Miksa was charged with rolling out a new look at the company's restaurants, along with a menu emphasizing beef and chicken items.

As part of its new approach, in late 2002 Rubio's Restaurants did away with the Rubio's Baja Grill brand name and replaced it with the name Rubio's Fresh Mexican Grill. According to Ralph Rubio, the change was made to eliminate any potential confusion among consumers, some of whom did not understand the meaning of "Baja." Around this time, a new prototype restaurant opened its doors in Ventura, California, featuring a copper-topped open grill, as well as an expanded salsa bar. Plans were formed to remodel existing restaurants in 2003.

LEADERSHIP CHANGES

Progress continued into the middle of the first decade of the 2000s. In November 2004 Miksa was promoted to CEO, and Rubio remained chairman. By early 2005 the company had 152 restaurants in operation. Rubio's ended 2005 with sales of $140.76 million, a five-year increase of 25 percent.

Beginning in 2006, the company had plans to grow 10 to 15 percent over the next three to five years. However, Miksa would not be at the helm to oversee the company's expansion. Following a fall in earnings throughout 2005, she resigned as CEO in December. On an interim basis, Ralph Rubio assumed the role of president and CEO.

A major leadership change occurred in August 2006, when Rubio named Daniel Pittard, a former executive with such companies as McKinsey & Co.,

PepsiCo Inc., and Amoco Corp., as the company's new president and CEO. Moving forward, Pittard revealed that Rubio's would focus on promoting high-quality food, as well as a unique atmosphere and reasonable prices. By mid-2007, Rubio's had grown to 160 locations. In July of that year, the company announced that it would begin using zero-trans-fat canola oil at all of its restaurants by mid-August.

In October 2008, Kelly Capital Investments LLC, which already held a 5.9 percent stake in Rubio's, offered to acquire the company in a deal worth $49.75 million. Rubio's, however, rejected the offer on the grounds that it was too low.

By late 2008, Rubio's consisted of approximately 180 owned and franchised locations. Difficult economic times, however, prompted the company to carefully consider its growth plans. For example, Rubio's indicated that it would avoid markets characterized by real estate and construction volatility. Rubio's approached the 21st century's second decade with 190 locations. Moving forward, the company continued to entice consumers by introducing cutting-edge menu items. For example, in mid-2009 it introduced the All-American Taco, a hybrid selection that combined a cheeseburger with a taco.

John W. Fiero
Updated, Paul R. Greenland

PRINCIPAL SUBSIDIARIES

Rubio's Restaurants of Nevada Inc.; Rubio's Promotions Inc.

PRINCIPAL COMPETITORS

Chipotle Mexican Grill Inc.; Del Taco LLC; Fresh Enterprises Inc.

FURTHER READING
Bagley, Chris, "Dining Chains Slow Expansions," *North County Times* (Escondido, Calif.), February 22, 2009.

Battaglia, Andy, "Rubio's Growth Plan: Become Biggest Fish Taco Purveyor in Each Pond," *Nation's Restaurant News,* August 23, 1999, p. 11.

Brune, Brett R. R., "Rubio's Deli-Mex Casts Line into Four New Market Areas," *San Diego Business Journal,* September 12, 1988, p. 8.

"Carlsbad, Calif.—Daniel Pitard Was Named President and Chief Executive Officer of Rubio's Fresh Mexican Grill, the 150-Unit Fast-Casual Chain Based Here," *Nation's Restaurant News Daily NewsFax,* August 22, 2006.

Casper, Carol, "Fishing for Customers: A Sub-Sub-Segment Builds Around Signature Fish Tacos," *Restaurant Business,* March 20, 1996, p. 102.

Cebrzynski, Gregg, "It's the Lobster That Got Away and the Tale of the Talking Bag," *Nation's Restaurant News,* July 27, 1998, p. 16.

Disbrowe, Paula, "Tacos of the Sea," *Restaurant Business,* October 1, 1997, p. 145.

Duchene, Lisa, "Rubio's Plays Up Steak, Chicken: Fresh Mexican QSR Backs Off National Expansion, Works to Boost Sales," *Seafood Business,* February 2002.

Fikes, Bradley J., "No Pesky Problems for the Rubio's Chain," *San Diego Business Journal,* February 22, 1993, p. 8.

Hardesty, Greg, "Orange County, Calif., Market Kings Plan to Take Fish Tacos Nationwide," *Knight-Ridder/Tribune Business News,* September 17, 1997.

"IT Director Says Function Always Triumphs Over Fashion at Rubio's," *Nation's Restaurant News,* May 24, 1999, p. 16.

Kragen, Pam, "Southern California Fish Taco Chain Expands, Stresses Baja Theme," *Knight-Ridder/Tribune Business News,* June 2, 1997, p. 602.

Rodrigues, Tanya, "Rubio's Names New CEO; Will Launch New Look," *San Diego Business Journal,* September 16, 2002.

"Rubio's Names Miksa CEO; Founder Rubio Still Chmn.," *Nation's Restaurant News,* November 22, 2004.

"Rubio's Turns to Franchisees: Second Franchised Location Opens This Month," *Seafood Business,* December 2001.

Spector, Amy, "Rubio's Files for IPO amid Expansion Push," *Nation's Restaurant News,* April 5, 1999, p. 8.

The Ryland Group, Inc.

—— ■ ——

24025 Park Sorrento, Suite 400
Calabasas, California 91302
U.S.A.
Telephone: (818) 223-7500
Fax: (818) 223-7667
Web site: http://www.ryland.com

Public Company
Incorporated: 1967 as James P. Ryan Company
Employees: 1,303
Sales: $1.98 billion (2008)
Stock Exchanges: New York
Ticker Symbol: RYL
NAICS: 233210 Single Family Housing Construction;
    522310 Mortgage and Non-mortgage Loan Brokers

■ ■ ■

One of the leading home builders in the United States, The Ryland Group, Inc., has operations in 19 markets in 15 states. With an average selling price of about $252,000 in 2008, the company's homes are geared toward entry-level buyers and first- and second-time move-up buyers, as well as active retirees. The Ryland Group also offers mortgage-related services, including title insurance, escrow, and various other insurance services. Since its inception in 1967, Ryland has built over 280,000 homes and financed over 235,000 mortgages. The company experienced rapid growth during the late 1990s and into the new millennium but has been hit hard by the housing and credit crisis. During 2007 it posted its first net loss in 12 years.

EARLY YEARS AS A HOME BUILDER

What became The Ryland Group was originally named after its founder, James P. Ryan, an energetic real estate entrepreneur who established the James P. Ryan Company in Columbia, Maryland, in 1967. Columbia was then a new, planned community of 220 single-family homes situated midway between Washington, D.C., and Baltimore, Maryland. Ryan created the name "Ryland Homes" when he chanced upon a sign that was supposed to say "Maryland," but on which the first two letters had been covered; "Ryland" struck him as the ideal name for his homes.

Operating in a dynamic and highly volatile housing market, Ryland developed a marketing strategy targeted toward the middle class or up-and-coming middle class: Homes were built with only brand-name construction materials and appliances and sold in the middle range, starting at $20,000. Ryland sought to be a highly focused home-building business rather than a development company speculating in land dealing or the development of "raw" land. In its first year of operation, the company concluded 48 sales and made a modest profit of $12.7 million.

In 1970 the company changed its name to The Ryland Group, Inc., and the following year the company went public. That same year Ryland broke ground on another planned community, Peachtree City, outside of Atlanta, Georgia. There Ryland Homes, with their careful attention to detail, frequent inspections at crucial phases of building, and use of only premium brand-name materials and appliances (Andersen windows,

Armstrong floor coverings, Owens Corning fiberglass, General Electric stoves and refrigerators), struck a balance between cost, quality, and choice that was extremely popular with consumers. The customer could select from 15 different floor plans and from a variety of different housing styles that often reflected regional tastes. Ryland also was building a variety of homes, from single-family dwellings to townhomes (the "townhome" concept was pioneered by Ryland) to condominiums, just as the last were growing in popularity. Ryland's building venture prospered, and more than 75 percent of its employees became stockholders.

The next several years saw further expansion into Texas. Ryland manufacturing centers, initially called Ryland Building Systems (later integrated into the Ryland Homes division in 1992), were also constructed at this time, providing preassembled, factory-supervised home-building components to the home site. By 1977 Ryland had penetrated the midwestern market as well as the Philadelphia area, and had completed its 10,000th home. A mere eight years later, in 1985, Ryland celebrated the completion of its 50,000th home.

DIVERSIFICATION AND CONTINUED GROWTH

The purchase in 1978 of Crest Communities in Cincinnati, Ohio, launched Ryland's mortgage operations, modestly begun through Crest's subsidiary Crest Financial Services. From there Ryland Mortgage Company (RMC) grew to become one of the nation's largest mortgage-finance companies, offering a full range of mortgage financing with branches in 18 states. In 1981, with the acquisition of Guardian Mortgage Company, RMC introduced full loan servicing. By the early 1990s, RMC was handling more than $2 billion in mortgage loans on an annual basis. In 1982 RMC formed Ryland Acceptance Corporation (which became a wholly owned subsidiary of RMC in 1987), an administrator and distributor of mortgage-backed securities.

During the 1990s Ryland entered the booming Florida and California home-building markets. In the latter, the M.J. Brock Corporation, with divisions in Los

Angeles and Sacramento, was acquired in 1986. Ryland homes were marketed in California under the Brock or Larchmont Homes labels, and by the early 1990s 40 percent of the company's business derived from Southern California. At that time, however, the savings and loan (S&L) scandal and the recession of the early 1990s struck California especially hard and moderated returns from land investment in the Golden State.

At the same time Ryland was expanding in California, it was also vigorously penetrating markets in Arizona, Colorado, Georgia, and North and South Carolina. In 1987 Ryland crossed the $1 billion mark in revenues; that same year founder Ryan retired from the board of directors. In 1989 Ryland established the Cornerstone Title Company, a wholly owned subsidiary of RMC in Columbia, Maryland, that administered real estate closings.

Market analysts gave Ryland credit for its geographical diversity, which enabled the company to compensate for difficulties in California and other local markets experiencing periodic difficulties. With mortgage interests declining during the recession, Ryland Mortgage Company had record profits, derived largely from entering the "spot loan" origination market. The S&L crisis, which culminated in the federal government taking over the ailing financial institutions and selling off their assets one by one, also became an advantage for RMC. Ryland's powerful mortgage servicing division, one of the largest in the country, benefited from the federal government's assumption of mortgage servicing contracts when S&L home mortgages were taken over by the government; by the early 1990s, they comprised approximately 50 percent of RMC's mortgage servicing portfolio.

EXPANSION EFFORTS

With the worst of the recession over by 1993, the company was stronger than ever. The housing market had recovered completely, with the exception of California and Florida. Thanks to Ryland's geographical diversity and its conservative business philosophy, it had not only weathered the recession (earnings climbed a phenomenal 191 percent between 1991 and 1992) but, unlike many of its competitors, company finances were in the black. Annual revenues still topped $1 billion. The company's four manufacturing centers, which produced the basic materials (lumber and trim) for all Ryland homes except those in the western states, were working over capacity. Ever attuned to the marketplace, the company shifted its marketing strategy in the 1990s to larger homes that did not necessarily cater to first-time home buyers. The average price of a Ryland home

KEY DATES

1967: James P. Ryan Company is formed in Columbia, Maryland.
1970: Company is renamed The Ryland Group, Inc.
1971: The Ryland Group goes public.
1978: Ryland Mortgage Company is founded.
1983: The company's stock moves to the New York Stock Exchange.
1987: The Ryland Group's revenues surpass the $1 billion mark.
2000: Corporate headquarters are relocated from Maryland to California.
2002: The company builds its 200,000th home.
2004: Ryland expands into Las Vegas.
2007: The company posts its first net loss in 12 years.
2008: Ryland's losses exceed $396 million during the housing crisis.

climbed to more than $150,000, with resulting larger profit margins.

In February 1991, Ryland Homes was asked to build single-family housing units in Israel because of that country's massive influx of immigrants from Russia. Unlike Israeli stone houses, which take an average of 18 months to build, Ryland homes could be assembled in a matter of weeks. Eventually, 1,300 housing shells were carefully packed in crates for assembling in Israel. In so doing, Ryland became the biggest American manufacturer of Israeli homes at that time, earning a profit of $13 million.

Also in 1991 the company formed a new subsidiary, Ryland Trading Ltd., to specialize in building Ryland homes for the overseas market, with a particular eye toward market opportunities in Eastern Europe and the former Soviet Union. The federal government even contributed $400,000 in two grants to Ryland Trading Ltd. to encourage it to study housing-market opportunities and the construction of housing factories in the former Soviet Union.

The result was the first U.S. housing project in newly renamed St. Petersburg, Russia, which had not seen the completion of new private housing in more than 70 years. In 1992 Ryland, in a joint venture with Russian companies, began a housing settlement outside of the city consisting of American-style homes priced at $150,000 and up. The homes were targeted toward the increasingly large contingent of foreign businessmen and women in Russia. In a very short time Ryland Trading Ltd. had also expanded its joint-venture portfolios with Mexico, Spain, Turkey, and Senegal.

FOCUS ON HOME CONSTRUCTION

Although Ryland appeared to be on track, the company struggled with the effects of its expansion efforts and the economic recession, and Ryland posted a net loss of $2.7 million for fiscal 1993. R. Chad Dreier, who joined Ryland in November 1993 as president and CEO and became chairman in 1994, implemented a restructuring strategy that turned Ryland's efforts back to its core business of building homes. Dreier planned to de-emphasize Ryland's mortgage banking operations, believing that over the long term, the company would meet with the highest profits and the most success by concentrating on home construction, managing costs more effectively, and establishing a strong national profile. Ryland also intended to increase customer satisfaction, which had declined from a high of about 85 percent in the late 1980s to less than 70 percent in the early 1990s, by introducing new home models and allowing more customer customization.

In 1995 Ryland sold its Institutional Financial Services division, which handled a $46 billion portfolio, to Norwest Bank Minnesota. The divestment of the division, a leading private issuer and administrator of mortgage-backed securities, was in keeping with Ryland's strategy to concentrate on home building and retail mortgage finance services. The following year Crestar Financial Corp. acquired Ryland's wholesale mortgage banking operations, known as Ryland Funding Group.

Ryland's streamlining began to pay off in 1996, when the company reported net earnings of about $16 million, up from a net loss of $2.6 million in fiscal 1995. Still, the company faced many challenges, including a relatively slow housing market that led to declines in both Ryland's number of homes built (8,388, a decline of 6.2 percent compared to closings in 1994) and new home orders (7,838, a fall of 14.2 percent). In 1997 Ryland increased its net income to $22 million, but the number of closings was flat, at 8,377 houses built.

Continuing to improve operations and sticking with its focus on the business of home construction, Ryland sold $2.7 billion in mortgages to PNC Mortgage Corp. of America in 1998, leaving Ryland with a loan servicing balance of about $800 million. The company planned to continue offering home loans to buyers of Ryland homes but felt increasing competition in the home financing business made remaining in the business risky and potentially unprofitable. While shedding some mortgages, Ryland also made some gains: the company acquired Regency Communities, a Florida home builder, and Thomas Builders of Baltimore. The Regency purchase provided Ryland with a strong foothold in the growing retirement market in Florida.

BACK ON TRACK

Net earnings for fiscal 1998 nearly doubled to $40 million, up from $22 million in fiscal 1997. The number of homes built rose to 8,994 homes, and Ryland appeared securely back on track. Earnings during the first quarter of 1999 jumped 116 percent compared to first-quarter earnings in 1998, marking the sixth consecutive quarter of increased earnings. In 1999 Ryland did even better, as the company reported record earnings of $66.7 million on revenues of $2 billion for the full year. The number of houses built surged 13 percent to 10,193 homes, and new orders increased by 10 percent.

The company made a major change in 1999 when it decided to move its mortgage subsidiary to Southern California. Corporate headquarters soon followed, completing the relocation in 2000. California was known as a leader in home-building innovation, and Ryland hoped to capitalize on the connection and keep a closer eye on home-building trends. The move apparently did not affect Ryland's bottom line, and the company continued to report record earnings and strong sales. For the first nine months of 2000, Ryland reported consolidated net earnings of $50.7 million, up from $45.9 million for the first nine months of 1999. The company planned to keep the momentum going in the 21st century by keeping in tune with customers' lifestyles and wishes. This included the possibility of building more town-house communities and retirement communities targeted toward "active adults" and expanding into new housing markets, such as the rapidly growing markets of Las Vegas, St. Louis, Detroit, and Nashville. "We're proud of our product now, of what we're doing," CEO Dreier told the *Baltimore Sun,* adding, "We've had bumps in the road and bad days, but we've now created a pride that we know we're going to do better in the future."

THE HOUSING BUBBLE BURSTS

Before the burst of the housing bubble, Ryland experienced unprecedented growth in the early years of the new millennium. As the number of homes being built increased along with the average price of a Ryland Home, the company secured record revenues and profits. The company opted to grow by moving into the

largest housing markets in the country. During 2002 the company expanded into Charleston, South Carolina; Greensboro, North Carolina; and the Central Valley of California. Ryland built its 200,000th home that year as it celebrated its 35th anniversary.

Growth continued in 2003 as Ryland moved into new markets in Florida and California. Mortgage rates were dropping and home builders were enjoying significant growth. The average price of a Ryland Home increased to $224,000 that year and the company built a total of 14,742 new homes.

By 2004 Ryland was operating as a *Fortune* 500 company and its stock was trading at nearly $100 per share. It revamped its Design Centers that year, allowing its customers to choose a range of items for their homes including countertops, ceilings fans, and doorknobs in a storelike setting. The company entered the Las Vegas market that year, hoping to capitalize on strong growth in the region. During 2005 the company secured its seventh consecutive year of record financial results as revenue topped $4.8 billion while net earnings reached $447 million. The number of new homes built for the year climbed to 16,673 while the average price of a new Ryland home reached $278,000.

While Ryland and many of its competitors in the housing industry had seen record growth over the past several years, a slowdown in the housing industry began to take its toll in 2006. New home sales in the United States began to fall and the number of unsold homes on the market began to increase. The industry's rapid expansion came to a screeching halt in 2007 and 2008 and Ryland began to feel the effects of rising interest rates and falling demand. The housing bubble in the United States had burst and the number of foreclosures was quickly rising.

STRUGGLING TO RECOVER

Subprime mortgage loans, offered to home buyers with little or poor credit history, were offered at a rapid rate during the early years of the new century. These loans came with higher interest rates due to the risk involved, which meant higher short-term profits for many of the lending companies. However, many of these subprime home buyers soon found themselves unable to make payments due to plunging housing values and high rates of unemployment. With the foreclosure rate rising, mortgage companies stopped offering risky loans and put in place stricter lending standards, which in turn made it more difficult for home buyers to secure financing.

The overall slowdown in the U.S. economy and the housing crisis had a significant impact on Ryland's bottom line. Indeed, the company reported its first net loss in 12 years in 2007. During 2008, revenues fell by over 34 percent over the previous year to $1.98 billion while the company posted a loss of nearly $397 million. Company stock was trading under $10 per share in November of that year. In response to market conditions, Ryland began an aggressive cost-cutting program, sold off excessive inventory and land, and exited several markets. It also began offering smaller homes that were priced within Federal Housing Administration loan limits. In 2009 Ryland partnered with Oaktree Capital, an investment manager with experience in distressed assets, to acquire and develop residential real estate projects.

Dreier retired from his CEO post in 2009, leaving Larry Nicholson at the helm. Dreier, considered to be one of the highest-paid executives during the housing boom, remained chairman. The company hoped to benefit from the new economic stimulus package passed in 2009 that included an $8,000 tax credit for first-time home buyers. While Dreier and Nicholson expected a very slow recovery in the housing market, the pair remained optimistic and believed Ryland had a solid strategy in place to weather the economic crisis.

Sina Dubovoj
Updated, Mariko Fujinaka;
Christina M. Stansell

PRINCIPAL OPERATING UNITS

North; Southeast; Texas; West; Financial Services; Corporate.

PRINCIPAL COMPETITORS

Centex Corp.; KB Home; Pulte Homes Inc.; Champion Enterprises Inc.

FURTHER READING

Blumenthal, Robyn G., "Ryland Group Inc. Indicates Net Rose in Third Quarter," *Wall Street Journal,* October 12, 1992, p. B6.

Corkery, Michael, "Housing Market Signals Slowdown," *Wall Street Journal,* February 28, 2006.

———, "Ryland's Departing CEO Will Be Paid $27 Million," *Wall Street Journal,* February 27, 2009.

Fink, Ronald, "Ryland Group: The Contracyclical Developer?" *Financial World,* March 3, 1992, p. 15.

Foust, Dean, and David Henry, "Homebuilders Are Stretched Thin," *BusinessWeek,* November 1, 2004.

Henry, Kristine, "Ryland Homes' Earnings Leap 128%," *Baltimore Sun,* July 24, 1998, p. 2C.

Kaplan, Peter, "Ryland Leads Home Builders in Work Abroad," *Baltimore Business Journal,* February 21, 1992, p. 3.

Kim, Queena Sook, "The Super-Model Home," *Wall Street Journal,* August 6, 2002.

Kyriakos, Marianne, "Getting Focused at Ryland," *Washington Post,* December 13, 1993, p. F8.

Marino, Vivian, "Home Builders, Preparing for Thaw," *New York Times,* April 26, 2009.

McQuaid, Kevin L., "Ryland Group Announces Sale of $2.7 Billion in Mortgages," *Baltimore Sun,* April 4, 1998, p. 12C.

———, "Ryland Posts Another Gain," *Baltimore Sun,* February 4, 1997, p. 1C.

———, "Ryland Raises Roof After Turnaround," *Baltimore Sun,* April 18, 1999, p. 1D.

———, "Ryland Undergoes Alterations," *Baltimore Sun,* January 15, 1995, p. 1D.

Salmon, Jacqueline L., "Ryland Group's Tough Year," *Washington Post,* November 15, 1993, p. F5.

Snow, Katherine, "Russian Houses to Carry 'Made in USA' Label," *Business Journal Charlotte,* September 21, 1992, p. 1.

Wells, Melanie, "Builders Still Falling as Market Hits Bottom (Washington Area Residential Real Estate Market)," *Washington Business Journal,* September 2, 1991, p. 13.

San Diego Gas & Electric Company

———■———

8326 Century Park Court
San Diego, California 92123
U.S.A.
Telephone: (619) 696-2000
Toll Free: (800) 611-7343
Fax: (585) 654-1515
Web site: http://www.sdge.com

Wholly Owned Subsidiary of Sempra Energy
Incorporated: 1905 as San Diego Consolidated Gas &
    Electric Company
Employees: 4,774
Sales: $3.25 billion (2008 est.)
NAICS: 221122 Electric Power Distribution; 221210
    Natural Gas Distribution

■ ■ ■

San Diego Gas & Electric Company (SDG&E) operates
as a regulated utility that serves San Diego County and
parts of southern Orange County. The company
provides electricity to 3.4 million customers and natural
gas to 3.1 million customers. The company generates
power at its Palomar and Miramar electric generation
facilities and through its 20 percent ownership in the
San Onofre Nuclear Generating Station. It also
purchases its energy from third parties. SDG&E operates as a subsidiary of Sempra Energy, which was formed
by the 1998 merger of Enova Corp. and Pacific
Enterprises.

EARLY HISTORY

SDG&E was founded in 1881 as the San Diego Gas
Company and incorporated as San Diego Consolidated
Gas & Electric Company in April 1905. Standard Gas
and Electric Co. owned the bulk of the utility's common stock. In 1910 San Diego Consolidated acquired
the United Light, Fuel & Power Co. of San Diego. The
utility also built its first principal electric generating
plant, Station B, that year. It had a monopoly on the gas
and electric business for San Diego and its suburbs. The
utility grew rapidly. The number of electricity customers
increased from 2,212 in 1906 to 14,321 in 1912; gas
customers multiplied from 4,594 in 1906 to 17,864 in
1912. Sales topped $1 million for the first time in 1912,
and surpassed $2 million in 1918.

In November 1923 the company, headed by
President Robert J. Graf and Chairman John J. O'Brien,
contracted to connect its transmission lines with those
owned by Southern Sierras Power Company of Pinon,
California. Through this agreement, the company assured Southern Sierras of an uninterrupted power supply in the Imperial Valley of Southern California should
Southern Sierras experience shortages or power failures.
By 1927 the company's system included two steam
electric generating stations, and it had signed an electric
power interchange agreement with Southern California
Edison Company (SoCal Edison). SoCal Edison was
based in Rosemead, California, and served parts of the
Los Angeles area. The 1920s were a time of booming
business throughout the United States and growth in
California especially, and this showed in San Diego
Consolidated's sales, which grew from $2.6 million in
1920 to $7.3 million in 1929.

In May 1932, under W. F. Raber, Graf's successor as president, the company applied to the California Railroad Commission, its regulating body, to replace manufactured gas with natural gas in its service area. The application was approved and the company contracted with a subsidiary of Pacific Lighting Company, the Southern Counties Gas Co., to provide 24 million cubic feet of natural gas daily. The necessary pipeline, covering 120 miles from Long Beach to La Jolla, California, was estimated to cost $1.7 million. At the time, the utility was serving a population of 222,000. The company began supplying natural gas in September 1932.

Two years later San Diego Consolidated bought a small share of the power produced by the Boulder Dam. The dam was erected by the U.S. government beginning in 1931 on the Colorado River. States, cities, and utilities bought or leased the output of the dam. The utility's sales dipped somewhat during the Great Depression, dropping to $6.8 million in 1934, but growth resumed the following year. The company remained profitable even in the Depression's worst years.

In June 1939 the company entered a new agreement to increase the amount of power it exported to its wholesale customers in Tecate, Mexico. San Diego Consolidated was authorized to export 3.6 million kilowatt hours per year. Previously, the Federal Power Commission had set its export limit at 700,000 kilowatt hours per year. Mexico figured prominently in the company's long-term strategic plan.

GOING PUBLIC

In 1940 as a result of the Public Utility Holding Company Act of 1935, the Securities and Exchange Commission ordered Standard Gas & Electric to sell all its utility holdings, including San Diego Consolidated, which changed its name to San Diego Gas & Electric Company and became publicly owned. In 1941 the last unit of the company's generating Station B was installed. During the 1940s, agriculture, mining, fishing, and aircraft manufacturing were important industries in San Diego. The population of the area had decreased slightly since the 1930s to 219,000. In 1942 Hance H. Cleland succeeded Raber as president. During World War II, army and navy bases became important to San Diego's economy, and the navy continued to influence the company's fortunes. In 1943 the Silver Gate steam electric generating station was completed. Operation began on January 27.

The population of SDG&E's service area had grown to 620,000 by 1949, and its sales were up to $23.3 million. In view of this growth, the company had installed another unit at the Silver Gate plant in 1948, and planned to add a fourth turbo-generating unit to the plant by 1952. Work also had begun on a generating station in Encino, California. SDG&E's first turbo-generator came into service in 1954. That year, SDG&E requested and received a rate increase. Unit 2 of the Encino station came online on July 26, 1956, and Unit 3 became operational in July 1958. The company also bid on 144 acres of land as the site of a possible future steam-generating plant.

SDG&E began research into nuclear power in the late 1950s. In 1961 it agreed to participate in a 350,000-kilowatt nuclear power plant with SoCal Edison. SDG&E owned 20 percent of the plant, located in San Onofre, California; SoCal Edison owned 80 percent. The plant went into operation in 1967.

SDG&E's new steam South Bay generating station was in operation by July 1960. H. G. Dillon became president in 1961, succeeding E. D. Sherwin, who remained on the board. Two years later, Dillon was chairman of the executive committee and J. F. Sinnott became president. The second South Bay unit began operation in June 1962. Unit 3 was put in service in September 1964.

SDG&E enjoyed the best earnings growth rate among California's four largest utilities from 1963 through 1968, averaging 9 percent annually. By 1970, its ninth consecutive year of record earnings, it was one of the fastest growing utilities in the United States. That year, San Diego became the nation's 15th largest city. San Diego County's economy was diversifying from a dependence on the aerospace industry and military installations to include recreation, electronics, oceanography, and education.

OVERCOMING CHALLENGES

By the late 1960s antismog ordinances were hindering the company's efforts to build plants to supply the

KEY DATES

1881: San Diego Gas & Electric Company (SDG&E) begins as the San Diego Gas Company.

1905: The company incorporates as the San Diego Consolidated Gas & Electric Company.

1910: San Diego Consolidated acquires the United Light, Fuel & Power Co. of San Diego; the company builds its first principal electric generating plant, Station B.

1923: The company contracts to connect its transmission lines with those owned by Southern Sierras Power Company of Pinon, California.

1932: The company begins supplying natural gas.

1940: The company changes its name to San Diego Gas & Electric Company and goes public.

1954: SDG&E's first turbo-generator comes into service.

1981: The company receives California Public Utilities Commission (CPUC) approval to construct the Southwest Powerlink.

1986: SDG&E receives conditional approval from the CPUC to diversify into real estate, utility services, and energy products.

1991: The Federal Energy Regulatory Commission rejects the merger of SoCal Edison and SDG&E.

1995: SDG&E forms parent company Enova Corp.

1998: Enova Corp. and Pacific Enterprises merge to form Sempra Energy; the retail power market in California begins to deregulate.

2001: California declares a state of emergency as it initiates rolling blackouts during an energy crisis.

2006: SDG&E settles a class-action lawsuit related to California's energy crisis in 2000 and 2001.

2008: The CPUC approves the company's Sunrise Powerlink transmission project.

at Kaiparowits, an oil-burning plant at Sycamore Canyon, and a nuclear plant at Sundesert, all in California. Stringent environmental regulations, however, made construction of the new plants prohibitively expensive, and SDG&E eventually canceled them all. From 1973 to 1978, SDG&E's cost of producing electricity increased by 250 percent while the rates it was permitted to charge increased only 145 percent. The company was in poor financial shape, its bond rating was lowered from AA to BBB, and $55 million spent on Sundesert before canceling the project was a complete loss. In December 1978 SDG&E resorted to buying power, signing a ten-year contract with Tucson Gas & Electric Co. for up to 500 megawatts of power annually. In March 1979, needing cash, it sold a generating unit to a group of banks to raise $132 million, then leased back the unit because it needed the output.

In 1980 inflation, a time lag following application for a rate increase, action by the California Public Utilities Commission (CPUC), and weather both warmer in winter and cooler in summer contributed to a disastrous year. Although sales rose to $960 million, 29 percent more than the previous year, net income fell 26 percent to $52 million. SDG&E's customers paid some of the highest rates in the United States because of the utility's dependence on high-priced oil, the cost of its canceled plants, and repairs at its nuclear plant. As 1981 began SDG&E focused on the future: the CPUC had suggested annual rate adjustments, instead of biannual, to more accurately reflect prevailing economic conditions; and a new fuel mix would be used in the 1980s, consisting of nuclear, purchased, and geothermal power.

Nuclear power from San Onofre Unit 1 was already available to SDG&E customers. Units 2 and 3 were nearing completion. The company was negotiating with Public Service Company of New Mexico for the purchase of coal-generated power. It already had several contracts for the purchase of geothermal power from companies in the United States and from Mexico's national utility, Comisión Federal de Electricidad. The proximity of San Diego to Tijuana, Mexico, encouraged cooperation between the two utilities. The experimental Heber binary geothermal plant was another avenue explored to reduce the use of oil. The binary cycle process used the hot brine found just beneath the surface in the Imperial Valley to produce high-pressure gas. The gas, in turn, ran a turbine that generated electricity. In June 1983, work began on the plant. At completion in 1985, energy produced at Heber would serve 45,000 residential customers. SDG&E was the majority owner of the plant. The U.S. Department of Energy paid for half of the project but was not an owner.

booming population. Fuel oil costs increased in 1970 due to local regulations that required the utility to burn higher-priced low-sulfur crude. The company began to look elsewhere for its power needs.

Between 1971 and 1976, SDG&E began three plants that would use lower-cost fuels: a coal-fired plant

DIFFICULT TIMES

SDG&E had another disappointing year in 1981. In April Robert Morris, president since 1975, was elected chairman of the board of directors, and Thomas A. Page, formerly executive vice-president and chief operating officer, was elected president. On October 1, Page also assumed the position of chief executive officer, and continued to emphasize SDG&E's goal of reducing its dependence on oil. Almost every part of the company suffered adverse affects during 1981. The San Onofre nuclear plant's Unit 1 was out of service for 14 months in 1980 and 1981 due to equipment failure and retrofitting required in the wake of the Three Mile Island disaster. In addition, SDG&E ran into problems with a fuel oil exchange. In the late 1970s the utility had excess oil and, rather than sell it at a loss, agreed to an oil exchange with United Petroleum Distributors Inc. of Houston, Texas, which later failed to deliver the oil it owed SDG&E when the utility needed it. SDG&E lost $31 million and was ordered by the CPUC to refund to its customers $4.4 million on the transaction, representing the price of the replacement oil it had to buy.

There was a positive development in December 1981, when the company received CPUC approval to construct the eastern interconnection transmission line, later named the Southwest Powerlink, which connected SDG&E with less expensive, coal-fired power generated in Arizona and New Mexico. The transmission line would extend 280 miles from the Palo Verde switchyard near Phoenix, Arizona, to SDG&E's Miguel substation southeast of San Diego. Cost of the Powerlink was estimated at $320 million.

By 1982 San Diego had grown into the eighth largest city in the country. Energy demand, however, had leveled off due to lower industrial energy consumption and energy conservation measures. SDG&E reaffirmed its decision to purchase more of its power. Utility networks were one way to mitigate the effects of variations in energy consumption. Work on the Southwest Powerlink began in mid-1982 with anticipated completion in 1984. At the same time, two new transmission lines to Mexico were under construction, with completion anticipated in 1983 and 1984. San Onofre Units 2 and 3 would boost power production. Both units were scheduled to begin full power production by the end of 1983. SDG&E hoped to sell a portion of the output of both units to help cover the costs of construction and keep rates down. Unit 1 was again out of service as questions about the plant's ability to withstand earthquakes had been raised.

FINANCIAL RECOVERY

After several difficult years, 1983 held the promise of improvement in SDG&E's financial health. The utility's bond rating was upgraded to A, making the cost of borrowing money much lower. San Onofre Unit 2 was put in operation while full power testing went on in Unit 3. Average fuel costs declined for the first time in ten years, and natural gas prices were stabilized. SDG&E closed its 60-year-old Station B generating plant and temporarily shut down its Silver Gate plant. Three-quarters of the Southwest Powerlink was completed. At this point, 44 percent of the company's electric energy was purchased from other utilities, and SDG&E began to define itself as an energy management company.

In 1984 both Moody's and Standard & Poor's upgraded SDG&E's bond ratings again. The company's short-term debt was eliminated, and common stock was trading at a ten-year high. The Southwest Powerlink became operational in May. San Onofre Unit 1 returned to operation in November for the first time since closing down for engineering modifications in 1982. A second transmission link with Mexico also was completed that month.

In 1985 the company had record earnings of $3.25 per share, and San Diego itself continued to enjoy record residential growth. The business community expanded to include information services companies, biomedical research, and other scientific industries. SDG&E's Heber geothermal plant was completed on schedule in May. Page sought approval from the CPUC to establish a holding company that would allow SDG&E to venture into unregulated industries. Stockholders approved the plan on November 1. In March 1986 SDG&E received conditional approval from the CPUC to diversify into real estate, utility services, and energy products. Pacific Diversified Capital Company, an SDG&E subsidiary since 1982, was activated to manage all nonutility operations. The subsidiary quickly acquired Phase One Development, Inc., a commercial real estate development company; Computer Solutions, Inc., a software company; and a majority holding in Mock Resources, Inc., a natural gas and petroleum products distributor.

Early in 1986, SDG&E's final single-fuel power plant, Encino, was converted to burn either gas or oil, allowing the company to purchase the less expensive of the two fuels. SDG&E signed a ten-year power purchase contract with Mexico's national electric utility. The U.S. Navy, SDG&E's largest single customer, announced in 1986 that it planned to withdraw from SDG&E's system and contract for a cogeneration plant to meet its power needs. SDG&E quickly began negotiations with the navy to prevent this from happening. In October, the CPUC decided to disallow $329.9 million in San Onofre Units 2 and 3 costs, about half of the original figure. The decision included $69.1 million in costs for SDG&E, owner of 20 percent of the plant. SDG&E vowed to appeal the ruling. In spite of this, SDG&E posted record profits while reducing customer rates in 1986.

PURSUING A MERGER AGREEMENT

Dividends went up for the 11th consecutive year in 1987. An employee incentive program begun in 1986 to encourage money-saving ideas helped the company save $2 million. The experimental Heber geothermal plant was shut down in 1987 because its production costs were too high. SDG&E established an environmental department to respond to concerns including the removal of polychlorinated biphenyls in its system.

In June 1988 SDG&E agreed in principle to merge with Tucson Electric Power Company (TEP), a company with which it had a long-term power sale agreement made possible by the Southwest Powerlink. TEP had excess capacity and SDG&E sought the merger as a way of ensuring its access to low-cost coal-fired power. Just a month after the merger was announced, SoCal Edison's parent company, SCEcorp, made an unsolicited $2.3 billion bid for SDG&E. If approved, the merger would join California's second and third largest utilities to create the largest investor-owned utility in the United States, with approximately $17 billion in assets. By August the city of San Diego called for hearings on the legality of a merger with SoCal Edison. SDG&E had not decided whether to accept the second merger offer. SCEcorp promised to reduce residential power rates by 10 percent within six months of completing the merger.

On September 1, the day SDG&E's board was to consider its previous offer, SCEcorp increased its bid to $2.36 billion. SDG&E's board voted unanimously to decline SCEcorp's new offer and merge with TEP. If SCEcorp's bid were successful, between 800 and 1,000 SDG&E employees would lose their jobs. In light of the vote, SCEcorp's Chairman and Chief Executive Officer Howard P. Allen did not rule out a hostile takeover. Any deal would have to be approved by the CPUC. Allen said he was willing to wait years for a merger to go through.

In November 1988 SDG&E ended its agreement to merge with TEP. The two utilities had disagreed over the best way to counter SCEcorp's efforts to stop their merger. SCEcorp continued to pursue SDG&E, raising its offer to $2.53 billion and offering Tom Page the

position of vice-chairman of SCEcorp and president of the San Diego division. On November 30, by a vote of six to two, SDG&E accepted SCEcorp's offer. The two directors who voted against the merger resigned from the board.

PROPOSED MERGER REJECTED BY CPUC

Apart from merger negotiations, 1988 was an active year for SDG&E. The U.S. Navy dropped plans to generate its own power and signed a ten-year contract with SDG&E. SDG&E applied for a rate decrease, which CPUC approved effective in January 1989. The company hooked up its one-millionth customer, and revenues rose to $2.1 billion from $1.9 billion in 1987.

SDG&E's merger into SoCal Edison was contingent on approval by the CPUC, the Federal Energy Regulatory Commission (FERC), and shareholders of both companies. The companies were sensitive to the politics of the approval process and promised rate reductions for commercial, industrial, and agricultural customers, in documents filed with the CPUC in April 1989. This pledge was in addition to the 10 percent rate cuts promised residential customers before the merger vote.

In December 1989 SDG&E approached the CPUC to begin the licensing process for a new two-unit, 460-megawatt, combined-cycle power plant. The plant would combine a natural gas turbine generator and a steam-producing unit to produce more cost-efficient power. If the merger did not take place, this plant would put SDG&E in a better position to generate more of the energy it needed in the future. In another move to augment its power resources, SDG&E anticipated returning its Silver Gate plant to service in 1992 due to a growing customer base.

In February 1990 California State Attorney General John Van de Kamp and an advocacy division of the CPUC stated their opposition to the merger. In November George P. Lewnes, an administrative law judge for the FERC, also opposed it on the basis that it was anticompetitive, but his decision was not binding on the FERC board, which was still considering the merger. SCEcorp Chairman Allen retired at the end of 1990 with a decision still pending. On February 1, 1991, two judges with the CPUC had not yet voted. SCEcorp and SDG&E both claimed they would rather cancel the merger than be forced to sell unregulated subsidiaries, which the CPUC judges had recommended should the merger go through.

The CPUC began its final hearings on the merger in March 1991. In May the five-member board handed down a unanimous decision rejecting the merger, citing a lack of long-term benefits and the lessening of competition. The two companies agreed not to appeal the CPUC's ruling and withdrew the application before the FERC. The decision meant that SDG&E needed to line up new sources for purchased power almost immediately. SoCal Edison was one of those sources.

DEREGULATION BRINGS CHANGE

Major changes were on the horizon for SDG&E as California began to set plans in motion to deregulate its utilities industry. The CPUC voted in favor of deregulation in 1995 and the legislative work began. In response to the coming market changes, SDG&E created Enova Corp., a holding company that would oversee its utility operations as well as its nonregulated businesses. The creation of Enova set the stage for the company's next big announcement: its plans to merge with Pacific Enterprises, the parent company of Southern California Gas Co. (SoCalGas).

The merger of Enova and Pacific Enterprises was announced in October 1996 and gained initial approval from the FERC in June 1997. The $6.2 billion merger was completed the following June and created Sempra Energy, one the largest energy companies in the United States with nearly $10 billion in assets. As a subsidiary of Sempra, SDG&E retained its identity and continued to operate independent of SoCalGas. As part of the requirements of the merger, SDG&E was forced to sell its fossil fuel–fired power plants.

Meanwhile, the retail power market in California began to deregulate in 1998. In 1999 market-based energy billing took effect when the CPUC stopped fixing rates for electricity customers. Local consumer advocacy groups spoke out against deregulation claiming SDG&E remained its only power source despite deregulation and went so far as to predict that demand would soon exceed supply, leaving the San Diego region in a perilous position. These fears would soon prove accurate as California experienced a major energy crisis in both 2000 and 2001.

A CHALLENGING START TO THE 21ST CENTURY

Advocates in support of California's electricity deregulation promised lower costs for consumers as well as energy providers. It soon became apparent, however, that the state's deregulation plan was flawed as wholesale prices began to skyrocket in 2000. Demand began to outstrip supply and on January 17, 2001, California instituted a policy of rolling blackouts in an attempt to

conserve energy. Governor Gray Davis declared a state of emergency in California that same day.

Two days later, Davis signed a $400 million bill to buy electricity and then resell it to California's utilities. In March, Davis announced the government had signed over $40 billion in contracts that would provide electricity to power nine million homes for the next ten years. Then in May, California initiated significant rate increases that included up to 40 percent increases for residential customers and up to 50 percent for industrial customers. The state of California eventually stopped buying electricity for its utilities in 2003.

SDG&E did not come through the energy crisis unscathed. Consumers filed an $8 billion class-action lawsuit against Sempra, claiming SDG&E and SoCal-Gas manipulated energy prices during the crisis of 2000 and 2001. The company eventually settled the case in 2006 while admitting no wrongdoing.

Attempting to put the crisis and problems with deregulation behind it, SDG&E moved ahead with plans to increase its generation capacity. As part of its plan to stabilize its energy industry after the crisis, California restored SDG&E's role as a full-service energy provider. In June 2004, the CPUC approved SDG&E's regional energy-reliability plan, which called for the acquisition of a new 550-megawatt natural gas–fired power plant constructed by Sempra Generation near San Diego. The company gained controlled of the plant, dubbed Palomar Energy Center, in 2006.

By this time, California had also mandated that 20 percent of its energy be renewable by 2010 and 33 percent by 2020. During 2008 the CPUC approved SDG&E's $1.9 billion Sunrise Powerlink project that included a transmission line that would link solar, wind, and geothermal power generation in East County and the Imperial Valley to its regional customers. The project was expected to be completed in 2012. In addition, the company began offering incentives to customers that practiced energy conservation. While California's deregulation and ensuing energy crisis had wreaked havoc on SDG&E's operations during the early years of the new millennium, the company appeared to be back on track as a reliable source of power for consumers in San Diego and southern Orange County.

Lynn M. Kalanik
Updated, Christina M. Stansell

PRINCIPAL COMPETITORS

Pacific Gas and Electric Company; PacifiCorp; Southern California Edison Company.

FURTHER READING

Beasley, Deena, "SDG&E Selling Carlsbad, Calif.–Gas Power Plant for $356 Million," *Reuters News,* December 14, 1998.

"California to Exit Business of Buying Power for Utilities Jan. 1," *Associated Press Newswires,* December 28, 2002.

Davis, Rob, "Sempra: Bankruptcy Was Too Big a Risk," *San Diego Business Journal,* January 9, 2006.

"Enova's and Pacific Enterprises' Merger into Sempra Energy Completed After SEC Grants Approval," *Foster Electric Report,* July 15, 1998.

"No Choice in San Diego, Consumer Group Claims," *Megawatt Daily,* November 2, 1999.

Rose, Craig D., "Paying the Light Bill," *San Diego Union-Tribune,* December 28, 2001.

————, "Regulated Rates Run Out of Energy," *San Diego Union-Tribune,* July 2, 1999.

Said, Carolyn, "The Energy Crunch/A Year Later," *San Francisco Chronicle,* December 24, 2001.

"Sempra, Utilities Settle Case with California PUC," *Gas Daily,* October 16, 2006.

Sharp, Tara, "SDG&E Powering Ahead," *San Diego Business Journal,* January 12, 2009.

Sutherland, Billie, "PUC Approves SDG&E Plan to Reorganize," *San Diego Business Journal,* December 11, 1995.

Toth, Simone, "Sempra Energy Switches On in San Diego," *San Diego Business Journal,* July 6, 1998.

sappi

Sappi Ltd.

Sappi House
48 Ameshoff Street
Braamfontein
Johannesburg, 2001
South Africa
Telephone: (27 11) 407-8111
Fax: (27 11) 403-8236
Web site: http://www.sappi.com

Public Company
Incorporated: 1936 as South African Pulp and Paper Industries
Employees: 17,000
Sales: ZAR 43.56 billion ($5.86 billion) (2008)
Stock Exchanges: Johannesburg New York London
Ticker Symbols: SAVVI; SPP (New York)
NAICS: 322121 Paper (Except Newsprint) Mills; 322122 Newsprint Mills; 322110 Pulp Mills

∎ ∎ ∎

South Africa's Sappi Ltd. is one of the world's leading manufacturers of coated fine papers used in a variety of applications including books, brochures, magazines, and catalogs. The company also stands as the world's largest producer of chemical cellulose, used primarily to manufacture viscose fiber, acetate tow, and consumer and pharmaceutical products. The company produces 3.3 million tons of paper pulp each year and has 23 manufacturing facilities in Europe, North America, as well as Southern Africa. The company has three main divisions: Sappi Fine Paper, which produces fine paper along with uncoated graphic and business paper and specialty papers; Sappi Forest Products, which has a production capacity of 830,000 tons of paper, 800,000 tons of chemical cellulose, and over one million tons of paper pulp per year; and Sappi Trading, a division based in Hong Kong that markets Sappi products to various regions not covered by the company's existing sales offices. Operations in Europe accounted for 40 percent of sales in 2008, followed by North America at 29 percent, and Southern Africa at 15 percent. Sappi began an aggressive acquisition strategy in the 1990s that positioned it as a global leader in the paper industry. The company has continued to bolster its coated fine paper business and completed its $1.1 billion purchase of M-real's coated graphic paper business in late 2008.

AFRIKAANS PULP AND PAPER PRODUCER

Sappi started out as South African Pulp and Paper Industries, registered in 1936 in Johannesburg, South Africa. The following year the company began construction of a pulp and paper mill, located near Springs. Because the mill used straw as its chief raw material, it was given the name Enstra, for "Enterprise Straw." That same flair for fantasy was to enable the company to weather the war years and eye further growth by the end of the 1940s.

South African Pulp and Paper Industries acquired two farms near the Tugela River in what was known as Zululand. The site was targeted for construction of a second paper mill. In the meantime, the company began its own plantation operations to ensure its raw materials

COMPANY PERSPECTIVES

Sappi's goal is to be the most profitable company in the paper, pulp and chemical cellulose sectors. Our goal is supported by a new global business strategy to significantly improve the company's profitability and returns. In this regard we have set ourselves very clear targets and measurements in terms of returns, customer satisfaction, employee satisfaction and engagement, as well as to ensure that Sappi is competitively positioned in all our core markets. We are committed to all our businesses and decided that growth and development will be our chosen route to success. In giving effect to our strategy, we will rely on, and remain true to our core values of excellence, integrity and respect.

supply. The decision to go ahead with construction of the Tugela Mill was made in 1950. Completed in 1954, the Tugela Mill was devoted to kraft packaging production, while the original Enstra location turned its specialty to the manufacture of fine papers.

By the end of the decade South African Pulp and Paper Industries sought further growth through acquisition, buying a controlling share of Union Corrugated Cases in 1959, then taking over Cellulose Products, which made tissue wadding products, the following year. South African Pulp and Paper Industries pursued organic growth as well; among the company's capital investments was the installation of a second machine at the Tugela Mill in 1963. The new machine was dedicated to the production of kraft linerboard products. By then South African Pulp and Paper Industries had celebrated its one millionth ton of paper produced since the company's inception.

South African Pulp and Paper Industries continued to seek organic growth during the decade, buying up farmland in the Elands River Valley. The company began construction of a new mill, completed in 1966, and called Ngodwana. This mill was dedicated to the production of unbleached kraft pulp. The site also gave the company expanded acreage for its raw materials plantation activities. By the end of that year South African Pulp and Paper Industries celebrated a new production milestone, reaching the two-million-ton production mark.

The company established a new dedicated timber division in 1968. That same year South African Pulp

and Paper Industries applied for a patent for a new bleaching process using oxygen instead of chlorine. The process, dubbed Sapoxyl, was put into production in 1970. The steady increases in production made by the company in the late 1960s could be seen with the passage of a new production milestone: South African Pulp and Paper Industries' three millionth ton of paper since its founding.

DOMESTIC EXPANSION AND REORGANIZATION

South African Pulp and Paper Industries changed its name to Sappi Limited in 1973. With the growth of its three core operation areas, the company moved to reorganize its operations in 1977, placing its activities into three new operating subsidiaries: Sappi Fine Papers, Sappi Kraft, and Sappi Forests. Each subsidiary operated with its own board of directors. Sappi itself came under control of Gencor, a conglomerate which itself was controlled by finance group Sanlam. This ownership gave Sappi the financial backing to pursue further expansion.

In 1979 Sappi acquired local market rival Stanger Pulp and Paper. The following year the company branched out into the operation of sawmills, forming a new subsidiary, Sappi Timber Products. That subsidiary acquired a new saw mill in Elandshoek, located near its parent company's Ngodwana mill. This mill was slated to undergo a vast expansion program, representing the company's largest capital investment program to date, to increase its capacity and add newsprint, linerboard, unbleached pulp, and bleached pulp production by 1985.

In the meantime, Sappi launched a new kraft linerboard mill in Cape Town. Called Cape Kraft, the new mill's production was based entirely on recycled raw material. Another new product line joined the group in 1982 when Sappi acquired Novobord, adding that company's production of particleboard. The following year the company acquired another particleboard manufacturer, Timberboard, which was merged into Novobord.

INTERNATIONAL MARKETING BEGINS

Sappi remained an entirely South African company. Nonetheless, exports represented an increasing percentage of the company's production, reaching 50 percent by the end of the 1980s. To encourage this development the company founded Sappi International, a subsidiary dedicated to international marketing of the company's

1936: The company registers as South African Pulp and Paper Industries Limited.

1937: The company builds the first paper mill at Springs, called Enstra Mill, for Enterprise Straw, after its chief raw material.

1950: Construction begins on a second paper mill, Tugela, in Zululand.

1959: A controlling stake in Union Corrugated Cases is acquired.

1960: Cellulose Products is acquired.

1966: Production begins at a new mill at Ngodwana.

1973: The company changes its name to Sappi Limited.

1982: The company acquires Novobord, entering production of particleboard.

1985: Expansion of the Ngodwana site finishes, adding production facilities for newsprint, linerboard, unbleached pulp, and bleached pulp.

1988: Sappi acquires Usutu Pulp Company, in Swaziland, gaining the world's largest producer of softwood kraft pulp.

1989: Saiccor, world leader in dissolving pulp production, is acquired.

1990: The company acquires five paper mills in the United Kingdom and establishes Sappi Europe subsidiary.

1992: Sappi acquires Hannover Papier, of Germany, becoming the European market leader in coated wood-free paper.

1994: Sappi acquires 75 percent of SD Warren (full control in 1996), giving it the leading position in the coated wood-free paper market in the United States.

1997: The company acquires KNP Leykam, European leader in wood-free paper production, making Sappi the world leader in the product segment.

1998: All Sappi operations are rebranded under a single Sappi name.

2000: Sappi Novobord is sold.

2001: Sappi Mining Timber is sold; the company announces its intention to close a number of U.S. paper mills.

2002: Sappi acquires Potlatch Corp.'s coated fine paper business and its Cloquet pulp and paper mill in Minnesota.

2004: The company buys a 34 percent stake in Jiangxi Chenming Paper Co. Ltd.

2008: The coated graphic paper business of M-real is acquired in a $1.1 billion deal.

products, in 1986. A year later, the company expanded its Sappi Novobord operation, adding particleboard manufacturing capacity. Then in 1988, Sappi acquired Usutu Pulp Company, based in Swaziland, giving it a world-leading producer of unbleached kraft pulp. The following year, Sappi acquired Saiccor, the world leader in dissolving pulp production.

With all of its production going to the export market, the Saiccor acquisition helped Sappi's own exports top half of the company's total production. These acquisitions helped Sappi gain a strong position in the industry as South Africa at last abandoned apartheid and rejoined the world community. Sappi was quick to expand beyond South Africa and the coming decade was to see the company transform itself from a company with 100 percent of its assets in South Africa to a truly globally operating company, with more than 75 of its assets located away from its home base.

POSTAPARTHEID GLOBAL MARKET LEADER

Among the company's first postapartheid acquisitions were those of five paper mills in the United Kingdom. Sappi followed up these purchases with the establishment of a new European headquarters, Sappi Europe. That office was soon joined by a new overseas subsidiary, Sappi Trading, which took over Sappi's international trading operations. Founded in 1991, Sappi Trading was formed around another key acquisition, Specialty Pulp Services, based in Hong Kong.

As Sappi moved into the 1990s, its sights were set on still higher growth. Led by Eugene van As, who joined the company in the late 1970s and took over as CEO and chairman in the 1990s, Sappi began making a small number of large-scale acquisitions. The first of these came in 1992 when Sappi acquired Hannover Papier, the leading manufacturer of coated wood-free paper in Germany. That purchase gave Sappi a position as one of the top three coated wood-free paper makers in the European market.

Capitalizing on its new scale, Sappi launched its stock on the London, Frankfurt, and Paris stock exchanges, while maintaining its chief listing on the Johannesburg exchange. A year later Sappi reorganized its European holdings under a new subsidiary, Sappi Europe S.A. At that time, Sappi became an independent operation as Gencor, as well as ultimate parent Sanlam, underwent drastic unbundling operations in an effort to streamline their businesses for the new postapartheid era.

MOVING INTO THE NORTH AMERICAN MARKET

Sappi turned its sights toward the North American market. In 1994 the company paid $1.6 billion to acquire a 75 percent share of SD Warren, the United States' leading coated wood-free paper producer. That acquisition placed Sappi in the worldwide leadership spot for that paper category. Although van As was criticized for having paid a premium price for SD Warren, the Sappi CEO was betting on a growing importance for wood-free paper products as the paper and publishing industries increasingly adopted high-technology applications.

Sappi completed its acquisition of SD Warren in 1996. In the meantime, it turned its attention toward renewing its industrial park. In 1995 the company began a ZAR 800 million expansion of its Saiccor subsidiary. The following year the company completed a modernization of all of its African pulp and paper mills.

Sappi returned to its external growth drive in the second half of the decade. In 1997 Sappi agreed to acquire KNP Leykam, the coated wood-free paper division of Burhmann, paying nearly $800 million. Again criticized for paying a premium price, Sappi with the Leykam acquisition had not only gained the European leader in the wood-free paper category, it had secured for itself the global leadership for that product segment. It also had pushed its debt levels to the limit, resulting in a deep drop in its share price.

Following the Leykam acquisition Sappi reorganized, splitting its operations into two principal subsidiaries. Sappi Fine Papers took London as its headquarters, grouping all of the company's paper production. Sappi Forest Products, which remained at the parent company's headquarters in Johannesburg, took over the company's pulp, particleboard, and cardboard production, as well as its forestry operations. This move was followed up in 1998 when the company rebranded its entire organization under the single Sappi name. That year Sappi's stock began trading on the New York Stock Exchange as well as the London, Frankfurt, and Johannesburg exchanges.

MOVING INTO THE NEW MILLENNIUM

Sappi came under pressure at the turn of the 21st century. On the one hand, the company remained burdened by a heavy debt load generated through its acquisition drive of the 1990s. On the other hand, Sappi was hard hit by a drop in world paper prices, and by the faltering of a number of markets, including Asia and Latin America. The weakening economic climate in the United States took a toll, as well. As a result Sappi's share price continued to be pelted, and the company was seen as a potential takeover target.

In 2000 the company began a sell-off of some of its assets, primarily from its Sappi Forest Products subsidiary. That company sold off Sappi Novobord in 2000, exiting the particleboard and mid-density fiberboard market. The following year the company sold off its Sappi Mining Timber division. The company also announced its intention to close a number of its U.S. paper mills in 2001 and 2002. The company's debt remained relatively high, more than $1.1 billion, equal to some 35 percent of its market value. Nonetheless, Sappi's share price was once again on the rise, while takeover rumors lulled.

As Sappi entered 2002 it suggested that its days of large-scale acquisitions were behind it, at least temporarily. Instead the company intended to continue growth through the acquisition of individual mills. In addition Sappi suggested that it would pursue growth through a series of greenfield initiatives, linking up with local partners. After transforming itself into a truly global company in just one decade, Sappi looked to continue its successful expansion drive into the Asian market as well.

In May 2002 the company acquired Potlatch Corp.Æs coated fine paper business and its pulp and paper mill in Cloquet, Minnesota. The $480 million deal signaled the company's intent to further grow its coated fine paper holdings and secured its foothold in the North American market. At the same time the purchase was in keeping with its strategy to purchase individual mills. The company strengthened its position in China in 2004 when it bought a 34 percent stake in

Jiangxi Chenming Paper Co. Ltd., a joint venture with two China-based paper firms, a South Korean firm, and the International Finance Corp.

Sappi's next big move came in 2008 when it announced plans to buy the coated graphic paper business of Finland-based M-real. At the time of the deal, the paper market in Europe was in turmoil as a result of falling demand and many companies were struggling to shore up profits. Sappi expected the merger to save the company EUR 120 million per year within three years. The $1.1 billion acquisition was finalized in late 2008 and included four coated graphic paper mills in Finland, Germany, and Switzerland.

The company and its competitors faced tough market conditions during this time as a result of weakening global economies and rising raw material costs. As such, the company set a stringent cost cutting plan in place and opted to shutter unprofitable mills. Sappi set plans in motion to reduce capacity at its mill in Muskegon, Michigan, in 2005. The mill was eventually shut down in 2009 as market demand for fine coated papers continued to fall. At the same time however, it expanded operations at its Saiccor Mill, which increased chemical cellulose capacity by over 225,000 tons per year.

Van As retired in 2008 as chairman of Sappi after 31 years of service. Daniel C. Cronjé was named as his replacement. With Ralph Boëttger, named as CEO in 2007, and Cronjé at the helm, Sappi was determined to succeed in the coming years. Along with its growth objectives, the company also focused on meeting its Black Economic Empowerment (BEE) targets, which had been set forth by the South African government. During 2008 the company completed the sale of a 25 percent undivided right to its forestry land to a BEE consortium led by Lereko Investments Pty. Ltd.

M. L. Cohen
Updated, Christina M. Stansell

PRINCIPAL DIVISIONS

Sappi Fine Paper; Sappi Forest Products; Sappi Trading.

PRINCIPAL COMPETITORS

Boise Inc.; International Paper Co.; Mondi plc.

FURTHER READING

Anderson, Robert, and Tom Burgis, "Sappi Sidesteps Turmoil to Buy European Paper Mills," *Financial Times,* September 30, 2008.

Brissett, Jane, "Duluth, Minn.–Area Paper Companies Eye Investments in China," *Duluth News-Tribune,* October 24, 2004.

Fine, Alan, "From Pariahs to Multinationals?" *Business Week,* November 7, 1994.

Innocenti, Nicol, "Sappi Shakes Off Takeover Rumours," *Financial Times,* November 10, 2002.

Kemp, Shirley, "No Mega-Deal for Sappi," *Moneyweb,* January 28, 2002.

Mittner, Martin, "'Paperless' van As Takes Sappi to New Heights," *Sake,* March 2, 2002.

Passi, Peter, "South African Company Takes Over Pulp, Paper Mill in Potlatch, Minn.," *Duluth News-Tribune,* May 11, 2002.

"Sappi Fine Paper North America to Suspend Operations at Muskegon Mill," *PR Newswire,* March 2, 2009.

"Sappi Signs Deal to Buy Potlatch Coated Business," *Graphic Arts Monthly,* April 2002.

"Sappi Successfully Concludes Acquisition of M-real's Coated Graphic Paper Business," *PR Newswire,* December 31, 2008.

"Sappi to Buy Potlatch," *In-Plant Graphics,* May 2002.

Sikhakhane, Jabulani, "Sappi's Paper Trail Leads Offshore," *Business Times* (New Zealand), November 23, 1997.

Walker, Julie, "Sappi Walks Tall Again Despite Heavy Weather," *Business Times* (New Zealand), December 5, 1999.

Selfridges Retail Ltd.

■

40 Dukes Street
London, W1A 1AB
United Kingdom
Telephone: (44 113) 369 8040
Web site: http://www.selfridges.com

Private Company
Incorporated: 1909 as Selfridges
Employees: 3,000
Sales: £655 million ($956 million) (2008)
NAICS: 452110 Department Stores

■ ■ ■

In business for more than 100 years, Selfridges Retail Ltd. remains a true department store pioneer. Long a fixture on London's Oxford Street, Selfridges opened its first branch in Manchester in 1998, followed within a few years by a second Manchester store and one in Birmingham.

In 1998, the company was spun off from former parent Sears Plc (not to be confused with the United States' Sears Roebuck and Co.). After spending the next few years as a public company, in 2003, it was acquired by Galen Weston, of the Canadian-Irish grocery and retail empire.

Selfridges has positioned itself as a "house of brands" and boasts 3,000 designer labels, giving them unprecedented autonomy in merchandizing. It also leases out up to half of its floor space to suppliers. Unlike most U.S. department store chains, the company eschews private labels.

A true department store, Selfridges sells much more than clothes. It is known for extensive dining operations as well as its public art installations and events, both of which establish it as a meeting place. Although it has few locations and is particularly dependent on the Oxford Street flagship, the company's wide range of product offerings gives it a broad appeal that seems to cushion it against economic downturns.

1909 ORIGINS

Selfridges is the brainchild of famed retailer Harry Gordon Selfridge, an American who came to England at the turn of the century. Described as an instinctive retailer, Selfridge belongs to the era of such retailing greats as Marshall Field. In fact, Selfridge started his career with Field, Leitner & Co., which operated the famed Chicago-based department store chain. At Field, Leitner, Selfridge was credited with a number of firsts in the retailing industry. Selfridge proposed the concept of the January sale as a means of reducing stock left over from the holiday season. Selfridge also introduced the "bargain basement" to the American shopper, and was later credited with the famous phrase: "The customer is always right."

However, Field, Leitner was not right for Selfridge. Denied a senior partnership with that company, Selfridge left his job and his country, moving to London at the age of 50. There he bought a piece of property on what was then the "dead end" of Oxford Street, paying £400,000. By the beginning of the 21st century, that same property was valued at more than £324 million. Selfridge devised a logo for his new company by combining the symbols for the U.S. dollar and the British pound.

The Selfridge department store opened in 1909 and represented a revolution in British retailing. While the United Kingdom had been credited with developing the department store concept in the early part of the 19th century, by the turn of that century, British retailing was seen as largely trailing its more innovative counterparts in Europe and the United States. The Selfridge store helped to return England to the forefront of retailing technology. Considered the world's largest department store at the time, Selfridge offered more than simply shopping counters. Inside the huge complex, shoppers found such amenities as a post office, a library, rooms dedicated to foreign visitors, and a department dedicated to selling items for clergymen.

Selfridge, a keen marketer, also had a sense of the visual, adding window displays to the outside of the department store and a rooftop garden. Inside the store, shoppers were treated to lavish displays and decorations. In 1913, the store added another innovation: a nursery for caring for customers' children while they shopped. Selfridge also began offering Christmas puddings to the bus drivers operating the routes past the Oxford Street store, encouraging the buses to stop and passengers to come into the store.

Buoyed by the store's success, Selfridge took the company public in 1921 and expanded its property holdings, giving the company one of the largest parcels of privately held land in the Oxford Street district of London. Later that same decade, Selfridges became the first department store in the world to open a department dedicated to a new invention: the television. However, the lavish decorations and upscale trimmings that had made Selfridges one of England's most prominent retailers also became the company's heaviest burden. With the stock market crash of 1929 and the worldwide depression of the 1930s, Selfridges found itself in increasing difficulties. The outbreak of World War II only exacerbated the company's troubles. H. Gordon Selfridge was finally forced to sell his company, to Lewis's Investment Trust, for £3.4 million. Selfridge, however, was to die in poverty.

MODERATE GROWTH THROUGH THE DECADES

In the mid-1960s, Selfridges caught the eye of another fast-rising retailing magnate, and the store was sold to Charles Clore in 1965. Clore had been responsible for building up the British Shoe Corporation as part of his Sears Plc retail empire. While Sears, unrelated to Sears Roebuck & Co. of the United States, built up its shoe division, which, by the late 1980s boasted more than 2,500 stores and accounted for one of every four pairs of shoes sold in the United Kingdom, it also began to invest in Selfridges. In the 1970s, Sears built the four-star Selfridge Hotel behind the department store, added a 500-car parking facility, and expanded its restaurant. While Selfridges remained an Oxford Street landmark, it also became a symbol for the dowdy department store by the late 1980s.

Selfridges also underwent a series of renovation attempts, which, in keeping with the fashion of the time, aimed to cover up the "old-fashioned" features of the building and to create a more modern appeal. This trend continued through the 1980s and into the 1990s, as Sears installed artificial ceilings and covered over such features as the huge solid bronze doors at the building's entrance, and removed much of its marble trim. Such decorative moves were nonetheless unable to counter the increasing association of "dowdy" with the Selfridges name.

In the 1990s, Sears began a new round of investments in Selfridges, including expanding its retail floor space, extending its range of restaurants, adding personal shopping services, and a beauty salon. Meanwhile, Sears was apparently neglecting its core British Shoe Corporation business. By the early 1990s, consumer shoe tastes and habits had changed, with people opting not only for sneakers instead of shoes, but also eschewing the small specialty shoe shops that made up the bulk of British Shoe Corporation's store chain in favor of buying their shoes in the same store they bought their clothing.

By the mid-1990s, Sears, once a dominant player in the United Kingdom retail market, had earned the prefix "struggling." The company seemed unable to counter its dwindling sales, despite successive reorganizations. By the second half of the 1990s, Sears's management saw no choice but to begin selling its holdings, including breaking up the British Shoe Corpora-

KEY DATES

1909: Harry Gordon Selfridge opens Oxford Street store.
1913: Adds nursery, window displays, and rooftop garden.
1921: Selfridges goes public.
1928: First dedicated television department.
1965: Acquisition by Sears Plc.
1970s: Adds four-star Selfridge Hotel and Food Hall.
1995: Opens first Heathrow Airport store; begins £100 million renovation of Oxford Street store.
1996: Opens second Heathrow Airport store.
1997: Closes both Heathrow stores.
1998: Selfridges spun off as public company; opens a second store, at Manchester's Trafford Centre.
1999: Oxford Street renovation completed; begins development of Birmingham store.
2002: Manchester Exchange Square store opens.
2003: Canadian department store entrepreneur Galen Weston acquires Selfridges for $1.1 billion; Birmingham store opens.
2009: Selfridges celebrates 100th anniversary.

chain of home furnishings stores. Since joining Selfridges in 1996, Radice had helped push through a massive seven-year, £100 million renovation plan meant to restore the Selfridges building to its previous splendor.

Radice also broke from Selfridges's long identification with the single Oxford Street store when he announced plans to build a new £43 million store in Manchester, in the north of England. At one-third the size of the Oxford Street store, the new Selfridges was also moving out of town, to a new £600 million shopping complex. While some observers were initially skeptical about the company's chances at this new location, which opened in 1998, the Manchester Selfridges quickly outpaced its projections, turning profitable by the end of 1999.

The public listing had immediately attracted the attention of British Land Corporation, led by John Ritblatt, which began acquiring stock in Selfridges. From an early position of more than 6 percent, British Land built up shares worth more than 13 percent of Selfridges stock by the end of the century. These moves fueled rumors that Selfridges might be taken over, or acquired outright. Radice, however, insisted on the company's determination to maintain its independence.

The renovation of the Oxford Street store reached completion in 1999 and immediately proved its worth, as shoppers returned to the store in force, raising company profits and sales. As Radice pointed out to the *Sunday Telegraph*, "Gordon Selfridge used to say this is not a store but a community centre. I believe this. It is not about selling goods but entertaining people." At the same time as entertaining the store's customers, however, Radice also took steps to increase their likelihood of buying. Among the company's initiatives was the introduction of a "house of brands" concept, separating departments into a collection of in-store boutiques for such famed brand names as Gucci, Calvin Klein, and Yves Rocher. "What you want is the feeling you get when you walk down Bond Street," Radice told the *Independent*, "You enter the Gucci store there or the Gucci space here and it is the same experience, the same ambience, staff with the same kind of knowledge of the product. But our big advantage is that here, if you want to return a Gucci jumper, you can pick up some Patrick Cox shoes instead."

With sales rising to £360 million and profits doubling over the previous year to top £27 million in 1999, Selfridges turned buoyantly to the future. By then, the company had started construction on a third store, tagging some £40 million for a venue that would be part of the revitalization of the Birmingham Bull Ring district. Selfridges also announced its intention to expand to as many as five stores, with Glasgow and

tion into its component brands to competitors. The company's Cable & Co. chain was purchased, for example, by the United States's Nine West. By the time the last of British Shoe Corporation had been sold, Sears had managed to lose more than £240 million on the breakup. Meanwhile, the company, criticized for holding on to Selfridges while shedding its core shoe business, was having troubles there, too. Its attempt to move beyond the London city center, notably with the opening of two new stores near Heathrow airport, first in 1995, with the second added in 1996, met with failure. The company was forced to abandon the Heathrow stores in 1997.

A NEW LOOK FOR A NEW CENTURY

By then, Sears was forced to begin looking for ways to shed the rest of its holdings. In 1997, the company decided to spin off Selfridges, a move that was completed in 1998 when Selfridges returned to a separate listing on the London stock exchange. By then, Selfridges had brought in Vittorio Radice, who had previously worked wonders turning around the Habitat

Newcastle among the company's top choices for its new locations. Selfridges announced ambitious plans for the recently renovated Oxford Street store as well. Seeking a real estate partner, with British Land among the favorites, to provide financing and expertise, Radice announced plans for a radical new extension of the Oxford site. In addition to adding 100,000 square feet of selling space, the new plans called for the construction of an office tower and residential complex above the site, as well as a new hotel and cinema.

Radice's initiatives helped Selfridges increase sales through some serious economic downturns. In 2001, the company posted pretax income of £45 million, the bulk of it attributed to the London store. Total sales were £402 million. Because Selfridges appealed to a broader cross section of the public than other high profile retailers like Harrods, it was less exposed to fall-offs in tourist traffic such as that following the September 11, 2001, terrorist attacks on the United States.

Some of Radice's most visible gestures were elaborate events staged to create a sense of spectacle to draw crowds. These were organized around such exotic themes as Tokyo (2001), Bollywood (2002), and Brazil (2004). One notorious stunt called Body Craze had dozens of nude people riding the venerable London store's escalators (2003).

CHANGES IN LEADERSHIP, OWNERSHIP

Department store rival Marks & Spencer lured away Radice in March 2003, assigning him to head its home furnishings unit. His successor as chief executive at Selfridges was Peter Williams, who had been with the company for about a dozen years, part of them as finance director. He continued the ambitious expansion program geared toward satisfying the growth expectations of the company.

With its valuable real estate holdings, Selfridges made a conspicuous takeover target as a public company. The Oxford Street location alone was estimated to be worth £358 million in 2001. Its property altogether was worth £383 million, which rivaled its entire valuation on the stock market.

Selfridges was ultimately acquired in 2003 by Canadian tycoon Galen Weston, who put forth a bid of £600 million ($1.1 billion), beating out other prominent entrepreneurs such as Tom Hunter and Robert Tchenguiz. The company's own chief executive, Peter Williams, had proffered a management buyout as well.

Through his holding company, Weston already owned department stores in Canada (Holt Renfrew) and

Ireland (Brown Thomas) and did not feel a pressing need for more geographic expansion. Weston canceled plans for stores in Bristol, Leeds, and Newcastle, preferring instead to refurbish existing ones.

The planned Glasgow store was also put on hold indefinitely, although Selfridges had acquired the land for that site. The company had also shelved its planned £300 million expansion for its Oxford Street site, which would have added a five-star hotel and office tower while increasing retail space.

Selfridges had opened a store at Manchester's Exchange Square in September 2002. There, it occupied part of a building put up by rival Marks & Spencer plc three years earlier, only ten miles away from Selfridges's existing Trafford Centre store.

Selfridges did proceed with the opening of a new, $64 million store in Birmingham in September 2003. At four stories and 270,000 square feet, it was a colossus and, like the Oxford Street store, did not require a sign outside for customers to identify it. It was shaped like a spacecraft and clad in thousands of metal discs.

Apparently frustrated with the curtailment of expansion plans, Peter Williams resigned in February 2004 and was replaced by Paul Kelly, who had led Weston's Dublin-based department store chain Brown Thomas for ten years. Members of Galen Weston's family held other key positions; he was said to work closely with his wife, Hilary. Their daughter, Alannah Weston, the new creative director, curtailed the annual spectacles established by Radice in favor of more frequent, smaller events. She was fond of incorporating contemporary art into displays.

The new management continued to update the store's presentation. In 2007 it installed a $20 million, 20,000-square-foot "Wonder Room" of luxurious gifts at a wide range of price points. True to Selfridges tradition, it was part entertainment, part sales. According to *WWD*, the company was responding to a shifting of the retail environment, which strengthened the lower end of the market at the expense of midpriced goods, while demand for premium luxuries remained high.

Selfridges had much to celebrate at the time of its 100th anniversary in 2009. Even in a dismal global economy, revenues were up 10 percent to £655 million ($956 million) in the fiscal year ended January 31, 2008. Income rose 30 percent to £84 million.

M. L. Cohen
Updated, Frederick C. Ingram

PRINCIPAL OPERATING UNITS

London; Manchester Trafford; Manchester Exchange; Birmingham.

PRINCIPAL COMPETITORS

Harvey Nichols Group Limited; House of Fraser Limited; John Lewis Partnership plc; Harrods Limited; Marks & Spencer p.l.c.

FURTHER READING

"American Store Pleases London," *New York Times*, April 18, 1909, p. C4.

Butler, Sarah, and Jenny Davey, "Selfridges Abandons £300m Oxford St Scheme," *Times* (London), Bus. Sec., May 12, 2004, p. 21.

Conti, Samantha, "Creating a New Selfridges," *WWD*, March 20, 2007, p. 3.

———, "Weston Freezes Selfridges' Expansion," *WWD*, October 29, 2003, p. 3.

Cope, Nigel, "Selfridges to Raise £360m from Flagship Store Deal," *Independent* (London), March 10, 2003, p. 17.

Dickson, E. Jane, "The Retail Therapist," *Independent* (London), April 24, 1999, p. 14.

Fanning, Aengus, "Every Day, in Retail, We Start All Over Again," *Sunday Independent* (Ireland), April 26, 2009.

Hardcastle, Elaine, "Selfridges in New Store, Development Plans," *Reuters*, February 16, 2000.

———, "Selfridges' Profits Eclipse Rivals," *Reuters*, March 30, 2000.

Honeycombe, Gordon, *Selfridges: Seventy-Five Years; The Story of the Store, 1909–1984*, London: Park Lane, 1984.

Kay, William, "Selfridges Wrestles with £600m Dilemma," *Independent* (London), May 12, 2003, p. 15.

Maier, Matthew, "The Department Store Rises Again: Wild Stunts and Clever Designs Have Transformed the Stuffy Selfridges Chain into a Collection of Hip and Happening Spaces," *Business 2.0*, August 2004, pp. 56f.

Menkes, Suzy, "100 Years of Seducing Shoppers," *International Herald Tribune*, April 28, 2009.

Patten, Sally, "Selfridges Squares Up Against Knightsbridge Rival—Head-to-Head—Harvey Nichols Versus Selfridges," *Times* (London), April 6, 2002, p. T47.

Potter, Ben, "Selfridges Lifted by Makeover," *Daily Telegraph*, October 1, 1999, p. 37.

Ravlin, Richard, "Selfridges Relishes Its New Liberty," *Sunday Telegraph*, June 21, 1998. p. 6.

Rozhon, Tracie, "From a London Retailer, Ways to Create a Sense of Theater," *New York Times*, December 1, 2003, p. C12.

———, "High Fashion, from Front Door to the Top Floor," *New York Times*, July 31, 2003, p. C1.

Staples, Laura, "A Century for Mr. Selfridge and His Spirit Lives On," *Spectator*, March 14, 2009.

Suff, Rachel, "Retail Therapy: Resourcing Staff at Selfridges," *IRS Employment Review*, January 14, 2005, pp. 47f.

Thomas, Helen, "Self-Assured," *PropertyWeek*, April 17, 2003, pp. 30–32.

Van der Post, Lucia, "The Idea That a Department Store Is for Buying Things Is Very Old Millennium Luxury," *Times* (London), September 6, 2002.

Woodhead, Lindy, *Shopping, Seduction & Mr Selfridge: The Extraordinary Rise and Fall of a Retail Prince*, London: Profile, 2008.

Worsley, Giles, "The Grande Dame of Shopping Gets Sexy," *Daily Telegraph*, December 17, 1999, p. 26.

Smiths Group plc

◼

765 Finchley Road
London, NW11 8DS
United Kingdom
Telephone: (44 20) 8458-3232
Fax: (44 20) 8454-4380
Web site: http://www.smiths-group.com

Public Company
Incorporated: 1914 as S. Smith & Sons (Motor Accessories) Ltd.
Employees: 22,600
Sales: $4.60 billion (2008)
Stock Exchanges: London
Ticker Symbol: SMIN
NAICS: 339112 Surgical and Medical Instrument Manufacturing; 339113 Surgical Appliance and Supplies Manufacturing; 334419 Other Electronic Component Manufacturing; 334513 Instruments and Related Products Manufacturing for Measuring, Displaying, and Controlling Industrial Process Variables

◼ ◼ ◼

Smiths Group plc is a diversified technology corporation that serves the threat and contraband detection, energy, medical devices, communications, and engineered components markets across the globe. The company operates five divisions including Smiths Detection, Smiths Medical, John Crane, Smiths Interconnect, and Flex-Tek. Smiths, formerly known as Smiths Industries, merged with the TI Group in 2000 and adopted the Smiths Group name shortly thereafter. With its corporate headquarters located on the north side of London, the company has gradually expanded its manufacturing and sales offices around the world and operates facilities and offices in more than 50 countries. The company sold its Smiths Aerospace division in 2007 to General Electric Company in a $4.8 billion deal.

EARLY HISTORY

The company roots date back to 1851, when Samuel Smith established a clock and watch business in London, not far from the landmark Elephant & Castle Pub. Because of his attention to detail and his friendly manner, gentlemen throughout London flocked to Smith's small shop, and by 1871 the proprietor had opened his second location. Smith's death in 1875 did not interrupt the prosperity of his enterprise, which was taken over by his son, Samuel Smith, Jr. In fact, the company was growing so rapidly that Samuel Smith, Jr., decided not only to move to a larger space in London, but also to open three new shops in different parts of the city.

By the dawn of the 20th century, the Smith family clock and watch business had become one of the notably successful enterprises in the imperial city of London. The company then turned its attention to the needs of the nascent automobile industry. Employing the skills of watchmaking learned from his father, Allan Gordon Smith diversified into the design and manufacture of automobile instruments and was one of the driving forces behind the creation of the odometer.

In just a few years Smith had garnered a reputation as one of the most innovative designers of instrumentation for the automobile industry. As a result, at the request of King Edward VII, Smith invented the speedometer and had the first one inserted in the monarch's Mercedes. By 1908 the family business was selling more than 100 speedometers each week.

With the company taking advantage of the increasing popularity of the automobile, Smith decided to incorporate the family enterprise as S. Smith & Sons (Motor Accessories) Ltd. in July 1914. Business was booming, and the firm employed more than 300 people. More than 50,000 Smith speedometers were being used in cars of various design and manufacture throughout the United Kingdom, while more and more orders were received at company headquarters every day. Nevertheless, it was the advent of World War I that not only increased the firm's productivity, but also earned it a reputation throughout Europe.

When the conflict began in August 1914, the British government immediately contracted Smith & Sons to design and manufacture a wide range of products for the war effort, including such items as wristwatches, kite balloon wind indicators, and tachometers. As the war progressed and the British Isles were drained of manpower and material goods, the government called upon Smith & Sons to expand its product line to include wire rope, signal lamps, spark plugs for airplane engines, and shell fuses. In 1917 the company originated the standard Clift airspeed indicator, which soon became the most widely used airspeed indicator within the aviation industry.

DIVERSIFICATION

When World War I ended in 1917, Smith & Sons continued the diversification program that it started during the conflict. Soon the company was selling ebonite batteries and spark plugs and manufacturing jacks for automobiles. Throughout the decade of the 1920s Smith & Sons continued its emphasis on manufacturing automotive accessories, such as speedometers. Allan Gordon Smith was well aware of the burgeoning demands of the aviation industry, however, and this led him to form Smiths Aircraft Instruments Division during the late 1920s. At approximately the same time, Smith established the All British Escarpment Company LTD to manufacture platform lever escarpments for clocks.

Although the company maintained its strong presence in the automotive accessories market, including the manufacture of ignitions, starters, and automotive lights, it was the Aircraft Instruments Division that came up with innovative designs throughout the decade of the 1930s. In 1932 the company produced the first electrical aviation fuel gauge, and not long afterwards the Aircraft Instruments Division established and opened its own aircraft manufacturing factory. Within this facility during the middle and late 1930s company engineers were at the forefront of experimenting with and developing oil pressure gauges for aircraft and electrical thermometers. By 1936 the company's system of remote indication had been installed on almost all aircraft built in Britain and soon would become the standard within the industry.

In 1937, war threatened the European continent and the aggressive expansionist policy and racism of Germany's Nazi regime began to concern many governments around the world. During this time, Allan Gordon Smith was invited to the United States to discuss developments in the aviation industry. Along with seven of his best engineers, Smith conducted a comprehensive analysis of U.S. aviation technology and manufacturing methods and also discussed how Britain and the United States could best share this technology in the event of another world war. Gathering as much information from the United States as he could, Smith and his management team upon returning to London decided to decentralize the company's operations in anticipation of Nazi aircraft raids on Britain. Management's first move was to relocate many of the company's manufacturing facilities to rural areas outside London.

When World War II started on September 1, 1939, as the Nazi war machine invaded Poland, S. Smith & Sons (Motor Accessories) Ltd. was well prepared for the conflict. Almost immediately, the company's manufacturing facilities were retooled to produce war materials and supplies, including large quantities of aircraft spark plugs, gauges, clocks, watches, speedometers, and a wide variety of aviation instruments. In May 1940, with the fall of France to the

KEY DATES

1851: Samuel Smith establishes clock and watch business in London.
1908: The family business is selling more than 100 speedometers each week.
1914: The family enterprise incorporates as S. Smith & Sons (Motor Accessories) Ltd.
1917: The company originates the standard Clift airspeed indicator.
1932: The first electrical aviation fuel gauge is produced.
1936: The company's system of remote indication has been installed on almost all aircraft built in Britain.
1944: Management reorganizes the entire firm and changes its name to S. Smith & Sons, Ltd.
1961: S. Smith wins a large contract to make aviation instruments for the Boeing Company.
1965: The company changes its name to Smiths Industries Ltd.
1987: Smiths buys Lear Siegler Holdings Corporation.
2000: Smiths merges with TI Group plc; the company adopts the Smiths Group plc name.
2001: TI Automotive Ltd. is spun off.
2004: The company lands a $1.6 billion supplier contract for Boeing's 787 Dreamliner aircraft.
2005: Medex Inc. is acquired.
2007: Smiths Aerospace is sold to General Electric Company.

Nazi regime imminent, the British government helped the company to open a new manufacturing facility for highly sophisticated aviation clocks in Cheltenham, England.

With high-volume production methods learned from the United States a short time earlier, Smith & Sons significantly contributed to the Royal Air Force's ability to prevent Nazi Germany from invading the British Isles. Pilots from Britain's famous Spitfire fighter aircraft relied heavily on the aviation instrumentation and accessories provided by Smith & Sons. As the tide of war turned in favor of Britain and its Allies, especially after the invasion of Nazi-occupied Europe on June 6, 1944, the company began to focus its attentions on the opportunities that would present themselves in the postwar period. Approving a comprehensive strategic plan near the end of 1944, management reorganized the entire firm, first by changing the name to S. Smith & Sons, Ltd., and then by dividing its commercial operations into four subsidiaries: Smiths Motor Accessories, Ltd., Smiths Aircraft Instruments Ltd., Smiths English Clocks, Ltd., and Smiths Industrial Instruments, Ltd. In addition, the company formed a joint venture to manufacture car radios, as well as another joint venture, the Anglo-Celtic Watch Company.

THE POSTWAR ERA

The late 1940s and the entire decade of the 1950s were years of rapid expansion and growth for the company. In 1947 management at the firm implemented a strategic plan that led to the establishment of the company's first subsidiaries outside the United Kingdom. A factory in Witney, Oxfordshire, was purchased in 1949 to enhance the company's automotive product line, while at the same time management decided to diversify product lines in its other operating divisions. One of the most important acquisitions during this time involved the purchase of Portland Plastics and its subsidiary, Surgical Plastics, two companies well positioned for growth in the burgeoning medical equipment business. As the company grew, it did not ignore the welfare of its workers. Sympathetic to the ideals and vision of the postwar socialist-leaning governments of Britain, the company joined with housing authorities near Smith & Sons factories to build a total of 192 employee dwellings.

By the early 1960s Smith & Sons had grown so large that management initiated a comprehensive reorganization strategy, including the decentralization of its operations, greater diversification of its product lines, and a broader delegation of authority. Although the primary source of revenue continued to be the automotive accessories division, the company was making a strong move to capture more of the aviation instruments market. This aggressiveness paid off handsomely in 1961 when the company won a large contract to make aviation instruments for the Boeing Company, one of the largest aircraft manufacturers in the United States.

During the middle of the decade the company expanded its capacity to produce automotive spark plugs through the acquisition of Lodge Plus, Ltd., and established a technical service center at Heathrow Airport, one of the first of its kind. The one engineering feat that brought the company international recognition was the design of an innovative autopilot equipment system that enabled a civil airliner to land in foggy weather with no more than 50 feet of visibility. From this time forward, the company's reputation in the civil aircraft instrumentation market was assured. To reflect the growing diversity of its product line, management changed the company name from Smith & Sons to Smiths Industries plc in 1965.

A NEW STRATEGIC POLICY

During the late 1960s the company's clock business suffered from the glut of Eastern European imports and low-cost components manufactured in Asia. Smiths Industries attempted to counterbalance these trends with a network of its own low-cost suppliers from foreign countries, but sales for the firm's clock business continued to decline throughout the 1970s. In 1979 management decided finally to discontinue the firm's clock business and permanently closed all related manufacturing facilities. Simultaneously, the automotive industry across Britain entered into a lengthy period of sluggish sales, and the firm's motor accessories production output dropped dramatically.

Traditionally, Smiths Industries revealed the talent and resourcefulness of its management at times when the company was confronted with major problems. Acting quickly and decisively, management implemented a new strategic policy that involved divesting all of the less profitable operations, while expanding the more lucrative and promising businesses. During the early 1980s the company sold its automotive instrumentation business and ceased operations in the automotive radio business. These two divestitures were followed by an announcement that Smiths Industries no longer would manufacture or supply original equipment to the automotive industry in Europe.

Building upon the foundation established in the 1950s and 1960s, management focused on developing the company's medical and aerospace businesses. Portex, formed from the firm's Portland Plastics and Surgical Plastics subsidiaries, quickly grew into the most lucrative operation within the company. An ever-increasing line of new products and an aggressive acquisitions strategy catapulted Portex into a leadership position within the medical supplies market. The company's newly created Smiths Industries Aerospace and Defense Systems Division also grew rapidly. Adhering to a similar aggressive acquisitions policy in the aerospace business, the company purchased Lear Siegler Holdings Corporation in 1987 and immediately skyrocketed to a leadership role within the American aerospace industry. By the end of the 1980s Smiths Industries had reorganized its operations into three divisions, including Aerospace and Defense, Medical Systems, and Industrial. In 1988 the company reported a rise in pretax profits of nearly 50 percent.

GROWTH CONTINUES

During the early 1990s Smiths Industries not only consolidated its share in the aerospace, medical systems, and industrial components markets, but continued an aggressive and unabated campaign to grow through strategic acquisitions, research and development, and new manufacturing technologies. The company placed particular emphasis on increasing its presence in the United Kingdom, Germany, Japan, and the United States. Two of the major achievements by the company at this time involved the acquisition of Japan Medico, a large medical equipment manufacturer that provided Smiths Industries with access to a burgeoning Asian market, and a contract with Boeing to supply electrical load management systems for the newly designed Boeing 777 commercial jumbo jet.

In the mid-1990s the company's Aerospace business had become known as one of the most innovative manufacturers within the industry. The company's Flight Management System, auto-throttles, standby instruments, and fully integrated satellite-based navigation system were purchased by commercial airlines around the world. Smiths Industries' Medical Systems Division, manufacturing a wide array of products such as disposable colostomy pouches, speaking aids for tracheostomy patients, and single use devices for administering anesthesia, also became known for its innovative approach to health care products. The Industrial Division, focusing on international ducting and hosing manufacturing, and air-moving products for consumer, industrial, and commercial applications, such as heating elements for clothes dryers, had developed into one of the most lucrative operations in the company's modern history, with an annual increase in sales of more than 20 percent from 1994 to 1997. Growth continued in 1998 and 1999 as the company continued its aggressive acquisition spree.

MOVING INTO THE 21ST CENTURY

Smiths Industries entered the new millennium on solid ground. It continued to grow at breakneck speed, adding several new companies to its arsenal in 2000. Its most notable move that year was its merger with TI Group plc, an engineering conglomerate based in Abingdon, England. The company changed its name to Smiths Group plc later that year, and then in 2001 spun off TI's automotive holdings as TI Automotive Ltd. Along with strategic acquisitions, Smiths also worked to secure lucrative contracts. In 2001, the company inked a $160 million deal with the U.S. Army to provide development services for Crusader, the army's artillery program. The terrorist attacks against the United States on September 11, 2001, and the ensuing wars in Afghanistan and Iraq prompted an increased demand for its defense-related products and services but also caused a sudden slowdown in its Aerospace Division.

The aerospace industry was experiencing a wave of consolidation and Smiths was poised to bolster this portion of its business. The company expected the downturn in the industry to be short-lived and spent most of 2004 making five key purchases that significantly increased its aerospace holdings. It also secured a $1.6 billion contract that year to supply landing gear and various other electronics systems to Boeing's new 787 Dreamliner, an aircraft that remained in development in 2009. The company's investments over the past several years paid off handsomely as the industry did indeed rebound. By 2006, Smiths Aerospace was securing revenues of $2.4 billion and the company had become an attractive suitor. General Electric Co., looking to expand its burgeoning aviation arm, made a play for Smiths' Aerospace Division in early 2007. The $4.8 billion purchase was finalized later that year.

Meanwhile, the company continued to expand its Smiths Medical Division. The company made one of its largest acquisitions to date when it purchased Medex Inc. in 2005 for $925 million. By adding Medex to its holdings, Smiths gained a stronger foothold in the safety devices market. Medex's product line included anesthesia equipment, infusion products used in intensive care units, and intravenous infusion catheters that prevented needle-stick injuries in health care workers.

Philip Bowman was named CEO of Smiths Group in 2007. Bowman had a reputation for splitting apart large companies, and many investors were beginning to speculate, according to an October 2007 *Daily Telegraph* article, that Smiths was no longer worth more than the sum of its parts. As investors urged for a breakup of the conglomerate-type company, both Bowman and Chairman Donald Brydon were determined to keep Smiths intact while restructuring group operations and cutting costs to shore up profits at its divisions.

Bowman worked to revamp Smiths Group's operating structure and by 2009, Smiths Group was organized into five divisions, including Smiths Detection, Smiths Medical, John Crane, Smiths Interconnect, and Flex-Tek. While company management remained confident Smiths Group and its divisions were on track for success

in the future, only time would tell if the company would succumb to its investors' wishes.

Thomas Derdak
Updated, Christina M. Stansell

PRINCIPAL DIVISIONS

Smiths Detection; Smiths Medical; John Crane; Smiths Interconnect; Flex-Tek.

PRINCIPAL COMPETITORS

B. Braun Medical Inc.; Flowserve Corporation; GE Security Inc.

FURTHER READING

Deveney, Paul J., "Smiths Industries PLC," *Wall Street Journal,* October 16, 1997, p. A15.

Endres, Gunter, "Toward the 'Intelligent' Aircraft," *Interavia Aerospace Review,* April 1991, p. 57.

Firn, David, "Smiths Expands Its Medical Footprint," *Financial Times,* December 7, 2004.

"GE Aviation Completes Acquisition of Smiths Aerospace," *Military Technology,* June 1, 2007.

The History of Smiths Industries Plc, London: Smiths Industries, Plc, 1994.

"Hi-Tech Engine Monitoring Systems," *Interavia Business & Technology,* June 1994, p. 51.

Hotten, Russell, "Will Smiths Vanish Like Other Icons?" *Daily Telegraph,* October 1, 2007.

Nordwall, Bruce D., "Glareshield Displays, Voice Control to Aid Pilots," *Aviation Week & Space Technology,* July 17, 1995, p. 59.

———, "New FMS to Offer 737 Fuel Savings," *Aviation Week & Space Technology,* March 27, 1995, p. 48.

———, "Smiths Industries Will Supply," *Aviation Week & Space Technology,* August 1, 1994, p. 64.

Pfeifer, Sylvia, "Revolution from the Top Sees Smiths Making More Cuts to Fit," *Financial Times,* August 11, 2008.

———, "Smiths Plans Two-Year Turnaround," *Financial Times,* March 20, 2008.

Proctor, Paul, "Sonic Fuel Measuring," *Aviation Week & Space Technology,* August 8, 1994, p. 13.

"Smiths Is Set for Defence Boom," *Gloucestershire Echo,* September 28, 2001.

Young, Jonathan, "Young Gun to Industry Bigshot," *Management Today,* June 1996, p. 96.

STIEBEL ELTRON

Stiebel Eltron Group

—————•—————

Dr.-Stiebel-Strasse
Holzminden, D-37603
Germany
Telephone: (49 5531) 702-0
Fax: (49 5531) 702-95480
Web site: http://www.stiebel-eltron.de

Private Company
Incorporated: 1924 as Eltron Dr. Theodor Stiebel
Employees: 3,000
Sales: EUR 460 million ($648.48 million) (2008 est.)
NAICS: 333414 Heating Equipment (Except Warm Air Furnaces) Manufacturing; 333415 Air-Conditioning and Warm Air Heating Equipment and Commercial and Industrial Refrigeration Equipment Manufacturing

■ ■ ■

Stiebel Eltron Group is one of Europe's leading manufacturers of heat pumps, water heaters, and other heating equipment and supplies almost 30 percent of all water heaters in Thailand. Stiebel Eltron also makes ventilation and air conditioning equipment for both residential and commercial buildings and maintains a special focus on renewable energy technologies. The company's range of products includes wall-mounted and freestanding electric heaters and water heaters, dehumidifiers and air conditioners, air source and ground source heat pumps (heat pumps that use thermal energy in the surrounding air or in the ground for heating purposes), solar thermal water heaters and compact solar heating systems as well as ventilation devices and systems. The company's subsidiary Geowell offers drilling services for heat pump projects.

Stiebel Eltron's main production facility is located at company headquarters in Holzminden, about 40 miles southwest of Hanover. Additional production plants are located in nearby Eschwege, in Slovakia, Thailand, and China where the company's shower units (compact wall-mounted water heaters with an attached adjustable shower head and a wall-mounted holder kit) and wall-mounted hand dryers are produced. Stiebel Eltron products are distributed globally through about 15 subsidiaries and 20 sales offices, mainly in Western and Eastern Europe, but also in Asia, the United States, Australia, and Africa. Foreign sales account for over 40 percent of the total. Organized under the umbrella of Dr. Theodor Stiebel Werke GmbH & Co. KG, the family business is owned and run by the company founder's two sons.

HEAD START WITH IMMERSION HEATERS

It was the first half of the 1920s in Berlin, when a young mechanical engineer by the name of Theodor Stiebel worked on his dissertation on the construction and manufacturing principles of immersion heaters, short metal wands used to bring small amounts of water to a boil, for example, for a cup of tea. The models already on the market were heavy and needed a very long time to heat up and cool down again, and a great deal of electrical energy was wasted heating the appliance instead of the water. Stiebel's goal was to develop a new kind of immersion heater with a much better performance. In contrast to the then common piston-shaped models, Stiebel gave the heating element of his immersion heater the shape of a hollow cylinder. This way the area available for heating the water was greatly enlarged. The wall of the cylinder was less than three millimeters thick, making it much lighter than conventional models.

Convinced that his new invention would be a market success, Stiebel built 100 samples of his immersion heater and rented a booth at the Leipzig Spring Fair, a popular consumer trade show in Germany at the time. Not only did Stiebel sell all his samples, he received orders for 600 more. Encouraged by this immediate success, Stiebel decided to set up his own company. On May 5, 1924, the young engineer founded Eltron Dr. Theodor Stiebel in Berlin. For the next three years, Stiebel's ring-type immersion heaters were manufactured in a small workshop in a Berlin courtyard.

By 1927 Eltron Dr. Theodor Stiebel employed 30 workers and was grossing 185,000 reichsmarks. In that year Stiebel began adding new products to his line, starting with a wall-mounted electric unit in which water was instantaneously heated as it flowed through—in German, a *Durchlauferhitzer*. In the following years the company put out water heaters and boilers of different sizes and specifications, including high-pressure boilers and water heaters that could hold up to 600 liters. With 200 workers on the payroll by 1934, Stiebel's enterprise had outgrown its premises and was therefore moved to a much larger factory building in Berlin's Tempelhof district. Four years later Eltron

launched a large *Durchlauferhitzer,* which was mounted on a base equipped with rollers. The beginning of World War II in 1939, however, put a sudden end to the company's rapid growth as a manufacturer of consumer goods.

A NEW START AT A NEW LOCATION DURING WARTIME

When the Nazis forbade the use of copper in hot water tanks in the late 1930s, Eltron's engineers feverishly experimented with alternatives, such as enameled steel tanks, to maintain the company's production. With the outbreak of World War II, however, civil production came to a sudden halt. Instead, Eltron became a part of the Nazi-controlled war economy and was ordered to manufacture a variety of war goods. In the beginning the company provided hot water tanks to military hospitals. Later, Eltron produced special heater ovens for air-raid shelters, defrosting devices for airplanes, electric heating devices for flak spotlight power units and for fur boots for pilots, as well as electric components for machine guns and ammunition detonators.

In 1943 the Eltron factory in Berlin was heavily damaged in a bombing raid. While a part of the production was moved temporarily to two other locations, the company founder immediately started looking for a new suitable site and, with the help of a relative, found it in Holzminden, a city of 20,000 in Lower Saxony. Leased at first, Stiebel later acquired the large property, where the construction of new production facilities began immediately. Renamed Eltron Werk G.m.b.H. in spring 1944, the company began to manufacture tail units for the V-1 flying bomb, an early German version of a cruise missile. As the war progressed, a rising number of women, prisoners of war, and forced laborers worked at the company. Accounts of the company's total workforce in the last war year varied from several hundred to approximately 2,500.

STARTING OVER WITH WATER HEATERS

After the war had ended in early spring 1945, the city of Holzminden and Eltron came under the administration of the U.S. military. By the summer the company had attained a production permit and Eltron manufactured what was most desperately needed in German households: pots and frying pans, irons, and laundry sprinklers. With the Holzminden factory fully functional again, Eltron, once again, began to produce immersion heaters. The company, which employed a few hundred workers at the time, also produced convection ovens and hot plates. After the British military

KEY DATES

1924: Mechanical engineer Theodor Stiebel founds his own company in Berlin.
1927: The production of water heaters begins.
1943: A new start is made in Holzminden after the Berlin factory is damaged during the war.
1953: The new company name, Stiebel Eltron, is introduced as a brand name.
1968: Stiebel Eltron's so-called night storage heater is launched.
1976: The company starts manufacturing heat pumps.
1977: Solar panels are added to Stiebel Eltron's product range.
1990: The first Stiebel Eltron air conditioners are launched.
2001: A brand-new factory is built in Thailand.
2002: German competitor Elektrolux Haustechnik is acquired.
2004: The company takes over Slovakian water heater manufacturer Tatramat.
2007: A state-of-the-art heat pump factory is built in Holzminden.
2008: An additional manufacturing plant for electric heaters is opened in China.

government had replaced the American, Eltron supplied the Brits with hot water boilers and heaters, tea kettles and irons, toasters, and hot plates. Nevertheless, despite all efforts to prevent the dismantling of the production equipment, the Allied forces confiscated Eltron's machinery and left the company with one option—to make a brand-new start.

With no public financial help the company, which was renamed Stiebel Eltron in 1952, evolved as a market leader in the area of electric hot water appliances in the 1950s. In particular, Stiebel Eltron achieved great commercial success with large water heaters and boilers during the postwar economic boom in Germany. Launched in 1949, the company's DH 18 hydraulic controlled *Durchlauferhitzer* became a bestseller as well. In 1950 Stiebel Eltron launched a combined electric-and-coal-powered hot water heater for domestic use, followed by a small wall-mounted water heater for kitchens or bathrooms. The company's over-the-sink wall-mounted water boiler EBK 5 became another bestseller.

In addition to its growing range of electric appliances for heating water, the company ventured into a

new market when it began to manufacture galley kitchens for commercial aircraft in 1952. Later in the decade Stiebel Eltron developed and manufactured large coffee makers for commercial aircraft as well. As the company's product range and output grew rapidly during the 1950s, new production facilities and administrative buildings sprang up like mushrooms in Holzminden. By the late 1950s Stiebel Eltron was grossing over 40 million deutschmarks. With about 160 patents to his name, company founder Theodor Stiebel passed away at age 66 in 1960.

SUCCESS WITH STORAGE HEATERS AND HEAT PUMPS

The passing of the company founder marked the end of the postwar boom period and opened a new chapter in Stiebel Eltron's history. In the 1960s the demand for modern household appliances that made life more convenient and comfortable rose in West Germany. In 1964, the year when the company grossed more than DEM 100 million for the first time, Stiebel Eltron introduced a convection oven that emitted heat instantly at the push of a button.

Diversification of the company's product range continued with the manufacture of domestic and commercial ironing machines and other electric appliances such as dishwashers, coffeemakers, and egg boilers. When German power companies significantly lowered their prices for electricity during the night hours because of overcapacities in the late 1960s, Stiebel Eltron's engineers developed a "night storage heater" that drew power from the grid during the night and stored the heat until it was needed during the day. Supported by a massive television advertising campaign that communicated the slogans "Cosy heat" and "Always hot water," output and sales skyrocketed in the decade that followed.

By 1973 Stiebel Eltron was grossing over DEM 240 million annually and the company began developing gas-powered heaters. The oil price shock of that year left its mark on the German economy. The costs of fuel and electricity went through the roof and ushered in the era of more fuel and energy efficient heating equipment. Stiebel Eltron jumped on the new trend and within two years developed its own model of a so-called heat pump. Reversing the technical principle of refrigerators, heat pumps drew heat from the surrounding air and used it to heat rooms. Stiebel Eltron's first model for domestic and commercial air source heat pumps was launched in 1976. In addition to ambient air heat pumps, the company also developed ground source heat pumps that absorb heat from the ground to provide heating. In 1979 the company launched its first heat pump model that was used for heating water. In the following decades Stiebel Eltron evolved as the leading supplier of heat pumps in Germany.

Another important renewable energy source that Stiebel Eltron put to use in the 1970s was solar power. The company developed high-performance flat-plate solar panels and the accompanying equipment for storing the generated energy and for heating water with it when needed in compact do-it-yourself installation kits.

FOCUS ON ELECTRIC HEATING, AIR CONDITIONING, AND VENTILATION

In the 1980s Stiebel Eltron made a strategic decision to focus on its core business (heating appliances and equipment) and discontinued the production of other household appliances. At the same time the company made a concerted effort to strengthen its marketing and distribution organization. The number of sales offices throughout Germany grew while the existing ones were enlarged. A brand-new education and training center was built at Holzminden headquarters where some 25,000 visitors—architects and craftsmen, building supplies wholesalers, and special retailers—were informed about Stiebel Eltron's products and trained in how to install and maintain them. In 1987 the company launched another innovative product, an electronically controlled instantaneous flow-through water heater that maintained the exact water temperature the user had preprogrammed. By the mid-1990s Stiebel Eltron's line of water heaters included models with a capacity ranging from 30 to 700 liters.

The growing emphasis on energy-saving construction principles in the 1980s opened up new growth opportunities for Stiebel Eltron. As buildings, including walls, doors and windows, were much better thermally insulated to minimize heating energy losses, the natural air exchange was greatly diminished. Due to insufficient ventilation, the perfectly sealed walls began to sweat, resulting in moist areas and, consequently, in the growth of fungi on inside walls. Stiebel Eltron sensed a new market and began to develop and manufacture air conditioning equipment in the 1990s. In 1990 the company launched the first Stiebel Eltron air conditioners that produced a perfect climate indoors through the combination of cooling, heating, ventilation, and dehumidifying functions. One year later Stiebel Eltron introduced its first electronically controlled ventilation system for residential buildings.

ENVIRONMENTALLY FRIENDLY TECHNOLOGIES STIR GROWTH

In the following decades the company further refined its air conditioning and ventilation products. Stiebel Eltron's line of air conditioners included models that were installed in suspended ceilings, mounted on walls, or housed in compact cabinets that blended into the room's interior design. The more sophisticated, remote-controlled units could even be used as heat pumps during the spring and fall seasons. Stiebel Eltron's state-of-the-art ventilation systems recovered up to 90 percent of the heat the units produced, which was then used for heating rooms and water.

To demonstrate the company's commitment to environmentally friendly technologies, Stiebel Eltron published "eco-balance sheets" for its line of water heaters that informed consumers about materials and energy used during the product's life cycle as well as about the emissions of substances into the environment in the mid-1990s. Stiebel Eltron's focus on innovative, energy efficient and environmentally friendly technologies paid off. In 1991 the company reported over DEM 500 million in sales for the first time. By the middle of the decade revenues had climbed to DEM 650 million. In 1998 Stiebel Eltron sold its gas technology subsidiary Hydrotherm, which accounted for roughly one-sixth of total sales.

Toward the end of the 1990s the company developed integrated heating, water heating and ventilation systems for residential and commercial buildings, a promising growth market. On the occasion of the World Expo in Hanover in 2000, Stiebel Eltron initiated a long-term research project on advanced technologies to ensure the highest possible energy efficiency as well as a healthy living environment. For that purpose, the company built a residential subdivision of 40 homes using environmentally sound concepts and materials, and equipped with different types of heating and ventilation appliances, in a Holzminden suburb. The pilot project's main goal was to cut annual energy consumption for heating purposes by about two-thirds.

NATIONAL AND INTERNATIONAL EXPANSION AND ACQUISITIONS

As the German market for heaters and water heaters stagnated in the 1990s, Stiebel Eltron ventured into new markets abroad. Almost from the very beginning, company founder Theodor Stiebel had taken steps to expand his enterprise beyond its main market. As early as in 1937 Stiebel traveled to Argentina to present his products at a trade show in Buenos Aires. In the 1950s Stiebel also presented his electric water heaters at trade shows in the United States. Thereafter, the company continuously expanded its international network of sales offices and associates. By the end of the 1990s Stiebel Eltron's international activities had spread to most of Western and Eastern Europe, the United States, Australia, and South Africa, but also to Colombia, Morocco, Namibia, Georgia, and the United Arab Emirates. In addition, the company had built a strong foothold in Asia, including Japan, Hong Kong, Singapore, the Philippines, Vietnam, Taiwan, and Thailand.

Nevertheless, Stiebel Eltron's national and international expansion reached a new level after 2000 when the company grew by leaps and bounds through massive investment in additional production capacity and through major acquisitions. In 2001 Stiebel Eltron opened a brand-new factory in Bangkok, Thailand, where simple models of instantaneous flow-through water heaters for the Asian market were produced. A major international acquisition followed in 2004 when the company took over Slovakian water heater manufacturer Tatramat, the market leader in Slovakia and the Czech Republic. Two years later Stiebel Eltron doubled its production capacity in Thailand. The company's internationally most successful products were a compact wall-mounted water heater with an attached adjustable shower head and a wall-mounted holder kit, the shower unit, and a compact wall-mounted hand dryer.

A major event in Stiebel Eltron's history was the acquisition of the European home comfort division of Swedish appliances manufacturer Electrolux, including one of the company's main competitors, Elektrolux Haustechnik GmbH, in 2002. The deal included a range of water heaters, heating appliances, air conditioning and ventilation equipment, and the well-known brand names AEG and Zanker. The takeover boosted Stiebel Eltron's sales by roughly 30 percent. Despite its international activities, Stiebel Eltron emphasized the company's commitment to keeping most of its production in Germany. As the demand for Stiebel Eltron's heat pumps continued to grow at two-digit rates in the first decade of the 2000s, Stiebel Eltron invested heavily in additional production capacity. In 2007 and 2009 the company built two state-of-the-art factories for heat pumps with a combined capacity of about 60,000 units per year in Holzminden. In 2008 a new manufacturing plant for electric heaters for the Asian and Australian markets was opened in Tianjin near Beijing.

By the end of the first decade of the 2000s exports accounted for roughly 40 percent of Stiebel Eltron's total sales, compared to 20 percent a decade earlier. Named one of Germany's Superbrands, Stiebel Eltron, with its strong focus on renewable energy sources and energy efficiency, and with a strong foothold in the growth markets of Southeast Asia and Eastern Europe, seemed well positioned for sustained future growth. In 2009 the company was aiming at becoming the number one producer of water heaters in Southeast Asia and a leading manufacturer of solar technology.

Evelyn Hauser

PRINCIPAL SUBSIDIARIES

Stiebel Eltron GmbH & Co. KG; Stiebel Eltron International GmbH; Stiebel Eltron (Guangzhou) Technology Development Co. Ltd. (China); Stiebel Eltron Asia Ltd. (Thailand); Stiebel Eltron SK (Slovakia); Stiebel Eltron Ges.m.b.H. (Austria); Stiebel Eltron AG (Switzerland); Geowell GmbH; Nihon Stiebel Co. Ltd. (Japan); Stiebel Eltron UK Ltd.; Stiebel Eltron S.A.S. (France); Stiebel Eltron Sprl. (Belgium); Stiebel Eltron Nederland B.V. (Netherlands); Stiebel Eltron, Inc. (U.S. A.); Stiebel Eltron Australia Pty Ltd; Stiebel Eltron sp. z o.o (Poland); Stiebel Eltron s.r.o. (Czech Republic); Stiebel Eltron LLC (Russia); Stiebel Eltron Kft. (Hungary).

PRINCIPAL COMPETITORS

Vaillant Group; Bosch Thermotechnik GmbH; Viessmann Werke GmbH & Co KG; Panasonic A.P. Sales (Thailand) Co., Ltd.

FURTHER READING

"Electrolux Divests Home Comfort Business," *Nordic Business Report,* November 1, 2001.

"Heater Firm to Expand Operations in Thailand," *Nation* (Thailand), January 19, 2004.

"Market Battle Hots Up," *Nation* (Thailand), September 19, 2007.

McDonough, Tony, "Energy Firm Chief's Passion for the 'Green Revolution,'" *Daily Post* (Liverpool), September 10, 2008, p. 3.

"Stiebel Eltron Aiming to Be Asia's No 2 in Water Heaters," *Nation* (Thailand), November 1, 2002.

"Stiebel Eltron erneut als 'Superbrand' ausgezeichnet," *News Aktuell Schweiz,* November 6, 2007.

"Stiebel Eltron sieht seine Zukunft in der Systemtechnik," *Frankfurter Allgemeine Zeitung,* March 27, 1999, p. 22.

"Stiebel Eltron to Sell Hydrotherm," *Welt,* October 27, 1998, p. 18.

Stiebel Eltron von 1924 bis heute, Holzminden, Germany: Stiebel Eltron GmbH & Co. KG, 2004, 109 p.

"Stiebel-Eltron will in Osteuropa expandieren," *Frankfurter Allgemeine Zeitung,* March 30, 1995, p. 25.

"Stiebel Eltron will werk in Berlin schließen," *Berliner Morgenpost,* October 28, 2005, p. 7.

"Stiebel Water-Heater Sales Steaming," *Nation* (Thailand), October 6, 2006.

"Von der Therme zum Pkw," *Automobil Industrie,* September 8, 2004, p. 87.

❖ SUMITOMO RUBBER

Sumitomo Rubber Industries, Ltd.

3-6-9 Wakihama-cho
Chuo-ku
Kobe, 651-0072
Japan
Telephone: (+81 78) 265-3004
Fax: (+81 78) 265-3113
Web site: http://www.srigroup.co.jp

Public Company
Incorporated: 1917
Employees: 5,491
Sales: ¥604.97 billion ($6.64 billion) (2008)
Stock Exchanges: Tokyo
Ticker Symbol: 5110
NAICS: 326211 Tire Manufacturing (Except Retreading)

■ ■ ■

Sumitomo Rubber Industries, Ltd., Japan's second largest automobile, truck, and race-car tire producer, manufactures tires under the Dunlop, Falken, and Goodyear brands. The company merged with Ohtsu Tire & Rubber Co. Ltd. in 2003 and created SRI Sports Ltd. and SRI Hybrid Ltd. All three companies make up the Sumitomo Rubber Group, which celebrated its 100th anniversary in 2009.

EARLY HISTORY

Sumitomo Rubber Industries, Ltd., is part of the Sumitomo group, one of Japan's largest *keiretsu*, or conglomerates. The Sumitomo group originated in a 17th-century book and medicine shop founded by Masatomo Sumitomo, a former samurai. Another Sumitomo family member perfected a method of extracting silver from crude copper by using lead, and by the late 17th century, the family ran a prominent copper mine and refinery. By the time of the Meiji Restoration in 1868, which initiated Japan's industrialization, Sumitomo's investments and development of copper mines made it one of Japan's largest companies.

The Sumitomo group owned an interest in Dunlop Japan, a unit of the British company Dunlop, when it was established in Kobe in 1909. Dunlop produced its first tires in Japan in 1913, and Sumitomo Rubber was established shortly thereafter, in 1917. A close relationship developed and continued between the two companies. By the early 1940s, the Sumitomo group had matured into one of Japan's leading *zaibatsu*, huge industrial concerns tightly controlled by a central board. When Japan went to war against the United States in 1941, all Sumitomo enterprises were pressed into military production. By the end of World War II in 1945, Sumitomo's industrial facilities had been substantially damaged by air raids, but the company was slated for rehabilitation during the postwar occupation and restoration period.

All *zaibatsu* were disbanded at that time under antimonopoly laws, so each Sumitomo unit became an independent company. When antitrust legislation was eased in the early 1950s, Sumitomo associates began reestablishing former business ties. Like other former *zaibatsu*, Sumitomo gathered its former companies together again through its family-owned bank, which facilitated cross-ownership of shares between the companies. These looser, but still powerful, industrial groups were called *keiretsu*, with Sumitomo ranking third among them, after Mitsubishi and Mitsui.

Sumitomo Electric Industries, another member of the Sumitomo group, bought a majority share of Dunlop Japan in 1963, and changed Dunlop's name to Sumitomo Rubber Industries, Ltd. (SRI). The rubber concern remained one of Sumitomo's smaller ventures, selling mostly within Japan, and ranking 12th in the world market as of 1985. By 1987, however, SRI ranked sixth in the global tire market, with tire-manufacturing bases in Europe, the United States, and Japan, the world's three centers of automobile production. With a 6 percent share of the market, it was creeping up on fourth-place Firestone and fifth-place Uniroyal; in the lead was Goodyear with 20 percent, followed by Michelin with 17 percent and Japan's Bridgestone with 8 percent.

SRI's change in standing came about through the company's acquisition of additional Dunlop operations. During the early 1980s, a growing number of Japanese companies realized that to compete in the world market, they must buy into foreign companies, thus overcoming a static home economy and trade barriers abroad. SRI became a trendsetter when it purchased a 98 percent interest in Dunlop's tire production in France, Germany, and the United Kingdom for $240 million in 1984.

THE DUNLOP PURCHASE

Dunlop was on the verge of bankruptcy when the friendly takeover was initiated. The British company had made a critical error in the early 1960s when it deemed steel-belted radial tires a passing fad. Instead of developing a steel-belted radial like pioneer Michelin, the company opted to produce lower-cost textile radial tires. These wore longer than traditional cross-ply tires, but could not perform like steel-belted radials. By the 1970s, when it was clear that steel-belted radials had superseded conventional tires, Dunlop did not have the capital to initiate steel-belted radial production.

Another of Dunlop's miscues was its acquisition of an interest in the Italian tire maker Pirelli in 1971. Pirelli had significant losses that year, and Dunlop had to write off its £40 million investment in the Italian company. The highly inflationary period of 1974–75 dealt a blow to Dunlop's borrowing power precisely when it should have been stepping up radial production. Although 1978 was one of its most profitable years to date, Dunlop's debt soon absorbed all its profits, and by 1983 the company was losing money. The company opted to reduce its product range, a mistake in the highly specialized tire market. Lack of cash meant that production facilities were in disrepair and design and development programs were canceled. Several factories were shut down as employees were cut from 5,000 to fewer than 3,500 in the United Kingdom. Morale was abysmal and even top executives quit. Finally in 1984, the British company found itself unable to refinance its French subsidiary's losses, and had to let it go into receivership.

SRI had maintained close technical and commercial links with Dunlop. Its investment in the operation was massive, and the Japanese company did not want Dunlop to fall into competitors' hands. Also, SRI saw that the Dunlop operations could be highly profitable if given the proper financial and managerial backing; so, at Dunlop's behest, it acquired most of the company's tire business in 1984. Dunlop's U.S. tire business was bought out by its management in 1984, but was acquired by SRI two years later.

DUNLOP RECOVERY PLAN

SRI changed the name of the U.K. company to SP Tyres, and the German one to SP Reifenwerke, but retained the Dunlop brand name. SRI officials predicted that the heavily loss-making U.K. operations would be profitable within three years. That appeared to be an audacious claim, but by 1986 SP Tyres achieved an operating profit, and by 1987 made after-tax profits, which increased the following year.

SRI renovated its newly acquired plants and cut the workforce by about 20 percent. The company established a ten-point recovery plan focusing on communication, training, employee participation in company goal-setting, equality among workers, cleanliness, job security, capital expenditure, staff flexibility,

KEY DATES

1909: The British company Dunlop establishes Dunlop Japan in Kobe.

1913: Dunlop produces its first tires in Japan.

1917: Sumitomo Rubber is established.

1963: Sumitomo Electric Industries buys a majority share of Dunlop and changes Dunlop's name to Sumitomo Rubber Industries, Ltd. (SRI).

1984: SRI purchases a 98 percent interest in Dunlop's tire production in France, Germany, and the United Kingdom.

1986: Dunlop's U.S. tire operations are purchased by SRI.

1999: SRI forms a $1 billion alliance with the Goodyear Tire & Rubber Company.

2003: The company merges with Ohtsu Tire & Rubber Co. Ltd.; SRI Sports Ltd. and SRI Hybrid Ltd. are created.

2006: SRI Sports lists on the Tokyo Stock Exchange.

2007: The Enasave 97 tire, made from 97 percent nonpetroleum-based materials, is launched.

The company ended the century by forming a global alliance with Goodyear Tire & Rubber Company based in the United States. The $1 billion deal called for the creation of four joint ventures in North America, Europe, and Japan, and was designed to increase sales and profits while cutting costs.

MOVING INTO THE 21ST CENTURY

Sumitomo Rubber Industries went through a major restructuring effort during the early years of the new millennium. In 2003 the company acquired the remaining shares of Ohtsu Tire & Rubber Co. Ltd. it did not already own and set plans in motion to create two new companies comprising its sports and industrial rubber products business. That year, SRI Sports Ltd. and SRI Hybrid Ltd. were created. SRI Sports was listed on the first section of the Tokyo Stock Exchange in 2006 and then acquired U.S.-based Cleveland Golf Co. the following year. All three companies—Sumitomo Rubber, SRI Sports, and SRI Hybrid—became known as the Sumitomo Rubber Group.

The merger with Ohtsu secured SRI's position as Japan's second largest tire manufacturer. The company moved forward with expansion efforts, opening a new facility in China in 2004 and then new factories in Thailand and Vietnam in 2006. At the same time, it remained focused on creating more fuel efficient and eco-friendly tires. In 2007 it launched its Enasave 97 tire, which was made from 97 percent nonpetroleum-based materials. It planned to create a tire made entirely from nonpetroleum materials by 2013. In addition, it had plans in the works to create a tire with 50 percent less rolling resistance by 2015, which would improve fuel efficiency of the vehicles on which the tires were used.

During 2008 the company experienced a sharp price increase in its raw materials while demand for tires was falling, especially in the United States. As global economies weakened, SRI was forced to cut costs to shore up profits. It began to reduce its capital spending, moved production to overseas facilities in an attempt to cut distribution costs, and curtailed management bonuses. The company celebrated its 100th anniversary in 2009 and was confident in its ability to withstand the economic pressures of the times.

Elaine Belsito
Updated, Christina M. Stansell

improved production methods, and compensation. The Japanese company, believing that local people would know their plants better than the new parent company personnel, allowed each of its newly acquired factories to maintain its own management, with Japanese advisers standing by as consultants. A massive capital investment was directed at improving quality and production efficiency, and by 1989 SP Tyres was making 40 percent more tires than before the acquisition with 30 percent fewer workers.

SRI headed into the 1990s with growth in all three of its divisions: tires, sports equipment, and allied goods. Total sales climbed 14 percent in 1990, although a depressed market for automobile tires contributed to an 81 percent decrease in profits. The drop also reflected heavy capital investment in its overseas plants. SRI looked to new technologies and improved coordination of its operations. In December 1990, it incorporated Sumitomo Rubber Europe B.V. in the Netherlands to oversee its European operations and to help prepare for the integration of the European market in 1992. It launched two new factories in 1996 and 1997 in Ichijima, Japan, and Indonesia, respectively. It was forced to close its Kobe facility after the Great Hanshin-Awaji Earthquake in 1995.

PRINCIPAL SUBSIDIARIES

SRI Sports Ltd.; SRI Hybrid Ltd.; Dunlop Falken Tyres Ltd.; Goodyear Japan Ltd.; Dunlop Goodyear Tires

Ltd.; SRI Tire Trading Ltd.; Dunlop Sports Ltd.; Dunlop Sports Enterprises Sumigomusangyo, Ltd.; Dunlop Home Products, Ltd.; Sumitomo Rubber (Changshu) Co., Ltd.; Sumitomo Rubber (Suzhou) Co., Ltd.; P.T. Sumi Rubber Indonesia; Sumitomo Rubber (Thailand) Co., Ltd.; Sumirubber Malaysia Sdn. Bhd.; Zhongshan Sumirubber Precision Rubber Ltd.; Sumirubber Vietnam, Ltd.

PRINCIPAL COMPETITORS

Bridgestone Corp.; Compagnie Générale des Établissements Michelin; The Yokohama Rubber Co. Ltd.

FURTHER READING

Arbose, Jules, "What's Behind the Rebirth of Dunlop in Europe? The Japanese," *International Management,* July–August 1987.

"IPO Profile: SRI Sports Ltd.," *Jiji Press English News Service,* October 6, 2006.

McNulty, Mike, "Goodyear No. 1 After Sumitomo Deal," *Rubber & Plastics News,* December 13, 1999.

———, "Goodyear Sells Majority of Stake in Sumitomo," *Rubber & Plastics News,* April 14, 2003.

Radford, G. D., "How Sumitomo Transformed Dunlop Tyres," *Long Range Planning,* June 1989.

"Sumitomo Rubber Industries Ltd. Plans to Reform Its Group Structure in July," *Rubber World,* February 1, 2003.

"Sumitomo Rubber Outlines Plan to Tackle Global Warming," *Japan Chemical Week,* December 4, 2008.

"Sumitomo Rubber to Develop Fuel-Efficient Tires," *Jiji Press English News Service,* October 23, 2007.

"Sumitomo to Swallow Ohtsu in Reorganization," *European Rubber Journal,* February 3, 2003.

suntron.
Quality Customer Service. Cost Reducing Solutions.

Suntron Corporation

■

2401 West Grandview Road
Phoenix, Arizona 85023
U.S.A.
Telephone: (602) 789-6600
Toll Free: (888) 520-3382
Fax: (602) 789-6200
Web site: http://www.suntroncorp.com

Private Company
Incorporated: 1984 as Electronic Fab Technology
   Corporation
Employees: 1,510
Sales: $183.2 million (2008 est.)
NAICS: 334418 Printed Circuit Assembly (Electronic
   Assembly) Manufacturing

■ ■ ■

Based in Phoenix, Arizona, Suntron Corporation is a provider of electronics manufacturing services. In addition to providing design and engineering services, the company assembles and tests printed circuit boards, cables, and harnesses, and also assembles complete systems. Suntron serves customers from the aerospace, defense, industrial, medical, network and telecommunications, and semiconductor capital equipment sectors. The company relies on more than 1,500 employees at manufacturing facilities in Phoenix; Manchester, New Hampshire; Lawrence, Massachusetts; Newberg, Oregon; Sugar Land, Texas; and Tijuana, Mexico.

FORMATIVE YEARS

Suntron's roots stretch back to 1981, when the company was established as Electronic Fab Technology Corp. After its first several years of operation, Electronic Fab Technology incorporated in the state of Washington in February 1984. By the early 1990s Electronic Fab Technology was "little more than a mom-and-pop shop that was struggling to stay afloat," according to an article by Diane Trommer in the August 25, 1997, issue of *Electronic Buyers' News.* Things changed in August 1996, however, when Jack Calderon was chosen to lead the company. In September, he implemented a 100-week plan to turn things around. His strategy included several key objectives, including plans to double the company's size, grow through acquisitions, expand its customer base, gain additional skills, and outperform the competition. The company capped off the year with sales of approximately $50 million.

By 1997 Electronic Fab Technology Corporation was headquartered in Greeley, Colorado, and serving a variety of markets as a contract manufacturer. Specifically, the company was providing design-for-manufacturability engineering services, developing prototypes, and performing circuit card assembly for original equipment manufacturers in the communications, instrumentation/avionics, high-end storage, industrial products, and medical industries.

The company grew through acquisitions in 1997. Early in the year, the company parted with $10.3 million to acquire Oregon-based Current Electronics Inc. and Current Electronics (Washington) Inc. Midway through 1997, Electronic Fab Technology shortened its name to EFTC Corp. and established a new 10,000-square-foot corporate center in Denver, Colorado. The new facility was part of the company's planned evolution from a regional player to a national one. In August, the company broke ground on a new 65,000-square-foot operations facility in Newberg, Oregon. Around the same time, EFTC purchased the assets of AlliedSignal Inc.'s Tucson Circuit Assembly Operation and Ft. Lauderdale Circuit Assembly Operation and began providing circuit board assembly services to AlliedSignal's aerospace business.

The company also acquired three additional companies in September: Circuit Test Inc., Airhub Service Group L.C., and CTI International L.C. Collectively known as the CTI Companies, the $29.3 million deal gave EFTC additional operations in Tampa, Florida; Memphis, Tennessee; and Louisville, Kentucky; and pushed the size of its workforce to 1,800 people. By this time, the company had developed a proprietary manufacturing system that it called asynchronous process manufacturing, which enabled it to produce many different kinds of circuit boards in a short time. Operations then included four facilities in the states of Washington, Colorado, and Oregon. EFTC rounded out 1997 with sales of $110 million.

A PERIOD OF GROWTH

Growth continued in 1998. Early in the year, EFTC acquired Manchester, New Hampshire-based RM Electronics Inc. (Personal Electronics), in a stock deal worth approximately $24 million. Midway through the year, the company announced plans to offer three million shares of its common stock, which it expected to generate $22.4 million. By this time EFTC was serving companies such as IBM, Hewlett-Packard, and Cisco Systems, and had begun to leverage the Internet to maximize the efficiency of its operations in areas such as procurement. To support its growing technology initia-

tives, the company hired Val Avery as its chief information officer.

The Wilmington, Massachusetts-based circuit card assembly operations of Bayer Corp.'s Agfa Division were acquired in September, at which time EFTC cemented a deal to continue supplying circuit cards to Agfa. In October 1998, EFTC completed the acquisition of Ottawa, Kansas-based Business & General Aviation Enterprise, which was part of the Electronics & Avionics Systems unit of AlliedSignal Inc. The following month, plans were made to shutter the company's Greeley-based Rocky Mountain Operation as part of a plant consolidation initiative that aimed to improve capacity utilization and cut costs. EFTC ended 1998 with sales of $226.8 million.

EFTC kicked off 1999 by shipping its 20,000th LifeBook computer, which the company had begun manufacturing for Fujitsu PC Corp. some seven months before. In March, the company agreed to acquire Honeywell Corp.'s Phoenix-based Commercial Aviation Systems business in a $2.5 million deal. Midway through the year, EFTC revealed plans to sell its repair and warranty service business, which employed about 500 people, to Jabil Circuit Inc. Looking forward, the two companies planned to work together, with EFTC continuing to market repair services. The $28.1 million deal was finalized in September.

By this time EFTC was struggling to turn a profit. In September 1999 the company rolled out a new initiative called Expedition 20/20, which intended to focus the organization on goals in five main areas: customers, profits, inventory turns, growth, and vision. In addition, a reorganization effort led EFTC to announce the closure of its Fort Lauderdale, Florida-based manufacturing plant in the fall of 1999. The company rounded out the year with a $67.6 million net loss, on revenues of nearly $221.9 million.

LEADERSHIP CHANGES

In early 2000, EFTC secured a $45 million revolving loan from the Bank of America. In addition, two private-equity firms, Blum Capital Partners LP and Thayer Equity Investor IV LP, agreed to joint together to invest $68 million in EFTC. Following the equity investments from Thayer and Blum, several management changes were instituted. The company's chief financial officer, Stuart Fuhlendorf, left the organization after an eight-year career. Midway through the year, former Sony Corp. executive James K. Bass was named EFTC's new president and CEO, and President and Chief Operating Officer Chuck Tillet announced plans to leave the organization. Calderon remained with EFTC as chairman.

KEY DATES

1981: The company is formed as Electronic Fab Technology Corporation.

1996: Jack Calderon is chosen as the company's new leader.

1997: Electronic Fab Technology shortens its name to EFTC Corporation and establishes a new corporate center in Denver, Colorado.

2000: James K. Bass is named EFTC's new president and CEO while Calderon remains chairman; EFTC announces plans to relocate its corporate headquarters from Denver to Phoenix, Arizona.

2001: Calderon steps down as chairman.

2002: EFTC merges with K*TEC Electronics Corporation, and both companies move forward as subsidiaries of Suntron Corporation.

2005: Paul Singh succeeds Bass as president and CEO.

2007: Thayer-Blum Funding LLC, which holds a 90 percent ownership stake in Suntron, acquires full ownership and takes the company private.

2009: Ed Wheeler is named chief operating officer.

In July, EFTC announced that it was relocating its corporate headquarters from Denver to an existing 146,000-square-foot facility in Phoenix. The following month, operations ceased at the company's facilities in Greeley. EFTC finished off the year with record net sales of $101.7 million. Furthermore, the company had its first profitable quarter since late 1998, generating net income of $0.2 million.

In January 2001, Calderon stepped down as the company's chairman but continued to serve on its board through April of that year. The company acknowledged his role in transforming EFTC from a small regional operation to a highly specialized national player. In February, EFTC received a merger proposal from K*TEC Electronics Corporation, the former contract manufacturing division of Sugar Land, Texas-based electronic component distributor Kent Electronics Corporation, which Thayer and Blum had acquired in a $225 million deal. A definitive merger agreement was signed in May that outlined the formation of a holding company, of which EFTC and K*TEC would be wholly owned subsidiaries.

FORMATION OF SUNTRON

EFTC began 2002 by announcing plans to relocate its operations in the northeastern United States from Wilmington, Massachusetts, to a new 75,000-square-foot facility in Lawrence, Massachusetts. On February 28, 2002, the merger of EFTC and K*TEC was finalized. On that date, EFTC's common stock was delisted from the NASDAQ National Market. The combined companies moved forward as subsidiaries of Suntron Corp., which began trading on the NASDAQ on March 1. Thayer-Blum Funding LLC held a 90 percent ownership stake in Suntron. The formation of Suntron allowed the company to expand its customer mix. Prior to the deal, EFTC had relied upon one customer (Honeywell International Inc.) for about 80 percent of its revenues.

In March 2002, Suntron acquired Midwestern Electronics Inc. in a deal with Olathe, Kansas-based Mercury Electronic Manufacturing Services Inc. Later in the summer, the company shuttered operations at its facilities in Fremont, California, and Ottawa, Kansas, as part of an effort to cut costs and consolidate operations.

Another acquisition took place in mid-2003, at which time Suntron acquired the Wilmington, Massachusetts-based manufacturer Trilogic Systems LLC in a deal worth approximately $855,000. By this time, Suntron's workforce had grown to include about 1,650 employees, as well as 150 contract workers. Services at this time included everything from cable and harness production, plastic injection molding, and product design to engineering services, full systems integration and testing, and printed circuit card assembly.

In early 2004 the company signed an agreement with Brillian Corporation for the assembly and production of high-definition televisions at its facilities in Phoenix and Tijuana. That year, the company continued to expand its customer base by establishing multiyear contracts with clients in the aerospace and defense sectors. To support its continued growth, Suntron revealed plans to expand its facility in Tijuana from 35,000 square feet to 110,000 square feet. The expansion came at a time when Suntron was transitioning more labor-intensive production work to Mexico.

In 2005 Paul Singh succeeded Bass as president and CEO of Suntron. Another senior leadership change took place in September of that year, when Chief Financial Officer Peter W. Harper left the company. The company ended the year with a net loss of $11.3 million on net sales of $328.7 million, compared to a loss of about $4.5 million on net sales of $475.4 million in 2004.

COMPANY TAKEN PRIVATE

Early in 2006 Suntron announced that it had sold its facility in Sugar Land for $16.8 million. The company used the proceeds to pay down its debt, and signed a seven-year lease for about half of the building. Midway through the year, Suntron announced plans to relocate certain operations within its facility in Lawrence, Massachusetts, resulting in the loss of approximately 60 jobs. That September, overcapacity resulted in plans to shutter the company's Midwest Operations, leading to the closure of its facility in Olathe, Kansas, and the elimination of about 182 jobs. At this time Suntron was carrying $47 million in bank debt, and Honeywell still accounted for about one-quarter of its business. The company capped off the year with net sales of $320.8 million and a net loss of $11.9 million.

In early 2007 Suntron finished bringing its operations in line with capacity. At that time, the company's facility in Garner, Iowa, was sold to Nortech Systems Inc. Key personnel changes that year included the naming of Brian Throneberry as vice-president of sales and marketing, and Glenn Hunter as vice-president of human resources and corporate services.

Suntron rounded out 2007 with a string of important developments. In October, the company revealed that Thayer-Blum, which continued to hold 90 percent of its stock, planned to take Suntron private. The transaction was completed in December, when Thayer Blum Funding LLC acquired the remainder of Suntron in a $3.1 million cash deal. One final highlight occurred when Suntron received the Frost & Sullivan Award for 2007 North American Competitive Strategy Leadership. The award acknowledged the company's leadership role within the electronic manufacturing services market.

Suntron continued to make progress in 2008. That year, the company extended an aerospace manufacturing contract with longtime customer Honeywell International. Other new business included an agreement to manufacture radio-frequency identification systems (technology used for tracking assets) with Awarepoint Inc., as well as an agreement to design and manufacture products for Wurldtech Security Technologies.

A number of key leadership changes took place at Suntron in 2009. In March, Jeff A. Wanago was named chief financial officer, succeeding Thomas Sabol. Ed Wheeler was named chief operating officer in late July, joining Singh, who continued to lead Suntron as president and CEO as the company prepared for operations during the second decade of the 21st century.

Paul R. Greenland

PRINCIPAL SUBSIDIARIES

Cathio LLC; Current Electronics Inc.; EFTC Operating Corporation; K*TEC Operating Corporation; RM Electronics Inc.; Rodnic LLC; Suntron GCO L.P.; Suntron-Iowa Inc.; Suntron-Kansas Inc.

PRINCIPAL COMPETITORS

Flextronics International Ltd.; Hon Hai Precision Industry Co. Ltd.; Jabil Circuit Inc.

FURTHER READING

"EFTC Announces Corporate Relocation to Phoenix," *Business Wire,* July 10, 2000.

"EFTC Announces Successful Completion of Combination with K*Tec; Suntron Common Stock to Begin Trading on the NASDAQ National Market on Friday, March 1, 2002," *Business Wire,* February 28, 2002.

"EFTC Closes Sale of Repair/Warranty Service," *Business Wire,* September 1, 1999.

"EFTC Launches Expedition 20/20," *Business Wire,* September 10, 1999.

"EFTC Reports Chairman to Depart," *Business Wire,* September 21, 2000.

"Electronic Fab Technology Corp. Changes Name to EFTC," *Business Wire,* May 29, 1997.

Serant, Claire, "Cash-Strapped EFTC Secures Aid from Investment Firms," *Electronic Buyers' News,* April 10, 2000.

———, "Suntron Hopes to Leave Rocky Past Behind—With Investor in Its Corner, EFTC-K*Tec Merger Maps Ambitious Course," *EBN,* March 18, 2002.

"Suntron Corporation Announces Initiation of 'Going Private' Transaction," *PrimeZone Media Network,* October 3, 2007.

"Suntron Corporation Names Ed Wheeler Chief Operating Officer," *Internet Wire,* July 20, 2009.

"Suntron to Close Midwest Operations," *America's Intelligence Wire,* September 13, 2006.

Trommer, Diane, "EFTC Makes Big Strides on 100-Week Journey," *Electronic Buyers' News,* August 25, 1997.

Svenska Spel AB

Norra Hansegatan 17
Visby, S-621 80
Sweden
Telephone: (46 0498) 26 35 00
Fax: (46 0498) 26 36 30
Web site: http://www.svenskaspel.se

State-Owned Company
Incorporated: 1997
Employees: 1,558
Sales: SEK 9.74 billion ($946.6 million) (2008)
NAICS: 713210 Casinos (Except Casino Hotels);
    713990 All Other Amusement and Recreation
    Industries

■ ■ ■

Svenska Spel AB holds the monopoly on legal gambling in Sweden. The state-owned company is one of the only gaming companies in the world to span nearly all forms of legal gambling. The company's operations include the Swedish national lottery, casinos, sports and odds betting, video lottery terminals (VLTs), and Internet gambling. The group's Retail Outlet business area is its largest, generating 54 percent of total revenues. This unit operates through a network of more than 6,800 retail outlets, including retail stores, supermarkets, department stores, and betting agencies.

The company's Restaurant Gaming and Bingo Halls business area, which produces 21 percent of group sales, operates through a network of nearly 2,300 restaurants and 90 bingo halls, including seven bingo halls directly owned by Svenska Spel. Most of this area's revenues come through the placement of Svenska Spel's VLTs, and especially its core product, the Jack Vegas VLT lottery game. The company has also rolled out its own bingo format, BingoLive, at its seven bingo halls.

Svenska Spel's Casino business area operates four international-style casinos in Göteborg, Malmö, Sundsvall, and Stockholm. This unit provided 12 percent of group revenues in 2008. Since 2002 Svenska Spel has been authorized to operate online betting and gambling sites. This unit added 12 percent to the company's revenues, which neared SEK 9.75 billion ($946 million) in 2008. The Swedish government has faced growing pressure from the European Commission (EC) to abolish Svenska Spel's gambling monopoly. The government was expected to respond to the EC's demands in 2009. Leading Svenska Spel is Meta Persdotter, who became CEO in February 2009.

SWEDISH GAMBLING HISTORY

Like many countries, Sweden had long regarded gambling with a certain ambivalence. Dice games were popular in Viking times; by the Middle Ages, however, gambling had begun to take on a negative image. The first legislation in Sweden governing gambling, and the oldest known gambling law in the world, was promulgated in 14th century under King Magnus Eriksson.

Gambling proliferated nonetheless. Playing cards and card games were introduced into the country in the 16th century, joining a variety of other types of luck- and skill-based forms of gambling. Lotteries also became

COMPANY PERSPECTIVES

Mission: To sell a range of exciting and entertaining games with cash winnings in a convenient, responsible and secure manner. Vision: We shall, in a responsible manner, create the most attractive games which provide entertainment to players and are of benefit to the community. Values: Commitment; Professionalism; Responsibility; Awareness.

a popular form of gambling, and in 1742 the court under Gustaf III introduced the country's first state-controlled lottery. By the 19th century, a number of Swedish health spa resorts had added their own casinos.

The beginning of the 19th century marked a new period of antigambling sentiment, led by the religious movements, as well as a growing temperance movement in Sweden. By 1841 the antigambling movement had succeeded in ending the state lottery. By 1846 the antigambling sentiment had led to a ban on casino operations as well.

Over the next several decades, however, the Swedish state's attitude toward gambling was inconsistent. While there were periods in which the government enforced a ban on gambling, at other times the creation of legal gambling venues was encouraged. A new lottery, Penninglotteriet, was instituted in 1896, for example, to help raise funds for the Swedish Exhibition at the dawn of the new century. Casinos were reintroduced at the beginning of the 20th century as well, but lasted only briefly. The last of these casinos opened in Nynäshamn, on the Swedish coast south of Stockholm, in 1911, but shut its doors just one year later.

SPORTS BETTING MONOPOLY

Gambling, while forced underground, nevertheless remained prevalent. Betting on horse races was finally legalized in 1923. The appearance of organized sports at the beginning of the century and the rise of professional sports teams and leagues in the 20th century encouraged new forms of sports and odds betting. Sports betting had come to prominence in the United Kingdom before arriving in Sweden in the 1920s. With no legalized structure, however, this new gambling category quickly gave way to criminal behavior.

By 1934 the Swedish government felt compelled to step in and regulate the sports betting market. In that year, the government authorized the creation of a privately held betting pool operator, called Tipstjänst, literally "Tip Service." The new company, which was granted the monopoly in Sweden on sports betting, quickly rolled out its first three products: Stryktipset, Siffertipset, and Pooltipset. From the start, Tipstjänst also became responsible for helping to prevent compulsive gambling, which at the time was still considered a largely a behavioral issue, rather than a psychological disorder. In 1935 Tipstjänst instituted a minimum age of 18 years for its betting pool products.

Profits from both Tipstjänst and Penninglotteriet remained in private hands until the late 1930s. In 1939 the Swedish government nationalized the Penninglotteriet. Tipstjänst's turn came in 1943, when the government passed legislation that transformed the sports betting operator into a state-owned company.

The two companies remained separate from each other, each developing a range of products and operations over the next several decades. In 1954 Penninglotteriet introduced its Dramatenlotteriet, which later became known as Kulturlotteriet, as its proceeds were used to support cultural initiatives. The company also introduced its first number lottery in 1970. In the meantime, Tipstjänst had replaced its original Pooltipset with a new Poängtipset, or "Credit Tips" product, in 1963. By 1969 the company had also launched its first television program, Tipsextra.

ADDING PRODUCTS

Both state-owned companies faced increasing competition in the postwar era. Betting on horse racing had remained a popular form of gambling in Sweden, although this sector too was placed under a state monopoly, AB Trav & Galopp, in 1974. In the 1950s, the country saw the introduction of the first roulette tables and mechanical gaming devices, such as slot machines, in a number of Swedish hotels and nightclubs.

Bingo was introduced into the country in 1961, and ultimately grew into a network of more than 90 bingo clubs throughout the country. By 1973 the government had passed new legislation permitting the installation of slot machines in restaurants. One year later, the government commissioned its first report on the possibility of allowing international-style casinos in Sweden. These would not be authorized for another 25 years, however.

In 1975 the Swedish government launched an investigation into the proposal of creating a single state-owned monopoly controlling all of the various gambling and gaming activities in Sweden. The proposal was

KEY DATES

1896: Penninglotteriet is established as a privately owned state lottery in Sweden.

1934: The Swedish government authorizes the creation of a privately held sports betting pool operator, Tipstjänst.

1939: Penninglotteriet is nationalized and becomes a state-owned company.

1943: Tipstjänst becomes a state-owned company.

1961: Bingo is introduced into the country.

1980: Penninglotteriet introduces the popular Lotto numbers game.

1986: Tipstjänst launches the world's first online betting pool.

1997: Svenska Spel is created through the merger of Tipstjänst and Penninglotteriet.

2001: Svenska Spel creates the subsidiary Casino Cosmopol, which opens its first casino in Sundsvall.

2002: The government expands Svenska Spel's mandate to include the operation of online gaming sites.

2005: Svenska Spel is authorized to launch online poker games.

2008: Svenska Spel introduces the Spelkort customer card as part of its prevention operations.

quickly dropped, however. The government nonetheless developed a more restrictive attitude toward gambling, and in 1978 instituted a ban on slot machines from the country's hotels and restaurants. Lottery enthusiasts did not feel the restrictions, however, and in 1980 Penninglotteriet introduced the highly popular Lotto numbers game. In 1986 Penninglotteriet added another highly popular product, the Triss instant lottery game. This was followed by a Keno game in 1990.

Tipstjänst also added to its range of products during the 1980s. The company launched two new betting pools in 1983, Maltipset and Poängtipset. In 1984 it added its own Joker and Lotto games. Two years later, the company became the first in the world to launch an online gambling pool, Oddset, which enabled Swedish gamblers to place wagers on foreign sports events. Tipstjänst also increased its television presence, adding Flax, a televised lotto game. By 1990 the company had begun broadcasting its Lotto and Joker games as well.

MERGER OF LEGAL GAMBLING OPERATIONS

By the middle of the 1990s, Tipstjänst had increasingly begun to eclipse Penninglotteriet as the country's major lottery operator, as well as its monopoly betting pool operator. Tipstjänst had also begun developing a number of international relationships. In 1992, for example, the company joined the Euro Tips alliance, together with its state-owned counterparts in Austria, Denmark, and Iceland. The following year, the group joined another multinational partnership, launching the online Viking Lotto game for the Nordic region. Both Tipstjänst and Penninglotteriet also ventured into the bingo market during this time, with the former launching Tip Bingo and the latter introducing Triss-Bingo, both in 1994.

The Swedish government once again took up the question of casino operations in the mid-1990s. One result of the new investigation was the authorization of electronic video lottery terminals (VLTs), despite the opposition from Tipstjänst, which argued that VLTs were a major factor behind the rise of compulsive gambling, particularly among youth. Nonetheless, control of the new market was given to Tipstjänst. In 1996 the company placed the first of its highly popular Jack Vegas VLT machines in a number of Swedish restaurants.

By 1997 the government recognized the need to form a new monopoly body with control of nearly all of the legal gambling varieties in the country. The new body would then be given the mandate to develop preventive measures to reduce the risk of compulsive gambling and related problems. Tipstjänst and Penninglotteriet were merged together that year, forming Svenska Spel.

The new company was unique in the world in that its operations included nearly every form of legalized gambling, ranging from sports betting and betting pools to lotteries and bingo. This list soon grew to include casinos, as the company received authorization to open up to four casinos to cover the Swedish market. For this, the group created a new subsidiary and brand, Casino Cosmopol, in 2001.

The first casino opened in Sundsvall in July 2001. This establishment was followed by the launch of a casino in Malmö in December of that year. By 2002 the company had added a casino in Göteborg, Sweden's second largest city. In 2003 Casino Cosmopol opened its fourth casino, in the capital city Stockholm.

POSSIBLE BREAKUP IN THE 21ST CENTURY

Svenska Spel had also moved to counter the growing strength of foreign-based online gaming web sites, which were becoming increasingly popular especially after the launch of broadband Internet services at the beginning of the 21st century. Indeed, in 2001 Ladbrokes, a leading United Kingdom-based player in this market, attempted to enter the Swedish market directly, setting up a web site there. Ladbrokes was forced to abandon the new site, however, after the Sweden government refused to grant it an operating license.

The government nevertheless recognized the impact of online gaming. In 2002 the government expanded Svenska Spel's mandate to include the operation of online gaming sites. By the end of the year, Svenska Spel had introduced its first online site, for bingo games. By 2005 Svenska Spel had been authorized to launch an online poker site as well.

Toward the end of the decade, the Swedish government faced increasing pressure from the EC to liberalize its gaming market and abandon Svenska Spel's monopoly. Svenska Spel also entered a period of uncertainty with the arrival of a new center-right government, which promised to break up the company at the end of the decade. The government nevertheless proved reluctant to dismantle the gaming monopoly, in large part in fear of a potential surge in compulsive gambling problems.

The EC offered a loophole of sorts for the European Union's state-owned gambling monopolies, allowing their continued existence with the stipulation that the primary mandate for the monopoly remained the control and prevention of gambling addictions and other social consequences of gambling. In order to meet this requirement, Svenska Spel stepped up the rollout of a range of initiatives designed to track customer gambling behavior and detect and prevent potential compulsive gambling behavior.

One part of this effort was the 2008 introduction of a new customer card, Spelkort. The company expected to expand the free card, restricted to Swedish residents 18 year and older, across the full range of its products. Use of the card was made compulsory on the group's gaming web site. Despite this effort, Svenska Spel continued to suffer criticism, in part because of its highly active marketing program. Indeed, with yearly spending rates of SEK 700 million and more, Svenska Spel was one of Sweden's leading advertisers. Given Sweden's long history of intense state involvement in every aspect of society, Svenska Spel appeared assured of maintaining most, if not all, of its gambling monopoly for the years to come.

M. L. Cohen

PRINCIPAL SUBSIDIARIES

AB Svenska Spels Internetservice; AB Svenska Spels Servicecenter; Casino Cosmopol AB; Casino Cosmopol Fastighets AB; CC Casino Restaurang AB; Svenska Spels Förvaltnings AB.

PRINCIPAL DIVISIONS

Retail Outlet Business Area; Restaurant Gaming and Bingo Halls Business Area; Casino Business Area; Internet Business Area.

PRINCIPAL COMPETITORS

AB Trav & Galopp; Folkspel; Svenska Postkodlotteriet; Betsson AB; Net Entertainment NE AB; Ladbrokes PLC; Unibet Ltd.

FURTHER READING

de Ru, Jochem, and Franka Pals, "Sweden," *Novamedia,* June 2, 2004.

McQueen, Patricia A., "Playing Monopoly & Winning," *IGWB: International Gaming & Wagering Business,* August 2008, p. 1.

Moshinsky, Ben, "EU Obligations Shackle Swedish Gambling Reform," *Gambling Compliance,* July 28, 2009.

"NYX Interactive and Svenska Spel Unveil New Bingo and Lottery Platforms," *Wireless News,* September 24, 2008.

O'Connor, Niall A., "Sweden's Gambling Industry and the Long Road to Liberalisation," *Bettingmarket.com,* 2008.

"Retail Exec Tapped to Take CEO Reins at Svenska Spel," *IGWB: International Gaming & Wagering Business,* March 2009, p. 11.

"Svenska Spel Buckling Under Pressure from EC," *IGWB: International Gaming & Wagering Business,* October 2007, p. 20.

"Svenska Spel Posts 9 Percent Increase in Revenues for '07," *IGWB: International Gaming & Wagering Business,* April 2008, p. 9.

"Svenska Spel Safe as New Government Reconsiders Breakup," *IGWB: International Gaming & Wagering Business,* July 2007, p. 7.

"Sweden's Monopoly Is Over—If the Governing Party Has Its Way," *IGWB: International Gaming & Wagering Business,* December 2007, p. 7.

"Swedish Gambling Monopoly Spends Big Money on Advertising," *Nordic Business Report,* July 13, 2004.

"Swedish Government to Look at Limit in Casinos," *Nordic Business Report,* October 22, 2003.

THE SWATCH GROUP SA

The Swatch Group Ltd.

Seevorstadt
Biel, 6CH-2502
Switzerland
Telephone: (41 32) 343 68 11
Fax: (41 32) 343 69 11
Web site: http://www.swatchgroup.com

Public Company
Incorporated: 1984 as Société Suisse de Microelectron-
ique & d'Horlogerie
Employees: 23,000
Sales: $5.38 billion (2008)
Stock Exchanges: Swiss
Ticker Symbol: UHR
NAICS: 334518 Watch, Clock, and Part Manufacturing;
421940 Jewelry, Watch, Precious Stone, and Pre-
cious Metal Wholesalers

■ ■ ■

The Swatch Group Ltd. is one of the world's largest
suppliers of watch movements and finished watches. In
addition to its flagship Swatch brand, the company also
offers many of the world's most prestigious names in
watch design, including Breguet, Tiffany & Co.,
Omega, Jaquet Droz, and Blancpain (luxury); Rado,
Union Glashutte, and Longines (high end); Tissot, Cer-
tina, Mido, Balmain, Hamilton, and ck watch & jewelry
(mid-market); and Flik Flak and Swatch in the "basic"
or low-end market. In addition, the company's exclusive
Endura label crafts custom-designed watches. Swatch

also produces jewelry through its Dress Your Body SA
subsidiary created in 2000.

Swatch remains a tightly vertically integrated
company, manufacturing not only watches but also their
movements and motors and other basic components.
The company produces components through a range of
subsidiaries, including ETA S.A. Manufacture Horlogère
Suisse. Its 156 production centers are located in
Switzerland and throughout the world. Beyond watches
and their components, Swatch has long been associated
with high technology, fabricating semiconductors, quartz
oscillators, and lasers used in telecommunications and
other electronics. It is also one of the largest producer's
of radio-frequency identification technology. The chief
architect behind the Swatch group's success has been
company Chairman Nicolas Hayek. Hayek is credited
with leading Swatch from the bankruptcy of its founding companies to more than $5.8 billion in annual sales
in 2008.

ORIGINS

Switzerland's traditional dominance of the international
watchmaking market foundered in the 1970s. The arrival of digital technology and the use of quartz-based
timing in so-called quartz analog watches gave rise to a
new breed of inexpensive Asian watches and to a new
generation of giant Japan and Hong Kong-based
industrial manufacturers. The Swiss market, with its
tradition of small, often family-owned firms, and its
continued focus on more expensive, labor-intensive
mechanical movements, was caught by surprise by the
gains made by such brands as Seiko and Citizen.

While Swiss watchmakers had been among the first to debut digital watches (priced at the high end of the market at their debut in the late 1960s) most of the Swiss industry considered these and quartz-based timing a fad that would swiftly pass. Instead, demand for these easily produced watches (in contrast to the meticulous craftsmanship needed for most mechanical watches) encouraged a whole new crop of worldwide competitors to enter the field.

By the mid-1970s, the market had become glutted, prices plunged, and the entire industry underwent a crisis, even as demand for digital watches and their LED or LCD faces vanished. The appearance of the first quartz analog watches, which supplanted mechanical movements with quartz-based "modules" while retaining traditional analog watch-faces, however, would prove more enduring. Here again, however, the Swiss industry clung to mechanical movements, convinced that the quartz fad would soon end as well.

By the end of the 1970s, the Swiss watchmaking industry was in serious trouble. Many spoke of exiting the watchmaking market altogether, or limiting craft-based production to the high-end and luxury markets. Two of the largest Swiss watchmakers were among those facing collapse. Both Allgemeine Schweizerische Uhren-industrie (ASUAG) and Société Suisse pour l'Industrie Horlogère (SSIH) had been formed in the 1930s Depression era, grouping, in SSIH's case, such long-revered names in watchmaking as Omega and Tissot. Omega, founded in the mid-19th century, had achieved prominence as one of the world's top luxury brands, with its mechanical watches and timepieces not only an Olympic Games standard, but also the choice of U.S. astronauts.

JOCKEYING FOR POSITION IN THE EUROPEAN MARKET

As French-speaking SSIH concentrated on watches, its German-speaking rival ASUAG focused on movements and other component parts, while also adding watchmaking subsidiaries and brands. By the 1960s, both ASUAG and SSIH were among the world's largest watchmaking firms. ASUAG itself had built a position as one of the Swiss industry's chief suppliers of movements and watch components. However by the beginning of the 1980s, faced with an onslaught of cheaply produced quartz-based and digital watches, both ASUAG and SSIH were facing bankruptcy proceedings. In addition to the glut of low-cost watches, ASUAG and SSIH had suffered from important economic factors: the devaluation of the U.S. dollar in the mid-1970s vastly increased the cost of importing Swiss watches into what had been one of the industry's chief marketplaces; at the same time, Switzerland could not hope to compete with the low wage and production costs available in the Far East.

In the late 1970s, both companies, joined by the Swiss industry as a whole, attempted to reverse their fortunes, investing massively in quartz module production facilities. By the end of the decade, the industry had succeeded in bringing all quartz component manufacture needs within the country's borders. ASUAG had been among the earliest to adopt this new manufacturing trend, and had succeeded in becoming an important supplier of quartz movements. Yet the move proved too late. As the decade closed, more than half of the 1,600 Swiss watchmakers present at the start of the decade had gone out of business. SSIH, which had become the country's largest watchmaker, was bleeding: After suffering large losses in 1980, it received a $150 million bailout from its banks. Nevertheless, its losses continued.

By 1982 it was the turn of ASUAG and SSIH to face liquidation procedures. Foreign competitors hovered around the two companies, eager to buy up such famous watch brands as Longines, Hamilton, Tissot, Rado, and Omega. Observers of the Swiss industry seemed resigned to see watchmaking fade into the fabric of Swiss history.

THE HAYEK ERA

Many credit the survival of ASUAG and SSIH's operations to the actions of one Nicolas Hayek. (Hayek himself would claim to have rescued the entire Swiss watchmaking industry, to the indignation of many of his competitors.) Hayek was the head of Hayek Engineering, which had built a reputation in the 1970s as a leading manufacturing consultant. In 1982 Hayek was hired by ASUAG and SSIH's creditors to investigate the Swiss watchmaking industry and, as Hayek claimed, according to a 1997 article by David Short in *European*, "produce a report saying it's impossible to produce in

KEY DATES

1982: Allgemeine Schweizerische Uhrenindustrie (ASUAG) and Société Suisse pour l'Industrie Horlogère (SSIH) face liquidation procedures; Nicolas Hayek is hired by ASUAG and SSIH's creditors to investigate the Swiss watchmaking industry.

1983: ASUAG and SSIH merge; Hayek buys 51 percent of the merged company and it Société Suisse de Microelectronique & d'Horlogerie, or SMH.

1986: SMH's revenues climb to CHF 1.25 billion thanks to sales of the popular Swatch watch.

1991: The company acquires the renowned Blancpain brand of luxury watches.

1998: The company adopts The Swatch Group name.

2000: Swatch branches out in jewelry design and sales with the creation of its Dress Your Body SA subsidiary.

2008: Tiffany Watch Co. Ltd. is created.

Switzerland because the Japanese are much cheaper, labor is cheaper."

Despite the banks' desire to shut down the Swiss watchmaking industry, and sell off its jewels to recoup some of their losses, the so-called Hayek Study would lead the Swiss industry into a new era. Chief among Hayek's recommendations was to merge the two longtime rivals into a single company. Hayek's second recommendation proved perhaps still more radical: the production of a new type of watch directed at the low-cost (under $50) watch market. The banks agreed to the merger, creating the ASUAG/SSIH entity in 1983. However, the banks refused Hayek's idea for the new type of watch. Instead, they offered to sell 51 percent of the merged company to Hayek for CHF 151 million. Hayek accepted the gamble, renaming the company as Société Suisse de Microelectronique & d'Horlogerie (SMH).

Hayek counted on an innovation made by the company's ETA watch movement subsidiary, led by Ernst Thomke. At the height of the watch market explosion in the 1970s, a great deal of competition had focused on making the thinnest watch in the world. ETA would win, developing the technology to produce a watch that was less than one millimeter in thickness. The watch, marketed as the Delirium, proved a success,

with sales of more than 5,000, despite a price tag of nearly $5,000. At the start of the 1980s, Thomke's attention too turned toward rescuing not only parent company ASUAG but also SSIH, as a means of rescuing ETA itself as the failure of these two watchmaking powerhouses would mean the failure of ETA as well. Thomke devised a radically new watch concept, based on the technology developed for the Delirium, and to be manufactured entirely by automated production methods. It was this concept that Hayek brought to SMH's creditors as the means to rescue the newly merged company.

THE INTRODUCTION OF THE SWATCH

This watch was, of course, the Swatch. More than a watch, the Swatch represented a entirely new marketing concept, featuring colorful designs and flashy advertising that not only broke from the conservative mold of the Swiss industry, but also caught its Asian competitors entirely off guard. Greeted by industry skepticism, the Swatch proved a huge success. The automated production process had succeeded in keeping costs down, propelling SMH into profitability by mid-decade. By 1986 SMH's revenues had climbed to CHF 1.25 billion. The Swatch's colorful designs encouraged customers to purchase multiple watches, and inspired an entire collecting craze consciously fueled by the company itself. In the late 1990s, rare Swatch designs would sell for nearly $20,000, for a watch that cost less than $50 when it was first produced.

The Swatch success would inspire the Swiss watchmaking industry as a whole; meanwhile, SMH scored a new hit in the second half of the decade with the introduction of the Rock-Watch, again conceived by Thomke, and released by SMH brand Tissot. Similarly, SMH introduced the children's watch Flik Flak, inspired by the Swatch with its multiple designs. SMH's success proved infectious for its other units, as brands such as Omega and Hamilton revitalized and refocused. Not all of SMH's initiatives were so fortunate: The company's attempt to move into merchandising, introducing a line of Swatch-inspired clothing and accessories, and a chain of in-store Swatch Boutiques, met with little interest. The company abandoned this project and returned its focus to watches and watch movements.

INDUSTRY LEADERSHIP

By the beginning of the 1990s, SMH was well on its way to becoming the world's largest producer of watches and watch movements. Under Hayek and Thomke, the company had made substantial gains, and the once-scoffed-at Swatch had sold more than 250 million watches worldwide. Thomke left the company in 1991, after helping reestablish such brands as Tissot, Rado, and Omega. These brands were joined by the 1991 acquisition of the renowned Blancpain brand of luxury watches. The Swatch success story seemed to have a strange side effect: renewed interest in mechanical watches, and especially in the high end and luxury category of watches.

Hayek, meanwhile, was looking in new directions for SMH. In the 1990s, the company would begin investigations on entering the portable telephone market—with announcements of a Swatch watch with built-in telephone. Hayek had also begun searching for a partner for a project that seemed as radical as the Swatch had been: a new type of car. The so-called Swatchmobile was to be an ecologically friendly vehicle based on a new type of car engine inspired in part by watch technology. SMH originally entered an agreement with Volkswagen to begin designing the proposed automobile. This agreement fell through, however.

In the mid-1990s, SMH found a new partner for its Swatchmobile in Daimler Benz. In 1994 the two companies announced the creation of the joint partnership Micro Compact Car for the production of the Smart car. Initially scheduled for shipping in October 1997, the Smart car would finally enter production in June 1998, with initial sales in October 1998. The car's minuscule design and Swatch-like design features, as well as an innovative sales approach, caused a sensation at its launch. The company however, sold its 19 percent stake in the venture to Daimler Benz later that year.

The late 1990s would bring to fruition other of SMH's projects. In May 1998, the company planned to launch its Swatch Talk, a new Swatch design featuring a built-in portable telephone. The Swatch Talk was joined by two other products, the Swatch Telecom and Swatch Access, designed to launch the company into the telecommunications market at a time of the European market's deregulation. Many of these projects proved short-lived though as the company focused on building its watch business. SMH began building a new distribution channel for its expanding Swatch brand, opening the first of a proposed 15-store chain of Swatch Megastores in New York and Geneva.

In 1998 SMH adopted the new name of the Swatch Group in recognition of its world-renowned product. The company had grown into an industry powerhouse representing more than 25 percent of total watch and watch component sales, while capturing 10 percent of global watch revenues. The Swatch Group, with its forays into automobile production and telecommunications, had also developed a strong vertically integrated organization, producing the full range of watches and watch components, including batteries and microprocessors. In 1997 Swatch posted revenues of CHF 3.05 billion, and net profits of CHF 332 million. The company purchased Groupe Horloger Breguet and Favre & Perret in 1999.

GROWTH AND ACQUISITIONS

Swatch's success continued into the early years of the new millennium. In April 2000, the company branched out into the design, manufacture, and sales of jewelry through the creation of its Dress Your Body subsidiary. The company also grew through a series of acquisitions including German luxury watchmaker Glashutter Uhrenbetrieb and the Swiss luxury brand Jaquet Droz in 2000. The following year Aliki Perri S.A. was added to the company's arsenal followed by Rubattel & Weyermann SA in 2002. Hayek turned CEO activities over to his son Nicolas Jr. on January 1, 2003, while he remained chairman.

With record sales and profits in 2005, Swatch stood secure in its position one of the largest watch companies in the world. Growth continued in 2006 with the purchase of watch dial manufacturer MOM Le Prelet S.A. That same year Swatch partnered with retailer Tourneau to open stores in luxury outlet malls in the United States. At this time, Swatch decided to focus on its watch, jewelry, and accessories business and began to shed noncore assets including its automobile parts manufacturing subsidiaries.

During 2008 the company acquired a stake in Rivoli Group, a Dubai-based luxury goods retailer. Tiffany Watch Co. Ltd. was created that same year by Swatch and Tiffany & Co. As part of the partnership, Swatch was responsible for the manufacture, branding, and distribution of Tiffany watches outside of the United States. The new collection would retail between $1,500 and $10,000 and made its debut at Baselworld 2009, the world's largest watch and jewelry trade show.

The Swatch Group continued to experience financial success in 2008 despite the global economic downturn. Chairman Hayek, known for his eccentric and outspoken style, described his take on the current economic climate in the Swatch Group's 2008 annual report. Describing the financial economic sky in America as darkening, he went on to write, "Little by little these clouds formed into a veritable hurricane approaching with frightening speed, a gigantic roll of thunder whose mighty bolt struck, also touching our major banks, in particular UBS and Credit Suisse. The populations and governments of the whole world were affected with a brutal and massive impact unimaginable before this disaster."

As a result of this described hurricane, sales of luxury items including watches and jewelry began to falter. Indeed, Swatch experienced a decline in sales during November and December 2008, and 2009 promised to bring additional challenges. Despite this, both Hayek and his son believe the company, with its growing arsenal of popular and luxury brands, had positioned itself to weather any storm that might come its way.

M. L. Cohen
Updated, Christina M. Stansell

PRINCIPAL SUBSIDIARIES

ETA S.A. Manufacture Horlogère Suisse; Dress Your Body S.A.; Tiffany Watch Co. Ltd.

PRINCIPAL COMPETITORS

Citizen Holdings Co. Ltd.; Compagnie Financière Richemont S.A.; Seiko Holdings Corporation.

FURTHER READING

Dobrian, Joseph, "Swatch Group, Tiffany Alliance Expected to Pay Off—In Time," *National Jeweler Network,* January 20, 2008.

Domberg, John, "Up from Swatch," *Business Month,* March 1988, p. 54.

Fuhrman, Peter, "Jewelry for the Wrist," *Forbes,* November 23, 1992, p. 173.

"The Many Faces of Swatch," *Harvard Business Review,* March–April 1993, p. 108.

Michelson, Marcel, "Swatch's Hayek Set Pace of Swiss Watch Sector," *Reuters News,* June 7, 2002.

Short, David, "At the Court of the King of Swatch," *European,* June 19, 1997, p. 28.

Steiner, Ruper, "Eccentric Time Lord Who Makes the Swiss Tick," *Sunday Times,* October 15, 2000.

"Swatch: Ambitious," *Economist,* April 18, 1992, p. 74.

"Swatch Group Buys Watch Dial Maker MOM Le Prelet," *Reuters News,* October 19, 2006.

"Swatch Group Takes Stake in Dubai-Based Retailer Rivoli," *Dow Jones International News,* July 23, 2008.

"Swatch, Tourneau Partner for U.S. Mall Venture," *National Jeweler,* April 6, 2006.

Tokyu Department Store Co., Ltd.

24-1, Dogenzaka 2-chome
Shibuyaku
Tokyo, 150-8019
Japan
Telephone: (81 3) 34773111
Web site: http://www.tokyu-depart.co.jp

Wholly Owned Subsidiary of Tokyu Corporation
Incorporated: 1919 as Shirokiya Gofukuten Co., Ltd.
Employees: 3,720
Sales: $2.68 billion (2008)
NAICS: 45211 Department Stores

■ ■ ■

Tokyu Department Store Co., Ltd., operates a chain of department stores in Japan and is the core of the retail division of Tokyu Corp. With a flagship department store in Shibuya, Tokyo, Tokyu runs 11 stores in Japan, primarily situated in the Tokyo region. The company was forced to restructure during the late 1990s and early years of the new millennium due to falling consumer demand and weakening of the Japanese economy. Tokyu has shuttered stores and sold most of its holdings unrelated to its department store activities including its real estate and restaurant businesses. The company became a wholly owned subsidiary of Tokyu Corp. in 2005.

FROM DRAPES TO RAILWAYS: EARLY HISTORY

Tokyu Department Store's most venerable antecedent dates back to the 17th century. This ancestor was a drapers' shop, Shirokiya, founded in 1662 by Hikotaro Omura in the Nihonbashi area of Tokyo, or Edo as the city was then called. In 1919 this business was incorporated as the Shirokiya Drapery Shop Co., Ltd. Four years later, the store, like most others in Tokyo, was devastated by fire following the Great Kanto Earthquake. Operating under the new trading name of Shirokiya Co., Ltd., the company redeveloped the old site to create a new and more up-to-date store, which opened in June 1933.

The evolution of Shirokiya constitutes one strand of the Tokyu Department Store's history. The other principal strand began in the 1930s, a boom period for Japanese department stores. At this time Tokyo's suburbs were growing rapidly, and railway lines were stretching out from the center to serve them. The railway companies often used the land adjacent to their commuter stations to build department stores, which they financed with money from their transport activities. One of the earliest railway companies to spot this opportunity was the Tokyo Yokohama Electric Railways Co., Ltd., owned by entrepreneur Keita Gotoh's Tokyo Corporation. In 1934 the Tokyo Yokohama Electric Railways Co. opened Toyoko Department Store, the first department store to be sited at a railway station; "Toyoko" was a portmanteau word formed from "Tokyo" and "Yokohama."

KEY DATES

1662: Shirokiya, a drapery shop, is founded in Tokyo.

1919: Shirokiya incorporates as Shirokiya Gofuku-ten Co., Ltd.

1934: Tokyo Yokohama Electric Railways Co. opens the first Toyoko Department Store.

1948: Toyoko Department Store Co., Ltd., forms.

1951: Toyoko opens Tokyo's first shopping arcade.

1958: Toyoko Department Store and Shirokiya merge and form Toyoko Co., Ltd.

1959: The company establishes Shirokiya Inc. in Hawaii.

1967: Toyoko changes its name to Tokyu Department Store Co., Ltd.; the company opens a new store in Shibuya.

1973: Tokyu opens its first store outside Tokyo, in Sapporo.

1989: Tokyu completes the building of the Bunkamura cultural center in Tokyo.

1993: Restructuring plan announced to strengthen the company's operations includes reducing workforce by about 20 percent.

1999: 330-year-old Nihonbashi store closes.

2005: Tokyu Corp. acquires all remaining shares of the company.

2007: The company forms a business partnership with Isetan Co.

After World War II the Allied occupying forces pursued a policy of dismantling the large combines or *zaibatsu*, which in the Allies' opinion had contributed to Japan's entry into the war. Many Tokyu operations were reconstituted as semi-independent companies. One such company, Toyoko Kogyo, assumed control of Tokyu's department store business in 1948, shortly afterward becoming known as Toyoko Department Store Co., Ltd.

Another company originating in 1948 and later affiliated with Tokyu Department Store was Tokyu Foods. Forty years after its foundation, Tokyu Foods became a significant manufacturer and retailer of bakery goods, operating 140 bakeries in Japan and elsewhere under the name "St-Germain," also selling delicatessen-style meats. Tokyu Department Store's other important food-manufacturing affiliate, Gold Pak, whose award-winning products were all based on fresh fruit and vegetable juices, began trading in 1966.

POSTWAR GROWTH

After the immediate postwar hardships, Japan's prosperity grew rapidly. Department stores flourished because they offered convenient one-stop shopping; from being primarily dry-goods suppliers before the war, they came to supply everything from food to consumer durables. They also catered to the westernization of Japanese tastes by bringing in imports in a way that smaller retailers could not afford to do. Department stores were typically situated at railway stations, as were Toyoko's stores.

It was against this promising background that Toyoko Department Store opened its Ikebukuro store in 1950, which was to close after only 14 years of trading. In 1951 the company inaugurated Tokyo's first shopping arcade under the name Toyoko Norengai. The west wing of the main Toyoko store was also extended during the early 1950s.

The two strands of Tokyu Department Store's history came together in the late 1950s. Shirokiya Co. joined the Tokyu group of companies in 1956. Two years later, after a period of intensive modernization and expansion of the Shirokiya main store, Shirokiya and Toyoko Department Store merged, adopting the name Toyoko Co., Ltd. The company took an initial step toward globalization with the creation of Shirokiya Incorporated in 1959. In the same year, this new affiliate opened Tokyu's first overseas store, the Hawaii Shirokiya in the Ala Moana Shopping Center. Over the years Shirokiya Incorporated opened another three stores in Hawaii, two of them in shopping centers and one in a hotel. That Shirokiya became a valued part of Hawaiian life was indicated by the fact that the city of Honolulu designated October 15, 1989, as "Shirokiya Day" in honor of the original store's 30th anniversary.

CONTINUED GROWTH

On the domestic front, the early 1960s found department stores facing unprecedented demand for household goods such as televisions and washing machines. However, the stores were also presented with growing competition from the newly arrived supermarkets and superstores that, sited away from town centers as they tended to be, could often provide shoppers with a more relaxed environment and lower-priced goods. Despite this competition, Toyoko continued to grow, both through acquisition and through construction of attractive new stores. In 1966 Toyoko formed a joint venture with Nagano Maruzen, which in 1970 would change its name to the Nagano Tokyu Department Store Ltd.

The company adopted its current name of Tokyu Department Store Co., Ltd., in 1967, the year in which it opened a new main store in Shibuya at one of Tokyo's largest railway stations. Both this and the original Toyoko Store nearby were to undergo an important expansion program in the late 1960s. Also in 1967, the 300-year-old Shirokiya shop changed its name to the Nihonbashi Tokyu Department Store. Its advantageous site, adjacent to the intersection of three subway lines and in an important shopping and business district, continued to make it one of Tokyu's busiest enterprises.

The 1973 oil shock precipitated a period of stagnation in the department-store sector. In spite of this, the 1970s were notable for the opening of several new Tokyu stores. In 1973 came the new Sapporo Tokyu Department Store, situated across the road from Sapporo Station in Hokkaido. This was the first Tokyu store to open outside the capital, and Tokyu made a point of staffing it locally to ensure a strong rapport with shoppers and a thorough understanding of their preferences. Initially a company in its own right, Sapporo Tokyu Department Store merged with Tokyu Department Store in 1978.

The Kichijoji store opened in 1974 at the Japan Railways Kichijoji Station in Musashino City, Tokyo. In 1980 the Machida Tokyu Department Store Co. began trading; it became part of the Tokyu Department Store Co. in 1989. Machida was one of Tokyo's most rapidly growing residential suburbs, and the store offered mainly sporting and leisure equipment to local shoppers.

During the 1970s and 1980s there was a trend toward specialization among Japanese department stores. A store catered to specific groups of customers, such as newly married women or teenagers. In 1979 Tokyu Department Store affiliate T.M.D. opened Shibuyu 109, a center aimed at the fashion-conscious woman and which by the 1990s contained 93 separate shops. Its success sparked off a series of similar enterprises, including the KOHRINBO 109 in Kanazawa, opened in 1985; One-Oh-Nine, opened in 1986; and 1092, opened in 1987.

EXPANSION AND DIVERSIFICATION

In 1990 Tokyu launched the first of a new style of fashion store, 1 2 3 (pronounced "un deux trois") in Shibuya. Among the boutiques it comprised was Trans Continents, an outlet for Tokyu affiliate Millennium Japan Ltd., also founded in 1990 as a retailer of fashion clothing and accessories. This exemplified Tokyu's participation in the trend for Japanese retailers to develop private-label fashion products, appealing to consumers in the way that designer-labeled goods do, but undercutting designer-label prices.

In the 1980s Tokyu added energetically to its overseas interests, starting with the opening of the Hong Kong Tokyu store in 1980 when it became the principal tenant of the then recently completed New World Center in Kowloon on the Chinese mainland. Then came stores in Bangkok and Thailand in 1985, and in Singapore in 1987. In each case Tokyu made a point of integrating itself into the local community—the slogan of the Singapore store was "Born and Raised in Singapore"—while offering shoppers a taste of Japanese courtesy and quality. Outside Asia, the OK Gift Shop 109 opened in Auckland, New Zealand, in 1990.

As well as opening new stores, Tokyu expanded overseas through acquisition. It bought the Dragon Seed Co. Ltd., a Hong Kong department store company, in 1988 from investment company First Pacific. With Dragon Seed, Tokyu gained a valuable building in the central area of Hong Kong Island, as well as a ten-store chain. Tokyu bought an equity participation in the Ever Green Department Store Corporation of Taiwan in 1990.

Tokyu's overseas operations were not confined to its retail outlets. International buying operations and joint ventures became increasingly important. Tokyu acquired the monopoly for Jim Thompson Thai silk in 1985, opening a Jim Thompson boutique in its main store. In 1988 it formed an alliance with Williams-Sonoma, a U.S. catalog sales company, to establish Williams-Sonoma Japan. Williams-Sonoma specialties included household goods and furnishings.

Overseas buying was not exclusively a quest for the unusual. Like many of its competitors, Tokyu Department Store sought to reduce its unit costs through imports and adopted a "develop and import" system whereby it joined forces with local interests to produce goods for sale initially in the local marketplace and, when a sufficiently high standard had been attained, for import to Japan. Goods imported in this way included knitwear from China, clothing from Hong Kong, and fruit from Thailand.

BUILDING AND RENOVATION

The 1980s was a period of recovery in the Japanese consumer market. Tokyu's expansion in the 1970s had left it well placed to benefit despite continued fierce competition from supermarkets. New Tokyu department stores continued to open. The Kitami Tokyu began trading in 1982 and the Komoro Tokyu store in Nagano prefecture, part of the Nagano Tokyu Department Store Co., began trading the following year, as did the Tama Plaza Tokyu department store. The Tama Plaza Shopping Center, constructed by Tokyu Corporation, was adjacent to Tama Plaza station in Yokohama, and the department store was its principal occupant. The Tama Plaza Tokyu Department Store Co. became the Seinan Tokyu Department Store Co. in 1989, although the store itself continued to be known as Tama Plaza.

Remodeling of stores was a keynote of Tokyu's activities throughout the 1980s. In 1984 it celebrated the 50th anniversary of the opening of Toyoko Department Store with a radical remodeling of the main store in Shibuya. By then the store contained a range of specialty shops under one roof. The Shibuya store's food department in the basement was greatly extended in 1990. The Toyoko store was refitted in 1985 and 1986. This, too, housed a mall of specialty shops, including concessions such as Benetton and the first Williams-Sonoma Japan retail outlet, which opened in 1988. The store's exterior was renovated in 1989.

Outside Tokyo, too, shops were constantly being restyled to keep abreast of consumer preferences. The Nagano Tokyu store was extended in 1986 and a new annex called Cherchez was added, making this the largest urban department store in the Nagano prefecture.

In 1988 the Kichijoji store was redecorated, and the Sapporo store embarked on an extension and renewal program. Thanks to the opening of a new subway line, the store's food floor in the basement was directly connected to Sapporo station. The Nihonbashi store, too, underwent a dramatic transformation, reopening complete with La Plasis, a huge customer service mall offering postal, travel, and other facilities. The renovated store also boasted a greatly expanded women's clothing department. Several years later the Nihonbashi store was crowned with the imaginative addition of a rooftop golf school.

NEW SYSTEMS FOR MEETING NEW CHALLENGES

During the 1970s and 1980s the Japanese department store sector, which had previously dominated the retail industry in terms of both sales and profitability, began to lag behind the supermarket companies with their out-of-town superstores. This tendency was attributed partly to the supermarkets' faster conversion to information technology. In 1988, however, Tokyu introduced a point-of-sale system to all its department stores to automate stock control and keep track of local customer preferences.

Tokyu was also innovative in finding ways to woo the shopper back from the superstores. In February 1987, for instance, the *Economist* reported that four Tokyu stores had introduced door-to-door sales teams of housewives selling on commission. This personal ap-

proach was so successful that several other department stores quickly followed suit.

Japanese stores tried to lure shoppers through their own doors by helping to improve the area of the city in which they operated; for example, an adjunct of the Toyoko Store renovation in 1985 was a project to improve and promote the whole street in cooperation with local government. This form of competition became known as the "Commercial Block War."

Tokyu played a major role in the revitalization of the Shibuya area, where its headquarters and largest stores were situated. Perhaps Tokyu's most spectacular contribution was the Bunkamura, or Tokyu Culture Village. A cooperative venture between a number of Tokyu companies, it involved the construction of a large complex, including art gallery, concert hall, and theater. It opened in 1989 on a site adjacent to Tokyu's main store, and the *Japan Company Handbook* soon reported that takings at the main store were shooting up under the influence of the Bunkamura.

In the early 1990s, healthy turnover of goods such as jewelry and fine art reflected the luxurious ambience that Tokyu endeavored to project in its stores and malls. New stores continued to open, usually in the proximity of stations. In 1990, for instance, Nagano Tokyu Department Store Co., Ltd., opened its Nagano Tokyu Life Store at the Japan Railways Kita–Nagano Station. Tokyu also pursued an active policy of expansion in and beyond the Pacific Rim area. There were four Hawaii stores and one each in Hong Kong, Bangkok, and Singapore, as well as a further six representative offices worldwide by the early 1990s. A second Thai store opened in 1993.

PROMOTION OF A WELL-BALANCED LIFE

During this time Tokyu Department Store was one of the most important of the Tokyu Group, a complex group of businesses of which Tokyu Corporation was the nucleus. These companies, of which there were nearly 400, were divided into four main groups: retailing and distribution; development; transportation; and recreation and leisure. Tokyu Department Store was the nucleus of the retailing and distribution group, which represented almost 40 percent of the Tokyu Group's total sales in 1990.

The retailing and distribution group also comprised a supermarket chain and the Tokyu Store Chain, with more than 100 stores in the greater Tokyo area. Like the department stores, most of these adjoined the Tokyu Corporation's railway lines. Tokyu also operated specialty stores such as Tokyu Time Co., started in 1965 to sell and repair watches, and Sports Tokyu Co., started in 1970. Both of these were affiliates of Tokyu Department Store Co., while a number of other specialty stores, such as Top Shoes, were more closely linked with the Tokyu Store Chain Co. All these specialty stores were available for inclusion in Tokyu Department Store's shopping malls.

The slogan of the Tokyu Group was "Creating a well-balanced life for the 21st century." This aspiration was reflected in Tokyu Department Store's community and lifestyle-oriented approach to its customers. The stores did not simply try to sell individual products and services; they offered lectures, cultural events, and educational programs to the public to reinforce the sales message and at the same time improve the quality of life. The stores used local staff to emphasize that the business was rooted in the customer community.

Writing in an August 1990 *Business Japan,* in his capacity as chairman of the Japan Department Stores Association, Tokyu Department Store's president, Mamoru Miura, discussed legislative changes and warned that Japan was about to encounter an "increasingly sinister" economic environment with labor shortages, rising interest rates, and unstable stock and foreign exchange markets. He identified the internationalization of the marketplace and the need for better information management as the two main challenges facing the department store industry in the coming decade. In contrast, analyst Ken Egusa of Morgan Stanley & Co. predicted continued growth and success for Japanese department stores in the 1990s. Egusa told *HFD—The Weekly Home Furnishings Newspaper:* "The 1990s will see consumer demand remaining firm and the marketplace as a whole will be driven, starting in the mid-1990s, during the period when the first and second baby boomers will become full members of the labor force." Egusa also indicated that changes in the Large-Scale Retail Store Law would open up opportunities for larger stores and shopping outlets in suburban areas.

Soon after these predictions were made, Japan's economy began to deteriorate, creating difficult conditions for Tokyu and other Japanese retailers. For the fiscal year that ended January 31, 1992, Tokyu indicated that although sales grew 8.2 percent over the previous year, its pretax profit declined 18 percent. The higher-end merchandise that consumers so readily sought in the late 1980s and early 1990s became less desirable as people tightened their spending budgets, and Tokyu's marketing expenses and management costs grew more quickly than sales. Tokyu fared no better the following year, and pretax profit slid 27 percent. Net profit was affected by a new land tax, which required Tokyu to pay ¥670 million in land taxes alone.

As a result of slumping revenues, Tokyu devised a three-year restructuring plan in 1993 to strengthen the company's operations. As part of the restructuring, Tokyu announced plans to reduce its workforce by about 20 percent, about 1,000 jobs, over a three-year period. Tokyu planned to accomplish the task by refraining from hiring new recruits, including high school and university graduates, in spring as was traditionally done, as well as through attrition.

INCREASED CHALLENGES IN 1995

Tokyu experienced a brief respite in 1995 as consumer spending picked up slightly. The company reported a net profit of ¥1.84 billion for fiscal year 1996, and during the first half of 1996 sales rose 1.1 percent over the same period a year earlier. Increased sales promotions and extended store hours in the Tokyo region helped generate revenues. Tokyu announced that clothing sales increased 1.8 percent and food sales rose 1.5 percent.

Despite increased revenues, Tokyu noted that sales were still relatively weak and complete recovery could not be anticipated in the near future. Indeed, Tokyu's upturn was brief; the company announced pretax profit for 1997 of ¥1.7 billion. Tokyu blamed continued slow personal consumption as well as the weather; an unseasonably warm winter resulted in poor clothing sales, and stores failed to meet sales targets in December and January.

To battle the poor economic conditions, Tokyu endeavored to better serve its clientele, hoping its efforts might translate into improved sales. After a five-year moratorium, Tokyu announced it would hire about 100 new employees beginning in the spring of 1998. The company believed introducing a younger employee to its personnel would create a better age balance. New recruits were also needed to accommodate Tokyu's extended hours. Although the Large-Scale Retail Store Law recommended that department stores take a minimum of 24 holidays per year, many ailing department stores believed offering more hours was the key to increasing sales. Tokyu hoped to decrease its holiday closures from 22 to 18 days at three stores in the Tokyo metropolitan area beginning in the summer of 1998.

In addition to the sluggish economy, Tokyu had suburban shopping centers to blame for its struggles. Once the ultimate destination for shoppers, urban department stores began to lose customers to shopping malls and superstores that cropped up in the suburbs. The convenience of suburban shopping appealed to the increasingly car-oriented shopper, and statistics indicated that suburban shopping was not a fluke. The *Asian Wall Street Journal* reported that between 1985 and 1994, the market share of six superstore chains increased from 4.6 percent to 5.3 percent in the overall retail industry. The market share of eight major department store chains, however, dropped from 2.9 percent to 2.6 percent. While most of the major department store operators shunned expansion into suburbs, Tokyu hoped to capitalize on the new trend and began making plans to open stores in suburban shopping centers. The company announced plans to build a shopping mall in the Tokyo suburb of Kohoku New Town with a Tokyu Department Store as a key retailer.

Hard times continued for Tokyu as the economic recession persisted. In 1998, after ten years in Japan, Williams-Sonoma announced it would end its joint venture with Tokyu. Slow expansion was believed to be one of the reasons for the break as there were only 15 Williams-Sonoma stores in Japan. Tokyu posted its first pretax loss since 1949 and sales fell 12 percent for the six-month period ending July 1998, spurring the company to develop a five-year restructuring plan. The plan called for the liquidation or sale of most of its international subsidiaries, including the Hong Kong operations, Merchandising Development USA Inc., a real estate company in the United States, and some operations in Thailand. Tokyu also announced it would close the Nihonbashi store. The Nihonbashi store was the third largest of Tokyu's department stores in terms of sales and contributed about 11 percent of Tokyu's revenues in fiscal 1998. The company also planned to eliminate about 900 jobs by 2002, many through voluntary early retirement.

The closure of the Nihonbashi store was significant news in Japan. The store, which had existed for more than 330 years, held a monthlong closing sale in January 1999 that generated unprecedented sales. On the sale's first day on January 2, the store reached record sales of ¥739 million. On the final day of business about 160,000 consumers visited the store. January sales reached a total of ¥16.5 billion, about half of the store's total 1998 sales. In September Tokyu indicated it had found a buyer for the Nihonbashi building; Mitsui Fudosan Co. planned to convert the store into a high-rise office building, with stores on the lower levels.

Although Tokyu shed unprofitable businesses to streamline operations, earnings continued to be bleak throughout 1999. Sales in fiscal 1999 dropped 6.3 percent, and during the first half of 1999 the company reported an unconsolidated pretax loss of ¥713 million, nearly double its year-earlier loss of ¥361 million. Net losses also increased, from ¥1.04 billion during the first half of 1998 to ¥5.07 billion in 1999. Closure of the Nihonbashi store contributed to poor sales, which fell

14 percent. Tokyu hoped to offset losses with the sale of the Nihonbashi building.

In April 1999 Miura stepped down from his post as chairman to signal his responsibility in Tokyu's poor performance. Miura had previously resigned his role as president in 1992 and assumed the chairmanship when Tokyu suffered large losses in investments. Tokyu predicted it would continue to rack up losses and forecast an after-tax loss of ¥2.9 billion for fiscal 2000. With the company's efforts to pare down overhead and its openness to take risks—plans to develop suburban shopping centers and to explore the community antenna television industry continued—Tokyu appeared armed for the coming millennium.

MOVING INTO THE 21ST CENTURY

The company faced challenges, however, as Japan's economy weakened and consumer demand slowed during the early 2000s. In response, Tokyu continued to cut costs and reduce personnel while revamping its existing stores in an attempt to lure new customers. As part of its strategy to shed noncore assets, the company sold its stake in Shibuya Development Inc. to its parent, Tokyu Corp. It also jettisoned another holding, Restaurant Monterosa Co., selling it to SHiDAX Co. and using the proceeds to pay down debt.

In 2003 the company announced plans to cut an additional 500 jobs through early retirement programs. It also sold the land and building that housed its flagship Shibuya store, allowing it to post a profit for the first time in three years. Despite the change to the company's bottom line, it failed to make dividend payments to its shareholders for the fifth consecutive year.

Revenue and profits dropped again in 2004, as store sales remained sluggish. Tokyu Corporation set plans in motion that year to make Tokyu Department Store Co. a wholly owned subsidiary. The transition was completed in 2005 and the department store firm was delisted from the Tokyo Stock Exchange.

Tokyu and its competitors were operating in a unique environment during this time period. Japan's population was aging and declining, and retailers were for the first time forced to cater to younger shoppers. At the same time, intense competition from specialty stores as well as suburban shopping malls was eating into traditional department stores sales. Overall, department stores sales in Japan fell for the 12th consecutive year in 2008.

As part of its strategy to secure new customers, the company partnered with Japanese department store operator Isetan Co. Ltd. in 2007. The two companies planned to share ideas on marketing, merchandising, and customer retention programs. While the partnership was slated to last through 2010, Isetan merged with Mitsukoshi Ltd. in 2008, creating the largest department store company in Japan. Isetan claimed the merger would have no effect on its partnership with Tokyu.

During 2008 Tokyu refurbished its women's fashion department at its Shibuya store for the first time in eight years. It also had plans in the works to expand and renovate its Tama Plaza store in Yokohama by 2010 and construct a new store at Shibuya Bunka Kaikan by 2012. Hirokazu Mizuta was at the helm of Tokyu as president and CEO and Hideo Fukushima was senior managing director. While conditions remained harsh for many department stores in Japan, both Mizuta and Fukushima were confident the company was laying the foundation for growth in the years to come.

Alison Classe
Updated, Mariko Fujinaka; Christina M. Stansell

PRINCIPAL COMPETITORS

The Diamaru Inc.; Mitsukoshi Ltd.; Takashimaya Co. Ltd.

FURTHER READING

"Department Stores Set to Freshen Up," *Nikkei Weekly,* August 25, 2008.

Diamond's Japan Business Directory 1991, Tokyo: Diamond Lead Co., Ltd., 1991.

"Doorsteps, the New Point of Sale," *Economist,* February 28, 1987.

Gilbert, Les, "Analyst Looks at Japan, 1990s Style," *HFD—The Weekly Home Furnishings Newspaper,* April 9, 1990, p. 14.

"Isetan Co.: Japanese Retail Chains to Forge Business Links," *Wall Street Journal,* March 28, 2007, p. C8.

"Japanese Department Stores Isetan, Tokyu Tie Up," *Reuters News,* March 27, 2007.

"Japan's Department Stores Report Dismal Earnings," *Asian Wall Street Journal,* April 26, 1993, p. 4.

Miura, Mamoru, "Department Stores Must Act As Integrated Life Industries," *Business Japan,* August 1990.

Ostrom, Douglas, "Consumer Spending in the Dumps, Poised to Get Worse," *JEI Report,* October 2, 1998.

Retail Distribution in Japan, Tokyo: Dodwell Marketing Consultants, 1988.

Shirouzu, Norihiko, "In Retailing, Risk Takers May Be Japan's Safest Bets," *Asian Wall Street Journal,* September 26, 1997, p. 15.

Terai, Shintaro, "Tokyu Department Store Frets," *Nikkei Weekly,* February 25, 2008.

"Tokyu Department Store Co. Incurs Net Loss for Restructuring," *Knight-Ridder/Tribune Business News,* March 31, 2004.

"Tokyu Department Store Expects Loss of $141.5 Million for the Year," *Asian Wall Street Journal,* January 26, 1998, p. 4.

"Tokyu Dept. Store to Close Major Tokyo Retail Outlet," *Japan Economic Newswire,* September 16, 1998.

"Tokyu Dept. Store to End 330-Year History with a Bang," *Japan Economic Newswire,* January 25, 1999.

"Tokyu Dept. to Cut Workforce by 500," *Jiji Press English News Service,* September 27, 2004.

"Tokyu to Take Full Control of Tokyu Department in April," *Jiji Press English News Service,* September 27, 2004.

"Tokyu to Turn Tokyu Dept. Store into Wholly Owned Unit," *Japan Weekly Monitor,* October 4, 2004.

Tree of Life, Inc.

405 Golfway West Drive
St. Augustine, Florida 32095-8839
U.S.A.
Telephone: (904) 940-2100
Toll Free: (800) 260-2424
Fax: (904) 940-2553
Web site: http://www.treeoflife.com

Wholly Owned Subsidiary of Royal Wessanen nv
Incorporated: 1972
Employees: 3,204
Sales: $1.18 billion (2008 est.)
NAICS: 422210 Drugs and Druggists' Sundries Wholesalers; 422490 Other Grocery and Related Products Wholesalers

■ ■ ■

Tree of Life, Inc., is the world's leading marketer and distributor of natural and specialty foods, serving thousands of retailers in the United States, Canada, and the Caribbean. During the later years of the first decade of the 21st century, the company operated ten distribution centers throughout the United States, as well as three Canadian distribution centers. Tree of Life is a wholly owned subsidiary of Royal Wessanen nv, a Dutch company with more than two centuries of experience in the food industry. The company serves as Royal Wessanen's North American distribution business. Royal Wessanen also operates a separate subsidiary named Tree of Life UK Ltd., through which it distributes products in Europe.

FORMATIVE YEARS

Tree of Life was founded by Irwin Carasso in St. Augustine, Florida, in 1970 as a natural foods retailer. Having incorporated in 1972, the company soon developed into a successful regional wholesale distribution company with $30 million in annual sales. The rapid growth of the natural foods industry in the 1980s enabled Tree of Life to establish operations in key markets across the country. Carasso sold Tree of Life in 1982 to Wilson Financial Corporation, a company based in Jacksonville, Florida, and controlled by Jacksonville financier J. Steven Wilson. Annual sales had reached $40 million by 1985, when the company was sold to Koninklijke Wessanen (which became Koninklijke Bols Wessanen in 1993, and later Royal Wessanen). The sale included another Wilson Financial unit, American Natural Snacks Inc., which was making items such as roasted nuts and carob- or yogurt-coated pretzels in St. Augustine.

The growth of Tree of Life was piecemeal. For example, it purchased Midwest Natural Foods Distributor, an Ann Arbor, Michigan, company with distribution outlets throughout the country by the late 1980s. This company was moved to Bloomington, Indiana, and combined with another division to form Tree of Life's midwest unit. Customers included health food and specialty foods stores, some grocery store chains carrying natural foods, and some food cooperatives. Gourmet Award Foods, a specialty foods distributor supplying ethnic and fancy food products from around the world, was created in 1988 from specialty foods distributors Tree of Life had added earlier. Consumer demand was a significant factor in the growth of both the natural products and specialty foods businesses, because shoppers in supermarkets increasingly were demanding niche products.

Tree of Life's sales reached $370 million in 1991 and $410 million in 1992 (of which Gourmet Award Foods contributed $60 million). By late 1993 it was operating nationwide, with ten distribution centers stretching from Miami to Seattle. Aside from American Natural Snacks, the company at this time included Atlanta area-based Swan Gardens, which was manufacturing a soy-based cheese substitute. Tree of Life had outgrown its 85,000-square-foot distribution center near its corporate headquarters and was planning a new 70,000-square-foot facility in St. Augustine. With 280 staffers, the company was the second largest employer in Saint Johns County, Florida.

Tree of Life's sales reached $540 million in 1995, and it held a 30 percent share of the natural foods market in the United States that year, making it the largest distributor of natural foods and health supplements in the nation. In 1996 Tree of Life made its tenth acquisition since being purchased by Wessanen, adding McLane America, Inc., the Salt Lake City-based specialty foods distribution subsidiary of McLane Co., Inc. With annual sales of about $60 million, McLane America was supplying supermarkets west of the Mississippi with gourmet, ethnic, and health food items. The operation was attached to Gourmet Award Foods, and its Salt Lake City facility added to Gourmet Award's distribution centers in Albany, New York; St. Paul, Minnesota; and Dallas, Texas. Tree of Life was then supplying 12,000 different natural/organic foods and food supplements to more than 5,000 retailers in the United States, Canada, and the Caribbean.

FOCUS ON SPECIALTY FOODS

Tree of Life strengthened its national distribution network by acquiring Specialty Food Distributors, Inc., of Plant City, Florida, in 1997, and Ray's Food Service, Inc., of Portland, Oregon, in 1998. The latter, with an-

nual sales of $80 million, was the leading marketer and distributor of specialty foods in the Pacific Northwest. This enterprise was combined with Tree of Life's Northwest division to form Tree of Life/Gourmet Award Foods Northwest, allowing it to offer a full assortment of natural and specialty foods products and services and one-stop shopping to all natural foods stores and supermarkets in the region.

Tree of Life introduced a new proprietary-branded vitamin and supplement line in 1998. By 1999 it had raised its market share in natural foods to 35 percent. About 60 percent of its business, however, was being generated by specialty foods, compared with 40 percent a few years earlier. The specialty foods category, which had grown both autonomously and by acquisitions, was more attractive to the company because it offered higher profit margins than natural foods. In all, sales reached $916.6 million in 1998, and operating income came to $31.3 million. These figures represented an increase from two years prior when sales and operating income were $724.9 million and $26.2 million, respectively.

Tree of Life announced in February 1999 the acquisition of Wine & Schultz, Inc., a specialty foods distributor based in Louisville, Kentucky, servicing Illinois, Indiana, Kentucky, Ohio, and Tennessee, and providing sales, marketing, and distribution services to supermarket retailers throughout the region. The operation was added to the Midwest division of Tree of Life/Gourmet Award Foods in Bloomington, which Norman Wine, the company's president, joined as director of specialty foods marketing. In the same month parent Koninklijke Wessanen announced the acquisition, for Tree of Life, of the North American-based Specialty Foods Group of Hagemeyer N.V., a Dutch company. The purchase consisted of the marketing and distribution companies Liberty Richter in New Jersey; MBC Foods in Milwaukee; Fine Distributing in Atlanta, Georgia, and Fort Lauderdale, Florida; and Ashley Koffman in Calgary and Toronto, Canada. Annual sales of these companies came to more than $300 million.

STATE-OF-THE-ART MARKETING

By 1999 Tree of Life's national system of distribution centers and the industry's largest tractor-trailer fleet were strategically positioned to serve every major metropolitan market in the United States with next-day delivery. This same distribution and transportation network allowed the company to present any new product from coast to coast in a single day. It also allowed Tree of Life's retail customers to efficiently coordinate product introductions and promotions at all levels, from local to national. Electronic communication was making it possible for retailers to use such online

KEY DATES

1970: The first Tree of Life store, a natural foods retailer, is established by Irwin Carasso in St. Augustine, Florida.

1972: Company is incorporated.

1982: Carasso sells Tree of Life to Wilson Financial Corp.

1985: The company is sold to Koninklijke Wessanen.

1988: Gourmet Award Foods, a specialty foods distributor supplying ethnic and fancy food products from around the world, is created.

1995: Tree of Life holds 30 percent of the U.S. natural foods market, making it the nation's largest distributor of natural foods and health supplements.

1999: Tree of Life acquires Wine & Schultz, Inc., a specialty foods distributor based in Louisville, Kentucky.

2003: The company's operations receive certified organic status from the U.S. Department of Agriculture's Natural Organic Program; Tree of Life becomes the nation's largest certified organic distributor.

2004: Chairman and CEO Rick Thorne announces plans to retire, ending a 20-year career with the company.

2005: Tree of Life and Gourmet Award Foods are merged into Tree of Life Inc.

2009: Parent company Royal Wessanen reveals plans to put its U.S. companies on the market.

ordering systems as MSI, Telzon, POS, and electronic data interchange (EDI). They also had instant access to the company's real-time pricing, catalogs, and promotions.

Tree of Life had 11 distribution centers in 1999. Its warehouse technology included radio-frequency picking and smart conveyors to expedite the fulfillment processes. The company offered to deliver daily or weekly to stores, using electronic routing and dispatching. Tree of Life's inventory of more than 25,000 products offered a broad assortment of premium imported, kosher, fat-free, natural, and organic foods; ethnic specialties; personal care items; vitamins and herbal supplements; and frozen and refrigerated items. The foods it was carrying ranged from Mexican salsas to Mandarin oranges, pasta to peanut butter, cookies to crackers. The more than 1,000 items in Tree of Life's family of proprietary products included fat-free, reduced-fat, and all-natural and all-organic products; foods for consumers with allergy and dietary restrictions; frozen entrees and side dishes; instant single-serve products; and gourmet and ethnic specialties.

Tree of Life and Gourmet Award Foods also were offering marketing and distribution services in 1999. These were available to small and large retailers alike, from natural foods stores and gourmet grocers to supermarket chains and major drugstores. Retail services included shelf management, back door check-in, ordering/receiving services, and store/department set design. Marketing and merchandising expertise were offered in the areas of product assortment, monthly merchandising guides, co-op advertising, product demonstrations, and category management.

Tree of Life's retail service programs offered to write and receive orders, maintain store shelves, set up and break down promotional displays, add new departments or reset existing ones, and even to help design a new store from the ground up. The company also offered a series of unique in-store training programs to help maximize retail merchandising efforts and improve the overall performance of the retailer's staff. A monthly merchandising guide was circulated to all customers, packed with exclusive purchasing opportunities and merchandising tips, in-depth information on new products, and emerging consumer trends. Other merchandising programs ranged from co-op advertising and product demonstrations to national promotions, endcaps, and impulse displays. Gourmet Award Foods was holding an annual international food festival for retailers and vendors.

ENTERING THE 21ST CENTURY

Growth continued at Tree of Life during the early years of the new century. By this time the company employed more than 6,000 people and had sales of approximately $1.7 billion. In 2001 Tree of Life agreed to acquire most of Food for Health Co. Inc.'s assets in a deal with that company's parent, Omaha, Nebraska-based AMCON Distributing Co.

In early 2002 Tree of Life acquired Better Than Milk, home to such brands as Soy Amazing, Hearty Life, Better Than Milk, and Better Than Ice Cream, from Fuller Life Inc. Midway through the year, Aurora, Ontario, Canada-based BEC Trading Ltd., a natural and specialty foods distributor with annual sales of CAD 13.5 million, was acquired. Tree of Life's operations received certified organic status from the U.S. Department of Agriculture's Natural Organic Program in late 2003. The certification was noteworthy in that the company became the largest certified organic distributor in the United States.

A major leadership change occurred in early 2004, when Tree of Life Chairman and CEO Rick Thorne announced plans to retire, ending a 20-year career with the company. Thorne had assumed the role of president and CEO in 1987, and guided the company as it grew from a regional player into a national one. While the company searched for a new leader, Wessanen Executive Board Chairman Ad Veenhof agreed to spend at least half of his time providing leadership for Tree of Life.

During the middle years of the decade, Tree of Life outlined a strategy that called for the company to focus on its core competencies. Along these lines, it agreed to sell its sales and marketing subsidiary, Specialty Partners Inc., to Natural/Specialty Sales Inc. By early 2005, Alec Covington had been named Tree of Life's new president and CEO. He was at the helm when the company completed the reorganization of its operations. A new East Region was established, which included the company's corporate headquarters, as well as the Northeast Region and the Southeast Region. Tree of Life at this time was serving customers from regional offices in Bloomington, Indiana; St. Augustine, Florida; and Dallas, Texas. More change followed in August, when Tree of Life and Gourmet Award Foods were merged into one organization named Tree of Life Inc.

FACING NEW OWNERSHIP

Progress continued as the company headed into the later years of the decade. This was especially true in the area of new technology. For example, software for transportation planning and warehouse replenishment was purchased from Scottsdale, Arizona-based JDA Software in 2006. By early 2007, Tree of Life was introducing the first phase of an EDI supply chain and marketing automation solution for its customers, providing features such as electronic invoices, electronic purchase orders, and purchase order acknowledgments.

Growth continued as Tree of Life acquired the Miami-based organic and select specialty foods distributor Organica USA in 2007. That deal was followed by the acquisition of the Sarasota, Florida-based specialty and organic wine/beer distributor Apple a Day Inc. By

this time, Richard Lane was serving as Tree of Life's president and CEO.

A significant development took place in April 2009, when Tree of Life parent company Royal Wessanen revealed plans to put its U.S. companies on the market. The move was part of a realignment of Royal Wessanen's business portfolio, which called for focusing on its European operations. The announcement came at a time when Tree of Life was on strong footing. Despite an economic recession, the company had experienced sales increases for nine consecutive quarters.

In May 2009, Tree of Life announced that a new Northeast Region Distribution Center would open its doors in August. Based near Allentown, Pennsylvania, the new facility spanned 311,000 square feet. Once that facility was open, Tree of Life revealed that it would close its existing distribution center in Albany, New York. In 2010 the company also planned to consolidate the operations of its distribution center in North Bergen, New Jersey, into the new Pennsylvania location. Rather than expressing concern over an uncertain future, the company's management was optimistic about the prospect of continued growth under new ownership.

Robert Halasz
Updated, Paul R. Greenland

PRINCIPAL COMPETITORS

C&S Wholesale Grocers, Inc.; Kehe Food Distributors Inc.; United Natural Foods Inc.

FURTHER READING

Everage, Laura, "Tree of Life, Inc., Completes Reorganization," *Gourmet Retailer*, April 2005.

Horak, Kathy, "Tree of Life Buys Land for $3 Million Expansion," *Business Journal–Jacksonville*, November 26, 1993, p. 3.

Orgel, David, "McLane to Sell Unit to Tree of Life," *Supermarket News*, February 26, 1996, p. 4.

"Thorne Announces Retirement from Tree of Life," *Gourmet Retailer*, February 2004.

"USDA Certifies Tree of Life's Operations as Organic," *Gourmet Retailer*, October 2003.

Zelade, Richard, "Healthy Merger," *International Business*, May 1996, p. 56.

Trinchero Family Estates

P.O. Box 248
St. Helena, California 94574
U.S.A.
Telephone: (707) 963-3104
Fax: (707) 963-2381
Web site: http://www.tfewines.com

Private Company
Incorporated: 1874 as John Thomann Winery and
    Distillery
Employees: 600
Sales: $375 million (2008 est.)
NAICS: 312130 Wineries

■ ■ ■

Trinchero Family Estates, which does business as Sutter Home Winery, is one of the leading producers of varietal wines in the United States. Based in the Napa Valley for decades, the company came to prominence for originating a light, slightly sweet, inexpensive lower-alcohol type of wine known as white Zinfandel, which was the nation's most popular premium wine in the 1980s and 1990s and spawned an entire new market of emulative "blush" wines. The owner of more than 6,000 vineyard acres in California, Trinchero manufactures a wide range of varietals under some two-dozen brand names, including Sutter Home, Folie à Deux, Soleo, Trinity Oaks, and the leading nonalcoholic wine, Fre. The company also owns the Australian-made Reynolds and Little Boomey labels and handles distribution for other niche wineries.

EARLY HISTORY

The founder of the company was a Swiss-German immigrant named John Thomann, who established a small winery and distillery in California's Napa Valley in 1874. After Thomann died, in 1906 his heirs sold the winery and the Victorian home he had built to another Swiss family, the Leuenbergers, for a reported $10. The new owners renamed the estate Sutter Home, in honor of Lina Leuenberger's father, John Sutter; they had formed the Sutter Home Winery and Distillery Company 11 years earlier in San Francisco. For the next half century, the Leuenberger family maintained control of the modest winery.

In 1947, John and Mario Trinchero, two Italian immigrant brothers whose family had been involved in the wine business in Italy for six generations, purchased the dilapidated winery. When the Trincheros took over, the Napa Valley region was a long way from becoming the thriving tourist attraction it would be in the 21st century: prunes, tomatoes, and walnuts were, in fact, more plentiful than wine grapes. Having immigrated to the United States in the 1920s, the aspiring winemakers moved their families from New York City to test their fortunes in a California rural area that seemed to be populated by as many cattle as people.

During the early years, the fledgling winery operated strictly as a "mom-and-pop" operation. Almost two-thirds of the wine sold was purchased at the front door. As Mario Trinchero's son Bob, who was only 12 years old when the family settled in St. Helena, recalled, "If you could carry or roll a container through the door, we'd fill it for you." In those days, during the 1950s, the company struggled to break even, and as the elder Trincheros neared retirement, the future of the wine business did not look favorable. Despite the tireless efforts of the Trincheros, their operation failed to turn a profit, and by 1960 they were in desperate need of a loan to keep the winery afloat.

When Mario Trinchero retired that same year, he managed to persuade his son Bob, who had left at age 18 for a four-year stint in the U.S. Air Force, vowing never to return to the Napa Valley region again, to carry on the family business and buy out his uncle's half share. However, before Bob could comply he first had to acquire the capital needed to rebuild the company. Bank of America, the only bank in town at the time, turned the company down for a loan, and the Trincheros were forced to put the winery on the market. As it happened, they found no takers at their asking price, and a new bank moved into town that was willing to lend them the money they needed. With their bills paid and $5,000 in fresh capital, the Trincheros were ready to rebuild their winery and their product.

FIRST SIGNS OF SUCCESS

Although Bob learned the art of winemaking from the ground up, handling such duties as barrel washing and pomace shoveling during his teenage years, he had no formal training. His efforts to improve the quality of the wine would be a matter of trial and error. While he was working on upgrading his product—he later told Robyn Bullard of the *Wine Spectator* that the wine was "actually drinkable by the late 1960s"—he made a discovery that would give him a secure foothold in the industry. In

1968, he paid a visit to Sacramento retailer Darrell Corti, who insisted that he try a homemade Zinfandel produced from grapes grown in the Sierra foothills' Amador County, a historic grape-growing region that had lain dormant since Prohibition. Immediately taken by the wine's intensity of flavor, Trinchero, who owned no fields of his own, contacted the grower and contracted to purchase grapes from him the following year. Not only would the change enable him to avoid the high cost of Napa Valley grapes, he would also get an opportunity to make his mark on the industry.

Trinchero's first experience with the Amador County grapes suggested that he had made a wise decision and that his winemaking skills were improving. The 1969 vintage of Amador County Zinfandel, produced from the century-old vines grown at the Deaver Ranch Vineyard in Amador's Shenandoah Valley, earned Sutter Home its first accolades and paved the way for future recognition.

Encouraged by the critical success of his Amador Zinfandel, Trinchero looked for ways to make the wine more robust and more appealing to a wider market. In 1972, while experimenting with his Zinfandel, he made a serendipitous discovery that would one day make him a multimillionaire and change the face of the American wine industry at the same time. Immediately after crushing a batch of Zinfandel grapes, he drained some free-run juice from the must (the juice pressed from grapes before it has been fermented) in an attempt to increase the ratio of skins, which impart most of a red wine's color and body. Modeling his creation after the French rosés he greatly admired, Trinchero then fermented the drawn-off juice like a dry white wine. Just for fun, he bottled 220 cases of the pale pink elixir after a period of barrel aging and offered the novel "blanc de noir" table wine to his tasting room clientele as a curiosity item.

A NEW PRODUCT FOR THE AMERICAN PALATE

The wine was originally called "Oel de Pedrix" (eye of the partridge), but the Bureau of Alcohol, Tobacco and Firearms (BATF) insisted that there be an English translation on the label. Trinchero reluctantly complied with the government's request and provided his customers with an easier name to remember, white Zinfandel. As Trinchero told the *Wine Spectator,* "It was white, and it was Zinfandel, and if anyone wants to know where the name came from, it was from the BATF forcing me to do it."

Although Trinchero's novelty item created some interest in his tasting room, enough for him to increase production the following year, its popularity was not

KEY DATES

1874: Swiss immigrant John Thomann establishes a small winery in Napa Valley, California.

1906: The Leuenberger family acquires the winery, renames it Sutter Home.

1947: Italian immigrants John and Mario Trinchero acquire Sutter Home.

1968: The Trincheros begin using Amador County grapes as an alternative to costly Napa County fruit.

1972: Trinchero discovers white Zinfandel as a result of a fermenting accident.

1981: Sutter Home is producing 25,000 cases a year of white Zinfandel.

1985: Sutter Home produces 850,000 cases of white Zinfandel.

1988: Sutter Homes buys Amador County winery Montevina.

1992: Fre nonalcoholic wine is introduced as part of the company's diversification effort.

1998: The winery celebrates its 50th year by launching a new brand, M. Trinchero, named after the company's founder.

1999: The company begins trading as Trinchero Family Estates.

2001: Trinity Oaks superpremium brand debuts.

2004: Trinchero Family Estates buys Folie à Deux of Napa Valley and Australian brands Reynolds Vineyards and Little Boomey.

2008: New flagship winery, Trinchero Napa Valley, opens on former Folie à Deux site.

widespread. It would take another "accidental" adjustment to the recipe for that to occur. In 1975, while working on a batch of 1,000 gallons, he discovered that the wine had stopped fermenting, a phenomenon known in the industry as a "stuck fermentation." Not knowing what else to do and busy with other more pressing concerns, Trinchero simply topped the tank and put his new concoction aside for a few weeks. When he returned to the tank to sample what he had produced, he noticed that the wine was a bit pink, taking on a kind of blush hue. The critical difference, Trinchero would later discover, lay in the 2 percent residual sugar the wine contained, which gave it a slightly sweeter flavor.

At this point, Trinchero's white Zinfandel was a long way from becoming America's most popular wine.

For a few years, the wine remained little more than a novelty item; most of it was sold in the Sutter Home tasting room on Napa Valley's Highway 29. Furthermore, Trinchero had plans to convert the entire 7,000-case production into his more established product, red Zinfandel. As it happened, however, the process that might have brought an end to the promising new wine was not occurring rapidly.

By the late 1970s, Trinchero, along with his younger brother, Roger, realized that a new marketing strategy was needed. Despite their efforts, the company was struggling to survive while the rest of the industry seemed to be booming. After one particularly difficult day, the two sat down to discuss their predicament over a couple of glasses of wine. The conclusion they reached, as Bob later told Bullard, was a simple one: "It seemed the consumer wanted something besides what we were giving them." Searching for a way to rectify this problem, the two took an inventory of all the wines they were making and discovered that the experimental wine they called white Zinfandel was the only wine in short supply.

NEW STRATEGY VAULTS SUTTER HOME TO THE TOP

Going against the rest of the industry, which was dominated by jug wines, the Trincheros channeled their efforts and resources on the product that seemed most in line with their customers' taste preferences. They doubled the production of their white Zinfandel, hoping that the strawberry fruitiness of the product would appeal to the American masses. Their gamble paid off: They were forced to double production the following year, and again the next. By 1981, the Trincheros, while fine-tuning their white Zinfandel over several vintages, had escalated production to 25,000 cases a year. Four years later, that number would jump to 850,000.

The explosive growth in white Zinfandel production and the expansion of the California wine industry made the task of maintaining an adequate supply of grapes a major concern for the first time, and the company's long held dependence on outside vineyards in the Napa Valley region no longer viable. In 1984, having strengthened its financial base through white Zinfandel sales, the company made its first purchase: a 300-acre vineyard in Lake County, located to the northeast of Napa Valley. Although the Trincheros initially planned to graft the vineyard entirely to Zinfandel, they decided to retain the existing varieties (Sauvignon Blanc, Chenin Blanc, and Cabernet Sauvignon) after discovering their high quality. This decision would provide Sutter Home with a base for future expansion of its line of premium varietal wines. Other purchases in the Sacramento Valley and the Sacramento Delta added another 2,500 acres by the end of the decade, bolstering the production capability for white Zinfandel and other premium wines.

Sutter Home's decision to focus its energies on varietal wines helped to redefine the American wine industry and allowed it to prosper during the remainder of the decade. As late as 1980, the market was dominated by what was known in the industry as "The Gang of Five": Gallo, Almaden, Masson, Inglenook, and Taylor, all of whom sold primarily generic wines simply by color and in four-liter jugs. Sutter Home's introduction and successful marketing of white Zinfandel, and the host of other wineries who later came up with their own, played a significant role in changing the dynamics of the industry. While jug wine sales dropped from $930 million in 1980 to $840 million in 1990, varietal wine revenue skyrocketed from $22.4 million to $1.4 billion over the same period.

A number of factors were responsible for this dramatic shift in the industry and for Sutter Home's tremendous success in the 1980s. According to Bob Trinchero, the enormous popularity of his white Zinfandel lay in its ability to break down the "wall of intimidation" that kept many Americans from drinking wine. Realizing that many people were apprehensive about ordering sophisticated, hard-to-pronounce wines in restaurants, the Trincheros attempted to develop a product that appealed to the majority of wine-drinking Americans who were not connoisseurs. Accordingly, instead of tailoring their wines to fit their own tastes, they asked their customers for their advice. "If you think all you've got to do is make a good wine to have people line up at the door," Roger, in charge of sales and marketing, told Bullard, "you're kidding yourself." White Zinfandel, an affordable varietal wine characterized by its light, slightly sweet taste and visually attractive pink hue, proved to be a perfect match. By 1989, it had become, on sales of 2.9 million cases, the most popular wine in the United States.

DIVERSIFICATION

As Sutter Home entered the 1990s, it found itself facing increasingly strong competition. Its unprecedented success with white Zinfandel had spawned a host of emulative "blush" wines, many of which helped to turn around the struggling wineries that produced them. An extremely cost-effective product, white Zinfandel was easy to manufacture and required very little aging, enabling wineries to generate revenue just a few months after the harvest. While Sutter Home remained at the top, it needed to diversify its marketing strategy for growth to continue into the new decade.

Again, Sutter Home focused its attention on the majority of American wine drinkers rather than on the exclusive tastes of the elite. This time, however, the innovation came in the form of a package instead of a new wine. In April 1989, the company introduced the "Classic Single," a 187-milliliter single-service wine packaged in a Bordeaux-style bottle. The brainchild of Roger Trinchero, the Classic Single package was designed to take advantage of a "less but better" market trend, the result of the country's growing health consciousness and its emphasis on moderation. The smaller portion size was also targeted to the increasing population of Americans living alone, or with a companion with differing beverage preferences. Sales of over a million cases of Classic Single bottles of white Zinfandel, Cabernet Sauvignon, Sauvignon Blanc, and Chardonnay in 1990 and two million the following year suggested that the company had again correctly read the preferences of the American wine consumer.

In 1992 Sutter Home again led the industry on sales of 5.2 million cases, or $145 million. The company and the entire premium wine industry benefited from several reports from the medical community, publicized most notably on a *60 Minutes* special, that praised the possible health benefits of drinking red wine in moderation. That same year the company tried to further capitalize on the good news for the wine industry by introducing a new chillable premium red wine, Soleo, a proprietary blend combining Zinfandel, Barbera, Pinot Noir, and Napa Gamay. The light, fruity, easy-drinking wine was designed for white-wine drinkers seeking the lower cholesterol levels promised by red wines.

That same year, Sutter Home made its boldest attempt to lead the industry in meeting the needs of the health-conscious consumer. Going against the conventional wisdom of the industry, the Trincheros became the first major winery to introduce a nonalcoholic wine. The innovative product, called Fre, was developed primarily by Bob Trinchero's daughter Gina and received accolades for its resemblance in taste to wine rather than grape juice. Produced using an Australian-developed de-alcoholizing process that retained more of the wine's essence instead of adding water, Fre proved to be another successful innovation for the company. In 1993, for instance, sales jumped to 200,000 cases, a fourfold increase from the year of its release.

As Sutter Home entered the second half of the decade, it remained in 100 percent control of the innovative Trinchero family, who had built the company into a $140 million operation. It looked to maintain its position of leadership in the industry by continuing to increase its diverse complement of wines. Increased competition in the premium wine market had made the company more dependent on its nonalcoholic wines, competitive pricing, and aggressive advertising in supermarkets. Vowing to "never stop experimenting," the Trincheros hoped to fuel future growth with the same type of innovative products and marketing strategies that allowed for their expansion during the previous four decades.

GROWING MORE SOPHISTICATED

Chardonnay eclipsed white Zinfandel as the country's most popular varietal in 1998. Sutter Home continued to produce 4.5 million cases a year of white Zinfandel as various other trends, such as Syrah and Merlot, emerged in the industry, competing for growing space as well as end consumers. Sutter Home was producing about ten million cases of all types of wine per year, worth about $300 million. The winemaker celebrated its 50th year in 1998 by launching a new brand, M. Trinchero, named after the company founder. These new wines represented a step into the market for serious, superpremium wines of the type that probably would not have been accepted under the populist Sutter Home label. Other superpremium brands followed, such as Trinity Oaks, launched in 2001. Around this time the initial M. (for Mario) was dropped from the M. Trinchero label with the launch of a new line of single-vineyard wines.

In mid-1999 the company began trading as Trinchero Family Estates. Within a year Constellation Brands, Inc., which through its Canadaigua Wine Company unit was one of the world's top three leading vintners, reportedly offered to buy out the Trincheros for $500 million. The business was particularly valuable for its ability to process grapes brought in from outside Napa Valley. The Trincheros, however, elected to keep the business within the family, although the next generation did not possess much interest in running it themselves, as noted in *Harvesting the Dream: The Rags-to-Riches Tale of the Sutter Home Winery.*

In 2002, U.S. wine consumption reached record levels, with nearly 600 million gallons consumed. The $21 billion domestic wine industry remained very competitive, with 1,800 wineries (more than half of them in California). Sutter Home was the fifth largest in the country, making more than nine million cases of wine a year. The company was exporting to the United Kingdom as well and in 2004 announced its first supermarket distribution deal there, offering white Zinfandel, Fre, and several other varieties. Around 2001 Trinchero Family Estates entered a joint venture to make wine in New South Wales, Australia, under the

Reynolds label. Its partner was Cabonne Limited. Trinchero bought Reynolds, and associated brand Little Boomey, in 2004.

By this time, Trinchero Family Estates owned 6,000 acres of vineyards in California, including 200 acres in Napa Valley. In 2004 the company added Folie à Deux, a small, highly regarded Napa Valley winery known for its Cabernet Sauvignon, made from grapes raised on its own 13-acre site in St. Helena.

In 2007, Trinchero Family Estates sold its 16-acre Sutter Home Winery south of St. Helena to entrepreneur Joel Gott, who converted it to a facility for producing a number of niche labels under contract while the Trincheros continued to use part of the former egg farm for wine storage. Two years later, Trinchero Family Estates joined a venture to distribute Joel Gott Wines internationally. Gott had a long history with the Trincheros, having sold them his own Montevina winery in Amador County almost 20 years earlier in 1988.

A new flagship vineyard, Trinchero Napa Valley, opened in 2008 on the former Folie à Deux site in St. Helena. As the flagship of the group's vineyards, it was devoted to making small batches of high-quality wines. The Trincheros were also building a new facility for their bread-and-butter product, the white Zinfandel, in Lodi, California. The new winery, called Westside, incorporated state-of-the-art energy-saving features such as a $5 million solar power system.

Jason Gallman
Updated, Frederick C. Ingram

PRINCIPAL OPERATING UNITS

Sutter Home Winery; Trinchero Napa Valley; Westside.

PRINCIPAL COMPETITORS

Constellation Brands, Inc.; E. & J. Gallo Winery; Beringer Blass Wine Estates Holdings Inc.; Kendall-Jackson Wine Estates, Ltd.

FURTHER READING

Bird, Laura, "Scanner Data Sauvignon: The American Palate Is Changing," *Adweek's Marketing Week,* August 19, 1991, pp. 18–19.

Bonné, Jon, "The Ranch Revamped; Joel Gott Turns Sutter Home's White Zinfandel Facility into a Haven for Top-Dollar Cabs," *San Francisco Chronicle,* June 20, 2008, p. F1.

A Brief History of Sutter Home Winery, St. Helena, Calif.: Sutter Home Winery, Inc., 1995.

Bullard, Robyn, "The House That White Zinfandel Built," *Wine Spectator,* May 15, 1994, pp. 52–60.

Campanelli, Melissa, "Going for the Gold," *Sales and Marketing Management,* June 1992, pp. 160–61.

"CEO Interview: Roger Trinchero—Trinchero Family Estates," *Wall Street Transcript Digest,* January 27, 2003.

Emert, Carol, "From Rags to Riches to Recycling Regimen; Trinchero Family Estates Shows the Wine Industry How to Save Money by Conserving Resources," *San Francisco Chronicle,* August 19, 2004, p. F5.

Gordon, Andrew, "Corporate Case Study: Trinchero Grows Its Stature by Pouring Effort into PR," *PR Week* (U.S.), October 27, 2003, p. 10.

Graebner, Lynn, "Sutter Home Buys 400 Acres," *Business Journal Serving Greater Sacramento,* October 23, 1995, p. 4.

Heyhoe, Kate, and Stanley Hock, *Harvesting the Dream: The Rags-to-Riches Tale of the Sutter Home Winery,* New York: Wiley, 2004.

Murphy, Linda, "White Zinfandel, Now 30, Once Ruled the U.S. Wine World; The Wine Snobs Won't Touch It, but That's Their Loss," *San Francisco Chronicle,* July 3, 2003, p. D2.

"Pair Game," *Caterer & Hotelkeeper,* June 24, 2004, p. 26.

Saekel, Karola, "The People's Winery: The Creators of White Zinfandel Still Holding Strong," *San Francisco Chronicle,* June 15, 2007, p. F2.

———, "Sutter Home Withstands over a Century of Change," *San Francisco Chronicle,* Food Sec., November 10, 1999.

Sinton, Peter, "Vino for the Masses; Sutter Home's Easy-to-Drink Varietals Make It Popular with Everyone Except Wine Aficionados," *San Francisco Chronicle,* August 9, 2001, p. B1.

Vizard, Frank, "Grapes Without Wrath," *Popular Mechanics,* March 1993, pp. 29–32.

Truworths International Ltd.

─────■─────

P.O. Box 600
Cape Town, 8000
South Africa
Telephone: (27 021) 460 7911
Fax: (27 021) 460 7132
Web site: http://www.truworths.co.za

Public Company
Incorporated: 1917 as Alliance Trading Company
Employees: 9,000
Sales: ZAR 5.65 billion ($773 million) (2008)
Stock Exchanges: Johannesburg
Ticker Symbol: TRU
NAICS: 448120 Women's Clothing Stores; 448110 Men's Clothing Stores; 448140 Family Clothing Stores; 448150 Clothing Accessories Stores

■ ■ ■

Truworths International Ltd. is one of South Africa's leading clothing retailers. The company operates more than 452 stores throughout southern Africa, including in Namibia, Ghana, Zimbabwe, Swaziland, Lesotho, Botswana, and Zambia. The company also operates a small franchise network of 24 stores across Africa and the Middle East. Truworths International operates through two primary divisions, Truworths and YDE (Young Designers Emporium). Truworths comprises the company's core women's wear retail brand Truworths, which includes 247 stores and generates 56 percent of the group's total sales. Truworths MAN operates 25 stores, adding 17 percent to sales, while the Identity retail accessories format includes 122 stores for 12 percent of group revenues. Other clothing brands in the Truworths family include Italian-design inspired Uzzi; Parisian-flavored Daniel Hechter; the youth-oriented Inwear, and leisure brand LTD.

Since 2004 Truworths has been converting a number of its stores into a new multibranded Emporium format. This format was inspired by the group's acquisition of a 75 percent stake in YDE, which operates 11 stores as a fashion collective for young and upcoming South African clothing designers. Truworths has also developed three non-clothing retail formats, Truworths Elements, for perfume sales; Truworths Fine Jewellery; and home furnishings brand Truworths Living. Truworths is listed on the Johannesburg and Namibia stock exchanges and is led by CEO Michael Mark. The company posted total revenues of ZAR 5.65 billion ($773 million) in 2008.

WHOLESALER ORIGINS

Truworths originated as a wholesale company called Alliance Trading Company, founded in Cape Town, South Africa, in 1917. Alliance's original focus was on the distribution of women's clothing, which it imported from Europe and the United States and sold through its own shop. In the 1930s, the company adopted a new name for the Cape Town store, Truworths Fashion House. The new name was more in keeping with its focus on women's clothing and later grew into one of the leading names in the South African retail sector. This growth began in 1935, when the company opened its first store in Johannesburg. The company formally

COMPANY PERSPECTIVES

Our Philosophy. The Truworths business model is driven by a philosophy that has been developed and refined over many years in pursuit of a unique approach to achieve sustainable growth in the complex and fast moving retail fashion environment.

A major asset in this pursuit is the strength of the Truworths brand that represents to youthful, fashionable consumers an innovative South African interpretation of fashion trends and attractive styling, competitive with the highest international standards.

We strive to: Make the Truworths brand of fashion merchandise the most aspirational, innovative and adventurous blend of colour, fabric, value and fashion styling. Make the Truworths store, the brand destination, the most enticing, visually appealing and effortless retail shopping environment. Engage and energise our people who personify the brand. Lead and motivate our staff to deliver consistently in the context of our value system so that we continue to build brand integrity. We measure our success in terms of how customers respond to our retail offering and how shareholders rate our capacity to execute innovative strategies that deliver significant real growth year after year.

changed its name to Truworths that year, and then opened a second Cape Town store.

In the late 1930s, Truworths continued its evolution beyond its wholesale roots. Instead of relying on imported garments, the company increasingly turned to the local market. Starting in the mid-1930s, Truworths took charge of its fabric sourcing, supplying a network of local manufacturers to produce its own clothing designs. The move helped establish the company as a major South African fashion brand. Starting in 1944, the company entered manufacturing, setting up its own factories in South Africa. Two years later, the company listed its shares on the Johannesburg Stock Exchange.

The public offering enabled the company to step up the expansion of its retail store network. By 1950 the company had opened 40 stores throughout South Africa. Supporting this growth was a new factory, added that year. By the end of the decade, the company had doubled its retail store network. The Truworths brand also moved beyond South Africa proper into neighbor-

ing territories. The presence of the Truworths brand in Zimbabwe, for example, dated from 1957.

JOINING WOOLWORTHS

A major factor in the growth of Truworths was its decision in 1955 to launch credit-based sales. The availability of credit encouraged customers to make larger and more frequent purchases. Interest-generating credit sales also provided higher profit margins than cash-based sales. In addition, the installation of a credit system provided Truworths with a growing customer database, allowing the company to develop more targeted marketing and communication programs. Truworths countered the risks inherent in credit sales by adopting a carefully conservative credit acceptance strategy. In this way, the company was able to minimize its bad debt portfolio. By the end of the 20th century, the company's credit-based sales routinely accounted for more than three-fourths of its total sales.

By 1959 Truworths had topped the symbolic ZAR 1 million mark. Through the 1960s, the company continued to develop its retail network. Truworths developed a new retail format, called Truworths Boutique, which provided new success for the company. Truworths operated more than 270 stores throughout South Africa by the end of the 1970s.

This growth caught the attention of another major South African retailer group, Woolworths, which operated supermarkets and other retail formats in that country. In 1981 Woolworths and Truworths agreed to merge. The merger involved the creation of a new publicly listed holding company, Wooltru, which became the parent for the Truworths, Woolworths, and Massmart retail networks. As a result, the Truworths listing was removed from the stock exchange.

Backed by its powerful parent, Truworths launched a new expansion drive during the 1980s. The company began to respond to a growing trend in the retail market. The rise of designer labels and retail brands had begun to turn customers away from traditional retailers like Truworths. In response to this trend the company began to develop its own range of designer-styled retail formats. In 1984, for example, the company teamed up with Parisian designer Daniel Hechter, developing a new retail format and clothing line for the South African market.

Truworths targeted a younger market in 1986, launching the Inwear label. In the meantime, the interest in designer labels had also led to a surge in interest in men's fashions. Truworths recognized an opportunity to extend its own operations into that market, launching the Truworths MAN retail store format in 1988. The Truworths MAN retail network grew to include 25

KEY DATES

1917: The Alliance Trading Company is founded as a women's clothing wholesaler, with a store in Cape Town, South Africa.

1935: First store opens in Johannesburg; the company becomes Truworths Fashion House.

1944: The company enters manufacturing, setting up its own factories in South Africa.

1946: Truworths goes public on the Johannesburg Stock Exchange.

1955: Truworths introduces credit-based sales.

1981: Truworths merges with Woolworths, forming Wooltru; Truworths listing is removed from the stock exchange.

1984: Truworths begins expanding its retail brand range, launching Daniel Hechter.

1988: The Truworths MAN retail store format is launched.

1998: Truworths is spun off as a publicly listed company, Truworths International, which lists its shares on the Johannesburg Stock Exchange.

2003: Truworths acquires Young Designers Emporium (YDE).

2004: Truworths launches multibranded Truworths Emporium retail format.

2006: Truworths opens its first Ginger Mary store; Italian-style brand Lucia Rosati is introduced.

stores, producing 17 percent of the company's total sales. Truworths continued to add new labels and retail formats through the 1990s. In 1989 the company branched out into jewelry, developing the Truworths Jewellery brand. This business segment remained only a small part of the group's total operations, however.

GOING PUBLIC AGAIN

The arrival of Michael Mark as company CEO in 1991 marked a new milestone in the company's history. Then 38 years old, Mark had entered the retail fashion industry in 1982, after a stint working in the pharmaceuticals industry. Mark initially worked at Foschini, another prominent South African retailer. In 1988, Mark joined Wooltru at another of the retail giant's companies, Topics, which later became part of Truworths. Under Mark, Truworths grew strongly, becoming one of South Africa's largest and most profitable clothing retailers.

Truworths continued to build its brand portfolio through the 1990s. The company added the LTD brand, a family-oriented leisurewear format, in 1992. In 1996 the company created a new, although shorter-lived format, Made in the World.

Wooltru began dismantling its structure in 1998. As part of that process, Truworths was spun off as a publicly listed company, called Truworths International, listing its shares once again on the Johannesburg Stock Exchange. The company also placed its shares on the Namibian Stock Exchange at the same time. Wooltru, however, remained a major shareholder in the company.

The public offering fueled the further growth of Truworths through the end of the decade and into the next century. The company extended into cosmetics, launching the Elements brand in 1999. Also that year, Truworths added a new and highly successful retail accessories format called Identity. This chain grew rapidly through the first decade of the new century, and by the end of 2009 expected to have nearly 150 stores in its network.

Less successful for Truworths was an attempt to enter the Australian retail market. For this, the company acquired that country's Sportsgirl-Sportscraft fashion group. However, the purchase appeared to stretch the company too thin. The Australian chain slipped into losses, as its debt mounted to more than AUD 91 million. By the end of 1999, Sportsgirl-Sportscraft was placed into receivership, and then sold to the Sussan Group.

EMPORIUM FOCUS

The overall Truworths business, however, remained sound. The company continued to look for new horizons in the new century. Truworths by this time operated directly in most of the southern African markets, including in Namibia, Ghana, Zimbabwe, Swaziland, Lesotho, Botswana, and Zambia. In order to expand farther abroad, the group launched a new franchising model, building up a secondary network of 24 stores through the end of the decade. The franchise model enabled the company to enter such distant markets as Bahrain, through the Al Jazira group.

Truworths launched a redesign of its core retail fashion operation, introducing its New Millennium Concept in 2002. Truworths also introduced a new cosmetics format that year, called MAC, opening a first store at the Cavendish Square shopping mall. The year 2002 also marked the completion of the group's unbundling from the Wooltru group.

In 2003 Truworths expanded again, through the acquisition of YDE (Young Designers Emporium). That company had been founded in 1994 by young designer

Paul Simon as a kibbutz-style designers' collective. YDE, which grew into an 11-store chain, provided Truworths with an extension into cutting-edge fashion. Truworths initially acquired 75 percent of YDE; by 2005 the company had acquired full control of YDE.

The YDE purchase also provided Truworths with the inspiration to develop its own multibranded Truworths Emporium retail format, launched in 2004. Truworths then began converting a number of its existing stores into the Emporium format, while rolling out a number of new Emporium stores through the end of the decade.

Truworths grew strongly through the decade, outpacing most of its retail rivals. By 2005 the company's revenues had topped ZAR 3 billion. Just one year later, the company's sales neared ZAR 5 billion, and despite the economic downturn, soared to ZAR 5.6 billion by the end of 2008. Part of this success was due to the rollout of credit sales facilities to a number of the group's retail operations, including Identity and YDE in 2004.

Truworths also extended its brand portfolio during this time. In 2004 the group launched the clothing brand Ginger Mary. The strong consumer welcome for the range encouraged the group to develop a dedicated retail format for the brand as well. In 2006 Truworths opened its first Ginger Mary store. In that year also the company introduced the Italian-style brand, Lucia Rosati. At the same time, Truworths acquired a 51 percent stake in the small high-end retail fashion label, Uzzi.

Truworths continued to build up its various retail chains. The Identity chain topped 100 stores in 2007 and reached 122 at the end of 2008, with another 20 slated to open by the end of 2009. YDE also grew to include 16 stores by 2008. The core Truworths women's shops also expanded, with expectations to top 250 stores before the end of 2009. Truworths also moved to acquire full control of Uzzi, buying the minority stake in that business in 2008. Despite the economic difficulties at the end of the decade, Truworths had successfully positioned itself as one of South Africa's leading and financially solid clothing retailers.

M. L. Cohen

PRINCIPAL SUBSIDIARIES

Truworths Limited; Truworths (Namibia) Ltd.; Truworths (Swaziland) Ltd.; Young Designers Emporium (Pty) Ltd.

PRINCIPAL DIVISIONS

Truworths; Young Designers Emporium (YDE).

PRINCIPAL OPERATING UNITS

Daniel Hechter; Elements; Identity; Inwear; LTD; Truworths; Truworths Jewellery; Truworths Living; Truworths MAN; Uzzi.

PRINCIPAL COMPETITORS

Woolworths Holdings Ltd.; Mr Price Group Ltd.; Delswa (Proprietary) Ltd.; Miladys; Rex Trueform Clothing Company Ltd.; Levi Strauss S.A. (Proprietary) Ltd.

FURTHER READING

Emond, Marie-Lais, "Companies in Focus," *Investor,* August 16, 2006.

Gilmour, Christopher, "Dressed for Success," *Financial Mail,* April 21, 2006.

Hall, Wendy, "Upbeat Truworths Buys Out YDE, Aims for Uzzi," *Business Day,* February 23, 2006.

Mawson, Nicola, "Truworths Says Space Growth Expected to Slow as Malls Stall," *Business Day,* February 24, 2009.

Morris, Ronnie, "Truworths Makes a Pretty Penny Across All Areas of Its Business," *Star,* August 24, 2007, p. 3.

Robbins, Tom, "Fashion Sense Is Truworths' Strong Suit," *Star,* August 21, 2008, p.1.

———, "Truworths Cashes In on Strict Credit Policy," *Star,* August 25, 2006, p. 4.

Stafford, Linda, "A Good Fit," *Financial Mail,* May 7, 2004.

Temkin, Ben, "Market Got It Wrong on Truworths, Then Right," *Africa News Service,* July 29, 2009.

Toffoli, Hilary Prendini, "Tru Grit," *Financial Mail,* June 17, 2005.

"Truworths Delivers Good Performance," *Star,* January 16, 2009, p. 18.

"Truworths Shoots Down Rumour of Private Buyout," *Star,* February 15, 2007, p. 5.

"Truworths Wears a Smile in Difficult Conditions," *Star,* August 21, 2008.

Wray, Quentin, "Truworths Has a Head for More Than Just Fashion," *Star,* August 21, 2008, p. 2.

UAL Corporation

—■—

77 West Wacker Drive
Chicago, Illinois 60601
U.S.A.
Telephone: (312) 997-8000
Web site: http://www.united.com

Public Company
Incorporated: 1934 as United Air Lines Transportation Company
Employees: 55,000
Sales: $20.19 billion (2008)
Stock Exchanges: NASDAQ
Ticker Symbol: UAUA
NAICS: 481111 Scheduled Passenger Air Transportation; 481112 Scheduled Freight Air Transportation

■ ■ ■

UAL Corporation is the holding company for United Airlines, Inc., one of the world's largest passenger and cargo carriers, which flies nearly 3,000 flights to over 200 U.S. and international destinations. The company lost employees and passengers aboard United Airlines Flights 93 and 175 in the terrorist attacks against the United States on September 11, 2001. That year proved both tragic and costly for UAL as it posted a $2.1 billion loss and filed for Chapter 11 bankruptcy protection the following year. The company completed its $23 billion restructuring and emerged in 2006. UAL and Continental Airlines Inc. announced plans to form a marketing alliance in June 2008.

ORIGINS

United Airlines was created in the early 1930s by Bill Boeing's aeronautic conglomerate to exploit demand for air transport and to serve as an immediate market for Boeing aircraft. At first United was similar to a consortium, involving the participation of several independent airline companies. One of those companies was Varney Air Lines, credited with being America's first commercial air transport company. Varney's 460-mile network between Pasco, Washington, and Elko, Nevada, was linked with Boeing Air Transport, which operated an airmail service between Chicago and San Francisco. This route crossed Vernon Gorst's Pacific Air Transport network, which ran mail between Seattle and Los Angeles. The National Air Transport Company, operated by New York financier Clement Keys, connected with Boeing in Chicago, flying mail south to Dallas. Stout Air Services, which had the financial backing of Henry and Edsel Ford, operated an air service between Chicago, Detroit, and Cleveland with Ford tri-motor airplanes.

These airline companies cooperated with Boeing, which manufactured aircraft in Seattle, and Pratt & Whitney, an aircraft engine manufacturer in Connecticut operated by Frederick Rentschler. Together they formed a vertically integrated aeronautic monopoly, restricting the delivery of new aircraft to its constituent partners and devoting its resources to eliminating competition on its air services. The airline group became known as United Air Lines in 1931. Among other things, the group was responsible for introducing air-to-ground radio, which improved communication and safety, and stewardesses, the original all eight of whom were registered nurses hired to allay passengers' fear of flying. A United executive at the time commented, "How is a man going to say he's afraid to fly when a woman is working on the plane?"

In 1934 National, Varney, Pacific, and Boeing officially merged under the name United Air Lines Transportation Company. Pat Patterson, a banker and Boeing official, was placed in charge of the airline at the age of 34. That year, however, congressional legislation outlawed the type of monopoly United had formed with Boeing and Pratt & Whitney, and the airline was forced to divorce itself from the conglomerate. It subsequently became an independent company based at Chicago's Old Orchard (later O'Hare) airport.

In 1936 after several airplane accidents, a series of syndicated newspaper stories sensationalized the horror of airplane crashes and incited a virtual state of panic, which drove passengers back to railroads by the thousands. The airline industry was so deeply affected that many smaller companies were faced with bankruptcy. United responded by retaining a popular military test pilot named Major R. W. Schroeder to oversee the company's implementation of new safety codes. With this action United helped to rebuild the public's confidence in air travel.

POSTWAR INNOVATION

As one of the nation's larger airline companies United maintained a position of leadership in the industry, constantly demanding newer, more advanced aircraft. United funded many of the developmental costs of the Douglas DC-4, the first four-engine passenger plane. However, when the United States became involved in World War II, all DC-4s were devoted to the war effort before ever having carried a commercial passenger. The company's name was shortened to United Air Lines in 1943 and new plans were made for the airline in anticipation of the end of the war. Two years later United redeployed its aircraft and resumed commercial flying.

In 1954 United became the first airline to employ flight simulators as part of its training and pilot testing programs. The following year United placed an order with Douglas Aircraft for DC-8s, the airline's first passenger jetliners. Although Boeing's 707 jetliner actually became available a few months before the DC-8, United preferred the DC-8 because of its seating arrangement and other cost advantages.

In spite of United's favorable position in the industry, its competitors were growing rapidly and in many cases outperforming United, which had entered a brief period of decline. However, when United acquired Capital Airlines in 1961 its network in the eastern United States was strengthened, helping the company to regain its position as the nation's number one airline.

United President Pat Patterson retired in 1966 and was replaced by George Keck, an engineer who rose to the top position from the company's maintenance department. Keck was generally regarded as arrogant and secretive. According to some reports, his abrupt manner and authoritarian personality offended many people within the company and its unions as well as in the Civil Aeronautics Board, severely limiting his effectiveness and ability to manage the airline in many ways. In 1971 Keck was forcibly removed in what was described as a "corporate coup" instigated by two members of the company's board, Gardner Cowles and Thomas Gleed. In 1967, during Keck's first year, United became the first airline to surpass $1 billion in annual revenue. On December 30, 1968, United created a subsidiary called UAL to operate its non-airline businesses, and the following year United Air Lines became a subsidiary of UAL.

NEW LEADERSHIP

Western International Hotels was acquired by the UAL holding company in 1970. Western's name was later changed to the Westin Hotel Company and linked to another UAL subsidiary that arranged travel packages. Westin's operations later grew to represent about one-twelfth of UAL's total business. Eddie Carlson, who had a record of success while in charge of the Westin Hotel subsidiary, was named to succeed Keck as UAL's new chief executive officer. Carlson's warm and personable demeanor motivated individuals in every division and level at UAL. He flew 186,000 miles one year inspecting the facilities and terminating the employment of what he regarded as redundant company bureaucrats. Despite his lack of experience in the airline industry, Carlson was successful in reversing the company's discouraging trends. Anticipating his own retirement, Carlson chose Richard Ferris, whom he had promoted from the Westin Hotel subsidiary, to succeed him. When Carlson was

KEY DATES

■

1934: Three airlines merge with Boeing to form United Air Lines Transportation Company.

1943: The company's name is shortened to United Air Lines (UAL).

1954: United becomes first to train pilots with flight simulators.

1967: Annual revenues exceed $1 billion.

1970: UAL acquires Western International Hotels (later Westin Hotel Company).

1987: "Allegis" becomes short-lived name for UAL's diverse travel interests.

1994: Employees take 55 percent stake in UAL in exchange for pay cuts.

2000: UAL announces its plan to acquire US Airways Group, Inc., a proposed $4.3 billion merger that faces several obstacles.

2001: The UAL/US Airways merger is called off; United loses two planes in the terrorist attacks against the United States on September 11; the company posts $2.1 billion loss for the year.

2002: UAL files for Chapter 11 bankruptcy protection.

2006: The company emerges from Chapter 11.

2008: UAL and Continental Airlines Inc. announce a marketing alliance.

named chairman of UAL and United, Ferris was made president of the airline; and in 1978 Ferris was promoted to chairman of United and president of UAL. Carlson remained as chairman of UAL until his retirement in 1983.

Notwithstanding efforts to improve the relationship the company had with its unions, which had deteriorated during the leadership of George Keck, United remained on cautious terms with its employee representatives. In 1976 the airline agreed to a $1 million payback settlement with women and minority employees in an antidiscrimination suit. In 1979 United lost $72 million, largely as the result of a monthlong labor strike.

Under the leadership of Richard Ferris the airline reached a compromise with its pilots' union. The agreement guaranteed that layoffs would not be authorized in return for more flexible work rules. The lower operating costs that resulted from the agreement were passed on to the consumer with the formation of a discount air

service called "Friendship Express." The service was also intended to allow the company to more effectively compete with cut-rate airlines such as People Express and New York Air.

NEW FRONTIERS AFTER DEREGULATION

In 1978 and 1979 UAL continued to diversify its operations when it acquired Mauna Kea Properties and the Olohana Corporation in Hawaii for $78 million. As resort developments, these acquisitions allowed UAL to take better advantage of the tourist business in the airline's most popular destination.

Under the Airline Deregulation Act, airline companies were free to enter new passenger markets without prior government approval. United was the first major airline to support deregulation; however, when Congress passed the legislation in 1978 United was forced to scale down its operations to compete profitably. Ferris later commented, "If we did make a mistake, it was in not recognizing the intensity of pricing competition that deregulation would bring, and getting structured to cope with it." Executives with smaller airline companies expressed their fear that the larger airlines would concentrate their resources on contested markets with the goal of forcing the smaller companies out of business. One executive remarked, "What Ferris wants is to have us for lunch, and I don't mean at McDonald's."

In 1985 United acquired Pan Am's Asian traffic rights for $715.5 million. The agreement also included 18 jets, 2,700 Pan Am employees, and all of Pan Am's facilities in Asia. The addition of 65,000 route miles and 30 destinations to United's network made other acquisitions pale in comparison. Ferris said, "We could spend two or three lifetimes and never get all the traffic [rights] we're buying from Pan Am."

Ferris joined the board of directors at Procter & Gamble in 1979 with the intention of studying its successful marketing formulas and applying them at UAL. He restructured UAL to reduce costs and improve marketing. After 1982, costs were controlled, productivity rose, and profits were stabilized. Part of the new marketing strategy involved the establishment of additional passenger transfer points, or "hubs." In addition to its main facility at Chicago's O'Hare airport, United operated secondary hubs in Denver, San Francisco, and Dulles airport near Washington, D.C.

In 1986 United's purchase of the bankrupt Frontier Airlines unit from People Express was canceled when the United pilots' union failed to reach an agreement with management over the manner in which Frontier pilots were to be absorbed by United. The $146 million acquisition promised to ease competition at Denver's Stapleton airport, where United, Frontier, and Continental were engaged in a costly battle for passengers. People Express closed Frontier in August 1986, declaring it bankrupt; less than a month later, however, Frank Lorenzo's Texas Air Corporation acquired People Express and liquidated Frontier. The following February People Express was absorbed into Continental Airlines. Still competing with United in Denver, Texas Air then controlled airlines with 20 percent of the domestic airline market, compared to United's 16 percent share.

United started to replace its fleet of B-727s with newer wide-body B-767s on more heavily traveled routes. Although United was the last major airline company to still operate the DC-8, federal regulations on noise pollution forced the company to replace the engines on its DC-8s with quieter models. In addition to these aircraft, United flew large numbers of B-737s, B-747s, and DC-10s.

NAME CHANGES

Early in 1987, UAL was renamed Allegis, a computer-generated choice that combined portions of the words *allegiance* and *aegis*. With an airline, a hotel chain, the Hertz car rental company, and the Apollo computerized reservations system to coordinate them all, Allegis had become an integrated full-service travel company. Shortly afterward, Allegis encountered a number of problems with Ferris's strategy to create a travel conglomerate. Several investor groups noted that Allegis's subsidiaries would be worth more as separate companies than as divisions of Allegis. On May 26, Coniston Partners announced that it had acquired a 13 percent share of Allegis stock, and that it would be purchasing more in an attempt to gain control of the board and remove Ferris. The Allegis board initialed an antitakeover defense in which the Boeing Company was given a 16 percent stake ($700 million) in the company in return for a $2.1 billion aircraft order. The defense failed in June, forcing Ferris and several other board members to resign. The new board appointed Frank A. Olson chairman of Allegis.

The Allegis name was retired in June 1988. After a brief transition period, the UAL board named Stephen M. Wolf, an airline veteran with executive experience at American, Pan Am, and Continental airlines, as CEO of United. Wolf inherited numerous business troubles, including a contract dispute over company ownership with United's three major employee unions, which went unresolved until 1990.

As the U.S. economy weakened going into the 1990s, United began to feel the effects of recession, which reduced the amount of passenger traffic, and fuel prices, which rose in the late 1980s and jumped sharply during the 1990–91 Persian Gulf War. These factors cut into the earnings of all carriers, and in 1991, UAL Corporation suffered a net loss of $331.9 million. United's losses, as well as those of other major U.S. carriers, were exacerbated by recurrent "fare wars," often launched by bankrupt airlines, such as TWA and Continental, whose Chapter 11 protection exempted them, unlike relatively well-off airlines, from paying interest on the debt that they incurred as a result of their sharp promotional price cuts. In 1992 United followed the lead of American Airlines in adopting a four-tiered fare-simplification program in an attempt to eliminate these restricted fares. Both carriers, however, scrapped this within a few months as budget carriers undercut them in droves.

Nonetheless, United treated the industry's lean period as an opportune time to expand. Such financially troubled airlines as Pan Am and TWA began in the late 1980s to sell routes to raise funds, and governments became increasingly willing to allow foreign carriers air rights within their countries; these two factors prompted United to embark on a strategy of globalization. United's 1985 purchase, for $715 million, of Pan Am's routes to Asia had left the airline well-poised to enter what many industry analysts described as a transition toward a global free market in transportation. Even Robert Crandall of American Airlines, who had rejected the Pan Am Asian routes as too expensive, later conceded that the purchase was an excellent move. In 1990 United placed a record $22 billion order for new airplanes. In 1991 the company purchased six Pan Am routes to London for $400 million, and late that same year finalized a $135 million deal to take over a portion of Pan Am's Latin American operations.

EMPLOYEE OWNERSHIP

Wolf resigned in July 1994 and was replaced by Gerald Greenwald. Later that month, United management and employees reached a historic agreement designed to stave off competition from low-cost, low-wage carriers. In exchange for pay cuts totaling $5 billion and more flexible work rules, employees received a 55 percent stake in UAL Corporation. This made UAL one of the world's largest employee-owned companies. The 20,000 flight attendants chose not to participate in the buyout.

In October 1994, the company launched a "shuttle" service to compete in the California Corridor in particular. It mimicked the low-cost, low-fare ways of Southwest Airlines but kept traditional major airline amenities such as assigned seating, a first class section, and a frequent flier club with global travel rewards. However, the pilots' union was skeptical of the lower paying "Shuttle by United" and contractually limited the operation's scope. After losing more than $1 billion dollars between 1991 and 1993, UAL posted a profit of $51 million in 1994. It had invested heavily in information technology, and was a pioneer in the use of paperless tickets. The company even sold its proprietary E-Ticket software to other international airlines.

United began flying dedicated cargo aircraft again in 1997 after a 13-year lapse. The DC-10 freighters operated exclusively on Pacific routes. Its charter membership in the Star Alliance with Lufthansa and SAS helped open hundreds of new markets. It upgraded in-flight amenities to recapture high-yield business travelers. It provided electrical outlets for laptop computers, in-flight entertainment systems, and bigger seats. These factors helped UAL outperform the industry.

In a controversial move, the carrier cut travel agency commissions in September 1997. Bookings from online brokers cost airlines an average $10, as opposed to $50 each for traditional travel agents. With the proliferation of online travel sites such as Expedia, Travelocity, Cheap Tickets, and later, Priceline, UAL began offering the chance to reserve seats on other airlines at its own web site. The strategy sought to appeal directly to the online bargain hunter.

In January 1999, UAL increased its flight frequencies to match moves by US Airways. It had previously boosted operations at its San Francisco, Denver, and Chicago hubs and created a new hub in Los Angeles. United added a daily nonstop flight from Los Angeles International Airport to Paris's Charles de Gaulle International Airport in April 2000. To retain frequent flier and full-fare economy class patrons, United installed roomier Economy Plus seating for them. James E. Goodwin followed Greenwald as chairman and CEO in July 1999. Both were known for their relatively good relationship with labor, and Goodwin had been with United for 32 years.

Later in the year, United launched an ad campaign in gay newspapers to woo gay and lesbian travelers back onto its planes. Moreover, American Airlines, Delta, and US Airways also initiated domestic partner benefits. The carrier's protest of a San Francisco ordinance mandating domestic partner health insurance benefits had resulted in a two-year boycott. American Airlines had created a "Rainbow TeAAm" to market to the gay community.

A major announcement came in May 2000, when UAL shared its plans to acquire competitor US Airways Group, Inc. Numerous questions about the proposed $4.3 billion merger remained, including antitrust and union objections, as well as whether US Airways might be the target of a separate offer from another industry heavyweight. The deal was eventually called off in 2001 amid antitrust concerns.

OVERCOMING TRAGEDY AND LOSS IN THE 21ST CENTURY

The year 2001 proved devastating for UAL. The company lost 18 employees and 93 customers aboard United Airlines Flights 93 and 175 on the morning of September 11, 2001. In the months following the terrorist attacks, UAL and its peers in the industry found themselves dealing with the worst crisis in airline history to date. With costs rising and passenger travel dwindling, UAL posted a $2.1 billion loss for the fiscal year—the largest loss ever recorded by a single carrier at the time.

UAL reduced its workforce by nearly 24 percent during the latter half of 2001 and into 2002 but still found itself struggling to gain financial footing as low-cost carriers ate into its market share. UAL tapped Glenn F. Tilton, an oil industry executive with crisis management experience, to head the company in 2002. Hoping to avoid bankruptcy, the company sought $1.8 billion in loan guarantees from the Air Transportation Stabilization Board (ATSB), which was formed on September 22, 2001, to aid struggling airline companies. The ATSB, however, denied its loan request after deeming its restructuring plan unviable. With debt surpassing $875 million, UAL was forced to file for Chapter 11 bankruptcy protection in December 2002.

The company worked diligently during its bankruptcy reorganization to cut costs and revamp its business model. While the operating environment remained challenging, the company believed its efforts would pay off. UAL emerged from its $23 billion restructuring in 2006 and immediately set out to find a merger partner. With competitors Delta Air Lines Inc. and Northwest Airlines Corp. announcing their own plans to join forces, analysts speculated UAL would follow suit. As predicted, UAL found itself in talks with Continental Airlines Inc. as well as US Airways Group Inc. The talks initially failed to produce results. Instead, UAL continued to reduce capacity, cut additional jobs, and trim overall costs. With fuel prices reaching record levels and global economies faltering, UAL was facing an uphill battle. During 2008 it shuttered Ted, the low-fare carrier it had launched during 2004.

The company and Continental Airlines announced in June 2008 that instead of a merger, they would form a unique marketing alliance in which both companies would benefit from complementary flight routes. A June

2008 *Wall Street Journal* article reported the positive aspects of the deal and claimed, "Such a deal also avoids the labor tensions, service disruptions and high upfront costs of merging." As part of the agreement, Continental would join the Star Alliance global marketing group made up of 20 airlines including United and Deutsche Lufthansa AG. The U.S. Transportation Department granted preliminary approval of Continental's admittance into Star Alliance in April 2009. UAL continued to face challenges but company management was optimistic that the Continental alliance was a step in the right direction.

John Simley and James Poniewozik
Updated, Frederick C. Ingram; Christina M. Stansell

PRINCIPAL SUBSIDIARIES

Air Wis Services, Inc.; Four Star Insurance Company, Ltd. (Bermuda); UAL Benefits Management, Inc.; United Airlines, Inc.

PRINCIPAL COMPETITORS

AMR Corporation; British Airways plc; Delta Air Lines Inc.; Air France-KLM S.A.

FURTHER READING

Bailey, Jeff, "United Plans to End Stay in Bankruptcy," *New York Times*, February 1, 2006.

Biederman, Paul, *The U.S. Airline Industry: End of an Era*, New York: Praeger, 1982.

Carey, Susan, "UAL Continental Pair, but Won't Merge," *Wall Street Journal*, June 20, 2008.

———, "UAL Names Goodwin Chairman, CEO; Strong Support from Unions Helped," *Wall Street Journal*, March 26, 1999, p. B9.

———, "UAL to Increase Flights from Hub at Dulles Airport," *Wall Street Journal*, January 6, 1999, p. A10.

Carey, Susan, and Joann S. Lublin, "New UAL Chief Faces Struggle to Cut Costs, Keep Airline Aloft," *Wall Street Journal*, September 3, 2002.

Flint, Petty, "United in Battle," *Air Transport World*, October 1994.

Harrar, George, "United's Soft Landing," *Forbes*, December 4, 1995.

Irvine, Martha, "United Airlines Trying to Boost Image with Gay, Lesbian Travelers," *San Francisco Examiner*, March 16, 2000.

Laibich, Kenneth, "Winners in the Air Wars," *Fortune*, May 11, 1987.

Lee, Connie J., "Airline Stocks Advance on Cut in Commissions—Analysts Say Lower Fees for Agents to Aid UAL, but Fallout Is a Concern," *Wall Street Journal*, September 22, 1997, p. B18.

Maynard, Micheline, "In Cost-Cutting Moves, United Will Close Low-Fare Carrier Ted and Ground Planes," *New York Times*, June 5, 2008.

Maynard, Micheline, and Andrew Ross Sorkin, "After a Failed Continental Deal, an Impasse for United and US Air," *New York Times*, May 28, 2008.

Nelms, Douglas W., "Giant Step in a Small Way," *Air Transport World*, June 1997, pp. 125–27.

Oneal, Michael, "Dogfight! United and American Battle for Global Supremacy," *Business Week*, January 21, 1991.

Ott, James, "United Remakes Itself for Global Competition," *Aviation Week & Space Technology*, July 7, 1997.

Petzinger, Thomas, Jr., *Hard Landing: The Epic Contest for Power and Profits That Plunged the Airlines into Chaos*, New York: Times Business, 1995.

Pletz, John, "Bumpy Ride Ahead for United," *Crain's Chicago Business*, May 5, 2008.

Smith, Timothy K., "Why Air Travel Doesn't Work," *Fortune*, April 3, 1995, pp. 42ff.

Warner, Bernhard, "Prepare for Takeoff," *Brandweek*, January 19, 1998, pp. 38–40.

Zuckerman, Laurence, "United Airlines' Loss for 2001 Breaks Record," *New York Times*, February 2, 2002.

W.S. Badcock Corporation

200 North Phosphate Boulevard
Mulberry, Florida 33860-2328
U.S.A.
Telephone: (863) 425-4921
Fax: (863) 425-7591
Web site: http://www.badcock.com

Private Company
Incorporated: 1926
Employees: 1,200
Sales: $519.7 million (2008 est.)
NAICS: 423220 Home Furnishings Merchant Wholesalers

■ ■ ■

The W.S. Badcock Corporation is a family-owned, regional furniture retailer based in Mulberry, Florida. About 80 percent of the company's more than 300 stores located in Alabama, Florida, Georgia, Mississippi, North Carolina, South Carolina, Tennessee, and Virginia are dealer owned. In 2009 the company was also looking to expand into Kentucky and West Virginia. Rather than employing a traditional franchise model, Badcock maintains a consignment relationship with dealers, providing merchandise to them for sale on a commission basis.

Like a franchiser, the company offers site selection help, store design and consultation, in-store training, shared advertising costs, and in-store customer financing. Badcock stores carry furniture for every room in the house and for the patio, as well as mattresses and bedding, appliances and home electronics, lamps, décor, flooring and rugs, grills and smokers, and mowers and other lawn equipment. The parent company also sells merchandise via its web site. Although the Badcock family has turned to outsiders to serve as chief executive officers, a fourth-generation member of the family serves as chairman. Fifth-generation members are also involved in the management of the company.

IMMIGRANT ORIGINS

The man who brought the Badcock family to the United States was Henry Stanhope Badcock, born in England in 1867 the fifth son of a country vicar. At the age of 16 he began an apprenticeship as a bank clerk but soon developed a dream of moving to the United States to make his fortune. In April 1889, shortly before the completion of his apprenticeship, the 21-year-old Badcock sailed from Liverpool and about two weeks later arrived on the docks of New York City. He soon took another ship bound for Jacksonville, Florida, where he hoped to use a letter of introduction to find work with a citrus grower and invest his funds to take an interest in the business. His involvement as a grower came to an end in 1895 when a killer freeze ruined the crop and his finances, a turn of events that caused Badcock to turn his attention to retailing.

Badcock moved to Bushnell, Florida, to serve as a clerk in a general store. He soon took a similar position at a general store in Fort Meade, Florida, and in 1900 was able to purchase the establishment. The area was dependent on the phosphate industry and when it suffered a downturn, Badcock relocated in 1904 to

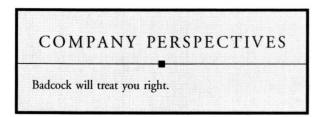

Mulberry, Florida, a community that was about to enjoy an economic boom due to the discovery of phosphate. It was there that Badcock turned his attention from general merchandise and began to sell furniture; he also sold coffins and served as an undertaker.

WOGAN BADCOCK GROWS THE BUSINESS

In 1915 Henry Badcock opened the Badcock Economy Furniture Store in West Palm Beach, Florida, leaving his 18-year-old son, Wogan Stanhope Badcock, to run the Mulberry store. Three years later the young man joined the army after the United States entered World War I, and his parents ran both stores. After the war, Wogan decided to stay in the furniture business after briefly consider considering college and a possible career in law. In 1920 he bought the Mulberry store from his father for $9,000. Because Wogan Badcock had less than $2 in his pocket at the time, his father also gave him $100 for working capital. The Mulberry furniture store then took the name W.S. Badcock.

Young Badcock struggled to make his store profitable but proved willing to try anything that might work, including sending salesmen out on the road to sell furniture from a truck. He also began placing furniture for sale on a consignment basis at other businesses. Slowly Badcock established his furniture business, and in 1926 W.S. Badcock was incorporated. The consignment arrangement soon developed into a slate of dealer-owned-and-operated associated stores. The first was located in Fort Meade followed by Plant City and Fort Myers, Florida. In 1928 Henry Badcock turned over the Badcock Economy Furniture Store to his daughter and her husband, and moved to Plant City to manage his son's new associated store. He returned to West Palm Beach in 1931 and eventually died in 1939.

In addition to the stores, Badcock established a furniture repair shop and several warehouses, and in 1937 acquired the Polk County Mattress Factory to begin supplying his operations with bedding. Badcock managed to survive the difficult years of the Great Depression that encompassed all of the 1930s and only came to an end in the early 1940s when the economy was stimulated by military spending necessitated by World War II. By 1943 the furniture chain totaled 15

stores. It continued to expand at a strong pace during the economic boom of the postwar years. Most of the dealers were either friends of the Badcock family or Badcock dealers. The small-town stores relied on small-town relationships, as well as easy financing and revolving credit accounts, to generate repeat business.

POSTWAR CHANGES IN LEADERSHIP

During the postwar period, the third generation of the Badcock family became involved in the business through Wogan S. Badcock, Jr., who had helped out his father while growing up. After graduating from high school in 1950, he enrolled at the University of Florida as well as joining the Air Force Reserve Officer Training Corps. He graduated with a degree in business in 1954 and spent the following three years on active duty with the Air Force as part of his military commitment. He then returned home to join his father in running W.S. Badcock, which at that time consisted of 57 stores. In 1962 he became executive vice-president and a year later was named president of the corporation. In 1965 his father turned over complete control of the business to him. The number of furniture stores in the network soon swelled to about 160. The first store outside of Florida opened in Valdosta, Georgia, in 1967.

The 100th Badcock store opened in 1970. To support the growth of the retail chain, a second warehouse and distribution center was opened in Live Oak, Florida, in 1972. By 1984 the number of stores reached the 200 mark, serving markets in Florida, Alabama, Georgia, North Carolina, and South Carolina. In that same year, to support the growth of the chain beyond the Florida borders, a third distribution operation was established in Thomson, Georgia. The 1980s were also a time of transition for the company. In 1984 Wogan, Jr., succeeded his father, who would die in 1987, as chairman while staying on as chief operating office and president. A year later he named his three sons, Wogan S. III, Henry C., and Ben M. Badcock, vicepresidents. Making plans for succession was important for Wogan, Jr., because in 1970 he had been diagnosed with ataxia, a neurological disorder. Increasingly he began to display effects of the disease, so that by 1990 his speech and mobility were greatly compromised. Unable to fulfill his duties, in 1992 he turned over day-to-day responsibilities to Wogan III ("Wogie"). Wogan, Jr., died in November 1996.

When Wogan III took the helm the Badcock network of furniture stores reached the 300 level, some of that expansion the result of the 1990 opening of a fourth distribution center in Cullman, Alabama, which opened up markets in Mississippi and Tennessee. The

KEY DATES

1904: Henry Stanhope Badcock opens furniture store in Mulberry, Florida.

1915: Badcock opens second store in West Palm Beach, Florida.

1920: Wogan S. Badcock buys Mulberry store from his father.

1926: W.S. Badcock Corporation is formed.

1937: Badcock acquires Polk County Mattress Factory to begin supplying his operations with bedding.

1939: Founder Henry Badcock dies.

1967: First store outside of Florida opens in Valdosta, Georgia.

1970: The 100th Badcock store opens.

1984: Wogan S. Badcock, Jr., succeeds father as chairman.

1990: Fourth distribution center opens in Cullman, Alabama, opening up markets in Mississippi and Tennessee.

1993: The business is reorganized into three units.

1998: Donald C. Marks becomes first nonfamily member to serve as chief executive.

1999: The company revamps its logo and begins developing Badcock & More format.

2004: Home Now rent-to-own concept is introduced.

2009: Marks retires as CEO.

business was reorganized in 1993 into three units, the responsibilities for which fell to the sons of Wogan, Jr. Wogan III was put in charge of administration and warehousing; Ben handled merchandising and advertising; and Henry became responsible for customer relations. Moreover, the three sons agreed to rotate two-year terms as president of the corporation. Under this arrangement, a new 300,000-square-foot distribution center opened in Mulberry in 1995, large enough to permit the closure of the Live Oak facility.

FIRST NONFAMILY MEMBER CEO

Following the death of Wogan, Jr., in 1996 the company's board of directors decided the time had come to bring in an outsider to run the business. Following a yearlong search, Donald C. Marks was hired as chief executive officer and president in September 1998. Marks came to Badcock following an extensive career with the Rent-A-Center chain and its parent company,

Thorne-EMI. He took over Badcock at a time when the furniture business had changed and Badcock, still wedded to its small-town approach, had failed to keep up with the times. Moreover, he had to deal with dissatisfaction within the dealer ranks. In early 1999 a group of 19 dealers, which collectively operated 28 stores, sued Badcock, alleging they had been overcharged for advertising, computers, and insurance. The lawsuit was soon thrown out because the dealer contracts called for arbitration, and eventually 15 of the dealers signed confidential agreements. A new contract was also developed to provide Badcock dealers with better terms.

Marks also had to contend with changing demographics. Rather than cater almost exclusively to rural, middle-aged white families of modest means, Badcock stores had to appeal to younger, middle-class Hispanics and African Americans. In 1999 the company revamped its logo and developed a new Badcock & More format that was more upscale than the old Badcock Home Furnishings Centers. A prototype was unveiled in 2000 and a five-year plan commenced to convert the stores to the new format and update the chain's image. In 2003 the chain also targeted for expansion new markets in eastern North Carolina, Kentucky, Virginia, and West Virginia, and laid plans to establish a new distribution center to support the effort. Because of the design and layout changes to the stores, customer traffic increased and annual sales that had reached a plateau around $374 million in the late 1990s began to rise steadily in the new century, reaching $395.8 million in 2000 and $480.9 million in 2004, when the number of stores totaled 333. (Another dozen Babcock stores, owned and operated by a separate branch of the family in south Florida, were not included in these numbers.)

PURSUING NEW CONCEPTS

While continuing the effort to convert its stores to the Badcock & More format, the company pursued two other new concepts, introduced in late 2004. One focusing on youth furniture was called Kids & More, while the other, Home Now, was a rent-to-own concept that made use of the Badcock distribution system. The first of these stores, which carried a smaller selection of what a regular Badcock store had to offer, opened in Clearwater, Florida, in 2005. Two other test stores would follow. If they were successful, the hope was that Home Now could serve as a franchise vehicle. The Kids & More introduction, in the meantime, was pushed back to 2006 due to changing business conditions. Also in 2005 a new 220,000-square-foot distribution center opened in Mebane, North Carolina, part of an effort to expand into new markets and add 170 stores over the next six years.

With a number of irons in the fire, manufacturing mattresses no longer fit into Badcock's future. The mattress business had been strong, doubling in the previous decade, but a new facility was needed and it did not make economic sense to invest in a new building. The $10 million it would cost, management decided, could be put to better use opening new stores or bolstering the company's infrastructure. In 2007 the Mulberry plant, after almost 77 years in operations, was shut down, and Badcock outsourced mattress manufacturing to International Bedding Corporation, which could supply the furniture retailer with mattresses at about the same cost as if produced in-house.

After ten years at the helm, Marks retired as CEO at the start of 2009. He was replaced by Chief Operating Officer Mike Price, who was very familiar with the Badcock business. He had been with the company since 1997 when he was hired as chief financial officer. The University of North Carolina graduate also brought nine years of experience with the Food Lion supermarket chain. By this time members of the fifth generation of the Badcock family were involved in running the company. Having shown that the Badcock chain was capable of changing with the times, there was every reason to expect the regional company to continue to enjoy success in the years to come.

Ed Dinger

PRINCIPAL SUBSIDIARIES

Badcock Ws Corp. Distribution; Ws Badcock Corp. Warehouse.

PRINCIPAL COMPETITORS

Bassett Furniture Industries, Incorporated; Ethan Allen Interiors Inc.; Rooms To Go, Inc.

FURTHER READING

"Dealers File Suit vs Badcock Corp.," *Tampa Tribune,* February 13, 1990, p. 3.

Driver, Raymond L., "Badcock Family Furnished Polk County with 100 Years of History," *Polk County Historical Quarterly,* December 2004, p. 1.

Gott, Gilbert, *Remembering Plant City,* Charleston, S.C.: History Press, 2007, 189 p.

Heery, Bill, "Badcock Benchmark," *Tampa Tribune,* January 14, 2004, p. 1.

Maready, Jeremy, "Mulberry, Fla.-based Furniture Supplier Badcock Picks Next CEO from Its Ranks," *Lakeland (Fla.) Ledger,* August 26, 2008.

McCormick, Elizabeth, "Mulberry, Fla.-based Furniture Retailer Plans Northward Expansion," *Lakeland (Fla.) Ledger,* September 10, 2002.

Miracle, Barbara, "Makeover: One of Florida's Oldest Retailers Is Midway Through a Rebranding," *Florida Trend,* February 2005, p. 56.

Schroeder, Angel, "W.S. Badcock Modernizes Image, Tests New Concept," *HFN,* March 13, 2000, p. 8.

Wakefern Food Corporation

600 York Street
Elizabeth, New Jersey 07207
U.S.A.
Telephone: (908) 527-3300
Fax: (908) 527-3397
Web site: http://www.shoprite.com

Member-Owned Cooperative
Founded: 1946
Employees: 50,000
Sales: $10.6 billion (2008)
NAICS: 422410 General Line Grocery Wholesalers; 311999 All Other Miscellaneous Food Manufacturing; 445110 Supermarkets and Other Grocery (Except Convenience) Stores

■ ■ ■

Wakefern Food Corporation is the wholesale purchasing and distributing cooperative for over 200 ShopRite supermarkets that operate in New Jersey (where it is the dominant grocery chain), New York, Connecticut, Pennsylvania, Delaware, and Maryland. Owned by 45 independent grocers, it is the largest such co-op in the United States and the largest employer in New Jersey. To provide goods at competitive wholesale prices for its member stores, the co-op purchases foods and other items both at home and abroad and distributes them from its warehouses in New Jersey, where it maintains its corporate headquarters.

Using 2.5 million square feet of warehousing, most of it located within one mile of the Port of New York docks, Wakefern distributes goods, packaged under national brands as well as private labels, to its member stores. To accomplish this, it uses one of the largest private transportation fleets on the East Coast, consisting of over 400 tractors and 2,000 trailers, which provide day-to-day deliveries of its various goods throughout its fairly concentrated network of ShopRite stores. Wakefern also offers centralized services to its member stores, including advertising, group insurance, and marketing.

STARTING OUT WITH A RISKY ENTERPRISE

The end of World War II brought an end to food rationing and price controls in the United States, but it also created problems for independent grocers who faced quickly stiffening competition from such rapidly growing supermarket chains as A&P. The problem was that such chains were able to undercut the retail prices of the independent grocers by volume buying at the wholesale level and by using more efficient marketing strategies.

In New Jersey in the summer of 1946, Ed Casson, a representative of Del Monte Foods, repeatedly heard the same complaint from independent grocers in the Newark area, that as individuals the independents had to purchase wholesale canned foods for retailing at the same prices customers at the chain stores were paying for them. Casson suggested that the independent grocers meet together to try to find a solution to the problem. Two of them, Abe Kesselman and Sam Aidekman, began doing so on a regular basis and were soon joined by five others: Al Aidekman, Dave Fern, Sam Garb, Albert Goldberg, Bill Kesselman, and Louis Weiss. The group then started experimenting, making some bulk wholesale purchases and splitting them for retail sale in their grocery stores, storing some items in their homes until they were depleted. It was a system that seemed to work well, so they formalized their cooperative venture on December 5, 1946, when each of them put up $1,000 and incorporated their association as the Wakefern Food Corporation. The Wakefern name, an acronym, was developed from the *w* from Weiss, the *a* from Aidekman, the *k* from Kesselman, and *fern* from Dave Fern. The extra *e* was added to make the name both agreeable and pronounceable.

The founding members were fully aware that other grocers had attempted to form co-ops and had failed, and they expected problems. They knew that they would have to put a lot of extra time and effort into the enterprise, rotating the responsibility of accepting deliveries at their first storage facility, a 1,000-square-foot storefront on Miller Street in Newark. They used their own cars and pickup trucks to transport food to that "warehouse" and took turns paying for deliveries and keeping the company's books. They operated without any long-range plan, just trying to stay afloat and not be beaten out by the chain giants.

Their first problem was to get credit from major food manufacturers. They were considered too risky an enterprise by most large food producers because they lacked sufficient capital, but they got a break when a loyal customer's husband, who worked for Campbell's Soup Company, persuaded that manufacturer to extend credit to Wakefern. Del Monte and other companies soon followed suit.

INCREASING MEMBERSHIP

The next need was for an immediate expansion of Wakefern's membership to help improve the cooperative's wholesale buying strength. The founders all undertook the task of enlisting new members, a difficult and frustrating effort. At the time, $1,000 or more was a lot of money to put at risk for most independent grocers, but the members' persistence and the donation of their free time to help prospective members paid off. Over the first five years, growth was gradual but steady.

In 1949 the company moved into a 15,000-square-foot warehouse in Port Newark, hired a warehouse manager, and contracted the services of a trucking company for the delivery of purchased goods. It was still a marginal operation, however, not very efficient and rather costly. At the time it forced member grocers to sell some items at a loss to remain competitive with the chain supermarkets.

In the next year, 1950, membership grew to 28. Annual sales reached $2.2 million, and a full-time office staff was doing the managing and accounting work the founders had originally undertaken themselves get the enterprise established. The change allowed for some longer range planning, including modifications designed to improve the cooperative's efficiency and to enhance its market image.

RAPID GROWTH AND CHANGE

Wakefern took the first important step the next year. On March 15, 1951, it began advertising in the *Newark Evening News* under a new name, ShopRite, a name that the co-op's members finally decided upon after careful deliberation. The $1,500 ad was a calculated risk, and only nine members were willing or able to participate in financing it. All of them, adding "ShopRite" to their stores' names, logged a significant increase in sales. They continued to advertise under the new name, and other Wakefern members, seeing the important benefits, soon joined in and changed their stores' names as well. The change also attracted other independent grocers, and within a year Wakefern's membership grew to over 50, almost doubling.

Wakefern's new advertising and merchandising program became "the cornerstone of its success." New memberships that resulted from it spurred an important

KEY DATES

■

1946: Consortium of New York and New Jersey grocers form the Wakefern cooperative.

1949: Co-op moves into 15,000-square-foot warehouse in Port Newark and hires professional staff.

1951: Seeking a more competitive industry image, Wakefern begins using "ShopRite" name in its marketing and advertising and institutes the ShopRite brand of foods.

1953: The company builds first large warehouse in Cranford, New Jersey, and adds more staff members.

1956: Wakefern members elect to cut retail food prices 10 percent rather than issue trading stamps.

1966: Supermarkets General Corporation forms and subsequently leaves Wakefern to form Pathmark.

1989: ShopRite institutes its Supermarket Careers training program.

1992: Wakefern member Big V Supermarkets opens PriceRite mini-warehouse club.

2002: The Big V Supermarket chain is acquired for $185 million.

2005: Thomas Infusino retires; Joseph Colalillo takes over as chairman.

2007: Wakefern expands its wholesale sales operations.

increase in volume, and that resulted in some significant developments, including a move to a larger warehouse, a growth in trucking operations, and enlarged stores with a complete line of products. Also, Wakefern began marketing foods packaged under ShopRite's own private label, a strategy that started as a promotional ploy in October 1951, when, for the Halloween season, its stores sold doughnuts packaged under the ShopRite name. It soon evolved into a whole line of ShopRite labeled foods, some processed by the cooperative itself.

The advertisements also helped the member grocers keep in touch with their customers by including biographical information about new members and announcing such events as the opening of new warehouses or the renovation or remodeling of any of its members' stores. Thus, even as their stores grew in size and number, the ShopRite owners continued a tradition of personal community involvement that characterized the

"mom and pop" corner groceries from which their stores evolved.

In addition to using ads to provide information about the local store owners and their ShopRite stores, for four years, from 1952 to 1956, the co-op published and distributed a newsletter called the *ShopRite Ladies Home News*. In it, a fictional character named Sally Rite shared tips on saving money and preparing foods.

By its tenth anniversary in 1956, Wakefern's membership had climbed to over 70, and its sales volume had reached $100 million, made possible by its bold warehouse and distribution strategies. These started in 1953, when Wakefern built the first of its large warehouses in Cranford, New Jersey, and took on additional staff members. Survival seemed certain, even though the members still had to face difficult decisions, an important one being whether or not to succumb to a major marketing trend, the issuing of trading stamps, which, by the mid-1950s, had become a national craze. In 1958, after a heated meeting, the members opted not to do so. Instead, they voted to cut their retail prices by 10 percent. The decision at first caused a decline in sales, but after a few months ShopRite's "low price leader" concept took hold, and their sales started a new upward swing.

At the same time, many of the ShopRite stores were expanding in size, either remodeled or relocated to accommodate the self-service system that was replacing the older, less-efficient full-service system. By 1960 some of the old stores, a few originally only 2,000 to 3,000 square feet in size, had been transformed into much larger operations up to ten times their original size.

PROFESSIONAL STAFF AND TEMPORARY SETBACKS

Through the 1960s and 1970s, Wakefern completed the task of turning over its management to a professional staff, freeing its members of direct involvement in any of the day-to-day operations of the co-op. The staff directed its volume buying, merchandising, warehousing, and distribution, always with an eye to improving efficiency and thereby cutting costs.

There were obstacles, including two problematic setbacks in the 1960s. The first occurred in 1962 when several smaller members sued Wakefern and what were then its two largest members: General Supermarkets and Supermarkets Operating Co. Their complaint was that the larger member companies wielded too much power and grabbed up the best store locations. Then, in 1966, the sued companies merged to form Supermarkets General Corporation, which subsequently took its 65-store chain out of the cooperative and formed Pathmark, cutting Wakefern's volume in half and effectively closing its Long Island market. The loss, however, prompted the remaining members to redouble their expansion efforts, opening new stores and improving their marketing and purchasing strategies. It took only three years for the changes to allow the cooperative to again reach the sales volume it had enjoyed before the withdrawal of Supermarkets General.

It was during the 1970s that Wakefern adopted the principle that each of its members would have just one vote in major decision making, regardless of the number of ShopRite stores each owned. The rule "One Member, One Vote" helped ensure member input in shaping policies. That attracted new members and enough financial backing to continue Wakefern's ongoing expansion, especially the addition of new warehousing facilities in the 1980s. By that time, Wakefern could confidently claim that ShopRite "had become the recognized market leader." It had also become the largest surviving retailer-owned cooperative in the nation.

COMMUNITY SERVICE AND CONTINUED SUCCESS

Throughout the last two decades of the 20th century, Wakefern compiled a significant record of achievements, not just as a successful cooperative in a business sense but as an enterprise profoundly committed to helping the host communities of the ShopRite stores. By 1996 the year in which Wakefern reached it 50th anniversary, those stores were serving over three million customers per week in a five-state network, and in sales the co-op was ranked 14th in the nation among supermarket chains. It had 36 member companies, each of which was an independent corporation. All together, they employed over 35,000 associates in retail outlets and another 3,000 in staff positions in Wakefern's purchasing, merchandising, warehousing, and distributions operations and administrative roles. To service the stores in its network, in 1997 alone, Wakefern's distribution fleet logged 23 million miles.

The ShopRite stores also reflected Wakefern's commitment to staying abreast of industry changes, to employing technological advances, and to promoting change through its own innovations, as in its Supermarket Careers program. Initiated in 1989, Supermarket Careers was created to help special needs students train for work in ShopRites or other stores. By 1999 the award-winning program was offered in the curriculum of 42 schools in five states.

In the 1990s, Wakefern adopted computer-generated ordering, fully automating the stock-replenishing process in the majority of its stores;

electronic data interchange; and computer-based training for its employees. The larger ShopRite stores also began offering the full line of services and departments that typifies the chain giants' megamarkets, including pharmacies, delis, catering, salad bars, coffee shops, and banking services. In 1992 one of its largest members, Big V Supermarkets, opened the first PriceRite mini-warehouse club, hoping to get a share of a market dominated by Sam's Wholesale Clubs.

Despite such up-sizing tendencies, Wakefern took pride in the fact that its members maintained an ongoing commitment to their respective communities and the continued participation of family members in their businesses. In projects such as the Community Food Bank of New Jersey and the Special Olympics, ShopRites played a very significant and highly publicized role, constant reminders that the stores were locally owned and operated by people who care about their community. Wakefern's record of assisting charities has been noteworthy throughout its history.

CHANGING LEADERSHIP

By the early years of the 21st century, Wakefern decidedly remained the largest retailer-owned cooperative in the United States. Its leadership status, however, did not come without complications. Big V Supermarkets, the company's largest member, filed for Chapter 11 bankruptcy protection in 2000 and set plans in motion to end its relationship with Wakefern. The company took action and in 2002 bought Big V's assets, which included 27 ShopRite stores, for $185 million.

Another potential snag came in 2005 when Thomas P. Infusino ended his reign as chairman of Wakefern after 34 years of service. Under his tenure, Wakefern's sales had grown from $969 million to approximately $9 billion. Average weekly store volume had grown from $473,000 in 1991 to $864,000 by 2005. Throughout his career, Infusino became known for his integrity and commitment to community by his colleagues and was considered to be in the upper echelon of grocery retailers. Seton Hall University awarded him an honorary doctorate for notable business ethics practices shortly before his retirement. Infusino's replacement, Joseph Colalillo, was a second-generation Wakefern member operating three ShopRite stores of his own. His father had joined the cooperative in the 1950s and Colalillo took over the family business when his father died in 1990. Upon Infusino's departure, Colalillo was charged with the formidable task of leading Wakefern into its next chapter of history as it faced stiff competition and a weakening U.S. economy.

Colalillo proved ready for the challenge and explained his strategy in a June 2005 *Supermarket News* article claiming, "We have to focus on whatever we have to do to give our customers the best possible shopping experience. We have to have good customer service, good prices and good perishables to compete. We will focus on our customers and associates—that's what Wakefern has always helped us do." With harsh competition coming from nontraditional supermarkets including Target Corporation, Wal-Mart Stores Inc., and CVS Caremark Corporation, Wakefern was indeed revamping its strategy to stay on top of its game. During 2007 the company began to expand its wholesale operations and began aggressively promoting and selling its products to nonmember supermarkets. It landed a wholesale agreement with New York-based Gristedes, a 40-store chain that began to carry ShopRite private-label branded products.

At the same time, the company acquired ten Stop & Shop Supermarkets from the Stop & Shop Supermarket Company. The stores adopted the Shop-Rite name shortly thereafter. During 2008 Wakefern entered the Baltimore, Maryland, market when Klein's Family Markets joined the cooperative. The company operated seven stores and became Wakefern's 44th member.

With sales on the rise, Colalillo's strategy was paying off. The cooperative planned to expand its presence not only in New York but throughout the entire Northeast. Management believed its focus on its wholesale business would prove lucrative as well and expected revenues to continue their upward climb. While Colalillo was only a few years into his chairmanship, it appeared he was on track to succeed much like his predecessor.

John W. Fiero
Updated, Christina M. Stansell

PRINCIPAL COMPETITORS

The Great Atlantic & Pacific Tea Company, Inc.; SUPERVALU Inc.; Wal-Mart Stores, Inc.

FURTHER READING

Brookman, Faye, "The ShopRite Superstore," *WWD*, August 28, 1998, p. 9.

"Can Can Alive and Kicking," *Progressive Grocer*, September 1991, p. 28.

Duff, Mike, "At ShopRite, They're Taking Quality on the Road," *Supermarket Business*, April 1992, p. 39.

Fensholt, Carol, and Kenneth Partch, "ShopRite's PriceRite: For Predators Planning to Pounce, a Poison Pill?" *Supermarket Business*, December 1992, p. 28.

Garry, Michael, "Protecting Its Turf," *Progressive Grocer*, November 1995, p. 84.

"Gristedes Becomes Wakefern Wholesale Customer," *Progressive Grocer*, January 3, 2008.

Hamstra, Mark, "Unifying Force: ShopRite Has Grown to Become a Regional Power Under Thomas Infusino's Leadership," *Supermarket News*, June 27, 2005.

"How America's Largest Retailer-Owned Cooperative Took Form 50 Years Ago," *Supermarket News*, May 13, 1996, p. 2S.

Interview with Wakefern CEO Thomas Infusino, *Supermarket News*, May 13, 1996, p. 4S.

Madigan, Nick, "Klein's Family Markets Is Joining ShopRite Group," *Baltimore Sun*, October 31, 2008.

McGintyk, Tony, "Wakefern's ShopRite Takes on All Comers in Nonfoods," *Supermarket Business*, November 1987, p. 55.

Millstein, March, Denise Zimmermann, and Chris O'Leary, "Automation's in Order at Wakefern," *Supermarket News*, December 4, 1995, p. 22.

Snyder, Glen, "Wakefern/ShopRite Thinks BIG," *Progressive Grocer*, January 1992, p. 61.

Turcsik, Richard, "MMI Hired to Handle Wakefern Store Brands," *Supermarket News*, December 26, 1994, p. 41.

"Wakefern Announces Expanded Wholesale Sales Operations," *Food Logistics*, July/August 2007.

"Wakefern Wraps Big V Acquisition," *Record* (Bergen County, N.J.), July 26, 2002.

Weinstein, Steve, "Wakefern: A Co-op That Works," *Progressive Grocer*, October 1991, p. 27.

———, "Wakefern Gives More Than Money," *Progressive Grocer*, December 1991, p. 23.

———, "Wakefern Operations: Overcoming Obstacles," *Progressive Grocer*, November 1991, p. 38.

World Wrestling Entertainment, Inc.

———— ■ ————

1241 East Main Street
Stamford, Connecticut 06902
U.S.A.
Telephone: (203) 352-8600
Fax: (203) 359-5151
Web site: http://www.corporate.wwe.com

Public Company
Incorporated: 1963 as World Wide Wrestling Federation
Employees: 564
Sales: $526.5 million (2008)
Stock Exchanges: New York
Ticker Symbol: WWE
NAICS: 711320 Promoters of Performing Arts, Sports, and Similar Events Without Facilities; 711190 Other Performing Arts Companies

■ ■ ■

Stamford, Connecticut-based World Wrestling Entertainment, Inc. (WWE), is one of the global entertainment industry's leading players. A publicly traded, integrated media company, the company produces and distributes original, PG-rated content via television, digital media, pay-per-view, and print publishing. WWE distributes its content in approximately 145 countries, reaching some 500 million homes throughout the world. In addition to its Connecticut headquarters, the company also has offices located in Chicago, New York, Los Angeles, London, Toronto, Sydney, Shanghai, and Tokyo.

ORIGINS

Vincent K. McMahon, Jr., represented the third generation of McMahons to earn a living by promoting professional wrestling. His grandfather, Jesse McMahon, established the trend, forgoing his career as a boxing promoter during the 1940s to try his hand at performing the same function for professional wrestling. Jesse McMahon's son, Vincent K. McMahon, joined his father in the business during the 1950s, when the popularity of professional wrestling was on the rise. Vincent McMahon formed his own promotion company in 1963, naming the enterprise the World Wide Wrestling Federation. The global implication of the company's name belied the realities of the professional wrestling business, which was composed of a patchwork of promoters who were geographically isolated. Far from worldwide, the World Wide Wrestling Federation operated within well-defined boundaries, promoting professional wrestling matches in northeastern cities of the United States.

Although the company's territory was restricted, it included heavily populated metropolitan areas, including New York City and Philadelphia. Popular wrestlers such as Gorgeous George had helped professional wrestling gain a loyal following among television viewers during the early years of television. However, not long after McMahon formed the World Wide Wrestling Federation, the half-sport, half-entertainment attraction began to lose its appeal. It was during the business downturn in the late 1960s and early 1970s that the third generation of McMahons entered the professional wrestling promotion business. Vincent K. McMahon, Jr., a pioneer in a decades-old business, entirely transformed the world of professional wrestling.

In a business that was a hybrid of sports and entertainment, McMahon excelled by being half-innovator, half-renegade. His unquestionable marketing skills may have surprised some, considering his less-than-exemplary past, but his iconoclasm probably struck longtime acquaintances as the natural progression of a troubled childhood. As a child, McMahon was exceedingly disruptive in school. Eventually, authorities were forced to present him with two alternatives: enroll in a state reform school or in a military academy. McMahon opted for the latter, becoming the first cadet in the history of the Waynesboro, Virginia, Fishburne Military School to be court-martialed.

McMahon's academic career only moderately improved after his truncated stay at Fishburne. He spent five years attending college, all the while petitioning professors to raise his grades while attending summer school each of the five years. After college, McMahon tried to make his mark in sales, hawking paper cups and adding machines before deciding to join his father in the promotion of professional wrestling. From his undistinguished background, McMahon emerged to create one of the most successful marketing organizations in the country.

In 1971, McMahon began working for his father's organization, shuttling throughout the Northeast promoting local shows and serving as an announcer at the matches. A 6′ 3″ amateur bodybuilder, McMahon fit the mold of a wrestler, but it was never his inclination to blend into the world of professional wrestling. As he had during his years as a schoolboy, McMahon reportedly wanted to be a disruptive force. He worked for the company (which dropped "Wide" from its title in 1979) for a decade, before acquiring the World Wrestling Foundation (WWF) in 1982 from his ailing father.

TAKING CHARGE

With full control over the organization, McMahon was able to shape the company into a formidable force, the

likes of which had never been seen in the business. The difference between McMahon and other promoters was his disregard for the traditions of professional wrestling. He ignored the geographical boundaries that divided the industry and began buying out regional promoters, emerging as a consolidator bent on amalgamating the smaller tours into a national company. Along with the territory he gained from other promoters, McMahon also took other promoters' top wrestling personalities, including a fellow amateur bodybuilder named Terry Bollea. Bollea, whom McMahon lured away from a Minneapolis promoter in 1983, wrestled under the name Hulk Hogan, the most popular professional wrestling star of the 1980s. To provide greater exposure to his motley collection of wrestlers, McMahon purchased time on local television stations to air WWF's matches, hoping to stimulate interest in a spectacle whose popularity had been on the wane for nearly 15 years.

Nothing contributed more to WWF's startling success, however, than an industry-shaking announcement McMahon made during the early 1980s. He acknowledged that the winners of professional wrestling matches were predetermined, sparking furor among other promoters and some fans. Aside from freeing WWF from state regulations, which was particularly important in light of the company's aggressive geographic expansion, McMahon's concession pushed professional wrestling headlong into the realm of show business. No longer forced to masquerade as a legitimate sport, professional wrestling could embrace the concept of entertainment wholeheartedly and throw away the trappings of bleak gymnasiums for something more akin to Las Vegas.

Presenting wrestling as pure entertainment unleashed McMahon's marketing talents, transforming WWF's live events into bawdy extravaganzas that titillated crowds. In the scripts that governed the live events, McMahon developed and accentuated rivalries between his wrestlers, creating story lines that carried the actions of one event to their denouement in later events. Marketing, brash and glitzy in its tone, was highly effective, transforming the image of such wrestlers as Andre the Giant, the Iron Sheik, and Hulk Hogan into superheroes or detestable villains. In essence, McMahon amplified the intensity of everything under his control, making Titan Sports, Inc., the company he created in 1982, and WWF, the wholly owned subsidiary of Titan Sports, a rousing success a few short years after leadership was passed from father to son.

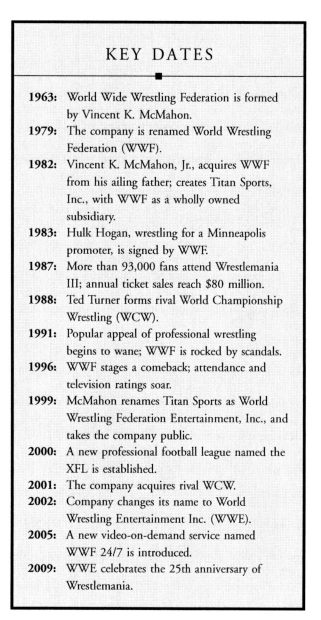

KEY DATES

1963: World Wide Wrestling Federation is formed by Vincent K. McMahon.

1979: The company is renamed World Wrestling Federation (WWF).

1982: Vincent K. McMahon, Jr., acquires WWF from his ailing father; creates Titan Sports, Inc., with WWF as a wholly owned subsidiary.

1983: Hulk Hogan, wrestling for a Minneapolis promoter, is signed by WWF.

1987: More than 93,000 fans attend Wrestlemania III; annual ticket sales reach $80 million.

1988: Ted Turner forms rival World Championship Wrestling (WCW).

1991: Popular appeal of professional wrestling begins to wane; WWF is rocked by scandals.

1996: WWF stages a comeback; attendance and television ratings soar.

1999: McMahon renames Titan Sports as World Wrestling Federation Entertainment, Inc., and takes the company public.

2000: A new professional football league named the XFL is established.

2001: The company acquires rival WCW.

2002: Company changes its name to World Wrestling Entertainment Inc. (WWE).

2005: A new video-on-demand service named WWF 24/7 is introduced.

2009: WWE celebrates the 25th anniversary of Wrestlemania.

FACING COMPETITION

By 1987, McMahon no longer had to pay television stations to broadcast WWF matches; advertisers were more than willing to sponsor his version of professional wrestling. WWF sold $80 million worth of tickets to live shows in 1987, including the proceeds from the more than 93,000 fans who attended Wrestlemania III in Pontiac, Michigan's Silverdome, setting the attendance record to date for an indoor event in the United States. Beyond ticket sales, there were a handful of other revenue sources, including merchandise sold at the live shows, television advertising sales, programs, videos, albums, and the 3 percent licensing fee awarded to WWF for the $170 million in sales racked up by retailers selling items such as professional wrestling lunch boxes and caricature action figures. Accounting

for all revenue, *Forbes* magazine estimated that Titan Sports was grossing $145 million in sales annually.

WWF, and with it professional wrestling, had become a business phenomenon. WWF distributed four of the top-selling sports videos on the market, besting Jane Fonda's workout video, and produced five television shows internally, three of which were syndicated nationally. Further, pay-per-view cable television had emerged as a potentially lucrative source of revenue. Wrestlemania IV was held at a much smaller venue than the Silverdome, yet grossed a record $30 million thanks to the one million pay-per-view customers who paid $15 per household to watch the event. McMahon, who oversaw all aspects of the WWF marketing machine, was worth in excess of $100 million, having catapulted into the country's business elite in roughly five years.

As the popularity of professional wrestling exploded, it developed into much more than an arena show. National television syndication, pay-per-view television events, and licensing deals for everything from action figures to wrestling-themed air fresheners were indicative of a booming business whose boundaries were stretching beyond precedent. WWF's core audience of children and teens expanded to embrace more and more adults, blue-collar and white-collar alike. Celebrities such as Sylvester Stallone, Madonna, and Cyndi Lauper began making appearances, performing as referees and timekeepers and, more importantly, helping professional wrestling become a mainstream phenomenon. With a fan base increasing by the droves and steady streams of revenue filling its coffers, WWF basked in the glow of the popularity it had created.

However, the company did not stand by itself for long. Attracted by the enormous financial potential of professional wrestling, media mogul Ted Turner decided he wanted a stake in the business. In 1988, he created World Championship Wrestling (WCW), forming a formidable rival to WWF. Backed by Turner's sizable fortune and TNT and TBS, the two cable television networks owned by Turner, WCW enjoyed an easy and swift entry into the business, securing a sizable market presence almost overnight. Wrestlers were easy to come by in the frenzy sweeping the country, as WWF and WCW hired "almost anyone off the street," according to John Wendt, director of the MBA sports and entertainment program at the University of St. Thomas. "If you're big, mean, and ugly," Wendt continued in his May 12, 1997, interview with *Marketing News*, "you're a world wrestler." The emergence of too many unknown wrestlers in the ring, however, delivered a crippling blow to the popularity of professional wrestling. By the end of the 1980s, the flamboyant world created by McMahon had begun to turn stale.

STRUGGLES AND SCANDALS

The overabundance of unknown wrestlers was just part of the problem affecting WWF. Licensing had proliferated out of control and marketing had grown too pervasive, saturating the appeal of Hulk Hogan and his cohorts to a detrimental extent. The same overblown aggrandizement of professional wrestling that fueled its meteoric rise led to its downfall by the beginning of the 1990s, as the hype surrounding the entertainment spectacle eventually suffocated its popularity. By the early 1990s, the celebrities who had once circled the wrestling ring at WWF events were nowhere to be found, fleeing the scene of what was rapidly coming to be perceived as a joke. A substantial portion of the fans went with them, causing attendance at live events to fall and television ratings to slip as well.

To make matters worse for McMahon, Titan Sports was the object of scandal during the early 1990s. Federal charges were lodged against McMahon and WWF's parent company for homosexual harassment and illegal steroid use, further deteriorating professional wrestling's image. McMahon and Titan Sports were acquitted of both charges, but damage had already been done, damage that made WWF vulnerable in Turner's mind. Turner took the opportunity presented to him to do what McMahon had done to regional promoters during the early 1980s. The WCW chief began luring WWF star wrestlers into his organization, including Randy Savage, Rowdy Roddy Piper, and, to complete the circle of events, Hulk Hogan.

Lawsuits and counter-lawsuits between WWF and WCW ensued, providing a litigious backdrop to professional wrestling's waning market appeal. Hobbled by the highly publicized scandals and the departure of some its most popular personalities, WWF lost ground to WCW, but McMahon was ready for another fight. He and his management team made pervasive changes to all facets of the company's operation. Methods governing staffing, licensing, touring, and marketing were altered, and marketing representatives were sent into the field. "We wanted to get back to grassroots efforts," explained WWF's senior vice-president of event booking and operations *to Amusement Business* in a May 13, 1996, interview.

Licensing was approached more methodically, with the company choosing its licensees after careful examination. Outside the United States, where WWF had registered considerable success in England and Germany in particular, the company was mindful of oversaturating markets. Company officials emphasized cultivating followings in new markets instead, leading to WWF tours in India, Kuwait, and South Africa during the mid-1990s.

As the company tightened its control over operations, pursuing a general strategy of reigning in corporate functions that had careened out of control during the late 1980s, McMahon amplified the scripted performances of WWF live events. To differentiate WWF from WCW, McMahon stepped up the violence and sexual innuendo contained in WWF shows, casting WWF as the edgier alternative to the tamer WCW. Matches between wrestling personalities were presented as parts within larger plots, following story lines that grew darker and more elaborate in style and content. The live events became chapters in a never-ending saga pitting factions of wrestlers against one another, each victimized by betrayals that spawned endless subplots.

In WWF's two-hour television program, 36 minutes of airtime was devoted to wrestling, with the remainder focusing on soap-opera-style feuds and "behind-the-scenes" intrigue. The response from the public left little doubt as to the effectiveness of McMahon's changes. Attendance figures rose, highlighted by the highest gross ever to date for a WWF event at Madison Square Garden in 1996, and television ratings climbed upward, with WWF eclipsing the figures reported by WCW in each category.

SUCCESSFUL COMEBACK

By the mid-1990s professional wrestling had overcome the problems of the early 1990s. By the end of the decade, professional wrestling exuded more strength than it had at its peak in the late 1980s. Personalities such as Stone Cold Steve Austin and the Undertaker performed in front of capacity crowds, while WWF programming, which aired in 120 countries in 11 languages, earned record ratings and attracted a different ilk of sponsors. During the 1980s, professional wrestling drew sponsorship deals generally from snack food companies and automotive products makers; however, by the late 1990s the broadening of WWF's fan base attracted sponsors such as Warner Bros., Hasbro, Procter & Gamble Co., Western Union, and the U.S. Army. The celebrities had returned as well, no longer fearing the stigma that had prompted their departure earlier in the decade.

In 1998, two of the National Basketball Association's most popular players, Karl Malone and Dennis Rodman, battled against one another in the ring, the same year a former WWF wrestler, Jesse "The Body" Ventura, was elected governor of Minnesota. In terms of revenue-generating capability, professional wrestling demonstrated remarkable prowess. The cornucopia of merchandise, ranging from toys and temporary tattoos to hot sauces, constituted a business valued in excess of $1 billion annually.

As McMahon prepared to lead WWF into the 21st century, his objectives were not limited to beating back the advances of rival WCW. Considering the popular appeal of the more than 200 live events staged by WWF annually and the company's consistent ranking as the highest-rated program on cable television, McMahon could entertain the prospect of mounting an assault against the purveyors of legitimate sport: the National Basketball Association, the National Football League (NFL), and Major League Baseball.

The WWF ended its 1999 fiscal year on a high note, generating revenues of $251.5 million. This figure was nearly double 1998 revenues of $126.2 million. In one of the last developments of the 1990s, McMahon renamed Titan Sports as World Wrestling Federation Entertainment, Inc., and took the company public. The debut of the WWFE ticker symbol on the NASDAQ in October 1999 marked the beginning of a new era in the company's history.

ENTERING THE 21ST CENTURY

WWF rang in the new millennium by announcing plans to establish the XFL, a new professional "off-season" football league that took to the field for a ten-week schedule following the NFL's Super Bowl. Working in partnership, NBC and the WWE invested $35 million in the new league, which played games on Saturday nights. Midway through the year, the company acquired ownership of WWF New York, an entertainment complex located in New York's Times Square that had been operated under license by a separate company.

In early 2001, WWF agreed to acquire rival and AOL Time Warner unit WCW. The deal brought many of the wrestlers who had been lured away by Ted Turner back within McMahon's organization. Difficult economic conditions had a negative impact on WWE during the early years of the new century. As ticket sales for live events struggled, and retail sales declined, the company implemented a restructuring plan and revealed plans to eliminate 9 percent of its workforce. WWE's restructuring plan resulted in the resignation of President and Chief Operating Officer Stuart Snyder. In addition, Senior Vice-President of Planning and Administration Pete DiNicola was named executive vice-president and chief operating officer. By this time, Linda McMahon served as CEO.

In 2002 WWF settled a lawsuit brought several years before concerning the use of its initialism, which was shared by the international nonprofit organization World Wildlife Fund. Under the terms of the settlement, "Federation" would no longer be used in any part of the business, which was renamed World Wrestling Entertainment Inc.; the company's logo was also redesigned, and it became known informally as WWE.

The XFL struggled with poor ratings during its first season. In May 2002, WWE agreed to buy out NBC's share of XFL—which the network referred to as one of the worst blunders in its history during a 75th anniversary special—for $27.7 million. The following year, WWE acquired Viacom's ownership interest in the company, which consisted of two million shares valued at approximately $19.2 million. Viacom indicated that its stake in WWE was no longer in alignment with its corporate strategy.

EXPANDED CONTENT OFFERINGS

Heading into the middle of the decade, WWE was focused on international expansion, particularly in Europe. In late 2004 the company hired former Hasbro executive Jonathan Sully to lead its international expansion efforts. In particular, Sully was tasked with leading a global licensing campaign that sought to increase awareness about wrestling. In early 2005, WWE cemented the first deal with a cable operator for WWF 24/7, a new video-on-demand service. For between $6 and $10 per month, subscribers could view 20 hours of content that included everything from classic wrestling matches to profiles of wrestlers dating back to the 1950s.

By early 2006, the WWE was making preparations to launch a new mobile portal, via which subscribers could access exclusive videos and other content from mobile devices such as cell phones. Early the following year, WWE promoted Chief Financial Officer Michael Sileck to the role of chief operating officer. At this time, Vince McMahon continued to lead the company as chairman, and his wife, Linda, remained CEO. Sileck was succeeded by Senior Vice-President, Finance, and Chief Accounting Officer Frank Serpe, a 20-year company veteran.

By 2007 WWE offered online programming and e-commerce sites in 120 different countries. The company continued to further its international expansion, selling localized content in markets such as Italy, Spain, Japan, and Portugal. The WWE recorded sales of $526.5 million in 2008. Early the following year, former U.S. Tennis Association Chief Marketing Officer Michelle Wilson was named the company's new executive vice-president of marketing, assuming responsibility for its global marketing and integrated brand strategies.

In 2009 WWE celebrated the 25th anniversary of Wrestlemania. The company held Wrestlemania XXV on April 5, 2009, at the Reliant Stadium in Houston,

Texas. On the promotional front, WWE partnered with Kmart, which supported the occasion with a number of marketing tactics including in-store displays of licensed products, point-of-purchase advertising, and a micro site on the Internet. By 2009, however, WWE was facing a difficult economic climate marked by reduced consumer spending. Just as it had done during the early years of the decade, the company took steps to reduce costs, launching an initiative to reduce its budget by up to $20 million. Moving forward into the second decade of the 21st century, WWE seemed well positioned for continued success as a leading entertainment enterprise.

Jeffrey L. Covell
Updated, Paul R. Greenland

PRINCIPAL SUBSIDIARIES

WWE Studios; WWE Canada Inc.; WWE EMEA (UK); WWE China; WWE Australia; WWE Japan.

PRINCIPAL OPERATING UNITS

Live and Televised Entertainment; Consumer Products; Digital Media; WWE Studios; Sales & Sponsorships.

PRINCIPAL COMPETITORS

National Association for Stock Car Auto Racing Inc.; National Basketball Association Inc.; National Football League.

FURTHER READING

Authors, John, "Wrestling Elbows Its Way into Big Money," *Financial Times,* May 31, 1999, p. 4.

Brown, Rich, "WWF Tries Out New Holds," *Broadcasting & Cable,* September 2, 1996, p. 50.

Chamish, Barry, "WWF Riding Wave of Popularity in Israel," *Amusement Business,* January 17, 1994, p. 12.

Collins, James, "Lords of the Ring," *Time,* June 29, 1998, p. 66.

Farrell, Mike, "WWF IPO Gets Big Rating," *Multichannel News,* October 25, 1999.

Fisher, Eric, "World Wrestling Federation Parent Mulls Public Offering," *Knight-Ridder/Tribune Business News,* May 20, 1999.

Fromm, Emily, "Good, Clean Entertainment," *Adweek Eastern Edition,* January 25, 1999, p. 3.

Jensen, Jeff, "Wrestling Goes Mainstream, Draws Big Ratings, Sponsors," *Advertising Age,* August 17, 1998, p. 3.

Katz, Richard, "Grappling with Success," *Variety,* June 14, 1999, p. 17.

"Let's Wrestle," *Delaney Report,* February 26, 2007.

McDonald, Michael, "Wrestlers Get the First Down; New Football League Seeks Fans, Legitimacy," *Crain's New York Business,* December 11, 2000.

Melvin, Mary Kay, "WWF Officials: This Year's Grosses Prove the Lull Is Over," *Amusement Business,* May 13, 1996, p. 10.

Palmen, Christopher, "'We Want to Be Like Disney,'" *Forbes,* October 17, 1988, p. 133.

Quinton, Brian, "Kmart Climbs into the Ring with Wrestlemania XXV," *Promo,* March 10, 2009.

"Ring Masters," *Economist* (U.S.), August 12, 1995, p. 74.

Rosellini, Lynn, "Lords of the Ring," *U.S. News & World Report,* May 17, 1999, p. 52.

Schmuckler, Eric, "Steel-Cage Legal Wrangle," *Mediaweek,* March 1, 1993, p. 20.

Sheraiach, Kelly, "Wrestling on a Peak; Keeps One Eye on Valley," *Marketing News,* May 12, 1997, p. 24.

Sorkin, Andrew Ross, "Smackdown! W.W.F. to Buy Wrestling Rival," *New York Times,* March 24, 2001.

Stanley, T. L., "Grapplin' for Dollars," *Brandweek,* April 19, 1999, p. 48.

"Titan Sports Inc., the Owner of the World Wrestling Federation, Has Acquired the Debbie Reynolds Hotel and Casino in Las Vegas," *Broadcasting & Cable,* August 10, 1998, p. 80.

Trigoboff, Dan, "Wrestling with the Competition," *Broadcasting & Cable,* August 12, 1997, p. 76.

Young Chang Co. Ltd.

178-55 Kajwa-Dong Seo-Gu
Incheon, 404714
Republic of Korea
Telephone: (82 32) 570 1000
Fax: (82 32) 576 2340
Web site: http://www.youngchang.com

Private Company
Incorporated: 1956
Employees: 200
Sales: $45.5 million) (2008 est.)
NAICS: 339992 Musical Instrument Manufacturing

■ ■ ■

Young Chang Co. Ltd. is one of the world's largest-selling piano manufacturers. The company is also the leading piano manufacturer in Korea, holding a 50 percent market share. Founded in 1956, Young Chang has developed one of the world's most vertically integrated musical instrument manufacturing operations. The company operates its own sawmills in Korea and China, produces its metal plates or soundboards at its own foundry in Korea, and produces much of its metal and other parts in its own machine shop facilities. The company's vertical integration strategy enables it to maintain control over the entire production process, which in turn has built the company's reputation as a producer of some of the world's finest quality pianos.

Young Chang's manufacturing operations are based in its Incheon, South Korea, home and at a 750,000-square-foot integrated manufacturing facility in Tianjin, China. The company operates a distribution subsidiary in the United States, which remains its largest single market. In addition to its acoustic piano sales, Young Chang also owns Kurzweil Digital Pianos, one of the world's leading makers of high-end electronic pianos. Hyundai Development Company (HDC), formed from the breakup of Korean automotive and industrial conglomerate Hyundai, owns 57.33 percent of Young Chang. Byung Jae Park, one of the founding forces behind the success of Hyundai Motors, serves as Young Chang's CEO.

PIANO IMPORTER ORIGINS

Young Chang Company was founded by three brothers, Jai-Young Kim, Jai-Chang Kim, and Jai-Sup Kim, in 1956 as an importer and distributor of Yamaha pianos for the South Korean market. The Kims combined their varied educational backgrounds—Jai-Chang majored in music, while Jai-Young studied finance, and Jai-Sup earned an engineering degree—to form a potent force in the musical instrument industry, both in Korea and in the world. The devastated South Korean economy provided only a modest market for pianos in the late 1950s. Nevertheless, the country's determination to transform itself into one of the Asian region's industrial and economic powerhouses provided strong growth prospects for the Kim brothers' company.

Sales rose steadily through the middle of the 1960s. In 1965, however, the South Korean government imposed heavy import duties on products arriving from Japan. This provided the signal to the Kims to set up

COMPANY PERSPECTIVES

All of us at Young Chang consider ourselves a family. Our confidence that Young Chang will not only maintain but improve its international status is based on the commitment of this Young Chang family. To create a truly outstanding instrument, each member in the manufacturing process must consider him or herself an artist, and their product a work of art. Such is the attitude at Young Chang; fine craftsmen skillfully creating a musical work of art ... A World Class Piano. Understanding that those who enjoy our instruments are themselves artists, we will never cease our efforts, constantly striving to satisfy their highest expectations.

their own piano manufacturing operation. For this, the Kims initially teamed up with Yamaha, forming a joint-venture company that year. The Kim brothers chose a Korean name, Young Chang, for their piano brand. This choice helped to establish the company's unique identity. As one Young Chang representative told the *Korea Times* that the "trend at the time we began to export was to label all products with foreign names. But the product was most definitely Korean, so we decided to give it a Korean label to show that we were proud of it."

EMPHASIS ON VERTICAL INTEGRATION

From the start, the Kims sought to develop a vertically integrated operation, to maintain control of quality levels. The company also set the entry-level, student, and nonprofessional segments as its primary target. In this way, the company initially avoided direct competition with Yamaha, which focused its own piano production largely on the professional market. The company built its first factory in Incheon, on the South Korean coast near Seoul.

Young Chang launched production of its first upright piano models by 1968. The company's initial production stood at just 150 pianos per year. With assistance from Yamaha, however, the company rapidly ramped up its manufacturing operations to supply the growing domestic demand for pianos. South Korea was in the midst of the first phase of its dramatic economic transformation, and the growing affluence led to the rapid adoption of luxury items, including pianos.

By the end of the 1970s, Young Chang's production topped 15,000 pianos per year. These included the company's first grand piano models. By then, Young Chang had taken over its own instrument development effort, having ended its relationship with Yamaha in 1974. The Kim brothers then gained complete control over the company. The Kims, however, nearly lost their business when a fire destroyed 90 percent of its production facility in 1976. The company, by then with 600 employees, set to work to rebuild the factory, succeeding in relaunching production in less than two months. By the end of that year, the company had opened a second, larger factory in Incheon.

The new facility came as part of Young Chang's vertical integration strategy. The company added its first sawmill, giving it control over its wood supply. The group then became one of the few piano makers to produce its own metal plates (essential for the piano's resonance and tonal quality) with the opening of a vacuum-press foundry in 1977. The company also invested in a sophisticated metal shop as part of its effort to produce nearly every component of their pianos, including the screws.

INTERNATIONAL EXPANSION

Young Chang's strong manufacturing investments allowed the company to branch out into other business areas. The company began developing other musical instruments, especially electric guitars and bass guitars. This production enabled the company to secure a supply contract with Fender Musical Instrument to supply guitars under that company's entry-level Squier brand, introduced in the 1980s.

Young Chang also attempted to develop its own guitar brand, Fenix. These guitars, like many Asian guitars of the period, were heavily based on, if not directly copies of, existing guitar designs from companies such as Fender and Gibson. When these companies successfully defended their copyrights, Young Chang was forced to end production of the Fenix line. A more successful business line for the company was its production of woodworking machinery, also launched during the decade.

The company had far more success, both in sales and in building its reputation, with its pianos. By the late 1970s, Young Chang was ready to tackle the export market, going head-to-head with former mentor Yamaha. The company began shipping pianos to the German, Dutch, Spanish, and Swiss markets during the decade. In 1979 the group set up its first North American subsidiary, in the United States. This was

---

KEY DATES

1956: The Kim brothers found a business importing Yamaha pianos into South Korea.

1965: The Kims and Yamaha form a Korean-based piano manufacturing joint venture, launching the Young Chang brand.

1974: The Kims take full control of Young Chang, ending its relationship with Yamaha.

1979: Young Chang enters North America with a subsidiary in the United States.

1984: Young Chang opens a subsidiary in Canada.

1990: Young Chang acquires digital piano maker Kurzweil in the United States.

1997: Young Chang defaults on its loans and is taken over by the Korean Exchange Bank.

2004: Samick Music Corp. acquires Young Chang but the merger is voided by the Korean Fair Trade Commission.

2006: Hyundai Development Company acquires 87 percent of Young Chang, rescuing it from bankruptcy.

2008: Young Chang announces new strategy focused on the high-end piano market.

---

followed by the creation of a Canadian subsidiary in 1984.

Young Chang's initial entry into the North American market, however, was nearly disastrous. Within months of its arrival, the early shipments of the company's pianos developed a number of problems with their internal components. Improper shipping methods, as well as the effect on the wood components of the change in climatic conditions, were blamed for the problems. In response, Young Chang instituted a major quality-improvement program, investing in new equipment and technologies throughout the full production system. The new commitment to quality helped establish Young Chang as a new and major force in the North American and worldwide piano markets.

INVESTMENTS IN GROWTH

Demand surged, and the company rose to become one of the best-selling piano brands in the United States and elsewhere. Domestic sales proved a strong driver for the company's sales as well. South Korea's fast-growing affluence in the 1980s in turn led to fresh surges in piano purchases, as the instrument increasingly served as an

important status symbol. By the end of the decade, the South Korean piano market was one of the most vibrant in the world, with nearly 150,000 pianos purchased each year. Young Chang's share of that market quickly reached 57 percent. By the 1990s, with annual sales of more than $200 million, Young Chang's sales outpaced even those of Yamaha.

Supporting this growth was a new investment program launched in 1986. Over a three-year period, the company spent almost $60 million to add some 633,000 square feet of production space to its main Incheon site. The investment also included a vast new technology upgrade, as the company installed some 400 new pieces of specialized manufacturing machinery. Following completion of the upgrade, Young Chang's total production capacity reached impressive levels; with an annual capacity of over 100,000 upright and 12,000 grand pianos per year, Young Chang then ranked among the world's largest. By 1989, also, the company's total guitar production reached 180,000.

Young Chang then launched a new expansion program. In 1990 the company stepped in to rescue Kurzweil Music Systems, a major U.S. manufacturer of electronic pianos and organs. Kurzweil had fallen into difficulties during the 1980s, resulting in its filing for bankruptcy protection in 1989. The purchase of Kurzweil, for $3 million, gave Young Chang a position in the young and fast-growing digital piano market. Unlike acoustic pianos, where the company was forced to compete against large numbers of piano makers, the digital piano market remained confined to just a handful of players, including Roland, Yamaha, Korg, Solton, and Kawai.

In 1992 Young Chang stepped up its U.S. presence, establishing its own sawmill in Tacoma, Washington, with an investment of $32 million. In this way, the company procured its own supply of hard maple and Sitka spruce for its piano production. The new sawmill also provided the company with the foundation for its move into a new musical instrument category; the company established the Tacoma acoustic guitar factory and brand in 1995. By 1998 Young Chang had moved its North American headquarters, including its Kurzweil operations, to Washington as well.

FACING FINANCIAL CRISIS

Young Chang continued its investment program through the middle of the decade. In response to rising wages in South Korea, the company launched construction of a new $40 million factory in Tianjin, China. That site, with a production space of 750,000 square feet, became one of the most vertically integrated piano

---

manufacturing facilities in the world, including its own on-site sawmill and metal workshop.

While the Chinese site provided the group with a significant potential cost reduction, Young Chang also set its sights on the high end of the piano market. In 1997 the company developed a partnership with Joseph Pramberger, one of the icons of modern piano manufacturing, who had spent much of his career with the famed Steinway Piano Company. Pramberger led a redesign of Young Chang's PG series, introducing a number of important innovations, resulting in the launch of the signature Pramberger PG-185 grand piano.

The new model established Young Chang among the world's highest-quality piano brands. It also attracted the interest of Steinway itself, as that company had begun expanding its own brand family. In 1999 Steinway's Boston Piano Company, maker of the company's midpriced Boston brand, signed on Young Chang to produce an entry-level piano line, called Essex.

These successes in piano design, however, could not mask a financial crisis that nearly ended Young Chang itself. The company's massive investment program through the middle of the 1990s had left the company heavily in debt, with much of its debt in foreign currency. This left the company highly vulnerable to the financial crisis that swept through much of the Asian region, with South Korea at its epicenter. Young Chang's sales suddenly dried up even as its debt load, due to the collapse of the Korean won, nearly doubled. As a result, Young Chang defaulted on its loans and was taken over by its main creditor, Korean Exchange Bank, which put the company up for sale.

NEW OWNER IN THE 21ST CENTURY

Young Chang struggled to find a buyer and for the next six years the company remained under the bank's control. The company restructured, shedding most of its non-piano operations. By 2002 Young Chang had succeeded in regaining its financial footing, and had launched a number of new pianos, including two from its high-end Pramberger line, and a new Bermann model, the brand produced at the group's Tianjin facility. Also in 2002, cofounder Jai-Sup Kim died at the age of 83.

In February 2004, Samick Music Corporation agreed to buy a 46 percent stake in Young Chang, paying $74 million. Samick, a diversified musical instrument maker and the world's largest producer of guitars,

was also Young Chang's main Korean rival. At the same time, Samick had built up its own portfolio of international brands, including Samick, Kohler & Campbell, Sohmer, and Bechstein. Immediately following the acquisition, Samick moved to restructure its piano operations, merging much of Young Chang's distribution, service, and similar operations into Samick's own operations.

In November of that year, however, the deal came under the review of Korea's Fair Trade Commission (FTC), which voided the merger on antimonopoly grounds. Samick was ordered to separate Young Chang from its operations, including restoring the company's self-standing distribution subsidiaries. Immediately following the FTC decision, however, Samick dropped its financing of Young Chang. In turn, Young Chang defaulted on some KRW 460 million ($4 million) in bank payments, declaring bankruptcy.

Young Chang once again appeared headed toward oblivion, as the company faced possible liquidation. In July 2006, however, the company caught the attention of HDC, which agreed to buy 87 percent of Young Chang for $74.3 million. HDC itself had been founded as a property development company amid the breakup of the Hyundai Motors conglomerate following its own financial crisis. HDC saw the acquisition of the Young Chang brand as a means of enhancing the image of its residential developments. HDC then called on Byung Jae Park, one of the members of the founding team that had transformed Hyundai into one of South Korea's leading companies, to lead Young Chang.

With Park's leadership and backed by HDC's financial muscle, Young Chang entered a new and promising phase in its growth. Park carried out an extensive reorganization of the group's manufacturing operations, tightening the group's production standards and upgrading its machinery and production facilities. This investment came in 2008 as part of the decision to abandon the lower-priced piano segments—where the company was forced to compete with such low-cost Chinese up-and-comers as Pearl River in favor of a focus on the high-end piano range.

The company would have to do this without its flagship Pramberger line. During the few months it had been part of Samick, and following Pramberger's death, Samick had negotiated the acquisition of the rights to the Pramberger brand name. Nevertheless, Young Chang retained sole control of the designs and technologies developed by Pramberger himself. The company promised to continue to produce these designs, under a new brand name. Young Chang in the meantime had regained its status as one of the world's most respected piano makers.

M. L. Cohen

PRINCIPAL SUBSIDIARIES

Tianjin Young Chang Akki., Ltd.; Tianjin Young Chang Piano Plate Foundry Co., Ltd.; Young Chang North America Inc.

PRINCIPAL DIVISIONS

Kurzweil Digital Pianos.

PRINCIPAL OPERATING UNITS

Sawmills; Foundry; Pianos.

PRINCIPAL COMPETITORS

Jiujiang Instrument Factory; Kaman Corp.; Roland Corp.; Guangzhou Pearl River Piano Group Ltd.; Kawai Musical Instruments Manufacturing Company Ltd.; Steinway Musical Instruments Inc.; Yamaha Corporation; Samick Musical Instruments Company Ltd.; Baldwin Piano Inc.

FURTHER READING

"Choi to Head Young Chang North America," *Music Trades,* March 2009, p. 138.

"Driving Hard to Become Number One!" *Music Trades,* February 2008, p. 128.

Dunmire, Jeffrey, "The Samick/Young Chang Controversy ... an Inside Perspective," *Music Trades,* May 2005, p. 8.

"Hyundai Pays $74 Million for Control of Young Chang," *Music Trades,* July 2006, p. 60.

"Jai-Sup Kim: Founder of Young Chang Akki," *Music Trades,* October 2002, p. 154.

"Ki Young Hong Takes Helm at Restructured Young Chang," *Music Trades,* November 2006, p. 124.

Majeski, Brian T., "The Korean Wrecking Crew," *Music Trades,* March 2005, p. 24.

"Rejuvenated Young Chang Marks 50th Year at NAMM," *Music Trades,* March 2007, p. 116.

"Samick & Young Chang Merge U.S. Operations," *Music Trades,* June 2004, p. 22.

"Will the Real Young Chang Distributor Please Stand Up?" *Music Trades,* March 2005, p. 26.

"Young Chang Files Bankruptcy," *Music Trades,* November 2004, p. 24.

"Young Chang Piano: Riding High on Sound Success," *Korea Times,* April 9, 1999.

"Young Chang Takes Back U.S. Distribution from Samick," *Music Trades,* May 2006, p. 32.

Zaro Bake Shop Inc.

138 Bruckner Boulevard
Bronx, New York 10454
U.S.A.
Telephone: (718) 993-5600
Fax: (718) 292-9353
Web site: http://www.zaro.com

Private Company
Incorporated: 1949
Employees: 110
Sales: $23.1 million (2008 est.)
NAICS: 311812 Commercial Bakeries

■ ■ ■

Zaro Bake Shop Inc. is a family-owned commercial bakery, also doing business as Zaro's Bread Basket, that operates a dozen retail stores in New York City and the surrounding area, best known for its locations at major transportation hubs. Catering to hurried commuters as well as area office workers, the company prides itself on quick service, operating on the theory that long lines dampen business and that transactions need to take 30 seconds or less. Zaro maintains four shops in Grand Central Terminal, a pair of shops at Pennsylvania Station, a single unit at the Port Authority Bus Terminal, as well as a unit at Penn Station in Newark, New Jersey. In addition, Zaro shops are found at four other Manhattan locations, and the company also sells its products online. In Manhattan, customers can order items online for delivery or pickup at four locations.

Primary baking is done at a central facility in the Bronx and the shops complete the process. Products include a wide variety of breads, bagels, chocolate babka, cookies (in particular Black & White iced cookies), rugelach, and birthday cakes. Zaro also sells gift baskets and operates a wholesale division that serves customers throughout the United States. The Zaro brand is well established in New York City, and is perhaps best known for its longtime presence in Grand Central Terminal and its fast service.

IMMIGRANT ORIGINS

Baker Joseph Zaro emigrated from Poland to the United States in 1927 and soon established a small bakery in Newark, New Jersey. He was successful enough that two years later he was able to send for his wife and children. During the 1930s, in the midst of the Great Depression, he and his sons William and Philip moved the bakery to the Bronx, where it operated under the Zaro's name for the first time. Over the next 30 years the family expanded their operation, opening other bakeries in the borough, including a flagship unit that combined a production and retail operation. All told, the Zaro chain numbered 21 Bronx locations by the mid-1960s. Of the two brothers, the elder, William, was primarily the baker, while Philip spent most of his time in the stores, serving as the public face of the company.

Once home to numerous middle-class neighborhoods, the Bronx deteriorated in the 1960s and early 1970s, leading to the closure of many of the Zaro's bakery shops. Eventually there would be just one store in the Bronx, located in the Parkchester section. There was also a changing of the guard. William Zaro retired

COMPANY PERSPECTIVES

Zaro's New York Bakery, more commonly known as Zaro's Bread Basket in Grand Central Station has been New York City's premiere bakery for over 75 years.

as co-president of the company in 1974 and Philip Zaro's sons, Andrew, Stuart, and Joseph, joined the company. According to *Forbes* magazine, Andrew Zaro was the one responsible for taking Zaro to Grand Central Terminal. At the time, the train station was in decline. Opened in 1913, the ornate Grand Central had enjoyed its golden age in the 1920s when more than 500 long-distance trains departed each day.

Following World War II, however, as train travel became less prevalent, the station fell into disrepair, and by the 1970s had become a haven for the homeless and rife with panhandlers and pickpockets. In the waiting area there was little food for consumers to buy other than hot dogs, pretzels, and soda. The Zaro family conducted some crude market research, which Stuart Zaro told *Crain's New York Business* "consisted of standing at the bottom of the escalators for weeks and watching what kind of people were walking by." They liked what they saw, apparently. "Smelling opportunity," according to *Forbes,* Andrew Zaro "wrangled a cheap lease on 2,100 square feet; his office was a 5-foot by 6-foot cubby carved into one of the station's load-bearing columns."

GRAND CENTRAL STORE OPENS TO GREAT SUCCESS

Zaro's Bread Basket, as the Grand Central shop was called, opened in 1977, occupying space below the terminal's west balcony where the lost and found department had been housed. Operating Monday through Saturday from 6:00 A.M. to 10:00 P.M., the store sold eastern European breads, Irish soda bread, bagels, and Danish pastry baked in Zaro's ovens, as well as French bread and croissants and Italian bread from other bakeries. The Zaro family hoped to serve 2,000 customers a day, but their projection proved to be much too conservative. The shop was an instant success and was soon serving 5,500 customers a day. The bakery was reviewed in July 1977 by Mimi Sheraton of the *New York Times,* who said the success of the bakery was "more a matter of convenience than distinction. Bagels were soft, white, tasteless and squashy. The challah had

so little body it was squashed pancake flat in the package by the time we got it back to the office. ... Irish soda bread was as sweet as cake and had none of the snowy, soda-accented lightness that is its chief characteristic."

Nevertheless, Zaro's Bread Basket was a major success for Zaro Bake Shop. Over the next few years, Zaro's Bread Basket evolved into Zaro's Market Place at Grand Central, with six carryout shops on the station's main level, catering to commuters as well as area office workers. The outlets included the Potato Sack, serving stuffed baked potatoes; the Vegetable Patch, offering soups, quiches, and salads; the Pita Pocket, specializing in pocket breads and fillings; the Juice Booth, offering fresh juices; the Yogurt Yard, serving frozen yogurt; and the French bakery. Together they served as many as 15,000 customers each day.

Zaro's success did not escape the notice of local real estate companies, which began calling on the Zaro family soon after the Grand Central unit opened to excellent business, offering potential sites for new bake shops. The company eschewed residential locations, believing that the rents were too high in relation to the foot traffic. Given Zaro's experience with Grand Central, it was not surprising that the company turned to other transportation hubs, leasing space at Pennsylvania Station and the Port Authority Bus Terminal. The company also targeted Manhattan locations where a large number of people passed by, leading to the opening of a Zaro's Bake Shop in the midtown Gimbels department store. Although the store generated $2.5 million in annual sales, the operation was terminated when Gimbels went out of business in 1986. Another Zaro's unit opened in the South Street Seaport, a popular tourist destination in Lower Manhattan.

CENTRAL BAKERY IN THE BRONX

To support the shops, Zaro Bake Shop built a 40,000-square-foot facility on Bruckner Boulevard in the South Bronx in 1982. The company grew further when it began franchising in 1986, leading to the opening of six franchised units by 1988. The company also made an attempt to leverage its name to create a wholesale operation by developing a line of frozen goods for sale to area hotels and restaurants. An attempt using an outside distributor, New Jersey-based A Bohrer Inc., was made in the late 1980s but failed because of problems with product freshness. The wholesale idea was not abandoned, however, but would be revived only when Zaro was able to control distribution and be assured of quality control. The company hoped to develop a wholesale channel in the early 1990s, but would have to wait another decade before the business was set up.

KEY DATES

1927:	Immigrant Joseph Zaro opens New Jersey bakery.
1977:	Zaro's Bread Basket opens in Grand Central Terminal.
1982:	Central facility opens in the Bronx.
1986:	The company begins franchising.
1996:	William Zaro dies.
2002:	Wholesale business is launched.
2004:	Philip Zaro dies.

Zaro tried its hand at importing in the late 1980s, the result of improving relations with the Soviet Union. An effort to import Russian bread garnered some publicity at the time because a squabble ensued and the incongruity of a fight over so-called peace bread created too much irony to be ignored by the press. Zaro had worked with a retired businessman and neighbor of Philip Zaro to import two-pound loaves of dark rye. The two parties argued over travel expenses to the Soviet Union and soon became rivals, each developing a separate source for the Russian loaves that then became competitive products in New York City. There was some talk of reciprocation— shipping a product to the Soviet Union or opening a Zaro's in Moscow—but nothing ever came of the idea, and "peace bread" became little more than a curious episode in Zaro's history and U.S.-Soviet relations.

GRAND CENTRAL RENOVATIONS

By 1990 Zaro Bake Shop consisted of 15 stores generating $30 million. Around this time Andrew Zaro left the family business, selling his interest to strike out on his own, creating a debt-buying business called National Loan Investors. His brothers Stuart and Joseph remained with Zaro Bake Shop, but the previous generation soon passed away. William Zaro died at the age of 81 in 1996 and his brother Philip, who had stayed on as chairman of the board, died of a stroke eight years later, at the age of 82.

In 1991 a new store opened in Rockefeller Center. By the mid-1990s the Zaro's chain included 12 total units and had spread beyond Manhattan and the Bronx to Yonkers in Westchester County and Penn Station in Newark. The Grand Central Terminal store remained the flagship operation and became increasingly important as Grand Central underwent extensive renovations in the second half of the 1990s, part of a master plan developed in the 1980s to add more upscale shops and eateries. Improvements did not come without difficulties, however, not the least of which were the interminable delays and secrecy of the Metropolitan Transit Authority (MTA).

In the 1980s Andrew Zaro complained to the *New York Times* that his family had been ready to spend $750,000 on renovations to upgrade Zaro's Bread Basket but felt constrained because they were not certain about the MTA's plans for their location beneath the west balcony. The family's caution was justified. In 1996 the MTA launched a two-year renovation project that forced about three-dozen businesses to close their doors. Zaro's was fortunate to be relocated to a temporary site, called Renovation Marketplace, while the work was done, but at the very least the shop was inconvenienced. Moreover, the project lasted well beyond the two-year estimated time of completion. While a number of former tenants were not issued new leases to become part of Grand Central's new retail area, Zaro's was able to receive four sites in the building; however, the company had to contend with further delays before launching its new operations.

WHOLESALE UNIT OPENS

As the new century dawned, Zaro maintained shops in Grand Central's New Market Place as well as locations near tracks 29, 34, and 103. Three of them were 800 square feet in size and the fourth occupied 400 square feet. The company's other high-profile locations at Pennsylvania Station, the Port Authority Bus Terminal, and Penn Station in Newark placed Zaro in a position to be passed by 1.5 million people each day. To take advantage of its recognizable brand, the company launched a wholesale operation in 2002, which generated $2 million in sales the first year. Initially the company tried to make multiple deliveries of small orders to accounts each week, but when this proved not to be a profitable approach, Zaro began to focus on higher volume accounts.

To the company's surprise the small accounts stayed with them but began placing larger orders just once a week. Less timely deliveries created packaging concerns, forcing Zaro to acquire horizontal flow machines that formed, filled, and sealed packages, as well as shrink-wrap machines. A year later wholesale revenues reached $3 million and continued to grow at a 20 percent rate in the next few years. The Bronx production facility that 20 years earlier had been ample in size for Zaro was becoming cramped, especially with freezer and office space. However, the site included another 17,500 square feet on which to build to keep up with growing demand.

Dependent on commuters, normally the company's core business, Zaro's operations were adversely impacted by a transit strike in December 2005. Not only were sales down sharply at Grand Central and Pennsylvania Station, employees who depended on mass transit had a difficult time getting to work, exacerbating the situation. When the strike was settled, business picked up again for Zaro. The renovations on the lower level of Grand Central were also paying dividends, as Zaro and the other stores in the Grand Central market enjoyed a robust business from commuters as well as area office workers and tourists.

As the first decade of the new century came to a close, Zaro faced challenges, such as the elimination of trans fats in baked goods, resulting in a significant increase in costs. By this time, however, the Zaro brand was well entrenched in the New York City area and that brand awareness was reinforced as millions of commuters walked by its outlets each day. There was every reason to expect the company to prosper and remain family-owned well into the future.

Ed Dinger

PRINCIPAL SUBSIDIARIES

Zaro Bread Basket.

PRINCIPAL COMPETITORS

ABP Corporation; Mr. Hot Bread Inc.; Panera Bread Company.

FURTHER READING

Elder, Martin, "Upscale Take-Out," *Restaurant Business,* November 1, 1987, p. 169.

Fabricant, Florence, "Soviet Bread Sets Off Capitalist Struggle," *New York Times,* May 24, 1989, p. C14.

Feron, James, "For Its Importers, Soviet 'Peace Bread' Proves Divisive," *New York Times,* June 4, 1989, p. A1.

Glassman, Mark, "Philip Zaro, 82, Who Founded Popular Bagel and Muffin Stores," *New York Times,* May 19, 2004.

Lang, Joan, "Take-Out," *Restaurant Business,* May 20, 1984, p. 206.

McCain, Mark, "Grand Central Terminal; Replace a Retail Hodgepodge with Urban Chic," *New York Times,* August 20, 1989.

Nelson, Brett, "A Betting Man," *Forbes,* September 29, 2003, p. 72.

Rigg, Cynthia, "The Mark of Zaro: Customers Roll In," *Crain's New York Business,* April 16, 1990, p. 1.

Sheraton, Mimi, "A Bakery That Gets Them Coming and Going," *New York Times,* July 2, 1977.

"William Zaro, 81, Baker Chain Founder," *New York Times,* August 1, 1996.

Cumulative Index to Companies

*Listings in this index are arranged in alphabetical order under the company name. Company names beginning with a letter or proper name such as Eli Lilly & Co. will be found under the first letter of the company name. Definite articles (The, Le, La) are ignored for alphabetical purposes as are forms of incorporation that precede the company name (AB, NV). Company names printed in **bold** type have full, historical essays on the page numbers appearing in bold. Updates to entries that appeared in earlier volumes are signified by the notation* **(upd.)**. *This index is cumulative with volume numbers printed in bold type.*

A

Abu Dhabi National Oil Company, IV
363–64; 45 6–9 (upd.)

Academic Press *see* Reed Elsevier plc.

Academy of Television Arts & Sciences,
Inc., 55 3–5

Academy Sports & Outdoors, 27 6–8

Acadia Realty Trust, 106 6–10

Acadian Ambulance & Air Med
Services, Inc., 39 7–10

Access Business Group *see* Alticor Inc.

ACCION International, 87 1–4

Acciona S.A., 81 1–4

Acclaim Entertainment Inc., 24 3–8

ACCO World Corporation, 7 3–5; 51
7–10 (upd.)

Accor S.A., 10 12–14; 27 9–12 (upd.);
69 3–8 (upd.)

Accredited Home Lenders Holding Co.,
91 1–4

Accubuilt, Inc., 74 3–5

Accuray Incorporated, 95 10–13

AccuWeather, Inc., 73 6–8

ACE Cash Express, Inc., 33 3–6

Ace Hardware Corporation, 12 6–8; 35
11–14 (upd.)

Acer Incorporated, 16 3–6; 73 9–13
(upd.)

Acergy SA, 97 1–4

Aceros Fortuna S.A. de C.V. *see* Carpenter
Technology Corp.

Aceto Corp., 38 3–5

Aché Laboratórios Farmacéuticas S.A.,
105 1–4

AchieveGlobal Inc., 90 9–12

Acindar Industria Argentina de Aceros
S.A., 87 5–8

Ackerley Communications, Inc., 9 3–5

Ackermans & van Haaren N.V., 97 5–8

ACLU *see* American Civil Liberties Union
(ACLU).

Acme-Cleveland Corp., 13 6–8

Acme United Corporation, 70 3–6

ACNielsen Corporation, 38 6–9 (upd.)

Acorn Products, Inc., 55 6–9

Acosta Sales and Marketing
Company,Inc., 77 1–4

ACS *see* Affiliated Computer Services,
Inc.; Alaska Communications Systems
Group, Inc.

Acsys, Inc., 44 3–5

Actavis Group hf., 103 1–5

Actelion Ltd., 83 5–8

Actia Group S.A., 107 1–5

Action Performance Companies, Inc., 27
13–15

Activision, Inc., 32 8–11; 89 6–11
(upd.)

Actuant Corporation, 94 1–8 (upd.)

Acuity Brands, Inc., 90 13–16

Acushnet Company, 64 3–5

Acuson Corporation, 10 15–17; 36 3–6
(upd.)

Acxiom Corporation, 35 15–18

Adam Opel AG, 7 6–8; 21 3–7 (upd.);
61 6–11 (upd.)

Adams Childrenswear Ltd., 95 14–19

The Adams Express Company, 86 1–5

Adams Golf, Inc., 37 3–5

Adams Media Corporation *see* F&W
Publications, Inc.

Adani Enterprises Ltd., 97 9–12

Adaptec, Inc., 31 3–6

ADC Telecommunications, Inc., 10
18–21; 30 6–9 (upd.); 89 12–17
(upd.)

Adecco S.A., 36 7–11 (upd.)

Adecoagro LLC, 101 1–4

Adelman Travel Group, 105 5–8

Adelphia Communications Corporation,
17 6–8; 52 7–10 (upd.)

ADESA, Inc., 71 7–10

Adia S.A., 6 9–11 *see also* Adecco S.A.

adidas Group AG, 14 6–9; 33 7–11
(upd.); 75 12–17 (upd.)

Aditya Birla Group, 79 1–5

ADM *see* Archer Daniels Midland Co.

Administaff, Inc., 52 11–13

Administración Nacional de
Combustibles, Alcohol y Pórtland, 93
23–27

Admiral Co. *see* Maytag Corp.

ADNOC *see* Abu Dhabi National Oil Co.

Adobe Systems Inc., 10 22–24; 33
12–16 (upd.); 106 11–17 (upd.)

Adolf Würth GmbH & Co. KG, 49
13–15

Adolfo Dominguez S.A., 72 3–5

Adolor Corporation, 101 5–8

Adolph Coors Company, I 236–38; 13
9–11 (upd.); 36 12–16 (upd.) *see also*
Molson Coors Brewing Co.

Adolphe Lafont *see* Vivarte SA.

ADP *see* Automatic Data Processing, Inc.

ADT Security Services, Inc., 12 9–11;
44 6–9 (upd.)

Adtran Inc., 22 17–20

Advance Auto Parts, Inc., 57 10–12

Advance Publications Inc., IV 581–84;
19 3–7 (upd.); 96 1–7 (upd.)

Advanced Circuits Inc., 67 3–5

Advanced Fibre Communications, Inc.,
63 3–5

Advanced Marketing Services, Inc., 34
3–6

Advanced Medical Optics, Inc., 79 6–9

Advanced Micro Devices, Inc., 6
215–17; 30 10–12 (upd.); 99 12–17
(upd.)

Advanced Neuromodulation Systems,
Inc., 73 14–17

Advanced Technology Laboratories, Inc.,
9 6–8

Advanced Web Technologies *see* Miner
Group Int.

Advanstar Communications, Inc., 57
13–17

Advanta Corporation, 8 9–11; 38 10–14
(upd.)

Advantica Restaurant Group, Inc., 27
16–19 (upd.) *see also* Denny's
Corporation

Adventist Health, 53 6–8

The Advertising Council, Inc., 76 3–6

The Advisory Board Company, 80 1–4
see also The Corporate Executive Board
Co.

Advo, Inc., 6 12–14; 53 9–13 (upd.)

Advocat Inc., 46 3–5

AECOM Technology Corporation, 79
10–13

AEG A.G., I 409–11

Aegean Marine Petroleum Network Inc.,
89 18–21

Aegek S.A., 64 6–8

Aegis Group plc, 6 15–16

AEGON N.V., III 177–79; 50 8–12
(upd.) *see also* Transamerica–An
AEGON Company

AEI Music Network Inc., 35 19–21

AEON Co., Ltd., V 96–99; 68 6–10
(upd.)

AEP *see* American Electric Power Co.

AEP Industries, Inc., 36 17–19

Aer Lingus Group plc, 34 7–10; 89
22–27 (upd.)

Aero Mayflower Transit Company *see*
Mayflower Group Inc.

Aeroflot - Russian Airlines JSC, 6
57–59; 29 7–10 (upd.); 89 28–34
(upd.)

AeroGrow International, Inc., 95 20–23

Aerojet-General Corp., 63 6–9

Aerolíneas Argentinas S.A., 33 17–19;
69 9–12 (upd.)

Aeronca Inc., 46 6–8

Aéroports de Paris, 33 20–22

Aéropostale, Inc., 89 35–38

Aeroquip Corporation, 16 7–9 *see also*
Eaton Corp.

Aerosonic Corporation, 69 13–15

The Aérospatiale Group, 7 9–12; 21
8–11 (upd.) *see also* European
Aeronautic Defence and Space
Company EADS N.V.

AeroVironment, Inc., 97 13–16

The AES Corporation, 10 25–27; 13
12–15 (upd.); 53 14–18 (upd.)

Aetna, Inc., III 180–82; 21 12–16
(upd.); 63 10–16 (upd.)

Aetna Insulated Wire *see* The Marmon
Group, Inc.

AFC Enterprises, Inc., 32 12–16 (upd.);
83 9–15 (upd.)

Affiliated Computer Services, Inc., 61
12–16

Affiliated Foods Inc., 53 19–21

Affiliated Managers Group, Inc., 79
14–17

Affiliated Publications, Inc., 7 13–16

Affinity Group Holding Inc., 56 3–6

Affymetrix Inc., 106 18–24

AFLAC Incorporated, 10 28–30 (upd.);
38 15–19 (upd.)

African Rainbow Minerals Ltd., 97
17–20

Africare, 59 7–10

After Hours Formalwear Inc., 60 3–5

Aftermarket Technology Corp., 83
16–19

AG Barr plc, 64 9–12

Ag-Chem Equipment Company, Inc., 17
9–11 *see also* AGCO Corp.

Ag Services of America, Inc., 59 11–13

Aga Foodservice Group PLC, 73 18–20

Automated Sciences Group, Inc. *see* CACI International Inc.
Automatic Data Processing, Inc., III 117–19; 9 48–51 (upd.); 47 35–39 (upd.)
Automobiles Citroën, 7 35–38
Automobili Lamborghini Holding S.p.A., 13 60–62; 34 55–58 (upd.); 91 25–30 (upd.)
AutoNation, Inc., 50 61–64
Autoridad del Canal de Panamá, 94 45–48
Autoroutes du Sud de la France SA, 55 38–40
Autostrada Torino-Milano S.p.A., 101 47–50
Autotote Corporation, 20 47–49 *see also* Scientific Games Corp.
AutoTrader.com, L.L.C., 91 31–34
AutoZone, Inc., 9 52–54; 31 35–38 (upd.)
Auvil Fruit Company, Inc., 95 32–35
AVA AG (Allgemeine Handelsgesellschaft der Verbraucher AG), 33 53–56
Avado Brands, Inc., 31 39–42
Avalon Correctional Services, Inc., 75 40–43
AvalonBay Communities, Inc., 58 11–13
Avantium Technologies BV, 79 46–49
Avaya Inc., 104 22–25
Avco Financial Services Inc., 13 63–65 *see also* Citigroup Inc.
Avecia Group PLC, 63 49–51
Aveda Corporation, 24 55–57
Avedis Zildjian Co., 38 66–68
Avendt Group, Inc. *see* Marmon Group, Inc.
Aventine Renewable Energy Holdings, Inc., 89 83–86
Avery Dennison Corporation, IV 251–54; 17 27–31 (upd.); 49 34–40 (upd.)
Aviacionny Nauchno-Tehnicheskii Komplex im. A.N. Tupoleva, 24 58–60
Aviacsa *see* Consorcio Aviacsa, S.A. de C.V.
Aviall, Inc., 73 42–45
Avianca Aerovías Nacionales de Colombia SA, 36 52–55
Aviation Sales Company, 41 37–39
Avid Technology Inc., 38 69–73
Avionics Specialties Inc. *see* Aerosonic Corp.
Avions Marcel Dassault-Breguet Aviation, I 44–46 *see also* Groupe Dassault Aviation SA.
Avis Group Holdings, Inc., 6 356–58; 22 54–57 (upd.); 75 44–49 (upd.)
Avista Corporation, 69 48–50 (upd.)
Aviva PLC, 50 65–68 (upd.)
Avnet Inc., 9 55–57
Avocent Corporation, 65 56–58
Avon Products, Inc., III 15–16; 19 26–29 (upd.); 46 43–46 (upd.)

Avondale Industries, Inc., 7 39–41; 41 40–43 (upd.)
AVTOVAZ Joint Stock Company, 65 59–62
AVX Corporation, 67 41–43
AWA *see* America West Holdings Corp.
AWB Ltd., 56 25–27
Awrey Bakeries, Inc., 56 28–30
AXA Colonia Konzern AG, III 210–12; 49 41–45 (upd.)
AXA Equitable Life Insurance Company, 105 21–27 (upd.)
Axcan Pharma Inc., 85 25–28
Axcelis Technologies, Inc., 95 36–39
Axel Johnson Group, I 553–55
Axel Springer Verlag AG, IV 589–91; 20 50–53 (upd.)
Axsys Technologies, Inc., 93 65–68
Aydin Corp., 19 30–32
Aynsley China Ltd. *see* Belleek Pottery Ltd.
Azcon Corporation, 23 34–36
Azelis Group, 100 44–47
Azerbaijan Airlines, 77 46–49
Azienda Generale Italiana Petroli *see* ENI S.p.A.
Aztar Corporation, 13 66–68; 71 41–45 (upd.)
AZZ Incorporated, 93 69–72

B

B&G Foods, Inc., 40 51–54
B&J Music Ltd. *see* Kaman Music Corp.
B&Q plc *see* Kingfisher plc.
B.A.T. Industries PLC, 22 70–73 (upd.) *see also* Brown and Williamson Tobacco Corporation
B. Dalton Bookseller Inc., 25 29–31 *see also* Barnes & Noble, Inc.
B.F. Goodrich Co. *see* The BFGoodrich Co.
B.J. Alan Co., Inc., 67 44–46
The B. Manischewitz Company, LLC, 31 43–46
B.R. Guest Inc., 87 43–46
B.W. Rogers Company, 94 49–52
B/E Aerospace, Inc., 30 72–74
BA *see* British Airways plc.
BAA plc, 10 121–23; 33 57–61 (upd.)
Baan Company, 25 32–34
Babbage's, Inc., 10 124–25 *see also* GameStop Corp.
The Babcock & Wilcox Company, 82 26–30
Babcock International Group PLC, 69 51–54
Babolat VS, S.A., 97 63–66
Baby Lock USA *see* Tacony Corp.
Baby Superstore, Inc., 15 32–34 *see also* Toys 'R Us, Inc.
Bacardi & Company Ltd., 18 39–42; 82 31–36 (upd.)
Baccarat, 24 61–63
Bachman's Inc., 22 58–60
Bachoco *see* Industrias Bachoco, S.A. de C.V.
Back Bay Restaurant Group, Inc., 20 54–56; 102 34–38 (upd.)

Back Yard Burgers, Inc., 45 33–36
Backus y Johnston *see* Unión de Cervecerias Peruanas Backus y Johnston S.A.A.
Bad Boy Worldwide Entertainment Group, 58 14–17
Badger Meter, Inc., 22 61–65
Badger Paper Mills, Inc., 15 35–37
Badger State Ethanol, LLC, 83 33–37
BAE Systems Ship Repair, 73 46–48
Bahamas Air Holdings Ltd., 66 24–26
Bahlsen GmbH & Co. KG, 44 38–41
Baidu.com Inc., 95 40–43
Bailey Nurseries, Inc., 57 59–61
Bain & Company, 55 41–43
Baird & Warner Holding Company, 87 47–50
Bairnco Corporation, 28 42–45
Bajaj Auto Limited, 39 36–38
Baker *see* Michael Baker Corp.
Baker and Botts, L.L.P., 28 46–49
Baker & Daniels LLP, 88 17–20
Baker & Hostetler LLP, 40 55–58
Baker & McKenzie, 10 126–28; 42 17–20 (upd.)
Baker & Taylor Corporation, 16 45–47; 43 59–62 (upd.)
Baker Hughes Incorporated, III 428–29; 22 66–69 (upd.); 57 62–66 (upd.)
Bakkavör Group hf., 91 35–39
Balance Bar Company, 32 70–72
Balchem Corporation, 42 21–23
Baldor Electric Company, 21 42–44; 97 63–67 (upd.)
Baldwin & Lyons, Inc., 51 37–39
Baldwin Piano & Organ Company, 18 43–46 *see also* Gibson Guitar Corp.
Baldwin Richardson Foods Company, 100 48–52
Baldwin Technology Company, Inc., 25 35–39; 107 33–39 (upd.)
Balfour Beatty Construction Ltd., 36 56–60 (upd.)
Ball Corporation, I 597–98; 10 129–31 (upd.); 78 25–29 (upd.)
Ball Horticultural Company, 78 30–33
Ballantine Books *see* Random House, Inc.
Ballantyne of Omaha, Inc., 27 56–58
Ballard Medical Products, 21 45–48 *see also* Kimberly-Clark Corp.
Ballard Power Systems Inc., 73 49–52
Ballistic Recovery Systems, Inc., 87 51–54
Bally Manufacturing Corporation, III 430–32
Bally Total Fitness Corporation, 25 40–42; 94 53–57 (upd.)
Balmac International, Inc., 94 58–61
Bâloise-Holding, 40 59–62
Baltek Corporation, 34 59–61
Baltika Brewery Joint Stock Company, 65 63–66
Baltimore & Ohio Railroad *see* CSX Corp.
Baltimore Aircoil Company, Inc., 66 27–29
Baltimore Gas and Electric Company, V 552–54; 25 43–46 (upd.)

Greene King plc, 31 223–26
Greene, Tweed & Company, 55 170–72
GreenMan Technologies Inc., 99 190–193
Greenpeace International, 74 128–30
GreenPoint Financial Corp., 28 166–68
Greenwood Mills, Inc., 14 219–21
Greg Manning Auctions, Inc., 60 145–46
Greggs PLC, 65 164–66
Greif Inc., 15 186–88; 66 154–56 (upd.)
Grendene S.A., 102 154–57
Grévin & Compagnie SA, 56 143–45
Grey Global Group Inc., 6 26–28; 66 157–61 (upd.)
Grey Wolf, Inc., 43 201–03
Greyhound Lines, Inc., I 448–50; 32 227–31 (upd.)
Greyston Bakery, Inc., 101 220–23
Griffin Industries, Inc., 70 106–09
Griffin Land & Nurseries, Inc., 43 204–06
Griffith Laboratories Inc., 100 196–99
Griffon Corporation, 34 194–96
Grill Concepts, Inc., 74 131–33
Grinnell Corp., 13 245–47
Grist Mill Company, 15 189–91
Gristede's Foods Inc., 68 31 231–33; 180–83 (upd.)
The Grocers Supply Co., Inc., 103 201–04
Grohe see Friedrich Grohe AG & Co. KG.
Grolier Inc., 16 251–54; 43 207–11 (upd.)
Grolsch see Royal Grolsch NV.
Grossman's Inc., 13 248–50
Ground Round, Inc., 21 248–51
Group 1 Automotive, Inc., 52 144–46
Group 4 Falck A/S, 42 165–68
Group Health Cooperative, 41 181–84
Groupama S.A., 76 167–70
Groupe Air France, 6 92–94 see also Societe Air France.
Groupe Alain Manoukian, 55 173–75
Groupe André, 17 210–12 see also Vivarte SA.
ARES see Groupe Ares S.A.
Groupe Bigard S.A., 96 151–54
Groupe Bolloré, 67 196–99
Groupe Bourbon S.A., 60 147–49
Groupe Bull see Compagnie des Machines Bull.
Groupe Caisse d'Epargne, 100 200–04
Groupe Casino see Casino Guichard-Perrachon S.A.
Groupe Castorama-Dubois Investissements, 23 230–32 see also Castorama-Dubois Investissements SCA
Groupe CECAB S.C.A., 88 131–34
Groupe Crit S.A., 74 134–36
Groupe Danone, 32 232–36 (upd.); 93 233–40 (upd.)
Groupe Dassault Aviation SA, 26 179–82 (upd.)
Groupe de la Cité, IV 614–16
Groupe DMC (Dollfus Mieg & Cie), 27 186–88

Groupe Dubreuil S.A., 102 162–65
Groupe Euralis, 86 169–72
Groupe Flo S.A., 98 172–75
Groupe Fournier SA, 44 187–89
Groupe Genoyer, 96 155–58
Groupe Glon, 84 155–158
Groupe Go Sport S.A., 39 183–85
Groupe Guillin SA, 40 214–16
Groupe Henri Heuliez S.A., 100 205–09
Groupe Herstal S.A., 58 145–48
Groupe Jean-Claude Darmon, 44 190–92
Groupe Lactalis, 78 128–32 (upd.)
Groupe Lapeyre S.A., 33 175–77
Groupe LDC see L.D.C. S.A.
Groupe Le Duff S.A., 84 159–162
Groupe Léa Nature, 88 135–38
Groupe Legris Industries, 23 233–35
Groupe Les Echos, 25 283–85
Groupe Limagrain, 74 137–40
Groupe Louis Dreyfus S.A., 60 150–53
Groupe Monnoyeur, 72 157–59
Groupe Open, 74 141–43
Groupe Partouche SA, 48 196–99
Groupe Pinault-Printemps-Redoute see Pinault-Printemps-Redoute S.A.
Groupe Promodès S.A., 19 326–28
Groupe Rougier SA, 21 438–40
Groupe SEB, 35 201–03
Groupe Sidel S.A., 21 252–55
Groupe Soufflet SA, 55 176–78
Groupe Vidéotron Ltée., 20 271–73
Groupe Yves Saint Laurent, 23 236–39 see also Gucci Group N.V.
Groupe Zannier S.A., 35 204–07
Grow Biz International, Inc., 18 207–10 see also Winmark Corp.
Grow Group Inc., 12 217–19
GROWMARK, Inc., 88 139–42
Groz-Beckert Group, 68 184–86
Grubb & Ellis Company, 21 256–58; 98 176–80 (upd.)
Gruma, S.A.B. de C.V., 31 234–36; 103 205–10 (upd.)
Grumman Corp., I 61–63; 11 164–67 (upd.) see aslo Northrop Grumman Corp.
Grunau Company Inc., 90 209–12
Grundfos Group, 83 171–174
Grundig AG, 27 189–92
Gruntal & Co., L.L.C., 20 274–76
Grupo Aeroportuario del Centro Norte, S.A.B. de C.V., 97 186–89
Grupo Aeroportuario del Pacífico, S.A. de C.V., 85 160–63
Grupo Aeropuerto del Sureste, S.A. de C.V., 48 200–02
Grupo Algar see Algar S/A Emprendimentos e Participações
Grupo Ángeles Servicios de Salud, S.A. de C.V., 84 163–166
Grupo Brescia, 99 194–197
Grupo Bufete see Bufete Industrial, S.A. de C.V.
Grupo Carso, S.A. de C.V., 21 259–61; 107 163–67 (upd.)
Grupo Casa Saba, S.A. de C.V., 39 186–89

Grupo Clarín S.A., 67 200–03
Grupo Comercial Chedraui S.A. de C.V., 86 173–76
Grupo Corvi S.A. de C.V., 86 177–80
Grupo Cydsa, S.A. de C.V., 39 190–93
Grupo Dina see Consorcio G Grupo Dina, S.A. de C.V.
Grupo Dragados SA, 55 179–82
Grupo Elektra, S.A. de C.V., 39 194–97
Grupo Eroski, 64 167–70
Grupo Ferrovial, S.A., 40 217–19
Grupo Ficosa International, 90 213–16
Grupo Financiero Banamex S.A., 54 143–46
Grupo Financiero Banorte, S.A. de C.V., 51 149–51
Grupo Financiero BBVA Bancomer S.A., 54 147–50
Grupo Financiero Galicia S.A., 63 178–81
Grupo Financiero Serfin, S.A., 19 188–90
Grupo Gigante, S.A. de C.V., 34 197–99
Grupo Herdez, S.A. de C.V., 35 208–10
Grupo IMSA, S.A. de C.V., 44 193–96
Grupo Industrial Bimbo, 19 191–93
Grupo Industrial Durango, S.A. de C.V., 37 176–78
Grupo Industrial Herradura, S.A. de C.V., 83 175–178
Grupo Industrial Lala, S.A. de C.V., 82 154–57
Grupo Industrial Saltillo, S.A. de C.V., 54 151–54
Grupo Leche Pascual S.A., 59 212–14
Grupo Lladró S.A., 52 147–49
Grupo Martins, 104 175–78
Grupo Mexico, S.A. de C.V., 40 220–23
Grupo Modelo, S.A. de C.V., 29 218–20
Grupo Omnilife S.A. de C.V., 88 143–46
Grupo Planeta, 94 218–22
Grupo Portucel Soporcel, 60 154–56
Grupo Posadas, S.A. de C.V., 57 168–70
Grupo Positivo, 105 196–99
Grupo Sanborns, S.A. de C.V., 107 168–72 (upd.)
Grupo TACA, 38 218–20
Grupo Televisa, S.A., 18 211–14; 54 155–58 (upd.)
Grupo TMM, S.A. de C.V., 50 208–11
Grupo Transportación Ferroviaria Mexicana, S.A. de C.V., 47 162–64
Grupo Viz, S.A. de C.V., 84 167–170
Gruppo Coin S.p.A., 41 185–87
Gruppo Riva Fire SpA, 88 147–50
Gryphon Holdings, Inc., 21 262–64
GSC Enterprises, Inc., 86 181–84
GSD&M Advertising, 44 197–200
GSD&M's Idea City, 90 217–21
GSG&T, Inc. see Gulf States Utilities Co.
GSI Commerce, Inc., 67 204–06
GSU see Gulf States Utilities Co.
GT Bicycles, 26 183–85
GT Interactive Software, 31 237–41 see also Infogrames Entertainment S.A.
GT Solar International, Inc., 101 224–28

Monster Worldwide Inc., 74 194–97 (upd.)

Montana Coffee Traders, Inc., 60 208–10

The Montana Power Company, 11 320–22; 44 288–92 (upd.)

Montblanc International GmbH, 82 240–44

Montedison S.p.A., I 368–69; 24 341–44 (upd.)

Monterey Pasta Company, 58 240–43

Montgomery Ward & Co., Incorporated, V 145–48; 20 374–79 (upd.)

Montres Rolex S.A., 13 353–55; 34 292–95 (upd.)

Montupet S.A., 63 302–04

Moody's Corporation, 65 242–44

Moog Inc., 13 356–58

Moog Music, Inc., 75 261–64

Mooney Aerospace Group Ltd., 52 252–55

Moore Corporation Limited, IV 644–46 *see also* R.R. Donnelley & Sons Co.

Moore-Handley, Inc., 39 290–92

Moore Medical Corp., 17 331–33

Moran Towing Corporation, Inc., 15 301–03

The Morgan Crucible Company plc, 82 245–50

Morgan Grenfell Group PLC, II 427–29 *see also* Deutsche Bank AG.

The Morgan Group, Inc., 46 300–02

Morgan, Lewis & Bockius LLP, 29 332–34

Morgan Motor Company, 105 304–08

Morgan's Foods, Inc., 101 352 |B5–55

Morgan Stanley Dean Witter & Company, II 430–32; 16 374–78 (upd.); 33 311–14 (upd.)

Morgans Hotel Group Company, 80 256–59

Morguard Corporation, 85 287–90

Morinaga & Co. Ltd., 61 222–25

Morinda Holdings, Inc., 82 251–54

Morningstar Inc., 68 259–62

Morris Communications Corporation, 36 339–42

Morris Travel Services L.L.C., 26 308–11

Morrison & Foerster LLP, 78 220–23

Morrison Knudsen Corporation, 7 355–58; 28 286–90 (upd.) *see also* The Washington Companies.

Morrison Restaurants Inc., 11 323–25

Morrow Equipment Co. L.L.C., 87 325–327

Morse Shoe Inc., 13 359–61

Morton International, Inc., 9 358–59 (upd.); 80 260–64 (upd.)

Morton Thiokol Inc., I 370–72 *see also* Thiokol Corp.

Morton's Restaurant Group, Inc., 30 329–31; 88 262–66 (upd.)

The Mosaic Company, 91 330–33

Mosinee Paper Corporation, 15 304–06 *see also* Wausau-Mosinee Paper Corp.

Moss Bros Group plc, 51 252–54

Mossimo, 27 328–30; 96 288–92 (upd.)

Mota-Engil, SGPS, S.A., 97 290–93

Motel 6, 13 362–64; 56 248–51 (upd.) *see also* Accor SA

Mothercare plc, 17 334–36; 78 224–27 (upd.)

Mothers Against Drunk Driving (MADD), 51 255–58

Mothers Work, Inc., 18 350–52

The Motley Fool, Inc., 40 329–31

Moto Photo, Inc., 45 282–84

Motor Cargo Industries, Inc., 35 296–99

Motorcar Parts & Accessories, Inc., 47 253–55

Motorola, Inc., II 60–62; 11 326–29 (upd.); 34 296–302 (upd.); 93 313–23 (upd.)

Motown Records Company L.P., 26 312–14

Mott's Inc., 57 250–53

Moulinex S.A., 22 362–65 *see also* Groupe SEB.

Mount *see also* Mt.

Mount Washington Hotel *see* MWH Preservation Limited Partnership.

Mountain States Mortgage Centers, Inc., 29 335–37

Mouvement des Caisses Desjardins, 48 288–91

Movado Group, Inc., 28 291–94; 107 273–78 (upd.)

Mövenpick Holding, 104 328–32

Movie Gallery, Inc., 31 339–41

Movie Star Inc., 17 337–39

Moy Park Ltd., 78 228–31

Mozilla Foundation, 106 299–303

MPI *see* Michael Page International plc.

MPRG *see* Matt Prentice Restaurant Group.

MPS Group, Inc., 49 264–67

MPW Industrial Services Group, Inc., 53 231–33

Mr. Bricolage S.A., 37 258–60

Mr. Coffee, Inc., 15 307–09

Mr. Gasket Inc., 15 310–12

Mr. Gatti's, LP, 87 321–324

Mrchocolate.com LLC, 105 309–12

Mrs. Baird's Bakeries, 29 338–41

Mrs. Fields' Original Cookies, Inc., 27 331–35; 104 333–39 (upd.)

Mrs. Grossman's Paper Company Inc., 84 277–280

MS&L *see* Manning Selvage & Lee.

MSC *see* Material Sciences Corp.

MSC Industrial Direct Co., Inc., 71 234–36

MSWG, LLC, 105 313–16

Mt. *see also* Mount.

Mt. Olive Pickle Company, Inc., 44 293–95

MTA *see* Metropolitan Transportation Authority.

MTC *see* Management and Training Corp.

MTD Products Inc., 107 279–82

MTel *see* Mobile Telecommunications Technologies Corp.

MTG *see* Modern Times Group AB.

MTI Enterprises Inc., 102 279–82

MTN Group Ltd., 106 304–07

MTR Foods Ltd., 55 271–73

MTR Gaming Group, Inc., 75 265–67

MTS *see* Mobile TeleSystems.

MTS Inc., 37 261–64

Mueller Industries, Inc., 7 359–61; 52 256–60 (upd.)

Mueller Sports Medicine, Inc., 102 283–86

Mulberry Group PLC, 71 237–39

Mullen Advertising Inc., 51 259–61

Multi-Color Corporation, 53 234–36

Multimedia Games, Inc., 41 272–76

Multimedia, Inc., 11 330–32

Munich Re (Münchener Rückversicherungs-Gesellschaft Aktiengesellschaft in München), III 299–301; 46 303–07 (upd.)

Munir Sukhtian Group, 104 340–44

Murdock Madaus Schwabe, 26 315–19

Murphy Family Farms Inc., 22 366–68 *see also* Smithfield Foods, Inc.

Murphy Oil Corporation, 7 362–64; 32 338–41 (upd.); 95 283–89 (upd.)

Murphy's Pizza *see* Papa Murphy's International, Inc.

The Musco Family Olive Co., 91 334–37

Musco Lighting, 83 276–279

Museum of Modern Art, 106 308–12

Musgrave Group Plc, 57 254–57

Music Corporation of America *see* MCA Inc.

Musicland Stores Corporation, 9 360–62; 38 313–17 (upd.)

Mutual Benefit Life Insurance Company, III 302–04

Mutual Life Insurance Company of New York, III 305–07

The Mutual of Omaha Companies, 98 248–52

Mutuelle Assurance des Commerçants et Industriels de France (Macif), 107 283–86

Muzak, Inc., 18 353–56

MWA *see* Modern Woodmen of America.

MWH Preservation Limited Partnership, 65 245–48

MWI Veterinary Supply, Inc., 80 265–68

Mycogen Corporation, 21 385–87 *see also* Dow Chemical Co.

Myers Industries, Inc., 19 277–79; 96 293–97 (upd.)

Mylan Laboratories Inc., I 656–57; 20 380–82 (upd.); 59 304–08 (upd.)

MYOB Ltd., 86 286–90

Myriad Genetics, Inc., 95 290–95

Myriad Restaurant Group, Inc., 87 328–331

MySpace.com *see* Intermix Media, Inc.

N

N.F. Smith & Associates LP, 70 199–202

N M Rothschild & Sons Limited, 39 293–95

Northwest Airlines Corporation, I
112–14; 6 103–05 (upd.); 26 337–40
(upd.); 74 204–08 (upd.)
Northwest Natural Gas Company, 45
313–15
NorthWestern Corporation, 37 280–83
Northwestern Mutual Life Insurance
Company, III 321–24; 45 316–21
(upd.)
Norton Company, 8 395–97
Norton McNaughton, Inc., 27 346–49
see also Jones Apparel Group, Inc.
Norwegian Cruise Lines *see* NCL
Corporation
Norwich & Peterborough Building
Society, 55 280–82
Norwood Promotional Products, Inc.,
26 341–43
Nova Corporation of Alberta, V 673–75
NovaCare, Inc., 11 366–68
Novacor Chemicals Ltd., 12 364–66
Novar plc, 49 292–96 (upd.)
Novartis AG, 39 304–10 (upd.); 105
323–35 (upd.)
NovaStar Financial, Inc., 91 354–58
Novell, Inc., 6 269–71; 23 359–62
(upd.)
Novellus Systems, Inc., 18 382–85
Noven Pharmaceuticals, Inc., 55 283–85
Novo Nordisk A/S, I 658–60; 61
263–66 (upd.)
NOW *see* National Organization for
Women, Inc.
NPC International, Inc., 40 340–42
The NPD Group, Inc., 68 275–77
NPM (Nationale Portefeuille
Maatschappij) *see* Compagnie Nationale
à Portefeuille.
NPR *see* National Public Radio, Inc.
NRG Energy, Inc., 79 290–93
NRJ Group S.A., 107 300–04
NRT Incorporated, 61 267–69
NS *see* Norfolk Southern Corp.
NSF International, 72 252–55
NSK *see* Nippon Seiko K.K.
NSP *see* Northern States Power Co.
NSS Enterprises, Inc., 78 262–65
NSTAR, 106 324–31 (upd.)
NTCL *see* Northern Telecom Ltd.
NTD Architecture, 101 373–76
NTK Holdings Inc., 107 305–11 (upd.)
NTL Inc., 65 269–72
NTN Buzztime, Inc., 86 308–11
NTN Corporation, III 595–96; 47
278–81 (upd.)
NTTPC *see* Nippon Telegraph and
Telephone Public Corp.
NU *see* Northeast Utilities.
Nu-kote Holding, Inc., 18 386–89
Nu Skin Enterprises, Inc., 27 350–53;
31 386–89; 76 286–90 (upd.)
Nucor Corporation, 7 400–02; 21
392–95 (upd.); 79 294–300 (upd.)
Nufarm Ltd., 87 345–348
Nuplex Industries Ltd., 92 280–83
Nuqul Group of Companies, 102
311–14

Nutraceutical International
Corporation, 37 284–86
The NutraSweet Company, 8 398–400;
107 312–16 (upd.)
Nutreco Holding N.V., 56 256–59
Nutrexpa S.A., 92 284–87
NutriSystem, Inc., 71 250–53
Nutrition 21 Inc., 97 307–11
Nutrition for Life International Inc., 22
385–88
Nuveen *see* John Nuveen Co.
NV Umicore SA, 47 411–13
NVIDIA Corporation, 54 269–73
NVR Inc., 8 401–03; 70 206–09 (upd.)
NWA, Inc. *see* Northwest Airlines Corp.
NYK *see* Nippon Yusen Kabushiki Kaisha
(NYK).
NYMAGIC, Inc., 41 284–86
NYNEX Corporation, V 311–13 *see also*
Verizon Communications.
Nypro, Inc., 101 377–82
NYRG *see* New York Restaurant Group,
Inc.
NYSE *see* New York Stock Exchange.
NYSEG *see* New York State Electric and
Gas Corp.

O

O&Y *see* Olympia & York Developments
Ltd.
O.C. Tanner Co., 69 279–81
Oak Harbor Freight Lines, Inc., 53
248–51
Oak Industries Inc., 21 396–98 *see also*
Corning Inc.
Oak Technology, Inc., 22 389–93 *see also*
Zoran Corp.
Oakhurst Dairy, 60 225–28
Oakleaf Waste Management, LLC, 97
312–15
Oakley, Inc., 18 390–93; 49 297–302
(upd.)
Oaktree Capital Management, LLC, 71
254–56
Oakwood Homes Corporation, 13 155;
15 326–28
OAO AVTOVAZ *see* AVTOVAZ Joint
Stock Co.
OAO Gazprom, 42 261–65; 107 317–23
(upd.)
OAO LUKOIL, 40 343–46
OAO NK YUKOS, 47 282–85
OAO Severstal *see* Severstal Joint Stock
Co.
OAO Siberian Oil Company (Sibneft),
49 303–06
OAO Surgutneftegaz, 48 375–78
OAO Tatneft, 45 322–26
Obagi Medical Products, Inc., 95
310–13
Obayashi Corporation, 78 266–69
(upd.)
Oberoi Group *see* EIH Ltd.
Oberto Sausage Company, Inc., 92
288–91
Obie Media Corporation, 56 260–62
Obrascon Huarte Lain S.A., 76 291–94
Observer AB, 55 286–89

Occidental Petroleum Corporation, IV
480–82; 25 360–63 (upd.); 71
257–61 (upd.)
Océ N.V., 24 360–63; 91 359–65 (upd.)
Ocean Beauty Seafoods, Inc., 74 209–11
Ocean Bio-Chem, Inc., 103 308–11
Ocean Group plc, 6 415–17 *see also* Exel
plc.
Ocean Spray Cranberries, Inc., 7
403–05; 25 364–67 (upd.); 83
284–290
Oceaneering International, Inc., 63
317–19
Ocesa *see* Corporación Interamericana de
Entretenimiento, S.A. de C.V.
O'Charley's Inc., 19 286–88; 60 229–32
(upd.)
OCI *see* Orascom Construction Industries
S.A.E.
OCLC Online Computer Library
Center, Inc., 96 324–28
The O'Connell Companies Inc., 100
306–09
Octel Messaging, 14 354–56; 41 287–90
(upd.)
Ocular Sciences, Inc., 65 273–75
Odakyu Electric Railway Co., Ltd., V
487–89; 68 278–81 (upd.)
Odebrecht S.A., 73 242–44
Odetics Inc., 14 357–59
Odfjell SE, 101 383–87
ODL, Inc., 55 290–92
Odwalla Inc., 31 349–51; 104 349–53
(upd.)
Odyssey Marine Exploration, Inc., 91
366–70
OEC Medical Systems, Inc., 27 354–56
OENEO S.A., 74 212–15 (upd.)
Office Depot, Inc., 8 404–05; 23
363–65 (upd.); 65 276–80 (upd.)
OfficeMax Incorporated, 15 329–31; 43
291–95 (upd.); 101 388–94 (upd.)
OfficeTiger, LLC, 75 294–96
Officine Alfieri Maserati S.p.A., 13
376–78
Offshore Logistics, Inc., 37 287–89
Ogden Corporation, I 512–14; 6
151–53 *see also* Covanta Energy Corp.
Ogilvy Group Inc., I 25–27 *see also* WPP
Group.
Oglebay Norton Company, 17 355–58
Oglethorpe Power Corporation, 6
537–38
Ohbayashi Corporation, I 586–87
The Ohio Art Company, 14 360–62; 59
317–20 (upd.)
Ohio Bell Telephone Company, 14
363–65; *see also* Ameritech Corp.
Ohio Casualty Corp., 11 369–70
Ohio Edison Company, V 676–78
Oil and Natural Gas Commission, IV
483–84; 90 313–17 (upd.)
Oil-Dri Corporation of America, 20
396–99; 89 331–36 (upd.)
Oil States International, Inc., 77
314–17
Oil Transporting Joint Stock Company
Transneft, 92 450–54

Peter Piper, Inc., 70 217–19
Peterbilt Motors Company, 89 354–57
Petersen Publishing Company, 21 402–04
Peterson American Corporation, 55 304–06
Pete's Brewing Company, 22 420–22
Petit Bateau, 95 327–31
PetMed Express, Inc., 81 305–08
Petrie Stores Corporation, 8 425–27
Petro-Canada, IV 494–96; 99 342–349 (upd.)
Petrobrás see Petróleo Brasileiro S.A.
Petrobras Energia Participaciones S.A., 72 278–81
Petroecuador see Petróleos del Ecuador.
Petrof spol. S.R.O., 107 352–56
Petrofac Ltd., 95 332–35
PetroFina S.A., IV 497–500; 26 365–69 (upd.)
Petrogal see Petróleos de Portugal.
Petrohawk Energy Corporation, 79 317–20
Petróleo Brasileiro S.A., IV 501–03
Petróleos de Portugal S.A., IV 504–06
Petróleos de Venezuela S.A., IV 507–09; 74 235–39 (upd.)
Petróleos del Ecuador, IV 510–11
Petróleos Mexicanos (PEMEX), IV 512–14; 19 295–98 (upd.); 104 373–78 (upd.)
Petroleum Development Oman LLC, IV 515–16; 98 305–09 (upd.)
Petroleum Helicopters, Inc., 35 334–36
Petroliam Nasional Bhd (Petronas), 56 275–79 (upd.)
Petrolite Corporation, 15 350–52 see also Baker Hughes Inc.
Petromex see Petróleos de Mexico S.A.
Petron Corporation, 58 270–72
Petronas, IV 517–20 see also Petroliam Nasional Bhd.
Petrossian Inc., 54 287–89
Petry Media Corporation, 102 326–29
PETsMART, Inc., 14 384–86; 41 295–98 (upd.)
Peugeot S.A., I 187–88 see also PSA Peugeot Citroen S.A.
The Pew Charitable Trusts, 35 337–40
Pez Candy, Inc., 38 355–57
The Pfaltzgraff Co. see Susquehanna Pfaltzgraff Co.
Pfizer Inc., I 661–63; 9 402–05 (upd.); 38 358–67 (upd.); 79 321–33 (upd.)
PFSweb, Inc., 73 254–56
PG&E Corporation, 26 370–73 (upd.)
PGA see The Professional Golfers' Association.
Phaidon Press Ltd., 98 310–14
Phantom Fireworks see B.J. Alan Co., Inc.
Phar-Mor Inc., 12 390–92
Pharmacia & Upjohn Inc., I 664–65; 25 374–78 (upd.) see also Pfizer Inc.
Pharmion Corporation, 91 379–82
Phat Fashions LLC, 49 322–24
Phelps Dodge Corporation, IV 176–79; 28 352–57 (upd.); 75 319–25 (upd.)

PHH Arval, V 496–97; 53 274–76 (upd.)
PHI, Inc., 80 282–86 (upd.)
Philadelphia Eagles, 37 305–08
Philadelphia Electric Company, V 695–97 see also Exelon Corp.
Philadelphia Gas Works Company, 92 301–05
Philadelphia Media Holdings LLC, 92 306–10
Philadelphia Suburban Corporation, 39 326–29
Philharmonic-Symphony Society of New York, Inc. (New York Philharmonic), 69 293–97
Philip Environmental Inc., 16 414–16
Philip Morris Companies Inc., V 405–07; 18 416–19 (upd.); 44 338–43 (upd.) see also Kraft Foods Inc.
Philip Services Corp., 73 257–60
Philipp Holzmann AG, 17 374–77
Philippine Airlines, Inc., 6 106–08; 23 379–82 (upd.)
Philips Electronics N.V., 13 400–03 (upd.) see also Koninklijke Philips Electronics N.V.
Philips Electronics North America Corp., 13 396–99
N.V. Philips Gloeilampenfabriken, II 78–80 see also Philips Electronics N.V.
The Phillies, 106 364–68
Phillips Foods, Inc., 63 320–22; 90 330–33 (upd.)
Phillips International, Inc., 78 311–14
Phillips Lytle LLP, 102 330–34
Phillips Petroleum Company, IV 521–23; 40 354–59 (upd.) see also ConocoPhillips.
Phillips-Van Heusen Corporation, 24 382–85
Phillips, de Pury & Luxembourg, 49 325–27
Phoenix AG, 68 286–89
Phoenix Footwear Group, Inc., 70 220–22
Phoenix Mecano AG, 61 286–88
The Phoenix Media/Communications Group, 91 383–87
Phones 4u Ltd., 85 328–31
Photo-Me International Plc, 83 302–306
PHP Healthcare Corporation, 22 423–25
PhyCor, Inc., 36 365–69
Physician Sales & Service, Inc., 14 387–89
Physio-Control International Corp., 18 420–23
Piaggio & C. S.p.A., 20 426–29; 100 348–52 (upd.)
PianoDisc see Burgett, Inc.
PIC International Group PLC, 24 386–88 (upd.)
Picanol N.V., 96 335–38
Picard Surgeles, 76 305–07
Piccadilly Cafeterias, Inc., 19 299–302
Pick 'n Pay Stores Ltd., 82 280–83

PictureTel Corp., 10 455–57; 27 363–66 (upd.)
Piedmont Investment Advisors, LLC, 106 369–72
Piedmont Natural Gas Company, Inc., 27 367–69
Pier 1 Imports, Inc., 12 393–95; 34 337–41 (upd.); 95 336–43 (upd.)
Pierce Leahy Corporation, 24 389–92 see also Iron Mountain Inc.
Piercing Pagoda, Inc., 29 382–84
Pierre & Vacances SA, 48 314–16
Pierre Fabre see Laboratoires Pierre Fabre S.A.
Piggly Wiggly Southern, Inc., 13 404–06
Pilgrim's Pride Corporation, 7 432–33; 23 383–85 (upd.); 90 334–38 (upd.)
Pilkington Group Limited, II 724–27; 34 342–47 (upd.); 87 375–383 (upd.)
Pillowtex Corporation, 19 303–05; 41 299–302 (upd.)
Pillsbury Company, II 555–57; 13 407–09 (upd.); 62 269–73 (upd.)
Pillsbury Madison & Sutro LLP, 29 385–88
Pilot Air Freight Corp., 67 301–03
Pilot Corporation, 49 328–30
Pilot Pen Corporation of America, 82 284–87
Pinault-Printemps-Redoute S.A., 19 306–09 (upd.) see also PPR S.A.
Pindar see G A Pindar & Son Ltd.
Pinguely-Haulotte SA, 51 293–95
Pinkerton's Inc., 9 406–09 see also Securitas AB.
Pinnacle Airlines Corp., 73 261–63
Pinnacle West Capital Corporation, 6 545–47; 54 290–94 (upd.)
Pioneer Electronic Corporation, III 604–06; 28 358–61 (upd.) see also Agilysys Inc.
Pioneer Hi-Bred International, Inc., 9 410–12; 41 303–06 (upd.)
Pioneer International Limited, III 728–30
Pioneer Natural Resources Company, 59 335–39
Pioneer-Standard Electronics Inc., 19 310–14 see also Agilysys Inc.
Piper Jaffray Companies, , 22 426–30 ; 107 357–63 (upd.)
Pirelli & C. S.p.A., V 249–51; 15 353–56 (upd.); 75 326–31 (upd.)
Piscines Desjoyaux S.A., 84 310–313
Pitman Company, 58 273–75
Pitney Bowes, Inc., III 156–58, 159; 19 315–18 (upd.); 47 295–99 (upd.)
Pittsburgh Brewing Company, 76 308–11
Pittsburgh Plate Glass Co. see PPG Industries, Inc.
Pittsburgh Steelers Sports, Inc., 66 255–57
The Pittston Company, IV 180–82; 19 319–22 (upd.) see also The Brink's Co.
Pittway Corporation, 9 413–15; 33 334–37 (upd.)

Smith Barney Inc., 15 463–65 *see also* Citigroup Inc.

Smith Corona Corp., 13 477–80

Smith International, Inc., 15 466–68; **59** 376–80 (upd.)

Smith-Midland Corporation, 56 330–32

Smithfield Foods, Inc., 7 477–78; **43** 381–84 (upd.)

SmithKline Beckman Corporation, I 692–94 *see also* GlaxoSmithKline plc.

SmithKline Beecham plc, III 65–67; **32** 429–34 (upd.) *see also* GlaxoSmithKline plc.

Smith's Food & Drug Centers, Inc., 8 472–74; **57** 324–27 (upd.)

Smiths Group plc, 25 429–31; **107** 406–10 (upd.)

Smithsonian Institution, 27 410–13

Smithway Motor Xpress Corporation, 39 376–79

Smoby International SA, 56 333–35

Smorgon Steel Group Ltd., 62 329–32

Smucker's *see* The J.M. Smucker Co.

Smurfit-Stone Container Corporation, 26 442–46 (upd.) ; **83** 360–368 (upd.)

Snap-On, Incorporated, 7 479–80; **27** 414–16 (upd.); **105** 423–28 (upd.)

Snapfish, 83 369–372

Snapple Beverage Corporation, 11 449–51

SNC-Lavalin Group Inc., 72 330–33

SNCF *see* Société Nationale des Chemins de Fer Français.

SNEA *see* Société Nationale Elf Aquitaine.

Snecma Group, 46 369–72 *see also* SAFRAN.

Snell & Wilmer L.L.P., 28 425–28

SNET *see* Southern New England Telecommunications Corp.

Snow Brand Milk Products Company, Ltd., II 574–75; **48** 362–65 (upd.)

Soap Opera Magazine *see* American Media, Inc.

Sobeys Inc., 80 348–51

Socata *see* EADS SOCATA.

Sociedad Química y Minera de Chile S.A.,103 382–85

Sociedade de Jogos de Macau, S.A.*see* SJM Holdings Ltd.

Società Finanziaria Telefonica per Azioni, V 325–27

Società Sportiva Lazio SpA, 44 386–88

Société Air France, 27 417–20 (upd.).

Société BIC S.A., 73 312–15

Societe des Produits Marnier-Lapostolle S.A., 88 373–76

Société d'Exploitation AOM Air Liberté SA (AirLib), 53 305–07

Société du Figaro S.A., 60 281–84

Société du Louvre, 27 421–23

Société Générale, II 354–56; **42** 347–51 (upd.)

Société Industrielle Lesaffre, 84 356–359

Société Luxembourgeoise de Navigation Aérienne S.A., 64 357–59

Société Nationale des Chemins de Fer Français, V 512–15; **57** 328–32 (upd.)

Société Nationale Elf Aquitaine, IV 544–47; **7** 481–85 (upd.)

Société Norbert Dentressangle S.A., 67 352–54

Société Tunisienne de l'Air-Tunisair, 49 371–73

Society Corporation, 9 474–77

Sodexho SA, 29 442–44; **91** 433–36 (upd.)

Sodiaal S.A., 19 50; **36** 437–39 (upd.)

SODIMA, II 576–77 *see also* Sodiaal S.A.

Soft Sheen Products, Inc., 31 416–18

Softbank Corporation, 13 481–83; **38** 439–44 (upd.); **77** 387–95 (upd.)

Sojitz Corporation, 96 395–403 (upd.)

Sol Meliá S.A., 71 337–39

Sola International Inc., 71 340–42

Solar Turbines Inc., 100 402–06

Solarfun Power Holdings Co., Ltd., 105 429–33

Sole Technology Inc., 93 405–09

Solectron Corporation, 12 450–52; **48** 366–70 (upd.)

Solo Cup Company, 104 424–27

Solo Serve Corporation, 28 429–31

Solutia Inc., 52 312–15

Solvay & Cie S.A., I 394–96; **21** 464–67 (upd.)

Solvay S.A., 61 329–34 (upd.)

Somerfield plc, 47 365–69 (upd.)

Sommer-Allibert S.A., 19 406–09 *see also* Tarkett Sommer AG.

Sompo Japan Insurance, Inc., 98 359–63 (upd.)

Sonae SGPS, S.A., 97 378–81

Sonat, Inc., 6 577–78 *see also* El Paso Corp.

Sonatrach, 65 313–17 (upd.)

Sonera Corporation, 50 441–44 *see also* TeliaSonera AB.

Sonesta International Hotels Corporation, 44 389–91

Sonic Automotive, Inc., 77 396–99

Sonic Corp., 14 451–53; **37** 360–63 (upd.); **103** 386–91 (upd.)

Sonic Innovations Inc., 56 336–38

Sonic Solutions, Inc., 81 375–79

SonicWALL, Inc., 87 421–424

Sonnenschein Nath and Rosenthal LLP, 102 384–87

Sonoco Products Company, 8 475–77; **89** 415–22 (upd.)

SonoSite, Inc., 56 339–41

Sony Corporation, II 101–03; **12** 453–56 (upd.); **40** 404–10 (upd.)

Sophus Berendsen A/S, 49 374–77

Sorbee International Ltd., 74 309–11

Soriana *see* Organización Soriana, S.A. de C.V.

Soros Fund Management LLC, 28 432–34

Sorrento, Inc., 19 51; **24** 444–46

SOS Staffing Services, 25 432–35

Sotheby's Holdings, Inc., 11 452–54; **29** 445–48 (upd.); **84** 360–365 (upd.)

Soufflet SA *see* Groupe Soufflet SA.

Sound Advice, Inc., 41 379–82

Souper Salad, Inc., 98 364–67

The Source Enterprises, Inc., 65 318–21

Source Interlink Companies, Inc., 75 350–53

The South African Breweries Limited, I 287–89; **24** 447–51 (upd.) *see also* SABMiller plc.

South Beach Beverage Company, Inc., 73 316–19

South Dakota Wheat Growers Association, 94 397–401

South Jersey Industries, Inc., 42 352–55

Southam Inc., 7 486–89 *see also* CanWest Global Communications Corp.

Southcorp Limited, 54 341–44

Southdown, Inc., 14 454–56 *see also* CEMEX S.A. de C.V.

Southeast Frozen Foods Company, L.P., 99 423–426

The Southern Company, V 721–23; **38** 445–49 (upd.)

Southern Connecticut Gas Company, 84 366–370

Southern Electric PLC, 13 484–86 *see also* Scottish and Southern Energy plc.

Southern Financial Bancorp, Inc., 56 342–44

Southern Indiana Gas and Electric Company, 13 487–89 *see also* Vectren Corp.

Southern New England Telecommunications Corporation, 6 338–40

Southern Pacific Transportation Company, V 516–18 *see also* Union Pacific Corp.

Southern Peru Copper Corporation, 40 411–13

Southern Poverty Law Center, Inc., 74 312–15

Southern Progress Corporation, 102 388–92

Southern States Cooperative Incorporated, 36 440–42

Southern Sun Hotel Interest (Pty) Ltd., 106 435–39

Southern Union Company, 27 424–26

Southern Wine and Spirits of America, Inc., 84 371–375

The Southland Corporation, II 660–61; **7** 490–92 (upd.) *see also* 7-Eleven, Inc.

Southtrust Corporation, 11 455–57 *see also* Wachovia Corp.

Southwest Airlines Co., 6 119–21; **24** 452–55 (upd.); **71** 343–47 (upd.)

Southwest Gas Corporation, 19 410–12

Southwest Water Company, 47 370–73

Southwestern Bell Corporation, V 328–30 *see also* SBC Communications Inc.

Southwestern Electric Power Co., 21 468–70

Southwestern Public Service Company, 6 579–81

Index to Industries

Northwest Airlines Corporation, I; 6 (upd.); 26 (upd.); 74 (upd.)
Offshore Logistics, Inc., 37
Pakistan International Airlines Corporation, 46
Pan American World Airways, Inc., I; 12 (upd.)
Panalpina World Transport (Holding) Ltd., 47
People Express Airlines, Inc., I
Petroleum Helicopters, Inc., 35
PHI, Inc., 80 (upd.)
Philippine Airlines, Inc., 6; 23 (upd.)
Pinnacle Airlines Corp., 73
Preussag AG, 42 (upd.)
Qantas Airways Ltd., 6; 24 (upd.); 68 (upd.)
Qatar Airways Company Q.C.S.C., 87
Reno Air Inc., 23
Royal Brunei Airlines Sdn Bhd, 99
Royal Nepal Airline Corporation, 41
Ryanair Holdings plc, 35
SAA (Pty) Ltd., 28
Sabena S.A./N.V., 33
The SAS Group, 34 (upd.)
Saudi Arabian Airlines, 6; 27 (upd.)
Scandinavian Airlines System, I
Sikorsky Aircraft Corporation, 24; 104 (upd.)
Singapore Airlines Limited, 6; 27 (upd.); 83 (upd.)
SkyWest, Inc., 25
Société d'Exploitation AOM Air Liberté SA (AirLib), 53
Société Luxembourgeoise de Navigation Aérienne S.A., 64
Société Tunisienne de l'Air-Tunisair, 49
Southwest Airlines Co., 6; 24 (upd.); 71 (upd.)
Spirit Airlines, Inc., 31
Sterling European Airlines A/S, 70
Sun Country Airlines, 30
Swiss Air Transport Company, Ltd., I
Swiss International Air Lines Ltd., 48
TAM Linhas Aéreas S.A., 68
TAME (Transportes Aéreos Militares Ecuatorianos), 100
TAP—Air Portugal Transportes Aéreos Portugueses S.A., 46
TAROM S.A., 64
Texas Air Corporation, I
Thai Airways International Public Company Limited, 6; 27 (upd.)
Tower Air, Inc., 28
Trans World Airlines, Inc., I; 12 (upd.); 35 (upd.)
TransBrasil S/A Linhas Aéreas, 31
Transportes Aereos Portugueses, S.A., 6
Turkish Airlines Inc. (Türk Hava Yollari A.O.), 72
UAL Corporation, 34 (upd.); 107 (upd.)
United Airlines, I; 6 (upd.)
US Airways Group, Inc., I; 6 (upd.); 28 (upd.); 52 (upd.)
VARIG S.A. (Viação Aérea Rio-Grandense), 6; 29 (upd.)
Virgin Group Ltd., 12; 32 (upd.); 89 (upd.)

Volga-Dnepr Group, 82
Vueling Airlines S.A., 97
WestJet Airlines Ltd., 38
Uzbekistan Airways National Air Company, 99

Automotive

AB Volvo, I; 7 (upd.); 26 (upd.); 67 (upd.)
Accubuilt, Inc., 74
Adam Opel AG, 7; 21 (upd.); 61 (upd.)
ADESA, Inc., 71
Advance Auto Parts, Inc., 57
Aftermarket Technology Corp., 83
Aisin Seiki Co., Ltd., 48 (upd.)
Alamo Rent A Car, Inc., 6; 24 (upd.); 84 (upd.)
Alfa Romeo, 13; 36 (upd.)
Alvis Plc, 47
America's Car-Mart, Inc., 64
American Motors Corporation, I
Amerigon Incorporated, 97
Andretti Green Racing, 106
Applied Power, Inc., 32 (upd.)
Arnold Clark Automobiles Ltd., 60
ArvinMeritor, Inc., 8; 54 (upd.)
Asbury Automotive Group Inc., 60
ASC, Inc., 55
Autobacs Seven Company Ltd., 76
Autocam Corporation, 51
Autoliv, Inc., 65
Automobiles Citroen, 7
Automobili Lamborghini Holding S.p.A., 13; 34 (upd.); 91 (upd.)
AutoNation, Inc., 50
AutoTrader.com, L.L.C., 91
AVTOVAZ Joint Stock Company, 65
Bajaj Auto Limited, 39
Bayerische Motoren Werke AG, I; 11 (upd.); 38 (upd.)
Belron International Ltd., 76
Bendix Corporation, I
Blue Bird Corporation, 35
Bombardier Inc., 42 (upd.)
BorgWarner Inc., 14; 32 (upd.); 85 (upd.)
The Budd Company, 8
Bugatti Automobiles S.A.S., 94
Caffyns PLC, 105
Canadian Tire Corporation, Limited, 71 (upd.)
CarMax, Inc., 55
CARQUEST Corporation, 29
Caterpillar Inc., 63 (upd.)
Checker Motors Corp., 89
China Automotive Systems Inc., 87
China FAW Group Corporation, 105
Chrysler Corporation, I; 11 (upd.)
Commercial Vehicle Group, Inc., 81
CNH Global N.V., 38 (upd.); 99 (upd.)
Consorcio G Grupo Dina, S.A. de C.V., 36
Crown Equipment Corporation, 15; 93 (upd.)
CSK Auto Corporation, 38
Cummins Engine Company, Inc., I; 12 (upd.); 40 (upd.)
Custom Chrome, Inc., 16

Daihatsu Motor Company, Ltd., 7; 21 (upd.)
Daimler-Benz A.G., I; 15 (upd.)
DaimlerChrysler AG, 34 (upd.); 64 (upd.)
Dana Holding Corporation, I; 10 (upd.); 99 (upd.)
Danaher Corporation, 77 (upd.)
Deere & Company, 42 (upd.)
Delphi Automotive Systems Corporation, 45
D'Ieteren S.A./NV, 98
Directed Electronics, Inc., 87
Discount Tire Company Inc., 84
Don Massey Cadillac, Inc., 37
Donaldson Company, Inc., 49 (upd.)
Dongfeng Motor Corporation, 105
Douglas & Lomason Company, 16
Dräxlmaier Group, 90
DriveTime Automotive Group Inc., 68 (upd.)
Ducati Motor Holding SpA, 30; 86 (upd.)
Eaton Corporation, I; 10 (upd.); 67 (upd.)
Echlin Inc., I; 11 (upd.)
Edelbrock Corporation, 37
Europcar Groupe S.A., 104
Faurecia S.A., 70
Federal-Mogul Corporation, I; 10 (upd.); 26 (upd.)
Ferrara Fire Apparatus, Inc., 84
Ferrari S.p.A., 13; 36 (upd.)
Fiat SpA, I; 11 (upd.); 50 (upd.)
FinishMaster, Inc., 24
Force Protection Inc., 95
Ford Motor Company, I; 11 (upd.); 36 (upd.); 64 (upd.)
Ford Motor Company, S.A. de C.V., 20
Fruehauf Corporation, I
General Motors Corporation, I; 10 (upd.); 36 (upd.); 64 (upd.)
Gentex Corporation, 26
Genuine Parts Company, 9; 45 (upd.)
GKN plc, III; 38 (upd.); 89 (upd.)
Group 1 Automotive, Inc., 52
Groupe Henri Heuliez S.A., 100
Grupo Ficosa International, 90
Guardian Industries Corp., 87
Harley-Davidson Inc., 7; 25 (upd.); 106 (upd.)
Hastings Manufacturing Company, 56
Hayes Lemmerz International, Inc., 27
Hendrick Motorsports, Inc., 89
The Hertz Corporation, 9; 33 (upd.); 101 (upd.)
Hino Motors, Ltd., 7; 21 (upd.)
Holden Ltd., 62
Holley Performance Products Inc., 52
Hometown Auto Retailers, Inc., 44
Honda Motor Company Limited (Honda Giken Kogyo Kabushiki Kaisha), I; 10 (upd.); 29 (upd.); 96 (upd.)
Hyundai Group, III; 7 (upd.); 56 (upd.)
Insurance Auto Auctions, Inc., 23
Isuzu Motors, Ltd., 9; 23 (upd.); 57 (upd.)
INTERMET Corporation, 77 (upd.)
Jardine Cycle & Carriage Ltd., 73

Kawasaki Heavy Industries, Ltd., 63 (upd.)
Kelsey-Hayes Group of Companies, 7; 27 (upd.)
Key Safety Systems, Inc., 63
Kia Motors Corporation, 12; 29 (upd.)
Kolbenschmidt Pierburg AG, 97
Kwik-Fit Holdings plc, 54
Lazy Days RV Center, Inc., 69
Lear Corporation, 71 (upd.)
Lear Seating Corporation, 16
Les Schwab Tire Centers, 50
Lithia Motors, Inc., 41
LKQ Corporation, 71
Lookers plc, 71
Lotus Cars Ltd., 14
Lund International Holdings, Inc., 40
Mack Trucks, Inc., I; 22 (upd.); 61 (upd.)
The Major Automotive Companies, Inc., 45
Marcopolo S.A., 79
Masland Corporation, 17
Mazda Motor Corporation, 9; 23 (upd.); 63 (upd.)
Mel Farr Automotive Group, 20
Metso Corporation, 30 (upd.)
Midas Inc., 10; 56 (upd.)
Mitsubishi Motors Corporation, 9; 23 (upd.); 57 (upd.)
Monaco Coach Corporation, 31
Monro Muffler Brake, Inc., 24
Montupet S.A., 63
Morgan Motor Company, 105
National R.V. Holdings, Inc., 32
Navistar International Corporation, I; 10 (upd.)
New Flyer Industries Inc. 78
Nissan Motor Company Ltd., I; 11 (upd.); 34 (upd.); 92 (upd.)
O'Reilly Automotive, Inc., 26; 78 (upd.)
Officine Alfieri Maserati S.p.A., 13
Oshkosh Corporation, 7; 98 (upd.)
Paccar Inc., I
PACCAR Inc., 26 (upd.)
Park-Ohio Holdings Corp., 17; 85 (upd.)
Parker-Hannifin Corporation, III; 24 (upd.); 99 (upd.)
Pennzoil-Quaker State Company, IV; 20 (upd.); 50 (upd.)
Penske Corporation, V; 19 (upd.); 84 (upd.)
The Pep Boys—Manny, Moe & Jack, 11; 36 (upd.); 81 (upd.)
Perusahaan Otomobil Nasional Bhd., 62
Peterbilt Motors Company, 89
Peugeot S.A., I
Piaggio & C. S.p.A., 20;100 (upd.)
Pirelli & C. S.p.A., 75 (upd.)
Porsche AG, 13; 31 (upd.)
PSA Peugeot Citroen S.A., 28 (upd.)
R&B, Inc., 51
Randon S.A., 79
Red McCombs Automotive Group, 91
Regal-Beloit Corporation, 18; 97 (upd.)
Regie Nationale des Usines Renault, I
Renault Argentina S.A., 67
Renault S.A., 26 (upd.); 74 (upd.)
Repco Corporation Ltd., 74

Republic Industries, Inc., 26
The Reynolds and Reynolds Company, 50
Rheinmetall AG, 9; 97 (upd.)
Riviera Tool Company, 89
Robert Bosch GmbH., I; 16 (upd.); 43 (upd.)
RockShox, Inc., 26
Rockwell Automation, I; 11 (upd.); 43 (upd.)
Rolls-Royce plc, I; 21 (upd.)
Ron Tonkin Chevrolet Company, 55
Rover Group Ltd., 7; 21 (upd.)
Saab Automobile AB, I; 11 (upd.); 32 (upd.); 83 (upd.)
Safelite Glass Corp., 19
Safety Components International, Inc., 63
SANLUIS Corporación, S.A.B. de C.V., 95
Saturn Corporation, 7; 21 (upd.); 80 (upd.)
Sealed Power Corporation, I
Servco Pacific Inc., 96
Sheller-Globe Corporation, I
Sixt AG, 39
Skoda Auto a.s., 39
Sonic Automotive, Inc., 77
Spartan Motors Inc., 14
SpeeDee Oil Change and Tune-Up, 25
SPX Corporation, 10; 47 (upd.)
Standard Motor Products, Inc., 40
Strattec Security Corporation, 73
Superior Industries International, Inc., 8
Suzuki Motor Corporation, 9; 23 (upd.); 59 (upd.)
Sytner Group plc, 45
Titan International, Inc., 89
Toresco Enterprises, Inc., 84
Tower Automotive, Inc., 24
Toyota Motor Corporation, I; 11 (upd.); 38 (upd.); 100 (upd.)
CJSC Transmash Holding, 93
TransPro, Inc., 71
Triumph Motorcycles Ltd., 53
TRW Automotive Holdings Corp., 75 (upd.)
TRW Inc., 14 (upd.)
Ugly Duckling Corporation, 22
United Auto Group, Inc., 26; 68 (upd.)
United Technologies Automotive Inc., 15
Universal Technical Institute, Inc., 81
Valeo, 23; 66 (upd.)
Van Hool S.A./NV, 96
Vauxhall Motors Limited, 73
Volkswagen Aktiengesellschaft, I; 11 (upd.); 32 (upd.)
Wagon plc, 92
Walker Manufacturing Company, 19
Webasto Roof Systems Inc., 97
Wilhelm Karmann GmbH, 94
Winnebago Industries, Inc., 7; 27 (upd.); 96 (upd.)
Woodward Governor Company, 13; 49 (upd.); 105 (upd.)
The Yokohama Rubber Company, Limited, V; 19 (upd.); 91 (upd.)
ZF Friedrichshafen AG, 48
Ziebart International Corporation, 30; 66 (upd.)

Beverages

A & W Brands, Inc., 25
A. Smith Bowman Distillery, Inc., 104
Adolph Coors Company, I; 13 (upd.); 36 (upd.)
AG Barr plc, 64
Ajegroup S.A., 92
Allied Domecq PLC, 29
Allied-Lyons PLC, I
Anadolu Efes Biracilik ve Malt Sanayii A.S., 95
Anchor Brewing Company, 47
Andrew Peller Ltd., 101
Anheuser-Busch InBev, I; 10 (upd.); 34 (upd.); 100 (upd.)
Apple & Eve L.L.C., 92
Asahi Breweries, Ltd., I; 20 (upd.); 52 (upd.)
Asia Pacific Breweries Limited, 59
August Schell Brewing Company Inc., 59
Bacardi & Company Ltd., 18; 82 (upd.)
Baltika Brewery Joint Stock Company, 65
Banfi Products Corp., 36
Baron de Ley S.A., 74
Baron Philippe de Rothschild S.A., 39
Bass PLC, I; 15 (upd.); 38 (upd.)
Bavaria S.A., 90
BBAG Osterreichische Brau-Beteiligungs-AG, 38
Belvedere S.A., 93
Beringer Blass Wine Estates Ltd., 22; 66 (upd.)
The Bernick Companies, 75
Blue Ridge Beverage Company Inc., 82
Boizel Chanoine Champagne S.A., 94
Bols Distilleries NV, 74
The Boston Beer Company, Inc., 18; 50 (upd.)
Brauerei Beck & Co., 9; 33 (upd.)
Britannia Soft Drinks Ltd. (Britvic), 71
Bronco Wine Company, 101
Brown-Forman Corporation, I; 10 (upd.); 38 (upd.)
Brouwerijen Alken-Maes N.V., 86
Budweiser Budvar, National Corporation, 59
Cadbury Schweppes PLC, 49 (upd.)
Cains Beer Company PLC, 99
Cameron Hughes Wine, 103
Canandaigua Brands, Inc., 13; 34 (upd.)
Cantine Giorgio Lungarotti S.R.L., 67
Caribou Coffee Company, Inc., 28; 97 (upd.)
Carlsberg A/S, 9; 29 (upd.); 98 (upd.)
Carlton and United Breweries Ltd., I
Casa Cuervo, S.A. de C.V., 31
Central European Distribution Corporation, 75
Cerveceria Polar, I
The Chalone Wine Group, Ltd., 36
The Charmer Sunbelt Group, 95
City Brewing Company LLC, 73
Clearly Canadian Beverage Corporation, 48
Clement Pappas & Company, Inc., 92
Click Wine Group, 68
Coca Cola Bottling Co. Consolidated, 10

Conglomerates

Construction

Containers

Drugs & Pharmaceuticals

American Pharmaceutical Partners, Inc., 69
AmerisourceBergen Corporation, 64 (upd.)
Amersham PLC, 50
Amgen, Inc., 10; 89 (upd.)
Amylin Pharmaceuticals, Inc., 67
Andrx Corporation, 55
Angelini SpA, 100
Astellas Pharma Inc., 97 (upd.)
AstraZeneca PLC, I; 20 (upd.); 50 (upd.)
AtheroGenics Inc., 101
Axcan Pharma Inc., 85
Barr Pharmaceuticals, Inc., 26; 68 (upd.)
Bayer A.G., I; 13 (upd.)
Berlex Laboratories, Inc., 66
Biovail Corporation, 47
Block Drug Company, Inc., 8
Boiron S.A., 73
Bristol-Myers Squibb Company, III; 9 (upd.); 37 (upd.)
BTG Plc, 87
C.H. Boehringer Sohn, 39
Caremark Rx, Inc., 10; 54 (upd.)
Carter-Wallace, Inc., 8; 38 (upd.)
Celgene Corporation, 67
Cephalon, Inc., 45
Chiron Corporation, 10
Chugai Pharmaceutical Co., Ltd., 50
Ciba-Geigy Ltd., I; 8 (upd.)
D&K Wholesale Drug, Inc., 14
Discovery Partners International, Inc., 58
Dr. Reddy's Laboratories Ltd., 59
Egis Gyogyszergyar Nyrt, 104
Eisai Co., Ltd., 101
Elan Corporation PLC, 63
Eli Lilly and Company, I; 11 (upd.); 47 (upd.)
Endo Pharmaceuticals Holdings Inc., 71
Eon Labs, Inc., 67
Express Scripts Inc., 44 (upd.)
F. Hoffmann-La Roche Ltd., I; 50 (upd.)
Fisons plc, 9; 23 (upd.)
Forest Laboratories, Inc., 52 (upd.)
FoxMeyer Health Corporation, 16
Fujisawa Pharmaceutical Company Ltd., I
G.D. Searle & Co., I; 12 (upd.); 34 (upd.)
Galenica AG, 84
GEHE AG, 27
Genentech, Inc., I; 8 (upd.); 75 (upd.)
Genetics Institute, Inc., 8
Genzyme Corporation, 13, 77 (upd.)
Glaxo Holdings PLC, I; 9 (upd.)
GlaxoSmithKline plc, 46 (upd.)
Groupe Fournier SA, 44
Groupe Léa Nature, 88
H. Lundbeck A/S, 44
Hauser, Inc., 46
Heska Corporation, 39
Hexal AG, 69
Hikma Pharmaceuticals Ltd., 102
Hospira, Inc., 71
Huntingdon Life Sciences Group plc, 42
ICN Pharmaceuticals, Inc., 52
ICU Medical, Inc., 106
Immucor, Inc., 81
Integrated BioPharma, Inc., 83

IVAX Corporation, 55 (upd.)
Janssen Pharmaceutica N.V., 80
Johnson & Johnson, III; 8 (upd.)
Jones Medical Industries, Inc., 24
The Judge Group, Inc., 51
King Pharmaceuticals, Inc., 54
Kinray Inc., 85
Kos Pharmaceuticals, Inc., 63
Kyowa Hakko Kogyo Co., Ltd., 48 (upd.)
Laboratoires Arkopharma S.A., 75
Laboratoires Pierre Fabre S.A., 100
Leiner Health Products Inc., 34
Ligand Pharmaceuticals Incorporated, 47
MannKind Corporation, 87
Marion Merrell Dow, Inc., I; 9 (upd.)
Matrixx Initiatives, Inc., 74
McKesson Corporation, 12; 47 (upd.)
Medicis Pharmaceutical Corporation, 59
MedImmune, Inc., 35
Merck & Co., Inc., I; 11 (upd.); 34 (upd.); 95 (upd.)
Merial Ltd., 102
Merz Group, 81
Miles Laboratories, I
Millennium Pharmaceuticals, Inc., 47
Monsanto Company, 29 (upd.), 77 (upd.)
Moore Medical Corp., 17
Murdock Madaus Schwabe, 26
Mylan Laboratories Inc., I; 20 (upd.); 59 (upd.)
Myriad Genetics, Inc., 95
Nadro S.A. de C.V., 86
Nastech Pharmaceutical Company Inc., 79
National Patent Development Corporation, 13
Natrol, Inc., 49
Natural Alternatives International, Inc., 49
Nektar Therapeutics, 91
Novartis AG, 39 (upd.); 105 (upd.)
Noven Pharmaceuticals, Inc., 55
Novo Nordisk A/S, I; 61 (upd.)
Obagi Medical Products, Inc., 95
Omnicare, Inc., 49
Omrix Biopharmaceuticals, Inc., 95
Par Pharmaceutical Companies, Inc., 65
PDL BioPharma, Inc., 90
Perrigo Company, 59 (upd.)
Pfizer Inc., I; 9 (upd.); 38 (upd.); 79 (upd.)
Pharmacia & Upjohn Inc., I; 25 (upd.)
Pharmion Corporation, 91
PLIVA d.d., 70
PolyMedica Corporation, 77
POZEN Inc., 81
QLT Inc., 71
The Quigley Corporation, 62
Quintiles Transnational Corporation, 21
R.P. Scherer, I
Ranbaxy Laboratories Ltd., 70
ratiopharm Group, 84
Reckitt Benckiser plc, II; 42 (upd.); 91 (upd.)
Recordati Industria Chimica e Farmaceutica S.p.A., 105
Roberts Pharmaceutical Corporation, 16
Roche Bioscience, 14 (upd.)
Rorer Group, I
Roussel Uclaf, I; 8 (upd.)

Salix Pharmaceuticals, Ltd., 93
Sandoz Ltd., I
Sankyo Company, Ltd., I; 56 (upd.)
The Sanofi-Synthélabo Group, I; 49 (upd.)
Santarus, Inc., 105
Schering AG, I; 50 (upd.)
Schering-Plough Corporation, I; 14 (upd.); 49 (upd.); 99 (upd.)
Sepracor Inc., 45
Serono S.A., 47
Shionogi & Co., Ltd., III; 17 (upd.); 98 (upd.)
Sigma-Aldrich Corporation, I; 36 (upd.); 93 (upd.)
SmithKline Beecham plc, I; 32 (upd.)
Solvay S.A., 61 (upd.)
Squibb Corporation, I
Sterling Drug, Inc., I
Stiefel Laboratories, Inc., 90
Sun Pharmaceutical Industries Ltd., 57
The Sunrider Corporation, 26
Syntex Corporation, I
Takeda Chemical Industries, Ltd., I
Taro Pharmaceutical Industries Ltd., 65
Teva Pharmaceutical Industries Ltd., 22; 54 (upd.)
UCB Pharma SA, 98
The Upjohn Company, I; 8 (upd.)
Vertex Pharmaceuticals Incorporated, 83
Virbac Corporation, 74
Vitalink Pharmacy Services, Inc., 15
Warner Chilcott Limited, 85
Warner-Lambert Co., I; 10 (upd.)
Watson Pharmaceuticals Inc., 16; 56 (upd.)
The Wellcome Foundation Ltd., I
WonderWorks, Inc., 103
Zentiva N.V./Zentiva, a.s., 99
Zila, Inc., 46

Education & Training
ABC Learning Centres Ltd., 93
American Management Association, 76
Benesse Corporation, 76
Berlitz International, Inc., 13; 39 (upd.)
Career Education Corporation, 45
ChartHouse International Learning Corporation, 49
Childtime Learning Centers, Inc., 34
Computer Learning Centers, Inc., 26
Corinthian Colleges, Inc., 39; 92 (upd.)
Council on International Educational Exchange Inc., 81
DeVry Inc., 29; 82 (upd.)
Edison Schools Inc., 37
Educate Inc., 86 (upd.)
Education Management Corporation, 35
Educational Testing Service, 12; 62 (upd.)
GP Strategies Corporation, 64 (upd.)
Green Dot Public Schools, 99
Grupo Positivo, 105
Huntington Learning Centers, Inc., 55
ITT Educational Services, Inc., 39; 76 (upd.)
Jones Knowledge Group, Inc., 97
Kaplan, Inc., 42; 90 (upd.)
KinderCare Learning Centers, Inc., 13

Electrical & Electronics

Engineering & Management Services

Entertainment & Leisure

Financial Services: Banks

Financial Services: Excluding Banks

Food Products

Food Services & Retailers

Health & Personal Care Products

Health Care Services

Hotels

Insurance

Materials

Mining & Metals

Nonprofit & Philanthropic Organizations

Paper & Forestry

Pope & Talbot, Inc., 12; 61 (upd.)
Pope Resources LP, 74
Potlatch Corporation, 8; 34 (upd.); 87
   (upd.)
PWA Group, IV
Rayonier Inc., 24
Rengo Co., Ltd., IV
Reno de Medici S.p.A., 41
Rexam PLC, 32 (upd.); 85 (upd.)
Riverwood International Corporation, 11;
   48 (upd.)
Rock-Tenn Company, 13; 59 (upd.)
Rogers Corporation, 61
The St. Joe Company, 8; 98 (upd.)
Sanyo-Kokusaku Pulp Co., Ltd., IV
Sappi Ltd., 49; 107 (upd.)
Schneidersöhne Deutschland GmbH &
   Co. KG, 100
Schweitzer-Mauduit International, Inc., 52
Scott Paper Company, IV; 31 (upd.)
Sealed Air Corporation, 14
Sierra Pacific Industries, 22; 90 (upd.)
Simpson Investment Company, 17
Smurfit-Stone Container Corporation, 83
   (upd.)
Sonoco Products Company, 8; 89 (upd.)
Specialty Coatings Inc., 8
Stimson Lumber Company 78
Stone Container Corporation, IV
Stora Enso Oyj, IV; 36 (upd.); 85 (upd.)
Svenska Cellulosa Aktiebolaget SCA, IV;
   28 (upd.); 85 (upd.)
Sveaskog AB, 93
Tapemark Company Inc., 64
Tembec Inc., 66
Temple-Inland Inc., IV; 31 (upd.); 102
   (upd.)
Thomsen Greenhouses and Garden
   Center, Incorporated, 65
TJ International, Inc., 19
U.S. Timberlands Company, L.P., 42
Union Camp Corporation, IV
United Paper Mills Ltd. (Yhtyneet
   Paperitehtaat Oy), IV
Universal Forest Products, Inc., 10; 59
   (upd.)
UPM-Kymmene Corporation, 19; 50
   (upd.)
Wausau-Mosinee Paper Corporation, 60
   (upd.)
West Fraser Timber Co. Ltd., 17; 91
   (upd.)
West Linn Paper Company, 91
Westvaco Corporation, IV; 19 (upd.)
Weyerhaeuser Company, IV; 9 (upd.); 28
   (upd.); 83 (upd.)
Wickes Inc., 25 (upd.)
Willamette Industries, Inc., IV; 31 (upd.)
WTD Industries, Inc., 20

Personal Services

Adelman Travel Group, 105
ADT Security Services, Inc., 12; 44 (upd.)
Alderwoods Group, Inc., 68 (upd.)
Ambassadors International, Inc., 68 (upd.)
American Retirement Corporation, 42
Aquent, 96
Bidvest Group Ltd., 106

Blackwater USA, 76
Bonhams 1793 Ltd., 72
The Brickman Group, Ltd., 87
CareerBuilder, Inc., 93
Carriage Services, Inc., 37
CDI Corporation, 6; 54 (upd.)
Central Parking System, 18; 104 (upd.)
CeWe Color Holding AG, 76
Chubb, PLC, 50
Correctional Services Corporation, 30
CUC International Inc., 16
Curves International, Inc., 54
eHarmony.com Inc., 71
Franklin Quest Co., 11
Gold's Gym International, Inc., 71
Greg Manning Auctions, Inc., 60
Gunnebo AB, 53
Hair Club For Men Ltd., 90
Herbalife Ltd., 17; 41 (upd.); 92 (upd.)
I Grandi Viaggi S.p.A., 105
Imperial Parking Corporation, 58
Initial Security, 64
Jazzercise, Inc., 45
Kiva, 95
Lifetouch Inc., 86
The Loewen Group Inc., 16; 40 (upd.)
Mace Security International, Inc., 57
Manpower, Inc., 9
Martin Franchises, Inc., 80
Match.com, LP, 87
Michael Page International plc, 45
Orkin, Inc., 104
PODS Enterprises Inc., 103
Prison Rehabilitative Industries and
   Diversified Enterprises, Inc. (PRIDE),
   53
Regis Corporation, 18; 70 (upd.)
Rollins, Inc., 11; 104 (upd.)
Rosenbluth International Inc., 14
Screen Actors Guild, 72
Service Corporation International, 6; 51
   (upd.)
Shutterfly, Inc., 98
SOS Staffing Services, 25
Spark Networks, Inc., 91
Stewart Enterprises, Inc., 20
Supercuts Inc., 26
24 Hour Fitness Worldwide, Inc., 71
UAW (International Union, United
   Automobile, Aerospace and Agricultural
   Implement Workers of America), 72
Weight Watchers International Inc., 12;
   33 (upd.); 73 (upd.)
The York Group, Inc., 50

Petroleum

Abraxas Petroleum Corporation, 89
Abu Dhabi National Oil Company, IV;
   45 (upd.)
Adani Enterprises Ltd., 97
Aegean Marine Petroleum Network Inc.,
   89
Agway, Inc., 21 (upd.)
Alberta Energy Company Ltd., 16; 43
   (upd.)
Alon Israel Oil Company Ltd., 104
Amerada Hess Corporation, IV; 21 (upd.);
   55 (upd.)

Amoco Corporation, IV; 14 (upd.)
Anadarko Petroleum Corporation, 10; 52
   (upd.); 106 (upd.)
ANR Pipeline Co., 17
Anschutz Corp., 12
Apache Corporation, 10; 32 (upd.); 89
   (upd.)
Aral AG, 62
Arctic Slope Regional Corporation, 38
Arena Resources, Inc., 97
Ashland Inc., 19; 50 (upd.)
Ashland Oil, Inc., IV
Atlantic Richfield Company, IV; 31 (upd.)
Atwood Oceanics, Inc., 100
Aventine Renewable Energy Holdings,
   Inc., 89
Badger State Ethanol, LLC, 83
Baker Hughes Incorporated, 22 (upd.); 57
   (upd.)
Basic Earth Science Systems, Inc., 101
Belco Oil & Gas Corp., 40
Benton Oil and Gas Company, 47
Berry Petroleum Company, 47
BG Products Inc., 96
BHP Billiton, 67 (upd.)
Bill Barrett Corporation, 71
BJ Services Company, 25
Blue Rhino Corporation, 56
Boardwalk Pipeline Partners, LP, 87
Boots & Coots International Well
   Control, Inc., 79
BP p.l.c., 45 (upd.); 103 (upd.)
Brigham Exploration Company, 75
The British Petroleum Company plc, IV;
   7 (upd.); 21 (upd.)
British-Borneo Oil & Gas PLC, 34
Broken Hill Proprietary Company Ltd.,
   22 (upd.)
Bronco Drilling Company, Inc., 89
Burlington Resources Inc., 10
Burmah Castrol PLC, IV; 30 (upd.)
Callon Petroleum Company, 47
Caltex Petroleum Corporation, 19
Calumet Specialty Products Partners, L.P.,
   106
CAMAC International Corporation, 106
Cano Petroleum Inc., 97
Carrizo Oil & Gas, Inc., 97
Chevron Corporation, IV; 19 (upd.); 47
   (upd.); 103 (upd.)
Chiles Offshore Corporation, 9
Cimarex Energy Co., 81
China National Petroleum Corporation,
   46
Chinese Petroleum Corporation, IV; 31
   (upd.)
CITGO Petroleum Corporation, IV; 31
   (upd.)
Clayton Williams Energy, Inc., 87
The Coastal Corporation, IV; 31 (upd.)
Compañía Española de Petróleos S.A.
   (Cepsa), IV; 56 (upd.)
Compton Petroleum Corporation, 103
Comstock Resources, Inc., 47
Conoco Inc., IV; 16 (upd.)
ConocoPhillips, 63 (upd.)
CONSOL Energy Inc., 59
Continental Resources, Inc., 89

Publishing & Printing

Real Estate

Retail & Wholesale

Rubber & Tires

Telecommunications

Textiles & Apparel

Tobacco

Transport Services

Utilities

Entergy Corporation, V; 45 (upd.)
Environmental Power Corporation, 68
EPCOR Utilities Inc., 81
Equitable Resources, Inc., 6; 54 (upd.)
Exelon Corporation, 48 (upd.)
Florida Progress Corporation, V; 23 (upd.)
Florida Public Utilities Company, 69
Fortis, Inc., 15; 47 (upd.)
Fortum Corporation, 30 (upd.)
FPL Group, Inc., V; 49 (upd.)
Gas Natural SDG S.A., 69
Gaz de France, V; 40 (upd.)
General Public Utilities Corporation, V
Générale des Eaux Group, V
GPU, Inc., 27 (upd.)
Great Plains Energy Incorporated, 65 (upd.)
Gulf States Utilities Company, 6
Hawaiian Electric Industries, Inc., 9
Hokkaido Electric Power Company Inc. (HEPCO), V; 58 (upd.)
Hokuriku Electric Power Company, V
Hong Kong and China Gas Company Ltd., 73
Hongkong Electric Holdings Ltd., 6; 23 (upd.); 107 (upd.)
Houston Industries Incorporated, V
Hyder plc, 34
Hydro-Québec, 6; 32 (upd.)
Iberdrola, S.A., 49
Idaho Power Company, 12
Illinois Bell Telephone Company, 14
Illinois Power Company, 6
Indiana Energy, Inc., 27
International Power PLC, 50 (upd.)
IPALCO Enterprises, Inc., 6
ITC Holdings Corp., 75
The Kansai Electric Power Company, Inc., V; 62 (upd.)
Kansas City Power & Light Company, 6
Kelda Group plc, 45
Kenetech Corporation, 11
Kentucky Utilities Company, 6
KeySpan Energy Co., 27
Korea Electric Power Corporation (Kepco), 56
KU Energy Corporation, 11
Kyushu Electric Power Company Inc., V; 107 (upd.)
LG&E Energy Corporation, 6; 51 (upd.)
Long Island Power Authority, V; 102 (upd.)
Lyonnaise des Eaux-Dumez, V
Madison Gas and Electric Company, 39
Magma Power Company, 11
Maine & Maritimes Corporation, 56
Manila Electric Company (Meralco), 56
MCN Corporation, 6
MDU Resources Group, Inc., 7; 42 (upd.)
Middlesex Water Company, 45
Midwest Resources Inc., 6
Minnesota Power, Inc., 11; 34 (upd.)
Mirant Corporation, 98
The Montana Power Company, 11; 44 (upd.)
National Fuel Gas Company, 6; 95 (upd.)
National Grid USA, 51 (upd.)
National Power PLC, 12

Nebraska Public Power District, 29
N.V. Nederlandse Gasunie, V
Nevada Power Company, 11
New England Electric System, V
New Jersey Resources Corporation, 54
New York State Electric and Gas, 6
Neyveli Lignite Corporation Ltd., 65
Niagara Mohawk Holdings Inc., V; 45 (upd.)
Nicor Inc., 6; 86 (upd.)
NIPSCO Industries, Inc., 6
North West Water Group plc, 11
Northeast Utilities, V; 48 (upd.)
Northern States Power Company, V; 20 (upd.)
Northwest Natural Gas Company, 45
NorthWestern Corporation, 37
Nova Corporation of Alberta, V
NRG Energy, Inc., 79
NSTAR, 106 (upd.)
Oglethorpe Power Corporation, 6
Ohio Edison Company, V
Oklahoma Gas and Electric Company, 6
ONEOK Inc., 7
Ontario Hydro Services Company, 6; 32 (upd.)
Osaka Gas Company, Ltd., V; 60 (upd.)
Österreichische Elektrizitätswirtschafts-AG, 85
Otter Tail Power Company, 18
Pacific Enterprises, V
Pacific Gas and Electric Company, V
PacifiCorp, V; 26 (upd.)
Panhandle Eastern Corporation, V
Paddy Power plc, 98
PECO Energy Company, 11
Pennon Group Plc, 45
Pennsylvania Power & Light Company, V
Peoples Energy Corporation, 6
PG&E Corporation, 26 (upd.)
Philadelphia Electric Company, V
Philadelphia Gas Works Company, 92
Philadelphia Suburban Corporation, 39
Piedmont Natural Gas Company, Inc., 27
Pinnacle West Capital Corporation, 6; 54 (upd.)
PNM Resources Inc., 51 (upd.)
Portland General Corporation, 6
Potomac Electric Power Company, 6
Power-One, Inc., 79
Powergen PLC, 11; 50 (upd.)
PPL Corporation, 41 (upd.)
PreussenElektra Aktiengesellschaft, V
Progress Energy, Inc., 74
PSI Resources, 6
Public Service Company of Colorado, 6
Public Service Company of New Hampshire, 21; 55 (upd.)
Public Service Company of New Mexico, 6
Public Service Enterprise Group Inc., V; 44 (upd.)
Puerto Rico Electric Power Authority, 47
Puget Sound Energy Inc., 6; 50 (upd.)
Questar Corporation, 6; 26 (upd.)
RAO Unified Energy System of Russia, 45
Reliant Energy Inc., 44 (upd.)
Revere Electric Supply Company, 96

Rochester Gas and Electric Corporation, 6
Ruhrgas AG, V; 38 (upd.)
RWE AG, V; 50 (upd.)
Salt River Project, 19
San Diego Gas & Electric Company, V; 107 (upd.)
SCANA Corporation, 6; 56 (upd.)
Scarborough Public Utilities Commission, 9
SCEcorp, V
Scottish and Southern Energy plc, 66 (upd.)
Scottish Hydro-Electric PLC, 13
Scottish Power plc, 19; 49 (upd.)
Seattle City Light, 50
SEMCO Energy, Inc., 44
Sempra Energy, 25 (upd.)
Severn Trent PLC, 12; 38 (upd.)
Shikoku Electric Power Company, Inc., V; 60 (upd.)
SJW Corporation, 70
Sonat, Inc., 6
South Jersey Industries, Inc., 42
The Southern Company, V; 38 (upd.)
Southern Connecticut Gas Company, 84
Southern Electric PLC, 13
Southern Indiana Gas and Electric Company, 13
Southern Union Company, 27
Southwest Gas Corporation, 19
Southwest Water Company, 47
Southwestern Electric Power Co., 21
Southwestern Public Service Company, 6
Suez Lyonnaise des Eaux, 36 (upd.)
SUEZ-TRACTEBEL S.A., 97 (upd.)
TECO Energy, Inc., 6
Tennessee Valley Authority, 50
Tennet BV 78
Texas Utilities Company, V; 25 (upd.)
Thames Water plc, 11; 90 (upd.)
Tohoku Electric Power Company, Inc., V
The Tokyo Electric Power Company, 74 (upd.)
The Tokyo Electric Power Company, Incorporated, V
Tokyo Gas Co., Ltd., V; 55 (upd.)
TransAlta Utilities Corporation, 6
TransCanada PipeLines Limited, V
Transco Energy Company, V
Tri-State Generation and Transmission Association, Inc., 103
Trigen Energy Corporation, 42
Tucson Electric Power Company, 6
UGI Corporation, 12
Unicom Corporation, 29 (upd.)
Union Electric Company, V
The United Illuminating Company, 21
United Utilities PLC, 52 (upd.)
United Water Resources, Inc., 40
Unitil Corporation, 37
Utah Power and Light Company, 27
UtiliCorp United Inc., 6
Vattenfall AB, 57
Vectren Corporation, 98 (upd.)
Vereinigte Elektrizitätswerke Westfalen AG, V
VEW AG, 39
Viridian Group plc, 64

Geographic Index

Germany

Toyoda Automatic Loom Works, Ltd., III
Toyota Motor Corporation, I; 11 (upd.);
    38 (upd.); 100 (upd.)
Trend Micro Inc., 97
Ube Industries, Ltd., III; 38 (upd.)
ULVAC, Inc., 80
Unicharm Corporation, 84
Uniden Corporation, 98
Unitika Ltd., V; 53 (upd.)
Uny Co., Ltd., V; 49 (upd.)
Ushio Inc., 91
Victor Company of Japan, Limited, II; 26
    (upd.); 83 (upd.)
Wacoal Corp., 25
Yamada Denki Co., Ltd., 85
Yamaha Corporation, III; 16 (upd.); 40
    (upd.); 99 (upd.)
Yamaichi Securities Company, Limited, II
Yamato Transport Co. Ltd., V; 49 (upd.)
Yamazaki Baking Co., Ltd., 58
The Yasuda Fire and Marine Insurance
    Company, Limited, III
The Yasuda Mutual Life Insurance
    Company, III; 39 (upd.)
The Yasuda Trust and Banking Company,
    Ltd., II; 17 (upd.)
The Yokohama Rubber Company,
    Limited, V; 19 (upd.); 91 (upd.)
Yoshinoya D & C Company Ltd., 88

Jordan
Arab Potash Company, 85
Hikma Pharmaceuticals Ltd., 102
Munir Sukhtian Group, 104
Nuqul Group of Companies, 102

Kenya
Kenya Airways Limited, 89

Kuwait
Kuwait Airways Corporation, 68
Kuwait Flour Mills & Bakeries Company,
    84
Kuwait Petroleum Corporation, IV; 55
    (upd.)
Zain, 102

Latvia
A/S Air Baltic Corporation, 71

Lebanon
Blom Bank S.A.L., 102
Middle East Airlines - Air Liban S.A.L. 79

Libya
National Oil Corporation, IV; 66 (upd.)

Liechtenstein
Hilti AG, 53

Luxembourg
ARBED S.A., IV; 22 (upd.)
Cactus S.A., 90
Cargolux Airlines International S.A., 49
Elite World S.A., 94
Esp ???? ito Santo Financial Group S.A.
    79 (upd.)

Gemplus International S.A., 64
Metro International S.A., 93
RTL Group SA, 44
Société Luxembourgeoise de Navigation
    Aérienne S.A., 64
Tenaris SA, 63

Malaysia
AirAsia Berhad, 93
Berjaya Group Bhd., 67
Gano Excel Enterprise Sdn. Bhd., 89
Genting Bhd., 65
IOI Corporation Bhd, 107
Malayan Banking Berhad, 72
Malaysian Airlines System Berhad, 6; 29
    (upd.); 97 (upd.)
Perusahaan Otomobil Nasional Bhd., 62
Petroliam Nasional Bhd (Petronas), IV; 56
    (upd.)
PPB Group Berhad, 57
Sime Darby Berhad, 14; 36 (upd.)
Telekom Malaysia Bhd, 76
Yeo Hiap Seng Malaysia Bhd., 75

Mauritius
Air Mauritius Ltd., 63

Mexico
Alfa, S.A. de C.V., 19
Altos Hornos de México, S.A. de C.V., 42
América Móvil, S.A. de C.V., 80
Apasco S.A. de C.V., 51
Bolsa Mexicana de Valores, S.A. de C.V.,
    80
Bufete Industrial, S.A. de C.V., 34
Casa Cuervo, S.A. de C.V., 31
Celanese Mexicana, S.A. de C.V., 54
CEMEX S.A. de C.V., 20; 59 (upd.)
Cifra, S.A. de C.V., 12
Cinemas de la República, S.A. de C.V., 83
Compañia Industrial de Parras, S.A. de
    C.V. (CIPSA), 84
Consorcio ARA, S.A. de C.V. 79
Consorcio Aviacsa, S.A. de C.V., 85
Consorcio G Grupo Dina, S.A. de C.V.,
    36
Controladora Comercial Mexicana, S.A.
    de C.V., 36
Controladora Mabe, S.A. de C.V., 82
Coppel, S.A. de C.V., 82
Corporación Geo, S.A. de C.V., 81
Corporación Interamericana de
    Entretenimiento, S.A. de C.V., 83
Corporación Internacional de Aviación,
    S.A. de C.V. (Cintra), 20
Desarrolladora Homex, S.A. de C.V., 87
Desc, S.A. de C.V., 23
Editorial Television, S.A. de C.V., 57
Empresas ICA Sociedad Controladora,
    S.A. de C.V., 41
El Puerto de Liverpool, S.A.B. de C.V., 97
Ford Motor Company, S.A. de C.V., 20
Gruma, S.A.B. de C.V., 31; 103 (upd.)
Grupo Aeroportuario del Centro Norte,
    S.A.B. de C.V., 97
Grupo Aeroportuario del Pacífico, S.A. de
    C.V., 85

Grupo Aeropuerto del Sureste, S.A. de
    C.V., 48
Grupo Ángeles Servicios de Salud, S.A. de
    C.V., 84
Grupo Carso, S.A. de C.V., 21; 107
    (upd.)
Grupo Casa Saba, S.A. de C.V., 39
Grupo Comercial Chedraui S.A. de C.V.,
    86
Grupo Corvi S.A. de C.V., 86
Grupo Cydsa, S.A. de C.V., 39
Grupo Elektra, S.A. de C.V., 39
Grupo Financiero Banamex S.A., 54
Grupo Financiero Banorte, S.A. de C.V.,
    51
Grupo Financiero BBVA Bancomer S.A.,
    54
Grupo Financiero Serfin, S.A., 19
Grupo Gigante, S.A. de C.V., 34
Grupo Herdez, S.A. de C.V., 35
Grupo IMSA, S.A. de C.V., 44
Grupo Industrial Bimbo, 19
Grupo Industrial Durango, S.A. de C.V.,
    37
Grupo Industrial Herradura, S.A. de C.V.,
    83
Grupo Industrial Lala, S.A. de C.V., 82
Grupo Industrial Saltillo, S.A. de C.V., 54
Grupo Mexico, S.A. de C.V., 40
Grupo Modelo, S.A. de C.V., 29
Grupo Omnilife S.A. de C.V., 88
Grupo Posadas, S.A. de C.V., 57
Grupo Sanborns, S.A. de C.V., 107 (upd.)
Grupo Televisa, S.A., 18; 54 (upd.)
Grupo TMM, S.A. de C.V., 50
Grupo Transportación Ferroviaria
    Mexicana, S.A. de C.V., 47
Grupo Viz, S.A. de C.V., 84
Hylsamex, S.A. de C.V., 39
Industrias Bachoco, S.A. de C.V., 39
Industrias Peñoles, S.A. de C.V., 22; 107
    (upd.)
Internacional de Ceramica, S.A. de C.V.,
    53
Jugos del Valle, S.A. de C.V., 85
Kimberly-Clark de México, S.A. de C.V.,
    54
Mexichem, S.A.B. de C.V., 99
Nadro S.A. de C.V., 86
Organización Soriana, S.A. de C.V., 35
Petróleos Mexicanos (PEMEX), IV; 19
    (upd.); 104 (upd.)
Proeza S.A. de C.V., 85
Pulsar Internacional S.A., 21
Real Turismo, S.A. de C.V., 50
Sanborn Hermanos, S.A., 20
SANLUIS Corporación, S.A.B. de C.V.,
    95
Sears Roebuck de México, S.A. de C.V.,
    20
Telefonos de Mexico S.A. de C.V., 14; 63
    (upd.)
Tenedora Nemak, S.A. de C.V., 102
Tubos de Acero de Mexico, S.A.
    (TAMSA), 41
TV Azteca, S.A. de C.V., 39
Urbi Desarrollos Urbanos, S.A. de C.V.,
    81

Leidy's, Inc., 93
Leiner Health Products Inc., 34
LendingTree, LLC, 93
Lennar Corporation, 11
Lennox International Inc., 8; 28 (upd.)
Lenovo Group Ltd., 80
Lenox, Inc., 12
LensCrafters Inc., 23; 76 (upd.)
Leo Burnett Company Inc., I; 20 (upd.)
The Leona Group LLC, 84
Leprino Foods Company, 28
Les Schwab Tire Centers, 50
Lesco Inc., 19
The Leslie Fay Companies, Inc., 8; 39
   (upd.)
Leslie's Poolmart, Inc., 18
Leucadia National Corporation, 11; 71
   (upd.)
Leupold & Stevens, Inc., 52
Level 3 Communications, Inc., 67
Levenger Company, 63
Lever Brothers Company, 9
Levi, Ray & Shoup, Inc., 96
Levi Strauss & Co., V; 16 (upd.); 102
   (upd.)
Levitz Furniture Inc., 15
Levy Restaurants L.P., 26
The Lewin Group Inc., 104
Lewis Galoob Toys Inc., 16
Lewis-Goetz and Company, Inc., 102
LEXIS-NEXIS Group, 33
Lexmark International, Inc., 18; 79 (upd.)
LG&E Energy Corporation, 6; 51 (upd.)
Libbey Inc., 49
The Liberty Corporation, 22
Liberty Livewire Corporation, 42
Liberty Media Corporation, 50
Liberty Mutual Holding Company, 59
Liberty Orchards Co., Inc., 89
Liberty Property Trust, 57
Liberty Travel, Inc., 56
Life Care Centers of America Inc., 76
Life is Good, Inc., 80
Life Technologies, Inc., 17
Life Time Fitness, Inc., 66
LifeCell Corporation, 77
Lifeline Systems, Inc., 53
LifeLock, Inc., 91
LifePoint Hospitals, Inc., 69
Lifetime Brands, Inc., 73 (upd.)
Lifetime Entertainment Services, 51
Lifetime Hoan Corporation, 27
Lifeway Foods, Inc., 65
Ligand Pharmaceuticals Incorporated, 47
Lillian Vernon Corporation, 12; 35
   (upd.); 92 (upd.)
Lilly Endowment Inc., 70
The Limited, Inc., V; 20 (upd.)
LIN Broadcasting Corp., 9
Lincare Holdings Inc., 43
Lincoln Center for the Performing Arts,
   Inc., 69
Lincoln Electric Co., 13
Lincoln National Corporation, III; 25
   (upd.)
Lincoln Property Company, 8; 54 (upd.)
Lincoln Snacks Company, 24

Lincoln Telephone & Telegraph Company,
   14
Lindal Cedar Homes, Inc., 29
Lindsay Manufacturing Co., 20
Linear Technology Corporation, 16; 99
   (upd.)
Linens 'n Things, Inc., 24; 75 (upd.)
LinkedIn Corporation, 103
Lintas: Worldwide, 14
The Lion Brewery, Inc., 86
Lionel L.L.C., 16; 99 (upd.)
Liqui-Box Corporation, 16
Liquidity Services, Inc., 101
Liquidnet, Inc. 79
Litehouse Inc., 60
Lithia Motors, Inc., 41
Littelfuse, Inc., 26
Little Caesar Enterprises, Inc., 7; 24
   (upd.)
Little Tikes Company, 13; 62 (upd.)
Littleton Coin Company Inc., 82
Litton Industries, Inc., I; 11 (upd.)
LIVE Entertainment, Inc., 20
Live Nation, Inc., 80 (upd.)
LivePerson, Inc., 91
Liz Claiborne Inc., 8; 25 (upd.); 102
   (upd.)
LKQ Corporation, 71
Lockheed Martin Corporation, I; 11
   (upd.); 15 (upd.); 89 (upd.)
Loctite Corporation, 8; 30 (upd.)
Lodge Manufacturing Company, 103
LodgeNet Interactive Corporation, 28;
   106 (upd.)
Loehmann's Holdings Inc., 24; 107 (upd.)
Loews Corporation, I; 12 (upd.); 36
   (upd.); 93 (upd.)
Logan's Roadhouse, Inc., 29
Logicon Inc., 20
LoJack Corporation, 48
London Fog Industries, Inc., 29
Lone Star Steakhouse & Saloon, Inc., 51
The Long & Foster Companies, Inc., 85
Long Island Bancorp, Inc., 16
Long Island Power Authority, V; 102
   (upd.)
The Long Island Rail Road Company, 68
Long John Silver's, 13; 57 (upd.)
The Longaberger Company, 12; 44 (upd.)
Longs Drug Stores Corporation, V; 25
   (upd.); 83 (upd.)
Longview Fibre Company, 8; 37 (upd.)
Loos & Dilworth, Inc., 100
Loral Space & Communications Ltd., 8;
   9; 54 (upd.)
Los Angeles Turf Club Inc., 102
Lost Arrow Inc., 22
LOT$OFF Corporation, 24
Lotus Development Corporation, 6; 25
   (upd.)
LOUD Technologies, Inc., 95 (upd.)
The Louis Berger Group, Inc., 104
The Louisiana Land and Exploration
   Company, 7
Louisiana-Pacific Corporation, IV; 31
   (upd.)
Love's Travel Stops & Country Stores,
   Inc., 71

Lowe's Companies, Inc., V; 21 (upd.); 81
   (upd.)
Lowrance Electronics, Inc., 18
LPA Holding Corporation, 81
LSB Industries, Inc., 77
LSI Logic Corporation, 13; 64
The LTV Corporation, I; 24 (upd.)
The Lubrizol Corporation, I; 30 (upd.);
   83 (upd.)
Luby's, Inc., 17; 42 (upd.); 99 (upd.)
Lucasfilm Ltd., 12; 50 (upd.)
Lucent Technologies Inc., 34
Lucille Farms, Inc., 45
Lucky Stores, Inc., 27
Lufkin Industries Inc. 78
Luigino's, Inc., 64
Lukens Inc., 14
Lunar Corporation, 29
Lunardi's Super Market, Inc., 99
Lund Food Holdings, Inc., 22
Lund International Holdings, Inc., 40
Lutheran Brotherhood, 31
Lydall, Inc., 64
Lyman-Richey Corporation, 96
Lynch Corporation, 43
Lynden Incorporated, 91
Lyondell Chemical Company, IV; 45
   (upd.)
M&F Worldwide Corp., 38
M. Shanken Communications, Inc., 50
M.A. Bruder & Sons, Inc., 56
M.A. Gedney Co., 51
M.A. Hanna Company, 8
M.H. Meyerson & Co., Inc., 46
M.R. Beal and Co., 102
Mac Frugal's Bargains - Closeouts Inc., 17
Mac-Gray Corporation, 44
MacAndrews & Forbes Holdings Inc., 28;
   86 (upd.)
MacDermid Incorporated, 32
Mace Security International, Inc., 57
The Macerich Company, 57
MacGregor Golf Company, 68
Mack Trucks, Inc., I; 22 (upd.); 61 (upd.)
Mack-Cali Realty Corporation, 42
Mackay Envelope Corporation, 45
Mackie Designs Inc., 33
Macklowe Properties, Inc., 95
Macmillan, Inc., 7
MacNeil/Lehrer Productions, 87
The MacNeal-Schwendler Corporation, 25
Macromedia, Inc., 50
Macrovision Solutions Corporation, 101
Macy's, Inc., 94 (upd.)
Madden's on Gull Lake, 52
Madelaine Chocolate Novelties, Inc., 104
Madison Dearborn Partners, LLC, 97
Madison Gas and Electric Company, 39
Madison-Kipp Corporation, 58
Mag Instrument, Inc., 67
MaggieMoo's International, 89
Magma Copper Company, 7
Magma Design Automation Inc. 78
Magma Power Company, 11
MagneTek, Inc., 15; 41 (upd.)
MAI Systems Corporation, 11
Maid-Rite Corporation, 62
Maidenform, Inc., 20; 59 (upd.)

Thermadyne Holding Corporation, 19
Thermo BioAnalysis Corp., 25
Thermo Electron Corporation, 7
Thermo Fibertek, Inc., 24
Thermo Fisher Scientific Inc., 105 (upd.)
Thermo Instrument Systems Inc., 11
Thermo King Corporation, 13
Thermos Company, 16
Things Remembered, Inc., 84
Thiokol Corporation, 9; 22 (upd.)
Thomas & Betts Corporation, 11; 54 (upd.)
Thomas & Howard Company, Inc., 90
Thomas Cook Travel Inc., 9; 33 (upd.)
Thomas H. Lee Co., 24
Thomas Industries Inc., 29
Thomas J. Lipton Company, 14
Thomas Nelson, Inc., 14; 38 (upd.)
Thomas Publishing Company, 26
Thomaston Mills, Inc., 27
Thomasville Furniture Industries, Inc., 12; 74 (upd.)
Thomsen Greenhouses and Garden Center, Incorporated, 65
Thor Industries Inc., 39; 92 (upd.)
Thorn Apple Valley, Inc., 7; 22 (upd.)
ThoughtWorks Inc., 90
Thousand Trails, Inc., 33
THQ, Inc., 39; 92 (upd.)
3Com Corporation, 11; 34 (upd.); 106 (upd.)
The 3DO Company, 43
3M Company, 61 (upd.)
Thrifty PayLess, Inc., 12
Thumann Inc., 104
TIBCO Software Inc. 79
TIC Holdings Inc., 92
Ticketmaster, 76 (upd.)
Ticketmaster Group, Inc., 13; 37 (upd.)
Tidewater Inc., 11; 37 (upd.)
Tiffany & Co., 14; 78 (upd.)
TIG Holdings, Inc., 26
Tilia Inc., 62
Tillotson Corp., 15
Timber Lodge Steakhouse, Inc., 73
The Timberland Company, 13; 54 (upd.)
Timberline Software Corporation, 15
Time Warner Inc., IV; 7 (upd.)
The Times Mirror Company, IV; 17 (upd.)
Timex Corporation, 7; 25 (upd.)
The Timken Company, 8; 42 (upd.)
Tishman Speyer Properties, L.P., 47
The Titan Corporation, 36
Titan International, Inc., 89
Titan Machinery Inc., 103
Titanium Metals Corporation, 21
TiVo Inc., 75
TJ International, Inc., 19
The TJX Companies, Inc., V; 19 (upd.); 57 (upd.)
TLC Beatrice International Holdings, Inc., 22
TMP Worldwide Inc., 30
TNT Freightways Corporation, 14
Today's Man, Inc., 20
TODCO, 87
Todd Shipyards Corporation, 14

The Todd-AO Corporation, 33
Todhunter International, Inc., 27
Tofutti Brands, Inc., 64
Tokheim Corporation, 21
TOKYOPOP Inc. 79
Toll Brothers Inc., 15; 70 (upd.)
Tollgrade Communications, Inc., 44
Tom Brown, Inc., 37
Tom Doherty Associates Inc., 25
Tom's Foods Inc., 66
Tom's of Maine, Inc., 45
Tombstone Pizza Corporation, 13
Tone Brothers, Inc., 21; 74 (upd.)
Tonka Corporation, 25
Too, Inc., 61
Tootsie Roll Industries, Inc., 12; 82 (upd.)
Topco Associates LLC, 60
The Topps Company, Inc., 13; 34 (upd.); 83 (upd.)
Tops Appliance City, Inc., 17
Tops Markets LLC, 60
Torchmark Corporation, 9; 33 (upd.)
Toresco Enterprises, Inc., 84
The Toro Company, 7; 26 (upd.); 77 (upd.)
The Torrington Company, 13
Tosco Corporation, 7
Total Entertainment Restaurant Corporation, 46
Total System Services, Inc., 18
Totem Resources Corporation, 9
TouchTunes Music Corporation, 97
Tower Air, Inc., 28
Tower Automotive, Inc., 24
Towers Perrin, 32
Town & Country Corporation, 19
Town Sports International, Inc., 46
Townsends, Inc., 64
Toy Biz, Inc., 18
Toymax International, Inc., 29
Toys 'R Us, Inc., V; 18 (upd.); 57 (upd.)
Tracor Inc., 17
Tractor Supply Company, 57
Trader Joe's Company, 13; 50 (upd.)
TradeStation Group, Inc., 83
Traffix, Inc., 61
Trailer Bridge, Inc., 41
Trammell Crow Company, 8; 57 (upd.)
Trane 78
Trans World Airlines, Inc., I; 12 (upd.); 35 (upd.)
Trans World Entertainment Corporation, 24; 68 (upd.)
Trans-Lux Corporation, 51
Transaction Systems Architects, Inc., 29; 82 (upd.)
Transamerica–An AEGON Company, I; 13 (upd.); 41 (upd.)
Transammonia Group, 95
Transatlantic Holdings, Inc., 11
Transco Energy Company, V
Transitions Optical, Inc., 83
Transmedia Network Inc., 20
TransMontaigne Inc., 28
Transocean Sedco Forex Inc., 45
Transport Corporation of America, Inc., 49
TransPro, Inc., 71

The Tranzonic Companies, 37
Travel Ports of America, Inc., 17
The Travelers Corporation, III
Travelocity.com, Inc., 46
Travelzoo Inc. 79
Travis Boats & Motors, Inc., 37
TRC Companies, Inc., 32
Treadco, Inc., 19
Treasure Chest Advertising Company, Inc., 32
Tredegar Corporation, 52
Tree of Life, Inc., 29; 107 (upd.)
Tree Top, Inc., 76
TreeHouse Foods, Inc. 79
Trek Bicycle Corporation, 16; 78 (upd.)
Trend-Lines, Inc., 22
Trendwest Resorts, Inc., 33
Trex Company, Inc., 71
Tri-State Generation and Transmission Association, Inc., 103
Tri Valley Growers, 32
Triarc Companies, Inc., 8; 34 (upd.)
Tribune Company, IV; 22 (upd.); 63 (upd.)
Trico Products Corporation, 15
Trico Marine Services, Inc., 89
Tilcon-Connecticut Inc., 80
Trident Seafoods Corporation, 56
Trigen Energy Corporation, 42
TriMas Corp., 11
Trimble Navigation Limited, 40
Trinchero Family Estates, 107 (upd.)
Trinity Industries, Incorporated, 7
TRINOVA Corporation, III
TriPath Imaging, Inc., 77
Triple Five Group Ltd., 49
TriQuint Semiconductor, Inc., 63
Tripwire, Inc., 97
Trisko Jewelry Sculptures, Ltd., 57
Triton Energy Corporation, 11
Triumph Group, Inc., 31
The TriZetto Group, Inc., 83
TRM Copy Centers Corporation, 18
Tropicana Products, Inc., 28; 73 (upd.)
Troutman Sanders L.L.P. 79
True North Communications Inc., 23
True Religion Apparel, Inc. 79
True Temper Sports, Inc., 95
True Value Company, 74 (upd.)
The Trump Organization, 23; 64 (upd.)
TruServ Corporation, 24
Trustmark Corporation, 106
TRW Automotive Holdings Corp., 75 (upd.)
TRW Inc., I; 11 (upd.); 14 (upd.)
TTX Company, 6; 66 (upd.)
Tubby's, Inc., 53
Tucson Electric Power Company, 6
Tuesday Morning Corporation, 18; 70 (upd.)
Tully's Coffee Corporation, 51
Tultex Corporation, 13
Tumaro's Gourmet Tortillas, 85
Tumbleweed, Inc., 33; 80 (upd.)
Tupperware Corporation, 28; 78 (upd.)
TurboChef Technologies, Inc., 83
Turner Broadcasting System, Inc., II; 6 (upd.); 66 (upd.)

Turner Construction Company, 66
The Turner Corporation, 8; 23 (upd.)
Turtle Wax, Inc., 15; 93 (upd.)
Tuscarora Inc., 29
Tutogen Medical, Inc., 68
Tuttle Publishing, 86
TV Guide, Inc., 43 (upd.)
TVI, Inc., 15
TVI Corporation, 99
TW Services, Inc., II
Tweeter Home Entertainment Group,
 Inc., 30
Twentieth Century Fox Film Corporation,
 II; 25 (upd.)
24 Hour Fitness Worldwide, Inc., 71
24/7 Real Media, Inc., 49
Twin Disc, Inc., 21
Twinlab Corporation, 34
II-VI Incorporated, 69
Ty Inc., 33; 86 (upd.)
Tyco Toys, Inc., 12
Tyler Corporation, 23
Tyndale House Publishers, Inc., 57
Tyson Foods, Inc., II; 14 (upd.); 50
 (upd.)
U S West, Inc., V; 25 (upd.)
U.S. Aggregates, Inc., 42
U.S. Army Corps of Engineers, 91
U.S. Bancorp, 14; 36 (upd.); 103 (upd.)
U.S. Borax, Inc., 42
U.S. Can Corporation, 30
U.S. Cellular Corporation, 31 (upd.); 88
 (upd.)
U.S. Delivery Systems, Inc., 22
U.S. Foodservice, 26
U.S. Healthcare, Inc., 6
U.S. Home Corporation, 8; 78 (upd.)
U.S. News & World Report Inc., 30; 89
 (upd.)
U.S. Office Products Company, 25
U.S. Physical Therapy, Inc., 65
U.S. Premium Beef LLC, 91
U.S. Robotics Corporation, 9; 66 (upd.)
U.S. Satellite Broadcasting Company, Inc.,
 20
U.S. Silica Company, 104
U.S. Timberlands Company, L.P., 42
U.S. Trust Corp., 17
U.S. Vision, Inc., 66
UAL Corporation, 34 (upd.); 107 (upd.)
UAW (International Union, United
 Automobile, Aerospace and Agricultural
 Implement Workers of America), 72
UGI Corporation, 12
Ugly Duckling Corporation, 22
UICI, 33
Ukrop's Super Markets, Inc., 39; 101
 (upd.)
Ulta Salon, Cosmetics & Fragrance, Inc.,
 93
Ultimate Electronics, Inc., 18; 69 (upd.)
Ultra Pac, Inc., 24
Ultra Petroleum Corporation, 71
Ultrak Inc., 24
Ultralife Batteries, Inc., 58
Ultramar Diamond Shamrock
 Corporation, 31 (upd.)
Umpqua Holdings Corporation, 87

Uncle Ben's Inc., 22
Uncle Ray's LLC, 90
Under Armour Performance Apparel, 61
Underwriters Laboratories, Inc., 30
Uni-Marts, Inc., 17
Unica Corporation, 77
Unicom Corporation, 29 (upd.)
Unifi, Inc., 12; 62 (upd.)
Unified Grocers, Inc., 93
UniFirst Corporation, 21
Union Bank of California, 16
Union Camp Corporation, IV
Union Carbide Corporation, I; 9 (upd.);
 74 (upd.)
Union Electric Company, V
Union Pacific Corporation, V; 28 (upd.);
 79 (upd.)
Union Planters Corporation, 54
Union Texas Petroleum Holdings, Inc., 9
UnionBanCal Corporation, 50 (upd.)
Unique Casual Restaurants, Inc., 27
Unison HealthCare Corporation, 25
Unisys Corporation, III; 6 (upd.); 36
 (upd.)
Unit Corporation, 63
United Airlines, I; 6 (upd.)
United Auto Group, Inc., 26; 68 (upd.)
United Brands Company, II
United Community Banks, Inc., 98
United Dairy Farmers, Inc., 74
United Defense Industries, Inc., 30; 66
 (upd.)
United Dominion Industries Limited, 8;
 16 (upd.)
United Dominion Realty Trust, Inc., 52
United Farm Workers of America, 88
United Foods, Inc., 21
United HealthCare Corporation, 9
The United Illuminating Company, 21
United Industrial Corporation, 37
United Industries Corporation, 68
United Jewish Communities, 33
United Merchants & Manufacturers, Inc.,
 13
United National Group, Ltd., 63
United Nations International Children's
 Emergency Fund (UNICEF), 58
United Natural Foods, Inc., 32; 76 (upd.)
United Negro College Fund, Inc. 79
United Online, Inc., 71 (upd.)
United Parcel Service of America Inc., V;
 17 (upd.)
United Parcel Service, Inc., 63; 94 (upd.)
United Press International, Inc., 25; 73
 (upd.)
United Rentals, Inc., 34
United Retail Group Inc., 33
United Road Services, Inc., 69
United Service Organizations, 60
United States Cellular Corporation, 9
United States Filter Corporation, 20
United States Pipe and Foundry
 Company, 62
United States Playing Card Company, 62
United States Postal Service, 14; 34 (upd.)
The United States Shoe Corporation, V
United States Steel Corporation, 50 (upd.)

United States Surgical Corporation, 10;
 34 (upd.)
United Stationers Inc., 14
United Talent Agency, Inc., 80
United Technologies Automotive Inc., 15
United Technologies Corporation, I; 10
 (upd.); 34 (upd.); 105 (upd.)
United Telecommunications, Inc., V
United Video Satellite Group, 18
United Water Resources, Inc., 40
United Way of America, 36
UnitedHealth Group Incorporated, 103
 (upd.)
Unitil Corporation, 37
Unitog Co., 19
Unitrin Inc., 16; V
Univar Corporation, 9
Universal Compression, Inc., 59
Universal Corporation, V; 48 (upd.)
Universal Electronics Inc., 39
Universal Foods Corporation, 7
Universal Forest Products, Inc., 10; 59
 (upd.)
Universal Health Services, Inc., 6
Universal International, Inc., 25
Universal Manufacturing Company, 88
Universal Security Instruments, Inc., 96
Universal Stainless & Alloy Products, Inc.,
 75
Universal Studios, Inc., 33; 100 (upd.)
Universal Technical Institute, Inc., 81
The University of Chicago Press 79
Univision Communications Inc., 24; 83
 (upd.)
Uno Restaurant Corporation, 18
Uno Restaurant Holdings Corporation, 70
 (upd.)
Unocal Corporation, IV; 24 (upd.); 71
 (upd.)
UnumProvident Corporation, 13; 52
 (upd.)
The Upjohn Company, I; 8 (upd.)
The Upper Deck Company, LLC, 105
Urban Engineers, Inc., 102
Urban Outfitters, Inc., 14; 74 (upd.)
URS Corporation, 45; 80 (upd.)
US Airways Group, Inc., I; 6 (upd.); 28
 (upd.); 52 (upd.)
US 1 Industries, Inc., 89
USA Interactive, Inc., 47 (upd.)
USA Mobility Inc., 97 (upd.)
USA Truck, Inc., 42
USAA, 10; 62 (upd.)
USANA, Inc., 29
USF&G Corporation, III
USG Corporation, III; 26 (upd.); 81
 (upd.)
UST Inc., 9; 50 (upd.)
USX Corporation, IV; 7 (upd.)
Utah Medical Products, Inc., 36
Utah Power and Light Company, 27
UTG Inc., 100
UtiliCorp United Inc., 6
UTStarcom, Inc., 77
Utz Quality Foods, Inc., 72
UUNET, 38
Uwajimaya, Inc., 60
Vail Resorts, Inc., 11; 43 (upd.)